The McGraw-Hill Homeland Security Handbook

The McGraw-Hill Homeland Security Handbook

David G. Kamien, Editor

With a Foreword by Professor Richard Falkenrath
Former White House Deputy Homeland Security Advisor

New York Chicago San Francisco Lisbon London Madrid
Mexico City Milan New Delhi San Juan Seoul Singapore
Sydney Toronto

The McGraw·Hill Companies

2 3 4 5 6 7 8 9 10 DOC/DOC 0 9 8 7 6

ISBN 0-07-144665-6

McGraw-Hill books are available at special quantity discounts to use as premiums and sales promotions, or for use in corporate training programs. For more information, please write to the Director of Special Sales, Professional Publishing, McGraw-Hill, Two Penn Plaza, New York, NY 10121-2298. Or contact your local bookstore.

 This book is printed on recycled, acid-free paper containing a minimum of 50% recycled, de-inked fiber.

Library of Congress Cataloging-in-Publication Data

Kamien, David G.

    The McGraw-Hill Homeland Security Handbook / David G. Kamien.

    p. cm.

    ISBN 0-07-144665-6 (hardcover : alk. paper)

1. Terrorism—United States—Prevention. 2. Emergency management—United States. 3. Civil defense—United States. 4. National security—United States. 5. United States. Dept. of Homeland Security. 6. Preparedness. I. Title: Homeland security handbook. II. Title.

HV6432.K36 2005
363.32'0973–dc22   2005004735

CONTENTS

Chapter 6

SECTION THIRTEEN **POLITICS AND ACCOUNTABILITY**

CONTRIBUTORS

Don Adams   VP, Chief Technology Officer–Government and Chief Security Officer, TIBCO Software (CHAP. 62)

Thurman J. Allard   Director of Homeland Security, Sandia National Laboratories (CHAP. 59)

Major General Donna F. Barbisch, C.R.N.A., M.P.H., D.H.A.   Director, Chem Bio Radiological and Nuclear Defense Programs Integration, Department of Defense; Adjunct Professor, George Washington University; President, Global Deterrence Alternatives, LLC (CHAP. 41)

The Honorable Scott D. Bates, J.D.   Senior Fellow, Center for National Policy; Former Senior Policy Advisor, U.S. House Select Committee on Homeland Security (CHAP. 54)

Carl Bentzel, J.D., LL.M.   Advisor for Homeland Security, DCI Group LLC; Former Senior Advisor, U.S. Senate Committee on Commerce Science, and Transportation Committee (CHAP. 39)

Anthony Beverina   President and Chief Operating Officer, Digital Sandbox, Inc. (CHAP. 28)

Mark Braverman, Ph.D.   Prinicipal, The Braverman Group, LLC (CHAP. 51)

Terry A. Bresnick   President and Senior Principal, Innovative Decisions, Inc. (CHAP. 29)

Dr. Daniel Byman   Associate Professor, Walsh School of Foreign Service, Georgetown University; Nonresident Senior Fellow, Saban Center for Middle East Policy, Brookings Institution (CHAP. 13)

Dr. James Jay Carafano   Senior Fellow, The Heritage Foundation (CHAP. 31)

Sidney J. Caspersen   Director, Office of Counter-Terrorism, State of New Jersey (CHAP. 24)

Fred H. Cate, J.D.   Distinguished Professor and Director, Center for Applied Cybersecurity Research, Indiana University; Senior Policy Advisor, Center for Information Policy Leadership at Hunton and Williams (CHAP. 68)

Sharon L. Caudle Homeland Security and Justice Team, U.S. Government Accountability Office (CHAP. 16)

Jean-Francois Cloutier   CTO, Mind-Alliance Systems (CHAP. 63)

Leonard A. Cole, Ph.D.   Adjunct Professor, Department of Political Science, Rutgers University (CHAP. 11)

Senator Susan M. Collins   Chairman U.S. Senate Committee on Homeland Security and Governmental Affairs (CHAP. 15)

David Cook, Ph.D.   Assistant Professor, Department of Religious Studies, Rice University (CHAP. 3)

James D. Cunningham Science Applications International Corporation (SAIC) (CHAP. 35)

Sara Daly   International Policy Analyst, The RAND Corporation (CHAP. 5)

Gijs de Vries Counterterrorism Coordinator, European Union (CHAP. 23)

Dr. Robin L. Dillon-Merrill   Professor, Georgetown University; Principal, Innovative Decisions, Inc. (CHAP. 29)

William Donnelly Chairman, Morris County Infrastructure Advisory Group (CHAP. 52)

C. Patrick Duecy   Partner, Homeland Solutions, LLC. (CHAP. 26)

Steve Emerson Executive Director, The Investigative Project on Terrorism (CHAP. 14)

Fred Facemire Director, System Integration, Smiths Detection (CHAP. 60)

Richard A. Falkenrath, Ph.D.   Senior Fellow, Foreign Policy Studies, The Brookings Institution; Former White House Deputy, Homeland Security Advisor (FOREWORD)

Dr. Baruch Fischhoff Howard Heinz University Professor, Department of Social and Decision Sciences, Carnegie Mellon University (CHAP. 30)

Admiral Cathal "Irish" Flynn (Retired) TranSecure, Inc. (CHAP. 38)

Abraham H. Foxman National Director, Anti-Defamation League (CHAP. 66)

Scott Gerwehr Associate Policy Analyst, The RAND Corporation (CHAP. 5)

Governor James Gilmore Partner, Kelley Drye & Warren LLP (CHAP. 47)

Karen J. Greenberg Executive Director, Center on Law and Security, New York University (CHAP. 22)

Rohan Kumar Gunaratna, Ph.D. Head of Terrorism Research and Associate Professor, Institute for Defense and Strategic Studies, Singapore (CHAP. 1)

Elin A. Gursky, Sc.D. Principal Deputy for Biodefense, National Strategies Support Directorate, ANSER/Analytic Services, Inc. (CHAP. 45)

Jack R. Harrald, Ph.D. Codirector, George Washington University, Institute for Crisis, Disaster, and Risk Management (CHAP. 43)

Ahmed S. Hashim, Ph.D. Professor of Strategic Studies, United States Naval War College (CHAP. 2)

Nigel Hey Sandia National Laboratories (CHAP. 59)

John Horgan, Ph.D. C. Psychol., Lecturer, Department of Applied Psychology, University College, Cork, Ireland (CHAP. 10)

Terry Janssen Chief Technologist for Knowledge Management, Lockheed Martin Corporation (CHAP. 58)

Brian Michael Jenkins Senior Advisor to the President of The RAND Corporation; Director of the National Transportation Security Center at the Mineta Transportation Institute (CHAP. 8)

David G. Kamien CEO, DGK LLC Homeland Security Management Consulting (INTRODUCTION and CHAP. 63)

Mark V. Kauppi   Program Director, Counterterrorism Training for Analysts, Joint Military Intelligence Center, U.S. Army (CHAP. 27)

Ronald J. Kelly   Director, IBM Corporate Security (CHAP. 48)

Anne M. Khademian   Associate Professor, Center for Public Administration and Policy, Virginia Polytechnic University (CHAP. 70)

Michael G. Knapp   Middle East Analyst, U.S. Army National Guard Intelligence Center (CHAP. 6)

Noel Koch   Chairman and CEO, TranSecur, Inc.; Former Director of Special Planning, U.S. Department of Defense; Former Special Assistant to the President (CHAP. 7)

Art Kosatka   CEO, TranSecure, Inc. (CHAP. 38)

Michael Kraft   Counterterrorism Consultant; Former Senior Advisor for Legislative and Budget Affairs in the State Department Office of the Coordinator for Counterterrorism; Former Staff Director of the Senate Foreign Relations Committee Middle East Subcommittee (CHAP. 21)

Richard C. Larson, Ph.D.   Professor of Civil and Environmental Engineering and of Engineering Systems, Massachusetts Institute of Technology (CHAP. 57)

Mark Laustra   Smiths Detection (CHAP. 60)

Ray Lehr   Northrop Grumman Corporation, Assistant Chief (Retired), Baltimore City Fire Department (CHAP. 42)

James F. McDonnell   Vice President and Chief Information and Security Officer, USEC, Inc. (CHAP. 33)

Paul McHale   Assistant Secretary of Defense, Homeland Defense Office, U.S. Department of Defense (CHAP. 18)

Gerald Metz   Chief Engineer, C2 Infrastructure Programs, Northrop Grumman Mission Systems (CHAP. 61)

Newton N. Minow   Senior Counsel, Sidley Austin Brown and Wood (CHAP. 68)

Laura W. Murphy   Director, Washington Legislative Office, American Civil Liberties Union (ACLU) (CHAP. 67)

Rania Nader School of Public and Environmental Affairs, Indiana University (CHAP. 71)

Harold W. Neil, Jr. Executive Assistant, Office of Transportation Security, Department of Transportation, State of New Jersey (CHAP. 40)

Patrick N. Newman, J.D. Program Manager, Marine Transportation System Initiative, U.S. Coast Guard Academy (CHAP. 56)

William C. Nicholson, Esq. Adjunct Professor, Widener University School of Law (CHAP. 53)

The Honorable Martin O'Malley Mayor, City of Baltimore, Maryland (CHAP. 20)

Alan Orlob Vice President, Corporate Security, Marriott International Lodging (CHAP. 50)

Terrence M. O'Sullivan Homeland Security Center for Risk and Economic Analysis (CREATE), University of Southern California (CHAP. 12)

Wiliam H. Parrish Associate Professor, L. Douglas Wilder School of Government and Public Affairs, Virginia Commonwealth University (CHAP. 36)

Dr. Gregory S. Parnell Professor of Systems Engineering, United States Military Academy at West Point; Senior Principal, Innovative Decisions, Inc. (CHAP. 29)

Dennis A. Pluchinsky Senior Threat Analyst, TranSecur, Inc.; Terrorism Analyst, U.S. Department of State (Retired) (CHAP. 25)

Dr. Lion Poles Deputy Director General, Kaplan Medical Center (CHAP. 46)

Denis Ranger Product Architect, Mind-Alliance Systems (CHAP. 63)

Xavier Raufer Director of Studies, Department for the Study of the Contemporary Criminal Menace, Criminology Institute, University of Paris II–Panthéon-Assas (CHAP. 9)

K. Jack Riley Associate Director of RAND, Infrastructure, Safety, and Environment, The RAND Corporation (CHAP. 37)

David Robertson Executive Director, Metropolitan Washington Council of Governments (CHAP. 19)

William Rosenau Political Scientist, The RAND Corporation, Washington Office; Adjunct Professor, Security Studies Program, Georgetown University (CHAP. 72)

Paul Rosenzweig Senior Legal Research Fellow, The Heritage Foundation, Adjunct Professor of Law, George Mason University, School of Law (CHAP. 65)

Claire B. Rubin President and Principal, Claire B. Rubin & Associates, Disaster Research and Consulting; Senior Research Scientist, George Washington University, Institute for Crisis, Disaster, and Risk Management (CHAP. 43)

The Honorable Warren Rudman Counsel, Paul, Weiss, Rifkind, Wharton & Garrison LLP; Former U.S. Senator from New Hampshire (CHAP. 69)

Marc Sageman, M.D., Ph.D. Senior Fellow, Foreign Policy Research Institute; Lecturer, Solomon Asch Center for the Study of Ethnopolitical Conflict, University of Pennsylvania (CHAP. 4)

Donald L. Schmidt Emergency Response Planning Practice Leader, Marsh Risk Consulting (CHAP. 49)

Frank Sesno Professor of Public Policy and Communication, School of Public Policy, George Mason University; CNN Special Correspondent (CHAP. 32)

Shmuel C. Shapira, M.D. Deputy Director General, Hadassah Medical Organization (CHAP. 46)

Congressman Christopher Shays Chairman, House Subcommittee on National Security, Emerging Threats, and International Relations (CHAP. 17)

Bradley D. Stein, M.D., Ph.D., M.P.H. Natural Scientist, Associate Director for Mental and Behavioral Health, Center for Domestic and International Health Security, The RAND Corporation (CHAP. 44)

Todd I. Stewart Major General U.S. Air Force (Retired); Executive Director, National Academic Consortium for Homeland Security (CHAP. 55)

Dr. Boaz Tadmor   Director, Cerberus Enterprises, LLC (CHAP. 46)

K. A. Taipale   Executive Director, Center for Advanced Studies in Science and Technology Policy, World Policy Institute (CHAP. 64)

Terri L. Tanielian, M.A.   Senior Research Analyst, Associate Director for Mental and Behavioral Health, Center for Domestic and International Health Security, The RAND Corporation (CHAP. 44)

Commander Joseph E. Vorbach III, Ph.D.   Associate Professor of International Relations and Director, Marine Transportation System Initiative, U.S. Coast Guard Academy (CHAP. 56)

Charles R. Wise   Professor, School of Public and Environmental Affairs, Indiana University (CHAP. 71)

Randall Yim, Esq.   Director, Homeland Security Institute (CHAP. 16)

Rae Zimmerman, Ph.D.   Professor of Planning and Public Administration; Director, Institute for Civil Infrastructure Systems (ICIS), Wagner Graduate School of Public Service, New York University (CHAP. 34)

ACKNOWLEDGMENTS

My deep thanks go to the contributors whose introductions, chapters, and illustrations make up *The McGraw-Hill Homeland Security Handbook*. I am also grateful for the expert editorial assistance provided by Susan Gamer, Aileen Torres, and my publisher: Jeffrey Krames, Laura Libretti, Maureen Walker, and the rest of the staff at McGraw-Hill.

I received many forms of assistance and encouragement from a great many institutions and people, including David Afhauser, Victor Anderes, Caroline Barnes, Mia Bloom, Sharon Caudle, Elizabeth Clausen, Jean-François Cloutier, Elissa Davidson, Amanda Dory, Lee Ewing, Al Felzenberg, Larry Halloran, Michael Hopmeier, Rosanne Hynes, Andrew Lauland, Don Kettl, Anna Khademian, Ray Lehr, Tony Moore, Harold Neil, John Paczkowski, Brad Penuel, Bob Poole, Tim Raducha-Grace, Edna Reid, Lisa Shields, Matthew Statler, Howard Steinberg, Paul Wilkinson, Dave Zolet, and others.

Several of the contributors—Mike Kraft, Claire Rubin, Dennis Pluchinsky, and Jack Riley—were exceptionally helpful in introducing me to other contributors and providing feedback. They deserve special thanks.

I also appreciate the efforts of government employees and the staff of the 9/11 Commission, and the work of numerous think tanks and task forces that have studied terrorism, have worked in the area of homeland security, and have passed on their knowledge in reports and studies.

The warm support provided by my wife, Felice Maranz; my children, Daniel and Amalia; and my parents, Anita and Roger Kamien, was essential to the completion of this book, and I dedicate it to them with love.

FOREWORD

Richard A. Falkenrath, Ph.D.
Senior Fellow, Foreign Policy Studies, The Brookings Institution;
Former White House Deputy, Homeland Security Advisor

Before the terrorist attacks of 9/11, there was no field called "homeland security" and hence no need for a handbook such as this. Today, homeland security is a multibillion-dollar enterprise and the motivating force behind countless reforms across dozens of heretofore separate government activities. The need for this enterprise is not tied to the fate of al-Qaida or any other particular terrorist group; instead, it derives from the structural—and hence, for all intents and purposes, permanent—vulnerability of free and open societies to catastrophic terrorist attacks. This vulnerability existed before 9/11 and will continue to exist indefinitely. Because all governments are charged with safeguarding their civilian population from deliberate large-scale death and destruction, homeland security has become a permanent mission for responsible governments worldwide.

Homeland security is a composite of many different fields that individually have some bearing on the terrorist threat to modern societies, the vulnerability of these societies to various forms of terrorist attack, and the techniques to combat these threats and vulnerabilities. Each individual field is supported by the knowledge and experience of an established community of experts and practitioners. As yet there is no community of individuals with the interdisciplinary breadth needed to manage the field of homeland security comprehensively and effectively.

The contrast between homeland security and national security (another even broader interdisciplinary field) is instructive. National security describes many different kinds of measures—diplomatic, economic, military, covert, overt, legal, illegal, etc.—taken by a state to ensure its survival and security. National security has been practiced by governments for centuries, and over time has emerged as a distinct field supported by a community of individuals with similar educational and practical backgrounds. Individuals from this community are able to coalesce quickly into effective work groups because they share a frame of reference, an understanding of established national security processes, and a general familiarity with each other's areas of profound expertise. This collection of national security experts represents what social scientists call an "epistemic community."

Homeland security has no epistemic community to speak of, but needs one. Men and women from dozens of different disciplines— regional experts, terrorism analysts, law enforcement officials, intelligence officers, privacy specialists, diplomats, military officers, immigration specialists, customs inspectors, specific industry experts, regulatory lawyers, doctors and epidemiologists, research scientists, chemists, nuclear physicists, information technologists, emergency managers, firefighters, communications specialists, and politicians, to name a few—are currently involved in homeland security, but it is not enough merely to aggregate specialists. The tendency to organize around disciplines, to adopt "stovepiped" approaches to problems, and to optimize solutions for part but not all of the problem is too strong among loose collections of unadulterated specialists. Only a team of individuals with genuine crosscutting knowledge and experience will be able to understand the complexity of any particular homeland security challenge, devise an efficient and viable strategy for dealing with the problem, and implement this strategy effectively.

There is an acute national and indeed international need for professionals who can think and operate across the breadth of homeland security while at the same time contributing expertise in one or more of the disciplines that comprise the field as a whole. There are only a few such individuals today, so more must be trained. Governments worldwide have already created a demand for such individuals, but the educational system in the United States has only just begun to provide the knowledge base and training capabilities needed to meet the government's demand for the genuine homeland security professional. Educational systems outside the United States are even farther behind.

This volume is long, and for a reason: its length is indicative of the substantive breadth of homeland security itself. Each individual chapter deals with a different and important aspect of the field as a whole. Together, the chapters provide a first-rate overview of a new and exceedingly complex field—a perspective that is broad, deep, and cognizant of the interrelationships among the disparate disciplines that make up homeland security. In that respect, this handbook is the first of its kind and an invaluable resource.

This handbook represents an important step toward creating the professional community that governments require to implement a comprehensive homeland security agenda effectively and efficiently. As such, the book makes a rare contribution not just to a professional literature but also to a noble public purpose: securing a nation from catastrophic terrorist attack while preserving the freedom and openness that make the homeland vulnerable in the first place.

P R E F A C E

The McGraw-Hill Homeland Security Handbook takes a broad view of the challenges involved in enhancing domestic security and emergency preparedness. Our goal is to contribute to the discussion of this national issue and heighten readers' awareness of the importance of integrating policies, strategies, and initiatives across different areas into a cohesive national and international effort.

The book provides a comprehensive introduction to the subject for university students, policy makers, and industry professionals. Several assumptions underlie the selection of chapters. First, although homeland security and national preparedness now encompass "all hazards," including events such as natural disasters, the focus of the book is on terrorism and security, areas where an understanding of the human element of the terrorist threat is critical. Second, with or without Usama bin Ladin as its leader, al-Qaida and radical fundamentalist Islam will remain a threat. An entire section is devoted to understanding this dominant terror threat to the United States. Third, regardless of specific types of attacks and the affiliation of their perpetrators, many of the principal missions and challenges that homeland security policy makers, operational managers, and analysts face will remain the same.

KEY FEATURES

The McGraw-Hill Homeland Security Handbook has several important features:

- The text provides extensive thematic coverage, encompassing analysis of al-Qaida and related terrorist threats, and of homeland security as part of the United States' response. There are more than 70 original chapters and case studies about a wide range of subjects, providing an opportunity to understand how homeland security challenges are interconnected. The book is the first in the literature to combine such a comprehensive array of topics, creating a basis for a shared understanding of homeland security.

- The contributors include distinguished members of Congress; senior federal, state, and local government officials; industry professionals; and academics, many of whom combine theory with practical experience in homeland security and are active in educating the next generation of national security leaders.
- The book includes chapters on practical matters and chapters that present theoretical models and concepts.
- The book covers recent developments, such as the July 2005 bombing in London and the restructuring of the Department of Homeland Security as a result of the Second Stage Review initiated by Secretary Chertoff, the Intelligence Reform and Terrorism Prevention Act of December 2004, the vote to create a permanent Committee on Homeland Security, and the appointment of Michael Chertoff as the secretary of the Department of Homeland Security.
- The Web site www.HomelandSecurityBook.com provides valuable resources for further study of homeland security.

ORGANIZATION

This book is divided into 13 sections, each preceded by a brief introduction to set the stage for the chapters that follow. These sections group the components of what many consider core homeland security subject matter into thematic units that provide a framework for study and discussion. Preceding Section 1 is an introductory chapter, "Homeland Security in Context," that places the subject in the setting of other policy frameworks and identifies some of its principal components.

Section 1: Al-Qaida and Global Jihad

In order to confront the threat posed by Usama bin Ladin, the al-Qaida network, and affiliated fundamentalist Islamist terrorist groups, one must understand their ideology, vision, strategy, recruiting methods, and use of the Internet. Al-Qaida's goals are to force occupying "infidels" off Muslim land; topple illegitimate apostate Arab regimes; drive U.S. forces out of Iraq, Saudi Arabia, and Afghanistan; and destroy Israel. Jihadists see their effort as an apocalyptic struggle, a righteous war of defense of the very existence of Islam and the Muslim world from attack and disintegration by a Zionist-Crusader conspiracy of infidels—Israel and the Jews, America, and "puppet" secular Arab regimes.

The most profound development related to al-Qaida since 9/11 is its transformation from a group to the self-proclaimed vanguard of Islamic movements, galvanizing Islamists worldwide to fight two battles: against their own governments and against the United States and its allies. Many extremist Muslims see bin Ladin as a figure of hope who can restore their dignity and save the Islamic world. According to bin Ladin's interpretation of the Muslim religion and its history, a violent jihad is justified and indeed noble.

The main Islamist terrorist threat to the United States comes not from a monolithic al-Qaida organization but from the broader, violent Islamist revivalist social movement, united by bin Ladin's utopian vision of justice and fairness. The threat from al-Qaida and its affiliates will remain even if bin Ladin is killed; and several of the contributors to this book think that the threat has been nourished by conflict in Iraq.

By analyzing biographical data on the terrorists and the topology of Islamist terrorist networks, as is done in one chapter, one can better understand how and why people join Islamist terror networks. For instance, one chapter in Section 1 describes various models al-Qaida may be using to recruit new members, including the "net," "funnel," "infection," and "seed crystal," along with psychographic or "state" factors. This section also explains how the Internet is central to the strategy of al-Qaida and the global jihad, which clearly appreciate its value as a weapon of psychological warfare, perception management, recruitment, and fund-raising.

Section 2: Terrorism Beyond al-Qaida

The second section looks beyond the topic of al-Qaida to study terrorism as a phenomenon, associated threats, and other groups. There is no universal definition of *terrorism*; rather, terrorism is a generalized construct derived from our concepts of morality, law, and the rules of war. Terrorism is a hugely complex social problem—what we see in an attack is only the tip of the iceberg—which must be understood in a broad sociocultural global context of chaos at the intersection of lawless places, dangerous flows, and extreme ideology.

Terrorism is an "asymmetric" form of warfare: a low-cost means of attacking civilian populations and national infrastructures when the enemy has superior economic and military might and therefore cannot be struck at with conventional tactics and weapons. However, terrorism is not only a matter of physical attacks but it is a mental game used to erode citizens' morale and their faith in their government, and to demonstrate strength to the terrorists' constituencies.

Important trends in terrorism over the past decades are presented in Section 2, but readers are cautioned against forecasting by extrapolation. Terrorist groups vary in culture, ideology, and priorities. Tomorrow's terrorism will surely be different from today's; and even at present it is misleading to lump all groups that use terrorist tactics into a notionally homogeneous group called "terrorists." This section includes a chapter on Hizballah, which aspires to transform Lebanon into an Islamic state and receives funding, training, and intelligence from Iran, a country that depicts the United States as the "great Satan" and aspires to build nuclear weapons. Readers are also presented with some of the limitations of psychology in understanding terrorists and terrorism. One chapter discusses terrorists' financing and efforts to counter it.

Another topic addressed in Section 2 is perhaps the most troubling terrorist threat: weapons of mass destruction (WMD) such as nuclear bombs, as well as weapons of mass effect such as biological and chemical agents and radiological dispersal devices (dirty bombs). Although attacks with unconventional weapons are relatively rare compared to attacks using explosives, and despite the fact that the "anthrax letters" of October 2001 resulted in only five fatalities, the possibility of WMD attacks implies a need for constant vigilance. Therefore, this section analyzes biological weapons in some detail, discussing their history and considering their potential future use by terrorists.

Section 3: The Role of Government

Section 3 introduces the role of various levels of government in homeland security. For the federal government, homeland security is a complex set of overlapping national missions. One chapter recommends ways to build capabilities and develop oversight so as to achieve those missions. Other chapters discuss the roles of the House and Senate (which not only exercise oversight but are of course responsible for federal appropriations for homeland security) and the Department of Defense (in this regard, one chapter describes the mission of the Northern Command and National Guard). The section also takes up regional planning organizations in cities and counties, which provide important support to the federal and state governments in homeland security management. Municipalities are likely to bear the brunt of terrorist attacks because such attacks typically occur in cities. At the municipal level, the primary challenges have to do with managing first responders: firefighters, police, emergency medical services, and citizens.

Still other chapters in Section 3 discuss law and intergovernmental counterterrorism. Terrorism has traditionally been addressed in the international community with treaties, such as those condemning hijacking and hostage-taking. One chapter considers new legal instruments such as the PATRIOT Act, emphasizing the need for effective, concerted implementation. Another chapter suggests that the United States could learn lessons about counterterrorism from Europe. It is also important to establish communication channels with foreign countries to share information and to foster trust and personal working relationships. Strategies for apprehending terrorists, such as standards and norms for extradition, should also be established internationally. One chapter stresses the importance of frameworks for international cooperation provided by the European Union and the United Nations. Ultimately, there can be no homeland security without international security.

Section 4: Counterterrorism Intelligence and Analysis

Arguably, counterterrorism must begin with analysis. In Section 4, one chapter provides a valuable typology of terrorism and an anatomy of the stages in planning offensive or logistical operations, although the reader is cautioned that despite any similarities in weapons and tactics, each terrorist offensive is unique. Another analysis in this section contrasts intelligence during the Cold War with intelligence today, when the intelligence community must deal with global, transnational groups that are difficult to detect, observe, and counter. With responsibility for different functions and phases of the intelligence cycle divided among many agencies, cooperation and information sharing must override bureaucratic turf wars. The Intelligence Reform and Terrorism Prevention Act of 2004 aims to align the 15 agencies of the intelligence community to achieve effective counterterrorism, but the unique bureaucratic culture of these semiautonomous agencies remains a formidable obstacle to cooperation. In one chapter, readers will be introduced to a five-step "intelligence process" and will learn that we actually have too much, not too little, intelligence—and that intelligence analysts must determine what information to feed into the process. The need for information sharing is emphasized, and the expanded role of law enforcement since 9/11 is addressed.

Section 5: Risk: Management, Perception, and Communication

The introduction to Section 5 notes that risk management is a never-ending process. Efforts made to achieve security and preparedness must be adjusted to changing levels of threat. One chapter in this section explores decision-making frameworks for antiterrorism planning, development, and implementation, including resource allocation; the authors maintain that risk assessment and risk management must accord with an organization's broader goals, objectives, and missions. To support their decisions, organizations need an unbiased, traceable process based on techniques of decision making and risk analysis.

Communicating warnings and other information about risks requires considerable sensitivity. Terrorism is meant to instill fear and anxiety; thus leaders must communicate in ways that inspire confidence, demonstrating that risk is being well managed. Citizens must trust their government enough to listen to its messages and respond effectively. How officials manage and communicate risk in a crisis will determine citizens' reaction to future communications. One chapter in this section examines the Homeland Security Advisory System (HSAS), which issues color-coded warnings. The broadcast media also play a significant role in disseminating information to the public. As is noted in one chapter, public officials need to be fluent in the "language of live"—that is, live broadcasting—so as to convey information about unfolding, confusing situations as clearly, transparently, and calmly as possible.

Section 6: Securing Critical Infrastructure and Cyberspace

In order to secure critical infrastructure, one must know what constitutes infrastructure, what makes it critical, and what functions of critical infrastructure are interdependent. Section 6 includes that information; it also provides a historical context for the evolution of policies regarding infrastructure, noting how policy has been influenced by experience—normal wear and tear, accidents, and natural hazards as well as terrorism. Readers will learn what fundamental attributes of infrastructure contribute to vulnerability, will be introduced to techniques for evaluating interdependence and vulnerability, and will learn about new developments in infrastructure technology that can reduce the consequences of terrorist attacks.

The Internet is a critical infrastructure that terrorists are unlikely to overlook as a potential target. Section 6 addresses problems of protecting cyberspace and offers a risk-management approach to cyberthreats. One chapter describes efforts by the federal government to assess risks and vulnerability in cyberspace; disseminate warnings; develop antiterrorist measures; coordinate the response to incidents; and provide technical assistance to organizations before, during, and after an incident. The chapter also offers guidelines for a robust information security program.

Section 7: Border and Transportation Security

This section covers security at borders, in immigration, in aviation, and in maritime settings—essential components of a nationwide counterterrorism strategy. "Porous" borders contributed to the defeat of the Soviet Union at the hands of the mujahideen in Afghanistan and as of this writing were enabling fighters to cross into Iraq to join the insurgents. Securing land, sea, and air borders—through which millions of people, planes, trucks, and containers pass annually—is a formidable challenge, especially if the necessary personnel are lacking.

Comparing civil aviation security in the United States before and after 9/11 can provide insight into the dynamics of homeland security. For example, the Transportation Security Administration (TSA) has given a high priority to screening baggage and passengers; but the rate of detection of explosives is still unsatisfactory, and airline cargo, shoulder-fired antiaircraft missiles, and other threats remain a concern.

In maritime security (as, typically, in homeland security in general), responsibility is fragmented among multiple agencies and the private sector. As a result, coordination and information sharing are crucial. The U.S. Coast Guard is the primary administrator of the Maritime Transportation Safety Act (MTSA), which one chapter in this section discusses in some detail.

This section also includes a case study of an envisioned statewide virtual network of transportation information to support decision making at all phases of homeland security.

Section 8: Emergency Management, Public Health, and Medical Preparedness

In the United States there is no national strategy to unify emergency management, public health, and medical preparedness. Here, a "system of systems" approach to risk management for homeland security is clearly needed. This approach must acknowledge the complexity of public health and the relationship among threats, vulnerabilities, and systems to understand specific weaknesses, allocate resources, and improve protection. In a large-scale emergency, it is necessary to move from a system of individual care to a system based on principles of public health and disaster management.

Section 8 provides an overview of the role of local first responders: emergency managers, firefighters, emergency medical personnel, and law enforcement officers. The Incident Command System (ICS) and the importance of reliable interoperable communications are discussed, as are the National Response Plan (NRP) and the National Incident Management System (NIMS). These are frameworks for managing and responding to domestic incidents that have "national significance," such as terrorist threats, major disasters and emergencies, and catastrophic incidents.

One chapter takes up pre- and postattack mental health strategies, which are another crucial aspect of preparedness.

The section also includes a chapter about emergency management and preparedness procedures at hospitals in Israel. The authors share their experience treating casualties of suicide bombings and preparing for the effects of WMD.

Section 9: Role of the Private Sector

Public-private partnerships are crucially important in homeland security because, for one reason, the private sector owns or operates more than 85 percent of the nation's critical infrastructure. This section provides practical advice for private-sector corporate security, risk and vulnerability assessment, emergency planning, crisis management, and planning. It includes an overview of the National Fire Protection Association (NFPA) standard on disaster and emergency management and business continuity programs.

One chapter in this section is a case study—a firsthand account of security measures taken by JW Marriott at its hotel in Jakarta—that provides an example of corporate crisis management in action. The section also covers two aspects of private-sector homeland security that are neglected by many companies. The first is the "human impact planning" to address the psychological health of employees and mitigate posttraumatic stress disorder; the second is legal issues that relate to homeland security and businesses, and measures that private industry can take to protect itself against liability in relation to a terrorist threat or incident.

Section 10: Academe

Academe played a vital role in determining how the Cold War would be fought. Now the academic sector must respond and restructure to meet new national security challenges. With regard to homeland security, academe can develop solutions through science and technology and can also offer education, training, outreach, and service. Academe is itself a potential target and resource for terrorists.

Homeland security is rapidly evolving as an academic course of study. One chapter in Section 10 suggests an interdisciplinary core curriculum for homeland security studies, to include such topics as resource optimization and management, classic national security and international relations theory and practice, interfaces between technology and policy, organizational behavior, cultural understanding, strategic and scenario-based (futures) planning, and risk-based decision making. Operations research (OR) is an academic discipline that uses the scientific method to assess the consequences of alternative decisions involving long-term strategic planning and shorter-range tactics and operations. One chapter provides examples of how OR can be useful in emergency response plans and strategies, especially for first responders.

Section 11: Science, Technology, and Information Sharing

Inputs from many types of sensors, people, and software in homeland security produce a flood of information—and thus a challenge to "knowledge management." Technology plays many roles in counterterrorist strategies for the private and public sectors. One role is combating chemical, biological, radiological, nuclear, and high-explosives (CBRNE) threats: for example, using systems to detect radiation at ports of entry. Technology also enables modeling, simulation, and analysis at each phase of emergency management. Data fusion, another tool of counterterrorism, gives decision makers and other public officials access to intelligence and analysis from the CIA, the FBI, and other government agencies.

Science and technology are particularly applicable in screening passengers and cargo for explosives—a capability that is essential for effective border and transportation security. However, many practitioners warn that simply "throwing technology" at a problem will not provide the desired security. One instance where this holds true is checkpoint security. Screening technologies must be integrated with a wider, holistic network, or security regime, within an organization, industry, region, or state and, ultimately, nationwide. Such integration requires wise technology policy and cooperation between the public and private sectors in order to result in increased efficiency and lower systemwide operational costs over the long term.

Many aspects of homeland security use information technology. One chapter in Section 11 explains why simply fusing data and information is unlikely to achieve the desired support for decision making. New IT "architecture" is needed to shift information sharing from "need to know" to "need to share" in the face of cultural barriers. The section examines new IT concepts such as using computer systems with monitoring software and an array of sensors to identify a threat rapidly and provide a "predictive response." One chapter presents a new paradigm for analyzing homeland security information-sharing needs by having distributed groups assess their needs collaboratively on an ongoing basis, using scenarios. This paradigm would constitute a key enabler for creating a broad-based information-sharing environment.

Section 12: Domestic Security and Civil Liberties

Security and liberty are both obligations of society. This section addresses various aspects of civil liberties in the context of homeland security. Topics include theoretical constructs and principles as well as actual and hypothetical examples. One chapter approaches the subject through three case studies (a proposed national identification card, bioterrorism, and the issue of racial and ethnic profiling). Data mining and surveillance raise special concerns about the invasion of privacy and are discussed in one chapter. These topics have become subjects of significant debate. Another chapter discusses the sensitive issue of balancing individual liberty and national security. When and where should free speech end in a post-9/11 world?

Section 13: Politics and Accountability

Homeland security gives rise to political questions that must be addressed—questions regarding values, principles, doctrine, the distribution of power, historic constitutional challenges, and account-ability. All participants in homeland security must be accountable to the American people for a realistic set of performance measures. The three chapters in Section 13 address these issues and challenges.

David G. Kamien

CEO, DGK LLC Homeland Security
Management Consulting

Homeland Security in Context

David Kamien
CEO, DGK LLC Homeland Security Management Consulting

*T*he *McGraw-Hill Homeland Security Handbook* explores both the threat of terrorism and the role of homeland security in dealing with this threat. This opening chapter surveys and contextualizes some of the key concepts and analytical frameworks used in the text.

HOMELAND SECURITY: KEY CONCEPTS

Homeland security is a policy framework for organizing the activities of government and all sectors of society to detect, deter, protect against, and, if necessary, respond to domestic attacks such as 9/11. Homeland Security is defined in the National Strategy for Homeland Security as "a concerted national effort to prevent terrorist attacks within the United States, reduce America's vulnerability to terrorism, and recover from and minimize the damage of attacks that do occur" (Office of Homeland Security 2002, p. 2).

In the context of this National Strategy, prevention means action at home and abroad to deter, prevent, and eliminate terrorism. Vulnerability reduction means identifying and protecting critical infrastructure and key assets, detecting terrorist threats, and augmenting defenses, while balancing the benefits of mitigating risk against economic costs and infringements on individual liberty. Response and recovery means managing the consequences of attacks, and building and maintaining the financial, legal, and social systems to recover.

The National Strategy for Homeland Security categorized homeland security activities into six critical mission areas. The

White House Office of Management and Budget (OMB) 2003 Annual Report to Congress on Combating Terrorism described these missions as follows:

Mission Area 1: Intelligence and Warning

Terrorism depends on surprise. The first mission area includes intelligence programs and warning systems that can detect terrorist activity before it manifests itself in an attack so that proper preemptive, preventive, and protective action can be taken. Specifically, this mission area is made up of efforts to identify, collect, analyze, and distribute source intelligence information or the resultant warnings from intelligence analysis. As part of the homeland security category, this excludes funding for intelligence activities of the national security community that are focused overseas.

Mission Area 2: Border and Transportation Security

This second mission area includes border and transportation security programs designed to fully integrate homeland security measures into existing domestic transportation systems. Since current systems are intertwined with the global transport infrastructure, virtually every community in America is connected to the world by seaports, airports, highways, pipelines, railroads, and waterways that move people and goods into, within, and out of the nation. This mission area focuses on programs to promote the efficient and reliable flow of people, goods, and services across borders, while preventing terrorists from using transportation conveyances or systems as weapons, or to deliver implements of destruction.

Mission Area 3: Domestic Counterterrorism

The third mission area incorporates federal funding for any law enforcement programs (including state, local, or regional) that investigate and prosecute criminal activity to prevent and interdict terrorist activity within the United States. It includes all homeland security programs that identify, halt, prevent, and prosecute terrorists in the United States. It also includes pursuit not only of the individuals directly involved in terrorist activity but also of their sources of support: the people and organizations that knowingly fund the terrorists and those that provide them with logistical assistance.

Mission Area 4: Protecting Critical Infrastructures and Key Assets

An attack on one or more pieces of our critical infrastructure could disrupt entire systems and cause significant damage. Programs that improve protection of the individual pieces and the interconnecting systems that make up our critical infrastructure belong in this fourth mission area. Programs associated with the physical security or cybersecurity of federal assets also belongs in this mission area. This area also includes programs designed to protect America's key assets, which are those unique facilities, sites, and structures whose disruption or destruction could have significant consequences, including national monuments and icons.

Mission Area 5: Defending against Catastrophic Threats

The fifth mission area includes homeland security programs that involve protecting against, detecting, deterring, or mitigating terrorists' use of weapons of mass destruction (WMD). It includes understanding terrorists' efforts to gain access to the expertise, technology, and materials needed to build chemical, biological, radiological, and nuclear (CBRN) weapons. In addition, this mission area includes funding for planning and efforts to decontaminate buildings, facilities, or geographic areas after a catastrophic event.

Mission Area 6: Emergency Preparedness and Response

This sixth mission area includes programs that prepare to minimize the damage of and recover from any future terrorist attacks that may occur despite our best efforts at prevention. This area includes programs that help to plan, equip, train, and practice the needed skills of the various first-responder units, including such groups as police officers, firefighters, emergency medical providers, public works personnel, and emergency management officials. This mission area also includes programs that will consolidate federal response plans and activities to build a national system for incident management in cooperation with state and local government.

The National Strategy describes four foundations for these six mission areas crossing all levels of government and sectors of society. These foundations are law, science and technology, information sharing and systems, and international cooperation. (See Figure I-3.)

Clearly these missions are all interrelated in many multi-dimensional ways. By imposing conceptual boundaries between these mission areas, one gains clarity for management and budgeting purposes. However, effective and viable plans and strategies can only be developed by acknowledging the complex reality that homeland efforts must cross mission areas, involve all levels of government and the private and public sectors, and coalesce into integrated, cross-cutting capabilities.

The last mission area—Emergency Preparedness and Response—merits special discussion, and is one area of homeland security where the notion of capabilities-based planning is being advanced. It also provides the context for discussing a macro-level tension in the field of homeland security. The December 2003 Gilmore Commission (formally known as the Advisory Panel to Assess Domestic Response Capabilities for Terrorism Involving Weapons of Mass Destruction) report defines preparedness as "the measurable demonstrated capacity by communities, States, and private sector entities throughout the United States to respond to acute threats with well-planned, well-coordinated, and effective efforts by all of the essential participants, including elected officials, police, fire, medical, public health, emergency managers, intelligence, community organizations, the media, and the public at large" (Gilmore Commission 2003, p. 8).

The National Strategy for Homeland Security established a "National Vision for Emergency Preparedness and Response" that made emergency response for terrorist attacks, no matter how unlikely or catastrophic, as well as all manner of natural disasters, a national requirement. Homeland Security Presidential Directive 8 (HSPD-8) refers to preparedness for major events as "all-hazards preparedness." It defines major events as "domestic terrorist attacks, major disasters, and other emergencies." It presented a "National Preparedness Goal" to help achieve this vision of preparedness.

It defines *preparedness* as the "existence of plans, procedures, policies, training, and equipment necessary at the federal, state, and local level to maximize the ability to prevent, respond to, and recover from major events" (The White House 2003, p. 2). As a result, homeland security policy must manage a tension between preparing for terrorism per se and the broadly scoped "national preparedness" construct (for any major disaster or emergency event, including terrorist attacks, as part of "all-hazards" planning (e.g., planning for natural disasters).

That is not to say that the capabilities required to prepare for terrorism and other emergencies are wholly separate. The Office of Domestic Preparedness (ODP), Universal Task List (UTL) Manual (Version 1.0 draft of July 31, 2004) divides preparedness tasks into four levels: (1) national strategic tasks; (2) planning, coordination, and support tasks; (3) incident management tasks; and (4) incident prevention and response tasks, as follows:

1. National strategic (primarily federal departments and agencies)

   - Develop national strategic intelligence
   - Manage national preparedness activities
   - Conduct national prevention operations
   - Provide command and management of incidents of national significance
   - Provide national incident support
   - Manage national resources
   - Provide national communications and information management support
   - Develop supporting national technologies

2. Planning, coordination, and support (primarily single states or groups of states, regions within states or counties, federal regions)

   - Conduct intelligence operations
   - Conduct preparedness activities
   - Conduct prevention operations
   - Command and manage incidents of national or state significance

- Provide incident support
- Manage regional and state resources
- Provide communications and information management support

3. Incident management (mayor, city manager, county executive, or emergency operations center)

  - Coordinate transportation operations
  - Operate and/or manage telecommunications and information technology
  - Manage and/or direct public works and engineering
  - Coordinate firefighting operations
  - Coordinate incident management operations
  - Coordinate mass care, housing, and human services
  - Coordinate resource support
  - Coordinate public health and medical services
  - Coordinate urban search and rescue
  - Coordinate oil and hazardous materials response
  - Coordinate agriculture and natural resource recovery
  - Coordinate energy recovery
  - Coordinate public safety and security
  - Coordinate community recovery, mitigation, and economic stabilization
  - Coordinate emergency public information and external communications

4. Incident Prevention and Response (incident site personnel)

  - Provide transportation
  - Operate telecommunications and information technology
  - Conduct public works and engineering
  - Conduct firefighting
  - Conduct incident management
  - Provide mass care, housing, and human services
  - Provide resource support
  - Provide public health and medical services
  - Conduct urban search and rescue

   • Conduct oil and hazardous materials response
   • Support agriculture and natural resource recovery
   • Support energy recovery
   • Provide public safety and security
   • Support community recovery, mitigation, and economic stabilization
   • Provide emergency public information and external communications

Clearly terrorism-focused homeland security programs and broader all-hazards preparedness efforts require sets of capabilities that overlap to a significant degree. Still, in a world of limited time and financial resources, efforts made in a preparedness context or framework that tries to be too all-encompassing may run the risk of being ineffective.

HOMELAND SECURITY: A POLICY FRAMEWORK

The National Strategy for Homeland Security is one of a set of national strategies that interrelate. (See Figure I-1.)

Homeland security needs to be understood in the context of the broad spectrum of policy, frameworks, and instruments of national power for combating terrorism and national preparedness. According to the Office of Management and Budget (OMB), homeland security is a subset of "combating terrorism," a policy framework that also includes "overseas combating terrorism" (OCT). Combating terrorism includes both antiterrorism (defensive measures used to combat terrorism) and counterterrorism (offensive measures used to combat terrorism), both domestically and abroad. (See Figure I-2.) Combating terrorism encompasses defense against WMD, improvements to critical infrastructure protection (CIP) to enhance the security of those physical and cyber-based systems essential to national security, national economic security, and public health and safety; and provision for federal "continuity of operations" (COOP—those activities of federal agencies that ensure that the "mission-essential" functions of each agency continue no matter the cause of the disruption, even in the face of a catastrophic event.

F I G U R E   I-1

Relationships between and among national strategies
related to combating terrorism

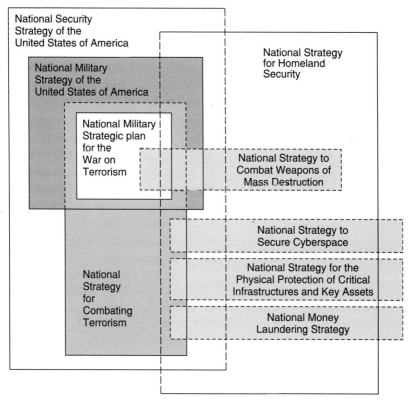

Source: GAO-03-5191 Combating Terrorism

Note: This graphic is intended to show relationships and overlaps among these
national strategies. The sizes and shapes of the boxes are not meant to imply the
relative importance of all the strategies.

Homeland security programs focus on activities within the
United States and its territories, or on activities in support of
domestically based systems and processes. The Homeland Security
Council (HSC) coordinates these activities governmentwide. OCT
includes activities that focus on combating and protecting against
terrorism that occurs outside the United States and its territories. Such
activities include efforts to detect, deter, protect against, and, if
needed, respond to terrorist attacks. OCT does not include funding

F I G U R E   I-2

Combating terrorism.

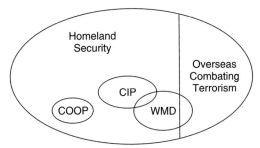

Source: Office of Management and Budget 2003 Report to Congress on Combating Terrorism (www.whitehouse.gov/omb/infreg/2003_combat_terr.pdf.).

Note: Not drawn to funding scale.

in support of the war on terrorism or other international conflicts. The National Security Council (NSC) coordinates these activities governmentwide. Together, the two areas account for the overall combating terrorism budget for the federal government.

Homeland security includes activities that focus on combating and protecting against terrorism that occur within the United States and its territories (this includes CIP and COOP), or outside the United States and its territories if they support domestically based systems or activities (e.g., prescreening high-risk cargo at overseas ports). Such activities include efforts to detect, deter, protect against, and, if necessary, respond to terrorist attacks.

HOMELAND SECURITY MUST BE INTEGRATED WITH OVERSEAS POLICY FRAMEWORKS

The center of gravity of homeland security is domestic and defensive. Yet terrorism is a transnational phenomenon, with roots and branches of recruiting, indoctrination, fund-raising, training, and attacking spread across the globe. Therefore, the counterterrorism "battle space" has "neither front lines nor geographic definition." As the *Final Report of the 9/11 Commission* noted:

> In this sense, 9/11 has taught us that terrorism against American interests "over there" should be regarded just as we regard terrorism

against America "over here." In this same sense, the American homeland is the planet.[1]

Because our society and economy are linked to and interdependent with the rest of the world, measures to defend the United States from threats such as a bomb in a cargo container extend internationally and depend on security efforts at foreign facilities. Many presumably domestic homeland security missions—border security and immigration, aviation and maritime security, intelligence, and law enforcement are some obvious examples—simply cannot be successful without international cooperation. Terrorists are finely attuned to differences in security regimes and will exploit seams between domestic and international counterterrorism.

Effective defensive measures influence a terrorist's choice of targets or mode of attack but fail to deter terrorists who are smart, adaptive, and willing to undertake suicide attacks. Although homeland security does aim to prevent terrorists from reaching American soil and attacking, and domestic counterterrorism may succeed in apprehending terrorists in the United States, proactively confronting terrorists before they even attempt to reach the United States is preferable.

The National Strategy for Homeland Security is a subset of the National Strategy for Combating Terrorism, which emphasizes that all instruments of U.S. power are needed in combating international terrorism, both "at home" and "overseas." In its final report the 9/11 Commission said:

> The first phase of our post-9/11 efforts rightly included military action to topple the Taliban and pursue al Qaeda. This work continues. But long-term success demands the use of all elements of national power: diplomacy, intelligence, covert action, law enforcement, economic policy, foreign aid, public diplomacy, and homeland defense. If we favor one tool while neglecting others, we leave ourselves vulnerable and weaken our national effort (pp. 363–364).

Homeland security, as a policy instrument, mostly does not address the intricate root causes that give rise to terrorism in the first place and the broader context of dangerous global "chaos" described in this book. Only economic policy, foreign aid, various types of diplomacy and conflict resolution, education and time can affect the root causes of terrorism; and ultimately it is foreign governments and civilian communities, as well as the United States, that will

FIGURE I-3

Homeland security in context.

The Global Context:
- Terrorism
- Religious fanaticism
- Emerging infectious diseases
- WMD proliferation
- Failed states, lawless territories and massacres
- Organized crime and trafficking in people, drugs, arms, toxic substances, gems
- Piracy
- Cyberattacks

National Guidance Documents:
- Legislation and Congressional Oversight
- National Strategies
- Homeland Security Presidential Directives (HSPD)
- National Security Presidential Directives (NSPD)
- National Response Plan (NRP)
- National Incident Management System (NIMS)

Policy Tools for Combating Terrorism:
- Homeland security
- Homeland defense
- Military force
- Diplomacy
- Foreign aid
- Economic policy
- Law enforcement
- Intelligence
- Covert action

National Strategy for Homeland Security:

Critical Mission Areas
- Intelligence and warning
- Border and transportation security
- Domestic counterterrorism
- Protecting critical infrastructures and key assets
- Defending against catastrophic threats
- Emergency preparedness and response

Political Context:
- Government organizational structure
- Funding
- Resource allocation
- Accountability
- Federalism
- Civil liberties (privacy, torture, speech)
- Role of military

Foundations
- Law
- Science and technology
- Information sharing and collaboration
- International cooperation

• Awareness	• Threat/hazard assessment (terrorism/natural/human-made) • Risk communication; information sharing and coordination; emergency notification • Vulnerability assessment/criticality assessment/preparedness assessment
• Prevention	• Detection (asset monitoring, screening people/baggage/cargo) • Threat elimination through counterterrorism law enforcement (apprehension of suspects; prosecution of terrorists, disrupt support, seize materials)
• Protection	• Secure assets (disperse/guard assets; target hardening/antiterrorism) • Mitigate risk (public health; asset protection; business continuity planning)
• Response	• Incident management (evacuation and shelter; isolation; assess emergency; decontamination) • Consequence management (victim care; hazard mitigation hazard; prophylaxis) • Assist victims (healthcare, social services)
• Recovery	• Restore/reconstitute/rebuild infrastructure, utilities, government services, economic institutions and property

Analytical Frameworks:

Results Management
- Capabilities–based–planning
- Program performance assessment
- Strategic planning
- Scenario-based planning
  - Mission area analysis
  - Universal task list
- Risk management

Figure courtesy of DGK LLC Homeland Security Management Consulting (www.kamien.com)

need to make hard decisions and take action in order to undermine support for terrorist ideology. Clearly, the success of overall counter-terrorism depends on internal and external integration of all national and international policy tools, strategies, and measures—including homeland security—into a carefully orchestrated global effort leaving no gaps in security that terrorists can exploit. (See Figure I-3.)

Whether or not the broader counterterrorism strategy is achieving its aims, delegitimizing terrorism and reducing the influence of the economic, political, religious, social, and psycholo-gical factors that motivate a person's decision to use terror tactics is beyond the scope of this text. Regardless, it is unlikely that Islamist terrorists will cease to view the United States as an enemy anytime soon.

As long as the threat of terrorism and other disasters exists, as evidenced by the recent bombing in London, homeland security will remain relevant and important.

See also Chapter 16 **Homeland Security's National Strategic Position: Goals, Objectives, Measures Assessment** and Chapter 18 **The Department of Defense: Defending the Homeland and Defeating Enemies Abroad**.

N O T E S

1. The National Commission on Terrorist Attacks Upon the United States, Final Report - Chapter 12: "What To Do? A Global Strategy," p. 362

Al-Qaida and Global Jihad

CHAPTER 1

Introduction to Section 1

Rohan Kumar Gunaratna, Ph.D.
Head of Terrorism Research and Associate Professor
Institute for Defense and Strategic Studies, Singapore

Section 1 serves as an introduction to al-Qaida's worldview, shared by the radical Salafi Islamist groups engaged in global jihad. This perspective is particularly important as al-Qaida evolves from a terror network to a movement, with or without Usama bin Ladin at its helm.

Al-Qaida and its affiliates are gaining as violence in Iraq radicalizes Muslims, inspiring new groups and bolstering existing ones. Exploiting porous borders, neighboring Islamist groups, notably in Saudi Arabia, are increasingly participating in the Iraqi campaign; and, as in Afghanistan during the occupation by the Soviet Union, the fighting is drawing Muslims from as far away as North America, Europe, and Africa. Just as fighting in Afghanistan incubated al-Qaida, the fighting in Iraq is likely to produce new radical Islamists. Images from Iraq may have a greater impact on Muslims, both in their native Middle East and Asia and in the migrant communities of the West, than even pictures of the Israeli-Palestinian conflict.

New al-Qaida cells are growing in various parts of the world. Having no operational contact with definable groups, these cells are hard to detect. In addition to mounting attacks within Iraq, new groups in North America and Europe will probably be inspired to attack their host countries.

Al-Qaida offers operational know-how to Salafi jihad groups, such as Algeria's Salafi Group for Call and Combat; various Pakistani groups; and Abu Mus'ab al-Zawkari's "al-Qaida in Iraq," the most active Islamist group affiliated with al-Qaida. Al-Zawkari is also heading parts of al-Qaida's global network, left leaderless after successful operations by the Coalition. (This is the U.S.-led military Coalition to disarm Iraq of its weapons of mass destruction and enforce 17 UNSC resolutions.) His network is becoming multinational by aggressively using the Internet and wealthy western Europeans to recruit poor Muslims from Eastern Europe and the Balkans seeking to fight in Iraq. Although al-Zawkari's attacks in Germany, France, and Great Britain have been prevented, he maintains a network of hundreds in Europe. Despite 150 arrests in 10 European countries, he continues to receive funds and recruits from Europe and Canada. Al-Zawkari will probably continue to strike both within and outside Iraq, possibly using unconventional agents. A chemical attack sponsored by al-Zawkari, which was meant to kill several thousand U.S. and Jordanian nationals, was frustrated in Amman, Jordan, in the spring of 2004.

As Ahmed Hashim discusses in Chapter 2 on al-Qaida's goals, strategies, and operational art, its radical Islamic jihad involves the use of force to eject all occupying infidels from any land which is, or ever was, under Muslim rule. Usama bin Ladin casts this jihad as an apocalyptic struggle to defend the Muslim world against the conspiracy of Americans, "puppet" secular Arab regimes, and Jews. In Chapter 3 David Cook explores the role of Islam and other motivating factors in the appeal of bin Ladin to his constituencies. He explains that this charismatic scholar-warrior appears to his constituency as an "incorruptible loner" who speaks the truth that Muslim tyrants and foreign infidels refuse to hear and points the way to a return to the glorious days of the first century, when Islam was a leading empire. In Chapter 4 Marc Sageman debunks the common stereotype of terrorism as perpetrated by poor, naive young men from the third world who are vulnerable to brainwashing. The terrorists he examined were either upwardly mobile men studying abroad or second-generation residents in the West, separated from their original culture and social origins. These lonely, alienated men were marginalized and prevented from advancement in their new society. They drifted to mosques and found a new sense of self through religious affiliation, which strengthened fraternal bonds that continued to intensify over time as they became increasingly part of the context of the mosque and its ideology.

In Chapter 5 Sara Daly and Scott Gerwehr detail various models al-Qaida may be using to attract new members; approaches to recruitment; characteristics of potential recruits; and *nodes*—centers of activity, such as mosques, universities, and charities—where al-Qaida's recruiters seek new members and where potential recruits are likely to become acquainted with the radical jihadist worldview.

Michael Knapp in Chapter 6 sheds light on how central the Internet is to the strategy of al-Qaida and the global jihad against Muslim governments and populations as well as against the United States and its western allies, and to the spread of its violent message of global jihad to sympathetic Islamic audiences. Al-Qaida has proved to be a wily, creative, and adaptive adversary that appreciates the value of the global electronic and print mass media as a primary weapon of psychological warfare or perception management, recruitment, and fund-raising.

The most profound development related to al-Qaida since 9/11 is its transformation from a group to the self-proclaimed vanguard of Islamic movements, galvanizing Islamists worldwide to fight two battles: against their own governments and against the United States and its allies. Al-Qaida's members work with three dozen Islamist groups that they financed and trained in Afghanistan in the 1990s. Through the Internet, using couriers, visiting combat tacticians and expert trainers, al-Qaida is sharing its expertise to reinforce the multinational mujahideen campaign in Afghanistan against the United States and its allies. Like-minded groups copy al-Qaida's tactics and techniques, such as coordinated, simultaneous suicide attacks. For instance, in August 2004 a car bomb circuit recovered in London was identical to the design used in Saudi Arabia and Iraq. Imitating al-Qaida's tactics, Chechen groups conducted spectacular attacks against a theater in Moscow, blew up two flights in midair, and attacked a school in Beslan. Another local jihad group that was willing to follow al-Qaida's prescriptions was a separatist Muslim group that beheaded a Buddhist teacher in southern Thailand.

Without cooperation between governments, al-Qaida's affiliated groups in the Middle East, the former Soviet Union, Asia, and Africa will grow and tap into the resentment of Muslims, drawing support and recruits. The dispersal of its members and associates has increased the threshold of violence significantly. In place of Afghanistan, Pakistan and Iraq have emerged as new centers of international terrorism.

The intent to strike "crusader and Jewish" targets has not diminished. Al-Qaida's planners are probing the loopholes and gaps in the post-9/11 security architecture to strike once again on western soil. Between 2001 and 2004, nearly 100 medium- to large-scale terrorist attacks against U.S., European, and Australian targets were thwarted by heightened public vigilance, unprecedented security, intelligence, law enforcement, military cooperation, and the proactive targeting of cells planning and preparing attacks. For example, in 2004 British authorities were able to neutralize cells planning theatrical attacks against British and American targets, meant as a fully transferable template for attacking other target countries. However, because al-Qaida's capabilities have suffered, the bulk of the attacks will be on the scale of Madrid, Bali, Casablanca, Riyadh, Istanbul, Karachi, Beslan, and Jidda and will continue to focus on the Middle East, Asia, and Africa.

Today, over 95 percent of terrorist groups originate in the Middle East and Asia. Nonetheless, Islamists have recruited and raised funds in North America, Europe, Australia, New Zealand, and Japan—liberal democracies where they can operate more freely.

At the same time, under threat of retaliation by the United States, Arab state sponsorship of terrorism has declined. Only Iran and Syria continue to support groups that engage in terrorism. Rather than isolate Iran, it is imperative for the West to engage Tehran. The removal of Saddam Hussein, who was a buffer between the Shia and the Sunni Muslims, has created the conditions for them to work together. The western failure to engage Iran against al-Qaida will strengthen the hand of the Iranian hard-liners who want to destabilize Iraq and assist anti-American Shia and Sunni Islamists.

The United States' most serious counterterrorist failures regarding al-Qaida have been diverting to Iraq resources that are needed to neutralize al-Qaida, and not maximizing the opportunity to rebuild Afghanistan into a model Muslim country. In 2003–2004, al-Qaida, the Taliban, and Hezb-i-Islami reemerged as a credible force in Afghanistan. Unless these threatening groups are neutralized, they will strike periodically, seeking to assassinate President Hamid Karzai.

The immediate threat of terrorism can be reduced by targeting operational cells and advancing intergovernmental collaboration by establishing common databases and sharing personnel and other resources. However, as the terrorists' operational infrastructures become more compartmentalized, they become harder to detect. Armed conflict generates new terrorists and supporters, and the failure to target ideology ensures that the threat will remain. The ideology that underpins radical Islamic activities around the world must be countered. (See Figure 1-1.) To end the violence, governments will have to think beyond the traditional counterterrorism practitioners' tool kit.

While authoritarian regimes such as Saudi Arabia aggressively target violent Islamists, democracies such as Malaysia should search for political solutions to contain or coexist with the Islamists. Some groups that practice political violence, including terrorism, are willing to negotiate, so it is essential to bring warring parties together and sustain protracted conflict-management dialogue with politically marginalized groups. The international community should facilitate negotiation between warring factions in Palestine, Chechnya, Kashmir, Mindanao (Philippines), Maluku and Poso (Indonesia), Algeria, Afghanistan, and Iraq. A lesson from Israel is that even with the best intelligence and strike capabilities, terrorism cannot be ended without containing extremism and targeting conceptual as well as operational infrastructures. As jihad organizations misrepresent the Quran, it is necessary for society to develop powerful countering visions. Such a response can be formulated not by the United States or Europe, but by the Muslim world, with the steadfast support of western nations.

FIGURE 1-1

Key areas of radical Islamic activities since 1992.

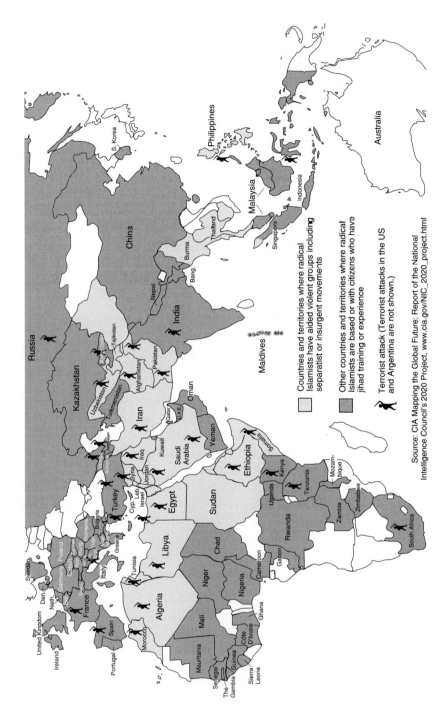

Countries and territories where radical Islamists have aided violent groups including separatist or insurgent movements

Other countries and territories where radical Islamists are based or with citizens who have jihad training or experience

Terrorist attack (Terrorist attacks in the US and Argentina are not shown.)

Source: CIA Mapping the Global Future: Report of the National Intelligence Council's 2020 Project, www.cia.gov/NIC_2020_project.html

CHAPTER 2

Al-Qaida: Origins, Goals, and Grand Strategy

Ahmed S. Hashim
Professor of Strategic Studies, United States Naval War College

INTRODUCTION

About a year after 9/11—though without actually assuming responsibility for it—Usama bin Ladin wrote a letter to the American people outlining the reasons for al-Qaida's vehement opposition to the United States and presenting advice and a warning. His argument ran as follows:

- First, "You attacked us in Palestine." This territory had been occupied for 80 years; it was seized from the Ottoman Empire by the British and then given to the Jews, who killed or scattered the Palestinians; and the "creation, nurturing, and protection of Israel is a great crime and you are the leaders of this crime." The crime "has to be erased. . . . Everyone who has polluted him- or herself with this crime has to pay for it, and pay for it heavily."

- Second, "You attacked us in Somalia"; and elsewhere in the Muslim world, the United States encouraged others to kill Muslims (e.g., Russia in Chechnya and India in Kashmir).

- Third, the United States supports puppets in the Arab and Islamic worlds, thereby precluding legitimate Islamic

---

Note: This chapter is based on a forthcoming book. The views expressed are the author's and do not necessarily represent those of the Naval War College, the Department of the Navy, or the Department of Defense.

governments and the implementation of the sharia (Islamic law based on the Quran).

+ Fourth, the United States has a neocolonial policy of exploiting the Islamic countries—"You ransack our lands, stealing our treasures and oil.... This theft is indeed the biggest theft ever witnessed in the history of the world."

+ Fifth, "Your forces occupy our lands, spreading your ideology and thereby polluting the hearts of our people."

By now, there is a vast literature on 9/11 and al-Qaida. I will not summarize it; rather, this chapter is intended to correct some erroneous ideas about Usama bin Ladin and al-Qaida, particularly regarding ideology, which make it difficult to combat him and his organization. For instance, one political scientist described al-Qaida as a sort of doomsday cult:

> What we are up against is apocalyptic nihilism. The nihilism of their means—the indifference to human costs—takes their action not only out of the realm of politics, but even out of the realm of war itself. The apocalyptic nature of their goals makes it absurd to believe that they are making political demands at all.[1]

This is inaccurate; it suggests either a misunderstanding of al-Qaida or a superficial analysis. I would argue that bin Ladin is political: he has defined goals, a worldview, and a strategy that assumes that violence is effective against an enemy. Ideology is central to his methods of warfare. Accordingly, this chapter is based on analysis of the statements and rhetoric of al-Qaida's leadership in order to analyze its origins, objectives, and grand strategy.[2]

ORIGINS OF AL-QAIDA[3]

Usama bin Mohammed bin Ladin was born in Riyadh, Saudi Arabia, in 1957. He was the seventeenth of 52 children (and the seventh son) of Sheikh Mohammed bin Ladin, who came to Saudi Arabia, destitute, in 1930 from the Hadramawt region of Yemen and died a billionaire in 1968, in an airplane crash.[4] The family had become the wealthiest in the construction industry in Saudi Arabia, associated financially and personally with the royal family.

It is difficult to get a clear picture of Usama bin Ladin's early years. His father was evidently dominating and domineering, and imposed discipline and a strict social and religious code on his children. According to some accounts Usama was quite religious, living in a city—Jeddah—where he was exposed to the thoughts of many Islamic scholars. Others maintain that he was not at all religious and had absorbed liberal ideas from his Syrian mother, a progressive woman who was his father's fourth wife. Usama attended King Abdul Aziz University in Jeddah and in 1979 earned a degree in economics and management, or perhaps in civil engineering. He never lived or studied in the West. He apparently took up radical politics out of a distaste for, and frustration with, the conditions prevailing in his own society.

The year 1979 marked a transformation in Usama bin Ladin's life. Early that year, an Iranian revolution led by an ascetic cleric, Ayatollah Ruhollah Khomeini, toppled the shah, Muhammad Reza Pahlavi, who had been a pillar of the United States' security and economic interests in the Persian Gulf. On March 26 Egypt and Israel made a peace that was denounced by many Arabs and Muslims worldwide. In December, the Soviet Union invaded Afghanistan, a Muslim country with an unstable Marxist puppet government. This last event, at least, had a profound impact on bin Ladin. He later said in an interview, "When the invasion of Afghanistan started, I was enraged and went there at once. I arrived within days, before the end of 1979."[5]

Bin Ladin may not actually have reached Afghanistan that soon, but he did indeed consider the invasion an act by an external, infidel enemy and thus directed his wrath against the invaders rather than against the internal oppressors. Also, the jihad in Afghanistan— in which he and a contingent of Muslim volunteers from Arab countries fought the Soviet troops to a standstill—confronted him with the military and technological strength of a superpower. He was at once impressed (by the invaders' ruthlessness) and disdainful: "The myth of the superpower was destroyed not only in my mind but also in the minds of all Muslims."[6]

In Afghanistan bin Ladin began to develop his concept of the outside enemy. He told a French journalist in 1995, "I did not fight against the communist threat while forgetting the peril from the west.... I discovered that it was not enough to fight in Afghanistan, but that we had to fight on all fronts against communist or western oppression. The urgent thing was communism, but the next target was America.... This is an open war up to the end, until victory."[7]

That is, he and the Afghan guerrillas had been aligned with the Americans solely because they were fighting a common enemy. It is not clear what relationship, if any, he had with the Central Intelligence Agency (CIA), which was pouring money and arms into Afghanistan; if he did accept funds and weapons, that simply indicated his willingness to collaborate operationally with one ideological enemy against another.

The war in Afghanistan revealed bin Ladin's modus operandi, political and organizational skills, flexibility, and opportunism. Contrary to popular belief, he did not rush into Afghanistan, AK-47 in hand, to do battle. The jihad was not simply a matter of fighting, dying, and killing in the name of God. It also required extensive preparation, a logistical infrastructure, political support for the Afghan fighters, funds, and the recruitment of Muslim volunteers from other parts of the Islamic world. Between 1979 and 1982, in fact, bin Ladin was in Afghanistan for only short periods. He made several trips out to collect money and materiel for the guerrillas. In late 1982 he took back construction and earth-moving machinery; a friend, an Iraqi engineer, used it to dig tunnels and caves in the mountains in Bakhhar Province for hospitals and weapons depots.

In 1984 bin Ladin formalized his role in the Afghan conflict, establishing a guest house in Peshawar for Muslim volunteers, and co-founding (with the Palestinian Islamist 'Abdullah 'Azzam) a propaganda and charity organization, Maktab al Khidamat, or Jihad Service Bureau, whose publications attracted thousands of Arabs and other Muslims to fight in the war. At the height of the conflict the "Afghan Arabs" included 15,000 from Saudi Arabia, 5,000 from Yemen, 3,000 to 5,000 from Egypt, 2,000 from Algeria, 1,000 from the Arab states of the Gulf, 1,000 from Libya, and several hundred from Iraq. Apparently bin Ladin facilitated their entry into Afghanistan.[8] He commanded some of the Afghan Arabs, and in 1986 he entered the battle himself. Among the fighters under his command were former senior military officers from Egypt and Syria, with combat experience and with training in the Soviet Union.[9]

Bin Ladin continued to address preparations and infrastructure and cultivated people in high places as a source of funds. In 1988, realizing that he needed better documentation of the activities of the Afghan Arabs and a formalized structure to keep track of their movements and casualties, he set up *al-Qaida* ("the base").

It developed into a clearinghouse for many loosely aligned radical Islamic organizations.[10]

Thus if bin Ladin entered Afghanistan as a dilettante, he left as a committed believer—though apart from expressing his view of the enemy and realizing that the enemy was not "ten feet tall," he set down little in the way of political philosophy or worldview. In 1989 the Soviets, defeated, withdrew from Afghanistan. Bin Ladin believed that the Afghan Arabs had contributed in no small measure to the collapse of the Soviet Union.

When bin Ladin returned to Saudi Arabia in 1989, he focused on another enemy, Saddam Hussein of Iraq, whom he saw as a greedy, aggressive secular Arab nationalist threatening Mecca and Medina. In August 1990 Iraq invaded Kuwait. Bin Ladin suggested that Saudi Arabia augment its defense with thousands of former Afghan Arabs, but to his dismay the royal family called on the Americans, infidels, to defend the holy places. In 1998, in his declaration of a "World Islamic Front for Jihad against the Jews and Crusaders," he said:

> Since God laid down the Arabian Peninsula, created its desert, and surrounded it with its seas, no calamity has ever befallen it like these Crusader hosts that have spread in it like locusts, crowding its soil, eating its fruits, and destroying its verdure; and this at a time when the nations contend against the Muslims like diners jostling around a bowl of food.[11]

Consequently, in 1995 he made his first major critique of the Saudi regime, in an "Open Letter to King Fahd," accusing the royal family of being uncommitted to Islam, squandering public funds and oil revenues, failing to develop a viable defense policy, and depending on non-Muslims for protection. In fact, he came close to denying the political legitimacy of the al-Sauds. He also advocated small-scale attacks against U.S. forces in the kingdom. The royal family stripped him of his nationality and exiled him, first to Sudan and then to Afghanistan. Not long afterward, there were attacks on U.S. facilities in Dhahran (1995) and Khobar (1996). Bin Ladin did not claim responsibility, but (as he would later typically do) he applauded the perpetrators: "What happened...when 24 Americans were killed in two bombings is clear evidence of the huge anger of Saudi people against America. The Saudis now know their real enemy is America."[12]

The political basis for bin Ladin's confrontation with the United States is found in the so-called Ladinese Epistle: "Declaration of War against the Americans Occupying the Land of the Two Holy Places," issued on 23 August 1996.[13] Muslims, he said, from Palestine to Iraq, from Chechnya to Bosnia, have been slaughtered, their lands expropriated, and their wealth looted by non-Muslims:

> The people of Islam [have] suffered from aggression, iniquity, and injustice imposed on them by the Zionist-Crusaders alliance and their collaborators, to the extent that the Muslims' blood became the cheapest and their wealth was loot in the hands of enemies. Their blood was spilled in Palestine and Iraq. The horrifying pictures of the massacre of Qana, in Lebanon, are still fresh in our memory. Massacres in [Tajikistan, Burma, Kashmir, Assam, the Philippines, Somalia, Chechnya, and Bosnia-Herzegovina] took place, massacres that send shivers in the body and shake the conscience.[14]

America was said to be implicated because it had provided arms; for example, American weapons were used in the killing of hundreds of Lebanese civilians in Qana in 1996 after the Israeli Operation Grapes of Wrath. Also, America was accused of standing passively by as Muslim civilians were massacred in the Yugoslav civil war, and as the Russians slaughtered Chechens; and of supporting the depredations of Arab and Muslim rulers against their own people.

However, the focus of bin Ladin's anger in the epistle of 1996 was the continued American "occupation"—permitted by the corrupt royal family at a time when Saudi Arabia was demoralized and economically distressed—of the land of the holy places:

> Everyone [has] agreed that the situation cannot be rectified ... unless the root of the problem is tackled. Hence it is essential to hit the main enemy who divided the *umma* [the Islamic community] into small and little countries and pushed it, for the last few decades, into a state of confusion. The Zionist-Crusader alliance moves quickly to contain and abort any "corrective movement" appearing in the Islamic countries.[15]

Therefore, one of the most important duties of Muslims is to "push the Americans out of the holy land." To lend weight to his argument, bin Ladin quoted a medieval Islamic jurist, Ibn Taymiyyah, who had said when Muslims face a serious threat, they must ignore minor differences and collaborate to get the enemy out of *dar al-Islam* ("the abode of Islam"). Bin Ladin said:

> If there [is] more than one duty to be carried out, then the most important one should receive priority. Clearly after belief (*imaan*) there is no more important duty than pushing the American enemy out of the holy land.... The ill effect of ignoring these [minor] differences, at a given period of time, is much less than the ill effect of the occupation of the Muslims' land by the great *kufr* [unbelief].[16]

If the Muslims fight one another instead of the great *kufr*, they will incur casualties, exhaust their own economic and financial resources, destroy their infrastructure and oil industries, and expose themselves to even greater control by the Zionist-Crusader alliance.

This epistle of 1996 also expresses bin Ladin's disdain for the United States. According to bin Ladin, after the attacks on American installations in Saudi Arabia, William Perry (who was then the secretary of defense) said that the explosions had "taught him one lesson: that is, not to withdraw when attacked by coward terrorists." Bin Ladin's response indicates his mindset: "We say to the defense secretary that his talk can induce a grieving mother to laughter!...Where was this false courage of yours when the explosion in Beirut took place in 1983?...You [were] turned into scattered pits and pieces at that time.... The extent of your impotence and weaknesses became very clear."

Bin Ladin, then, sees the United States as a paper tiger—and this assumption may be a crack in the edifice of his goals and worldview.

AL-QAIDA'S GOALS

Goal 1: Remove U.S. Forces from the Arabian Peninsula and the U.S. Presence from the Islamic World

Nothing seems to have infuriated Usama bin Ladin more than the United States' presence in the Arabian Peninsula; he once described its entry there as "arbitrary and a reckless action."[17] Removing the Americans from the land of the "two holy mosques" (i.e., Saudi Arabia) has been a goal since the early 1990s. After two attacks on U.S. installations, bin Ladin told a western journalist that "every day the Americans delay their departure, they will receive a new corpse."[18] The presence of U.S. forces in the land of the two holy mosques is considered sacrilegious: "Now infidels walk everywhere on the land where Muhammad was born and where the Koran was revealed to him."[19] In an interview after the attacks on the U.S. embassies in Nairobi and Dar es Salaam in 1999, bin Ladin said that the "International Islamic Front for Jihad against the U.S. and Israel has issued a crystal-clear fatwa calling on the Islamic nation to carry on *jihad* aimed at liberating holy sites. The nation of Muhammad has responded to this appeal."[20] Moreover, the American presence humiliates the Muslims of the peninsula, is morally corrupting, is socially and economically destructive, and threatens the entire Islamic world because the United States uses the peninsula to launch "aggressive crusades" against other Muslim territories (i.e., Iraq and Afghanistan).[21]

Contrary to what most western observers assume, bin Ladin is not only interested in the foreign presence in Saudi Arabia he is also concerned about the rest of the Islamic world. He and others believe that Muslims are still suffering from neocolonialism. Thus his discourse is anticolonial as well as Islamic. He believes, for instance, that the West wants to keep Iraq weak and unstable, a sentiment echoed by his lieutenants:

> The campaign against Iraq has aims that go beyond Iraq to target the Arab and Islamic world. It aims at crushing any effective military force neighboring Israel. It also aims to confirm Israel's uncontested monopoly over weapons of mass destruction in the region, so as to ensure the submission of Arab and Islamic states to its wishes and ambitions.[22]

Goal 1 was reinforced and disseminated in late 2002 by al-Qaida's official media person, Suleiman Abu Ghaith: "The liberation of our holy places and countries headed by Palestine and the land of the two holy mosques is the sublime aim, to which all efforts and energies must be devoted."[23]

Goal 2: Overthrow Illegitimate Regimes in Arab and Islamic Countries and Establish Islamic Systems

Usama bin Ladin considers himself a social commentator on the Arab state system and believes that the regimes in the Arab and Islamic countries have been failures and must be overthrown so as to establish pristine Islamic systems.

First, these regimes have failed their people. Bin Ladin said in 1998: "For the enforcement of Shariat (sic), it is essential for all Muslims that they should establish an Islamic system on the basis of the teachings of the Prophet Mohammed."[24] Especially, the house of Saud in Saudi Arabia has failed the tests of legitimacy— application of Islamic law and meeting the people's needs:

> The regime started under the flag of applying Islamic law and under this banner all the people of Saudi Arabia came to help the Saudi family take power. 'Abdul Aziz (the founder of the modern Saudi state in 1932) did not apply Islamic law; the country was set up for his family.[25]

Bin Ladin continues, referring to the American presence after Operation Desert Storm:

> At the same time, the financial crisis happened inside the kingdom, and now all the people suffer from this.... Prices are going up and people have to pay more for electricity, water and fuel.... Education is deteriorating and people have to take their children from government schools and put them in private education, which is very expensive.
>
> The ordinary man knows that his country is the largest oil producer in the world, yet at the same time he suffers from taxes and bad services. Now the people understand the speeches of the ulemas in the mosques—that our country has become an American colony.[26]

The second failure is that the "region's states are in one way or another agents for the United States and Israel."[27] According to bin Ladin, the ostensible leaders of the Muslim countries are either collaborationists or too cowardly to stand up against the despoliation of their peoples and lands. Those who support the United States "are apostates and outside the community of Muslims. It is permissible to spill their blood and take their property."[28] Therefore, he exhorts Muslims to overthrow these regimes:

> We also stress to honest Muslims that they should move, incite, and mobilize the (Islamic) nation, amid such grave events and hot atmosphere so as to liberate themselves from those unjust and renegade ruling regimes, which are enslaved by the United States. They should also do so to establish the rule of God on earth.[29]

In an interview with Al-Jazeera in 2003, Ayman al-Zawahiri excoriated the Pakistani leader Pervez Musharraf for allowing the United States to use Pakistan as a base from which to attack the Afghan Taliban regime and al-Qaida. And in 2004, regarding the plan of the Bush administration to promote democratic reform in the Middle East, he said:

> America has nothing to do with reform. The truth of what it is seeking is to replace the current regimes with new regimes. The alleged American reforms can never achieve for us our independence or pride. The human rights they are advocating are the rights of the criminal to humiliation of the Muslim. The true reform plan begins from within us.[30]

Many people in the Middle East—such as those from western-ized and secularized social strata—who reject al-Qaida's ideo-logy would nevertheless agree with al-Zawahiri that U.S. policy is inequitable and hypocritical. Even those who believe that the United States is a democracy characterized by the rule of law do not believe that Americans sincerely want to spread such values. Al-Qaida's second-in-command has said that "Iraq does not enjoy freedom and security. All that has happened is that Iraq moved from the tyrannical control of a secularist despotic anti-Islam ruler to a Crusader occupation that fights Islam, that kills, arrests, and tortures whomever it wants."[31]

Goal 3: Liberate al-Aqsa Mosque in Jerusalem and Recover Palestine

Israel, which al-Qaida (among other Islamist groups and Arab nationalists) refers to as the "Zionist entity," is considered a per-manent enemy with which no compromise is possible. In bin Ladin's words: "He who claims there will be a lasting peace between us and the Jews is an infidel.... We are in a decisive battle with the Jews and those who support them from the crusaders and the Zionists."[32]

There are several reasons for this attitude. First, bin Ladin sees the enmity between Muslims and Jews as historical and deep-rooted. Second, according to modern ideology, Israel as a state exists at the expense of Muslims. It has dispossessed the Palestinians and has occupied al-Aqsa mosque, a holy shrine of Islam. Thus Israel is illegitimate and must be destroyed. Third, Israel is a dagger pointed at the Islamic community. It was established with the help of the West and has been supported politically, financially, and militarily by the United States. Fourth, Israel is a launching place for assaults by Zionists and neocrusaders against the Islamic *umma*. Bin Ladin has declared: "Let the whole world know that we shall never accept that the tragedy of Andalucia [i.e., the loss of Spain to the infidel] would be repeated in Palestine. We cannot accept that Palestine will become Jewish."[33]

Goal 4: Save the Arab Countries, Particularly Iraq and the Islamic World, from Disintegration at the Hands of the "Zionist-Crusader" Conspiracy

There is a theory that U.S. forces and the "Zionist entity" in the Middle East are intended (among other things) to break up the most important and powerful Arab countries—specifically, Egypt, Iraq, and Saudi Arabia—into controllable "statelets" that cannot threaten Israel. This was first expounded by Arab nationalists in the 1960s and 1970s and has since been adopted by Islamists. Six months before the U.S. military campaign in Iraq, Ayman al-Zawahiri presented what he considered the "hidden" reasons for it:

> The campaign against Iraq has aims that go beyond Iraq into the Arab Islamic world. Its first aim is to destroy any effective military force in the proximity of Israel.
>
> Its second aim is to consolidate the supremacy of Israel with weapons of mass destruction in the region without any rival. This is to ensure that subjugation of the Arabic Islamic countries is complete, to the wishes and greed of Israel. America without any shyness aids the refusal of Israel to commit itself to any agreement that will terminate its weapons of mass destruction.... The attack on Iraq is expected to extend to Iran and Pakistan....
>
> Its third and biggest aim is to split the Arab world into smaller states that are incapable of protecting themselves. The whole incursion is being executed to protect the security of Israel....
>
> We implore the Muslim nation to act immediately.[34]

His reasoning would be found persuasive by many people in the Middle East, including some with no sympathy for al-Qaida.

AL-QAIDA'S GRAND STRATEGY

"Grand strategy" refers to the theory and practice of attaining or implementing goals. It emerges from the relationship between goals and means[35] and, I would argue, has three components: (1) a world-view that implies goals, (2) a philosophy of action, and (3) means or resources to implement the goals. Individuals, organizations, states, and nonstate actors such as al-Qaida all have goals.

Al-Qaida's Worldview

Al-Qaida sees a dire threat to *dar al-Islam* ("the abode of Islam"). Its worldview includes two fundamental ideas: first, that the war between Islam and America is a conflict between good and evil; second, that the present threat to Islam is the most vicious and most concentrated in its history. Although the Christian West has attacked *dar al-Islam* in the past, the contemporary assault is unprecedented. Usama bin Ladin said in 1997:

> I emphasize that this war will not only be between the two people of the sacred mosques and the Americans, but it will be between the Islamic world and the Americans and their allies, because this war is a new crusade led by America against the Islamic nations.[36]

Christendom and Islam: From Crusade to Crusade?

Since the Middle East has a long memory, it is instructive to review the historical relationship between Christendom and Islam. Christian and Muslim states and empires have engaged in regular commercial intercourse, have often eyed each other warily, and have sometimes warred with each other.[37]

The battle of Tours, in France, halted the northward expansion of the Arab-Muslim armies into Europe, but the most significant interaction in medieval times was the Crusades in the Holy Land—religious wars that lasted for two centuries.[38] The Crusaders established and ruled little principalities or enclaves, but eventually the Muslims expelled them. Today, the Crusades have enormous symbolic importance in the Islamic world. Many Muslims believe that they are under a new crusader assault by the Christian West. This is a major theme for Usama bin Ladin, who holds that the U.S. and western political and military presence, technological dominance, and attacks on Arab and Islamic lands are part of the new crusade. He expressed this idea in an interview with Al-Jazeera in October 2001, when the United States was assaulting Afghanistan in order to destroy al-Qaida and overthrow the Taliban. Later that year he described the United States' operations in Afghanistan as a "fierce crusade" by an enemy with an "unspeakable hatred for Islam."[39] Still later, when the United States and its coalition were about to invade Iraq, bin Ladin urged the Muslim peoples not to "think that the war will be between the United States and Iraq or between Bush and Saddam. It is between you, all our Muslim brothers, and us on one side and the crusaders and Jews on the other."[40]

The Rise of the West and the Decline of Islam

In the early modern and modern eras, the competition between Christians and Islam continued; ultimately, the military balance of power would tilt in favor of the West, with profound consequences.

However, before that happened—although the Arabs faded from prominence and their place was taken by the Ottoman Turks—the political and military balance of power had remained stable for centuries. At the battle of Lepanto in 1571, a Christian fleet annihilated an Ottoman fleet, but the Christian West remained fearful of Turkish military prowess, especially after the Turks tried to seize Vienna in 1525 and 1683.

In the sixteenth and seventeenth centuries, the Christian West experienced profound political, ideological, socioeconomic, technological, and military changes. These changes included a decisive separation of church and state—so that we must now talk of "the West" rather than of "Christendom"—and the emergence of uncontested military and technological superiority, which enabled the West to invade and colonize its rivals. This was symbolized by Napoleon's ephemeral but historically significant invasion of Egypt. Sadik al-'Azm has noted that "the massive difference between the effects of the Crusades and the results of the French expedition of 1798 distills the essence of European modernity."[41]

The rise of the West and the decline of the East occasioned much discussion by eastern ruling circles and intellectuals, for whom reform became a rallying cry. The Egypt of Muhammad Ali and the Ottoman and Persian empires strove, though unsuccessfully, to close the gap between them and the West.[42] The collapse of the Ottoman Empire in 1918 following its defeat in World War I meant the end of the last major Muslim power. The Arabic-speaking peoples who had been a part of the Ottoman Empire then sought to found an independent Arab state, or states.

Colonialism, Nationalism, and Modernization

Despite the persistence of European colonialism after World War I, Arabs were optimistic. Many Arab thinkers accepted European notions of secular nationalism and modernity and objected to colonialism specifically because it resulted in underdevelopment and illegitimate puppet regimes. Others rejected secular, liberal nationalism, because of its association with Britain and France; espoused radical nationalism and far-right ideologies; and were sympathetic to Nazi Germany and fascist Italy. In either case Arabs saw their salvation in western ideas; very few advocated a return to the precepts of Islam.

Even when independence came, in the 1950s and 1960s, many Arab thinkers and some rulers continued to believe in modernization through a nationalist, socialist agenda. The "enlightened" Arab dictators of these years wanted—but did not get—a modern society, a dynamic economy, and a powerful army. According to Fouad Ajami, Israel's victory in the Six-Day War of 1967 was the Waterloo of Arab secular nationalism. That war was a sad commentary on the entire Arab world, particularly the modernizing regimes, which were revealed as corrupt and futile:

> Syria had the worst army of all the Arab countries bordering Israel. The reason was that it was not designed to fight. Its specialty was politics.... The military became the dominant force in the country.... Training for war with Israel came in a very distant second. Army officers concentrated on the art of seizing and then keeping power.[43]

A generation of intellectuals and politicians debated the causes of this defeat. Secularists argued that the Arabs had failed to modernize and must now do so; and some conservatives wanted to blend Arab and Islamic culture with western technology. But the thinkers known as Islamic fundamentalists became most prominent.

Islamic fundamentalism is not new, and it gains strength whenever Arab or Muslim societies are under stress, as in 1967. Some Islamic fundamentalists argued that Israel had won because, unlike the Arab world, it had remained true to its faith. Others went further, arguing that Arabs needed to abandon *hulul mustawrada*— "imported solutions," such as the secular nation-state—and return to Islam.[44]

The Egyptian Sayyid Qutb had considerable influence. He was executed for sedition in 1966, before the Six-Day War; and his critique of the contemporary Islamic world became even more relevant afterward. To understand his views, it is necessary to realize that unlike Christianity, Islam is both a religion and a sociopolitical system, with no separation between church and state. The Prophet Muhammad was both a religious figure, who received the Quran as a divine revelation, and a political ruler. Islam had nothing analogous to the Protestant Reformation—such a concept is alien to the *umma* because for most of their history Muslims have not really lived under an Islamic order. (The Ottoman Empire was not such an order; the sultans in Istanbul were often corrupt, dissolute usurpers who were incapable of preventing foreign depredations.)

That there is no separation between religion and politics in Islam was stressed by the first modern Islamist thinker, the Indian Abu'l-A'la al-Mawdudi (1903–1979), who lived through a separation of religion and politics in Turkey after the collapse of the Ottoman Empire and participated in the debates over modernizing Islamic societies. Mawdudi argued that Islam was a complete political and socioeconomic system, which represented a better way than either capitalism or communism, and that a Muslim "should concentrate all his effort upon wresting leadership from unbelieving and corrupt men to entrust it to the righteous."[45]

Qutb was influenced by Mawdudi but went further, condemning all things western. Qutb called for *hakimiyat Allah*—"God's rule"—and divine law, the sharia. An Islamic head of state exercises power legitimately only insofar as he carries out the sharia, the will of God. In the Islamic order, God alone is sovereign; thus western political philosophy, in which humans are sovereign, is blasphemy, and Muslims in a human-made political order live in *jahiliyyah*— "ignorance and barbarism." This Quranic term originally referred to Arabia before Muhammad; it now refers to societies antithetical to the Islamic order. Not long after 9/11, *The Economist* remarked:

> The past three decades have provided fertile ground for [Islamic fundamentalism]. Nearly every Muslim country has experienced the kind of social stress that generates severe doubt, discontent and despair. Populations have exploded. Cities, once the abode of the privileged, have been overrun by impoverished, discontented provincials. The authoritarian nature of many postcolonial governments, the frequent failure of their great plans, and their continued dependence on western money, arms and science has discredited their brand of secularism. The intrusion of increasingly liberal western ways, brought

by radio, films, television, the Internet and tourism, has engendered schism by seducing some and alienating others.[46]

The Economist later printed a survey that reiterated these points: "Arab Human Development Report 2002," written by Arabs under the auspices of the United Nations Development Program.[47] The continued failures of all Arab regimes since 1967 have provided a rationale for the *nizam Islami*, or "Islamic order," advocated by the fundamentalists.

Al-Qaida's Philosophy of Action

Al-Qaida's leaders do not believe that their goals can be attained by peaceful methods. Their reasoning derives from their worldview, from their experiences of fighting enemies, and from three activist Islamist thinkers: Abdel Salam al-Farag, an Egyptian radical who was a member of al-Jihad; 'Abdullah 'Azzam; and Ayman al-Zawahiri— the modern men of "violent action."[48]

Mohammad Abdel Salam al-Farag's manifesto *Al-Faridah Al-Gha'ibah* ("The Neglected Duty") is critical to an understanding of Usama bin Ladin's concept of world order and direct confrontation. Al-Farag asks, "Do we live in an Islamic state?" Muslims live in an Islamic polity if its ruler follows Islamic law; otherwise they are in the *dar al kufr* ("abode of infidels") and are permitted to rebel. Al-Farag quotes the Prophet Muhammad: "If you have proof of infidelity [you] must fight it."[49] He dismisses all the proposed peaceable ways to establish an Islamic polity;[50] the only—and imperative—way is jihad.

The term *jihad* has been controversial in the West. It does not mean "holy war" (the term for that is *harb mukaddasah*).[51] *Jihad* conveys three kinds of striving or exertion (fighting) in the way of God: against the evil in oneself, against Satan, and against apostates (*murtadd*) and infidels. For al-Farag, the third *jihad* is most important and should be the sixth pillar of the Islamic faith, in addition to the five pillars (individual and social obligations) prescribed by the Prophet Muhammad. According to al-Farag, jihad allows all kinds of tactics, including deceiving and lying to an enemy, and infiltrating the enemy's ranks. Al-Farag also mentions the importance of detailed planning before battle is joined.

Usama bin Ladin may have read al-Farag, but it is more likely that al-Farag's ideas were passed on to him by a fugitive Egyptian surgeon, Dr. Ayman al-Zawahiri. In any case, al-Qaida's philosophy of action is based on the following three ideas.

Concept 1: Peaceful Means Cannot Attain Goals

As Lenin once asked, with respect to bringing about the Marxist state, "What is to be done?"[52] The political views of many Islamic fundamentalists imply violent confrontation with the state. Fighting an Arab state poses major problems. Despite its decay and corruption, the Arab nation-state has formidable paramilitary forces and security services—which may account for its survival.

Given this disparity in power, some Islamic fundamentalists have focused on the individual within society, or on society itself—a form of Basil Liddell Hart's strategy of "indirect approach," which avoids confronting the state and seeks to re-Islamize individuals in their daily lives, in the hope that they will break with "impious" manners and customs. Other fundamentalists have taken a broader, more peaceful approach that seeks to re-Islamize society through such institutions as the media, the judiciary, and entertainment. Both indirect strategies ultimately undermine secular foundations of the nation-state, and neither is easy to combat, as the secular Turkish state has learned. But Usama bin Ladin, influenced by Abdel Salam al-Farag and Ayman al-Zawahiri, rejects peaceful methods:

> Any thief or criminal or robber who enters another country in order to steal should expect to be exposed to murder at any time. For the American forces to expect anything from me, personally, reflects a very narrow perception. Muslims are angry. The Americans should expect reactions from the Muslim world that are proportionate to the injustice they inflict.[53]

Al-Zawahiri remains adamant that violence is the only way and has in fact felt vindicated by the violence with which Egypt put down an Islamist insurgency in the 1990s, and by the United States' onslaught against al-Qaida after 9/11. In October 2002 he declared in an interview that his organization's "message to our enemies is that America and its allies must realize that their crimes will not go unpunished."[54] In May 2003 he stated:

> Protests will not do you any good, neither will demonstrations nor conferences. Nothing will do you good, but toting arms and taking revenge against your enemies, the Americans and

the Jews.... The crusaders and the Jews do not understand but the language of killing and blood. They do not become convinced unless they see coffins returning to them, their interests being destroyed, their towers being torched, and their economy collapsing.[55]

Concept 2: Offensive and Defensive Jihad Are Two Sides of the Same Coin

In an offensive jihad, as the term implies, the Islamic community goes on the offensive against its enemies. This jihad is conducted by professional soldiers and volunteers under the command of the ruler. A defensive jihad is undertaken when the Islamic community is attacked; every Muslim is obligated to contribute to a defensive jihad.

A defensive jihad is the ideological justification for violence. In his famous "Declaration of War against the Americans Who Occupy the Land of the Two Holy Mosques" (August 23, 1996, quoted above), bin Ladin stated unequivocally that the community was under attack: "The people of Islam had suffered from aggression, inequality and injustice imposed upon them by the Zionist-Crusader alliance."[56] Thus all Muslims must take up arms or contribute in any way they can to the struggle, as he pronounced in "Declaration of the World Islamic Front for Jihad against the Jews and the Crusaders"(February 22, 1988):

> To kill Americans and their allies, both civil and military, is an indi-vidual duty of every Muslim who is able, in any country where this is possible, until the al-Aqsa Mosque and the Haram Mosque are freed from their grip and until their armies, shattered and broken-winged, depart from all the lands of Islam, incapable of threatening any Muslim.[57]

Concept 3: Attacking the Enemy Afar and the Enemy Who Is Near Are Two Sides of the Same Coin

Al-Farag argues that Islamists must focus first on the enemy at home: "We must begin...by establishing the rule of God in our nation.... The first battlefield for *jihad* is the uprooting of these infidel leaders and replacing them with an Islamic system from which we can build";[58] only afterward can we combat the enemy "who is afar." For bin Ladin and al-Qaida, targeting both sets of enemies simultaneously or nearly simultaneously is not only permissible but necessary and feasible. After 1982, when al-Farag was executed, the situation changed. By the 1990s the United States had established a presence in the Arabian Peninsula. Thus bin Ladin, who focuses on the United States and its "puppets," the al-Sauds, sees the enemy who is near and the enemy who is afar as closely linked.

Al-Qaida's Means, Instruments, and Resources

We now return to the traditional concept of grand strategy: the relationship of goals to means. What does al-Qaida have in the way of means, instruments, and resources? Clearly, it has enough at its disposal to be comparable to a mid-size corporation and more than a failing or failed state; but it cannot compete in this regard with its prime enemy, the United States—a powerful, efficient state. How does al-Qaida deal with this imbalance?

The Problem of Facing a Superior Foe

If you have a philosophy of action that requires violence, you must develop violent instruments or means. A comparative political scientist has observed that "Islam is the most martial of the world's great religions. Alone among the prophets, Muhammad was...a victorious commander on the battlefield and the founder of a state that was soon to become an empire."[59] Pagan enemies threatened the Islamic state from its inception, but in the Arabian Peninsula, and against the Byzantine and Persian armies, the outnumbered Muslims won out; and they ascribed these victories to faith in God. Over time the Islamic empire developed into a formidable military power; but in the modern era it declined. Despite attempts by Islamic rulers to modernize their armed forces in the nineteenth century, the West penetrated and colonized the Islamic world. This was a source of dismay throughout the twentieth century and into the twenty-first, but people like Usama bin Ladin were not content to remain dismayed.

Bin Ladin does not underestimate the difficulty of fighting the United States; he is aware of its technological superiority and its vast economic power. But he does not feel that these considerations should lead to paralysis or fatalism:

> The difference between us and our adversaries in terms of military strength, manpower and equipment is very huge. But, for the grace of God, the difference is also very huge in terms of psychological resources, faith, certainty and reliance on the Almighty God.[60]

In Afghanistan, there was an enormous disparity between the mujahideen and their Muslim supporters on one side and the Soviets on the other, yet mujahideen eventually triumphed—an outcome that "cleared from Muslim minds the myth of super-powers"[61] and helped destroy an atheist entity, the Soviet Union. During the United States' assault on Afghanistan in October 2001, bin Ladin emphasized his belief that the presence of God on the side of the Muslims would again give them the strength to win:

> Praise be to God, I say that the battle is not between al-Qaeda and the world crusade. The battle is between Islam and Muslims on the one hand and the world crusade on the other. With God's grace, . . . the Soviet Union has vanished into oblivion. . . . God Almighty will give us the support once again to defeat the Americans on the same land and with the same people.[62]

But bin Ladin does not just trust in God. For him and his sub-ordinates, the United States is not "ten feet tall": it suffers from overweening pride and arrogance, and its self-confidence has blinded it to its own weaknesses and to its opponents' strengths. He seems to doubt the staying power of the United States: "We were surprised by the U.S. soldier's psychological level in the Somali war. There was nothing for him to fight for. It was just a media show."[63]

Another weakness of the United States is its disdain for the combat abilities of others. In the words of "Abu 'Ubayd al-Qurashi," presumably an al-Qaida adherent, who writes extensively on the Internet, the U.S. military is:

> . . . among the armies that have not paid much attention to the past experience of others, particularly in the wake of this army's euphoria following its victory in World War II. With its pride smeared in the dirt after the Vietnam War, the U.S. Army revised its calculations and started to study the unchanging laws of war. . . . However, following their victory in the second Gulf War, it seemed that the Americans once again turned their back on the lessons learned

from the wars of the past and, instead, focused on modern technology as a decisive tool to win wars that is unparalleled in their views.[64]

An al-Qaida Web site, the Center for Islamic Studies, professes disdain for U.S. military superiority and argues that it can be neutralized:

> We know that you are still deluded by your power and think that your fortresses and destroyers and aircraft carriers will protect you. But we will remind you that these are worth nothing in our eyes. You have seen how we have taken the war technology which you possess out of the battle using simple, basic methods, as your chief of staff has admitted, so that we can face you one-on-one and make you taste the despair of those who have put their faith in this world. We say to you that neither your wealth nor your military forces will be of any help to you.[65]

Guerrilla Warfare under Conditions of Inferiority

Bin Ladin was prepared to wage war under conditions of inferiority, using guerrilla tactics, because the Islamic world cannot wage war by conventional means. In addition to the technological disparity, its regular armies, he argues, are under the control of puppets of the United States.

Al-Qaida exhorts Muslims to conduct guerrilla warfare against the enemies of Islam. Guerrilla warfare as defined by bin Ladin is useful against projected U.S. power or military forces within the lands of Islam. While acknowledging the loss of Afghanistan as a sanctuary and a site for training bases and logistical infrastructure, al-Qaida claims to be heartened by the continuation of guerilla warfare against the United States and its allies there. This has hindered the United States' ability to establish hegemony in Afghanistan, and it has led to the expenditure of vast resources on an enterprise whose success is still doubtful. Shortly before the United States invaded Iraq, bin Ladin urged the Iraqis to prepare for guerrilla warfare and suicide attacks. "Iraq in Jihad—Hopes and Risks," a handbook, presents commonsense strategic, operational, and tactical advice: the coalition forces must be attacked daily and everywhere so that they will be stretched thin; attacks that drive a wedge between the United States and its partners should be undertaken; and "preparation and planning are the bases of the success of any project."[66]

Al-Qaida evidently also believes that small, well-trained professional cadres continue to be necessary for mega-strategic attacks
against the United States' economic activities and infrastructure.

Permissibility of and Justification for Terrorism

Obviously, bin Ladin commends terrorism and has made considerable efforts to justify it, as an ineluctable aspect of interstate and
intrastate relations. In an interview with ABC's correspondent
John Miller, bin Ladin said:

> Terrorism can be commendable and it can be reprehensible. Terrifying
> an innocent person and terrorizing him is objectionable and unjust, also
> unjustly terrorizing people is not right. Whereas, terrorizing oppressors
> and criminals and thieves and robbers is necessary for the safety
> of people and for the protection of their property.... Every state
> and every civilization and culture has to resort to terrorism under
> certain circumstances for the purpose of abolishing tyranny and
> corruption.... The terrorism we practice is of the commendable kind,
> for it is directed at the tyrants and the aggressors and the enemies of
> Allah....[67]

Moreover, in his mind terrorism against the West, and particularly against the United States, is justified because Americans are
themselves terrorists:

> After World War II, the Americans grew more unfair and more oppres-
> sive towards people in general and Muslims in particular.... Those
> who threw atomic bombs and used the weapons of mass destruction
> against Nagasaki and Hiroshima were the Americans. Can the bombs
> differentiate between military and women and infants and
> children? America has no religion that can deter her from extermi-
> nating whole peoples.... We believe that the worst thieves in the
> world today and the worst terrorists are the Americans. Nothing
> could stop you except perhaps retaliation in kind. We do not have to
> distinguish between military or civilian.[68]

A year after 9/11, al-Qaida produced a long justification of
the attacks: "The Reality of the New Crusaders' War," by a senior
operative, Ramzi Binalshibh, who was captured in late 2002.
Binalshibh argues that "it is permissible for Muslims to kill infidels
under a principle of reciprocity, because if those infidels are targeting
Muslim women, children, and the elderly, then the Muslims can do
the same." In late 2002, after several acts of terror by al-Qaida and

associated groups, bin Ladin returned to the principle of reciprocity and argued that the Muslims will cease their operations only if aggression against them ends: "The road to safety begins by ending the aggression. Reciprocal treatment is part of justice."[69]

The controversial Abu Mus'ab al-Zawkari has had the greatest impact on the jihadist approach to warfare in Iraq. In an audio message at a jihadist Web site, al-Zawkari gives a sense of his vicious but rational approach to warfare. He begins by saying that the United States' presence in Iraq requires a puppet or set of puppets and the supporting structures—a view similar to the arguments of Marxist and other critics of western imperialism:

> Instead of having the infidel foreigner assume the task of looting the nation, plundering its resources, and enslaving it, this must be done by the hypocrites who claim to belong to this nation. The Arab countries that are around us are being administered from the White House through brokers who are extremely loyal to their masters.... Therefore, let the experience be repeated in Iraq.[70]

He then states that he is fighting to implement God's will on earth and adds that any local leader who provides the infidel with support or infrastructure "is our enemy and a target for our swords, regardless of his name and kinship."

A significant subcategory of terrorism is suicide terrorism,[71] which has existed at least since the early 1980s. The Tamil Tigers of Sri Lanka—not al-Qaida—have conducted the greatest number of suicide terrorist attacks; in fact, other Islamist groups in the region have also conducted more suicide attacks than al-Qaida. But al-Qaida's suicide attacks have been the most costly and have had the greatest strategic impact. Clearly, the organization has put a great deal of effort into making its suicide operations successful.

Permissibility of and Justification for Weapons of Mass Destruction

Bin Ladin believes that it is incumbent on Muslims to acquire whatever weapons are necessary for the *umma* to deter enemies, defend itself against attack, and retaliate. Traditional Islamic warfare has the concept of a balance of power between the community and its enemies, and of maintaining adequate deterrent power.

This raises the issue of weapons of mass destruction (WMD). Recently, particularly since the nerve gas Sarin was released in Tokyo in 1995, there has been considerable literature within terrorism studies on WMD, or chemical, biological, radiological, and nuclear (CBRN) weapons. Analysts have asked whether modern terrorist groups intend to acquire such weapons; whether they have the necessary organizational, scientific-technological, and financial resources; and how they would use WMD. What we need to address here is whether al-Qaida seems to intend to acquire or develop CBRN weapons.[72] The short answer is yes; and although—as of 2005—it did not seem to have capability in this regard, it will evidently keep trying to develop or acquire capability. (We may also ask what al-Qaida would do with CBRN capability—but an answer could only be speculative, and none will be offered here.[73])

There is no doubt about al-Qaida's intention to obtain CBRN weapons. In a June 1998 interview, bin Ladin congratulated the "Muslim" state of Pakistan for its successful tests of atomic weapons:

> The explosions conducted by Pakistan over recent days have caused a disruption in the international balance and a change in the balances of conflict (*muwazin al-sira'*), which the nations of atheism have been eager to prevent the Islamic nation and all its peoples from influencing.[74]

He then urged other Muslims "not to be lax in possessing nuclear, chemical, and biological weapons." Six months later, in an interview with *Time*, he said that, from a religious perspective, Islamic peoples were obligated to acquire WMD and nuclear, biological, and chemical (NBC) weapons: "Acquiring weapons for the defense of Muslims is a religious duty.... It would be a sin for Muslims not to try to possess the weapons that would prevent the infidels from inflicting harm on Muslims."[75] In still another interview he rejected as hypocritical the charges that he was seeking unconventional weapons and asserted that the *umma* has the right to possess WMD in self-defense.

Al-Qaida's purported capability for CBRN has been a source of controversy and misinformation.[76] It has been stated, on the basis of considerable evidence, that al-Qaida began seeking CBRN weapons in 1993.[77] But if so, the organization has little to show for its efforts. This conclusion can be drawn, not because al-Qaida has not used such weapons (capability does not necessarily mean used), but because the overwhelming evidence is that the effort was poorly coordinated, insufficiently funded, and ineffectively implemented.

CONCLUSION

Ideology and concepts of warfare are keys to understanding Usama bin Ladin and al-Qaida. The initial avalanche of commentary on al-Qaida either downplayed the role of ideas or repeated such platitudes as "they hate our values." It is true that Islamists hate the secular, material values of the United States and the West in general, and that even many Muslims who are not religious fundamentalists hate the United States' policies in the Islamic world. But to assert this plausibly we need to know why, and in order to know why we need to know what their own values are. Bin Ladin and his followers have focused on the presumed inequities of American and western policies in the Islamic world—and this focus has provided an enduring message and has attracted adherents. One purpose of this chapter has been to show how their ideology has been shaped to ensure broad appeal.

N O T E S

1. Michael Ignatieff, *Guardian* (10 October 2001). Also quoted in Thomas Scheffler, "Apocalyticism, Innerworldly Eschatology, and Islamic Extremism" (online).
2. The operations and tactics of al-Qaida will be included in my forthcoming larger work.
3. For more on al-Qaida's origins and evolution, see the following. Anon., *Through Our Enemies' Eyes: Osama Bin Laden, Radical Islam, and the Future of America* (Washington, D.C: Brassey's, 2002), pp. 77–195. Peter Bergen, *Holy War, Inc: Inside the Secret World of Osama Bin Laden* (New York: Free Press, 2001). Thomas Wandinger, "Das Terrornetzwerk El Kaida unter Usama bin Laden," *Politische Meinung*, No. 385 (December 2001): 57–65.
4. For biographical details see Al-Watan al-Arabi, "A Biography of Osama Bin Laden," *Frontline* (12 September 2001) at www.pbs.org/wgbh/pages/frontline/shows/Binladen/who/bio.html. See also Florent Blanc, *Ben Laden et l'Amerique* (Paris: Bayard, 2001).
5. Quoted in *Independent* (6 December 1993): 1.
6. Quoted in "Osama bin Laden v. the U.S.: Edicts and Statements," *Frontline*, at www.pbs.org/wgbh/pages/frontline/shows/Binladen/who/edicts.html.
7. Ibid.
8. See Olivier Roy, "Une fondamentalisme sunnite en panne de projet politique," *Monde Diplomatique* (October 1998): 8–9. See also Ahmed Rashid, "Les Talibans au coeur de la déstabilization regionale," *Monde Diplomatique* (November 1999): 4–5.
9. See Mark Huband, *Warriors of the Prophet: The Struggle for Islam* (Boulder, Col.: Westview, 1998), pp. 1–4.
10. Ahmed Hashim, "Al-Qaeda's Operational Art and Tactics" (unpublished).

11. Bernard Lewis, "License to Kill: Usama Bin Laden's Declaration of Jihad," *Foreign Affairs* (November–December 1998): 14.

12. "Osama Bin Laden v. the U.S.: Edicts and Statements."

13. *Declaration of War* (1, 2, 3) at www.msanews.mynet.net/MSANEWS/199610/19961012.3.html/19961013.1.0.html/19961014.2.html.

14. Ibid.

15. Ibid.

16. Ibid.

17. *Al Quds al-Arabi* (27 November 1996): 5.

18. John Miller, "A Conversation with the Most Dangerous Man in the World," *Esquire* 131 (February 1999): 96.

19. *Time* (11 January 1999): 16.

20. Ibid.

21. Quoted in Lewis, "License to Kill," p. 15.

22. Doha Al-Jazeera Television (8 October 2002).

23. Jihad Online News Network (8 December 2002).

24. *Jang* (18 November 1998): 1, 7.

25. *Independent* (10 July 1996): 14 (interview).

26. Ibid.

27. *Al Quds al-Arabi* (27 November 1996): 5.

28. Al-Jazeera (Doha) (11 February 2003) (accessed online).

29. Ibid.

30. Dubai Al-'Arabiyah Television (11 June 2004).

31. Doha Al-Jazeera Television (24 February 2004).

32. "Transcript of Bin Laden's October Interview (5 February 2002) (accessed online).

33. Quoted in *Washington Post* (7 October 2001).

34. *Qoqaz* (Internet) (11 October 2002).

35. This is a superficial analysis of a topic as complex as grand strategy, but it suffices for our purposes in this chapter. I have relied heavily on the following works. Richard Rosecrance and Arthur Stein (eds.), *The Domestic Bases of Grand Strategy* (Ithaca, N.Y.: Cornell University Press, 1993), pp. 3–21. Lars Skalnes, *Politics, Markets, and Grand Strategy: Foreign Economic Policies as Strategic Instruments* (Ann Arbor: University of Michigan Press, 2000), pp. 1–14.

36. Gwynn Roberts, interview with Osama bin Laden, Channel 4 Network (London) (20 February 1997).

37. For early interactions between Christendom and Islam, see Bernard Lewis, *The Muslim Discovery of Europe* (New York: Norton, 1982).

38. For the history of the Crusades, see Peter Partner, *God of Battles: Holy Wars of Christianity and Islam* (Princeton, N.J.: Princeton University Press, 1997). See also Stanley Lane-Poole, *Saladin and the Fall of Jerusalem* (London: Greenhill, 2002).

39. Agence France Presse (27 December 2001).

40. *Al Quds al-Arabi* (28 November 2002): 1.

41. Sadik al-'Azm, "Time Out of Joint: Western Dominance, Islamist Terror, and the Arab Imagination," *Boston Review* (October–November 2004): 7.

42. For Muslim reformism in the nineteenth and early twentieth centuries, see Antony Black, *The History of Islamic Political Thought: From the Prophet to the Present* (New York: Routledge, 2001), pp. 255–307. For military reform in Egypt and the Ottoman Empire in the nineteenth century, see David Ralston, *Importing the European Army: The Introduction of European Military Techniques and Institutions into the Extra-European World, 1600–1914* (Chicago, Ill.: University of Chicago Press, 1996), pp. 43–79.

43. Jeremy Bowen, *Six Days: How the 1967 War Shaped the Middle East* (London: Simon and Schuster, 2004), pp. 13–14, 39–40.

44. See Bassam Tibi, *The Challenge of Fundamentalism: Political Islam and the New World Disorder* (Berkeley: University of California Press, 1998), p. 7.

45. Quoted in Black, *The History of Islamic Political Thought.*

46. "Enemies Within, Enemies Without," *Economist* (22 September 2001): 20–21.

47. "Self-Doomed to Failure," *Economist* (6 July 2002): 24–26. See also *Washington Post* (27 February 2003): 20.

48. I will discuss the writings of the two other important Islamist men of action— 'Abdullah 'Azzam and Ayman al-Zawahiri—in my forthcoming book.

49. Quoted in Asaf Hussain, *Political Terrorism and the State in the Middle East* (London: Mansell, 1988), p. 86.

50. For a study of al-Farag, see Johannes Jansen, *The Neglected Duty: The Creed of Sadat's Assassins and Islamic Resurgence in the Middle East* (New York: Macmillan, 1986), pp. 182–190.

51. See Sami Hajjar, "Political Violence in Islam: Fundamentalism and Jihad," *Small Wars and Insurgencies* (Winter 1995): 335.

52. The same analogy is encountered in Gilles Kepel, *Muslim Extremism in Egypt: The Prophet and the Pharaoh* (Berkeley: University of California Press, 1993), p. 12.

53. Quoted in *Time* (11 January 1999): 16.

54. Quoted in "America Must Leave the Lands of Islam," at http://www.megastories.com/attack/alqaeda/ayman02oct08.shtml.

55. Doha Al-Jazeera Television (21 May 2003).

56. *Declaration of War* (1).

57. Cited in Lewis, "License to Kill," p. 15.

58. Quoted in Hussain, *Political Terrorism and the State in the Middle East.*

59. Dankwart Rustow, "Political Ends and Military Means in the Late Ottoman and Post-Ottoman Middle East." In V. J. Parry and M. E. Yapp (eds.), *War, Technology, and Society in the Middle East* (London: Oxford University Press, 1975), p. 386.

60. Al-Jazeera (Doha) (18 April 2002) (accessed online).

61. Quoted in Miller, "A Conversation."

62. The text of the interview appeared later on Jihad Online News Network (21 January 2003) (accessed online).

63. *Al Quds al-Arabi* (27 November 1996), p. 5. See also his interview with Robert Fisk: *Independent* (22 March 1997): 1 (in which he expresses the Maoist idea that "America is a paper tiger").

64. Abu 'Ubayd al-Qurashi (pseudonym), "Al-Qaeda and the Art of War," *Al-Ansar* (15 January 2002): 11–15. From Foreign Broadcasting Information Service—Near East/South Asia (15 January 2002) (accessed online).

65. Center for Islamic Studies and Research, posted on the Web (6 December 2002), accessed at http://www.megastories.com/attack/alqaeda/lessons02-dec06.shtml.

66. Quoted in Yassin Musharbash, "Change of Strategy: The New Al-Qa'ida Doctrine," *Spiegel* (18 March 2004) (accessed online).

67. "Interview: Osama Bin Laden," May 1998, at http://www.pbs.org/wgbh/pages/frontline/shows/binladen/who/interview.html.

68. Ibid.

69. Al-Jazeera (Doha) (12 November 2002) (accessed online).

70. See Ahmed S. Hashim, "Insurgency and Counterinsurgency in Iraq" (2004) (unpublished).

71. The burgeoning literature on suicide terrorism includes the following studies, from which I have drawn. Robert Pape, "The Strategic Logic of Suicide Terrorism," *American Political Science Review* 97:3 (August 2003): 1–19. "La question des attentats suicides: Tactique ou théologie?" *Religioscope* (14 May 2002) at http://www.religioscope.com/info/articles/009_attacks.html. See also Michael Taarnby, "Profiling Islamic Suicide Terrorists," *Research Report for the Danish Ministry of Justice* (27 November 2003).

72. For this discussion of terrorists and WMD, I have relied extensively on the following sources. Roberta Wohlstetter, "Terror on a Grand Scale," *Survival* 18:3 (1976): 98–104. Gavin Cameron, "The Likelihood of Nuclear Terrorism," *Journal of Conflict Studies* 18:2 (Fall 1998): 5–28. Stanley Jacobs, "The Nuclear Threat as a Terrorist Option," *Terrorism and Political Violence* 10:4 (Winter 1998): 149–163. "WMD Terrorism: An Exchange," *Survival* 40 (Winter 1998–1999): 168–183. Richard Falkenrath, "Nuclear, Biological, and Chemical Terrorism." In *Studies in Contemporary History and Security Policy* 3 (Berne: Peter Lang, 1999) (chapter accessed online at http://www.fsk.ethz.ch/publ/studies/volume_3/Falkenrath.html. Charles Ferguson and William Potter, *The Four Faces of Nuclear Terrorism*, Monterey Institute—Center for Nonproliferation Studies. Bill Keller, "Nuclear Nightmares," *New York Times Magazine* 26 (May 2002). Morten Bremer Maerli, "Relearning the ABCs: Terrorists and Weapons of Mass Destruction," *Nonproliferation Review* (Summer 2000): 108–119. Morten Bremer Maerli, *Nuclear Terrorism: Threats, Challenges and Responses*. Norwegian Atlantic Committee, 2002.

73. I touch on this speculative issue in "Al-Qaeda's Operational Art and Tactics" (forthcoming, 2005).

74. *Al Quds al-Arabi* (1 June 1998): 2.

75. *Time* (23 December 1998) (accessed online).

76. See *Daily Telegraph* (London) (24 December 2001): 1. See also *Washington Times* (4 March 2002): 1.

77. For details, see Stefan Leader, "Osama bin Laden and the Terrorist Search for WMD," *Jane's Intelligence Review* (June 1999): 34–37. See also Kimberley McCloud and Matthew Osborne, "WMD Terrorism and Usama Bin Laden," Center for Nonproliferation Studies, Monterey Institute of International Studies (October 2000) at http://cns.miis.edu/pubs/reports/binladen.htm. See also Paul Mann, "Terrorist Mass Murder: New Weapon of Choice," *Aviation Week and Space Technology* 17 (September 2001): 15.

CHAPTER 3

The Role of Islam as a Motivating Factor in Usama bin Ladin's Appeal within the Muslim World

David Cook, Ph. D.
Assistant Professor, Department of Religious Studies,
Rice University

INTRODUCTION

The actions of Usama bin Ladin have made him notorious; however, his ideology has rarely been analyzed in comparison with normative Sunni Islam. This chapter will take his publications— which include his so-called fatwas, his letters to King Fahd of Saudi Arabia, his correspondence with Shaykh 'Abdallah bin Baz (the late grand mufti of Saudi Arabia), and his published interviews[1]—as a basis for examining his ideology and his appeal throughout the Muslim world.

Bin Ladin was born in 1957 into an emigrant Yemeni family in Riyadh, Saudi Arabia. As one of perhaps 54 children, he hardly knew his father, the owner of a successful construction company. Bin Ladin's education was a traditional religious one (he attended Abdul Aziz University in Jiddah); he also had secular pleasures in Saudi Arabia and western Europe. With the Islamic revival of the mid-1970s, his life changed dramatically. After the Soviet Union invaded Afghanistan in 1979, when he was in his mid-twenties, he volunteered for the mujahideen, together with young religious men from all over the Muslim world. This formative experience made him a pan-Islamic radical, with a considerably wider vision than that of others who had stayed in the Arabian Peninsula. He also fell under the influence of 'Abdallah 'Azzam, a radical Palestinian, who, frustrated with the lack of progress in fighting Israel,[2] had come to Afghanistan to fight the Soviet occupation.[3] They had a close ideological association, and after 'Azzam was assassinated in 1989, bin Ladin continued to think of him as a mentor. However, 'Azzam and bin Ladin differed over strategies for the future: 'Azzam focused narrowly on the two areas closest to his heart—Israel-Palestine and Afghanistan—whereas bin Ladin took a more international view.

After the Soviet occupation of Afghanistan ended, bin Ladin (like many men who became used to violence as youths) found it impossible to settle down and live peaceably. Apparently he tried to reintegrate himself into Saudi Arabia during 1989–1990 but was unable to do so because of his grand pan-Islamic vision. During the Gulf War (1990–1991), he tried to persuade the Saudi authorities that his mujahideen could protect the kingdom from Iraqi aggression better than the American outsiders,[4] but he was rejected with some contempt. Apparently feeling that his experience in Afghanistan gave him both military and religious authority, he took to writing a number of epistles to a political leader (King Fahd) and a religious leader (Sheikh 'Abdallah bin Baz, the chief mufti of the kingdom).[5] These epistles are bin Ladin's principal prose documents and shed considerable light on his thought.

During the 1990s he wandered from place to place, searching for a haven from the wrath of the Saudi Arabian government and later the United States. In 1991 he left Saudi Arabia, first for Afghanistan and then for the Sudan. In 1994 his passport was canceled; in 1996 he was stripped of his citizenship and was asked to leave the Sudan. He then made his way to Afghanistan, immediately after most of it had been taken over by the Taliban. There he assembled a coalition of radical Muslims with the object of attacking the United States, and issued the "Declaration of War against the American Occupation of the Land of the Two Holy Places" on 23 August 1996.[6] This rather verbose declaration was supplemented by a terser "World Islamic Front for *Jihad* against Jews and Crusaders" published by the pro-Iraqi newspaper *al-Quds al-Arabi* on 23 February 1998. By this time bin Ladin had succeeded where so many other radical Muslim leaders had failed, in uniting Muslims from Egypt, Saudi Arabia, Pakistan, and Bangladesh for a single grandiose goal: to expel foreigners from the Arabian Peninsula.[7]

Following this declaration, bin Ladin instigated or participated in the planning of a series of escalating attacks on American interests in the third world, culminating in the attacks on the World Trade Center in New York and the Pentagon in Washington, D.C., on 11 September 2001. However, since the American invasion of Afghanistan and the downfall of the Taliban regime that had given him refuge there, bin Ladin has remained elusive. Periodically he has called for jihad or made threats, but he has made no public appearance since 2001. Probably, he continues to live in secrecy somewhere along the Afghani-Pakistani border, guarded by his closest followers and relatives.

USAMA BIN LADIN'S ISLAM

Bin Ladin's Islam is best characterized as a Wahhabi globalist radical Islam. Its roots are in the thought of Muhammad bin 'Abd al-Wahhab (d. 1797), whose alliance with the ancestors of the Saudi Arabian dynasty marked the beginnings of Wahhabism. For the Wahhabi, there is only one version of Islam. Wahhabism, "returning" to a stark legalistic version of Islam, rejects Sufism (mystical Islam) and any other spiritual interpretations. Bin Ladin's support of this worldview is illustrated by a statement in his interview with Taysir Alwani (of Al-Jazeera):

> Our Lord is one, our Prophet is one, our Qibla is one, we are one nation (*umma*), and our Book [the Qur'an] is one. And this blessed Book, with the tradition (*sunna*) of our generous Prophet, has religiously commanded us with the brotherhood of faith.[8]

This accords closely with Ibn 'Abd al-Wahhab, many of whose works were based on a sharp differentiation in creed between Islam and non-Islam. These ideas are conveyed in his list of 10 "nullifiers of Islam": (1) associating other deities with God; (2) allowing for intermediaries between the Muslim and God; (3) not calling unbelievers infidels (*kuffar*), or doubting their infidelity; (4) believing that a revelation other than that accorded to Muhammad is perfect; (5) hating something that Muhammad taught or did; (6) having contempt for any part of the religion of Islam; (7) engaging in magic; (8) helping infidels against Muslims; (9) believing that any part of the Muslim community could leave the bounds of the sharia and still be Muslim; and (10) turning away from the religion of God.[9] Bin Ladin cites these "nullifiers" repeatedly, and they are important for his own vision of Islam.[10] According to bin Ladin, the Saudi regime is guilty of at least three of these "nullifiers": numbers 3, 8, and 9.

This is a powerful indictment based entirely on Wahhabi sources, and avers that large numbers of apparent Muslims are in effect non-Muslims and should be so labeled (*takfir*). Although this idea in its contemporary manifestation is associated with the Egyptian radical Sayyid Qutb (executed in 1966), bin Ladin focuses on classical sources such as Ibn 'Abd al-Wahhab and the earlier Ibn Taymiyya (d. 1328). From the concept of *takfir* most of bin Ladin's ideas proceed naturally. They begin with the need for demarcating a clear boundary between Islam and infidelity. (In this regard Sufis, to whom most conversion and cross-religious interaction in Islam must be ascribed, had the opposite view. They felt that blurring the boundary would attract people to Islam.) For this reason it is necessary to identify as outright infidels any groups, activities, and individuals that can be labeled as having non-Muslim influence or as contributing to the rise or predominance of non-Muslim influence among Muslims. The breadth of this accusation is amazing. As Taysir Alwani listened to bin Ladin in the interview of 21 October 2001, he exclaimed "But a big part of the *umma* [Muslim community] falls into this category!" Bin Ladin's answer was to ignore this accurate comment and simply take the *takfir* interpretation of Islam as God's will.

Other elements of bin Ladin's ideology also flow from the general *takfir*. Since any Muslim who allows for something that can promote non-Muslim influences, or who has non-Muslim friends or associates, must be labeled a non-Muslim, it is easy to see why Saudi Arabia is his primary focus. Saudi Arabia sets the standard for the rest of the Muslim world, containing as it does the two holy sites of Mecca and Medina, as well as being the financial support for many Sunni religious organizations. But since Saudi Arabia has had a close political and financial relationship with the United States, has allowed American troops to be stationed on its soil, and has experienced a pervasive Americanization of its culture, it is clearly open to the accusations made by bin Ladin and other globalist radical Muslims.

Bin Ladin has been especially clever in choosing to attack Saudi Arabia, because of the widespread perception (at least in the Arabic-speaking world) that Saudi Arabians are hypocrites, and because by attacking the religiosity of the Saudi Arabian regime he attacks its legitimacy. By framing this attack as a jihad he puts the Saudi regime on the defensive. Portraying the religious elites of Saudi Arabia, especially the late 'Abdallah bin Baz, as collaborators with a "non-Muslim" regime is necessary for bin Ladin, in order to gain spiritual and political legitimacy for waging jihad. Otherwise he would be merely an autodidact, comparatively ignorant of Islam. But bin Ladin can always use his most powerful argument: he is willing to speak about Islamic issues, such as jihad, that they are unwilling to address. Thus he can conclude: "It has been established through what has followed, O king [Fahd], that your regime has committed [actions] that nullify Islam in such a manner as to make void your right to rule in the eyes of God."[11] This is a statement that bin Ladin could have made about all Muslim regimes. And since all are non-Muslim, they must be fought by a jihad until they become Muslim again.

For bin Ladin, jihad is paramount. In all his writings, he sees it as a panacea—the answer to all the problems the Muslim world faces. Jihad provides social cohesion; it makes non-Muslims vulnerable and makes them want to leave the Muslim world; it exposes nominal or "hypocritical" Muslims to a charge of treason; and it holds out the possibility of recovering territory and people lost to Islam. Bin Ladin also sees jihad as a missionary tactic: people will respond to victory and convert to Islam.[12] Therefore, he is willing to stake everything on the idea that jihad is systematically ignored by collaborationist religious elites and their westernized political masters. This message could, potentially, drive a wedge between the rulers and the ruled throughout the Muslim world, where many seek solutions to obvious social, political, and religious problems.

Part of this interpretation of Islam is the idea that the non-Muslim world hates Muslims for the sole reason that they are Muslims and will use any excuse to move aggressively against them. In the traditional literature this idea is given powerful support by the "Hadith of Thawban":

> The Messenger of God said: The nations are about to flock against you [the Muslims] from every horizon, just as hungry people flock to a kettle. We said: O Messenger of God, will we be few on that day? He said: No, you will be many as far as your number goes, but you will be scum, like the scum of the flash-flood, since fear will be removed from the hearts of your enemies, and weakness (*wahn*) will be placed in your hearts. We said: O Messenger of God, what

does the word *wahn* mean? He said: Love of this world and fear of death.[13]

Bin Ladin cites this tradition in the first paragraph of his "World Islamic Front Declaration" (1998), and it appears in many of his published works. It promotes his theory of jihad as the panacea for the problems of contemporary Islam and of the innate hostility of the outside world toward Muslims—implying that Muslims need to divide themselves completely from the non-Muslim world. It also appeals to the feeling that something is basically wrong with the political state of Islam in the contemporary world. This wrong can be summed up as either general weakness or the avoidance of jihad. Thercfore, he sees a necessity to proclaim to the people and to overthrow or at least undermine the authority of the elites. To do that he undercuts the basis of their authority: their knowledge of Islamic tradition and their interpretation of Islamic history.

ISLAMIC ROOTS OF USAMA BIN LADIN'S THOUGHT

Bin Ladin is best seen in the tradition of the ascetic jihad fighter, exemplified by (among others) 'Abdallah bin al-Mubarak (d. 797) and Ibn al-Nahhas (d. 1414), who were personally ascetic and gained prominence through their reputation as ascetics by forcing central governments to heed their message. Both of them abandoned successful positions to live in areas (Syrian and Egyptian coastlands) that were under attack by non-Muslims, and thus put pressure on the central governments to follow their aggressive jihad. Similarly, bin Ladin disavowed his comparatively privileged upbringing in Saudi Arabia to fight the jihad, and his fame is enhanced because Muslims seek a religious leader who does not depend on local Muslim governments for support, is not tainted by relations with non-Muslims, and is fighting solely for Islam. Whatever Usama bin Ladin does will be seen by many Muslims in terms of his ascetic behavior; consequently there is a reservoir of tolerance for his actions—which are perceived to be solely for Islam, not for his personal gain.

Other than standard Wahhabi teaching, bin Ladin is most influenced by the medieval Islamic doctrine of *al-wala' wa-l-bara'* (roughly, "love-loyalty and hatred-disassociation"), which polarizes all social relations as those that exemplify either love or hatred for Islam. It has two ideological precedents in Islam. One precedent, ironically, is Shiism. *Al-wala' wa-l-bara'* was first developed by Shiites because there was a stark distinction between the words that they were required to say in public and what they truly believed in private. Therefore, one had to manifest love or loyalty toward the imams and hatred or disassociation for the enemies of the imams in one's heart.[14]

This doctrine was never important in classical Sunnism until the thirteenth century because there was only rarely a divide between one's words or actions and one's true beliefs. For the most part the Sunni could rely on being part of the majority and could express their faith openly. However, starting with Ibn Taymiyya (d. 1328) we find the beginnings of the Sunni doctrine of *al-wala' wa-l-bara'*, which are much more important for bin Ladin's thought. According to Ibn Taymiyya, a Muslim is not necessarily (or merely) one who recites the *shahada* but rather is one who manifests loyalty and love for the Muslims and disassociates himself from any aspect of the unbelievers.[15] It is easy to see why this doctrine is central to radical Islam; those who have written on the subject are a veritable who's who of globalist radical Muslims.[16] According to the contemporary interpretation of this doctrine, those who imitate an unbeliever or maintain positive social relations with an unbeliever are themselves non-Muslims. As bin Ladin stated in the "Open Letter to King Fahd" (1995):

> There is no doubt among the *ulama* [religious leadership of Islam] that loyalty to the infidels (*kuffar*) and rendering them aid against the Muslims constitutes a total nullifier of Islam. Ibn Taymiyya and Muhammad b. 'Abd al-Wahhab listed this as one of the nullifiers of Islam ... and loyalty to the infidels, as the people of knowledge have recounted, is honoring them, praising them, helping them, rendering them aid against the believers, associating [with them], and refusing to disassociate from them publicly.[17]

Given this analysis of *al-wala' wa-l-bara'* it is clear that bin Ladin's beliefs do have roots in a strain of Muslim thought.

Beyond this starting point, bin Ladin is careful to root all his major doctrines in Quranic as well as traditional (hadith) and legal sources. This attention to religious references has grown more obvious with each passing year until at present documents issued under his name that do not contain a substantial stock of Quranic and hadith citations must be considered spurious. In the letters to King Fahd and to Ibn Baz (especially the latter), such citations are numerous; but there are far fewer in the "Proclamation of Jihad" (1996). Although that document starts with a number of Quranic references, they are artificially attached and are not part of the standard radical Islamic fare. Throughout the "Proclamation" bin Ladin cites only 13 additional verses, most of which are to be found in other radical Muslim publications. Citations of traditions indicate knowledge of all six canonical collections of hadith, plus several subsidiary ones. His legal knowledge is confined to the standard radical Muslim citation of Ibn Taymiyya, who is often considered the spiritual ancestor of this tendency in Islam.

The "World Islamic Front Declaration of War against Zionists and Crusaders" (1998), though considerably shorter than the "Proclamation," is much more firmly grounded in traditional jihad teachings from all perspectives. It starts out with a pertinent Quranic verse (9:5, the "Verse of the Sword") and the two strongest traditions in the radical Muslim repertoire: "Behold! God sent me [Muhammad] with a sword, just before the Hour of Judgment . . . " and the "Hadith of Thawban" (cited above) that illustrates the worldwide conspiracy against Islam and jihad as the panacea needed to combat this conspiracy. Bin Ladin cites four mainstream Sunni authorities—Ibn Qudama al-Maqdisi (d. 1223), al-Kasani (d. 1191), al-Qurtubi (d. 1273), and Ibn Taymiyya—all from the Crusader-Mongol period. Probably this attempt to ground himself in the Muslim legal tradition was a result of criticism that he had faced for his prior forays into the world of fatwas. Most of the contemporary authorities mentioned by bin Ladin are Saudi, including Hamud bin 'Uqla al-Shu'aybi (d. 2002), Sulayman al-'Ulwan (who wrote on the "nullifiers of Islam"), and Yusuf al-'Ayyiri (killed in June 2003); but there are several others, such as the Egyptian 'Umar 'Abd al-Rahman and the Pakistani Nizam al-Din Shamzi.[18] They all have impeccably radical credentials, and he never cites anyone who is not fully committed to the cause.[19]

Since these two foundational proclamations, bin Ladin has confined himself to shorter statements and interviews, all of which continue the trends described above. He cites Quranic verses whenever he can, and hadiths, and usually starts his statements with a standard radical Muslim citation, to set the tone.

It is interesting to consider what precisely constitutes proof for bin Ladin, since he allows himself considerable freedom in interpreting classical material. As he said in his interview with Hamid Mir (7 November 2001), "The *fatwa* [religious opinion] of an official *'alim* [leader] has no value for me."[20] However, despite his relative lack of learning and his occasional mistakes, he maintains his spiritual prestige because his pronouncements are so revolutionary. Other Muslims, especially the educated religious elites he despises, occasionally laugh at his simplistic interpretations, but these interpretations are popular because they express what many Muslims believe and have not heard from any other source.

THE APPEAL OF USAMA BIN LADIN TO MUSLIMS WORLDWIDE

From bin Ladin's published works, it is easy to see the reasons for his appeal. First, he says what people want to hear in a way that is based on one (obviously not the only possible) interpretation of classical Islamic thought and history. Bin Ladin's appeal is that of a scholar-ascetic who is outside the system. He is David against Goliath; the hopelessness of his cause romanticizes it. For instance, he regularly speaks of his followers (and sometimes Muslims as a whole) as the *mustada'fin* (those considered weak) described so often in the Quran. Since God supports those who are weak, the use of this term implies that God will aid the radical Muslims in their fight for justice.

Second, bin Ladin and his supporters frame their struggle as a re-creation of the struggle of the Prophet Muhammad against his pagan opponents. Most of bin Ladin's examples are taken directly from the Quran or the traditional literature (hadith) and appeal to symbols that are well known to Muslims worldwide.

Third, bin Ladin's ideas are clear and focused. All his published works focus on a few basic ideas, which he pounds home effectively. These include the need to remove foreign (American) influences from Saudi Arabia, the jihad as a panacea for the Muslim world, and the need to reform Muslim societies and end corruption. With the possible exception of removing foreign influences, none of these ideas are original; but he can point to the example of the Prophet Muhammad, who described himself as merely a reminder (e.g., Quran 88:21).

Fourth, bin Ladin's language and examples are those of the common people. Often he starts his thoughts by saying that they are "clear" (*wadih*, *bayyin*), which is usually true. His themes are easily comprehensible and rooted in traditional ideas of self-sacrifice, asceticism, honor, and vengeance. The descriptions are polarized—absolute victory or abject defeat—and he delights in pouring scorn on his enemies, often in the form of poetry or pithy characterizations.

Fifth, his ideas are pan-Islamic and egalitarian. He represents the larger world of Islam, and appears to be willing to accept people solely on the basis of their belief in Islam, rather than their Arab (or other) heritage. This is clear from his critiques of Arab Islam, and from his willingness to accept Mullah 'Umar, the Taliban leader of Afghanistan, as the legitimate *amir al-mu'minin* (commander of the faithful, a caliphal and messianic title), even though Mullah 'Umar was not ethnically Arab.

Fundamentally, bin Ladin tells a certain section of the Muslim world what they want to hear, and he gives them the message that faith can overcome the technology of the larger powers that are the targets of globalist radical Muslims. Faith and the willingness to die, according to bin Ladin in his "Final Address," can overcome all the technology of the United States, Europe, and Israel.[21] This is an inspiration to Muslims who feel that their faith should be victorious and dominant on earth in order to manifest God's truth. Bin Ladin's appeal is sufficiently strong that many are willing to overlook the problems and tension inherent in his doctrine.

DIFFERENCES AND TENSION BETWEEN BIN LADIN'S ISLAM AND NORMATIVE SUNNISM

Wahhabism has been critiqued by a number of Muslim thinkers during the past 200 years, and all of their critiques are useful in dealing with bin Ladin's version of Islam.[22] From the beginning of radical Islam (in its contemporary manifestation, from the 1960s) the most potent critiques of its doctrines have focused on authority and on who has the authority to make the categorical and global judgments exemplified by *takfir*. For all of bin Ladin's occasional veneration of the category of *ulama* (which he idealizes)—as opposed to the actual *ulama* (which he excoriates)—very few religious leaders have supported his doctrines. Thus while bin Ladin in his pronounce-ments appears to believe that the *ulama* should support every-thing he has said, in actuality he is forced to arrogate to himself the right to make pronouncements and has become increasingly hostile toward the religious leadership as their collective rejection of him has been manifest. At every point in his doctrine there is tension, in that he believes the *ulama* should be supporting him. Since they do not (for the most part), they must therefore be compromised by their association with apostate rulers. In general, although he harshly criticizes these governmental *ulama*, such as Ibn Baz, the grand mufti of Saudi Arabia, he has not actually labeled them "non-Muslims."

Bin Ladin's general classification of other Muslims as infidel (using *takfir*)—since almost every Muslim who does not actively support radical Islam must be an apostate according to his doctrines—is also a serious weakness. Although this doctrine is necessary in order to explain how Islam came to be in its present position, the idea has not proved a good selling point to Muslims worldwide. Most Muslims are influenced by Sufism, which Wahhabism has made its principal target, and some (especially in India, Africa, and Indonesia) practice forms of syncretism, and thus find themselves part of the larger group of enemies that bin Ladin has identified.

There are also serious problems with bin Ladin's interpretation of jihad. In classical Islam *jihad* is regulated warfare that can be declared only by an authoritative Muslim figure against a certain defined objective (usually to repel an invader). Since bin Ladin's goals are too grand to be supported by the classical theory of jihad, his rationale is open to criticism. He often justifies tactics, such as the extensive use of suicide attacks against civilians and targets that include Muslims, on the grounds that whatever is done to Muslims should be done to their enemies (see Quran 3:140). This argument is quite weak, relying on the disputable perception that the Muslim world is being attacked by a global conspiracy bent upon wiping out Islam. Suicide attacks, the favored tactic of radical Islam, have also been criticized by Muslims (though not when such attacks are used against Israel). Bin Ladin is often ridiculed as someone whose knowledge of Islam is not deep, and his writings do not demonstrate a real grasp of the nuances of Islamic law and tradition.

Still, it is comparatively rare for Muslims to criticize bin Ladin. His popularity mutes criticism, since he is known to say what many people believe. Also, many of his would-be critics are deterred by their lack of spiritual prestige to match his; or they are employees of governments, and thus lack legitimacy.

CONCLUSION

Bin Ladin has managed to achieve greatness not because of any original ideas—with the possible exception of his fixation on American troops in Saudi Arabia—but because of the simplicity, directness, and clarity of his beliefs and vision for the Muslim world. His image is that of an incorruptible loner, speaking the truth that (Muslim) tyrants and foreign infidels refuse to hear. This is symbolized more than anything else by the apocalyptic tradition:

> Abu Sa'id al-Khudri said: It was said, O Messenger of God, who is the best of people? The Messenger of God said: A believer who fights in the path of God, expending himself and his wealth. They said: Then who? He said: A believer who exists in one of these mountain paths, fearing God and exhorting the people from their evil.[23]

To many in the Muslim world, this extremely popular tradition, which has dozens of variants and is cited in hundreds of compilations, is precisely fulfilled by bin Ladin. He fought in the war against the Soviet Union (1979–1989), expending himself and his wealth, and then afterward against the separatists in the Sudan. He gave aid to beleaguered Muslims in Bosnia and Herzegovina (when many Muslims were ashamed that their governments refused to do anything about the slaughter taking place there), in Kashmir, in the Philippines, and in Chechnya, as well as in other, lesser-known areas. For this (according to the perception) and for speaking the truth about Muslim tyrants he was exiled to Afghanistan (recalling the "mountain paths" of the tradition). From this distant land he continued to speak truth to the Muslims and to their illegitimate rulers. Although nominally he had no power, his spiritual prestige was immense.

He also has charisma. One can admire his ability to bring rival extremist organizations together to work for a common goal. These groups—like other extremists the world over—do not easily give up their petty differences. Muslim radicals are torn by doctrinal, tactical, and sometimes strategic disagreements (some are committed absolutely to a pan-Islamic vision; others feel that their individual causes are most important and fear to take on a goal too large for them). There are frequent personality clashes and prejudices inherited from the different peoples, regions, or even versions of Islam from which they originate. (Even if they are all committed to the radical Muslim cause, sometimes these attitudes can persist and emerge in times of stress.) Yet bin Ladin has forged (and continues to forge) a coalition of the most disparate groups. This says much about his charismatic appeal and the simplicity of his vision. For all these disparate groups bin Ladin, as a figure larger than life, represents unity rather than division.

Although his vision is derivative, it has power and coherence, and above all relevance for a significant segment of the Muslim world. Even those who profoundly disagree with either the man or his vision recognize that they are both forces to be reckoned with, and cannot be simply relegated to the lunatic fringe. One should not ignore the large number of Muslims who have responded negatively to bin Ladin or have remained passive: their response suggests that most believe it unlikely that there will ever be a pan-Islamic caliphal messianic state, or that if one were to arise embracing part of the Muslim world, it would be unworkable. Still, the evidence suggests that bin Ladin has a powerful messianic vision and has constructed a method of aggressive jihad to achieve it.

Probably bin Ladin counts on divine aid more than any other single factor to realize what others see as a hopeless venture. He seems to see his situation as precisely re-creating that of the Prophet Muhammad in the seventh century. Bin Ladin promotes a radical reinterpretation of core Muslim doctrines, and arrogates to himself authority to modify teachings in accordance with his own (and his perception of the *umma*'s) exigencies. Is this ideology a cover-up for anti-Israel or anti-American attitudes, and would bin Ladin really be satisfied if the political issues he raises (the American "occupation" of Saudi Arabia, the Israeli occupation, the heavy-handed western policies toward Muslims) were solved? I think the evidence is clear that bin Ladin sees these political issues as manifestations of rot at the core of the Muslim world. He sees allowing illegal monetary practices and immorality to pervade the *umma* as laying the foundation for more political issues such as aiding and associating with infidels. Therefore, bin Ladin—true to his radicalism—seeks to deal with issues at what he perceives as the root of the problem.

NOTES

1. These include interviews with *Nida ul-Islam* (October–November 1996), with Robert Fisk (June 1996), with Peter Arnett (late March 1997), with John Miller (28 May 1998), with Salih Najm and Jamal Ismail (June 1999), with *Ummat* (16 October 2001), with Taysir Alwani of Al-Jazeera (21 October 2001), and with Hamid Mir (7 November 2001).

2. This was before the formation of HAMAS (founded in August 1988); during the 1970s and early 1980s the radical Palestinian Muslims of the West Bank, the Gaza Strip, and the Hashemite kingdom of the Jordan were of a comparatively quietistic bent.

3. His complete writings can be found at www.cybcity.com/azzamjihad; selections are translated into English at www.azzam.com.

4. See Abu Umamah (trans.), *What the Kuffar Say about Usama b. Ladin* (Khurasan Press, 1998), p. 23; Jason Burke, *al-Qaeda* (London: I. B. Tauris, 2003), p. 124.

5. Bin Baz answered Bin Ladin, and his rather dismissive return epistle has been translated into English "The Advice of Shaykul-Islaam Ibn Baz (d. 1420H) to Usaamah Ibn Laadin al-Khaarijee" (at www.troid.org, trans. Maaz Qureshi). Bin Ladin's response was a personal attack upon Bin Baz published in his interview with *Nida'ul-Islam* (October–November 1996).

6. Although Bin Ladin claims to have participated in operations against the American army in Somalia, there is no evidence that he did anything other than inspire the Somalians from afar.

7. In accordance with the tradition "expel the polytheists from the Arabian Peninsula"; see al-Bukhari, *Sahih* (Beirut: Dar al-Fikr, 1991), Vol. 4, p. 78 (Nos. 3167–3188); also Malik bin Anas, *al-Muwatta* (Beirut: Dar al-Fikr, n.d.), p. 597 (Nos. 1650–1652).

8. "Interview with Taysir al-'Alwani," original at alneda.com, trans. jehad.net (Part 2), p. 2.

9. Taken from Sulayman al-'Ulwan (the well-known Saudi supporter of al-Qaida), *al-Tibyan fi sharh nawaqid al-Islam* ('Amman: Dar al-Barayiq, 1999).

10. For example, "Open Letter to King Fahd" (1995), p. 7; "Proclamation" (1996) pp. 10, 13; "Interview with al-'Alwani," Part 2, pp. 3, 5.

11. "Open Letter to King Fahd," p. 13, see also p. 7.

12. "Videotape of Usaama b. Ladin," p. 3 (CNN edition, 11 December 2001).

13. Sources cited in al-Silafi, *al-Fawa'id al-hisan fi hadith Thawban* (Casablanca: Dar Ibn 'Affan, 2001), pp. 7–14.

14. Etan Kohlberg, "*Bara'a* in Shi'i Doctrine," *Jerusalem Studies in Arabic and Islam* 7 (1986), pp. 139–175.

15. For development in Wahhabi Islam, see Elizabeth Sirriyeh, "Wahhabis, Unbelievers, and the Problems of Exclusivity," *British Society for Middle Eastern Studies* 15–16 (1988–1989), pp. 123–132.

16. See Muhammad al-Qahtani, *Al-Wala' wa'l-Bara' According to the 'Aqeedah of the Salaf* (London: al-Firdous, 1999); Salih b. Fouzan al-Fouzan, *al-Walaa' wal-Baraa'* (trans. Abu Abdur Rahman Bansfield, Ipswich: Jami'at Ihya Minhaj al-Sunna, 1997); Hamud b. 'Uqla al-Shu'aybi, *al-Wala' wa-l-bara'* (available at aloqla.com); and Ayman al-Zawahiri, *al-Wala' wa-l-bara'* (available at e-prism.com).

17. "Open Letter," p. 7.

18. In his "Open Letter to King Fahd" he also cites Muhammad b. Ibrahim Al Shaykh (former grand mufti of Saudi Arabia), Ahmad Muhammad Shakir (d. 1959), and the Egyptian Sufi al-Shanqiti (from the end of the nineteenth century).

19. He also mentions Salman al-'Awda and Safar al-Hawali (both Saudis), but not as authorities.

20. *Dawn* (Internet version), p. 2 (10 November 2001).

21. "Final Address of the Noble Shaykh Usama b. Ladin," pp. 4–5 (2001, available at alneda.com).

22. Below is a summary of the principal critiques contained in Sulayman b. 'Abd al-Wahhab, *al-Sawa'iq al-ilahiyya fi al-radd 'ala al-Wahhabiyya* (Damascus: Dar Ghar Harra, 2000); Ahmad b. Zayni Dahlan, *Fitnat al-Wahhabiyya* (Istanbul: Hakikat Kitabevi, 1991); and for contemporary critiques, Nasir al-Din al-Albani, *Fatawa al-Shaykh al-Albani* (Beirut: Dar al-Jil, 1995), pp. 13–18, 117–125, reprinted in *Fitnat al-takfir* (Casablanca, n.d.), and trans. Malik al-Akhdar, *In Defense of Islam in Light of the Events of September 11* (Toronto: TROID, 2002), pp. 115–131. See also al-Hasan b. Ahmad al-Damadi, *Hukm takfir al-mu'ayyin* (Riyad: al-Dibaji, 2001); and Hamid Algar, *Wahhabism: A Critical Essay* (Oneonta, NY: Islamic Publications, 2002).

23. Al-Bukhari, *Sahih*, Vol. 3, p. 264 (No. 2786); note the citation of a variant in "A Message from the Mujahid Usama b. Ladin to Ibn Baz," p. 1 (1994).

Understanding Al-Qaida Networks

Marc Sageman, M.D., Ph.D.
Senior Fellow, Foreign Policy Research Institute
Lecturer, Solomon Asch Center for the Study
of Ethnopolitical Conflict, University of Pennsylvania

Today, the main terrorist threat to the United States comes from a violent Islamist revivalist social movement, united by a utopian vision of justice and fairness. The effort to deal with this threat is hampered by common beliefs about terrorists: for example, that they are products of poverty and broken families, ignorant, lacking skills and opportunities, without occupational or family responsibilities, weak-minded and vulnerable to brainwashing, mentally ill (psychopaths or sociopaths), outright criminals, religious fanatics, or simply evil. This chapter attempts to test the conventional wisdom by analyzing biographical data on the terrorists.[1]

Similarly, studies of terrorism have in general been hampered by the difficulty of defining it. A common observation is that one person's terrorist is another's freedom fighter. So in this case a crucial task is to delineate the sample by (1) identifying who belongs in it, (2) defining the threat to the United States, and (3) understanding the social movement that poses this threat. First, since this study was concerned only with terrorists connected to the perpetrators of the attacks of 9/11, it excluded other terrorists, such as the Palestinians or Tamil Tigers, who are often lumped together with those anti-American terrorists but who are not in fact linked to them. Second, the terrorists who hijacked the airplanes that flew into the World Trade Center and the Pentagon and crashed in a field in Pennsylvania on 9/11 were part of al-Qaida. Third, the term *al-Qaida* is confusing, because it refers both to a specific organization and to a more diffuse global social movement at war with the United States. The formal organization al-Qaida is the vanguard of the violent Islamist revivalist social movement. I chose to include in my sample people who belonged to this terrorist social movement, which I called the global Salafi jihad, because many of the terrorists are not formally in al-Qaida, in the sense of swearing an oath of loyalty to Usama bin Ladin, its leader, but are nevertheless fellow travelers with it. To determine who belongs to this social movement, we need to understand its nature—in particular, its inception and history. That is the topic of the following two sections.

THE EVOLUTION OF THE GLOBAL SALAFI JIHAD IDEOLOGY

This terrorist social movement is held together by a common vision. This arose in the context of gradual Muslim decadence over the past 500 years, during which Islam fell from its dominant position in the world. Because Islam claims to be the last and perfect revelation from God, this decline presents a problem. Many explanations, secular and religious, have tried to deal with the obvious mismatch between claim and reality. One of the more popular religious explanations is simply that Muslims have strayed from the righteous path. The source of strength of the original and righteous Muslim community was its faith and its practices, which pleased God. Recapturing the glory and grandeur of the Islamic golden age requires a return to the authentic faith of the ancient ones, namely the Prophet Muhammad and his companions, the *Salaf* (from the Arabic word for "predecessor" or "ancient one"). The revivalist versions of Islam advocating such a return are called *Salafi*. Their strategy is the creation of a pure Islamist state, which would in turn create the conditions for the reestablishment of such a community.

Most Salafists advocate a peaceful takeover of the state, either through face-to-face proselytizing or by forming legitimate political parties. Their peaceful strategy was undermined by President Nasser's brutal crackdown in the name of a pan-Arabist socialist project. Some Islamists, such as Sayyid Qutb,[2] concluded that Nasser would never give up power peacefully and preached his violent overthrow. Qutb argued that Muslim countries had reached a condition of decadence, injustice, and unfairness similar to *jahiliyyah*, the barbarism prevailing in the Arabian Peninsula just before the revelations of the Quran. This was due to a "crisis of values"— specifically greed, corruption, and promiscuity—which could be redressed only from above, by capturing the state. The rulers of these countries were accused of apostasy, of having abandoned true Islam; and the Quranic punishment for apostasy was death. Mohammad 'Abdal Salam Faraj[3] claimed that the violent overthrow of these rulers, the "near enemy," was the forgotten duty of each Muslim, a sixth pillar of Islam.

The invasion of Afghanistan by the Soviet Union international-ized the militant Islamist movement. Sheikh 'Abdullah Azzam preached a traditional jihad against the Soviet invaders. Many mili-tants from all over the Muslim world answered his call. As the Soviets withdrew, Azzam extended the defensive jihad into a more global one. He preached that all former Muslim lands dating back to the fifteenth century, from the Philippines to Spain, had to be liberated from the infidels. After the Soviet Union withdrew from Afghanistan, these militants focused on the other lands under infidel occupation. They gathered in the Sudan, where they held intense discussions about their failure to capture a core Arab state and transform it into an Islamist state. Some militants, led by Usama bin Ladin, argued that this failure was due to the United States' propping up the local regimes. The strategy advocated by the most militant was to switch priorities and fight the "far enemy" (the United States and Jews) in order to expel them from the Middle East; then, it would be possible to overthrow the "near enemy," the Muslim regimes. This argument split the Islamist militant community, for many did not want to provoke or confront a powerful enemy like the United States. However, Usama bin Ladin and his followers returned to Afghanistan and declared war on the United States.[4] In February 1998, bin Ladin extended his "Jihad against Jews and Crusaders"[5] to civilians outside the Middle East, declaring that "to kill the Americans and their allies—civilians and military—is an individual duty for every Muslim who can do it in any country in which it is possible to do it."

With the evolution of this ideology and social movement in mind, we may select the terrorists that belong in this sample: they are those who use violence against any foreign or non-Muslim govern-ment or population (the far enemy) to establish an Islamist state in a core Arab region.

THE HISTORY OF THE GLOBAL SALAFI JIHAD

The historical roots of the present terrorist Islamist revivalist social movement go back to Egypt in the 1970s, when President Anwar al-Sadat encouraged the formation of Islamic societies at the universities to counter the leftist supporters of Nasser. Some of these militants adopted the radical views of Qutb and al-Farag and turned against Sadat himself when he made peace with Israel. They were responsible for his assassination in 1981. Most of these militants were arrested and tortured in a crackdown after the assassination. Those not directly involved were released three years later and found their way to Afghanistan, in support of Sheikh Azzam's jihad against the Soviet Union.

The presence in Afghanistan and Peshawar of so many Islamist militants from all over the world transformed the jihad from a collection of local attempts to overthrow local governments to a more international movement reclaiming former Muslim lands lost to the infidels over the past five centuries. After the victory in Afghanistan, most of the Islamic foreigners went back to their own countries. But those who could not, usually because of earlier terrorist activities at home, stayed behind and became the nucleus of the organization al-Qaida. After many middle eastern countries complained to Pakistan that it was harboring terrorists, Pakistan expelled them. The most militant went to the Sudan, invited by the new militant regime of Hassan al-Turabi, who tried to unify the disparate local Islamist terrorist movements under one umbrella. His greatest supporter in this enterprise was Usama bin Ladin, who set up camps in the Sudan and Afghanistan for the training of terrorists who came from around the world. During this Sudanese episode, the most militant terrorists switched priorities to target a common enemy—the United States. The imposition of international sanctions on the Sudan after its support for a serious attempt to assassinate President Mubarak of Egypt during a state visit in Addis Ababa forced the Sudan to expel the terrorists. The few who agreed with bin Ladin's strategy of going after the far enemy returned to Afghanistan, and within two months of their arrival declared war on the United States. So the threat to the United States came from a process of self-selection, in which the "most militant of the most militant of the most militant" switched their target from their own government to the United States.

The return to Afghanistan heralded the start of a close collaboration with the Taliban leader Mullah Omar, who provided sanctuary to the now global Salafi jihad. That allowed Usama bin Ladin to gain control over the social movement through his monopoly of training and funding for the various local Islamist terrorist groups scattered around the world. The result was an apparently hierarchical organization, with al-Qaida (Usama bin Ladin's organization) at the top, exercising strong command and control over the whole movement. During the five years leading to 9/11, this was mostly true, as bin Ladin and his lieutenants provided training for local Islamist terrorists, housed them and their families in protected areas in Afghanistan, supported them with logistics and funds, and gave advice on their operations. In a sense, for about five years, Usama bin Ladin achieved in Afghanistan what al-Turabi had tried to do in the Sudan.

The reaction of the United States to 9/11 changed the movement. The elimination of sanctuaries in Afghanistan, the destruction of the training camps, and the disruption of the financial "golden chain" for the jihad undermined bin Ladin's and al-Qaida's control over the social movement, which degraded back into smaller local networks of operatives, now linked through the Internet. To the extent that these smaller clusters of terrorists respond to the Salafi vision and general guidance from al-Qaida, they are still part of the global Salafi jihad. There is no more need for a strong command and control structure. Now, this social movement is self-generated from below, very similar in structure and behavior to the World Wide Web itself, which shows that a network can grow and prosper with no need for top-down control.

METHODOLOGY OF THE STUDY

The present study is based on biographical details about people who belong to the global Salafi jihad. There is a paralyzing assumption in research on terrorism that no good data are available, for at least three reasons: (1) to preserve their own security, terrorists would not grant interviews, even to serious researchers; (2) to preserve national security, the state would not grant access to captured terrorists; (3) one could never be sure whether terrorists would be honest with an interviewer. This assumption has prevented empirical research—i.e., research based on evidence. However, with the development of the Internet, open-source data have become more available, even in one's home.

All the data collected for this study came from the public domain. I did not have direct access to the terrorists or to any government's secret reports. Despite the problems listed above, there is enough information in open sources to support an empirical analysis of the global Salafi jihad. My sources included documents and transcripts of legal proceedings involving global Salafi terrorists and their organizations, government documents, articles in the press and in scholarly periodicals, and Internet articles. The information was often inconsistent. In assessing it, I considered its source. In decreasing order of reliability, I favored (1) transcripts of court proceedings subject to cross-checking, (2) government documents such as the 9/11 Commission Report, (3) reports of court proceedings, (4) corroborated information from people with direct access to the information provided, (5) uncorroborated statements from people with such access, and finally (6) statements from people who had heard information secondhand. "Experts" fall into the last category, for their reliability as a source of information depends on their diligence as historians.

The collected information suffers from several limitations. First, the terrorists selected are hardly representative of the global Salafi jihad as a whole. Journalists and scholars tend to focus on the atypical: leaders, people they can investigate, and unusual cases. This bias toward leaders and unusual cases tends to ignore those who cannot be investigated and downplays the rank and file. Second, reliance on journalistic accounts is fraught with danger. In the rush to publish, the information initially reported may not be reliable. Lack of direct access to information leads to wild rumors, and journalists are born storytellers, who fill in the gaps in knowledge. These initial inaccuracies need to be corrected by following the developing stories over time. Third, retrospective accounts from principals and witnesses are subject to the biases of self-reports and flawed memory. These accounts were often the only available information, though very occasionally they could be corroborated with existing contemporaneous documents. Finally, there was no relevant control group that would allow the generation of statements specific to the terrorists. It is difficult to make specific statements about these terrorists without comparing them with some group of

Muslims of similar background and involved in similar activities that had an opportunity to participate in terrorism but did not do so.

Nevertheless, the hope is that even though each piece of information may be of questionable validity, the emerging pattern will be accurate, given the large numbers involved. A description of the potential sample might be able to support or refute the conventional wisdom about al-Qaida's terrorism. Using the definition of a terrorist indicated above, I was able to identify 394 terrorists, on whom there existed enough background information to include them in empirical generalizations as to age, origin, religious commitment, and education. I was able to codify them into a matrix with 34 variables, most of which dealt with their relationships to each other and are not relevant to this article.

PROFILES OF THE AL-QAIDA TERRORISTS

As mentioned above, the common stereotype is that terrorism is perpetrated by poor, desperate, naive, single young men from the third world, vulnerable to brainwashing and recruitment into terror. This formula implies that the mujahideen should have originated in the third world, and specifically in some of the poorest countries of the third world. It also implies that they come from the lowest socioeconomic strata. Naïveté and vulnerability imply that they either are brainwashed early into hatred of the West or are relatively uneducated and susceptible to such brainwashing as young adults. In this sense, they are relatively unsophisticated and local in their outlook, since a broad experience of the world might be protective against the presumed brainwashing that led to their conversion to terrorism. Desperation implies that their occupational opportunities are extremely limited. Singleness is implied by the assumption that any strong family responsibilities might preclude total dedication to a cause that demands their ultimate sacrifice.

In fact, however, most of the global Salafi terrorists come from core Arab countries, from immigrant communities in the West, from Indonesia, or from Malaysia. They do not come from the poorest countries in the world, including Afghanistan. Surprisingly, there is no Afghan in my sample. As regards socioeconomic background, three-fourths come from upper- and middle-class families. Nor do they come from broken families; they grew up in caring intact families, mildly religious and concerned about their communities.

As regards education, more than 60 percent have some college education. Most are in technical fields, such as engineering, architecture,
computers, medicine, and business. This is all the more remarkable
because college education is still relatively uncommon in their countries or immigrant communities. Far from being immature teenagers,
the men in my sample joined the terrorist organization at age 26,
on average. Most of the terrorists have some occupational skills.
Three-fourths are either professionals (physicians, lawyers, architects,
engineers, or teachers) or semiprofessionals (businessmen, craftsmen,
or computer specialists). Furthermore, they are solidly anchored in
family responsibilities. Three-fourths are married, and the majority
have children. There was no indication of weak minds brainwashed
by the family or by education. About half of the sample were religious
as children; but only 13 percent of the sample, almost all of them
in southeast Asia, were educated in a madrassa. The entire sample
from the North African region and the second-generation Europeans
went to secular schools. About 10 percent were Catholic converts to
Islam, who could not have been brainwashed into Islam as children.

Another popular set of explanations for terrorism centers on
mental illness or innate criminality. These popular explanations are
based on the belief that "normal" people do not kill civilians indiscriminately. Such killing, especially when combined with suicide, is
viewed as irrational. The notion of mental illness is dealt a strong
blow by the fact that only 1 percent of the sample had hints of
a thought disorder; that percentage is below the base rate for thought
disorders worldwide. A variant of the notion of abnormality is
that terrorists are sociopaths, psychopaths, or people with antisocial
personality disorder. These terms are used to mean that terrorists
are recidivist criminals, owing to some defect of personality. Such
recidivism implies that the personality defect had some antecedents
in childhood. Among the third of my sample for which I had some
fragmentary childhood data, less than 8 percent showed evidence of
a conduct disorder. The rest of this group seems to have had a normal
childhood with no evidence of getting into trouble with the law.

Logically, although antisocial people might become individual
terrorists, they would not do well in a terrorist organization. They
would not fit into the organization, would not get along with other
members, and indeed would be unlikely to join any organization
that demanded great sacrifices from them. If they did attempt to join,
they would be weeded out early. Likewise, very few people in my

sample had any criminal background. Those who did came from the excluded North African immigrant community in Europe and Canada, where they resorted to petty crime in order to survive. But there were no previously violent criminals in this sample. Therefore, it is more parsimonious to argue that in an organized operation demanding great personal sacrifice, those least likely to do any harm individually are best able to do harm collectively.

That mental illness fails to explain terrorism is consistent with three decades of research in which no significant pattern of mental illness could be detected in terrorists. Indeed, these studies have indicated that terrorists are surprisingly normal in terms of mental health.[6]

GROUP DYNAMICS

The above findings refute the conventional wisdom about terrorists. The global Salafi terrorists were generally middle-class, educated young men from caring, religious families, who grew up with strong positive values of religion, spirituality, and concern for their communities. They were truly global citizens, conversant in three or four languages, and skilled in computer technology. A striking finding in this sample is that three-fourths of the terrorists joined the jihad as expatriates, mostly as upwardly mobile young men studying abroad. At the time, they were separated from their original environment. An additional 10 percent were second-generation residents in the West, who felt a strong pull toward the country of their parents. So 84 percent (a remarkably high figure) were cut off from their culture and social origins. They were homesick, lonely, and alienated. Although they were intellectually gifted, they were marginalized, underemployed, and generally excluded from the highest status in the new society. Although they were not religious, they drifted to mosques for companionship. There, they met friends or relatives, with whom they moved in together, often for dietary reasons. As their friendship intensified, they became a "bunch of guys," resenting society at large, which excluded them; developing a common religious collective identity; and egging themselves on to greater extremism. By the time they joined the jihad, there was a dramatic shift in devotion to their faith. About two-thirds of those who joined the jihad did so collectively with their friends or had a longtime childhood friend already in the jihad. Another fifth had close relatives already in the jihad. These friendship or kinship bonds predated any ideological commitment. Once inside the social movement, they cemented their mutual bonds by marrying sisters and daughters of other terrorists. There was no evidence of "brainwashing." The future terrorists simply acquired the beliefs of their friends.

Joining this violent social movement was a bottom-up activity. Al-Qaida had no top-down formal recruitment program. There was neither a central committee with a budget dedicated to recruitment nor any general campaign of recruitment. There was no need for either. There were plenty of volunteers who wanted to join the jihad. Al-Qaida's problem was never recruitment but selection. Joining al-Qaida was somewhat like applying to a very selective college— many apply but few are accepted. Al-Qaida was able to assess and evaluate potential candidates who showed a desire to join by coming to Afghanistan for training. It invited only about 15 to 25 percent of that group to join the jihad. However, this reliance on self-recruits had a drawback: there were gaps in the distribution of the jihad. One of the gaps was the United States. The few volunteers from the United States who came to Afghanistan to join the jihad were shocked by the anti-Americanism in the training camps, which was based on beliefs and ideas about the United States that they knew from personal experience to be false. Some, like the Lackawanna Six, tried to leave early or simply forget about this experience. Because of this gap, al-Qaida had to import terrorists from elsewhere to wage its war on American soil. This was easier to do before 9/11, when there was easy access for Saudi citizens. But since 9/11, the United States has hardened entry to the country and increased its vigilance against suspicious foreign activities, making such operations much more difficult. The lack of an indigenous terrorist population ("sleeper cells") in the United States and the hardening of the United States as a target account for the lack of major al-Qaida operations there. In contrast, most of the global Salafi jihad operations conducted else-where in the world after 9/11 relied heavily on indigenous global Salafi terrorists.

The process just described is grounded in social relations and dynamics. To look at it as an individual phenomenon—as a narrative like that of Robinson Crusoe on his deserted island—is to miss its fundamentally social nature. And this is where women play a critical role. So far the account of the global Salafi jihad seems to be a purely male story of heroic warriors fighting the evil West. Yet women are also involved. They provide the invisible infrastructure of the jihad. As an influential part of the social environment, they often encourage their relatives and friends to join the jihad. Many Christian converts or secular Muslims joined because of marriage to a committed wife. Indeed, an invitation to join the Indonesian Jemaah Islamiyah depends on the background of the applicant's spouse. And once in the jihad, single members often solidify their participation by marrying the sisters of other members. This further separates a new recruit from the rest of society and increases his loyalty to the social movement.

So far, this account has neglected the contribution of religious ideology in the transformation of alienated young Muslims into fanatic terrorists. The specific interpretation of Islam that promoted this violent strategy with respect to the United States played a crucial role in the transformation. It provided a script for the cliques of distressed men to follow. Very few mosques worldwide preached this aberrant strategy to transform society using the utopian Salafi community as a model. Indeed, only about ten mosques worldwide generated about 50 percent of my sample. This is a very small number, suggesting that the global Salafi jihad is a small collection of localized networks of people rather than being more widely and randomly distributed.

This script, stressing the justice and fairness of the original Muslim community, appeals to gifted young men who are excluded from the higher rewards of society. Combined with natural group processes, it transforms their values to conform to those of their ever-closer friends. Faith and commitment are grounded and sustained in intense small-group dynamics as friends and peers provide support and strength to help each other cope with any potential hardship. These born-again believers welcome struggles in this life as a test of their faith. Over time, "authentic" Islamic spirituality and religious growth replace dominant "western" values of career advancement and material wealth, which had contributed to their original feelings of exclusion, frustration, unfairness, and injustice. They embrace Qutb's diagnosis that society faces a "crisis of values," for its main problems are not material but spiritual. The progressive detachment from the pursuit of material needs allows them to transcend their realistic frustrated aspirations and promotes satisfaction in terms of spiritual goals more consistent with their limited resources and opportunities, relieving the malaise arising from their exclusion and marginalized status. Their sacrifice and participation in this Islamist vanguard provide them with a sense of moral superiority, optimism, and faith in the collective future. Their activism and firm belief in the righteousness of their mission generate a sense of efficacy that enables them to overcome the apathy and fear that would otherwise inhibit high-risk terrorist operations. Over time, there is a general shift in values: from the secular to the religious, from the material to the spiritual, from short-term opportunity to long-term vision, from individual concerns to communitarian sacrifice, from apathy to active engagement, from traditional morality to specific group morality, and from worldly gains to otherworldly rewards. This transformation is possible only within intense small-group face-to-face interactions. The values and fellowship of these groups not only forge intense bonds of loyalty and a collective identity but also give a glimpse of what a righteous Islamist society could be like. The small size of these cliques and the mutual dedication of their members allow them to spontaneously resolve their problems among themselves. The quality of these small, dense networks promotes in-group love, transforming self-interest into self-sacrifice for the cause and comrades. The militants' experience in these groups deludes them into believing that social problems would also be spontaneously resolved in a righteous Islamist society; and this delusion accounts for their curious lack of concern about what the ideal society would actually look like or how it might function politically or economically.

Less positively, these same group dynamics account for their hatred of Jews and the United States, as revealed by the police wiretaps of their apartments in Montreal, Hamburg, and Milan. This hatred is grounded in their everyday experience of humiliating exclusion from society at large and promoted within the group by a vicious process of one-upmanship in complaints about the alienating society. The "bunch of guys" phenomenon escalates resentment into hatred and rejection of the ambient society itself. The militants expressed their hatred of it by cursing its symbols and legitimizing myths and by endorsing a conspiracy theory of Jews corrupting a now totally degenerate and unredeemable society. The wiretaps give a hint of this visceral hatred that seeks to destroy society even at the cost of the destroyers' own lives. The virulent rejection of society finds a home in the doctrine of *takfir*, or excommunication of society, which is popular in militant circles and sanctions the commission of crimes against infidels in the pursuit of the jihad.

This trajectory from low-risk participation with an increasingly closer set of friends, to medium-risk proselytism for an ideal way of life, and then to high-risk terrorist activities is progressive and insidious. The progression embraces an ideology that frames activism as a moral obligation demanding self-sacrifice and unflinching commitment to the jihad. This particular interpretation of Islam stands apart in challenging the validity of mainstream Islamic faith and practices, and it isolates new adherents to the doctrine. Their self-sacrifice is again grounded in group dynamics. The terrorist is ready to show his devotion to his now exclusive friends, their group, and their cause by seeking death. Love of the in-group combined with hatred for the out-group is a strong incentive for committing mass murder and suicide.

NETWORK ANALYSIS

The above analysis suggests that this form of terrorism is an emergent quality of dense networks rather than an aberration based on individual pathology. A qualitative social-network analysis of the sample generates insights that simply cannot be generated from a more individualistic perspective.

The topology of the network representing the interpersonal links in the global Salafi jihad is divided into four major clusters of terrorists that evolved individually into four different structures. There are many links between members within a specific cluster, but very few links spanning any two large clusters. See Figure 4-1.

First, there is the central staff cluster, which used to connect to the rest of the clusters before the autumn of 2001, when the United States' campaign against al-Qaida dramatically interfered with its communication to the social movement and broke its operational links to the other clusters. This central staff consists mostly of Egyptian Islamist militants who were released from prison after Sadat's assassination and went to Afghanistan to join the jihad against the Soviet Union. They formalized their bonds of friendship and kinship in al-Qaida proper after the Soviet Union announced its intention to withdraw. They provide the movement with leadership, training, and ideological guidance. The structure of this cluster is difficult to describe, as most of its relationships date back to the 1970s in Egypt. It is both an informal self-organizing group of friends forged during their militant activities in Egypt and their fight against

F I G U R E   4-1

Salafi terrorist network topology.

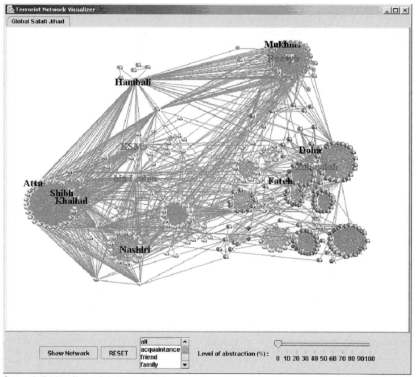

Source: Artificial Intelligence Lab, University of Arizona. Data supplied by Dr. Marc Sageman.

the Soviets and a hierarchical organization with bin Ladin as its emir, supported by a *shura* composed of about a dozen members and dominated by Egyptians. The al-Qaida staff is divided into four committees: finances, military affairs, religious affairs, and public relations.

A second cluster consists of the Southeast Asian part of the social movement, dominated by the Jemaah Islamiyah, which is hierarchically organized around the leadership of Abu Bakar Baasyir. This cluster evolved out of recruitment of Baasyir's students at his two schools: Pondok Ngruki in Indonesia and Pesentren Luqmanul Hakiem in Malaysia. As would be expected from top-down recruitment of former disciples, this cluster looks like a rigid pyramid, where all the significant decisions are made at the top and there is very little local initiative. This cluster is vulnerable to decapitation if the political will to destroy it existed. The cluster has been mostly eliminated in Malaysia through aggressive governmental counterterrorism but still exists in Indonesia, for internal political reasons. This type of structure may also promote the formation of splinter groups in the future, as has been the case in the Philippines.

The third and fourth clusters constitute the great majority of the global Salafi terrorist social movement. They consist of core Arabs coming out of core Arab countries from the Arabian Peninsula, Jordan, and Egypt; and Maghreb Arabs coming out of Tunisia, Algeria, and Morocco and their expatriate communities, mostly in France. These clusters organized themselves spontaneously around local charismatic members, often in the vicinity of very radical Salafi mosques. This preferential attachment to the jihad resulted in a small-world or cellular structure, which is decentralized with much local initiative and flexibility. As such, it is very robust, resistant against random attacks, such as random arrests of its members or decapitation of its leadership.

This small-world structure provided for rapid diffusion of terrorist innovation through popular social hubs and for flexible communication in all directions rather than the slow, vulnerable vertical communication required in strict hierarchical organizations. This communicative flexibility, based on preexisting social bonds (kinship, friendship, and later informal cliques), was a major factor contributing to the successful execution of terrorist operations. The informal communications bypassed the various rules of tradecraft advocated in the terrorist manuals, which reflected a more theoretical orientation to operational security, based on the "need to know" principle. This principle implies a hierarchical topology, with strict vertical communication. Such a communicative topology would ensure the failure of any operation because it would flood the vertical links of communication and prevent people in the field from talking to each other to overcome the inevitable obstacles arising there during the execution of a terrorist operation. Informal communications among intimates who knew each other, often from birth, that bypassed this security regulation violated this rule of tradecraft. This explains an apparent inconsistency found when the actual execution of global Salafi terrorist operations is compared with policies stated in their manuals. The execution of their operations was characterized by very poor tradecraft on the part of the terrorists—leaving behind documents which would immediately identify them, using real names rather than aliases, using their personal telephones when they knew they could be monitored, and so on. Paradoxically, it is this poor use of tradecraft that made their success possible, especially when the authorities were not paying attention to the threat. In the new post-9/11 environment, this poor tradecraft makes detection possible and hampers their operations.

After the United States' intervention in Afghanistan eliminated al-Qaida's command and control, this social movement reverted back to its original morphology. Now, its boundaries have become very fuzzy. These new terrorists no longer formally belong to a terrorist organization. They are often a bunch of guys inspired by al-Qaida messages on the Internet. There is no fixed number of terrorists. The pool of potential terrorists fluctuates according to local grievances and the world situation. Activated cliques of militant friends swarm together for a specific operation. They no longer respond to central command and control but are self-organizing from the bottom up, fueled by local initiatives. Like the Internet, they function very well with little coordination from the top. Gaps in the network do not last long; such a gap becomes an opportunity for the most aggressive to step up and fill the void created by the elimination of the old leadership. While the old leadership has been gradually eliminated through death and capture, a complete and different new leadership has been reconstituted. Aggressive new leaders, lacking the training and support of their predecessors, conduct more frequent, reckless, and hurried operations. Often, the time between conception and final execution of an operation is just a few weeks—not years, as was true before 9/11. The difficulty of communication between the central staff and these local groups has degraded the ability of the social movement to mount operations with the same degree of sophistication and coordination as the hijackings of 9/11 and the bombing of the embassies in east Africa in 1998. The wave of future terrorist operations will be similar in scale and execution to the bombings in Saudi Arabia, Casablanca, Istanbul, and Madrid.

The distribution of the global Salafi jihad is based on the presence of militant mosques preaching the specific script advocating violence against western civilians. This script interprets the United States' foreign political actions and transforms local grievances into global ones. Groups of friends, who had no previous connection or only a very distant connection to the movement, may elect to answer these exhortations for violence and carry out terrorist operations. This makes them very difficult to detect beforehand, for the first indication of their participation in the jihad might very well be the successful execution of their operation. This has been the scenario in Casablanca, Istanbul, and Madrid.

The global Salafi jihad is a unique terrorist social movement. Traditionally, terrorist organizations consist of people from country A, living in country A, and attacking the government of country A. The global Salafi jihad consists of people from country A, living in country B, and targeting country C. That imparts very different dynamics to this terrorist social movement as opposed to more traditional movements. One major difference is that because the terrorists are completely disconnected from their target, they are not socially embedded in the targeted society as more traditional terrorist organizations are. *Embeddedness* refers to the rich nexus of social and economic linkages between the terrorists and the society they live in. These multiple bonds act as a limit to the damages the terrorists can bring to their environment. The lack of such bonds frees them from such responsibility and from local concerns. Unrestrained by any responsibility to their target, this free-floating network is able to follow the logic of its abstract ideology and escalate terror (a culmination was the operation of 9/11). Lack of embeddedness in the target society makes possible a strategy of vast devastation and damages, including the use of weapons of mass destruction, which more traditional terrorists would avoid in order not to destroy their own society. This makes the global Salafi jihad especially dangerous to the United States and its allies.

New information technology has made the global Salafi jihad possible. Before the Sudanese exile of 1991, Usama bin Ladin and his lieutenants could not have led this social movement from the remoteness of Afghanistan. By the time he returned in 1996, technology had solved his communications problems. Satellite telephones allowed him to speak extensively with his followers in Yemen, England, and Saudi Arabia; facsimiles carried his press releases to his public relations firm in London; laptops and e-mail made quick and extensive communication possible. The Internet also had a strong impact on the new, more sophisticated recruits by diffusing the violent Salafi message of the jihad, bypassing traditional imams. Since most of these computer-savvy recruits had little prior religious training, they were most vulnerable to the appeal of sites that encouraged a very aberrant interpretation of Islam and rejected traditional interpretations. The more traditional religious teachers simply could not compete with the sophisticated militant Web sites, which did not require much knowledge of religion but did require a great deal of technical knowledge. The egalitarianism of chat rooms on these sites also fostered a feeling of unity with other members, creating a virtual Muslim community on the Web, sustaining and encouraging extreme interpretation of the Quran and of world events.

The vulnerability of the new electronic devices to interception has given the Internet more prominence in the global Salafi jihad. After the bombing of the embassies in 1998, bin Ladin discovered through a media leak that the United States was monitoring his satellite phone conversations. He abandoned these and communicated with his followers through his lieutenants. The post-9/11 crackdown further eroded his ability to communicate with his subordinates in the field. The old al-Qaida leadership started using Islamist Web sites on the Internet as indirect means of communication. These Web sites allow the leaders to continue to provide general guidance even if they no longer exert direct command and control over operations. For instance, the bombings in Madrid were evidently inspired by a document anonymously posted on the Internet advocating the use of bombs just before the Spanish election in order to influence the government to withdraw its troops from Iraq. In the future, this trend will continue and the leadership of the global Salafi jihad will rely more and more on the Internet to broadcast its message and to discuss tactics, as is already done in the proliferating virtual magazines. Since it is difficult to detect people who read these postings, identification of future terrorists will become even more difficult.

CONCLUSION

The global Salafi jihad has now become a fuzzy idea-based network, self-organized from below, inspired by postings on the Internet. It will expand spontaneously from below according to international political developments, without coordination from above, except for general, blind guidance. From a counterterrorist perspective, such a loose, ill-defined network does not present hard targets for military options. More subtle methods should be used to disrupt the formation of these networks by changing the social conditions that promote them and challenging the ideas that encourage mobilization into them.

Fighting such a network requires the United States to address the ideology uniting this social movement. This is something that the American public is loath to do, as it believes in transparency—believes that the facts speak for themselves. Any attempt to engage in a war of ideas raises the specter of disinformation or propaganda. But the United States cannot afford to concede this ideological war, waged on the battlefield of interpretations, to the militant Islamists. It needs to develop a coherent, comprehensive strategy to deal with this new and unique threat. Such a strategy involves discrediting the legitimacy of the leaders and the ideology behind the global Salafi jihad and replacing it with an inspiring vision of a just and fair partnership with Islam. Unfortunately, the United States is poorly set up to wage such a war. Our free media broadcasts statements intended for domestic consumption which anger international audiences, for in politics the domestic agenda will always trump foreign concerns. Such an ideological war would also require the United States to regain the credibility that it has lost in the Muslim world in the past four years because of its lack of evenhandedness in the Israeli-Palestinian problem, its invasion of Iraq on false premises, and its support of repressive Muslim regimes. Its words and its public diplomacy would need to be matched with deeds to regain this lost trust and credibility. Otherwise, any statement, no matter how laudable, would simply be dismissed as hypocritical and would further encourage the spread of the global Salafi jihad.

See also Chapter 10, **Psychology of Terrorism.**

N O T E S

1. Marc Sageman, *Understanding Terror Networks* (Philadelphia: University of Pennsylvania Press, 2004).
2. Sayyid Qutb. (Undated.) *Milestones.* (Cedar Rapids, Iowa: Mother Mosque Foundation).

3. Muhammad 'Abdel al-Salam Faraj, "Al-Faridah al Ghaibah." In Johannes Jansen, *The Neglected Duty: The Creed of Sadat's Assassins and Islamic Resurgence in the Middle East* (New York: Macmillan, 1986), pp. 159–234.

4. Osama bin Laden, "Declaration of War against the Americans Occupying the Land of the Two Holy Places," *Al-Quds al-Arabi* (London, 23 August 1996).

5. Osama bin Laden et al., "Jihad against Jews and Crusaders" (23 February 1998).

6. Andrew Silke, "Cheshire-Cat Logic: The Recurring Theme of Terrorist Abnormality in Psychological Research," *Psychology, Crime, and Law* 4 (1998): 51–69. Andrew Silk (ed.). *Terrorists, Victims, and Society: Psychological Perspectives on Terrorism and Its Consequences* (Chichester, England: Wiley, 2003). Also see article by Horgan in this text.

BIBLIOGRAPHY

Bin Laden, Osama, "Declaration of War against the Americans Occupying the Land of the Two Holy Places," *Al-Quds al-Arabi* (London, 23 August 1996). See www.pbs.org/newshour/terrorism/international/fatwa_1996.html.

Bin Laden, Osama, et al., "Jihad against Jews and Crusaders" (23 February 1998). See www.fas.org/irp/world/para/docs/980223-fatwa.html.

Faraj, Muhammad 'Abdel al-Salam, "Al-Faridah al Ghaibah." In Johannes Jansen, *The Neglected Duty: The Creed of Sadat's Assassins and Islamic Resurgence in the Middle East* (New York: Macmillan, 1986), pp. 159–234.

Qutb, Sayyid. n.d. *Milestones.* (Cedar Rapids, Iowa: Mother Mosque Foundation).

Sageman, Marc, *Understanding Terror Networks.* (Philadelphia: University of Pennsylvania Press, 2004).

Silke, Andrew, "Cheshire-Cat Logic: The Recurring Theme of Terrorist Abnormality in Psychological Research," *Psychology, Crime, and Law* 4 (1998): 51–69.

——— (ed.). *Terrorists, Victims, and Society: Psychological Perspectives on Terrorism and Its Consequences* (Chichester, England: Wiley, 2003).

Al-Qaida: Terrorist Selection and Recruitment

Scott Gerwehr
Associate Policy Analyst, The RAND Corporation

Sara Daly
International Policy Analyst, The RAND Corporation

September 11 was, obviously, a seminal event for al-Qaida. Historically, terrorists' and insurgents' successes have had two kinds of effects on recruiting: the positive effects of the action, measured in more recruits and approbation by state sponsors; and the negative effects of the reaction, measured in arrests, compromise of intelligence assets, etc. Thus when there is a significant development in a terrorist or insurgent campaign, there are almost always significant changes in recruiting. Al-Qaida and its affiliates have had to adapt since September 11 and since the loss of their training base in Afghanistan, and to incorporate new and more clandestine methods of recruitment.

A priority of the American-led campaign against global terrorism is to move beyond responding to attacks and threats and take proactive steps to cripple al-Qaida. One prong of this proactive strategy is to diminish the ability of al-Qaida and its affiliated terrorist organizations to recruit new members. Manpower for carrying out attacks and sustaining operations is a critical resource for terrorist organizations; therefore, hindering recruitment strikes a blow at their ability to function.

A first step toward hindering al-Qaida's recruitment is to understand how it works—where al-Qaida recruits, what tools it uses, whom it targets, and why. A clearer picture of this recruitment process could help the United States and its allies develop strategies and interventions to counter terrorist groups' ability to replenish and increase their numbers.

This chapter focuses on the structure of the recruitment process; models al-Qaida may be using to attract new members; approaches to recruitment; characteristics of potential recruits; and *nodes*—centers of activity, such as mosques, universities, and charities—where al-Qaida's recruiters seek new members and where potential recruits[1] are likely to become acquainted with the radical jihadist worldview.

A NOTE ON METHODOLOGY

To better understand who al-Qaida and its affiliated organizations are recruiting as well as what types of individuals are attracted to al-Qaida, we examined the social-psychological and sociological literature on recruitment into extremist and totalist organizations to identify recruitment models al-Qaida may be using in various regions. We then looked at the persuasive instruments that al-Qaida uses to attract potential recruits, whether through the media or personal contacts in a closed setting, such as a prison or paramilitary training camp. Finally, we examined various recruitment nodes that may be used for recruiting by al-Qaida and its affiliated groups. This chapter does not include any data that comment empirically on whether or not al-Qaida is actually using these particular strategies or models to recruit new members. Most of our conclusions are drawn from open-source, academic, and journalistic accounts of how al-Qaida has sought recruits in the past and an assessment of those who seek to join al-Qaida.

THE STRUCTURE OF THE RECRUITMENT PROCESS

It has long been known that effective recruitment "pitches" are tailored to the audience and its cultural, social, and historical context. For example, encouraging a youth to leave home and join a military or paramilitary organization can be (1) couched in patriotic terms if the youth's family is a member of a privileged class, or (2) framed as a step in social advancement if the family is immigrant and struggling, or (3) characterized as a revolutionary act of self-discovery if the family is disapproving and must be circumvented. These are simple generic examples of "tuning" the pitch to the psychographic[2] and demographic[3] particulars of the audience and its environment. This tuning is especially necessary for marginal or illicit groups, whose recruiting is often undertaken in the teeth of governmental or other opposition. There is little room for error, and the consequences of failure can be severe. Less well appreciated than tuning is how these groups alter or adapt their own shape and patterns of activity to facilitate recruitment. For instance, when religious terrorist[4] groups are banned from evangelizing on school campuses, they may disguise their activities by changing their names, dress, meeting places, use of language, types of activities, and timetable to avoid interference from authorities and yet maintain access to the target population. This organizational adaptation occurs across both regions and nodes[5] (e.g., prisons, schools, direct-mail solicitations).

Two guiding principles follow directly from the preceding discussion. First, there is no single, uniform recruitment process for a group; rather, there are as many recruitment processes as there are distinct regions and nodes in which the group operates. While there may be overlap and similarity between the recruitment techniques in one location and those in another, there will as often be stark differences. For example, in one forum (e.g., a training camp) recruiters may enjoy open, public access to the target population while in another (e.g., a prison) they may have to operate more clandestinely. Moreover, the characteristics of any regional or nodal recruitment process will change over time, as circumstances warrant.

Second, and correspondingly, the recruitment efforts of a group will not be mitigated, shaped, hindered, or halted by a one-size-fits-all prescription. Different recruitment patterns will necessitate different counterrecruitment interventions. Some counterrecruitment methods may be effective in more than one locale, but just as often what works in one situation will prove ineffective (or counterproductive) in another. Thus breaking up prayer meetings and discussion groups with armed force might be an effective intervention if the potential recruits are enlightenment-seekers (as is the case with many new recruits to al-Qaida) but may polarize and strengthen the will of antigovernment revolutionaries [as might be the case with the LTTE (Liberation Tigers of Tamil Eelam) in Sri Lanka].

MODELS OF RECRUITMENT

The specific characterization of any recruitment process may be called its *shape*—a combination of overall pattern and specific descriptors. As suggested above, counterrecruitment interventions should be matched to the pattern and descriptors.

What kinds of patterns are there? How much variety is there in the overall pattern? There is tremendous variety, but a review of the empirical literature on terrorist groups' recruiting reveals a few common structures.[6] Some examples follow.

The Net

In the "net" pattern a target population may be engaged equitably (for example, every member of a congregation may be sent a videotape or every student invited to a weekend retreat). Some members will respond positively, others negatively; but in general the whole population is viewed as primed for recruitment. See Figure 5-1. More specifically, the target audience is viewed as homogeneous enough and receptive enough to be approached with a single undifferentiated pitch. This is often the approach used when there is little serious opposition to the group in the audience's environment, or in conjunction with other approaches (e.g., beginning with the net and moving on to the "infection"). Among the key variables to be investigated in this model are geography (where is the net cast?) and demographic-psychographic similarities and contrasts among

F I G U R E   5-1

The net.

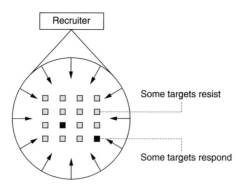

members of the targeted audience (Who is caught? Who slips out of the net?).

An example of a node where this approach may work best for al-Qaida is a mosque headed by an imam widely recognized as "radical." Those who attend are ready to receive the recruiting pitch without additional preparation. Regionally, this model would be most effective in locations such as the Northwest Frontier Province of Pakistan, which is known to have a population widely sympathetic to al-Qaida.

The Funnel

A recruiter may use an incremental, or phased, approach when he or she believes a target population is ripe for recruitment yet requires a significant transformation in identity and motivation. As the term *funnel* implies, potential recruits start at one end of the process and are transformed, after some culling[7] along the way, into dedicated group members when they emerge at the other end. See Figure 5-2. This approach can be characterized by milestones such as hazing rituals and group identity-building exercises or, in the case of al-Qaida, validation of commitment to its principles through the recruits' demonstrated knowledge of radical Islam and the use of violence to achieve its goals. These milestones capitalize on a wealth

F I G U R E   5-2

The funnel.

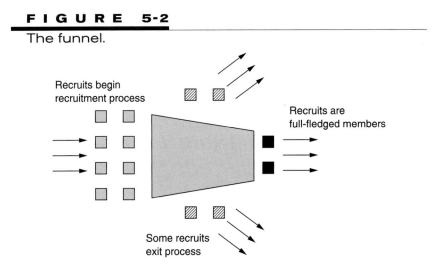

Recruits begin recruitment process

Recruits are full-fledged members

Some recruits exit process

of techniques well studied in cognitive, social, and clinical psychology. These techniques can result in radically polarized and altered attitudes among those who successfully navigate them, usually along the lines desired by the recruiting group. Even those who fall out of the process can still be affected in ways beneficial to the recruiter: for example, by developing a positive outlook toward the group and serving as intermediaries for further recruitment.

The Infection

Frequently a target population is so insular or so difficult to reach that the most effective method is to recruit from within. A trusted agent can be inserted into the target population to rally potential recruits through direct, personal appeals. This method leverages the significant persuasive strength of (1) source credibility, (2) social comparison and validation,[8] and (3) specifically tailored appeals. At least in its early stages, this method of recruiting suits groups that are actively opposed by governments, lending itself to clandestinity and operational security. See Figure 5-3. As recruits rally, the reach of the recruiting effort grows, as does its ability to exert conformational pressure.[9] Among the most critical variables to be investigated in this type of recruiting is time. How long does it take to insert an agent into the target population, and how long does it take for the infection to spread to a level hazardous to the body politic?

FIGURE   5-3

The infection.

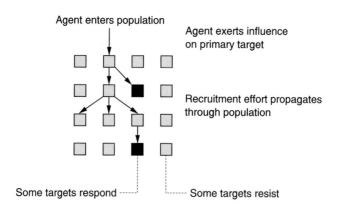

Agent enters population

Agent exerts influence on primary target

Recruitment effort propagates through population

Some targets respond ----- ----- Some targets resist

Infection is likely to be most successful for a terrorist group in an organization such as the police or the military, where most members are not extremists. In this case, an infiltrator may be able to convert selected members who are dissatisfied with their jobs or have a grudge against the police or military organization, or the government. Regionally, it may be most successful in an environment such as Kenya or Tanzania where the majority of the population is unsympathetic to al-Qaida's cause, but selected individuals could be recruited for al-Qaida operations.

The Seed Crystal

Often a target audience is so remote or so inaccessible that a trusted agent cannot be put into it, nor can a media net be cast over it (see Figure 5-4). In this case recruiters may seek to provide a context for self-recruitment. This may be compared to lowering the temperature of a glass until the water inside it cools and then ice crystals form as the seeds of a complete freeze. Once individuals emerge within the population as new recruits, they will often follow the pattern of the infection. In "seed crystal" recruitment, critical variables include the type of environmental forces being used to "chill the glass," and the durability of the "freeze." (In other words, how long must the environmental manipulation be applied in order to produce self-recruitment? Or does the process occur inevitably once it is initiated?)

F I G U R E   5-4

The seed crystal.

Agent self-recruits, begins proselytizing

Recruitment effort propagates through population

Some targets resist

Some targets respond

In terms of al-Qaida, the seed crystal approach may be most successful in diasporas or populations where open recruiting is difficult or impossible—as with the plotters of September 11 who constituted the Hamburg cell.

This is by no means an exhaustive list of patterns. It merely serves to illustrate that common patterns of recruiting can be quite different in their details, and those differences imply different responses for counterrecruitment efforts. Moreover, these shapes should be taken as simplified hypotheses to be investigated in collecting intelligence rather than foregone conclusions or analytic straitjackets.

RECRUITMENT APPROACHES

Any attempt at recruitment makes use of persuasive instruments, direct (e.g., a face-to-face invitation to participate in paramilitary training) or indirect (e.g., political pronouncements and exhortations posted on a Web site). These instruments include every form of mass media in use today (e.g., newspapers, radio, television, and the Web) as well as interpersonal social influence (e.g., sermons, rumors, education, and training). Often a group with some reach and resources will use several instruments in concert for added effect, such as writing textbooks that support the ideology of the group and then creating a school in which those textbooks may be made required reading.

How can the vast space of possible instruments be usefully bounded, and what can be gained by such an exercise? One sociologist[10] observed two cardinal dimensions along which recruiting communications can be measured at any given time (keeping in mind that this is a snapshot in time, and the recruiting pattern will evolve):

1. *Public versus private forums:* Is the interaction taking place in or out of the public eye? Clearly the prevailing laws of the region, rules of the local institutions, and attitudes toward the group will all greatly affect where recruitment efforts fall on this spectrum.

2. *Proximate versus mediated contact.* Is the source of the recruitment effort physically close to the target audience? Cultural norms, available technology, and socioeconomic

F I G U R E   5-5

One perspective on types of communication in recruiting.

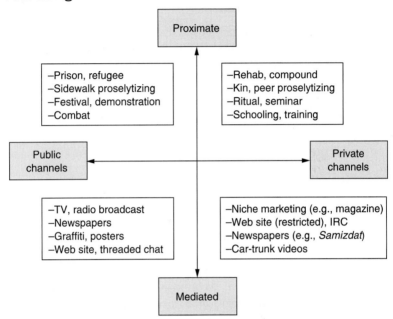

status are just three of the variables that will dictate how the persuasive message can be passed to the intended target audience.

When these two dimensions are placed at right angles, a simple but useful figure is generated that can put common recruitment vectors into distinct quadrants (see Figure 5-5). A brief discussion of each quadrant will illustrate the actionable differences among various forms of recruiting instruments.

Public and Proximate

Recruiting in this quadrant is conducted face to face or in small groups, in a setting visible to the general public or authorities. Prisons, refugee camps, and large-scale wartime experiences (e.g., life during an occupation) are prime examples of this setting. Recruiters commingle with the population and target individuals or small groups that they deem ripe for recruitment. This activity takes place irrespective of (or despite) any opposition by authorities—often because of political sensitivity, insufficient legislation, or fear of negatively polarizing the audience's attitudes. With regard to the shapes of recruitment, this quadrant is most amenable to infection-type efforts because the recruiter has face-to-face access to the audience, with few restrictions. For the purposes of counterrecruiting, the work does not end once the terrorist is arrested and put in prison. Recruitment can occur in the prison setting and can negate the success of the arrest by creating a number of new recruits.

Public and Mediated

In this quadrant recruiting tends to be broader, more akin to propaganda than to a sales pitch. Mass media is used, including those within the reach of legislation and government (e.g., television) as well as the more illicit media (e.g., graffiti). Media channels can include Web sites that are not password-protected and whose domain name is not a secret. The target for these media efforts is usually some stratum of the regional demographic or psychographic, such as young, single men gathering in a particular café, or devout members of a particular religious congregation. The indirectness of this quadrant of communications may be necessary because physical immediacy is not possible or sustainable. Though such indirectness sacrifices the persuasive power of more intimate, tailored appeals, it does have a much broader reach. As regards the shapes of recruitment, this quadrant very much suits a net or seed crystal approach because personal access to the target audience is not available, but communication is still relatively unrestricted. For example, al-Qaida periodically releases jihadist or martyrdom videos and makes statements to various newspapers in the Arab world decrying the United States and its role in Iraq and Israel. These demonstrate how the organization uses public channels to prime specific segments of the population for recruitment.

Private and Proximate

Communication techniques in this quadrant are used out of the public eye and in intimate settings, as a rule. Individuals recovering from addictions in private clinics, attending prayer sessions in a neighbor's living room, attending a paramilitary training program (such as potential al-Qaida recruits attending training camps in Afghanistan), or receiving vocational instruction from a tutor are all examples of venues where these types of recruiting are undertaken. This suits those groups who are operating out of sight or in opposition to local authorities. Moreover, these techniques rely heavily on personal appeals tailored specifically for a targeted individual or small group. They often use peers, including relatives, in making the pitch. This strategy effectively leverages the influential power of conformity (peer pressure) and related phenomena. This quadrant suits an infection or funnel approach because the power of one-on-one persuasive communication is brought to bear at an individual level, and new recruits can be directly manipulated.

Private and Mediated

Recruitment in this quadrant combines a mass-media approach with intimacy or clandestinity. Techniques include producing dissident literature on someone's basement printing press and circulating it covertly to a broad audience. In terms of more recent technology, this quadrant includes password-protected Web sites, restricted Internet chat groups, and the clandestine propagation of digital video.

Since September 11, al-Qaida has made use of these new technologies to recover from the loss of private and proximate channels provided, for example, by the training camps in Afghanistan and the experience of building personal networks through fighting various jihads in Chechnya, Iraq, etc. Al-Qaida's use of password-protected Web sites and restricted Internet chat groups has led policy makers to describe these methods as "virtual jihad," and has made it more difficult for intelligence and law enforcement to track their activities and understand who is moving into and out of the organization. These methods are often very effective when aimed at a population that is already primed to accept al-Qaida's message, because a large number of people can be affected at once, while at the same time counterpersuasion (such as government propaganda) is excluded and the environment can be controlled. It is difficult, however, to measure how virtual jihad affects the number of recruits that al-Qaida and like-minded terrorist groups are able to attract. It is probably best used to maintain the current membership rather than to recruit new personnel. The techniques in this quadrant would best serve net approaches because large audiences are reached, although the communication is largely out of the sight and control of adversarial authorities.

Why does classifying recruitment techniques along these axes matter? There are two simple reasons. First, an appreciation of the variety, necessity, and utility of different recruitment techniques in general will lead to an improved understanding of any specific recruitment effort. It will result in a more empirical, systematic approach to both collection and analysis. The quadrants can be used as a basis for organizing the collection effort, and filling in the quadrants is the equivalent of mapping the psychological battlefield of recruitment and counterrecruitment. This is much more useful and timely than understanding the recruitment process of an adversary retrospectively (e.g., through interrogations). Second, a more detailed understanding of the recruitment process will make counterrecruitment more precise and more effective. To take another simple example, if a target population is seen as insular and more receptive to persuasion by peers than persuasion by the mass media, then countering the recruitment of an adversary group such as al-Qaida among that population should rely on infiltrators and credible proxies, not radio and television ads extolling the virtues of the United States.

CHARACTERISTICS OF THOSE TARGETED FOR RECRUITMENT AND HOW THEY ARE MANIPULATED

There is surprisingly little rigorous, scientific study on the vulnerability of individuals to recruitment by terrorist groups.[11] There is empirical work on the operational side (e.g., collection and analysis by the intelligence community), but this tends to focus on demographic variables, primarily because they are the easiest to collect. The science of changes in attitude and of group dynamics suggests that demographics are less important than other variables. What empirical studies have been conducted find that the variables which seem to matter most in the success or failure of recruitment are psychographic variables[12] and "state" variables.[13] Attitudes, ideas, reasoning, and physical experiences of individuals weigh more heavily in their ability to resist recruitment than do such factors as their age, profession, and gender.[14] Here is a synopsis of some psychographic and state variables:[15]

A high level of current distress or dissatisfaction (emotional, physical, or both)

Cultural disillusionment in a frustrated seeker (i.e., unfulfilled idealism)

Lack of an intrinsic[16] religious belief system or value system

Some dysfunctionality in family system (i.e., family and kin community exert "weak gravity")

Some dependent personality tendencies (e.g., suggestibility, low tolerance for ambiguity)

These data suggest that efforts to map (i.e., collect against) a group's recruitment structure will need to measure far more than just plain demographics to truly understand, within a given population, who is at risk, who is likely to join, and who is likely to become radicalized. This level of collection is all the more necessary in counterrecruitment—which usually involves manipulating variables similar or identical to those affecting recruitment. That is, if a recruiter attempts to weaken targets' family or community bonds in order to get them to join (e.g., by emphasizing a religious duty to go to war), an effective countermeasure is to strengthen or preserve those social networks (e.g., by emphasizing the religious imperative to protect and preserve one's family).

One example of someone recruited into al-Qaida who had many of the aforementioned characteristics was Richard Reid, the "shoe bomber," who attempted to bring down an American Airlines flight in December 2001 by detonating explosives hidden in his shoes. Since his incarceration in January 2003, it has come to light through various police and intelligence investigations into his life that Reid had at least four of the five characteristics listed above. According to his father, Reid did not receive adequate attention at home as a child because the father was incarcerated for most of that time, and his parents separated when he was young—this suggests some level of dysfunctionality in the family system. Reid also felt a sense of cultural disillusionment living in the United Kingdom as a person of mixed race in an all-white family and attending all-white schools where he felt that he did not fit in.[17] He lacked an intrinsic value system, falling into a life of petty crime before he converted to Islam in prison in his twenties. According to the imam at the mosque he attended in the United Kingdom, Reid was a "weak character" and "very, very impressionable."[18] Finally, one could argue that because of his experiences—a life of crime, imprisonment, a broken family, and a sense of being part of an outgroup because of his mixed race—Reid was undergoing severe distress or dissatisfaction.

Though vulnerability to recruitment is not a fully understood phenomenon, there are common techniques used by terrorist groups to induce the psychographic or state variables necessary and sufficient in encouraging (1) an initial contact between potential recruit and recruiter resulting in subsequent and more intense contacts, and (2) subsequent contacts leading to identity transformation by the recruit (i.e., joining the group as a self-identified member). The common theme of all these techniques is that they exploit or create physical and mental trauma to produce a dissociative state in the target individual—a condition in which identity, memory, consciousness, awareness, and rational thought are in flux. Coupled with that dissociation is the creation of a new identity and new thought processes—a transformation—along the lines sought by the recruiter. A full discussion of the process of identity transformation (also known as thought reform or brainwashing) is beyond the scope of this chapter, but it is the logical next step after the forced dissociation.[19]

CHALLENGES IN IDENTIFYING AND MITIGATING AL-QAIDA'S RECRUITMENT

A serious limitation to any detailed understanding of how new members come to al-Qaida is the confusing and sometimes contradictory definitions of what al-Qaida is and who is affiliated with it. This definitional predicament makes it challenging to distill recruitment patterns and trends that transcend regional dynamics. Having a more disciplined understanding of what al-Qaida is and who the adversaries are in each specific region, based on an assessment of the terrorist threat posed in that region to the United States' interests, will help the U.S. government and its allies craft a more accurate and focused counterrecruitment plan. If the United States is uncertain who its adversaries are in a specific region, using general counterrecruitment techniques—as opposed to developing a targeted, region-specific counterrecruitment plan—may not work, and could even backfire. Moreover, using the models of recruitment discussed above to understand the types of individuals that al-Qaida and related organizations are trying to recruit, and the tools and models they are using for recruitment, could serve to reveal gaps in information that need to be filled in each region where al-Qaida and its affiliates are operating.

CONCLUSION

In general more data need to be collected on the types of recruits al-Qaida and related organizations are seeking, how al-Qaida is using specific nodes to recruit new members, and what precisely is the nature of the relationship between al-Qaida and other Islamic extremist organizations. This empirical effort can be usefully married to the scientific literature on recruitment, changes in attitude, conversion, and radicalization in crafting more effective countermeasures to combat al-Qaida's recruitment.

N O T E S

1. For the purposes of this chapter recruits are considered to be individuals who have gone beyond exposure to terrorist messages and have been both indoctrinated and incorporated into the organization, whereas potential recruits—the primary focus of this chapter—are either those who are assessed by terrorist organizations as ripe for recruitment or those who self-select for terrorism on the basis of various personal and environmental factors.
2. Measurements of attitudes, opinions, emotions, perceptions, interests, etc.
3. Measurements of education, race, gender, occupation, etc.
4. In this chapter, we use the phrase *terrorist groups* to refer to violent groups or institutions such as al-Qaida that are totalist: that is, they seek to completely transform and dominate the lives of members. Our examination of the literature focused on the most destructive and demanding totalist groups (e.g., Aum Shinrikyo, the People's Church, and Chinese "thought reform" of American POWs during the Korean War) for illustrative patterns. Al-Qaida is at the high end of the spectrum of totalism.
5. We will use the term *node* to refer to the context of recruitment. This may be a prison, a school campus, a medical clinic, a religious center, the living room of the recruiter's home, or any other milieu used as a stage by the recruiting organization.
6. These are shorthand models to characterize the recruitment process. For ease of reference we have given them descriptive names, but these are not meant to be rigid or comprehensive categorizations.

7. Culling or weeding-out usually enhances the reputation of the group and its members by giving them elite status.

8. Individuals tend to model themselves on or seek guidance from those like them, not alien outsiders.

9. Surrounding potential recruits with peers who are already established recruits.

10. E. Goffman, *Behavior in Public Places: Notes on the Social Organization of Gatherings* (Glencoe, Ill.: Free Press of Glencoe, 1963).

11. Good studies include: P. Zimbardo and C. Hartley, "Cults Go to High School: A Theoretical and Empirical Analysis of the Initial Stage in the Recruitment Process," *Cultic Studies Journal* 2:1 (1985): 91–147. J. Lofland and R. Stark, "Becoming a World Saver," *American Sociological Review* 30 (1965): 862–875. I. Yalom and M. Lieberman, "A Study of Encounter Group Casualties." In Sager, Singer, and Kaplan (eds.), *Progress in Group and Family Therapy* (New York: Brunner/Mazel, 1972), pp. 223–254. S. Moscovici, "Toward a Theory of Conversion Behavior," *Advances in Experimental Social Psychology* 13 (1980): 209–239.

12. For example: opinions, attitudes, emotions, preconceptions, motivation, self-efficacy, stereotypes.

13. For example: sickness, fear, disorientation, depression, hunger.

14. S. Ash, "Cult-Induced Psychopathology, Part One: Clinical Picture," *Cultic Studies Journal* 2:1 (1985): 31–90. A. Bloomgarden and M. Langone, "Preventive Education on Cultism for High-School Students: A Comparison of Different Programs' Effects on Potential Vulnerability to Cults," *Cultic Studies Journal* 1:2 (1984): 167–177.

15. S. Ash, 1985; M. Zerin. 1982. "The Pied Piper Phenomenon: Family Systems and Vulnerability to Cults," unpublished doctoral dissertation, The Fielding Institute, Santa Barbara, Calif.

16. Self-chosen and strongly held as part of identity.

17. Keme Nzerem, "At School with the Shoe Bomber," *Guardian Unlimited* (February 28, 2002). Available at http://www.guardian.co.uk/g2/story/0,3604,659184,00.html.

18. BBC News, "Who Is Richard Reid?" (December 28, 2001), Available at http://news.bbc.co.uk/1/hi/uk/1731568.stm.

19. We are implying not that every recruit to al-Qaida is brainwashed or coerced, but rather that many techniques used in classic, predatory thought reform are used by al-Qaida. Moreover, most of the recruiting techniques used by predatory totalist groups (e.g., cults) are shared by al-Qaida.

BIBLIOGRAPHY

Ash, S., "Cult-Induced Psychopathology, Part One: Clinical Picture," *Cultic Studies Journal* 2:1 (1985): 31–90.

Ash, S., 1985; M. Zerin, 1982, "The Pied Piper Phenomenon: Family Systems and Vulnerability to Cults," unpublished doctoral dissertation, The Fielding Institute, Santa Barbara, Calif.

Bloomgarden A. and M. Langone, "Preventive Education on Cultism for High-School Students: A Comparison of Different Programs' Effects on Potential Vulnerability to Cults," *Cultic Studies Journal* 1:2 (1984): 167–177.

Goffman, E., *Behavior in Public Places: Notes on the Social Organization of Gatherings* (Glencoe, Ill.: Free Press of Glencoe, 1963).

Lofland, J. and R. Stark, "Becoming a World Saver," *American Sociological Review* 30 (1965): 862–875.

Moscovici, S., "Toward a Theory of Conversion Behavior," *Advances in Experimental Social Psychology* 13 (1980): 209–239.

Nzerem, Keme, "At School with the Shoe Bomber," *Guardian Unlimited* (28 February 2002). Available at http://www.guardian.co.uk/g2/story/0,3604,659184,00.html.

"Who Is Richard Reid?" BBC News (28 December 2001). Available at http://news.bbc.co.uk/1/hi/uk/1731568.stm.

Yalom, I. and M. Lieberman, "A Study of Encounter Group Casualties." In Sager, Singer, and Kaplan (eds.), *Progress in Group and Family Therapy* (New York: Brunner/Mazel, 1975), pp. 223–254.

Zimbardo, P. and C. Hartley, "Cults Go to High School: A Theoretical and Empirical Analysis of the Initial Stage in the Recruitment Process," *Cultic Studies Journal* 2:1 (1985): 91–147.

"The War of the Ether": Al-Qaida's Psychological Warfare Campaign Against the Western and Muslim Worlds

Michael G. Knapp
Middle East Analyst, U.S. Army National Ground Intelligence
Center (NGIC)

Anyone who knows the media will discover that the mujahideen have been able to move from the defensive to the offensive in the field of psychological warfare. Unlike previous decades, when it was possible to play completely with the news, the leap in communication technology has made it impossible for anyone to monopolize information. This factor in particular has given the mujahideen broad scope to launch their counterattack, which has been able to bring fear to the other side to an unprecedented degree.

—Abu-'Ubayd al-Qurashi, "The War of the Ether," *Al-Ansar*, 20 November 2002.[1]

Al-Qaida has proved to be a wily, creative, and adaptive adversary that appreciates the mass media as a primary weapon of psychological warfare in its unconventional conflict against the West and in the Arab and Muslim worlds. Moreover, its success in using the mass media to shape the global information environment underscores the corresponding ineffectiveness of western information warfare and psychological operations (PSYOP) efforts in the global war on terrorism (GWOT).

This chapter analyzes a moving target: al-Qaida as a global cellular terrorist network with ever-changing methods of operation, but with a consistent ideology and culture. My purpose is to shed more light on what messages the al-Qaida transnational terrorist network is sending, over the mass media, to spread its concept of violent global jihad and to strategically counter our greater conventional military and media capabilities. That is, the media serve as a "window" to influence sympathetic Islamic audiences, as a weapon against Muslim governments and populations, and as a weapon against the United States and its western allies. I will also note the centrality of the global electronic and print mass media for al-Qaida in disseminating its messages.

This study covers more than 200 documents from January 2002 to January 2004. It is based mostly on English translations of online al-Qaida articles and Internet books but also includes translations of selected articles in Arab and Muslim news media. The primary source is the U.S. government's Foreign Broadcast Information Service (FBIS), but a few translations from commercial research centers were consulted when FBIS analyses were not available. My analysis is also buttressed by selected material in western professional journals and the western press.

INFOWAR AND PSYOP DEFINED

What kinds of virtual warfare are Islamic terrorist groups such as al-Qaida conducting against us? The forms that are apparently most relevant for this discussion include information warfare, or infowar, and a primary subset of infowar called psychological operations, or PSYOP. *Infowar* is defined by the U.S. Joint Chiefs of Staff as "the range of actions taken during conflict to achieve information superiority over an adversary while defending one's own information, information processes, and information systems."[2] What this boils down to is using information to create such a mismatch between us and an opponent that the opponent's strategy is defeated before its first forces can be deployed or its first shots can be fired. Infowar has to do with how humans think and with influencing how they make decisions; the target of infowar, therefore, is human minds, especially those minds that make key decisions of war or peace. The primary medium through which infowar is waged is the communications networks of a society or its military.[3]

PSYOP (also called psychological warfare) are "operations taken to convey selected information and indicators to foreign audiences to influence their emotions, motives, objective reasoning, and, ultimately, the behavior of foreign governments, organizations, groups and individuals. [Their] purpose is to induce or reinforce foreign attitudes and behavior that are favorable to the originator's objectives."[4] In essence, PSYOP are an attempt to project a false view of reality, to warp the opponent's view of reality, or to influence its will to engage in hostilities. Martin Libicki, an expert on infowar, has proposed four categories of psychological warfare: (1) operations designed to impose a particular culture on another nation; (2) operations against the adversary's national will; (3) operations against opposing commanders; (4) operations against their troops.[5]

THE IMPORTANCE OF THE INTERNET FOR AL-QAIDA

For several reasons, the Internet is optimal for transnational terrorist groups such as al-Qaida. It is perfect for command and control (C2), since it allows for a globally dispersed network, unhindered by distance. It can be a secure channel for such a group, with easily available encryption software, steganography for graphic images, and coded words or phrases in open text.[6] Information-savvy irregular adversaries such as al-Qaida find this medium very effective for fund-raising and recruiting. The Internet has served to ensure the network's continuity of operations despite the capture or death of some of its leaders and the breakup of many of its cells. Al-Qaida also uses the Internet to disseminate propaganda and disinformation and has used the Internet for PSYOP—to intimidate targeted populations and spread fear and hate among its adversaries. Al-Qaida's extensive use of Internet-based media, and its careful defense and preservation of those capabilities, indicates that it knows it must remain engaged in order to dominate the ideological debate, and even to survive.

Open societies such as the United States place a lot of information about ourselves on the Internet to serve our members, but this information is just as easily retrieved by our adversaries. As will be demonstrated later in this chapter, al-Qaida has proved adept at collecting and exploiting our open-source information against us. Some of it provides a good window into our political, military, economic, and cultural vulnerabilities, and such a window can be a distinct advantage to those who do not wish us well. The almost limitless size and scope of the Internet make it a source of and repository for information, and its sophisticated search and retrieval capabilities make much of its contents easily available to anyone. The nature of the worldwide net provides and promotes anonymity and deception. Thus governments find it difficult to identify or monitor users, or to control the content or use of what is posted.

For terrorist networks, the Internet is a tool of the weak. It allows nonstate groups with limited resources and unsophisticated capabilities to compete with or even outmatch the huge media machines of advanced nations. The Web also provides operational flexibility (since there is no physical state to defend), and a long-range strike capability that puts distance between planners and the targets they attack. As a protective capability, the Internet can be used to divert attention from a real attack scenario or to confuse or disrupt defense or security efforts, since terrorists know that when their Internet chatter increases, western officials tend to issue warnings of possible attacks.[7]

The Internet is also effective for mobilization. It can create solidarity and brotherhood within the larger community (in the Muslim case, the *ummah* or *umma*—the diaspora) and between groups.[8] It has also been a way to maintain morale within the network in the face of reverses since the attacks of 11 September 2001 (particularly al-Qaida's loss of its training facilities and planning base as a result of the United States' campaign in Afghanistan). Al-Qaida has used the Internet to promote and support "franchise operations," in which affiliated regional or local extremist groups (portions of its "network of networks") can be influenced to achieve the aims of the "parent" group. Because these groups share the radical ideology as well as the fluid structure and adaptive methods of al-Qaida, they represent a comparable threat.

Recently, al-Qaida has transformed itself from an operational structure to a common ideology (in order to survive and continue to influence other Islamist groups as well as Muslims worldwide). Its more intense use of the mass media has helped it advance its traditional mission by nonmilitary means and build a committed worldwide support base.

WHY ARE TERRORISTS' MOTIVES IMPORTANT?

Examining al-Qaida's motives tells us much about how its leaders think, and why they operate as they do. First, these motives provide a rationale for the group's pursuit of political power through violence. Second, they justify risks (to be considered rational, violence requires a congruent purpose). Third, the motives of a terrorist group serve to recruit followers—true believers, opportunists, people who like action, and people who seek a feeling of belonging. Fourth, motives develop a sense of camaraderie that ensures group loyalty, solidarity, and self-protection.[9]

Terrorist groups' motives tend to reflect one overriding theme: injustice from a repressive political authority that is denying the terrorists their due, which is an independent system organized by their ideology. This is an important point. If we can undertand how injustice is perceived, then we can remove or alter that perception (by redressing grievances), thus decreasing the pool of recruits available to the terrorists and possibly creating divisions in their present ranks.[10]

AL-QAIDA'S MASS MEDIA DOCTRINAL PLATFORMS

The two main platforms that al-Qaida has used to disseminate its doctrinal and strategic messages are *Al-Ansar* ("The Followers") and *Alneda* ("The Call"). *Al-Ansar* was the network's first "online magazine" and was posted every two weeks from January 2002 to April 2003. According to an introductory article, this publication was created to provide "a correct view of the conflict" between the "international crusade" and the "Islamic *ummah*," and to revive the path of jihad that had been taken by the first generation of Muslims.[11] *Al-Ansar* had a standard four-section format: normally, a one-page unattributed editorial; a religiously oriented article in the section "Vision of Faith" (usually four to seven pages), by Sayf al-Din al-Ansari; a military analysis in the section "Strategic Studies" (usually six to eight pages), by Abu 'Ubayd al-Qurashi; and a politically focused article in the section "Political Analyses" (also six to eight pages), by Abu Ayman al-Hilali. (All of the authors' names in al-Qaida's online publications are thought to be pseudonyms, and more than one writer may sometimes share the same pen name.)

In September 2001 al-Qaida began publishing longer, more in-depth treatises (called "books") on political, military, and religious topics as Internet "zip" files, initially in *Al-Ansar*; these are still available on some jihadist Web sites. These were first published at four-month intervals, but since the summer of 2003 they have become available more frequently (one or two per month). As of January 2004, eight volumes had been published over 15 months; some of them are cited in the endnotes.

Alneda is considered al-Qaida's official Web site, and from March 2002 to April 2003 it was a repository for single essays (up to one or more per day) that were not published on a regular schedule. The site was closed down three times between April and September 2003 (reportedly by western government action) but had been attempting to reappear within a few months before July 2004. As with *Al-Ansar*, *Alneda*'s contents have been keyed to current developments concerning the "depressed situation" in the Muslim world, and developments in the American-led global war on terrorism.

Al-Qaida's official media organ is the Center for Islamic Studies and Research (CISR), but within the last two to three months (all time references are as of July 2004) it may have been renamed the Global Islamic Media Center. This center has been hosted by numerous legitimate Internet Service Providers as well as several jihadist Web sites, has sometimes used the *Alneda* Web address, and has had to move frequently because it has been subject to many shutdowns. Like *Al-Ansar*, CISR is thought to provide strategic guidance, theological arguments, and moral inspiration ("virtual leadership") to al-Qaida elements worldwide; it may also be used to direct the network's operational cells. CISR's Web content consists of 11 sections that include the CISR's own reports of fighting in Afghanistan and other theaters; a regular digest of world media coverage of these conflicts; books of jihad theology to download; poetry about the virtues of jihad; videos such as testaments from some of the 9/11 hijackers; and information about the trials of mujahideen prisoners in custody at Guantánamo and in Pakistan.[12] CISR has also been a main source for the series of Internet "books" (zip files).

Al-Qaida's leaders evidently feel that a biweekly "professional journal" is still an important part of their mass media arsenal. From mid-October 2003 to November 2004, a new online magazine, *Sawt al-Jihad* ("Voice of Struggle"), was published on jihadist Web sites; it focused on ideology and appeared to be a replacement for *Al-Ansar*. *Sawt al-Jihad* was more narrowly focused than its predecessor, stating that it is concerned with the situation of mujahideen and the jihad in the Arabian Peninsula.[13] Its content includes interviews with al-Qaida's leaders; firsthand "battle stories" from participants in recent prominent attacks; the wills of martyred mujahideen; religious justifications for jihad (articles and religious rulings favorable to al-Qaida's ideology); and critical coverage of international cooperation and domestic antiterror activities of the Saudi regime. The magazine has also posted excerpts from earlier al-Qaida books, such as Ayman al-Zawahiri's *Knights under the Prophet's Banner*.[14]

The most recent addition to al-Qaida's mass media arsenal is *Ma'askar al-Battar* ("Al-Battar Training Camp"), which, like *Sawt al-Jihad*, was published by "mujahideen in Arabia." This online magazine appeared in January 2004, was posted to jihadist Web sites approximately every two weeks, and disappeared in November 2004; each issue contained five or six articles and sophisticated graphics. It differed from its companion magazine, however, in that it focused on military matters and was published "in support of Muslims in several lands of Islam."[15] Its announced goal was to spread "military culture among the youth of Islam" by providing lessons in physical exercise and jihad preparedness, proficiency in the use of light weapons and "guerrilla group actions in the cities and mountains," and "important points in security and intelligence."[16] This publication appeared to be designed as a "virtual training camp" to promote home study of jihad (away from the Saudi security forces' grasp and America's "eyes in the skies," and to compensate for the lack of conventional military training); to recruit new militants; and possibly to send messages to sleeper cells affiliated with al-Qaida. The appearance of, and the considerable effort invested in, a second such publication, from an organization trying to sustain operations and avoid discovery and destruction by the Saudi authorities, indicates the importance for al-Qaida of reaching its youthful (but not uninitiated) audience.[17] Particularly noteworthy were a series of articles on operational security measures and the principles of conducting guerrilla warfare.

KEY POLITICAL THEMES

Political themes are prominent (and often repeated) in al-Qaida's mass media articles. This is not unexpected, given the political dimension of terrorist violence and the fact that political affairs are an integral part of Islamic movements. The Palestinians' plight and their "liberation" from Israeli domination and oppression have been a central cause for Muslims, as is fighting against the anti-Islamic campaigns in Bosnia, Chechnya, Afghanistan, Kashmir, and other theaters. Usama bin Ladin is presented not only as the leader of al-Qaida but as the imam (religious leader) for all Muslims; therefore, the Islamic nation (*ummah*) should rally around him and fully embrace his cause.[18] Similarly, Muslims worldwide need to wake up to the "depressed condition" of their community and not stand passively by while infidels and apostates dominate and oppress them. Active participation in the jihad to free all Muslim lands is thus required.

The complicity of Arab and Muslim regimes (which are friendly to infidels) in the oppression of their populations makes them a legitimate target of this global jihad. The United Nations is also a target for the mujahideen (literally, "fighters for God's cause"), since it is held to be clearly a lackey of the United States and thus a tool for injustice, and is itself against Islam.[19] Al-Zawahiri's warning in *Knights under the Prophet's Banner*—that the "far enemy" must be targeted first but that the mujahideen must still beware of the continuing threat from the "near enemy" at home—also appears from time to time.

One of the most interesting assertions in al-Qaida's writings concerns good versus bad terrorism. The network claims that it practices "commendable" terrorism as part of the fight to stop the United States' oppression of and injustice toward Muslims, and to halt American support for the aggression of the Zionists (Israel). By contrast, there is "abhorrent" terrorism: what Israel is practicing in Palestine, and what the United States is doing in Iraq, Afghanistan, and all over the world.[20]

Al-Qaida zeroed in on President Bush's mention, immediately after 9/11, of a "crusade" against terrorism, and since then has claimed that this American crusade against the entire Islamic world is doomed to fail. The reasons are that Muslims adhere more closely than Christians or Jews to the principles of their faith, that the Muslim *ummah* is more cohesive domestically and internationally, that al-Qaida and the Taliban are now a "major presence on the world political and psychological map," that the "crusaders' enemy front" is in conflict and disintegrating.[21] Articles in the mass media show that more recent events can be exploited equally well: the fall of Baghdad to the invading "coalition" marked the return of "direct colonialism" in the Arab world and recalls the earlier conquests of Jerusalem, Beirut, and Kabul by the infidels.[22]

In the aftermath of the attacks of 9/11, al-Qaida has consistently maintained that these *ghazwah* (or "raids," referring to pre-Islamic Arabian military expeditions) were legitimate and justified, in light of the United States' continuing "occupation" of Saudi Arabia, the use of this sacred territory to launch attacks on other Muslim states (such as Iraq), and American support of Israel's anti-Islamic aggression. Al-Qaida also points out that the United States is clearly bent on controlling the region's oil and dominating Muslim territories, through its use of regional surrogates (i.e., through "veiled colonization").[23] The United States is also the enemy because it is illegally holding (in subhuman conditions), and mistreating, the mujahideen prisoners at Guantánamo. Since these brother Muslims are suffering for a noble cause, al-Qaida explains, Muslims must do everything in their power to free them.[24]

Another recurrent political theme is that Usama bin Ladin is still alive, and that al-Qaida will "stay the course" in its fight against the United States, despite the losses in personnel, training facilities, and base of operations that the network has sustained since the American campaign in Afghanistan. A recent and more unusual claim (allegedly made by a female commander of the "women's *mujahidat*"—the feminine form of mujahideen) is that women fighters are being mobilized for the jihad.[25] Less believable to westerners (but plausible to the Arab and Muslim worlds) was al-Qaida's claim of responsibility for the blackout that struck the eastern United States and part of Canada in August 2003. Still, the claim was noteworthy because the network emphasized the weakness of the United States' power infrastructure, and the initial confusion and ineffectiveness of civil responses to the crisis.[26]

KEY MILITARY THEMES

The prominence of military subjects in al-Qaida's mass media articles demonstrates that this aspect of the conflict is also of high importance for the network. Al-Qaida stresses that it is familiar with the art of war (as described in Sun Tzu's *The Art of War* and other classical Chinese military works), but that the American military has chosen to ignore the past lessons of others and to rely on modern technology: the United States is arrogant and thus is ignorant of its current mujahideen foes.[27] An early essay by al-Qurashi boasts that al-Qaida is familiar with American writings on fourth-generation warfare and asymmetric warfare and is using these strategies effectively against the American military, which is still stuck in a cold war mentality.[28] Another al-Qaida article tells Muslims that guerilla warfare is the best weapon they have and that it is the best way to prolong the conflict with the "crusader enemy."[29] In a revealing admission, a spokesperson for the group indicates that the frequency of strikes has changed from one major operation every two years (before the 9/11 attacks) to two or more operations per year.[30] Iraq is also mentioned, as the highest-priority battlefield for the global jihad.

An analysis by al-Qurashi of Americans' "nightmares" indicates that al-Qaida's leaders have studied our societal fears and weaknesses through our own mass media. Threats that al-Qaida believes the United States is most concerned about include weapons of mass destruction (WMD); "naval jihad" attacks, such as that against the USS *Cole* in Yemen in October 2000; attacks against oil supplies and other aspects of the American economy; "Internet jihad," as has already been used by both sides in the Israeli-Palestinian conflict; and the forging of interests and operational links between "jihad groups and organized criminal groups."[31] In another article, a jihadist writes that the United States is losing the "information war" because it does not understand Arab, middle eastern, or Muslim culture.

Al-Qurashi (as al-Qaida's military writer) favors historical comparisons and selective "lessons learned." In some of his *Al-Ansar* articles he points out negative qualities of his adversaries or vulnerabilities that can be exploited by the mujahideen. For example, the attack on Israeli athletes at the Munich Olympics in 1972 is compared to the 9/11 attacks in New York and Washington, D.C., and both episodes are hailed as "great propaganda victories."[32] According to another article by al-Qurashi, the surprise achieved against the United States in the 9/11 "conquest" exceeded that of the Japanese attack against Pearl Harbor.[33] Another case study analyzes the Soviet victory at Stalingrad against the Nazi invaders during World War II and the "victory" of Palestinian irregulars against invading Israeli soldiers in the Jenin refugee camp. Both were "decisive battles" that revealed the weakness of the apparently stronger side. This study also identifies "urban jihad operations" as a strategic choice for Islamic fighters, since it is an Israeli center of gravity (COG).[34] Another article focusing on Israeli aggression claims that the al-Aqsa Intifada is Israel's "Vietnam," since winning the battles does not necessarily win the war.[35] In another analysis of military trends, al-Qurashi attempts to show that the American military has a history of barbarity and war crimes against civilians; the reason for targeting civilians is to give the United States a "political pressure card" and to wage psychological warfare.[36] A spokesperson for al-Qaida also insinuates that Iraq fell to America in the second Gulf War not because the United States was proficient in combat but because of the "treachery of the Baathist regime."

There has been much speculation about whether the al-Qaida network possesses and can deploy WMD against the West. In June 2002, in an installment of "In the Shadow of Spears"—a series of articles in *Alneda*—al-Qaida's spokesman Sulayman Abu-Ghayth stated that the network had a right to use "chemical and germ weapons" against the United States.[37] Next, Hashim al-Makki's online "book" about the experiences of the Afghan Arabs in Afghanistan, published in September 2002, included references to a sharp divergence within al-Qaida between "hawks" and "doves" on the issue of possession and use of WMD.[38] This was followed by the release in May 2003 of a fatwa (religious ruling) formulated by the pro-jihadist Saudi cleric Nasir bin Hamd al-Fahd, which defended the use of WMD against infidels supposedly on the basis of Islamic law.[39] This indicates that al-Qaida may be laying the groundwork to justify its use of WMD, even if it does not yet possess any.

Another instance of the issuing of detailed online guidance for terrorists following a theoretical military discussion is an article by al-Qurashi in October 2002 on the overlooked value of snipers against infidel forces.[40] This article was apparently influenced by the widespread fear in the United States during the sniper attacks in the area of Washington, D.C., from 2 to 22 October 2002; it was published on the date of the last attack, just before two men were arrested and charged with the attacks. Three months after al-Qurashi's article appeared, a jihadist Web site published an online snipers' training manual providing detailed tactics, techniques, procedures, and technical standards.[41]

Al-Qurashi demonstrated the depth of al-Qaida's open-source research in a review and analysis of the weaknesses—said to be both systemic and current—of U.S. intelligence. This article was published in *Al-Ansar* on June 26, 2002; it states that even though U.S. intelligence was surprised by the 9/11 attacks, no real changes have been made in our intelligence system after those attacks (in contrast to the changes made after World War II as a result of the Japanese attack on Pearl Harbor, and the passage of the National Security Act of 1947). Further, al-Qurashi claims that American intelligence will continue to fail against the mujahideen, because of interagency competition, "bureaucratic obesity," and failure to understand a "determined and creative enemy." Al-Qaida's advantages over us in the conflict (which it claims we are unable to counter) include the unconventional structure and methods of the mujahideen, their strong religious faith, and the network's decentralized operations and continually changing military doctrine.[42]

Another interesting article by al-Qurashi in *Al-Ansar* reviews the center of gravity (COG)—a concept used by Carl Von Clausewitz in *On War* to describe conventional land warfare—and goes on to analyze the United States' failed attempts to apply this theory to unconventional foes such as al-Qaida. Al-Qurashi alleges that the United States has misidentified al-Qaida's COG as a moral one (its hatred of infidelity), and that because al-Qaida is decentralized, such efforts by the Americans to find its decisive points will not succeed. Al-Qurashi points out that, although the United States does not understand al-Qaida's COG, the network knows the United States' COG very well (our economy) and is targeting those interests not only within the continental United States but all over the world.[43] Two more recent military items worthy of note are al-Qaida's admission that it has been recruiting "blue-eyed foreign fighters" for operations in the West, since they can move more freely and disappear in those targeted societies,[44] and the reported publication of a new kidnapping manual that provides tactics for snatching Americans, especially in Muslim countries, in order to force the release of the mujahideen detainees.[45]

KEY RELIGIOUS THEMES

Religious propaganda appears to rank as highly with al-Qaida's leadership as political and military ideas. Here again, some significant themes recur in the media articles. Al-Ansari argues that there is indeed a Quranic basis for perpetual hostility between Muslims and unbelievers and that (armed) jihad against the infidels is obligatory and an individual duty for all.[46] Another writer argues that Islamic law permits the killing of infidels (seven grounds are cited) and also of fellow Muslims (six grounds are provided).[47]

Al-Qaida's writers stress that the West is conducting a "new crusade" against all of Islam, not a "war against terrorism" as it proclaims. Thus jihad is important as a means of destroying the infidel countries: "annihilation of the infidels is a divine decree."[48] Al-Qaida recognizes that it must influence the population against some Islamic scholars in the societies it targets, and it warns that not all these *ulama* truly represent Islam; Muslims must beware of those who are under the control of the "agent regimes." Some appeals are also directed toward these scholars; those *ulama* not under "apostate government" control are urged to support the jihad to free Muslims from injustice. The network also directs some of its messages toward the larger Muslim *ummah*: a frequent warning in mass media articles is that all who cooperate with the "crusaders" are themselves infidels, and al-Zawahiri exults that the "Islamic awakening" (for which al-Qaida is supposedly responsible) is frightening the enemies of Islam.[49]

Another threat, according to these writers, is that western intellectuals are helping to "psychologically mobilize" public opinion against Muslims and to justify the waging of a long-term crusade against Islam. The most prominent of these alleged inciters of hatred against the Muslim world are Thomas Friedman, Samuel Huntington, Bernard Lewis, and Daniel Pipes.[50] The state of Israel and Shiite Muslims are also painted as enemies of the *ummah*. Israel's Jews, al-Qaida claims, intend to expand their territorial aggression beyond Palestine to make Iraq part of "greater Israel," and Shiite "renegades" in Iran and Iraq are said to be as much of a threat as the Christians and Jews are to Sunni Muslims.[51]

A primary aim of this westernization campaign, according to one of al-Qaida's authors, is the forcible imposition by the United States of secularism on the region and the implementation of this throughout the Islamic world after the occupation of Iraq. Al-Qaida warns its readers that separation of religion and state is dangerous because it transforms the human being from a servant of God into a base animal driven by self-interest. Something else to beware of is democracy, readers are told, since it is one of the "fruits of secularism" that take ultimate authority away from God and place the people's will above God's.[52]

AL-QAIDA LAYS OUT ITS STRATEGY

A particularly significant aspect in some of al-Qaida's mass media writings is that the network is laying out (and justifying) a strategy against the West as well as against the governments and populations within its own areas of operations. For the terrorists, the attacks of 9/11 appear to constitute a dividing line. Before the attacks, al-Qaida's primary mission was to inspire, train, arm, and finance as many mujahideen as possible and to assist radical Islamist groups worldwide. The objectives of the attacks themselves, according to a western expert, were to provoke a massive western response, revealing that the West is really at war with Islam, and to force westerners and Muslims to take sides against each other, since their fundamental values are incompatible. Both Muslims and westerners will thus be convinced that they are in a fight to the death, and this would make Samuel Huntington's violent "clash of civilizations" a reality.[53] Other benefits of these attacks were, first, that they showed the impotence and ineffectiveness of the West as well as the "high treason" of the Arab governments which expressed support for the United States; and, second, that (in the network's eyes) they "globalized" the Islamist war against the West by negating regional perceptions and the nationalist dimension of the conflict. The current focus of al-Qaida's strategy also becomes more evident from its recent communiqués. Al-Qaida admits that it is seeking to "expand the battlefield and exhaust the enemy," in the hope that targeting American interests everywhere will overstretch our resources and spread fear.[54] Also, the network is evidently increasing its investment in PSYOP to compensate for the loss of its physical capabilities.

Although al-Qaida has not publicly revealed its infowar strategy, al-Qurashi did spell out (in an article in *Al-Ansar* of 20 November 2002) its plans for "counterpropaganda" operations. After reviewing the United States' many alleged failures in "political propaganda and . . . informational and psychological warfare" from the Spanish-American War up to the current conflicts in Afghanistan and Iraq, al-Qurashi lists the "scientific foundations and principles" for al-Qaida's campaign against the Americans' use of the media and psychological warfare. These principles are to determine the strongest elements of the enemy's propaganda, so they can be "isolated and divided according to their degree of importance" and then refuted; remove the enemy's ideas from their symbolic and emotional framework, so they can be attacked and the contradictions among them identified; "strongly attack...the weak points in the enemy's propaganda"; "avoid...confronting the enemy's propaganda while it is at its strongest"; "respond...to the enemy's propaganda with events"; turn people's eyes toward their leaders, "aiming always at putting the enemy on the defensive"; and "take...the initiative, because it always produces a powerful effect on public opinion."[55]

Al-Qurashi then acknowledges the importance for al-Qaida of al-Jazeera's broadcasts of the network's series of audio- and videotapes since 9 September 2002. As an example of the events referred to above, al-Qurashi first discusses Usama bin Ladin's audiotape released on the first anniversary of the 9/11 attacks, in which bin Ladin acknowledges the network's responsibility for those attacks. Second is Ayman al-Zawahiri's audiotape of October 2002, which heralded a series of attacks such as the killing of American marines in Faylaka, Kuwait; the bombing of the French oil tanker *Limburg*; and "the bombing of the dens of corruption in [Bali] Indonesia." In the author's view, this second message by al-Zawahiri is "psychological warfare," which is "the beginning of a strategic counterattack." Last, al-Qurashi disparages the United States' strategy of "information dominance," which he claims consists of failed "plans to control the sources of information, both as regards educational curricula and as regards audio, video, and cable broadcasting." The author concludes that this American strategy must be "understood and opposed forcefully," and that the mujahideen are "on their way to winning the war of the ether."[56] Finally, another article concerning the "U.S.-*Alneda* Internet War" states that al-Qaida will persevere in its use of the Internet no matter how many of its sites are hit, and urges Muslim technical experts to "break the U.S. companies' monopoly" of program software and "operation systems" even though this will take several years, so that the infidels will no longer know the mujahideen's secrets.[57]

An Israeli expert's analysis of an article of 30 November 2002 by Lewis Atiyyatallah—a prominent jihadist (and interpreter of al-Qaida)—identifies four strategic stages in the conflict between Islamist radicals and the West. (1) Continue the current guerrilla and information war against the "external enemy," since the West cannot be defeated in a traditional confrontation. (2) Defeat the Arab "agent regimes" by influencing or removing the United States as their

patron: Getting the United States to limit its power and direct its
actions removes its legitimacy, and undermining American support
makes its allies more vulnerable. (3) During the "stage of isolation,"
the network will remove the United States' administration from its
own citizens and from its allies (for example, by exploiting difficulties
in the American campaigns in Afghanistan and Iraq). (4) Directly
confront the United States, defeating the "great crusader" on its own
soil; this will lead to loss of the conflict by the West and will shift the
international center of gravity back to the Islamic world. There is a
gaping hole in this strategy, however. Nowhere in al-Qaida's mass
media works is there a real political vision of how the modern Islamic
world would look at the conclusion of this conflict against western
domination and injustice. Global jihad and the resulting utopian
sharia-based, unified Islamic society are the only well-defined goals.[58]
This is one area where more effective western infowar operations
could potentially do much to decrease the attraction of the
global jihadist ideology for the world's increasingly impressionable
Muslim youth.

SHIFTS IN TARGETS AND AUDIENCES

Al-Qaida has shown its ability to move quickly from compromised or
blocked Web sites to others so as to continue spreading its venom in
the mass media. It has also been creative in its shifts in targets for
physical attacks and in audiences for virtual influence. From its initial
primary focus on physically attacking the United States, Israel, and
the Arab-Muslim "agent regimes," al-Qaida has moved increasingly
to non-Arab and non-Muslim allies such as the United Kingdom,
France, Russia, Australia, and Japan. Its targets have also changed
from "hard" (targets high in political, economic, or military value but
generally better defended) to "soft" (less well-defended infrastructure and support assets), and its attacks have expanded into less
developed regions such as Africa and southeast Asia. Al-Qaida has
also expanded its targeting of fellow Muslims to anyone who is aiding
infidels.

With regard to the audiences it has sought for virtual influence,
al-Qaida focused first on Muslims in the Arabian Peninsula and
throughout the Middle East and south Asia. This focus was initially
broadened to Muslims living in central and southeast Asia, and
Europe (especially those in the Balkans), and then to the Muslim

ummah (diaspora) worldwide, particularly Islamist "brethren" in Palestine and Iraq, and to Muslim youth everywhere. Mujahideen networks, both those affiliated with al-Qaida and those with only indirect or very loose ties to the group, have also been targeted for mass media influence. Of most interest have been al-Qaida's direct approaches to the public in countries involved in one way or another in the GWOT or in various alliances with the West. Usama bin Ladin has twice made personal appeals to the American public, for example, to either embrace Islam and repudiate American leaders who are anti-Islamic and whose policies and campaigns in Afghanistan and Iraq are doomed to fail or prepare for more attacks like those of 9/11.[59] Even the public in countries that are allies of the United States and the public in nonaligned nations have been a focus of al-Qaida's media campaign.

CONCLUSION

Although al-Qaida's methods continue to change and its targets continue to shift, its underlying goals and ideology have been constant. Its mass media writings also reveal that even as al-Qaida's operational capabilities have suffered, its intention to attack has not diminished. Further, perception management remains central to its war strategy against the West and the Arab and Muslim societies it seeks to change. In their articles on the Internet and in Arabic news media, Usama bin Ladin and other leaders of al-Qaida have consistently chosen to publicly describe their organization's doctrine, its strategy, and even some of its tactics. However, even though anniversaries of its significant "victories" are exploited for propaganda, they are not tied to the network's physical strikes (which are assessed to occur when all preparations for an attack have been completed, and when the security posture of the target is optimal).

Al-Qaida's mass media writings and addresses provide significant, detailed insight into the cultural and religious "language" that it is applying against the West and against its own governments and populations. As Americans, we must better understand our adversaries in the global war against terrorism. Knowledge of Islamic terrorists' political, military, and religious goals matters, since it can help frustrate their objectives and protect our own diplomatic and military forces and society. We must learn to get inside their heads to discern what motivates them, how they think, and why they think that way.

It is evident that the lack of a counterideology among regional Arab and Muslim governments has tilted the political environment in favor of radical Islamism and violence, and is thus inflicting long-term damage on the Muslim world. We can also see that poorly planned and inappropriately conducted information warfare and psychological operations by the West have so far allowed al-Qaida's extremists to define and shape the global information environment to their advantage. We must start to turn this around if the United States is to realize its goals of isolating the terrorists from the "sea of injustice" they thrive in, and of supporting our Arab and Muslim allies as they begin to make the meaningful changes in their societies that will address the long-term conditions on which terrorism thrives.

N O T E S

1. FBIS, "Commentator Analyzes Recent Bin Ladin Tapes, Sees U.S. as Losing 'Information War' Against al-Qa'ida,"*Al-Ansar* in Arabic (20 November 2002): 9–15, GMP20021126000154. Internet. (*Note on format and security*: All FBIS translations used are unclassified but were accessed through a U.S. government information system; therefore, Web site addresses are normally not included. FBIS Document Identification Number is provided at the end of each such reference. When jihadist Web site addresses are provided, readers are cautioned to avoid accessing these sites directly.)

2. Chairman of the Joint Chiefs of Staff Instruction (CJCSI) 3210.01, quoted in Department of the Army Field Manual 100–6, Information Operations (27 August 1996), p. 2–2. (*Note*: Hereafter this source is referred to as FM 100–6.)

3. George J. Stein, "Information Warfare," *Airpower Journal* (Spring 1995): 2. Accessed at www.airpower.au.af.mil/airchronicles/apj/stein.html on 28 May 2003.

4. U.S. Department of Defense Joint Publication 3–53, quoted in FM 100–6, pp. 3–4.

5. Yael Shahar, "Information Warfare: The Perfect Terrorist Weapon," p. 4. International Policy Institute for Counterterrorism (ICT) Web site, www.ict.org.il Accessed from (30 May 2003).

6. Timothy L. Thomas, "Al Qaeda and the Internet: The Danger of 'Cyberplanning,'" *Parameters* (Spring 2003): 112–123.

7. Ibid.

8. Ibid.

9. Nicholas Berry, "Effective Counter-Terrorism Deals with Motives," Center for Defense Information (CDI) Terrorism Project (2 November 2001), pp. 1–2.

Accessed from CDI Web site www.cdi.org/terrorism/motives-pr.cfm (28 June 2002).

10. Ibid., pp. 2–4.

11. FBIS, "Editorial Discusses Name 'al-Ansar,'" *Al-Ansar* in Arabic (15 January 2002), p. 3, GMP20020220000169. Internet.

12. Paul Eedle, "Terrorism.com," *Guardian* (London) (17 July 2002). Available through FBIS as "UK Daily Says Website 'Central' to Al-Qa'ida Strategy to Continue War against U.S." (17 July 2002), EUP20020717000203.

13. "New Al-Qa'ida Online Magazine Features Interview with a 'Most Wanted' Saudi Islamist, Calls for Killing of Americans and Non-Muslims," Middle East Media Research Institute (MEMRI) Special Dispatch No. 591 (17 October 2003). Accessed at www.memri.org 10 November 2003.

14. See Reuven Paz, "Dark Side: Sawt al-Jihad," published by PRISM Web site (26 October 2003), and available from www.ocnus.net Web site; accessed 11 December 2003. See also Jonathan R. Galt, "Al-Qaeda Publishes Third Issue of Magazine," SITE Institute Web site (7 November 2003); accessed at http:// 216.239.37.104, (11 December 2003).

15. "Al-Battar Training Camp: The First Issue of Al-Qa'ida's Online Military Magazine," MEMRI Special Dispatch No. 637 (6 January 2004), accessed from www.memri.org (6 January 2004).

16. Ibid.

17. "'Al-Qaeda' Training Manual Deconstructed," Stratfor (23 January 2004). Accessed from www.stratfor.com.

18. FBIS, "Writer Examines Bin Ladin's Political 'Vision,' Support for Palestinian Cause," *Al-Ansar* in Arabic (15 January 2002), pp. 16–20, GMP20020220000194. Internet.

19. FBIS, "'Text' of Al-Qa'ida Statement on Baghdad UN Headquarters Bombing," London *Qods Press* in Arabic (25 August 2003), GMP20030825000179. Internet.

20. FBIS, "Writer Analyzes Political Thinking in 'Imam' Bin Ladin's Latest Speech," *Al-Ansar* in Arabic (28 January 2002), pp. 22–29, GMP20020223000091. Internet.

21. FBIS, "Commentator Sees U.S, as Failing in Its War on Terrorism and in Neutralizing Islamic and Jihadist Movements," *Al-Ansar* in Arabic (22 September 2002), pp. 18–24, GMP20021001000099. Internet.

22. FBIS, "Reasons behind Fall of Baghdad Analyzed," *Al-Ansar* in Arabic (17 April 2003), GMP20030422000163. Internet.

23. FBIS, "Islamic Research Center Publishes Book on 12 May Riyadh Operation," www.cybcity.com in Arabic (1 August 2003), pp. 3–5, GMP20031004000119. Internet.

24. See FBIS, "Letter by al-Qa'ida Spokesman Abu-Ghayth Appealing for Release of Prisoners," www.almuslimun.com in Arabic (2 September 2002), GMP20020902000041; Internet. See also Abu Ayman al-Hilali, "Guantanamo Bay: A Mirror of Our Ummah's Reality," accessed (in English) at www.jihadun-spun.net (20 September 2002).

25. FBIS, "Al-Qa'ida's Women Organization 'Commander' on Women's Role in 'Jihad,'" London *Al-Sharq al-Awsat* in Arabic (12 March 2003), p. 3, GMP20030312000069.

26. FBIS, "Al-Qa'ida Group Claims Responsibility for U.S., Canada Electricity Outage," London *Al-Quds al-Arabi* in Arabic (18 August 2003), p. 4, GMP20030818000073.

27. FBIS, "Pro-Al-Qa'ida Writer Notes Mujahidin's Tactics against U.S. Forces in Afghanistan," *Al-Ansar* in Arabic (15 January 2002), pp. 11–15, GMP20020220000183. Internet.

28. FBIS, "Writer Says New Type of Wars Suits Mujahidin's Fight against Western War Machine," *Al-Ansar* in Arabic (28 January 2002), pp. 15–21, GMP20020223000086. Internet.

29. See the following two English translations of the *Alneda* document. "Al-Qaida on the Fall of Baghdad: Guerilla Warfare 'Is the Most Powerful Weapon Muslims Have, and It Is the Best Method to Continue the Conflict with the Crusader Enemy," MEMRI Special Dispatch No. 493 (11 April 2003), accessed at www.memri.org (27 April 2003). "Al-Qaida on the Fall of Baghdad," trans. Jihadunspun; accessed from www.jihadunspun.net (12 April 2003).

30. FBIS, "Islamic Research Center Publishes Book on 12 May Riyadh Operation," www.cybcity.com in Arabic (1 August 2003), p. 14, GMP20031004000119. Internet.

31. FBIS, "Strategies, Targets for Jihad against U.S. Discussed," *Al-Ansar* in Arabic (13 February 2002), pp. 15–21, GMP20020620000172. Internet.

32. FBIS, "Pro-Al-Qa'ida Writer Views Similarities between Munich, New York Operations," *Al-Ansar* in Arabic (27 February 2002), pp. 9–14, GMP20020307000169. Intenet.

33. FBIS, "*Al-Ansar* Writer Views Reasons for U.S. Intelligence 'Failure' against Mujahidin," *Al-Ansar* in Arabic (26 June 2002), pp. 10–14, GMP20020702000138. Internet.

34. FBIS, "Battle of Janin Seen as Palestinian Victory, Turning Point in Palestinian-Israeli Conflict," *Al-Ansar* in Arabic (14 April 2002), pp. 9–14, GMP20020422000135. Internet.

35. FBIS, "Commentator Sees al-Aqsa Intifada as Israel's Vietnam, Calls for Support of Mujahidin," *Al-Ansar* in Arabic (8 October 2002), pp. 9–15, GMP20021020000227. Internet.

36. FBIS, "*Al-Ansar* Writer Reviews U.S. Military 'Barbarity,' 'War Crimes' against Civilians," *Al-Ansar* in Arabic (24 July 2002), pp. 9–14, GMP20020805000114. Internet.

37. See the following two English translations of this article. FBIS, "Al-Qa'ida's Abu-Ghayth Notes Right 'to Use Chemical, Germ Weapons' against U.S.," *Alneda* in Arabic (8 June 2002), GMP20020608000060; Internet. "'Why We Fight America': Al-Qa'ida Spokesman Explains 11 September and Declares Intentions to Kill 4 Million Americans with Weapons of Mass Destruction," MEMRI Special Dispatch No. 388 (12 June 2002), accessed at www.memri.org (4 November 2002).

38. FBIS, "Al-Qa'ida 'Ideologue' Reveals Years-Long Controversy on Using WMD against U.S.," London *Al-Sharq al-Awsat* in Arabic (12 September 2002), p. 7, GMP20020912000159.

39. FBIS, "Use of Weapons of Mass Destruction Defended on Basis of Islamic Law," Internet text in Arabic (1 May 2003) (18 trans. pp.), GMP20030602000454.

40. FBIS, "*Al-Ansar* Article Views Overlooked Role of Snipers in Wars of 'Mujahidin,'" *Al-Ansar* in Arabic (22 October 2002), pp. 9–14, GMP20021024000088. Internet.

41. FBIS, "Jihadist Website Posts Sniper Training Manual," www.arabforum.net in Arabic (28 January 2003) (25 trans. pp.), GMP20030221000172. Internet.

42. FBIS, "*Al-Ansar* Writer Views Reasons for U.S. Intelligence 'Failure' against Mujahidin," *Al-Ansar* in Arabic (26 June 2002), pp. 10–14, GMP20020702000138. Internet.

43. FBIS, "Commentator Faults U.S. Identification of al-Qa'ida's 'Center of Gravity'; Sees Economy as U.S.'s Vulnerable 'Center of Gravity,'" *Al-Ansar* in Arabic (19 December 2002), pp. 10–16, GMP20030122000038. Internet.

44. FBIS, "Report Details Rise of 'Foreign Fighters' to Al-Qa'ida Command," London *Al-Majallah* in Arabic (3–9 August 2003), pp. 10–14, GMP20030805000138.

45. FBIS, "DEBKAfile Views Al-Qa'ida Manual for Kidnapping Americans, Plans to Attack in U.S.," Jerusalem DEBKAfile in English (25 November 2003), GMP20031126000083. Internet.

46. See the following three FBIS translations of al-Ansari articles. "Koranic Basis for Perpetual Hostility, Fighting Between Muslims and Unbelievers Supported," *Al-Ansar* in Arabic (15 January 2002), pp. 4–9, GMP20020220000172; Internet. "Fighting in Jihad against Unbelievers Seen as Duty of Every Individual Muslim," *Al-Ansar* in Arabic (27 February 2002), pp. 4–8, GMP20020307000167; Internet. "Guidelines for Armed Conflict between the 'Muslim Nation' and Its 'Enemies' Explored," *Al-Ansar* in Arabic (14 May 2002), pp. 4–8, GMP20020522000129; Internet.

47. FBIS, "Al-Qa'ida Issues Statement on 'Legitimacy' of New York, Washington Attacks," *Alneda* in Arabic (24 April 2002), GMP20020424000171. Internet.

48. "Al-Qa'ida Affiliated Magazine: On the Importance of Jihad," MEMRI Special Dispatch No. 418 (4 September 2002). Accessed from www.memri.org (4 September 2002).

49. FBIS, "Al-Zawahiri Article Says 'Islamic Awakening' Frightening Enemies of Islam," London *Al-Hayah* in Arabic (18 February 2003), pp. 1, 6, GMP20030218000075.

50. FBIS, "Future of Iraq, Arabian Peninsula after the Fall of Baghdad," www.cybcity.com in Arabic (1 August 2003) (50 trans. pp.), GMP20030929000003.

51. For the intrafaith threat from the Shia, see the following two sources. FBIS, "Future of Iraq, Arabian Peninsula . . ." "Al-Qa'ida Affiliated Web site: The Shi'a Threat to Sunni Islamists Is No Less Than the 'Judeo-Christian' Threat," MEMRI Special Dispatch No. 498 (2 May 2003); accessed from www.memri.org (12 May 2003).

52. FBIS, "Future of Iraq, Arabian Peninsula . . ."

53. Paul Eedle, "Al-Qaeda Takes Fight for 'Hearts and Minds' to the Web," *Jane's Intelligence Review* (1 August 2002). (Online version, posted 10 July 2002.)

54. FBIS, "Islamic Research Center Publishes Book on 12 May Riyadh Operation," www.cybcity.com in Arabic (1 August 2003), p. 15, GMP20031004000119. Internet.

55. FBIS, "Commentator Analyzes Recent Bin Ladin Tapes, Sees U.S, as Losing 'Information War' against al-Qa'ida," *Al-Ansar* in Arabic (20 November 2002), pp. 9–15, GMP20021126000154. Internet.

56. Ibid.

57. FBIS, "Center for Islamic Studies and Research on U.S.-Alneda Internet War," *Alneda* in Arabic (3 October 2002), GMP20021003000145. Internet.

58. FBIS, "Expert Analyzes Article by Bin Ladin 'Interpreter' for Keys to Al-Qa'ida Plans," Herzliyya GLORIA e-mail text in English (6 March 2003), GMP20030307000119.

59. Both of Bin Laden's mass media messages to the American public have been translated by FBIS. "Islamist Site Publishes Bin Ladin's 'Letter to the American People,'" *Waaqiah* in English (26 October 2002), GMP20021026000053; Internet. "Al-Jazirah Carries Bin Ladin's Audio Messages to Iraqis, Americans," Doha Al-Jazirah Satellite Channel Television in Arabic (18 October 2003), GMP20031018000194.

Terrorism Beyond Al-Qaida

Introduction to Section 2

Noel Koch
Chairman and CEO, TranSecur, Inc.
Former Director of Special Planning
U.S. Department of Defense

Since 9/11, everyone's primary focus has been on al-Qaida, in the person of Usama bin Ladin, along with his deputy Ayman al-Zawahiri, as representing the threat to global security. But if bin Ladin and al-Zawahiri were to be killed or captured, that would not end radical Islamic terrorism: al-Qaida is a network that has spread throughout the Islamic world. Raising any expectation of victory over such an organization, which cannot be subdued by military means, could lead to a loss of public confidence in the United States' counterterrorist policies. Instead, to calm or "cure" Islamic terrorism, we must profoundly alter the environment in which it develops—an environment characterized by a sense of humiliation, personal powerlessness, economic deprivation, indignity, and despair.

The chapters in Section 2 remind us that terrorism did not begin with al-Qaida and that counterterrorism must go beyond this specific threat. They can help us understand that it is futile to try to quell Islamist terrorism by force alone, rather than by fostering for the disaffected a better economic and social future—a sentiment also expressed in the Intelligence Reform and Terrorism Prevention Act of 2004.

In Chapter 8 Brian Jenkins offers a perspective on significant trends in terrorism over the past four decades. Terrorism has become bloodier, is less dependent on state sponsors, has evolved new models of organization, has become adept at exploiting new communications technologies, involves global campaigns, and has had a strategic impact. Jenkins notes, however, that none of these trends will allow prediction or extrapolation. Also, terrorists have yet to achieve their stated long-range goals, and terrorists' use of weapons of mass destruction (WMD) have not materialized.

Xavier Raufer considers in Chapter 9 how groups that are in conflict with the established order defy standard organizational concepts. He discusses terrorism in a broad context of the cultural, social, political, and economic dynamics of distress and "chaos," as well as the emerging relationship between terrorism and crime. Raufer offers insights on the development of cities as war zones effectively off-limits to established authority, the leading edge of a threat to the nation-state. He helps us see beyond the issues that dominate the media day by day, and to locate terrorism on a continuum of conflict that reaches beyond the immediate threat.

John Horgan also offers a challenge to conventional thinking in Chapter 10, insisting that we should not uncritically attribute certain qualities, capabilities, and motives to terrorists on the basis of political rhetoric. He argues that counterterrorist policy makers should instead use academia more effectively and rely on empirical analysis. Horgan's article should be required reading not only for policy makers but also for counterterrorist analysts and operators.

In Chapter 11 Leonard Cole discusses the history of chemical, biological, and nuclear weapons (WMD), considering, notably, sub-stances such as anthrax spores. It is difficult to assess the actual threat of WMD by terrorists, or to explain why—despite popular fears—these devices have not been generally deployed. It is speculated that terrorists hesitate to unleash a biological attack because, since the consequences are unpredictable, it might undermine their own interests. Terry O'Sullivan also discusses the threat of bioterrorism and presents a history of its use as a weapon in Chapter 12.

In Chapter 13 Daniel Byman offers a look at Lebanese Hizballah, a group funded, trained, and supported by Iran that aspires to transform Lebanon into an Islamic state. Iran and Hizballah are further examples of troubling entities that cannot be adequately addressed by military force.

In Chapter 14 Steven Emerson reviews terrorist financing and the legislative instruments devised after 9/11 to track and cut off such funds. Since terrorism is not a costly venture, one can ask whether cutting off the fund-raising efforts of middle eastern philanthropies will indeed have the desired effect.

CHAPTER 8

The New Age of Terrorism

Brian Michael Jenkins
Senior Adviser to the President of the RAND Corporation
Director of the National Transportation Security Center
at the Mineta Transportation

The purpose of this chapter is to consider how terrorism has changed over the past four decades. The word *terrorism* dates from the eighteenth century, but as recently as 1971—when Rand published my essay "The Five Stages of Urban Guerrilla Warfare"—the term had not yet acquired its present currency. Nor did it then refer to a distinct mode of armed conflict. That meaning would be added subsequently, by terrorists themselves and by analysts of terrorism; and in my view the latter impart more coherence to the phenomenon than the former.

We should be careful not to think of terrorism or terrorists as monolithic. Terrorism is a generalized construct derived from our concepts of morality, law, and the rules of war, whereas actual terrorists are shaped by culture, ideology, and politics—specific, inchoate factors and notions that motivate diverse actions. But although terrorists are not monolithic, neither are they isolated. They innovate; exploit new technology; learn from one another; imitate successful tactics; produce manuals of instruction based on experience; debate tactics, targets, and limits on violence; and justify their actions with doctrines and theories.

Thus we can, cautiously, identify apparent trends:

- Terrorism has become bloodier.
- Terrorists have developed new financial resources, so that they are less dependent on state sponsors.

- Terrorists have evolved new models of organization.
- Terrorists can now wage global campaigns.
- Terrorists have effectively exploited new communications technologies.
- Some terrorists have moved beyond tactics to strategy, although none of them have achieved their stated long-range goals.

These trends do not allow prediction or extrapolation; analysis is not prophecy. Neither do they imply inexorable progress. Terrorists have not done many of the things we worried about 30 years ago—our worst fears have not been realized. On the other hand, no amount of analysis can cover every conceivable terrorist scenario, every form of attack, or every angle. The future, like the past 40 years, will probably bring surprises and shocks.

TERRORISM HAS BECOME BLOODIER

Perhaps the most striking development is that terrorism has become bloodier, in terms of what acts are committed and how many victims are involved. The order of magnitude has increased almost every decade. In the 1970s the bloodiest incidents caused fatalities in the tens. In the 1980s, fatalities from the worst incidents were in the hundreds; by the 1990s, attacks on this scale had become more frequent. On 9/11 there were thousands of fatalities, and there could have been far more. We now contemplate plausible scenarios in which tens of thousands might die.

At one time, I wrote that terrorists wanted a lot of people watching, not a lot of people dead. They were limited not only by access to weapons but by self-constraint. Mayhem as such was seldom an objective. Terrorists had a sense of morality, a self-image, operational codes, and practical concerns—they wanted to maintain group cohesion, avoid alienating perceived constituents, and avoid provoking public outrage, which could lead to crackdowns. But these constraints gave way to large-scale indiscriminate violence as terrorists engaged in protracted, brutal conflicts; as the more squeamish dropped out; as terrorism became commonplace and the need for headlines demanded higher body counts; and as ethnic hatred and religious fanaticism replaced political agendas.

Some terrorists still operate below their capacity. Even the most fanatic jihadists, who believe that God mandates the slaughter of infidels, debate, pragmatically, the acceptability of collateral Muslim casualties, whether Shiite Muslims are potential allies or apostates, and whether beheadings are counterproductive. Overall, though, jihadists seem ready to murder millions, if necessary. Many of today's terrorists want a lot of people watching and a lot of people dead.

To repeat, though, some fears about what terrorists might do have not been realized. In a poll conducted in 1985, most experts predicted chemical terrorism by the end of the twentieth century; but when nerve gas was released on the subway in Tokyo in 1995, the consequences were less severe than had been imagined. Biological warfare has taken place only on a small scale, as in the anthrax letters of 2001.

During the 1960s and 1970s there were fears of nuclear black markets and nuclear terrorism. This fear was heightened by the collapse of the Soviet Union and the exposure of its nuclear arsenal to corruption and organized crime. But although nuclear terrorism remains a concern, it has not yet happened, nor have cities been held hostage with weapons of mass destruction.

Although accurate surface-to-air missiles are widely available and have been in some terrorists' arsenals for years, they have not been used against commercial aircraft outside conflict zones. Terrorists, so far as we know, have not attacked agriculture. Terrorists have not attempted to seize or sabotage nuclear reactors.

Also, there are no more terrorist organizations today than 10 or 20 years ago; and the annual number of international incidents has remained in the hundreds, not the thousands.

What conclusion can we draw? Although not all our fears have been realized, some may materialize in the future. Scenarios that seemed far-fetched in the 1970s are now plausible; in fact, 9/11 redefined plausibility. In present attempts to anticipate and prepare for what terrorists might do next, virtually no scenario is dismissed. Analysts and the public seriously consider the possibility that terrorists may send waves of suicide bombers to America's shopping malls; wipe out Boston's waterfront with a hijacked liquid-natural-gas carrier; topple the George Washington Bridge in New York City; crash planes into the Houses of Parliament in London, the Capitol in Washington, or a nuclear reactor; spray anthrax over a city; sink tankers to block narrow straits; release hoof-and-mouth disease; sabotage the banking system; spread smallpox; or destroy Manhattan with a nuclear bomb. Terrorists' own chatter, echoing this speculation, may be picked up by intelligence services and taken as confirmation.

These concerns are due partly to 9/11 and partly to a new basis for analysis. Whereas traditional threat-based analysis assessed an enemy's intentions and capabilities, today's vulnerability-based analysis identifies a weakness and hypothesizes a terrorist and a worst-case scenario. Vulnerability analysis is useful for assessing consequences and preparedness, but it relegates the terrorist to a secondary role: the scenario is driven by the vulnerability. Often, such a scenario is reified and becomes a threat: it is successively considered possible, probable, inevitable, and imminent. In vulnerability-based assessment, consequences trump likelihood. Terrorists' actual capabilities, ambitions, and fantasies blur with our own speculation and fears to create what the terrorists want: an atmosphere of alarm.

By contrast, "red team" exercises, in which analysts actually plan terrorist operations, put terrorists (or their red team surrogates) back in the main role. This approach narrows the spectrum of potential attacks. From a terrorist's assumed perspective, some operations appear less attractive, or planning them seems more challenging. This may indeed happen in real-life terrorist groups. Actual terrorists may contemplate many modes of attack but keep returning to common forms such as vehicle attacks.

TERRORISTS HAVE DEVELOPED NEW WAYS OF FINANCING THEIR OPERATIONS

Since terrorists are outlaws, unable to hold territory and openly collect taxes, their finances are necessarily clandestine and often depend on criminal activity. Terrorist organizations that have survived for long periods have developed various financial resources. In the 1960s, rival superpowers and their local allies were willing to finance terrorism; but this support (with some exceptions) declined at the end of the Cold War, and terrorists had to seek other means.

One innovation of South American urban guerrillas in the early 1990s was kidnapping for ransom. Terrorists had previously avoided such kidnapping because its criminal connotations might tarnish a group, but its use spread as it brought in tens of millions of dollars.

Some groups engaged in extortion and protection rackets, gradually adding fraud and even legitimate investments. Drug trafficking also offered large-scale returns that benefited groups in South America, central Asia, and the Middle East.

Ethnic diasporas, émigré communities, and coreligionists could also be a source of contributions, especially when charity was presumably ordered by a religion. Such groups may sometimes have been unwitting supporters. In some cases, they were duped; in other cases, their contributions were ostensibly meant for humanitarian efforts by the recipients—schools, medical supplies, assistance to widows and orphans. However, some private contributors knew that their money financed terrorist operations.

Collecting money from various foreign sources and disbursing it to scattered operational units and operatives require clandestine transfers of funds. Some terrorist organizations are skilled at moving money from charitable organizations and criminal operations through informal banking systems, money order and cash wire services, and regular banks. Some authorities have reduced high-volume transactions, but it is not clear that they have severely impeded terrorists' cash flows, which may simply move into less regulated areas. We know the sums that have been blocked, but it is difficult to estimate the amounts moving in ways governments cannot monitor.

Terrorists benefit from uneven enforcement. Many financial institutions and some countries remain reluctant to interfere with suspect transfers, not because they support terrorism but because strict controls could interfere with lucrative transactions deriving from tax evasion, white-collar crime, and political corruption.

TERRORISTS HAVE BECOME LESS DEPENDENT ON STATE SPONSORS

Even during the Cold War, there was less and less enthusiasm for backing guerrillas so as to wage surrogate warfare. The Soviet Union became disenchanted with national liberation movements and especially with the Palestinians: by the mid-1980s, Europe's colonial empires had been dismantled; the Americans had been driven from Indochina; Cuba was bankrupt; Marxist guerrillas in Latin America seemed stalled; and in 1985 Soviet diplomats were kidnapped in Lebanon. Similarly, in the United States support faded for clandestine projects to topple Fidel Castro in Cuba, an enterprise of the 1960s; and Congress restricted further funding for the contras in Nicaragua—although support continued for the mujahideen fighting against Soviet forces in Afghanistan. Also, both the United States and the Soviet Union were becoming increasingly concerned about terrorism.

With the departure of the Soviet Union from Afghanistan and the end of the Cold War, local conflicts no longer had strategic significance. This development facilitated the resolution of a few armed struggles—guerrillas and governments made peace. Others in the field were left to their own devices. Some, like the old Palestinian groups, became toothless; some, like those in Central America, turned to local banditry. But certain others, like the Afghan veterans, survived and created new, more autonomous enterprises.

The end of the Cold War also altered the calculations of the few nations identified by the United States as sponsors of terrorism. It reduced support from and protection by the Soviet Union—as in Syria, a patron of the Palestinians. Iraq, involved in a costly war with Iran, had sought assistance from the West, but that was ended when Iraq invaded Kuwait in 1990. Libya was bombed by the United States, and although it continued to support terrorist operations (notably sabotage of American and French airliners), it became more circumspect and eventually sought rapprochement with the West. Sanctions eventually had their effect. Gradually, therefore, state-sponsored terrorism became less of a problem.

However, state sponsorship had provided a means of monitoring terrorists, and its decline entailed less influence over terrorist movements and a loss of intelligence sources within them. With the severance of these links, we knew less. This was demonstrated on 9/11. Not only American intelligence but also other intelligence services had missed the preparations. They knew bits but lacked a complete picture.

TERRORISTS HAVE EVOLVED NEW MODELS OF ORGANIZATION

Commenting on terrorists' organization requires distinguishing among groups that use terrorist tactics. Guerrilla groups, governments, and armies differ from urban guerrilla gangs and from groups like Germany's Red Army Faction, Italy's Red Brigades, or the

Japanese Red Army for which terrorism was the primary (or only) activity. When we talk about the evolution of terrorist organization, we mean the latter—organizing to do terrorism. And even in this category, terrorist groups range from primitive gangs to sophisticated organizations.

The guiding principle of all terrorist organization is survival, which depends on maintaining secret membership and operational security, preventing infiltration, punishing betrayal, and limiting damage.

Larger organizations and more ambitious operations have functional specialization, with individuals devoted to recruiting, training, intelligence, reconnaissance, planning, logistics, finance, propaganda, and social services (e.g., support for widows, orphans, and families of suicide attackers). Functional specialization would normally lead to hierarchy and bureaucracy, as in al-Qaida before 9/11. Some groups are organized as miniature armies with general staffs, brigades, and battalions. But hierarchies are open to penetration and may stifle initiative.

Al-Qaida seems to be one of the first groups to pattern itself on a lean international business model: hierarchical but not pyramidal, loosely run, decentralized but linked, able to assemble and allocate resources and coordinate operations, but hard to depict organizationally or penetrate. Networks provide numerous operational benefits: they are quick to learn, adaptive, and resilient—hard to break. To work well, networks require strong shared beliefs, a collective vision, some original basis for trust, and excellent communications. Networks have become an object of intense analysis in the intelligence community. Whether the global jihadist network created by al-Qaida is unique or can be replicated by future groups remains a question.

The online monthly manuals to exhort and instruct would-be terrorists seem close to a concept suggested by Louis Beam—"leaderless resistance"—in which self-proclaimed combatants are linked by common beliefs and goals and wage a common terrorist war, but operate autonomously. This model may be possible for isolated actions, such as those by animal-rights activists and ecoguerrillas; but organizational continuity and major operations still require cooperation, coordination, and structure, which in turn require a basis for trust that is difficult to establish on the Internet.

TERRORISTS ARE ABLE TO MOUNT GLOBAL CAMPAIGNS

Contemporary terrorism transcends national frontiers; in fact, this is what initially made it a subject of international concern. There are two ways in which terrorism can be international.

First, terrorists can attack foreign targets: foreign airliners, embassies, and local offices and employees of multinational corporations—a growing body of entities whose activities in a country, inadvertently or by design, make them participants (and thereby targets) in local conflicts. To draw international attention, embarrass, increase their leverage over local governments, or compel international intervention, terrorists have bombed embassies, assassinated or abducted diplomats, and held corporate executives for ransom. Most incidents of international terrorism fall into this first category.

Second, terrorists can cross national frontiers to carry out attacks abroad, again to gain international attention, or to isolate their foes from their hosts—or simply because distant targets are not as well guarded as targets at home. The Palestinians, inspired by the Algerian FLN's (Front de Libération Nationale) terrorist campaign in mainland France, were the first to systematically adopt this approach, but others soon followed.

Many terrorists have seen their struggles as global. Marxist revolutionaries are an example. In the late twentieth century, for instance, Marxist leaders considered themselves beyond borders and united in revolution. In 1966, the Tri-Continental Conference in Havana was intended to bring together the world's guerrilla movements. No coordinated revolutionary movement emerged, but some interesting alliances eventually evolved, such as that between the Japanese Red Army—rebels looking for a cause—and the Popular Front for the Liberation of Palestine (PFLP), which was both Palestinian and Marxist and cultivated foreign recruits and relationships. The brief coalescence of Europe's left-wing terrorist groups led to concerns about "Euroterrorism," and the Irish Republican Army (IRA) and Spain's Euskadi Ta Askatasuna (ETA) exchanged technical know-how.

The jihadists, inspired and guided by al-Qaida's ideology, represent a further and apparently more durable development. Historically, al-Qaida was never a centrally directed, disciplined organization, even when it operated training camps in Afghanistan. It remained a loose association, capable of centrally directed action and of assembling resources for specific operations, but always more of a network than a hierarchy. Its nature proved to be its strength at a time when survival required decentralization. Al-Qaida is truly a global enterprise, drawing recruits and funding from all over the world, maintaining connections in 60 countries, and carrying out operations in perhaps 20. It may properly be called a global insurgency—a phase that implies both scale and reach.

Lesser movements that are global in cause and ambition, though far below the jihadists in operational capabilities, include neo-Nazis, animal-rights extremists, and some segments of the disparate antiglobalization movement.

TERRORISTS HAVE EFFECTIVELY EXPLOITED NEW COMMUNICATIONS TECHNOLOGIES

For terrorists, the most significant technology is not weapons but direct communication with their multiple audiences. Terrorism, to repeat, was originally aimed at the people watching. Victims were threatened or killed to make a point, not only to the terrorists' foes but above all to the terrorists' own constituents. Technological developments in the 1960s and 1970s—the ubiquity of television, more portable television cameras, communications satellites, uplinks to remote news crews, global news networks—allowed terrorists to reach audiences worldwide almost instantaneously. By carrying out visually dramatic acts of violence, terrorists could virtually guarantee coverage, intensifying the terror and inflating their own importance.

It should be noted that terrorists have not always communicated effectively. For example, the dramas that draw the attention of the news media have often obscured the terrorists' political message: whatever they had to say was lost in the anguish caused by the attack itself. Moreover, terrorists' writings have frequently been incomprehensible to all but a few; and some terrorists have issued voluminous manifestos and strategic directives that mostly remain unread. Sometimes they have failed to use the media pragmatically, as when terrorists who had kidnapped a prominent figure released a photo of the victim holding a placard on which they had written not a short, bold slogan but a message of 50 words or more that was too small to be legible. Also, news editors, rather than the terrorists themselves, determine what will be covered on television. Images considered too gruesome may not be shown; and except for a sound bite, terrorists' messages may be omitted. Videotape permitted terrorists to substitute motion pictures for still shots, so that they and their hostages could speak directly into the camera, but access to the media was still controlled by others. Not until the development of the Internet did terrorists have unmediated access to their audiences.

On the Internet, terrorist violence, performed on-camera, can be webcast directly and unedited. The Internet also allows direct communication between terrorists' public affairs departments and various audiences: recruits, sympathizers, broader constituencies, enemy states, and citizens who may disagree with their own governments' policies. A bombing no longer needs to be followed by a telephone call to a wire service. Today's terrorists have Web sites, publish online magazines, explain their causes, debate doctrine, and provide instruction in making explosives. They may use these same channels to clandestinely communicate with operatives through coded messages or, according to some reports, steganography.

Some of the jihadists' recruiting videos, emphasizing atrocities at the hands of infidels, are of high quality and probably appeal to potential adherents. And after a webcast of an execution appears on the Internet, mainstream media are more likely to show at least short edited segments. Such material may not spread significant alarm, but its appeal to violence-prone young men who harbor fantasies of revenge should not be underestimated. Iraq represents the latest phase in this evolution. Videos of beheadings of hostages circulate in Iraqi markets, and al-Qaida has reportedly compiled them in an exultant film.

This development suggests a democratization of extremism, whereby people can in a sense shop for belief systems and submerge themselves in "virtual groups" that encourage violence.

TERRORISTS HAVE ACHIEVED STRATEGIC RESULTS

Through dramatic acts of violence, terrorists have always attracted attention, evoked alarm, caused disruption, instigated crises, and obliged governments to divert resources to security and occasionally to make concessions. Strategically, though, they were less effective. They could sometimes upset negotiations and impede the resolution of conflicts. In fragile democracies they could sometimes provoke an overthrow of a government by those, usually the armed forces, who were determined to take a stronger line against terrorism. But terrorists rarely created powerful political movements. They were not able to fundamentally alter national policies, and they brought down no governments directly.

However, terrorists have gradually developed ways to achieve strategic results. Scale was one way. The best example is 9/11, which not only killed nearly 3,000 people, caused hundreds of billions of dollars in damage, and is still affecting the American economy but also has had a profound influence on U.S. policies. It made the "global war on terror" the framework for future policy, provoked two invasions, and led to some profound changes in government organization.

Another example of strategic effects is found in Iraq. In 2004, Iraqi insurgents kidnapped and beheaded or threatened to behead foreign nationals—aid officials, contract workers, journalists—and, despite the overall high level of violence in Iraq, were able to create political crises in countries participating in the multinational coalition, especially where there was strong domestic opposition to the war. In return for releasing the hostages, the kidnappers demanded, among other things, that governments withdraw forces or that companies cease operations. Only one government, the Philippines, pulled out; but, coming at a time when the United States was attempting to persuade additional countries to join the coalition, the kidnappings, more than the intensification of the conflict, persuaded others to stay away—not one new country joined. The kidnappings also forced aid organizations to suspend or reduce their activities, thereby slowing economic reconstruction and prolonging the misery that facilitated further recruiting by the insurgents.

Terrorist strategy is based not on achieving military superiority but rather on making the enemy's life unbearable by attacking incessantly (this contributed to Israel's decision to withdraw from Lebanon); by inflicting endless casualties (the strategy of the Palestinians' suicide bombings); by destroying tourism and discouraging investment, and thus inflicting economic pain; and by carrying out spectacular operations like 9/11.

Yet although terrorists have escalated their violence, developed new methods of financing their operations, exploited new communications technologies, created new organizational models, and undertaken global enterprises, they have yet to achieve their own stated long-range objectives.

TERRORISTS HAVE NOT ACCOMPLISHED THEIR LONG-RANGE GOALS

The South American urban guerrilla groups that initiated the wave of kidnappings and bombings in the 1970s were wiped out in a few years, having achieved no political result except brutal repression. Their counterparts in Europe, Japan, and North America were also suppressed, although offspring of Italy's Red Brigades reemerge from time to time. The IRA has made peace; apart from a few diehards, it is no longer a fighting force—its contest has been resolved politically. In Europe, only Spain's ETA, now in its fourth decade, fights on for Basque independence.

The death of Yasir Arafat symbolized the end of an era in the Palestinians' struggle. If a viable, independent Palestinian state is ultimately formed, much credit will be given to him. It cannot be denied that terrorism kept the Palestinians' hopes alive when Arab governments were defeated on the battlefield, that terrorism galvanized the Palestinian population and contributed to the concept of the Palestinian state, and that terrorism compelled international intervention. But today, the violence continues. Different militants have taken the field. Suicide bombings have been elevated to a strategy. Walls have been erected. Peace initiatives are renewed. War-weary populations await some kind of resolution. What that will be remains uncertain.

Meanwhile, today's jihadists speak of driving the infidels out of the Middle East, of toppling the exposed apostate regimes that depend on their support, of then going on to destroy Israel and ultimately reestablishing the caliphate. They have proved to be dangerous terrorists, have achieved some strategic results, are determined to continue attacking, and are resilient survivors, capable of recruiting despite adversity. Destroying their terrorist enterprise will take years. And until that happens, they might prevail in Afghanistan or Pakistan and might make it too costly for the United States to remain in Iraq. But they have not yet achieved these successes, and the verdict on their movement must await the judgment of future historians.

This is a paradox of terrorism. Terrorists often succeed tactically and thereby gain attention, cause alarm, and attract recruits. But their struggle has brought them no success measured against their own stated goals. In that sense, terrorism has failed, but the phenomenon of terrorism continues.

CONCLUSION

The course of terrorism over the next few decades cannot be predicted, just as the actual evolution of terrorism over the last 30 years could probably not have been predicted.

Suppose that at the beginning of the 1970s, when contemporary terrorism was still in its early stages and formal research had just begun, I had, with remarkable prescience, outlined its future course. Take as the starting date President Nixon's creation of the Cabinet Committee to Combat Terrorism in October 1972.

It would have been easy to forecast hundreds of airline hijackings, since many had already occurred; but the screening of all passengers, let alone the elaborate security measures that have now become routine, would have been considered very unlikely. A terrorist attack had just occurred at the Munich Olympics; still, it would have been far-fetched to predict that in 2004, more than $1 billion would be spent on security at the games in Athens.

Suppose that I had predicted the terrorist assassinations of the former prime minister of Italy, the former president of Argentina, the presidents of Lebanon and Egypt, two prime ministers in India, and one in Israel; and the attempted assassinations of the pope and the heads of government of Pakistan, Egypt, and the United Kingdom.

Suppose that I had predicted hundreds of suicide bombings; the release of nerve gas on subways; a Senate office building shut down by letters containing anthrax spores; and the destruction of the World Trade Center (which was still being built in 1972). Suppose that, with regard to the United States, I had predicted its military retaliation against terrorism; a global war on terror as the framework for its foreign policy; its bombing of Libya; its invasions of Afghanistan and of Iraq; its creation of a new Department of Homeland Security; its detention of American citizens without trial; and its arguments supposedly justifying the use of torture.

Such predictions would have been dismissed as fiction, not sober analysis. Who, then, can say with confidence what will or will not happen over the next 30 years?

See also Chapter 25 **A Typology and Anatomy of Terrorist Operations.**

Chaos, Terrorism, and Beyond

Xavier Raufer
Director of Studies, Department for the Study of the
Contemporary Criminal Menace, Criminology Institute,
University of Paris II—Panthéon-Assas

FROM DISORDER TO CHAOS

From November 1989 to September 2001, the developed world lived in relative peace. Although it felt some repercussions from disorder and violence elsewhere, it was not affected by any serious conflict. The West tended to see this tranquillity as an acquired and permanent situation and took little interest in global disorder, but the period was actually an interlude preceding a chaotic phase of world history. When the lull was brought to an abrupt end by the attacks of 11 September 2001, westerners suddenly glimpsed the huge strategic threat posed globally by a new—or perhaps ancient—form of conflict: terrorist and criminal war.

This kind of terrorist and criminal war is completely different from the bloody wars of the twentieth century. In classic international law, the state has a monopoly on legitimate violence, so that in a world dominated by states, the only "real" wars are those between states. Such wars have, however, largely ceased to exist, for at least three reasons: (1) Nuclear weaponry is a deterrent; it makes them too dangerous, especially when superpowers are involved. (2) Democracies are now more numerous than before, and democracies tend not to war among themselves. (3) Economic and technological development makes the acquisition of territory by military means less essential than it was in the past.

Until the end of the Cold War, the utmost limit of warfare between states was indirect strategy: a complex pattern of ruses and maneuvers intended to break up an enemy's order of battle. At the beginning of the twenty-first century the logic of indirect strategy has become outdated and inapplicable in a world where previously clear distinctions—between attack and defense, the state and civil society, the public and private sectors, civilians and the military, war and peace, police and army, legality and illegality—are being blurred. New forms of confrontation have emerged, in which the determining factor is no longer nation or ideology but race, tribe, greed, or religious fanaticism.

The Advent of Wars of Chaos, Terror, and Criminality

When a new era begins, the greatest difficulty is to identify, sufficiently early, the enemy, the battlefield, and the rules—if any— of engagement. What conclusions can we reach about the real dangers of the present world?

First, in today's chaotic world, wars are no longer fought between one state and another and so are becoming increasingly ferocious. Often, our opponents are fighting for things that represent a visceral attachment and are held sacred, such as a bloodline (them- selves and their descendants, kin, and clan) and land (their homes and territory).

Second, this chaotic warfare is characterized by crime, tribalism, and terrorism. The adversary is increasingly a sort of hybrid, part common criminal and part political. A warlord, tribal leader, or fanatical fundamentalist might head a militia or terrorist network funded by extortion rackets and trafficking in human beings, arms, drugs, protected species, and toxic waste. For example, several sub- Saharan African countries have plunged into a downward spiral in which the nation-state fails; armed gangs and guerrillas lacking any ideology proliferate; gang warfare occurs and recurs; organized crime becomes pervasive; tribalism and warlord rule predominate; and a culture of impunity develops.

Oswaldo de Rivero, a high-ranking UN official, commented in *Le Monde Diplomatique* of April 1999: "Civil war goes hand in hand with the worst level of criminality." As he put it, the "national nonviability of many developing countries" causes the nation-state to implode into "ungovernable chaotic entities" dominated by an "alliance of general anarchy and various forms of delinquency."

Characteristics of Wars of Chaos

One characteristic of chaotic war is the abolition of the clearly defined geostrategic space in which major countries once developed their national defense.

A second characteristic is a decrease in the number of nation-states that have continuous, controlled frontiers and comply with current international law. Consequently, a growing number of participants in criminal or terrorist wars are resolutely indifferent to states and to state boundaries.

Third, no distinction can be made between civil and military authority or front line and rear; and militia forces wearing any sort of regular uniform are rare.

Fourth, the opponent is dispersed among the population, often mixing with friendly forces.

Fifth, "classic" combat in an open field of battle is replaced by massacres, bloody vendettas (as in Albania, Algeria, Chechnya, and the former Yugoslavia), and terrorist attacks.

These phenomena are part of a web of criminality of all kinds: trafficking in drugs, toxic waste, human beings (either whole as illegal migrants, or piecemeal in the human organ trade), "sensitive" electronic components, precious stones ("war diamonds"), and arms. We also find clashes between religious fanatics, ethnic and tribal conflict, civil war and famine, and piracy at sea and in the air.

A New Form of Terror: Undefined and Unexpected

From 1989 to 2001, the nature and pace of terror changed. Previously, the enemy was known, stable, and familiar. Today the enemy is evasive, strange, and incomprehensible—but just as dangerous, if not more so. During the Cold War, strategic threats (such as the Warsaw Pact) were heavy, stable, slow, identifiable, almost familiar. Even the terrorist threat was stable and explicable. Abu Nidal's Fatah Revolutionary Council is an example. Its hideout, protectors, and weapons were known to all; and deciphering the acronyms it chose for its actions was child's play. Now, by contrast, terror offers but a fleeting glimpse of a brutal, irrational face, as with the Aum Shinrikyo sect or the Groupes Islamique Armés (GIA) in Algeria.

What, then, are the real threats we face today? What has terrorism become?

TERROR ARISING FROM WORLD CHAOS
General Observations

Since its first appearance in the nineteenth century, terrorism has been studied within a specific frame of reference, that of terrorism itself. Today, this concept has become too narrow. With the end of the bipolar world order (marked by the fall of the Berlin Wall), terrorism mutated and moved outside the domain within which it used to be analyzed. The broader domain of the threats, criminal and other, that now menace society provides a more suitable framework for conceptualizing and defining terrorism and understanding its extent.

Today, the real menace is posed by hybrid groups that are opportunistic and capable of rapid transformation. The real conflicts (in the Balkans, in Africa, and elsewhere) are essentially civilian and are often ethnic or tribal. They are melting pots of crime; religious fanaticism; massacres; piracy; and trafficking in human beings, drugs, arms, toxic substances, or gems.

Thus for the foreseeable future warfare will have a criminal dimension, a terrorist dimension, or both. Civilians—cities, corporations, the population at large—will be increasingly affected, as they were by the attacks of September 2001 and by the anthrax scares in New York that same autumn. The wars, whether inspired by terrorism or criminality, will originate in two types of lawless zones: (1) failed states that have become temporarily or permanently anarchic (Afghanistan, Albania, Liberia, Sierra Leone, etc.) and (2) vast anarchic urban sprawls in the developing world (Karachi, Lagos, Rio de Janeiro, etc.), where entire districts and suburbs are effectively controlled by organized criminal groups, terrorists, and traffickers. Karachi and Rio de Janeiro are striking examples of urban sprawls as terrorist or criminal strongholds. Karachi—referred to in the press as a city like, say, Paris or Rome—is actually a gigantic shantytown approximately as large in area and population as the whole of Belgium. In Karachi, fanatical Islamist supporters of Usama bin Ladin have organized demonstrations by more than

300,000 protestors. Rio has perhaps 800 hillside shantytowns called *favelas* that take up one-third of the metropolitan area and have a population of 1 million, almost all squatters. In these favelas, according to local nongovernmental organizations (NGOs), one youngster in four aged 10 to 19 belongs to a criminal gang, and gunshot wounds are the leading cause of death in this age group. According to the police, 3 to 4 tons of cocaine are moved through the favelas each month, and 80 percent of it is destined for Europe or North America.

From bases such as these,[1] dangerous groups can easily strike at symbolic targets in the developed world.

New Hybrid Forms of Terrorism

Today, terrorism is a major component in warfare, which it has slowly but steadily contaminated over the past three decades. Terrorism is now the central security concern for our governments. It may even be said that terrorism has *become* war. However this all-pervasive terrorism—daily, somewhere in the world, for one reason or another, bombs are exploding—has itself undergone a significant mutation.

The state terrorism of the Cold War, whether political or ideological, has almost disappeared. New terrorists have emerged. The hard core are fanatics such as Islamist terrorists, but there are also nonpolitical criminals such as mafia gangs, doomsday sects, and other irrational and violent groups.

The "New Menace"

An understanding of reality in the actual danger zones since the end of the bipolar world order, with objective assessment of where attacks originate, where conflicts occur, and how the flow of illegal goods and services (human beings, narcotics, arms, stolen vehicles, etc.) is organized, leads to the conclusion that the real menace comes from militias, mutant guerrilla groups, and hybrid groups combining terrorists, fanatics, so-called patriot thugs, and army deserters. These are under the orders of dissident generals and warlords, lunatics, or outright criminals. They are often unknown and obscure groups, capable of swift mutation and shifting alliances. They are contemptuous of international law, particularly humanitarian law.

They are symbiotically linked to the criminal economy: narcotics, the arms trade, and dirty money.

The "Biology" of Dangerous Groups

The end of the bipolar world order has brought about mutations in groups that previously were solely terrorist or criminal—and a sudden, unpredictable slide from the "technomorphous" to the "biomorphous" domain. In the technomorphous domain, transnational terrorism was carried out by groups involved in special services on behalf of states; such groups were salaried and under orders and acted, in a sense, mechanically, on a stop-start basis. In today's biomorphous domain, complex dangerous groups proliferate, in a sense, organically—and so far uncontrollably. They are difficult to identify, define, or understand, emerging in flows and territories that are barely charted.

The new dangerous groups have at least seven characteristics in common. In the first place, they are not really organizations at all, as the West generally uses that term. That is, they are not solid, rigid structures. On the contrary, they are fluid, liquid, or even volatile. For example, let us consider what the United States government refers to as al-Qaida and insists on presenting as a formal hierarchical organization (with a "No. 2" and a "No. 3"). The United States has alleged that "two-thirds of the command structure has been eliminated," implying some sort of stable or permanent membership. Such fictions are spread by various presumed experts, one of whom blithely estimated the "membership of al-Qaeda" as 1,200. But al-Qaida is not an organization in the way that (to confine our example to terrorism) the IRA is an organization. It is easy to show that al-Qaida is not simply an Islamic militant counterpart of the Roman Catholic IRA.

Since August 1998 and its first attacks against the U.S. embassies in Nairobi and Dar es Salaam, al-Qaida has been subjected to fierce repression. According to the database of this author and his colleagues, some 5,000 individuals referred to as its "members," nationals of 50 or more countries, have been interrogated in 58 countries worldwide; and hundreds of additional arrests have taken place secretly, especially in the Arab world. Moreover, there has been a worldwide freezing of al-Qaida's funds. According to a report of July 2003 by UN experts responsible for monitoring the application of UN resolutions on the fight against terrorism, since al-Qaida's first attacks in August 2001 $59.2 million held by al-Qaida, by linked companies or other entities, or by individuals identified as its members has been frozen or confiscated in 129 countries: 70 percent in Europe, Eurasia, or North America; 21 percent in the Middle East (Saudi Arabia, Emirates, etc.); and 8 percent in southeast Asia. All this, it should be noted, took place before the war in Iraq began in spring 2003 and before the subsequent attacks in the following countries:

> Riyadh, Saudi Arabia (May 2003, 35 killed; November 2003, 17 killed)
>
> Casablanca, Morocco (May 2003, 45 killed)
>
> Jakarta, Indonesia (August 2003, 12 killed)
>
> Istanbul, Turkey (November 2003, 69 killed)
>
> Madrid, Spain (March 2004, 202 killed)

A second characteristic that the new dangerous groups have in common is their hybrid nature—part political, part criminal. Considerable exchanges between criminal and terrorist groups are currently being reported: the Neapolitan camorra with the Basque group ETA and the GIA in Algeria; the Dawood Ibrahim gang in Karachi with Islamist groups close to bin Ladin such as Jaish-i-Muhammad and Mujahedin-e Khalq (MEK). Similar contacts link the IRA with the degenerate, protocriminal Fuerzas Armadas Revolucionarias de Colombia (FARC) guerrilla movement in Colombia.

A third shared characteristic of these dangerous groups is their mutability. As noted above, they are capable of very rapid mutations, as a function of the now crucial "dollar factor."

Fourth, typically, they are nomadic, deterritorialized (or located in inaccessible areas), and transnational.

Fifth, they are cut off from the world and civilized society. Their objectives may be criminal, fanatical, based on notions of doomsday, or entirely spurious—in reality they seem determined to hoodwink the larger world [examples, in Liberia and Sierra Leone, are the murderous bands led by Foday Sankoh under the name of the Revolutionary United Front (RUF)]. In some cases their goals may simply defy understanding (an example is the Aum sect).

Sixth, these dangerous groups generally have no state sponsorship of any kind; this lack makes them still more unpredictable and uncontrollable.

Seventh, they inflict massacres widely, with the intention of killing as many people as possible (examples include bin Ladin, the GIA in Algeria, and the Aum sect).

TWO CRUCIAL ELEMENTS IN FIGHTING MUTATING TERRORISM
Element 1: Criminal and Terrorist Money—Ending the Confusion

What would be a realistic assessment of attempts so far by states to contain money laundering by terrorists or criminals? There is no doubt that such efforts have been ineffectual: states, their laws, their police forces, and their judiciary seem to move in one dimension while terrorists, mafias, and networks of arms, narcotics, explosives, and currency trafficking move in another. The two dimensions intersect only rarely, in the form of seizures, arrests, and confiscations that are no more than a nuisance to the malefactors. Islamist terrorists are fatalistic about such losses of material or imprisonment of personnel. They believe they are in the hands of God; they will continue their holy work in prison or wherever Allah sees fit to lead them. Organized crime can afford to take setbacks even more philosophically. The amounts confiscated are far lower than regular corporation taxes. Also, police crackdowns serve as a stimulus to criminal elites. In a Darwinian struggle, the hunters impose a steep learning curve on their prey. Without ever exterminating the prey— the fittest will always survive. And state campaigns against crime are announced in a blaze of publicity, well before the troops move—ever so slowly—into the field. For its part, the world of crime acts swiftly, counterattacking perhaps on the very same day, closing down offshore operations at risk and transferring funds to other, safer front companies.

Thus terrorist or criminal money must be tracked down in both space and time. One battlefield of world chaos is "uncontrolled spaces"—lawless zones or "gray areas," intermediate spaces between the territories effectively policed by true nation-states, and neglected zones between ministries, or between the "territories" of particular services (narcotics, human trafficking, terrorism, smuggling, etc.).

There is also a battle against time. Aggressive, dangerous groups equipped with the latest technology have gained a huge advantage in time over states that are top-heavy, slow, paralyzed by administrative and legal inertia. How and why is this so?

Today, terrorist or criminal groups mostly operate from bases in uncontrolled, no-go areas (such as mountain ranges and urban sprawls). There they accumulate cash, which has to be recycled in a legitimate economy in order for it to be circulated electronically. Terrorist and mafia organizations recruit experts in high finance for this purpose. Working with lawyers and financial consultants, these banking professionals constantly seek international legal loopholes, studying legislative developments with a single aim in mind: to disguise the true origin of the funds they manage. For every major transaction, a new offshore corporate identity may be created and then instantly erased. Business is conducted smoothly and in record time. The launderers have a powerful incentive not to make mistakes, since the penalty for misuse of mafia or network funds is death (this is doubtless a better motivator than an annual bonus or a medal for productivity).

A money launderer also knows that states and international organizations have short memories, and that they soon tire of issues. Politicians are so close to the virtual reality of the media that they end up believing that by merely raising a problem they have actually solved it. We need only think of the periodic showpiece global conferences on ecological or social issues: "greenhouse gas emissions to be reduced by 50 percent in five years"; "extreme poverty to be cut by half worldwide in five years." And in five years, what changes? Nothing.

In the real world, far from the sound bites and headlines, what can be done to combat the shifting, mutating crime of money laundering? Before any treatment is attempted, a realistic prognosis of the disease must be obtained. The enormous difficulties involved in the operation must be faced. Failure to recognize these difficulties is a main conceptual obstacle to the tracking of terrorist money.

In the United States at present, tracking terrorist money is based first and foremost on attempts to freeze the circulation of money, or else on the seizure of accounts and funds belonging to individuals and entities on the terrorist watch lists. The approach of the U.S. government is thus premised on the notion that the individuals and entities being tracked are stable and have a fixed, permanent identity like their counterparts in the West. This may well have been true, or most often true, during the Cold War; but today—at any rate outside Europe—nothing could be further from the truth.

As far as the Middle East is concerned, the notion is patently absurd. An Arabian resident might, for instance, have ten local identification cards and permits, one permanent visa, etc.—none of which is an accurate transcription of his real registered identity. Let us suppose that the man's name is John Stephen Mackay. Then (with no exaggeration) one local permit may be in the name of Mr. Jon McQuay and another in the name of Mr. Stefan Mikey; a third may be made out to Mr. Mackie Stephens; and so on. There is no way that a computer trace, in any office, embassy, or airport, will pick up Mr. Mackay, who can easily open a local checking account, take out a credit card, etc., in the name of, say, Mr. Mikey. The same applies to his accomplices. So much for the watch list and the authorities' hopes of tracking their money! And these are Europeans, with fixed surnames. Imagine the situation if we repeat the exercise for a certain Ali bin Mohammad al-Baghdadi ("Ali, son of Mohammed, born in Baghdad").

Element 2: Understanding the Incubators and Battlefields of Terrorism

The entities described above are damaging enough in general, but in urban contexts—especially in the urban sprawls of the Southern Hemisphere—they pose a mortal threat.

A "mega urban sprawl" is an immense, chaotic agglomeration of apartment blocks and projects, escalators, markets, malls, highways, airports, severe pollution, shantytowns, rampant crime—and terrorism.

Outbreaks of war and violence in the mega urban sprawls of the Southern Hemisphere are reported almost daily on television; in particular, these take place in Gaza (the Gaza Strip is in effect a gigantic shantytown), in Baghdad and Bassora in Iraq, in Karachi, in Rio de Janeiro, and elsewhere. In Gaza and Baghdad, crack troops are in the field, equipped with the latest technology and equipment; furthermore, the current governments of both armies have suspended de facto the Geneva Conventions (regarding treatment of prisoners and suspects, long-term internment without trial, destruction of civilian targets, etc.). Yet both Gaza and Baghdad have proved a fatal trap—physically and morally—for the occupying forces; and both armies are facing the need for withdrawal in the future, with no decisive or permanent gains.

Before war is waged in a mega urban sprawl or a shantytown, there are more than just the specifics of the terrain to consider:

1. The local population may be organized in tribes or clans, and its reflexive reactions to attack or invasion will be driven by concepts of honor and vengeance.

2. Explosive population growth is an important factor. Gaza long had the world's highest rate of growth, with a birthrate of 6.8 children per woman of childbearing age. The second Intifada has caused 4,000 deaths—roughly three-quarters on the Palestinian side and the rest Israelis. But can the tolls of 3,000 and 1,000 be compared in terms of the ability of the respective populations to sustain (we might almost say "absorb") them? Certainly not.

3. A populace may be ripe for the temptations of religious fanaticism (Islamist in the case of Gaza and Baghdad) because the vast majority has been reduced to abject poverty. A promise of paradise in the afterlife is at least as realistic as the prospects for improving their current existence.

4. A society could be living as a "parallel economy," partly criminal (trafficking in human beings, drugs, vehicles, arms, etc.).

CONCLUSION

It is clear that the violence and conflicts ravaging the mega urban sprawls and shantytowns concern not only these places but the entire world, first and foremost the developed world. Everything we have learned about dangerous territories and entities since the fall of the Berlin Wall shows that criminal chaos, wherever it appears, is virulent and contagious. For instance, Iraq has already become a center of criminal trafficking in the Middle East. The independent Palestinian administration and police force, hounded by the Israeli army, have disappeared, allowing criminal disorder to prosper on a scale extending beyond the Independent Territories to involve the Palestinian diaspora, in the whole of the Middle East and even beyond. Furthermore, the same disorder is today beginning to gain ground in the Israeli settlements in the occupied territories. A recent report by the Israeli government's National Audit Office[2] exposed corruption and a rising "opacity index" in the settlements—the first, classic symptoms of a slide into criminality.

This is the reality that the developed nations must soon face up to. Criminal chaos may be less spectacular and less newsworthy than the media-conscious terrorism of bin Ladin and his kind. But it is precisely criminal chaos that is the real menace, both to the developed world and to the world which, in order to develop, has an immense, paramount need for the opposite of chaos—for peace and stability.

NOTES

1. On Karachi, see Anne-Line Didier and Jean-Luc Marret, *Etats échoués, mégapoles anarchiques*, PUF, coll. Défense et Défis Nouveaux, 2001. For Brazil's "criminal strongholds," see the Web site of the Department for the Study of the Contemporary Criminal Menace, www.drmcc.org, "Note d'Alerte" No. 2, headed *Cocaïne sur l'Europe: L'inondation approche* (*Cocaine in Europe: The Flood Is Coming*).
2. "Israël: Existerait-il deux états juifs?" ("Israel: Are There in Fact Two Jewish States?") *Ha'aretz-Courrier International* (13 May 2004).

The Psychology of Terrorism: Future Directions and Potential Implications for Counterterrorist Policy

John Horgan, Ph.D.
C. Psychol., Lecturer, Department of Applied Psychology,
University College, Cork, Ireland

INTRODUCTION

Anyone who spends even a short time studying terrorism, and political violence more generally, quickly discovers that it is an onerous task. There is more information in print on the subject than even the most enthusiastic student or analyst could read in a lifetime, and it is becoming increasingly difficult to assess the validity, reliability, and usefulness of much of this voluminous work, let alone keep up with the new analyses emerging each week. Also, there is a steadily increasing tendency for what might be expected to be reliable analyses of terrorism to mix fact and fiction in varying quantities. That this happens at the levels of both policy and basic research may not be news to some, but it is one major reason for the poor sustainability of developments in our knowledge and for a broader failure to develop the conceptual structures from which meaningful advances may emerge in the future. Much of what has been written since 9/11 pays little if any attention to the efforts of researchers before that date, and supposedly new arguments are produced almost daily in the contemporary literature on terrorism.

Since 9/11, we have seen how the drama and emotion associated with terrorism have hindered the emergence of systematic, coherent strategies to prevent future terrorist attacks and have also hindered any clear sense of what general issues drive and sustain terrorism. Paul Wilkinson has often said that terrorism is too important a problem to leave to politicians, and while this is a valid sentiment, the bulk of the academic community has been slow to respond with suggestions of how input from academia might contribute to counterterrorism (in the broadest possible sense). Indeed, a wider issue is the now obvious failure by any agency or community to assert even a remote sense of ownership of particular facets of the problem of terrorism. Certainly the time has come for the academic community to assert its relevance to understanding terrorism in ways perhaps not considered helpful in the past; moreover, it is time to begin critically assessing what contributions any analysis of terrorism can offer. Surely the question "Is it useful?" has never before been so relevant.

PSYCHOLOGICAL RESEARCH ON TERRORISM

Jerrold Post once remarked that the psychology of terrorism could be described as "primitive,"[1] and although his comment was made in 1987, it still holds true. Unless psychological research on terrorism begins to develop systematically, we are unlikely to achieve either the evidence or the perspective necessary to properly and reliably inform policy. However, there are some attempts to redress this situation; some newer commentaries on the psychology of terrorism make a detailed case for sound, sustained investment in objective, independent, empirical, data-driven research on terrorists' behavior.[2]

While it is easy to criticize the shortcomings of existing research, it is heartening to discover that the challenges posed by such problems are not as insurmountable as we might imagine or as some commentators may suggest. Psychological research on terrorism to date has been plagued by many issues, such as an unfortunate lack of reliable data to support or refute its elementary theories or test its basic hypotheses. More disturbingly (apart from the issue of data), much psychological research has been rather shortsighted,[3] with little sense of its own limitations. We essentially lack perspective, space, and clear priorities as we try to make sense of the relevance and applicability of psychology to terrorism and to related broader processes. One relevant lesson of the war on terrorism—a lesson we have failed to grasp—is that it is wrong for us to uncritically attribute certain qualities (and notions of sophistication) to terrorist movements and individuals. The capacities, abilities, and presumed intentions of terrorist movements (as well as what terrorism can and does realistically achieve—indeed what we perhaps allow it to achieve) should be neither over- nor underestimated, but examined critically using what valuable conceptual tools we already have at our disposal. This is not to say that the problem is the sole remit of psychological analyses, but it is one that, as Reich[4] warned, psychologists tend to be associated with more often than others.

Specifically, many researchers unfortunately still believe that psychopathology and limited theories of individual psychology are the keys to understanding the complex origins, development, and sustenance of terrorism. One main reason for the persistence of what should be exposed as a weak analysis is that it is based on belief, when what we need is for all of our analyses to be based on evidence. Only evidence will settle the disputes that arise so regularly and so vociferously when we tackle issues of how best to understand terrorism, let alone try to respond to it. Many analyses continue to be shrouded in pseudopsychology, frequently nothing more than cozy conjecture masquerading as informed expertise, with no evidence (or the incorrect use of facts) provided in support of notions that, for example, we could explain terrorism with reference to personality traits. (This could perhaps be linked to a broader sentiment that an alliance with an extremist ideology is in itself indicative of some sort of pathology). A major problem in psychological analysis to date, therefore, has been that it is reductionist—various psychological concepts (including personality) are being pushed far beyond their limitations, in an attempt to explain a hugely complex social problem.

The violence associated with terrorism is a factor in the persistent idea that terrorism is pathological. Much psychological analysis is founded on a misinformed, inappropriate use of psychometric assessment and clinical diagnosis as a supposed way of making informed, testable judgments about terrorism and terrorists. The notion that terrorists' behavior can be explained away by character analysis (often in terms of inadequacies) is supported by no evidence whatsoever and remains seriously misleading; within contemporary psychology it would quickly be exposed as deeply flawed. The following points will serve to summarize the limitations of such research:

Point 1. Explanations of terrorism (particularly at the level of the individual) in terms of personality traits are insufficient to let us understand why people become involved in terrorism. These arguments take numerous forms; some of them (such as equating terrorism with "psychopathy") seem clumsy, but others have varying degrees of subtlety. In any case, though, personality-based explanations do not acknowledge that terrorism is a complex, multifaceted activity, with many different roles and many different kinds of involvement for many different people, not all of whom are necessarily engaged in the end product of violent terrorist acts. What we see in an actual attack is only the tip of the iceberg. If we consider the composition of some large terrorist movements, for instance, it becomes apparent that the number of active terrorists is minuscule compared with the overall size, capacity, and membership of the movement. Thus while all the members serve important functions in sustaining terrorism (as well as providing the pool from which terrorists emerge), actual acts of terrorism are limited to a relative few.

Point 2. Many psychological explanations attempt to support the concept of terrorism as pathology by considering why some people become directly engaged in terrorist activity while many others (who may engage in related activities) do not. But in reality, contained and focused membership reflects organizational concerns and issues of leadership (e.g., security and strategy) as well as serving more diffuse psychological objectives. For one thing, it ensures that there is a psychological "premium" associated with key roles. In other words, if the leadership puts recruits into key roles without severe restrictions, the premium associated with those roles would diminish (and the roles would be less attractive and would confer less status); moreover, operational effectiveness would ultimately diminish as well. A related argument, often reflected in the literature, is that people seek out a role in terrorist movements because attaining the role would serve some personal need. This is, admittedly, part of the reason, since involvement with a terrorist group does have positive aspects such as status, excitement, and a sense of purpose. However, it is unhelpful to interpret such a role as redressing some deficiency in personality or as indicating some personality type.

The tendency to make this interpretation is common in psychological analyses of terrorism; we assume that if something makes sense to us as onlookers, or is significant to us, it must therefore have the same significance or meaning to the people who are engaged or involved with a terrorist group. In fact, though, in this regard each member of a terrorist group—or even each member of the same cell—is unique.

Point 3. A broader problem emerges in individual psychological theories of terrorism. In trying to suggest why (when all other situational factors are presumed more or less similar) some people but not others become terrorists, such theories suffer from many conceptual, theoretical, and methodological difficulties. Thus, as asserted (and testable) hypotheses, these explanations are weak; furthermore, they are internally flawed and inconsistent, and demonstrate a lack of understanding of basic psychological concepts. There are various reasons for this; perhaps the most obvious is that at present, few psychologists are engaged in this type of research. Of course, a larger number of researchers does not necessarily imply higher-quality research, but at least within psychology it might serve to distinguish basic issues more effectively. For the moment, then, we may have to ask more sophisticated questions about terrorism, the better to test psychological theories. For instance, we might do well to distinguish questions about *why* people become terrorists from questions about *how* they become terrorists. In truth, questions about any occupational choice (terrorism, accountancy, or anything else) are essentially impossible to answer; more often than not, the choice has to do with idiosyncrasy and accident. (This quickly becomes apparent when we consider such questions outside the context of terrorism.) Nevertheless, such choices can be understood in terms of developmental processes—but they cannot be understood in terms of theories that assume a set of stable, consistent terrorist traits.

The purpose of these three points is not necessarily to comment on psychological theories of personality or motivation, but to convey some sense of the limitations incurred by a preoccupation with individual psychological research on terrorists. Ideas about the apparent usefulness of terrorist profiles are equally plentiful and are often said to be on firmer footing. While a profile may be attractive to administrators at policy-making levels, it too is largely unhelpful. At the heart of the profile approach is an attempt to reduce the complexity of terrorism into something more manageable,[5] and there are implicit (though rarely explicit) assumptions about what such profiles suggest about counterterrorism. The evidence that does exist tells us that we need to appreciate how heterogeneous terrorists are and how many forms engagement in terrorism can take. It also tells us that many of the personal traits or characteristics we attempt to attribute to terrorists are not specific to terrorists and do not serve to distinguish one type of terrorist from another (even within the same movement, let alone across categories, such as "Islamist," that we assume to be meaningful). There is, moreover, no evidence to suggest the existence of a priori qualities of the terrorist that could enable us to predict, with any validity or reliability over a meaningful period of time, the likelihood of involvement and engagement by any person or any social group.[6] Not only does no such evidence exist—none could exist.

There is some room for optimism, however. While individual approaches to understanding terrorism have largely floundered, other potential approaches are available for further exploration. These other routes have practical benefits, allowing us to think about how counterterrorism could develop in newer, more effective ways. This author,[7] in developing a model for the understanding of involvement in terrorism and engagement in terrorist incidents, has argued that until psychological research considers terrorism in a fundamentally different way, we should at least recognize the limitations of psychological perspectives alone (as we should with any discipline) and begin to encourage the integration of, for example, psychological and criminological frameworks. This might help us recognize the value of seeing terrorism as a process.

Rather than seeing involvement and engagement in terrorist violence (and in nonviolent related activities) as indicative of a psychological state, it may be more useful to analyze their complexity in terms of a discrete, identifiable process with incremental stages of increasing intensity, culminating in violence. The focus changes from thinking about terrorists less in terms of inclination and more in terms of engagement with activities and incidents. Implications for counterterrorism then become more obvious, and the boundaries of individual psychological explanations of terrorism become much clearer. By viewing terrorism as a process that people seek to enter and work through, we can see that, for example, the reasons for becoming involved with a terrorist movement have little or no relevance to understanding the nature, extent, and direction of terrorist attacks.

There are at least three identifiable psychological phases of involvement: (1) initial involvement, (2) continued or sustained involvement, and (3) disengagement. Each phase has unique implications for prevention. I have suggested these phases as potential intervention points and have encouraged a metaphor—risk assessment—to help us think about the psychology of terrorism in different and ultimately more beneficial ways. Psychological analysis in this sense can let us reframe complex questions such as "What makes a terrorist?" in ways that open up more practical avenues for research. For example, if we consider the complexity of terrorists' behavior in a slightly more sophisticated psychological sense, we can see that "becoming a terrorist" does not raise issues having to do with hidden, internal mental qualities; rather, it raises any or all of the following questions:[8]

1. Why do people want to become involved in a group that engages in terrorist violence? Here we will have to rely on individual accounts by terrorists themselves, in interviews or autobiographical material, to supplement our own efforts to develop plausible, verifiable explanations. We may not find truth or accuracy in such accounts, but we might identify common themes that illustrate the effects of ideological control (a common element of sustained membership of a terrorist group).

2. How do people become involved? (The distinction between *how* and *why* will be of critical importance in advancing research.)

3. What roles or functions do members fulfill and what meaning do individuals associate with the acquisition and retention of a specific role? (However, there may be a hidden assumption here that it is possible to identify criteria for membership as having reached some clear state or position.)

4. How and why does a person move within and through a terrorist group?

5. How and why do individuals assimilate the shared values and norms of the group, and how and why do they then accommodate to qualities of engagement that were unconsidered

or unexpected before membership? Also, how and why do members assimilate and accommodate at varying rates, and does this difference relate to individual qualities as opposed to individuals' experiences postrecruitment?

6. How and why do members commit specific acts of violence, e.g., do people become hardened by experience, or do leaders apply crude psychometric measures to select aggressive people for violent roles? (Al-Qaida has used propaganda videos showing massacres, filmed in Algeria by the Armed Islamic Group, for this latter purpose.)

7. How and why do members affect one another at various stages of their own and others' involvement?

8. How and why might terrorists eventually want to, or have to, disengage from violence, move into nonviolent but relevant support activities, or leave the organization altogether?

Although these psychological distinctions may seem academic, a critical conceptual point, which would inform strategies of response, prevention, and control (at whatever stage they may be focused), is that the eight questions are not necessarily related to each other, and answering one may not necessarily reflect on any other. In addition, although developing questions in this way reveals gaps in our knowledge (in terms of what we have yet to do), each issue has a unique implication for prevention. We will not know this, however, unless we develop psychological research into each of the issues. At present, our knowledge of them is incomplete.

Another area for potential psychological research is terrorists' selection of targets. When one thinks of practical counterterrorism informed by psychology, negotiating with terrorists who have taken hostages naturally comes to mind, but there are other interesting areas. For example, we know from analysis of terrorists' behavior that every operation has predictive, logical, and above all environmental behavioral qualities, regardless of its size, capacity, and scope—and regardless of the implications of the operation (or attack) itself and of those who conduct it. However, little attention is currently paid to the specific environmental cues (discriminative properties) associated with decision making by terrorist organizations in planning attacks. Understanding of the environment in which terrorists operate does not make that environment invulnerable, but it may limit opportunities once we are able to quantify these issues and apply their predictive qualities. The enormous implications of this knowledge and what they can bring about are not obvious to policy makers or planners—a situation that needs immediate redress.

As of this writing, research at the department of applied psychology at University College, Cork (UCC), is establishing and developing environmental and contextual cues that might facilitate the prediction of vehicular suicidal terrorist attacks.[9] In particular, the author and his associates are developing a series of experiments to identify and classify discriminative cues of environments in which suicidal terrorist attacks develop or may develop. The results will form the basis of counterterrorism training modules and feed into higher-level environmental planning to control the levels of risks and vulnerability associated with terrorist attacks.

To begin with, the research at UCC has identified from open-source material predictive qualities of vehicular suicidal terrorist attacks in several conflict zones. The identified predictive qualities, or environmental cues, then form the basis of reconstructing, through scenario-based simulations (or virtual environments), accounts to be used in the series of experiments. These accounts are supplemented with data from interviews of police officers and military personnel who have firsthand experience of suicidal terrorism.

One practical implication of such research is examining the capacity of experienced and inexperienced personnel to identify, and be alert to, probable targeting cues relevant to understanding the location of specific vehicular suicidal terrorist attacks. The identification of some cues by police officers might seem obvious in hindsight, but only in the context of an actual attack can these cues be identified as significant. For this reason, the research is also applying the experimental method as a basis for identifying useful ways to train counterterrorists.

Although the idea behind it is simple, such research could be groundbreaking. Its purpose is to develop a more solid conceptual framework for a psychology of terrorism (or perhaps psychologies of terrorism), but it can also serve to move the psychological research beyond issues concerning terrorist personalities and into more operationally relevant notions.

THINKING BROADLY, YET CONCISELY

A related issue is a dogmatic preoccupation with the term *terrorism*, and our failure to appreciate how this preoccupation affects the possibility of developing a psychological perspective. Obviously, there is little point in trying to replace the word, but its inconsistent, muddied use has skewed the nature and scope of analysis of those who engage in terrorism and has impeded a fuller understanding of the broad processes that give rise to and emerge from political violence. Psychological analysis has yet to identify all the behaviors associated with all stages and aspects of terrorism. For example, it has not clearly identified the behaviors associated with initially becoming involved, being or remaining involved (or escalating one's commitment), engaging in terrorist events, and disengaging. However, whatever label we attach to those who participate in these behaviors—and regardless of short-term policy shifts and of politically creative uses of language (in particular, any attempts to fundamentally alter our thinking about who or what is a terrorist)— the behaviors themselves, and the ways in which they develop, do not change. They remain consistent (and this is a major reason behind the development of the virtual environment research by the author and his associates). Becoming a terrorist, as noted above, is a cumulative, incremental process that culminates in an increased, sustained, focused commitment to a group ideal. As more integrative and beneficial analyses develop (e.g., see the analysis by Sageman in Chapter 4), such behaviors and the dynamics affecting them are becoming more predictable.

However, there are changes in policy makers' ideas about the appropriate focus and scope of preventive measures or control. An additional complication is that counterterrorism itself is rarely based on evidence or outcomes; as a result, there is even more confusion. The behaviors constituting or related to terrorism are always in flux, and there is little or no sense of what factors drive them. Ultimately we must consider belated responses to what we have inadvertently allowed to become a massively complex problem.

All these points reflect a pressing problem facing researchers in psychology and counterterrorist officials: a lack of clear priorities. Apparent prioritization of practical counterterrorist measures often has little relevance to real-world issues: where terrorism comes from (not in a geographical or technical sense), how it develops, and what we might do to disrupt it. This is not cynical criticism of the already battered and bruised intelligence services. In fact, serious analysts rarely appreciate how law enforcement and intelligence agencies can strategically respond to the broad terrorist threat in ways that enable them to develop their own agenda. Problems regarding the collection of evidence are not, of course, unique to terrorism; they have to do with criminology in general. But after a terrorist attack, a political sensitivity develops that allows for arguments about changing rules, protocols, language, and the very meaning of terrorism—arguments that would hardly be made about, say, automobile theft.[10]

We therefore find a situation that ultimately affects everyone involved in counterterrorism: in this area the political process is almost completely ineffective, in many ways. Moreover, when its weaknesses are exposed, it predictably tries to find solutions elsewhere—for example, in the intelligence services or law enforcement. A vicious circle then develops in which police officers (or other first responders) accept (or are encouraged to accept) ownership of the problem as a means of obtaining increased resources and attaining increased importance, but eventually acknowledge that they too cannot solve the problems posed by terrorism. The search for solutions is then pushed back to the structural and systems-level vulnerabilities: in other words, the problem once again becomes political. Sometimes, frustration leads governments to admit that, say, the war on terrorism is essentially unwinnable. Here, once again, the choice of words is self-defeating. It implies thinking of the problem as a war to be won, rather than—more usefully—as a process to be managed and a situation to be controlled. If we are to break this vicious circle, we must be prepared to challenge traditional, comfortable views that security is the most appropriate and effective solution to terrorism. But this challenge will inevitably result in greater pressure on the academic community to assert its relevance, limitations, strengths, and broader potential.

CONCLUSION

It is unfortunate that within the discipline of psychology, and sometimes within other academic disciplines, we continue to speak about terrorism in such polarized ways. Terrorism continues to be viewed as either mysteriously complicated or devastatingly clear.

Often, which view is adopted depends on access to information, or on a worldview influenced, or even dictated, by education, background, or professional training. The seemingly chance use of a particular word or phrase in a presentation, an article, or a document can betray the user's allegiance, political leanings, or academic perspective. And given the overwhelming volume of materials now coming out of the revitalized terrorism industry, we can too easily respond by castigating a work or, because of our own ignorance, by assuming that it is irrelevant. The issue is not "What works?" but "How do we know if it works?" or "What is its relevance?" or "How can we assess its value?" These questions now represent major challenges for psychological analyses, but at least we are beginning to realize that the potential for psychological analyses of terrorism goes far beyond ideas of profiling or personality assessment.

One way to move forward is for both academia and policy makers to demonstrate the practical applicability and mutual relevance of their work. This would help us ascertain more precisely the quality and potential of academic research, and that assessment would in turn give focus to psychological analyses of terrorism as well as help to develop the agendas needed for short- to medium-term future intelligence analysis.[11] The academic community needs to show how its analyses are relevant in the real world; the intelligence community needs to address—in routine ways, and in ways perhaps not considered before—issues of assessing value. Recognizing the value of reliable, validated information is at the heart of useful collaboration. Often, collaboration and the sharing of information give rise to mistrust, suspicion, and poor experiences. But most of the time—and this has never really changed—collaboration gives rise to issues of power and control. Because we live in a bureaucratic society that has certain rules and expectations, it is probably natural to expect the academic community to become the vanguard and demonstrate relevance and some form of ownership; but those responsible for responding to terrorism (at whatever level) must voice their needs through appropriate, responsible channels. In short, neither side can truly benefit the other, or in turn the wider community, unless each side knows what the other wants, needs, and is willing to be clear about—what each can, in practice, deliver. When such knowledge is lacking, opportunities are wasted.

See also Chapter 4 **Understanding al-Qaida Networks.**

N O T E S

1. J. M. Post, "Group and Organisational Dynamics of Political Terrorism: Implications for Counterterrorist Policy," in P. Wilkinson and A. M. Stewart (eds.), *Contemporary Research on Terrorism* (Aberdeen: Aberdeen University Press, 1987), pp. 307–317.

2. For example, see J. Horgan, *The Psychology of Terrorism* (London: Routledge, 2005). Some of the arguments in the present article are developed more fully in this book.

3. See W. Reich (ed.), *Origins of Terrorism: Psychologies, Ideologies, Theologies, States of Mind* (New York: Cambridge University Press, 1990).

4. Ibid.

5. See M. Taylor, *The Terrorist* (London: Brassey's, 1988).

6. See especially the various chapters on this topic in A. Silke (ed.), *Terrorists, Victims, and Society: Psychological Perspectives on Terrorism and Its Consequences* (London: Wiley, 2003).

7. Horgan, *The Psychology of Terrorism.*

8. See also J. Horgan, "The Social and Psychological Characteristics of Terrorism and Terrorists," in T. Bjorgo (ed.), *Root Causes of Terrorism* (London: Routledge, in press).

9. For information, please contact the author.

10. Horgan, *The Psychology of Terrorism*, Chapter 7.

11. Horgan, *The Psychology of Terrorism*, discusses this in detail.

CHAPTER 11

WMD and Lessons from the Anthrax Attacks

Leonard A. Cole
Adjunct Professor of Political Science, Rutgers University

The anthrax mailings in the aftermath of 9/11 demonstrated how varied a terrorist's arsenal can be and increased Americans' anxiety about terrorism. Especially worrisome are weapons of mass destruction (WMD), which include biological agents like anthrax, as well as chemical, radiological, and nuclear weapons. Any of these materials can cause extensive damage and widespread fear. But while they are commonly lumped together as WMD, each is distinct. Differences among them include the nature of the materials, the difficulty and cost of production, potential effectiveness, and means of protection. Still, although germ weapons are distinct from other WMD, some aspects of bioterrorism are also relevant to other forms of terrorism involving WMD. After summarizing various weapons, this chapter reviews the biological attack of 2001 and the lessons it has taught.

THE SPECTER OF TERRORISM

An ironic aspect of 9/11 and the anthrax mailings is that although anthrax is commonly deemed a WMD and an airliner is not, the letters resulted in only five deaths whereas 9/11 resulted in some 3,000. But the small number of casualties from anthrax in this particular case does not diminish the catastrophic potential of bioterrorism. Many additional deaths were avoided by appropriate health-care responses and simply by good luck: relatively few anthrax letters were mailed, and the organism was responsive to antibiotics. Even so, the mailings caused serious disruptions, including the closing of government buildings and the quarantine of tens of thousands of pieces of mail. Attacks with other WMD are likely to be no less disruptive.

Obviously, 9/11 made a deeper impact on the national consciousness than the anthrax mailings. In fact, few people now recall the specific dates of the anthrax attack: 18 September, when the earliest recovered anthrax letters were postmarked; 4 October, when the first case of anthrax was diagnosed; and 21 November, when the last case was diagnosed.

Thus far, apart from turning airliners into missiles, al-Qaida apparently has used only conventional munitions, even for suicide bombings, but it is seeking biological and other nonconventional weapons. In 2002, George Tenet, director of Central Intelligence, cited a declaration by bin Ladin that acquiring weapons of mass destruction was "a religious duty."[1] Two years later the staff of the federal commission investigating 9/11 reported that al-Qaida "remains extremely interested in conducting chemical, biological, radiological, or nuclear attacks" against the United States.[2]

In June 2004 Deputy Attorney General James Comey declared that Jose Padilla and other al-Qaida operatives had revealed to U.S. authorities their intention to detonate a radiological device in the United States.[3] It was not clear whether they had come close to realizing the plan.

Palestinian groups that have dispatched suicide bombers against Israel have also sought biological and chemical weapons. One of these organizations, HAMAS, acknowledged experimenting with chemical weapons for attacks against Israel. Israeli officials contend that HAMAS may have already tried to use cyanide and rat poison in suicide bombings.[4]

Keeping these weapons out of the hands of Palestinian terrorists, bin Ladin's minions, and other rogue groups should be a preeminent goal of the United States and its allies. But it is clear that despite dedicated efforts, unsavory groups might well acquire WMD. An essential requirement of preparedness is to understand the nature of these different weapons and the challenges they pose.

NUCLEAR WEAPONS

Nuclear arms, unlike other weapons, originated on a precise date: 16 July 1945, when the first atomic bomb was detonated at a desert site in Alamogordo, New Mexico. This event was the culmination of three years of secret work by 130,000 American-led scientists and other workers. The Manhattan Project, as the program was called, arose from fear that Nazi Germany would try to develop an atomic bomb. In 1938, scientists in Germany had bombarded a uranium atom with neutrons that split its nucleus, releasing energy. It was then understood that splitting numerous nuclei of uranium atoms could release an immense amount of energy. The challenge was to harness that division, or fission, into a controlled blast. Only after the war did the United States and its allies learn that Germany had failed to embark on a similar effort. German scientists apparently considered the technical challenge too formidable.[5]

By the time the atom bomb was developed, Germany had surrendered. But Japan had not yet capitulated, and military planners estimated that invading Japan would cost tens of thousands of American lives. In hopes of ending the war quickly, President Harry Truman ordered the use of the two available atomic bombs. One was dropped on 6 August over Hiroshima, and the other on 9 August over Nagasaki. Both cities were leveled. Some 70,000 people in Hiroshima and 40,000 in Nagasaki were killed instantly. Many more died later from effects of the blasts, the resulting fires, and the radiation released by the explosions. The Japanese sued for peace, and the war ended on 3 September.

The destructive force of the atom bomb is produced by a chain reaction within a mass of uranium 235, a scarce isotope of the element. Bombarding the uranium with neutrons causes nuclei to split and release more neutrons, which cause more nuclei to split, and so on. The amount of energy released depends on the mass of uranium and the frequency of neutron bombardment. At predictable levels, the nuclear energy transforms into heat, which can generate electricity. But with enough uranium and neutron bombardments, the energy can cause a huge explosion. The explosive force of each bomb dropped on Japan was about 15 kilotons (15,000 tons) of TNT. After World War II, far more powerful nuclear arms were developed, including hydrogen bombs whose force could exceed 1 million tons of TNT.

The number of countries with nuclear weapons has been limited by the technical challenges of development and by international agreements aimed at curbing nuclear proliferation. Nine countries are now believed to have nuclear arms—China, France, India, Israel, North Korea, Pakistan, Russia, the United Kingdom, and the United States.[6] Others, especially Iran, are suspected of trying to develop them.

Developing even a low-level atomic bomb requires sophisticated technology and materials not readily available. Expertise from several disciplines is necessary: nuclear physics, nuclear chemistry, materials chemistry, mathematics, and mechanical and electrical engineering. But developing a bomb is not the only way to acquire one. Although guarded by the countries that have them, nuclear arms ultimately might be acquired by theft or illicit purchase. Especially troubling in this regard are recent disclosures that Pakistani scientists sold nuclear know-how and materials to Libya and possibly to North Korea and others.[7]

RADIOLOGICAL WEAPONS

A complicating feature of nuclear reactions is that they are radioactive: they release radiation, which itself can be harmful. Although radioactivity was discovered in the 1890s, the potential danger was not initially appreciated. In time, it was understood that radiation can destroy human cells, and exposure to very high levels can kill a person quickly. But lower levels also affect the DNA in cells and make them prone to cancer. Only uranium and a few other elements, notably plutonium, can be turned into explosive weapons, but many more elements emit radiation.

Several radioactive materials are used in legitimate biological and medical work. Others are unwelcome by-products of nuclear power reactors. Radioactive carbon and potassium, for example, are used routinely as markers in biological laboratory research. Radioactive iodine is used to treat certain thyroid conditions. Radiation is also integral to some medical equipment, notably X-ray machines. The waste from nuclear power plants includes highly radioactive cesium, tritium, and strontium. In short, radioactive materials are plentiful. They are in hospitals, research institutions, universities, and other locations throughout the country. Even if radioactive items are monitored, their sheer quantity increases the chance that a terrorist could acquire them.

This possibility raises the specter of a "dirty bomb" in which radioactive material is mixed with conventional explosives. A detonation could release radiation over large areas. According to one study, if a casket of spent fuel from a nuclear power plant was exploded in downtown Manhattan, more than 2,000 people might die quickly and thousands more would suffer from radiation poisoning.[8]

Although brief contact with low-level radioactive material causes little harm, extended exposure increases the likelihood of cellular destruction and illness. The dispersal of even modest quantities of radioactive materials in a populated area could cause panic. Droves of fearful people might try to flee. Many might seek medical attention and overload hospitals and other health-care facilities. Anxiety would be rampant. The challenge to the medical responders would be to differentiate people most at risk from those least at risk. One approach would be to quickly develop a grid to help establish who had been closest to the point of release and for how long.

CHEMICAL WEAPONS

Unlike nuclear and radiological weapons, chemical and biological weapons extend back thousands of years. Until the nineteenth century, when microorganisms were found to be the cause of disease, little distinction was made between toxic chemical and biological materials. The ancients understood that arsenic—just like water polluted by animal carcasses—could cause illness and death. No matter how a poison was made up, it could be used to kill and debilitate. But by the early twentieth century, chemical and biological warfare agents were recognized as being in different categories.

The first large-scale use of chemical weapons was in World War I. Germany introduced chlorine on the battlefield in 1915; it was followed later in the war by other agents, including mustard gas. By the end of war all the major powers had used chemicals, resulting in more than 1 million casualties. These agents caused painful blisters, blindness, burned lungs, and tortured deaths. The horrible effects prompted the Geneva Protocol of 1925, an international agreement prohibiting chemical weapons in war. Beyond chemicals, which are inanimate, the protocol also prohibited "bacteriological" agents.[9]

Despite the prohibition, countries continued to develop and stockpile chemical arms. In the 1930s, the Germans developed nerve agents, including sarin. A small drop of sarin absorbed by the skin, or a whiff of its vapor, can impair the nervous system and cause death in minutes. In the 1950s, the United States and the United Kingdom developed an even more potent nerve agent, VX. Still, after World War I chemicals were rarely used as battlefield weapons. The major exception was Iraq's extended use of chemicals against Iran in the 1980s. Inspectors under the auspices of the United Nations Security Council repeatedly reported between 1983 and 1988 that Iraq was attacking with mustard and possibly nerve agents, though neither the Security Council nor individual nations offered vigorous protests.[10]

A spectacular terror attack with chemicals occurred in 1995, when the Japanese cult Aum Shinrikyo released a nerve agent in the subway in Tokyo. On 20 March, using sharp umbrella tips, cult members punctured 11 plastic pouches filled with sarin. As the liquid and its vapor leaked out, people began to suffocate and collapse. Twelve people died, and more than 1,000 became ill. An investigation by the staff of a U.S. Senate committee found that the sarin had been impure and was poorly disseminated. If not for these mistakes, "tens of thousands could have easily been killed," the committee's report concluded.[11]

Several countries are in the process of destroying their chemical arsenals in accordance with the Chemical Weapons Convention of 1933, which bans the development or possession of these weapons.[12] Still, at least three countries—Iran, Syria, and North Korea—maintain chemical arsenals, and more than a dozen others are suspected of continuing their chemical programs.[13]

A chemical poison is far easier to produce than a nuclear bomb. For some agents, advanced knowledge of chemistry would be required; but the equipment and ingredients are readily available, since precursor chemicals are often used for commercial purposes. Mustard agent, for example, can be made by combining hydrochloric acid with thiodiglycol, a chemical used in the manufacture of dyes and inks. Sarin, like other nerve agents, is an organophosphate. Its chemical structure resembles that of insecticides which kill by breaking down an insect's nervous system. Production requires special apparatus, and dispersing an agent with, say, a low-explosive grenade, would need additional expertise. But as Aum Shinrikyo demonstrated in Tokyo, releasing a chemical in a populated area can also be very simple.

BIOLOGICAL WEAPONS

Biological weapons—bacteria, viruses, and other microorganisms that cause disease and death—pose a unique threat. Unlike any other category of weapons, most biological agents can reproduce and make an environment more dangerous over time. Among the biological agents deemed likely weapons, some, like anthrax and botulinum toxin (a poisonous bacterial product), are not transmitted from person to person. But others, including plague bacteria and smallpox viruses, are highly contagious. People infected with a contagious agent can spread the disease, in effect themselves becoming biological bombs. Further, the potential to genetically engineer an organism toward greater virulence and resistance to drug treatment creates additional concern.

Still, biological agents as weapons of war or terror have been even rarer than chemical agents. In the twentieth century, the only known biowarfare against humans occurred in the late 1930s and early 1940s, when Japanese aircraft dropped porcelain bombs filled with plague-infected fleas. The germs reportedly caused epidemics that killed thousands.[14]

Various groups, including American right-wing extremists, have sought biological poisons. In 1991, members of the Minnesota Patriots Council produced the toxin ricin from castor beans, but were arrested before using it.[15] In fact, until the anthrax attacks in 2001, the only large-scale bioterrorism incident in the United States took place in 1984 in Oregon. Members of the Rajneesh cult poured a liquid containing salmonella bacteria onto salad bars and into coffee creamers in several restaurants. At least 750 people became ill, though none died.[16]

The salmonella incident demonstrated how easily and unobtrusively a biological attack could be launched. But the Rajneeshees had also released bacteria on earlier occasions, with no apparent effect. Similarly, in the early 1990s Aum Shinrikyo tried to infect people with anthrax but did not succeed. These unsuccessful efforts underscore the variables that can affect the outcome of a biological attack: type of organism, susceptibility of targeted victims, weather and other environmental conditions, and availability of appropriate antibiotics and vaccines.

The variability extends as well to the nature of the particular agent species. In a natural habitat, anthrax spores may lie dormant under the soil indefinitely. But in the human lungs they can transform to an active state in which they reproduce and release a lethal toxin. Unless the victim is treated promptly with appropriate antibiotics, death can follow in days.

The smallpox virus poses a different kind of biological threat. Smallpox was eradicated in the 1970s after a global public health campaign. Samples of the virus are now legitimately preserved at only two locations: one in the United States and the other in Russia. But analysts believe that rogue states or terrorists are interested in acquiring the virus and that some may have already succeeded. Concern that Iraq might have developed smallpox as a weapon prompted the vaccination of American troops on the eve of the invasion in March 2003. (After Iraq was occupied, neither smallpox nor other WMD were found there.) Since the terror attacks in 2001, the United States has acquired a stockpile of 300 million doses of smallpox vaccine and has developed plans for quick distribution.

Other possible biological weapons, such as the Ebola virus, offer their own variations. A cause of hemorrhagic fever, Ebola is contagious, untreatable, and deadly. Yet Ebola does not survive long outside a living host; thus storing and disseminating it are especially challenging.

Despite the Biological Weapons Convention, a treaty that bans germ weapons,[17] perhaps a dozen countries are suspected of main-taining illegal biological programs. Among the most worrisome are some that have chemical weapons programs, including, again, Iran, Syria, and North Korea.[18]

Moreover, a formidable biological weapon might be developed through genetic engineering. The result could be a drug-resistant hybrid that is as hardy as an anthrax spore, as contagious as a flu virus, and as deadly as a virulent plague bacterium. According to scientists who worked in the biological weapons program of the former Soviet Union, efforts there included trying to produce such nightmarish concoctions.[19]

COMPARATIVE EFFECTIVENESS OF WMD

The distinctive qualities of weapons of mass destruction—biological, chemical, radiological, nuclear—bear on their comparative effectiveness and likelihood of use. Figure 11-1 makes comparisons in six categories: (1) complexity of production, (2) difficulty of acquisition, (3) cost of production, (4) difficulty of delivery or dispersal, (5) likelihood of effectiveness, and (6) worst-case consequences. For each category, 1 denotes "lowest or least," and 5 "highest or most." These rankings are partially subjective because some categories encompass a range of agents. This is especially true of biological and chemical agents. For example, the smallpox virus and the anthrax bacterium are both potential bioweapons, but they differ in accessibility, the symptoms they produce, and the anticipated manner of delivery. Still, as a group, biological agents are typically distinct from any other agent, as their numerical ranking suggests.

Similarly, the complexity of producing a chemical weapon varies from one chemical to another. Making VX nerve agent is more complicated than, say, making hydrogen cyanide or chlorine gas. Thus a chemical weapon is given a 3 for complexity—somewhere between rather simple and somewhat complicated. In contrast, producing a nuclear weapon, which is indisputably complicated, warrants a 5.

FIGURE   11-1

Characteristics of weapons of mass destruction.

	Biological	Chemical	Radiological	Nuclear
Complexity of production	2	3	1	5
Cost of production	2	3	3	5
Difficulty of acquisition	2	2	2	5
Difficulty of delivery or dispersal	1	2	1	4
Likelihood of effectiveness	3	3	3	5
Worst-case consequences	5	4	4	5

Note: 1 = lowest or least; 5 = highest or most.

The designations are based on literature that has compared various WMD as well as information relevant to the individual agents.[20] As Figure 11-1 indicates, the weapon most likely to be effective (in general) and most devastating (in a worst-case scenario) is a nuclear bomb. But it is also very costly, complicated to produce and handle, and difficult to acquire. Radiological and chemical weapons are less likely to cause mass destruction, though in worst-case scenarios they certainly would cause many illnesses and deaths.

Of all WMD, biological agents are the most problematic. As with chemical weapons, their effectiveness varies markedly. Virulence varies not only between species but also within species. Thus certain strains of anthrax kill quickly whereas others are quite harmless. Growing any of the organisms, whether virulent or not, is easy and inexpensive, but transforming them into optimal weapons may be more complicated. The anthrax spores sent in the mail were dried and manipulated to reduce clumping. This enhanced their danger because individual organisms are more likely than larger clumps to reach deep into the lungs, where they can be lethal. Even the more easily produced moist spores, though, could be sprayed from an atomizer and pose a deadly danger to anyone who inhaled them.

The release of a biological agent is less certain to produce an effect than the detonation of a nuclear weapon. But in worst-case scenarios, some biological agents could be devastating. A virulent strain of smallpox or flu virus, both highly contagious, could cause widespread illness and death.[21] Finally, biological weapons evoke a particular horror for many people. The Biological Weapons Convention of 1972, which prohibits their development or production, describes the use of biological weapons as "repugnant to the conscience of mankind." As the episode with the anthrax letters demonstrates, a small volume of spores can cause widespread fear and anxiety.

MAILED ANTHRAX[22]

The anthrax attack in 2001 was the only known deliberate bioattack in the United States that resulted in loss of life. The powdered anthrax spores sent through the mail infected 22 people, five of them fatally. The experience moved fears and expectations about an intentional germ assault from theory to reality. It upset many earlier assumptions and has left a trail of uncertainties. Indeed, as of the summer of 2005 the mailer or mailers had still not been identified and it remained unclear whether there was any connection to the 9/11 terrorists.

The first victim, Bob Stevens, age 63, was a tabloid photograph editor in Florida. A presumptive diagnosis of anthrax was confirmed on 4 October, and he died the next day. The last victim was Ottilie Lundgren, age 94, who had been active in her Connecticut community until her death on 21 November. All 11 who contracted the skin form of the disease survived, as did six of those who became ill from inhaling the germs.

Although the death toll was only five, the letters and their trail of contamination terrorized much of the nation. During the anthrax scare, congressional sessions were suspended, buildings on Capitol Hill were closed, the U.S. Supreme Court was evacuated, media studios were sealed off, the postal system was disrupted, and many people were afraid to open mail.

An estimated six or seven threatening letters, each containing 1 or 2 grams of powdered anthrax, had been mailed. Four letters were later found. The recovered letters were addressed to media and political figures, including NBC's anchorman Tom Brokaw and the Senate majority leader, Tom Daschle. The postmarks, "Trenton NJ," meant that the letters had been mailed in the Princeton-Trenton area and processed at the postal sorting facility in Hamilton Township. Two of the recovered letters were processed on 18 September and two on 9 October.

Not until the third week of October did anyone realize that anthrax had been leaking from the sealed envelopes. By then, some 85 million pieces of mail had been processed at the sorting center in New Jersey and another sorting center in Washington, D.C. Perhaps millions of letters carried some spores after having been contaminated in those anthrax-infected facilities. Subsequently at least 30,000 people who were considered at risk of exposure took Cipro or other appropriate antibiotics, an action that doubtless saved lives.

The anthrax bacterium exists in two forms. In spore form, the bacterium is a durable kernel so tiny that 1,000 spores side by side would hardly reach across the thin edge of a dime. In warm, moist environments like the human lungs, the bacterium can transform into an active state, reproduce, and release toxin that may kill untreated victims. A single spore is about 1 micron wide. Only in hindsight was it realized that spores apparently were leaking through envelope paper whose pores, though microscopic, were 20 times larger than the width of a spore.

The effectiveness of the mail as a bioterror vehicle was a surprise to security experts, although many other delivery scenarios had been devised by weapons planners through the years. During the 1950s and 1960s, the U.S. Army conducted hundreds of germ warfare tests in populated areas throughout the United States. Mock biowarfare agents were released from boats, slow-flying airplanes, automobiles, germ-packed lightbulbs, perforated suitcases, and wind-generating machines. The test agents included the bacteria *Serratia marcescens* and *Bacillus subtilitis*, and the chemical zinc cadmium sulfide. (Although less dangerous than real warfare agents, the test bacteria and chemicals did pose risks.) Cities and states including San Francisco, Minneapolis, St. Louis, and parts of Illinois, Ohio, and Hawaii were blanketed with these agents. Some attacks were more focused, such as those in which bacteria were released in the New York subway and on the Pennsylvania Turnpike. In each instance, the spread and survivability of the bacteria were measured to assess the country's vulnerability to a germ attack.[23] But apparently the testers never considered the U.S. mail as a possible vehicle.

Inhalation anthrax is so rare that proposed treatment protocols were in part speculative. Only 18 cases of anthrax from inhaled spores in the United States were recorded in the twentieth century. Until the attack in 2001, the supposition was that if antibiotics were not administered before symptoms (such as a headache and difficulty breathing) appeared, almost all victims would die. The reality proved less grim. All six survivors received antibiotics only after they became ill. However, three years later, only one victim had fully recovered and returned to work—Ernesto Blanco, a mail room clerk at American Media in Boca Raton, where Bob Stevens worked. At 73, Blanco was also the oldest of the survivors. The other five continued to tire easily and suffered from memory loss.

NATIONAL PREPAREDNESS AND LESSONS FROM THE ANTHRAX ATTACK

Is the United States better prepared now than in 2001 for an attack with biological or other weapons of mass destruction? Yes and no.

The nation now could surely deal better with another attack by mail. In September 2003, postal officials announced the successful testing of a system that sets off an alarm if anthrax spores are detected near mail-handling equipment.[24] And officials would doubtless act more quickly to close facilities now than they did in 2001. The medical community is also more alert to threats from biological and chemical agents. Physicians are more aware of symptoms caused by anthrax, smallpox, sarin, and other prospective killer agents.

Of course, if a drug-resistant strain of a lethal bacterium or virus was mailed or otherwise dispersed, it could cause havoc. Nor can protection ever be guaranteed against terrorism from any possible weapon. But advances have been made in both detection and response capabilities. Radiation monitors, including Geiger counters, can indicate the presence of radioactive material. Spectrophotometers, which measure the wavelength of molecular structures, can identify particular chemical or biological agents. None of these methods is foolproof, but research is under way to improve the speed and accuracy of the devices as well as other means of coping with terrorist threats.

In the area of biodefense alone, government spending on preparedness has risen more than tenfold since the attacks in 2001. Civilian biodefense funding was $414 million in fiscal year 2001 and $5.5 billion in 2004. The largest share went to the Department of Health and Human Services, which in 2004 received $3.5 billion, while the Department of Homeland Security (DHS) received $1.6 billion.[25] Money was being spent on a variety of projects to enhance preparedness, including improving detection capabilities; developing more effective antibiotics, antidotes, and vaccines; enhancing strategic stockpiles of medical supplies; strengthening the public health system; and enhancing coordination and education among responders. Instruction has also included understanding the different responses required for a biological, chemical, radiological, or nuclear attack.

The increased budget for bioterrorism preparedness may be better appreciated by relating it to the dollar cost of an actual attack. Figure 11-2 shows estimated costs for several activities associated with the anthrax attack in 2001. The overall total, which probably exceeds $6 billion, would be greater than the annual total now being spent on biopreparedness.

F I G U R E   1 1 - 2

Estimated costs associated with the anthrax attack in 2001.

Source of Cost	Basis of Calculation	Total
Tests by laboratories associated with Centers for Disease Control and Prevention (CDC) on 125,000 clinical specimens and 1 million environmental specimens[a]	$25–$30 per test	$30 million
CDC personnel[b]	5,000 individuals at $800 per week for 6 weeks	$24 million
Prophylactic antibiotics and associated medical care[c]	30,000 individuals, $10 each per day for 60 days	$18 million
Federal Bureau of Investigation (FBI) personnel[d]	251,000 person-hours (through January 2004) at $25 per hour	$6 million
Decontamination of Hart Senate Office Building[e]	Publicly reported	$42 million
Decontamination of U.S. postal facilities plus preparedness measures[f]	Publicly reported	$1.7 billion
Reduced mail revenue[g]	October 2001–June 2002 compared with equivalent period 1 year later	$2.7 billion
Additional costs:[h] State and local health and law enforcement Clinical and environmental tests at military laboratories Medical and hospital care for victims and the "worried well" Lost work time and relocations associated with affected facilities Lawsuits by victims and families Ongoing FBI investigation		$1–$2 billion (?)
Grand Total (likely): >$6 billion		

Note: Estimates are based on personal communications with officials from CDC, the FBI, the U.S. Postal Service, and the following references.

[a] James M. Hughes and Julie Louise Gerberding, "Anthrax Bioterrorism: Lessons Learned and Future Directions," *Emerging Infectious Diseases* 8:10 (October 2002): 1013.

[b] Personal communications with CDC officials. The figure of 5,000 personnel is somewhat arbitrary. One official told me that at times all 8,000 CDC personnel were working on anthrax-related matters.

[c] Judith Miller and David Johnston, "Investigators Liken Anthrax in Leahy Letter to That Sent to Daschle," *New York Times* (21 November 2001).

[d] Michael D. Lemonick, "Homegrown Terror," *Time* (16 February 2004): 41.

[e] Scott Shane, "Cleanup of Anthrax Will Cost Hundreds of Millions of Dollars," *Baltimore Sun* (18 December 2002).

[f] John E. Potter, Postmaster General, U.S. Postal Service Emergency Preparedness Plan for Protecting Postal Employees and Postal Customers from Exposure to Biohazardous Material. . .(6 March 2002), http://www.usps.com/news/2002/epp/emerprepplan.pdf. David Firn, "U.S. Spends $800 Million on Clean-Up after Anthrax Scare," *Financial Times* (22 April 2004).

[g] U.S. Postal Service, Financial Operating Statements (by Month), http://www.usps.com/financials/fos/welcome.htm.

[h] Reference sources unavailable.

CONCLUSION

Four salient lessons from the experience with anthrax bear on terrorism preparedness in general and should inform the nation's counterterrorism and response plans. First, the volume of agent can be very small and still have an enormous effect. Even if a material was not as broadly dispersed as the anthrax, anxiety might still be widespread. If a shopping mall in, say, Ohio was the target of sarin or low-level radiation, exposure would be limited to people in the area. But anxiety could spread from coast to coast and affect the daily routines of millions. Reluctance to travel and to visit malls and other public locations might well be the result. Coping with such a collapse of public activity and services should be part of a national plan.

Second, the effectiveness of the U.S. mail as a disseminator of anthrax was a surprise. Initially, testing for the presence of the bacteria in postal and other facilities was not a consideration, because no one understood that the germ could leak from sealed envelopes. The applicable lesson here is to be wary of conventional assumptions. Most colleagues of Dr. Larry Bush, the physician who first suspected that Bob Stevens had anthrax, were dubious. Had Bush not ignored the skeptics and pushed for more tests, confirmation of Stevens's anthrax might have come later, if at all. The lesson: remain open to seemingly far-fetched possibilities and be prepared for the unexpected.

Third, in almost every instance, the first professional to see each anthrax victim was a primary care or emergency room physician. Understandably, the anthrax attack initially eluded officials who are thought likely to address a terrorist incident, such as police, fire, hazmat, FBI, or military personnel. The lesson, again, is to prepare for likely scenarios, but also be open to the possibility of the unlikely. Rehearsing for terrorist incidents by law enforcement and emergency responders is a must. But many others in public roles should receive instruction about WMD terrorism. Besides health care workers, they should, for example, include postal workers, teachers, store managers, bus drivers, and train conductors.

Fourth, the anthrax attack victimized people not only in large cities but also in remote communities. People became infected in New York City and Washington, D.C., but also in Boca Raton, Florida; Hamilton Township, New Jersey; and Oxford, Connecticut.

Responsible preparedness must not be limited to heavily populated areas. A similar lesson was taught in 1984 when the Rajneeshees disseminated salmonella bacteria. The germs had been placed in restaurants in a small Oregon town called The Dalles. The lesson is clear: the target of a terrorist attack, whether with conventional or nonconventional weapons, can be anywhere.

In sum, recognizing the differences among WMD is essential to preparing for an attack with each weapon. Such recognition will indicate the appropriate techniques for protection and response. Some weapons, such as a nuclear bomb, could be so devastating that any response plan would scarcely be effective. But proper plans to address most types of WMD attacks could lessen their threat and severity. Still, the unanticipated effectiveness of the anthrax letters stands as a reminder that however prepared we think we are, surprises are always possible.

N O T E S

1. Worldwide Threat – Converging Dangers in a Post 9/11 World, testimony of Director of Central Intelligence George J. Tenet, before the Senate Armed Services Committee, 19 March 2002.

2. National Commission on Terrorist Attacks Upon the United States, Overview of the Enemy, Staff Statement No. 15, presented at public hearing, May 18, 2004, http://www.9–11commission.gov/hearings/hearing12/staff_statement_15.pdf. Also see Joshua Sinai, "How to Forecast and Preempt al-Qaeda's Catastrophic Terrorist Warfare," *Journal of Homeland Security* (August 2003), http://www.homelanddefense.org/journal/Articles/sinaiforecast.htm.

3. Remarks of Deputy Attorney General James Comey Regarding Jose Padilla, June 1, 2004, http://www.usdoj.gov/dag/speech/2004/dag6104.htm.

4. World Tribune.com, "HAMAS Threatens to Use Chemical Weapons Against Israel," (June 17, 2002), http://216.26.163.62/2002/me_palestinians_06_17.html.

5. For discussion of possible reasons that the Germans did not try to develop an atomic bomb see Stanley Goldberg and Thomas Powers, "Declassified Files Reopen 'Nazi Bomb' Debate," *The Bulletin of the Atomic Scientist* (September 1992).

6. Federation of American Scientists, accessed June 11, 2004 at http:www.fas.org/irp/threat/wmd_state.htm.

7. Raymond Bonner and Craig S. Smith, "Pakistani Said to Have Given Libya Uranium," *The New York Times* (February 21, 2004): A–1.

8. Center for Defense Information, accessed April 6, 2004 at www.cdi.org/terrorism/nuclear-pr.cfm.

9. Protocol for the Prohibition of the Use in War of Asphyxiating, Poisonous or Other Gases, and of Bacteriological Methods of Warfare (signed at Geneva 17

June 1925), United Nations Department for Disarmament Affairs, *Status of Multilateral Arms Regulation and Disarmament Agreements*, (2nd ed.) (New York: United Nations, 1983).

10. Leonard A. Cole, *The Eleventh Plague: The Politics of Biological and Chemical Weapons* (New York: W.H. Freeman, 1998), pp. 87–91.

11. U.S. Senate Permanent Subcommittee on Investigations, Minority Staff Statement, "A Case Study on the Aum Shinrikyo," Washington, D.C., October 31, 1995, p. 52.

12. Convention on the Prohibition of the Development, Production, Stockpiling and Use of Chemical Weapons and on Their Destruction. Signed in 1993, entered into force in 1997. Accessed June 28, 2004 at www.opcw.org/html/db/cwc/eng/cwc_frameset.html.

13. Monterey Institute of International Studies, "Chemical and Biological Weapons: Possession and Programs Past and Present," accessed June 25, 2004 at http://cns.miis.edu/research/cbw/possess.htm.

14. Wendy Orent, *Plague: The Mysterious Past and Terrifying Future of the World's Most Dangerous Disease* (New York: Free Press, 2004), p. 213.

15. Jonathan B. Tucker and Jason Pate, "The Minnesota Patriots Council (1991)," in Jonathan B. Tucker, ed., *Toxic Terror: Assessing Terrorist Use of Chemical and Biological Weapons* (Cambridge, Mass: MIT Press, 2000), pp. 159–83.

16. W. Seth Carus, "The Rajneeshees (1984)," in Tucker, ibid., pp. 115–37.

17. Convention on the Prohibition of the Development, Production and Stockpiling of Bacteriological (Biological) and Toxin Weapons and on Their Destruction. Signed in 1972, entered into force in 1975. Accessed June 28, 2004 at www.state.gov/t/ac/trt/4718.htm.

18. "Chemical and Biological Weapons: Possession and Programs Past and Present," op cit.

19. Ken Alibek, *Biohazard: The Chilling Story of the Largest Covert Biological Weapons Program in the World* (New York: Random House, 1999), pp. 258–62.

20. U.S. Congress, Office of Technology Assessment, *Proliferation of Weapons of Mass Destruction: Assessing the Risks* (Washington, D.C.: Government Printing Office, August 1993); U.S. Congress, Office of Technology Assessment, *Technologies Underlying Weapons of Mass Destruction* (Washington, D.C.: Government Printing Office, December 1993); Richard A. Falkenrath, Robert D. Newman, and Bradley A. Thayer, *America's Achilles' Heel: Nuclear, Biological, and Chemical Terrorism and Covert Attack* (Cambridge, Mass: MIT Press, 2001).

21. A mock bioterrorism exercise in 2002, titled "Dark Winter," created a scenario in which a smallpox attack resulted in thousands of deaths, www.homelandsecurity.org/darkwinter/index.cfm.
    The naturally occurring flu pandemic in 1918 killed an estimated 40 million people worldwide. See Gina Kolata, *Flu: The Story of the Great Influenza Pandemic of 1918 and the Search for the Virus That Caused It* (New York: Touchstone Books, 2001).

22. This section is largely drawn from Leonard A. Cole, *The Anthrax Letters: A Medical Detective Story* (Washington, D.C.: Joseph Henry Press/National Academies Press, 2003), http://www.anthraxletters.com.

23. Leonard A. Cole, *Clouds of Secrecy: The Army's Germ Warfare Tests Over Populated Areas* (Lanham, Md.: Rowman and Littlefield, 1990).

24. "Postal Service Completes Test of New Anthrax Detection System," *Global Security Newswire* (September 9, 2003), accessed October 10, 2003 at www.govexec.com/dailyfed/0903/090903gsn1.htm).

25. Ari Schuler, "Billions for Biodefense: Federal Agency Biodefense Funding, FY2001-FY2005," *Biosecurity and Bioterrorism: Biodefense Strategy, Practice, and Science*, 2:2 (2004): 87.

Biological Terrorism: Risks and Responses

Terrence M. O'Sullivan
Homeland Security Center for Risk and Economic Analysis
(CREATE), University of Southern California

This chapter discusses the dynamics of bioterrorism (BT) and biowarfare (BW), their historical context, their practical aspects, and benefit-cost calculations for attackers and vulnerable targets.

BIOLOGICAL THREATS TO CIVILIAN POPULATIONS

Bioweapons—a category of weapons of mass destruction (WMD)—offer terrorists considerable versatility and pose a unique challenge for possible targets. BT, even if it does not cause widespread casualties, can elicit anxiety, panic, and even chaos; thus counterterrorism must take into account the psychological as well as the physical threat. In addition, BT is not static: the earlier practical, technological, and ethical barriers against it have been eroding.

The military can be protected, at some cost, against most bioweapons; also, military use of BT is unwieldy and would probably be intended mainly to harass or slow modern, well-equipped western troops. By contrast, civilian populations are difficult (and expensive) to protect. There are few completely safe, simple, or uncontroversial means of protecting civilians before exposure, as can be seen in the ongoing debates about smallpox and anthrax.[1] And even when

post-exposure treatment—such as an antibiotic for inhalation of
anthrax—is available, an attack must, ideally, be detected before
victims are symptomatic, because thereafter the prognosis deterio-
rates rapidly. Moreover, although BioWatch and other programs of
the Department of Homeland Security (DHS) are making real-time
biodetection feasible for major urban areas, there are still formidable
logistical barriers to distributing large amounts of antibiotics quickly
enough. One difficulty is distinguishing, within a tight response
window, between people who have actually been exposed and the
"worried well." Three years after 9/11, DHS instructed American
cities to be capable of delivering antibiotics to all residents (6–10
million in Los Angeles County, for instance) within 48 hours of an
anthrax alarm; this goal remains highly improbable for overstretched
public health and emergency medical response systems.

Genetically engineered—and perhaps antibiotic-resistant or
vaccine-resistant—pathogens are a sobering future threat. In a
laboratory, diseases that may normally be harmless, subject to
immunization, or treatable could be transformed into bioweapons.
For example, an American research team inserted a gene for the
immune system molecule IL-4 into the mousepox virus, creating a
pathogen that killed 100 percent of even mice that had been
vaccinated against mousepox.[2] Other researchers manipulated a
single protein derived from a relative of smallpox, and by doing so
synthesized an actual smallpox protein that they soon discovered
would disarm human immune system molecules in laboratory tests.[3]
In 2002, researchers at SUNY Stony Brook ordered pieces of the
poliovirus DNA sequence from a commercial supply company and
demonstrated that it was possible to reconstruct them as a complete
DNA chain, sufficient to create effective poliovirus particles able to
paralyze and kill experimental mice.[4] And bioweapons scientists from
the former Soviet Union have claimed that during the 1980s they
developed genetically engineered vaccine-resistant and antibiotic-
resistant germs, such as smallpox and anthrax.

Another factor in the rising threat of BT is the globalization
of trade, travel, economics, and terrorism itself. Still another factor
is the ideology of "antigovernmentalism." Arguably, the current
emphasis in the United States on domestic and international
economic privatization has worsened global public health, emergency
medical infrastructures, and overall preparedness and response
capabilities.[5]

THE HISTORICAL CONTEXT OF BIOLOGICAL THREATS

Deliberate, human-caused outbreaks of infectious disease have a long history. Until the nineteenth century, nothing was known about microbes, but people were still able to use disease as a weapon. Early methods of BT could be as simple as throwing a diseased corpse down a water well. BT has been used by nonstate groups and by organized armies as an aspect of total warfare extending to civilians. Today, it is a threat posed mostly by nonstate groups unfettered by geographic boundaries or diplomatic constraints.

Early Bioterror

In the fourteenth century, the Black Death (bubonic plague) may have been abetted by BW. According to some accounts, during their siege of the Crimean city of Caffa in 1346 the Mongols, who had been struck by the plague, used catapults to hurl their corpses over the walls. Plague then broke out in Caffa, spread with refugees fleeing eastward, and eventually killed perhaps one-third to two-thirds of the infected European and Asian populations.[6] There are numerous reports of this use of infected corpses, continuing into the late eighteenth century.

In 1495, the Spanish tried to deliver wine laced with leprous blood to the French in Naples. At about that time a Polish artillery officer tried to arm hollow cannon projectiles with saliva from rabid dogs. The smallpox virus, variola, has also played a role in BW. Around 1519, when Cortez arrived in the new world, clothing contaminated with variola was evidently delivered to native Meso-Americans by Spanish conquistadors; and during the French and Indian Wars of 1754–1767, British soldiers may have distributed contaminated blankets among the opposing Native Americans, initiating epidemics that wiped out more than half of the affected tribes.[7] During the American Civil War, a Confederate physician, Luke Blackburn (who later became the governor of Kentucky), sold clothing infected with smallpox to Union troops and was said to have killed one officer.

After the "germ theory" of disease became established in the nineteenth century, the related new technologies could be used for BW. During World War I, the Germans made several unsuccessful attempts at this, including efforts to inoculate cavalry horses with glanders.[8] World War I led to a temporary taboo against "bacteriological" weapons; in the West, this taboo persisted through World War II, even though the Soviet Union, the United States, and Germany had bioweapons programs. However, Unit 731 of the Japanese army used thousands of prisoners for biological experiments and dropped canisters filled with plague-infected fleas on cities and towns in China; the ensuing epidemics are believed to have killed some 250,000 civilians. (Members of Unit 731 turned over the results of their secret research to the American military and thus avoided being tried for war crimes.)

Bioweapons Programs During and After the Cold War

Among the nations with bioweapons programs during the Cold War, the Soviet Union was most notable. It started Biopreparat ("the Concern") around 1973, just after the signing of the Biological Weapons Convention (BWC).[9] At its peak in the 1980s, this program may have employed as many as 60,000 scientists, technicians, and others at some 100 secret sites, with an annual budget of almost $1 billion. The Soviet Union produced and stockpiled tons of smallpox virus, anthrax, plague, etc.; experimented with perhaps 80 bioagents; and loaded some agents onto ballistic missiles aimed at American cities. One plant, in Stepnogorsk, had the capacity to produce within months 300 tons of dried anthrax, enough to kill the entire U.S. population.[10] Russia inherited most of this program [including stores of smallpox virus sanctioned by the World Health Organization (WHO)] and may still maintain a smaller-scale bioweapons effort.

By 2003, North Korea was known to have a program, probably maintaining smallpox virus stores. South Africa had a program, and since the 1980s there have been rumors that during apartheid it used bioagents against the African National Congress and other dissenting groups.

The American bioweapons program—based at Camp Detrick (later Fort Detrick) in Maryland—continued after World War II and peaked in the 1960s. Over 20 years, $700 million may have been invested in it; and hundreds of tests were conducted, including many using a live bioagent simulant, over cities such as New York and San Francisco. At least one U.S. civilian is believed to have died.[11] In 1969 monkeys and farm animals were exposed to actual airborne biological agents released over the Pacific Ocean. From 1955 through the mid-1960s, the U.S. Army's Operation Whitecoat ("CD-22") conducted live aerosol tests of Q-fever and other pathogens on volunteers (Seventh-Day Adventist conscientious objectors).

The original U.S. program ended in 1970; but in 2001 the *New York Times* reported secret bioweapons research and held that the government had crossed the line between defensive and offensive efforts and had violated BWC. One covert U.S. program was intended to re-create, for counterterrorist purposes, technology (such as BW "bomblets") developed in the former Soviet Union; but it actually produced offensive weapons. Another U.S. program bought used off-the-shelf equipment and assembled a laboratory capable of making anthrax bioweapons (although only a simulant was actually produced).

The Rising Threat of Bioterrorism

In modern U.S. history, the incident of BT involving the most casualties was in The Dalles, Oregon, in 1984, when a cult called Bhagwan Shree Rajneesh attacked 10 salad bars with salmonella, which it had acquired legally from a commercial supplier. Though no one died, at least 751 people became ill and 45 were hospitalized.[12] Initially, the contamination was attributed to poor hygiene among restaurant workers. In 1985, the true cause was discovered, but (to prevent similar attacks) it was not publicly disclosed for 10 years thereafter.[13]

As of the present writing, this attack and the anthrax letters of 2001 were the only major publicly documented incidents of BT in the United States, although there had been some anthrax hoaxes and small-scale use of ricin toxin since the 1990s. Still, since about 1995 there has been a perception among policy makers that the threat of BT is increasing.

In March 1995, Aum Shinrikyo, a doomsday cult based in Japan, released a nerve gas, sarin, in the subway in Tokyo. This was a chemical attack, but the cult was found to have developed a bioweapons program as well, and to have experimented with anthrax and botulinum toxin. In 1993, the cult had made a series of unsuccessful biological attacks, including at least one on a suburb of Tokyo; apparently, these attacks failed only because the cult had inadvertently used a harmless animal-vaccine-grade strain of anthrax.[14] Also, before the chemical attack of 1995, the cult had placed a timed device to disperse botulinum bacilli near a subway station and several government buildings. Aum Shinrikyo was probably the first nongovernmental organization to have used such a wide range of bacilli, viruses, and lethal chemicals for terrorism.[15]

Also in 1995, UN inspectors found that at about the time of the Gulf War of 1991, Iraq had an extensive covert program to develop biological and chemical WMD.

In March 1998, officials from several U.S. federal agencies conducted war games involving BT. In this simulation, terrorists spread what appeared to be a smallpox virus along the U.S.–Mexican border near California; the Americans rushed existing stores of smallpox vaccine into the area; but the hypothetical (fictional) virus was specified to be a worst-case, genetically engineered, incurable "Ebola-pox" hybrid—as transmissible as smallpox and as lethal as Ebola hemorrhagic fever—and the result was chaos and frustration. This simulation suggested that the United States was, at the time, incapable of responding to such BT.[16]

Preparedness and Counterterrorism

In June 1995, President Bill Clinton signed PDD-39 (Presidential Decision Directive-39), asserting that for the U.S. government there was "no higher priority" than preventing WMD, including bioweapons, from falling into the hands of terrorists. In 1998, Clinton read a fictional thriller about BT, Richard Preston's *The Cobra Event*, and was so impressed that he asked the Pentagon and intelligence agencies to evaluate Preston's assumptions. They found the assumptions plausible, and Clinton and his cabinet then invited several scientists to a meeting to assess "opportunities and the national security challenges posed by genetic engineering and biotechnology." The scientists recommended developing and stockpiling antibiotics, vaccines, and other pharmaceuticals; developing a rapid deployment system; pressuring international negotiators to create a mechanism for verifying compliance with BWC; improving the United States' public health infrastructure; allotting federal funds for medical research related to BT; coordinating the complicated, inefficient tangle of competing agencies that were then responsible for preparation and response; and protecting "critical infrastructure."[17]

One result of all this was the creation of the National Pharmaceutical Stockpile (NPS), which since 2003 has been called the Strategic National Stockpile (SNS). To deal with the initial stages of a biological event, SNS is capable of transporting emergency medical supplies, antibiotics, and other drugs to any major American city within less than a day. These "push packs" are stored at various secret sites in the continental United States, where they can be quickly loaded onto military transport planes.

Legislation since 9/11 has included BioWatch, created in 2002 to detect any aerosol release of bioagents in 30 U.S. cities; this program was adapted from the Biological Aerosol Sentry and Information System (BASIS's) DNA-based hardware and software system to analyze samples of air. BioShield, a $5.6 billion program (for fiscal years 2004–2012), was created in 2003 to fund research on and development of vaccines, antimicrobials, and other counter-BT materiel for use by SNS.

Both before and after 9/11, assessments by government and private entities regarding counterterrorism had noted duplication of efforts, gaps in preparation, insufficient coordination, and a lack of accountability. These evaluations included reports by the U.S. General Accounting Office (GAO) on counterterrorist spending (1997)[18] and on bioterrorism (2001). After the anthrax attacks of 2001,[19] the Bush administration put billions of dollars into countering bioterrorism. One initiative was the Frist-Kennedy Act of 2001. Also, under the auspices of the Office of Homeland Security (later DHS), elements of several existing cabinet offices were combined; this was the largest government reorganization since World War II. Nevertheless, as of late 2004 biosecurity under DHS was still subject to serious criticism.

MOTIVES AND METHODS OF BIOTERRORISM

By the late 1990s, motives for terrorism were changing from primarily economic and territorial to ideological and religious. This change has serious implications, because whereas economic and territorial grievances can often be redressed, ideologically motivated groups such as al-Qaida may be implacable—and thus willing to kill civilians indiscriminately. The methods available to terrorists have also become more diverse and now include WMD.

Bioweapons range from very simple to very complex. Their effect depends on factors such as the quality of the bioagent, environmental conditions, the delivery system, and the method of dispersal. If all these variables are optimal, a bioweapon can have a tremendous impact; but if any of them is inadequate or fails, the attack may be partly or wholly ineffective.[20]

Biological Agents

The bioagent is obviously the most important factor. If the strain used is relatively harmless, its dispersal will be ineffective; and even a highly pathogenic agent may be comparatively harmless if it is not in an optimal form for efficient dissemination. Liquid forms of many bioagents can be produced relatively easily, but wide aerosol dissemination is still difficult. In contrast, an optimally produced, dried, and processed agent is difficult to make but comparatively easy to disperse.[21]

As the anthrax letters of 2001 illustrated, the condition of the bioagent is critical to aerosol dispersal and inhalation by the victims. For a dry agent, the ideal size, 1 to 5 microns (as found in the letters sent to Senators Leahy and Daschle), is achieved only by proper drying and milling techniques that avoid damaging most of the spores. At this size the particles behave like a gas, floating freely in the air for long periods, depending on various environmental factors. Effective anti-electrostatic treatment prevents clumping, enabling more particles to float independently. In addition to wide dispersion, this size also allows particles to be inhaled and lodge deep in the lungs, thereby decreasing the number of particles, or amount of agent, required for maximum effect. (At optimal size and with optimal characteristics, a potent strain of anthrax can kill 50 percent of untreated victims who have inhaled 2,200 to 55,000 spores. There is evidence that 100 spores will lead to anthrax in 10 percent of those infected, and that as few as one, two, or three spores can cause disease. Daschle's letter contained roughly 2 grams of bacilli, i.e., 200 billion to 2 trillion spores.[22])

Environmental Conditions

Atmospheric conditions are crucial for an outdoor release of airborne bioweapons.[23] These conditions include humidity, airflow (wind speed and direction, etc.), and sunlight. Because bioterrorism can include release into enclosed buildings or enclosed spaces such as malls and stadiums, I will refer to this category more broadly as environmental conditions.

Humidity can make bioagent particles more likely to stick together, and thus less likely to remain airborne and less likely to be inhaled deeply, if at all. If the wind is strong, an agent may simply blow away and disperse too rapidly to be effective; if there is little or no wind the agent may not disperse widely enough. Most biological organisms are vulnerable in varying degrees to ultraviolet radiation, including sunlight, making nighttime attacks optimal. Exceptions include anthrax spores and *Coxiella burnetii* (Q-fever rickettsia), which are comparatively hardy even in prolonged sunlight. Anthrax can live for decades in soil.[24]

Delivery System

Delivery of a bioagent might be accomplished with a missile or an aircraft emitting clouds of agent in its wake (a "line source" dispersal)—a method widely publicized when some of the 9/11 terrorists were said to have expressed an interest in crop-duster planes. Delivery may also be as simple as mailing a letter, as in the anthrax attacks of 2001.

Dispersal Method

There must be a mechanism for optimal dispersal of a bioagent once it has been delivered to the target. Bioweapons developed by a national military biological program could range from a bomblet that explodes in the air or on the ground (referred to as a "point source" dispersal) to a jet aircraft specially equipped to disperse a dried agent. Dispersal can also be accomplished by a garden pesticide sprayer. Essentially, dispersal is accomplished by any method that puts a bioagent into a free-floating form that drifts on the wind, so the device need not be complicated. Anti-electrostatically treated dry particles of the proper size (1 to 5 microns) may not even require a device; they may be dispersed by only minimal kinetic energy, such as flinging a flask full of agent into a light breeze. In contrast, a pathogenic agent in liquid "slurry" form, while easier to produce, is much more difficult to aerosolize and disperse.

Lessons of 2001

The anthrax attacks of 2001 seem to have been very clever. For the perpetrator or perpetrators, the greatest challenge would have been acquiring the deadly Ames strain of anthrax and successfully processing it (by incubation, drying, milling, and application of silicon-based antistatic treatment to avoid clumping and sticking); or, as may have been the case, stealing a preprocessed agent from a covert laboratory.

In this episode, environmental conditions, delivery method, and dispersal technique were nonproblematic and effective:

* Environmental conditions in most office buildings are ideal for such a bioattack: dry, with a light flow of air (because of modern air conditioning).
* The delivery system was a porous paper mailing envelope transported by the U.S. Postal Service.
* The dispersal method was the Postal Service's sorting machines or an act performed by someone at the target destination—opening the envelope and removing the letter. The ensuing kinetic energy was more than enough to release spores into the air.

RISK VARIABLES: ADVANTAGES AND DISADVANTAGES OF BIOWEAPONS FOR PERPETRATORS AND TARGETS

Compared with other methods, bioweapons have distinct potential advantages and disadvantages. Bioweapons offer unique opportunities to a terrorist; they also impose certain limitations, but as a general category of WMD, they can be considered quite attractive. Because they are unseen and their effects may be delayed, bioweapons—pound for pound—can cause more fear and confusion, and tie up more resources, than conventional or chemical weapons.

It should be noted, of course, that not all bioweapons are alike. Some, such as anthrax, are similar to chemical weapons, in that they might sicken and kill anyone who comes into contact with the dispersed agent, but are limited in geographic impact. Even airborne anthrax spores, while highly lethal if inhaled in sufficient quantity and not treated by antibiotics, and certainly capable of killing millions in a major urban area, will not amplify beyond the immediate extent of the windblown spores. Anthrax victims, like victims exposed to sarin gas, are not contagious; but victims of smallpox and pneumonic plague can be.

Potential Advantages of Bioweapons

It is often assumed that relative to conventional, chemical, and nuclear weapons, bioweapons are prohibitively costly for terrorists and even for nations. But in fact they are inexpensive to produce, and bioweapons have already proved effective in inspiring fear and causing disruption and havoc. Following are their main advantages.

Bioweapons are easy to conceal and smuggle.   A tiny amount of a bioagent can be grown into virtually limitless quantities, with the proper equipment and enough time. Seed quantities could easily be concealed in a tiny glass vial, easily evading airport metal detectors; and larger amounts could be smuggled in sealed containers, as illegal drugs are. Even the biodetection devices currently being developed might not pick up such shipments.

Bioweapons are cheap to produce, relative to the casualties they can inflict.   Compared with other WMD or with conventional weapons, bioweapons are cheap, offering a favorable cost-to-casualty ratio and cost-to-terror ratio. Airborne pathogenic agents could kill many victims per dollar invested in production and dispersal; and in the worst case, aerosol human-to-human transmissible microbes could create destructive, self-sustaining epidemics.

Production technology is easily available.   Although creating a viral agent can be fairly difficult, because viruses need living tissue such as human cells or chicken eggs in order to reproduce, it is often comparatively easy to produce bacterial bioagents from a small amount of seed stock. The technology, equipment (new or used), and expertise required to produce and process a bioagent such as anthrax are readily available on the open market for commercial biological technology and research. Therefore, monitoring and restricting the sale of a growth medium or production equipment are problematic.

The equipment and much (though not all) of the expertise required for bioweapons overlap with civilian biological technology—including the production (especially fermentation, used for anthrax production), freeze-drying or lyophilization, and milling, all of which can get bioagents to a dry, uniform consistency. A bio-weapons production facility can be indistinguishable from a civilian pharmaceutical factory, and can even be used for dual purposes with minimal conversion, especially if workers' safety is ignored:

> Advances such as computer-controlled, continuous-flow fermenters and hollow-fiber bioreactors have greatly reduced the size of a facility capable of producing large quantities of BW agents. Moreover, fermentation tanks equipped with "clean-in-place" technology make it possible to remove the telltale residues of BW agent production in a matter of hours. The equipment...suitable for growing anthrax [is] routinely used to produce legitimate...vaccines, vitamins, food supplements, biopesticides, and fermented beverages. A multitude of companies manufacturing this equipment has grown up to service the burgeoning biotechnology industry, complicating attempts to impose restrictive export controls.[25]

The expertise involved in preparing and handling many bioagents does not go much beyond the level of a master's degree in biology; and no more than a few people may be required to oversee each stage. And although "weaponization" for dispersal can be more difficult, advanced commercial pharmaceutical technologies (such as freeze-drying to make a powdered agent in optimal-size clumps from a liquid "slurry") are increasingly available.

Bioweapons can inflict mass casualties. It may be possible to kill thousands or millions of people even with a nontransmissible agent such as anthrax, if an attack is not discovered before the first victims become symptomatic. But the bioagents most capable of mass destruction and disruption are any that might become airborne, through human intervention or passed from one person to another. Most notable are viruses such as variola (smallpox); microbes such as Ebola, Marburg, and Nipah that cause hemorrhagic fever; and bacterial microbes such as plague. Even influenza might be used to cause an epidemic.

Bioweapons can cause disruption and fear. This may be the great-est advantage of bioweapons over other methods. It is impossible to predict the public reaction to a catastrophic outbreak of an infectious disease, but factors that might contribute to increased anxiety and disorder include a highly contagious agent, a large number of cases, a perceived low chance of survival, a belief that the disease is untreatable or incurable, the possibility that vaccines or drugs are unavailable (either because they do not exist or because they cannot be adequately supplied or distributed), and confusion and fear on the part of doctors.[26] In, say, a smallpox attack, all these factors might be present.

Many experts in public health and BT policy believe that even a smallpox attack would not cause mass panic; they base this conclusion on the typical reaction to natural disasters and the reaction to the anthrax attacks of 2001. But although the public remained calm during the anthrax incident, official communication was inadequate, the official reaction was sometimes contradictory, and in one poll only about 60 percent of the respondents believed that the Centers for Disease Control and Prevention (CDC) could protect them from anthrax or correctly assess the danger in their work-places—suggesting reasons for concern about future incidents. One researcher believes that Americans will not be very forgiving if another BT attack occurs and the United States is unprepared.[27]

Bioweapons are unseen and stealthy.   Because pathogens have an incubation period, the perpetrators have an opportunity to escape. Also, the initial zone of infection could rapidly expand as the first wave of victims spread a transmissible pathogen to others; such potential for epidemic growth is a significant aspect of BT.

In this regard, bioweapons also offer deniability. If foot-and-mouth disease broke out in the United States, how would anyone know if it was accidental or deliberate? Certain patterns could suggest the latter—such as multiple, simultaneous outbreak points or other syndromes not normally seen in nature. But if an agent is a naturally occurring pathogen, such an event could plausibly be either natural or deliberate. When the Rajneeshee cult spread salmonella in Oregon, the perpetrators were eventually turned in by their own leadership; otherwise, no one might ever have discovered the facts.[28] And for more than a decade the Soviet Union was able to deceive western public health experts and defense analysts about the nature of an outbreak of anthrax in Sverdlovsk in 1978 and an outbreak of smallpox in Aralsk, Kazakhstan, in 1971. Certain agents and patterns may be recognizable as BT; but virtually any epidemic that can break out naturally might be due to mischief.

Bioweapons may be untraceable.   Even with techniques such as genetic fingerprinting, it may be impossible to trace a pathogen to bioterrorists unless there is some other direct evidence. This is true especially if the strain used is commonly available from a central seed-culture research repository. In the anthrax attacks of 2001, the agent had been kept and used in the United States, and the strain was at one time readily available to any laboratory in the world; as of this writing, no perpetrator has been identified. Inability to find the perpetrators can make BT even more fearsome.

Deterrence may be ineffective. If the international community cannot identify bioterrorists, there can be no punishment; and without the possibility of punishment, there is no deterrence.

Potential Disadvantages of Bioweapons

Following are some difficulties of bioterrorism—though it should be noted that many of these hurdles are becoming easier to surmount.

Biological agents may be difficult to acquire. In the late 1980s and early 1990s, Iraq managed to obtain potent strains of anthrax and other agents through commercial biological supply companies, but it may not yet be easy for nonstate terrorist organizations or individuals to acquire bioagents. Global standards have been raised since 1995, when the extent of Iraq's program was discovered, and access to seed samples of agents for civilian research has been further restricted since 9/11, especially in the United States under the PATRIOT Act.

Expertise is needed to produce large quantities of bioagents. Generally, a microbiologist trained in graduate school is needed to produce and process quantities of dangerous bioagents. (For instance, care must be taken not to contaminate a slurry with competing microbes.[29]) However, many people have such training; supplemental knowledge specific to BT is becoming easier to acquire; and in any case, advances in genetic engineering are making microbiological expertise less important. Compared with nuclear weapons, crude bioweapons are easy to develop.

Bioagents may be difficult to handle safely. There is a risk of self-infection or accidental release, unless those working with bioagents have been, say, vaccinated against smallpox or are taking prophylactic antibiotics against anthrax. And even such self-protection would not prevent accidental or premature infection of nearby people if a bioterrorist was sloppy in handling an agent before the intended attack. Moreover, the dangers to terrorists would exist at all stages of the preparation and attack. Production, processing (drying, milling, etc.), delivery, and dissemination each present logistical problems for safe handling. Smallpox properly prepared for an aerosol attack might be even more potent than that coughed up by a victim who had been infected naturally. Even one or two inhaled virus particles might cause a clinical case.

Bioagents may be difficult to "weaponize" or disseminate widely. It is not easy to mill and process microscopic bacterial spores or dried virus so that significant quantities are of the proper size. Improper milling could leave too many large particles—particles that cannot float freely or be inhaled deep enough into the lungs to stick. It could also leave particles that are too small, so that the spores are damaged or not large enough to stick in the lungs.[30]

Similarly, it is not easy to spread a bioagent over a wide enough area to maximize exposure. Even if the mechanism for dispersal is effective, environmental conditions must also be favorable. And hypothetically, at points far from the initial drop the agent would be diluted too much by the wind and overall dispersal to have a significant effect. This may be true of anthrax, for instance, which seems to need hundreds if not thousands of particles to be successfully embedded in the lungs to produce symptoms in most people.

Dissemination can be difficult. A bioterrorist must be able to disseminate an agent widely for maximum impact and casualties. Crop dusters are often mentioned as an example of a simple technique, but a terrorist cannot simply jump into a crop duster and perpetrate a major attack. Without specially engineered nozzles on the spraying devices, standard crop dusting equipment would quickly become clogged by the bioagent.[31]

Biodefense might reduce the impact. A target nation might develop effective countermeasures before or after an attack. Counterbioterrorism could be as simple as a fully functional public health and emergency medical system capable of quickly diagnosing, treating, and isolating large numbers of victims and the worried well to minimize death and social disruption (though such a system would be expensive). Other measures include immunization of vulnerable populations against anthrax, smallpox, or plague (before or after an attack), and placement of bioweapons detectors in especially vulnerable cities or locations (subways, government buildings, stadiums, etc.). American officials believe that they could isolate and selectively vaccinate any potential victims of smallpox, eliminating the need for mass vaccination, especially since smallpox vaccine can be used after exposure to prevent or reduce illness. Such civil defense measures might discourage a bioterrorist.

In April 2004, the DHS Advanced Research Projects Agency (HSARPA) funded an 18-month, $48 million research and development project aimed at producing low-cost, reliable systems to identify multiple bioagents. BioWatch equipment installed in major U.S. cities up to then required hand carrying for lab analysis, slowing the alert process.[32] New Instantaneous Bio-Aerosol Detector Systems (IBADS) equipment offers three approaches: (1) Biological Fast Aerosol Countermeasure System (BioFACS) would identify airborne bioagents nearly instantaneously at a high level of detection; (2) Biological Confirmation and Detection System (BioCADS) would provide similar detection capabilities but would trigger a fast confirmation step, greatly reducing false alarms; (3) Volumetric Bio-Aerosol Instantaneous Detection Systems (VBAIDS) would rapidly survey large indoor and semioutdoor enclosed spaces such as auditoriums, airport terminals, and shopping malls to provide warnings before alerts from point sensors like BioFACS and BioCADS.

With bioweapons, terrorists' gratification is delayed. The impact of a bioterrorism attack may take days, weeks, or even months to be fully felt; this might be a disincentive for terrorists who want to see immediate, dramatic effects.

Bioweapons have a risk of physical blowback. Especially with a highly transmissible agent, there is a risk of infecting distant or untargeted populations. If a virulent, transmissible pathogen was used on the American population, for instance, at least one infected victim—say, a tourist or businessperson—might travel to the terrorists' homeland, endangering their family and friends. "Blowback" is often cited as a reason why terrorists would never use smallpox; that reasoning might not apply to religious terrorists intent on widespread loss of life but would probably deter anyone well-informed and politically motivated.

Bioweapons have a risk of political blowback. Regarding bioweapons (unlike conventional weapons), there is little moral ambiguity. International law is clear on the stockpiling of bioweapons: BWC prohibits their production and possession for use against anyone, combatant or civilian. Whatever potential military usefulness they may have, biological agents are considered taboo. Thus, if BT is traced to a particular group, that group could lose political support even among its sympathizers, further alienate its opponents, and perhaps incur retaliation. Here again, though, these considerations might not apply to millennialists.

CONCLUSION

In October 2004 a report by the British Medical Association found an "alarming gap between the quickening pace of scientific discoveries that could be misused and the desperately slow development of international arms control" and commented that "the biggest threat remains...the development of state level biological weapons."[33] Russia, Iraq, North Korea, and other states are already believed to have produced and stockpiled bioweapons, and less-developed countries seem likely to do the same. Regarding bioweapons, surveillance and oversight are difficult, and it is fairly easy to violate the spirit of the Biological Weapons Convention, with either successful commercial biotechnology or active defensive bioweapons programs.

The threat of bioweapons could also emanate from nonstate terrorists: individuals or terrorist organizations like al-Qaida. These weapons can be acquired, produced, and used by anyone with the right agent, equipment, knowledge, and resources. In fact, it may be more likely that bioweapons will be used against civilians—"soft targets"—than on the battlefield.

A significant aspect of counterbioterrorism is public expectations of preparedness, compared with reality. Law enforcement and defense establishments are becoming better-coordinated, and overall planning is improving; still, it will probably be impossible to prevent all BT. In 2003, according to the American Hospital Association, some 1,700 hospitals in the United States—one-third of the total—were on the verge of bankruptcy, and about the same number were operating at a loss. This situation, given the crisis in the health care system, seems unlikely to improve; and it would clearly affect the nation's ability to deal with a bioweapons attack. Such an attack, then, could shatter Americans' trust in their governmental and private public health institutions.

See also Chapter 45, **Moving Target: Biological Threats to America**.

NOTES

1. Though the microorganism is b. anthracis, it has become a convention to refer to it and the disease it causes both as anthrax. See, e.g., Christian Davenport, "Fears About Smallpox Shots May Put Public at Risk," *Washington Post* (12 September 2004), p. C1. See also Marc Kaufman, "U.S. Barred from Forcing Troops to Get Anthrax Shots," *Washington Post* (28 October 2004): A1.

2. Deborah McKenzie, "U.S. Develops Lethal New Viruses," *New Scientist* (29 October 2003).

3. Ariella M. Rosengard, Y. Liu, Z. Nie, and R. Jimenez, "Variola virus immune evasion design: Expression of a highly efficient inhibitor of human complement," *Proceedings of the National Academy of Science, USA* 99 (25 June 2002): 8808–13.

4. J. Cello, A. V. Paul, and E. Wimmer, "Chemical Synthesis of Poliovirus cDNA: Generation of Infectious Virus in the Absence of Natural Template," *Science* 297 (2002): 1016–8.

5. See Laurie Garrett, *Betrayal of Trust: The Collapse of Global Public Health* (New York: Hyperion, 2000).

6. Mark Wheelis, "Biological Warfare at the 1346 Siege of Caffa," *Emerging Infectious Diseases* 8:9 (September 2002).

7. See the following: Michael S. Bronze, M. M. Huycke, L. J. Machado, et al., "Viral Agents as Biological Weapons and Agents of Bioterrorism," *American Journal of Medical Science* 323:6 (2002): 316–25. Elizabeth A. Fenn, *Pox Americana: The Great Smallpox Epidemic of 1775–1782* (New York: Hill and Wang, 2001). E. W. Stearn and W. E. Stearn, *The Effect of Smallpox on the Destiny of the Amerindian* (Boston, Mass.: Bruce Humphries, 1945).

8. Ali S. Khan and David A. Ashford, "Ready or Not: Preparedness for Bioterrorism," *New England Journal of Medicine* 345:4 (26 July 2001): 287.

9. Convention on the Prohibition of the Development, Production, and Stockpiling of Bacteriological (Biological) and Toxin Weapons and on Their Destruction. BWC was opened for signature on 10 April 1972 in London, Moscow, and Washington, D.C.; it entered into force on 26 March 1975.

10. Judith Miller, Stephen Engelberg, and William Broad, *Germs: Biological Weapons and America's Secret War* (New York: Simon and Schuster, 2001), pp. 166–7.

11. Ibid.

12. John Cramer, "Oregon Suffered Largest Bioterrorism Attack in U.S. History, 20 Years ago," *Bulletin* (Bend, Oregon) (14 October 2001). Accessed 16 June 2003 at www.bendbulletin.com.

13. Miller, Engelberg, and Broad, *Germs*.

14. Paul Keim et al., "Molecular Investigation of the Aum Shinrikyo Anthrax Release in Kameido, Japan," *Journal of Clinical Microbiology* 39:12 (December 2001): 4566–7.

15. Akihiko Misawa, "Aum Bio-Attacks Opened Pandora's Box," *Daily Yomiuri* (26 October 2001). Cited by Center for Studies of New Religions (CENSUR), www.censur.org.

16. Judith Miller and William J. Broad, "Exercise Finds U.S. Unable to Handle Germ War Threat," *New York Times* (26 April 1998): A1, A10.

17. Ibid., p. A10. See also Miller, Engelberg and Broad, *Germs*, pp. 223–6.

18. GAO, *Combating Terrorism: Spending on Governmentwide Programs Requires Better Management and Coordination* (GAO/NSIAD-98-39) (December 1997), p. See also Richard Falkenrath, *America's Achilles Heel* (Cambridge, Mass.: MIT Press, 1998).

19. See Elin Gursky et al., "Anthrax 2001: Observations on the Medical and Public Health Response," *Biosecurity and Bioterrorism* 1:2 (2003).

20. Frederick Sidell, William C. Patrick III, T. R. Dashiell, et al., *Jane's Chem-Bio Handbook* (2nd ed.) (Alexandria Va.: Jane's Information Group, 2002), pp. 153–71.

21. Ibid., p. 158.

22. Thomas Inglesby et al., "Anthrax as a Bioweapon, 2002: Updated Recommendations for Management," *Journal of the American Medical Association (JAMA)* 287:17 (May 2002): 4.

23. Sidell et al., *Jane's Chem-Bio Handbook*, pp. 165–9.

24. Ibid., pp. 165–6, 172, 186.

25. Jonathan B. Tucker, "The Proliferation of Chemical and Biological Weapons Materials and Technologies to State and Sub-State Actors," testimony before the Subcommittee on International Security, Proliferation, and Federal Services of the U.S. Senate Committee on Governmental Affairs, Washington, D.C., Office (7 November 2001).

26. Ceci Connolly and David Brown, "Survey Finds Major Misconceptions About Smallpox," *Washington Post* (20 December 2002): A38.

27. Robert J. Blendon et al., "The Impact of Anthrax Attacks on the American Public," *Medscape General Medicine* 4:2 (2002); accessed 5 December 2002 at www.medscape.com/viewarticle/430197.

28. Miller, Engelberg, and Broad, *Germs*, pp. 15–33.

29. Bill Patrick, address at UCLA Berkle Center Conference, 2002.

30. Ibid.

31. Ibid.

32. Joe Pappalardo, "Scientists Seek Breakthroughs in Bio-Detection," *National Defense* (July 2004).

33. "BMA Say Scientists Should Take Part in Bioterrorism Debate," *British Medical Journal (BMJ)* 329:30 (October 2004), www.bmj.com.

CHAPTER 13

Hizballah

Daniel Byman
Associate Professor, Walsh School of Foreign Service
Georgetown University; Nonresident Senior Fellow
at Saban Center for Middle East Policy, Brookings Institution

The Lebanese Hizballah is perhaps the world's most skilled terrorist group, highly disciplined and capable of sophisticated attacks not only in the Middle East but also as far away as Europe and Argentina. The group works closely with Iran and at times with Syria, acting as perhaps the leading proxy of both countries, which have used it to harry Israel and advance their interests in Lebanon. Today, the Lebanese Hizballah is also a guerrilla movement, a sponsor of Palestinian rejectionists, a source of skillful propaganda, a social welfare movement, and a political party. These functions affect its use of violence, making it a complex, multidimensional actor.

This chapter reviews the origins and lethal record of the movement; describes how it developed and became more involved in Lebanese politics, in promoting social welfare, and in other activities that are not typical of terrorists; and concludes by arguing that Hizballah today, although potent and dangerous, is far more cautious than the zealous revolutionary movement of the 1980s.

Adapted by permission of FOREIGN AFFAIRS, (Vol. 82, No. 6). Copyright (2003) by the Council on Foreign Relations, Inc.

THE EMERGENCE OF HIZBALLAH

Hizballah grew out of Lebanon's largest religious sect, the Shiite community. The Lebanese political system had traditionally marginalized the Shia in favor of the Maronite Christians and, to a lesser degree, the Sunni Muslims. The Lebanese Shia began to organize in the 1960s, under the leadership of a Shia cleric, Musa al-Sadr. Al-Sadr politicized and organized Lebanon's Shia community and—like all other major political movements in Lebanon—formed a militia, the Lebanese Resistance Detachments, or Amal.

Lebanon collapsed into civil war in 1975, just as the Shia were emerging. The war involved not only Lebanon's many religious and ethnic communities but also its neighbors—particularly Syria and Israel—and the large Palestinian refugee community in Lebanon.[1] To end the Palestinian militant presence in Lebanon, Israel invaded in 1982, quickly overrunning much of the country.[2]

At first, Lebanon's Shia welcomed the Israeli tanks, feeling that these forces would liberate them from the Palestinian militants, who had often treated Shia areas like private fiefdoms—extorting money, lording it over the locals, and incurring retaliation by Israel.[3] But the Shia soon soured and came to see the Israelis as occupiers. Israel was also widely resented for trying to install its Maronite Christian allies in power in Beirut. The United States, France, and other countries sent peacekeepers to Lebanon to facilitate the departure of Palestinian fighters from Lebanon and to help maintain order.

This mix of Israeli occupation, western intervention, and the imposition of a perceived puppet government in Beirut elicited anger in Lebanon—and also in Syria, which saw itself as the natural hegemon in Lebanon, and in Iran, whose revolutionary regime vehemently opposed Israel and sought to empower its Shia coreligionists. Moreover, the new leader of Amal, Nabih Berri, cooperated with the new pro-Israel government, infuriating many other Amal leaders, some of whom were also inspired by the Iranian revolution and by Iran's new leader, Ayatollah Khomeini, and his call to spread the Islamic revolution. Damascus and Tehran both encouraged this resentment, hoping to disrupt the new government and, in the process, exploit the Shia wrath against Israel.

Tehran, with Syrian support, gradually brought together many Shia factions, helping them arm, organize, and otherwise work together. This new organization was Hizballah. After Israel invaded

Lebanon in 1982, Tehran seized the opportunity and sent 1,000 members of the Islamic Revolutionary Guard Corps (IRGC)—the revolutionary vanguard of Iran's military—to the Bekaa valley in Lebanon; this number later leveled off at between 300 and 500.[4] IRGC worked with Iranian intelligence and Iranian diplomats as well as Syrian officials to create Hizballah from a motley assortment of small Shiite organizations. Iran helped the fledgling movement train and indoctrinate new members in the Bekaa valley and developed a social services and fund-raising network there.[5]

Hizballah found it easy to recruit among the Lebanese Shia. Under Iran's guidance, it worked through Lebanon's Shia network, using existing religious leaders and their local ties to attract supporters. Iranian financial support also gave Hizballah an advantage in recruiting, enabling it to offer financial compensation to attract fighters and to build hospitals, schools, and other elements of a broader social network that enhanced its stature while giving it access to the community. Hizballah's terrorist wing also worked through family and neighborhood ties. Most important, Hizballah's spectacularly successful terrorism and its impressive military resistance to Israel demonstrated its dedication and capabilities to potential supporters.

Hizballah issued its first official proclamation in 1985, though it was active well before then. It had three primary goals: the destruction of Israel, the end of western influence in Lebanon, and the transformation of Lebanon into an Islamic state. At this time, Hizballah was a committed revolutionary organization that sought to bring the Iranian model of government to Lebanon.

HIZBALLAH'S BLOODY PAST

Hizballah led the effort to expel the Americans, other western peacekeepers, and the Israelis from Lebanon. It captured Americans' attention with devastating and, at the time, innovative suicide attacks on the U.S. embassy in Beirut in April 1983 (63 people died, including 17 Americans) and on the U.S. Marine barracks in October 1983 (killing 241 marines; another attack at the same time killed 58 French peacekeepers). The suicide attacks fostered an image of Hizballah as fanatical and zealous. In addition, defenders despaired of fending off a bomber who gave no thought to his own escape.

These attacks, and the sense that the peacekeepers had little peace to keep, led President Reagan to withdraw U.S. troops in February 1984.

Hizballah's use of terrorism continued after the Americans left. During the 1980s Hizballah took numerous hostages: 17 Americans, 15 French, 14 Britons, 7 Swiss, 7 West Germans, and 27 others.[6] Its operatives also hijacked TWA 847, an incident in which one American hostage was brutally killed.[7] In the 1980s and 1990s, Hizballah and Iran worked together to kill dissident Iranians, such as members of Kurdish and other opposition groups living in Europe. In March 1992, Hizballah worked with Iran to bomb the Israeli embassy in Argentina, killing 29; in July 1994 it attacked the Jewish Community Center in Buenos Aires, killing 86. Hizballah also aided other groups that shared its agenda. A member of the Lebanese Hizballah was indicted for helping design the truck bomb that flattened a U.S. military facility, Khobar Towers, in Saudi Arabia in 1996, killing 17 Americans.[8]

There were also repeated truck bombings and other terrorist attacks against Israel's facilities. In November 1983, Hizballah destroyed the headquarters of the Israeli Defense Force in Tyre, killing 141. Hizballah also conducted a long, bitter guerrilla war against Israel; initially, this was carried out by local, relatively autonomous fighters in the south, but over time it became more organized and effective. Many of the Hizballah's initial tactics, such as driving truck bombs into Israeli convoys and facilities, represented a mixture of terrorism and guerrilla strategy.

IRAN AND SYRIA: HIZBALLAH'S BACKERS

Iran and Syria both use Hizballah as a proxy to advance their interests, particularly against Israel. Both countries have encouraged Hizballah to attack Israeli targets but, because they are not acting directly, have been able to shield themselves from what might otherwise be a ferocious Israeli response. Yet Iran and Syria have different objectives with regard to Hizballah and offer different forms of support.

Syria is hardheaded, using Hizballah to advance its own strategic interests yet being careful not to give the organization too much rope. For Syria, Hizballah's exceptionally skilled guerrilla forces are a lever against Israel, demonstrating that Israel must accommodate Damascus. It is also a pro-Syrian voice within Lebanese politics.

Although Iran is allowed to arm Hizballah via Syria, Syria's most important contribution is giving Hizballah a sanctuary in Lebanon, which Syria dominates. Damascus disarmed all the Lebanese groups at the end of the civil war in 1991, but allowed Hizballah to continue to keep its fighting forces intact. Damascus can also keep the lid on Hizballah when it fears escalation by Israel or other unwanted consequences.

Damascus does not tightly control Hizballah's activities, but it probably is able to veto operations in Lebanon that might hurt its own position. According to Human Rights Watch, "By controlling Hizballah's prime access to arms, Syria appears to hold considerable influence over Hizballah's ability to remain an active military force in the south."[9] Syria's potential influence is even greater. Damascus fears unrest in Lebanon, so its intelligence on that country is superb. Damascus knows the identity and location of Hizballah's core membership and many of its sympathizers. Moreover, Syria has repeatedly proved its ruthlessness: to root out opposition, it is willing to inflict thousands of civilian casualties. Syrian intelligence personnel remain in Lebanon even after the 2005 withdrawal, which followed the 2005 assassination of president Rafi Hariri.

While Syria's support consists primarily of allowing Hizballah to act, Iran, as noted above, helped build the movement from the ground up and still plays a major role in sustaining it from day to day. Iranian sponsorship of Hizballah is much of the reason why Iran consistently heads the United States' list of state sponsors of terrorism. Although exact figures are hard to verify, Tehran provides perhaps $100 million per year to Hizballah. In addition, Iranian forces train the movement and provide it with intelligence. Moreover, Hizballah's operatives have close ties to Iranian intelligence and the Islamic Revolutionary Guard Corps, which is in turn tied directly to Iran's supreme leader Ali Khamenei. Hizballah's senior terrorist, Imad Mugniyieh, reportedly has Iranian citizenship and regularly travels in Iran. Hizballah proclaims its loyalty to Khamenei, and he is said to be an arbiter for group decisions. Iran is particularly influential with regard to Hizballah's activities overseas. Hizballah, for example, stopped its attacks in Europe as part of a broader Iranian decision to halt attacks there.

In exchange for this aid, Iran gains a weapon against Israel and influence far beyond its borders. Because of Hizballah, Iran has defied geography and is able to disrupt the Middle East peace process. Iran has also used Hizballah's operatives to kill Iranian dissidents and attack U.S. forces, including strikes in Saudi Arabia and Germany. Iran also uses terrorism as a form of deterrence, "casing" U.S. embassies and other facilities to give it a response should the United States step up pressure.[10] Finally, Tehran has an ideological bond with Hizballah, formed by a similar view of the role of Islam in government and by historically close ties between Lebanon's and Iran's clerical establishments.

Hizballah's foreign backers are both a source of its strength and a brake on its activities. Iran and Syria use Hizballah's operations to further their own foreign policy, and in the process they make the movement far more dangerous. Yet their close ties to Hizballah make them vulnerable to retaliation, leading them to rein Hizballah in if they feel threatened. The limits imposed by Hizballah's foreign backers are best observed by what Hizballah does not do. Hizballah walks a fine line between provocation and retaliation, and it has shown itself to be particularly careful when any escalation on its part would jeopardize Syria's or Iran's position.

A GLOBAL NETWORK

In conjunction with Iran, Hizballah also developed a truly global network. In the 1980s and early 1990s, Hizballah's operatives struck in France, Kuwait, and Germany, and elsewhere against western targets. In 1992 and 1994, Hizballah attacked Israeli and Jewish targets in Argentina.

Hizballah cells have been found in Europe, Africa, South America, North America, and Asia. Operatives in these cells provide logistical support for global attacks, raise money, recruit local operatives, and collect intelligence, among other duties.[11] In Africa, for example, Hizballah has worked with people in the Lebanese Shia diaspora—some of whom support Hizballah while others simply fear it—to raise money and identify potential operatives who receive further training in Iran and Lebanon.[12] In 2001, U.S. investigators uncovered a Hizballah cell in Charlotte, North Carolina, that was raising money through the arbitrage of tobacco sales tax differentials and using the profits to buy sophisticated equipment for the movement.[13]

HIZBALLAH TODAY: A MULTIDIMENSIONAL THREAT

Hizballah today is far more sophisticated and complex than the motley collection of militants that grabbed the world's attention in 1983. Now, it focuses more on guerrilla war than on terrorism, though it still retains a terrorist capacity. It is also an important political actor in Lebanon and in the region, exporting its model to Palestinians in particular.

Hizballah as a Guerrilla Force

In its effort to expel Israel from Lebanon, Hizballah engaged in a constant guerrilla campaign. Initially, the attacks were remarkable for morale and enthusiasm, but unskilled. At times, Israel would be forced to withdraw in the face of Hizballah's attacks, but only after inflicting tremendous casualties. Hizballah had perhaps 5,000 guerrilla fighters under its banner in the 1980s.[14]

Hizballah's attacks were one reason why Israel withdrew to a "security zone" carved out of Lebanese territory on the Israel–Lebanon border in 1985. Once in this zone, however, Israel initially was able to repel repeated Hizballah attacks with few losses. Hizballah, recognizing that many of its fighters were poorly trained and that its large numbers made clandestine operations more difficult, deliberately shrank the size of its fighting cadre while expanding its professionalism.

Hizballah's elite nature has enabled it to weather losses. It can easily recruit new fighters to replace those who fall, drawing on its wide network among the Shiite population. By the time of the Israelis' withdrawal, Hizballah had greatly reduced the casualty ratio with Israel. Israel withdrew from Lebanon in May 2000, in large part because it had suffered continued casualties and appeared to have little chance of defeating Hizballah.

Exporting the Hizballah Model

The nature of Hizballah's involvement in terrorism has changed fundamentally. In the 1980s, Hizballah was perhaps the world's most active terrorist organization, assassinating anti-Iranian figures, bombing targets around the world as well as in Lebanon, holding hostages, and otherwise targeting noncombatants. In the 1990s, however, the movement decreased its direct involvement in terrorism, focusing more on its guerrilla war against Israel.

Still, with Iran's encouragement, over time Hizballah has itself become a sponsor of terrorism, often seeking to build other radical groups instead of conducting its own activities. Hizballah's direct attacks on Israel decreased after Israel withdrew from Lebanon in May 2000. But after the second intifada broke out in September 2000, Hizballah began to export to Palestine what the journalist James Kitfield called the "Hizballah model." Hizballah has trained members of HAMAS and the Palestine Islamic Jihad (PIJ) and worked with officials of the Palestinian Authority to establish cells, as well as trying to develop its own network and contacts inside Israel. In January 2002, Iran and Hizballah worked together to send a boatload of arms aboard the *Karine-A* to the Palestinian Authority for its struggle against Israel. In May 2003 the Israeli navy stopped a boat that had missile ignition switches and a Hizballah expert, which Israel claims were intended to help Palestinian militants increase the accuracy of their Qassam rockets.[15]

In addition to direct training and the provision of arms, Hizballah has tried to promote itself as a model for others. It runs a popular satellite television station, a Web site, and other sophisticated means of reaching people throughout the region. Its leaders argue that sacrifice and violent resistance will lead to success, particularly against Israel.

Hizballah as a Political Movement

After the end of the Lebanese civil war in 1990, Hizballah steadily expanded its political role. In the 1980s, the revolutionary organization advocated an Islamic republic, rejecting Lebanon's political system, which explicitly tied politics to religious identity and gave the Shia only marginal power. Today, realizing that the movement cannot forcibly impose its vision of an Islamic republic on other communities, Hizballah's leadership is willing to work with other religious communities in Lebanon and has deemphasized its hope of an Islamic republic.[16] In addition, it has offered candidates for Lebanon's parliament in order to ensure its political voice, even though the system still discriminates against Lebanon's Shia. Hizballah also has a large social service network that is both efficient and honest, unlike the services of the Lebanese government. This network enhances the movement's political role and its popularity.

Participation in politics has gentled Hizballah. Many of its political constituents seek prosperity and peace and are uneasy with any violence that might again bring strife to Lebanon.[17] Particularly now that Israel has left Lebanese soil, there are far fewer pretexts for continued violence. As a result, Hizballah has in general tried to justify its more limited continued attacks, usually claiming that they are in response to provocations by Israel or are intended to regain territory. (For instance Syria has tried, with little backing elsewhere, to claim that Shebaa Farms is part of Lebanon; this is Hizballah's justification for its attacks on Israeli positions there.)

Hizballah's Greater Caution

Hizballah is far more cautious today than it was in the past, largely because its triumphs have reduced the need to take risks. Having forced American and other western troops out—and then expelling Israel in 2000—Hizballah enjoys remarkable prestige. Much of its popularity among the Lebanese comes from removing what was widely perceived as a foreign occupier. If Hizballah conducted a sustained campaign outside Lebanon that led to retaliation by Israel or the United States, it would not be so popular.

September 11 has also had a limiting effect. The attacks occurred over a year after the Israelis withdrew from Lebanon. Because of the tremendous worldwide concern about terrorism, and the active U.S. campaign against al-Qaida, Hizballah's leaders are cautious about any attacks that would make them seem comparable to al-Qaida. Perhaps more important, Hizballah's sponsors—Iran and Syria—were cautious in their use of Hizballah because they feared that they would be targets of "regime change." The United States' invasion of Iraq heightened that concern.[18]

Hizballah now is best characterized not as a purely terrorist group but as a guerrilla and political movement that at times uses terrorism. Hizballah has reduced its direct involvement in terrorism in recent years, though it has retained the potential to act and has helped the Palestinians in their terrorist attacks. Indeed, Hizballah has been cautious even with regard to guerrilla war. It has not used all the available weapons, saving long-range rockets that might strike larger Israeli cities such as Haifa for use to deter escalation by Israel. Hizballah made this shift in part because it recognized that attacks on civilians which could be described as terrorism hurt its image among potential supporters in the region and elsewhere.[19]

Thus, in essence, Hizballah's priorities and its very nature have changed. It still seeks Israel's destruction, but it will take fewer risks and endure fewer sacrifices to achieve this now that Israeli forces are no longer on Lebanese soil. Instead, Hizballah sees itself as a model for and partner to the Palestinians in their own struggle against Israel, rather than as the tip of the spear.

In many ways, the idea of Hizballah is as dangerous as any operations it conducts. Hizballah is dramatic proof that for a political movement, violent resistance—including terrorism—can produce impressive results. Hizballah can be described, without exaggeration, as one of the most lauded and respected movements in the Middle East because of its successes. In the Palestinian territories in particular, but also in much of the Arab world, Hizballah is being held up as a model rather than as a violent terrorist group to be shunned.

CONCLUSION

Hizballah remains a serious threat to several U.S. interests, particularly the security of Israel. In addition, it is a tremendous latent threat. It remains capable of devastating terrorist attacks against U.S. targets worldwide, and it is establishing a strong and growing presence in Iraq.

Hizballah's political and media activities, and its sponsorship of various Palestinian groups, also demonstrate the potential multidimensionality of a terrorist group. Hizballah today is both a terrorist group and an idea: it stands for the success of violent resistance, including attacks on noncombatants. In the Palestinian territories (and perhaps in Iraq), this idea has gained credence, inspiring others to follow Hizballah's example. Effectively countering Hizballah entails more than just stopping its actual use of terrorism.

Direct military strikes against Hizballah would be exceptionally difficult, however. As Israel has discovered, Hizballah's members blend in easily with the Lebanese populace, making it difficult to target only the terrorists. In addition, an attack by the United States would anger many Lebanese, increasing Hizballah's popularity.

The best way to counter Hizballah is indirectly, by putting pressure on its sponsors, Iran and Syria. Iran has considerable influence over Hizballah's activities outside Lebanon, which are of most concern to the United States. Damascus has excellent intelligence on Hizballah and probably could shut it down if that seemed desirable. Both Iran and Syria are sensitive to how Hizballah's actions affect their own standing and have a healthy respect for American power.

N O T E S

1. For accounts of the collapse of Lebanon into civil war, see Dilip Hiro, *Lebanon: Fire and Embers* (New York: St. Martin's Press, 1992); and Michael Hudson, "The Breakdown of Democracy in Lebanon," *Journal of International Affairs* 38 (Winter 1985): 277–92. The steady politicization of the Shia is described in Augustus Richard Norton, *Amal and the Shia* (Austin: University of Texas Press, 1987).

2. For an excellent account of the military campaign, see Kenneth Pollack, *Arabs at War* (Lincoln: University of Nebraska Press), pp. 524–51. See also Thomas Collelo, *Lebanon: A Country Study* (Washington, D.C.: Federal Research Division, Library of Congress, 1989), p. 204.

3. Fouad Ajami, *The Vanished Imam* (Ithaca, N.Y.: Cornell University Press, 1986), p. 200; and Hala Jaber, *Hezbollah: Born with a Vengeance* (New York: Columbia University Press, 1997), p. 14.

4. Augustus Richard Norton, "Hizballah and the Israeli Withdrawal from Southern Lebanon," *Journal of Palestine Studies*, 30:1 (Autumn 2000), electronic version; Shimon Shapira, "The Origins of Hizballah," *Jerusalem Quarterly*, 46 (Spring 1988): 123.

5. Initially, these included the Islamic Amal movement (a splinter of the overall Amal organization founded by al-Sadr), the Association of Muslim Ulema in Lebanon, the Lebanese Da'wa, and the Association of Muslim Students, among others. Over time, the movement spread to Beirut, where it incorporated the many followers of Shaykh Fadlallah, a leading Lebanese religious scholar who at the time endorsed many of the ideas of the Iranian revolution. From there, the movement spread to the Amal stronghold of southern Lebanon, where it incorporated many local fighters who were battling the Israelis largely on their own. Magnus Ranstorp, *Hizb'allah in Lebanon: The Politics of the Western Hostage Crisis* (New York: St. Martin's, 1997), pp. 25–3. See Shapira, "The Origins of Hizballah," p. 124; Martin Kramer, "The Moral Logic of Hizballah," in W. Reich (ed.), *Origins of Terrorism: Psychologies, Ideologies, Theologies, States of Mind* (Cambridge: Cambridge University Press, 1990), pp. 131–57; Carl Anthony Wege, "Hizbollah Organization," *Studies in Conflict and Terrorism* 17 (1994): 154; Sami G. Hajjar, "Hizballah: Terrorism, National Liberation, or Menace?" (August 2002) (Carlisle, Pa.: Strategic Studies Institute), pp. 6–9 (available at www.carlisle.army.mil/usassi/welcome.htm).

6. Jaber, *Hezbollah*, p. 113.

7. For a review of the impact of this hijacking on the United States, see George P. Schultz, *Turmoil and Triumph: My Years as Secretary of State* (New York: Scribner, 1993), pp. 655–64.

8. Iran sponsored Saudi Hizballah, which carried out the bombing, and also trained cell members. One suspect detained by the FBI and later deported to Saudi Arabia noted that IRGC recruited him and that an IRGC leader directed several operations in the kingdom. The suspects also worked with the Iranian embassy in Damascus for logistical support. For a review, see Elsa Walsh, "Louis Freeh's Last Case," *New Yorker* (14 May 2001).

9. Human Rights Watch, *Civilian Pawns: Laws of War Violations and the Use of Weapons on the Israel-Lebanon Border* (New York: Brookings Institution Press, May 1996), p. 22.

10. Paul Pillar, *Terrorism and U.S. Foreign Policy* (Washington, D.C.: Brookings Institution, 2001), p. 159.

11. See "Terrorist Group Profiles," Naval Postgraduate School, from *Patterns of Global Terrorism* (available at http://library.nps.navy.mil/home/tgp.hizballah.htm); and Yoram Schweitzer, "A Transnational Terrorist Organization" (1 September 2002, available at www.ict.org.il/articles/articledet.cfm?articleid=448).

12. Matthew Levitt, "The Hizballah Threat in Africa," *Policywatch 823* (2 January 2004).

13. "*United States of America v. Mohamad Youssef Hammoud et al.*, United States District Court, Western District of North Carolina, Charlotte Division.

14. Hizballah has admitted that these organizations are not separate entities. Ranstorp, *Hizb'allah in Lebanon*, p. 53. See also A. Nizar Hamzeh, "Islamism in Lebanon: A Guide," *Middle East Review of International Affairs* 1:3 (Spring 1997), electronic version. Other experts report that Hizballah had 5,000 fighters and 5,000 more reservists by the end of the 1980s. Wege, "Hizbollah Organization," p. 155.

15. International Crisis Group, "Hizballah," p. 10; Schweitzer, "Hizballah: A Transnational Terrorist Organization"; Kitfield, "The Iranian Connection," p. 1469.

16. Amal Saad-Ghoreyeb, *Hizbu'llah: Politics and Religion* (Sterling, Va.: Pluto, 2002), pp. 23–36; Jaber, *Hizballah*, pp. 56–77; Judith Harik, "Between Islam and the System: Sources and Implications of Popular Support for Lebanon's Hezbollah," *Journal of Conflict Resolution* 40:1 (March 1996): 58.

17. Steven N. Simon and Jonathan Stevenson, "Declawing the 'Party of God': Toward Normalizing in Lebanon," *World Policy Journal* (Summer 2001): 39; International Crisis Group, "Hezbollah," p. 7.

18. As of this writing, Hizballah's role in Iraq is one of the most important issues that will determine the future course of the movement. The movement appears to be helping organize Iraqi Shia and otherwise building a capacity for action in Iraq to serve Iran's interests there because of the Hizballah leadership's historic ties to Iraq and because of the movement's continued anti-Americanism and its sense that the United States' role in Iraq is imperialistic. Whether Hezbollah will be content to help Iraqi Shia organize politically or whether it will actively encourage them to use violence against U.S. forces and other Iraqis is unclear at this time. Such a move, however, could set the movement and Iran on a collision path with the United States.

19. Judith Palmer Harik, *Hezbollah: The Changing Face of Terrorism* (New York: Tauris, 2004), pp. 2–4.

CHAPTER 14

Terrorist Financing

Steve Emerson
Executive Director, The Investigative Project on Terrorism

Money is the lifeblood of terrorist operations. Today, we're asking the world to stop payment.
—President George W. Bush, 24 September 2001

Of all the objectives laid out by U.S. officials following 9/11, perhaps the most important—and ambitious—was to declare war on the individuals and entities that fund Islamic terrorism worldwide. Before 9/11, inability to grasp the complexities of terrorist financing remained a glaring weakness among U.S. intelligence and governmental agencies: the CIA, FBI, and Department of Treasury were all unable to fully recognize the diverse sources behind al-Qaida's funds. For instance, al-Qaida, much like HAMAS and other leading Islamic terrorist organizations, regularly diverted funds from so-called Muslim charitable organizations—some in the United States—as well as wealthy donors in the Persian Gulf region (particularly in Saudi Arabia), to finance its operations. Although these illicit activities have not ceased altogether since the war on terror began in late 2001, they have been hampered considerably by a vigorous international effort—spearheaded by the United States—to freeze the assets of terrorists and their supporters. A key to this success, especially in the United States, has been an increased commitment by governments to provide the resources necessary to combat terrorist financing.

Before we discuss efforts to combat terrorist financing since 9/11, a brief review of governmental power to do so is in order.

GOVERNMENTAL POWER TO COMBAT TERRORIST FINANCING

The U.S. government derives its power to combat terrorist financing on the national and international levels primarily from (1) the International Emergency Economic Powers Act; (2) United Nations Security Council Resolutions 1267, 1333, and 1390; (3) the USA PATRIOT Act; and (4) the Intelligence Reform and Terrorism Prevention Act of December 2004.

International Emergency Economic Powers Act (IEEPA)

IEEPA is the legislation giving the president authority to disrupt terrorist financing. It confers on him the power to freeze assets and prohibit trade with individuals, entities, or states known or suspected to be associated with "an unusual and extraordinary threat to national security, foreign policy, and the economy of the U.S."

President George W. Bush called on the powers of his office under IEEPA on 22 September 2001 by issuing an executive order intended to disrupt the underlying processes of terrorist financing and to strike at the root of the problem: international financiers and enablers. This executive order pins culpability for terrorist financing not only on conscious bankers of terrorism, but also on the managers (i.e., directors, officers, and employees) and fiduciaries (i.e., trustees, counselors, and shareholders) of nongovernmental organizations (NGOs), particularly foreign financial institutions. Economic sanctions are the penalty for both conscious and unconscious bankers of terrorism.

In a keynote address of 27 March 2003 to the Securities Industry Association's Anti-Money Laundering Compliance Conference, David Aufhauser, a former treasury general council, distilled the following main points of the executive order:

- It is global in scope.
- It is expressly aimed at terrorist financing.

- It implicates in acts of terror knowing and active participants and, more important, those "otherwise associated with" the financing of terrorism.
- No intent, mens rea, or showing of *scienter* is required for the latter.
- It is as broad a standard of culpability as can exist in jurisprudence—strict liability for failing to know what is going on.

The executive order gives both the president and the secretary of the treasury the authority to find and penalize all witting and unwitting agents of terrorist financing. The threat of economic sanctions is intended to be a powerful deterrent to current and potential financiers of terrorism and to prompt increased vigilance in legitimate financial institutions: i.e., these institutions are expected to detect and prevent the use of their infrastructure for the financing of terrorism.

United Nations Security Council Resolutions (UNSCRs) 1267, 1333, and 1390

Once the executive order authorizing the president to use his powers under IEEPA was issued, the United States sought to build an international coalition to bolster its efforts to combat terrorist financing globally. It approached coalition building via the UN, which responded positively by creating UNSCRs 1267, 1333, and 1390, all of which are based on that executive order. These three resolutions condemn terrorist financing as an international crime and require the establishment of an international regime to prevent, detect, and deter the movement of such funds.

The three resolutions are also a step toward a global counterterrorist strategy because they shift counterterrorism toward the international community and away from an American perspective and an American responsibility. They emphasize the idea that terrorism affects all states and therefore requires a global countereffort. Aufhauser has said, "Without international cooperation and coordination, an order to freeze assets borders on political theater." To date, more than 169 nations have officially agreed to freeze terrorist assets and bring terrorist financiers and their enablers to justice.

It is not sufficient, however, to have international laws in place to disrupt and thwart terrorist financing. If a truly international coalition is to work toward this goal, economic aid must be provided to countries whose political and financial infrastructure, or lack thereof, is already being exploited by terrorists or is in danger of being exploited. To this end, the World Bank and the International Monetary Fund (IMF) have been effective in their country assessments, intended to strengthen counterterrorist regimes and provide technical assistance when needed, particularly to many countries in the Persian Gulf, Africa, and Southeast Asia that do not have the regulatory infrastructure to monitor the financial systems and behavior of NGOs, money remittance providers, and banks in their territory. Combating terrorist financing globally requires trust between states, which can be encouraged and sustained by assistance from such institutions as the World Bank and IMF.

USA PATRIOT Act

The PATRIOT Act focuses narrowly on halting terrorist financing within the borders of the United States. It places responsibility on fiduciaries of U.S. financial institutions to be aware of the nature of the people and groups with whom they conduct business. Compared with the executive order on terrorist financing, this act is "soft" legislation because it relies on financial institutions and their trustees to police themselves. In essence, the act is a "best practices" model, or guide, for the U.S. financial community as that community regulates its own commercial interactions with foreign persons and entities. The act also encourages the private sector to share with the government details of such interactions. The act is based on principles of risk management, implying that there is an inherent risk whenever a U.S. financial institution chooses to do business with a foreign person or group, and it is the responsibility of the financial institution to mitigate that risk.

In addressing terrorist financing, the act includes the following key points, as articulated by Aufhauser soon after the legislation was created:

- It prohibits transactions with shell banks.
- It requires offshore banks to nominate agents for service of process.

- It authorizes interbank accounts to be frozen, so as to reach suspected terrorists' assets maintained abroad in correspondent banks.
- It requires enhanced due diligence for private banking accounts in excess of $1 million and in dealings with prominent political figures and their families.
- It further requires U.S. financial institutions to examine the quality of the regulatory regime abroad and publicly available information about institutions seeking to establish correspondent relationships.
- It empowers the U.S. Treasury Department to subpoena records held abroad by any correspondent bank.

Critics of the PATRIOT Act argue that there is an inherent problem of motivation associated with effective implementation, or, more simply, that there is no incentive for the private sector to police itself. To carry out the implied demands of the act, the underlying values and principles of self-regulation for the sake of counter-terrorism must be internalized by the private sector.

Intelligence Reform and Terrorism Prevention Act

In December 2004, under the Intelligence Reform and Terrorism Prevention Act, the U.S. government was granted additional means to combat terrorist financing. This act updated the International Money Laundering Abatement and Financial Antiterrorism Act of 2001 and appropriated funds to strengthen the detection and prevention capabilities of the intelligence community regarding financial crimes and terrorism. In addition, the act required the president, acting through the secretary of the treasury, to submit to Congress a report—to be released sometime in 2005—evaluating the United States' efforts to curtail international financing of terrorism. The report was to evaluate the following and make recommendations:

- Governmental efforts toward detecting, tracking, disrupting, and stopping terrorist financing
- The relationship between terrorist financing and money laundering, including the laundering of funds from illegal narcotics or foreign political corruption

- Governmental efforts to coordinate intelligence and agency operations to detect, track, disrupt and stop terrorist financing
- Efforts to protect the critical infrastructure of the U.S. financial system, and ways to make financial institutions more effective
- Ways to improve multilateral and international governmental cooperation regarding terrorist financing
- Ways to improve coordination and the setting of priorities, including recommendations for changes in executive branch organization or procedures, legislative reforms, additional resources, or use of appropriated funds

EFFORTS TO COMBAT TERRORISM FINANCING SINCE 9/11

Since 9/11, through investigative work and a worldwide network of contacts, U.S. intelligence officials have identified, and sometimes neutralized, primary routes by which terrorists have raised or laundered funds, including corporate "front" entities, financial institutions, and Islamic charitable organizations.

Corporate Entities

The use of for-profit corporations and entities for funneling money has been uncovered as a part of terrorists' support infrastructure. These for-profit entities can alter their balance sheets and financial statements to hide the fact that profits from various commercial enterprises (including real estate deals, Internet ventures, and other seemingly innocuous business transactions) have been used to finance terrorism. Thus a corporate model allows terrorists to transfer money between branches around the world with little public or governmental scrutiny.

The Hawala System

For terrorists, keeping their money trail hidden allows a constant flow of funds. By contrast, financial transactions that are heavily documented—as in the United States—hinder terrorists who are trying to maintain anonymity. To overcome this obstacle, al-Qaida and other terrorists have relied on the hawala banking system.

A hawala transaction involves paperless movement of money, with one individual sending funds to a target individual through a hawala dealer. The hawala dealer communicates with another hawala dealer near the target individual and has that dealer give the money to the target individual. No money is sent or wired. Records of the transaction are thereby minimized; and if any records are kept, they are often unclear, since there is no standard for record keeping. More important, these transactions can occur at any time of the day or night, allowing a rapid transfer of money. Stopping the proliferation of hawala transactions remains an ongoing challenge for the United States.

Islamic Charities

To terrorists, charities can represent a perfect cover for collecting large amounts of money and arms. Because charities face far less scrutiny than for-profit corporations or individuals from the Internal Revenue Service (IRS), some charities that fund terror have actually succeeded in receiving financial assistance from government-sponsored grant programs, such as the U.S. Agency for International Development (USAID).

Holy Land Foundation

For example, the Holy Land Foundation for Relief and Development (HLFRD), whose assets were ordered frozen in 2001 and which was indicted in 2004 for allegedly funding HAMAS, was approved by USAID to receive supplemental funding. Since 9/11, the United States has been able to avoid such missteps, owing to its active efforts to freeze, seize, interrupt, and otherwise interdict the flow of funds to terrorists, and to identify terrorists' enablers. In fact, HLFRD itself represents a notable success for the United States in this regard.

HLFRD began in 1989 as the Occupied Land Fund, a nonprofit, tax-exempt charitable organization that ostensibly aided needy people in the West Bank and Gaza.[1] In 1992, the group changed its name to HLFRD and established headquarters in Richardson, Texas, and branches in several U.S. cities.[2]

In October 1993, the FBI surveilled a meeting at a Marriott hotel in Philadelphia at which five HAMAS leaders met with the top three executives of HLFRD. According to the FBI, "It was decided that most or almost all of the funds collected in the future should be directed to enhance the Islamic Resistance Movement and to weaken the self-rule government."[3] Additionally, the participants agreed that "in the United States, they could raise funds, propagate their political goals, affect public opinion, and influence decision-making of the U.S. government."[4]

On 6 May 1997, HLFRD's offices in Israel were closed by Israeli authorities after they connected the organization's fund-raising to HAMAS.[5] Furthermore, the chairman of its office in Jerusalem, Muhammad Anati, was arrested and eventually convicted on charges of aiding and abetting a terrorist organization.[6] In December 1997, Anati told his Israeli interrogators:

> I remember I used to send to the United States pictures of orphans, photos of projects that we did, photos of refugee camps and also videos.... They used to present the movies and the photos in front of the people in the United States. ... During these conferences, they used to describe the organization—the Holy Land Foundation— ... as an Islamic organization which helps people. They did not say directly that the organization supported Hamas, they told the people that the institute—the Holy Land Foundation—is an Islamic institute, which was connected and was supporting Hamas.[7]

On 4 December 2001, the U.S. Treasury Department froze the assets of HLFDR, stating that the organization "provides millions of dollars each year that is used by Hamas."[8]

In July 2004, HLFRD and seven of its leaders were named in a 42-count indictment for providing material support to HAMAS, engaging in prohibited financial transactions with a "Specially Designated Global Terrorist," money laundering, conspiracy, and filing false tax returns.[9] According to the indictment, after 1995 HLFRD and its members illegally sent $12.4 million to support HAMAS and the goal of creating an Islamic Palestinian state by eliminating the state of Israel through violent jihad.[10] Between 1988 and 1995, HLFRD sent an additional $24 million to people and groups linked to HAMAS.[11]

SAAR Foundation
The case against HLFRD was complex enough—the prosecutors needed years to unravel the money trail—but the investigation of another U.S.-based fund-raising entity, the SAAR network, has involved an even more challenging financial maze.

The SAAR network is a sophisticated arrangement of nonprofit and for-profit organizations that serves as fronts for Islamic terrorist organizations, including Palestinian Islamic Jihad (PIJ) and HAMAS.[12] On 20 March 2002, federal agents raided homes, businesses, and charities associated with the SAAR Foundation in northern Virginia as part of the government's investigation into, according to the search warrant, "a criminal conspiracy to provide material support to terrorist organizations."[13]

According to the affidavit filed by a Customs special agent, David Kane, in support of the search warrant, the:

> ...many organizations in the [SAAR network] dissolve and are replaced by other organizations under the control of the same individuals. Most of these [SAAR network] organizations, which present themselves as Islamic educational and charitable organizations, are "paper" organizations that are registered at common addresses, but have no apparent physical presence on the premises.[14]

Most of these organizations are located at 555 Grove Street, Herndon, Virginia.[15]

Components of the SAAR network, which officially began with the incorporation of the SAAR Foundation in Herndon, Virginia, as a 501(c)(3) nonprofit corporation on 29 July 1983,[16] include for-profit businesses such as Mar-Jac Poultry and Mena Estates. The SAAR network also includes charitable, educational, and cultural entities, such as the International Institute for Islamic Thought (IIIT) and the Fiqh Council of North America.[17]

SAAR is thought to be an acronym for Sulaiman Abdul-Aziz al-Rajhi, head of the al-Rajhi family in Saudi Arabia and one of the wealthiest men in the world.[18] Yaqub Mirza, an officer in the SAAR network, once stated that the al-Rajhi family is the foundation's biggest donor.[19]

Muslim Brotherhood

The SAAR network is closely linked to the Muslim Brotherhood,[20] which is the ideological underpinning for all modern Islamic terrorist groups. In October 2003, in testimony before the Senate Committee on Banking, Richard Clarke—who had been the national coordinator for Security, Infrastructure Protection under presidents Clinton and Bush—discussed HAMAS, al-Qaida, and the Islamic Jihad. He stated that "the common link here is the extremist

Muslim Brotherhood—all of these organizations are descendants of the membership and ideology of the Muslim Brothers."[21]

In July 2004, in the indictment of HLFRD and seven of its leaders, federal prosecutors stated that "Hamas was founded.... as an outgrowth of the Muslim Brotherhood.... The Muslim Brotherhood.... is committed to the globalization of Islam through social engineering and violent *jihad* (holy war)."[22]

Alternative Methods of Financing

Terrorists also have alternative ways of obtaining funds, such as counterfeiting goods, smuggling cigarettes, devising coupon schemes, stealing baby formula, trafficking in narcotics, and trafficking in human beings.

The most lucrative avenue is the counterfeit goods market, which the secretary general of Interpol, Ronald Nobel, has estimated to be as large as $450 billion annually.[23] In November 2003, Christophe Zimmerman, a customs expert from the European Commission, told a conference that "counterfeiting has become the preferred method of financing for terrorist organizations."[24] Nobel believes that counterfeiting appeals to terrorists because it is "a low-risk, high-profit crime area that for most governments and most police forces is not a high priority."[25]

Terrorists have been involved with counterfeiting a broad range of goods, including soap, perfume, pharmaceuticals, cigarettes, shampoo, car parts, software, and music CDs.[26] For example, a ring that dealt in counterfeit T-shirts helped finance the bombing of the World Trade Center in 1993.[27] And in May 1996, the FBI seized 100,000 counterfeit T-shirts that were to have been sold that year during the summer Olympics in Atlanta. This operation had been masterminded by followers of Sheikh Omar Abdel Rahman,[28] who in January 1996 was sentenced to life in prison without parole for his role in plotting to bomb New York City landmarks.[29]

In 2002, Danish customs seized a container filled with counterfeit shampoos, creams, colognes, and perfumes, along with 8 tons of fake Vaseline petroleum jelly, allegedly sent by a member of al-Qaida.[30] Investigators were unable to determine how much of the profits went directly to al-Qaida.[31] Likewise, in October 2003 authorities in Beirut intercepted counterfeit brake pads and shock absorbers valued at $1.2 million. According to Interpol, the profits were intended for supporters of Hizballah.[32]

Cigarette smuggling has also proved quite profitable for terrorists, as they can make nearly $3 per pack by purchasing large quantities of cigarettes in a state with a low tax rate and a correspondingly low retail price and selling them in a state with higher taxes and higher retail prices.[33] In July 2000, authorities dismantled a cell that had operated in North Carolina, Michigan, and Canada and had sent money earned through cigarette smuggling to Hizballah for the purchase of night vision devices, global positioning systems, stun guns, etc.[34] By the time of their arrest, the smugglers had earned close to $8 million; officials estimated that more than $100,000 was funneled to Hizballah.[35]

In upstate New York in 2001, proceeds from another cigarette smuggling ring were used to fund the travel of the "Lackawanna Six" to an al-Qaida training camp in Afghanistan. Five defendants were convicted in New York of felony charges as a result of their activities in this smuggling ring.[36] According to an article in the *Washington Times* in February 2004, federal agents were continuing to investigate other terrorist-linked cigarette smugglers as well.[37]

As the authorities put more and more pressure on the more visible financing mechanisms, it is likely that terrorists will turn increasingly to these alternative sources.

CONCLUSION

Since 9/11, the United States has been at the forefront of an international effort to identify and neutralize terrorist financiers and freeze their assets. The U.S. government now fully recognizes the vital importance of following the terrorist money trail; accordingly, it has given intelligence officials the resources necessary to identify an often surprisingly broad array of sources for terrorists' funds. This has enabled the United States to disrupt the plans and operations of terrorist networks worldwide, particularly al-Qaida. For example, before and after 9/11, Saudi Arabia—largely by way of monies diverted from mosques and charitable organizations—served as the primary source of funding for al-Qaida worldwide. But as a result of considerable pressure from the United States, and of repeated attacks by al-Qaida on Saudi targets since May 2003, the Saudi government has slowly begun to take steps to cut off the flow of money to al-Qaida from within its kingdom. Financiers of terrorism in Saudi Arabia and around the world are now more hesitant to funnel money to al-Qaida, for fear of being caught.[38] As a result of this and other factors (in particular, the fall of the Taliban and the killing or capture of several high-profile al-Qaida leaders since 9/11), al-Qaida's budget has taken a severe hit in recent years.[39]

Nevertheless, significant challenges remain for counterterrorism. A pair of reports released by the United States and the United Nations in 2004 indicated the relatively low cost of launching devastating terrorist attacks. For example, the bombings of the embassies in Africa in 1998 cost only approximately $10,000; and the bombing of the nightclub in Bali in 2002 cost only approximately $20,000.[40] These figures, however, do not include overhead such as training at camps, evaluation of trainees, and recruitment.[41]

Attention will need to be paid to the recruitment pipeline, as terrorism is the intended result of extensive indoctrination. Arguably, radical Islam—largely propagated by the Saudi government's well-funded Wahhabi machine—is spread daily throughout the world's mosques and madrassahs, influencing the minds of young Muslims and preparing them for jihad. To dismantle the terrorist infrastructure and prevent future generations of terrorists, it is crucial not only to stem the flow of direct aid to terrorists but also to drain this pool of recruits.

NOTES

1. Occupied Land Fund, IRS Form 1023, filed 19 July 1989.
2. Holy Land Foundation (HLFRD), IRS Form 990, 1992.
3. Action Memorandum, HLFRD International Emergency Economic Powers Act. From Dale Watson, Assistant Director, FBI Counterterrorism Division, to Richard Newcomb, Director of the Office of Foreign Assets Control, Department of Treasury (5 November 2001).
4. Ibid.
5. *State of Israel v. Mahmud ben Mahagna (a.k.a. Abu Samra) et al.*, District Court of Haifa, 23 July 2003.
6. Statement by Muhammad Anati to Israeli authorities, Petach Tikva, Israel, 17 December 1997.
7. Ibid.
8. "Shutting Down the Terrorist Financial Network," U.S. Treasury Department, 4 December 2001, accessed 8 July 2004 at www.ustreas.gov/press/releases/po841.htm.
9. *U.S. v. Holy Land Foundation* (N.D. Texas), indictment filed 27 July 2004.
10. Ibid.

11. Ibid.
12. Redacted Affidavit in Support of Application, in the Matter of Searches Involving 555 Grove Street, Herndon, Virginia, and Related Locations, in the United States District Court for the Eastern District of Virginia, No. 02-114-MG.
13. Ibid.
14. Ibid.
15. Ibid.
16. SAAR Foundation, Inc., Virginia Secretary of State, Corporate Record.
17. Redacted Affidavit, op. cit., Attachment C.
18. Redacted Affidavit.
19. Ibid.; and Harry Jaffe, "Unmasking the Mysterious Mohamed Hadid," *Business Dateline* (October 1998).
20. John Mintz and Douglas Farah, "In Search of Friends among the Foes," *Washington Post* (11 September 2004).
21. Testimony of Richard Clarke before Senate Committee on Banking, Housing, and Urban Affairs (22 October 2003).
22. *U.S. v. Holy Land Foundation*, op. cit.
23. Statement of Ronald Noble, Interpol Secretary General, before House Committee on International Relations, "The Links between International Property Crime and Terrorist Financing" (16 July 2003), p. 3.
24. Laz Baguioro, "Terrorists 'Selling Pirated Goods to Get Money," *Straits Times* (21 November 2003).
25. Brooks Boliek, "Interpol IDs Piracy Link to Funding of Terrorism," *Reuters* (10 June 2004).
26. Ibid.
27. John Solomon and Ted Bridis, "Feds Track Sales of Counterfeit Goods, Money to Terror Groups," *Associated Press* (25 October 2002).
28. Ibid.
29. "Sheik Gets Life Sentence in Terror Trial," *CNN* (17 January 1996).
30. Noble, statement, op. cit; Baguioro, op. cit.
31. Noble, statement.
32. "'Terror' Groups Cashing in on Fake Goods—Interpol," *Reuters* (7 April 2004).
33. S. A. Miller, "Smoking Out Smugglers," *Washington Times* (29 February 2004), www.washingtontimes.com/specialreport/20040229-124325-8213r.htm.
34. *United States v. Hammoud* (W.D. North Carolina), No. 00CR147, superseding bill of indictment filed 28 March 2001.
35. "Homegrown Terrorists: How a Hezbollah Cell Made Millions in Sleepy Charlotte, N.C.," *US News and World Report* (10 March 2003).
36. Dan Herbeck, "Defendant Accused of Funding Al-Qaida," *Buffalo News* (4 March 2004).
37. Miller, "Smoking Out Smugglers," op. cit.
38. National Commission on Terrorist Attacks upon the United States, Terrorist Financing Staff Monograph, pp. 21–2.
39. Ibid., p. 29.
40. Ibid., pp. 27–8.
41. Ibid., p. 28.

The Role of Government

CHAPTER 15

Introduction to Section 3

Senator Susan M. Collins
Chairman, U.S. Senate Committee on Homeland Security and
Governmental Affairs

The fundamental obligation of government—of any government—is to protect its citizens. Democratic governments have an additional obligation: to balance security concerns with the civil liberties our citizens cherish.

The attacks of 9/11 made clear the challenge posed by these dual and inseparable obligations. Nineteen terrorists were able to organize, plan, and train in our midst. They used our freedoms as a weapon against us, at the cost of some 3,000 innocent lives.

Our response has been, and must always be, not to restrict freedom, but to defend it. At the heart of the concept of homeland security is the principle that freedom is not our weakness. The energy and innovation that freedom unleashes are our strength.

As chairman of the Senate Committee on Homeland Security and Governmental Affairs, I am keenly aware that this strength can be brought to bear only through cohesiveness of government at all levels: federal, state, and local. In the detection and deterrence of terrorist plots, in the protection of critical infrastructure, in the response to an attack, the vast resources of the federal government are vital, but so are the specific knowledge and expertise of state and local governments.

This partnership is unprecedented but achievable. It is absolutely necessary. After all, in an emergency, people want to call 911, not Washington, D.C.

This section provides a wide-ranging and comprehensive look at the issues involved in creating this partnership. In Chapter 16 Sharon Caudle and Randall Yim provide a definition of homeland security and describe a system with which we can measure the effectiveness of our efforts. In Chapter 17 Congressman Christopher Shays explores the evolving nature of congressional oversight of homeland security and the dynamics—often vexing and always complicated—of appropriations. The role of the Department of Defense in national security and its partnership with the Department of Homeland Security are described by Paul McHale in Chapter 18. Dave Robertson (Chapter 19) and Mayor Martin O'Malley (Chapter 20) offer comprehensive views of prevention and response from regional and municipal perspectives.

In Chapter 21 Mike Kraft discusses counterterrorism legislation and the use of the rule of law. Two chapters provide insight into international aspects of homeland security. In Chapter 22 Karen Greenberg provides recommendations for enhancing transatlantic counterterrorism. Lastly, in Chapter 23 Gijs de Vries, counterterrorism coordinator for the European Union, presents an introduction to transatlantic cooperation in the war against terrorism.

Although the subject areas are diverse, these essays are unified by the fundamental obligation democratic governments have to protect both life and liberty. Just as the power inherent in free societies rose to the threats posed by tyranny throughout the twentieth century, it now is surging up against the emerging threats of the twenty-first. And it will prevail.

CHAPTER 16

Homeland Security's National Strategic Position: Goals, Objectives, Measures Assessment

Sharon L. Caudle, Ph.D.
Homeland Security and Justice Team, U.S. Government
Accountability Office

Randall Yim, Esq.
Director, Homeland Security Institute

OVERVIEW

This chapter discusses homeland security: missions, recommendations for achieving those missions, approaches to building the capabilities needed to accomplish the missions, and oversight. Specifically, it identifies principles for decision making and expectations for homeland security and preparedness. It also discusses the elements of management system standards, scenario-based planning, risk management, and capabilities development to set strategies for homeland security and assess progress as part of a basic results management system. It concludes with challenges to oversight.

INTRODUCTION

What are we seeking to accomplish in homeland security? The process of answering this question is shaping America's future. Difficult choices made now will initiate programs and investments with intended and unintended consequences, and certainly with opportunity costs. These choices will set courses of action which may

---

Note: This chapter represents the views of the authors, not necessarily those of the Homeland Security Institute or the U.S. Government Accountability Office.

be difficult to change, particularly in a time of structural fiscal deficits exacerbated by disturbing demographic trends that will make the government less flexible in dealing with continually changing threats. Also, emerging technologies may promise solutions but may actually expose even more dangers. Anticipating an uncertain future, and avoiding failures in imagination, will require new approaches.

A movement in government called "managing for results," "managing for performance," or "results management" has shifted attention from inputs, processes, and outputs to what is accomplished with them: outcomes or results. The primary theory underlying this movement is that effectiveness, efficiency, and accountability will improve as agencies focus on what programs should achieve.[1] Advocates of results management argue that its benefits should include increased public satisfaction with government, improved quality of services, and reduced costs.[2]

Results management relies primarily on defining the mission, on the commitment of those responsible for funding and actual "mission delivery," on guidelines for choosing strategies, on implementation of strategies, on assessment of results, and on what remains to be done—so that implementation may evolve in response to changing circumstances or new or additional information. For example, Wholey defines results-oriented management or performance-based management as "the purposeful use of resources and information to achieve and demonstrate measurable progress toward outcome-oriented agency and program goals."[3] Such management consists, he says, of three processes: (1) securing key stakeholders' agreement on missions, goals, and strategies; (2) developing systems for measuring performance; and (3) using information about performance for improvement, accountability, and decision making.

Results management can and should be a flexible, nonlinear approach. Its emphasis on outcomes requires continual evaluation of assumptions and the assessment of new information so that programs are continually refined to achieve the desired outcomes. This approach can take several directions. For example, outcomes that are desired or outcomes to avoid can be "reverse-engineered" to create strategies that maximize the chance of positive results, minimize the impact of unavoidable negative outcomes, or both.

Today, homeland security has become an object of results management. The attacks of 9/11, and subsequent international events, have resulted in intense efforts toward homeland security, with considerable costs. There have been continued calls for improvement—for example, from the 9/11 Commission (formally the National Commission on Terrorist Attacks upon the United States). Overall, managers in the public sector—federal, state, and local—face increasing demands from funders and the public to concretely define performance expectations, explain how their homeland security programs should be assessed, document progress, and continually plan for the future. Managers in the private sector also feel pressure from their customers, employees, and insurance companies. Failure, or misallocation of finite resources, can have tragic consequences.

Results and accountability are, of course, not new concerns. In congressional testimony shortly after 9/11, David Walker, the U.S. comptroller general and head of the Government Accountability Office (GAO, formerly the General Accounting Office), highlighted several issues for current and future decision making regarding homeland security:[4]

1. What national vision and objectives will make the homeland more secure?
2. What leadership is needed to guide our efforts and leverage resources within and outside government?
3. What approach to risk management will identify threats, vulnerabilities, and the critical assets that we must protect?
4. What federal tools and programs provide the most cost-effective approaches for homeland security?
5. What organization of the executive branch and the Congress will address these issues?
6. What approach will assess the effectiveness of implementation to address the spectrum of threats?

As of 2005, these questions—all related to strategy, accomplishments, and accountability—still bedeviled policy makers. Perhaps most important are questions 1 and 6, which largely guide decisions concerning the other four. Overall, the questions emphasize the importance, complexity, and challenge of accountability in homeland security.

This chapter offers observations on the "homeland security mission," and specifically on expected results. It also defines principles to guide policy and operational decisions and elements of results management for homeland security.

THE HOMELAND SECURITY MISSION

The starting point for results management in homeland security is the response to Walker's first question, regarding vision and objectives— or what many would call the mission. Early on, the Bush administration's *National Strategy for Homeland Security*[5] defined homeland security as "a concerted national effort to prevent terrorist attacks within the United States, reduce America's vulnerability to terrorism, and minimize the damage and recover from attacks that do occur." More fully:

- *Prevention* means action at home and abroad to deter, prevent, and eliminate terrorism.
- *Reducing vulnerability* means identifying and protecting critical infrastructure and key assets, detecting terrorist threats, and augmenting defenses, while balancing the benefits of mitigating risk against economic costs and infringements on individual liberty.
- *Response and recovery* means managing the consequences of attacks and building and maintaining the financial, legal, and social systems to recover.

The Homeland Security Act of 2002 that created the Department of Homeland Security (DHS) used this definition to set the primary mission of DHS. However, the term *homeland security*—essentially defined as combating terrorists and their threat to domestic targets, including secondary effects on the economy or other social functions—is often used interchangeably with a broader concept: national preparedness. National preparedness is intended to address any major disaster or emergency event. For example, Homeland Security Presidential Directive 8 (HSPD-8) defines preparedness as the "existence of plans, procedures, policies, training, and equipment necessary at the federal, state, and local level to maximize the ability to prevent, respond to, and recover from major events."[6] This definition encompasses all-hazards preparedness to respond to domestic terrorist attacks, major disasters, and other emergencies. Similarly, the Gilmore Commission of December 2003 (formally, the Advisory Panel to Assess Domestic Response Capabilities for Terrorism Involving Weapons of Mass Destruction) describes homeland security as preparedness: "the measurable demonstrated capacity by communities, States, and private sector entities throughout the United States to respond to acute threats with well-planned, well-coordinated, and effective efforts by all of the essential participants, including elected officials, police, fire, medical, public health, emergency managers, intelligence, community organizations, the media, and the public at large."[7]

For both concepts—the narrower homeland security mission or the broader national preparedness—there are many expectations for what should be accomplished and how the goals are to be achieved. For example, *National Strategy for Homeland Security* was intended to define homeland security and its missions, define what should be accomplished and the most important goals, assess current accomplishments, and make recommendations for nonfederal governments, the private sector, and citizens. The strategy defined six critical mission areas to address prevention, vulnerability, response, and recovery:

1. *Intelligence and warning*: Deter terrorist activity before it manifests itself in an attack, so that preemptive, preventive, and protective action can be taken

2. *Border and transportation security*: Promote the efficient and reliable flow of people, goods, and services across borders while preventing terrorists from using transportation conveyances or systems to deliver implements of destruction

3. *Domestic counterterrorism*: Identify, halt, and (where appropriate) prosecute terrorists in the United States, including those directly involved in terrorist activity and their sources of support

4. *Protection of critical infrastructure and key assets*: Levels of protection should be appropriate to each target—i.e., should depend on how critical and how vulnerable the target is

5. *Defense against catastrophic threats*: Develop new approaches, a focused strategy, and a new organization to address chemical, biological, radiological, and nuclear terrorism

6. *Emergency preparedness and response*: Develop a comprehensive national system to bring together and coordinate all necessary "response assets" quickly and effectively

The strategy also describes four foundations necessary for all six mission areas, at all levels of government and in all sectors of society: (1) law, (2) science and technology, (3) information sharing and systems, and (4) international cooperation.

National Strategy for Homeland Security and presidential directives such as HSPD-8 are only part of many executive-branch strategies and directives that present goals for homeland security or issue calls for action. *National Strategy for Homeland Security* is joined by many other national strategies for combating terrorism and achieving homeland security. Drawing on GAO, the following paragraphs describe these other strategies.

National Security Strategy of the United States of America provides a framework for strengthening security in the future. It identifies goals, describes the foreign policy and military capabilities necessary to achieve them, evaluates the current status of these capabilities, and explains how national power will be structured to utilize the capabilities. In one chapter it focuses on disrupting and destroying terrorist organizations, on winning the "war of ideas," on strengthening homeland security, and on cooperating with allies and international organizations to combat terrorism.

National Strategy for Combating Terrorism elaborates on *National Security Strategy* as regards the need to destroy terrorist organizations, win the "war of ideas," and strengthen security at home and abroad. Unlike the *Homeland Security* strategy, which focuses on preventing terrorist attacks within the United States, *Combating Terrorism* focuses on identifying and defusing threats before they reach the borders of the United States. In that sense, although it has defensive elements, this strategy is offensive, complementing the defensive *Homeland Security* strategy.

National Strategy to Combat Weapons of Mass Destruction presents a threefold national strategy against weapons of mass destruction (WMD): nonproliferation, counterproliferation, and "consequence management" if WMD are deployed. It addresses the international production and proliferation of WMD and the threat of terrorists using such weapons.

National Strategy for the Physical Protection of Critical Infra-structures and Key Assets is based on eight principles, including establishing responsibility and accountability, encouraging and facilitating partnerships among all levels of government and between government and industry, and encouraging market solutions whenever possible and governmental intervention when needed. The strategy also establishes three strategic objectives: (1) Identify and ensure the protection of the most critical national assets, systems, and functions, in terms of public health and safety, governance, economic and national security, and public confidence; (2) Ensure the protection of infrastructures and assets facing specific, imminent threats; and (3) Pursue collaborative measures and initiatives to ensure the protection of other potential targets that may become attractive.

National Strategy to Secure Cyberspace is intended as a framework for organizing and prioritizing efforts to protect cyberspace. Also, it is intended to provide direction for federal departments and agencies involved in cyberspace security and to identify steps that state and local governments, private companies and organizations, and individual Americans can take to improve the nation's collective cybersecurity. The strategy is organized according to five national priorities, with major actions and initiatives identified for each: (1) a National Cyberspace Security Response System, (2) a National Cyberspace Security Threat and Vulnerability Reduction Program, (3) a National Cyberspace Security Awareness and Training Program, (4) Securing Governments' Cyberspace, and (5) National Security and International Cyberspace Security Cooperation. In describing threats to, and the vulnerabilities of, our nation's cyberspace, the strategy highlights the potential for damage from attacks by terrorists.

The *2002 National Money Laundering Strategy* (updated in 2003) as per author is intended to support planning for the efforts of law enforcement agencies, regulatory officials, the private sector, and overseas entities to combat the laundering of money generated from criminal activities. Although the strategy does address general criminal financial activity, it outlines a specific governmentwide strategy against the financing of terrorists. It discusses the need to adapt traditional methods of combating money laundering to unconventional tools used by terrorist organizations to finance their operations.

In addition, as of September 2004, the administration had issued 12 presidential directives that provide additional expectations for homeland security:

- HSPD-1 (October 2001) Organization and Operation of the Homeland Security Council
- HSPD-2 (October 2001) Combating Terrorism through Immigration Policies
- HSPD-3 (March 2002) Homeland Security Advisory System
- HSPD-4 (December 2002) National Strategy to Combat Weapons of Mass Destruction
- HSPD-5 (February 2003) Management of Domestic Incidents
- HSPD-6 (September 2003) Integration and Use of Screening Information
- HSPD-7 (December 2003) Critical Infrastructure Identification, Prioritization, and Protection
- HSPD-8 (December 2003) National Preparedness
- HSPD-9 (January 2004) Defense of United States Agriculture and Food
- HSPD-10 (April 2004) Biodefense for the Twenty-First Century
- HSPD-11 (August 2004) Comprehensive Terrorist-Related Screening Procedures
- HSPD-12 (August 2004) Policy for a Common Identification Standard for Federal Employees and Contractors

More recently, there have been security directives and new executive orders in response to the recommendations of the 9/11 Commission. Through these, the president strengthened the authority of the director of Central Intelligence, created a National Counterterrorism Center and the President's Board on Safeguarding Americans' Civil Liberties, asked for strategies to strengthen requirements for terrorist-related screening, and mandated a common identification standard for federal employees and contractors. Virtually all of the commission's recommendations have been enacted in new intelligence reform legislation.

The Gilmore Commission and the 9/11 Commission are two of several commissions chartered by Congress that provide general and specific recommendations. Other well-known commissions included the Bremer Commission (formally the National Commission on

Terrorism) and the Hart-Rudman Commission (formally the U.S. Commission on National Security/Twenty-First Century). The reports of these four commissions provide a more complete picture of issues, needs, and possible actions. The table shown in Figure 16-1 lists the major areas of recommendations, with examples.[8]

GAO has been a significant factor in expectations regarding homeland security. In 2004, GAO[9] issued a report listing 173 selected recommendations from itself and the Gilmore, Bremer, and Hart-Rudman commissions, organized by critical mission areas. The mission areas include those in *National Strategy for Homeland Security*, such as intelligence and warning, protection of critical infrastructure and key assets, defense against catastrophic events, and emergency preparedness and response. The recommendations were further categorized into topics, including (1) changes in general approach or priorities; (2) creation of, or consolidation of, organizations and systems; (3) assignment of specific functions to DHS and other departments or agencies—and the need for (4) operational and technological improvements; (5) increased readiness; (6) additional studies or analyses; (7) improved management; (8) increased coordination between federal, state, and local governments and the private sector; and (9) enhanced or clarified federal or state authorities. For example, for intelligence and warning, several recommendations covered specific operational or technical improvements to allow better collection, analysis, reporting, and dissemination of information on terrorists, or on potentially related matters such as infectious diseases.

Arguably, addressing all the objectives and recommendations from these sources might be seen as success, responding to the last issue posed by Walker: assessment of effectiveness. However, there is no agreed-upon definition of success in homeland security. One could argue that implementing all the goals and objectives would add up to success; but some people argue that many of the expectations are tantamount to laundry lists of activities that may do little to significantly improve homeland security. The difficulty of defining and determining success was highlighted during the presidential election of 2004, as controversy arose over whether it was possible to "win" the war on terrorism.

Even before 9/11, Falkenrath[10] identified problems with assessing homeland security, such as setting reasonable, measurable goals for preparedness. He also asked whether preparedness could be sustained over time and how the preparedness program might be leveraged to fulfill multiple government priorities. He recognized that a lack of measurable objectives prevented the rational allocation of resources and the ability to quantify progress. In addition, he noted

F I G U R E   16-1

Recommendations by homeland security—related commissions.

Recommendation Areas	Examples
Border and transportation security	Integrate the United States' border security into a larger network of transportation screening points Complete biometric entry-exit screening system
Domestic counterterrorism	Track and confront terrorist financing and travel Make homeland security a primary mission of the National Guard
Protection of critical infrastructure and key assets	Set risk-based priorities Designate DHS as the lead and USDA as the technical advisor on food safety and agriculture and emergency preparedness
International antiterrorism	Identify and prioritize terrorist sanctuaries Make long-term commitment to Pakistan and Afghanistan Confront problems in the United States' relationship with Saudi Arabia Negotiate more comprehensive treaties and agreements with Canada and Mexico for combating terrorism
Roots of terrorism	Provide moral leadership and action; define and defend ideals abroad Encourage economic development and open societies Develop a comprehensive coalition strategy against Islamist terrorism
State and local assistance	Reform homeland security grants and funding; base assistance on risk assessment Develop comprehensive processes for training and exercise standards Revise Homeland Advisory System; adopt Incident Command System
Private sector	Promote the adoption of a recommended standard for private preparedness

Recommendation Areas	Examples
Weapons of mass destruction	Prevent proliferation of WMD
	Use authority to designate foreign governments as not fully cooperating
	Establish DOD unified command structure to combat catastrophic terrorism
Intelligence and information sharing	Establish National Counterterrorism Center, built on TTIC, for joint operational planning and joint intelligence
	Replace DCI with a National Intelligence director
	Aggressively recruit human intelligence sources on terrorism
	Develop and disseminate continuing comprehensive strategic threat assessments
	Designate authorities to grant clearances recognized by all federal agencies; develop a new regime of clearances and classification of intelligence for dissemination to states, localities, and the private sector
	Establish a specialized, integrated national security workforce
	Establish comprehensive procedures for sharing information with relevant state and local officials

that the operation and maintenance of new preparedness capabilities might deteriorate because of the uncertainty of support.

After 9/11, Kettl[11] also wondered what kind of performance systems might work for homeland security. He identified possible approaches based on outcomes (the presence or absence of a terrorist attack), basic thresholds of preparedness (such as response plans, mutual aid compacts, and equipment availability), and a statistical index of preparedness based on variables (such as the availability of basic equipment and supplies, training and exercises, and external assessments). Falkenrath also advocated a "preparedness index."

Defining success may call for a more basic approach that centers on risks and capabilities to address them. In its final report issued in December 2003, the Gilmore Commission identified managing risk as the measure of responding to terrorist threats. It warned that total security could not and should not be the measure of success:

> There will never be an end point in America's readiness. Enemies will change tactics, citizens' attitudes about what adjustments in their lives

they will be willing to accept will evolve and leaders will be confronted with legitimate competing priorities that will demand attention.... In the end, America's response to the threat of terrorism will be measured by how we manage risk. There will never be a 100 percent guarantee of security for our people, the economy, and our society. We must resist the urge to seek total security—it is not achievable and drains our attention from those things that can be accomplished.[12]

More recently, the 9/11 Commission also focused on risk and the sustainability of efforts. It asked what Americans should expect from their government[13] and advocated concrete objectives for homeland security so that the White House, Congress, the media, and the general public could assess their effectiveness. Setting priorities and making hard choices in allocating limited resources, the commission said,[14] revolved around two questions: first, how much money should be set aside for criteria not directly related to risk; second, what criteria for risk and vulnerability should be developed. The 9/11 Commission recommended that assistance with homeland security should be based strictly on assessing risks and vulnerabilities and factors such as population, population density, vulnerability, and critical infrastructure within each state. The commission envisioned a panel of security experts to develop written benchmarks for evaluating community needs, with federal funds for homeland security allocated accordingly. The Homeland Security Grant Program has consolidated several grants and the Urban Area Security Initiative (UASI) has some of its allocations based on population. The UASI discretionary allocations are distributed based on threats, critical infrastructure, vulnerability, population, population density, law enforcement investigative and enforcement activity, and mutual aid agreements.

The challenge for policy makers is finding tools and approaches that can set specific objectives for homeland security and assess achievement in managing risk within an environment of competing priorities, lack of clarity about what level of security is appropriate, constrained resources, and many opinions about what the objectives and strategies should be. In the following sections, we present observations on principles to guide decision making in setting objectives and developing approaches to assessment, core elements in results management, and challenges in congressional oversight.

GUIDING PRINCIPLES FOR HOMELAND SECURITY

We believe that several major principles should guide national homeland security as a normal part of management: clarity, sustainability, integration, balance, and accountability.

Clarity requires actions to set expectations for prevention, for reducing vulnerability, for preparedness, and for responses to threats and hazards. Clarity relies on developing a risk profile that would include (1) identifying current, emerging, and evolving characteristics and impacts of threats and hazards; (2) defining critical needs, priorities, and milestones for preparedness; (3) identifying what should be protected; and (4) characterizing acceptable risk and tolerances. Clarity also would include a gap analysis to assess current and needed capabilities, and the development of strategies or countermeasures to address the risk profile and the gap analysis. Last, clarity would answer who, what, when, where, and how with regard to responsibilities and capabilities.

Sustainability requires actions to leverage interdependent current and expected funding. Sustainability means stressing multiple use or all-hazards use of resources and using a mix of the tools of government, from voluntary approaches to prescriptive approaches intended to leverage resources and stimulate results. Moreover, decision making should respond to fiscal constraints, the demands of other programs, and human capital (staffing and skills). Sustainability should be built on baselines and benchmarks for affordable and sustainable goals. And it should sustain the attention of top leadership despite pressures to invest in other programs and despite simple complacency.

Integration requires identifying opportunities and approaches to bring concepts and activities together seamlessly in ongoing programs and business processes. Integration considers common policy and operational points of intersection for homeland security and efforts other than homeland security. It should structure security within overall mission or program goals, priorities, and final decision making. Integration also means leveraging shared capabilities through integrated planning, operations, and use of resources by involved parties. Policy makers should find opportunities for integration in adjustments in legislation; executive regulations, directives, or guidance; and program functions or operations, such as addition, change, or removal. Security can be integrated as infrastructure is recapitalized or modernized. And emerging technology or new infrastructure should be analyzed for potential weaknesses in all future applications and then designed to be secure.

Balance requires assessing the costs and benefits of homeland security and the impact on goals unrelated to homeland security, and striking an appropriate equilibrium. It considers (1) direct costs such as personnel, machinery, materials, and information technology; (2) indirect costs such as dealing with security measures and delays; and (3) collateral or unintended consequences for other priorities (such as free trade or civil liberties) or reduction in resources available for other critical national priorities (such as education, health care, and the environment). Balance would "make visible" the net benefits and costs for decision making.

Accountability involves more than ensuring that resources are spent for intended purposes, or preventing fraud, waste, and abuse or misallocation of resources. Accountability requires rigorous performance management: identifying points of accountability, measuring results, and assessing progress. Accountability calls for establishing a playbook to guide action: Who is in charge? When? Who needs to do what? Who pays? Who holds whom accountable? It also requires a system for performance and measurement that will (1) link the goals of homeland security with the day-to-day activities of "delivery partners," organizations, and individuals; (2) assess shared capabilities and actions; and (3) provide standards for reliable, timely data. Most important, accountability should provide incentives for foresight, anticipation, and adaptation so that strategies can immediately change and evolve along with, or ahead of, threats and hazards.

CORE ELEMENTS FOR RESULTS MANAGEMENT

The challenge for homeland security is to craft a results-management system with elements that (1) incorporate prevention, response, and recovery and reduce vulnerability; (2) set goals for and assess programs to combat domestic terrorism and other hazards; (3) facilitate integrating the capabilities of many organizations; (4) choose investments to close any gap between current and needed capabilities; (5) continually evaluate results and strategies; and (6) balance elements 1 through 5 in terms of sustainability. It should produce, through national goals or standards for performance, specific goals for security and preparedness and priorities for all major involved organizations that can "nest" within national goals.

Results management normally works well in a stable environment; but for homeland security it must accommodate dramatic shifts in threats or in operations, quickly revisiting goals, priorities, activities, partnerships, and allocations of resources. A new terrorist weapon or capability threatening domestic targets, or major changes in technological tools for reducing threats, should immediately be fed into results management.

Problems with a Traditional Approach

One option for results management in homeland security is a traditional approach: formal goal-setting, budgeting, measurement, and assessment as part of strategic planning. Typically, traditional strategic planning has several parts.[15] One part is defining the mission from legislation, stakeholders' expectations, mission statements, or mandates. For homeland security, this might cover prevention, preparedness and response, or reduction of vulnerability, depending on the organization or program and its primary function.

Second is clarifying strategic and shorter-term goals and objectives, for everything an organization or program might try to achieve. Long-term programmatic, policy, and management goals set the stage for expected performance levels between two points in time, creating a "vital few" performance goals and specific objectives. For homeland security, an organization might define specific expectations for critical infrastructure, response and preparedness, levels of readiness, or reduction of vulnerability.

Third is developing measures of processes and outcomes. For each vital goal and related objectives, an organization defines what has to happen and possible measures to evaluate progress and compares them with existing measures. A final set of measures are selected and incorporated into a measurement system from the "activity level" to the "enterprise level."

Fourth is putting the measures to work: measures are communicated to an organization, baselines and benchmarks are defined, strategies (programs, resources, policies, actions) are put in place, and progress is rated and reinforced. Goals, strategies, and assessment across organizational boundaries may be included, but not often as a main feature.

However, it is not easy to address homeland security solely through the traditional process. For example, there may be no consensus among sources of mission statements that would define a clear mission for all. Rather, there may be multiple missions in the sources, with varying priorities. Homeland security relies on many interdependent efforts, and even within an organization there will be differing views of goals, objectives, threats, and hazards, all operating within a political environment involving roles and power. Different actors will evaluate costs and trade-offs differently. In government, programs also may conflict or overlap, creating even more complexity in setting shorter-term goals and objectives. The aims of governmental or nongovernmental organizations may run counter to those of the private sector. Most significantly, the traditional approach is best suited to a stable, more homogeneous environment where a deliberate, slow process defines ends and means. This approach is less useful when shifts in policy and operations require immediate changes, especially in responding to an aggressive, lethal opponent such as a terrorist network.

Even if goals are consensual and there are no organizational conflicts or overlaps, coordinating and integrating efforts remain a problem. In strategic and annual plans, organizations may refer to the efforts of others, but integrated goals and capabilities are not the norm. For instance, with regard to national drug control policy and outcomes, Murphy and Carnevale[16] said that federal strategic and annual performance planning requirements focus on individual departments, implying that a single government organization or program would affect measures. However, the national policy involved coordinating more than 50 federal agencies and departments, and often their goals, objectives, and measures were developed independently.

Another difficulty is measuring homeland security, which is still in its infancy. Little is known about cause-and-effect that could guide measurement. In assessing prevention, "proving a negative" becomes an issue. Also, deterrence may reduce the number of possible terrorist events, but not to zero. And if terrorists fail to execute an attack as planned, the reason may be something other than the preventive efforts the nation has in place.

We believe that the traditional approach by itself will not be sufficiently effective for homeland security. Instead, we believe that four core elements would create more effective results management for homeland security, to either supplant or enhance a traditional approach: (1) management standards for homeland security, (2) short- and long-term scenario-based planning, (3) a risk-management tool, and (4) capabilities-based planning and assessment. Management standards would be benchmarks for a homeland security management system, with specific operational performance objectives and actions left to the organization. Scenario-based planning would identify possible events and outcomes for short- and long-term planning. Risk management would involve analysis and decision making to achieve an affordable, acceptable level of risk. Capabilities-based planning and assessment would identify what is needed for all parties to accomplish their homeland security missions, while retaining the flexibility needed to respond to continually evolving threats and conditions.

Management Standards for Homeland Security

In our view, voluntary national management standards (or management system standards, but we will use the briefer term here) are a key to results management in homeland security. Standards are generally consensually defined, uniform measures, agreements, conditions, or specifications for performance. These standards address what an organization does to manage its processes or activities—in this case, those associated with homeland security.

Management standards are applicable to any organization in any sector and are independent of an organization's products or services. Performance is assessed as conformance with the standards. National management standards have been effective in various settings, in developing agreements, rules, or characteristics for activities or the results of those activities.[17] Adherence to management standards could strengthen homeland security missions and support strategic goals and objectives—and thus security. GAO has promoted standards for homeland security, focusing on capabilities that can deal with many possible terrorist events and impacts.[18]

Management standards generally do not state specific performance criteria. Instead, they provide general guidance for an organization to develop its own specific performance criteria and management system. One well-known standard is ISO 9000, which provides a model for quality assurance in the production, delivery, and servicing of either manufactured goods or services. Examples of quality management standards include (1) determining the sequence and interaction of identified processes; (2) determining criteria and methods to ensure the effective operation and control of the identified processes; (3) ensuring the availability of information necessary to support the operation and monitoring of the identified processes; and (4) measuring, monitoring, and analyzing the identified processes.

Another example is the ISO 14000 environmental management standard. This emerged to help organizations prevent activities, products, or services from adversely affecting the environment. It includes (1) ensuring that environmental policy is appropriate to the nature, scale, and environmental impact of activities, products, or services; (2) establishing and maintaining documented environmental objectives and targets at each relevant function and level within the organization; (3) establishing and maintaining programs for achieving objectives and targets; and (4) developing the capabilities and support mechanisms necessary to achieve environmental policy, objectives, and targets.

A more focused standard for homeland security and national preparedness is that of the National Fire Protection Association, called NFPA 1600. It provides a common set of criteria for disaster management, emergency management, and business continuity programs. It is intended to give those responsible for these programs criteria to assess current programs or to develop, implement, or maintain a program to mitigate, prepare for, respond to, and recover from disasters and emergencies. The standard covers elements such as program administration and evaluation, hazard identification, risk assessment, impact analysis, hazard mitigation, mutual aid, resource management, planning, and operations and procedures. Examples of standards include (1) establishing performance objectives and conducting periodic evaluations; (2) identifying hazards, the likelihood of their occurrence, and the vulnerability of people, property, the environment, and the entity itself to those hazards; (3) developing and implementing a strategy to eliminate hazards or mitigate the effects of hazards that cannot be eliminated; and (4) developing the capability to direct, control, and coordinate response and recovery operations.[19]

Working with DHS, the American National Standards Institute (ANSI) recommended to the 9/11 Commission that NFPA 1600, with adjustments recommended by a working group, be recognized as the national preparedness standard.[20] The planned adjustments include (1) emphasizing an all-hazards approach, (2) emphasizing prevention and deterrence, (3) expanding mitigation strategies, (4) leveraging existing preparedness programs and capabilities, and (5) including partnership relationships and incentives, particularly with those outside the organization involved in an interdependent, coordinated network.[21] The 9/11 Commission recommended the national preparedness standard in its final report, and urged DHS to promote that standard. The new intelligence reform act directs DHS to establish a program to promote private-sector preparedness for terrorism and other emergencies, including promoting the adoption of a voluntary national preparedness standard.

While we emphasize conformance to a specific standard such as NFPA 1600, the next step may be full integration of security into other standards, so that security is built into normal activities. Standard-setting bodies and other groups[22] are proposing an integrated risk-management and security-management approach that would include standards for disaster management, emergency management, business continuity, occupational safety, life safety, and environmental safety. The U.S.-Israel Science and Technology Foundation (USISTF) is testing such an approach in pilot sites in Israel and the United States. The USISTF project will result in guidelines for other organizations wishing to implement an integrated security management system. The pilots may also result in a proposal for an international integrated security management standard.[23]

Organizations implementing requirements such as NFPA 1600 will face some challenges. Implementation is hampered by the unit of analysis for adopting a standard—traditionally an organization or facility. The addition of elements such as partnership roles and relationships for national preparedness will better reflect interdependencies in homeland security. The international and national standards are also voluntary, with various means to certify conformance. That may make standard coverage spotty. Further, the standards are normally adopted by private-sector entities, not public organizations. Additional leverage—such as encouragement and training by DHS, reductions in insurance rates and in liability (or, conversely, the imposition of liability), and supply-chain management—can provide incentives for their adoption. Last, even though NFPA 1600 is expected to expand beyond a primary focus on response, recovery, and reducing vulnerability, in the near term after-the-event preparedness will remain the focus. Efforts to address prevention will lag behind.

Scenario-Based Planning

Scenario-based planning operates within the framework defined by the management standard. The risk-management tool and the capabilities-based approach described below rely heavily on scenarios. Scenario-based planning traditionally has been used for individual organizations and their specific projects.

Long-term scenario planning (over many years) was originally designed to deal with how managers can chart a course into the future despite uncertainty.[24] Scenario planning asks what the future might hold and considers many possible futures of developments and related outcomes. Not knowing which scenario or variation of a scenario might develop, managers craft strategies to address all the scenarios. The intent is to plan actions or projects that will work and have a positive return under any of them.

The following steps are used in developing scenarios:[25]

- Identify the specific decision or issue. This could include what organizational decision makers should be thinking about in the near future and what decisions must be made that will have a long-term influence on the organization's outcomes.
- List key factors or forces influencing the success or failure of the decisions. For example, this could include what will be seen as success or failure and what considerations will shape those outcomes.
- List forces that drive the key factors. For example, these could include major trends and unpredictable forces.
- Rank the key factors and driving forces. They are ranked according to their uncertainty and their importance for the success of the decision or issue.
- Select the scenarios that will make a difference to decision makers, given the rankings.
- Flesh out the scenarios by more fully defining each key factor and trend.
- Discuss the implications of the scenarios for the issues or decisions. In other words, how does each decision look in each scenario? What are the vulnerabilities? Is the decision robust

across all the scenarios? If not, how could it be adapted to be more robust?

- Select leading indicators and signposts to monitor and identify which of the several scenarios might be closest to reality.
- Feed the scenarios back to those who were consulted for this purpose.

The scenarios then can be used in strategic planning in a traditional approach. For example, Ringland[26] describes (1) reviewing scenarios to identify opportunities and threats in each scenario and across all scenarios; (2) determining what the organization should and should not do in any case; (3) selecting a "planning focus" scenario which is generally the most probable one; (4) developing a coherent strategy for this scenario; (5) testing this strategy against the remaining scenarios to assess their resilience or vulnerability; and (6) reviewing the results of this test to determine the need for modifying strategy, hedging, and contingency planning. An implementation plan will cover strategies and options.[27] In addition, scenario development can help identify patterns and common actions across the scenarios, or identify one scenario that may be most likely to occur.

Longer-term scenario development can help officials understand variables in homeland security and how these variables are interrelated. For example, the U.S. Coast Guard[28] has used scenario planning to describe five alternative futures in 2025 in developing core shorter-term strategies for annual planning and budgeting. These scenarios range from "Forever War"—with characteristics such as continued terrorist attacks, long-term occupation of Arab countries, and a growing rivalry with China—to "Code Quebec," in which the world experiences a series of epidemics that weaken economies, and medical certification is used to control travel and commerce. The scenarios informed specific objectives for the Coast Guard, leading to strategic goals and mission programs that could be presented in formal planning and budget documents.

The Gilmore Commission[29] took a scenario approach for homeland security and highlighted three specific alternative scenarios, called threat scenarios, over a five-year planning horizon. Five years is a short time for normal scenario planning, but the commission's scenarios do provide a sense of the threats and environment that homeland security management might address. They included:

- *Very infrequent attacks*: This scenario is characterized by few or no significant terrorist attacks in the United States, or against U.S. assets or bases overseas. It assumes eventual success in the Iraqi war and a reduction in tension between Israel and Palestine. In retrospect, 9/11 is seen as unique, or as less and less likely to be repeated as time goes by.
- *A continuum of post-9/11 threats levels:* The country continues on, basically, today's course, anticipating a long-term, slow-motion, highly episodic strategic threat. There might be some major terrorist incidents, but most likely not with the impact of 9/11.
- *A rise in terrorist attacks and lethality:* Despite the effort led by the United States to combat terrorism, the overall terrorist threat stays ahead of national and international preparedness. Independent terrorist groups are increasingly in league with nations hostile to the United States. In this scenario, successful attacks continue worldwide, and Americans are killed or injured at home and abroad.

The Gilmore Commission used the threat scenarios to define four strategic visions for homeland security.[30] Under "complacence," resources were moved away from combating terrorism and generally there was a pre-9/11 state of preparedness, even though it was recognized that the terrorists' interest in attacking had not diminished. "Reactive" was characterized by steady funding but no major increases in the resources and assets committed to homeland security. While reaction to an attack would be strong, general priorities were unchanged. "Fortress America" was characterized by general skepticism about whether terrorist threats could be significantly curtailed without draconian measures. Insurance and government programs were similar to those for a natural disaster, and ever-increasing resources were committed to combating terrorism. The commission highlighted its last scenario, "the new normalcy," under which terrorism was treated as a crime, subject to domestic and international action. It also called for clear roles and responsibilities at all levels of government, in the private sector, and among citizens. According to the commission, this strategic vision could serve as a benchmark for reasonable, measurable, attainable preparedness.

"Nonevent" scenarios such as those proposed by the Gilmore Commission, even if they anticipate events only a few years out, are not widely used in governmental strategic or operational planning for homeland security. More common are specific-event, short-term scenarios that can help test national preparedness. Detailed threat scenarios are used in exercises and planning for preparedness, most often in responding to an emergency such as a terrorist attack. For example, scenarios that test participants' ability to anticipate and respond to problems include a dirty bomb detonated in a shopping mall, a chemical attack in a subway system, a cyberattack on energy control systems, an agroterrorism event, and an explosion in a port. Considering multiple scenarios can also help identify strategies common across the scenarios, in a form of nonlinear planning. DHS sponsors numerous scenario-based exercises each year, for local officials.

For results management, long-term scenarios require considerable expertise and a commitment by managers to define possible futures and consider how to deal with them. "Futures planning" or "foresight planning" is infrequently used in the public sector and is hampered by very brief attention from managers, two- to five-year budget cycles, and immediate demands for allocating resources. Also, public managers rarely develop expertise and rarely provide incentives for foresight, anticipating threats and risks. Short-term scenarios help entities prepare for a specific event, but learning may not be carried over to other events that are not covered in the exercises. Successful response to one event may also create a false sense of security, an assumption that all scenarios will be the same. The event scenarios normally involve responding to and recovering from an emergency, not prevention or protection. Other mechanisms or approaches, or expansion of the scenario technique, would be necessary to cover this gap in homeland security.

Risk Management Approach

The risk-management tool discussed here uses scenarios and addresses several elements of the management standard for homeland security: risk profiles, hazard identification, risk assessment, and risk analysis. Nationally, a major emphasis has been comprehensive assessments of the vulnerabilities of key resources and critical infrastructure. DHS is still attempting to conduct risk assessments, however, the July 2005 results of the Second Stage Review indicate DHS will more forcefully emphasize preparedness based on risk and performance. The first priority will focus on catastrophic consequences, not addressing threats and risks for all critical infrastructure. That said, the new intelligence reform act requires reports on DHS progress in completing vulnerability and risk assessments of critical infrastructure and the adequacy of government plans to protect such infrastructure. As mentioned earlier, the 9/11 Commission has recommended that assistance for homeland security be based strictly on an assessment of risks and vulnerabilities.

Risk-management tools are often used at a facility level but can have a larger scope, such as use by an organization or a community. Risk management involves evaluating assets (including people), ranking priorities, and executing decisions under uncertainty to achieve an acceptable level of risk at an affordable cost supporting the organization's mission. Drawing on the work of others, we propose a four-part risk-management process: (1) assessing risk and capability, (2) developing a risk profile, (3) using risk-based decision making, and (4) evaluating results and adjusting actions accordingly.[31]

In part 1, risk and organizational capabilities to address risk—long- and short-term—are assessed separately. Assessing risk normally involves three components: threats (and hazards), vulnerability, and criticality. These are the same components emphasized in DHS's Second Stage Review. First, threats and hazards are evaluated, as is the exposure of assets to them. Second, in assessing the vulnerability of assets, possible weaknesses and damage—and options for countering them—are noted. Assessment of criticality determines the importance of vulnerable assets and thus what priorities should be established. Assessing capability to address risk involves examining the components and culture of risk management, such as governance and decision-making structures, human and financial resources, and planning processes.

In part 2, a risk profile is developed. Officials define key risks by developing credible scenarios, ranking the risks, and characterizing the ability to control them. The scenarios may not exhaust all possible undesirable events, but each valid threat is represented in at least one scenario. The long-term scenarios would emphasize longer-term threats and possible futures. The characterization of risks also includes a description of uncertainty, both in the information used in risk assessment and in the final results of the assessment. Officials also use the process of risk control to clarify risk tolerances by describing stakeholders' comfort with various risk levels and with risks related to policies, plans, programs, and operations. The officials also describe the organization's capability to manage risk. For example, how is risk control aligned with organizational objectives at all levels, strategic planning and operational processes, and defined roles and responsibilities?

In part 3, officials develop, select, and implement strategies for anticipating and responding to risks more capably and flexibly. These are actions that can eliminate the causes or reduce the effects of one or more vulnerabilities, such as implementing new physical security controls. For the longer term, strategies might be of broader scope. Strategies are inserted into a scenario, and the risk rating for that scenario is recalculated to account for the effect of the countermeasures. Officials should develop and implement an action plan to include (1) the mission and goals appropriate to address the scenario and related strategies; (2) objectives, milestones, and measures for achieving objectives; (3) resources to address the strategies, including leveraging the resources of other actors; and (4) formation of a risk-control or risk-management function integrated with overall organizational management.

In part 4, officials evaluate and adjust risk management. Active monitoring determines if milestones are reached and policies and programs are operating as intended. Results flow continuously into informed decision making and priority setting. The longer term is continually reviewed. Costs and benefits are considered and balanced. Reassessment should occur if there are significant changes, such as changes in facilities for security, new information about credible threats to an organization's assets, or emerging patterns that might indicate a new or growing threat.

The normal unit of analysis of a facility is one challenge in using risk management for homeland security. It also calls for accurate and timely intelligence, effectively defining risks and stakeholders' tolerance for risk, and determining to what extent other entities outside the organization or facility are responsible for and capable of reducing risk. Risk management also calls for considerable analysis, information on threats and hazards, and continual updating as threats and hazards change. If used as part of a mutual aid approach, whether public or private, risk management can help define roles and responsibilities and integrate activities. Finally, risk management most often addresses specific events, not longer-term scenarios. The approach will need to explicitly address both short- and long-term scenarios.

Capabilities-Based Planning and Assessment

Capabilities-based planning and assessment (CBP) is the element most operationally demanding for homeland security. CBP stresses the ability to accomplish clearly defined missions, such as preventing terrorists from hijacking airplanes. As described by Kelley and others[32] and Davis,[33] CBP is planning under uncertainty to develop the means—capabilities—to perform effectively and efficiently in response to a wide range of potential challenges and circumstances. In addition, Davis emphasizes that CBP does not ignore issues of costs and sustainability.

Davis's CBP model starts with intelligence, strategic studies, and experiences that result in what he calls "plausible worries." Those in turn produce specific and generic scenarios for specific events or longer-term visions. Thus the model can incorporate both short- and long-term scenarios.

The scenarios produce a sense of needs and related capabilities, which are then defined in an analytical framework. The framework (1) defines an operational challenge (mission objectives, metrics of strategic and operational success); (2) considers a set of options (forces, weapons, command and control, logistics, doctrine, plans, skills, readiness) for meeting the operational challenge; (3) analyzes mission-system capabilities across a wide range of highly uncertain circumstances ("scenario spaces"); and (4) generates an assessment of options that distinguish among situations, characterize risk, and evaluate flexibility, adaptiveness, and robustness. The end point is making choices about mission requirements and how to meet them, including considering trade-offs in capabilities and issues such as the impact on others (allies, for instance).

For results management, the end product might be measures or metrics of success from what Davis calls "envelopes of capability."[34] One envelope of capability he mentions is the number of cities that can be simultaneously supported with rescue and decontamination teams. In his framework, goals, requirements, and metrics should be conceived in terms of these capability envelopes rather than particular scenarios. His framework also considers the potential benefits of a new capability, how much "mission capability" is needed, and how the "capability building blocks" can be identified, tailored, and assembled at different levels of organizations and through networks. Overall, CBP expands on the management standard for homeland security, scenario-based planning, and the risk-management tool. It provides the policy and operational details for standard elements such as training, communication during a crisis, operations and procedures, and mutual aid.

CBP is being adopted by the Department of Defense (DOD) for its strategic planning and by DHS in defining national preparedness under HSPD-8.[35] Initially, DHS's Office of State and Local Government Coordination and Preparedness (OSLGCP) asked for comments on a draft goal of national preparedness: "Federal, State, local, and tribal entities will achieve and sustain a risk-based standard of national preparedness within 3 years (by September 30, 2008) that provides assurance of the Nation's capability to prevent, prepare for, respond to, and recover from major events, especially terrorism."[36]

Under HSPD-8, the national preparedness goal is to establish measurable priorities and targets that balance the potential threat and magnitude of terrorist attacks, major disasters, and other events with resources required to prevent, respond to, and recover from them. In March 2005, DHS issued an Interim National Preparedness Goal that no longer set an explicit national preparedness goal, but established a national vision and list of priorities. Emphasizing capabilities, still to come will be indentifying the level of capabilities various types of jurisdictions should have for national preparedness. DHS continues to evolve the goal and its metrics and supporting elements, such as standards for assessments and strategies, and a system for assessing the nation's overall preparedness.

DHS's Office of Domestic Preparedness (ODP) used various strategic and planning documents and 15 scenarios developed under the leadership of the Homeland Security Council to define a universal task list (UTL) for achieving national preparedness. The December 2004 UTL identifies approximately 1,800 tasks at all levels of government to prepare for, prevent, respond to, and recover from the events described in the scenarios as part of a national response. Wisniewski-Biehn[37] reported that DHS planned to use scenarios identified by the Homeland Security Advisory Council in concert with CBP to

(1) define a national strategy for all-hazards preparedness, (2) identify what investments to make, and (3) deploy a national system of training and exercises to develop the capabilities. Later, DHS planned to address tasks for the private sector, nongovernmental organizations, and citizens. However, recent national preparedness goal documents remain mostly silent on task development for these three areas.

The scenarios that ODP used to define UTL addressed a number of probable threats: terrorism, natural disasters, and other emergencies. For example, the scenarios included a biological attack with aerosol anthrax dispersed in a large urban setting during rush hour, synchronized vehicular and suicide bombings, and an earthquake along a fault line in a metropolitan area. The scenarios define the type and scope of incidents for national preparedness and were intended to serve as a planning tool for defining capability requirements. ODP conducted a workshop in June 2004 to define the tasks for each scenario. The major areas of awareness, preparedness, prevention, response, and recovery were further organized into many subareas such as command, control, coordination, critical infrastructure, and resource management. Then tasks were defined for the subareas. For example, tasks for the anthrax scenario included identifying the emergency response plan for one's place of employment and its role in community, state, and regional plans; developing plans and procedures for emergency operations; and establishing mutual aid agreements at all levels of government.[38]

ODP revised UTL to include every unique task identified from the analysis of tasks required to prevent and respond to the events in the scenarios. The UTL was used to develop what ODP calls a target capabilities list (TCL), which defines capabilities for coping with diverse homeland security scenarios. ODP has drafted conditions and measures of performance. Conditions will be environmental variables that affect task performance, such as weather or casualties. Measures and performance criteria establish how well a task must be performed and a basis for varying levels of acceptable performance.[39] Homeland security agencies can use the performance criteria to assess their ability to perform tasks for which they are responsible. For the goal of national preparedness, DHS is considering a scorecard approach, with ratings ranging from "capable" to "partially capable."[40]

In October 2004, DHS—ODP and OSLGCP—conducted a workshop to select critical capabilities by scenario and propose quantitative measures for each of them. At that workshop, DHS provided a prototype for CBP using a scenario involving explosives. The scenario included critical tasks in 10 mission areas, ranging from prevention and deterrence to recovery and remediation. At the workshop, state and local officials voiced concerns about CBP, such as its intent, its impact on state and local funding, and administrative and technical issues, such as requiring all localities to have the same capabilities regardless of individual risk.

These issues required quick resolution. The House-Senate conference report on the DHS appropriation for fiscal year 2005, citing HSPD-8 implementation, called for DHS to (1) provide state and local jurisdictions with nationally accepted first responder preparedness levels no later than January 31, 2005, (2) include in the fiscal year 2005 formula-based grant guidance guidelines for state and local jurisdictions to adopt national preparedness standards in fiscal year 2006, and (3) issue final guidance on the implementation of the national preparedness goal no later than March 31, 2005. DHS officials are using CBP to meet these congressional requirements. For example, DHS issued an interim national preparedness goal on March 31, 2005. Fiscal Year 2005 funding guidance targeted preparedness for an improvised explosive device scenario as a starting point. The new intelligence reform act also calls for DHS to set national performance standards and ensure that homeland security plans are in conformance with those standards.

In our view, CBP offers a framework for defining capabilities for prevention, response, recovery, and reducing vulnerability that goes beyond one organization and has very broad goals. However, we have concerns about DHS's approach to CBP. At this point it is not clear to what extent or how DHS will address (1) the full scope of homeland security; (2) the interdependence of responsibilities and roles of organizations, whether public or private, not under DHS's control; (3) the integration with existing planning and budgeting approaches and the traditional give-and-take of funding; (4) achieving results rather than achieving the tasks represented by UTL; and (5) long-term scenarios.

Scope of Homeland Security
Our first concern has to do with full homeland security coverage. The first line of defense is prevention and deterrence. While ODP's

draft UTL includes prevention efforts such as developing intelligence and providing strategic and threat intelligence, it focuses much more on response, recovery, and reducing vulnerability. Emergency response—after an event—appears to take the lion's share of analysis and preparation; and, clearly, the roles and responsibilities of first responders are emphasized. Moreover, DHS appears to assume that preparing for terrorist events, representing the vast majority of the planning scenarios, will prepare jurisdictions for all-hazards events. Many would argue that it might make more sense to develop capabilities for more probable all-hazards events that can be "ramped up" for large-scale terrorist events, natural disasters, or inadvertent human-caused disasters. Capabilities then can be scaled to what is affordable and sustainable (and more likely to be used) at the state and local level, and then supplemented by regional or federal capabilities (or both) if an event overwhelms state and local capabilities.

Interdependence of Responsibilities

Our second concern has to do with the interdependencies of organizational roles and responsibilities in homeland security. We are concerned that DHS's CBP does not adequately guide analysis when the assets and capabilities needed to accomplish a mission are not under one jurisdiction, are unknown, or ebb and flow over time. DHS's draft rating scheme for national preparedness indicates that a group of organizations can be rated collaboratively under a mutual aid or assistance compact to perform prevention, response, or recovery tasks for a specific scenario, but the devil will be in the details.[41] However, CBP is always tied to sustainability analyses, and funding support favors multiple-use capabilities and multiple sources of capabilities to reduce the funding burden on any one organization. Much more work is needed to better understand how to use the framework where there are networks of organizations that work on homeland security issues, or discrete sets of organizations that handle specific homeland security functions. As we have suggested earlier, national management standards can guide organizations in linking desired capabilities, across jurisdictional and sector boundaries, into an effective and efficient network. This will be even more important when CBP is expanded to address the private sector, nongovernmental organizations, and nonprofit entities that are critical players in prevention, response, recovery, and the reduction of vulnerability.

Integration with Planning, Budgeting, and Funding

Third, it is not clear how CBP will be seamlessly integrated with existing planning, budgeting, and funding. Managers and others in the organization have to be comfortable, and have the skills, for example, to identify plausible scenarios, understand needed generic capabilities and operational challenges, and think in terms of missions that might be necessary in diverse circumstances. In addition, funders such as boards of directors, city councils, state legislatures, and Congress have to accept the analytical framework. The failure point will be reached if organizations—government, nonprofit, and private—do not identify, fund, and sustain the capabilities.

Achieving Results

Fourth, we are concerned that CBP might get bogged down in a checklist mentality, responding to UTL and not focusing on results for an organization and its partners in homeland security. State and local officials at the capabilities workshop in October 2004 noted that the task lists and defined capabilities can easily become a standard of care for which they will become accountable. A defensive posture might be to "manage to" the lists, not to the overall results that must be achieved within a risk assessment process. Our approach in blending management standards, scenario-based planning, risk-management tools, and capabilities-based planning and assessment might alleviate that possibility.

Long-Term Scenarios

Fifth, we do not see that the CBP model which DHS is using will produce processes and results that can anticipate, adapt, and evolve for alternative futures, say, 20 years from now. The power of long-term scenario planning is that it demands more imagination—called for by the 9/11 Commission—and strategies that look beyond the immediate present.

DHS's Second Stage Review recommendations and changes in priorities and organizational structure may address some of these concerns. The Review indentified new management tools, for example, to centralize and improve policy development and coordination and enhance coordination and development of preparedness assets. Specifically, there should be more emphasis on long-range strategic policy planning, oversight of national preparedness efforts, and coordination with state and local governments and the private sector.

CHALLENGES TO OVERSIGHT

Here, we briefly discuss challenges and issues of oversight in homeland security. Oversight is a well-known tool of policy makers and funders. Simply, it is the review, monitoring, and supervision of organizations, most often government agencies.[42] The Congressional Research Service[43] writes that congressional oversight of the executive branch, for example, is designed for several purposes, such as ensuring executive compliance with legislative intent; improving the efficiency, effectiveness, and economy of governmental operations; evaluating program performance; and protecting individual rights and liberties. Oversight processes include shaping the federal budget, creating and shaping government programs and agencies, examining and passing on the budget requests of agencies, conducting investigations, confirming nominees to public positions, and impeaching executive officials.

At present, congressional oversight for intelligence and homeland security is widely dispersed. For intelligence, authorization oversight is done through the current House Permanent Select Committee on Intelligence (established in 1977) and the Senate Select Committee on Intelligence (established in 1976). According to Kaiser,[44] these two committees emerged after extensive, detailed congressional and executive investigations had found widespread abuses in the intelligence community and ineffective congressional oversight, in disparate standing committees. These select committees hold exclusive authorizing and legislative powers for the Central Intelligence Agency, the director of Central Intelligence, and the National Foreign Intelligence Program. Oversight of the intelligence components in DOD, DHS, and the Department of Justice, among other agencies, is shared with appropriate standing committees.

For homeland security, as described by Schneider and Rundquist,[45] the House created, in January 2003, a new Select Committee on Homeland Security to serve during the 108th Congress as its focus for legislative and oversight coordination for homeland security issues, while other House committees retained their more limited legislative and oversight authority over homeland security.

The Senate has continued to consider homeland security issues within its existing committee structure. The structure of the House and Senate Appropriations Committees changed once DHS was created, with the House abolishing the former Subcommittee on Treasury and Postal Service Appropriations and transferring its responsibilities to a renamed Subcommittee on Transportation, Treasury, and Independent Agencies Appropriations. A new thirteenth Subcommittee on Homeland Security was established and assigned jurisdiction over appropriations for the new department and for bureaus in other departments transferred to it. The Senate took the same action to ensure that the subcommittee structures of the two committees were parallel.

According to Schneider and Rundquist,[46] critics say that Congress has not shifted the focus of its committee system toward new policy areas. Consequently, they say, there are questions about duplication, overlap, and neglect of issues, and ill effects on policy making. Many members have already endorsed further changes to the committee system, such as establishing a new temporary select, permanent select, or standing committee on homeland security; altering the appropriations process; or making other changes in congressional structures dealing with homeland security. The 9/11 Commission[47] recommended that Congress create a single, principal point of oversight and review for homeland security in the form of a permanent standing committee in both the House and the Senate.

Despite these structural issues, congressional oversight of homeland security has been fairly rigorous since 9/11, in many areas. However, much of that oversight has focused on individual programs, not on larger objectives and progress. In addition, concerns have been raised about the effectiveness of oversight in intelligence programs. Recently, Congress did make some changes in its oversight structure.

However, oversight in homeland security goes beyond the role of Congress. Decision makers—small county commissions, large city councils, state legislatures, and Congress itself—are interested in oversight. For state and local government, oversight is also complex. States and localities have established central homeland security authorities or offices, prepared emergency management plans, requested federal funding through a variety of programs, and established mutual aid pacts. Each jurisdiction will have its own oversight authorities and processes, and if federal funding is involved, the expectation that there will be federal oversight. For the private sector, oversight is more diffuse. The private sector is responsible for protecting most critical infrastructure in the country, most of which is not subject to governmental oversight. In large part, oversight comes in the form of assessments by stockholders and insurers that address risk management findings and liabilities.

Those responsible for oversight should not forget that homeland security is a result of an integrated, interdependent response by all parties, not just one level of government or one private firm. For homeland security, oversight must address a national response and extend beyond the federal environment to what is happening at other levels of government and in the private sector.

Strengthening homeland security in the context of results management will mean strengthening oversight. Establishing the four components of results management that we have suggested should help clarify what is expected, how expectations can be met, and how progress can be measured and assessed. Moreover, oversight of decision making in results management should also use the five principles of homeland security that we have highlighted for setting objectives and assessment approaches—clarity, sustainability, integration, balance, and accountability. Was there clarity in setting expectations for preparedness? Was sustainability considered in leveraging funding? Have opportunities for integration been seized to bring concepts and activities of homeland security together in ongoing programs and processes? Were there actions that struck a balance between costs and benefits? Were there actions to implement a rigorous performance management system? These questions should be asked of individual homeland security programs at all organizational levels, and of their totality in providing national results.

CONCLUSION

While some would argue that our homeland security strategies would not result in "Fortress America," we clearly lack the resources to protect everything, no matter what its value, from every contingency. Instead of managing risk responsibly, we are in danger of losing the larger goal in a fog of voluminous activities not structured for what should be accomplished. As we seek homeland security we should apply our finite resources in innovative ways that emphasize clarity, sustainability, integration, balance, and accountability, creating a safer America that prevents and survives terrorism without compromising other essential national goals and principles.

N O T E S

1. M. Aristigueta, *Managing for Results in State Government* (Westport, Conn.: Quorum, 1999).

2. M. Aristigueta, L. J. Cooksy, and C. W. Nelson,"The Role of Social Indicators in Developing a Managing for Results System," *Public Performance and Management Review* 24:3 (March 2001): 254–69.

3. J. Wholey, "Making Results Count in Public and Nonprofit Organizations: Balancing Performance with Other Values." In K. Newcomer, E. T. Jennings, C. Broom, and Al Lomax (eds.), *Meeting the Challenges of Performance-Oriented government* (Washington, D.C.: American Society for Public Administration/ Center for Accountability and Performance, 2002), p. 14.

4. D. Walker. 2001a. *Homeland Security: A Framework for Addressing the Nation's Efforts.* GAO-01-1158T. Washington, D.C.: U.S. General Accounting Office (21 September). See also 2001b. *Homeland Security: Challenges and Strategies in Addressing Short- and Long-Term National Needs.* GAO-02-160T. Washington, D.C.: U.S. General Accounting Office (7 November).

5. Office of Homeland Security. 2002. *National Strategy for Homeland Security.* Washington, D.C.: Executive Office of the President (July), p. 2.

6. White House. 2003. Homeland Security Presidential Directive/HSPD-8. Washington, D.C. (17 December), p. 2.

7. Gilmore Commission, *V. Forging America's New Normalcy.* Fifth Annual Report to the President and the Congress, Advisory Panel to Assess Domestic Response Capabilities for Terrorism Involving Weapons of Mass Destruction (Arlington, Va.: Rand, 2003) p. 8.

8. U.S. General Accounting Office. 2004a. *Evaluation of Selected Characteristics in National Strategies Related to Terrorism.* GAO-04-408T. Washington, D.C. (3 February), table 2, pp. 5–6.

9. U.S. General Accounting Office. 2004b. *Homeland Security: Selected Recommendations from Congressionally Chartered Commissions and GAO.* GAO-04-591. Washington, D.C. (31 March). See also Government Accountability Office. 2004c. *Homeland Security: Observations on the National Strategies Related to Terrorism.* GAO-04-1075T. Washington, D.C. (22 September).

10. R. Falkenrath, "Problems of Preparedness: U.S. Readiness for a Domestic Terrorist Threat," *International Security* 25:4 (2001): 147–86.

11. D. Kettl, *Promoting State and Local Government Performance for Homeland Security* (New York: Century Foundation Homeland Security Project, 2002).

12. Gilmore Commission, p. 2.

13. 9/11 Commission. 2004. *The 9/11 Commission Report.* Final Report of the National Commission on Terrorist Attacks upon the United States. Washington, D.C.: U.S. Government Printing Office, p. 364. See also R. Grimmett. 2004. *Terrorism: Key*

Recommendations of the 9/11 Commission and Recent Major Commissions and Inquiries. Report RL32519. Washington, D.C.: Congressional Research Service (11 August).

14. 9/11 Commission, pp. 395–6.

15. H. Hatry, *Performance Measurement: Getting Results* (Washington, D.C.: Urban Institute, 1999). See also J. Bryson. *Strategic Planning for Public and Nonprofit Organizations*, rev. ed. (San Francisco, Calif.: Jossey-Bass, 1995).

16. P. Murphy and J. Carnevale, *The Challenge of Developing Cross-Agency Measures: A Case Study of the Office of National Drug Control Policy* (Arlington, Va.: PricewaterhouseCoopers Endowment for the Business of Government, 2001).

17. S. Spivak and F. Brenner, *Standardization Essentials: Principles and Practice* (New York: Marcel Dekker, 2001).

18. R. Yim. 2003. "Homeland Security: The Need for National Standards." Testimony before the National Commission on Terrorist Attacks upon the United States, Princeton, N.J. (19 November). See also R. Yim and S. Caudle, "Homeland Security: Using Standards to Improve National Preparedness." *ISO Management Systems* 4:1 (2004): 15–8.

19. National Fire Protection Association, *Standard on Disaster/Emergency Management and Business Continuity Programs 2004 Edition* (Quincy, Mass.: NFPA, 2004).

20. American National Standards Institute. 2004. "9-11 Commission Presented with Recommendation on Emergency Preparedness." (News release, 29 April.)

21. ANSI-HSSP Workshop on Private Sector Emergency Preparedness and Business Continuity. 2004. *Recommendations to the NFPA 1600 Committee.* (Internal document dated 22 March.)

22. J. Milliman, J. Grosskopf, and O. Paez. 2003. "Responding to New Security and Environmental Threats: The Integrated Security, Environment, Health and Safety Management System Approach." Unpublished paper provided by the authors (9 December).

23. U.S.-Israel Science and Technology Foundation. 2004. *Request for Applications in Integrated Security Management Systems Approach Pilot Studies*, accessed 18 May at www.usistf. org/04_A_RFPs.html.

24. P. Schwartz and J. Ogilvy, "Plotting Your Scenarios." In L. Fahey and R. M. Randall (eds.), *Learning from the Future: Competitive Foresight Scenarios* (New York: Wiley, 1998), p. 2.

25. Ibid.; and P. Schwartz, *The Art of the Long View* (New York: Doubleday, 1991), pp. 241–8. See also G. Ringland, *Scenarios in Public Policy* (Chichester, U.K.: Wiley, 2002).

26. G. Ringland, *Scenario Planning: Managing for the Future* (Chichester, U.K.: Wiley, 1998), p. 115.

27. Ringland, 2002.

28. D. McClellan, "Delivering Strategic Intent." Presentation to the World Future Society, Washington, D.C. (2 August 2004).

29. Gilmore Commission, p. 12.

30. Ibid., pp. 12–3.

31. ASIS International. 2003. *General Security Risk Assessment Guideline*. Alexandria, Va. See also Treasury Board of Canada. 2001. *Integrated Risk Management Framework*, www.tbs-sct.gc.ca.

32. C. Kelley, P. Davis, B. Bennett, E. Harris, R. Hundley, E. Larson, R. Mesic, and M. Miller, *Metrics for the Quadrennial Defense Review's Operational Goals* (Santa Monica, Calif.: RAND National Defense Research Institute, 2003).

33. P. Davis, *Analytical Architecture for Capabilities-Based Planning, Mission-System Analysis, and Transformation* (Santa Monica, Calif.: RAND, 2002).

34. Ibid., p. 18.

35. Ibid.; and Office of Domestic Preparedness (ODP). 2004a, b. *Request for Input on Universal Task List*. Washington, D.C.: ODP, Department of Homeland Security (12 July and 13 August).

36. Office of State and Local Government Coordination and Preparedness (OSLGCP). 2004. *Draft National Preparedness Goal*. Washington, D.C.: OSLGCP, Department of Homeland Security (September), p. 6.

37. B. Wisniewski-Biehn. 2004. "Department of Homeland Security Office of Domestic Preparedness Training and Technical Assistance Division." Presentation to American National Standards Institute Homeland Security Standards Panel, Falls Church, Va. (29 April).

38. ODP, 2004a.

39. ODP, 2004b.

40. OSLGCP, 2004.

41. Ibid.

42. F. Kaiser. 2001. *Congressional Oversight*. Report 97-936 GOV. Washington, D.C.: Congressional Research Service (2 January).

43. Congressional Research Service. 2002. *Congressional Oversight Manual*. Report RL30240, updated. Washington, D.C.: Congressional Research Service (17 January), pp. 1–3.

44. F. Kaiser. 2004. *A Joint Committee on Intelligence: Proposals and Options from the 9/11 Commission and Others*. Report RL 32525. Washington, D.C.: Congressional Research Service (25 August).

45. J. Schneider and P. Rundquist. 2004a. *Department of Homeland Security: Options for House and Senate Committee Organization*. Report RS21360, updated. Washington, D.C.: Congressional Research Service (13 August).

46. Ibid.; and J. Schneider and P. Rundquist. 2004b. *House Committee System: Jurisdiction and Referral Reform Options*. Report RS21643, updated. Washington, D.C.: Congressional Research Service (24 March).

47. 9/11 Commission, p. 421.

CHAPTER 17

Congressional Oversight over Homeland Security and the Dynamics of Appropriation

Congressman Christopher Shays
Chairman, House Subcommittee on National Security,
Emerging Threats, and International Relations

Before 9/11, there was little systematic congressional oversight of homeland security. A search for the term *homeland security* in the online House and Senate legislative database for the 106th Congress (1999–2000) produces no results.[1] To the extent that the topic came up in hearings, it was primarily in the context of questions about the technical capabilities of the proposed missile defense. Despite the earlier bombing of the World Trade Center, the bombing in Oklahoma City, a series of deadly attacks abroad, and the jihadists' publicly stated desire to strike on American soil, the myth of a secure "fortress America" persisted.

This is not to say that oversight on any number of related topics was not conducted. In 1995, when the Republicans took control of the House of Representatives, we reinstated a requirement for all standing committees to promulgate two-year oversight plans.[2] The committee oversight agendas vary in scope and specificity, with some simply defining jurisdictional boundaries while others convey their oversight inquiries more explicitly. But the plans provide some sense of overall direction and scope.

The House Government Reform Committee, which may exercise oversight "without regard" to House rules conferring the same jurisdiction on another committee, reviews the reports and can fill gaps noted by committee and House leaders. The same rules changes in the House attempt to link oversight findings with legislative and appropriations activities by directing that oversight findings and recommendations be transmitted to other committees with jurisdiction over the matter, and by requiring that any report on legislation in the same area contain a reference to the oversight.[3] The Senate Governmental Affairs Committee can play a similar role in coordinating and disseminating oversight results.

In 1998 the National Security Subcommittee—whose chairman was then Dennis Hastert (Republican, Illinois)—asked several federal agencies how they coordinated plans and spending for counterterrorism. When Hastert became House Speaker, the National Security Subcommittee continued those inquiries. Between January 1999 and September 2001, the National Security Subcommittee held 20 hearings on terrorism and homeland security, including national preparedness programs, the role of the National Guard, pharmaceutical stockpiles, data sharing, and the need for a coordinated federal response and a retooled national strategy.[4]

It was lonely work. Media coverage was minimal. Other committees brought much narrower jurisdictional interests to topics touching on homeland security. Judiciary focused on terrorism as a domestic crime and looked to the five-year plan of the Department of Justice for strategic momentum. Armed Services committees were simultaneously resisting demands on military assets to play a greater role in civil support and funding the formation of National Guard Rapid Assessment and Initial Detection (RAID) teams, later renamed WMD Civil Support teams; the funding process reflected past political practices more than an assessment of emerging threats. The Transportation committees jealously guarded their "all-hazards" jurisdiction over first-responder grants and authorization of the Federal Emergency Management Administration (FEMA).

The National Commission on Terrorist Attacks upon the United States (9/11 Commission) called congressional oversight "dysfunctional" and said that:

> ... attention to terrorism was episodic and splintered across several committees. Congress gave little guidance to executive branch agencies, did not reform them in any significant way, and did not systematically perform oversight to identify, address, and attempt to resolve the many problems in national security and domestic agencies that became apparent in the aftermath of 9/11.[5]

The 9/11 Commission faulted Congress for delegating oversight of important national security questions to serial national commissions, then all but ignoring their recommendations.

That criticism was on target. In response to intermittent pressure to address terrorism, but with little time or impulse to do so, Congress did often delegate terrorism and homeland security to high-level study commissions. In sequence, panels chaired by L. Paul Bremer,[6] Governor James Gilmore of Virginia,[7] and the former senators Gary Hart and Warren Rudman[8] came to increasingly sophisticated, strikingly similar conclusions about security and the role of Congress. Each commission analyzed current terrorist threats to the United States, found a lack of official assessments of threat, and called for a comprehensive counterterrorist strategy. Each saw a need for some reorganization of the federal government, including Congress, to meet the challenge of global, transnational terrorism.[9,10,11]

The Hart-Rudman Commission concluded, "Congress should establish a special body to deal with homeland security issues, as has been done effectively with intelligence oversight,"[12] to "develop a comprehensive understanding of the problem of homeland security, exchange information and viewpoints with the Executive branch on effective policies and plans, and work with standing committees to develop integrated legislative responses and guidance."[13] This commission also suggested:

> Congress should rationalize its current committee structure so that it best serves U.S. national security objectives; specifically, it should merge the current authorizing committees with the relevant appropriations subcommittees. . . . This is to ensure both that important issues receive sufficient attention and oversight and [that] the unnecessary duplication of effort by multiple committees is minimized.[14]

Contributing to the weaknesses of executive or legislative management in addressing terrorism and homeland security was a definitional morass—a problem that persists today. Terrorism—as a crime, a form of warfare, a threat, and a budgetary issue—is relatively new. It poses the most significant challenge since the Cold War to governments' duty to provide for the common welfare and protect human life. But each sphere defines terrorism differently; so far, there is no overarching strategic definition to unify national counterterrorism. With only varied and vague definitions of terrorism as a starting point, it remains difficult to define with any precision the program to secure the homeland against terrorists. The Homeland Security Act[15] contains no definition of the term *homeland security*.

The Government Accounting Office (GAO) has been concerned about this. In a report of June 2002 it said:

> ... key terms such as "homeland security" have not been officially defined; consequently, certain organizational, management, and budgetary decisions cannot currently be made consistently across agencies. In the interim, the potential exists for an uncoordinated approach to homeland security that may lead to duplication of efforts or gaps in coverage, misallocation of resources, and inadequate monitoring of expenditures.[16]

A definition is a crucial element in any attempt to coordinate international and domestic counterterrorism. Until now Justice Potter Stewart's attitude toward pornography has been applied: one need not go to great lengths to define it, because one knows it when one sees it.[17] However, in the future the United States should set an example for the international community and come to a common understanding of homeland security. Obviously, we should specify what we are fighting against. Ambiguity of purpose among agencies, and in the international community, will breed dissension and defeatism.[18]

Separate definitions scattered throughout the U.S. Code give House and Senate committees and subcommittees with jurisdictional claims over those titles a legitimate assertion of the right to conduct oversight.[19] The lack of international consensus on terrorism also leads to conflicting perceptions of congressional purview over foreign affairs. This helps produce the long list of panels to which the Department of Homeland Security (DHS) must answer. Estimates put the number at more than 80 committees and subcommittees before which DHS can be called.[20] Secretary Ridge often complains about this fractured, diffuse oversight, noting the people and resources required to prepare and deliver DHS's testimony 145 times in 2003, before panels containing all 100 senators and all but 20 representatives.[21]

In the 1990s—reluctantly concluding that national and domestic (i.e., homeland) security would have to merge in order to confront jihadist terrorism—federal policy makers began to reshape the flow chart of federal responsibilities. Presidential Decision Directives designated federal agencies for crisis management (solving the crime) and consequence management (mitigating deaths and property damage). The Department of Justice, Federal Bureau of Investigation (FBI), was to coordinate the use of additional federal resources in figuring out what had happened and who had done it. FEMA leads the postattack cleanup. The Federal Response Plan, the procedural document through which FEMA administers the Stafford Act[22] and other assistance programs for national disasters, was augmented with a Terrorism Annex.[23]

This approach is based on the "all-hazards" theory: since bomb blasts, hurricanes, earthquakes, and industrial accidents leave similar devastation, similar response mechanisms should serve. It has the advantage of building on existing policies, procedures, and relationships. But its disadvantage is that an all-hazards response to terrorism will involve the tangled tendrils of existing oversight mechanisms, developed from preceding natural disasters and bombings, but will not necessarily avoid the impulse to devise new schemes to meet the "new" threat.

Grants from the Department of Justice, firefighters, the police, and other emergency response personnel suddenly became counterterrorism programs. Drug enforcement and coastal interdiction programs underwent similar transformations. Even before 9/11, agencies and programs understood the value of labeling a request to Congress "counterterrorism." Understandably, and sometimes justifiably, eager to address what was by then acknowledged as a serious issue, authorizers and appropriators did not discourage that practice.

A further complication in the congressional approach to counterterrorism is that attacks have to be viewed as more than just very violent crimes. Even when individuals or subnational groups took or were given credit for attacks, their ability to operate, lethally, across international borders—largely considered a trait of established nations subject to the incentives and pressures of traditional statecraft—required a military assessment and response. That in turn required defense committees in the House and Senate to consider the implications of new military roles in domestic preparedness and response.

In the past, disaster response beyond a certain level often involved military assets, primarily National Guard units dispatched by a governor under state authority. In extraordinary circumstances, such as forest fires (often on federal lands), the president would direct active-duty units to assist. Also, the capacity of the Department of Defense (DOD) for rapid transport and heavy lift was built into larger-scale domestic response scenarios; and national command authorities and military elements always had primary authority in the event of a nuclear incident. But various legal, fiscal, and cultural firewalls limit or block DOD's participation in some homeland security activities. Those firewalls bound the jurisdictional maze of congressional oversight of domestic security.

Preparation for, and operational roles in, response to a terrorist act of war on U.S. soil were strategic and legal issues not often confronted after the Cold War put the enemy at some distance. Under U.S. law, "the term 'act of war' means any act occurring in the course of—(A) declared war; (B) armed conflict, whether or not war has been declared, between two or more nations; or (C) armed conflict between military forces of any origin."[24] It is clear from DOD's general policy on military assistance to civilian authorities, articulated in 1997, that DOD views civilian support as a secondary undertaking. Requests for help will be evaluated for the legality of the task, the lethality of the threat, the risk posed, cost and reimbursement, appropriateness, and the impact "on DOD's ability to perform its primary mission."[25]

When homeland security was viewed as a distraction, DOD and Congress, perhaps unintentionally, deferred to the constitutional and geographic primacy of the National Guard. Beginning in fiscal year 1999, funding was provided to equip and train one specialized unit in each of the 10 FEMA regions to assist in "WMD response" scenarios. As noted above, these units were initially called RAID teams; but the "ID" did not really describe a team that would arrive on the scene hours after "initial detection" would have to be done. Also, the unfamiliar and improbable politics of sharing those units across state lines produced pressure to fund at least one unit in each state. The process of certifying the renamed WMD Civil Support Teams continues; but the role of the units has not been fully validated in integrated field exercises, and many mayors and first responders remain uncertain where such units fit into the Incident Command System.

When terrorism and homeland security were clearly becoming growth industries, the federal government and many state and local agencies set up programs and teams designed to handle domestic terrorism and manage the consequence of unconventional attacks.

As a result, duplicative, confusing, ill-defined federal response capabilities emerged. Often these programs were designed in the absence of any specified end state or level of preparedness. No one could tell if the new units were ready, because no one had adequately defined what they needed to be ready for.

Efforts to revise federal response mechanisms, including an expanded domestic role for the military, further complicated an already daunting intergovernmental situation. An attack and its aftermath would in all likelihood entail not just mass destruction but mass confusion as local first responders, state officials, and follow-on federal agencies jostled to figure out who was in charge. After the bombing in Oklahoma City, some officials there were quite vocal about all the "help" Washington provided, confirming fears and stereotypes of heavy-handed federal law enforcement and patronizing emergency assistance staffs.

In 1997, as federal spending on homeland security began to grow, Congress directed the Office of Management and Budget (OMB) to establish a reporting system for executive agencies' spending on counterterrorism and issue an annual report of government-wide expenditures. Spending by more than 40 separate departments, agencies, and programs was aggregated in five major categories:

1. Law enforcement and investigative activities
2. Preparing security of government facilities and employees
3. Physical security of government facilities and employees
4. Physical protection of the national populace and national infrastructure
5. Research and development

But GAO found OMB's reports plagued by the same definitional vagaries that confounded the threat assessments and strategies.[26] The lack of strategic guidance suggested that funds were being wasted on invalidated requirements and on programs not directly addressed to a current threat.[27] Subsequent reports by OMB have captured more categories of spending, but evolving methodologies, by design or by accident, still prevent meaningful year-to-year trend analysis.

The path of the legislation establishing DHS is a cautionary tale on the difficulty of focusing congressional oversight. In the House, the bill was referred to 11 standing committees and two select committees,[28] with the new select panel on Homeland Security created specifically to re-form the misshapen distributed pieces of the legislation into some coherent whole. In the Senate, the companion bill was referred to the Governmental Affairs Committee, and several other committees influenced the proposal during a lengthy amendment process on the floor.

As DHS was being assembled, Congress attempted to ease the fears of the executive branch about "armies of midwives in the birthing room" by giving one committee in each chamber primary oversight. In the 108th Congress, the Senate Governmental Affairs Committee and the reconstituted House Select Committee on Homeland Security were to monitor the vast new undertaking. But the presence on the House panel of standing committee chairs with jurisdictional equities at stake did little to smooth the way for DHS or the Select Committee.

Jurisdictional territoriality (turf) may be inevitable and perhaps necessary when legislative authority is divided over a vast federal bureaucracy and a trillion-dollar annual budget. This competition was sharpened in the case of homeland security, with its potential to reach into every jurisdictional nook and cranny, and with the explosive growth of funding for it.

Although DHS consolidated numerous agencies, programs, functions, and staffs from throughout the federal government, significant pieces of the federal effort remain outside it, notably public health surveillance and research programs conducted by the Department of Health and Human Services. Security at energy plants and nuclear facilities remains under the Department of Energy (DOE). The Department of Veterans Affairs continues to play a major role in managing the national pharmaceutical stockpiles. Control of exports remains the responsibility of the departments of State, Commerce, and Defense. The Environmental Protection Agency (EPA) continues to monitor urban air quality and regulate chemical plant safety. As a result, House and Senate authorizing committees and appropriations subcommittees with a tradition of authority over those non-DHS functions conclude that they retain some measure of homeland security oversight.

Nevertheless, the House Select Committee and Senate Governmental Affairs have tried to lead in oversight, often by securing the first testimony on a day's hot topic from the secretary or another prominent DHS official, so as to dissuade others from holding "me too" hearings. In 2003–2004, the House Select Committee and its subcommittees convened 56 hearings and the Senate Governmental Affairs Committee held 20 oversight hearings.[29] Topics included agroterrorism threats, grants for first-responder preparedness, and the role of the broadcast media in combating terrorism.

Perhaps significantly, only six hearings by the House Select Committee were convened jointly with other standing committees or their subpanels. Given the legacy of jurisdictional coverage by the permanent committees, some people expected the Select Committee to collaborate more often, at least initially, with other committees in an effort to build support for whatever jurisdictional realignment might be recommended later. In some cases, Homeland Security subcommittees chose to proceed alone in shared areas, to demonstrate autonomy and expertise. In others cases, joint oversight appears to have been resisted by standing committees not much interested in helping the Select Committee establish its credibility or authority.

At the same time, other committees of both chambers also proceeded with their own oversight. The Budget and Appropriations committees had a legitimate role regarding DHS because of their interest in its economy and efficiency. Panels on transportation continued to examine the security of critical infrastructure, aviation, and the railroads (after Madrid), and emergency preparedness programs. Border security and immigration policy remained of interest to foreign relations committees. Intelligence panels continued to keep a close hold on reviews of efforts to connect the dots. Bioterrorism—preparedness, detection, and countermeasures—was the object of inquiries by tax panels and of committees on small businesses, public health, and commerce.

Oversight is often defined and motivated by the interests of members' constituencies. Members from coastal districts are likely to be attuned much more to port security than to land borders. Those representing urban areas, where critical infrastructure is likely to be more concentrated, will favor risk-based grant formulas—whereas members from rural areas, whose constituents also feel at risk, need to be sure that every area gets a fair share of homeland security funding. Consequently, in the 108th Congress, homeland security oversight focused on a long list of perceived weaknesses and vulnerabilities. As a result of local concerns and overt partisanship, this oversight at times became characterized by posturing—both parties tried to highlight vulnerabilities, claim credit for progress, and avoid the damaging charge of being soft on terrorism. No real bipartisan consensus emerged on how to focus federal grant funding more effectively.

Regarding several issues, homeland security oversight did succeed in focusing and accelerating DHS's activities. In others, oversight merely underscored the intractability of complex problems requiring unprecedented interagency and intergovernmental coordination.

COORDINATING INTELLIGENCE AND SHARING INFORMATION

For example, Christopher Cox, as chairman of the House Homeland Security Select Committee, examined widely noted barriers to information sharing between the federal intelligence community and others, including state and local law enforcement agencies. The Terrorist Threat Integration Center (TTIC) was created to address the failure, before 9/11, to connect the dots that might have given officials a clearer picture of the terrorists' plans. But TTIC was outside DHS; thus there was suspicion that DHS would be a second-class customer of intelligence with no real ability to shape the collection of evidence by specifying targets or practices.

Dissatisfaction with TTIC echoed congressional criticisms of intelligence coordination and foreshadowed the later debate over reforming intelligence, including long-simmering complaints about limited—some might say lax—oversight by House and Senate Permanent Select Committees. Shielded by closed hearings and an expansive interpretation of their exclusive jurisdiction over sources and methods, the intelligence committees and the entities they were overseeing formed a closed loop. Some believe that the relationship has become too comfortable, losing the healthy skepticism needed for effective oversight. Staff members migrate from committees to intelligence agencies and back again. As a result, the Central Intelligence Agency (CIA) felt able to take what it described as a "hard line" against oversight inquiries by other committees.

For example, on 17 July 2001 the CIA wrote to Stephen Horn, chairman of the Government Reform Subcommittee, in response to his request for testimony on the security of information technology and on the results of a survey by GAO to which other intelligence agencies but not the CIA replied. The director of Central Intelligence

(DCI) informed Horn that no testimony would be provided and that his decision "was fully compatible with the wishes of the Chairman of the House Permanent Select Committee on Intelligence who urged me not to testify." DCI relied on the broadest possible interpretation of House rules regarding the Select Committee's exclusive jurisdiction over intelligence sources and methods.

The glacial pace of the interagency integration of terrorist "watch" lists also drew criticism, and raised doubts about the ability and willingness of traditionally wary law enforcement entities to share information more broadly. Senate hearings raised similar questions about the clear goal of the Homeland Security Act of 2000 to put DHS at the center of domestic intelligence, and about the extent to which TTIC advanced that goal. At least in part as the result of these criticisms, when the administration and Congress approached broader intelligence reforms after the 9/11 Commission report, TTIC was subsumed into the structure of the Director of National Intelligence (NID).

NUCLEAR SECURITY

Prodding by House oversight committees helped build, and sustain momentum for, efforts by DOD and DOE to strengthen post-9/11 security at the nation's sprawling nuclear weapons complex. The interagency process to update the facility security standard, called the "design basis threat" or DBT, took almost two years. Meanwhile, rigorous force-on-force exercises were suspended and so-called iterative site assessments produced idiosyncratic improvements but no systemwide program to deny terrorists access to nuclear weapons and fissile materials. At the same time, reflexively augmenting security through the traditional approach of adding gates, guns, and guards was wearing on a workforce laboring under the demanding requirements of intermittent code orange alerts.

Some people suspected that the lengthy process reflected bureaucrats' unwillingness to confront the fiscal implications of the threat or to acknowledge that the reformulated DBT was intentionally watered down to require only as much security as DOE could afford. Sustained, constructive engagement by oversight panels gave DOE an opportunity to refocus security management, launch initiatives to strengthen the protective force, and revisit DBT periodically in order to keep it calibrated to current threat assessments.

CRITICAL INFRASTRUCTURE

Governors, senators, representatives, and mayors do not want to be told that nothing in their area is critical to homeland security. So oversight of DHS efforts to inventory and prioritize critical infrastructure has yet to move much beyond unranked vulnerability assessments. This is particularly true with regard to industrial chemical facilities, a sector easily portrayed as vulnerable. Testimony on voluntary efforts by private plant owners to strengthen internal safety and external security practices left members of Congress unconvinced that safeguards were being made diligently or consistently upgraded.

Linkage between EPA, which already regulates plant safety in terms of accidental discharges, and DHS's critical infrastructure directorate sparked a debate over whether DHS could or should assume a parallel role as regulator of security for chemical facilities. Some thought that giving DHS sector-specific regulatory responsibilities would draw it into a bureaucratic thicket and distract it from its own core missions. Others feared an attempt to repackage environmental policies (e.g., substitution of potentially less dangerous but more expensive chemicals) as homeland security mandates.

Environmental politics aside, oversight of critical infrastructure—of which some 80 percent is privately owned—could not bridge the chasm between governmental security policy and the capacity of the private sector to meet new domestic threats. The 9/11 Commission recommended formulating standards of preparedness for the private sector that could serve as underwriting tools for insurers and give governments a nonintrusive look at response capabilities now beyond their view. This area will draw considerable attention in the future.

TRANSPORTATION AND BORDER SECURITY

After 9/11, nothing received more oversight attention than aviation security and related transportation issues. GAO's database of open recommendations currently lists 52 separate reports containing more than 100 prescriptions for reform not yet acted on by various homeland security agencies.[30] Half of those reports and recommendations deal with transportation and border security.

Baggage screening continues to be a contentious issue, with critics accusing the Transportation Security Administration (TSA) of slow-rolling or loosely interpreting requirements to subject all checked luggage to some form of inspection. Oversight helped identify appropriate technologies, and technical solutions not yet ready for broad deployment, to meet deadlines.

People who shipped themselves into the United States, and a television news crew that shipped a block of depleted uranium through a seaport, served as starting points for congressional scrutiny of border security. Led by the Judiciary and Transportation panels in both chambers, oversight of border security and immigration continued to monitor executive management of, for instance, policies on waiving and revoking visas and on screening seaport cargo, and technologies for securing porous land borders. Reflecting oversight findings on the low volumes of cargo inspected before being loaded onto passenger airliners, the Homeland Security Appropriations Act for fiscal year 2005 directs DHS to triple the current screening rate, strengthen the "known shipper" program, and develop more robust systems as soon as possible. As the largest single component of DHS, and the directorate with the most visible and complex mission, TSA will continue to be scrutinized by the inspector general, GAO, and congressional oversight committees.

TECHNOLOGY DEVELOPMENT

After 9/11, members of the House and Senate were inundated with proposals for building a better mousetrap, from companies and individuals seeking federal help. Some proposals were technically sophisticated and accompanied by a sound business plan; many were not. But how DHS proposed to deal with this growing mountain of paper on homeland security became, and remains, an important question for members.

Again, even in this specific area of homeland security, oversight revealed that not all roads led to DHS. The Technical Support Working Group, an interagency team headed by the Department of State but housed in DOD, had an established process for the scientific review of proposed counterterrorism technology. This group was trying to review the flood of submissions received in response to "broad area announcements" after 9/11 soliciting ideas for counter-measures. The Defense Advanced Research Projects Agency (DARPA) also funds innovative concepts. DHS established a parallel organization, HSARPA. How DHS sets technology goals, and how these other organizations assess proposals to address those priorities, will be an object of continuing congressional interest.

FIRST-RESPONDER GRANTS

Many people in Congress remain frustrated over incomplete, inconsistent accounts of federal spending on homeland security; similarly, oversight of grants for homeland security is impeded by the apparent inability of DHS and others to follow the money once it has left Washington. DHS says that billions in grants are in the pipeline. State and local officials say that only a trickle is coming out at the other end. This political dissonance invites oversight by authorizers and appropriators.

In fact, however, both perceptions may be right. Differences in fiscal calendars and accounting methods between federal, state, county, and local governments can mask or delay funding flows, making end-to-end visibility all but impossible. A grant for equipping or training first responders may go into a state fund, mix with other federal or state funds, wait for state and local budget approval, and come out in forms and amounts unrecognizable to all but the most astute, patient auditor.

Finding ways to measure the effectiveness and impact of federal spending on homeland security should receive sustained attention from Congress, along with ways to link oversight findings and appropriations effectively and more formally. That linkage is now only informal and episodic, with some appropriators reaching out to other investigative panels and using their work as a basis for decisions on funding and on the language of reports, while others merely acknowledge oversight findings, as required by the rules.

Legislative proposals to focus funding criteria on risk, as opposed to more familiar geographic or population-based formulas, reflect a desire to establish measurable standards against which expenditures can be judged. Similarly, implementation of proposals requiring DHS to accelerate standards for preparedness and for first responders' capability would enable Congress to apply oversight criteria more systematically.

CONCLUSION

The 9/11 Commission concluded that "Congress needs dramatic change ... to strengthen oversight and focus accountability."[31] The commission (which was bipartisan but unanimous) said:

> The oversight function of Congress has diminished over time. In recent years, traditional review of the administration of programs and the implementation of laws has been replaced by "a focus on personal investigations, possible scandals, and issues designed to generate media attention." The unglamorous but essential work of oversight has been neglected, and few members past or present believe it is performed well.[32]

While the bulk of its criticism is aimed at intelligence oversight, the commission included homeland security in a more general indictment of Congress's balkanized approach to security issues. The commission recommended a single, principal point of oversight and review for homeland security in each house of Congress, preferably a standing committee with a nonpartisan staff.[33]

On January 4, 2005 Congress established a permanent standing committee on homeland security with authorizing authority over DHS and primary oversight authority. The move followed the 9/11 Commission's recommendation that both the House and the Senate should create a single, principal point of oversight and review for homeland security across the federal government. While falling short of that sweeping recommendation—which would include all aspects of immigration, Coast Guard, FBI, and intelligence—the change to the House Rules established a committee with primary jurisdiction over government-wide counterterrorism policy, and primary jurisdiction over the counterterrorism mission of the Department of Homeland Security. Rep. Christopher Cox, R-Calif., chair of the new committee called its creation "the most significant reorganization of national security, jurisdiction in the Congress in 58 years, since the creation of the Committee on Armed Services on January 2, 1947."

Unquestionably, oversight will be improved by having just one committee in each chamber responsible for DHS authorization, and one appropriations subcommittee responsible for allocating funds to DHS. The question remains whether that formulation can allow the robust oversight that the 9/11 Commission said was lacking. Partisanship remains a barrier. When passed through the prism of harsh partisanship, the illuminating power of oversight is refracted into clashing bands of color. Structural fixes alone will not repair the congressional oversight function without a corresponding consensus, or truce, to depoliticize inquiries about homeland security.

Oversight must overlap somewhat, in order to offer a more three-dimensional view of large, complex undertakings by the executive branch. Given the pervasiveness of homeland security issues, and the volume of unglamorous work to be done, it seems inevitable, and probably beneficial, that other committees will continue to engage in the oversight of counterterrorism and domestic security programs. But to meet the reform mandate of the 9/11 Commission, rules will have to be clarified, jurisdictions realigned, and greater purpose and focus brought to the broader oversight effort.

NOTES

1. Accessed 1 September 2004 at www.house.gov/.
2. Rules of the House of Representatives, Rule X, Clause 2 (d)(1); Rule XI, Clause 1 (d)(1).
3. Ibid., Clause 4 (c)(1) & (2).
4. Combating Terrorism: Federal Counterterrorism Spending (11 March 1999); Combating Terrorism: National Domestic Preparedness Office (26 May 1999); Combating Terrorism: National Guard Response Teams (23 June 1999); Combating Terrorism: Medical First Responders (22 September 1999); Combating Terrorism: Assessing the Terrorist Threat (20 October 1999); Combating Terrorism: Medical Stockpiles (8 March 2000); Combating Terrorism: Research Coordination (22 March 2000); Combating Terrorism: Domestic Preparedness (CT Field) (27 March 2000); Force Protection: DOD Chemical/Biological Defense Plan (2 May 2000); Force Protection: Individual Protective Equipment (21 June 2000); Combating Terrorism: Threats, Risk, and Priorities (20 July 2000); Biological Weapons Convention Protocol (13 September 2000); Combating Terrorism: National Strategy (26 March 2001); Combating Terrorism: Protecting Interests Abroad (3 April 2001); Combating Terrorism: Federal Response (Joint with Trans. Cmte.) (24 April 2001); Combating Terrorism: Medical Stockpiles (1 May 2001); Biological Weapons Convention Protocol (5 June 2001); Biological Weapons Convention Protocol (10 July 2001); Dark Winter (23 July 2001); Inter Agency Data Sharing and National Security (24 July 2001).
5. *The 9/11 Commission Report*, Final Report of the National Commission on Terrorist Attacks upon the United States (24 July 2004) at www.9-11commission.gov/, p. 106.
6. www.gpo.gov/nct/.

7. www.globalsecurity.org/security/library/report/2003/gilmore-commsion_vol5_15dec2003.htm.

8. Charter of U.S. Commission on National Security/Twenty-First Century, Department of Defense (2 September 1999).

9. National Commission on Terrorism (Bremer Commission), *Countering the Changing Threat of International Terrorism* (June 2000), accessed 15 September 2004 at www.mipt.org/bremerreport.asp.

10. Advisory Panel to Assess Domestic Response Capabilities for Terrorism Involving Weapons of Mass Destruction (Gilmore Commission), II. *Toward a National Strategy for Combating Terrorism* (15 December 2000), p. 17.

11. U.S. Commission on National Security/Twenty-First Century (Hart-Rudman Commission), III. *Road Map for National Security: Imperative for Change* (31 January 2001) at www.cfr.org/pdf/Hart-Rudman3.pdf, p. viii.

12. Ibid., p. 28.

13. Ibid.

14. Ibid., p. 112.

15. P.L. 107–296.

16. United States Government Accounting Office (GAO), Report to Congressional Requesters, *Homeland Security Key Elements to Unify Efforts Are Underway but Uncertainty Remains*, GAO-02-610 (June 2002) at www.gao.gov/.

17. Justice Stewart in *Jacobellis v. Ohio*, 378 U.S. 184, 197 (1964).

18. Congressional Research Service, Issue Brief: Terrorism and National Security—Issues and Trends, IB10119, 5 (October 2004).

19. Federal law contains two major definitions of terrorism. The criminal code defines international terrorism as activities that: "A. involve violent acts or acts dangerous to human life that are a violation of the criminal laws of the United States or of any State, or that would be a criminal violation if committed within the jurisdiction of the United States or of any State; B. appear to be intended—to intimidate or coerce a civilian population; to influence the policy of a government by intimidation or coercion; or to affect the conduct of a government by mass destruction, assassination, or kidnapping; and C. occur primarily outside the territorial jurisdiction of the United States, or transcend national boundaries in terms of the means by which they are accomplished, the persons they appear intended to intimidate or coerce, or the locale in which their perpetrators operate or seek asylum." A provision of the statutory title on U.S. foreign relations defines the terms somewhat differently, to mean: "(1) ... terrorism involving citizens or the territory of more than 1 country; (2) the term "terrorism" means premeditated, politically motivated violence perpetrated against noncombatant targets by subnational groups or clandestine agents; and (3) the term 'terrorist group' means any group practicing, or which has significant subgroups which practice, international terrorism."

20. "National Security: The Ultimate Turf War," *National Journal* (4 January 2003).

21. Ibid. Congressional committees with homeland security jurisdiction: Senate—Committee on Agriculture, Nutrition, and Forestry, Subcommittee on Marketing, Inspection, and Product Promotion, Subcommittee on Research, Nutrition, and General Legislation; Committee on Appropriations, Subcommittee on Agriculture, Rural Development, and Related Agencies, Subcommittee on Commerce, Justice, State, and the Judiciary, Subcommittee on Defense, Subcommittee on District of Columbia, Subcommittee on Energy and Water Development,

Subcommittee on Interior and Related Agencies, Subcommittee on Labor, Health and Human Services, Education, Subcommittee on Transportation, Subcommittee on Treasury and General Government, Subcommittee on Veterans, Housing and Urban Development; Committee on Armed Services, Subcommittee on Emerging Threats and Capabilities, Subcommittee on Personnel; Committee on Banking, Housing, and Urban Affairs, Subcommittee on Financial Institutions; Committee on Commerce, Science, and Transportation, Subcommittee on Aviation, Subcommittee on Communications, Subcommittee on Consumer Affairs, Foreign Commerce, and Tourism, Subcommittee on Oceans, Atmosphere, and Fisheries, Subcommittee on Science, Technology, and Space, Subcommittee on Surface Transportation and Merchant Marine; Committee on Energy and Natural Resources, Subcommittee on Energy, Subcommittee on National Parks, Subcommittee on Water and Power; Committee on Environment and Public Works, Subcommittee on Transportation, Infrastructure, and Nuclear Safety; Committee on Finance, Subcommittee on International Trade; Committee on Governmental Affairs, Subcommittee on International Security, Proliferation, and Federal Services, Subcommittee on Oversight of Government Management, Restructuring, and the District of Columbia; Committee on Health, Education, Labor, and Pensions, Subcommittee on Public Health; Committee on Judiciary, Subcommittee on Immigration, Subcommittee on Technology, Terrorism, and Government Information; Committee on Veterans' Affairs; Select Committee on Intelligence. *House*—Committee on Agriculture, Subcommittee on Livestock and Horticulture; Committee on Appropriations, Subcommittee on Agriculture, Rural Development, FDA, and Related Agencies, Subcommittee on Commerce, Justice, State, and the Judiciary, Subcommittee on Defense, Subcommittee on District of Columbia, Subcommittee on Energy and Water Development, Subcommittee on Interior, Subcommittee on Labor, Health and Human Services, and Education, Subcommittee on Transportation, Subcommittee on Treasury, Postal Service, and General Government, Subcommittee on VA, HUD, and Independent Agencies; Committee on Armed Services, Subcommittee on Military Research and Development; Committee on Energy and Commerce, Subcommittee on Commerce, Trade, and Consumer Protection, Subcommittee on Energy and Air Quality, Subcommittee on Health, Subcommittee on Oversight and Investigations; Committee on Financial Services, Subcommittee on Capital Markets, Insurance, and Government-Sponsored Enterprises; Committee on Government Reform, Subcommittee on National Security, Emerging Threats, and International Relations; Committee on Judiciary, Subcommittee on Crime, Terrorism, and Homeland Security, Subcommittee on Immigration, Border Security, and Claims; Committee on Resources, Subcommittee on National Parks, Recreation, and Public Lands; Committee on Science, Subcommittee on Energy, Subcommittee on Research; Committee on Transportation and Infrastructure, Subcommittee on Aviation, Subcommittee on Coast Guard and Maritime Transportation, Subcommittee on Economic Development, Public Buildings, and Emergency Management, Subcommittee on Railroads, Subcommittee on Water Resources and Environment; Committee on Veteran's Affairs, Subcommittee on Health; Committee on Ways and Means, Subcommittee on Trade; Committee on Permanent Select Committee on Intelligence, Subcommittee on Terrorism and Homeland Security.

22. www.fema.gov/pdf/rrr/frp/frp2003.pdf.
23. www.fas.org/irp/offdocs/pdd39_frp.htm.
24. 18 U.S.C. 2331.

25. Department of Defense Directive 3025.15, *Military Assistance to Civilian Authorities* (9 February 1997), p.1.

26. *Combating Terrorism: Spending on Governmentwide Programs Requires Better Management and Coordination* (GAO/NSIAD-98-93) (1 December 1997).

27. *Observations on Federal Spending to Combat Terrorism* (GAO-T-NSIAD-99-107) (11 March 1999).

28. Standing committees: Agriculture, Appropriations, Armed Services, Energy and Commerce, Financial Services, Government Reform, International Relations, Judiciary, Science, Transportation, Ways and Means. Select committees: Intelligence, Homeland Security.

29. U.S. House of Representatives, Select Committee on Homeland Security, accessed 8 October 2004 at hsc.house.gov/schedule.cfm.

30. U.S. General Accounting Office, *Status of Open Recommendations*, accessed 21 October 2004 at www.gao.gov/docdblite/openrecs.php?fy = &recflag = 2&query = 1&subhead = Homeland +Securit.

31. *9/11 Commission Report*, p. xv.

32. Ibid., p. 105.

33. Ibid., p. 421.

CHAPTER 18

The Department of Defense: Defending the Homeland and Defeating Enemies Abroad

Paul McHale
Assistant Secretary of Defense, Homeland Defense Office,
U.S. Department of Defense

INTRODUCTION

Protecting the United States homeland from attack is the highest priority of the Department of Defense (DOD). The department has the responsibility not merely to respond to enemies who attack the U.S. homeland but, more importantly, to deter and defeat them. In my judgment, the fundamental nature of the national security environment changed in many ways at the end of the twentieth century; the reality of that change was imposed brutally upon our nation on September 11, 2001. It has become tragically clear that asymmetric threats—transnational terrorist groups—can now acquire the destructive capacities that had only been associated with nation-states in the past. Emerging technology—such as weapons of mass destruction (WMD) technology—enables small groups of transnational terrorists, and even individuals, to possess the kind of destructive force that formerly required the collective resources of a country. After September 11 we recognized that, as the threat

---

Note: Mr. McHale would like to acknowledge the assistance of his staff in helping to research and prepare this chapter. Neither the U.S. government nor the Department of Defense nor any of its components endorses the McGraw-Hill Companies, Inc., David Kamien, *or The McGraw-Hill Homeland Security Handbook.*

had changed, our defenses had to change. Our defenses must now be equally capable of defeating hostile countries as well as the known and emerging asymmetric capabilities of transnational terrorist groups, in particular al-Qaida.

The concept of an active, layered defense, predicated on seizing the initiative from adversaries, underpins DOD's approach to national defense. Multiple barriers to attack must be deployed across the globe—in the forward regions, the approaches to the United States, in the U.S. homeland, and in the global commons. An effective homeland defense begins overseas. To implement such an active, layered defense, DOD must be capable of decisive power projection, bringing the fight to the terrorists where they live, train, plan, and recruit. A second line of defense also lies beyond the borders of the nation—combat operations in the air and maritime avenues of approach, where we will engage terrorists before they reach our borders. Within the United States, the Department of Homeland Security and the domestic law enforcement community are primarily responsible for countering terrorist threats; DOD stands ready to provide assets and capabilities in support of civil authorities, consistent with U.S. law. In addition, DOD is prepared to conduct combat operations within the United States when directed by the president or the secretary of defense. Examples of such missions include combat air patrols, U.S. Navy missions within our territorial waters, and land-based rapid response operations under extraordinary circumstances. And finally, an active, layered defense requires the ability to defend the global commons, such as space and cyberspace.

With a sense of urgency and focus, DOD continues to implement substantial improvements in homeland defense capabilities, in order to achieve and enhance the safety of our nation. There is no basis for complacency. We fully recognize that even though global terrorism has been dealt a severe blow, significant challenges still lie ahead. As President Bush has said, we may be safer, but we are not yet safe.

THE ROLE OF DEFENSE IN NATIONAL SECURITY

After 9/11, President Bush, Congress, and DOD moved quickly to establish new organizations focused on homeland security, homeland defense, and civil support: the Department of Homeland Security (DHS); the Office of the Assistant Secretary of Defense for Homeland Defense (OASD-HD); and the combatant command, U.S. Northern Command (NORTHCOM).

At the request of the secretary of defense, OASD-HD was established by Congress in the Bob Stump National Defense Authorization Act for Fiscal Year 2003. This act recognized the need for the secretary of defense to have a focal point for improving policy and providing guidance to combatant commanders regarding air, ground, and maritime defense of U.S. territory and the conduct of support to civilian authorities. As specified in the establishing statutory language, OASD-HD provides overall supervision of DOD's homeland defense activities.

On 1 October 2002, DOD activated NORTHCOM, with head-quarters in Colorado Springs, Colorado. This is the first combatant command with the primary mission to defend the land, sea, and air approaches to the United States. NORTHCOM conducts operations within its assigned area of responsibility to deter, prevent, and defeat threats and aggression aimed at the United States, its territories, and its interests. Accordingly, as directed by the president or secretary of defense, NORTHCOM directs military operations within its area of responsibility, to include combat operations. In addition, when directed by the president or secretary of defense, it provides military assistance to civil authorities to mitigate the results of disasters and catastrophes, including those resulting from an attack with weapons of mass destruction.

NORTHCOM's area of responsibility includes the continental United States, Alaska, Canada, Mexico, and the surrounding water out to approximately 500 nautical miles. The defense of Hawaii and U.S. territories and possessions in the Pacific remains the responsibility of U.S. Pacific Command (PACOM). The commander of NORTHCOM is also the commander of the binational U.S.-Canada North American Aerospace Defense Command (NORAD).

In the air domain, NORAD guards, patrols, and monitors the skies over Canada and the United States. Daily, the U.S. Air Force, U.S. Air Force Reserve, and Air National Guard secure the skies over major U.S. metropolitan areas, historic monuments, and critical national infrastructure. Since 9/11, these forces have executed more than 40,000 air defense sorties. During that period, planes have been scrambled from the ground or diverted from patrols to investigate suspicious aircraft about 2,000 times, as of mid-2005.

In the maritime domain, similarly, NORTHCOM and PACOM guard the sea approaches to the United States and work with the U.S. Coast Guard to patrol international waters and our territorial seas. Daily, the U.S. Navy monitors the blue-water approaches to our territorial seas, operating under new and expanded authority to interdict vessels potentially bearing terrorists or their weapons before they reach our shores. Further, under Operation Noble Eagle, naval maritime surveillance and engagement forces are designated for transfer to NORTHCOM's command and control when directed by the secretary of defense. We are working to ensure greater awareness in the maritime domain through sharing and, ultimately, fusing intelligence. This will assist the development of future maritime defense systems necessary to defeat transnational terrorists on the high seas, long before their reach can extend to American coastal waters.

In the land domain, the Homeland Security Act of 2002 assigns DHS the responsibility for the security of the nation's borders. That responsibility includes protecting our ports of entry; enforcing laws regarding immigration; ensuring the speedy, orderly, efficient flow of lawful traffic and commerce; and preventing terrorists and instruments of terrorism from penetrating our borders. DOD's role in this border security mission is to provide support to civil authorities, principally DHS, when appropriate. To that end, we are prepared to respond swiftly when required. For example, DOD has established and maintains "quick reaction forces" and "rapid reaction forces," which, when deployed, will operate under NORTHCOM's command and control. These highly trained U.S. Army and Marine Corps personnel are positioned to respond to the full range of potential threats to the United States.

In the event of an attack with WMD on U.S. territory, Joint Task Force Civil Support (with headquarters in Norfolk, Virginia), Joint Task Force Consequence Management East (with headquarters at Fort Gillem, Georgia), and Joint Task Force Consequence Management West (with headquarters at Fort Sam Houston, Texas), under the command and control of NORTHCOM, are charged with providing consequence management support to civil authorities. Also, the Joint Force Headquarters National Capital

Region (JFHQ-NCR) has been established to conduct planning and to direct the military response in defense of our nation's capital.

NORTHCOM, as an evolving unified command, continues to address the challenge of intelligence sharing and interoperable communications systems to include communication with other agencies at the federal, state, and local level. NORTHCOM and NORAD are both working to improve our air defense system and to explore the development of collaborative approaches to maritime and land security.

DOD applies the "total force" concept to ensure that the right forces with the right tools are used for the right missions. The active and reserve components are both fundamental to fighting expeditionary wars and to homeland defense. The seven reserve components (Army National Guard, Army Reserve, Marine Corps Reserve, Navy Reserve, Air National Guard, Air Force Reserve, and Coast Guard Reserve) now make up almost 50 percent of the total force and are a partner in all military operations. The National Guard, in particular, is well suited for homeland defense missions. National Guard forces are uniquely positioned to act within the United States and its territories by virtue of their geographic dispersal and their relationship to state and local governments. The National Guard plays a critical role in the planning for, and any response to, future terrorist attacks in the United States, including "mass-casualty" attacks. It is no accident that a National Guard general officer serves as NORTHCOM's chief of staff.

Developing clear, coherent agreements and relationships between combatant commands and state and territorial National Guard organizations was a top priority for DOD following the establishment of NORTHCOM. To accomplish their homeland defense and civil support missions, NORTHCOM and PACOM coordinate closely with the 54 state and territorial National Guard organizations through the National Guard Bureau.

It is important to understand that relationships between combatant commands with homeland defense support to civil authorities missions and the National Guard are not static. They are based on specific scenarios and the particular legal authorities invoked in managing a contingency.

In addition to active duty forces, the president or the secretary of defense may authorize the use of activated National Guard forces in federal status, also known as Title 10 status (federal control, federal funding). The commander of NORTHCOM would have direct command-and-control authority over such forces assigned to NORTHCOM, as would the commander of PACOM in that area of responsibility.

NORTHCOM and PACOM have no command-and-control relationship with the National Guard when these forces are in state active duty (state control, state funding) or in Title 32 status (state control, federal funding). Under both of these circumstances National Guard forces are under the exclusive command and control of the state governor. In either status, members of the National Guard are not subject to the provisions of the Posse Comitatus Act and may engage in activities related to law enforcement if authorized to do so under applicable state law.

In the event of a domestic attack, forces under state command and control and federal forces under the command and control of NORTHCOM or PACOM could find themselves operating within a common area. Unity of effort requires close coordination and cooperation among all forces, even if they are not part of the same command structure. The commanders of NORTHCOM and PACOM, the National Guard Bureau, the Army, the Air Force, and other relevant components of DOD are currently working to refine such unity of effort in the domestic context. Unity of effort is also an inherent element of NORTHCOM's exercise program.

THE COMMITMENT OF DEFENSE TO MISSION ASSURANCE

DOD is committed to maintaining the readiness of military forces to execute the full spectrum of homeland defense operations and to support civil authorities when needed. To this end, DOD has hosted exercises or participated in exercises sponsored by other government entities. Exercise scenarios have addressed a range of potential threats to the United States, including cyberattacks, bioterrorism, radiological attacks, and a large-scale nuclear detonation. Such exercises support the DHS National Homeland Security Exercise Program established by Homeland Security Presidential Directive 8 on National Preparedness (HSPD-8, December 2003). DOD's recent exercises for homeland defense and civil support involving interagency and international partners include Unified Defense '04 and Determined Promise '03, the second in a series of exercises designed to evaluate and enhance NORTHCOM's ability to manage multiple operations in homeland defense and civil support.

Within DOD, OASD-HD is also responsible for the continuity of DOD's operations and DOD's support to the continuity of government (COG) mission—the ability of the federal government to carry out its constitutional responsibilities in the event of a national emergency or catastrophe. These responsibilities include planning for enduring communications capabilities to ensure national command and control of military forces as well as the execution of crisis management functions.

DEFENSE AND CRITICAL INFRASTRUCTURE

Public Law 107–296 (the Homeland Security Act of 2002) assigned DHS the responsibility for developing a comprehensive national plan to protect our nation's critical infrastructure and important assets. The National Strategy to Secure Cyberspace (February 2003) and the National Strategy for the Physical Protection of Critical Infrastructure and Key Assets (February 2003), as well as Homeland Security Presidential Directive 7 on Critical Infrastructure Identification, Prioritization, and Protection (HSPD-7, December 2003), designate DOD as the Sector Specific Agency for the Defense Industrial Base. This designation recognizes DOD's important role in the protection of critical infrastructure, which sustains our capability to defend our nation and fight its wars. In this capacity, DOD must work closely with private-sector owners of critical defense infrastructure and assets to deter, mitigate, or neutralize terrorist attacks in order to sustain military operations.

In September 2003, OASD-HD was assigned the responsibility for Defense Critical Infrastructure Protection (CIP) by the secretary of defense. A newly established Defense Program Office for Mission Assurance consolidates CIP funding and conducts focused research and development using a systems approach for CIP activities supporting DOD missions. We have also taken steps to protect critical defense installations and facilities from chemical, biological, radiological, and nuclear threats, to include development of DOD-wide installation protection standards and requirements for application at key installations over the next few years.

This is an immense undertaking because defense infrastructure is obviously a complex, interdependent, decentralized network of systems, services, people, and processes. Defense infrastructure includes private-sector and other government functions, crosses organizational and political boundaries, and provides goods and services to meet DOD-wide operational and business requirements. It is composed of assets that provide the operational and technical capabilities essential to mobilize, deploy, and sustain military operations in peacetime and during a war. DOD must ensure that national and international infrastructure dependencies do not adversely affect the military's ability to fulfill its mission of national defense and global force projection.

DOD is generally concerned with two main classes of infrastructure and assets. The first includes infrastructure and assets owned by DOD that support the National Defense Strategy. The second includes non-DOD infrastructures and assets that support the National Defense Strategy:

- The Defense Industrial Base (DIB) provides defense-related products and services that are essential to mobilize, deploy, and sustain military operations.
- Selected civil and commercial infrastructure provides the power, communications, transportation, and other utilities that DOD war fighters and support organizations must rely on to meet their respective operational needs.

Although critical industries, services, and systems may be found in both the public and the private sector, DHS estimates that more than 85 percent fall within the private sector. In the private sector, asset owners have an inherent responsibility to protect their infrastructure. This constitutes the first level of protection. As the threat escalates, local authorities will assist the asset owner in meeting protective responsibilities, the second level of protection. If the response from local authorities does not provide the necessary protection, state or federal law enforcement authorities may be brought in to address the situation, the third level. In more serious situations, a state governor may request federal support or employ the National Guard under his or her command and control to enhance protection. At the fifth level, the president may direct the employment of U.S. military forces to protect threatened DIB assets.

Certain critical infrastructures and resources in the private sector, although not required to support DOD missions, are so vital that their incapacitation, exploitation, or destruction could have a debilitating effect on the nation's security and economic well-being. Federal departments and agencies will take necessary measures to identify, prioritize, and protect these critical assets. For example, on 18 February 2004 DHS announced that it was launching the Protected Critical Infrastructure Information (PCII) program. PCII enables the private sector to voluntarily submit information about infrastructure to the federal government to assist in reducing the United States' vulnerability to terrorist attacks. Identification and protection of these national assets and high-profile national special security events is a joint responsibility, with DHS in the lead. DOD works closely with DHS to ensure that DOD's capabilities are leveraged to support national security concerns.

In a comprehensive effort, DOD has developed a CIP risk-management strategy, composed of five major elements: metrics, information sharing, burden sharing for fixing vulnerabilities, and approaches to program acceleration, as well as education and training. Each element contributes to managing the risks to DOD's critical infrastructure and to providing mission assurance or protection for infrastructures and assets critical to DOD's missions or to national security. DOD, DHS, and other interagency partners are continuing to work closely together to enable the successful implementation of the strategy. We fully recognize the necessity of ensuring resolution in these areas. Such an integrated approach is necessary to ensure that, in the event of an attack, military commanders and DOD policy makers are able to effectively manage the consequences of cascading infrastructure failures.

DEFENSE AND CIVIL AUTHORITIES

DOD has a long tradition of support to civil authorities, while maintaining its primary mission of fighting and winning the nation's wars. DOD continues to lend assistance to civil authorities when they are overwhelmed or faced with challenges necessitating DOD's unique capabilities. From January 2004 to December 2004 the DOD acted on 99 requests for assistance from more than 20 civilian agencies, including DHS; the departments of Justice, Health and Human Services, Transportation, and State; the National Air and Space Administration (NASA); the U.S. Marshals Service; and the National Interagency Fire Center. For example, the DOD provided support to communities in New Mexico that needed water supplies; gave assistance in firefighting to western states; and supported relief to Florida after four hurricanes in 2004.

Additionally, in 2004 DOD successfully assisted civil authorities with the conduct of national special security events, including the president's State of the Union address in January; the Super Bowl in Houston in February; the G8 Economic Summit at Sea Island, Georgia, in June; the U.S. Olympic track and field trials in Sacramento, California, in June; and the Olympic Games in Greece in August. DOD also supported both the Democratic and the Republican national conventions and the UN General Assembly in October.

THE HOMELAND SECURITY COUNCIL

The president established the Office of Homeland Security (OHS) and the Homeland Security Council (HSC) on 8 October 2001 to develop and implement a comprehensive national strategy against terrorist threats. DOD coordinates with the assistant to the president for homeland security, and any staff, as appropriate. The secretary of defense is, along with the president, vice president, secretary of homeland security, attorney general, and other cabinet officials, a member of HSC. DOD worked closely with OHS from October 2001 to March 2003, and it continues to do so with its successor, the HSC staff.

The assistant secretary of defense for homeland defense is DOD's principal representative to the HSC staff and represents DOD at committee meetings of HSC's principals and deputies. OASD-HD represents DOD on HSC's interagency policy coordination committees (PCCs) and in subordinate working groups, with the participation of other DOD offices as appropriate. HSC has become a key forum for interagency communication on homeland security and homeland defense, including the evaluation of terrorist threats and the development of responses to crises. For example, HSC worked effectively throughout the tense weeks of a code orange alert during the December holiday season in 2003 and through an elevated-threat period through the November 2004 presidential election.

INTELLIGENCE AND INFORMATION SHARING

DOD works closely with elements of the intelligence community to maintain maximum awareness of potential attacks against and emerging threats to the United States. OASD-HD engages actively with the undersecretary of defense for intelligence—USD(I)—established in 2003 by Public Law 107–314, on all matters of intelligence regarding homeland defense. USD(I) is charged with ensuring that the senior DOD leadership receives the warning, actionable intelligence, and counterintelligence support needed to pursue all the objectives of the updated defense strategy, including defense of the homeland. USD(I) also provides a single point of contact for coordination of national and military intelligence activities with the community management staff under the director of Central Intelligence (DCI) and strengthens the relationship between DCI and the secretary of defense.

Additionally, DOD is a full partner in the National Counterterrorism Center (NCTC), a multiagency joint venture launched by Executive Order 13354, dated 27 August 2004. The NCTC serves as the primary organization in the United States for analyzing and integrating all intelligence related to terrorism, conducts strategic operational planning for counterterrorism activities, and, while serving as the central knowledge bank on known and suspected terrorists, ensures that agencies have access to intelligence support. On a daily basis, NCTC coordinates assessments of terrorist threats with its partner agencies, including DOD, DHS, the Federal Bureau of Investigation (FBI), the Central Intelligence Agency (CIA), and the Department of State.

USD(I) is working with DHS and other federal departments and agencies to perform the tasks set forth by Executive Order 13311, Homeland Security Information Sharing (July 2003), to establish procedures for the horizontal sharing of information between federal agencies and the vertical sharing of information with authorities at the state and local levels. We are likewise supporting intelligence initiatives contained in the executive orders issued by President Bush in August 2004 to address recommendations of the 9/11 Commission.

THE PARTNERSHIP OF DEFENSE AND DHS

DOD's responsibility for homeland defense focuses on the protection of the United States' sovereignty, territory, domestic population, and critical defense infrastructure against external threats and aggression, or other threats as directed by the president. It also includes routine, steady-state activities designed to deter aggressors and to prepare U.S. military forces for action if deterrence fails. DHS, by contrast, focuses on homeland security, which is defined in *National Strategy for Homeland Security* (2002) as "a concerted national effort to prevent terrorist attacks within the United States, reduce the vulnerability of the United States to terrorism, and minimize the damage and assist in the recovery from terrorist attacks."

In simpler terms, DOD provides the military defense of our nation against attacks by foreign enemies, including hostile nation-states and transnational terrorists, while DHS protects the nation against, and prepares for, acts of terrorism within or attempting to penetrate the United States. DOD is also prepared, at the direction of the president and the secretary of defense, to play a vital role in support of the DHS mission, with a particular focus on chemical, biological, radiological, nuclear, or high-yield explosive (CBRNE) consequence management.

The two departments have worked closely together since the establishment of DHS in 2002. Under a memorandum of agreement, DOD provides on a detail basis some 64 personnel to DHS to fill critical specialties, principally in the areas of communications and intelligence. We have also established a 24/7 DOD presence in the DHS Homeland Security Operations Center with a direct connection back to DOD for rapid response and a DOD advisory and liaison office—the Homeland Defense Coordination Office— within DHS headquarters. Additionally, we established planning teams to assist the DHS Interagency Incident Management Group, consisting of senior interagency officials who focus on "incident response."

Public Law 107–396 (Homeland Security Act of 2002), Section 502, directed DHS to consolidate existing federal emergency response plans—the Federal Response Plan, the U.S. Government Interagency Domestic Terrorism CONOPS Plan, the National Contingency Plan, and the Federal Radiological Emergency Response Plan—into a single, coordinated National Response Plan. According to Homeland Security Presidential Directive 5 (HSPD-5), "the Secretary of Homeland Security is the principal federal official for domestic incident management." DOD has been fully engaged in the interagency development of the National Response Plan and the National Incident Management System.

TECHNOLOGY TRANSFER

In accordance with Section 1401 of Public Law 107–314, the Assistant Secretary of Defense for Homeland Defense (ASD-HD) serves as the "Senior official of the Department of Defense to coordinate all Department of Defense efforts to identify, evaluate, deploy, and transfer to Federal, State, and local first responder technology items and equipment in support of homeland security." Recent examples of technology transfer initiatives include information-sharing systems, such as the Disaster Management Interoperability Services; biometrics identification technologies; ground sensors and their application in border security; and unmanned aerial vehicle experimentation. Additionally, new efforts in Advanced Concept Technology Demonstration (ACTD) are under way that have the potential to deliver capabilities supporting both DOD missions abroad and DHS missions at home. These include the high-altitude airship, a prototype untethered platform that could provide wide area surveillance and communications capabilities, and air transportable cargo screening, designed to detect explosive threats in pallet cargo loads moving through military transportation systems.

Finally, DOD invests nearly $100 million yearly in the Technical Support Working Group (TSWG), a U.S. national forum that brings together more than 85 federal agencies, including DHS, to identify, prioritize, and coordinate interagency and international research and development requirements for combating terrorism. TSWG rapidly develops technologies and equipment to meet the high-priority needs of the combating terrorism community. These technologies typically are also applicable to first responders and other homeland security missions.

Funding for TSWG has increased from $8 million in fiscal year (FY) 1992 to approximately $180 million in FY 2003. This increase reflects heightened concern over terrorist activity and a perceived need to accelerate the development of technology to effectively address the threat. DOD provides the bulk of funding for TSWG's activities. The Department of State contributes annually to TSWG's core funding, while other departments and agencies share the costs of selected projects and provide personnel to act as project managers and technical advisors. To date, TSWG has successfully "transitioned" capabilities to the departments of Agriculture, Defense, Justice, State, and Treasury; the intelligence community;

the Transportation Security Administration; the Public Health Service; and other departments and agencies.

CONCLUSION

Throughout the history of the United States, its military forces—active-duty and reserves—have defended our country against enemies on land, at sea, and in the air, adapting continuously to address specific threats. Today we face a particularly serious challenge. We must cope not only with the threat of adversarial nation-states and the proliferation of weapons of mass destruction and missile technology but also with asymmetric threats posed by individual terrorists and transnational terrorist organizations.

Abraham Lincoln said, "As our cause is new, we must think and act anew." DOD is continuously transforming itself to improve agility, flexibility, technical knowledge, and operational capabilities designed to execute an effective homeland defense, while continuing its long-standing tradition of support to civil authorities. We are finalizing a comprehensive strategy of homeland defense and civil support for the twenty-first century, the first such strategy in American history. This strategy will support the National Security Strategy, the National Strategy for Homeland Security, and the National Defense Strategy. It will also provide a framework for pursuing operational capabilities to prepare for tomorrow's challenges.

The citizens, institutions, and armed forces of the United States have repeatedly demonstrated patriotism, toughness, innovation, resilience, and a determination to defeat our enemies while retaining an unwavering commitment to our freedoms. Although there is little doubt that we will be sobered and challenged by this newest threat, there must be no doubt that we will prevail.

CHAPTER 19

Emergency Planning: The Evolving Role of Regional Planning Organizations in Supporting Cities and Counties

David Robertson
Executive Director, Metropolitan Washington Council
of Governments

Planners have long been responsible for helping to shape the communities they serve, but do they have a role in emergency planning and preparedness? In many regions across the country, the answer is yes. In typical years, work programs have traditionally focused on projects to improve transportation infrastructures, protect the environment, and enhance housing and community services. But 9/11 changed the role of many planning organizations in their communities, shifting the focus to public safety and security.

The challenges of this new role quickly became clear to municipalities in the National Capital Region (NCR). Regional coordination was essential, and both the necessity of, and the obstacles to, developing a regionwide system for cooperation became evident to the Metropolitan Washington Council of Governments (COG), an agency representing the diverse interests of 19 governments in three states.

9/11

The mutual aid agreements that had already been developed under COG's auspices were put to use on 9/11, when the Pentagon was attacked. One of COG's oldest programs, a mutual aid and support system for local police and firefighters, allowed first responders to cross jurisdictional lines in an organized way to help one another.

On 9/11 there were attempts to bridge communication gaps among local officials, but other gaps appeared between federal, state, and local officials at the site of the attack. Some of the police and fire officials were using incompatible radios, phones, and pagers. Gridlock ensued on the roads because of a lack of coordination in releasing federal office workers. The Office of Personnel Management released 180,000 federal employees without realizing that the U.S. Secret Service had cordoned off streets around the White House, the Department of State, and Capitol Hill. When workers headed home to Maryland and Virginia, they found two of the major thoroughfares closed. Commuters who decided to walk home found the sidewalks overcrowded.

COG contacted local officials from around the region and sponsored a conference call that resulted in a joint decision to close schools and many offices the next day. This decision eased the minds of many families and underscored the critical importance of regional communication to safety and security. But the conference call did not take place until six o'clock in the evening, more than 10 hours after the attack. The region was unable to get the appropriate leaders on call quickly; and no procedure was in place to share accurate information with them instantly, or to communicate to the public.

Local governments realized that terrorism and disasters do not respect municipal or state lines and that a lack of interjurisdictional communication could perilously impede the communication of vital information to officials and the public. Combating threats to security would require innovative solutions. Thus municipal leaders invited state and federal officials to join them on a new Task Force on Homeland Security at COG. The task force later became the Emergency Preparedness Council and now assists local governments, state agencies, and key federal officials in prioritizing and implementing regional emergency plans, coordinating new resources and technologies, and conducting exercises and training.

A NEW REGIONAL PLAN

The task force's first responsibility was to develop a regional emergency coordination plan (RECP) that would draw on traditional planning roles, access to data, and technical tools to eliminate problems of communication and coordination. Such a plan had no precedent and so was costly and time-consuming to develop.

COG's initial financial support was a $75,000 award from the Washington Regional Association of Grant Makers; later there was a $5 million appropriation from the federal government.

By pooling staff resources from multiple agencies, COG delivered the final RECP on 11 September 2002. At its core was an understanding that effective regional coordination goes beyond individual roles of participating local governments, and emergency management involves more than just public safety organizations. RECP has become an important resource for coordinating responses to any hazard or threat and now involves businesses, transportation and health entities, utilities, educators, volunteer groups, and government officials at all levels.

As the task force began its meetings, the federal Office of Homeland Security was established, so the group saw the importance of aligning any plans with the structure used by the government. It addressed 12 specific emergency support functions (ESFs) based on the response plan developed by the Federal Emergency Management Agency (FEMA). The ESFs included transportation, mass care, food, donations, managing volunteers, and dealing with hazardous materials. COG's task force added law enforcement, media relations, and community outreach.

To create a plan encompassing two states and the District of Columbia, municipalities first had to identify—and agree on—the "go-to" agencies and organizations implied by the ESFs to help assemble information needed for each sector. This entailed a fundamental shift in the way the region's stakeholders would be determined during preparation for emergencies. Cities and counties would be supported by planning organizations not as separate entities but as part of a larger group. For COG, the planning process involved all member jurisdictions as well as emergency management agencies, road and transit entities, schools, utility companies, medical institutions, community associations, and volunteer organizations. The new plan was to prepare the region not only for terrorism but also for any emergencies, including natural disasters (e.g., tornadoes and snowstorms), major transportation incidents, and widespread power outages.

The task force was organized into six major functional areas: (1) transportation, (2) health, (3) communications, (4) solid waste and debris management, (5) public safety, and (6) energy and water supply. Health, for example, included plans for public health services as well as private-sector organizations such as hospitals and the American Red Cross. Later, an emergency evacuation annex was added, with procedures for sheltering in place (remaining safely indoors during a bioterrorist attack). Other comprehensive guidelines were for mass care, food supplies, law enforcement, volunteer management, community outreach, and communication.

The Emergency Preparedness Council inspired new procedures for joint decision making among stakeholders spread throughout the region. After the initial strategic preparedness plan was in place, senior officials representing various agencies and COG member jurisdictions began regular meetings of committees formed to discuss and update each emergency support function of the plan. A communication system was also put in place, to be used when in-person meetings were impossible because of inclement weather or other factors.

COMMUNICATION CAPABILITIES

An important part of implementing RECP is the use of modern technology to communicate effectively. A new Regional Incident Communication and Coordination System (RICCS) provides timely notification of emergencies or regional incidents.

RICCS is built on the Roam Secure Alert Network, a software emergency communication system used by governments, emergency management agencies, and first responders to send alerts and updates to cell phones, pagers, PDAs, and e-mail accounts. It is meant to facilitate coordination and communication among government authorities and ensure an effective response to emergencies. It is managed through emergency operations centers 24 hours a day, seven days a week, allowing decision makers and experts to be notified of incidents, share information, and coordinate decisions. RICCS-assisted communication focuses on dealing with the effects of an emergency on regional transportation and public health and safety. Examples of collaborative messages include notifying the public of evacuation routes and of nearby shelters, activating special teams within local communities, and notifying public officials of conference calls.

Throughout the development of a regional plan and communication system, it became clear that local governments would need to alter individual approaches to preparedness and encompass cooperative methods. In emergency planning, each stakeholder would begin to have equal footing with its neighbors. Thus COG came to oversee 80 percent of the infrastructure required in emergency response and recovery in NCR. Such administration is necessary because the key players vary depending on the nature of each incident. The plan created through COG has local decision makers working with federal authorities, state officials, and the private sector.

This concentration on combating terrorism as a region in metropolitan Washington became part of a larger federal policy that resulted in appropriations to first responders in individual jurisdictions and counties. In 2004 a report from the Government Accountability Office (GAO) stated that the most effective responses are not jurisdiction-specific but coordinated and planned across regions. GAO's study of six metropolitan areas found that including a wide range of stakeholders greatly increased the ability to solve shared problems. The report stressed regional planning organizations and the development of strategic plans with quantifiable goals for preparedness.

The importance of bringing together participants from 19 jurisdictions became clear as RECP and RICCS were put to use. Disasters and events have rarely affected just one entity, but instead tend to ripple from one city or county to the next.

This is true for most metropolitan areas, where the downtown area is relatively close to the suburbs. Tropical storms that caused flooding in Alexandria also affected residents of the District of Columbia who commuted there. A sniper attack in northern Montgomery County in Maryland spread fear and a call for law enforcement throughout the region down to Virginia. Planning for routes to evacuate residents during an emergency would require input from various governments and agencies, as would decisions regarding public health policies. For these reasons, the role of regional planning organizations in supporting cities and counties is changing rapidly.

COLLABORATIVE DECISION MAKING

In emergencies caused by weather, traffic incidents, political demonstrations, or terrorism, planners in NCR can use RICCS to arrange a conference call. They can discuss whether local schools and offices will remain open, and they can quickly develop unified messages regarding public health and evacuation.

During the sniper attacks of 2002, senior officials from around the region were able to use RECP and RICCS to make a unified decision to have schools remain open with increased security (see case study 1, below). Officials were also able to quickly unify a message asking for public support that eventually led to the arrest of John Allen Muhammad and Lee Boyd Malvo.

Within one year after 9/11, decisions regarding response to disasters were being made far more quickly, competently, and—most important—effectively.

OBSTACLES

The new plan in Washington, D.C. had to surmount barriers that could confront any regional planning organization. The greatest initial challenge for COG was creating a strong administrative plan that would not be seen as interfering with the ability of states, cities, and counties to administer their own emergency plans during a terrorist attack or another disaster. To forestall problems, EPC created a plan that would help COG jurisdictions coordinate activities such as communications while leaving implementation of the separate state, city, and county emergency operations plans to the discretion of state and local authorities.

Similar consideration must be given to managerial plans already in place in various jurisdictions. GAO has noted that in such circumstances collaboration can be beneficial, by integrating the plans of various agencies and municipalities. Such was the case in Dallas–Fort Worth, where Dallas contracted with the North Central Texas Council of Governments to develop a strategy for using federal funds. Similar efforts take place in the Washington, D.C., area through COG's chief administrative officers' committee and the Office of National Capital Region Coordination in the Department of Homeland Security (DHS).

REGIONAL PLANNING AT THE MUNICIPAL LEVEL

In a crisis, there is a tremendous need for communication among local first responders, policy makers, and the state and federal sectors.

The administrative framework for regional communications is necessary for regional coordination but is difficult to accomplish.

NCR's new emergency plan has been used many times since 9/11 and has proved effective on several occasions. The incident command center was valuable during the sniper shootings in 2002, a snowstorm in early 2003, and dangerous weather created by hurricane Isabel. The system has been utilized to notify officials of events such as demonstrations in downtown Washington and the failure at the wastewater treatment plant; in some cases, these communications have been credited with saving lives.

CASE STUDY 1: SNIPER

In October 2002, a mysterious sniper opened fire on civilians in 12 separate, deadly attacks. The shootings began in Silver Spring, Maryland, a suburb 14 miles north of downtown Washington. The attacks terrorized the entire region, spreading to the District of Columbia and to jurisdictions in suburban Maryland and northern Virginia.

Throughout this episode, the region's chief administrators, law enforcement, and school officials used conference calls arranged through RICCS to coordinate decisions on school closings and community activities. Should schools close? How should drivers react to traffic delays created by police roadblocks? Conference calls took place almost daily to monitor the unfolding events in Silver Spring and Rockville, Maryland; the District of Columbia; and Falls Church and other parts of Virginia. Officials from the affected areas joined authorities from COG's other member jurisdictions and participating agencies, who were alerted about the many communications calls through RICCS. The alerts were sent to participants, instructing them to call a common number at a specified time.

The system was extensively used and allowed police, school, and community officials from several jurisdictions to discuss their plans in real time and evaluate the effect their actions would have on the entire region. As a result, the officials avoided having to make critical decisions under the glare of television lights, in front of an already frightened public. By the time John Allen Muhammad and Lee Boyd Malvo were arrested after a three-week shooting spree, this tool for regional emergencies and incidents had been reported on national news: Montgomery County's police chief, Charles Moose, mentioned it in a press conference.

CASE STUDY 2 : HURRICANE ISABEL

The forecasts regarding hurricane Isabel in September 2003 were so ominous that the U.S. military deployed ships and aircraft when Isabel made landfall in North Carolina, as a category 2 hurricane, and wreaked havoc on the coast. As it headed toward Washington, D.C., officials prepared for possible calamities well in advance.

RICCS was essential throughout this episode. Stakeholders collaborated, sharing the steps they were taking to prepare for the hurricane, and how they were going to handle school and office closings. RICCS made it easy for the National Weather Service to join an important conference call that included regional chief administrative officers, emergency management directors, federal officials, school superintendents, and public transit authorities. During that call, the weather service notified participants that the storm would hit with winds of at least 40 miles per hour by midafternoon the following day, 18 September 2003.

The decisions prompted by that call were thought by many to have protected residents and saved lives. The Washington Metropolitan Area Transit Authority (Metro) advised that with such powerful winds, the system could not operate safely; it alerted the public that it would close all train and bus services beginning at eleven in the morning, so riders would be able to get home by one o'clock in the afternoon, before the worst of the storm. The decision to shut Metro down in the interest of public safety was made multilaterally after all city and county officials joined in a discussion about local suburban feeder systems, Metrorail schedules, and the expected timing of the unsafe conditions.

Similarly, governments, schools, and businesses coordinated their reactions. Each individual decision was made separately, but with full knowledge of the actions taken by surrounding jurisdictions and businesses. The result was consistent, coordinated decisions across the region: members of the public were advised to stay home as school systems and governments closed.

Although Isabel had been downgraded to a tropical storm by the time it actually hit the region, it still downed trees and caused floods and extensive power outages. Flash floods forced the evacuation of thousands of local residents, and presidential disaster declarations were issued for the District of Columbia and most of Maryland and Virginia. In the following days, stakeholders continued to come together for discussions of school and office closings, damage, and methods being implemented to handle aftereffects of the storm.

The need for a supporting agency to guide regional coordination was made clear by the successful use of RICCS. Not a single death occurred in the region as a result of Isabel.

LESSONS LEARNED
Benefits of Regional Coordination

In the months after 9/11, advanced domestic security measures were viewed as a necessity. As plans for preparedness were developed, the benefits of regional cooperation became clear to municipalities and their planning organizations. In many cases, working jointly opened the door to greater funding for cities and counties, gave access to new technologies and equipment, improved training capabilities, and enhanced the ability to react and make decisions.

After Congress passed the budget for fiscal year 2003, DHS's Office of Domestic Preparedness made billions of dollars available to local public sectors working together to protect communities. Today, there is an Urban Area Security Initiative (UASI) allowing for greater access to funding for regional planning. Through this program and the State Homeland Security Grant Program, nearly $4 billion was distributed in 2003 alone to state and local governments to help first responders and to offset local governments' costs associated with extra security measures needed to prevent, respond to, and recover from terrorism and disasters. UASI funds totaling $1.4 billion were provided to address the unique needs for equipment, training, planning, and exercises in urban areas at high risk. At the core of the federal department's mission is a declaration that "funding the capabilities of local first responders requires a strategy of shared responsibility, shared accountability, and shared leadership."

In NCR, regional coordination led to a grant by UASI of about $60.5 million in fiscal year 2003 and $29 million in fiscal year 2004. The funds were dedicated to various security measures that had not previously been available to COG's member jurisdictions, such as domestic preparedness training exercises and a campaign for educating citizens. The UASI funds allowed for the purchase of personal protective equipment for first responders in participating cities and counties, as well as a regional supply of 800-megahertz radios allowing firefighters and police responding to emergencies from outside the area to communicate quickly and directly across jurisdictional lines. Recognizing the need for the cities and counties that are today an important part of the nation's capital to come together, Congress appropriated a combined $300 million in 2001 alone for the District of Columbia, northern Virginia, and suburban Maryland—and for Metro to buy equipment and improve safety for residents and visitors.

GAO, in its report of 2004, heralded the distribution of UASI grants to address regional emergency preparedness. The federal government, it says, should continue to provide funds as an incentive for developing strategic plans with measurable goals and objectives, much as metropolitan planning organizations mandated by federal law have been doing for years. Regional working groups like COG's Emergency Preparedness Council and the chief administrative officers' committees are best able to handle the coordination needed to secure federal funding and determine its use.

Comprehensive training also has been made available for first responders throughout the region. A new goal for the U.S. Fire Administration is to train state and regional incident management teams (IMTs) for large-scale, high-impact disasters through a new all-hazards approach. COG was able to coordinate the nation's first all-hazards regional IMT to include several states through its fire chiefs' committee, a group that includes members from the Federal Bureau of Investigation (FBI), DHS, and Washington's naval district as well as chiefs of member agencies' fire departments. Pilot training for the course through COG began in April 2004.

Another benefit of regional emergency planning (as noted in the two case studies above) is the development of new procedures and shared tools that enable immediate decisions and actions. Following the implementation of RICCS, the need for a second, more specialized system led to another tool to help the area's public information officers (PIOs) unify messages. A virtual Joint Information Center was created in the summer of 2004 as a secure Web-based portal allowing regional representatives to share information in real time during emergencies. The customized site includes pages of information specific to the needs of PIOs, such as maps, shared documents, and round-the-clock contact with all participants.

CONTINUING CHALLENGES

The initial stages of domestic preparedness were put in place by DHS after 9/11, but the role of planning organizations continually evolves as solutions are revealed for each new or recurring challenge. Ideally, stakeholders with different interests would find a middle ground for agreement at the close of each conference call, meeting, or virtual encounter. But in practice, interjurisdictional consensus-building is often delayed by foreseen or unpredictable complications. A successful multijurisdictional approach to preparedness is often the product of numerous meetings, discussions, and compromises.

With few exceptions, the power given to cities and counties is determined by the states. Therefore, emergency planners and decision makers in one municipality can connect with nearby towns and cities much more easily when all of them are located in the same state. In metropolitan areas such as New York, Los Angeles, Cincinnati, St. Louis, and Washington, D.C., the process of preparing government authorities, emergency personnel, and health officials for emergencies entails dealing with different laws. This is especially significant in planning for bioterrorist attacks or public health incidents, which may involve problems such as the need for physicians to practice in states other than the state where they have credentials—a situation that may leave these physicians unprotected against claims of malpractice.

There is no quick way to unify conflicting laws. The only practical way to deal with the complex issues is through regional councils and similar groups, where attorneys, health officials, police officers, firefighters, and other decision makers can come together to determine the best solutions for specific areas. Convening stakeholders from neighboring jurisdictions to determine the best practices for emergency planning may be necessary even in areas where no planning organization exists. At COG, determinations are made through various committees, such as a public safety policy committee, an attorneys' committee, and a health officers' committee. (The last of these has developed a regionwide system to track diseases and their early symptoms; this committee includes pharmacists, representatives of hospital emergency rooms and medical schools, veterinarians, laboratory technicians, and emergency medical services.)

In emergency planning, coordinating the work of various disciplines can be difficult. In the nation's capital, learning to work with law enforcement personnel was a new territory for health officials. Likewise, transportation officials had to decide how much detail public information officers should disseminate to residents and the media when an evacuation "annex" was being developed.

Another challenge is shared funding. Although coordinated planning can increase the resources available to individual municipalities, at times the advantages of shared aid can have divisive consequences. Frederick County, Maryland, for instance, plays a crucial role in emergency planning supported by COG, but because it does not fall under the federal definition of the "metropolitan Washington area," it remains ineligible for any direct financial assistance provided through UASI's grants. Similar hindrances could affect other regions, if geographical determinations differ from actual coordination among interlocking municipalities and surrounding counties.

While some obstacles faced by planning organizations and the communities they serve are unique to the process of domestic planning for preparedness, many others are typical of multilateral decision making in general. Among the latter is the basic process of facilitating group decisions. Planning organizations must take into account not only the diverse communities that make up any region but also the varying interests of leaders and the differing regulations of local governments. Cooperation regarding any group purchase, for instance, incurs the often lengthy process of considering how each participant will use the services rendered. Often, the more participants there are, the more difficult it is for organizations to guide them all to a consensus on how to best plan for their multifaceted needs during an emergency.

TIPS FOR MUNICIPAL PLANNING

Regional planning for emergency preparedness is a time-consuming ongoing process. In NCR, as in many other regions implementing new policies and strategies for preparedness, lessons are continually being learned. Since the planning process began in the Washington, D.C., metropolitan region after 9/11, several guiding principals have been formulated.

Keep the Public Informed

Emergency plans should be user-friendly and capable of being explained to the public at large. Cooperation from all citizens is essential for a successful response to any emergency, whether that response involves an order to evacuate or simply instructions to remain indoors until further notice. If residents cannot trust official emergency planning, all other efforts will be inadequate.

Ensure That Local Anticrime Programs Do Not Suffer as a Result of an Emergency

Preparing for natural disasters and terrorism should not replace or overshadow the need for crime-fighting and safety programs. Regionwide public safety programs like those in COG's region are vital to ensuring residents' everyday safety. The staffing needed to facilitate emergency preparedness should not take away from priorities such as law enforcement, corrections initiatives, and emergency medical assistance.

Assess Measures According to the Threat Level in an Area

The potential for a terrorist attack in Washington, D.C., is about the same as that in New York City or Los Angeles. In other areas of the country, though, natural disasters such as hurricanes and tornadoes may be more likely. Before moving forward, planning organizations should conduct a local risk assessment and prioritize responses accordingly.

Include Local Businesses

The private sector controls an estimated 80 percent of the infra-structure required in responding to and recovering from emergencies. A vast majority of workers are employed by the private sector; and this sector also makes the equipment and provides many of the services on which most people in a region rely. For these reasons, no plan would be fully effective without active participation by local businesses. Contributing portions of security funds to this sector can facilitate employees' drills and instruction, plans to provide emergency care and support, and restarting operations quickly after a shutdown during an emergency.

CONCLUSION

The National Strategy for Homeland Security, announced in July 2002, recognized the vital role of state and local governments in public safety. As many cities and counties initiated significant efforts toward preparedness of individual jurisdictions after 9/11, the need for more comprehensive and coordinated regional activity became clear. Emergency preparedness at the municipal level requires communication and coordination across jurisdictional boundaries and, in some cases, across state lines.

BIBLIOGRAPHY

Government Accountability Office (GAO), Homeland Security: Effective Regional Coordination Can Enhance Emergency Preparedness (October 2004). GAO-04-1009.

Metropolitan Washington Council of Governments, Chief Administrative Officers Committee. www.mwcog.org/committee/committee/default.asp?COMMITTEE_ID=137.

Metropolitan Washington Council of Governments. 2004. Partners in Preparedness: The Regional Emergency Coordination Plan at Work.

Metropolitan Washington Council of Governments, Regional Emergency Coordination Plan. www.mwcog.org/security/security/plan.asp.

Metropolitan Washington Council of Governments, The Regional Emergency Coordination Plan Summary (September 2002).

CHAPTER 20

Preparing a City for Terrorism

The Honorable Martin O'Malley
Mayor, City of Baltimore, Maryland

AMERICA'S CITIES AND THE WAR ON TERRORISM

On 9/11 it became clear that America's cities were the second front in a new kind of war. As major population centers, hubs of cultural and economic activity, focal points for the nation's critical infrastructure, and home to symbolic national institutions, cities are, and will continue to be, the most likely targets of foreign terrorism on American soil.

Also, 9/11 proved that local law enforcement, firefighters, and emergency medical technicians are the new soldiers in this new war on the home front. The federal government and state governments do not have fire departments or medical units, and there is no time to bring personnel and equipment in from elsewhere when terror strikes—911 is a local call.

To date, much of the burden of preparing these home-front soldiers and protecting the frontlines in America's cities has fallen on local first responders, their governments, and local elected officials. Although some of these new challenges are inevitable, some are the result of failures by other levels of government to "provide for the common defense."

While other levels of government may choose to take time to adjust, local government does not have that luxury. Local elected officials must make the decision to invest—now—in their city's security. They must identify and attempt to defend likely and vulnerable targets within their borders, regardless of whether the ownership is in the private sector or other public entities. A city must find ways to protect its personnel, for their own safety and to improve their ability to protect the public, learning from the past. It must find ways to break through long-standing institutional barriers within and across government to ensure that all available resources are brought to bear as efficiently and effectively as possible. And finally, it must find a way to pay for this new mission. This chapter provides some lessons that one city has learned along the way.

IDENTIFYING (AND HARDENING) TARGETS

Every American city must conduct a thorough assessment of its potential vulnerabilities. Mechanically, this is a difficult but achievable task. Local government has a variety of experts at its disposal internally—security professionals in the police department; hazardous materials experts in the fire service; public health officials who can identify critical facilities for medical care; and public works personnel who are well-versed in the area's critical transportation, power generation, water infrastructure, and major facilities under the government's control. The private sector can and should also play a role—businesses that may be potential targets such as the chemical, financial, and hotel industries generally have their own security professionals and already know their facilities and understand their vulnerabilities. Community groups, including religious institutions, such as mosques, synagogues, and churches, should also be brought into the loop. Last, this work cannot be begun soon enough; and if necessary, various professional security firms can be brought in under contract to speed the process.

The far more difficult task faced by local government is determining what to do about the multitude of potential targets likely to be found in any major metropolitan area.

Lesson 1

Cities do not control all the targets they must be concerned about, particularly when these targets are part of larger systems, such as port and rail.

Many of the worst-case scenarios a local elected official must be concerned with involve facilities or systems not under his or her direct control. The attacks on the World Trade Center and the Pentagon involved airplanes originating in other jurisdictions; the attack in Madrid involved passenger trains that had passed through several jurisdictions; the increasingly commonly discussed scenario of a weapon of mass destruction in a cargo container could hinge on the performance of security agents in another country. Even locally, there is often no single entity responsible for oversight; or the responsible entity may not be the municipal government, even though the city would suffer the consequences of an attack.

There is no simple solution. Local government must reach out to the public and private entities that control key facilities. Although steering committees and work groups organized around a common concern (e.g., maritime security) can be helpful, the most effective and practical means to create working coordination may be taking concrete real-world steps:

1. Establish and refresh contact information among key operational personnel (to avoid an often-cited peril—"exchanging business cards for the first time at an incident").
2. Sponsor and regularly conduct joint drills.
3. Offer resources—including intelligence information, expertise, and funding—to these partners. [In Baltimore, the city and the chemical industry have united under the South Baltimore Industrial Mutual Aid Pact (SBIMAP) to conduct regular drills with industry and city responders to achieve these goals.]

Local government does have the power to pass regulatory ordinances to influence protection of some critical systems. Baltimore worked with the chemical industry to pass a local ordinance requiring firms to adhere to industry-established security standards and allowing the fire department to enforce compliance through inspections and fines. However, additional federal action will be the only means to improve many aspects of security.

Ultimately, it is an inescapable fact that key aspects of the security of some facilities and modes of transit will remain outside local control. Responders must be aware of potential hazards involving these facilities and must be trained to deal with them.

Lesson 2

Some targets are inherently difficult to harden.

In the case of ports and railroads, many traditional physical countermeasures are impossible. To take an oversimplified example, rail generally cannot be fenced in at two ends. So-called soft targets such as hotels, apartment buildings, and shopping malls are increasingly seen as attractive targets for terrorists, but are too abundant and, by definition, accessible to the general public to effectively secure. Even individual gas stations could be objects of terror plots, but there are far too many to secure or monitor them all.

Targets that can never be secured completely can still be hardened enough to deter an attack; this is done through multiple layers of defense, particularly through surveillance and awareness. Baltimore is investing substantially in closed-circuit camera technology for large open areas such as the inner harbor and facilities that are difficult to secure, such as rail lines. Surveillance technology must be paired with real monitoring—for example, there must be rapid and reliable consequences to trespassing.

Awareness must be fostered among the general public and partners to increase the likelihood that suspicious activity will be noticed and reported. The Baltimore police department (BPD) has preestablished contact lists for various sectors so that during industry-specific alerts from the federal government, BPD can contact local firms to discuss the alert and share information.

Lesson 3

Threats change; technology is developed; data need to be updated.

Immediately after 9/11, Baltimore conducted a wide-ranging assessment of its potential targets and outstanding vulnerabilities. However, vulnerability assessment is an ongoing process, and the city assessment is a "living" document (or, more correctly, database)—information is updated constantly, and new categories of facilities are added as intelligence emerges.

One example of an ever-changing aspect of Baltimore's defenses is its biosurveillance network. This network was created within days of 9/11, in an atmosphere of urgency. There were few or no outside models that could be used for guidance, and only limited local funding was available. Today, what began as a rudimentary system to bolster Baltimore's short-term defenses against chemical or biological weapons of mass destruction (WMD)—largely using data that were already being collected, but not collated or analyzed for this purpose—has grown to an invaluable asset with applications beyond preventing terrorism.

Baltimore's network is designed to detect—as early as possible—anomalous biological events associated with the use of biological or chemical agents, by using a combination of data already collected by city agencies, the private sector, and medical care providers: EMS calls reported by the fire department, recovery of animal carcasses reported by the department of public works, data on syndromes from city hospital emergency rooms, and over-the-counter sales of sentinel pharmaceuticals from local businesses. Data are collated every 24 hours and reviewed for any anomaly or unusual pattern compared with previous and seasonal trends, compared with expected patterns, and relative to world events or developing threats. Since its creation the network has also grown to be an invaluable tool for detecting, monitoring, and responding to a range of traditional and unanticipated (nonterrorist-related) public health concerns.

PROTECTING YOUR FIRST RESPONDERS

Local government now faces the extraordinary challenge of combining the traditional missions of public safety—fighting fires, preventing crime, and providing emergency medical care—with the new and ever-evolving mission of being prepared to respond, without notice, to massive and deliberate attacks that may involve deadly chemical or biological agents. First responders themselves may be targets. It is the duty of local government to take every measure possible to protect these public safety personnel, regardless of whether resources are available from outside. Funding issues will be covered below, but there are other challenges that local government must first address.

Lesson 4

Necessary levels of protection must be established and implemented.

It is impossible to state definitely what package of protective equipment is sufficient or appropriate for local first responders.

However, there are some reasonable and logical starting points: protection against inhaled hazards and skin and eye protection. Fire departments are well versed in the use of breathing apparatus and protective equipment, and local governments should draw on this knowledge to build a protective program for their other personnel. Consider the experience in Baltimore.

Baltimore expanded on the traditional gear of the fire department by providing every company with a "WMD equipment box" containing a protective chemical suit, gloves, boots, etc., for each firefighter. The boxes also contain antidotes for nerve agents, materials for testing chemical agents, and devices for testing radiation. Each EMS unit has the same equipment, as well as face masks and self-contained breathing apparatus (SCBA) identical to that carried by the firefighters. Every police officer in Baltimore will be issued a 5-pound pouch, containing the same face mask and chemical suit that can be carried during a heightened alert. This equipment has also been distributed to a smaller subset of personnel in other key agencies and stored in caches ready for quick transport to incident scenes.

Equipment must be readily available (because in many cases, it will be used only in a worst-case, no-warning scenario), identical, and interoperable so that it can be shared or damaged pieces can be swapped during an incident; and there must be regular drills in its use. Knowledge—of what might be encountered in the field, and whether to approach a scene—is also power: there are various "train the trainer" courses in WMD awareness for public works and other personnel that can be accessed through federal grant funds.

Issuing protective gear to agencies that have not traditionally used it will raise numerous issues: obtaining the medical clearances required by OSHA; significant ongoing maintenance, replacement, and training costs; and institutional resistance. However, all these obstacles can be overcome by introducing the program in a disciplined manner, and the cost of these efforts pales in comparison with the alternative of leaving your personnel unprotected.

Lesson 5

It is necessary to define who is a first responder and to understand what other personnel may be at risk.

By definition *first responders* are limited to those individuals who will arrive first at an incident scene to provide emergency assistance, often with little or no information about the conditions or hazards they will encounter. Without question, these responders need immediate and constant access to a variety of detection equipment and protective gear previously restricted only to specialized units such as bomb squads and hazardous materials teams.

However, a broader class of personnel and agencies may not have traditionally been considered part of the public safety apparatus, or may not be first responders, but may be called on to serve critical roles during a terrorist attack. These include, for instance, public health personnel now needed in field capacities, public works personnel who may need to operate a critical water facility, and transportation engineers to troubleshoot evacuations. These individuals may be called on to perform their jobs under hazardous or uncertain conditions and need to be protected.

Baltimore decided that every one of its police officers and paramedics must be provided with the same level and type of personal protection equipment against chemical and biological hazards that were being provided to its firefighters. The likelihood that these individuals could be placed in a dangerous situation—and the need to have them available to provide assistance—was simply too great to ignore.

All levels of government have long maintained lists of essential employees. These lists now need to be revisited—to the extent possible, in advance of a crisis—under the auspices of response to a terrorist attack to determine who would be needed in a potentially catastrophic situation. Government must consider questions such as these: How would nonuniformed personnel (such as public works employees) physically get into work? Should they be issued additional credentials to allow them to bypass road closures? Will they require transport? How will they be notified when and where to report?

Lesson 6

An interoperable radio is a piece of protective equipment.

First responders, other critical personnel, and all levels of the command staff across agencies must have interoperable communications equipment. This equipment, and protocols governing and guaranteeing communications between agencies, must be used daily.

COORDINATING HORIZONTALLY, VERTICALLY, AND ACROSS TRADITIONAL BOUNDARIES

Institutionalizing the incident command system to pull together disparate agencies and levels of government, though critical, need not be covered here. However, there is a great need for coordination apart from and before the on-scene response. In many ways coordination is a leadership issue for local government. In some situations, local officials have information or resources to share and are in a natural position to offer them to foster coordination. In other cases, others have resources (or share problems), and the challenge is to ensure that information is flowing to your jurisdiction. Because there is probably no such thing as too much coordination, this section will focus on only a few areas that are most within the control of local governments and are most critical to successful operations:

Lesson 7

Information can be shared across traditional boundaries.

The terrorist threat to the United States breaks through traditional barriers: first responders' jobs have changed; ordinary citizens face risks in situations previously believed to be safe (e.g., going to work); and the next attack could involve a chemical or biological agent never seen in our streets. Just as the threat shatters old boundaries, to address it effectively our country must do no less. In many cases this means that the circle of who "needs to know" information previously restricted within a single profession may have to be redrawn to reflect roles that world events are thrusting on new players. In some cases the challenge is overcoming established frames of mind with regard to simple notifications regarding when an event has occurred.

Internally, local government needs to consider sharing information in nontraditional ways, particularly the following: for police departments, sharing information related to law enforcement with the fire and health departments (e.g., thefts involving hazardous or exotic materials that could be "weaponized"); for fire and health departments, sharing information about responses (e.g., hazmat incidents or ER visits by patients with suspicious patterns). In many cases, agencies may need to help each other know what to look for (for example, law enforcement can identify injuries associated with failed attempts to make bombs).

Data from the local vulnerability assessment should be shared with first responders in advance, if necessary in an edited format that at least still provides information on facility content and access. This type of information sharing has almost no downside and will generally improve routine operations and responses. Cities need to reorient themselves to recognize that every response is potentially a multiagency response.

Local—and nonlocal—intelligence networks must be developed. The agencies of local government need to develop and practice the habit of sharing information, and different law enforcement jurisdictions must do the same. In Maryland this has been operationalized through an intelligence fusion center staffed by officers from the various city, county, and state law enforcement organizations. City government should be a voracious consumer of intelligence and a prolific producer of raw data. On the consumption side, intelligence networks provide the best hope that local government will receive actionable or operational information as soon as possible. Be alert for particular suspicious behavior patterns observed elsewhere, or events elsewhere such as industrial accidents of unknown cause that could signal a temporary need for heightened vigilance locally. On the production side, the raw data collected daily by local law enforcement, whether through traffic stops or noncriminal interactions with the public, can be a crucial source of information for other levels of government, including the professional intelligence service in the federal government. There is still much to be done to improve the distribution of federal "watch list" information to local law enforcement so that it may be used proactively rather than reactively.

Lesson 8

Major incidents require regional response, so planning and prevention must be regional as well.

An event of the magnitude of 9/11 will be too large for any single jurisdiction to handle. Potential incidents may also involve shared assets—highways, airports, or ports. Issues that have already been discussed with regard to internal coordination among local responders must also be applied to regional partners; neighboring fire departments should not arrive at the same scene with the intention of providing mutual aid only to find that they have incompatible breathing apparatus or radio systems. However, coordination must extend deeper than this to involve planning as well. If nothing else, there are inherent economies of scale to equipment (bulk purchases at lower prices; ensuring that expensive and seldom called-for apparatus is not duplicated); but regions need to truly embrace a philosophy of posing a united front.

A first step is extending mutual aid pacts beyond their traditional scope. Although robust agreements have historically existed across jurisdictional lines to provide relief for firefighting and emergency medical services, other forms of response and service, particularly law enforcement activities, should be added to these pacts. Law enforcement operations present specific difficulties—Will powers of arrest transfer across jurisdictional lines? How will liability be managed?—but can be solved if the political will is present.

One way to foster regionalism is to formally tie together the spending decisions of different agencies and jurisdictions. In Baltimore, the city and its two surrounding counties jointly received a grant from the Urban Area Security Initiative (UASI). Although the three jurisdictions could have easily exhausted the grant without meeting all their priority needs, the three governments elected to share these funds with four other mutual aid jurisdictions, both in recognition of the historic mutual aid between the jurisdictions and as a means to foster regional cooperation. As a result, a robust multijurisdictional working group has been formed that has been able to jointly determine priorities for developing the region's capabilities and joint training exercises.

Communications interoperability must not stop at city lines. Achieving interoperability within a jurisdiction can be difficult and expensive, and doing this across city and county lines can be almost prohibitively so. The Baltimore metropolitan area (the cites of Baltimore and Annapolis and their five adjacent counties) solved this problem by building out the capability in each jurisdiction to access a set of radio channels reserved by the federal government for emergency use. In 1986 the National Public Safety Planning Advisory Council (NPSPAC) established one national calling channel and four tactical channels to be reserved for use in support of regional mutual aid agreements. The Baltimore metro region applied jointly for a competitively awarded grant from the U.S. Department of Justice to facilitate access to these channels in each jurisdiction, eliminating the need for the unwieldy and imperfect patches that had previously been the only alternative to link disparate systems.

MANAGING THE MONEY

A primary reason for the establishment of the federal government by our founding fathers was to provide for the common defense. However, although terrorism represents a challenge to our nation's defense, to date the federal government has picked up only a portion of the costs of preparing our common domestic defenses. As a result, local governments face a difficult choice: to take on a new, largely unfunded mandate; or to hold out hope that nothing will happen within their city or town.

Of course, in reality this is no choice at all—as Baltimore did in the War of 1812, local governments must muster their own defenses. Unlike the federal government (but like a household), local governments must balance their operating budgets; and taking on a new and unexpected expense puts considerable strain on local budgets. There are various federal aid programs for homeland security, but they are changing and are likely to continue to evolve, and the ones that do currently exist leave significant gaps and problems:

Lesson 9

Personnel costs associated with homeland security largely fall on local government.

Federal grant programs have been created to provide some relief for law enforcement over time associated with national orange alerts, but grant funds currently cannot be used for permanent new personnel costs associated with expanding the basic mission of local law enforcement. Local governments must make a difficult choice: add to the bottom line or redirect personnel away from traditional duties. Other nonpersonnel costs associated with building out newly essential functions—such as office equipment—must also be borne locally.

Following 9/11 the Baltimore police department increased the size of its intelligence unit from 6 detectives to 36. The unit has proved indispensable, serving as liaison to the FBI Joint Terrorism Task Force (JTTF) and other intelligence services, assessing incoming intelligence for operational implications on a daily basis, and conducting vulnerability assessments. However, these services have come at a cost—several million dollars in salaries over the unit's three-year existence, and the diversion of key personnel away from traditional law enforcement. It can be hoped that in the future, grant programs may be designed to accommodate this type of need; but as of this writing the forecast is not promising.

Many cities have outdated facilities for coordinating the operations of support agencies and maintaining city services during a major response, and must develop modern emergency operations centers (EOCs). While grant funds are available for response equipment, they are often not available for the more mundane things that make an EOC run—telephone and fax lines, computers, and office equipment. There are some limited grant programs for improving EOCs, but by and large local government will probably need to invest its own time and resources. Redundancy is also expensive but necessary. Perhaps the best practical advice is that where possible, cities should try to develop dual-use equipment and facilities. Baltimore developed EOC redundancy by upgrading the capabilities of an existing department of transportation facility for managing snowstorms.

Lesson 10

Most federal grant funds are passed through state capitals and are not paid in advance.

Most federal homeland security grant funds are provided on a formula basis rather than being based on a competitive application. Almost without exception, these formula funds are passed through the state government to local government, often with the state having the option to retain 20 percent or more of the funds. The local government is then required to submit to the state for approval an application for use of its allocation, which the state then forwards to DHS for final approval. Once these approvals have been obtained, the local government must front the money for its purchases and request reimbursement through the state. Without question, this can create a significant delay between the time a new grant allocation is announced and the time that equipment actually reaches the local first responders on the front lines. Short of reforming the process, local governments can spend their own funds (as Baltimore did, spending millions in local resources before DHS was even created) and can attempt to engage in multiyear planning with the state so that the approval process can be streamlined.

Lesson 11

It is incumbent on local government to be aggressive.

There is often more latitude in federal programs than an initial reading of grant rules may suggest, and the timing of your request may make a difference. Baltimore asked DHS for permission to spend federal homeland security grant funds on a generator that did not seem to be allowed under the basic rules of the program; however, the city asked the day after the regional blackout of August 2003, asked the state to support the request, and received approval. The lesson is that it doesn't hurt to ask, and you should make the grantor tell you "no."

Federal grant programs changed significantly in three years preceding this writing and are likely to continue to change. The first federal grants for homeland security generally restricted funds to equipment needed to respond to an attack. These programs were also formula grants based on state population, then further allocated by the state government to local government, again often on a per capita basis. New programs focus more on allowing funds to be used for prevention—surveillance, hardening targets, sharing information— and some funds are now directed to urban areas on the basis of risk rather than simply population. However, there is much room for improvement—funds should be provided directly to cities, and allocations should be based on threat assessments, not formulas. In this uncertain environment local government cannot predict or plan for specific funds to be available, even in the next fiscal year. Accordingly, the best option is to identify critical needs now, prioritize them, and maintain an updated list—detailed down to the make, quantity, and unit cost—ready to be used on the day when funds become available or a new program is announced.

CONCLUSION

As disturbing as the threat to our home front is, it is not without precedent. During the War of 1812 America's cities were also the front lines of a war with a foreign adversary, as the nation's capital itself fell before British invaders. Nearly 200 years later, the second front is here at home once again, and the War of 1812 holds powerful lessons for today's leaders.

Baltimore's defenders in the War of 1812 had the wisdom to understand a reality that local officials would be wise to take to heart today: when the enemy is at the gates, the usual recourses of waiting for help or hoping that someone else will get the job done are not options. If the unusual coalition of local government, citizens (including large numbers of immigrants and freed slaves), and owners of private businesses had not risen up to form a united defense, Baltimore might have burned, just as Washington, D.C., burned 40 miles to the south. During the War of 1812, Congress was scattered throughout the woods around Washington, but the British forces were turned back from Baltimore by local militias and a fort built with private funds. That fort was Fort McHenry, the birthplace of the "Star-Spangled Banner."

Today, we can do no less. Local elected officials must confront the challenging reality that the next terrorist attack could occur tomorrow. They must rally every available resource and make the decision to invest their time, personnel, and financial resources. Doing so is not easy—resources are scarce, the challenge is immense, and overcoming institutional barriers represents a major organizational and leadership challenge. However, it can be done, and it must be done.

Like Baltimore's defenders almost 200 years ago, we must dig our own trenches, and arm our own modern-day militias.

Legal Issues

Michael Kraft
Counterterrorism Consultant; Former Senior Advisor for Legislative and Budget Affairs in the State Department Office of the Coordinator for Counterterrorism; Former Staff Director of the Senate Foreign Relations Committee Middle East Subcommittee

INTRODUCTION

Because most terrorism against Americans in the past three decades occurred overseas, counterterrorist legislation initially focused on foreign terrorists and their state supporters. After the attack on the World Trade Center in 1993 and the bombing in Oklahoma City in 1995, the United States also enacted criminal laws specifically covering offenses related to terrorism. (Until then, many such offenses—for example, murder and assault, were already covered by the criminal code.) Both kinds of counterterrorist legislation are important to homeland security. This chapter reviews their evolution, some highlights, applications to homeland security, and practical issues of enforcement. It also notes some of the counterterrorism provisions, primarily refining earlier legislation, that were wrapped into the Intelligence Reform Act of 2004, but received little press or public attention.

FIRST STEPS

The first phase was the development of international treaties against such crimes as hijacking aircraft and taking hostages. By 1971 there were four international conventions dealing with the security of civil aircraft; and in the 1970s three international conventions against taking hostages were enacted.

In the 1980s, after terrorist attacks on airports and the hijacking of the Italian cruise ship *Achille Lauro*, international conventions were negotiated against attacks on civilian airports, passenger vessels, and offshore platforms. In the 1990s the United States and other countries, working at the United Nations, successfully drafted international conventions against terrorist bombings and against funding terrorism.

These treaties usually required implementing legislation. For example, the Anti-Hijacking Act of 1974 prohibits the hijacking of aircraft in the jurisdiction of the United States and provides jurisdiction over offenders who hijack other civil aircraft in other countries if those hijackers are subsequently found in the United States.

Two themes are clear: these international treaties were responses to terrorism, and they embodied the "extradite or prosecute" principle. That is, parties to the conventions are obligated to extradite suspects to the country that had primary jurisdiction over the crime, or to prosecute the suspects in their own courts.

Apart from the Convention for the Suppression of Financing of Terrorism (1999), the conventions do not define terrorism but consider actions such as blowing up aircraft a criminal act and an extraditable offense regardless of motivation. This approach was reflected in numerous statements by high-level U.S. government officials that terrorist acts are criminal regardless of motivation. It also reflected the realties of the difficulties in achieving an international consensus on a definition of terrorism.

Sanctions and State Sponsors

In the late 1970s, when Congress passed its first counterterrorist laws, it focused on imposing sanctions against countries that supported terrorism. Thus—in the wake of the terrorist killings of Israeli athletes at the 1972 Olympics in Munich, and other terrorism overseas—one early law, enacted in 1976, cut off foreign assistance to "any government which aids or abets, by providing sanctuary from prosecution, any group or individual which has committed an act of international terrorism."[1] It was logical for Congress to use foreign aid to exert pressure, since Americans might well ask why the United States should give aid to countries that support terrorism.

The Terrorism List

Congress also became concerned in the late 1970s that tighter scrutiny and controls were needed over the export of dual-use equipment to countries supporting terrorism. Some types of equipment, such as certain trucks, aircraft, and boats, could be used for military purposes and terrorism. Also, several influential members of the House Committee on Foreign Affairs were concerned about the political implications of approving licenses for military and dual-use equipment. They felt that approving export licenses for dual-use equipment without serious consideration at high levels could send the wrong signal—that the United States was willing to do business as usual even with regimes engaged in terrorism or supporting terrorists. These concerns emerged in 1978, when the Commerce Department approved export licenses for exporting dual-use equipment to Libya and Syria; the approvals had been made by low- and mid-level Commerce and State Department officials.

The sale to Libya involved 400 heavy-duty off-road trucks of the type used by the American and Canadian armies for transporting tanks into a battle zone. In Syria's case, the State Department Near East Bureau approved the export of six so-called civilian versions of the Lockheed C-130 transport plane, at a time that Syria was enmeshed in the Lebanese civil war. Shortly after the license was approved, Syria stepped up its shelling of Christian suburbs of eastern Beirut.

Representative Millicent Fenwick (Republican, New Jersey), a junior member of the House Foreign Affairs Committee, introduced an amendment to require closer scrutiny of such sales. Working with Representative Jonathan Bingham (Democrat, New York), the chairman of the Economic subcommittee, she won passage of an Export Administration Act amendment requiring the executive branch to notify Congress 30 days before export licenses are issued for goods or services valued at more than $7 million that would significantly enhance the military capability or the ability to support acts of international terrorism of a government of a country that the secretary of state determined had repeatedly supported acts of terrorism.[2]

This was intended to ensure that decisions about licensing with regard to state sponsors of international terrorism would be approved at the top levels of the State Department and reviewed for foreign policy implications, rather than for primarily commercial considerations. Quickly, what was intended as an export control mechanism became known as the "terrorism list" or "state sponsors list" and developed into an important counterterrorist tool. The countries initially designated were Libya, Iraq, Syria, and South Yemen. Later, Iran, Cuba, North Korea, and the Sudan were added. South Yemen was dropped after it merged with North Yemen. The State Department removed Iraq in 1982, but redesignated it after Saddam Hussein's invasion of Kuwait in 1991. Then on 20 October 2004, the State Department announced, after providing Congress with advance notification, that Iraq had been taken off the terrorist list, following the procedures in a 1989 law (see below). The list currently includes Cuba, Iran, Libya, North Korea, Sudan, and Syria.

In piecemeal fashion over the years after the Export Administration Act of 1979 was enacted, Congress passed half a dozen "piggyback" amendments imposing sanctions on the designated countries. One such provision amended the U.S. tax code to discourage investments by denying American companies and individuals federal income tax credits for income earned in the listed countries. Other provisions included cutting off military and economic assistance to countries on the list and suspending American assistance to countries that supplied lethal military equipment to listed countries.

Major legislation also followed the Iran-contras scandal during the Reagan administration and the congressional investigations into whether Oliver North, a National Security Council (NSC) staffer, had violated U.S. laws by selling missiles to Iran and using the proceeds to finance the contras in Nicaragua. Congress passed the Anti-Terrorism and Arms Export Control Act of 1989, which codified procedures for designating "state sponsors" of terrorism under the foreign assistance and military assistance laws as well as under the Export Administration Act.

The 1989 law also laid out specific criteria and advance notification procedures that had to be followed before a country could be taken off the terrorism list. The procedures require the president to certify to Congress that the government of the country in question has not supported acts of international terrorism for the previous six months and has given assurances that it will not do so in the future. The rescission has to lie before Congress for 45 days before taking effect. This provision was a reaction to a congressional outcry that had arisen when the State Department removed Iraq from the list in 1982 without consulting or informing Congress in advance. The removal was perceived as an effort by the Reagan administration to tilt toward Iraq in the Iran-Iraq war.

The second removal of Iraq in October 2004, followed congressional procedures and assurances given by the interim Iraq government. The effect was largely symbolic because after the overthrow of Saddam Hussein, the Bush administration already had used special authorities Congress enacted a year earlier, permitting the lifting of sanctions that had been triggered by the 1991 designation.

The Long-Arm Statute

In October 1985, a Palestinian terrorist group hijacked the Italian cruise liner *Achille Lauro* in an effort to enter Israel during a port call. The terrorists intended to take hostages after landing and force the Israelis to release other group members who had been arrested for previous terrorist acts, including one in which a terrorist smashed a toddler to death against a rock. However the plotters were accidentally discovered aboard the ship, and they quickly hijacked it.

During the hijacking, which lasted for several days while the American, Italian, and Israeli navies were trying to locate the ship, the hijackers threw overboard Leon Klinghoffer, an elderly American passenger who was in a wheelchair. Abu Abbas, the leader of the group, was later arrested after the ship finally docked in Alexandria, Egypt. Italian authorities forced his release when the American military plane transporting him to the United States landed at an Italian air base for refueling. Abu Abbas fled to Yugoslavia, then took refuge in Iraq, was eventually recaptured by U.S. forces after the 2003 invasion, and died of a heart attack while in custody.

This episode, in which terrorists killed an American overseas and were released by one country to take refuge in another, prompted the Justice Department to draft the long-arm statute, making it a federal crime to murder, attempt to murder, conspire to murder, or cause serious bodily injury to Americans if the attorney general determined that the violence was terrorism, rather than an

ordinary nonpolitical criminal offense.[3] This legislation allowed the
United States to prosecute terrorists who attacked Americans overseas even if the attack did not take place on American territory,
such as in an embassy. In singling out terrorist crimes from ordinary
crimes the legislation defined the criteria to be used by the attorney
general as action intended to coerce, intimidate, or retaliate against
a government or civilian population.

The long-arm statute did more than provide additional grounds
for prosecuting terrorists. To facilitate investigations overseas, the
Justice Department greatly expanded its assignment of legal attachés
(LEGATs) abroad. Although this sometimes caused friction with the
State Department, whose embassies were already strained to provide
logistical support for other agencies, the LEGATs did facilitate U.S.
investigations and in some cases also helped host countries pursue
investigations and improve their own laws. Currently, 54 LEGATs
are assigned overseas and more are expected.

Aviation and Maritime Security

The hijackings of airplanes in the 1970s and 1980s and the attacks on
airports in Rome, Vienna, and Karachi in the mid-1980s prompted
a series of aviation and security-related laws long before the term
homeland security came into use.

This legislation was aimed at countries that had weak aviation
security. For example, Section 1115 of the Federal Aviation Act allows
the president to suspend air transportation between the United States
and any foreign state that acts "in a manner inconsistent" with the
antihijacking convention of The Hague (1970); or permits territory
under its jurisdiction to be used by terrorists for operations, training,
or sanctuary; or arms, aids, and abets any terrorist organization that
"knowingly uses the illegal seizure of aircraft or the threat thereof
as an instrument of policy." The president also is authorized to
suspend air transportation between the United States and any
country that maintains air service between itself and such a state.
The United States has banned direct air service to Lebanon because
of concerns about terrorist groups within anti-aircraft missile range
of flights using Beirut's international airport.

After the hijacking of TWA 847 and other aircraft in the 1980s,
Congress enacted Section 551 of the International Security and
Development Cooperation Act of 1985, which directs the Secretary

of Transportation to inspect security at foreign airports with air links to the United States. Travel advisories are to be issued if the security is substandard and has not been sufficiently improved after airport authorities are given 90 days' notice.

Such advisories have been issued for airports such as Lagos and Athens. Typically, the bans are lifted after a State Department antiterrorism training assistance team sends aviation security specialists overseas and works with the local airport authorities to improve security.

After the bombing of Pan Am 103 in 1988 with plastic explosives concealed in a radio, an international convention was drafted to require explosives manufacturers to incorporate a detection chemical. About a dozen countries (including Czechoslovakia, which had manufactured the explosive, Semtex, used in the bombing of flight 103) cooperated to identify chemicals that could be mixed into various plastic explosives. The United States passed its implementing legislation as part of the Antiterrorism and Effective Death Penalty Act of 1996 (AEDPA).[4]

One controversial provision of AEDPA required the Federal Aviation Administration (FAA) to impose on foreign air carriers serving a U.S. airport the same security measures required of American carriers serving that airport. This entailed considerable negotiations, as some countries claimed that their own measures were equivalent, if not exactly identical.

After the hijacking of the *Achille Lauro*, Congress added to the Omnibus Diplomatic Security and Antiterrorism Act of 1986[5] a program for protecting passenger liners against hijacking. This included developing International Maritime Organization security standards, inspecting U.S. and foreign ports, and issuing travel advisories against unsafe foreign ports. The Intelligence Reform Act, passed in December 2004, contained a provision requiring that cruise ship crews and passengers be checked against a comprehensive, coordinated database containing information about known or suspected terrorists and their associates.

THE CHANGING FOCUS: FIGHTING TERRORIST GROUPS

In the 1990s, the focus of new U.S. legislation changed. Republican and Democratic administrations had used economic sanctions against countries on the terrorism list, but experts now became concerned about terrorist groups that did not have state sponsors. For example, an unclassified CIA paper indicated that the Abu Nidal organization had set up front companies in Eastern Europe to raise and transfer funds.

The 1994 enactment of a "material support" provision made it a criminal offense to provide funds or other material support for specific acts of terrorism by a terrorist organization or an individual. Material support was defined as "currency or other financial securities, financial services, lodging, training, safe houses, false documentation or identification, communications equipment, facilities, weapons, lethal substances, explosives, personnel, transportation, and other physical assets, except medicine or religious materials." This provision was a refinement of the concept of aiding and abetting in criminal law and became part of the Violent Crime Control and Enforcement Act of 1994.[6]

However, to avoid the danger that more extensive proposals might get lost during the congressional deliberations of that large-scale crime act, the Clinton administration began working on a separate, more comprehensive counterterrorist bill to be introduced the following year. This legislation was prompted by a series of terrorist acts in Israel and the West Bank by the Palestinian group HAMAS, and a shooting of Arabs at a mosque in Hebron by an Israeli immigrant from the United States. As an interim measure, on 23 January 1995, the administration issued Executive Order 12947 freezing the assets subject to U.S. jurisdiction of 12 groups—10 Arab and 2 Jewish—whose support of violence was deemed to undermine the peace process in the Middle East.[7]

Foreign Terrorist Organizations

In January 1995, the Clinton administration submitted to Congress the broad counterterrorism bill drafted during 1994. It contained provisions to designate for foreign and domestic terrorist organizations for the purpose of prohibiting the provision of material support. But in revising the legislation, which passed as the Antiterrorism and Effective Death Penalty Act of 1996 (AEDPA),[8] Congress narrowed the scope to foreign organizations. AEDPA makes it a criminal offense for an American to knowingly provide funds and other material support to groups designated by the secretary of state (in consultation with the attorney general and the secretary of the treasury) as foreign terrorist organizations (FTOs).

The legislation against support by individuals or organizations for terrorist groups was a natural development from earlier legislation against maverick governments that supported international terrorism. It reflected the new threat from groups such as HAMAS and al-Qaida that were not state-sponsored but raised funds on their own.

Some of the target groups also did charitable work, but Congress noted in Section 301(7) of the act ("Findings and Purpose") that "Foreign organizations that engage in terrorist activity are so tainted by their criminal conduct that any contributions to such an organization facilitates that conduct." Also, even a contribution intended for legitimate charitable purposes would free up funds for terrorist activities, such as buying weapons. Some terrorist groups, such as HAMAS and those in Algeria and Egypt, attracted adherents by providing schools and medical facilities or assisting the families of active members or suicide bombers.

In the provisions regarding FTOs,[9] AEDPA defined material support as it had been defined in the crime act of 1994. The definition of material support was expanded in the Intelligence Reform Act of 2004, including a clarification of the meaning of training to include military-type training from or on behalf of a terrorist organization and training to impart specific skills as opposed to general knowledge. These modifications were enacted in the wake of court cases in which the definition of training was questioned. Overall, these material support provisions in law have been used in cases involving previously unknown and undesignated terrorist groups. As of mid-2004, 39 persons had been charged under the two material support provisions, and 14 had been convicted or had pleaded guilty (sometimes to other criminal charges).

The material support provisions do not define terrorism directly, but instead cite U.S. laws implementing various international conventions regarding terrorism, such as those concerned with destroying civilian aircraft and taking hostages, as well as U.S. laws concerning attacks on the president, cabinet officials, members of Congress, and government property. The provisions also cite the definitions used in the Immigration and Nationality Act and the Foreign Relations Authorization Act for fiscal years (FY)

1988 and 1989 that mandated the annual *Patterns of Global Terrorism* report to Congress.

AEDPA also authorizes the Treasury Department to seize assets in the United States of a designated FTO. This provision complements executive orders issued under the authority of the International Emergency Economics Powers Act (IEEPA); such orders have been used increasingly since 9/11.

Additionally, the FTO provision tightens the Immigration Nationality Act with regard to restrictions on visas for persons involved with terrorist groups. Under AEDPA, mere membership in a designated FTO was added to the grounds for denying a visa as well as previous restrictions against leaders or representatives of a terrorist group.

Administrative Record

While deliberating on AEDPA, some members of Congress, in both parties, expressed concern that groups might be designated FTOs for political reasons, or with insufficient justification. The final legislation compromise required the secretary of state to base the designations on a detailed administrative record that had to withstand scrutiny and could not be "arbitrary or capricious." As noted above, the attorney general and the secretary of the treasury had to be consulted; also, a group was allowed to challenge its designation within 30 days in the U.S. Court of Appeals for the District of Columbia. Congress also stipulated that a designation would expire after two years unless renewed; a renewal entailed using the same procedure required for the initial designation—including a detailed administration record.

Because the administrative record was the sole basis for the review process, the Justice Department decided that it should be equivalent to a court brief. This proved to be a labor-intensive matter, especially as redesignations had to be automatically reviewed every two years. Preparing administrative records even for groups that boasted of their terrorist activities turned out to be time-consuming and diverted government officials from other counterterrorism efforts.

Therefore, in 2003, the State Department Counterterrorism Office and Justice Department drafted amendments that would extend the review requirements to a four-year period. It first passed the House in 2003 and in early 2004, but the vehicle State Department

Authorization bill became bogged down in the Senate. Finally as part of the Intelligence Reform Act of 2004, Congress included an amendment extending the review period for all groups to five years, with a provision allowing a designated group to seek a review every two years.

The first designations were made in October 1997. As of late 2004, 39 groups are designated FTOs. Most of them were on the original list. Several groups have challenged their designations more than once—including the Mujahedin-e Khalq organization (MEK), an anti-Iranian group that actively lobbies Congress—but U.S. courts have upheld these designations.

Weapons of Mass Destruction

A growing concern over weapons of mass destruction (WMD) led to the Biological Weapons and Anti-Terrorism Act of 1989.[10] In 1992, the Weapons of Mass Destruction Act called on the Defense and Energy departments to maintain and improve their ability to monitor and respond to the proliferation of WMD and missile delivery systems. Although the nonproliferation effort originally was directed against nations, it has since also been directed against nonstate groups such as al-Qaida that are evidently seeking to obtain or develop chemical and biological agents.

Progressively tighter legislation has strengthened controls over chemical, biological, and radioactive (CBR) agents or has authorized sanctions against countries that use CBR weapons in violation of international law and against companies that aid in the proliferation of such weapons. For example, provisions in Title V of AEDPA refine and expand the definition of possession of CBR agents to cover unlawful possession of a substance whether or not the material is in the form of a delivery system, such as a bomb or missile. The Intelligence Reform Act of 2004 contained additional provisions to tighten controls over CBR agents. The provisions in Title VI include specific prohibitions against possession of CBR agents by persons who are acting on behalf of terrorist organizations and manufacture or possession of variola (the virus that causes smallpox).

The PATRIOT Act

The USA PATRIOT Act[11] was rushed through Congress and passed on 26 October 2001 in the wake of 9/11. Reflecting the focus of and impetus for the legislation, Title I was called "Enhancing Domestic Security against Terrorism." Many other titles also related to homeland security—for example, by facilitating investigations and surveillance. Some provisions had been drafted earlier, during the Clinton administration, by career officials in the Justice Department and other agencies but had been rebuffed by Congress before 9/11. One example is a "roving wiretap" provision (Section 206) under which federal officials may get a wiretapping order that would follow a suspect to any phone he or she uses. (Previously, a wiretap order had to apply to a specific phone number.) Roving wiretaps were already permitted in ordinary criminal cases.

The PATRIOT Act also permits the sharing of foreign intelligence (including information relating to protection against international terrorism or foreign attack, or concerning foreign activity and the conduct of foreign affairs) with officials of federal law enforcement, protective enforcement, immigration, national defense, and national security, for the performance of official duties. This removal of an earlier legal barrier is considered by some observers to be a major benefit of the PATRIOT Act. Others, however, say that the barrier had resulted not from law but from perceived restrictions and operating practices within the CIA and FBI. Regardless, the PATRIOT Act enhanced the government's ability to share intelligence with criminal investigators and prosecutors and has facilitated criminal prosecutions and helped in some court cases. The PATRIOT Act also allows the secretary of state (in order to counter terrorism and other crimes) to share with foreign governments information in the State Department's visa lookout system. The United States already had a working relationship on this database of terrorist suspects with Canada and with Australia in connection with the 2000 Sydney Olympic Games.

Addressing the funding of terrorism, the PATRIOT Act's provisions on money laundering established jurisdiction over foreigners who maintain a bank account in the United States. Also, U.S. financial institutions are required to terminate correspondent relationships with foreign banks that ignore U.S. subpoenas for records. Additionally, the money laundering provisions make terrorism subject to RICO (anti-racketeering legislation); and all assets of a person or entity that participates in or plans an act of domestic or international terrorism are subject to forfeiture. This provision includes a procedure for the owner of confiscated assets to contest the seizure.

The FTO designations of AEDPA were modified by the PATRIOT Act, which allows redesignation of a terrorist group after the initial two years even if no terrorist activities have been cited during that period, provided that the group retains the "capability and intent" to engage in terrorism. This change takes account of the fact that terrorist groups sometimes "lie low" and do not conduct an actual attack for some time, and that their planning and fund-raising may be undetectable.

The PATRIOT Act also broadens the denial of visas for prominent persons who use their position to endorse terrorism, or persuade others to support terrorism, in a way that the secretary of state considers detrimental to the United States' counterterrorism. This could apply to a local leader who encourages people to take part in terrorist activities or provide funds for terrorists, even though he or she does not do so.

The PATRIOT Act has critics outside the government and in Congress. Many members of Congress—although they were reluctant to be painted as obstructionists or as weak on terrorism—were perturbed when the voluminous bill was rushed through in the aftermath of 9/11 without enough time to read and study it. Librarians and civil libertarians campaigned against a provision allowing the FBI to obtain access to the records of who checked out books or visited particular Web sites. The original intent of that provision was to let investigators determine if a suspect was obtaining, say, books on how to make explosives; but the issue became something of a cause célèbre. The American Civil Liberties Union (ACLU) and others also charged that the act violated the Constitution by allowing investigators to obtain search warrants in a "sneak and peak" procedure and not disclose the fact to those subject to search. Some critics tried to get city councils to vote for repeal of the law.

The reaction against the act was to some extent fueled by distrust of former Attorney General Ashcroft's leadership of the Justice Department. On the other hand, many people in law enforcement consider the opposition unjustified and sometimes overwrought. Efforts to block repeal narrowly failed in the House of Representatives in autumn 2004, but disputes over the act are likely to continue.

Border Security

Reflecting a concern that terrorists could enter the United States across the land borders with Canada and Mexico, Title IV of the PATRIOT Act (called "Protecting the Borders") authorized tripling the number of Border Patrol personnel.

The authority to deny visas to prominent people who incite others to support terrorism (see above) is also relevant to border and homeland security. The Intelligence Reform Act of 2004 also required that visa applicants between the ages of 14 and 79 had to submit to a personal interview with a U.S. consular official unless certain waiver conditions were met.

The new law requires the administration to develop a comprehensive strategy for intercepting terrorists and constraining their mobility. The Department of Homeland Security also is directed to conduct a pilot study of the use of advanced technology to improve border security, including the use of unmanned aircraft to help monitor the long borders with Canada and Mexico. The Intelligence Reform Act also requires the State Bureau of Diplomatic Security to develop a strategic plan to improve the U.S. government's ability to prevent terrorist suspects from fraudulently using U.S. or foreign government passports to enter the United States.

Civil Suits

A new legal dimension is the filing of civil suits by victims of terrorism against terrorists or their supporters or both.

An early suit was brought by the family of Leon Klinghoffer, who was killed during the hijacking of the *Achille Lauro* in 1985. An Italian court had convicted the terrorist leader Abu Abbas in absentia; but a U.S. warrant was dropped two years after the hijacking when the Justice Department concluded that the evidence could not be used under U.S. legal procedures. Because Abu Abbas was a member of the Fatah ruling council, the Klinghoffer family filed suit in 1990 against the Palestine Liberation Organization (PLO), which had property in the United States. The case, brought under the Death on the High Seas Act,[12] was settled out of court in 1996; the terms were never publicly disclosed.

Several changes in the U.S. legal system made it easier to file civil suits against terrorists and their alleged supporters. Legislation initially enacted in 1990 with the support of the State Department, and of the Klinghoffer family and the families of those who died on Pan Am 103, allowed U.S. nationals or their survivors injured by acts of international terrorism to file civil suits to seize terrorists' assets.[13] The measure contained provisions that addressed the concerns of the Justice Department about protecting evidence that might be used in criminal prosecutions.

Another development was Section 221 of the Antiterrorism and Effective Death Penalty Act of 1996[14] amending the Foreign Sovereign Immunity Act to allow U.S. nationals to bring civil actions against terrorist states. Families of the victims of Pan Am 103 filed suit against Libya for its complicity in the attack, winning large settlements.

Americans who were taken hostage in Lebanon during the 1980s by the Iranian-backed organization Hizballah brought suits against Iran—as have the families of some American citizens killed by Palestinian terrorists affiliated with groups receiving Iranian material support. The implementation of favorable judgments became problematic, however, because in some cases the countries supporting terrorists had no assets in the United States, or those countries' assets had already been frozen and there were previous claims and agreements. The State Department has had difficulty persuading families and the public to accept its concerns about previous claims and agreements and about setting precedents that might be used by other countries to seize U.S. assets.

In July 2004, the U.S. District Court of Rhode Island ruled that the Palestinian Authority and PLO did not have sovereign immunity, because "Palestine" does not constitute a state under U.S. law. It awarded $116 million in damages to the family of Yaron Ungar, who had been shot and killed by Palestinian gunmen.

Another legal dimension of counterterrorism is the use of "material support" statutes—civil suits against entities accused of facilitating the transfer of funds to support terrorist operations. In a suit brought in 2002, families of the victims of 9/11 sought damages from banking institutions (including Saudi banks), charities, and other defendants that they say provided material support to al-Qaida in the form of financial services.

In July 2004 a civil case was filed against the Arab Bank of Jordan alleging that it had provided material support to terrorists by serving as a conduit for funds from Saudi contributors to families of Palestinian suicide bombers. Several Americans joined in the suit, including the widow of John Linde, one of three U.S. civilian contractors killed by a roadside bomb. Linde had been serving on a protective detail for U.S. diplomats who were visiting the West Bank to interview Palestinian candidates for scholarships.

In September 2004 Cantor Fitzgerald Securities, a bond trading firm that had lost many employees on 9/11, filed a civil suit against Saudi Arabia and dozens of banks and Islamic charities, alleging that charities authorized or controlled by the Saudi government provided funds to terrorist groups. The Port Authority of New York and New Jersey filed an analogous suit.

And in December 2004, a federal judge in Chicago ordered the Holy Land Foundation and two other American-based Islamic organizations that describe themselves as charities to pay $156 million to the family of David Boim, an American citizen who was fatally shot at an Israeli bus stop by members of HAMAS. A jury earlier ruled in favor of the Boim family who charged the groups and the alleged fund-raiser with providing material support to HAMAS, a Palestinian group formally designated as a foreign terrorist organization.

IMPLEMENTATION

Effective implementation of counterterrorist laws requires commitment by the law enforcement community and political leaders; otherwise, personnel, training, and financial resources will lag.

One example revealed by the 9/11 Commission and congressional committees was the FBI's antiquated computer system, which impeded the sharing of information between investigators and thus made it more difficult to "connect the dots." By contrast, Secretary of State Colin Powell made it a priority to upgrade the State Department's computer system; previously, many officers there had resorted to doing open unclassified research on the Internet at home.

The FBI has been criticized for being slow to respond to terrorist threats; but during a flurry of threats in the summer of 2001, when it made efforts to shift to counterterrorism, it was rebuffed. In May 2001, according to the 9/11 Commission report, Attorney General Ashcroft testified at a congressional appropriations hearing that "one of the nation's must fundamental responsibilities is to protect its citizens . . . from terrorist attacks"; yet the next day, his department distributed internal guidance for the fiscal year 2003 budget request to Congress that did not list fighting terrorism as a priority. The commission reported that Dale Watson, the FBI counterterrorism chief, "told us that he almost fell out of his chair when he saw the memo." As the summer wore on, the FBI submitted its request for an increase to the Justice Department for forwarding to the Office of Management and Budget (OMB), but on 10 September, according to the commission's report, Ashcroft turned down the request.

OMB and Congress have also short-changed international counterterrorism programs even though President Bush has repeatedly said we must fight terrorists overseas before they can hit us at home. The State Department's Antiterrorist Assistance (ATA) program is an example of the budget cutting that takes place behind the scenes despite the rhetoric. ATA strengthens the counterterrorism capabilities of foreign law enforcement personnel; it offers courses in subjects such as crisis management, airport security, detecting and defusing explosives, negotiating for the release of hostages, and protecting important individuals. Yet despite widespread terrorist attacks in Kenya, Tanzania, Yemen, Morocco, the Philippines, Indonesia, and elsewhere, OMB cut the State Department's ATA budget request by an average of 20 percent for fiscal years 2003, 2004, and 2005. Several smaller but important related programs such as the terrorist interdiction program and funding for foreign emergency support teams were cut even more. Then in November 2004, in a lame-duck session after the elections, Congress finally passed an Omnibus Appropriations Bill that cut the OMB-approved request for ATA training by 9.5 percent, from $128 to $120 million. The $8 million difference is peanuts compared to the millions of dollars in pork that members of Congress slipped into the same Omnibus Bill for pet projects in their home districts.

Another type of budget problem emerged after the State Department's counterterrorism office and officials of the Diplomatic Security Bureau in 1999 proposed a new training facility near Washington, D.C., for foreign participants in ATA and the State Department's own security agents. Budget officials in the State Department did not want the funding to be taken from the department's operating budget, and the congressional appropriations subcommittees that handle the foreign assistance bill said, "We don't do bricks and mortar." Eventually, in 2003, the Maryland congressional delegation obtained $5 million in start-up funds for the project at Army Proving Ground in Aberdeen, Maryland. Another $5 million was approved in the FY '05 budget. If the training facility, expected to cost over $55 million, had been approved when it was first proposed, it would have been operating by now.

Other agencies also have been affected. According to the *New York Times*, OMB and the Treasury Department cut the Internal Revenue Service's request for additional investigators to follow terrorists' complex funding trails. Government sources say the Office of Foreign Assets Control (OFAC), which takes the lead in seizing terrorists' assets, has not been able to increase its staff. Meanwhile the State Department's unit dealing with terrorism financing has had to cancel trips to help other countries because of the lack of travel funds.

There is also an imbalance in the Department of Homeland Security (DHS), which is expected to obtain $2.6 billion to protect the nation's infrastructure. By contrast, the Defense Department budget has allocated $7.6 billion for improved protection of military bases that already have some degree of protection.

In addition to budgetary constraints, a serious weakness of counterterrorism is a lack of strong international laws. The United Nations' Security Council Resolution 1373, passed after 9/11, requires member nations to take steps against the financing of terrorists. As part of this effort, the United States and other developed countries such as Britain, Germany, Australia, New Zealand, and Canada have worked with emerging nations; but there is still a long way to go.

For example, the State Department and Justice Department used ATA funding to hold six seminars for 36 countries in 2002 to provide suggestions for assessing and strengthening counterterrorist laws and regulations. Half a dozen countries took part in each week-long seminar, but because of time constraints, it was not a forum to discuss thoroughly each country's individual current legislation and needs. As a follow-up to the seminars, small teams that specialize in drafting legislation were supposed to be sent to countries that requested their assistance. In the next (the third) stage, assistance was to be provided for training investigators and prosecutors. However, these follow-up stages, which would cost only an estimated $800,000 a year for about half a dozen countries annually, were stalled because of budget and staff issues in the State Department's counterterrorism office and funding issues between the Antiterrorism Assistance Program and the Justice Department.

These budget issues and programs are important because a higher priority should be given to implementing the United States' existing counterterrorist laws and strengthening legislation in other countries. Passing laws is not enough. There must be enough financial resources and human resources—investigators, prosecutors, trainers, and security officials. And at the level of the White House and the NSC, priority should be given to implementing counterterrorist programs and pushing the bureaucracy and Congress to provide the necessary resources.

To some extent, there is a problem of mindset. OMB and congressional budget specialists tend to look at the previous year's budget as the baseline for the new fiscal year. Thus when they work out appropriations, they tend to think in terms of the relationship to the previous year's budget and add or subtract a certain percentage, instead of focusing on the actual needs of a program. They may then describe an appropriation as an increase of X percent over last year's budget instead of noting that it is, say, only 75 percent of the program's projected requirement.

NEW LEGISLATION

As law enforcement officials gain more experience with existing counterterrorism laws, they (or defense attorneys) find loopholes, and as the terrorism threat evolves, additional legislation may be desirable to fine-tune and build on the existing legal structure. Already some proposed new legislation has been drafted, intended to fill gaps that were discovered during the conflicts in Afghanistan and Iraq. For example, a bill to make it illegal for citizens or residents of the United States to receive military-type training from a designated FTO was incorporated in the Intelligence Reform Act.

Many other provisions the administration sought as a result of experiences following 9/11 were incorporated in the Intelligence Reform Act of 2004. Thus the legislative stage is at a consolidation and reevaluation rather than a new initiative stage. Some relatively minor provisions could be useful, such as specifically making attacks on mass transit subject to prosecution as terrorism. It would be useful to try to consolidate and rewrite the existing counterterrorism laws into one comprehensive package and resolve any inconsistencies or clarify any ambiguous passages. However, this would be a tremendously time-consuming undertaking. When State Department and Justice Department officials discussed the issue in the past, there was a reluctance to open up the door to what some officials worried might result in Congress writing in provisions that might be unworkable or counterproductive.

If there is another large-scale terrorist attack, there will be a scramble to "do something"—and that often involves introducing and passing new laws. Lawmakers and the executive branch must collaborate to ensure that such legislation is carefully drafted.

CONCLUSION

At one time—before the political tension between the Clinton administration and the Republican-controlled Congress, and before 9/11—fighting terrorism was mainly a bipartisan effort. That is no longer necessarily true. For example, although the Senate Intelligence Reform Bill implementing the recommendations of the 9/11 Commission was passed with a bipartisan consensus, the Republican leadership in the House pushed its 9/11 bill through in October 2004 without meaningful hearings or debate. The House conference report then ran into strong opposition from two key House committee chairs before pressure from the White House and 9/11 family organizations persuaded the House to pass the bill during the post-election lame-duck session.

If good legislation is to be passed in the future, the Senate model is preferable. A great deal will depend on whether the press and public pay attention when these often complicated measures are being considered. It also depends on whether Congress can change its habits and deal with these difficult issues in a more considered manner—not rushing during the immediate aftermath of an attack, when its members are scrambling to "do something." That will be the real test of leadership.

N O T E S

1. Section 303 of the International Security Assistance and Arms Export Control Act of 1976, which created Sec. 620A of the Foreign Assistance Act (since modified in 2002, Public Law 107-115: Stat. 3147, 2153. 2155).

2. Section 6(j) of the Export Administration Act of 1979 (P.L. 96-72. Codified as 50 U.S.C. App. Sec. 2405). In 1988, "would enhance" was changed to "could enhance." Also, the dollar threshold was lowered, making the provision more stringent.

3. Section 1202 of the Omnibus Diplomatic Security and Antiterrorism Act of 1986 (P.L. 99-399, 18 U.S.C 2332). Section 60022 of the Violent Crime Control and Law Enforcement Act of 1994 added a death penalty provision.

4. P.L. 104-132 (28 U.S.C. 1602 et seq.).

5. 46 U.S.C. App. §§ 1801–1805.

6. P.L 103-322, Sec. s12005a.

7. E. O. 2947 and executive orders freezing the assets of other terrorist groups after 9/11 were issued pursuant to the International Emergency Economic Powers Act (P.L. 95-223).

8. The provisions regarding FTOs and material support were signed into law on 24 April 1996 as part of AEDPA (P.L. 104-132, 110 Stat.). Although the bill had been drafted in response to terrorism overseas, it gained impetus after the bombing in Oklahoma City. The wording of the final draft suffered to some extent because the Clinton administration and the Republican-controlled Congress prodded each other to move quickly before various recesses.

9. 18 U.S.C. Sec. 2339B.

10. P.L. 101-298.

11. Uniting and Strengthening America by Providing Appropriate Tools Required to Intersect and Obstruct Terrorism Act of 2001 (P.L 107-56). USA PATRIOT is the acronym.

12. 46 U.S.C. Sec 761.

13. 18 U.S.C. Sec. 2333.

14. P.L. 104-132 (28 U.S.C. 1602 et seq.).

CHAPTER 22

Transatlantic Counterterrorism: Some Recommendations

Karen J. Greenberg
Executive Director, Center on Law and Security,
New York University

INTRODUCTION

The policing and judicial working alliances between the United States and the countries of Europe belie their fragile diplomatic relations. Much remains to be done to strengthen these ties as the western powers enhance their efforts to defeat Islamist terrorists. Following is a summary of some of the more important European law enforcement trends in counterterrorism, and a series of suggestions for strengthening the ties between American and European powers in the global war on terror.

BILATERALISM

The European nations pursue both bilateral and multilateral relationships with one another. Bilateral relationships are the central pillar of European counterterrorism. Police, prosecutors, and judges have a long history of relationships with one another and share information on a firsthand, frequent, and timely basis, especially between France, Spain, Germany, and England. These bilateral relations are increasingly formalized in the European context. In September 2004, for example, the French and Spanish police launched a new joint program to stem terrorism. The program involves joint efforts in enhancing information sharing, relations with Muslim communities, border security, extradition, and the implementation of the European arrest warrant.

There are a number of lessons to be learned from the bilateral relations among the European nations. They include the following important elements:

1. Structures and communication systems that encourage the sharing of timely information among agencies and police departments on a regular basis
2. Trust and good working relationships at the level of personal exchange
3. Sharing updated knowledge of known suspects whose activities may go on for years
4. Agreed-upon strategies for apprehending terrorists, including, for example, the use of surveillance over early arrest when circumstances and police capacity allow for this

With regard to the prosecution of terrorists, the following agreed-upon procedures are enhanced by bilateral relationships:

1. Understanding—e.g., between the United Kingdom and the Continent—of the differences between the common law system and the adversarial law system that exists, for example, in France
2. Standards or norms for evidence and preserving the chain of evidence that can be introduced in court
3. Standards or norms for extradition

MULTILATERALISM

Multilateralism among the European nations also exists, though with much less history than the bilateral ties. Particularly in the wake of the bombings that took place in Madrid in March 2004, the Europeans have poured energy and funds into fortifying their previously existing multilateral relationships in order to ensure swift transfers of information and rapid, coordinated policing responses. Europol and Interpol have both developed wide-ranging and effective responses in the aftermath of 9/11 and the bombings in Madrid. Interpol has decreased the time for responding to requests for information and activity so that the organization is utilized regularly as an effective means of apprehending terrorists. Europol has developed a database of information on alleged and known terrorists that has become an invaluable tool for the police in Europe. Meanwhile, in October 2004, the European Commission proposed a comprehensive antiterrorism package for coordinating information. In September 2004, Paris, London, Moscow, and Berlin formed an antiterror alliance coordinated at the level of the mayors' offices in each city.

RELATIONSHIPS WITH FOREIGN POLICE AND COURTS

Given all the energy and initiative abroad, how can the United States strengthen its involvement in bilateral and multilateral arrangements at the level of the police and the courts? The trend is definitely toward increased cooperation, as is evidenced by the fact that the United States has signed mutual legal assistance treaties (MLATs) with numerous European nations, including France, Austria, Switzerland, Luxembourg, the Czech Republic, Italy, Hungary, and the Baltic states. Treaties with Germany and Sweden have been signed but are awaiting ratification by the Senate. These treaties define activities and administrative procedures at the level of the police and the courts. They are important because of the strength of bilateral relations among European nations, which regularly share information about specific terrorist threats. Further, signs of increasing cooperation at the multilateral level are evident in the recent signing by the United States of an MLAT with the European Union (EU). This MLAT covers 25 nations and subsumes the individual country MLATs. This is an essential but by no means adequate measure.

On the level of the police, the United States has a long history of bilateral interaction. And today, the New York Police Department (NYPD), along with the intelligence services, has stationed police officers in one or two countries in Europe that are strategically important to the prosecution of terrorists. Yet these placements are few and far between. There are no NYPD officers, for example, stationed in Germany or Amsterdam, where they would be most valuable. The placement of NYPD officers in Singapore, Israel, and the United Kingdom, moreover, raises the question of language as an impediment to developing wider ties, particularly on the continent of Europe.

The FBI places legal attachés (LEGATs) in courts throughout Europe where trials of terrorists are taking place. But for the most part, experts in each of these countries live and work in the United States, from which they monitor events and persons abroad. As with the police, the main points of contact remain outside the European continent, in the United Kingdom and in Israel. Once again, both language and legal systems may account for this level of comfort. Outside the State Department, which has a political officer in each embassy assigned to watch issues of terrorism, and the Justice Department, the International Association of Prosecutors has begun to look into a more coordinated response to terrorism. Indeed, dealing with terrorism was the subject of its large international conference in Washington in the summer of 2003. Despite efforts at coordination, however, recent relations with European courts have been strained, as in the cases of Mzoudi and Mouttassedeq in Germany when the United States initially refused to turn over information from Ramzi bin al-Shibh. Now that the United States has agreed to provide excerpts from the transcripts in question, the allegations of coercive interrogation may render the information unusable in the foreign courts. A similar situation arose with the suspected terrorist Abu Hamza in England. After a prolonged effort to extradite him to the United States, the British, blocked from swift extradition because of the existence of the death penalty in the United States, decided to try him themselves. (In Hamza's case, the United States agreed not to seek the death penalty on conviction, but human rights activists delayed the extradition on the grounds that the promise could not be a guarantee.)

Finally, one of the more important aspects of counterterrorism is the relationship between law enforcement and the Muslim communities. The police in the United Kingdom have developed a coordinated outreach program; the French and the Spanish have yet to do so.

RECOMMENDATIONS
Recommendation 1

Establish programs to increase firsthand knowledge of European police and courts.

First, a program of regular appointments throughout Europe needs to be established for the purpose of bringing the United States directly into the exchange of information about terrorists. Police officers must be located in Brussels as well as in four or five of the European countries, including France, Germany, Spain, Italy, and Amsterdam. Lawyers from the Department of Justice (DOJ) must be present at every major international terrorist trial abroad.

Second, mandatory language programs are needed for lawyers and police involved in counterterrorism.

Third, mandatory courses in European law are needed for DOJ lawyers working in counterterrorism.

Fourth, the administration should include an adequate appropriations request to fund these activities.

Recommendation 2

Ensure that the United States will be able to share information in a way that is acceptable to European courts.

Programs for coordination of common law versus adversarial law courts need to be established. The use or prohibition of intelligence information in courts abroad must be understood by law enforcement officials in the United States so as to ensure the effective prosecution of terrorists abroad.

Issues of border security also must be understood within the requirements of European laws, particularly when guarantees of privacy are involved.

Recommendation 3

Increase the involvement of American police, prosecutors, and judges in the growing European counterterrorism effort.

Americans need to be involved in meetings such as the European Council's proposed efforts for coordinating the effective prevention of and response to terrorism.

Prosecutors would benefit from an organization devoted solely to coordinating efforts between American and European courts. Examples of such efforts under way include those by the International Association of Prosecutors, as well as the annual conference

"Prosecuting Terrorism: The Global Challenge" sponsored by the Center on Law and Security of the New York University (NYU) School of Law.

Recommendation 4

Create a program focusing on the relationship between law enforcement and the courts and the Muslim communities in each country.

American and European governments, including police, prosecutors, and judges, need to develop and coordinate their strategies with their Muslim communities. Specifically, the police forces, prosecutors, and court authorities in Tunisia, Algeria, and Morocco need to participate in the discussion of integrating North African Muslim communities into the European polities.

CONCLUSION

As the jihadists have declared war on the West, the West has little choice but to respond with as unified a "policy voice" as is possible. Coordination among policy-making officials, the police, and the judicial systems needs to be seamless in order to result in the effective apprehension and prosecution of terrorists. Until this coordination is improved, the fight against terror will not be as strong as it needs to be.

CHAPTER 23

International Cooperation in Counterterrorism

Gijs de Vries
Counterterrorism Coordinator, European Union

INTRODUCTION

Terrorism is not a new phenomenon; several member states of the European Union (EU) have experienced it. However, terrorism of the kind represented by 9/11 and by the attacks of 3/11 in Madrid is new, and neither America nor Europe was prepared for it. These events changed our perception of the threat we face. Terrorism is now considered a global threat that knows no borders and that must be countered globally. We are all targets, and to combat terrorism effectively we must work together.

The report of the 9/11 Commission revealed how the terrorists were able to circumvent America's defenses: how they had obtained documents and transportation and had relied on a network of facilitators. The Monograph on Terrorist Financing traced the means used by the hijackers to raise, move, and retrieve money through financial institutions based in the United States. This episode, then, holds important lessons for Europe as well as for America.

Cooperation is needed on many fronts. It is needed domestically with respect to law enforcement and prevention of attacks. Barriers must be broken down between all the different agencies involved in counterterrorism, especially with respect to sharing information. Cooperation is also needed internationally, in order to build the widest possible counterterrorist alliance, based on respect for human rights and the rule of law. Not all countries have the capacity to act against terrorism on their own. Concerted efforts are therefore necessary to give those countries political and technical support. Much has already been done along these lines, but there is still work to do.

EU is improving cooperation internally—i.e., among its 25 member states—and is fostering international cooperation. EU itself can be considered a very successful model of coordination and integration among sovereign states. Several steps can be identified in this process: establishment of a common legal framework; adoption of legislation; and, perhaps most important, implementation. I will note first what EU is doing internally, then comment on cooperation at the international level, within the framework of the United Nations (UN), with other organizations and countries, and in particular with the United States.

I was appointed counterterrorism coordinator for EU in March 2004. One of my tasks is to ensure that the appropriate structures and mechanisms are in place to facilitate cooperation among member states. I am not responsible for coordinating individual members' national counterterrorist structures or operations—that is a matter for the countries themselves. But much important work is being done at the level of EU. We are working to align the legislation of the 25 member states to improve the effectiveness of our common counter-terrorist effort. The challenge for the coming years will be to develop and fully implement a coherent strategy bringing together EU and national action.

EU responded strongly to 9/11, agreeing on a wide range of measures to enhance its ability to combat terrorism. The "European arrest warrant," for example, obliges the police of one member state to arrest a criminal on the basis of a warrant issued by a judge of another member state. This arrangement makes it more difficult for terrorists to exploit differences in national legal systems. EU has also created new agencies, such as Eurojust, which brings together prosecutors and magistrates from all member states to improve judicial cooperation. The criminal laws of the member states are being aligned so that terrorism is prosecuted and punished in the same manner throughout EU. Other measures have been initiated regarding border and transport security, health security, and civil protection. The ministers responsible for justice and home affairs have carried out an evaluation of national counterterrorism arrangements in order to identify the best practices and make recommendations for improvements. In response to this evaluation, a number of member states have already made changes to their national structures or legislation.

THE UN's ROLE

Coordination within national structures and international coordination are two sides of the same coin: the better national counterterrorist arrangements are, the greater the potential for effective international cooperation. The UN provides an essential legal framework for international cooperation in counterterrorism, and EU is fully committed to supporting that key role. To have a real impact, counterterrorism must be as nearly universal as possible. All countries should ratify and implement the UN's 12 conventions and protocols relating to counterterrorism. In recent years, the rate of ratification of these instruments has gone up. Still, of the 191 member states of the UN, only 57 are party to all 12 instruments, and 47 have ratified fewer than six. To improve this record is one objective of EU's common foreign and security policy.

Within the UN framework, the Counterterrorism Committee (CTC) established pursuant to UN Security Council Resolution (UNSCR) 1373 has a vital role to play. It has an important monitoring function as regards implementation of international obligations. A recent resolution has further strengthened its role and structure by enhancing its technical assistance function and calling for stronger cooperation with other international, regional, and subregional organizations. A key decision was the creation of an executive directorate to support the work of CTC. EU fully supports CTC, as well as other initiatives aimed at strengthening the multilateral framework for counterterrorism.

The UN is also active in other relevant areas. UNSCR 1540 deals with the link between terrorism and weapons of mass destruction. As stated in the European Security Strategy, "the most frightening scenario is one in which terrorist groups acquire weapons of mass destruction." Two draft conventions on international terrorism are currently being discussed in the UN: (1) a comprehensive convention that should include a definition of terrorism valid throughout UN member states and (2) a convention for the suppression of acts of nuclear terrorism. EU believes that their adoption would strengthen the international legal framework, develop a common ground for counterterrorism, and further mobilize international efforts. In November 2004, the General Assembly's High-Level Panel on Threats, Challenges, and Change released a report proposing a comprehensive strategy for counterterrorism. The aspects that would be included in such a strategy have much in common with the principles guiding EU in its counterterrorism.

EU's INITIATIVES

I will now touch briefly on EU's counterterrorist initiatives in the context of its relations with other countries. EU has an extensive network of relations with organizations and countries worldwide. In this network EU's instruments are political dialogue and the provision of technical assistance to countries whose capacity for counterterrorism needs to be enhanced. The challenge for EU is to coordinate its political messages and its action with other participants in counterterrorism. Synergy with like-minded countries, in particular with the United States, is being explored. Concerted efforts, especially in providing technical assistance, are desirable in order to promote synergy and avoid duplication. However, this coordination must be based on a thorough analysis of needs and on proper information from other donors. This is happening bilaterally now, through direct exchange of information between donor countries, and to some extent multilaterally. But there remains considerable room for improvement.

Internationally, transatlantic cooperation is crucial to counterterrorism. EU and the United States agree about the seriousness of the threat, and both believe that terrorism cannot be defeated without solidarity and collective action. A declaration adopted in June 2004 at a summit of EU and the United States has confirmed our common determination to collaborate in counterterrorism, while sharing a commitment to protect and respect human rights, fundamental freedoms, and the rule of law.

Since 2001, our cooperation has produced important results. Two agreements have been concluded between the European Police Office (Europol) and the United States on mutual legal assistance and on extradition. EU and the United States are working closely with Interpol to keep track of lost and stolen passports. In 2004 we established a "policy dialogue on border and transport security" that provides a forum for timely discussion of issues on which we might have different perspectives. Such different perspectives, however, should not—and do not—impede our cooperation, which is ongoing on a wide range of areas. Our systems do differ in some respects, and this implies that in some cases our responses might not be exactly alike. The agreements reached on the Container Security Initiative and on passengers' name records are examples of how we should handle these differences—working together in order to find acceptable solutions, even on sensitive issues.

UNDERLYING FACTORS

Countering terrorism is not only a matter of preventing attacks, punishing terrorists, and dismantling terrorist networks. It is also a struggle over values. This is a crucial dimension of our counterterrorist strategy. The UN General Assembly has stated that terrorism "is in any circumstances unjustifiable, whatever the consideration of a political, philosophical, ideological, racial, ethnic, religious, or other nature that may be invoked to justify" it. In this respect, ratification and implementation of all the relevant UN instruments will help build a global consensus in support of these principles, and a legal framework for specific action. The adoption of the comprehensive convention on terrorism would send an unequivocal message and further contribute to depriving terrorism of legitimacy.

However, our rejection of any justification for terrorism should not obscure the need to identify the underlying factors that may encourage support for terrorists and recruitment into their ranks; when these factors have been identified, strategies to address them must be developed. This issue is not easily resolved. There is no simple, causal link between social or political conditions and the decision of a particular individual to engage in an act of terrorism. Nevertheless, addressing issues such as poverty, bad governance, poor education, and unfavorable demographics will undoubtedly diminish the sense of deprivation, despondency, and despair that radicals seek to exploit. Politically, issues such as the Arab-Israeli conflict and the situations in Chechnya and Iraq cause anger and resentment throughout the Muslim world, and these feelings are exploited in extremist propaganda as examples of a global campaign against Muslims. Therefore, policies in support of peace, democracy, the rule of law, good governance, and human rights are essential.

PROTECTING HUMAN RIGHTS

Protecting human rights while fighting terrorism is fundamental to EU's counterterrorist strategy. Counterterrorism must respect international law, in particular international human rights, refugee, and humanitarian law. Civil liberties are at the heart of our societies, and we would be giving in to the terrorists if we gave up human rights. If we want to win the struggle of ideas, we have to show the world that whatever the circumstances, free societies will continue to respect human rights and human dignity. We must be careful not to give recruitment propaganda to al-Qaida and its supporters. Violating human rights and the rule of law is not only morally wrong but also ineffective against terrorism in the long run.

An active human rights policy must be an integral part of our policies to address the roots of terrorism. As Louise Arbour, the UN's high commissioner for human rights, has argued, there can be no genuine personal security if people's rights are in peril. Almost one-quarter of the UN's member states have still not joined the International Covenant on Civil and Political Rights, and almost one-third are not a party to the Convention against Torture and Other Cruel, Inhuman, or Degrading Treatment or Punishment. EU is committed to promoting the universal ratification of these instruments to protect human rights and strengthen the rule of law. EU is equally committed to the widest possible ratification of the Rome Statute of the International Criminal Court.

CONCLUSION

Terrorism will remain a long-term challenge with no quick or easy solutions. Even though there will be silent successes, there will also be setbacks. Close international cooperation, including across the Atlantic, remains crucial to counterterrorism and to defending the rule of law. EU and its member states are determined to play their full part.

Counterterrorism Intelligence and Analysis

CHAPTER 24

Introduction to Section 4

Sidney J. Caspersen
Director, Office of Counter-Terrorism, State of New Jersey

Since 9/11, *homeland security* has become a new catchphrase, and the responsibility for securing the homeland now belongs to many more entities than ever before. The United States has recognized that with regard to terrorism, what happens overseas has a direct impact on domestic security. Therefore, it is no longer realistic or useful to think of America's response as predominantly domestic or international— nor is it useful to apply such categories as "state or federal" and "law enforcement or intelligence." We must bring all available resources to bear.

This realization has raised challenges, many of which were articulated in the final report of the 9/11 Commission. How can we achieve preventive, rather than reactive, counterterrorism? How can we merge the capabilities of law enforcement with those of intelligence? How can we make intelligence analysis actionable? Perhaps most important, how can we ensure that information will be shared among all the entities that share responsibility for homeland security?

These challenges are nowhere more evident than at the state and local level, which may also be the most critical level of counterterrorism. It was not CIA operatives or FBI agents but state and local law enforcement officers who had contact, though unwittingly, with the 9/11 hijackers. In fact, just two days before 9/11 Ziad Jarrah, the hijacker who piloted United Airlines Flight 93, was stopped by a

Maryland state trooper for speeding on I-95. Moreover, terrorists lived among us as they prepared for 9/11 and, earlier, for the first bombing of the World Trade Center in 1993. Traditionally, state and local law enforcement officials have handled "evidence," not "intelligence." They have not hired intelligence analysts and have not themselves received training in counterterrorism. But at the state and local level, just as at the national level, analysis must drive investigations in order to achieve truly preventive counterterrorism. Local and state law enforcement officers should be our first line of defense against terrorist threats; to serve this function, they must have the necessary training and must have access to the necessary information.

In this regard, one model is the New Jersey Office of Counter-Terrorism (OCT), created by executive order in January 2002 to "administer, coordinate, and lead New Jersey's counterterrorism and preparedness efforts with the goals of identifying, deterring, and detecting terrorist-related activities." OCT, the state's primary counterterrorist agency, has four divisions: intelligence, investigations, critical infrastructure, and training. The intelligence division monitors data from all sources—local, state, federal, foreign, and open—to assess current threats and to help identify vulnerabilities and investigative resources. The investigations division works with the FBI and other law enforcement entities to conduct inquiries into reported suspicious activity and "precursor" crimes, in a proactive effort to discern and forestall terrorist threats. The critical infrastructure division liaises with some 20 private-sector groups to alert them to relevant information about threats, develop protective buffers, and establish "best practices" for security. The training division has instructed thousands of state, county, and local police officers in counterterrorism. In short, OCT is attempting to put into practice at the state level a strategy that will meet the challenges posed by terrorists.

The chapters in Section 4 capture the new reality and the attendant challenges in considerable detail, discussing counter-terrorist intelligence work in the law enforcement and intelligence communities, providing a framework for analyzing terrorist operations, describing the current threat, and describing the agencies that make up our response apparatus. In Chapter 25 Dennis Pluchinsky, though acknowledging that each terrorist offensive or operation is unique, offers a typology and anatomy of terror attacks. Because operational areas, triggers, organizational structure, membership, logistics, finances, and weapons change relatively slowly, it is valuable to study a group's preferences, tendencies, patterns, and conventions. In Chapter 26 C. Patrick Duecy contrasts the present period of transnational terrorism with the Cold War era and emphasizes the current challenge of gathering accurate, reliable, and timely intelligence. Mark Kauppi in Chapter 27 explains the "intelligence process" and the challenge of determining what information is necessary and accurate enough to feed into that process. He also considers the expanded role of law enforcement, which since 9/11 has come to include intelligence.

CHAPTER 25

A Typology and Anatomy of Terrorist Operations

Dennis A. Pluchinsky
Senior Threat Analyst, TranSecur, Inc.
Terrorism Analyst, U.S. Department of State, Retired

Attack! Attack! Attack! Terrorists must carry out attacks or operations, which are their primary reason for existence. Terror cannot be instilled by just threats and rhetoric; words must be backed up by action. Thus a terrorist group's daily activities— acquiring and using safe houses, traveling, recruiting, gathering intelligence, developing logistics, training, communicating, experimenting—all support the planning, preparation, and execution of operations.

There are essentially three types of terrorist operations: offensive, logistical, and psychological. Offensive operations are designed to inflict casualties, take hostages, or cause property damage. Logistical operations are carried out to acquire weapons, money, explosives, false documents, and to release imprisoned colleagues. Psychological operations are effected to have an emotional impact on the enemy and usually consist of threatening statements, false claims of responsibility, bomb threats, audio and video messages, and video clips showing offensive operations, hostages, and their executions and beheadings. Clearly, offensive operations also produce an emotional blow on the enemy, but psychological operations are intended to fill the lull between offensive operations in order to keep the enemy off balance and apprehensive.

OFFENSIVE OPERATIONS

There are basically seven types of offensive operations: (1) explosives attacks, (2) weapons attacks, (3) hostage-taking, (4) standoff weapons attacks, (5) materials attacks, (6) cyberattacks, and (7) combination attacks.

Explosives Attacks

Explosives attacks involve detonating explosives—hidden in various containers and using different fuses—and are designed to kill people or damage property. They are the most frequent type of attack because they are cheap and flexible as regards method of delivery, container, fusing system, explosive filler, and shrapnel attachments. Suicide, a tactical ingredient that enhances the psychological impact of an offensive attack, can of course be added. Suicide bombers detonate explosives worn on the body or hidden in objects in their possession, or drive a vehicle filled with explosives into a target. The choice of container and fusing system in particular makes the explosives attack an attractive operation for terrorists, allowing them to use their imagination. The attacks of 9/11 were an innovative method of delivery and container: the terrorists used commercial aircraft to deliver an explosives package into buildings.

Weapons Attacks

Weapons attacks involve only knives, handguns, rifles, machine pistols, and machine guns. The purpose is primarily to inflict casualties, but strafing can also be used to damage property. Weapons attacks have been used in both arm's-reach and remote assassinations. Here too, suicide can be added: in shooter suicides terrorists are armed with weapons that they fire until they are killed.

Hostage-Taking

Hostages are taken in order to extract concessions from an enemy or to publicize a group's grievances. Weapons and explosives are used in these attacks but are simply tools. Typical scenarios are kidnapping, hijacking, and barricading. In a kidnapping, the hostage is removed from the attack site and taken to a hidden location. A hijacking involves seizing hostages aboard a mode of transportation (bus, train, ship, airplane); the location of the hostages is known but can be changed. Most hijackings have involved airplanes. In a barricade situation, hostages are seized in a building such as an embassy, a consulate, a theater, a hotel, apartments, or a house; the location of the hostages is known and stationary. Most barricade situations have been at diplomatic facilities. If, in the context of terrorist operations, suicide is defined as the intentional death of the terrorist, it cannot be applied to hostage-taking. The objective of hostage-taking attacks is to extract concessions from a target government; the operatives are expected to escape or be allowed to leave unhindered.

Standoff Weapons Attacks

Standoff weapons attacks use only weapons designed to be fired at a safe distance from the target, so as to ensure surprise and escape. Such attacks are aimed at motorcades, buildings, and modes of transportation, primarily aircraft. Notable standoff weapons are antiarmor rockets, surface-to-air missiles, rifle grenades, and mortars. We may eventually see standoff weapons such as thermobarometric guns and electromagnetic pulse cannons.

Materials Attacks

Materials attacks use only chemical, biological, radiological, or nuclear (CBRN) materials, primarily against people and buildings, in order to kill and cause panic. Suicide can be an ingredient: a terrorist may be infected with a deadly biological agent, or CBRN materials can be packed around an explosive device to be detonated by a terrorist who will die in the explosion.

Cyberattacks

A cyberattack involves digitally targeting a computer information system so as to destroy, damage, or steal data and thereby disrupt or disable telecommunications, health, transportation, finances, utilities, food distribution, and other critical infrastructure systems. The primary target of a cyberattack is information, but such attacks can ultimately cause casualties, depending on the system targeted.

Combination Attacks

A combination attack involves more than one method. The most frequent combination is weapons and explosives; the next most frequent is weapons and standoff weapons.

LOGISTICAL OPERATIONS

Logistical operations are carried out to acquire money, false documents, weapons, explosives, and other things needed for offensive operations. Logistical operations also include attacks on prisons or jails to free imprisoned colleagues, or to execute traitors in the group so as to ensure discipline and security.

PSYCHOLOGICAL OPERATIONS

Offensive operations are designed to have a psychological impact; and psychological operations can be used between offensive operations, as a supplement. Such psychological operations are aimed at undermining the enemy's resolve and sense of security, and eroding citizens' confidence in their leaders.

Psychological operations primarily involve circulating stated textual, video, or audio threats. Since 9/11, mostly because global jihadists have recognized the value of the Internet, there has been a marked increase in threats posted there. Such threats are meant to keep the enemy unbalanced, cause it to expend resources on security (and thus reveal its security measures and response time), and create insecurity in the enemy population. Another component of psychological operations is to tape offensive operations and broadcast these on the Internet. Before 9/11 terrorist groups rarely filmed their attacks and seldom distributed such films to Internet sites; but since 9/11 Iraqi, Kashmiri, Pakistani, Saudi, and Palestinian terrorist groups have included combat cameramen in their attack teams. For example, when Chechen terrorists took schoolchildren hostage in the town of Beslan in the Russian republic of North Ossetia on 1–3 September 2004, combat cameramen filmed parts of the operation. This video was later recovered and shown on television around the world. In 2004 there was a significant increase in hostage-taking by terrorist groups, especially in Iraq and Saudi Arabia. Many of the hostages were filmed, and the videos were distributed on Internet sites belonging to the terrorists and their supporters. Some hostages were beheaded; these executions too were filmed and shown on Internet sites. Such filming of hostages was initiated by Lebanese Shia terrorist groups in the mid-1980s, when western hostages were being seized in Lebanon, but at that time the execution of hostages was rare and was not filmed. After 9/11 the first hostage whose execution was filmed was Daniel Pearl, who was seized by Pakistani global jihadists in Karachi in January 2002.

A disturbing trend since 9/11 is the global jihadists' increasing reliance on the Internet and their recognition that to instill fear in the enemy they must intensify terror. If the media pay less attention to terrorists' acts or refuse to publish or broadcast terrorist propaganda and threats, the terrorists feel compelled to attack a dramatic target, use dramatic tactics, or circumvent the media. Sooner or later, when Americans or Europeans are watching television, the broadcast signal will be hijacked by terrorists who will read a threatening statement or show a videotaped execution.

There was a new development in July 2004 when phantom or virtual terrorist groups—with names like Abu-Hafs al-Masri Brigades, Islamboli Brigades of Al-Qaida, Martyrs of the Nation Movement, Jama'at Abi-Bakr al-Libi, Supporters of the Islamic Holy War Group, Battalions of Islamic Jihad (Black Death) Brigade, and Muhammad Ata Brigades—issued threats on the Internet, saying that they would attack countries in western Europe and Latin America if these countries did not withdraw their troops from Iraq.[1] Threats from virtual groups are posted anonymously in Islamic forums and chat rooms. Also, virtual groups sometimes falsely claim responsibility for actual terrorist attacks; such claims become "ground clutter" for counterterrorist analysts. It is not known whether the threats and false claims from the various virtual groups are coordinated or are simply issued by individuals trying to make a contribution to the global jihad. In any case, the Internet is likely to become even more of a focal point as terrorist groups and their sympathizers take advantage of it, and of desktop publishing programs and audio-video editing programs. The Internet allows these groups to go around the target government and address the people directly—in effect, they are dropping virtual propaganda leaflets behind the enemy's lines.

STAGES OF A TERRORIST OPERATION

Each terrorist offensive or logistical operation is unique. Weapons and tactics may be similar, but attacks usually differ in timing, objectives, the experience and ability of the terrorists, the security around the target, and the ramifications. Each group has its own operational code, tactical playbook, targeting menu, operational rhythm, skill level, experience, worldview, and ideological mind-set. Despite these differences, there appear to be certain sequential stages that a terrorist group will confront when planning an offensive or logistical operation. (Because this is less true of psychological operations, henceforth *attack* will refer only to offensive and logistical operations.)

There are seven sequential stages of an attack: (1) the "trigger," (2) establishing targeting parameters, (3) researching the target, (4) selecting the target, (5) planning the operation, (6) executing the attack, and (7) postattack evaluation.

Stage 1: The Trigger

Spontaneous attacks are rare; usually, an attack has an internal or external "trigger." The trigger stage essentially initiates an operation by providing a reason to take action now. Triggers are generally events. An internal trigger could be a formal split or a power struggle within the group; an anniversary; impatience or discontentment among group members, sympathizers, supporters, or sponsors regarding the frequency of attacks; the discovery of a traitor; a need for money, weapons, explosives, documents, etc.; or maintenance of the group's operational tempo. The latter is designed to put constant pressure on the enemy by carrying out a certain number of attacks per week, month, or year. Human resources, logistics, law enforcement and intelligence in the host country, the targeting menu, and the operational area are factors in the frequency of attacks, as are the size and nature of the group. Larger groups carry out more attacks; and in general, ethnic and left-wing groups carry out more attacks than right-wing, single-issue, or religious groups. Operational tempos can change as a result of a voluntary decision by the group; or a change can be imposed if the police arrest members or discover safe houses or weapons caches.

An internal trigger can be a piece of intelligence sent to a terrorist group by a supporter or sympathizer. For example, when the separatist group Basque Nation and Freedom (ETA) assassinated Prime Minister Carrero Blanco of Spain in Madrid in December 1973, the attack originated with "a piece of information like many others that come our way."[2] According to the leader of the ETA commando that carried out the attack, "ETA was given a secret news report that in Madrid, Luis Carrero Blanco went to mass every morning at 9 in a Jesuit church on Serrano Street."[3] ETA's leadership sent a member to Madrid to check out the report. A more recent example is the kidnapping of an American, Paul Johnson, in Saudi Arabia on 12 June 2004 by al-Qaida's Arabian Peninsula affiliate: one operative stated that "the mujahidin received information about an American man who would make a good target for a kidnapping."[4]

Attacks can also be triggered by external events such as national elections, arrests of terrorists, visits by foreign dignitaries, hunger strikes by imprisoned terrorists, meetings of international organizations, domestic scandals, controversial domestic issues, or international events.

All terrorist groups have two types of qualitative operations: high-value and low-value. Low-value operations are aimed at soft, common targets such as the police, local politicians, businesses, soldiers, journalists, or local government officials. Decisions to attack such targets are usually made by local cells, without consultation with the higher leadership. Low-value operations account for most of a group's operational rhythm. In contrast, high-value operations are aimed at prominent people or facilities of the national government and foreign targets: national politicians; government leaders; high-ranking military officers; high-ranking police officials; corporate leaders; central government institutions; and foreign embassies, consulates, and diplomats. Most high-value operations take place in the capitals of targeted states. The prominence or notoriety of the targets usually means that they have some measure of security; thus the operations are more complicated and may require more planning and human resources. Because high-level attacks have political and security implications and ramifications, the decision to carry out these operations is usually made by a group's higher leadership. High-value operations are usually triggered by national events (such as elections), anniversaries, arrests of terrorist leaders, or a group's desire to demonstrate the seriousness of its threats.

Most terrorist groups carry out both low-value and high-value operations. Some groups establish special operational units, plant them in capitals, and use them for high-profile actions. The Irish Republican Army (IRA) had such a division of labor. Most of its cells in Northern Ireland carried out frequent attacks on low-value targets while its supreme leadership body, the Army Council, controlled special active service units that carried out attacks on the British mainland, in Ireland and Western Europe, or on high-profile targets in Northern Ireland. ETA had a similar arrangement: its leadership in southern France had more operational control over its special Madrid or España commando, which was planted in the capital. The Liberation Tigers of Tamil Eelam (LTTE) had high-value operations in the capital, Colombo, that were controlled by the leadership. However, LTTE understood the political and international ramifications of these attacks and rarely claimed responsibility for them; also, as of this writing, LTTE had not claimed responsibility for the assassination of the former Indian Prime Minister Rajiv Gandhi in Madras, India, in 1991. This pattern also seems to apply to the Islamic revolutionaries in Chechnya. Attacks outside Chechnya—especially attacks in Moscow—are considered high-value and are more tightly controlled by the leadership.

Some terrorist groups focus more on high-value than low-value operations. The Red Army Faction, a left-wing political group in Germany in the 1970s and 1980s, attacked mostly high-value targets.[5] Al-Qaida's attacks on and before 9/11 were orchestrated and approved by the central leadership in Afghanistan. Immediately after 9/11, evidently, the central leadership in Pakistan approved several high-value operations such as those in Tunisia, Morocco, and Kenya. After the arrest of Khalid Sheikh Mohammad in March 2003 in Pakistan, the decision making for high-value attacks seems to have been delegated by default to regional or local al-Qaida commanders.

By contrast, some groups focus primarily on low-value targets. The Communist Combatant Cells (CCC, a left-wing terrorist group) in Belgium and the Corsican National Liberation Front (FLC) are two examples. Both have carried out predominantly bombings designed only to damage property, going out of their way to avoid inflicting casualties. This is also true of several small left-wing terrorist groups active in Germany and Italy during the 1970s, like the Revolutionary Cells and the Popular Resistance Group.

Identifying potential triggers allows counterterrorist analysts to determine a "threat window" and take appropriate security measures.

Such triggers do not indicate a precise target, location, or time; they simply suggest the possibility of an attack and a need to go on an alert and dig for more information.

Stage 2: Targeting Parameters

Terrorist offensive attacks are constructed in order to convey a political message to the enemy. ("Throw-away" attacks, conducted simply for the sake of attacking, are illogical and rare.) In stage 2, the major question to be answered is what the specific political message should be. It can be subtle or blatant and can be aimed at one audience or several audiences; and it is decided primarily by the group or cell leadership.

The next question is what target will be most appropriate for transmitting the message. Should the target be a person or an object? Should there be one target or several? Should the target be within or outside the group's usual operational area? What sector should it represent—political, security, diplomatic, military, social, transportation, or economic? Should it be domestic or foreign? Should the attack be lethal, nonlethal, discriminate, or indiscriminate? Will the target be acceptable to group members, sympathizers, supporters, state sponsors, financial sponsors, and the community?

Not all terrorist groups address all these questions, but general guidelines regarding targets are often set when a group is first formed. Some conditions—lethal versus nonlethal attacks, domestic versus foreign targets, discriminate versus indiscriminate operations, and attacks within a group's region or country versus attacks outside it—are usually set by the group's founders. The guidelines may be altered as the group grows or declines in strength or the political environment changes; modifications will depend on situations that the group encounters as it evolves. Generally, however, terrorist groups are hesitant to revise their general conditions for targeting.

CCC made the following statements concerning targets:

> The choice of the targets we attacked was basically dictated by the political purpose of our campaign.... There were also other considerations; to what level of revolutionary violence could we take the attack, given the degree of consciousness of the class movement and the actual size of our forces?... Having examined the problem of class consciousness, we decided that for our first campaign, our action would not include the execution of enemy leaders.... Since mobility is

one of the tactical foundations of guerrilla warfare, we decided to attack "sector by sector." We decided, in other words, that we would "never look back" during our campaign. We undertook three actions against the economic sector, two against the political sector, and three against the military sector.[6]

Another question sometimes addressed at stage 2 is whether an attack will be "unlinked" or will initiate a terrorist campaign—that is, a series of political and armed attacks linked by a central theme. Such a theme is usually obvious but sometimes can be difficult to discern. For example, in 1984–1985 CCC carried out three campaigns against different economic sectors: the October Anti-Imperialist Campaign, Karl Marx Campaign, and Pierre Akkerman Campaign.[7] It explained its deliberations as follows:

> Contrary to the gossip in the media, which misrepresents our policy by presenting it as an accidental and anarchic congeries of operations by partisans, we always act after reflection and criticism, in a spirit of order and method, on the basis of precise analyses and as a function of the goals to be achieved, both political and organization, immediate or historical.[8]

Terrorist groups seldom reveal their decision-making processes. CCC provided more information about this than any other terrorist group that has emerged since 1968; al-Qaida is more typical, saying very little about how it thinks and how it establishes targets. Sulayman Abu Gayth, a reported spokesman for al-Qaida, said in July 2002 that it "functions according to a rigorous secret logic."

Stage 3: Researching the Target

Once the above target parameters are decided and a proposed target(s) is selected, a terrorist group will then initiate target research. There are two types of target research: tasked and continuing. *Tasked* target research is when a group's leadership or cell leader will specifically ask group members to gather information on specific targets or targeting sectors. As previously noted, the target or targeting sector is determined by the attack trigger and target parameters. *Continuing* target research is the ongoing process of collecting information on possible targets for future operations. An example of continuing target research would be the January 2003 discovery in Carrickfergus, Northern Ireland, of an Ulster Defense

Association, a Protestant loyalist terrorist group, safe house containing names, addresses, and car registration details of between 200 to 300 people in the greater Belfast area.[9] A more recent example is the October 2004 discovery in Italy of Red Brigade computer files with a very long list of 291 names of high-profile people from Italy's political circles, trade unions, and state bureaucracy.[10] Both of these examples underline the fact that terrorist groups are constantly collecting information on targets. To quote again the Belgian CCC: "Intelligence gathering is nothing to be ashamed of; it is a totally necessary activity. We devote a great deal of our actual work to spying on the economic, political, or military systems of the bourgeoisie. The more we do, the more we succeed in penetrating its 'secrets'."[11]

There are four components of the target research stage: (1) open-source research, (2) insider information or planting spies, (3) electronic surveillance, and (4) physical surveillance.

Open-Source Research

Open-source research involves acquiring relevant political and operational information on the target(s). It is generally the first phase of target research. If the proposed target is a person, then information will be collected on that person's political views, previous positions, associations, and actions. The purpose of this collection effort is to politically evaluate the target; assess its value to the group as a target; and to uncover any operational information on the target's residence and work locations, security measures, vehicle identification, family members, relatives, membership in clubs, places of worships, and favorite recreation sites. Some of this information could eventually be incorporated into the group's written claim of responsibility for the attack or the attack communiqué. In the attack communiqué, the terrorist group usually explains why it attacked the target. Terrorist groups have always used open-source research to acquire information on targets of interest. Before the advent of the Internet, open-source research was primarily conducted by reading newspapers, journals, and magazines; listening to radio and TV broadcasts; and visiting libraries and bookstores. Arrests of members of left-wing and ethnic terrorist groups in Western Europe in the 1970s and 1980s usually led the police to terrorist safe houses that contained voluminous files of newspaper and magazine clippings and microfiche printouts on prominent personalities. Many groups maintained political dossiers on potential targets for future use. The Red Army Faction, a left-wing terrorist group in Germany in the 1970s and 1980s, frequently carried out research on potential targets in German libraries. Open-source research has always been a key ingredient in terrorist target research. Sean MacStiofain, a former intelligence officer for the Irish Republican Army's (IRA) London unit in the 1940s and a former chief of staff for the breakaway Provisional Irish Republican Army (PIRA) in the 1970s, stated in his memoirs: "I issued instructions to IOs (intelligence officers) that they should study the daily and local newspapers carefully, and indeed read every serious magazine and periodical they could lay their hands on."[12] In a further testament for the value of open-source research, he noted:

> I quickly realized how much a shrewd intelligence organization can put together from systematic study of serious newspapers and military magazines, apart from the efforts of its agents and contacts. There was a case in the 'thirties in which one man was able to build up the accurate order of battle of the German army just by close analysis of the German provincial press down to reports of dinners and even engagement notices.... We used to spend a fair amount of time in the military section of Foyle's bookshop.[13]

More recently, a suspected global jihadist training manual that was discovered in Manchester, England, noted that:

> Using public sources openly and without resorting to illegal means, it is possible to gather at least 80% of the information about the enemy. The percentage varies depending on the government's policy on freedom of the press and publication. It is possible to gather information through newspapers, magazines, books, periodicals, official publications, and enemy broadcasts. Attention should also be given to the opinion, comments, and jokes of the common people.[14]

With the advent of the Internet, open-source research has been made easier for terrorist groups. They no longer have to spend time in a library or bookstore. They no longer need to clip out articles from newspapers, magazines, and professional journals. Government-sponsored or published studies and reports; academic articles; company Web sites; map and photo libraries; and newspaper, magazine, and journal articles can all be accessed on the Internet in a matter of minutes. The Internet is an open-source gold mine for terrorists conducting target research. The media in particular have been very helpful in pointing out vulnerabilities to terrorist groups.[15] Personal information on potential targets, detailed mention of potential target vulnerabilities, and follow-up reports on the status of those vulnerabilities are key ingredients that can be found in open sources and help terrorists gather information on a potential target. Media and academic censorship would be an extreme solution to plug up this vulnerability. The use of common sense by academia and media editors and an understanding of what type of information is valuable to terrorists would be a more appropriate, voluntary patch.

Insider Information

Another method of collecting research on a target is to plant a spy with or near the target. A terrorist group can use members, sympathizers, supporters, or nonaffiliated people to gain employment or vendor access to the target. This method is very valuable when the target has extensive security measures, thereby making it difficult to acquire information through open sources or electronic and physical surveillance. Information on the internal layout of a hard target, details on the inner security perimeter, and movement plans of the targeted person can be acquired with planted spies. Using this method, terrorists can acquire valuable operational information concerning the target. If the target is a building, information such as the internal security measures of the building, accurate floor plans, access passes to certain floors, identification badges, and the office location of specific personnel can be obtained. If the target is a person, a spy or informant could get information such as the schedule of meetings or movements, identification of relatives or friends, and favorite places to eat, etc. It is easier to plant spies or informants near targets if the agent has a clean background and no known associations with extremist groups. Of more value to the terrorists is to try and convince a long-time employee to cooperate with the group and provide insider information. The purpose of insider information is usually operational in nature and used to supplement open-source research and electronic and physical surveillance of the target. Insider information can be used to authenticate and reinforce information acquired through these other target research components. Insider information is the most prized source of target information for terrorist groups. Global jihadist training manuals frequently emphasize the recruitment of spies to collect information.[16]

The German RAF used insider information when they assassinated Juergen Ponto, the Chairman of the Board of the Dresdner Bank, on 30 July 1977. One of the RAF terrorists who was part of the commando that killed Ponto was a family friend of the Pontos and able to gain access to his house where the assassination took place. The Turkish left-wing group the Revolutionary People's Liberation Party/Front (DHKP/C) used insider information when they had a female member infiltrate the building where their assassination victim worked. This member got a job as a cleaning lady at the Sabanci headquarters building in Istanbul 4 to 5 months before the attack was carried out. The target of the attack was Ozdemir Sabanci, a leading Turkish industrialist. He was assassinated on 9 January 1996, in his office—purportedly one of the most secure buildings in Turkey.[17] This DHKP/C spy was eventually promoted and given security access to the executive suites where Sabanci was killed by a three-person DHKP/C commando. Another example of terrorists using insider information took place on 1 May 2004, when Islamic revolutionary terrorists attacked the offices of ABB Lummus Global in Yanbu, Saudi Arabia, killing two Americans, two Britons, one Australian, and one Canadian. Three of the four terrorists involved in the attack worked in the compound where ABB Lummus Global was located.[18]

Electronic Surveillance

Another component of terrorist target research is electronic surveillance. This consists of gathering information on the target by means of electronic equipment such as telephone taps, miniaturized video cameras, police scanners, global positioning systems, etc. The major characteristic of this component is that it can be carried out from a remote location and is not in the line of sight of the target. Terrorists have not to date taken full advantage of this component, and it has rarely been used. One example of terrorist electronic surveillance would be by the RAF in October 1986. The RAF had determined that their target, a German Foreign Ministry official named Gerold Von Braunmuehl, had the habit of working late at the foreign ministry. When he was ready to go home he would call a taxicab to come pick him up and take him home. The RAF, using a radio scanner, picked up the call for the taxi and waited for von Braunmuehl to arrive home. When he arrived the RAF killed him. Terrorist use of electronic surveillance will most likely increase as potential targets increase their capability to detect physical surveillance. This will force terrorist groups to rely more on electronic surveillance conducted from remote surveillance perches. This is a logical evolution of terrorist surveillance methods.

Physical Surveillance

The fourth component of terrorist target research is physical surveillance. Physical surveillance is the hostile systematic visual observation of a facility, location, person, or route with the intention of possibly attacking that target. There are four stages to physical surveillance: pilot, full, update, and final. Physical surveillance is also called casing, observation, gathering intelligence, investigation, or reconnaissance. In late July 2004, Pakistani and U.S. authorities, after a shoot-out with terrorists, discovered some 50 computer disks in an al-Qaida safe house in Gujrat, Pakistan. The disks contained extensive surveillance notes on several buildings in New York City and Washington, D.C.[19] Much of this information had been acquired through open-source research; physical surveillance was used to supplement and confirm the research and acquire more information on the targets.

Terrorists always conduct some form of physical surveillance before an attack. The purpose is to systematically analyze a potential target to discover security measures and patterns, and vulnerabilities. This information is then examined by the group's leaders or a cell leader to determine whether an attack can be successful and—if the target is chosen—to develop a plan of attack. Surveillance is obviously important, but it is not a process that requires a wide array of special skills; it simply involves logic and common sense. Its accuracy and completeness are enhanced when surveillants have been well instructed so that they know what to look for, how to use special equipment, how to write reports, and how to identify countersurveillance or surveillance detection teams. Only during surveillance do terrorists actually expose themselves to a target, or "telegraph" their interest in it, before an attack. But "interest" is not necessarily an intent to attack: other factors, events, or conditions may prevent a group from actually planning an attack. Surveillance should be considered an indicator but with the understanding that the attack may never materialize.

In constructing a surveillance mission, certain decisions must initially be made by the person in charge of the operation. It appears that in general, terrorists may send one or two persons to conduct a "pilot" surveillance of the target and its surrounding environs. This initial report will determine how many people should make up the surveillance team, what type of equipment should be used, whether the surveillance can be carried out from fixed positions, what are the best surveillance perches around the target, what is the nature of the movement of people around the target's area, what type of cover story should be constructed, and the type of security and law enforcement presence in the area. The answers to these questions will determine the "full" surveillance package that will be sent to observe the target. One of the axioms of surveillance is the harder the target, the more complicated and lengthy the surveillance mission. After a full surveillance of the potential target has been carried out, a report will be passed on to the operational leader of the cell or group. This detailed report will contain sketches, maps, photos, and suggested attack methods. This report will be used by the cell or group leaders to decide if this target will be selected for attack.

If the leaders decide to attack another target, the surveillance report(s) of those targets not selected would be filed away and addressed at a later date if needed. When a specific target is selected for attack, the group may carry out an update surveillance of the target to make sure there have been no changes to the target's security measures and patterns. The time between the full and update surveillance depends on the timing of the attack. If the attack will take place several weeks after completion of the full surveillance then an update surveillance may not be necessary. If the attack is scheduled to take place months or years after completion of full surveillance, then one or more update surveillances may occur. If the attack team is separate from the surveillance team, then the attack team may choose to carry out a final surveillance just before the attack.

Surveillance can be done by one or more persons, or by teams that rotate to avoid detection. It can be carried out from a fixed position such as an outdoor café or park bench, or in motion—by walking behind a human target, for instance, or following one vehicle in another vehicle. There are many methods and variations. The key is for the surveillant to avoid being noticed. Some hard targets will deploy countersurveillance or surveillance detection teams. Many soft targets do not have such security, but even so, surveillance may be detected by an observant security guard, a police officer, an employee, etc. Therefore, surveillants try to blend into the surroundings, to insert themselves into the rhythm and pattern of the environment without attracting attention; they may use ruses and disguises to accomplish this. In fact, terrorists sometimes carry out surveillance of an environment before they survey the target itself. Busy urban environments are easier to blend into than isolated rural environments; and the environment around soft targets is more favorable than the environment around hard targets. The pattern and intensity of pedestrian and vehicular traffic also affect how conducive an environment is to surveillance.

It is difficult for countersurveillance to determine whether surveillance is initial, follow-up, or final—that is, preattack—but unless this question is answered accurately, costly resources may be misallocated, because some terrorist surveillance may precede an actual attack by months or years. Identifying the source of the surveillance is also important: what terrorist group is carrying it out? The answer to this question will indicate the operational capability of the group, its possible approaches to the target, and its possible tactics. Unfortunately, terrorist surveillance is rarely detected, and very few terrorists have been arrested while conducting surveillance.

Stage 4: Selecting the Target

At stage 4, the political research and physical surveillance of the potential target(s) have been completed, and the targeting packages are given to the group or cell leaders to select the final target. During the target parameters stage, the group may have developed an initial wish list of potential targets. The target research stage would have examined the operational feasibility of attacking these targets. A desired target may not necessarily be a viable target. An evaluation would be made of the submitted targets to determine which of the targets has the appropriate political value to convey the intended message of the group, whether the target is vulnerable to an attack, and what risk the group will have to accept to attack the target. This is basically a cost-benefit analysis. It involves weighing the human resources, other resources, and political costs against the political-military benefits of attacking the target. For terrorist groups that do not add the suicide ingredient to their offensive operations, this cost-benefit analysis is very important in determining whether or not to attack a particular target. These groups must consider the possibility of losing members of the attack team to death or capture during the attack. Suicide attacks in a sense eliminate that consideration since the nature of a suicide attack is such that the human resources price is a front-end charge. No escape plans have to be devised. There is little fear of capture and possible compromise of the group.

Once the group or cell leaders decide on a particular target or several targets, the information on the targets not selected may be filed away for future consideration. If the group is embarking on a terrorist campaign, then the other targets may be attacked later on in the campaign. The target selection stage ends with the group or cell leadership picking the specific target or targets for attack. In general, most terrorist attacks involve a single target. However, the targeting pattern demonstrated by al-Qaida and its affiliates so far has been to hit two or more targets simultaneously. The targets, however, have been cluster targets in the sense that they are usually in the same city.[20]

Stage 5: Planning the Operation

What type of attack should be developed? How much money will the attack cost? How large should the attack team be? Will any special skills be needed? Who will the team leader be? When should the attack take place? How will the attack team communicate with the leadership? Who will make the final decision to attack? Will additional surveillance be needed? How many members should be aware of the plan? Will it be necessary to have a support structure? How will the attack team escape? What false documents, travel arrangements, weapons, or explosives are needed, and are they available? Who will acquire the safe houses? Will a communiqué be issued claiming responsibility for the attack? If so, how and when will this communiqué be issued? Who will draft it? What political points should it include? These are questions that must be addressed during the planning stage. In some cases the group's leadership will make the decisions; in others, cell leaders will make the decisions. Once the group's leaders approve the target and the general shape of the attack, the details may be delegated to the military commander of the group. Larger groups have a clearer and more extensive division of labor in planning operations. In smaller terrorist groups, responsibilities and duties frequently overlap.

Stage 6: Executing the Attack

After the operational plan is formed and the attack team is sent to the site of the target, the team may want to carry out a final surveillance to be sure that there have been no changes in routine or security measures. (For most groups, the personnel who carry out the initial and follow-up surveillance are not members of the attack team.) Until the day of the attack, the team leader can decide to abort or postpone it. Depending on the communication channels and the agreed-on instructions, the team leader may consult with the group's leaders. On the day of the attack, once the attack is deployed, it is extremely rare for a team to abort it.

Stage 7: Postattack Evaluation

Once the attack takes place the group or cell will begin the process of evaluating whether or not the intended objectives were met and if there were any unintended consequences. A successful attack can be defined as follows: (1) the attack was carried out; (2) the target was killed or damaged; (3) the attack team escaped; and (4) the attack had a political-military impact on the enemy. Questions considered at stage 7 include: Were any team members injured? Was the group's local logistical infrastructure affected? How did the domestic and international media cover the attack? The group will also monitor the government's response, and it may monitor newspaper coverage and commentary. Eventually, the group may get feedback from its sympathizers and supporters. If the attack was part of a campaign, the group or cell may try to determine when another attack can take place. Immediate police pressure will delay an immediate follow-up operation.

ANTICIPATING TERRORIST ATTACKS

A terrorist group devotes most of its time, energy, and resources to planning, preparing, and executing attacks. All this is clandestine. The group tries to ensure that its members are unknown to the police; if members are known, the group may have them use false documents and change their appearance. An inconspicuous safe house, where the terrorists live and plan, will be selected. The lifestyle of the terrorists should not attract the attention of neighbors. When possible, the terrorists' travel and communications are camouflaged with false documents, disguises, code words, and secure communication methods. The specifics of the attack plans are compartmentalized and distributed in fragments to various team members. The acquisition of weapons and explosives for the attack is concealed. The surveillance of the target is performed discreetly. In sum, everything the terrorist group does is designed to be hidden and subtle. A main objective of counterterrorism is to detect one or more of these covert activities to learn the target, location, timing, and perpetrators of the next attack. In this race between terrorists (who want to attack) and counterterrorists (who want to prevent or postpone the attack), the terrorists usually have the upper hand—offense always has an advantage over defense because the offense knows what its next action is whereas the defense must anticipate.

If a terrorist safe house is discovered, a terrorist is arrested, a terrorist's telephone call is intercepted, a terrorist's computer is acquired, or an undercover agent provides information, anticipating the next attack is somewhat easier. This depends on the scope and detail of the information attained. The best (and most commonly used) metaphor for this process is putting together a puzzle. While the terrorists are trying to hide the pieces of the puzzle and in some cases intentionally dropping damaged, deformed, and disparate pieces, the counterterrorist analyst is trying to acquire as many pieces as possible. The first disadvantage for the analyst is that there is no box top to show how the completed puzzle looks. The second disadvantage is not knowing how many pieces are in the puzzle. Third, the analyst is usually under a time constraint.

What are the elements of this puzzle? The first is timing: when will the attack take place? Second is location: where will the attack take place? Third is the target: who or what will be attacked? Fourth is the perpetrators: who will carry out the attack? Within each of these sections is a scale of specificity. This is a very important point.

- When *will the attack take place?* Scale of specificity: (1) year, (2) quarter, (3) month, (4) week, (5) day
- Where *will the attack take place?* Scale of specificity: (1) worldwide, (2) region of the world, (3) country, (4) region of the country, (5) city, (6) street address
- What *is the target of the attack?* Scale of specificity: (1) person or object, (2) nationality, (3) sector (business, diplomatic, military, etc.), (4) domestic or foreign interest, (5) name of target

- Who *will carry out the attack?* Scale of specificity: (1) name of movement, (2) name of group, (3) name of cell or unit, (4) names of terrorists

Another piece of the puzzle is tactics, or how the attack will be carried out. If this is known, security resources can be deployed to counter the tactics. Clearly, the more specific the information is, the more narrowly the security resources can be focused. The more general the information is, the more difficult it is to decide whether or not to allocate security resources at all, and if so for how long. This can be expressed as a sort of formula: *Timing + location + target + perpetrators + tactics = allocation of security.* Ideally, all the terms to the left of the equal sign should be at the highest level of specificity; but that is unlikely to be possible; in fact, it is rare for even a majority of these terms, or even one, to be at the highest level of specificity.

Also, although counterterrorism analysts can put some pieces of the puzzle together, they can seldom be confident that they have all the available pieces—all the information that the government has obtained. Is there another analyst in another agency who has different pieces? Is there another analyst in another agency who has a different take on the puzzle so far constructed? In most cases, when analysts lay out all the pieces in their possession, many gaps appear. These gaps can sometimes be partially filled by an analyst's expertise and hunches.

There is a race between the terrorist group that is planning, preparing, and executing the attack and the counterterrorist agencies that are trying to acquire and put together the pieces of the puzzle before the attack. Whenever an attack takes place, the race has been won by the terrorists. Moreover, al-Qaida and its global jihadist affiliates are becoming more aware of how we are collecting pieces of the puzzle and how we use them. They are studying our analytical methods just as we study their tactics, targeting patterns, operational codes, ideology, worldview, and surveillance methods. The purpose of their scrutiny is to identify what pieces of the puzzle we consider important and then to plant damaged or disparate pieces (disinformation) and to avoid giving us any valuable pieces. Here is a quotation taken from a global jihadist Web site in June 2003:

> It is known to all observers that the crusader enemy under the United States' leadership is exerting massive efforts to collect information from everywhere about the jihad and mujahidin, both the old and new ones.

The enemy has set up special bodies to analyze and correlate all this information and deduce the conclusions from them. If we know the importance of the information for the enemy, even if it is a small piece of information, then we can understand how important is the information that we know and how it can benefit the enemy by publishing it without being aware of this. If the enemy picks up a piece of information that the mujahidin are on the verge of carrying out a huge operation but this information does not indicate its timing and venue or how it will be carried out and the number of persons carrying it out, if he picks up another piece of information about the sale and purchase somewhere of a quantity of military equipment, weapons, ammunition, or food, and if he also picks another piece of information that a number of mujahidin are moving to the mountains around a city and then another piece of information calling on the mujahidin to remain quiet for a whole week, then when the enemy brings all this information together in one place, analyzes them minutely on the basis of the data base he already has and correlates them, he can deduce the details of what the mujahidin are intending to do.

We know that the enemy's analysis of this information does not mean that he is sure of it or of his expectations, but he takes precautions. If his expectations are wrong, he loses nothing other than the cost of alertness and preparations, and this is better for him than the loss of his personnel and equipment. The enemy daily analyzes dozens of such pieces of information and it sometimes leads him to something real.[21]

Further evidence that al-Qaida and the global jihadists are aware of the United States' effort to collect puzzle pieces is found in the following statement by al-Qaida, commenting on who was responsible for the suicide attack against a French oil tanker off the Yemeni coast on 6 October 2002:

Whether it was Al-Qa'ida that dealt this strike or one of the other "mujahidin bases" who belong to the same creed, ideology, and course ... [i]n order not to give free security advice to the enemy, we will not specify for him which of the two assumptions is correct. We will leave him to drown in all the assumptions and possibilities that have beleaguered him for two years without reaching any conclusion in the USS *Cole* destruction case.[22]

Mohammed al-Ablaj, a military trainer in al-Qaida, stated in June 2003: "The United States is spending heavily to understand how Bin Laden thinks, plans, and deals with events. They are trying to predict what Bin Laden has hidden in his bag for them and that is the big secret."[23]

It is clear that al-Qaida and its global jihadist affiliates are acutely concerned about the United States' efforts to acquire strategic and tactical information on the movement's activities, operational patterns, and attack mind-set. In 2004, there was a noticeable increase in warnings in Web sites, forums, and chat rooms to jihadists to be careful what they say. Additionally, al-Qaida's online military magazine *Camp al-Battar* frequently devotes one or two articles to security-related issues.[24] It is not unusual for a terrorist group to be concerned about the enemy's effort to collect information. However, in most cases this concern focuses on counterintelligence, such as enemy agents planted inside a group. It is unusual for a terrorist group to make a dedicated effort to understand how the enemy analyzes the group's intentions, or what pieces of the tactical puzzle it seeks and how it puts these pieces together. As noted above, Sulayman Abu Gayth, a frequent spokesperson for al-Qaida in 2002–2003, stated that "al-Qaeda functions according to a rigorous secret logic.... It will organize more attacks against American and Jewish targets, inside and outside American territory, at the moment we choose, at the place we choose, and with the methods we want."[25] The goal of the counterterrorism analyst is to understand as clearly as possible what that "rigorous secret logic" comprises.

CONCLUSION

The objective of this chapter has been to construct a basic analytical framework to apply to terrorist operations and the evolution of a terrorist attack. This framework should give the reader a better understanding of the type of operations that terrorist groups carry out and how they plan these operations. The main purpose, and the main activity, of a terrorist group is to carry out offensive operations or attacks. Although there may be setbacks—arrests, internal debates, external political events, and logistical problems—there is little downtime for a terrorist group: one attack leads to the next. It is important to recognize this operational persistence, especially in al-Qaida, its affiliates, its allies, and the global jihad movement in general.

It is easy to list the stages of a terrorist attack, but the critical task is to identify them as they are occurring. Preattack indicators are very difficult to detect without penetration of the group. Unless counterterrorist analysts have specific tactical intelligence concerning a group's plan of attack, they can only collect and assemble the available pieces of the puzzle. It is possible to deduce some pieces at stage 1, especially when the trigger is external. It is very difficult to deduce pieces at stage 2, because this stage primarily involves the message of a potential attack, which is typically developed during internal leadership meetings. It is also difficult to deduce the target (stages 3 and 4), although some general assumptions can be made, based on the group's previous attack patterns. And unless one knows what "targeting package" a group has considered, it is difficult to detect open-source research and physical surveillance by terrorists. Remember, too, that political research and physical surveillance, if detected, suggest only interest in a target, not an intent to attack it. Target selection and the development of the operational plan (stage 5) are the most difficult to deduce. This is where intercepting communications and penetrating a group's leadership are most important.

Stages 4 and 5 produce the specific name of the target, the exact timing of the attack, the identification of the perpetrators, the tactics to be used, and the exact location of the target. At these two stages a group's internal security comes into play. The specific information on the proposed attack is now limited to certain people; also, the details of the attack are partitioned and distributed to team members on a need-to-know basis. A good counterterrorism analyst can propose a general "window" when an attack is most likely to take place. The narrower the window, the more speculative the analyst must be. A general target menu can also be inferred from previous attacks, information on the terrorist Web site, group-related events, and current political conditions. However, this target menu will most likely be so large that efficient protective security resources cannot be deployed for a long period. A good counterterrorism analyst has already constructed a detailed tactical playbook for the group. A list of possible tactics to be used in the attack can be drawn up with a high degree of accuracy. A general location of the possible target can also be conceived, based on previous attacks, terrorist Web sites, group-related events, and—again—current political conditions. A very good counterterrorism analyst may be able to deduce the region or country where the attack may take place. It is impossible to guess the specific address of the target with any measure of accuracy. It is virtually impossible to guess who the specific perpetrators of the attack may be. Of course, the odds are improved if one is dealing with a small terrorist group like the left-wing groups that operated in Western Europe in the 1970s and early 1980s.

A terrorist group establishes general targets, tactics, and operational guidelines when it is founded. Modifications are made as the group develops; but for most groups, the impact and scope of these modifications are usually minor. Typically, the targeting and tactical menus are more subject to change than operational area, triggers, organizational structure, membership, logistics, finances, armaments, or weapons. Modifications are usually dictated by the evolving operational capability of the group, changes in leadership, and political conditions. The operational evolution of most terrorist groups is slow and uneven. Their tactical playbooks generally stay the same, and their targeting menus rarely expand. Consequently, it is possible to detect a group's preferences, tendencies, patterns, and conventions. Ultimately, the goal is to answer this question: are all places, all targets, and all methods legitimate in the eyes of the terrorist group? General operational profiles of terrorist groups are fairly common in the media and in governmental and academic literature. One can map, profile, chart, model, type, role-play, and "war-game" terrorist groups and their operations. However, the goal remains to understand the "rigorous secret logic" that groups use to determine when and what to attack.

NOTES

1. The most prolific and prominent such group as of this writing calls itself the Abu Hafs Al-Masri Brigades. In mid-July 2004 it issued a 15-day threat to the Italian people to get rid of Prime Minister Silvio Berlusconi. For example, see *La Repubblica* (Rome) (8 August 2004), p .2; and Middle East Media Research Institute, *Inquiry and Analysis* Series, Report No. 185 (10 August 2004).

2. Julen Agirre, *Operation Ogro: The Execution of Admiral Luis Carrero Blanco* (New York: Quadrangle, 1975), p. 3.

3. Ibid.

4. www.hostinganime.com/sout19, 19 June 2004. This Web site publishes online jihadist military and political magazines.

5. For example, see Dennis Pluchinsky, "An Organizational and Operational Analysis of Germany's Red Army Faction Terrorist Group (1972–1991)." In Dennis Pluchinsky and Yonah Alexander (eds.), *European Terrorism Today and Tomorrow* (Washington, D.C.: Brassey's, 1992). See also Dennis Pluchinsky and Yonah Alexander, *Europe's Red Terrorists: The Fighting Communist Organizations* (London: Cass, 1992).

6. CCC, "Concrete Answers to Concrete Questions" (communiqué, late April 1985). Document in author's possession.

7. CCC, "Communiqué on the Bombing of the Bank of America in Antwerp on 4 December 1985." Document in author's possession. (I have used many quotations from CCC, a fascinating left-wing terrorist group in the mid-1980s. I had personal friendships with several senior intelligence analysts in the Belgian GIA, or counterterrorism group, that was formed in 1984 as a result of CCC's terrorist campaign in Belgium. CCC's communiqués provided insights—rarely afforded by any terrorist group—into its operational methods and tactical and strategic thinking.)

8. Ibid.

9. The Irish News (Belfast) Internet version (14 February 2003).

10. FBIS EUP20041021000349, dated 21 October 2004.

11. CCC communiqué dated late April 1985—"Concrete Answers to Concrete Questions."

12. Sean MacStiofian, *Revolutionary in Ireland* (Edinburg: Gordon-Cremonesi, 1975), p. 103.

13. Ibid.

14. Al Qa'ida Terrorism Training Handbook, 180-page manual in Arabic seized in May 2000 in a global jihadist safe house in Manchester, England, translation, pp. 80–1.

15. See, for example, the author's commentary "They Heard It All Here, and That's the Trouble" in the *Washington Post* (16 June 2002): B03.

16. Manchester safe house handbook, pp. 92–8.

17. Information derived from the publication "Terrorist Tactics: Trojans, Trust Not the Horse" by the Office of Intelligence and Threat Analysis, Bureau of Diplomatic Security, U.S. Department of State, dated 24 September 2004.

18. Ibid.

19. *Time* (16 August 2004): 30–6; *Newsweek* (16 August 2004): 24–32.

20. The exceptions have been the August 1998 attacks on U.S. embassies in Kenya and Tanzania and the September 2001 attacks in Washington, D.C., and New York City.

21. "Do Not Be with the Enemy Against Us," statement issued by a Web site affiliated with al-Qaeda, Islamic Studies and Research Center (June 2003). Trans. FBIS report GMP20030611000061 (11 June 2003).

22. Statement commenting on the attack on the French oil tanker *Limburg* on 6 October 2004; issued by "Political Bureau of Al-Qaeda Organization," 13 October 2002, as reported in *Al-Quds al-Arabi* (London), 16 October 2002, p. 2. Trans. FBIS report GMP20021016000051.

23. Quoted in Movement for Islamic Reform in Arabia (Web site, www.myislah.org) (24 June 2003).

24. *Al-Battar* is a biweekly online magazine, first published January 2004. As of 17 September 2004, it was at Issue 18.

25. Statement of July 2002.

CHAPTER 26

Intelligence and Information Sharing in Counterterrorism

C. Patrick Duecy
Partner, Homeland Solutions, LLC

INTRODUCTION

Terrorism is difficult to counter partly because it differs from other threats. In general, the intelligence processes and information-sharing practices that were developed during the Cold War have proved inappropriate for terrorism, and the failure to forestall 9/11 has stimulated significant changes in the United States' internal security and intelligence structures.

The mainstream intelligence capabilities that have been applied against foreign states—divining national policies and strategies; assessing national economies; monitoring military industries; counting and evaluating ballistic missiles, tanks, and submarines—cannot be readily used to detect, observe, or counter terrorists. Al-Qaida, for instance, is transnational. No boundaries define its location, operations, range of movement, or affiliations; and it has no attributes that can be reliably and consistently observed by the sensors used against nation-states and conventional military forces. Al-Qaida and similar terrorist groups can adapt and mutate rapidly when they face changed conditions. Their methods and targets are often unpredictable; thus although al-Qaida may announce its broad intentions, it is highly secretive and ambiguous regarding operations, capabilities, and tactics. Also, terrorists are not inhibited by international law or conventions of warfare and are not deterred by diplomatic warnings or threats of military action. Nor, in principle, do they limit their choice of weapons; if al-Qaida, say, could use weapons of mass destruction, it probably would.

The 9/11 Commission noted that the intelligence community had not adjusted its imagination, strategy, or processes to deal effectively with terrorism. Specifically, the community had not shared intelligence adequately and so had been unable to "connect the dots." Fundamentally, intelligence sharing is about who gets to see the dots. The intelligence community has evolved very complex processes for gathering and distributing these dots, but most of its resources and capabilities pertained to the former Soviet Union and similar threats. Our national intelligence has been characterized by highly structured organizations, multiple chains of authority, assembly-line management, and rigidly regulated relationships between demand, suppliers, and consumers. By contrast, counterterrorist intelligence must resemble entrepreneurship, which is characterized by agility, flexibility, imagination, multiorganizational partnering, uniquely crafted products, and short times from production to market.

Effective counterterrorist intelligence is a matter of getting access to as many dots as possible, because the information is typically fragmentary and because even the smallest fragments are potentially valuable. Putting the dots together—through correlation, assessment, and application—is the job of "all-source" analysts. If the analysts are to do their job properly, the fragments must be reported in real time (or as near to it as possible), and, most crucially, the reports must be faithful to what the sources actually reveal. Information must not be denatured by "processing," "gisting," "characterization," "summarization," or overzealous protection of sources and methods. In this regard, today's intelligence is inadequate. To understand why, we need to consider the nature and machinery of the intelligence community.

THE INTELLIGENCE COMMUNITY
Background

During and immediately after World War II, U.S. intelligence was principally vested in the armed forces. The Cold War occasioned considerable debate about how to reorganize national security to serve new strategies, how to coordinate intelligence, whether intelligence should be managed by a military or a civilian organization, and how to consolidate and unify diverse intelligence capabilities and views.

The National Security Act of 1947 established the Central Intelligence Agency (CIA) and the post of director of Central Intelligence (DCI). The CIA was then the only named agency with a national-level strategic intelligence mission of directly supporting national security and, importantly, the president.

This act laid the foundation for an intelligence community. However, its description of the CIA's role and the DCI's authority was intentionally vague, partly because other entities, particularly the new Department of Defense (DOD) and the military services, were unwilling to subordinate their intelligence to the DCI, and partly because the nation was unwilling to create a very centralized, powerful intelligence service. Both factors have continued to influence the nation's attitude toward intelligence.

The growth of the intelligence community, the diversity of its members, and the development of specialized capabilities were driven by the imperatives of the Cold War. The result was a large, incredibly complex, loosely governed federation with member agencies capable of resisting the weak authority granted to the DCI.

The U.S. Intelligence Community comprises 15 federal agencies, offices, and elements of organizations within the Executive branch that are responsible for the collection, analysis, and dissemination of intelligence.[1] The members of the intelligence community are:

Independent Component

Central Intelligence Agency (CIA): CIA collects intelligence, principally through human means, and provides comprehensive, all-source analysis related to national security topics for national policymakers, defense planners, law enforcement officials, and the military services. CIA also conducts counterintelligence overseas and undertakes special activities at the direction of the President.

Department of Defense Components

Defense Intelligence Agency (DIA): DIA provides comprehensive, all-source, foreign-military intelligence for the military services, policymakers, and defense planners.

National Security Agency (NSA): NSA collects and processes foreign signals intelligence information for members of the policy-making and military communities and protects critical U.S. information systems from compromise.

National Geospatial-Intelligence Agency (NGA): NGA provides geospatial intelligence (described later) in support of national security and Department of Defense missions.

National Reconnaissance Office (NRO): NRO designs, builds, operates, and maintains the nation's reconnaissance satellites.

Army, Navy, Air Force, and Marine Corps intelligence organizations: Each service collects and processes intelligence relevant to its particular needs.

Non-Defense Department Components

Department of State/Bureau of Intelligence and Research (INR): INR provides analysis of global developments to the State Department and contributes its unique perspectives to the community's National Intelligence Estimates.

Department of Justice/Federal Bureau of Investigation (FBI): FBI takes responsibility for intelligence issues related to counterespionage, terrorism and counterintelligence inside the United States, threats to homeland security, and data about international criminal cases. Because of its law enforcement mission, the FBI is not, in its entirety, part of the intelligence community.

Department of Homeland Security/Directorate of Information Analysis and Infrastructure Protection: This component of DHS monitors, assesses, and coordinates indications and warnings of threats to the U.S. homeland; gathers and integrates terrorist-related information; and assesses and addresses the vulnerabilities of the nation's critical infrastructures.

Department of Homeland Security/U.S. Coast Guard Intelligence: Coast Guard Intelligence assesses and provides information related to threats to U.S. economic and security interests in any maritime region including international waters and America's coasts, ports, and inland waterways.

Department of Energy (DOE)/Office of Intelligence (IN): The Department of Energy's Office of Intelligence performs analyses of foreign nuclear weapons, nuclear nonproliferation, and energy-security related intelligence issues in support of U.S. national security policies, programs, and objectives.

Department of Treasury/Office of Terrorism and Financial Intelligence (INF): Treasury's intelligence component collects and processes information that bears on U.S. fiscal and monetary policy and threats to U.S. financial institutions.

All the responsibilities of the CIA, DIA, NSA, NRO, and NGA are related to intelligence, and therefore each of these organizations in its entirety is considered a member of the intelligence community. The other departments and military services listed earlier are concerned primarily with business and missions other than intelligence, and therefore only parts of their organizations are considered part of the intelligence community. For example, in the case of the U.S. Navy, only the Office of Naval Intelligence (ONI) is considered a member of the intelligence community.

The individual members vary in independence, influence, ambition, cooperativeness, and "community spirit." The intelligence community was charged with providing authoritative intelligence to guide and support national security strategy, foreign policy, defense strategy, and military capabilities. The DCI was responsible for leadership, policy, direction, and priorities, and for fostering cooperation.

The principal focus of the CIA is to provide intelligence for the president and for the policy levels of the executive branch. It has the authority to conduct covert operations. The other members of the intelligence community are generally organized and aligned to support the missions of their parent departments in the executive branch; consequently, their integration within the community and their contributions to overall national intelligence have been less than optimal. However, rarely if ever has there been a shortage of traditional intelligence; in fact, more intelligence is collected—especially by technical means—than can be analyzed. By contrast, there have been shortfalls in counterterrorist intelligence, which emphasizes highly specialized signals intelligence and covertly or overtly collected human intelligence.

The Intelligence Community and Counterterrorism

At least since 9/11, all agencies in the intelligence community are expected to contribute to counterterrorism. Its directives include the

National Security Strategy, the National Strategy for Countering Terrorism, the Homeland Security Strategy, and many implementing and departmental instructions that encompass preventing terrorist attacks; protecting the population, infrastructure, and national interests; and, if necessary, overseeing postattack management and recovery.

In this chapter, members of the intelligence community will be categorized as "all-source" agencies or "collection" agencies. (This categorization is somewhat arbitrary because CIA, DIA, and perhaps others fulfill both roles.) All-source agencies analyze all categories of collected intelligence and disseminate their findings as "products." Collection agencies gather and provide highly specialized intelligence in the form of images and geospatial products, signals intelligence, measurement and signatures intelligence, and human intelligence. The all-source agencies define their intelligence priorities and needs and set requirements for the collection agencies.

THE INTELLIGENCE CYCLE

The intelligence cycle involves identifying intelligence needs to guide collectors in acquiring and delivering intelligence to analysts who make sense of it and, in turn, deliver it in the form of analytical products to decision makers, planners, and other users. This cycle is essentially sound but has been weighed down by numerous policies, practices, and regulatory processes. The 9/11 Commission concluded that this complexity was a factor in the failure of intelligence sharing: "Over the decades, the agencies and the rules surrounding the intelligence community have accumulated to a depth that practically defies public comprehension."[2]

Intelligence Collection

Collection encompasses "technical collection" and "human collection." Within these two broad categories, specific capabilities are commonly called INTS. The major INTS include:

Signals intelligence (SIGINT)
Imagery intelligence (IMINT)

Measurement and signatures intelligence (MASINT)

Human intelligence (HUMINT)

Open-source Intelligence (OSINT)

INTs are departmentally managed, mostly by DOD; but ultimately the DCI, and now the director of national intelligence, is responsible for defining and prioritizing requirements and assigning tasks to collectors.

SIGINT

The National Security Agency (NSA) has authority over all SIGINT collection, processing, and reporting. SIGINT is global and involves technical collection: intercepting electronic signals and putting them into a form that can be analyzed or directly reported to users. The NSA is also responsible for devising measures such as encryption to protect U.S. intelligence.

IMINT

This is a generic term for intelligence in the form of images. It is managed by the National Geospatial Intelligence Agency (NGA, formerly the National Imagery and Mapping Agency, established in 2003) and encompasses imaging systems, related sensors, and derived products. Geospatial intelligence is gathered through a network of satellites, aircraft, and other sensor platforms. It normally requires postcollection processing and specialized analysis to make it useful for all-source analysis and other general purposes such as mapping.

MASINT

This function involves passively collecting information on targets of interest and measuring or identifying the unique characteristics—the "signatures"—of objects and activities. MASINT requires highly sophisticated technical processing and interpretation before it is of use to an all-source analyst. MASINT is still maturing, and its capabilities are expanding as new applications are found.

HUMINT

This is the oldest function, popularly associated with spies and secret agents. It is collected by and from people, overtly, covertly, or both.

CIA's Directorate for Operations (DO) is the preeminent HUMINT collector, supplying most of the covertly obtained intelligence on terrorists. DIA's Defense HUMINT Service is smaller and is closely coordinated with the DO to avoid duplication and conflicts. The collection of HUMINT by other agencies (including CIA and DIA) and the military is limited almost exclusively to operations outside the United States. The FBI collects and reports HUMINT within the United States.

HUMINT can provide information on an adversary's intentions, plans, and capabilities but may not be able to do so quickly. This is because sources may not always be available, collectors may have to return to sources for follow-up information, and contacts with sources require time-consuming precautions. Also, the identification and development of sources and the training and positioning of HUMINT case officers can take months or years. HUMINT is the most difficult and dangerous of the collection functions and the most vulnerable to human foibles and imperfections.

OSINT

This involves publicly available media. It is valuable in counter-terrorism but remains the least exploited and least appreciated source of information. OSINT is readily available and can offer insights on terrorists' intentions, ideology, and strategies, and on organizations supporting terrorism.

Intelligence Analysis

In theory, all-source agencies produce the most comprehensive intelligence if their analysts have access to a full array of intelligence; have the skills, experience, and time required to make sense of it; and are capable of presenting it as useful findings and sound judgments.

The concept of analysis as a focused, objective, intellectual effort to derive knowledge from fragments is accurate as far as it goes. However, today's all-source analysts are increasingly burdened by voluminous reports. They must be highly proficient in using multiple information systems and technologies and must be continuously responsive to departmental leaders' voracious appetites for dynamic, instant analysis in the form of "current intelligence." The time available for research and focused, in-depth analytical work has steadily diminished because there are competing demands for the work of the best analysts.

The major agencies performing all-source analysis of terrorism are the CIA and DIA. But most of the CIA's analysts are posted to the Counterterrorist Center (CTC) and the National Counterterrorism Center, which now encompasses the former Terrorist Threat Integration Center. DHS's Information Analysis Division and the FBI's nascent Directorate for Intelligence also do all-source analysis.

Technical collection agencies, such as the NSA and NGA, perform technology-intensive, time-sensitive analysis: processing, interpreting, and validating information and rendering it as products and databases to support the all-source agencies.

Analysts from across the intelligence community collaborate periodically. For example, the CTC and the newly established National Counterterrorism Center and National Counterproliferation Center are interagency centers designed to be manned by analysts from the intelligence community's member agencies. Analysts also come together temporarily to produce "national products" such as national intelligence estimates and, more often, "national warning products." These interagency centers alert federal agencies and contribute to DHS's national threat advisory levels and homeland security information bulletins. All "national intelligence products" are meant to distill the combined knowledge and judgments of the intelligence community to support policy making and decision making at the highest levels of government.

Intelligence Production

Intelligence products—the findings and judgments of analysts—may be written reports, databases, briefings, annotated images, or maps or a target graphic for conventional military operations, special operations, or paramilitary forces. Products are multifaceted and tailored to the users' requirements.

Intelligence Requirements

Most often, intelligence requirements have to do with collection and are stated formally. Registering and processing collection requirements is a highly structured management specialty.

Intelligence requirements also apply to intelligence analysis and production, although analysts have some latitude in the work they undertake. Production requirements are prioritized descriptions of categories of intelligence or specific products requested by users. Requirements may be long term, calling for continuing analysis and production. One example of an enduring requirement is the assessment of terrorist threats. However, many production requirements involve one-time, high-priority, time-sensitive "tasks" such as assessing the content of a new videotape issued by Usama bin Ladin.

Intelligence Dissemination

Dissemination involves distributing collected information reports and intelligence. If intelligence is to be effective, it must reach users on time and in an appropriate form.

As a result of the advent of secure digital intranets and Internets, digital networks and secure formal federal telecommunications networks are being used in parallel. The federal networks are still the "record" or official means of transmission; but the ease and speed of Internet-style communications have made them preferable for moving and storing information, communicating, collaborating, and coordinating.

One function of dissemination is regulating the flow of intelligence to authorized recipients on the basis of security clearance and "need to know." Typically, before collection reports and analytical products are disseminated, management specialists review them for proper classification, complete address lists, and instructions. These officers usually work with "release and disclosure" specialists who are authorized to apply national and departmental guidelines to determine what should be omitted from or left in an intelligence product; this depends on who will receive it. A collection report or analytical product is normally released at several classification levels so as to be shared as widely as possible. Generally, the higher the users' security clearance, the broader their need to know. With access to special compartments, the more intelligence they will see.

Dissemination involves a hierarchy of federal communications systems certified for the degree of security they provide. Some systems are certified only for unclassified but still sensitive information not to be publicly disclosed. For example, almost all threat-related information and advisories to state and local governments from DHS are currently disseminated by the Homeland Security Information Network (HSIN), an encrypted channel over the Internet. Other networks are certified to carry "secret" or "top-secret" information.

Protected Information

Classified

The federal government classifies certain material to prevent disclosure that might compromise national security. Intelligence is classified to protect sources, methods, and hard-won knowledge and to deny our adversaries certain information, since public disclosure or compromise of intelligence can cause adversaries to practice deception or change their means of communications or operations. There is always conflict between the need to protect intelligence and the need to make it available so that it can be used effectively. Ultimately, the director of national intelligence is responsible for policies and guidelines regarding classification and restrictions.

In addition to the national classifications—top secret, secret, and confidential—other means are used to regulate dissemination and access. Following are three examples:

- *Sensitive compartmented information (SCI)*: This most often further protects top-secret material by "compartmenting" or restricting access to persons with a certified need to know sensitive information. Someone with a top-secret clearance would not automatically also have access to information that is further categorized as SCI. Information that is top-secret SCI may be further compartmented into special access categories.

- *Dissemination and extraction of information controlled by originator (ORCON or OC)*: This means that any additional dissemination or inclusion of classified information marked ORCON or OC in another document must be approved by the originator of that information.

- *Not for release to foreign nationals (NOFORN)*: This designation denotes information that may not be shared with foreign nations or foreign nationals.

Other Categories

Some information that is not officially classified might still cause harm if publicly disclosed. Following are some categories commonly used for such information:

- ◆ "Sensitive but unclassified" (SBU), "for official use only" (FOUO), and "law enforcement sensitive" (LES) denote information that is not related to national security but might still cause harm if disclosed.
- ◆ "Sensitive homeland security information" (SHSI) generally means information that, if improperly disclosed, would be expected to significantly impair the ability of federal, state, local, or tribal agencies to prevent, protect against, or recover from incidents related to terrorism.
- ◆ "Unclassified" is not technically a classification, but this label clearly indicates that information is not sensitive and can be publicly disclosed. Some information previously classified is subject to automatic downgrading or declassification after a certain time and may eventually become unclassified.

PROBLEMS WITH INTELLIGENCE

Some inner workings of the intelligence cycle hamper the reporting and sharing of intelligence. Some examples follow.

Problem 1: Ownership

Ownership of intelligence is a distorted doctrine found in intelligence-collecting agencies and some analytical organizations. It fosters a culture of exclusivity, and it fatally narrowed information flows to analytical and operational counterterrorist forces before 9/11. In this regard, the 9/11 Commission identified *ownership* specifically: "The biggest impediment to all-source analysis—to a greater likelihood of connecting the dots—is the human or systemic resistance to sharing information." The commission also observed, regarding *need to know*: "This approach assumes it is possible to know, in advance, who will need to use the information. Such a system implicitly assumes that the risk of inadvertent disclosure outweighs the benefits of wider sharing. Those Cold War assumptions are no longer appropriate." That conclusion may also apply to "compartments"— the classic way to protect extremely sensitive sources and methods. Indeed, the commission continually returned to the issue of owner-ship as an impediment to intelligence sharing: "The culture of agencies feeling they own the information they gathered at tax-payer expense must be replaced by a culture in which the agencies instead feel they have a duty to the information—to repay the taxpayers' investment by making that information available" (pp. 416–7).

Problem 2: Processing Raw Intelligence

Information about terrorists is often difficult to process not only because its credibility is uncertain but also because it is fragmentary and is of value only when compared with other fragments. The significance, if any, of an isolated fragment is hard to assess. Putting fragments together is the specialty of all-source analysts, who see a broad range of intelligence; but ironically, collectors strongly resist sharing raw intelligence, which often contains crucial information "dots."

The potentially most important raw intelligence is gathered through SIGINT, HUMINT, and law enforcement. SIGINT and HUMINT collection agencies have well-developed ways of processing raw intelligence before disseminating it to analysts as reports; processing by law enforcement (principally the FBI) lags far behind them. But all three areas have problems.

SIGINT Processing

Here, technical processing is an initial task to derive intelligible information from an intercepted signal. Processing often includes transcribing and translation, which are beyond the capacity of most agencies. The next steps in processing are where the value of collected dots can be most seriously affected.

Collection specialists and the management staff evaluate raw SIGINT for its value in terms of intelligence priorities and require-ments. Without a "requirement" of appropriate priority, information may not be collected or, if it has already been collected, may not be shared. The 9/11 Commission noted: "In the 9/11 story ... we sometimes see examples of information that could be accessed—like the undistributed NSA information that would have helped identify Nawaf al Hazmi in January 2000. But someone had to ask for it. In that case, no one did" (p. 417).

If an intercept does match a requirement, the portion of the collected data that is considered valuable will be extracted, validated, edited, and put into a report format for dissemination. However, at each stage of SIGINT processing, some fidelity is lost. In the final stage, for example, reports to analytical organizations tend to be characterizations, descriptions, or narratives, not the raw text of what was actually intercepted. Expert, experienced analysts who are attuned to the nuances of terrorism would benefit from having access to the details in intercept transcripts early in the processing sequence.

Compartmentation of SIGINT reporting is commonplace. Analysts and users must be certified and cleared for a wide variety of special accesses to various compartments. This slows analysis, impedes integration of some SIGINT-derived information in all-source products, and complicates and narrows dissemination.

HUMINT Processing

With regard to collection, processing, and reporting, HUMINT is similar to SIGINT. Collected HUMINT generally follows a path from a field collector to a higher organizational echelon for predissemination processing by a reports officer, who determines if collected information is of intelligence value and should be rendered into a formal report for dissemination to analysts. This officer also excises sensitive information and renders the portions of the field report determined to be of intelligence value as a report that is disseminated to need-to-know users. As with SIGINT, what to take out and what to leave in are a matter of judgment. In any event, the final HUMINT report is normally a summary of the source's information. Capable analysts argue that access to field reports (from which truly sensitive methods and details of tradecraft have been deleted) is essential to obtain the full value of the content.

At the CIA—which is the most prolific collector and reporter of HUMINT—reports officers and DO managers sometimes keep field reports within operations channels and do not render them as reports to analysts. This may happen with fragmentary field reports considered to have little intelligence value. The collected but unreported information on the meeting of the 9/11 hijackers in Malaysia in 2000 is instructive.

Compartmentation is a problem at HUMINT. In CTC, where analysts are given some access to field reports, the reports officers and analysts following al-Qaida may not have access to field reporting on other groups and may have only restricted access to computerized files. As al-Qaida becomes less of a "group" and more a "movement" of loosely affiliated groups, compartmentation will become an increasingly artificial and dangerous practice.

Another long-standing issue is the access of intelligence and law enforcement to each other's information. This is the now-familiar "wall" between intelligence and criminal investigations. The PATRIOT Act and the clarification of certain earlier policies and regulations (e.g., concerning grand jury testimony) are said to have gone far toward improving this situation; but even so, the act did not address other chronic cultural problems that impede cooperation between law enforcement and intelligence.

The FBI

The 9/11 Commission found considerable mishandling of information by and between the CIA and FBI. The CIA bears its share of responsibility, but the FBI has long undervalued intelligence as a tool or avoided it as a contaminant in criminal investigations. The FBI seemingly remains focused on its familiar postincident or postcrime investigation and prosecution, rather than on sharing information that might disrupt, deter, or prevent mischief. Also, the FBI has been slow to invest in information technology, and not particularly successful when it does use such technology.

For this latter reason, even if the FBI wanted to share information related to terrorism, it would have great difficulty doing so in any efficient or effective way. The 9/11 Commission noted: "The poor state of the FBI's information systems meant that such access depended in large part on an analyst's personal relationships with individuals in the operational units or squads where the information resided" (p. 77). Before 9/11 the FBI had no effective collection capability, no reports officers, too few experienced professional analysts to render acquired information as intelligence, and insufficient technology to disseminate reports effectively.

By now, Congress has elevated intelligence within the FBI and has demanded that the FBI improve its intelligence capability and create a career field independent of traditional investigations. But unless the FBI develops a capability for domestic intelligence, effectively shares what it collects, and works more cooperatively with the intelligence community, with DHS, and with state and local law enforcement, counterterrorism inside the United States will remain problematic.

Problem 3: Classification and Controls

The classification system—particularly the associated practice of compartmenting and imposing dissemination controls on reports—complicates, slows, and may preclude information sharing and integration. The 9/11 Commission noted:

> Security concerns need to be weighed against the costs. Current security requirements nurture overclassification and excessive compartmentation of information among agencies. Each agency's incentive structure opposes sharing, with risks (criminal, civil, and internal administrative sanctions) but few rewards for sharing information. No one has to pay the long-term costs of overclassifying information, though these costs—even in literal financial terms—are substantial. There are no punishments for *not* sharing information. Agencies uphold a "need-to-know" culture of information protection rather than promoting a "need-to-share" culture of integration. (p. 417)

Problem 4: Information Technology

The United States excels in technology for sharing information securely over digital networks, and the intelligence community has invested heavily in new technology. But with regard to information and communication the community still has a tangled web of old systems, hundreds of duplicative databases, and different agency security standards and policies that hinder exchanges of intelligence and interagency collaboration. Untangling this web is a necessary step to advance counterterrorism. Moreover, dissemination of meaningful intelligence outside the community, particularly to the large new homeland security constituency of state and local governments, has been an impossible goal so far.

INITIATIVES SINCE 9/11 FOR REFORMING INTELLIGENCE

Intelligence Sharing and Homeland Security

The Homeland Security Act of 2002 is quite specific concerning intelligence sharing as an obligation of the intelligence community.

> The Secretary shall have access to all reports, assessments, and analytical information relating to threats of terrorism in the United States and to other areas of responsibility described in section 101(b), and to all information concerning infrastructure or other vulnerabilities of the United States to terrorism, whether or not such information has been analyzed, that may be collected, possessed, or prepared by any executive agency, except as otherwise directed by the President. The Secretary shall also have access to other information relating to the foregoing matters that may be collected, possessed, or prepared by an executive agency, as the President may further provide.

DHS will remain a work in progress for some years to come, and this work will involve developing a national information architecture and establishing new information-sharing relationships with federal, state, local, and private entities. It will also include physically connecting with the intelligence community and federal information systems and gaining access to information and intelligence. Establishing communications with the private sector and sharing and protecting proprietary industrial and commercial information concerning infrastructure will present new and unique issues of security and privacy, as well as legal issues. State laws and regulations regarding information and privacy must be taken into consideration in extending DHS networking to state and local jurisdictions. All these arrangements are still being established and formalized.

Meanwhile, DHS has initiated secure digital communications with state and local governments at the "sensitive but unclassified" and "law enforcement sensitive" levels. The DHS Homeland Security Information Network (HSIN) connects all 50 states and 50 major municipalities and will extend to the county level. Aside from its obvious benefits for information sharing, HSIN gives DHS an opportunity to build a strong intelligence capability, drawing on virtually unexploited resources available to state and local law enforcement, the emergency response community, and the private sector. A parallel DHS network, for sharing information classified up to "secret," is deployed to federal, state, and local jurisdictions in 2005.

The Terrorist Threat Integration Center was established to aggregate and fuse all foreign and domestic intelligence related to terrorism and homeland security. The administration, the 9/11 Commission, and the Intelligence Reform and Terrorism Prevention Act of 2004 have all given the FBI time to develop effective domestic intelligence, rather than empowering DHS to perform that role or creating a new domestic intelligence organization. These initiatives have diluted some of the roles and responsibilities originally envisioned for DHS, so that it must tailor intelligence produced by others to serve the needs of its own mission.

A division of DHS—Information Analysis (IA)—represents the department in the intelligence community. IA is charged with receiving and analyzing information related to terrorism, comparing threats with national vulnerabilities, and providing the resulting intelligence assessment to components of DHS, national agencies, and state and local authorities that can then take measures to deter, disrupt, and prevent terrorist attacks. As of this writing IA was still building its analytical staff and capabilities and was still serving more as an assimilator of intelligence collected and produced by others than as an originator of intelligence.

Reforming the Intelligence Community

Both the report of the Joint Inquiry of December 2002 and the recommendations of the 9/11 Commission included specific structural and doctrinal improvements for national counterterrorism and for the performance of the intelligence community in general.

In August 2004, the president signed an executive order[3] in response to the recommendations of the 9/11 Commission. Its main provisions are expected to guide the new director of national intelligence in reforming intelligence sharing. These provisions involve:

- Establishing common standards for sharing information about terrorism at the outset of the intelligence collection and analysis process
- Creating records and reporting, for both raw and processed information, in a manner that protects sources and methods

and allows information to be distributed at lower classification levels and in unclassified versions

- Distributing reports related to terrorism in multiple versions, including some at an unclassified level
- Maximizing terrorism reporting free of "originator controls," including controls requiring the consent of the originating agency prior to the dissemination of the information outside any other agency to which it has been made available
- Holding personnel accountable for increased sharing of information about terrorism
- Establishing collection and sharing requirements and procedures throughout the executive branch
- Establishing guidelines for collecting information about terrorism within the United States, including information from publicly available sources and nongovernmental databases
- Establishing a Systems Council and a plan for the establishment of an interoperable information-sharing environment to facilitate automated sharing
- Minimizing the applicability of information compartmentalization systems to terrorism

Many recommendations of the 9/11 Commission were incorporated into the Intelligence Reform and Terrorism Prevention Act of 2004. The director of national intelligence has considerable responsibility for implemention that will respect both the letter and the spirit of the law. Noteworthy provisions of the act relevant to counterterrorist intelligence include the following:

- Establishing a National Counterterrorism Center that will be independent of policy considerations or influences. The act transfers the Terrorist Threat Integration Center to the National Counterterrorism Center.
- Establishing a National Counterproliferation Center to interdict the trafficking of weapons of mass destruction, materials, technologies, and delivery systems to terrorists, terrorist organizations, and other state and nonstate actors.
- Directing the FBI to continue improving its intelligence capabilities, to maintain an intelligence workforce, and to

cross-train agents in intelligence. The act raises the standing of the intelligence component, and authorizes the establishment of an intelligence career service, within the FBI.

- Directing the establishment of a secure "trusted information network" to enable and promote information and intelligence sharing, communications, coordination, and collaboration across the federal, state, local, and private sectors.

- Requiring the president to issue guidelines for information sharing and to name a principal officer responsible for promoting information sharing across the federal government. The act establishes an Executive Council on Information Sharing to assist the principal officer and requires progress reports to Congress.

- The act calls for various improvements to secure U.S. borders against terrorists; requires a DHS strategy for closer integration of travel intelligence operations and law enforcement to intercept terrorists and restrict their mobility; and requires the integration of all data on aliens and relevant law enforcement and intelligence data to govern visa issuance, admissions, and deportation.

CONCLUSION

The reports of the Joint Inquiry and the 9/11 Commission include comprehensive and candid critiques of, and remedies for, intelligence and counterterrorism. The series of executive orders issued in response to the commission's findings and the codification of its key recommendations in the Intelligence Reform and Terrorism Prevention Act provide a sound foundation for reforming intelligence and improving homeland security. However, the effect of all these initiatives will not be known for some time and may actually depend more on personal factors—such as the leadership and political will of the director of national intelligence and the backing of the president— than on mandated structures and authorities. Also, if its history is any guide, the response from the intelligence community may be mixed or generally resistant.

The increased authority over intelligence budgeting and execution granted to the director of national intelligence is a step toward remedying the DCI's lack of budgetary and management leverage over the intelligence community. But the National Intelligence Program, over which the director of national intelligence has been given increased authority, is only one of several ways the overall intelligence budget is governed. Whether intelligence reform succeeds or founders may depend on the national intelligence director's exercising his budget authority and establishing practices and precedents.

Congress legislated intelligence reform precisely because the intelligence community had been unwilling or unable to reform and had resisted external pressures. Thus meaningful reform may be a struggle, despite the clear intent of the reform act. The fierce competition within the intelligence community over resources, mission share, and authority may continue to impede intelligence sharing and other forms of cooperation. There may also be unified resistance to congressional oversight, criticism, and reform efforts—and to the control of the director of national intelligence. Changes in the intelligence community have so far been evolutionary, not revolutionary, and this tendency can be expected to persist, despite calamitous events and groundbreaking legislation.

Setting the intelligence community on a new, unfamiliar course will take time and will entail some risk of breaking rather than adjusting the processes that foster a stable, reliable intelligence cycle. At the least, adjustments on the scale mandated by Congress may temporarily diminish the effectiveness of the community, until it finds a new equilibrium. Moreover, it remains to be seen if the present intelligence cycle can be modified to respond simultaneously to counterterrorism and any new threats to national security that might arise.

Among general reforms, broad sharing of intelligence is particularly critical as a way to remedy persistent imperfections in intelligence and law enforcement procedures and structures. The more information dots there are in the hands of more intelligence analysts in federal, state, and local intelligence centers, the better the chance of detecting plots and preventing attacks.

N O T E S

1. See Report of the Commission on the Intelligence Capabilities of the United States Regarding Weapons of Mass Destruction, Appendix C,

'An   Intelligence   Community   Primer'.   www.wmd.gov/report/report.
html#appendixc.
2. *9/11 Commission Report*, p. 410. For subsequent quotations from this report, page
    numbers will be noted parenthetically.
3. Executive Order 13356, Strengthening the Sharing of Terrorism Information to
    Protect Americans (27 August 2004).

CHAPTER 27

Counterterrorism Analysis and Homeland Security

Mark V. Kauppi
Program Director, Counterterrorism Training for Analysts,
Joint Military Intelligence Center, U.S. Army

INTRODUCTION

Since 9/11 there has been a dramatic increase in the number of government employees dedicated to counterterrorism (CT) analysis. Personnel have been drawn from three basic sources. First, at the federal level experienced analysts from other analytical offices were initially reassigned in order to respond to the new highest priority in national security. One day people are experts on African ports or drug smuggling; the next day they are reading message traffic on transnational Islamist extremists. Despite this shift in analytic focus, such people are experienced in the basic skills of intelligence analysis and are usually able to get up to speed in a relatively brief time.

Second, people are hired for newly created billets in the intelligence community as a result of budgetary largesse on the part of Congress. Many have military or government experience, but most arrive straight out of college. As these new hires come on board, training courses and mentoring programs begin the process of

---

Note: The views expressed in this chapter are those of the author and do not necessarily reflect the official policy or position of the Defense Intelligence Agency, Department of Defense, or the U.S. government.

socializing them into the culture of the intelligence community and the basics of intelligence analysis.

Third, there are people assigned to intelligence analytical duties in law enforcement agencies whose primary organizational mission, by definition, is not the analysis of terrorism. Some have worked as intelligence research specialists supporting an agent's casework, usually involving the analysis of crime and criminal organizations. Compared with national-level agencies, analysts at the state and local level are in a distinct minority within their organization and have little access to analytical training programs. Exceptions might be those assigned to the nationwide Joint Terrorism Task Forces (JTTFs) or law enforcement personnel who are also military reservists assigned to intelligence agencies. In the case of large police departments or U.S. attorneys' offices, however, the number of analysts is so small that in-house training programs would not be financially justifiable. As a result, such an office will try to have its personnel attend established training courses conducted by national-level agencies in Washington, D.C., will request mobile training teams, or will look to the private sector.

This chapter provides a brief overview of CT intelligence work for personnel in the law enforcement community at the state and local levels. As someone whose professional duties entail training CT analysts from various federal intelligence organizations, I have since 9/11 increasingly come into contact with individuals from law enforcement agencies. As I initially learned about the nature of their work beyond the Washington beltway and their organizational cultures and missions, differences from the intelligence community were evident. It quickly became apparent, however, that basic analytic thought processes are equally applicable to classic detective work and intelligence analysis. Furthermore, while the terminology may vary, particular tasks are essentially the same and common methodologies are applied to make sense of a large volume of information. Given that the imperative of improving homeland security has led to an exponential increase in contacts between national-level intelligence agencies and state and local entities involved in security, an appreciation of similarities and differences in the analysis of information is useful. To structure this discussion I will rely on what is called the *intelligence-cycle model*.

THE INTELLIGENCE PROCESS

The intelligence process is a cycle in which information is acquired, converted into intelligence, and made available to customers for action.[1] There are five steps:

1. *Planning and direction:* Managing the entire intelligence effort, from identifying the need for data (collection requirements) to delivering a finished intelligence product to a consumer (dissemination).

2. *Collection:* Gathering the raw information needed to produce the finished intelligence. Sources can include foreign broadcasts, newspapers, books, and agents working abroad.

3. *Processing:* Converting the massive amounts of collected data (for example, by decryption and translation) into a form usable by analysts.

4. *All-source analysis and production:* Converting basic information into finished intelligence. This step includes integrating, evaluating, and analyzing all available data and preparing intelligence products. Analysts have to consider the reliability, validity, and relevance of intelligence, integrate the data into a coherent whole, put the information into context, and create the final product.

5. *Dissemination:* Distributing the finished intelligence to consumers whose needs initiated the intelligence requirements. On the basis of the intelligence being provided, new requirements or follow-up requests for clarification and amplification can be expected, once again triggering the intelligence cycle.

We now turn to specific observations on steps 2 (collection) and 4 (all-source analysis and production).

COLLECTION
Collectors and Analysts

Counterterrorism analysts traditionally have spent most of their career working in a cubicle at their home agency. Temporary-duty assignments overseas may have been eagerly anticipated, but the typical day involved reading message traffic and preparing briefings and intelligence products for consumers. The analyst did not go into the field to collect intelligence; that is the job of the collector—whether a clandestine agent, an attaché, or a diplomat. A detective, by contrast, combines the traditionally distinct roles of the collector and the analyst. Once a detective has developed leads (such as the address on a victim's driver's license), he or she can go about gathering information firsthand and can also analyze its significance. But the CT analyst submits "collection requirements" and "requests for information" (RFIs) that are sent to collectors in the field; then, the CT analyst must wait for a response.

Evidence and Intelligence

The jigsaw puzzle is a popular analogy for both detective and intelligence work. In both cases information is collected, scrutinized, and fitted together in a logical manner. In both cases the picture may be incomplete. But how one views the nature of information is traditionally quite different in the law enforcement world and the intelligence world.

Law enforcement personnel generally collect evidence—information—which must meet a certain legal standard, concerning a crime or criminal conspiracy. In some cases the evidentiary bar may be set high; in other cases (such as a conspiracy investigation) it may be relatively low. To be considered evidence and to be admissible in a court of law, information must be handled in a specified manner (chain of custody). In collecting evidence, the ultimate objective is the successful prosecution of an individual charged with committing a criminal act.

This is quite different from intelligence. Intelligence analysts are increasingly aware that some intelligence may end up in a court of law, but their primary goal is to inform their consumers. In CT analysis, the content of the information is threats and developing trends in terrorist activity. It is up to the recipients of the intelligence—such as the president of the United States or an ambassador overseas—to decide what, if any, action should be taken. Another difference is that if a district attorney has insufficient evidence to charge someone with a crime, the case is dropped and attention turns to other, more promising cases and investigations. In the world of CT information, however, new intelligence is constantly integrated into ongoing assessments of threats.

ALL-SOURCE ANALYSIS
Reliability and Validity of Sources

It is sometimes assumed that CT analysis suffers from a dearth of intelligence. Actually the opposite is the problem: there is too much intelligence, most of it of questionable value. A flood comes in each day as message traffic, and then there is the vast amount of finished intelligence available through government intranets. An analyst could easily spend all day doing nothing but reading intelligence and not actually producing anything. But being an analyst, by definition, requires an effort to make sense of the pieces of the terrorist puzzle and provide value-added analysis. Otherwise, analysts are doing little more than repackaging intelligence that crosses their desks. As with all intelligence analysts, value-added analysis requires an ability to separate the wheat from the chaff, or the signals from the noise.

The starting point for analyzing human intelligence (HUMINT) is to critically assess the reliability and validity of a source. Reliability involves answering the question "To what extent should one believe the information this source provided?" Fortunately, HUMINT reports usually provide some guidance on the reliability of the original source based on a past track record, as well as can be determined. One's confidence in a source is increased or decreased depending on the answers to the following questions:

- Does the source have access? (In other words, can he reasonably be expected to have been in a position to gain access to this sort of information?)
- Is the information first- or secondhand? (That is, was the source personally in the room when a plot to attack was being hatched, or did she hear it from a friend who heard it from a cousin who heard it from . . . ?)
- Does the source have a good track record on issues related to terrorism? Or was his reliability assessed as good because he had a track record reporting other types of information, such as military order of battle?
- What is the likelihood of disinformation or fabrication?

Similar questions arise in assessing the reliability of reports from foreign services that might be providing intelligence in pursuit of their own agenda.

A single-source report of a threat cannot be summarily dismissed, but one will feel more comfortable with the information if it is validated or corroborated by other sources. These sources may be other HUMINT reports, signals intelligence (SIGINT), imagery, or even open sources. The more compatible one piece of information is with other evidence, the more confident one can be as to its validity.[2] Putting such pieces of information together is the essence of all-source analysis.

This process is not all that different from the work of detectives. Detectives also must assess the reliability of their sources, or informants. What is the motivation of informants? Why would they provide this information? Can their claims be corroborated by others or perhaps by electronic wiretaps? Thus detectives too may be engaged in all-source analysis. A major advantage for detectives, however, is that they can interview sources face to face, watching the sources' body language, listening to their tone of voice. In this sense a detective is more like an intelligence case officer working overseas and recruiting sources than like an intelligence analyst.

Patterns and Trends

Identifying patterns and trends is a time-honored element of intelligence analysis. A pattern is simply behavior repeated over time. A trend is a change in the pattern of behavior; a trend could be, for instance, an increase or decrease in the rate of activity or type of activity. Hence, analysts may come to identify particular patterns of military mobilization of various countries, or note a trend in a state's procurement of increasingly sophisticated weaponry.

Academics and analysts also look for patterns and trends in the behavior of terrorist groups. Bruce Hoffman, for example, notes that the classic pattern of a terrorist group is "a collection of individuals belonging to an identifiable organization that has a clear command-and-control apparatus and a defined set of political, social, or economic objectives." But the 1990s witnessed a new trend:

> The more traditional and familiar types of ethnic/nationalist and separatist as well as ideological groups have been joined by a variety of organizations with less-comprehensible nationalist or ideological motivations. These new terrorist organizations embrace far more

amorphous religious and millenarian aims and wrap themselves in less-cohesive organizational entities, with a more-diffuse structure and membership.[3]

Similarly, the U.S. Department of State, in *Patterns of Global Terrorism*, notes:

> U.S. counterterrorist policies are tailored to combat what we believe to be the shifting trends in terrorism. One trend is the shift from well-organized, localized groups supported by state sponsors to loosely organized, international networks of terrorists.[4]

Analysis of patterns and trends can reveal general tendencies over time. Hence, often it is a useful basis for strategic-level products in terms of an individual group (e.g., "HAMAS's targeting has expanded from the West Bank and Gaza to Israel proper") or reflects the analysis of aggregate data over time for terrorism as a general phenomenon (e.g., "Though the number of international incidents is generally down in recent years, the degree of lethality has gone up"). Furthermore, it is imperative to identify a group's pattern of behavior in order to establish a baseline for how terrorists go about doing what they do; unless you know what the traditional modus operandi is or pattern of terrorist activities, you cannot recognize an innovation in a group's behavior.

Analysis of patterns and trends is also found in works on crime such as the FBI's annual crime report, which tracks crimes such as homicide. The dramatic drop in crime in New York City over the past decade is an often-cited example of a trend. Many police departments in large cities use computer programs to track various crimes, plotting them on maps to identify neighborhoods where there should be a greater commitment of police resources.

Analytical methodologies to track organizations and identify patterns and trends actually developed in the business world, were adapted by the law enforcement community, and then spread to the intelligence community. In 1968, for example, the Los Angeles Police Department (LAPD) was asked to come up with a visual for the prosecution of Sirhan Sirhan, who had assassinated Senator Robert Kennedy. LAPD compared the symbols and terms of "performance evaluation review techniques" (PERT) and the "critical path method" (CPM) and then used them to visually depict concurrent activities. Three charts—one depicting Sirhan Sirhan's life, another depicting his activities five days before the assassination, and a third tracking Senator Kennedy's movements—were eventually used in the courtroom. Network analysis and link charts of criminal organizations are also staples of police work.[5]

PRODUCTION

What do CT analysts actually produce, and what are they trying to achieve with their products? At a minimum, CT intelligence analysis aims to:

- Provide timely warnings of impending terrorist attacks
- Improve consumers' awareness of threats
- Facilitate the disruption of terrorists' activities and the destruction of terrorist organizations

Let us examine each goal in turn and note how (if at all) they relate to law enforcement.

Warnings

Before 9/11, probably the single greatest difference between national-level CT analysts and law enforcement personnel was that warning was central to CT analysis. In fact, the number one job of the CT analyst is to provide timely warnings to consumers, whether in the field or in Washington, D.C.

There are three levels of warning. First and most important is tactical-level warning. Information at the tactical level is time-sensitive: it means that an attack is impending in a few days or even in a few hours. An example would be a warning that the U.S. embassy in Cairo will be bombed by a terrorist organization in the next 48 hours. This is the type of warning we wish we had received before 9/11. Second, operational-level warning involves a time frame of several weeks or months. An example would be intelligence that preparations are under way for an attack against U.S. interests somewhere in the Persian Gulf, but with no targets and no method of attack specified. On 6 August 2001 the presidential daily brief (PDB) included a warning about al-Qaida's interest in hijacking airplanes;

that was an operational-level warning. Third, strategic-level warning involves a time frame of perhaps six months to several years. The focus is regional or international, and the intelligence might address a topic such as the probable evolution of al-Qaida in the years ahead. Here are three examples of strategic-level warnings before 9/11:

> *Americans will become increasingly vulnerable to hostile attack on our homeland.... Americans will likely die on American soil, possibly in large numbers.*
> —Hart-Rudman Commission, September 1999

> *Today's terrorists seek to inflict mass casualties, and they are attempting to do so both overseas and on American soil.*
> —National Commission on Terrorism, June 2000

> *We have been fortunate as a nation. We are impelled by the stark realization that a terrorist attack on some level inside our borders is inevitable and the United States must be ready.*
> —Gilmore Commission, December 2000

To clarify the role and difficulties of warnings, consider the following example. Suppose that the body of a man is found in the lobby of a hotel. Initially, the police are able to identify the victim (by examining the driver's license in his wallet). Assume that they know what happened (the man has been shot in the head). They know where the shooting happened (the hotel), and when (shots were heard at 10 p.m. by hotel employees and patrons). The key task for the homicide squad is to solve the crime by answering the questions "Who did it?" and "Why?" and not to warn about potential future crimes.

My impression is that before 9/11, warning was not considered an important part of law enforcement and was not even part of the vocabulary of most law enforcement personnel. This is in striking contrast to the primary responsibility of a CT analyst—to warn of impending terrorist attacks. As CT analysts sift through message traffic and perhaps open-source material, they are faced with the daunting task of trying to determine who is planning or about to commit the attack, what the terrorists are intending to do, and when and where the attack will occur. Another question, though of less concern, is why the United States is being targeted by an individual or group. Whereas a detective is trying to solve a crime that has already occurred, the counterterrorism analyst is trying to prevent an attack from happening.

It is possible for a CT analyst to accurately forecast an impending attack but receive no credit. This is the "paradox of warning." Suppose you have done a masterly job of pulling together the pieces of a puzzle involving terrorism and feel confident that you can convincingly answer the questions *who, what, when, where, how,* and *why.* If your analysis is accepted, the threatened target—say, an embassy or a military post—would, logically, improve its security. As it did so, the terrorists' surveillance of the facility would reveal these changes. The terrorists may therefore call off the attack or seek a softer target; what they do depends on what we do. The paradox arises because nothing happens, and consequently you cannot know whether you were correct in your assessment or whether the terrorists never planned to attack in the first place. How do you prove that your assessment was correct? What are the criteria for success? The result is that intelligence failures make the headlines, but probable successes do not.[6]

This desire for tactical-level warning is not new, but such warnings are extremely difficult to achieve. This is a recurrent theme in reports that preceded the work of the 9/11 Commission. The Long Commission Report of 1983 examined in detail the bombing of the Marine Corps headquarters in Beirut in October of that year— a bombing that left 241 Marines dead. It concluded: "Although intelligence was provided at all levels that presented a great deal of general information on the threat, there was no specific intelligence on the where, how, and when of the 23 October bombing." The Air Force's report on the bombing of Khobar Towers in 1996 reached similar conclusions: "Although intelligence furnished a good picture of the broad threat facing U.S. forces in Southwest Asia, neither HUMINT nor counterintelligence provided specific tactical details on the threat." And the Crowe Commission on the bombing of U.S. embassies in Africa in 1998 noted: "There was no credible intelligence that provided immediate or tactical warning of the August 7 bombings."[7]

As noted by the 9/11 Commission, the FBI (and law enforcement in general) has had an advantage in that "performance in the Bureau was generally measured against statistics such as numbers of arrests, indictments, prosecutions, and convictions."[8] But now that the FBI is being transformed into an agency with a broader focus on national security and an emphasis on preventing terrorism, it will probably continue to receive harsh judgments, as in the report of the 9/11 Commission.

Awareness of Threats

Most of the product of CT intelligence has to do with awareness of terrorist threats. Products may take the form of a daily "threat summary," widely disseminated; or of briefings for commanders and policy makers that provide an overall assessment of a threat. Products also include the country "threat levels" of the U.S. Department of Defense (DOD) and the "post-threat levels" of the Department of State (DOS). It must be emphasized that these DOD and DOS threat levels are not tactical warnings: they do not have the specificity of such a warning. Rather, they characterize the "overall threat environment." In fact, the state levels are reviewed and adjusted only every six months.

The most familiar domestic example of a threat-level product designed to increase awareness is the color-coded national warning system: red, orange, yellow, blue, and green. This domestic system is similar to, if not inspired by, the DOD system and has been roundly criticized, even ridiculed. The problem may be partly due to the initial decision to call the color codes a "warning system"; perhaps "threat awareness system" would have been a better term. Before 9/11, local law enforcement agencies nationwide certainly undertook threat-awareness activities—for example by attending neighborhood "watch" meetings and informing the public of current concerns and trends in local crime.

Disruption and Destruction

Intelligence designed to facilitate the disruption or destruction of terrorist organizations is encapsulated by the stated mission of the director of Central Intelligence's (DCI) Counterterrorist Center (CTC): preempt, disrupt, and defeat terrorism.[9] In this case intelligence is produced and disseminated with the goal of aiding operators in the field as well as keeping policy makers informed. Since 9/11 the United States has made an aggressive military, intelligence, and

diplomatic effort to capture terrorists and destroy terrorist organizations or at least put pressure on them through such policies as
disrupting their sources of financing.

Al-Qaida as we knew it immediately after 9/11, for example, no
longer exists, having been severely incapacitated by the air and
ground war launched against the Taliban at the end of 2001.[10] But
completely eradicating its remnants and associated groups has
proved to be problematical. Pinpointing a handful of terrorists who
follow good operational security and operate in a foreign country is a
challenge to U.S. agents responsible for providing the intelligence
grist for the analysts' mill. Going to the Defense Language School at
Monterey, California, for 44 weeks will not turn you into a native-born
speaker of Pashtun or Urdu capable of infiltrating a terrorist
organization. Even if an American agent is a native-born speaker of
a relevant language, many terrorist groups are clan- or tribal-based,
and such affinities are part of the vetting process. Recruiting a local is
also a challenge in terms of judging his motivation. Technical means
of collection also have limitations. Imagery is not useful in trying to
pinpoint terrorists living in an apartment in Hamburg, Germany.
Collectors of SIGINT are challenged to locate and monitor terrorists
who use off-the-shelf communications technology available at any
electronics store. Commercially available encryption also complicates
the task.[11]

An appropriate analogy is that a law enforcement agency may
have the task of infiltrating criminal organizations as part of a
strategy to disrupt and destroy them. But the analogy is not exact. As
difficult as such infiltration may be, at least it is conducted on
American soil, with supportive personnel close at hand.

CONCLUSION

Even before 9/11, the distinction between the analysis of criminal
intelligence and the analysis of CT intelligence was questionable.
Although, owing to legal strictures, the procedures for handling
evidence may differ from those for intelligence, analysts in law
enforcement and analysts in the intelligence community are alike
in having to assess the reliability of sources, assess the relevance
of information, and determine how new intelligence fits into our
existing knowledge. Basic analytical tools and methods such as
association matrices, link diagrams, and time lines have long been

used by both law enforcement personnel and intelligence analysts to sort out information and reveal organizational structures and patterns of behavior.

Since 9/11, law enforcement and intelligence have come even closer together. To achieve homeland security, national-level agencies are directed to reach out to the state and local levels and develop protocols for exchanging information. Work has begun on developing an electronic infrastructure to support such exchanges, though certain legal and institutional issues remain to be addressed. Equally important, just as terrorism has officially been designated the FBI's number one priority, so, too, state and local law enforcement agencies have been forced to take terrorism into account in conjunction with their traditional focus on crime. As a result, the leading responsibility of the CT analyst—warning—has also become the highest priority for analysts and research specialists assigned to many new state and local CT entities.

NOTES

1. This discussion is drawn from Central Intelligence Agency, Office of Public Affairs, *Factbook on Intelligence*, www.cia.gov/cia/publications/facttell/index.html.

2. In the language of the counterterrorism analyst, you are trying to see how the report fits into "current streams of reporting."

3. Bruce Hoffman, "Terrorism Trends and Prospects." In Ian O. Lesser, et al. (eds.), *Countering the New Terrorism* (Santa Monica, Calif.: Rand, 1999), pp. 8, 9.

4. U.S. Department of State, *Patterns of Global Terrorism, 1999* (April 2000), p. iii.

5. See, e.g., Paul P. Andrews and Marilyn Peterson (eds.), *Criminal Intelligence Analysis* (Loomis, Calif.: Palmer, 1990).

6. There is a story that during a hearing, a congressman asked a counterterrorism manager, "How many terrorist incidents did your organization stop by timely intelligence?" This is akin to asking the border patrol, "How many undetected terrorists entered the United States last year?" The FBI is the one agency that publicly announces the number of terrorist incidents it has prevented; see *Terrorism in the United States 1999: 30 Years of Terrorism* (Washington, D.C.: U.S. Department of Justice, 2001), p. 3. But because of the "paradox of warning," even the FBI cannot be sure that it has not experienced more successes than it may suppose.

7. *Report of the DOD Commission on Beirut International Airport Terrorist Act, October 23, 1983* (20 December 1983), p. 63; Air Force Inspector General and Judge Advocates General, "Report of Investigation: The Khobar Towers Bombing, 25 June 1996: Background," at www.fas.org/irp/threat/khobar_af/tableof.htm.; "Report of the Accountability Review Boards: Executive Overview," at www.state.gov/www/regions/africa/board_overview.

8. 9/11 Commission, p. 74.

9. CIA, *DCI Counterterrorist Center: Preempt, Disrupt, Defeat*, n.d.

10. Jason Burke, "Think Again: Al Qaeda," *Foreign Policy* 143 (May–June 2004) ("Al Qaeda's dead: the organization of men whose deadly choreography of planes in the sky murdered 3,000 people on September 11 has been smashed into oblivion"). Corine Hegland, "Global Jihad: No End in Sight," *National Journal* (8 May 2004) ("A new generation of terrorists is emerging to take the place of elders who have been killed, captured, or forced deep underground"). Paul Havenand and Chris Tomlinson, "Al-Qaeda's New Guard," *Washington Times* (16 June 2004). www.washingtontimes.com/world/20040615-100822-2072r.htm

11. "The ships, planes, antennas, and satellites are the result of a triumph of Cold War engineering, designed to keep tabs on the Soviet Union and its allies. The question now is this: How useful is the system against terrorists who know not to trust their satellite phones? How effective can it be in an age when almost untappable fiber-optic lines carry information at stupefying rates and cheap, off-the-shelf encryption systems can stump the most powerful supercomputers on earth?" Stephen Cass, "Listening In," *IEEE Spectrum* (April 2003): 33.

Risk: Management, Perception, and Communication

CHAPTER 28

Introduction to Section 5

Anthony Beverina
President and Chief Operating Officer, Digital Sandbox, Inc.

One can debate whether or not the war on terrorism is winnable, but there is little doubt that the need to protect critical infrastructure will continue for the foreseeable future. Making prudent decisions and resource allocations aimed at deterrence, security, and mitigation is challenging and requires adaptive sensitivity to threats and vulnerability. Risk management is a powerful approach to the process of identifying and evaluating risks and selecting and managing techniques to adapt to risk exposures. In homeland security it involves determining which infrastructure and assets are to be defined as critical and rapidly assessing this list to determine individual and systemic vulnerabilities or risk. The ensuing effort to plug the holes and develop strategies for securing the critical infrastructure is a long-term process. This process must be affordable, sustainable, and easily implemented by organizations with a stake in the infrastructure. Given the scale of the problem, and the uncertainty of the threat environment, a systematic risk management approach provides the most complete and sustainable framework for maximizing the value of investments and minimizing the exposure of critical assets and citizens.

The building blocks of comprehensive risk management are (1) identifying risks; (2) measuring risks; and (3) controlling risks through actions that mitigate, avoid, or transfer them. Practitioners in different industries develop variations on the fundamental concepts—e.g., hazard (or threat), assets (and infrastructure), risk mitigation (security measures)—to best support the decisions that must be made. In homeland security the tailoring of these concepts to suit the decisions that must be made is unfinished business.

In contemplating the complexity and scope of homeland security, it is very instructive to study the practices of other industry sectors. In Chapter 29 Gregory Parnell, Robin Dillon, and Terry Bresnick offer a broad survey of available risk management techniques in use in homeland security as well as other sectors and provide insight into the factors that must be considered for the unique risk posed by terrorism.

One aspect of homeland security is that it involves protecting not only infrastructure and lives but also the public trust and confidence in leadership. Thus, in any calculation or analysis of risk, one must accommodate the potential impact of an event not only in terms of casualties, damage, and financial effects but also in terms of public trust, consumer confidence, and other intangibles. These effects must be considered and managed as well. Baruch Fischhoff, in Chapter 30 on risk perception, points out that risk communication is a balancing act which involves informing the public and enlisting the American people as part of the risk management strategy, but not unnecessarily alarming people or crying wolf. Competent, well-considered use of the tools of risk communication, such as the Homeland Security Advisory System and the news media, can have powerful results. But a tool can be a double-edged sword if the public does not trust the institution that is using it, or if people believe they are being misled or ill informed. In Chapter 31 James Carafano discusses the Homeland Security Advisory System, its promise, its early rough spots, and its future uses. Frank Sesno discusses the role of the media in risk communication in Chapter 32.

While many challenges in homeland security are formidable and some are unique, the basic need to analyze risk, make decisions, and communicate these decisions is shared by many other disciplines in many other industries. These other industries have a head start in dealing with such issues and have settled into a more steady-state approach to managing their risks. Careful study of these approaches, and application of their tenets and practices, will help us transform homeland security from a surge effort to a long-term sustainable strategy.

Integrating Risk Management with Security and Antiterrorism Resource Allocation Decision Making

Dr. Gregory S. Parnell
Professor of Systems Engineering,
United States Military Academy at West Point;
Senior Principal, Innovative Decisions, Inc.

Dr. Robin L. Dillon-Merrill
Professor, Georgetown University;
Principal, Innovative Decisions, Inc.

Terry A. Bresnick
President and Senior Principal, Innovative Decisions, Inc.

Terrorism is defined in the Code of Federal Regulations as "the unlawful use of force and violence against persons or property to intimidate or coerce a government, the civilian population, or any segment thereof, in furtherance of political or social objectives." ... [Fighting] terrorism includes both antiterrorism and counterterrorism activities. Antiterrorism refers to defensive measures used to reduce the vulnerability of people and property to terrorist acts, while counterterrorism includes offensive measures taken to prevent, deter, and respond to terrorism. Within the emergency management arena, antiterrorism is a hazard mitigation activity and counterterrorism falls within the scope of preparedness, response, and recovery.[1]

Note: The authors would like to acknowledge five colleagues who provided useful ideas and suggestions that influenced our thinking about this chapter: Vicki Bier, Don Buckshaw, Michael Cassidy, Bob Reynolds, and Ralph Semmel.

THE IMPACT OF TERRORISM ON NATIONAL, STATE, AND LOCAL RESOURCE ALLOCATION

Since 9/11, more resources have been made available to combat terrorism at the national, state, and local level, but this additional funding has raised the difficult issue of how to allocate them cost-effectively. At the national level, the global war on terrorism (with two major fronts in Afghanistan and Iraq) has resulted in significant budget supplements each year since 2001; in addition, a large-scale governmental reorganization resulted in the new Department of Homeland Security (DHS). Also, in the wake of the 9/11 Commission, changes have already occurred or are being contemplated in the intelligence community (IC). At the state and local level as well, many organizational changes and changes in resource allocation have been implemented.

A DECISION-MAKING FRAMEWORK FOR ANTITERRORISM

We have developed a framework (Figure 29-1) to describe decision making related to antiterrorism (AT): it shows levels, purposes, types, timing, and elements (or implementation) of decisions.

F I G U R E   29-1

Antiterrorism decision-making framework.

Level (Who)	Purpose (Why)	Type (What)	Timing (When)	Elements (How)
International	Prevent	Planning	Multiyear	Law
National	Deter	Programming	Annual	Policy
Nongovernmental organizations	Detect	Budgeting	Monthly	Procedures
Federal department	Warn	Executing budget	Real-time	People
State	Protect	Crisis management		Technology
County	Respond			
Local (community)	Recover			
Company				
Individual				

Decisions about allocating resources include planning, programming, budgeting, and execution of the budget: i.e., the first four types of decisions in Figure 29-1. The fifth type of decision in the figure is real-time crisis management. In such a situation the decision maker has time to respond only according to preexisting plans and programs. However, before an actual crisis, decisions about allocation of resources must include all levels of decision makers, all purposes, various time periods, and various elements so as to evaluate alternatives. Also, decisions at different levels will have different priorities. For example, local communities and county governments will serve primarily as first responders, so they may allocate more resources for response and recovery whereas the federal government may allocate more resources for detection and warning systems.

Funds provided for antiterrorism by the initial budget increases have been used—among other things—to upgrade facilities (e.g., add physical barriers), to increase personnel (e.g., hire air marshals), to change procedures (e.g., increase screening), to conduct research (e.g., on bioscreening), and to share information. With the availability of new funding, national, state, and community leaders must decide what is an appropriate focus for their level of decision making and how they can integrate budgetary decisions regarding AT into their general process of allocating resources.

THREE APPROACHES TO ALLOCATING RESOURCES FOR ANTITERRORISM

Antiterrorism has a profound impact on the funding available to, and the public services provided by, various governmental organizations. Funding AT involves trade-offs and opportunity costs because funds allocated to AT are not available for other projects. We have identified three major approaches to allocating resources for AT:

- *Approach 1—AT stands alone.* The organization (public or private) establishes a funding level for all projects intended to reduce the risk of terrorism, and all AT projects compete for these funds. Allocation involves identifying current risks and funding projects that reduce these risks. The key analytical tasks are risk assessment and risk management.

- *Approach 2—AT is integrated into "mission-assurance" allocations.* The organization establishes a funding level for all mission-assurance activities: i.e., projects that reduce risks that might impede the organization's mission. Such projects are designed to deter, protect against, or defend against natural disasters and human threats. A project might reduce the probability of an adverse event, reduce the vulnerability of the system to such an event, or reduce the consequences of an event that does occur. In this approach—which is consistent with the "all-hazards" approach advocated by the Federal Emergency Management Agency (FEMA)—AT projects compete with other mission-assurance projects for funding. The process encourages synergy with AT and other mission-assurance activities. Again, the key analytical tasks are risk assessment and risk management, but the scope is different: all mission-assurance projects.

- *Approach 3—AT is integrated into overall allocations.* In this approach AT is still considered necessary, but it must compete for funding with all other projects of the organization. Funding is based on the costs and benefits of each project. AT projects are assessed according to the "benefits" they provide in terms of reducing risk. Here too, risk assessment and risk management are key considerations, but the scope is the organization's entire project "portfolio."

In all three approaches there are significant trade-offs between mission, risk, and impact on the customer (the "stakeholder"). AT projects may have negative effects, such as inconveniencing customers and infringing on civil liberties. Since 9/11, Americans have been more willing to tolerate inconveniences and some impacts on their civil liberties. However, this attitude may change if significant time passes with no further terrorist attack.

Because of these trade-offs, we believe that allocating resources for AT should involve four tasks: (1) stakeholder analysis, (2) assessment of risk, (3) evaluation of multiple—often conflicting—goals, and (4) risk management. Organizations need an objective, traceable process to support their decisions. This process should be based on techniques of decision making and risk analysis. Kirkwood[2] offers a useful framework that applies multiple-objective decision analysis to quantify benefits and optimization so as to identify the maximum benefit for the resources available. Furthermore, organizations need to develop a culture of risk management that identifies, analyzes, and reduces "life-cycle" risks.

LESSONS FROM OTHER APPLICATIONS

Risk analysis and allocation procedures based on it have been successfully applied in various contexts that offer useful lessons for AT. These contexts include natural disasters, commercial nuclear power, space systems, and "information assurance."

Natural Disasters

Researchers interested in natural disasters have developed a knowledge base on many topics of importance to AT, including how to communicate warnings to the public[3]; how to prepare, respond to, and recover from disasters; and how to plan mass evacuations.[4] Wenger and his associates[5] examined several myths regarding individuals' behavior during disasters and found, for example, that panic and looting are rare: altruism is a more common response. They also found that most of the initial search-and-rescue activity is done by the victims themselves rather than by organizations generally categorized as first responders.

To share learning between the context of natural disasters and that of AT, FEMA advocates an "all-hazards" approach to planning for emergencies at the state and local levels. Because of the diversity of risks and targets, an all-hazards approach that focuses on preparedness and encompasses terrorism, natural disasters, and other environmental challenges will probably offer an optimal use of resources. FEMA's list of hazards includes those related to dams, earthquakes, extreme heat, fires, floods, hazardous materials, hurricanes, landslides, nuclear power, terrorism, thunderstorms, tornadoes, tsunamis, volcanoes, wildfires, winter storms, and "multihazard."[6] This approach is similar to approach 2 for allocating resources—in which AT competes for funds with all mission-assurance projects. FEMA has developed special software for benefit-cost analysis for "hazard reduction" projects.[7]

Commercial Nuclear Power

The nuclear power industry, notably, uses probabilistic risk analysis (PRA) in its risk analysis and risk management. PRA originated in the commercial nuclear power industry in the 1970s.[8] The U.S. Nuclear Regulatory Commission (USNRC) and the nuclear power industry jointly developed fundamental procedures and handbooks for PRA models.[9] Today, the industry is moving toward regulations based on risk, specifically using PRA to formulate lower-cost regulations without compromising safety.[10] Research in the industry has also supported advances in three other types of analysis: human reliability, external events, and "common cause failure."[11]

Space Systems

During the Apollo program, pessimistic risk estimates discouraged NASA's use of PRA. Furthermore, the notion of "failure risks" often clashes with an engineering culture that is primarily based on safety factors. The problem with safety factors is that they do not allow prioritization. But since the disaster that destroyed the *Challenger*, NASA has increasingly adopted PRA to identify and manage risks in the space shuttle program and in other projects.[12] PRA models are currently implemented with a software tool, Quantitative Risk Assessment System (QRAS), specifically designed for the requirements of space missions.[13] QRAS combines event-sequence diagrams to describe possible risk scenarios and fault trees to model the details of each event in the scenarios (see below).

Information Assurance

Information assurance (IA) is defined as activities that protect and defend information systems by ensuring their availability, integrity, authentication, confidentiality, and nonrepudiation.[14] It requires risk assessment and risk management that can deal effectively with life-cycle threats posed by adversaries. Cohen,[15] in his classification of information systems, lists 37 potential adversaries. In general, all commentators agree on a basic set of adversaries, but they differ with regard to specific subsets. One useful grouping identifies nine major classes of adversaries:[16]

1. Foreign intelligence services (FIS)

2. Information warriors
3. Cyberterrorists and activists
4. Hackers, crackers, script kiddies
5. Malicious insiders
6. The press
7. Organized crime and lone criminals
8. Law enforcement
9. Industrial competitors

Analysis of attack scenarios for information systems and networks is an important approach that can be applied far beyond IA.

Comparison of AT with Other Contexts of Risk

When we compare AT with these other situations, we find many similarities and some major differences. In Figure 29-2, shading

F I G U R E   29-2

Sources of risk in important application areas.

Sources of Risk		Anti-terrorism	Natural Disasters	Commercial Nuclear Power	Space Systems	Information Assurance
Primary sources of risk	Foreign countries	▓				▓
	Hostile groups	▓				▓
	Hostile individuals	▓				▓
	Environment (weather, earthquakes, etc.)		▓	▓		
	Technology			▓	▓	▓
Secondary sources of risk	Organizational issues	▓	▓	▓	▓	▓
	System design		▓	▓	▓	▓
	Human error	▓	▓	▓	▓	▓

indicates that a specific source of risk applies to a particular context. The major difference among applications is the primary source of risk. AT and IA have similar primary sources of risk: foreign governments, groups, and individuals. In both cases, the major risks are from attacks by intelligent, determined adversaries who can alter their strategies to circumvent protective measures.[17] IA differs from AT in that technology is also included as a primary source of risk for IA because even without malicious behavior and intelligent adversaries, hardware fails and software has bugs. Technology is identified as a primary source of risk for commercial nuclear power: e.g., valves and pumps fail in nuclear plants and require maintenance; and even though nuclear power plants are designed to withstand severe natural disasters, environmental factors can still pose risks. In natural disasters, the primary risks are entirely from environmental factors: hurricanes and earthquakes cannot become stronger in response to protective actions taken against them. For space systems, hostile environmental conditions and technology are primary risks: systems can be damaged by orbital debris, for instance, and parachutes can fail to open for space probes.

The secondary sources of risk are common to all applications. Organizational factors—an institution's culture and management practices—can always be secondary sources of risk. In the *Columbia* investigation report, the organizational practices of NASA were considered as much to blame as the foam debris.[18] One secondary factor common to all applications considered here is organizational barriers that prevent effective communication of critical information regarding safety and stifle professional differences of opinion. This problem is a risk for AT and was cited by the 9/11 Commission in discussing problems with the coordination of intelligence among the major agencies. Errors in system design also occur in all applications (this becomes apparent when there is a major event that a system should have been able to withstand but could not); similarly, all the applications are subject to human error.

TOOLS AND TECHNIQUES OF ANALYSIS

Here, we will focus on systems engineering, risk analysis (risk assessment and risk management), decision analysis, scenario analysis, game theory, and benefit-cost analysis. When applying any of these tools, one must remember that people's behavior is influenced by personal judgments, and by biases such as the following:

* *Availability:*[19] Events may be deemed frequent or probable because they are readily available in memory. People tend to consider an event likely or frequent if it is easy to imagine or recall—but availability in this sense depends on many factors besides actual frequency.

* *Invincibility:*[20] People may consider negative events less likely to happen to themselves or their peers ("It can't happen to me"). Also, people may consider themselves more effective than others at avoiding preventable risks.

* *Confirmatory bias:*[21] Given information favoring a focal hypothesis, people rarely select diagnostic data relevant to an alternative hypothesis. In the case of *Columbia*, the one analytical resource available, Crater, predicted damage deeper than the actual tile thickness. Rather than become concerned, NASA's engineers discounted the evidence because previous calibration tests with small projectiles had showed that Crater predicted deeper penetrations than were actually observed.[22] It was easier for the personnel involved to disregard the evidence than to consider an alternative hypothesis.

* *Disregard of independent events:* People may assume that when a disaster has recently occurred, it is less likely to recur soon ("Lightning doesn't strike twice in the same place").[23]

These and other biases contribute to the challenge of making decisions when risks and uncertainties are involved. Decision makers need to rely on tools to support planning, analysis, and allocation of resources.

Systems Engineering Techniques

Successful terrorists plan attacks from a systems perspective. They seek, and attack, the weakest link in a system. The attacks of 9/11 resulted from systems planning. The terrorists believed that the airline security systems could be defeated, and they took advantage of gaps in policy and procedures between the Federal Aviation Administration (FAA) and the military to simultaneously commandeer four airplanes, defeating policy, technology, procedures, and people.

To deter such threats, homeland security planners must also take a systems perspective. They must understand how the elements of the system operate, including organizations, hardware, software, and humans. Systems engineering offers many tools for understanding systems and system complexity,[24] such as stakeholder analysis, systems design, systems simulation, and systems analysis.

An example is an alternative-generation table. This tool is commonly used in systems engineering (and in decision analysis). The purpose of an alternative-generation table is to identify the dimensions of alternatives, list the various decisions that can be made for each dimension, and generate an alternative by combining one decision each from all the dimensions.

Figure 29-3 is a simple alternative-generation table for a response by a city to an elevated alert for the potential release of a chemical by a terrorist. Each alternative must address four functions: detection of the threat, warning, protection, and response. Each function can be performed by several means. Each alternative uses one or more means to perform each function. For example, the high-tech alternative uses ground and air sensors for detection, multimedia for warning, gas masks for protection, and the National Guard for response.

Alternative-generation tables have at least five advantages: (1) The table explicitly identifies the dimensions of the alternative. (2) It can be used to focus creativity on new ways of performing each function and the overall alternative. (3) It clearly defines the alternatives. (4) It generates many alternatives ($3^4 = 81$ in Figure 29-3). (5) It provides a way to communicate with stakeholders and decision

FIGURE   29-3

Example of an alternative-generation table for an elevated alert.

Alternatives	Detect	Warn	Protect	Respond
Humanpower-intensive	Patrols	Sirens	Containment	Citizens
High-tech	Ground and airborne sensors	Television	Gas masks	Emergency medical teams
Combined	Both	Multimedia	Both	National Guard

makers. However, if not all the functions are identified, the alternatives will be incomplete.

Risk-Analysis Techniques

The level of risk analysis should be sufficient for planning effective strategies to mitigate a risk. Often, a categorization or screening based on a risk matrix may suffice. In some cases, relative importance (as in a ranking of risks) is needed, requiring a more sophisticated technique.

Many definitions have evolved for several concepts related to risk. The following definitions of terms are relevant to our discussion.

- *Asset*: Infrastructure component of value to an organization or enterprise (facilities, hardware, software, information, activities, operations, and people).
- *Attack*: Action by an adversary or competitor aimed at degrading the operation of an asset, denying use of it, or destroying it.
- *Countermeasures*: Actions or devices that mitigate risk by affecting threats or vulnerabilities. Countermeasures include deterrence to keep adversaries from attempting attacks, protection to stop an adversary should deterrence fail, and mitigation to minimize the impact should protection fail.
- *Event*: Occurrence that has the potential to affect an asset (e.g., loss of power).
- *Impact; consequences*: Loss or effect on the system if a risk materializes.[25]
- *Probability*: Likelihood that a risk will occur.[26] In AT, probability is determined by both threat and vulnerability.
- *Risk*: Potential for some unwanted event to occur. If probabilistic definitions are used, the calculation is risk = consequence × threat × vulnerability.
- *Risk assessment*: Systematic analysis to determine the likelihood that a threat will harm an asset, and the consequences if it does.
- *Risk management*: Systematic analysis to identify and evaluate countermeasures to reduce risk and mitigate consequences of an attack or another adverse event.

- *Threat*: Capability and intention of an adversary or competitor to undertake actions that have consequences detrimental to an organization or enterprise. Threat is often measured as the probability of an attack by an adversary.[27]
- *Threshold for acceptable risks*: All the resources in the world cannot mitigate all possible risks; therefore, in most situations a level (threshold) must be determined such that risks whose severity falls below this level are simply accepted, and no resources are expended to mitigate them.
- *Time frame*: Period when action is required in order to mitigate a risk.[28]
- *Vulnerability*: Weakness that can be exploited by an adversary. Vulnerability is sometimes measured as the probability of success, given an attack.[29]

We can now consider several techniques of risk analysis: fault trees, threat-vulnerability-consequence tables, risk matrices, failure modes and effects analysis—critical items lists, and probabilistic risk analysis.

Fault Trees

Fault trees have been used in reliability analysis since the 1960s. They were originally developed by Bell Telephone Laboratories to evaluate the safety of the Minuteman Launch Control System.[30] Special applications of fault trees have been called threat trees, attack trees, and vulnerability trees.[31] In a fault tree, an undesirable event is postulated and the possible scenarios necessary for this event to occur are systematically identified.[32] Through the analysis, all possible component failures are identified that can contribute to the occurrence of the event.

Figure 29-4 is an example of an attack tree.[33] The analysis included paths that an adversary could use to defeat the confidentiality of an e-mail transmission. To obtain access to the e-mail information, the adversary would need to both intercept the e-mail and decrypt it. In the branch for intercepting the e-mail, the adversary could obtain the e-mail in one of two ways: by installing a sniffer to pick up the message, or by having an insider forward the message. Several options are shown for decrypting the message.

F I G U R E   29-4

Example of a fault, or attack, tree.

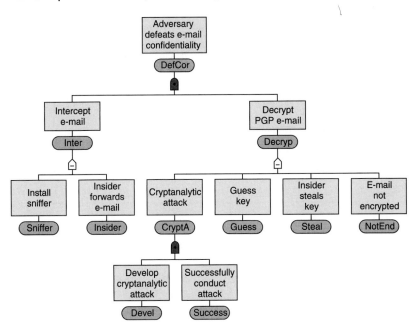

There are four primary advantages of fault trees. (1) A fault tree is focused on identifying paths in the system that can lead to failure. (2) The analyst can concentrate on one particular system failure at a time. (3) The results provide graphics to help managers visualize system weaknesses. (4) The trees can serve as a basis for more sophisticated risk analysis, such as PRA. But there are at least two disadvantages. First, only problems that contribute to the event in question are modeled; thus the model may have limited applicability in an environment where threats and vulnerabilities are continually changing. Second, in the traditional form, component outcomes are Boolean (i.e., failed state or not failed state), but a real situation may have many partial failure states.

Threat-Vulnerability-Consequence Tables

These allow a systematic consideration of each asset; they can be used to identify and assess critical assets, analyze vulnerabilities, and

F I G U R E   29-5

Threat-vulnerability-consequence assessment table.

Assets	Undesirable Events	Assessment of Loss
Key personnel	Loss of availability due to injury or death	High
File server	Loss of availability due to power disruption	Critical
Customer data	Loss of confidentiality due to unauthorized access	High
Principal production facility	Loss of availability due to natural disaster	Critical
Pipeline	Loss of availability due to sabotage	Medium

assess risks on the basis of consequences. An example is shown in Figure 29-5.

Threat-vulnerability-consequence tables are useful for screening or categorizing major assets. However, because of the focus on consequences and the lack of any estimates of likelihood, this method does not distinguish between low- and high-probability events. This focus on consequences can cause a misallocation of resources to very-low-probability events rather than to more likely events with less extreme consequences.

Risk Matrices

These are constructed ordinal scales used to "score" risks. A scale index associates specified levels with qualitative descriptions. Matrices can be used individually or in conjunction with other, more detailed methods. Figure 29-6 shows an example of this technique.

Risk matrices are useful for screening or categorizing major risks versus minor risks. But this method lacks any estimates of likelihood and thus does not distinguish between low- and high-probability problems. As a result, concern can be focused on low-probability issues rather than on more likely ones. If a budget is tight or complex decisions must be made (e.g., if risks must be ranked or there must be trade-offs in a design), more sophisticated risk analysis may be required. Also, when using risk matrices as a screening tool for a more quantitative analysis, one should be careful to note the overall

F I G U R E   2 9 - 6

Example of a risk matrix.

Probability of Occurrence	Severity Level			
	I Catastrophic	II Critical	III Marginal	IV Negligible
A Frequent	I A	II A	III A	IV A
B Probable	I B	II B	III B	IV B
C Occasional	I C	II C	III C	IV C
D Remote	I D	II D	III D	IV D
E Improbable	I E	II E	III E	IV E

Risk level

IA, IB, IC, IIA, IIB, and IIIA	☐	Unacceptable (reduce risk through countermeasures)	1
ID, IIC, IID, IIIB, and IIIC	▨	Undesirable (management decision required)	2
IE, IIE, IIID, IIIE, IVA, and IVB	☐	Acceptable with review by management	3
IVC, IVD, and IVE	▨	Acceptable without review	4

Source: Adapted from Military Standard 882C and multinational oil company.

magnitude of the risks that have, individually, been assumed to be negligible.

Failure Modes and Effects Analysis and Critical Items Lists

This technique—abbreviated FMEA/CIL—originated as a formal methodology in the 1960s when demands for improved safety and reliability extended studies of component failures to include the effects of the failures on the systems of which they were a part.[34] FMEA/CIL is an inductive analysis that systematically details all possible failure modes and identifies their resulting effects on the entire system. Possible single failure modes in a system are identified and analyzed to determine the effect on surrounding components and the system. In most cases there is a criticality component, and one of the most common methods is the risk priority number (RPN). RPN for a failure mode is determined from an ordinal scoring and multiplication of three components: likelihood of occurrence, severity, and likelihood of detection. For example, a high likelihood of occurrence might score 10; minor severity (minor effects) might score 4;

and a failure detectable with an instrument during regular operations might score 6. For this example, RPN $= 10 \times 4 \times 6 = 240$. RPNs for different system components are then compared, so as to prioritize risks.

In general, the steps in FMEA/CIL are as follows:[35]

1. Definition of system

2. Development of functional and reliability block diagram

3. Extraction of failure modes

4. Analysis on FMEA worksheet

5. Analysis of failure (causes and effects)

6. Identification of detection and probability of failure (optional)

7. Evaluation of criticality (optional)

8. Countermeasures and recommendations

Figure 29-7 provides an example of FMEA/CIL analysis for a component of a missile system.[36]

The main advantage of FMEA/CIL is its simplicity. In many situations statistical data are lacking, and so estimates of likelihood are often challenged; FMEA/CIL avoids this problem. The method is useful for analyzing risks that do not involve complex trade-offs—for example, in the development of inspection plans. Also, FMEA/CIL is

F I G U R E   29-7

Example of FMEA/CIL.

Item	Failure Modes	Cause(s) of Failure	Possible Effects	Criticality	Possible Action to Reduce Failure Rate or Effects
Motor case	Rupture	a. Poor workmanship b. Defective materials c. Damage during transportation d. Damage during handling e. Overpressurization	Destruction of missile	Critical	Quality control of manufacturing process and materials; inspection and pressure testing of completed cases; suitable packaging during transportation and handling
Etc.					

useful early in the design process when few data are available to highlight potential functional failure modes and the design is still easily changed. The primary shortcoming of this process is that the analysis generally does not include probabilities of failure. Also, it may not recognize the risks from a component that appears in several parts of the system, or the risk from external events that damage multiple components at once. CIL can be misleading because a "criticality 1" component with a low probability of failure may represent a smaller risk than a "criticality 3" component with a higher probability of failure. Also, numerical scales that are based not on the explicit assessment of the risk but rather on subjective, implicit combinations of frequencies and consequences can be misleading.

Probabilistic Risk Analysis

PRA seeks to measure the risks inherent in a system's design and operation by quantifying both the likelihood of various low-probability accident sequences and their consequences. PRA is based on a functional analysis of the system, identification of failure modes, and estimation of the probabilities of external events and component failures. PRA for a particular facility starts with an identification of the initiating events of accident sequences, computation of the probabilities of reaching different final systems states given the initiating events, and evaluation of the consequences of different degrees of system failure. PRA is usually based on event-sequence diagrams and fault trees. Its results are often represented by a distribution of the probabilities of different potential system states (i.e., a risk curve) based on best estimates of the model and parameter values.[37]

Figure 29-8 shows a high-level PRA for the failure of one Mars Rover in 2003.[38] The data shown are for illustrative purposes only; the format is that of an influence diagram. Major events with significant risks were modeled and included schedule failure, launch failure, failure in entry-descent-landing (EDL), and failure in operations. The success of these major events is influenced by other uncertain events including the height of rocks at the landing site, the weather, possible design errors, and the communications channels: direct-to-earth (DTE), UHF link, and the Mars Global Surveyor (MGS) link. On the basis of these illustrative data, the Rover had about a 1-in-4 chance of failure.

High-level PRA for failure of a Mars Rover.

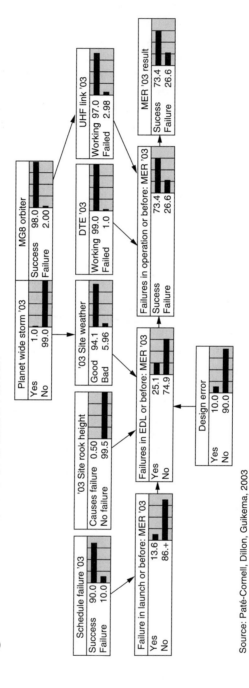

Source: Paté-Cornell, Dillon, Guikema, 2003

PRA allows problems to be ranked according to their probabilities (mean future frequencies) and consequences. This ranking is useful for setting priorities when budgets are limited. PRA is most useful when few statistical data are available to assess the probability of failure of a whole system. This technique focuses on decomposing the system into subsystems and components for which more data are generally available. The major criticism is that, depending on the level of detail, PRA may require large amounts of data and in most cases must rely on subjective estimates of probability.

Decision Analysis Techniques

The primary objective of decision analysis is to determine which alternative course of action will maximize expected utility for the decision maker. Decision analysis is based on a set of logical axioms and is a systematic procedure to aggregate probabilities and preferences based on those axioms.[39] Decision analysis provides the framework for including values and preferences to determine if the potential benefits are worth the associated risks, but one tool of risk analysis previously discussed is needed to quantify the risk of potential alternatives. Risk analyses are often carried out as part of a decision analysis: for example, for decisions affecting the likelihood that accidents or exposures will result in fatalities.[40]

Unique to decision analysis is the creation of a preference model to evaluate alternatives and possible consequences. This preference model includes information about value trade-offs, concerns regarding equity, and attitudes toward risk.[41] Figure 29-9 shows a hierarchy of values developed as part of an IA multiple-objective decision analysis model of how an adversary values an attack on an information system.[42] With decision analysis,[43] a complete mathematical model can be developed to evaluate the adversary's attacks. As shown, the hierarchy includes an overall objective and four measures. The adversary wants to maximize its attack value on the basis of four components: maximizing the likelihood of success, minimizing the likelihood of detection, minimizing the resources required, and maximizing the impact of the attack.

The advantage of decision analysis is its systematic treatment of preferences, alternatives, and uncertainty. The disadvantage is that it is time-consuming and requires support from others: the decision

F I G U R E   29-9

An adversary's hierarchy of values.

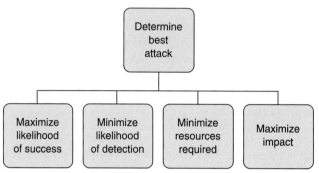

maker needs to obtain preferences (from senior leaders and key stakeholders), alternatives (from technical experts), and probabilities (again, from technical experts).

Scenario Analysis

A *scenario* is an "internally consistent story about how events relevant to your decision *might* develop over time."[44] Scenario analysis is an excellent technique for understanding the potential consequences of decisions when there are uncertainties about the future. Scenarios have been used for over 20 years by decision analysts[45] and risk analysts. Scenarios are often represented with tree structures. If a scenario tree includes key decision points, it is called a decision tree; if it includes only probabilistic events, it is often called an event-sequence diagram. Kirkwood[46] provides a summary of the literature on scenarios relevant to decision analysis. He recommends using scenarios to design and assess alternatives. Scenario analyses have been used to avoid strategic surprise[47] and to evaluate system concepts.[48]

Following are illustrative scenarios that could be used for risk analysis related to homeland security:

- ♦ A large truck bomb explodes in a tunnel in a city.
- ♦ A bioterrorism event occurs on a mass transit system.
- ♦ Coordinated information attacks are made on the telecommunications system.

- ◆ Several dams are destroyed.
- ◆ Simultaneous attacks are made on oil refineries and pipelines.

The major advantage of scenarios is that they help bound the decision space when we cannot reasonably identify all possible outcomes. The disadvantage of scenarios is that they take time to develop, and they may not include all the possible terrorist attacks.

Game Theory Models

A challenge arises when we can no longer model a problem simply from the decision maker's perspective but need to consider two competing sides. Game theory models can be constructed to include both an attacker and a defender.[49] In a game theory model, one considers how each side would respond to intelligence information about the other side's actions during the latest time period, and models each side's decisions regarding actions in the coming time period, on the basis of the information that each has accumulated so far.

The major advantage of game theory is that the models can include intelligent adversaries who would adopt different offensive strategies based on the actions taken by the defender. The disadvantage is that the models take time to develop, and at some point an arbitrary starting point and ending point need to be established.

Benefit-Cost Analysis

Benefit-cost analyses are often used as criteria for deciding which AT projects to fund. In its simplest form, benefit-cost analysis uses a ratio to rank projects.[50] This methodology is appropriate only if the project's benefits and costs are both independent and we have only one budget constraint. More often, the benefits from multiple projects are not independent. Projects can be substitutes or they can be complementary. Likewise, costs may be dependent. In addition, we usually have many constraints. For example, it may be cheaper to produce multiple projects that are bundled into a program. Even if independence exists within benefits and costs, the key issues are how to measure these benefits and costs. In commercial projects, the benefits and costs may both be measured in dollars. In many public applications, including AT, it may be difficult to quantify the benefits and, perhaps, the costs (e.g., loss of privacy) in dollars.

In many public decision-making applications, benefits (and sometimes costs) can be captured using multiple-objective decision analysis,[51] and costs can be life-cycle costs or acquisition costs. If we forgo the benefit-cost ratio and determine the highest-benefit projects for our budget, we no longer have to worry about the assumption that benefits and costs are independent. Using optimization techniques, we can develop a very flexible process.[52]

Figure 29-10 continues the example that was shown in Figure 29-9. Now, the decision analyst works with the system engineers to identify potential countermeasures that will reduce the adversary's attack value. The decision analyst then determines the set of countermeasures that would have the best combination of cost and impact on operational users of the information system. Figure 29-10 shows the impact of adding additional countermeasures.[53] At first the most effective countermeasures are used; then the curve reflects diminishing returns; then it reflects negative returns. The flat part of the curve is the low-risk solution.

The advantage of benefit-cost analysis is that it provides a common framework for comparing homeland security projects. Multiple-objective decision analysis can provide a credible objective and a defensible basis for measuring benefits. The time spent discussing AT countermeasures will be more objective and more focused. The disadvantage of benefit-cost analysis is that it takes support

FIGURE   29-10

Cost-benefit curve for information-system countermeasures.

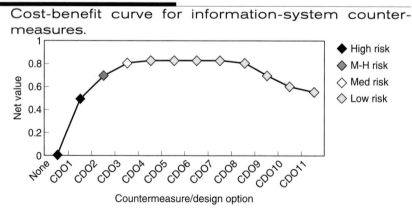

and time to quantify the benefits (by consulting senior leaders and key stakeholders) and to obtain credible cost data (from experts).

A METHODOLOGY FOR INTEGRATING RISK MANAGEMENT AND ALLOCATION OF RESOURCES IN ANTITERRORISM

DHS faces three formidable challenges. First, it must assess continuously what could go wrong (i.e., what are the risks) when assets, threats, vulnerabilities, and consequences are always changing. Second, it must prioritize risks by determining which are the most important. Third, it must implement cost-effective strategies to deal with those risks. To meet these challenges, we must identify key tasks of risk assessment, risk management, and resource allocation. Figure 29-11 shows the tasks that we believe must be included; they are described below.

Task 1: Identify Critical Assets

The key to our proposed methodology is identifying critical assets by applying a systematic process. Important stakeholders should be

F I G U R E   29-11

Tasks for integrating risk management and AT resource allocation.

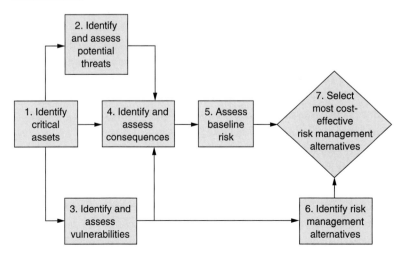

involved in the process. System architecture diagrams that show assets, systems flows, and interdependencies can be very useful. If no system architecture exists, developing this architecture should be the first step in the process. Once the major assets have been identified, screening is needed to determine the critical assets. The criteria may include potential casualties, potential economic disruption, and symbolic importance.

Task 2: Identify and Assess Potential Threats

The second step is to identify and assess threats to homeland security. A threat assessment can be based on types or sources of threats. The Office of Domestic Preparedness (ODP) focuses on the type of weapon that terrorists might use—chemical, biological, radiological, nuclear, and explosive.[54] The alternative is to focus on sources of threat—any organization with the motivation, capability, and opportunity to launch a successful attack on the system. It is essential to develop a range of scenarios that represent possible types of attacks. A scenario is a plausible (not necessarily probable) sequence of events that defines a potential threat. Each defined scenario should include targeted assets, weapons, and modes of delivery.

Task 3: Identify and Assess Vulnerabilities

The third step is to evaluate the vulnerability of the critical assets in the scenarios. For a given weapon and a given target, the probability that an attack will be successful depends on our ability to detect it, the warning time, the system's response, and the ability of the attacker to overcome the response. In evaluating these factors, it is important to consider, for each target, any current countermeasures, relevant physical layouts, geographical configurations, etc., that might prevent access to the target, ability to detect an attack in progress, or assistance in defeating a detected attack.

Task 4: Identify and Assess Consequences

If an attack has been successful, the next step is to assess its potential consequences for critical assets. This step is crucial because, with limited resources, we must concentrate on the vulnerabilities with the most significant consequences. Potential consequences may include casualties, economic disruption, and loss of public confidence.

Task 5: Assess the Baseline Risk

Once we have completed tasks 1 to 4, we have the information to assess the baseline (i.e., current) risk. This risk assessment must consider probability, consequences, and time frame (i.e., the period when action is required in order to mitigate the risk). This assessment provides the foundation for risk management. It also provides a total system risk assessment that allows decision makers and risk analysts to focus their efforts.

Task 6: Identify Alternatives for Risk Management

We need to involve stakeholders and technical experts in a structured process to identify potential actions in risk management. These actions can include all the aspects identified in the right-hand column in Figure 29-1. One useful decision analysis technique is the alternative-generation table.[55]

Task 7: Select the Most Cost-Effective Alternatives

Here, we assess the degree to which each action reduces risk. This is not necessarily an easy task. Unlike a natural disaster, a terrorist is intelligent and will change behaviors in response to the strategies that we implement. In addition, task 7 is a "portfolio" decision problem. We want to determine the most cost-effective portfolio of actions. As well as risk, other factors must be considered, including the impact of our actions on stakeholders and customers.

DEVELOPING THE INTEGRATIVE METHODOLOGY

To develop a methodology for integrating risk management and AT resource allocation, we must identify the techniques that are most applicable for each task. Figure 29-12 provides this information. The shaded boxes identify the potential use of each technique to perform

Applicability of techniques to risk-management tasks.

Techniques	Tasks for Risk Assessment and Risk Management						
	1. Identify Critical Assets	2. Identify and Assess Potential Threats	3. Identify and Assess Vulnerabilities	4. Identify and Assess Consequences	5. Assess Baseline Risk	6. Identify Risk Management Alternatives	7. Select the Most Cost-Effective Alternatives
Alternative generation table						Applicable	
Fault (attack tree)		Applicable			Applicable		
Threat-vulnerability-consequence table		Applicable	Applicable				
Risk matrix				Applicable			
Failure modes and effects analysis			Applicable	Applicable			
Probabilistic risk analysis			Applicable	Applicable			
Scenario analysis		Applicable	Applicable	Applicable		Applicable	
Decision analysis			Applicable			Applicable	
Game-theory models				Applicable	Applicable		
Benefit-cost analysis							Applicable

one of the risk-management tasks. For example, scenario analysis helps to identify threats, assess vulnerabilities, and identify consequences.

Each organization's methodology should be tailored to its unique challenges and circumstances. To develop a methodology, an organization should select at least one technique for each task. Most important, the techniques must be linked to provide consistent analysis. For example, probabilities obtained using PRA and consequences obtained from scenario analysis can all be used in decision analysis.

Also, the technique selected may depend on the number of threats and the potential consequences. For example, if the number of threats is very large and the consequences are small, the threat-vulnerability-consequence table may be appropriate. If the threats are fewer and the consequences are significant, a more detailed analysis, such as fault trees, may be appropriate.

CONCLUSION

Homeland security and antiterrorism are massive undertakings. The risk cannot be eliminated altogether, but it must be reduced. Risk analysis requires changes in organizational culture that take time and expertise if they are to succeed. The key is to use a systematic process to identify critical assets, assess risks, and make smart decisions for managing risk. It is important to tailor risk analysis techniques to potential consequences and to the resources involved. Major consequences of terrorism warrant more detailed risk analysis. On the basis of our experience with many applications, we recommend the following:

- ◆ *People*: People are crucial to risk assessment and risk management. Businesses and organizations need to acquire and train personnel in systems engineering, decision analysis, and risk analysis. Senior leaders must ensure that risk analysts have access to the best subject-matter experts.
- ◆ *Synergy*: We believe that AT has considerable synergy with other mission-assurance activities. For example, dispersing operations to multiple locations may reduce system vulnerabilities and potential consequences of terrorism and natural disasters.

- *Processes*: We have offered a framework for a general, flexible methodology. However, more detailed procedures will be needed. In fact, we believe a useful next step would be a handbook for risk analysis in homeland security, as a resource for analysts and managers in industry and government.
- *Timing*: The most cost-effective time to factor risk management into the decision process is when a system is being designed. Countermeasures made later are always more costly and typically less effective.
- *Culture*: We have focused on risk analysis, but to be successful an organization must develop a security culture that involves awareness, assessment, management, and communication of risks.

Through a resource allocation process based on detailed and thorough risk assessment, effective and efficient management of the risk of terrorism is possible.

See also Chapter 30, **The Psychological Perception of Risk.**

N O T E S

1. Federal Emergency Management Agency (FEMA). 2004. *Terrorism*, www.fema. gov/hazards/terrorism/.
2. Craig W. Kirkwood, *Strategic Decision Making: Multiobjective Decision Analysis with Spreadsheets* (Belmont, Calif.: Duxbury, 1997).
3. Dennis S. Mileti and Paul W. O'Brien, "Warnings during Disaster: Normalizing Communicated Risk," *Societal Problems* 39:1 (February 1992): 40–57.
4. Dennis S. Mileti, *Disasters by Design: A Reassessment of Natural Hazards in the United States* (Washington, D.C.: Joseph Henry Press, 1999).
5. Dennis E. Wenger, James D. Dykes, Thomas D. Sebok, and Joan L. Neff, "It's a Matter of Myths: An Empirical Examination of Individual Insight into Disaster Response," *Mass Emergencies* 1 (1975): 33–46.
6. FEMA. 2004. Hazards List, www.fema.gov/hazards/.
7. FEMA. 2004. *Benefit-Cost Analysis (BCA) of Hazard Mitigation Projects Appendix 1 to the Riverine Flood—Full Data Module User's Guide for Software Version 5.2.3,* www.fema.gov/pdf/fima/hmgp/bcmanual.pdf.
8. *Reactor Safety Study: Assessment of Accident Risk in U.S. Commercial Nuclear Plants.* 1975. WASH-1400 (NUREG-75/014). Washington, D.C.: U.S. Nuclear Regulatory Commission (USNRC).
9. *PRA Procedures Guide.* 1983. NUREG/CR-2300. Washington D.C.: USNRC. See also W. E. Vesely, *Fault Tree Handbook* (Washington D.C.: Office of Nuclear Regulatory Research, 1981).

10. Mark Davison and William Vantine, "Understanding Risk Management: A Review of the Literature and Industry Practice," *European Space Agency Risk Management Workshop, ESTEC* (30 March–2 April 1998): 253–6. See also Michael Frank, *A Survey of Risk Assessment Methods from the Nuclear, Chemical, and Aerospace Industries for Applicability to the Privatized Vitrification of Hanford Tank Wastes.* Report to USNRC (August 1998).

11. *Procedural and Submittal Guidance for the Individual Plant Examination of External Events (IPEEE) for Severe Accident Vulnerabilities.* 1991. Final Report. Washington, D.C.: USNRC. See also *A Technique for Human Error Analysis (Atheana).* 1996. Washington, D.C.: Division of Systems Technology, Office of Nuclear Regulatory Research, USNRC. And see Ali Mosleh. 1993. *Procedure for Analysis of Common-Cause Failures in Probabilistic Safety Analysis.* Washington D.C.: Division of Safety Issue Resolution, Office of Nuclear Regulatory Research, USNRC.

12. M. E. Paté-Cornell and Robin L. Dillon. "Probabilistic Risk Analysis for the NASA Space Shuttle: A Brief History and Current Work," *Reliability Engineering and System Safety* 74:3 (2001): 345–52.

13. F. Groen, C. Smidts, A. Mosleh, and S. Swaminathan, "QRAS: Quantitative Risk Assessment System," *Proceedings of RAMS 2002, Annual Reliability and Maintainability Symposium* (2002).

14. Joint Chiefs of Staff, Department of Defense, *Joint Doctrine for Information Operations.* Joint Publication (JP) 3-13 (Washington, D.C.: Pentagon, 1998).

15. Fred Cohen, "Information System Attacks: A Preliminary Classification Scheme," *Computer and Security* 16:1 (1997): 29–46.

16. D. L. Buckshaw, G. S. Parnell, W. L. Unkenholz, D. L. Parks, J. M. Wallner, and O. S. Saydjari, "Mission Oriented Risk and Design Analysis of Critical Information Systems." Technical Report 2004-03, Innovative Decisions, Inc. (August 2004).

17. Vicki Bier, "Should the Model for Security Be Game Theory Rather Than Reliability Theory?" *Fourth International Conference on Mathematical Methods in Reliability: Methodology and Practice,* Santa Fe, N.M. (21–25 June 2004).

18. Columbia Accident Investigation Board (CAIB) Report (Washington, D.C.: NASA, August 2003).

19. A. Tversky and D. Kahneman, "Judgment under Uncertainty: Heuristics and biases," *Science* 185:4157 (1974): 1124–31.

20. N. D. Weinstein, *Taking Care: Understanding and Encouraging Self-Protective Behavior* (Cambridge: Cambridge University Press, 1987).

21. M. E. Doherty, R. Chadwick, H. Garavan, D. Barr, and C. R. Mynatt, "On People's Understanding of the Diagnostic Implications of Probabilistic Data," *Memory and Cognition* 24 (1996): 644–54. See also P. C. Wason, "On the Failure to Eliminate Hypotheses in a Conceptual Task," *Quarterly Journal of Experimental Psychology* 12 (1960): 129–40. And see Wason, "Reasoning about a Rule," *Quarterly Journal of Experimental Psychology* 20 (1968): 273–281.

22. CAIB, 2003.

23. M. K. Lindell and R. W. Perry, *Behavioral Foundations of Community Emergency Planning* (Washington, D.C.: Hemisphere, 1992).

24. Dennis M. Buede, *The Engineering Design of Systems: Models and Methods* (New York: Wiley, 2000).

25. Software Engineering Institute (SEI), *Continuous Risk Management Guidebook* (Pittsburgh, Pa.: Carnegie Mellon University, 1996).

26. Ibid.

27. National Infrastructure Protection Center (NIPC), "Risk Management: An Essential Guide to Protecting Critical Infrastructure," Washington D.C. (November 2002).

28. SEI, 1996.

29. NPIC, 2002.

30. E. J. Henley and H. Kumamoto, *Probabilistic Risk Assessment: Reliability Engineering, Design, and Analysis* (New York: IEEE, 1992).

31. Buckshaw et al., 2004.

32. M. Modarres, *What Every Engineer Should Know about Reliability and Risk Analysis* (New York: Marcel Dekker, 1993).

33. Buckshaw et al., 2004.

34. John B. Bowles, "The New SAE FMECA Standard," *Proceedings of the Annual Reliability and Maintainability Symposium* (1998): 48–53.

35. Katsushige Onodera, "Effective Techniques of FMEA at Each Life-Cycle Stage," *Proceedings of the Annual Reliability and Maintainability Symposium* (1997): 50–6.

36. Adapted from Henley and Kumamoto, 1992.

37. M. E. Paté-Cornell, "Uncertainties in Risk Analysis: Six Levels of Treatment," *Reliability Engineering and System Safety* 54 (1996): 95–111.

38. M. E. Paté-Cornell, R. L. Dillon, and S. D. Guikema. "On the Limitations of Redundancies in the Improvement of System Reliability." *Risk Analysis* 24:6 (December 2004): 1423–36.

39. Samuel Bodily, "Introduction: The Practice of Decision and Risk Analysis," *Interfaces* 22:6 (November–December 1992): 1–4.

40. Ralph Keeney, "Decision Analysis: An Overview," *Operations Research* 30:5 (September–October 1982): 803–38.

41. Ibid.

42. Buckshaw et al., 2004.

43. Kirkwood, 1997.

44. Ibid.

45. R. L. Keeney and H. Raiffa, *Decision Making with Multiple Objectives: Preferences and Value Tradeoffs* (New York: Wiley, 1976).

46. Kirkwood, 1997.

47. J. A. Engelbrecht, Jr., R. L. Bivins, P. M. Condray, M. D. Fecteau, J. P. Geiss II, and K. C. Smith, "Alternate Futures for 2025: Security Planning to Avoid Surprise" (Maxwell Air Force Base, Ala.: Air University Press, April 1996).

48. J. A. Jackson, G. S. Parnell, B. L. Jones, L. J. Lehmkuhl, H. Conley, and J. Andrew, "Air Force 2025 Operational Analysis," *Military Operations Research* 3:4 (1997): 5–21.

49. M. Dresher, *Games of Strategy* (Englewood Cliffs, N.J.: Prentice Hall, 1961). See also M. E. Paté-Cornell and S. D. Guikema, "Probabilistic Modeling of Terrorist Threats: A Systems Analysis Approach to Setting Priorities among Countermeasures," *Military Operations Research* 7:4 (2002): 5–20. And see Bier, 2004.

50. Kirkwood, 1997.

51. Ibid.

52. Ibid.

53. Buckshaw et al., 2004.

54. Department of Homeland Security (DHS). 2003. *Office of Domestic Preparedness: Special Needs Jurisdiction Toolkit.*

55. Kirkwood, 1997.

FURTHER READING

General Accounting Office (GAO). 2003a. Critical Infrastructure Protection: Challenges for Selected Agencies and Industry Sectors. GAO-03-233. Washington, D.C. (February).

GAO. 2003b. Homeland Security: Information Sharing Responsibilities, Challenges, and Key Management Issues. GAO-03-1165T. (17 September).

Haimes, Y. Y., *Risk Modeling, Assessment, and Management* (New York: Wiley, 1998).

Kaplan, S., "The Words of Risk Analysis," *Risk Analysis* 17:4 (1997): 407–417

Kaplan, S., and B. J. Garrick, "On the Quantitative Definition of Risk," *Risk Analysis* 1:1 (1981): 11–27.

Keeney, R. L., *Value-Focused Thinking: A Path to Creative Decisionmaking* (Cambridge, Mass.: Harvard University Press, 1992).

Paté-Cornell, M. E., and P. S. Fischbeck.. "Risk Management for the Tiles of the Space Shuttle," *Interfaces* 24 (1994): 64–86.

The Psychological Perception of Risk

Dr. Baruch Fischhoff
Howard Heinz University Professor
Department of Social and Decision Sciences
Carnegie Mellon University

Risk communication: Provision of concise, comprehensible, credible information, as needed to make effective decisions regarding risks.

INTRODUCTION

The Challenge

Terrorists seek to undermine public morale, to the point where societies collapse or lose their momentum, at home and abroad. The direct route to this goal involves instilling terror, thereby undermining citizens' well-being, ability to function, and confidence in their way of life. One indirect route involves disrupting normal life, by interfering with economic activity, travel, education, leisure, elections, and the like. A second indirect route involves alienating people from their leaders, by throwing doubt on the two cornerstones of trust: competence and honesty. A successful attack (or even a false alarm) may leave citizens feeling that their authorities not only failed to protect them but also denied them the ability to protect themselves (including material resources and candid situation assessments). A third indirect route involves turning citizens against one another, by creating the feeling that they are receiving differential protection, or even that some are profiting from a situation in which others are suffering.

In these ways, terror is a continuous "mind game," punctuated by events with horrific physical consequences. As a result, counter-terrorism involves a battle of wits, for the hearts and minds of civilian populations. Communicating effectively about risks is one element of that battle. It requires accomplishing three tasks.

1. *Task 1: Manage risks well, so as to have a credible message to communicate.* Without reasonable progress, relative to the challenges, the authorities will find it difficult to inspire confidence in their messages. If terror seems to be managed poorly in other ways, then the credibility of communications will suffer. For example, if citizens believe that authorities have put their own interests ahead of those of the public, then they may suspect that communications are being "spun," complicating their ability to make life-and-death decisions. If the authorities have inconsistent policies (e.g., in alert levels or safety practices), then their messages may prompt further skepticism.

2. *Task 2: Create appropriate communication channels.* These channels not only deliver content but also are part of it. Improvised, fragmentary, and uncoordinated channels suggest poor execution in other, less visible aspects of terror risk management. Having appropriate channels should increase public confidence, by demonstrating that a common framework underlies preparation, alert, crisis, and recovery plans. The accepted standard for risk communication is creating two-way channels, in which recipients are treated like partners, shaping how risks are managed and sharing what is learned about them. In contrast, one-way channels tell recipients that they are being managed, learning no more than what someone wants them to know. Public relations, public affairs, and issues management are all legitimate activities. However, they are not risk communication, which must serve the public's interests.

3. *Task 3: Deliver decision-relevant information, concisely and comprehensibly.* Doing this requires rigorous analysis of the facts that citizens need to know in order to make the choices facing them. That analysis must be followed by empirical study of what they already know, and then the design (and evaluation) of communications bridging the critical gaps.

That design will face tension between condensation and expansion. On the one hand, it needs to use (and be seen as using) recipients' time efficiently. On the other hand, it must provide sufficient background to make the message meaningful, as interpreted within recipients' evolving "mental model" of the situation.

These three elements interact. Terror risk managers inevitably make assumptions about behavior that is shaped by their risk communications. For example, to what extent will people comprehend, trust, obey, and effectively execute instructions to evacuate, shelter in place, get (or avoid) medical treatment, leave children in school (or collect them), surrender personal data, report on neighbors' actions (or suspicious packages), maintain emergency supplies, and install computer firewalls? The answers to these questions will depend on the faith that the authorities have generated over time, as well as on the technical execution of specific communications.

Incompetent risk communications can further terrorists' short-term and long-term goals. For example, a common misconception is that people panic during a crisis, behaving irrationally at the individual and group level.[1] That belief is contradicted by a large body of research, which has found that people respond reasonably, even bravely, to such challenges.[2] People may act on the basis of poor information, making their reasonable actions ineffective. If so, however, the fault lies with the inputs to their choices, not with their decision-making processes. In hindsight, citizens will be critical of authorities who failed to collect the right information; they will be unforgiving of those who failed to disseminate it or misrepresented it for some unacceptable reason.

Deliberately ignoring behavioral research entails assuming that, somehow, everything is different with terror—or else preferring hunches to science. In the specific case of perpetuating the myth of panic, the likely result, in order to manage a public that is not trusted to behave responsibly, is the unwarranted use of coercive measures (e.g., hiding risks; sending soldiers rather than first responders, to emergency scenes). Doing so takes the short-term risk that coercion will be less efficient than relying on the self-organizing properties of a motivated, intelligent populace. It takes the long-term risk that needlessly coercive measures will be seen as violating the social contract between citizens and authorities. If not, then social fiber may be sacrificed, in a misguided attempt to protect physical well-being. Terror is a multiple-play game. Actions that undermine a society's cohesion reduce its ability to defend itself, as well as forfeiting some of what it values.

THE RESOURCES

The confrontation with terrorism has revealed new risks and changed the shape of old ones (e.g., risks to aviation and to shipping). The new risks and the new wrinkles are often intellectually and emotionally challenging. They involve complex, novel phenomena. They require expertise distributed over multiple disciplines and cultures. They are dynamic and uncertain. They pose difficult trade-offs: your money or your life, your life or your liberty, my freedom or yours. They require vigilance, from already weary people. They evoke social tension, in an already complex time.

Although the legacy of existing risks adds to the stress of managing the new ones, it also provides resources. These take several forms. One is providing people with knowledge about related risks and control mechanisms. A second is providing them with analytical strategies for extrapolating beyond direct evidence. These strategies have been documented in behavioral decision research and behavioral economics, overlapping fields which study behavior in ways that allow comparison with formal models defining optimal performance. Doing so shows how much specific imperfections matter, how they come about, and how they might be corrected (if need be). The basic research has been applied extensively with health, safety, and environmental risks. Many of these problems are intellectually and emotionally challenging, in ways like those of terrorism. Applying this research to terror constitutes a "defense dividend" from investments in research into these (peaceful) problems.

Given the urgency of terror risk communication, we can ill afford to reinvent this research—unless we have powerful evidence that the usual rules of behavior are repealed when people face terrorism. As a result, the remainder of this chapter begins with research into other risks, then proceeds to guarded extrapolations to terror. The next three sections deal with the three tasks facing risk communication, as listed above. We begin with the second task, creating appropriate channels. These channels determine the content and character of the communications. Within these constraints, decision-relevant facts must be communicated concisely and comprehensibly. We then consider the science relevant to this third task. It leads to treatment of what risk communication contributes to the first task, managing terror risks effectively.

CREATING APPROPRIATE COMMUNICATION CHANNELS

Other Risks

Health, safety, and environmental risk communications are a central social function, shaping relationships between citizens and authorities.[3] Experiences with them provide both lessons and expectations for terror risk communication. In the western democracies, the evolving standard calls for a high degree of shared responsibility. It reflects faith (and hope) that authorities can create the facts that the public needs for effective decision making and can deliver those facts in a comprehensible, credible form. The outcomes of this social experiment will depend on both institutional commitment and technical execution. By facilitating the technical execution, risk research may enhance institutional resolve, by showing that public engagement is possible.

Figure 30-1 shows how the Canadian Standard Association (1997) has conceptualized this process. On the right appear the standard steps of risk management. The scheme is unusual only in requiring an explicit evaluation at each transition. That is, the model recognizes the possibility of having to repeat the work until it has been performed adequately—and that this goal might not be achieved. The left-hand side shows a commitment to two-way risk communication at each stage of the process. Both the comprehensiveness and the reciprocity of this involvement are noteworthy. In this view, citizens have a right to hear and to be heard from the very beginning, when risk analyses are initially formulated. Moreover, citizens have expertise that should shape the terms of an analysis and inform its content. This is a striking departure from the one-way communication strategy, sometimes called "decide-announce-defend."

Similar policies have been advanced by the Presidential/ Congressional Commission on Risk (1998) and the Environmental

F I G U R E   30-1

Steps in the Q850 Risk Management Decision-Making Process—Simple Model.

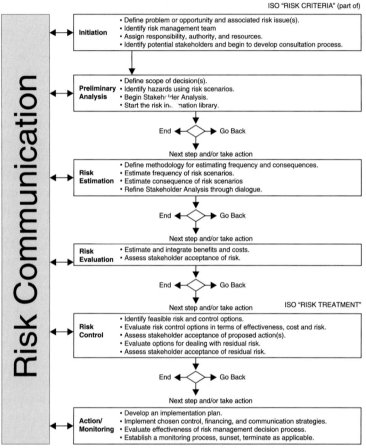

ISO "RISK CRITERIA" (part of)

Initiation
- Define problem or opportunity and associated risk issue(s).
- Identify risk management team
- Assign responsibility, authority, and resources.
- Identify potential stakeholders and begin to develop consultation process.

Preliminary Analysis
- Define scope of decision(s).
- Identify hazards using risk scenarios.
- Begin Stakeholder Analysis.
- Start the risk information library.

End ◄── ◇ ──► Go Back

Next step and/or take action

Risk Estimation
- Define methodology for estimating frequency and consequences.
- Estimate frequency of risk scenarios.
- Estimate consequence of risk scenarios
- Refine Stakeholder Analysis through dialogue.

End ◄── ◇ ──► Go Back

Next step and/or take action

Risk Evaluation
- Estimate and integrate benefits and costs.
- Assess stakeholder acceptance of risk.

End ◄── ◇ ──► Go Back

Next step and/or take action   ISO "RISK TREATMENT"

Risk Control
- Identify feasible risk and control options.
- Evaluate risk control options in terms of effectiveness, cost and risk.
- Assess stakeholder acceptance of proposed action(s).
- Evaluate options for dealing with residual risk.
- Assess stakeholder acceptance of residual risk.

End ◄── ◇ ──► Go Back

Next step and/or take action

Action/ Monitoring
- Develop an implementation plan.
- Implement chosen control, financing, and communication strategies.
- Evaluate effectiveness of risk management decision process.
- Establish a monitoring process, sunset, terminate as applicable.

Risk Communication

Source: CSA, July 1997. Risk Management: Guideline for Decision-Makers
(CAN/CSA Q850-97) Canadian Standards Association.

Protection Agency (2000) in the United States; and by the Royal Commission on Environmental Pollution (1998), Health and Safety Executive (2001), Parliamentary Office of Science and Technology (2001), and Cabinet Office (2002) in the United Kingdom. All endorse involving the relevant publics, focusing on their informational needs, and taking advantage of their expertise. All recognize the importance of trust for risk management, and the centrality of open, competent communication in securing it.

The evolution of this philosophy is reflected in a series of reports from the U.S. National Academy of Sciences. The "Red Book"[4] recognized that risk analysis inevitably reflects both science and politics. Even if scientists could scrupulously avoid the influence of vested interests, the choice of analytical topics and focal outcomes reflects what matters to those commissioning an analysis. So do the decisions to invest in creating data that could support or undermine particular concerns. The Red Book advocated recognizing these issues explicitly, thereby framing analyses in ways relevant to stakeholders. Doing so requires hearing stakeholders describe their concerns (through case-specific deliberations, supported by research into general concerns). Although this stance in the Red Book presaged the current (two-way) communication standard, the immediate response was a quest for fuller separation: scientists would assess the situation, while politicians would decide what to do about it. That separation was designed to keep scientists from spinning their results and politicians from claiming unwarranted expertise. It was naturally appealing to scientists hoping to perform purely objective research (and ignore how political power shapes research agendas).

Improving Risk Communication[5] asserted the public's right to know the results of risk analyses. That commitment envisioned a less passive public, doing more than just waiting for scientists and officials to manage risks. It reflected a view that the public can understand risks—contrary to many experts' belief in citizens' incompetence (captured in phrases like "real versus perceived risks," "hysterical public," or "panic"). The report concluded that citizens could fill a constructive role, if provided with diligently prepared communications.

One body of research evidence supporting this conclusion provided a richer context for interpreting disagreements between citizens and experts, rather than just assuming citizens' ignorance or stupidity. It showed that any account of disagreement between laypeople and experts must consider whether they (1) use terms differently (e.g., which outcomes they treat as the "risk" of a technology; how they weight catastrophic potential); (2) are prey to self-serving biases, assuming the worst about the others' motivation and biases; and (3) are insufficiently critical of their favored information sources. A common finding is that citizens are most skeptical of claims for which experts' evidence is weakest, such as assessments of low-probability, high-consequence events.[6]

Understanding Risk[7] revived the Red Book's intertwining of science and values. It challenged the assumption that scientists can simply do their work and leave the politics to others. Rather, it showed how the framing of a risk analysis must express some values. They are seen in its choice of topics (why some outcomes are studied and not others) and definition of terms. For example, *risk* could mean just mortality or also include morbidity; its definition must assign relative weights to different consequences. Even weighting all deaths equally expresses a value: not assigning greater weight to deaths among young people (with more lost years) or those exposed to a risk involuntarily.[8] The report argued that these definitional choices should be made explicitly, by stakeholders (those whose fate depends on them) or their representatives.

Involving citizens in priority setting was further endorsed by the congressionally mandated Committee on Setting Priorities for the National Institutes of Health.[9] It led to the creation of a Citizens Advisory Panel, chaired by the head of the institutes. *Toward Environmental Justice* called for "participatory science"[10] involving citizens in the design and conduct of studies affecting their community. That participation takes advantage of their expertise (e.g., in exposure processes), while seeing that they learn as much about their conditions as the outsiders examining them. It should improve citizens' scientific and policy-making sophistication, while increasing the chances of their accepting the results of risk analyses (which they now see as collaboratively produced).

Terror Risks

At this writing, terror risk communication is in its infancy, as is research into the efficacy of that communication. As a result, this section will focus on how a consultative process, integrating risk analysis and communication, could be adopted to the demands of several terror risks.

Smallpox Vaccination

In 2002–2003, the United States sought to vaccinate first responders and health care workers against vaccinia, a disease closely related to familiar strains of smallpox. The campaign generated considerable acrimony, over issues including the magnitude of the risks faced by health care workers and compensation for health problems that they suffered or caused, by transmitting diseases to others. A small fraction of the initial vaccination goal was achieved (with disagreement over whether this reflected a partial failure or reassessment of needs).

Whatever the lesson of this campaign, mass vaccination is a plausible prospect in the struggle against terror, not to mention pandemics of infectious diseases arising from natural causes.[11] The risks and benefits of such campaigns are sufficiently uncertain that responsible risk management must begin with a formal analysis of the anticipated impacts of alternative programs. A two-way risk communication process would begin by enlisting stakeholders to identify those consequences that matter to them. For health care workers, their personal health risks would obviously be on that list, as would the health benefits for others. Nonetheless, having them nominate those consequences would be an important courtesy. Their list might also include effects on their future insurability, ability to provide emergency services and legal liability for secondary infections. An analysis that neglected vital outcomes would be guilty of misplaced precision in its analyses of the factors that it did consider.

As the analytical process continues, healthcare workers (or their representatives) would be able to follow its work, ensuring that the results are comprehensible and credible. They would be able to contribute their knowledge about how things really work (e.g., needle stick rates and compliance with recommended precautions) and how they might be improved. Analogous consultations could shape the analysis to meet the informational needs of other stakeholders. For example, representatives of immunocompromised groups might want estimates of disease and side effects refined by populations. First responders' representatives might provide input into the roles and concerns of their members. Minority groups might identify their communities' special suspicions and ways to address them.

Domestic Surveillance

Managing terror requires police work. That means placing people under some degree of surveillance, reflecting some measure of suspicion. By design, the process reduces their privacy. Almost inevitably, some (if not most) suspicions will lead nowhere. Nonetheless, they will impose costs on the individuals involved. It might be as little as a note in their file (indicating a suspicion that was raised and dismissed), or as much as a lingering shadow of doubt complicating their jobs, health, etc. These risks to innocent civilians must be justified by reductions in terror risks. The cleared suspects (e.g., travelers who undergo airport screening) benefit from that reduction. Other benefits might include reducing the chance of discrimination against "people like them" following an attack. Thus, even at the individual level, the benefits may outweigh the risks, for all but the guilty. Even where that is not strictly true, most people will pay some personal price in order to protect their community.

Explaining the risks and benefits of surveillance programs is a familiar chore for police officials. Controversies over profiling show the difficulties of getting it right, played out against the history of relations between the police and the community, constrained by the limits to what can be revealed without compromising the operations. Approached as a risk communication task, terror-surveillance procedures would be accompanied by an ongoing dialogue with stakeholders. As elsewhere, the act of respectful, proactive communication would itself carry a message. Its content would improve understanding of both specific plans and general principles (e.g., how legal protections work). Content would flow in both directions (e.g., informing authorities about community sensitivities, discussing program designs that might address them without reducing effectiveness).

These communications must be grounded in formal analysis, no less than ones regarding hazardous technologies—especially given the challenges of conducting the conversation without revealing details that compromise a program's efficacy. In this case, the critical issues are likely to be the rates of true and false choices possible with surveillance methods of varying intensity and targets of varying frequency. Other things being equal, there will be more false positives (e.g., arrests of innocent people), with less discriminating procedures, rarer targets, and greater aversion to false negatives (missing guilty ones). For example, if there are very few guilty individuals, then the only chance of finding them all is with very intrusive procedures and arrest rates. These relationships are thoroughly understood by decision scientists.[12] However, applying them requires an institutional commitment to estimating the rates. Such quantification may be uncommon. It may be opposed by those who prefer to rely on intuition. Unfortunately, people intuitively exaggerate how well many diagnostic procedures work and underestimate how difficult it is to detect rare phenomena.[13] The authorities commissioning a program are, of course, also stakeholders. They need an ongoing communication process in order to shape programs to their needs, and create realistic expectations about its capabilities. It's important to know when the best possible program is still very porous.

Decontamination Standards

Attacks by chemical, radiological, and biological weapons impose both immediate and longer-term costs. The latter arise from their ability to disrupt everyday life. One determinant of that disruption is lost access to contaminated areas. The benefits of avoiding such areas come at an economic cost, from lost business, relocation, reduced property values, etc. There may also be health costs, arising from the stress of dislocation (e.g., lost income, inconvenient circumstances, family tension, and difficulty maintaining health care regimens). A comprehensive analysis of decontamination standards would consider all these effects, then determine acceptable trade-offs. There is no logical reason why the resulting exposure standards would be those adopted elsewhere, with differing control options and distributions of risks and benefits (e.g., for radiation exposure to patients and health care practitioners, or for nuclear power plants and hazardous waste sites). Moreover, all standards reflect an imperfect resolution of conflicting political and economic pressures and hence have inconsistencies, in terms of the protection bought per dollar spent.[14]

Homeland security situations require their own cleanup standards, informed by scientific research and social values. In the absence of explicitly developed and adopted standards, multiple competing ones may be advocated, adding confusion to an already stressful situation. The winners in this competition may reflect bureaucratic politics rather than public needs. In particular, they may be much more stringent than citizens want. In an emergency, a small increase in lifetime cancer risk might be an acceptable price to pay for returning to home and work.

Establishing cleanup standards requires a socially credible process, informed by research into the effects of both radiation and the disruptions caused by reducing radiation risks. None of the stakeholders will be familiar with all the technical issues. Neither will any of the experts (e.g., health physicists will know the effects of radiation, but not those of stress). As elsewhere, consultation is a communication act that lends credibility to subsequent communication of its conclusions. Materials developed for standard-setting deliberations can be adapted for broader distribution. Creating and disseminating sound explanations should reduce public anxiety over these risks—as should the observation of a deliberative, participatory approach.

DELIVERING DECISION-RELEVANT INFORMATION CONCISELY AND COMPREHENSIBLY
Other Risks

The logic of creating the content of risk communications is simple: (1) Analytically, determine the facts most relevant to predicting the outcomes that matter most to citizens. (2) Empirically, determine what citizens know already. (3) Design messages to close the most critical gaps, applying scientifically sound information-processing principles. (4) Evaluate the impact of the messages. (5) Repeat the process, as needed, until an acceptable level of understanding is achieved.[15]

Prioritizing information is important because the communication channel is often narrow. Citizens may have other things on their minds (e.g., they may be suffering from a medical condition or may be angry because they do not feel respected). Poorly chosen content can narrow the channel further: Why pay attention to experts who say things that are irrelevant or that don't need to be said? Why trust communicators who omit crucial facts or who treat people as if they are stupid and need to have obvious things explained?

People poised to make well-formulated personal or policy decisions need *quantitative* estimates of the probability and magnitude of each relevant consequence. Often, though, people also need *qualitative* information regarding the processes underlying those estimates, creating and controlling the risks. Such knowledge can give the quantitative estimates intuitive credibility, allow citizens to follow the discussions, and confer a feeling of competence.

Formally analyzing information needs is straightforward, if technically demanding.[16] A typical analysis examined the importance of knowing about each of the many possible side effects of carotid endarterechtomy, which involves scraping out the carotid artery, for patients with arteriosclerosis. Although successful surgery can reduce the risk of stroke, many things can go wrong. However, the analysis showed that only a few risks were sufficiently likely and severe to matter to many surgery candidates.[17] While no risks should be hidden, communication should focus on these critical ones (death, stroke, and facial paralysis).

In another typical study, we examined what teens need to know about HIV-AIDS, in order to make effective choices (reducing the risks, without unduly constraining their lives, ostracizing others who may be ill, etc.). To this end, teens need both quantitative information (e.g., prevalence, transmissibility), in order to evaluate options; and qualitative information (e.g., prevention strategies, modes of transmission), in order to fashion options. Interviews with teens revealed that they knew much of the relevant qualitative information. In part, that reflected general knowledge of infectious disease. In part, it reflected society's intensive HIV-AIDS education. However, there were significant gaps in their knowledge, reflecting omissions in that education. These gaps included both quantitative information, which is rarely presented anywhere; and qualitative information that some venues find too sensitive (e.g., explicit descriptions of safe sex practices or explanations of risk levels). We reduced these risks by plugging these gaps with an intervention that also stressed self-efficacy, the grounded feeling of being able to manage the risks.[18]

Although communications must address the specifics of particular decisions, they can draw on design principles, identified in the basic research literature.[19] For example, one long-standing focus of decision-making research has been how people's current beliefs shape their future understanding. Knowing about these processes is essential for effective communication. People's ability to process risk communications depends on their numeracy and literacy. Numeracy is required to understand how big risks are (and the cost-benefit trade-offs of risk-reduction measures). Language literacy is required to process written messages. Scientific literacy is needed to grasp the content of messages that, with terror, can span many domains. The greater the base, the further that communications can take them.

People's responses are also constrained by their cognitive capacity. Given its limits, they must either acquire domain-specific knowledge or rely on robust but imperfect heuristics. Such rules of thumb simplify problems and provide approximate answers, at the price of somewhat predictable biases. For example, people seem to count, almost automatically, how frequently they see events. Those estimates are useful for estimating frequencies—unless appearances are deceiving, making some events disproportionately visible. People often do not think about the representativeness of the evidence. When they do, they have difficulty adjusting adequately from what they have seen to what is actually out there.[20]

Researchers who rely on psychological theories and methods have found it possible to increase people's understanding of many risks. Some concepts require special efforts. One challenge is giving a feeling for very low probabilities. There are about 290 million people in the United States. It is hard to bear that denominator in mind, when thinking about a risk with a few highly salient casualties in the numerator. Another challenge is conveying how risks accumulate through repeated exposure. An improbable risk might merit attention, given enough chances to happen (e.g., driving without a seat belt). A third problem arises with verbal quantifiers such as "likely," which may mean different things to different people in one situation, and different things to one person in different situations. Communicating with words, instead of numbers, sets a trap for the audience.[21]

People have difficulty making decisions about events that they have never experienced. In effect, they do not really know what they want or what it would mean to them. Such uncertainty about values has methodological as well as practical and theoretical implications. Conventional survey research is ill suited to eliciting preferences among unfamiliar prospects. Rather, people need help to understand the options and how their basic values should be articulated for them. Such measurement, called constructive valuation, integrates behavioral decision research, which provides understanding of the factors shaping values, and decision analysis, which provides a disciplined approach presenting alternative perspectives in an unbiased way.

One aspect of that challenge is predicting personal emotions. A simple example is fully anticipating how one will feel if an investment goes bad or one becomes sick. Current emotions can color those predictions. For example, anger increases optimism, as well as the tendency to blame other people, rather than complex situations, for problems.[22] Those shifts might be useful in mobilizing for an immediate fight. They might undermine policy making by amplifying the natural tendency toward undue optimism.

Terror Risks

Although complex, these processes have been extensively studied in research that could be applied to communicating about terror risks. Ignoring it would fail to serve the public interest. However, there are institutional barriers to avoid this form of professional malpractice. Because terror is so new, many risks have yet to be analyzed at all, much less from the perspective of citizens' decision-making needs. New groups of experts are thrust into the front lines of communication, without knowing their audience or its problems. They must make rapid progress on the communication learning curve if they are to earn trust that is hard to restore, once lost.[23]

Unfortunately, many experts' first response is telling citizens to "go away while we figure things out." If people persist in wanting to hear something immediately, it is tempting to tell them what they ought to think, rather than leveling with them and providing the facts that they need for independent choices. It is tempting, at some times, to magnify risks in order to motivate citizens. It is tempting, at other times, to trivialize their worries, with comparisons like "why get so excited about terror, when you're still smoking" or "only five people have died from anthrax [so far], compared with 40,000 annually from motor vehicle accidents." The rhetorical tone of such comparisons puts many people off, especially when the options differ in other ways (benefits, alternatives).

One common institutional response is training experts in communication skills (like those in the appendix to this chapter). That training might reduce experts' misconceptions about the public, like the belief in panic. However, it is difficult to change behavioral patterns, especially when people tend to regress to old behaviors in stressful situations. Moreover, even if the training is successful, demeanor can go only so far, with an audience wanting to know "What is happening?" and "What should I do?" The best communicator is badly exposed if denied the staff work needed to provide the content of concise, comprehensible messages.

The rest of this section sketches the conclusions about content that might emerge from systematic treatment of the three examples. These speculations are no substitute for systematic analysis, design, and evaluation.

Smallpox Vaccination

Interest here could be prompted by various specific choices, such as whether to support legislation creating a national stockpile, to consider the 2003 vaccination campaign a success or failure, to seek vaccination proactively, to participate in an emergency campaign, and to help someone who has been exposed. Somewhat different information is critical for each choice and hence should be emphasized. Inferences about each will draw on a common set of beliefs, which will, in turn, be supplemented by the beliefs extracted from new messages. The more complete people's mental model, the less needs to be said in a new situation. As a result, each communication has a role in creating the background needed by later ones.

In the absence of directly relevant information, people will draw on seemingly related beliefs. In the case of smallpox, these might include beliefs about other infectious diseases and vaccines. Communicators should be particularly alert to cases where such inferences lead in the wrong direction. For example, a survey conducted by the United States during the run-up to the vaccination campaign of 2003 found that few people confidently believed that vaccination could be effective after exposure. That easily understandable fact was, obviously, not made salient (if it was said at all). A similar communication failure was not conveying the fact that anthrax is not easily transmissible, apparently buried in the massive reportage during the crisis.[24]

With health matters, mental models naturally include the other people involved, including those delivering and managing health care. Many vaccines are surrounded by controversy, including some childhood immunizations (in the civilian population) and anthrax vaccination (in the military). In our survey, most people endorsed the statement "If smallpox breaks out somewhere, we should quarantine the area." Thus, at that time, there was the trust needed to support such a draconian program. This valuable resource could be imperiled in many ways, including a tendency to disparage the public for failing to know facts that experts had communicated poorly.

Domestic Surveillance

Citizens evaluating domestic intelligence policies need both quantitative and qualitative information. On the one hand, they need to know the magnitude of the threat, the chance of identifying legitimate suspects, and the damage done by false positives. On the other hand, they need to know how the system works. For example, pulling in a class of individuals (e.g., male students from a given country) could yield valuable information about them, as individuals and as a class. However, it is a reactive form of measurement. It might deter some targets, while radicalizing others. It could have unpredictable effects on future visitors.

The attention that the authorities pay to civil liberties issues, when conducting such surveillance, will affect these processes. It might reduce the yield from questioning, by restraining interrogators; or increase the yield, by convincing participants that they can speak freely. It could alienate or draw in the target community. The attention that the authorities appear to be paying will inform people's beliefs. Of course, the methods and effects of these programs are, by their nature, incompletely visible. Outsiders cannot see the evidence supporting (or contradicting) the decision to question (or ignore) someone. Nor can they see problems averted or deterred by a program. Indeed, even the authorities cannot be sure of its effects. As a result, citizens need theory to supplement their observations, regarding both the effectiveness and the costs of such programs.

That theory will come from their mental models of how such matters work, supplemented by what they hear from various sources, weighted by their credibility and comprehensibility. A consultative process can help with both. It will have to overcome availability bias, arising from the observation of unrepresentative evidence. That could be incidents depicted as harassment or interceptions. Given the natural tendency for initial beliefs to shape later ones, proactive communication is important.

Decontamination Standards

At the time of a dirty bomb attack, citizens will want to know what to do in order to protect themselves and others. They will want to know whether to shelter in place or try to evacuate, what they can eat and drink, what to do with their clothing, and so on. Their inferences will shape their approach to subsequent decontamination, just as they will be shaped by previous encounters with radiation issues and the authorities managing them. Those may include beliefs about nuclear weapons, power, and medicine.

The research on these risk perceptions shows predictable misunderstandings, but also manageable ones, given proper communications.[25] People confuse radioactivity (the potential to do damage) and radiation (the release of energy that does damage). Treating the former eliminates the latter and is often possible (e.g., removing clothes and showering after exposure). As a result, it is critical to preserve the cleanup option (e.g., by avoiding the inhalation of particles and closing external air ducts). Without clear messages, citizens cannot know whether the dose is like medical X rays or domestic radon (which many accept, within reason) or like that of nuclear weapons or high-level radioactive waste.

As elsewhere, messages will be interpreted in the context of the messengers. The institutional legacy here is a difficult one. Managing nuclear materials has been among society's most contentious issues. The authorities involved with decontamination will have to distinguish themselves from those associated with Hiroshima, downwinders, Three Mile Island, Chernobyl, Yucca Mountain, and the like. That will be hard to do without a deliberative process involving stakeholders' representatives.

MANAGING RISKS WELL, SO AS TO HAVE A CREDIBLE MESSAGE TO COMMUNICATE
Other Risks

Experts are people, too, with uncertain beliefs and emotions. Complex, novel risks can draw them into areas that no one understands very well. They must interface with other experts, from unfamiliar disciplines. Decision makers (whether authorities or citizens) need the best expert judgment available. However, in order to use it well, they need to know how good it is. That trust is a function of (1) how completely the relevant topics are covered, (2) how well the pieces are integrated, and (3) how candidly they are qualified. To this end, experts need to have—and convey—a realistic assessment of their own competence, bounding their domain of expertise and coordinating with experts from other domains. That requires overcoming the territorial and commercial imperatives that lead disciplines and consultants to exaggerate their capabilities.

One way of disciplining expert judgment is to perform formal risk analyses. That involves identifying valued outcomes, the processes affecting them, and the experts for each. These experts must then pool their beliefs, uncertainties, controversies, and omissions and then subject their work to independent peer review. Although the basic formalisms of risk analysis are well established (and under constant refinement), their implementation is a human process, which requires attention to how groups are assembled and how their judgments are elicited.[26]

One statement of these issues emerged in a National Research Council report (1994) in the Red Book series. *Science and Judgment in Risk Assessment* recognized the central role of judgment in risk analysis—given the great uncertainty surrounding many novel issues, with complex conjunctions of environmental, industrial, social, psychological, and physiological processes. It offered standards for diagnosing and disclosing the role of expert judgment, and for eliciting it in a disciplined way. Further critiques have warned about risks of risk analysis. One is stifling creativity, by focusing on the justification of existing proposals. A second is emphasizing readily quantified factors (e.g., monetary costs) over more qualitative ones (e.g., impacts on public morale or minority groups' feelings). A third is disenfranchising those unfamiliar with model formalisms, even if they have or need substantive knowledge of risk topics.

Collaborative schemes, as in Figure 30-2, reflect recognition of risk communication needs, within expert communities, as well as between them and their clients. Figure 30-2 shows a risk analysis combining social, biological, and engineering knowledge, with a problem involving the role of communications when typically benign systems misbehave.[27] It looks specifically at outbreaks of *Cryptosporidium*, a protozoan parasite that can enter public water supplies through sewage effluent discharges and fecally contaminated storm runoff (e.g., from feedlots). Although many infected individuals are asymptomatic or recover within two weeks, the disease can be fatal to immunocompromised individuals (especially those with AIDS).

Figure 30-2 has the form of an influence diagram.[28] Each node represents a variable. An arrow connects two nodes, if knowing the value of the variable at the tail facilitates predicting the value of the variable at the head. For example, the greater the water utility's awareness of outbreak potential, the greater the chances that it

F I G U R E   30-2

Influence diagram for predicting risks from *Cryptosporidium* intrusion in domestic water supplies.

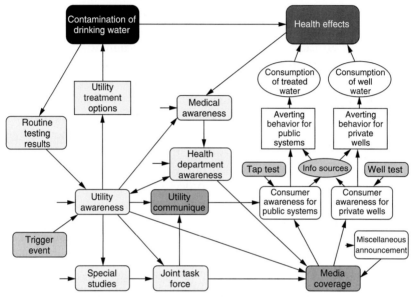

Source: Casman et al. (2000).

will conduct special studies or create a multiagency task force. Estimating the model requires inputs from multiple disciplines, including microbiology (dose-response relationships), engineering (filtration and testing), ecology (land use), communications (message penetration), and psychology (perceived risk, actual response). Applications specify values for each variable and dependency, then predict the risks and uncertainties.

This model was created as the integrating core of a project intended to reduce *Cryptosporidium* risks, by communicating with consumers. However, running the model revealed that current testing is so ineffective that an outbreak will probably have passed (or at least peaked) before its source is detected. Thus, even if every consumer got a perfect message and followed it precisely, an emergency system relying on "boil water" notices would not protect the most vulnerable. Such a system may threaten health by taking the place of more effective controls.

The same system might, however, be adequate for a readily detected pollutant, such as the many strains of *E. coli*. Even current *Cryptosporidium* testing may be adequate for decisions about land-use or filtration systems—if testing provides a (forensic) diagnosis of an outbreak's source. In descriptive research, to determine message content, citizens often raise questions about the system that creates (and controls) these risks (e.g., where did this problem come from, and who was issuing "boil water" notices). A satisfactory message might need to convey (1) why one's water is vulnerable, (2) how all uses pose danger (even brushing one's teeth), and (3) what "boiling water" entails.

Terror Risks

Research on risk perception and communication can contribute to terror risk management, both by improving performance and by clarifying its limits. Planning is ill served when citizens' abilities are overestimated (e.g., as with *Cryptosporidium*) or underestimated (e.g., in panic myths). An indirect contribution is that these researchers are sometimes the sole social scientists on risk management teams dominated by engineers, lawyers, and natural scientists. As a result, they may play a translational role, showing where social science research can replace intuitive theories, while helping social scientists make themselves more relevant. The following paragraphs briefly sketch issues that might emerge from systematically treating the three examples.

Smallpox Vaccination

The optimal allocation of vaccine resources will require people to understand their personal risk, in order to take proper action and accept the authorities' prioritization. One possible barrier is feeling an exaggerated sense of personal invulnerability, as has been found in many situations where people can imagine some sense of control: e.g., being able to tell who is a carrier;[29] surprisingly, adults are, if anything, more prone to this illusion than teens. A contrary barrier is not knowing that one could be vaccinated after exposure. Any plan for smallpox will make explicit or implicit assumptions about these behavioral variables. Those plans create, in turn, the circumstances on which laypeople's future inferences will be based.

Poor communication can itself undermine decision making, by undermining trust in authorities to manage supplies effectively (or fairly). The anecdotal reports of runs on ciprofloxin, during the anthrax attacks of 2001, were partially attributed to such distrust.[30]

Domestic Surveillance

People's ability to judge others is one of the most heavily studied topics in psychology. The overwhelming result is that making complex judgments (e.g., personality, dangerousness, propensity for taking risks) is a skill that is acquired slowly, even under favorable conditions for learning (concentrated trials with prompt, unambiguous feedback). However, people do not recognize their limits, exaggerating how well they (and others) can make such judgments. Indeed, the processes generating such exaggerated faith in intuition are extensively documented. For example, convincing stories and scenarios can have much greater impact than is warranted. Simple statistical models routinely beat even experts' intuition.[31] As elsewhere, policy makers need to know how good even the best evidence is.

Decontamination Standards

Expert panels are a natural way to set cleanup standards. Participants seek reasonable trade-offs between their detailed understanding of the residual risks of possible standards and their more intuitive understanding of the associated benefits. The recommendations of a successful panel both predict and shape public acceptance. Threats to success include (1) adopting standards from other domains with qualitatively different risks or benefits; (2) adopting standards that reflect political compromises, rather than cost-benefit trade-offs; (4) adopting unintuitive standards without explanation; (5) misreading citizens' concerns (e.g., the price of extended dislocation, or worries about profiteering); and (6) arousing suspicions—easy enough in a domain (radiation) fraught with controversy. A consultative process might reduce these risks by improving the standards, educating citizens, and demonstrating respect.

CONCLUSION

Terror risk communication faces some challenges. It requires diverse specialists to collaborate, in creating integrated risk models, combining theoretical understanding with historical statistics. It requires addressing citizens' hearts and minds, beliefs and emotions. It requires demonstrating competence and honesty, subjugating private motives to the national interest. However, although the details of these challenges are unique, the fundamental issues arise with communicating about many complex, uncertain threats. As elsewhere, terror risk communication must (1) manage risks well, so as to have a credible message; (2) create appropriate communication channels, and relations, with the public; and (3) deliver relevant information concisely and comprehensibly.

Given the experiences with other risks, implementing these practices is a known craft. There are many functionally equivalent guidelines for setting the tone for interacting with the public during difficult times. In effect, they interpret normal human relations for risk situations. (This one was written for, and disseminated by, the American Psychological Association, during the sniper attacks of 2002 in the area around Washington, D.C.). They require a consultative process, like that in Figure 30-1, for the tone to match the reality.

Selecting the content of messages is, however, inherently situation-specific. As described above, one must (1) determine the facts central to the decisions that citizens face, (2) determine what they know already, and (3) design messages closing the critical gaps—repeating until an acceptable level of understanding has been achieved. The design can (and should) draw on the extensive basic and applied research into judgment and decision making, showing which concepts are difficult and what is known about communicating them. Producing the messages will require a clear division of responsibility among these essential functions: (1) scientific accuracy of the content, (2) relevance of that content to the audience's decision-making needs, (3) comprehensibility of the content, (4) design of the material and delivery method, and (5) the institutional concerns (legal, political) of the source. Unless these roles are defined, the product and process will be incoherent.

Risk communication is a primary contact between authorities and citizens. It determines citizens' ability to make effective choices both during crises and between them. It shapes citizens' faith in the competence and trustworthiness of the authorities. As a result, risk communication can strengthen (or weaken) a society's ability not only to weather a protracted struggle with terror but also to emerge stronger for it.

NOTES

1. Fischhoff, B., R. Gonzalez, D. Small, and J. Lerner, "Evaluating the Success of Terror Risk Communication," *Biosecurity and Bioterrorism* 1:4 (2003): 255–8.

2. Glass, T. A, "Understanding Public Response to Disasters," *Public Health Reports*, Vol. 116 (Supplement 2) (2001): 69–73.

3. Cvetkovich, G., and R. Löfstedt (eds.), *Social Trust and the Management of Risk* (London: Earthscan, 1999). Fischhoff, B., S. Lichtenstein, P. Slovic, S. L. Derby, and R. L. Keeney, *Acceptable Risk* (New York: Cambridge University Press, 1981). Krimsky, S., and A. Plough (eds.), *Environmental Hazards: Risk Communication as a Social Process* (Dover, Mass.: Auburn House, 1988). Leiss, W., and C. Chociolko, *Risk and Responsibility* (Kingston and Montreal: Queens and McGill University Press, 1994).

4. National Research Council, *Risk Management in the Federal Government* (Washington, D.C.: National Academy Press, 1983).

5. National Research Council, *Improving Risk Communication* (Washington, D.C.: National Academy Press, 1989).

6. Fischhoff, B., S. Lichtenstein, P. Slovic, S. L. Derby, and R. L. Keeney, *Acceptable Risk* (New York: Cambridge University Press, 1981). Fischhoff, B., P. Slovic, and S. Lichtenstein, "Lay Foibles and Expert Fables in Judgments about Risk," *American Statistician* 36 (1983): 240–55. Fischhoff, B., A. Bostrom, and M. J. Quadrel, "Risk Perception and Communication," in R. Detels, J. McEwen, R. Beaglehole, and H. Tanaka (eds.), *Oxford Textbook of Public Health* (London: Oxford University Press, 2002).

7. National Research Council, *Understanding Risk* (Washington, D.C.: National Academy Press, 1996).

8. Fischhoff, B., S. Watson, and C. Hope, "Defining Risk," *Policy Sciences* 17 (1984): 123–39.

9. Institute of Medicine, *Scientific Opportunities and Public Needs* (Washington, D.C.: National Academy Press, 1998a).

10. Institute of Medicine, *Toward Environmental Justice* (Washington, D.C.: National Academy Press, 1998b).

11. Health Canada, *Canadian Pandemic Influenza Plan* (Ottawa: Public Health Agency of Canada, 2004).

12. Clemen, R, *Making Hard Decisions* (Belmont, Calif.: Duxbury, 1996). Hastie, R., and R. M. Dawes, *Rational Choice in an Uncertain World* (Thousand Oaks, Calif.: Sage, 2001).

13. Gilovich, T., D. Griffin, D. Kahneman (eds.), *The Psychology of Judgment: Heuristics and Biases* (New York: Cambridge University Press, 2002).

14. Tengs, T. O. and A. Wallace, "One thousand health-related quality-of-life estimates," *Medical Care* 38:6 (2000): 583–637.

15. Morgan, M. G., B. Fischhoff, A. Bostrom, and C. Atman, *Risk Communication: The Mental Models Approach* (New York: Cambridge University Press, 2001).

16. Fischhoff, Baruch, "Giving Advice: Decision Theory Perspectives on Sexual Assault," *American Psychologist* 47 (1992): 577–88. Fischhoff, Baruch, in press. "Decision Research Strategies." *Health Psychology.*

17. Merz, J., B. Fischhoff, D. J. Mazur, and P. S. Fischbeck, "Decision-Analytic Approach to Developing Standards of Disclosure for Medical Informed Consent," *Journal of Toxics and Liability* 15 (1993): 191–215.

18. Downs, J. S., P. J. Murray, W. Bruine de Bruin, J. P. White, C. Palmgren, and B. Fischhoff, "An Interactive Video Program to Reduce Adolescent Females' STD Risk: A Randomized Controlled Trial," *Social Science and Medicine* 59: 8 (2004): 1561–72.

19. Fischhoff, B., A. Bostrom, and M. J. Quadrel, "Risk Perception and Communication," in R. Detels, J. McEwen, R. Beaglehole, and H. Tanaka (eds.), *Oxford Textbook of Public Health* (London: Oxford University Press, 2002). Slovic, P. (ed.). *The Perception of Risk* (London: Earthscan, 2001).

20. Gilovich, T., D. Griffin, D. Kahneman (eds.), *The Psychology of Judgment: Heuristics and Biases* (New York: Cambridge University Press, 2002). Kahneman, D., P. Slovic, and A. Tversky (eds.), *Judgment under Uncertainty: Heuristics and Biases* (New York: Cambridge University Press, 2002).

21. Fischhoff, Baruch, in press. "Decision Research Strategies." *Health Psychology.* Morgan, M. G., B. Fischhoff, A. Bostrom, and C. Atman, *Risk Communication: The Mental Models Approach* (New York: Cambridge University Press, 2001).

22. Lerner, J. S., R. M. Gonzalez, D. A. Small, and B. Fischhoff, "Effects of Fear and Anger on Perceived Risks of Terrorism: A National Field Experiment," *Psychological Science* 14 (2003): 144–150.

23. Fischhoff, Baruch, "Risk Perception and Communication Unplugged: Twenty Years of Process," *Risk Analysis* 15 (1995): 137–45.

24. Fischhoff, B., R. Gonzalez, D. Small, and J. Lerner. "Evaluating the Success of Terror Risk Communication." *Biosecurity and Bioterrorism* 1:4 (2003): 255–8. Thomas, P., *The Anthrax Attacks* (New York: Century Foundation, 2003).

25. Maharik, M., and B. Fischhoff, "Public Views of Using Nuclear Energy Sources in Space Missions," *Space Policy* 9 (1993): 99–108. Morgan, M. G., B. Fischhoff, A. Bostrom, and C. Atman, *Risk Communication: The Mental Models Approach* (New York: Cambridge University Press. 2001).

26. Fischhoff, B., "Eliciting Knowledge for Analytical Representation," *IEEE Transactions on Systems, Man and Cybernetics* 13 (1989): 448–61. Fischhoff, B., "Scientific Management of Science?" *Policy Sciences* 33 (2000): 73–87. Morgan, M. G., and M. Henrion, *Uncertainty* (New York: Cambridge University Press, 1990).

27. Casman, E., B. Fischhoff, C. Palmgren, M. Small, and F. Wu, "Integrated Risk Model of a Drinking Water-Borne Cryptosporidiosis Outbreak," *Risk Analysis* 20 (2000): 493–509.

28. Clemen, R. *Making Hard Decisions* (Belmont, Calif.: Duxbury, 1996).

29. Gilovich, T., D. Griffin, D. Kahneman (eds.), *The Psychology of Judgment: Heuristics and Biases* (New York: Cambridge University Press, 2002).

30. Thomas, P., *The Anthrax Attacks* (New York: Century Foundation, 2003).

31. Hastie, R., and R. M. Dawes, *Rational Choice in an Uncertain World* (Thousand Oaks, Calif.: Sage, 2001).

BIBLIOGRAPHY

Cabinet Office, *Risk and Uncertainty* (London: B. Fischhoff, 2002).

Canadian Standards Association, *Risk Management Guidelines for Decision Makers* (Q850) (Ottawa: B. Fischhoff, 1997).

Casman, E., B. Fischhoff, C. Palmgren, M. Small, and F. Wu, "Integrated Risk Model of a Drinking Water-Borne *Cryptosporidiosis* Outbreak," *Risk Analysis* 20 (2000): 493–509.

Clemen, R., *Making Hard Decisions* (Belmont, Calif.: Duxbury, 1996).

Cvetkovich, G., and R. Löfstedt (eds.), *Social Trust and the Management of Risk* (London: Earthscan, 1999).

Downs, J. S., P. J. Murray, W. Bruine de Bruin, J. P. White, C. Palmgren, and B. Fischhoff, "An Interactive Video Program to Reduce Adolescent Females' STD Risk: A Randomized Controlled Trial," *Social Science and Medicine* 59:8 (2004): 1561–72.

Environmental Protection Agency, *Toward Integrated Environmental Decision Making* (SAB-EC-00-011) (Washington, D.C.: B. Fischhoff, 2000).

Fischhoff, B., "Eliciting Knowledge for Analytical Representation," *IEEE Transactions on Systems, Man and Cybernetics* 13 (1989): 448–61.

—. "Giving Advice: Decision Theory Perspectives on Sexual Assault," *American Psychologist* 47 (1992): 577–88.

—. "Risk Perception and Communication Unplugged: Twenty Years of Process," *Risk Analysis* 15 (1995): 137–45.

—. "Scientific Management of Science?" *Policy Sciences* 33 (2000): 73–87.

—. In press. "Decision Research Strategies," *Health Psychology.*

Fischhoff, B., A. Bostrom, and M. J. Quadrel, "Risk Perception and Communication," in R. Detels, J. McEwen, R. Beaglehole, and H. Tanaka (eds.), *Oxford Textbook of Public Health* (London: Oxford University Press, 2002).

Fischhoff, B., R. Gonzalez, D. Small, and J. Lerner, "Evaluating the Success of Terror Risk Communication," *Biosecurity and Bioterrorism* 1:4 (2003): 255–8.

Fischhoff, B., S. Lichtenstein, P. Slovic, S. L. Derby, and R. L. Keeney, *Acceptable Risk* (New York: Cambridge University Press, 1981).

Fischhoff, B., P. Slovic, and S. Lichtenstein, "Lay Foibles and Expert Fables in Judgments about Risk," *American Statistician* 36 (1983): 240–55.

Fischhoff, B., S. Watson, and C. Hope, "Defining Risk," *Policy Sciences* 17 (1984): 123–39.

Gilovich, T., D. Griffin, D. Kahneman (eds.), *The Psychology of Judgment: Heuristics and Biases* (New York: Cambridge University Press, 2002).

Glass, T. A., "Understanding Public Response to Disasters," *Public Health Reports* 116 (Supplement 2) (2001): 69–73.

Hastie, R., and R. M. Dawes, *Rational Choice in an Uncertain World* (Thousand Oaks, Calif.: Sage, 2001).

Health Canada, *Canadian Pandemic Influenza Plan* (Ottawa: Public Health Agency of Canada, 2004).

Health and Safety Executive, *Reducing Risks, Protecting People* (London: B. Fischhoff, Author, 1999).

Kahneman, D., P. Slovic, and A. Tversky (eds.), *Judgment under Uncertainty: Heuristics and Biases* (New York: Cambridge University Press, 2002).

Institute of Medicine, *Scientific Opportunities and Public Needs* (Washington, D.C.: National Academy Press, 1998a).

—. *Toward Environmental Justice* (Washington, D.C.: National Academy Press, 1998b).

Lerner, J. S., R. M. Gonzalez, D. A. Small, and B. Fischhoff, "Effects of Fear and Anger on Perceived Risks of Terrorism: A National Field Experiment," *Psychological Science* 14 (2003): 144–50.

Krimsky, S., and A. Plough (eds.), *Environmental Hazards: Risk Communication as a Social Process* (Dover, Mass.: Auburn House, 1988).

Leiss, W., and C. Chociolko, *Risk and Responsibility* (Kingston and Montreal: Queens and McGill University Press, 1994).

Maharik, M., and B. Fischhoff, "Public Views of Using Nuclear Energy Sources in Space Missions," *Space Policy* 9 (1993): 99–108.

Merz, J., B. Fischhoff, D. J. Mazur, and P. S. Fischbeck, "Decision-Analytic Approach to Developing Standards of Disclosure for Medical Informed Consent," *Journal of Toxics and Liability* 15 (1993): 191–215.

Morgan, M. G., B. Fischhoff, A. Bostrom, and C. Atman, *Risk Communication: The Mental Models Approach* (New York: Cambridge University Press, 2001).

Morgan, M. G., and M. Henrion, *Uncertainty* (New York: Cambridge University Press, 1990).

National Research Council, *Risk Management in the Federal Government* (Washington, D.C.: National Academy Press, 1983).

—. *Improving Risk Communication* (Washington, D.C.: National Academy Press, 1989).

—. *Science and Judgment in Risk Assessment* (Washington, D.C.: National Academy Press, 1994).

—. *Understanding Risk* (Washington, D.C.: National Academy Press, 1996).

Parliamentary Office of Science and Technology, *Open Channels: Public Dialogues in Science and Technology* (London: House of Commons, 2001).

Presidential/Congressional Commission on Risk, *Risk Management* (Washington, D.C.: B. Fischhoff, 1998).

Royal Commission on Environmental Protection, *Setting Environmental Standards* (London: B. Fischhoff, 1998).

Slovic, P. (ed.), *The Perception of Risk* (London: Earthscan, 2001).

Tengs, T. O., and A. Wallace, "One thousand health-related quality-of-life estimates," *Medical Care* 38:6 (2000): 583–637. Thomas, P., *The Anthrax Attacks* (New York: Century Foundation, 2003).

Tierney, K., "Disaster Beliefs and Institutional Interests: Recycling Disaster Myths in the Aftermath of 9–11," in L. Clarke (ed.), *Research in Social Problems and Public Policy* 11 (St. Louis, Mo.: Elsevier, 2003).

Treasury Board, *Communications Policy of the Government of Canada* (Ottawa: B. Fischhoff, 2002).

APPENDIX: A STRATEGY FOR THE CONTENT OF RISK COMMUNICATIONS

Note: Explanations are italicized.

1. Acknowledge the gravity of the events and the tragedy of those who have suffered.

2. Recognize the public's concerns, emotions, and efforts to manage the risk.

     Everyone is needed to keep society functioning in a time of stress, and all should be rewarded for doing the best they can. Emotions are an important and legitimate part of responding to extreme events. Recognizing their existence creates a human bond with the audience. Recognizing the legitimacy of emotions can help people take the steps needed to manage them. Individuals needing special attention should be afforded ready access. However, the tenor of the communication should be adult to adult, assuming the ability to cope.

3. Assure the audience that the relevant officials are doing all that they can.

     The communicator cannot vouch for the competence of all officials or for the adequacy of the resources at their disposal. However, it should be possible to attest to their commitment.

4. Express a coherent, consistent communication philosophy (for all risks):

     —We will do all we can to help you to make responsible decisions for yourself and your loved ones.

     —To that end, we will provide you the best relevant information that we can, along with an idea of how good that information is.

     —We will not engage in speculation.

     —We may need to withhold information that may aid or comfort the enemy. Recognizing our duty to inform, we are following a socially acceptable procedure for deciding what to withhold.

     The commitment is to a partnership, with officials attempting to empower citizens to master difficult and potentially protracted challenges. The communicator will leave speculation to others (e.g., news media, ordinary citizens), knowing that many ideas will be discussed in a democratic society, preserving the role of being the definitive source for vetted information.

We currently lack mechanisms for withholding information in a socially acceptable way. Although the social acceptability of mechanisms is an empirical question, I anticipate that it will include the involvement of ordinary citizens, serving in an advisory role.

I did not include withholding information that might cause panic. The disaster literature predicts little mass panic, unless officials behave in ways that erode trust in them. Withholding vital information might be construed as such behavior. People do not want to learn that they have exposed themselves and their loved ones to risks because they were not trusted to act like adults.

5. Provide quantitative risk estimates, including the attendant uncertainties.

People need to know how big risks are, in order to decide what to do about them. Often those numbers are missing, because the experts have not produced them or have not disseminated them. Sometimes the numbers are incomplete, as when people see the death toll but not the total number of people exposed. An intuitively appealing message is, "The risk of X is smaller than being struck by lightning." However, it often offends people by trivializing their concerns, and misrepresents the risk by ignoring the many ways in which X differs from lightning (e.g., the associated uncertainty). It often appears manipulative, undermining the credibility of the source. Just giving the numbers, and uncertainties, is safer. Doing so requires the staff work needed to produce those estimates.

6. Provide summary analyses of possible protective actions, considering all the expected effects.

People may ignore the fact that actions reducing one risk may increase other risks. They may not recognize the psychological costs and benefits of actions that reduce risk. They may not see the things they are losing (i.e., "opportunity costs") when they forgo activities in order to reduce risks. They may not be able to estimate the effects of their actions, exaggerating some, underestimating others. Presenting the best available understanding of these issues, in a standard format, should help people to develop coherent decision-making strategies. It respects individuals' right to make different choices, reflecting their personal values.

7. Lead by example, showing possible models for responsible bravery.

People expect leaders to conduct themselves professionally, including their own exposure to risk. Such behavior can have a calming effect and model the sort of quiet "soldiering on" that many people want to show, in their own way, appropriate to their own circumstances.

8. Commit to earning and keeping the public trust.

We want to achieve market share as the source of unbiased information. Having such a source is essential for social coordination, in both the long and the short run. Communication processes should be evaluated to ensure their continued success. They should solicit continuing input from the public to ensure their relevance.

CHAPTER 31

The Homeland Security Advisory System

Dr. James Jay Carafano
Senior Fellow, The Heritage Foundation

THE NEED FOR INTELLIGENCE AND EARLY WARNING

The 2002 National Homeland Security Strategy, established by President George W. Bush, defines six areas critical to protecting U.S. citizens from transnational terrorism.[1] The first critical mission area, intelligence and early warning, includes activities related to detecting terrorists and disseminating information and warnings. Central to its success is the development of programs for sharing intelligence across the public and private sectors. The Homeland Security Advisory System (HSAS), established by Presidential Homeland Security Directive 3 in March 2002, is designed to do just that. Designating various levels of national preparedness in anticipation of a terrorist attack, HSAS alerts government agencies, the private sector, and American citizens.

This chapter examines the origins, structure, and functions of HSAS. Because the system has been, and remains, under continuous development, assessments published by Congress's Government Accountability Office (GAO) and various studies on the implementation and coordination of public alert systems will also be considered.

THE HOMELAND SECURITY ADVISORY SYSTEM

In March 2002, the president established HSAS and the U.S. attorney general assumed overall responsibility for its implementation.[2] Soon after, the Homeland Security Act of 2002 shifted the responsibility for intelligence and early warning to the secretary of the Department of Homeland Security (DHS). Accordingly, DHS's assistant secretary for Information Analysis and Infrastructure Protection (IAIP) is responsible for the following:

> (1) To access, receive, and analyze law enforcement information, intelligence information, and other information from agencies of the Federal Government, State and local government agencies (including law enforcement agencies), and private sector entities, and to integrate such information in order to—(A) identify and assess the nature and scope of terrorist threats to the homeland; (B) detect and identify threats of terrorism against the United States; and (C) understand such threats in light of actual and potential vulnerabilities of the homeland.[3]

Section 201 of the law also assigns IAIP responsibility for administering HSAS.

Using color codes, HSAS designates five threat conditions: low, guarded, elevated, high, and severe. Each condition has corresponding suggested protective measures, with federal, state, and local agencies responsible for developing and implementing their own specific responses.[4] By establishing common terms for these levels and providing for homeland security intelligence to be communicated, HSAS enables DHS to integrate and disseminate information effectively.

INTELLIGENCE INTEGRATION AND WARNING (SUPPORT) SYSTEMS

An explanation of the auxiliary institutions and systems that inform and support HSAS is essential to an understanding of the role of the advisory system and its effect on national homeland security strategy and preparedness. The major contributors to HSAS include the Homeland Security Council (HSC), Homeland Security Operations Center (HSOC), Homeland Security Information Network (HSIN), Terrorist Threat Integration Center (TTIC), and DHS Web site: ready.gov.

Homeland Security Council

HSC and its staff provide oversight and guidance for the implementation of HSAS. HSC convenes when a threat condition is elevated to ensure an integrated, appropriate federal response. A steady stream of policy directives and strategy planning documents from HSC suggests ongoing and improving coordination under the direction of its staff. At the national level HSAS appears to be achieving its stated goal of ensuring the coordinated employment of protective measures across the federal government, thanks largely to the assistance and oversight of HSC.

Homeland Security Operations Center

Within DHS, HSOC is vital to the operations of HSAS. HSOC is responsible for consolidating information about homeland security and domestic terrorism, and for issuing advisories. Representing more than 35 agencies, the center is split between law enforcement and intelligence activities; however, the two sides exchange and fuse information daily. The consolidation of analysis capabilities is long overdue and enables DHS to see the "big picture" and manage implementation of HSAS.

Homeland Security Information Network

HSIN will link states, territories, and major urban areas to HSOC through the Joint Regional Information Exchange System (JRIES). Initially, HSIN will be limited to sensitive but unclassified information; in the future, it is intended to carry secret information to the state level. A collaborative tool such as HSIN is essential to establishing the interactive communications needed to implement HSAS.

Terrorist Threat Integration Center

TTIC, established by President Bush in 2003, is staffed by an interagency group responsible for gathering, assessing, and disseminating all terrorist-related information to federal agencies. TTIC is intended to be the place where correlations are identified and the right information gets to the right people at the right time. Over the long term TTIC will probably provide the key intelligence assessments determining changes in HSAS. Thus the management of TTIC is critical to the continued success of HSAS.[5]

On December 2004, President Bush signed into law the Intelligence Reform and Terrorism Prevention Act. Based on the recommendations of the National Commission on Terrorist Attacks Upon the United States (widely known as the 9/11 Commission), the legislation merged the TTIC with a newly established National Counterterrorism Center (NCTC). The NCTC will serve under the director of National Intelligence (DNI), a new independent oversight authority who replaces the director of Central Intelligence (DCI) as the head of the U.S. Intelligence Community.

Currently, the DCI provides oversight of TTIC, and most of the TTIC staff comes from the Central Intelligence Agency. DHS plays only a subordinate role. Policies on operations and the functions and duties of DHS personnel and other participating agencies are governed by an interagency memorandum of understanding. Over the course of 2005, all TTIC assets will fall under the DNI as part of the NCTC.

Establishing TTIC separate from DHS is problematic. The arrangement appears to conflict with the intent of the Homeland Security Act of 2002 to centralize responsibility in DHS and raises concerns about whether such an approach will optimize intelligence sharing overall and the implementation of HSAS specifically. It is troubling that DHS, as the primary consumer of intelligence relating to domestic security, does not have primary control over the mechanisms for fusing and disbursing information.[6]

TTIC and the intelligence functions of the DHS Information Analysis and Infrastructure Protection directorate (IAIP) should be merged into a single interagency staff under the supervision of DHS, whose secretary should have authority over all TTIC-related appropriations. DHS should have authority to approve, evaluate, and establish education and experience requirements for the TTIC staff.

Ready.gov

DHS has undertaken programs to make citizens more aware of their role in anticipating and responding to terrorist attacks. The DHS Web site ready.gov provides clear, jargon-free advice on how to respond to chemical, nuclear, biological, and radiological dangers. The recommendations also include practical daily measures to ensure public safety and prepare for all kinds of natural and technological (i.e., human-made) disasters. The Web site does not, however, suggest significant changes in behavior when the threat status shifts from one color to another. Thus citizens may still be puzzled over how to react to HSAS alerts.

PRECISION IS CRITICAL FOR A NATIONAL ADVISORY SYSTEM
Integration

HSAS provides a tool for exploiting the capabilities of federal, state, local, and private-sector responders and is essential to an effective national preparedness and response strategy.

The establishment of common terms and national performance and preparedness standards will allow integration of federal, state, local, and private-sector responders and their disparate capabilities. When these standards have been developed, they will help establish appropriate security measures for each threat condition and will help state and local governments determine how to counter terrorist threats and what assistance to expect from the federal government.[7]

Public and Specific Applications

Although HSAS can potentially integrate various responders and capabilities, the all-inclusive nature of its alerts has been an obstacle to the effective allocation of critical resources. The system attempts both to inform federal forces on global and national threats and to inform state, local, and private-sector responders for purposes of civil defense. Given the large, diverse population and infrastructure of the United States, this is a daunting task.

HSAS is moving away from its former "one size fits all" threat classifications and warnings. Formerly, when the HSAS threat condition was raised the whole nation had to ratchet up security— even where no credible threat existed. Such a response did little or nothing to inform state and local governments or the public of specific threats.[8]

On the federal level, Washington needs an integrated system to add to or subtract from security levels at our borders, at sea, and around key assets. The HSAS threat conditions are evolving into an appropriate instrument to accomplish that goal, but the application of HSAS to state and local governments and to the private sector is more problematic. State and local response organizations need more information on the type of attack, where it is likely to occur, and when.[9] Few of these organizations have the classified intelligence and the sophisticated analytical capabilities to evaluate threats. Without concrete assessments, many states, counties, and cities either do nothing or pile on layers of unneeded security, generating exorbitant overtime costs and other expenditures.

The nation does not require a standardized system that solicits uniform responses from every state and local government. In fact, research suggests that diversity is natural and desirable. Public safety and emergency response entities are more effective when they adapt their operations to local conditions.[10] HSAS must be flexible enough to serve all their needs.

Economic Impact

Any national system of this magnitude will have significant fiscal implications. Increased security resulting from changing the alert status in its first two years required an estimated $1 billion per week at the federal level. The additional costs incurred by state and local governments and the private sector, as well as the impact on the economy overall, such as reducing consumers' confidence or affecting business travel and tourism, are more difficult to estimate.[11]

According to a report from GAO in June 2004, federal agencies reported average daily costs between $190 and $3.7 million for the three code-orange alert periods covered in the study. For the first two code-orange alert periods, states reported additional costs ranging from approximately $7,900 to $8 million; localities reported additional costs of $2,800 to $28 million. Costs for the third period ranged from $2,000 to about $7 million for states, and from $3,000 to about $4 million for localities.[12]

Psychological Effects

Another consideration in evaluating HSAS is that it can have a psychological impact on the nation. Currently, many citizens appear perplexed by changes in threat conditions. Frequent or ambiguous shifts in threat levels could have a long-term effect on the mental health of the general population, although this is difficult to measure in the short term.

Despite the perception that HSAS is primarily a warning system for the general public, it has a wide range of purposes. When the national alert level is changed, local officials may take no publicly discernable action because they have no specific information on threats in their area, but incongruous responses to ambiguous alerts raise questions about the credibility of HSAS.

Public alerts must be credible, specific, and understandable, and must imply actions by individuals.[13] Changes in color codes, which dominate the public perception of what HSAS represents, meet none of these criteria. The lack of specific advisories and the absence of clear guidance on what actions individual citizens ought to take under each threat level ultimately detract from the positive role of HSAS.

It is doubtful that the color-coded alert elicits greater preparedness, and such alerts could have unintended adverse psychological consequences, fostering a "fortress America" mentality and increasing personal anxiety. Since age and socioeconomic and sociodemographic factors can significantly condition preparedness and public response to warnings,[14] additional research could help determine the long-term mental-health impact of HSAS and its capacity to reach a growing and increasingly diverse U.S. population. Carefully tailored, consistently reinforced prealert education is needed to persuade a significant number of Americans to take commonsense precautions during threat periods that may span several years between major attacks.

Responsible voices—including James Gilmore, a former governor of Virginia who chaired a prestigious national commission on terrorism, along with Representatives Christopher Cox (Republican-California) and Jim Turner (Democrat-Texas)—have called for revising the alert system. Some experts believe that HSAS has become marginalized as a result of "a lack of understanding of its intended use as well as the absence of a well-orchestrated plan to guide its implementation at all levels of government."[15] The Gilmore Commission has made useful suggestions for improving HSAS.[16]

LOOKING TO THE LONG TERM

The GAO report of June 2004 recommends specific actions for the DHS undersecretary for Information Analysis and Infrastructure Protection. First, the undersecretary should institute procedural standards for alerting federal agencies and states about changes in the national threat level, including guidance on recommended actions and methods of exchanging information. Second, the undersecretary should modify HSAS to provide the most specific information possible to states, localities, and industries regarding times, methods, and locations of possible attacks.[17]

HSAS must stay simple in order to remain relevant as threats and technologies develop. The public color-coded portion of HSAS should be replaced with a basic model to which the public is already somewhat conditioned to respond. Terrorist alerts should be merged into an "all-hazards" alert system with common formats and methods of dissemination. Public alerts should be issued in straightforward, clearly worded watch or warning reports that average people can understand. These reports must contain specific threats and specific actions to be taken.

DHS has undertaken a comprehensive risk-level ranking of all areas in the country, using criteria such as population, threat assessment, number of important sites, and vulnerability. Areas will then be classified as low-, medium-, or high-risk. As the department becomes more sophisticated in analyzing threats and communicating information, it should issue more audience-tailored warnings. HSAS should continue developing capabilities for regional alerts and specific warnings for different types of industries and infrastructure. More specific alerts will allow DHS, in cooperation with other federal agencies and state and local authorities, to better apply scarce resources to address higher threats.

As HSAS adopts new protocols and structural developments, officials must be extremely judicious in using it. Overuse could lead to public apathy. Although the response of the "internal" audience (public officials and emergency responders) to alerts can actually be strengthened by frequent alarms, some research suggests that the public "external" audience (individual citizens) can be adversely affected by alarms that are not followed by the appearance of an actual threat. Using the system provides opportunities for agencies and responders to test readiness and refine procedures, but most people who issue public safety alerts are afraid of false alarms. In fact, 54 percent of responders to a survey conducted by researchers at the University of Colorado at Colorado Springs said that fear of false alarms delays their decision to notify the public.[18]

Historically, public response to alarms has sometimes remained highly sensitive even when no threat has materialized, but these instances have generally followed large-scale attacks experienced by a majority of the general public. Furthermore, in each such instance, the public had a clear understanding of the threat and how to respond to it. In contrast, the United States may see long periods when terrorist threats represent "potential" rather than imminent dangers, and the overwhelming likelihood is that a majority of its citizens will not experience an attack firsthand. Thus, HSAS could be more prone than previous advisory systems to degraded public response over time.

Modern information technologies can enhance the public portions of HSAS. Currently, the government relies on an emergency broadcast system that interrupts television, radio, and cable programs.[19] But the system is not sufficiently robust to meet the needs of HSAS, nor does it exploit the Internet and multimedia and telecommunications capabilities of the information age. Additional research is required to determine how best to apply all these capacities, as well as the costs and benefits of integrating HSAS with other alert systems such as the AMBER alerts used by various states and the National Weather Service advisory system.

Finally, and perhaps most important, more attention must be given to how the emerging national preparedness system can best exploit the warnings that may be provided by an effective HSAS. Particular emphasis should be given to human capital and leadership programs that will train the next generation of homeland security professionals, public safety leaders, and government officials.[20] The actions of these men and women, not alerts as such, will determine whether the nation is safer in the years to come.

CONCLUSION

Continuing professional development for emerging senior leaders is also needed. A program focusing on homeland security, providing lectures and workshops for middle-grade professionals, would establish a base of knowledge from which the private sector could quickly and effectively enter and contribute to the national discourse on homeland security. The nation might also benefit from a national homeland security university modeled on the military's war college system. Any national leader development effort will have to include numerous state and local leaders. The present network of junior colleges, now the hub of continuing adult education, may provide the best venue for leader development.

Over the long term, the capacity of the national homeland security system to take advantage of intelligence and early warning will depend more on the quality of the decisions made by its leaders and the programs they implement than on the structure of HSAS. Equal attention must be given to both sides of the coin.

N O T E S

1. White House, National Strategy for Homeland Security (2002), pp. 15–46.
2. Presidential Homeland Security Directive–3, March 2002, at www.whitehouse. gov/news/releases/2002/03/20020312-5.html.
3. Public Law 107-296, Sec. 201.
4. Presidential Homeland Security Directive–3, March 2002, at www.whitehouse. gov/news/releases/2002/03/20020312-5.html.
5. For concerns over the TTIC's current operations, see Second Report of the Markle Foundation Task Force, *Creating a Trusted Network for Homeland Security* (2003), p. 3.
6. James Jay Carafano and Ha Nguyen, "Better Intelligence Sharing for Visa Issuance and Monitoring: An Imperative for Homeland Security," Heritage Foundation *Backgrounder* No. 1699, (27 October 2003), at www.heritage.org/ Research/HomelandDefense/BG1699.cfm.
7. James Jay Carafano, "Homeland Security Grant Bill Needs Revision, but a Step in the Right Direction," Heritage Foundation *Executive Memorandum* No. 909 (8 January 2004), at www.heritage.org/Research/HomelandDefense/EM909.cfm.
8. James Jay Carafano and Ha Nguyen, "Warning: We Need a Better Warning System," *Commentary* (8 January 2004), at www.heritage.org/Press/ Commentary/ed010804a.cfm.
9. "Advisory Panel to Assess Domestic Response Capabilities for Terrorism Involving Weapons of Mass Destruction," *Forging America's New Normalcy: Securing Our Homeland, Preserving Our Liberty,* Fifth Annual Report to the President and the Congress, Vol. 5 (15 December 2003), p. D-7-2, at www.rand.org/nsrd/terrpanel/volume_v/volume_v.pdf.
10. Russell. R. Dynes et al., "Disaster Analysis: Local Emergency Management Offices and Arrangements," Final Report, No. 34, University of Delaware, Disaster Research Center, 1986.
11. For example, the U.S. Conference of Mayors estimates the cost at approximately $70 million per week. New York City spends about $5 million per week when the alert level is raised. Boston estimated its costs at about $100,000 per day.

12. GAO Report, "Homeland Security: Communication Protocols and Risk Communication Principles Can Assist in Refining the Advisory System," pp. 36–7.

13. Kathleen J. Turner et al., *Facing the Unexpected: Disaster Preparedness and Response in the United States* (Washington, D.C.: Joseph Henry Press, 2001), p. 30.

14. Ibid., pp. 167–88.

15. Advisory Panel to Assess Domestic Response Capabilities for Terrorism Involving Weapons of Mass Destruction, *Forging America's New Normalcy: Securing Our Homeland, Preserving Our Liberty*, p. 27.

16. For concerns and recommendations on revising the system, see ibid., pp. 27 D-1 and D-7-2.

17. GAO Report, "Homeland Security: Communication Protocols and Risk Communication Principles Can Assist in Refining the Advisory System," p. 40.

18. Eve Gruntfest and Kim Carsell, *The Warning Process: Toward an Understanding of False Alarms*, at http://web.uccs.edu/geogenvs/ecg/falsealarms/understandingfalsealarms.html.

19. Partnership for Public Warning, "The Emergency Alert System (EAS): An Assessment," PPW Report 2004-1 (February 2004).

20. For an overview of homeland security training and education programs, see James Jay Carafano, "Homeland Security and the Trouble with Training," *CSBA Backgrounder* (3 October 2002).

CHAPTER 32

The Role of Broadcast Media in Homeland Security Communication

Frank Sesno
Professor of Public Policy and Communication,
School of Public Policy, George Mason University;
CNN Special Correspondent

Terrorism and homeland security represent a profound challenge to American journalism. Broadcast journalism bears an extra burden because it is on the front line of breaking news and plays a special real-time role in informing the public during a crisis. Since 9/11, new grim realities have confronted the media and redefined the responsibilities of the media as providers of information and holders of a public trust. Reporting in an emergency is not merely a matter of getting a story right or beating the competition; it is a matter of saving lives, conveying vital information, and contributing to an orderly response. Those who work in and with the media must understand and navigate in an uncertain landscape.

This chapter will examine the special pressures involved in coverage of terrorism and homeland security, how and why the media operate as they do, and steps that the media and public officials can consider so as to maximize their own preparedness and their ability to communicate.

HOMELAND SECURITY AND THE MEDIA ON 9/11

Journalists' role has always been to get information to the public. The news media represent a pipeline through which the public learns of events. The emergence of terrorism within the United States, in conjunction with a hypercompetitive 24/7 news cycle, suggests a new paradigm for how the media should work and for the impact of the media on social order. This paradigm includes public safety; a recognition that the information flow now is—and is expected to be—perpetual; a recognition that tone and content can influence how people judge and react to a crisis; and the fact that the media often disseminate information before official sources can act on or respond to it.

As a result, the media not only inform the public but also influence decision makers. Television monitors are standard equipment in city halls, police stations, and incident command centers. Officials often use media to communicate with one another. Information that comes over the airwaves is seen and heard by first responders and their commanders in the field. Bad information can be a distraction or even destructive.

After 9/11, for example, one news story involving bad information distracted first responders and brought unnecessary heartache to some victims' families: a local channel in New York reported that an SUV holding several firefighters who were still alive had been found in the rubble of the World Trade Center. The basis of the story was vague, and people in the fire department knew nothing about it except what they saw on television and what they heard in the barrage of phone calls that immediately followed the initial report. Still, the story generated an instant response: fire department officials tried to verify it; hospital emergency rooms prepared to treat the injured; the staff at the mayor's office was deployed to find the survivors; women whose husbands were still missing went to the hospitals. Frank Gribbon, deputy commissioner for public information in the New York Fire Department, was unable to confirm the story from within, so he went to several emergency rooms around the city. At Belleview Hospital, he encountered several staffers from Mayor Giuliani's office who were trying to determine if and when the mayor should come there. At the World Trade Center, a sector commander, Assistant Fire Chief Frank Fellini, had to take time away from more urgent tasks to answer questions from other fire officials about the story. But there was no SUV; there were no more survivors; and according to Gribbon, the origin of the story has never been determined.

Technology intensifies immediacy and emotion. Disturbing images can be shown on the air as events occur. Cell phones, Blackberries, and other wireless devices make news portable and make many citizens potential reporters. Eyewitness accounts and "man on the street" interviews can give voice to fears before officials have even assessed a situation. Thus real-time news can lead to rumors and errors and can undermine the traditional role of the editorial "gatekeeper," the responsible news professional who can consider a story and kill it if it does not meet certain criteria: solid reporting, accuracy, and appropriate confirmation and attribution. And terrorism magnifies all these effects, because of the stakes involved and the public's thirst for rapid information.

THE CHALLENGE OF TIMELY AND ACCURATE COVERAGE

Imminent danger not only produces fear and anxiety but also generates questions, which usually arise much faster than they can be answered. Thus a significant challenge related to the coverage of homeland security and terrorism is the need to convey information quickly, clearly, accurately, and responsibly. Lives and public order may hang in the balance. Determining what has happened, what to do, where to go, whether to shelter in place or move to safer ground, what route to take, whether to seek medical attention, what to do about vulnerable populations—e.g., children, the disabled, the elderly, the homeless—will be an urgent, early focus of the public and the media.

These unique pressures have prompted many news organizations to plan and prepare in new ways. Some have bought and tested new equipment and sent staffers to seminars on homeland security. Others, like CNN, have invested in homeland security beats, knowing that it can take years to build expertise and a solid relationship with informed sources. Senior news executives have met with officials from the Department of Homeland Security (DHS) and other government agencies to discuss contingencies and understand appropriate roles in an emergency. Professional organizations, such as the Radio and Television News Directors Association (RTNDA), have developed training tools and Web sites to provide information, guidance, and suggestions regarding the coverage of terrorism. RTNDA has offered workshops for local journalists and public officials in cities around the country. The Project for Excellence in Journalism has conducted training seminars in newsrooms nationwide, some of which focus on reporting during the "war on terrorism." But all this is just a start.

According to Tom Rosenstiel, director of the Project for Excellence in Journalism, most news executives understand that their newsrooms need specialized expertise and knowledge. He argues that new standards are now required, in order to determine what information to put on the air and what to withhold—since what may once have been merely a story about, say, lax security at a chemical storage facility can now be valuable information for potential terrorists. News organizations and the public must weigh the relative merits of vital information and a free press, on the one hand; and new notions of national security on the other. Rosenstiel's experience in newsrooms suggests that many broadcasters are not matching their rhetoric with actions. He has found that many stations relegate homeland security to a "part-time beat," which has to compete with whatever other news the reporter or producer is working on. And he makes this point: a newsroom's commitment to homeland security often reflects the community's commitment. If the governor, mayor, or police chief is not taking homeland security seriously—is not making it a sustained public priority—why should the station or the local newspaper do any of this?

Indeed, many newsrooms, especially in rural areas, reflect the attitude of local public officials: they do not consider themselves at high risk of terrorism and are not prepared for terrorism operationally, logistically, or editorially. Even large news organizations that have taken preparatory steps have probably not tested their readiness beyond holding meetings or writing a coverage plan that may or may not be widely read by the staffers who would actually be doing the work and reporting the story. Yet during a terrorist attack, these are the teams on which the public will depend to sort through and disseminate massive, confusing amounts of information.

Outside major markets, few television or radio stations have personnel who are experts in homeland security, who know anthrax from tularemia or plague from smallpox, or who could explain a "dirty bomb." Most broadcast news practitioners are generalists who are moved from story to story. They may report on terrorism and preparedness in their community, but they probably have had little experience or training in the details of that subject. Still, these are the journalists who will be expected to face a camera or a microphone and report to thousands, perhaps millions, of anxious citizens.

Many communities do not even have a local news team of consequence. Budget cuts and mergers have impeded local coverage; some rural and remote communities have no local news at all.

Whatever the particular circumstances of a news organization— a network, a big player in a major market, or a small-town operation—knowing the right sources of information and expertise will make the difference between good or responsible coverage and incomplete or irresponsible coverage. Where will reporters and news executives turn for advice? Who will help them shape their coverage? Who will appear on the air, perhaps offering guidance as well as information? How responsive will public officials be?

THE POTENTIAL FALLOUT OF BAD REPORTING

It is hard to overstate the consequences of getting a story wrong during a terrorist attack, because real-time reporting in the midst of such an event will drive behavior. Moreover, terrorism today is likely to be a global event that can spread fear and prompt responses over a wide area; and if it involves weapons of mass destruction, whole populations could be affected. In any case, large numbers of citizens will use whatever information they have to make decisions and take action. Terrorism is like an electric shock to the body politic, and the news media are the central nervous system that sends and receives information. Some people will be present at the scene of an attack and will base their actions on their own experiences; but for most people terrorism will be as a "mediated" experience that they absorb through television, radio, the Internet, photos, and print journalism. The danger of terrorism combined with continuous real-time reporting creates opportunities and also perils. The opportunities are obvious. More information can reach more people more quickly than ever before. It is easier to disseminate information. People can surf multiple platforms and multiple media to gather a vast amount of information and a variety of viewpoints. They can go online—to the mayor's community Web site, DHS's site (ready.gov), or the personal security site of the *Washington Post* (washingtonpost.com)—to get information for themselves. The perils are equally clear. If reporting is bad, irresponsible, or sloppy, the consequences can be staggering. People may evacuate when they should stay put. They may inundate hospitals in search of medication when there is no reason for them to do so. They may rush toward or away from a site where authorities are desperately trying to work. The public may be influenced by uninformed speculation, sensational or unnecessarily frightening coverage, or information that is simply wrong.

All this implies an unprecedented challenge for journalists and public officials. Television reporters often feel enormous pressure to get on the air and talk, even if they do not have all the facts or do not fully know what they are talking about. First responders, public health officials, and other officials who instinctively try to be cautious and deliberative before releasing information to the public often find themselves under siege by the media. This culture clash can be sharpened in a context of terrorism. Today, furthermore, information is flowing faster than ever; it is part of the media landscape.

Thus news organizations need to establish relationships with responsible, informed sources before an incident. They need to know where to go for expertise, who makes decisions, where the true experts are. Today, when rumors and misinformation can travel at the speed of an e-mail or text message, access to informed experts is critical to keeping the public properly informed. Similarly, public officials need to seek out and establish relationships with reporters and news executives in their communities. They need to explain their emergency preparedness plans and what the chain of command and information flow would be in the event of attack. They need to make personnel with specialized information available to reporters. All concerned need to make a genuine, ongoing commitment to maintain these relationships.

THE LANGUAGE OF LIVE

Because events unfold live and in real time, often before a global audience, journalists, public officials, and experts need to understand what I call the "language of live." This is the information lag that is the gap between the time when the media (or members of the public) ask a question and the time when a responsible official can answer it correctly. During a crisis, questions and the flow of information are relentless. The most difficult aspect of this kind of reporting—which the public and many public officials little understand—is the sheer volume of information that comes into a newsroom, and the daunting task of sorting out what to report and what to set aside. Official sources, eyewitnesses, informed sources, viewers, news conferences, and rumors compete for attention. Reporters take to the streets and to telephones, pursuing details large and small—anything relevant that they can find out. The first wave of information is often anecdotal or observational; witnesses say they saw what happened, cell phone callers claim to know something, public officials who have not been fully briefed provide what information they have. Cameras and satellite trucks are deployed. Anyone who may have knowledge is contacted and questioned. Reporters, as they learn elements of the story, are expected to go on the air with it, piecing it together as they proceed.

In this setting, no detail is too small to report and repeat. Relatively minor developments become the next piece of breaking news, set into the mosaic of the larger story. We may see a reporter at the White House telling us that the president has just received a briefing from his national security advisers (it would probably be bigger news if, in the midst of a crisis, the president did *not* get such a briefing). Or we are told that the police are looking for a white van, that bombing suspects appear to be middle eastern, or that electricity is expected to be restored within hours. Such information may be incremental—and it may be wrong. But it always, or almost always, is reported, because people in positions of authority pass it along.

This suggests another aspect of the language of live, that the time may be measured in minutes, hours, or in some cases—as with certain types of bioterrorism—days. Perhaps the most perilous part of a story is the point when information is lagging and speculation and rumor fill the void. Presumed experts offer insights and advice. Former officials are asked to explain, or offer opinions about, what is happening behind the scenes and why. While many of these "talking heads" can contribute to public understanding, many venture, or are asked to go, beyond their expertise or beyond the scope of their knowledge. Three words are often conspicuous by their absence: "I don't know." Guests who say that too much are unlikely to find themselves in a studio again.

Thus news organizations and public officials need to learn the language of live because that language recognizes the 24/7 world and permits real-time communication when some, perhaps many, facts are unknown. It is a transparent language that clearly informs the public. It explicitly states what is and what is not known, confirmed, or corroborated. It attributes information directly to sources. It labels speculation as such. When information turns out to be bad, it doubles back to correct the record. The language of live is a language that most journalists used in the days after 9/11. Mayor Rudolph Giuliani spoke it as well; in his public comments, he avoided offering more information than he had, but he acknowledged the need of the media and the public to know. He did not overpromise; he made it clear when his answers were based on incomplete information, or when he could not answer at all. Yet he responded to facts and reports as they developed. He conveyed emotion but was not emotional. He clearly demonstrated that he was in charge.

A commitment accompanies this language. It gives the public credit for being intelligent and for understanding what is at stake. It brings people into the process. For example, a news anchor may say, "We have only fragmentary information so far about what happened at city hall, but we believe this information to be solid and important, so we are passing it along to you. Keep in mind that it may change as we learn more about today's events. According to several eyewitnesses and preliminary police accounts...." This kind of explanation makes clear where the news is coming from, that the story is incomplete, and that the situation may change. It is deliberate and careful. In the midst of a crisis it brings a measured, calming tone to the delivery of the news and, as a result, it provides a degree of reassurance to the public and gives room to public officials who are both consuming and conveying news through the media.

There are some things the language of live should not be. It should not be breathless. It should not be hyped. It does not need to be accompanied by sensational graphics or music; the events themselves will be sufficiently alarming. But neither should this language be overly or unrealistically reassuring. Words and tone should be carefully chosen. Talk to the public straight, giving the facts. Citizens will see through spin or undue optimism; and they will appreciate straight talk that is clear and credible. Credibility is essential for news organizations and public officials during a crisis.

But credibility will be strained by bureaucratic infighting, competition, or a concerted effort on the part of first responders and public officials to suppress information. In numerous exercises and drills, federal, state, and local officials have practiced setting up a joint information center (JIC). Many officials think mistakenly that through the JIC they will be able to coordinate and manage the news, and speak with one voice. The JIC will surely be a central point of contact for public information officials, who will use it to share information and coordinate their messages. Reporters, too, will rely on the JIC for centralized, authoritative, on-the-record information. However, it is a mistake to think that the news can or should be managed. There are simply too many sources and too many avenues by which information flows. Also, efforts to manage news too often become efforts to manipulate it. Reporters are like an army that can be deployed more widely and can move information more rapidly than the first responders and public officials they are covering. In fact, as we have seen, first responders depend on the news media—on pictures, reporters, and eyewitnesses—for valuable information. Indeed, in antiterrorist exercises and in discussions with the media, public officials have learned that they will have to move faster, be more responsive, and provide more information to accommodate the realities and expectations of real-time media and popular culture.

HOMELAND SECURITY: PHASES OF A STORY

As events unfold and time passes, pressures and the type and speed of information will vary. It may be helpful to review what I consider the distinct phases of a story. On the basis of my own experience as a reporter, anchor, and behind-the-scenes decision maker, I would identify four distinct phases that apply to news stories in general and to the reporting of homeland security and terrorism in particular.

Information Phase

In the *information* phase, basic questions are asked and answered, often in the onrush of events and in an atmosphere of great uncertainty. What has happened? What are the consequences? Who did it? What is being done about it? What should the public do in response? Reporting at phase 1 represents the front line of information and often contains vital instructions to the public. There may be a hundred angles to a story at this stage, but these questions are most obvious and most immediate.

Examination Phase

The second phase can be thought of as *examination*. In this phase, the media—and often citizens—want to look deeper into events for meaning, perspective, and context. Phase 2 is a process of taking stock. Why has this happened? What does it mean for the future? Were there warning signs that should have alerted us? This is the point when the circumstances of—and possibly controversies about—an event are framed: Was this unexpected? Are events out of control? Were there missed signals?

Investigation Phase

In the *investigation* phase, these issues are pursued as reporters (and officials) try to get to the bottom of how this happened, what was going on behind the scenes, what public officials knew or should have known, what steps were—or were not—taken to prevent or deter the attack. At this point the media will step away from press conferences and observational reporting to piece together the puzzle, solve the mystery. Phase 3 can be difficult and time-consuming. Investigative reporting often depends on long-established relationships, anonymous sources, whistleblowers, internal memoranda, and other documentation that is generally not widely available to the public.

Recrimination Phase

Investigation may lead to the fourth phase, *recrimination*. In this phase, responsibility and blame are assigned—to an individual, an agency, an institution. In today's supercharged media environment, especially in talk television and radio, phase 4 can become a feeding frenzy, with media piling on, midnight stakeouts, finger-pointing, attacks, and criticism. More positively, however, at phase 4 public officials, institutions, and processes are held to account. It is the point when the media and the public consider who or what was responsible. This process may determine, in part, what price will be paid and how similar violent or tragic events can be avoided in the future. Phase 4 of a story is often feared or criticized, and we have seen it spin out of control many times. But often it is the way we determine accountability, fix a problem, learn from our mistakes, and move on.

RESPONSIBILITIES OF MEDIA

Appreciating these phases of a story is critical to understanding the role of the news media in homeland security and terrorism. Each phase has its own urgency and impact; each will convey a different set of information; each will unfold over time, and the later phases will depend on the information that emerges from the earlier phases.

Thus, given the new threats, journalists in the United States face a new responsibility, a public service in the true sense of the term, and an urgent challenge. Many news organizations have recognized the challenge and taken steps to meet it, but many others have not. News organizations—especially broadcasters—need coverage plans, to be sure they will get the story right. They need emergency plans, to look after their own personnel. They need contingency plans so that they can continue working if their broadcasting, publishing, or server capacities are damaged or destroyed. They need access to experts and expertise in the event of an attack.

RECOMMENDATIONS FOR NEWS ORGANIZATIONS

News organizations can take several steps to be better prepared for the story that no one wants to report. Some of the measures require the active cooperation of public officials. All should be done before the next crisis:

- ◆ Assemble, be familiar with, and be able to access relevant information from professional organizations and public health, academic, and government sources and Web sites.
- ◆ Know the emergency plans and the responsible officials in the community.
- ◆ Develop and keep current a list of sources and experts who can provide accurate, responsible information and advise the news organization about facts relating to it.
- ◆ Impress on sources, especially public officials, the need for rapid information in the event of a terrorist incident, and explain why that will benefit the public.
- ◆ Have a strong vetting process for information so that there is a deliberate, designated editorial chain of command to determine what goes on the air or is published and when.

This should include standards and practices for using sources, for attribution, and for reporting that involves issues of security.

- Master the language of live so that information about an unfolding, confusing situation can be conveyed as clearly, transparently, and calmly as possible.

- Train reporters, photographers, and other staff members in matters of personal and family safety; in the event of terrorism, they will be first responders, too, facing risks and personal pressures.

- Consider conducting exercises or drills that simulate a terrorist attack, to test the readiness of the staff, the editorial vetting process, the reach and redundancy of communications equipment, and the coverage plan that would be implemented in an actual event.

CONCLUSION

In the context of homeland security and terrorism, the media play a new and vital role. They are expected not only to inform the public but also to maintain a measured, responsible tone. The media must provide instructions by connecting citizens with their government while also scrutinizing government so that citizens can know whether they are being well served and their dollars are being wisely spent. Some commentators say that in this "new normal" situation the news media and government should recognize their common interests and pursue a partnership. That is not practical, is not a good idea, and will not happen. Nonetheless, there are common interests and even common responsibilities. Journalists and public officials serve the public and need to be sure that the information they disseminate is accurate, credible, timely, and relevant. Both should know that they will be held to account if they fail to do their jobs well.

Today, there is an acute need for clear, accurate, fast, responsible information. In this context, journalism represents a public service in the truest sense of the word—a public service on which millions of people and whole communities depend.

Securing Critical Infrastructure and Cyberspace

CHAPTER 33

Introduction to Section 6

James F. McDonnell
Vice President and Chief Information and Security Officer,
USEC, Inc.

"It will be our mission to protect the nation's critical infrastructure."

This simple statement, made by me and others in the early days of creating the Department of Homeland Security (DHS), raises a number of questions. First, what is critical infrastructure?

We all know what infrastructure is. Across America, when an alarm clock goes off to begin a workday, the energy infrastructure is at work. A hot shower and a healthy breakfast take advantage of public water systems and our agriculture and food systems. As millions of Americans commute to work by car or mass transit, their travel is coordinated by stoplights, rail switches, and ticketing systems. Employees in the retail sector might begin the day with inventory, ordering, and sales. Employees in the financial sector may begin computerized analysis of, say, market trends in Europe. Millions of people in all sectors settle in, with a cup of coffee, to read their e-mail. Thus by about eight o'clock each morning almost every American has used numerous infrastructures and has done so with the expectation that these infrastructures will work smoothly.

American businesses have always been involved in protecting infrastructures. As part of the normal course of doing business, owners and operators of facilities assess risks and make investments to mitigate those risks. Even the smallest business has recovery plans. I worked in a family business as a boy and remember my grandfather's discomfort with our first electric cash register.

He insisted that we have a manual calculator as a backup in case we lost power—we were not going to miss a sale because of a power outage.

If Americans know what infrastructure is, and if businesses already protect it, why did the government feel a need to consolidate federal efforts for the protection of critical infrastructure? Three questions remain: What is critical? To whom is it critical? Who decides what *critical* means?

These questions are complicated by the complexity of the behind-the-scenes aspects of our infrastructure. Millions of seemingly unconnected functions enable us to get to work in the morning. Computers running mass transit rail-switching networks depend on electric power generation, which may be fired by natural gas delivered through an interstate pipeline system that depends on another computer system to operate the pumping and compressor stations. Clearly, electricity is critical, but which transmission line is critical? Which generation plant? Which substation? When? This is the series of questions that government must answer. When the potential exists for a disruptive attack that would exceed the scope of a single company's assets, or an attack that would affect several systems, the government is obligated to take on the role of protector. Business owners do provide for business continuity; the bottom line demands that they protect their assets. But protection is based on the risks inherent in their environment, which is controlled by government.

The two chapters in Section 6 offer insights into parts of America's critical infrastructures that usually go unnoticed.

In Chapter 34 Rae Zimmerman addresses the complex issue of interdependence, offering ideas about the role of government in an interdependent space and ideas for future infrastructure planning. Interdependencies break down the normal model of business continuity. The loss of a particular component in a system can no longer be measured by the loss to that system or company alone; the downstream effects need to be understood and analyzed.

James Cunningham, in Chapter 35 on cybersecurity, delves into the next layer of the unseen: the digital backbone on which all of our systems depend but which nobody completely controls. An understanding of the vulnerabilities associated with using digital technologies is critical to any business today. During our morning commute, if the train stops running, we tend to think first of a power outage, not of the possibility that the control systems have been attacked by a virus. Cunningham reminds us how much of our life is controlled by digital systems and provides some thought-provoking comments on what we should be doing to protect ourselves.

Critical Infrastructure and Interdependency

Rae Zimmerman, Ph. D.
Professor of Planning and Public Administration; Director,
Institute for Civil Infrastructure Systems (ICIS),
Wagner Graduate School of Public Service, New York University

CRITICAL INFRASTRUCTURE AND ITS SECURITY

Infrastructure supports the economy, public health and welfare, and security, sometimes in ways that are not apparent. Depending on how infrastructure is defined, it contributes directly to about 10 percent (perhaps more) of the gross domestic product.[1] Infrastructure assets in the United States have been valued at several trillion dollars, or even tens of trillions.[2]

The security of infrastructure has become a major objective of national policy. Since the mid-1990s, regulations and guidelines regarding infrastructure—executive orders, reports, legislation, plans,

Note: This work was supported by several grants, including the National Science Foundation (NSF) Cooperative Agreement No. CMS-9728805 for the Institute for Civil Infrastructure Systems (ICIS) at New York University (in partnership with Cornell University, Polytechnic University of New York, and the University of Southern California); Urban Infrastructure in a Time of Crisis (grant number 0204660) and Bringing Information Technology to Infrastructure (grant number 0091482); and a grant from the U.S. Department of Homeland Security (DHS) through a subaward from the University of Southern California for the first Homeland Security Center of Excellence. The author's opinions, findings, and conclusions or recommendations are not necessarily those of NSF or DHS.

and strategies—have intensified. Infrastructure security in general evolved out of earlier concerns over protecting communications, and that theme continues to dominate infrastructure security policy.

As a collection of activities and facilities, infrastructure is complex, pervasive, and thus particularly open to terrorism. To make infrastructure secure, we need to understand its interdependencies and vulnerabilities.

Definitions: Infrastructure, Critical Infrastructure, and Interdependent Infrastructure

The current definition of the word *infrastructure* is relatively new, dating from the 1980s; earlier, the concept had to do mainly with military installations and public works.[3] In 1997, the President's Commission on Critical Infrastructure Protection (PCCIP) adopted a definition that refers to networks, processes, synergy, and continuity "to produce and distribute a continuous flow of essential goods and services."[4] In this chapter, infrastructure encompasses transportation, energy, water, environmental services (wastewater disposal), and telecommunications, all of which share certain features, such as their customers, the nature and configuration of the services they provide, and the type and location of their facilities.

The concept of critical infrastructure and interdependencies is even more recent; and a still newer concept is the link between infrastructure and security. Both ideas followed a national emphasis on the performance of infrastructure to promote health, safety, and welfare. In the mid-1990s, for example, Presidential Decision Directive (PDD) 63 defined critical infrastructure as "those physical and cyber-based systems essential to the minimum operations of the economy and government."[5] Section 1016(e) of the PATRIOT Act of 2001 defined critical infrastructure as "systems and assets, whether physical or virtual, so vital to the nation that the incapacity or destruction of such systems would have a debilitating impact on security, national economic security, [or] national public health and safety." As policies regarding critical infrastructure evolved, the scope of the concept evolved as well. Earlier laws, presidential directives, and executive orders list a more limited set of components than the detailed planning documents that emerged later. Present-day categories of critical infrastructure include agriculture, banking, hazardous chemicals, defense, emergency services, energy, mail and shipping, public health and health care, telecommunications, transportation, and water as well as certain key assets such as national monuments, commerce and manufacturing, dams, nuclear power plants, and the government. These categories are similar to those used in, say, lifeline engineering, which focuses on transmission and distribution systems.[6]

Policies Regarding Vulnerability

Condition and Performance

The need to address vulnerability first emerged as an aspect of the condition of infrastructure, which affects its ability to withstand disasters and in certain respects was considered life-threatening. Condition is often a function of design, operation, and maintenance. Prieto discussed the relationship between safety and the "core capacity" of infrastructure, specifically with regard to the transit infrastructure in New York City, which, he found, was in good condition and thus was able to respond to, and recover from, 9/11.[7] O'Rourke, Wang, and Shi discussed how the performance of lifelines (distribution and transmission lines) after an earthquake is related to their performance beforehand.[8] Damage to bridges, elevated roadways, and buildings as a result of storms indicates the ability of these structures to withstand earthquakes and floods. Also, engineering can be indicative. For example, the Schoharie Bridge in New York State was vulnerable to flood waters because its piers were embedded in sand; and the collapse of the Nimitz Freeway during an earthquake was attributed in part to differences in the reinforcement of the piers on the two sides of the roadway.[9]

Improving the condition of the nation's infrastructure was emphasized in the book *America in Ruins*.[10] Earlier, several failures of transportation infrastructure had prompted the creation of the National Transportation Safety Board in 1975; and failures of dams, such as the collapse of the Grand Teton Dam in 1974, had indicated a need for a national dam inspection program. Also, the electric power outages of 1965 and 1977 affected millions of customers,[11] and there have been numerous smaller outages along distribution and transmission lines. Such problems led to changes in national policy and legislation. For example, a state of good repair is a criterion for receiving federal transportation funds.

Some studies focused on the investment in infrastructure, arguing that budget allocations often fell short of needs. In the 1980s and 1990s, estimates of shortfalls were issued by government agencies such as the Joint Economic Committee in Congress and the Congressional Budget Office. The American Society of Civil Engineers (ASCE) has been assessing the condition of the nation's infrastructure since the 1980s.[12] The deterioration of infrastructure remains on the public agenda; in fact, in 2002 ASCE generally did not give any infrastructure sector a grade higher than C.

Natural Hazards

Concerns about natural hazards have created increasing pressure for protective rather than reactive public policy. In the late twentieth century and early twenty-first century, for instance, earthquakes and hurricanes revealed the fragility of many infrastructures. There was serious damage to infrastructure during the earthquakes of 1989 in Loma Prieta (California) and Kobe (Japan) and during the sequence of hurricanes that struck the Gulf Coast states in 2004. The National Incident Management System (NIMS) takes an all-hazards approach that includes natural disasters as well as terrorism. Experience with natural hazards is thus a basis for designing infrastructure security.

The "Security Age"

Since 9/11, policy regarding infrastructure has focused more intently on security. For instance, the National Research Council analyzed each infrastructure sector as a basis for assessing vulnerability.[13]

From the mid-1990s on, protecting critical infrastructure from intentional attacks has had a central place in federal policy, regulation, and fact-finding. Examples include Executive Order (EO) 13010 in 1996 and the report of the PCCIP in 1997. An initiative of the Critical Infrastructure Assurance Office (CIAO) increased awareness of infrastructure as a target of terrorism and began to develop a management structure for its security. PDD 63 also emphasized infrastructure. Examples since 2000 include EO 13231 in 2001; the PATRIOT Act of 2001; Homeland Security Presidential Directives (HSPDs) 7 and 8; the National Strategy for Homeland Security (2002), developed from the PATRIOT Act; and the National Strategy for the Physical Protection of Critical Infrastructures (2003). The report of the 9/11 Commission (2004) proposed reshaping security policy and management, and many elements of this report were related to infrastructure. Organizationally, infrastructure security management reflected the increased interest in infrastructure, and coordinating entities emerged at high levels of the federal government and in DHS. Specific federal offices have been opened to be responsible for homeland security, focusing on critical infrastructure and overlaying a complex existing organizational structure within traditional line agencies for managing various types of infrastructure.

Terrorism and Infrastructure Policy

Incidents of terrorism, sabotage, and vandalism throughout the world before and after 9/11 have been factors in shaping government policy with regard to the protection of infrastructure.

Examples

Transit systems outside the United States were targets of several hundred incidents during the twentieth century.[14] Notably, sarin gas was released in three subway lines in Tokyo in 1995; a subway car was bombed as it entered a station in Paris in 1995 (7 people were killed and 80 injured in that attack); a subway car was bombed in Moscow in 2004; and trains at several stations in Madrid were bombed simultaneously in 2004 (this attack killed hundreds of people). In the United States, the most symbolic attack on transit was the direct and indirect damage to the subway system in New York City on 9/11. Vandalism has also affected rail systems in the United States; for instance, Amtrak's Sunset Limited was derailed in Arizona in 1995.

Electric power has been a target of terrorism at several stages of production and consumption. Oil and gas pipelines have been particularly hard hit in Iraq. Between mid-2003 and September 2004, 112 attacks on oil and gas pipelines were reported. Domestic attacks have been more subtle. The U.S. General Accounting Office (GAO), citing the National Research Council, noted that in the first half of 2002, "security experts reported that 70 percent of energy and power companies experienced at least one severe cyber attack." Various components of transmission and distribution are vulnerable to attack. For example, vandalism caused a power outage in October 2004, when two bolts were removed from a transmission tower in Milwaukee, Wisconsin; a rail line was also disrupted, because the tower fell onto the tracks.[15]

Water systems worldwide have been affected by simple damage inflicted on small components, by break-ins, and by contamination. In 2003, break-ins were reported in Carpentersville, Illinois; Volusia, Florida; Willcox, Arizona; Grand Rapids, Michigan; Shelton, Washington; and Montreal, Canada.[16] In 1992, Kurdish rebels threatened to use potassium cyanide to poison the water system of a military base in Turkey; much earlier, in 1973, a German biologist had threatened to contaminate water supplies with biological toxins.[17] An actual incident was the sabotage of the Ta'Kandja water galleries in Malta: a pipe supplying chlorine was intentionally replaced by one containing fuel.[18] There have been fewer accounts of breaches of wastewater treatment, but one noted by GAO[19] involved a disgruntled employee of an Australian company who used a radio transmitter to hack the controls of a sewage treatment system and released about 264,000 gallons of raw sewage into parks and rivers in 2000.

GAO also notes an example in telecommunications. In 1997 a teenager in Worcester, Massachusetts, disabled switching stations, "disrupting telephone service for 600 residents and the fire department and causing a malfunction at the local airport." There are numerous examples of such breaches in software and hardware. It is often difficult to say how serious these are, but potentially they could have an enormous effect; for example, unintentional ruptures in fiber-optic cables during construction have caused not only small local outages but also very disruptive outages in airport systems.

Trends

There are serious indications that terrorist incidents may be increasing. Regarding transit, a database for 1920–1997 indicated a rise in terrorism.[20] Regarding energy fuels, attacks against oil and gas pipes in Iraq have escalated since mid-2003. Cyberattacks have also escalated.

INTERDEPENDENCIES AMONG INFRASTRUCTURES

Interdependence is a significant attribute of today's infrastructure, and this concept has been part of the relevant federal law since the 1990s. Before 9/11, PDD 63 had provisions for identifying and analyzing interdependence, and CIAO was expected to identify interdependence among key infrastructure sectors. Immediately after 9/11, EO 13231 contained a section (8 c viii) establishing a standing committee on infrastructure interdependencies.

Interdependency refers to a wide range of connections among physical facilities, services, and customers. Thus a related concept is interconnectedness:

> Interconnectedness refers to a formal linkage between two different systems. A related term, interdependence, connotes a stronger relationship in which two systems not only are connected, but depend upon one another in some way, such as functionally. Not all interconnected systems are interdependent, but all interdependent systems are interconnected.[21]

Other related terms are *interconnectivity* and *interoperability*. Many forms of interdependency exist at various scales, ranging from small components within a single infrastructure sector or facility to multiple infrastructure systems that can work sequentially or simultaneously.

Categories

Interdependence of infrastructure has been categorized in several ways. How it is categorized is important, because different categories imply different behaviors and analyses. Rinaldi, Peerenboom, and Kelly's categories are physical, cyber, geographic, and logical.[22] The author categorizes interdependence as functional and spatial.[23] EO 13010 implicitly categorizes it as physical and cyber threats. Actually, however, the basic concepts are consistent and can be distilled as follows:

+ Geographic, spatial, or physical interdependence typically refers to the collocation of two kinds of infrastructure that may or may not function together.
+ Functional interdependence (including cyber and logical interdependence) refers to two facilities or services that rely on each other in order to operate.
+ Economic and financial interdependence refers to the dependence of sectors on one another as sources or recipients of goods and services; these relationships are often captured by input-output methods or other techniques intended to compensate for the limitations of input-output.

Interdependence can be sequential, parallel, or a combination of both. Also, it can be unidirectional or two-directional, or multidirectional.

Mechanisms

Interdependence can affect the operations of infrastructure in many ways. On the one hand, connectivity is often intentional, having been designed for economic and technological reasons. On the other hand, reliance on deliberate interdependence or ignoring unintentional interdependence can have catastrophic effects.

Rinaldi, Peerenboom, and Kelly[24] describe failures associated with interdependence as cascading, escalating, and common-cause. In rare instances, there may be dampening effects. In a cascading failure, a disruption in one infrastructure causes a disruption in another; in an escalating failure, the effect on the next infrastructure increases in severity or recovery time; in a common-cause failure, two independent infrastructures are disrupted by the same cause, often at the same time. Time is important in assessing vulnerability; this factor includes response time, the duration of a disruption or outage, and the time required for repair and restoration.

The author has cited a number of interdependencies that led to system failures.[25] O'Rourke noted some dramatic cascading failures as a consequence of earthquakes.[26] Other interdependencies were revealed—or first appreciated—on 9/11.[27] Because of interconnections among various telecommunications and computing systems within the World Trade Center, for example, Internet outages had local effects as far away as South Africa.[28]

FACTORS CONTRIBUTING TO INTERDEPENDENCE

Interdependence typically develops in connection with patterns and rates of population growth that influence not only the use of infrastructure services but also the consumption of resources, such as land,[29] in ways that can increase vulnerability. That infrastructure has grown rapidly is apparent from general trends in consumption or usage. Despite efficiencies, the consumption of energy tripled, and the use of water doubled, from 1950 to 2000; there have also been significant increases in automobile travel and mass transit,[30] and in telecommunications (including cell phones).[31]

Also, growth in infrastructure is mainly characterized by a combination of fewer, centralized production facilities, and by very long networks in which services are delivered far from where they are produced or travelers' destinations are far from their points of departure. To cite two dramatic examples of long networks, there are more than 200,000 miles of oil pipeline and 2 billion miles of fiber-optic cable for telecommunication.[32]

Sites of production and consumption are critical nodes that vary by type of infrastructure. There are many such nodes: for instance, there are some 5,000 public airports and 4,000 offshore drilling platforms. The number of discrete sites (for production, processing, storage, etc.) is even more impressive: for example, there are nearly 600,000 highway bridges.

The following examples, all from the United States, convey the intensity of centralization; note that just nine states account for about half of the U.S. population.[33]

- ◆ 6.8 percent of all community water supply systems serve 45 percent of the population, and the proportions are similar for wastewater treatment systems.
- ◆ Of 225 petroleum refineries, 54 percent are located in only four states—Texas, California, Louisiana, and Pennsylvania.
- ◆ Of 2,776 electric power plants, 51.4 percent are located in 11 states.

- In transportation, 48.2 percent of 3.5 billion hours of delay surveyed in 85 areas in 2002 were concentrated in the six "very large" urban areas (defined as having populations exceeding 3 million).[34]

- Annual transit trips totaled 9 billion at the end of 2002; 49.8 percent were in only two states—New York and California.

- Total annual ridership (number of trips) reported by the American Public Transportation Association (APTA) increased by 8.1 percent between 2000 and 2003; but in the two top states—New York and California—the increase was 14.6 percent.

- In 1950, the average publicly owned treatment works (POTWs) served 7,790 people; in 1996, this figure had risen to 11,838.

ANALYZING INTERDEPENDENCE

Direct and indirect attacks on infrastructure seem to involve very simple means even if tactics and strategies are complex. For example, the derailment of Amtrak's Sunset Limited in Arizona in 1995 (an incident in which 1 person died and 65 were injured) was accomplished merely by removing some nuts and bolts from a piece of track at a crucial point—a trestle—and disabling a signal so that the train engineer was unaware of the damage. Yet, often, very complex measures and analytical methods are applied to such incidents.

Interdependency is not easily quantified. Analyses generally concentrate on assessing threats to infrastructure, vulnerability and risk of attack, or consequences of an incident. Although approaches differ in their use of engineering or economics, they are generally based on scenarios: scripts created to reflect the components, relationships, and behavior of interdependent systems. Methods currently in use or being developed for creating scenarios often begin with a set (or "suite") of indicators and conceptual models such as influence diagrams, followed by fault and event trees that provide a basis for quantitative analyses, risk analysis, and decision analysis. Influence diagrams show linkages at a single point in time, not necessarily implying sequences of events or decisions.[35] Decision trees or trees adapted to events, such as fault and event trees, show sequences of occurrences and are a basis for assigning probabilities to the phases.

Scenarios usually make implicit assumptions about outcomes, assumptions that are only as accurate as the scenario itself and are very difficult to scrutinize or test. An alternative is to base the scenario and the probability of outcomes on actual data.

Attack scenarios for infrastructure are different from those for other situations, and this fact also complicates analysis. For example, the impact of an incident can be deepened, and recovery can be slowed, if different kinds of attacks take place simultaneously—say, a cyberattack along with a physical attack or the release of a chemical used in infrastructure operations (e.g., chlorine, which is used in wastewater treatment plants) or conveyed by infrastructure. GAO calls such an incident a "swarming attack."[36]

Models

Economic and engineering models for interdependent infrastructure take various approaches. They often combine techniques such as risk analysis, event and fault tree analysis, game theory, and geographic information systems (GIS). Although economic and engineering models can be applied within a single infrastructure sector, they are usually applicable to other sectors as well.

Economic models can also be applied to interdependence between infrastructure and the rest of the economy. Such models have been developed by Haimes and Jiang,[37] who used databases of the U.S. Department of Commerce, Bureau of Economic Analysis; by Henry and Dumagen,[38] who used the same databases to identify linkages between information technology, other infrastructure, and the economy at large; and by Rose et al.,[39] who used equilibrium analyses to estimate economic and business impacts.

Engineering models use various techniques. Martz and Johnston[40] used event-tree analysis as the basis for a risk analysis of military installations involving munitions storage and the transport of a missile. Paté-Cornell[41] used an overall systems approach. GIS have been combined with lifeline engineering to estimate the reliability of infrastructure lifelines exposed to natural hazards, and with spatial overlays to analyze interdependencies statistically.[42] Risk analysis has been applied to the safety of infrastructure.[43] The risk-ranking technique developed by Haimes[44] has been applied to individual infrastructure systems, such as water distribution[45] and transportation;[46] it can be extended to multiple interactions. Mili, Qiu, and Phadke[47] apply risk assessment to scenarios associated with the failure of large-scale electrical systems; this analysis could be extended to interactions between electrical and nonelectrical systems.

Economic and engineering frameworks can often be combined, particularly in the work being done at the national laboratories, collectively known as the Civil Infrastructure Protection/Decision Support System (CIP/DSS).

In addition to economic and engineering models, a third category encompasses social-psychological dimensions of terrorism and the communication of risk. For example, some techniques apply the social-psychological behavior of decision makers and the general public to infrastructures such as electric power and railroads in situations that do not involve terrorism.[48] Other methods have focused on risk communication associated with terrorism.[49]

Indicators

Indicators are inputs to or outputs of a model. They are often expressed as ratios or rates derived externally—from other models or empirical research. (The examples of centralization listed above are simple indicators.) Indicators are easy to use and are a component of various models, but they are not designed, in themselves, to capture the complexity of interdependence.

Actual cases of failure and of recovery after failure are an important approach to the development of indicators. One indicator derived in this way is a ratio of two frequencies: how often one infrastructure causes failure in another, and how often it is affected by failure in another. When this indicator was applied to about 100 cases across the United States, water mains appeared to have the highest ratio of damage caused to damage incurred.[50] This result is supported by common sense: when a water main breaks, the consequences can literally spill over into other sectors.

INSTITUTIONAL INTERDEPENDENCE

How can interdependence be managed? Traditionally, each type of infrastructure is dealt with separately and views interconnectivity as add-ons to itself. But if dispersed systems are to achieve effective counterterrorism, interdependence must be integrated.

Government

GAO has summarized the proliferation of governmental organizations at the federal level to manage infrastructure security, identifying:

> ...at least 50 organizations involved in national or multilayer cyber CIP (civil infrastructure protection) efforts. These entities include 5 advisory committees; 6 Executive Office of the President organizations; 38 executive branch organizations associated with departments, agencies, or intelligence organizations; and 3 other organizations. These organizations are primarily located within 13 major departments and agencies mentioned in PDD 63. Other departments and agencies, in addition to the 13 mentioned in PDD 63, are also involved in CIP activities.[51]

Congress, too, has many committees and subcommittees addressing infrastructure security. In addition, under PDD 63, Information Sharing and Analysis Centers (ISACs) were created to bridge the gap between public- and private-sector infrastructures; this linkage was considered essential because 80 percent of the U.S. infrastructure is under the control of the private sector.[52] And NIMS formally incorporates many levels of government into incident responses, regardless of what caused an incident or what its impact is.

Concern for infrastructure security had caused changes in the organization of government even before 9/11. The responsibility for security began within councils and coordinating entities and gradually became part of line agencies. Following are some highlights.[53]

PDD 63 (1998) generally relied on existing line agencies for the security of specific types of infrastructure, but added several coordinating and cross-cutting layers to integrate them, and located them close to the executive office through agencies such as the National Coordinator for Security, Infrastructure Protection, and Counterterrorism, who chaired a Critical Infrastructure Coordination Group (CICG); a National Infrastructure Assurance Council; and a chief information officer. Communications were a pervasive element in programs intended to protect critical infrastructure; in this regard the National Infrastructure Protection Center (NIPC) and the ISACs—especially the warning system—are significant. PDD 63 also contains a planning function in the form of the National Infrastructure Assurance Plan; and research capabilities were provided, for example, by CIAO, within the Department of Commerce.

After 9/11 a Critical Infrastructure Protection Board cutting across many governmental functions was established by EO 13231. It was abolished in 2003 after the formation of the Office of Homeland Security and DHS (the latter was created under the Homeland Security Act of 2002). Critical infrastructure remained a focus, through two directorates: Information Analysis and Infrastructure Protection (IAIP) and Science and Technology. IAIP assumed many functions regarding protection and security.[54] The considerable reliance on the line agencies for infrastructure protection continued, although a number of functions associated with transportation security were transferred to DHS. The strong focus on information technology, distinct from other forms of critical infrastructure, is evident throughout the organizational history of homeland security. Infrastructure continues to be a focus of congressional legislation. In the 108th Congress more than one-fifth of the bills reported pertained to critical infrastructure, typically involving transportation.[55] Still, GAO noted in 2002 that many goals were not being met on schedule.[56]

The most dramatic structural changes in homeland security are likely to result from the 9/11 Commission report,[57] which emphasized communication and information transfer practices. Traditional agency controls over communication and infrastructure are part of the centralized intelligence structure proposed by the commission.

The Public

Policy, including organizational policy, is often driven by public concern, and surveys have found increasing public concern over the vulnerability of infrastructure to terrorism. In 2001, Herron and Jenkins-Smith[58] conducted a nationwide telephone survey of 935 people; in 2002, they did a panel survey of 474 of these respondents; a survey had also been done in 1997, and a follow-up to this included critical infrastructures. The results, some of which were statistically significant, were as follows:

- Threats to infrastructure were perceived as being greater from foreign sources than domestic sources.
- Perceived threats from both foreign and domestic sources increased between 1997 and 2001 but decreased between 2001 and 2002.
- When respondents ranked the threat to eight types of critical infrastructure (including banking and finance and emergency services), they placed water supply systems and oil and gas supplies and services first and second: that is, the percentage of respondents considering attacks an extreme threat was highest for these two types. These percentages also declined slightly between 2001 and 2002.

TECHNOLOGY AND INTERDEPENDENCE
Information Technology

The information technology (IT) revolution has pervaded almost every sector of the economy, including infrastructure; and the interdependence of IT and other infrastructures was underscored by the widespread anxiety over Y2K. In infrastructure, IT generally encompasses computing and communications, and the means to operate, control, monitor, and analyze other systems.[59] The connection between IT and other infrastructures has been enhanced on the supply side by the tremendous growth in the availability of IT in the form of wireless phones, cell phones, cell phone sites, the Internet, and broadband. On the demand side, infrastructure sectors have become important consumers of IT; nationwide, infrastructure is estimated to account for one-third of investment in IT.[60]

The use of IT to "enable" infrastructure provides enormous opportunities but can also increase vulnerability when IT does not perform as expected and infrastructure management is unprepared for that contingency. The extent to which other infrastructures rely on IT, and the implications of that reliance, have been the subject of studies and various specialized reports.[61] The vulnerability of critical infrastructures to cyberattack has motivated federal policy. The CERT Coordination Center (CERT/CC) at Carnegie Mellon University in

Pittsburgh, Pennsylvania, monitors such intrusions, and between 1999 and 2003 it reported an increase from 9,859 to 137,529 incidents. At least 70 percent of electric utilities have reported cyberintrusions.[62]

Energy

Energy (sometimes literally) drives other infrastructure and other sectors of the economy. Since the early 1980s, on average, about 50 electric power outages per year have been reported to the U.S. Department of Energy (DOE). Not all of these have affected customers, but large-scale outages seem to be increasing in frequency, extent, and duration. Large outages, such as those of January 1998 and August 2003 in the northeastern United States and Canada, have underscored the interdependence between electric power and the overall economy, as well as IT. In the outage of August 2003 (which is estimated to have cost $4.2 to $10 billion[63]), an initiating factor was a cyberfailure in critical operating areas, including software and emergency backup. The cyberfailure soon combined with weaknesses inherent in the network in Ohio, causing a rapidly spreading series of outages.[64] These outages then disrupted many other systems,[65] including transportation and water supplies.

REDUCING VULNERABILITY BY MODIFYING INTERDEPENDENCY

Commonly, in securing infrastructure to reduce the consequences of incidents, the emphasis is on "hardening" through design and operation and on providing short-term backup systems. Another way to provide security involves alternative infrastructure technologies, such as "green technologies." Proponents of sustainability and environmental protection have advocated such technologies, which are already influencing the design of energy, transportation, water, and communication systems. Concepts that were once tangential or marginal have entered the mainstream with regard to the planning and development of infrastructure. Renewable energy is an important part of public energy policy; for instance, in New York State a goal is that 20 percent of energy consumed should come from renewable sources.

These technologies offer opportunities to combine security with environmental protection and the conservation of energy, but certain limitations need to be recognized. The criteria for secure infrastructure generally include separability from heavily networked, centralized systems; locating services close to the users; flexibility in changing deployment patterns through mobility or other means; and the use of raw materials and other resources that are ubiquitous and not easily destroyed.[66] Green technologies meet many of these criteria; however, these technologies, especially those for producing energy, are built to operate intermittently, and when they are not operating they rely on networked systems for infrastructure. Also, the resources (such as fuel) that they use for operation are produced by centralized systems.

Renewable Energy Sources That Can Be Decoupled

Energy is often the first link in a critical infrastructure network. Therefore, renewable sources of energy are a critical factor in reducing the vulnerability of such a network. Renewable energy sources are those that can be regenerated or are not used up, and thus are not greatly threatened or disrupted by an attack, although they are vulnerable as regards their delivery to users. Renewable forms of energy include solar (photovoltaics), wind, geothermal, sea heat-gradient, and tidal. Usually, these energy sources are local or specific to a particular production process or cycle. According to DOE's Energy Information Administration,[67] a subset of renewable energy resources that included solar, biomass, geothermal, hydroelectric, and wind accounted for 6 percent of the United States' 98 quadrillion BTUs in 2003, and roughly half of that percentage was accounted for by biomass and hydroelectric. The proportion and level of consumption of renewable energy have generally been increasing—peaking in 1997, declining through 2001, then increasing through 2003. Electric power generation has used by far the largest amount of renewable energy, accounting for 60 percent of renewables, primarily from hydropower. Next comes the industrial sector, which draws most of its renewables from biomass. Two-thirds of the renewable energy consumed is used to generate electricity.

Although renewable energy is still a small share of total energy consumed, solar and wind energy are being increasingly used in local settings. For example, in New York City the redevelopment of the World Trade Center area has given considerable prominence to green energy, and Battery Park City in downtown Manhattan already relies on photovoltaic energy. A serious obstacle to local use of fuel cells has been constraints on space for energy storage, but new nanotechnology may overcome this problem.[68] Use of renewables in transportation has been less impressive; this sector accounts for only about one-third of the consumption of renewable energy, primarily alcohol fuels.[69] Also, there is debate over the net effect of environmentally friendly sources of power such as electric and hydrogen vehicles.

It should be noted, with respect to security, that many of these technologies ultimately connect back to centralized production facilities. Some systems that appear to be decoupled, such as backup units for electric power, may not in fact be independent of centralized energy production. For example, generators that run on diesel fuel are decentralized and decoupled from the grid when in use but they are not renewable resources and are produced at centralized sites. However, storage mechanisms such as fuel cells enhance the ability of infrastructure to decouple from large networks and reduce interdependence at least for a short time.

Renewables and other energy technologies are promising, but a thorough systems approach is needed to evaluate them fully.

Technologies for Rapid Recovery

The technology needed to repair infrastructure after destruction from any cause has been growing rapidly. Bridges are a notable example. For more and more bridges, a temporary bridge as well as permanent sections can be swung into place after a collapse. When a segment of the San Francisco Bay Bridge was destroyed in an earthquake, it was repaired in less time than it would have taken to build a new bridge. Rapid construction techniques can also be used for other bridge structures such as long spans and overpasses, at least for temporary repairs. The rapid (though temporary) repair of infrastructure at the World Trade Center showed that managers were able to adapt their services very quickly.

CONCLUSION

The interdependence of infrastructures, and thus their vulnerability, seems to be increasing. New approaches to designing, using, and managing infrastructure show promise, at least in reducing the consequences of terrorism; but security still represents a challenge to management. The challenge for line agencies is to organize themselves so as to address interdependence specifically.

The lessons learned so far include the ubiquity, diffusiveness, and complexity of infrastructure services—factors that are important for technology and for building institutions. The public has shown its concern for threats to infrastructure, and these concerns also need to be incorporated into institution building.

Incidents that threaten infrastructure have included terrorism but also other events and incidents. This history needs to be recorded and analyzed—particularly in terms of the operational issues associated with infrastructure and with human responses—to produce a comprehensive picture of how various elements interact during an event.

N O T E S

1. D. Henry and J. Dumagen, "Economics," in R. Zimmerman and T.A. Horan (eds.), *Digital Infrastructures: Enabling Civil and Environmental Systems through Information Technology* (London: Routledge, 2004), p. 155.

2. U.S. Department of Commerce, Bureau of Economic Analysis, table 3.1ES, Current-Cost Net Stock of Private Fixed Assets by Industry, 2001, www.bea.gov. See also J. P. Gould and A.C. Lemer (eds.), *Toward Infrastructure Improvement: An Agenda for Research* (Washington, D.C.: National Academy Press, 1994).

3. A. Altshuler, "Infrastructure Investment" (Book Review), *Journal of Policy Analysis and Management* 8 (1989): 506. See also D. C. Perry, "Building the Public City: An Introduction," in D. C. Perry (ed.), *Building the Public City. The Politics, Governance, and Finance of Public Infrastructure* (Thousand Oaks, Calif.: Sage, 1995), pp. 1–20.

4. S. M. Rinaldi, J. P. Peerenboom, and T. K. Kelly, "Identifying, Understanding, and Analyzing Critical Infrastructure Interdependencies," *IEEE Control Systems* (December 2001): 12.

5. U.S. Executive Office of the President, "The Clinton Administration's Policy on Critical Infrastructure Protection: Presidential Decision Directive 63" (22 May 1998).

6. T. D. O'Rourke, Y. Wang, and P. Shi, "Advances in Lifeline Earthquake Engineering," *Proceedings of the Thirteenth World Conference on Earthquake Engineering* (Vancouver, Calif.) (1–6 August 2004).

7. R. Prieto, "The 3Rs: Lessons Learned from September 11," presented at the Royal Academy of Engineering, 2002.

8. Op. cit.

9. R. Zimmerman, "Planning and Administration: Frameworks and Case studies," in John Ingleton (ed.), *Natural Disaster Management* (Leicester: Tudor Rose, 1999), pp. 225–7.

10. P. Choate and S. Walter, *America in Ruins* (Durham, N.C.: Duke University Press, 1983).

11. North American Electric Reliability Council (NERC), "Examples of Major Bulk Electric System Power Outages," n.d.; ftp://www.nerc.com, accessed 26 September 2004.

12. American Society of Civil Engineers (ASCE), *Scorecard: 2003 Progress Report*. Washington, D.C.: ASCE, 2003; http://www.asce.org/reportcard/, accessed 13 January 2004.

13. National Research Council (NRC), *Making the Nation Safer: The Role of Science and Technology in Countering Terrorism* (Washington, D.C.: National Academy Press, 2002).

14. Mineta International Institute for Surface Transportation Policy Studies, *Protecting Surface Transportation Systems and Patrons from Terrorist Activities* (Washington, DC: Mineta Institute, 1997), p. 23.

15. "Tampering Blamed for Power Outage," *USA Today* (12 October 2004): 3A.

16. R. Zimmerman, "Water," in R. Zimmerman and T. Horan (eds.), *Digital Infrastructures: Enabling Civil and Environmental Systems through Information Technology* (London: Routledge, 2004a), p. 80.

17. A. S. Khan, D. L. Swerdlow, and D. D. Juranek, "Precautions against Biological and Chemical Terrorism Directed at Food and Water Supplies," *Public Health Reports* 116 (2001): 7.

18. P. Cachia, "Saboteur Contaminates Water Supply at Ta' Kandja," *di-ve news* (10 November 2003), http://www.di-ve.com/dive/portal/portal.jhtml?id= 114070&pid= null, accessed 4 December 2003. See also Zimmerman, 2004a.

19. U.S. General Accounting Office (GAO), "Critical Infrastructure Protection: Challenges and Efforts to Secure Control Systems," GAO-04-354 (25 April 2004), p. 17.

20. Mineta Institute, 1997.

21. R. Zimmerman, "Social Implications of Infrastructure Network Interactions," in *Sustaining Urban Networks: The Social Diffusion of Large Technical Systems* (London: Routledge, 2005), p. 69.

22. Op. cit., 2001.

23. R. Zimmerman, "Decision-Making and the Vulnerability of Critical Infrastructure," *Proceedings of IEEE International on Systems, Man, and Cybernetics* (2004b).

24. Op. cit., 2001, p. 22.

25. Zimmerman, 2005.

26. T. D. O'Rourke, "Prospectus for Lifelines and Infrastructure Research," in B. Stenquist (ed.), *The Art and Science of Structural Engineering: Proceedings of the Symposium Honoring William J. Hal* (Upper Saddle River, N.J.: Prentice-Hall, 1993), 37–58.

27. R. Zimmerman, "Public Infrastructure Service Flexibility for Response and Recovery in the September 11th, 2001, Attacks at the World Trade Center,"

in Natural Hazards Research and Applications Information Center, Public Entity Risk Institute, and Institute for Civil Infrastructure Systems, *Beyond September 11th: An Account of Post-Disaster Research*, Special Publication 39 (Boulder: University of Colorado, 2003a), pp. 241–268.

28. NRC, *The Internet under Crisis Conditions: Learning from September 11* (Washington, D.C.: National Academy Press, 2003).

29. U.S. Environmental Protection Agency (EPA), *Development, Community, and Environment:—Our Built and Natural Environments* (Washington, D.C.: EPA, November 2000).

30. R. Zimmerman and T. Horan (eds.), *Digital Infrastructures: Enabling Civil and Environmental Systems through Information Technology* (London: Routledge, 2004); see the editors' article "What Are Digital Infrastructures?" p. 71.

31. Cellular Telecommunications and Internet Association (CTIA), "Semiannual Wireless Industry Survey" (Washington, D.C.: CTIA, 2003). See also Zimmerman, 2005, p. 71.

32. D. Bart, Presentation for the Defense Standardization Program Conference: An Update on ANSI Homeland Security Standards Panel (HSSP), ANSI-HSSP, Private Sector Cochair (17 March 2004).

33. Statistics are from, or were calculated from, the following: Zimmerman, 2004b, p. 81: U.S. Bureau of the Census, 1997, http://www.census.gov/prod/www/abs/manu-geo.html, accessed 29 October 2004; U.S. Department of Energy, Energy Information Administration (DOE, EIA), 2000, http://www.eia.doe.gov/cneaf/electricity/ipp/html1/ippv1te1p1.html, accessed 29 October 2004; D. Shrank and T. Lomax, *The 2004 Urban Mobility Report* (College Station: Texas A&M University, Texas Transportation Institute, 2004), p. 71; and U.S. Department of Transportation (DOT), National Transit Database.

34. Mineta Institute, 1997.

35. R. Clemen and T. Reilly, *Making Hard Decisions with Decsiontools* (Pacific Grove, Calif.: Duxbury, 2001), pp. 67–8.

36. GAO, "Critical Infrastructure Protection: Significant Challenges Need to Be Addressed," GAO-02-961T (24 July 2002), p. 14.

37. Y. Haimes and P. Jiang, "Leontief-Model of Risk in Complex Interconnected Infrastructures," *Journal of Infrastructure Systems* 7:1 (2001): 1–12.

38. Op. cit.

39. A. Rose, J. Benavides, S. Chang, P. Szczesniak, D. Lim, "The Regional Economic Impact of an Earthquake: Direct and Indirect Effects of Electricity Lifeline Disruptions," *Journal of Regional Science* 37:3 (1997): 437–58.

40. H. Martz and M. Johnston, "Risk Analysis of Terrorist Attack," *Risk Analysis* 7 (1987): 35–47.

41. E. Paté-Cornell, "Probabilistic Modeling of Terrorist Threats: A System Analysis Approach to Setting Priorities Counter Measures," *Military Operations Research* 7:4 (December 2002): 5–20.

42. O'Rourke, Wang, and Shi, 2004.

43. G. Apostolakis, "The Concept of Probability in Safety Assessments of Technological Systems," *Science* 250:7 (7 December 1990).

44. Y. Haimes, *Risk Modeling, Assessment and Management* (New York: Wiley, 2004).

45. B. Ezell, J. V. Farr, and I Wiese, "Infrastructure Risk Analysis Model" and "Infrastructure Risk Analysis of Municipal Water Distribution System," *Journal of Infrastructure Systems* 6:3 (2000): 114–17, 118–22.

46. M. Leung, J. H. Lambert, and A. Mosenthal, "A Risk-Based Approach to Setting Priorities in Protecting Bridges against Terrorist Attacks," *Risk Analysis* 24:2 (2004): 963–84.

47. L. Mili, Q. Qiu, and A. G. Phadke, "Risk Assessment of Catastrophic Failures in Electric Power Systems," *International Journal of Critical Infrastructures* 1:1 (2004): 38–63.

48. B. Fischhoff, P. Slovic, S, Lichtenstein, S. Read, and B. Combs, "How Safe Is Safe Enough: A Psychometric Study of Attitudes toward Technological Risks and Benefits," in P. Slovic (ed.), *The Perception of Risk* (London and Sterling, Va.: Earthscan, 2000): 80–103.

49. B. Fischhoff, "Assessing and Communicating the Risks of Terrorism," in A. H. Teich, S. D. Nelson, and S. J. Lita (eds.), *Science and Technology in a Vulnerable World* (Washington, D.C.: AAAS, 2002): 51–64. See also B. Fischhoff, R. M. Gonzalez, D. A. Small, and J. S. Lerner, "Evaluating the Success of Terror Risk Communications," *Biosecurity and Bioterrorism: Biodefense Strategy, Practice, and Science* 1 (2003): 255–8.

50. Zimmerman, 2004a.

51. GAO, 2002, p. 17.

52. Ibid., p. 26.

53. Ibid. For more detail, see also National Academy of Engineering, Computer Science, and Telecommunications Board (CSTB), *Critical Information Infrastructure Protection and the Law: An Overview of Key Issues* (Washington, D.C.: National Academy Press, 2003).

54. GAO, 2004, p. 27.

55. TheOrator.com, http://www.theorator.com/bills108/issues/homeland_security.html, accessed 30 October 2004.

56. GAO, 2002, p. 10.

57. National Commission on Terrorist Attacks upon the United States, *The 9/11 Commission Report* (New York: Norton, 2004).

58. K. G. Herron and H. C. Jenkins-Smith, *U.S. Public Response to Terrorism: Panel Study 2001–2002* (College Station: Texas A&M University, August 2003), pp. 3, 22–8; table 2.5.

59. Zimmerman and Horan, 2004, p. 6.

60. Henry and Dumagan, op. cit.

61. E.g., Zimmerman and Horan, 2004; NRC, 2002, 2003.

62. GAO, 2004, pp. 6, 12.

63. Electricity Consumers Resource Council, "The Economic Impacts of the August 2003 Blackout" (2 February 2004).

64. U.S.-Canada Power System Outage Task Force, *Final Report on the August 14th 2003 Blackout in the United States and Canada: Causes and Recommendations* (April 2004).

65. R. Zimmerman, "NYC Needs Systems to Blunt New Blackouts," *Newsday* (27 August 2003b): A31.

66. R. Truly, "New Energy Systems Enhance National Security," DOE, National Renewable Energy Laboratory, 14 March 2002; http://www.nrel.gov/director/trulyspeech_031402.html.

67. U.S. Department of Energy, Energy Information Administration (DOE/EIA), *Renewable Energy Trends 2003* (Washington, D.C.: July 2004): 1–2.

68. C. Lenatti, "Nanotech's First Block-busters," *Technology Review* (March 2004): 46–52.

69. DOE/EIA, op. cit., p. 6.

CHAPTER 35

Cybersecurity in Post-9/11 America

James D. Cunningham
Science Applications International Corporation (SAIC)

Our preeminent military status means that enemies know that they cannot attack us directly. No one will do what Saddam Hussein did and line up tanks in the desert to face the fury of the U.S. armed forces. Instead, our enemies will attack us where we are weakest: here, in the homeland.

—Richard A. Clarke, former head of counterterrorism at the National Security Council

THE UNITED STATES: A NATION DEPENDENT ON CYBERSPACE

Since 9/11, known and potential attacks on the Internet by hackers, criminals, and foreign or domestic terrorists—combined with the defenders' apparent inability to deter or even identify the attackers—have produced a sobering new term: *cyberwarfare*. Yet three years after 9/11, the cybersecurity community is divided over the basic questions that must be answered in order to mount a credible cyber-defense: Can America's enemies launch a catastrophic cyberassault against the homeland? What havoc could such an assault wreak? And if cyberterrorists can strike, why haven't they done so? Questions are more numerous than answers for the simple reason that the nation is not mobilized for war in cyberspace.

This chapter begins with some history and then reviews vulnerability and risks in cyberspace and how to integrate them into an effective security program. Terrorists' uses of, and threats against, the Internet are discussed, and cybersecurity by the U.S. government is examined. In conclusion, there are 10 guidelines for a robust security program.

The Internet—A Network of Networks

Since the Internet would be the battlefield of any cyberwar, its history and makeup are an appropriate beginning for this chapter.

Technologically, 1969 was a remarkable year. On 2 March Concorde 001 took off from Toulouse for its first test flight; on 20 July the astronaut Neil Armstrong announced, from the moon, "The Eagle has landed"; and on 21 November a small computer at UCLA was linked to a similar device at the Stanford Research Institute in Menlo Park, California, and the Internet's precursor was born.

The global Internet's first hesitant step was conceptually simple: the linking of several computers in a few scientific centers across the United States so that they could communicate with one another. As always, the devil was in the details; groundbreaking discoveries had to be coaxed from the new and still very theoretical realm of computer science. To turn theory into reality, the Pentagon's Advanced Research Projects Agency (ARPA) provided funding and support to a small academic and research community. Soon ARPANET, the world's first operational packet-switching network, began communicating. By the end of 1969 four host computers were connected to form the initial ARPANET.

Packet switching is now an indispensable underpinning of both data and voice communications worldwide. Earlier network communications, like telephone circuits in the predigital age, required a dedicated circuit that was tied up for the duration of the session and could communicate only with the single machine on the other end of the line. These new computer networks divided messages into slices called packets. The data bits independently followed different routes to the final destination, where the packets were reassembled into a coherent message. Much as a common mailbox is used to forward letters to different destinations, the computer's packet-switching communications link could now be shared.

For a long time scientists and academics had been essentially the only users of this revolutionary new communication medium. Usenet, the initial chat room for geeks, soon became a forum for free-ranging intellectual exchanges that would be recognized today as newsgroups. Each network, however, was managed separately and evolved with its own name, structures, procedures, and membership. Open-architecture networking, which allowed various individual networking "architectures" to work together, became an important concept. The Internet hosts—not ARPANET—became responsible for ensuring the reliable delivery of messages. With the network's role minimized, linking almost any networks became possible.

The migration from ARPANET to the packet-switched Internet was enabled by the development in the mid-1970s of Internet standards for connections and the transfer of data between two computing devices. This indispensable Internet protocol suite is often called TCP/IP after its two most important elements: the Transmission Control Protocol (TCP) and the Internet Protocol (IP). Any computer that spoke TCP/IP could utilize Internet applications such as Telnet, FTP, SMTP, and others that were also standardized. In 1972 the notation name@computer.xxx was introduced, and the e-mail application fueled the Internet's initial growth.

In 1984 the U.S. military portion of ARPANET was spun off as MILNET. The 1980s also saw network connections expand to more educational institutions and to some companies (such as Digital Equipment Corporation and Hewlett-Packard) that were participating in, or supporting others who were conducting, network research projects. The National Science Foundation (NSF), a branch of the U.S. government, became involved in the Internet during this period of growth. In 1986 the NSFNet backbone began connecting a number of supercomputing centers. By the end of the 1980s the U.S. Department of Defense determined that the network was developing on its own and stopped further funding of the core Internet. By 1989 the last ARPANET node was shut down and NSF became responsible for long-haul network connectivity in the United States.

By the early 1990s NSFNet was allowing commercial access to the Internet components initiated by NSF. In parallel with the actual Internet, other networks were growing too. Some were educational and centrally organized; others were a grassroots mix of school, commercial, and hobby; but all were independent. During the late 1980s the first Internet service providers had sprung up to service regional research networks and to provide alternative network access. Although commercial use of the Internet was forbidden, its potential for economic purposes became a topic of debate.

The World Wide Web

At the end of the 1980s the Internet was not user-friendly. This situation changed dramatically in 1989, when Timothy Berners-Lee at the Conseil Européen pour la Recherche Nucléaire (CERN) in Geneva, Switzerland, conceived the World Wide Web (WWW). Today, the Web is the second most popular Internet application, behind e-mail. The two keys to the WWW's instant success were the uniform resource locator (URL) and hypertext markup language (HTML). URL allowed ordinary computer users to specify the location of a document anywhere on the Internet by typing a simple, intuitive name such as http://www.whitehouse.gov. HTML soon provided an easy way to create Web text and graphics and to include links to other documents.

Although the Web was growing in the early 1990s, it was still difficult for most people to use. Most of the available browsers were Unix-based, expensive, and generally available only to academics and computer engineers. As with much of the Internet's initial development, Mosaic—the first graphical Web browser—was created by a university-based team, in this case led by Marc Andreesen in 1992.[1] In early 1993 Mosaic was posted for free downloading, and within weeks tens of thousands of new Unix-based users were surfing the Web. PC and Mac versions were released in late spring. With Mosaic now available for a much wider audience, its popularity soared, and more users inspired the creation of new content, which then brought more Web users on board—a cycle that continues to this day. After graduation, Andreesen and his fellow developer Eric Bina joined Jim Clark, a founder of Silicon Graphics, Inc. (SGI), and created Netscape Communications Corporation, making Netscape Navigator the first commercially successful browser. Microsoft acquired browser technology from SpyGlass and produced Internet Explorer.

As the Web's content continued its exponential growth, search engines were created so that people could find their way through the growing maze of documents. Lycos, the first search engine, was produced at Carnegie Mellon University, and by the end of 1993 it had indexed 800,000 Web pages.

By 1994 the network backbones and interconnections of a growing list of commercial providers were playing too critical a role to
be ignored any longer. NSFNet dropped out as the main Internet
backbone, and the doors to Internet commercialization opened wide.

It has taken 35 years to create today's worldwide network
of networks, but the growth has been astonishing. From the original
two host computers in 1969, the Internet Systems Consortium Internet
domain survey of January 2004 reported 233,101,481 Internet hosts;[2]
and in late 2004 the Google search engine tracked more than 4.2
billion Web pages.

Retrofitting the Internet for Security

The builders of the Internet did not intend it to be secure; they
focused on its utility. What we now see as a systematic shortcoming
was, initially at least, viewed as its best feature. Steve Crocker, who as
a graduate student at UCLA in the 1960s was one of ARPANET's
original architects, notes: "The environment we were operating in
was one of open research. The only payoff available was to have
good work recognized and used. Software was generally considered
free. Openness wasn't an option; it just was."[3]

Without much thought to security, therefore, America has
become a nation fully dependent on cyberspace. The process of
linking the entire world's computers into one hugely complex
mechanism has begun. The rapidly emerging Bluetooth wireless
technology could extend the Internet to almost every device on earth
capable of receiving a 10-meter radio signal—each with its own
security exposure to be managed.

OUR COMPLEX CRITICAL INFRASTRUCTURES

The fundamentally unsecure Internet has become the arteries and
veins of many an American entity, including—of particular interest
to this chapter—the national critical infrastructures, itself a hugely
complex network of activities. The United States attempts to secure
a nearly 7,500-mile border with Canada and Mexico, crossed each
year by more than 500 million people, 130 million motor vehicles,
and 2.5 million railway cars. Almost 9,500 miles of shoreline and
navigable waters are patrolled, as are 361 ports that annually see 8,000

foreign-flag vessels, 9 million containers of cargo, and nearly 200 million cruise and ferry passengers. There are 442 primary airports and 124 commercial service airports that see 3,000 flights and 1.8 million passengers every day. There are approximately 110,000 miles of highway and 220,000 miles of rail track crisscrossing the nation; and 590,000 bridges dot America's biggest cities and smallest towns. We have built 54,000 community water systems and 75,000 dams.

Add to this mix the U.S. system of government, in which state governments share power with federal institutions, shaping a structure of overlapping federal, state, and local governance—the United States has more than 87,000 different police jurisdictions, 26,000 fire departments, and some 6,000 hospitals.

Finally, include the war on terrorism declared in September 2001, and the stage is set for a cyberbattlefield.

Success in any war, including cyberwar, requires an understanding of the enemy's strengths and weaknesses, and how and where they can strike. The formula that is crucial to risk management is threat + vulnerability = risk.

Physical and Information Security Must Work Together

To older security professionals, cybersecurity is technically obscure and procedurally incomprehensible. Many veteran security managers have quietly surrendered the digital field to system administrators or to a new breed of information systems security professionals. But information security cannot be conveniently separated from more traditional forms of security: physical, personnel, and technical security, and counterintelligence.

Why and to what extent physical security and cybersecurity officers must work together is a persistent question. But physical security and information security have a long history of working together; they have been intertwined at least since the Romans used cipher systems to protect messages carried by armed couriers on horseback. Two thousand years later, in 1946, ENIAC, the world's first electronic digital computer, was assembled at the University of Pennsylvania and was soon moved to a more physically secure environment, the U.S. Army's Aberdeen Proving Grounds. And today, two-factor authentication for access to information systems is becoming an accepted tool of information security. Logging on to many high-security networks requires some information that one knows (a password) and something that one possesses (fingerprints, retina, or a hardware token such as a badge or smart card or SecurID). This concept of rigorous access control was first developed, tested, and deployed by physical security officers: approach the entrance to a high-security area and you will probably be facing a two-factor authentication system.

As a result of advances in information technology, the physical and cyber-based systems essential to the minimum operations of the economy and the government are increasingly automated and inter-linked. These advances have created new vulnerabilities to equipment failure, human error, weather and other natural disturbances, physical attacks, and cyberattacks. Addressing these vulnerabilities will have to span physical security and cybersecurity.

Why, then, do some people view cybersecurity and physical security as essentially different? Perhaps it is because physical security seems blue-collar whereas information security sees itself as white-collar and high-tech. Today, however, cybersecurity and physical security must succeed together, or both will fail.

CYBERRISK MANAGEMENT

Traditional security officers and cybersecurity officers have had the same national goals since computers moved out of the defense establishment and academia in the 1960s; but the role of an infor-mation systems security officer is arguably more difficult to define post-9/11. The national objective is to make information available while making it secure—helping intelligence, the military, and law enforcement to connect the dots but not aiding the enemy in the process. With regard to protecting national infrastructures, security must find the proper balance between, on the one hand, enabling an authorized community of information technology users and, on the other hand, deterring and detecting diverse groups bent on mischief or destruction.

Administering a cybersecurity program involves risk management—a discipline that has existed at least since security officers who supervised construction of the pharaohs' tombs pondered the threat of grave robbers. Whether the threat is a physical attack, cyberintrusion, or a natural disaster, the goal for all security professionals is to set an acceptable level of risk.

Cyberrisk management (CRM), like traditional risk management, involves three steps: (1) assess threats; (2) detect vulnerabilities; (3) gauge the risk and identify countermeasures.

Assessing Threats

First, CRM teams begin by assessing threats to information and systems. They must recognize what exploitation techniques could succeed with their systems and networks. To the extent they can, CRM analysts assess the methods, training, and motivation of people who threaten their data and systems. This step builds an appreciation of how other people could exploit weaknesses and how far aggressors will go to inflict damage. The apparent intelligence failures surrounding 9/11 and Iraq are reminders that threat assessments are inherently complex and seldom yield clear-cut conclusions.

Detecting Vulnerabilities

Second, CRM teams identify vulnerabilities in a computer program or network that can potentially harm the system. (It is useful to focus on problems that could affect the confidentiality, integrity, and availability of information.) CRM involves examining all aspects of a system's technology and configuration. The teams become familiar with their systems' business uses and policies governing system operation. Through interviews and by simply walking around, they learn who can access the information—typically employees, contractors, and vendors, but also service providers, partners, and in many cases the general public. The teams must assess the value of their information assets to both inside and outside attackers. Risk managers must know of any planned changes in the information systems and identify any interdependencies with other cybercomponents and physical components. This discovery phase enables a team to determine which assets are most valuable and vulnerable and provides an appreciation of how these systems could be exploited.

Gauging Risk

Third, the most difficult task of a CRM team is realistically gauging risk. The analysts combine their knowledge of system vulnerabilities with their review of a potential opponent's strengths, motivation, and determination and put themselves inside the enemy's head. Understanding the opposition's strong points and one's own weaknesses goes a long way toward anticipating consequences and determining where prudent changes are required. The following paragraphs explore some general vulnerabilities of the Internet and some current threats, particularly terrorism.

BROAD THREATS TO THE INTERNET

Poisoned software, or malicious code, on the Internet is often mentioned as a means of disrupting e-commerce, public health and safety, intelligence analysis and sharing, military operations, and other critical activities. What exactly is malicious code?

Since September 2001, disruptive and costly viruses and network worms such as NIMDA, Sapphire/Slammer, Blaster, and Sasser have made headlines. They can reveal a high degree of programming skill or merely reflect the spite of a novice. Malicious code can subvert, spy, and destroy, and has become the cyberterrorist's preferred weapon. Because viruses, worms, and Trojan horses can be quietly aimed at specific targets or launched indiscriminately at the Internet, they represent a significant threat to the information infrastructure. It is important, therefore, to understand how viruses, worms, and Trojan horses work and how they spread.

Viruses

A computer virus is a small piece of software that piggybacks on legitimate programs in order to execute. For example, a virus can attach itself to a spreadsheet. Each time the spreadsheet runs, the virus opens and reproduces by attaching to other programs— the infection phase. If viruses did nothing but replicate themselves, they would not be such a nuisance. But most viruses also have an attack phase—anything from displaying an annoying message to destroying data.

In March 1999 the Melissa virus introduced a malicious code delivered by e-mail. Downloading and opening a document infected with Melissa triggered a virus that would browse the victim's e-mail address list and then send up to 50 new infected messages. The virus spread quickly, seized sizable network bandwidth, and forced several large companies, including Microsoft and Intel, to temporarily shut down some e-mail services.

The ILOVEYOU virus, which appeared in May 2000, also contained a malicious code sent as an attachment; clicking it open allowed the code to execute. ILOVEYOU sent copies of itself to everyone in the victim's address book and corrupted the victim's files.

In summer 2004 the MyDoom.O virus hit the Web with denial-of-service attacks. This virus, a variation on the earlier MyDoom.A/Novarg, came as an attachment to an e-mail message with the file extension .bat, .cmd, .exe, .pif, .scr, or .zip. MyDoom.A/Novarg, which is still around, attacks by opening a port that allows an attacker to access the victim's computer and use it as a relay station. The invader can also install a keystroke logger that will record and transmit things like passwords, credit card numbers, and social security numbers.

Worms

A worm is a computer program that exploits software flaws to attack a computer. A newly infected machine uses a copy of the worm to scan the network to identify other machines that have a similar security hole and then copies itself to the new machines and begins reproducing from there as well.

NIMDA, a mass-mailing blend of a worm and a virus, discovered in September 2001, was an automated cyberattack. By using several methods to spread, NIMDA demonstrated that cyberweapons can now learn and adapt to their environment. NIMDA tried several different ways to infect targeted computer systems until it gained access and destroyed files. Propagating with enormous speed, it went from nonexistent to nationwide in an hour, lasted for days, and attacked 86,000 computers. (On 19 July 2001, two months before the NIMDA attack, the CodeRed worm reproduced itself more than 359,000 times in about nine hours.) Although NIMDA destroyed files, its impact on the cyber infrastructure was short-lived.

Sapphire/Slammer, released in January 2003, was at the time the fastest worm yet seen. Spreading throughout the Internet, it doubled in size every 8.5 seconds and infected more than 90 percent of the vulnerable hosts within 10 minutes. Although it did not contain a destructive payload, Sapphire/Slammer slowed the Internet to a crawl and significantly disrupted financial, transportation, and government institutions. Ironically, Microsoft had posted a patch the previous July.

The Blaster worm made headlines in August 2003 when it launched a denial-of-service attack against Microsoft's Windows Update Web. When executed, Blaster crashed operating systems and affected a wide range of systems, causing a worldwide disruption of Internet services. Blaster infected more than 120,000 computers within the first 36 hours.

Trojan Horses

A Trojan horse is a computer program that purports to do something beneficial but instead does harm when it is run. For example, the program may masquerade as a game but can erase a hard disk or open up a back door to a system. Trojan horses have no way to replicate automatically.[4]

Fueling the Spread of Viruses, Worms, and Trojan Horses

To appreciate today's untamed Internet environment, consider that the number of computer security incidents reported to CERT/CC[5] rose from fewer than 10,000 in 1999 to 137,529 in 2003. The director of CERT Centers estimates, moreover, that 80 percent of actual security incidents pass unreported because they are unnoticed or the victims are reluctant to admit their problems. Following are the main factors that have converged to fuel the spread of viruses, worms, and Trojan horses:

Computer Literacy
The number of computer-literate individuals has increased tremendously in the past decade. Regrettably, a small percentage of the people using cyberspace launch malicious code out of vanity, greed, criminal intent, political or religious convictions, or sheer cussedness.

Sophisticated Hacking
Hackers can now exploit program vulnerabilities within days, whereas a short time ago hackers' advanced tools took weeks or

months to refine and publicize. Today, with skilled programmers posting sophisticated do-it-yourself hacker kits on Internet sites, even inexperienced hackers can create a virus or worm and literally point and click to launch it. (The National Institute of Standards and Technology estimates that 30 to 40 new attack tools become available on the Internet each month.) Although the actual number of hacker sites is impossible to determine—guesses range from the low hundreds to the mid-thousands—the quantity is unimportant, since a handful of knowledgeable geeks sharing their tools can cause a disproportionate amount of trouble, and the most dangerous hackers do not necessarily frequent hacker Web sites.

Complex Codes

The increasing size and intricacy of software programs contribute significantly to vulnerabilities by spawning programming errors or omissions. For example, Microsoft Windows XP contains about 50 million lines of code, a 427 percent increase over Windows 95. After three years of incrementally plugging Windows XP security holes, Microsoft announced the release of Service Pack 2 (SP2) in late summer 2004. SP2 users download up to 265 megabytes of data for the upgrade. This complexity, combined with most vendors' perceived need to have their product reach the market first, practically guarantees that security and privacy flaws are lingering around waiting for hackers to exploit.

Avoidance of Patches

Microsoft—whose operating systems power 90 percent of the PCs that connect to the Internet—issues security patches about once a month, but corporations and home users simply cannot or will not install them promptly. Thus compromised PCs continually join a pool of machines that unwittingly spread spam, break into private networks, or support scams and identity theft.

Incompatibility

Security products do not work well together. Today's belea-guered network security administrator needs tools for intrusion detection, intrusion prevention, firewall, antivirus, antispyware, and site-blocking (antipornography). Despite vendors' claims, little true integration has occurred. Therefore few cybersecurity administrators have assembled the budget, the cooperation of skeptical network managers, and the infinite patience to install the full range of network defenses.

Technical Issues

Most security products are made for technical personnel such as systems administrators, not for the average security or law enforcement officer. As a result, these products seldom contribute to actually closing down Internet abusers.

Risk-free Environment

The rewards—criminal, political, or psychic—that hackers seek are worth the risk, because the chance of getting caught is slight. In fact, the attackers have a virtually risk-free environment. Weak U.S. and international laws, combined with a seeming reluctance to use the rulings that are on the books, have produced little deterrent effect.

Federal Reticence

The national security, intelligence, and military services are tight-lipped about chinks in the United States' cyberarmor. The Pentagon, for example, routinely asserts that anything beyond a vague discussion of cyberproblems is too sensitive for public discussion. The government also has a powerful incentive for perpetuating the fog surrounding cyberwar; it wants to prevent potential adversaries from refining their own defenses.

Vendors' Reticence

Vendors of computer systems and networks are not known for candor about how their products contribute to flaws in the post-9/11 information infrastructure. Consequently, media commentators either wildly overstate obvious problems or minimize potential issues. The technically challenged react to this posturing by ignoring the problem, and issues that are inadequately considered are seldom adequately addressed.

The Impact of Toxic Code

By definition, malicious software is created to cause harm of various kinds:

Information Disclosure

Mass-mailing viruses typically harvest e-mail addresses from the address books or files found on an infected system. Some viruses will also send data from an infected host to other potential victims or back to the virus author. These latter files may contain sensitive organizational or personal information.

Another favorite pursuit of hackers involves subverting a computer's security defenses. For example, "cracking programs" that run through millions of passwords until they hit on the right one are free and easily available on the Internet. Likewise, network sniffers that capture keystrokes—among which may be passwords or personal data such as social security or credit card numbers—are commonplace and available to even technically artless hackers.

Wormlike programs called "mass rooters" do not self-replicate. Hackers deploy mass rooters to automatically inspect thousands of machines for vulnerabilities. When the mass rooter discovers a weak point, it installs remote-control software and back doors so that the hacker can later access the compromised machine. Root kits, many of which are fully automated and capable of hiding their presence, are popular remote-control and backdoor tools.

Virus Effects on System Stability

Once a system is compromised, a virus could potentially add, modify, or delete files on the system. These files may contain personal information or may be required for the proper operation of the computer system. Viruses can consume significant amounts of computer resources, causing a system to run slowly or become unusable.

Attacks on Other Systems

Systems infected by viruses are frequently used to assault other systems. These attacks often involve attempts to exploit vulnerabilities on the remote systems or to launch denial-of-service attacks by creating a high volume of spurious network traffic. One of a network hacker's favorite tactics is a denial-of-service (DOS) attack: a digital mugging that deliberately overwhelms a computer network's resources. For instance, the hacker will flood a Web server so that the targeted server squanders its resources attempting to handle these bogus requests. The targeted device cannot respond to legitimate requirements and may even crash. An e-mail bomb is similar but seeks out the victim's mail server.

Installation of Back Doors

Many viruses install a back door such as Back Orifice on an infected system. A hacker can later use this program's system administrative privileges to open a surreptitious access route and to read, add, modify, or delete files. Back doors can also be used to download and control additional tools for use in distributed denial-of-service attacks against other sites.

Spam

Spam is unsolicited, unwanted e-mail sent indiscriminately to multiple mailing lists. About 80 percent of the approximately 5 billion e-mail messages handled by Microsoft's free Hotmail service each day are spam, and national estimates put the total deluge at 70 percent of all e-mail. Spam has also become a primary delivery system for viruses, often to gain control of a compromised system to send bulk e-mail. Frequently these contaminated systems are poorly protected home and small-business computers.[6]

Phishing

Cyberphishing—not a form of toxic code per se, but a scheme for tricking unwitting online customers into responding to requests for personal information—is the latest in a line of cybercrimes dating back to "phone phreaking" in the early 1970s. The spurious inquiry appears to come from a trusted bank or e-commerce site but is a clever forgery that leads the victims to provide their passwords, account numbers, social security numbers, and other data useful to criminals.

Phishing scams, which did not even have a name in 2002, have surged to record numbers: some 1,100 identity stings were launched in May 2004 alone. Transactions carried out using data gathered through phishing cost banks and credit card companies an estimated $1.2 billion in 2003. According to the research firm Gartner, Inc., about

57 million American adults had received a phishing e-mail as of May 2004. In a separate survey of 650 online banking customers conducted in summer 2004, 74 percent of the respondents said they were less likely to shop online because of concerns about being phished.

E-commerce security is open to exploitation. Security experts have repeatedly sounded the alarm over mounting evidence of Web activities in which illegal profit is the motive. In a Deloitte Touche 2004 Global Security Survey of 100 leading financial institutions, 83 percent of the respondents had experienced a security breach in 2004, up from 39 percent in 2003. Four of ten corporations that were attacked suffered financial losses.[7]

Know Thine Enemy

Almost everyone agrees that hackers come in several shades. White-hat hackers are hired by an organization to probe its digital security perimeter and are considered good guys. Gray-hat hackers are not authorized to break into systems or programs but do so anyway, they say, to publicize security vulnerabilities so that the holes can be patched. Gray hats argue that they are good guys too. (Security administrators who have spent time, effort, money, and goodwill recovering from a "benign" incursion may disagree.) Black-hat hackers are intruders, including criminals and terrorists. Black hats are bad guys, and their hacking is a felony in the United States and most other countries. *Crackers* is a derogatory term reflecting disgust at the theft and vandalism of the early hacking gangs.

TERRORISTS AND THE INTERNET

We now turn to the post-9/11, or terrorist, threats to the Internet, as they are currently understood. Defending cyberspace would be easier if terrorists operated within identifiable borders, wore distinctive uniforms, stood tall, and declared war. Instead, a defender must get inside the opponents' heads and understand their behavior. What motivates terrorists? How do they communicate and plan operations? Most important, can they coordinate a cyberwar? Terrorists project an image of hooded holy warriors brandishing assault rifles: deadly, powerful, totally committed, and in complete control. Why, then, do they find the fuzzy digital world of the Internet so appealing?

To remain relevant, all terror organizations must communicate among themselves and with the outsiders they seek to influence. To remain in existence, every group must raise funds, pay its members, supply itself, conduct training, and attract recruits. Let us consider first what role the Internet plays in terrorists' daily operations.

Al-Qaida and other terrorist groups are painfully aware that they cannot confront the United States' military on traditional battlefields. Disrupting its information infrastructure is considered far less risky: terrorists can be fairly sure that the U.S. Air Force will not be ordered to smart-bomb cybercafés around the world.

No geographic borders exist in cyberspace. To reach a target, a cyberterrorist does not have to pass an airport inspection or submit identity documents to immigration and customs scrutiny. Unlike physical terrain, the Internet gives terrorists a readily available, unguarded corridor where they can hide their location, select their entry path, and mask their identity.

Terrorists may borrow the ploys of e-commerce criminals, who steal people's identities and credit card data to run up bogus charges, and computer geeks, who pilfer unwitting victims' identities to get their Internet access bills paid. Even moderately sophisticated Internet attackers can wield these cyberweapons anonymously and with little personal risk. Terrorists can fund their activities similarly, while covering their tracks.

Limited information warfare does not require sizable financial resources or state sponsorship; an $800 laptop and a modem are sufficient. Even a coordinated cyberattack could be mounted with laptops that the terrorists already have. And possession of a laptop, unlike firearms or explosives, does not bring down the security forces. In fact, the still unsolved release of several MYDOOM worm variants in 2004 suggests a new reality of cyberspace. Not only will security forces not come and break the door down, but (1) no one may ever know who or where the attacker was, and (2) there is no agreement on which agency, bureau, or department is responsible for finding out.

Terrorists use the Internet continually to attract new recruits and supporters: Alan Cullison of the *Wall Street Journal* acquired one of the few al-Qaida computers in the possession of journalists (contrasted to the growing number captured by intelligence and security services) just as Afghanistan fell to coalition forces in November 2001. Cullison asserts that the desktop was used by

Ayman al-Zawahiri, Usama bin Ladin's top deputy. Together with nearly 1,000 text documents, photographs, and video files, it "contained hundreds of Web pages, many of which were part of the group's increasingly sophisticated efforts to conduct a global Internet-based publicity and recruitment effort." [8]

Muhammad Naeem Noor Khan, the alleged al-Qaida computer expert arrested in Pakistan in August 2004, told U.S. government investigators that al-Qaida members use e-mail and Web sites in Turkey, Nigeria, and the Pakistani tribal regions to communicate with one another. For particularly sensitive communications, an e-mail address is used only once. Al-Qaida, Khan stated, often used couriers to deliver encrypted CDs. (But lest we believe that all terrorists are trained security experts, Khan's hard drive stored a treasure trove of intelligence on terrorist cells, operations, and tradecraft that resulted in the arrest of numerous al-Qaida operatives.)

Our enemies are taking advantage of the free, open, information-rich American society to mine the World Wide Web for data: terrorists can "Google" too. Muhammad Khan's hard drives were filled with Web pages and images that were evidently gathered to conduct surveillance, pick targets, and plan attacks. But sanitizing the Web is not a straightforward proposition. Take natural gas pipelines, for example. One would assume that since the 180,000 miles of gas pipelines crossing the United States are an obvious high-risk target, information about their routes would be closely guarded. Private industry and local governments, however, have publicized the locations of natural gas pipelines to make them safer— misdirected backhoes and wayward boat anchors having caused scores of lethal explosions in past decades.

Since 9/11, security concerns have dictated a rethinking of this openness. Web sites are being scrubbed of the pipeline maps that contractors once consulted before excavating, and fewer nautical charts now show gas pipe routes. The new challenge of protecting the public from accidents while not inviting terrorist acts is being deliberated by water boards, bridge operators, small airports, and many other elements of the critical national infrastructures. On the government side, the secretary of defense, Donald Rumsfeld, has issued a directive ordering government agencies to carefully monitor what they publish on the Web.

Terrorists believe that they can access classified information by hacking into the Internet. Although this particular threat has been overstated for decades and has been even more improbable since 9/11, the Internet does contain data that are not classified when viewed alone but occasionally create a far more complete and potentially compromising picture when analyzed together with similar data. This "mosaic" principle is a long-standing security concern made infinitely worse by the Internet's billions of downloadable pages, which include, for example, photos of airports, bridges, federal buildings, and other potential terrorist targets.

CYBERWARFARE OR INFORMATION VANDALISM?

People who should know better often associate America's supposed vulnerability to an information infrastructure meltdown with more probable and truly horrific concerns such as suicide bombers and weapons of mass destruction. The specter of an electronic Pearl Harbor can still receive a page-one story even though the consequences of a domain-name-system root-server crash pale in comparison with the devastation that could be caused by a truck bomb in Times Square.

Since about 1996, the term *information warfare* has been used to explain everything from defaced Web pages to hacks on wide-open university computers, and from mailboxes overwhelmed with spam to deliberate denial-of-service attacks. The term *cyberwarfare* is so vaguely defined that a teenager at a keyboard in a Bronx walkup, a major in a war room at the Pentagon, or a holy warrior in a cybercafé in Kabul could be called a cyberwarrior. The only consistent aspect of information warfare is that it has not happened yet, and the public is increasingly reacting to Internet problems with a day or so of patient resignation followed by indifference.

Overheated rhetoric aside, cyberdefenders know that enemies are dedicated to hurting the United States, that tools for conducting cyberattacks are readily available, and that the nation's computer systems and networks are very vulnerable. Defenders know too that the nation's ability to analyze vulnerability and risk is immature and that CRM is woefully imprecise. Thus some form of cyberstrikes is a threat that must be taken seriously.

One possibility is use of the Internet to attack the U.S. economy. Within two months of 9/11, Usama bin Ladin had asserted:

> The Twin Towers were legitimate targets; they were supporting U.S. economic power. What were destroyed were not only the towers, but the towers of morale in that country. The towers were supposed to be filled with supporters of the economical powers of the United States who are abusing the world.[9]

Although bin Ladin did not succeed in destroying U.S. economic power on 9/11, the erosion of Americans' faith in the Internet as an engine of electronic commerce would indeed deal our economy a harsh blow.

In general, however, the threat is more a matter of cybervandalism than cyberwarfare. More disruption is caused on the Internet by system failures, flawed programming, and construction accidents than is ever likely to be caused by any cyberwarriors' attack. It is an absolute certainty that terrorists will unleash cyberattacks when and if they accumulate the technical savvy. But the result will not be coercion, intimidation, panic, and terror; for reasons discussed below, the worst that American cyberdefenders will have to deal with is weapons of mass annoyance.

The Doomsday View

Nevertheless, many debates about cybersecurity feature a terrorist with his finger poised just above the Enter key, ready to bring the Internet crashing down. What would happen if al-Qaida, Islamic Jihad, HAMAS, America's own homegrown Aryan Nations, or anyone else succeeded in launching an electronic bomb? The doomsday scenarios go somewhat as follows.

The cyberwar starts with an all-out, indiscriminate, highly visible assault on the Internet. The U.S. information infrastructure is hit broadly and hard by unguided, or "dumb," cyberbombs, and by more precise "surgical" cyberstrikes—perhaps integrated with physical attacks. The attackers do not distinguish between military and civilian targets. In the first hours they do everything possible to cripple the U.S. economy; state, local, and federal governments; and the military, law enforcement agencies, and first responders. They try to disable communications, impede recovery efforts, and sow panic.

In addition to brute-force assaults such as multiple denial-of-service attacks, cyberwarriors also attack specific critical targets with something analogous to precision-targeted, or "smart," bombs. Specific infrastructure such as America's fragile northeast electrical grid, telecommunications, transportation, water, and emergency operations are disrupted. The cyberterrorists remotely and quietly go after particular physical entities by seizing digital control of dam floodgates,[10] altering railway system track switches and traffic signals, or disrupting air traffic control radar. Predictable objectives include military and civilian command and control structures such as networked systems: telecommunications, power management, emergency services, public health, water resources, and air traffic control. Simultaneously, a detailed target list of specific stock exchanges, futures markets, and financial institutions is hit.

Such doomsday scenarios sound apocalyptic, but of course they are intended to. Most people realize that the Internet is vulnerable. But is Internet warfare really an electronic dagger aimed at the nation's heart? Fortunately, the chances for al-Qaida or anyone else to conduct a successful cyberwar are remote. After almost two decades of combating hackers, the tide of the Internet battle is shifting in favor of the defenders.

The Real-World View

The public still hears about Internet security problems with catchy names like Slammer, but it seldom appreciates that the victimized organizations had failed to take even basic security precautions. Today's reality is that alert system administrators, security officers, and (more recently) software developers have evolved responsive, workable defense strategies. Corporations with an Internet presence have been probed tens of thousands of times by now. The survivors have learned to update patches, respond quickly to holes punched in their cyberwalls, or, if all else fails, unplug their Internet connection.

To be effective, a dumb-bomb cyberweapon would have to simultaneously pierce the defenses of thousands of computer systems and networks. Think about this for a moment; then calculate the odds that the designer of a cyberweapon could gather enough data to break through every likely configuration of every possible firewall. (There are more than 400 firewalls on the market.) Even a spectacular success rate would only get the cyberwarriors through the door; they would still have to navigate unchecked inside thousands of ever-changing networks and programs.

Since builders of smart cyberbombs are not in an arms race with the larger hacker community, they can presumably spend more time doing research and developing weapons before going after specific victims. But effective smart cyberweapons require highly sophisticated programming, and there is no practical way to work out the inevitable bugs before they are launched. Furthermore, it is reasonable to assume that the cyberwarriors' intended victims will realize that they are attractive targets and will raise their security shields.

Defenders of information technology are often at a disadvantage, owing to the sheer size and intricacy of their networks. Fortunately, this complexity is even more troublesome to attackers. The defenders have open access to the systems' hardware and software configurations. They can refine their security measures by direct observation, by consultation with the designers and more experienced users, and by trial and error. The attackers have none of these advantages.

Cyberwarriors can make a broad-based attack only once. Even if their strike is successful, the Internet security community is now geared up to react quickly. To ensure prolonged disruptions and overcome continual new defensive countermeasures, the aggressors would have to exploit new flaws and introduce new tactics continuously.

What is the likelihood that a cyberwarrior can develop an attack so diabolical that there are no known defenses against it? Remote. Competition is fierce among hackers of all hat colors. Chances are good that while cyberwarriors are carefully guarding their top-secret cyberweapons for the planned attack date, a caffeine-crazed hacker will launch something similar and security defenders will develop a response. In what would be a double irony, the claims of some hackers that they are actually improving Internet security could indeed be realized.

A terrorist takeover of supervisory control and data acquisition (SCADA) or similar trusted digital control systems (TDCSs) is another threat that, although potentially serious, seems even less likely to occur. More and more owners and operators of critical infrastructure are aware of their SCADA/TDCS vulnerabilities and have taken steps to host their critical systems on networks isolated from the general public. Also, since the accident in 1979 at the Three Mile Island nuclear power plant, control room operations of all types have increasingly required redundant human intervention before a potentially catastrophic reconfiguring of pumps, valves, circuits, and similar equipment can occur. Control room computers do not operate in isolation. This greatly reduces the chance that a cyber-terrorist, operating alone across a remote network connection, can wreak havoc.[11]

Could digital warriors plant misinformation or corrupt data so that operations such as military movements or emergency responses would be disrupted? Almost certainly not. The attackers' limited knowledge of the computer systems' structure, documentation, and standard operating procedures would rule out a nonalerting intru-sion. (Let us not confuse hackers' joyriding with data manipulation.) Altering a database or issuing bogus reports and commands without raising the daily users' eyebrows requires insider information. A trusted insider—an inside agent—roaming around systems and networks replaces the need for remote computer sabotage and is every security officer's worst nightmare.

Cyberterrorists would need to attack multiple targets simulta-neously for long periods of time to have any significant effect. But the Internet is amazingly resilient; its networks exhibit all the healing powers of an immune system under constant assault. In October 2002 the 13 root servers that manage Internet addresses were hit by a distributed-denial-of-service attack. Even though eight of the root servers were forced offline, the attack itself was a nonevent to Internet users.[12]

Incidentally, one enduring myth about threats to the Internet is that ARPANET was designed by the Pentagon to survive a nuclear holocaust. The Internet Society addresses this misconception in *A Brief History of the Internet*[13]:

> It was from the [contemporary] RAND study [on the survivability of secure voice communications] that the rumor started claiming that the ARPANET was somehow related to building a network resistant to nuclear war. This was never true of the ARPANET; only the related RAND study on secure voice considered nuclear war.

Terrorists use the Internet themselves. Almost any radical Islamic Web site hosts inflammatory stories and photos of Abu Ghraib prison and of the bullet-, bomb-, and shell-scarred Imam Ali shrine

in Najaf, Iraq. A prolonged Internet collapse could have unanticipated and unwelcome consequences for the radical Islamists' own
propaganda operations.

Consider the terrorists' use of cyberweapons in the context of
their political goals and whether cyberweapons will achieve these
objectives. A cyberattack, which may not even be noticed by its
victims or may be attributed to routine delays or outages, will not
be their preferred weapon. Terrorism is violence used to create
shock and achieve political objectives. How useful will terrorists find
a weapon whose impact may be gradual, cumulative, and of limited
duration?

Perhaps a day will come when cyberwarfare is as effective and
deadly as today's pundits predict. Perhaps someday, when every
device has computer chips that communicate among themselves
wirelessly, a cyberweapon will cause a digital meltdown. But for the
time being, technology and logistics are overwhelmingly on the
side of the defender.

Cyberstrikes in Support of Physical Attacks

An Internet-based assault on the United States' critical infrastructure
could support physical attacks by disrupting communications and
the analysis of information and intelligence. By precluding the use of
the Internet at a critical time, the enemy would seriously disrupt the
response; affect the decision makers' situational awareness at all
levels; and delay the emergency responders, public health workers,
and disaster recovery personnel who would be essential following a
physical attack.

A cyberattack that might pass unnoticed in the normal clutter of
daily life could have useful multiplier effects in conjunction with a
physical attack. Assuming, for example, that a terrorist could penetrate and shut down the network that operates a city water supply,
such a hit might worsen the damage of a physical attack by hampering firefighters. This integration of physical and cyberattacks
might be the only way in which cyberweapons could be attractive
to terrorists. The prospect of integrated attacks reinforces the need of
information security officers to work closely with traditional security
officers.

Since terrorists hold the advantage of surprise, would al-Qaida
launch a digital assault as a preface to a physical attack? Or would it

avoid anything that might alert the target that the enemy is stirring and that a physical assault may be imminent? Common sense suggests that a surprise attack requires—well, surprise.

Actually, cyberassaults have been considerably less effective than physical terrorist attacks in causing panic and destroying morale. Thus far, the major advantage of cyberwarfare for terrorists is that it is cheaper and safer than a physical attack.

CYBERSECURITY BY THE U.S. GOVERNMENT

The U.S. government has been trying to carve out an information security role since the late 1970s, an effort that has obviously accelerated since 9/11. Initiatives by the Department of Homeland Security (DHS) for protecting critical information infrastructure are centered on the National Cyber Security Division (NCSD). Formed in June 2003, NCSD consolidated the information-assurance responsibilities of several existing federal offices and cybercenters.[14] NCSD's charter includes identifying, analyzing, and reducing cyberthreats and vulnerabilities; disseminating threat warnings and information; coordinating response to incidents; and providing technical assistance in continuity-of-operations and recovery planning.

NCSD's First Year

NCSD's first year was spent consolidating several previous cybersecurity and telecommunications programs and overcoming a legacy of bureaucratic issues and obstacles. With apologies for not spending more time on its accomplishments, I will move on to review the strengths and weaknesses of America's cybersecurity from NCSD's perspective.

Combining a number of existing infrastructure protection operations into DHS has not made the government's program for protecting information infrastructure an overnight success. Since 9/11—as was also the case before NCSD's formation—governmental efforts to counter threats to cybersecurity are slowly maturing. Meanwhile cybersecurity professionals, private-sector officials, and members of Congress are expressing frustration that cybersecurity is not getting enough attention from some senior department officials.

According to some outspoken information-assurance experts, NCSD itself lacks visibility and clout inside and outside DHS.

The assistant secretary who leads the Information Analysis and Infrastructure Protection Directorate, and to whom the cyberdivision reports, has stated publicly that giving cybersecurity special status would be a step backward. The physical threats and cyberthreats are closely related, and the predominant danger has been the physical threat. Not all tech industry leaders concur, and the debate continues.

With 9/11 still fresh in people's minds, a role of DHS is to calm the public by instilling confidence that the government stands squarely between it and cyberterror. The key is credibility—instilling a belief that DHS (together with the FBI, CIA, NSA, DOD, and others) has the threat of a digital infrastructure collapse under control. In this information-assurance world, unfortunately, *confidence* and *credibility* have never been words associated with the government's efforts. Today, fairly or unfairly, the perception is no different. Of course, this lack of government credibility did not happen overnight. From its first day, NCSD inherited a lot of the baggage that other public-sector cybercenters and emergency response teams have been dragging through cyberspace.

Impediments Facing DHS

Following is a summary of serious impediments facing DHS, since they illustrate the divided responsibilities and seams in critical infrastructure protection that a knowledgeable adversary could exploit.

Battles for Turf

Turf battles "inside the Washington beltway" are making life difficult for DHS, including NCSD. Now that three years have passed since 9/11 without a major incident, few experienced Washington bureaucrats are prepared to surrender their authority to DHS without a fight, or at least a prolonged delaying action. Which government department, for instance, has primary responsibility for releasing classified information to state and local governments? Who has the core duty of passing along to the private sector critical data on threats to the infrastructure? Who is in charge of protecting infrastructure or, more narrowly, assessing the vulnerability of the critical national infrastructure? (DHS, the FBI, the DOD, state and local agencies, the National Guard, the private sector, and many others have active vulnerability assessment programs. Few of these studies are shared; the players cannot even agree on common reporting formats.) Anyone knowledgeable about Washington recognizes that these are loaded questions. There are many players, and no one is yet in charge.

A report in June 2004 by DHS's inspector general on the department's cybersecurity efforts cited two shortfalls: (1) an apparent lack of communication and coordination with federal, state, and local governments and industry, and (2) a failure to set priorities.[15] Again, what is DHS's proper role? Prior to his resignation, former NCSD director Amit Yoran indirectly acknowledged the turf issues when he told *InformationWeek*:

> Any government mandate or forced action in the cyber realm is doomed to failure, so we are very much taking an entrepreneurial approach to cybersecurity. How do we attract and encourage collaboration and sell people on the concept that being part of our collaboration is worthwhile?[16]

How indeed? With no mandatory minimum standards for protecting critical national cyberassets,[17] DHS's encouragement of collaboration between the public and private sectors boils down to asking people nicely to cooperate. The strategy is not working.

Leading by Example?
Industry executives and security professionals point out that DHS has not followed many information-assurance practices that it encourages the private sector and other government agencies to adopt. For example, DHS still lacks an independent, dedicated cyber-security unit staffed by information security experts. Also, the highly publicized partnership with industry for addressing information technology security has yet to gain much traction. After meeting late last year, the partnership delivered five major reports and dozens of recommendations. But follow-up has been slow and unfocused, and a second meeting has not been scheduled. Even DHS's supporters are concerned that the department as a whole is not leading by example.

Lack of Experts
NCSD inherited the important task of issuing virus and worm alerts and coordinating a national response to cyberattacks. But it can acquire

credibility and instill confidence in the program only when independent observers acknowledge that DHS has a world-class cadre of experts shaping the agenda. To lead, the government needs to be out in front of the private sector. At present it is not.

For instance, there is a widespread perception that NCSD's U.S. Computer Emergency Readiness Team (US-CERT) rewrites private-sector advisories and reissues them too late to be useful. Yoran, acknowledging the reviews of the first-year performance of the national cyberalert system, which he said were "mixed," stated that "it is not the government's intention to be the first one out there to say, 'Hey, something is going on.' The private sector has a finely tuned machine" for that purpose, and the government works collaboratively with it.[18] Conventional wisdom now holds that the government is lagging behind private industry.

Poor Security Practices

Some of the worst computer security practices anywhere are found in the U.S. government. The Government Accountability Office (GAO, formerly the General Accounting Office) has been reporting for many years on the widespread negative impact of poor information security within federal agencies and has identified this as a governmentwide high-risk issue since 1997. In April 2004 the federal government released its Report Card on Computer Security at Federal Departments and Agencies. The average grade for fiscal 2003 was D, up from F in 2002.[19]

The same might be said of bureaucratic inertia regarding the government's failure to buy only trusted security products and to use its buying power to insist that vendors pay more attention to cybersecurity. The private-sector perception that the government is unwilling or unable to follow its own advice has been met with considerable cynicism.

The Focus on Cyberwar

By focusing on cyberterrorism, some observers assert, DHS is failing to lead the battle against routine abuse of the Internet. Frequent reports of Internet outages and cybercrimes are eroding citizens' confidence in electronic commerce, causing countless hours of lost productivity, and costing U.S. businesses hundreds of millions of dollars annually. Meanwhile, critics say, NCSD is devoting too much of its limited resources to cyberterrorism, to the exclusion of other threats. In fact, Yoran believed that the countermeasures one would put in place for cyberterrorism differ little from the measures to protect against other threats, but his message is not getting through to outsiders.

A worthwhile reference is *The National Strategy to Secure Cyberspace* (February 2003), which:

> ... outlines an initial framework for both organizing and prioritizing [national cyberspace security] efforts. It provides direction to the federal government departments and agencies that have roles in cyberspace security. It also identifies steps that state and local governments, private companies and organizations, and individual Americans can take to improve our collective cyber security.[20]

The national cyberspace security strategy sets five priorities: (1) creating a response system, (2) crafting a program to reduce threats and vulnerabilities, (3) developing awareness and training programs, (4) securing the government's computer networks, and (5) encouraging international cooperation. The strategy is well conceived and clearly prescribes what is needed. The critical priorities give a clear insight into the principal concerns of the White House and DHS for protecting the information infrastructure. It is instructive as a guidebook to high-level cybersecurity strategy and for its insights into the state of information security shortly after 9/11.

Unfortunately, however, the strategy is not getting sufficient attention. Richard Clarke, who as White House cybersecurity chief oversaw publication of the strategy in early 2003, stated: "I think the national strategy fell essentially on deaf ears. The president signed it, the president issued it, there was the usual amount of lip service, but then nothing ever happened for the better part of a year."[21] As of September 2004, there was no public timetable for updating the strategy.

On the positive side, the federal government supports some excellent information security centers. For example, the National Institute of Standards and Technology's Computer Security Resource Center (NIST CSRC)[22] and the National Security Agency's Information Assurance Directorate (NSA IAD)[23] both have active outreach programs that are an exceptional source of timely and useful information on cybersecurity.

TEN GUIDELINES FOR INFORMATION SECURITY PROGRAMS

This list of guidelines for building and administering a robust information security program was purposely limited to 10; but it can and should be reviewed and modified to include however many others, of the dozens of candidates, that apply to a given situation.

1. *Invest in cybersecurity training and education.* If you have $1 to spend on information systems security, spend it on educating and training your users and administrators in good security practices.

2. *Practice sound, ongoing CRM.* The heart and soul of every security program, and every cybersecurity program, should be sound risk management. The chance of receiving a warning in time to react to an attack is almost nil, and the time required to bolster defenses will probably be measured in days or weeks. Threats and vulnerability must be continually assessed.

3. *Develop and publish policies, standards, and guidelines for information handling and information security.*[24] The old saying "If people do not know where they are going, any road will get them there" surely applies to information security. A lack of policies is almost certainly the most consistent failure of corporate cybersecurity programs. (Lack of up-to-date network configuration diagrams runs a close second.) Establish what is required of people and educate them. Then require them to follow your organization's policies.

4. *Follow industry's best practices.* Most cybersecurity vulnerabilities can be mitigated through good security practices. The NIST Computer Security Division's Computer Security Resource Center (http://csrc.nist.gov) is a valuable source of free information on security tools and techniques. These are some of the topics discussed there:

   - Two-factor authentication, such as SecurID tokens or biometrics.
   - Early warning systems and patch management.
   - Encryption of e-mail, of desktop and laptop files, and of files on servers.

- Wireless security issues.
- Automated vulnerability and (policy) compliance tools.
- A listing of certified security products. The identification and use of security certified products are imperfect but are off to a positive start. (Two government sites for certified security products are www.commoncriteriaportal.org/ and http://niap.nist.gov/.)

5. *Pay particular attention to remote-access security issues.* Most viruses and worms are introduced through laptops, and nearly every organization now has people who routinely use broadband or dial-up connections to access internal networks.

6. *Factor the security of your partners, contractors, and supply-chain vendors into your information security program.* In government and industry, networks are only as strong as their weakest links. Also, work with your Internet service providers— having more than one is good insurance—and integrate their antivirus, antiworm, antispam, antispyware, and network availability measures into your information security program.

7. *Contingency and continuity-of-operations plans are essential.* Create realistic disaster recovery plans and test them periodically. Identifying critical business assets, including information assets, can ensure that they will either survive a disaster or be recoverable or replaceable. Design your networks to be robust. Also, insurance companies—which have realized the strong role insurance coverage can play in cyberbusiness recovery—have developed specialized policies that cover nonphysical losses from viruses, worms, and software bugs. Some insurers will also cover such current cyberspace issues as trademark and copyright infringement, and liability protection in case hackers use your systems to launch attacks.

8. *Join an information-sharing-and-analysis center (ISAC).* There is strength in numbers. If your sector does not have an ISAC, start one. DHS-NCSD can be of assistance.

9. *Investigate the opportunity cost your organization pays by operating an inadequate cybersecurity program.* Unaddressed vulnerabilities place more than transactions at risk: security defects can open intellectual property and business operations

to unauthorized exposure, put infrastructure assets and services at risk, and seriously erode consumers' trust. Estimating the cost of a critical cyberattack is not easy, but surveys repeatedly show that recovery is likely to cost more than the investment in an information security program to prevent attack. Persuade your management to invest in protection up front.

10. *Do not wait for the government to take the lead.* The following is some sound advice from *The National Strategy to Secure Cyberspace.*

The federal government could not—and indeed, should not—secure the computer networks of privately owned banks, energy companies, transportation firms, and other parts of the private sector. The federal government should likewise not intrude into homes and small businesses, into universities, or state and local agencies and departments to create secure computer networks. Each American who depends on cyberspace, the network of networks, must secure the part that they own or for which they are responsible.[25]

CONCLUSION

Terrorism will adjust, adapt, transform itself, and continue to threaten. It will not just go away. But the nation's information infrastructure has also been changing and becoming more secure ever since computer scientists at UCLA in 1969 linked two computers with a 15-foot cable and devised a new way to exchange data over networks. Phishing, unknown in 2002, is a huge problem today. But given a little more time, the Internet will be retrofitted so as to let recipients authenticate a sender's identity before opening e-mail.

Today some new applications are so data-intensive that they are unsuited for the present first-generation Internet. But next-generation networks such as LambdaRail and Internet2—100 times faster than the typical home broadband service—are already running. The fact that these semipublic networks are not connected to the World Wide Web is a powerful safeguard, isolating critical information infrastructures from cyberterrorists.

Many of the security tools needed to protect the information infrastructure are available today, but not enough people are using them. Other solutions will come forward to meet emerging threats. Although the process will be slow, disorganized, and frustrating, cybersecurity will improve.

Our free, open, capitalistic way of life brings levels of national vulnerability not found in other, more authoritarian societies. Consequently, the vulnerabilities must be managed carefully to ensure that the inevitable risks are acceptable, and that our enemies' work is not made easier because of poor risk management decision making. In the cyberworld, the struggle is to achieve balance— between openness and privacy, for example. Understanding of this equilibrium is only now dawning, and is therefore hard to identify and harder to achieve.

I began this chapter by noting that America is not yet mobilized for war in cyberspace, and perhaps it never will be. Cybersecurity will improve, though, because the stakes in Internet survival and growth are so high that failure is not an option.

NOTES

1. Mosaic was developed by a team at the National Center for Supercomputing Applications at the University of Illinois, Urbana-Champaign (NCSA-UIUC) by Marc Andreesen and Eric Bina. (Spyglass acquired their technology from NCSA.)
2. www.isc.org/ops/ds/reports/2004-01/.
3. History of ARPANET, Part IV: Conclusion, www.dei.isep.ipp.pt/docs/arpa–4.html.
4. Definitions were adapted from *How Computer Viruses Work* by Marshall Brain, http://computer.howstuffworks.com/virus.html.
5. CERT/CC® is a center of Internet security expertise at Carnegie Mellon University's Software Engineering Institute. See www.cert.org.
6. Derived from CERT® Advisory CA-2004-02 E-mail-borne Viruses, www.cert.org/advisories/CA-2004-02.html.
7. www.deloitte.com/dtt/research/0,2310,sid=1013&cid=48978,00.html.
8. Alan Cullison, "Inside al-Qaeda's Hard Drive," *Atlantic* (November 2004).
9. David Bamber, "Bin Laden: Yes, I Did It," news.telegraph.co.uk, 11 November 2001; www.portal.telegraph.co.uk/news/main.jhtml?xml=/news/2001/11/11/wbin11.xml.
10. These scenarios almost always involve the electronic hijacking of supervisory control and data acquisition (SCADA) systems connected to a data network via a wide area network. The sophistication of SCADA systems and their associated distributed control systems (DCSs) varies widely. But modern SCADA and DCS systems operate metropolitan water distribution networks, major water and wastewater treatment plants, and wastewater collection systems.
11. Dial-up connections to individual computers and to internal (private) networks for diagnostic and repair pose an entirely separate set of potential vulnerabilities.

12. Most DNS data needed to pass communications are stored locally and updated daily. Very few name resolution requests require root server assistance.

13. Internet Society, *A Brief History of the Internet*, www.isoc.org/internet/history/brief.shtml.

14. The former Critical Infrastructure Assurance Office, the National Infrastructure Protection Center, the Federal Computer Incident Response Center, and the National Communications System were transferred to DHS to become the nucleus of NCSD.

15. *Progress and Challenges in Securing the Nation's Cyberspace*, Department of Homeland Security Office of the Inspector General, OIG-04-29 (July 2004), www.dhs.gov/dhspublic/display? theme=89&content=3438.

16. George V. Hulme and Stephanie Stahl, "Q&A with Amit Yoran," *Information Week* 13 (February 2004), www.informationweek.com/shared/printable Article.jhtml? articleID=17603406.

17. Federal guidelines for protecting information are found in the Federal Information Management Act of 2002 (FISMA): http://csrc.nist.gov/policies/FISMA-final.pdf.

18. William New, "Homeland Security Has No Plans to Update Cybersecurity Strategy," *National Journal's Technology Daily* (10 June 2004), www.govexec.com/story_page.cfm? articleid=28729&printerfriendlyVers+1&.

19. www.computerworld.com/printthis/2004/0,4814,91899.00.html.

20. *The National Strategy to Secure Cyberspace* (February 2003), p. viii, www.whitehouse.gov/pcipb/.

21. William New, "Ex-Cybersecurity Czar Blasts Bush's Efforts," *National Journal's Technology Daily* (17 May 2004); www.govexec.com/story_page.cfm?articleid=28506&printerfriendlyVers=1&.

22. National Institute of Standards and Technology, Computer Security Resource Center (NIST CSRC), http://csrc.nist.gov/.

23. National Security Agency's Infrastructure Assurance Directorate (NSA IAD), www.nsa.gov/ia/.

24. Policies for handling information include how documents are created, revised, published, temporarily stored, archived, and destroyed. Policy for information security deals with information assets and how to ensure their confidentiality, integrity, and availability. Policies are high-level statements of broad intent, such as "Product development data will be protected at all times." Standards are used to interpret policies for individual departments and users and are typically written in plain, straightforward terms. Guidelines tend to be technical implementation rules.

25. *National Strategy to Secure Cyberspace*, p. 11.

Border and Transportation Security

CHAPTER 36

Introduction to Section 7

William H. Parrish
Associate Professor, L. Douglas Wilder School of Government
and Public Affairs, Virginia Commonwealth University

Section 7 includes chapters on issues of border security and transportation security, which can be considered two of the most critical areas being addressed today in response to 9/11. Strategic planners and policy makers in border and transportation agencies must realize that whenever they implement a protective measure or program to prevent terrorists from entering the United States, the terrorists will look for other avenues to penetrate our defenses. Americans must recognize that time is on the side of the terrorists, and they will use it to find seams, gaps, and other weaknesses.

With regard to the security of borders and transportation, there are lessons to be learned from the defeat of the Soviet Union in Afghanistan. The mujahideen from around the world who responded to the call of the jihad crossed easily over the borders of Afghanistan, with their materiel. An effective strategy for securing borders and transportation must therefore be a set of overlapping measures designed to leave no gaps, and also designed to complement the activities of all border and transportation agencies. The United States' border and transportation programs must include the international community—its support and its participation. Developers of these programs must take a balanced approach in order to preserve the integrity of our Constitution as well as provide security. Programs must be designed to facilitate people's legitimate entry and exit across our borders—land, sea, or air—and to support timely, secure processes for the movement of commerce into and out of the United States.

Issues regarding immigration are directly linked to programs for border and transportation security. As the screening of persons and materials at ports of entry becomes more effective, illegal aliens, including terrorists, will attempt to enter the country "in between" the usual ports. Border security programs must use applicable technologies, such as military technology, to cover areas where illegal border crossings are likely. Homeland security planning and programming must be done in partnership with the military's Northern Command (NORTHCOM), which can support border and transportation agencies with technology, equipment, and other resources. The Intelligence Reform Act will provide for additional resources to address challenges that arise concerning immigration. If we fail to provide adequate resources, including technology and people to monitor our borders for illegal aliens and terrorists, we will have ignored the lessons of Afghanistan.

Al-Qaida has made the United States' borders and transportation system two of its high-priority strategic targets. For this reason, and because borders and transportation can never be made completely or absolutely secure against another terrorist attack, there is a need for a wide range of overlapping preventive and protective measures in both the public and the private sector.

The federal government and state and local governments have a vital mission to provide a safe, secure, economically efficient border and transportation system; but that can be achieved only through a strong, committed partnership with the public and with private industry. A globally integrated and coordinated government and private-sector defense applying state-of-the-art technology along with aggressive investigation by border and transportation agencies, law enforcement and security agencies, and alert citizens can help us detect and disrupt terrorists' activities. Thwarting terrorists' attempts to plan operations, acquire weapons of mass destruction, and travel across our borders may well prevent another attack.

This section covers border and immigration, and maritime and aviation security domains. In Chapter 37 Jack Riley explains the formidable task of securing the nation's land, sea, and air borders through which millions of people, planes, trucks, and containers pass annually. In Chapter 38 Cathal Flynn and Art Kosatka give an overview of civil aviation security in the United States, both before and after the 2001 attacks, and the implications of that comparison are significant. In Chapter 39 Carl Bentzel discusses the Maritime Transportation Safety Act of 2002 (MTSA) and reviews the maritime security domain. In Chapter 40 Howard Neil presents a vision for a virtual network of transportation information to support decision making at all phases of homeland security.

CHAPTER 37

Border Control

K. Jack Riley
Associate Director of RAND Infrastructure, Safety, and Environment
The RAND Corporation

The borders of the United States can be conceptualized as four segments, or points of entry. Three segments—airports, ports, and guarded land points—are official. The fourth—unguarded land borders and shoreline—is unofficial and is used primarily by migrants, smugglers, traffickers, and perhaps terrorists. Each segment is to some degree porous, because of the volume of activity and the amount of physical space that must be protected. Physical space is particularly important at unofficial points of entry.

The need to improve control over the airport border was highlighted dramatically by 9/11, but the attacks also indicated a need for increased control over the other segments. Meeting that need will be complicated and probably expensive and will necessarily involve many "stakeholders," including foreign allies and trading partners, the private sector, and local governments that have a substantial interest in fees and revenues from ports and airports. This chapter reviews the main policies that have recently been created to strengthen our borders and suggests possible future issues.

THE PROBLEM OF BORDERS

The United States has more than 100 international airports, through which some 88 million foreign visitors pass annually. It also has numerous major ports; for instance, Los Angeles and Long Beach together constitute one of the world's largest container port facilities, handling approximately half of the seaborne trade entering or leaving the country. Every day more than 16,000 large shipping containers arrive at American ports. Also, the United States protects thousands of miles of land border with Canada and Mexico. Daily truck and passenger traffic at key land ports of entry, such as Detroit (Michigan), Vancouver (Washington), and San Diego (California), numbers in the millions.

The borders of the United States serve many vital functions. All legitimate cargo trade passes over these borders, generating customs and other revenues and duties. In this sense, the borders facilitate the flow of trade, which is increasingly important to the American economy. Borders are also a "choke point" for monitoring the arrival and departure of people. Although 9/11 necessarily focused our attention on terrorists seeking to enter the country, an equally challenging issue is appropriate action against people who have overstayed their visit to the United States. Currently, there are orders of deportation for some 400,000 people who are thought to have absconded and to be living here illegally.

As noted above, the volume of activity at the borders makes control very difficult, and the numerous stakeholders in the processes of control complicate the issue. Even in the atmosphere of caution that has developed since 9/11, other trends are putting strains on borders. For example, many manufacturers and retailers now use the "just-in-time" strategy: to reduce the costs of carrying and storing inventory. They want intermediate and retail goods delivered at the last possible moment. This business model has been facilitated by steep drops in shipping costs and by improvements in efficiency during the last two decades.[1]

An additional complication is that nobody "owns" the borders or segments. Despite the creation of the Department of Homeland Security (DHS), many federal agencies still have a role in border security, and many state and local governments have a role in financing and regulating border segments, particularly ports and airports. Also, private companies such as airlines, truckers, container shippers, and manufacturers—as well as companies whose employees travel over these borders—are stakeholders. These firms care about what the security procedures are and whether private firms are expected to pay for them directly or indirectly. Perhaps less obviously, various industry, labor, and trade associations have a role in determining work rules and dealing with related issues. Last but not least, there are the interests of our allies and trading partners.

THEMES OF BORDER SECURITY AFTER 9/11

Shortly after 9/11 the authorities took specific steps to improve border security. These programs are discussed in more detail below. Broadly, however, the post-9/11 philosophy has had two important themes:

1. *It is beneficial to push the border out.* After 9/11, security at the border was seen as necessary but insufficient. Accordingly, there was a strong effort to move certain security operations farther offshore to prevent threats from reaching our borders. Examples include requiring advance information on cargo and passenger manifests, positioning Customs and Border Protection (CBP) personnel at overseas ports, and developing means to track stolen passports and to make passports and visas tamper-proof or at least tamper-resistant.

2. *"Profiling out" reduces noise and focuses resources on trouble spots.* All programs that profile out have a common feature: identifying trustworthy people or entities that will be allowed to circumvent routine inspections (though, typically, not random inspections). At land borders, for example, Canadian and U.S. officials have a program called NEXUS that allows travelers who have passed a background check to bypass routine inspection lines. The Customs-Trade Partnership Against Terrorism (C-TPAT), under which manufacturers self-certify their security procedures for goods shipped to the United States, gives this commerce easier access into the country.

We will now consider specific procedures at the four border segments.

AIRPORTS

Because airplanes were used as weapons on 9/11, and because of al-Qaida's well-documented fascination with attacking planes and using planes for attacks, the security of airplanes has been a high priority.

However, securing the air border segment involves more than securing aircraft. Of the millions of foreigners who visit the United States each year, a few may intend to plan or facilitate terrorist attacks. They may travel with stolen or falsified passports, or they may enter the country using legitimate passports and visas and then not leave when required. A significant aspect of border security is preventing such people from entering the United States. Following are some major changes that have been implemented at airports.

Airport and Airline Security Measures

Many security measures at airports and on aircraft can be considered extensions of border protection. They include air marshals, CAPPS II, screening of baggage and passengers, and NORTHCOM.

Air Marshal Program[2]

In November 2003 responsibility for the U.S. Federal Air Marshal Service (FAMS) was transferred from one component of DHS, the Transportation Security Administration (TSA), to another component—Immigration and Customs Enforcement (ICE). FAMS agents are trained for surveillance, deterrence, and combat to protect American flights.

Computer-Assisted Passenger Prescreening System (CAPPS II)[3]

Responding to opposition from the travel industry, from advocates of privacy and civil liberties, and from other groups,[4] Secretary Ridge announced in June 2004 that CAPPS II was being abandoned. The system had been intended to verify travelers' identity and assess risk by checking passengers against "watch" lists provided to airlines by the government. CAPPS II would also have flagged suspicious patterns of purchasing and travel, such as buying a one-way ticket or paying in cash, as well as passengers with certain outstanding criminal warrants. Under Secure Flight, the replacement for CAPPS II, airlines will forward passenger data to TSA for comparison against watch lists. Secure Flight will not target passengers with outstanding criminal warrants and will not use statistical analyses to predict which passengers may be terrorists.

Screening of Checked Baggage

The Aviation and Transportation Security Act passed by Congress in November 2001 required all airports to screen all baggage checked by passengers; the date for compliance was 31 December 2002. The measure was intended to prevent terrorists from concealing an explosive or incendiary device in checked baggage and detonating it during a flight. Early in 2004, GAO reported that TSA had "collected limited performance data related to its baggage screening operations" and that "TSA deployed Explosive Detection Systems and Explosive Trace Detection equipment to all airports to screen checked baggage...[but] TSA has been unable to fully utilize this equipment to screen 100 percent of checked baggage due to screener shortages, and equipment out of service for maintenance and/or repairs."[5] Thus although airports appear to be meeting the requirement for screening checked baggage, there is concern about the cost and efficiency of the methods they are using.

Screening Passengers and Carry-on Luggage

The nearly simultaneous bombings of two Russian airplanes in August 2004 renewed concern about terrorists' ability to smuggle explosives onto flights. Certain explosives, such as the hexogene used in these two bombings, do not show up well under ordinary gamma-ray screening and may be easily concealed in luggage. Currently, several American airports, including those at San Diego and Tampa, are testing portals that use small blasts of air to dislodge trace particles of explosives. The particles are siphoned through a vacuum to laboratory equipment that rapidly compares the air sample with molecular-weight profiles of explosives. At least two firms, General Electric and Smiths Detecting, make such equipment. The equipment is also being tested at the Statue of Liberty in New York City.

Northern Command (NORTHCOM)

This was developed after 9/11 to fill a security gap in civil aviation— the inability to force down the flights that were used in the terrorist attacks.[6] Previously, American armed forces had focused primarily on flights, and threats, originating outside the country and had monitored relatively few civilian flights—partly because of radar limits and partly because there was no formal communication link to the Federal Aviation Administration (FAA) in the event of an emergency involving civil aviation.[7] NORTHCOM now monitors 100 percent of civil aviation traffic and maintains a direct link to FAA. Most significantly, NORTHCOM also has the authority to shoot down, as a last resort, flights that appear to threaten targets in the United States. According to press reports, NORTHCOM came perilously close to exercising this authority when a private plane carrying the governor of Kentucky (who was on his way to the funeral of the former president Ronald Reagan) failed to transpond on appropriate frequencies as it approached National Airport.[8]

Passengers' Entry and Exit

Perhaps the most far-reaching change in border controls is U.S. Visitor and Immigration Status Indication Technology (US-VISIT).[9] To speed up the comparison of arriving passengers against watch lists, US-VISIT captures electronic fingerprints, a digital photo, and visa and passport information from these passengers. The system was first tested in Atlanta in late 2003 and became operational at all 115 international airports in the United States on 5 January 2004. Simultaneously, it was introduced at 14 major seaports served by cruise liners.[10] US-VISIT can also be used to assess the extent of visa overstays and to track departures. At several locations, exit kiosks are being tested; foreign visitors check out through these kiosks as they leave the country. The increased monitoring of arriving and departing foreign travelers is a fundamental change in U.S. policy.

A related element is the U.S. Visa Waiver Program (VWP). Twenty-seven countries—mostly European—are part of VWP. Citizens of these countries do not need to have visas for most travel to the United States. Initially, these countries were exempt from US-VISIT: their residents were not fingerprinted or photographed. However, at the end of September 2004 residents of VWP nations were required to adhere to US-VISIT procedures. In addition, to remain eligible for VWP, participating nations were required to provide their citizens with machine-readable passports by 26 October 2004 and biometric-enabled passports by 26 October 2005.[11] The latter requirement was originally intended for 2004, but it was delayed until 2005 because of objections by the European Union (EU) and many member nations. Actually, as of this writing many European leaders thought that EU would not meet the 2005 deadline and expected another postponement.[12]

Monitoring of visas and exits is a critical element of security, as the 9/11 Commission noted in its report on travel by terrorists.[13] The commission pointed out that all 19 of the terrorists in the attacks on 9/11 had violated one or more provisions of U.S. immigration and visa laws:

> One [attacker]...overstayed his visa by less than six months. Without an exit system in place at the border tied to law enforcement databases, there was no way to establish with certainty that he remained in the United States. Thus, there was no risk that his immigration law violations would be visible to law enforcement, and there was no risk of immigration enforcement action of any kind.[14]

The report also found that before 9/11, all aspects of entry and exit enforcement were weak and uncoordinated and had been given a low priority. This included the State Department's consular procedures for visa management and enforcement activities by the Immigration and Naturalization Service (INS), now the U.S. Immigration and Customs Enforcement.

Airline Cargo

Carry-on bags and checked luggage are screened or manually inspected before being loaded onto planes; in contrast, the vast majority of cargo is not inspected before loading. Airport officials estimate that less than 10 percent of all this cargo is physically inspected, and most airports lack the equipment to conduct inspections, especially of large containers. As with port facilities (discussed below), there is considerable concern that mandated inspections would place an undue financial burden on the $4 billion airline cargo industry and reduce the competitive advantage—speed—that air cargo has relative to other modes of transportation.

Certain programs, such as the Known Shipper Program, which screens companies that send cargo, are designed in part to reduce the need for inspecting all air cargo. The Known Shipper Program is analogous to the Customs-Trade Partnership Against Terrorism (C-TPAT, also discussed below). The Senate passed a bill that would eventually require all cargo loaded onto passenger jets to be inspected. However, the House has yet to complete action on a similar bill. Some congressional observers believe that this is one of the biggest gaps in border security.

Gaps in Air Border Protection

Substantial progress has been made in securing the air border. The probability of another attack like those of 9/11 has been reduced by reinforced cockpit doors, the arming of some pilots, the presence of air marshals, and increased awareness on the part of passengers. Our ability to identify potential terrorists by using watch lists has also improved—although these security measures are by no means foolproof.

The most serious gaps in air border security appear to be in air cargo and the screening of passengers. Air cargo constitutes a substantial issue: screening it involves complicated problems of logistics, space, cost, and accuracy.

The other serious gap is in screening passengers and their carry-on luggage for explosive devices. Certain explosives are difficult to detect with ordinary screening mechanisms: some do not show up clearly; others, such as hexogene, look like ordinary harmless liquids and so are easily disguised. It seems inevitable that, eventually, airports will be required to have systems capable of detecting the "vapor signature" of traces of explosives on passengers and carry-on luggage. As mentioned, promising systems are currently being tested in several airports around the world; but until such systems are deployed, we will have to rely on the existing, unsatisfactory methods.

PORTS

When goods arrive at an American port, they are typically off-loaded at an intermodal transportation hub (on or near the port facilities) and are then transferred to rail cars and trucks for distribution throughout the United States. An attack *through* a port could be devastating, depending on the target. Terrorists could use the ports as a point of entry and deliver a weapon to virtually any place in the country. For example, the ports of Los Angeles and Long Beach together send goods to more than 400 of the nation's 435 congressional districts.

An attack *on* a port—and especially several such attacks occurring simultaneously—could also disrupt the American economy. Ports tend to be large and sprawling, so it is unlikely that any attack would destroy a port's infrastructure. But an attack could disrupt a distribution node for a considerable time and would probably lead to a slowdown at all ports until security measures were reviewed and upgraded.

The consequences of a slowdown undertaken for purposes of security are potentially severe. For example, the port of Los Angeles alone handled more than $140 billion in goods in 2003. How quickly would the costs of port closures mount up? There are at least two cases that provide information about this. In 2002 a brief lockout of longshoremen at ports in the western United States was estimated to have generated losses exceeding $1 billion per day. Given that this lockout was to some degree predictable (the labor dispute was widely publicized, and both sides had indicated their intentions), it could be argued that the losses from a surprise terrorist attack would be even larger. For example, it seems highly likely that after a terrorist attack, the movement of goods would be considerably slowed by increased inspections or by decreased efficiency resulting from damaged infrastructure. Such requirements did not result from the lockout. Second, a consulting firm conducted a "tabletop exercise" in 2002 that explored the consequences of a terrorist attack through several ports.[15] The Booz-Allen game generated several lessons, including the realization that emergency postevent security measures were not sustainable and that the restart and rebound capabilities of the port system were unknown.

Below are some major port-related security efforts.

Security of Port Facilities and Associated Infrastructure

The most important legislative step has been the passage of the Maritime Transportation Safety Act of 2002 (MTSA), which primarily addresses the physical security of ports and ships. MTSA is designed to help prevent breaches of maritime security, and to enable recovery from those that cannot be prevented. Among other requirements, it required facilities and ships to develop security and response plans.[16] The U.S. Coast Guard (USCG), a part of DHS, is the primary executive entity for MTSA.

Security of Trade Processes

Whereas MTSA and USCG focus primarily on the physical infrastructure of ports and ships, Customs and Border Protection (CBP) focuses primarily on the process of shipping and moving goods. CBP's overarching objective, with regard to homeland security, is to enhance security within a framework that facilitates the international movement of goods. CBP has led to significant changes in the thinking about security of the supply chain, and how the impact of these changes will be felt for many years to come.

Container Security Initiative

The extension of the borders has several aspects. Container Security Initiative (CSI) combines the presence of CBP personnel with the use of intelligence and other information to identify containers and ships for screening at the port of origination. It consists of four core elements:[17]

1. Using intelligence and automated information to identify and target containers that pose a risk of terrorism
2. Prescreening such containers at the port of departure—i.e., before they arrive at U.S. ports
3. Using detection technology to quickly prescreen these containers
4. Using "smarter" containers that give evidence of tampering

The first stage of CSI, which was implemented in 20 major world ports, covered nearly 70 percent of container traffic entering the United States. With the subsequent addition of other ports, more than 80 percent of the containers reaching the United States are covered by CSI procedures.

Customs-Trade Partnership Against Terrorism

In addition, CBP developed Customs-Trade Partnership Against Terrorism (C-TPAT), a joint initiative by government and business to build cooperative relationships that will strengthen the overall security of supply chains and borders. C-TPAT allows manufacturers and shippers to conduct a security self-assessment and implement a security plan that eases the entry of their goods into the United States.

By May 2003 more than 3,000 importers, carriers, freight forwarders, and other organizations had begun participating in C-TPAT.[18]

Remaining Issues at Ports

It is difficult to pinpoint gaps in the security of ports and supply chains, because to date there has been no comprehensive evaluation of security measures in these areas. As a result, there is very little evidence about how the different elements of security work together; how much security the measures actually provide; or what impact they have on the timing of movements of goods, on synchronization with links to other modes of transportation, or on just-in-time deliveries of manufacturing goods. Given the complexity of international trade and its importance to the U.S. economy, such an evaluation should be undertaken soon, while there are still opportunities to shape and refine the security program.

Even the costs and benefits of individual security programs are not clear. For example, are we better off using intelligence to target containers for inspection or randomly selecting them? What percentage of cargo should we try to screen? There are thousands of facilities and vessels that have had to develop security plans under MTSA, but many of these plans have not been evaluated. Similarly, verifying the accuracy of security self-assessments conducted under C-TPAT is problematic.

The basic issues of security are complicated by the issue of payment: it remains unclear who should bear the burden of upgrading security. Some European officials have objected to CSI, arguing that it fosters security competition among ports, putting small ports at a disadvantage. More generally, ocean shipping is highly competitive and cost-sensitive. Many elements of the private sector are reluctant participants in security upgrades.

The models of security used in ports vary widely. Some ports use local police; others maintain their own forces. The consequences of these different models are not clear. Moreover, whereas workers in aviation are accustomed to carrying identification and to encountering a great deal of visible security, the labor force in ports tends to resist such measures. For example, some staff members have objected to conducting background investigations of port workers.

Also, we know little about the fault tolerance of ports—the ability of the port and supply chain to resist system failure in the event of a disruption—or about resilience: how quickly the stopped system is able to return to normal operations.[19] Fault tolerance is a function of hardness (the resistance of the system to attack), shock absorption (the ability of the system to accommodate the disruption in its locality), and shock dispersion (the ability of the system to dissipate the shock through a network). Resilience, the system's ability to recover after it has failed, is measured by the time until a backup system starts functioning, the time until full capacity is restored and sustainable, and the time to clear all backlogs. We have little experience to help us understand how fragile the international supply chain would be in the face of an attack, and what it would take to reestablish the chain. Contingency planning in this area is important, and policies that promote fault tolerance and resilience should be explored.

REGULATED LAND BORDERS

Mexico and Canada offer dozens of land points of entry into the United States. Some border crossings, such as the one between Windsor (Ontario) and Detroit, are among the busiest in the world. Immediately after 9/11, the borders with Mexico and Canada were, for all practical purposes, closed. Federal officials rushed the National Guard and other security personnel to border crossings. Land crossings into the United States took hours longer than usual, affecting the movement of commerce and the production of import-dependent goods. Generally, this slowdown lasted for only a few months. However, this short-term disruption raised many longer-term issues that are still being addressed.

Border Trade and Commerce

Mexican maquiladoras are an example of the longer-term stakes of border security. *Maquiladoras* are factories, producing a wide variety of goods for export to the United States, that operate in Mexican territory but near the United States. They rely on Mexican labor that is cheap by U.S. standards but well-paid by Mexican standards. In the last decade maquiladoras have lost ground to Chinese manufacturers who have access to a larger, even less expensive labor pool and who have benefited from a tremendous decline in shipping and logistics costs. Maquiladoras recognize the need for increased security, and many border groups have experimented with or proposed such methods as Web-enabled cameras to monitor manufacturing and the loading of goods onto trucks; credentialed drivers, with satellite tracking of trucks to identify deviations from prescribed (and randomly selected) routes; electronic truck locks that can raise an alarm if improperly accessed; and FAST lanes[20] that allow for more rapid movement of goods over the border. The fear is that the cost of security measures may put Mexican manufacturers at a further disadvantage relative to the Chinese, but that ignoring security will preclude sales to the U.S. market. Maquiladoras are emblematic of the larger issues at stake in port security.

Smart Border Initiatives

The short-term consequences of the slowdown at land borders after 9/11—combined with fears about the impact of security measures on costs and jobs—led to the development of "smart border initiatives" with Canada and Mexico.

- *Canada*: In December 2001 the United States and Canada signed a 30-point border action plan, addressing the secure flow of people and goods, secure infrastructure, information sharing, and coordinated enforcement. The two countries are using dedicated NEXUS lanes that speed prescreened, preapproved, low-risk travelers and goods over the border. Once these travelers and goods have passed rigorous security checks and have provided biometric data for identification, they may cross the border without routine customs and immigration questioning, although they are still subject to random inspection. As of July 2005, NEXUS operated at over a dozen U.S.–Canadian border locations.
- *Mexico*: In February 2004 Secretary Ridge and Mexico's Secretary of the Interior Santiago Creel signed a "2004 U.S.–Mexico Action Plan for Cooperation and Border Safety," intended "to improve border safety and security along our shared border in order to prevent migrant deaths and combat

organized crime linked to human smuggling and trafficking."[21] Ridge and Creel also announced their intention
to expand another program—Secure Electronic Network
for Traveler's Rapid Inspection (SENTRI)—to six land ports
accounting for 90 percent of border crossings; and CBP
expanded the number of FAST crossings on the Mexican
border from seven to 14.

Technology

CPB agents have begun testing a Pulsed Fast-Neutron Analysis
(PFNA) system that lets border teams see individual contraband
items in large cargo vehicles.[22] PFNA is similar in principle to radar
and magnetic resonance imaging (MRI) but creates three-dimensional
views and can label the specific content of the cargo by comparing
the collected gamma-ray signature with a library of signatures. An
inspector would thus be able to guide or refine searches using the
visual image along with knowledge about the specific type of
contraband. A future demonstration for aircraft cargo scanning is
planned.

PFNA is one of several promising technologies that could allow
more cargo to be scanned more cheaply and efficiently at borders.
Other methods in use are X-ray scanning and gamma-ray scanning
(to develop an image of a container's contents), radiation detection,
and manual searching. However, additional refinements or breakthroughs are needed before any of these technologies can be used
to scan a significantly larger fraction of incoming cargo, vehicles,
or passengers. The three issues that must be addressed are as follows:

1. *Increasing the scanning rate*: Faster scanning will allow a
   greater proportion of cargo to be inspected without creating
   bottlenecks at the border.
2. *Lowering the cost of equipment*: Cheaper equipment cost will
   reduce the security tax that scanning imposes on commerce.
3. *Reducing false positives*: Reducing the number of false
   positives will further reduce the size of the security tax by
   decreasing the need for expensive, time-consuming hand
   searches.

Unresolved Border Issues

The remaining issues in land border security are much the same as in port security. It is difficult to know how much security we should be paying for, because little can be definitively said about how effective individual measures are. Our national experience with controlling illicit drug imports (discussed below) suggests that border enforcement is at best a weak deterrent. Increased border enforcement has led drug traffickers to find new smuggling routes and to develop methods that are more difficult for government authorities to police. Similar adaptations by terrorists can be expected.

Although terrorists' behavior will not be static in the face of increased border enforcement, several steps can be taken to make enforcement more effective. In particular, it seems important to invest in developing faster, cheaper, more reliable screening technologies. It would also be prudent to investigate whether the "smart border" procedures with Canada and Mexico will work as planned in the event of another attack. An untested assumption is that NEXUS, FAST lanes, and other programs will keep commerce flowing (or enable a rapid restart) after a disruptive incident. This assumption should be tested with games, simulations, and other exercises that can suggest unanticipated issues.

UNREGULATED LAND BORDERS

At this writing, elected officials and others had recently warned the public about al-Qaida's efforts to evaluate and defeat unguarded portions of the U.S. border,[23] which are primarily the responsibility of the Border Patrol. The Border Patrol uses fencing and other measures at key crossings, although there is evidence that such measures simply displace illegal crossings and activities to unguarded portions of the border. The Border Patrol supplements its efforts in the unguarded areas with unmanned aerial vehicles (UAVs), helicopters, and fixed-wing aircraft. The aerial methods are often used to direct land-based teams to trouble spots. In addition, the Border Patrol has been supplemented by the U.S. military. For example, marine reservists support the Border Patrol by flying helicopters equipped with sophisticated radar to search for illegal border crossings.

Adding to the complexity of this situation are certain factors related to our enforcement capabilities:

- *We have limited space for detention and limited capability for deportation.* At present, the U.S. government lacks the capability to handle deportations of convicted criminals who are being released from U.S. prisons and jails.
- *We have limited enforcement capacity.* This is particularly true of the borders themselves, where there are few immigration control personnel.
- *We do not have extensive cooperation with state and local enforcement agencies.* The first two problems necessitate cooperation with state and local agencies, but many such agencies have policies against arresting or detaining suspects simply on the basis of immigration status. That is, unless there are other indicators (such as an outstanding criminal warrant unrelated to immigration) local police must let such suspects go.

Congress, DHS, and other government entities have developed various responses to address these shortcomings. They include the following approaches.

Border Patrol

In 2003, the U.S. Border Patrol apprehended more than 900,000 illegal immigrants at the border. This figure does not include any who were deterred, were sent back, or made it over the border. Officials estimate that for every apprehension at the border, there may be as many as four successful illegal crossings.

The Border Patrol uses a wide variety of equipment and methods, such as fences and barriers around points of entry, observation towers that increase sight lines along a fence, and infrared cameras and other devices to make observation possible around the clock and in all kinds of weather.

In August 2004 DHS granted the Border Patrol a significant new power—to deport illegal aliens directly. Before that, all apprehended illegal aliens were allowed a hearing before an immigration judge; this process often took a year or longer and thus required a significant amount of detention space, or the release of aliens before the hearing. The new rule will apply primarily to the land borders with Mexico and Canada, because the authority to deport suspects, without judicial review, who are apprehended at airports and seaports, had already been granted in November 2002. The land border was seen as a necessary extension, given the volume of activity there.

In the post-9/11 environment, the Border Patrol reports concerns about its ability to secure borders. T. J. Bonner, president of the National Border Patrol Council, has remarked: "By a two-to-one margin, the protectors of our nation's borders do not believe that they have been given the proper tools, training, and support to be effective in stopping potential terrorists from entering the country and protecting it from terrorist threats."[24]

Problems of border control and illegal immigration have spawned several private and grassroots border patrol efforts. Perhaps the largest is the Minuteman Project, which claims more than 1,000 patrol volunteers who are "doing the jobs Congress won't do."[25]

Clear Law Enforcement for Criminal Alien Removal

Congress has proposed the Clear Law Enforcement for Criminal Alien Removal (CLEAR) Act, which would offer incentives to law enforcement agencies to increase their participation in the removal of aliens. Currently, many law enforcement agencies below the federal level have a policy of assisting immigration enforcement only if the immigration offense is accompanied by another criminal offense; otherwise, these agencies will not take action.[26] CLEAR, if enacted in its present form, would authorize state law enforcement agencies "to investigate, apprehend, detain, or remove aliens in the United States." Some commentators consider CLEAR misguided, arguing that it is superfluous (simply duplicating existing authorities), that it could distract the police from routine law enforcement, and that it could undermine immigrants' trust in law enforcement.[27] Others have hailed it as a potential breakthrough, arguing that participation would be voluntary and that the legislation would provide access to training, data, and other resources beneficial to homeland security.[28] Supporters also argue that the services of the 600,000 local law enforcement agents are needed, since there are only 2,000 federal immigration officers to handle more than 400,000 existing orders of final deportation; and that the participation of state and local law enforcement agencies is needed to create a credible deterrent at the border.

IMPLICATIONS FOR POLICY

The process of securing borders can never be complete, because the environment is too complex and the volume of activity is too great. Thus it is prudent to consider what the future of border security might hold. What trends and what issues of policy are we likely to confront?

Two significant issues stand out. First, as we improve our control of airports, ports, and guarded land borders, there will probably be pressure on the unguarded land borders. The 9/11 Commission highlighted this point in its report. Second, since the borders are in a sense a shared asset (because of commerce and tourism), there will be an increasing need to collaborate on border issues with our allies and trading partners. Therefore, this chapter concludes by discussing next steps.

The Push toward the Unregulated Borders

There are two main reasons for the growing concern about unregulated borders. First, as control over air, sea, and regulated land borders is tightened, there is the suspicion that terrorists will attempt entry at the unregulated border. We have seen such flexibility in the behavior of drug smugglers who seek the path of least resistance.

Second, there is increasing concern about Latin America as a potential recruiting ground for terrorist groups, and as a place where terrorist operatives may hide and from which illegal border crossings and drug smuggling can emanate. This concern is based on the region's history of weak, corrupt governmental and police institutions and lax, intractable border controls.

The suspicion that terrorists will eventually focus on the unregulated land borders is probably well founded. The United States' experience with narcotics trafficking at the borders provides some clues. Despite substantial efforts at control, drug traffickers have proved flexible, innovative, and capable of learning.[29] Decade after decade, quantities of cocaine, heroin, and marijuana sufficient to meet the demand have reached the U.S. market, as traffickers have adopted new techniques (light planes, small offshore boats, submarines, and individual carriers called "mules") and new routes (through the Caribbean islands, over the land border with Mexico, up to Canada and down to the United States). The drug traffickers have persevered because they have a financial incentive. Terrorists have a fundamentally different motivation, but they too are highly likely to circumvent new security measures.[30]

Also, although the border has played only a supporting role in actions against drugs, its role relative to terrorism is far more significant. Kleiman et al. note that "acceptable leakage rates are much lower for terrorism than for drugs.... Stopping 90 percent of the drugs entering the U.S. would be a spectacular success, but letting 10 percent of attempted major terrorist acts succeed would be a disaster." This is a crucial difference between border security against narcotics and border security against terrorism. Controlling narcotics at the border is a relatively narrow policy issue, affecting the relatively few countries that are thought to be the primary sources of drugs. Combating the drug trade remains, principally, a public-sector problem; the private sector has little motivation to assist in it. However, border enforcement against terrorism is a broader-based issue that might affect all of the United States' global trading partners. Moreover, after 9/11 the U.S. government demonstrated its willingness to clamp down on the border and to promote comprehensive, long-term programs such as CSI and C-TPAT that affect trade. Repeated border shutdowns, or new border protection measures, implemented unilaterally by the United States, might cost our allies and the private companies that use U.S. borders billions of dollars in lost revenue. In short, foreign governments and private companies have a far stronger incentive to be partners with the United States in protecting the border against terrorism than in protecting it against drugs.

International Relations

In May 2004 the United States imported and exported some $184 billion in goods.[31] Canada accounted for more than 20 percent of the imports; Mexico for approximately 12 percent; and four members of EU—Germany, the United Kingdom, France, and Italy—for

13 percent. The other countries among the top ten importers to the United States are China, Japan, Korea, and Taiwan. These statistics, which do not count passenger movements or dollars spent in the United States by foreign tourists, underscore the fact that the borders are a significant resource. Millions of jobs in the United States and abroad depend on movement of commerce across the border, and many of our consumer products and industrial inputs are obtained through trade.

Thus it is important to understand how our trading partners have been affected by the changes in border security since 9/11. The following paragraphs review issues that have arisen with Canada, Mexico, and EU.

Canada

According to the Canadian Security Intelligence Service (CSIS), "With the possible exception of the United States, there are more international terrorist organizations active in Canada than anywhere in the world."[32]—although Canada itself has suffered few terrorist attacks. Terrorist groups use Canada for fund-raising, mobilizing the diaspora, developing logistical and other support for operations, obtaining weapons, and facilitating transit to and from the United States and elsewhere. Chalk and Rosenau have noted:

> Over the past decade, terrorists linked to Hamas, Hizbollah, Egyptian Islamic Jihad, the GIA, al Qaeda, IRA, the Kurdish Worker's Party (PKK), the Liberation Tigers of Tamil Eelam (LTTE), Babbar Khalsa, and the Dashmesh Regiment are known to have entered Canada—generally posing as refugees—to engage in various front and organizational support activities.[33]

If relations between the United States and Canada are strained by border control, the issue has to do with the refugees who seek asylum in Canada. Canada's asylum system is considered generous.[34] Refugees seeking asylum often arrive with little or no documentation, or forged papers. They are allowed to enter Canadian society while their claims (which are infrequently rejected) are being adjudicated. A substantial proportion of those seeking asylum—estimated to be as much as one-third—come from countries such as Pakistan, Saudi Arabia, Iran, and Algeria.[35] Ahmed Ressamn, the would-be "millennium bomber," entered Canada with a fraudulent passport, claimed asylum, and then failed to show up for his hearing.[36] He subsequently obtained a Canadian passport through criminal means. He was caught by alert U.S. officials as he attempted to enter the United States. His case is typical in Canada (and in the United States): many outstanding deportation warrants are simply not enforced, because resources are lacking and absconders are hard to track down.

The United States' concern about the Canadian asylum system is understandable, given the very porous border, the high level of activity supporting terrorism in Canada, and the continuous flow of new refugees who may rely on their ethnic compatriots for support and acculturation. Still, despite the potential seriousness of this issue, relations between Canada and the United States do not seem to have been unduly damaged. Indeed, there is considerable collaboration between the two nations on border security.

Mexico

According to the U.S. Committee for Refugees, Mexico granted asylum to fewer than 50 of 2,900 refugees and applicants for asylum in 2003.[37] Moreover, Mexico, unlike Canada, is not thought to have many immigrants or nationals who are active in supporting terrorist activities. There is concern, however, about people who enter Mexico using fraudulent passports and visas, and their subsequent ability to surreptitiously make their way to the United States.[38] To combat these threats, Mexico has imposed additional screening requirements for visas and has established a digital passport security system.[39]

A larger issue between Mexico and the United States is the volume of illegal immigration from Mexico. As noted in "Patterns of Global Terrorism 2003":

> A continuing issue of strategic concern to U.S.–Mexico counter-terrorism efforts is the existence and continued exploitation of long-standing smuggling channels traversing the U.S.–Mexico border. These routes have existed for many years to facilitate movement across the border while avoiding U.S. and Mexican authorities. Despite active and prolonged cooperation by the Mexican Government to address these smuggling routes, many smugglers have avoided prosecution.[40]

Although these issues are complicated and always have the potential for conflict, at this point they are not impeding cooperation on border security between the United States and Mexico.

European Union

The United States' relations with EU have been strained by issues of border protection. Customs and border protection are generally a responsibility of EU rather than of the member nations, but EU is in the early stages of developing and consolidating its federal powers. The United States would generally characterize EU as slow to respond to the security threats and concerns that emerged after 9/11. EU, for its part, would generally characterize the United States' actions as unilateral and nonconsultative. On certain issues, the United States has worked at the bilateral or national level, as opposed to the multilateral or EU level. The issue has become very complicated. For example, EU filed suit in the European Court of Justice to overturn bilateral agreements between the United States and individual EU member states on the Container Security Initiative (CSI). EU won the suit and has since implemented an EU-level agreement with the United States.

There are other barriers to increased cooperation between the United States and EU on border security, although not all these barriers have actually developed in the context of border security:

- *Intelligence*: U.S. intelligence agencies want to be able to predict how European courts will handle intelligence issues. The United States feels that this has not yet been achieved and that much detailed work, some at the bilateral level, must still be done.

- *Law enforcement*: There is little or no "law enforcement" constituency among European nations generally or EU in particular. This creates a sense of imbalance in the relationship, with the United States often pushing enforcement issues.

- *Decision making by EU*: This is a slow process and generally conflicts with progress in the United States, particularly under DHS, which tends to move fast and be focused.

- *Role of the private sector*: The private sector has little involvement in EU's planning, relative to the role of the private sector in the United States. In the United States, the involvement of the private sector in homeland security ensures that initiatives receive extensive attention, lobbying, and resources.

More positively, DHS and EU have increased high-level contacts in an effort to ensure that potentially contentious policy issues are identified as far in advance as is practical and to create additional mechanisms for resolving future disputes.

CONCLUSION

Security at U.S. borders has been significantly increased. Much of policy implemented after 9/11 reflects the principles of "pushing the border out" to extend the reach of our security and "profiling out" less threatening people and cargo in order to focus on targets that require more scrutiny. These principles have made border control more manageable, though they have by no means resolved certain broader issues of security.

Underlying these themes, however, is the startling realization that we do not know very much about the effectiveness of individual border security programs, or about how various programs work together to affect commerce, costs, and security. The effectiveness of programs such as CSI, C-TPAT, and US-VISIT has not been evaluated. The leaders of such programs, however, are increasingly aware of the need to establish performance standards—for one reason, because representatives of the private sector are concerned about the cost of security.

There is also increasing need for evaluation above the program level, at the strategy level. As we enter the fourth year after 9/11, it is becoming increasingly clear that securing the homeland is expensive and potentially endless. How much we should spend on, say, airline security compared with rail and bus security will become increasingly relevant. We cannot begin to resolve broad issues of resource allocation until we know more about individual programs (such as airline security). Evaluating the effectiveness of individual programs will provide a basis for the more strategic allocation of resources across programs.

Finally, there is a need to develop a road map for investing in technology for border security.[41] Faster, cheaper, more reliable screening technologies are needed. Similar needs arise in many other areas of border security and of homeland security generally. When there is a pressing need for security, there can be an incentive to invest in any—or all—apparent technological solutions, regardless of the potential payoff. Inherent in technology development, however, is risk. Some technologies are simply not going to reach their expected potential; others will reach it, but perhaps over a time span that will not meet current needs. It is important to structure the investment pattern so that homeland security officials will invest in technologies that address mission-relevant functions and provide essential capabilities.

N O T E S

1. Michael Wolfe, "Freight Transportation Security and Productivity: Complete Report," Long Beach, Calif.: Intermodal Freight Security and Technology Workshop (27–29 April 2002). Wolfe provides details on logistical improvements.

2. For a more detailed review of the marshals' program, see *Aviation Security: Federal Air Marshal Service Is Addressing Challenges of Its Expanded Mission and Workforce, but Additional Actions Needed*, GAO (November 2003); and *Evaluation of the Federal Air Marshal Service*, Office of Inspections, Evaluations, and Special Reviews, Department of Homeland Security (August 2004).

3. The airlines had responsibility for administering the first prescreening program, CAPPS.

4. For opposed opinions, see "Business Travel Association Applauds GAO Report but Fears Potential CAPPS II Impact on Industry," Association of Corporate Travel Executives (12 February 2004); "CAPPS II: Government Surveillance via Passenger Profiling," Electronic Frontier Foundation, accessed at www.eff.org/Privacy/cappsii/background.php on 9 September 2004; and "Barr Submits Formal Objections to Passenger Profiling System," American Conservative Union (30 September 2003).

5. "Challenges Exist in Stabilizing and Enhancing Passenger and Baggage Screening Operations," GAO (12 February 2004).

6. Several GAO reports mention a lack of attention to general aviation as a potential terrorist threat. See, e.g., GAO-03-1150T, "Progress Since 11 September 2001 and the Challenges Ahead"; and GAO-04-592T, "Improvements Still Needed in Federal Aviation Security Efforts."

7. *The 9/11 Commission Report* reviews the positions of FAA and NORAD; see pp. 82–5, 352.

8. Spencer S. Hsu, "Plane that Caused Capitol Evacuation Nearly Shot Down," *Washington Post* (July 8, 2004; p. A1).

9. For an overview, see GAO-04-586, Randolph C. Hite, *First Phase of Visitor and Immigration Status Program Operating, but Improvements Needed* (Washington, D.C.: Government Accounting Office, 2004).

10. US-VISIT is expected to be operational at all land points of entry by the end of 2005.

11. "Extension of Requirement for Biometric Passport Issuance by Visa Waiver Program Countries," press release, U.S. Department of State (10 August 2004).

12. Personal interviews with EU and EC leaders (26–29 July 2004), Brussels, Belgium.

13. *9/11 and Terrorist Travel: Staff Report of the National Commission on Terrorist Attacks upon the United States,* 2004.

14. Ibid., p. 4.

15. Booz-Allen-Hamilton, "Port Security War Game: Implications for U.S. Supply Chains," Executive Summary (2002).

16. Other objectives and requirements included maritime safety and security teams, security assessments for foreign ports, and a common identity card for transportation workers.

17. www.cbp.gov/xp/cgov/enforcement/international_activities/csi/csi_in_brief.xml, accessed 3 September 2004.

18. *Container Security: Expansion of Key Customs Programs Will Require Greater Attention to Critical Success Factors,* GAO-03-770 (25 July 2003).

19. Henry H. Wills and David S. Ortiz, "Evaluating the Security of the Global Containerized Supply Chain," TR-214-RC, RAND (2004).

20. Free and secure trade (FAST) lanes. Manufacturers shipping by FAST lanes must agree to many of the security measures mentioned above. Secretary of Homeland Security, "Fact Sheet: U.S.-Mexico Bilateral Meeting" (20 February 2004).

21. Ibid. This agreement formalized a 22-point plan announced in March

22. Ryan Singel, "New Nukes at U.S. Border," www.wired.com/news/technology/0,1282,64735,00.html. See also www.ancore.com/ACI-PFNA_brochure.PDF.

23. See, e.g., Brad Olson, "Terrorists Probing U.S.-Mexico Border, Intelligence Suggests," *Corpus Christi Caller-Times* (3 September 2004); and Alan Caruba, "Is a Terrorist Army Massing in the U.S.?" *MichNews* (28 August 2004). According to the latter, "In July, Defense Watch reported that, in Arizona, an area called the Naco Strip has become a primary route of illegal entry by 'significant numbers of Arab-speaking males.' It took a small town weekly newspaper, the *Tombstone Tumbleweed,* to reveal that 'males of possible Syrian and Iranian descent have been detained in the past few weeks.' Since 1 October 2003, 5,510 illegal aliens designated 'Other Than Mexican' (OTM) have been apprehended while crossing the Arizona terrain."

24. "How Secure Are America's Borders? Front-Line Border Protection Personnel Speak Out," Statement by T. J. Bonner, president of National Border Patrol Council of the American Federation of Government Employees (23 August 2004).

25. Accessed July 25, 2005 at www.minutemanhq.com/project.

26. E.g., refer to LAPD special order No. 71.

27. James Jay Carafano, "No Need for the CLEAR Act: Building Capacity for Immigration Counterterrorism Investigations." Heritage Foundation, Executive Memorandum No. 925, 21 (April 2004).

28. U.S. Representative Charlie Norwood, "CLEAR Act Pointed to as Solution to Criminal Alien Crisis at House Hearing," news release (3 October 2003). According to the release, the bill (H.R. 2671) is supported by the National Sheriffs' Association, the Law Enforcement Alliance of America, the Southern States Police Benevolent Association, and Friends of Immigration Law Enforcement, and by more than 100 members of Congress.

29. For the evolution of drug trafficking, see K. J. Riley, "Snow Job? The War against International Cocaine Trafficking," *Transaction* (1996).

30. Mark A. R. Kleiman, Peter Reuter, and Jonathan P. Caulkins, "The 'War on Terror' and the 'War on Drugs': A Comparison," *FAS Public Interest Report*, (March–April 2002). See Vol. 55, No. 2 for a more complete comparison of drugs and terrorism.

31. Statistics are from U.S. Department of State International Information Programs accessed at www.census.gov/foreign-trade/top/dst/current/balance. html (10 September 2004).

32. "Operational Programs: Counter-Terrorism," Canadian Security Intelligence Service, rev. 9 (August 2002), accessed at www.csis-scrs.gc.ca/eng/operat/ ct_e.html (9 September 2004).

33. Peter Chalk and William Rosenau, *Confronting the "Enemy Within": Security Intelligence, the Police, and Counterterrorism in Four Democracies*, RAND, MG-100 (2004). See especially pp. 25–31.

34. James Bissett, *Canada's Asylum System: A Threat to American Security*, Center for Immigration Studies (May 2002). Bissett provides an overview of the issues. See also Stephen Gallagher, "Canada's Dysfunctional Refugee Determination System: Canadian Asylum Policy from a Comparative Perspective," *Public Policy Sources* 78 (December 2003) (Fraser Institute).

35. "Canada's Asylum System: A Threat to U.S. Security," Panel Discussion Transcript, Center for Immigration Studies (22 August 2002).

36. *9/11 and Terrorist Travel*, p. 53.

37. "World Refugee Survey 2003 Country Report," U.S. Committee for Refugees. Report, accessed at www.refugees.org/world/countryrpt/amer_carib/2003/ mexico.cfm (10 September 2004).

38. The United States' processing of Mexicans' requests for visas has also been questioned. See United States Embassy press release, "Temporary Suspension of Visa Processing in U.S. Consulate General in Ciudad Juarez," rev. 20 June 2003, accessed at www.fullerton.edu/international/TRAVELVISA/Mexico VisaProcessing.htm (10 September 2004).

39. "Patterns of Global Terrorism Report 2001," Office of Counterterrorism, Department of State (21 May 2002).

40. "Patterns of Global Terrorism 2003," Office of the Coordinator for Counterterrorism (29 April 2004).

41. See B. W. Boehm, *Software Engineering Economics* (New York: Prentice Hall, 1981); L. Putnam, *Measures for Excellence: Reliable Software on Time, within Budget* (New York: Yowder, 1992); Lance Sherry, *Four Habits of Highly Effective Software Development Managers*, Software Development (2001); R. S. Silberglitt and Lance Sherry, "A Decision Framework for Prioritizing Industrial Materials Research and Development," MR-1558-NREL (2002).

Civil Aviation in the United States: Security Before and After 9/11

Admiral Cathal "Irish" Flynn (Retired)
TranSecure, Inc.

Art Kosatka
CEO, TranSecure, Inc.

THE FOUNDATIONS OF AVIATION SECURITY AND THE PROLOGUE TO 9/11

Aviation security in the United States before 9/11 has been described as on a peacetime footing, suggesting that it might now be on a wartime footing. But such terms are inappropriate for civil aviation, which must have effective security, decade after decade, against attacks that occur infrequently and, as often as not, when the United States is not consciously engaged in an international conflict. This was the case in December 1988, when Pan Am 103 was destroyed; in January 1995, when the Bojinka plot to destroy perhaps 12 U.S. airliners in flight was foiled; and on 9/11.

The United States' aviation security programs in effect on 9/11, administered and regulated by the Federal Aviation Administration (FAA), had evolved over five decades. They were designed to protect passengers, the public, and airline and airport employees from armed attacks, hijackings, and bombings. They were also important in national security, to prevent the recurrence of attacks such as the bombing of Pan Am 103 and the prolonged hijacking of TWA 847 in 1985 three years earlier.

The programs covered domestic airports and flights within the United States, flights of U.S. airliners worldwide, foreign-carrier flights to and from the United States, and the security of the airports from which all these flights originated. Terrorism was the gravest threat, but the programs were also directed against the repetition of crimes such as hijacking to extort money from airlines, the planting of bombs in the luggage of unsuspecting family members (in order to collect their life insurance when they died as the airliner exploded), and the deliberate crashing of an airliner by a recently fired airline employee.

Aviation security was implemented through regulation of carriers, indirect air carriers (the regulatory term for cargo consolidators and freight forwarders), and airports. American law gave the regulated parties substantial protection against arbitrary action by FAA. The regulations came into effect through a process of public notice and comment, followed by FAA's exhaustive analysis of the comments and of costs and benefits, and occasionally by issuance of a revised notice and repetition of comment and analysis. During this long process, the public might question the necessity and appropriateness of a proposed rule; there might also be internal comment, from the Department of Transportation (DOT) and the Office of Management and Budget (OMB), both of which had in mind the views of Congress and the affected industries. Cost to the regulated industries was not the only point of interest to DOT and OMB; they were also concerned about public acceptance and effects on civil liberties (with the Justice Department commenting on impermissible discrimination, such as any based on ethnicity). In sum, the bar for new regulations was set high, and bureaucratic friction slowed the process to a crawl.

When the level of threat was high, FAA could avoid formal procedures by issuing emergency program amendments or security directives, which were intended to be used narrowly and for limited periods. They were not a legally permissible means of imposing long-term, costly demands on the regulated entities.

By 1995, FAA was increasingly aware of a threat by middle eastern terrorists to aviation within the United States and concluded that it could not maintain adequate security by depending on these emergency powers. The baseline of security—the content and effectiveness of the permanent carrier and airport programs—had to be raised. FAA also believed that a broad consensus was needed for permanent improvements, many of which would be expensive and burdensome. That consensus was achieved by the White House Commission on Aviation Safety and Security, also called the Gore Commission (after its chair, Vice President Al Gore). The commission was formed soon after the loss of TWA flight 800 on 17 July 1996 and delivered its final report on 17 February 1997. The report—which gave important direction, authority, and resources for FAA's work in the following years—concluded that protecting civil aviation was essential to national security, that the government therefore should pay at least part of the cost of new equipment, and that FAA's recommended baseline improvements should be implemented.

However, the report was in some respects disappointing. Even though the directors of the Central Intelligence Agency (CIA) and the FBI were among the commission's members, it rather discounted the threat to civil aviation from middle eastern terrorists such as Usama bin Ladin and his adherents (who had bombed the World Trade Center in 1993), seeming to suggest that individual American fanatics such as Timothy McVeigh (who bombed the federal building in Oklahoma City in 1995) posed an equal threat. It thus obscured the very different motivations, objectives, capabilities, and attributes of the two categories of terrorists. By 1996, all the credible intelligence that would be received before 9/11 about the interest of bin Ladin's adherents in using aircraft to attack buildings was already in the hands of the CIA and FBI; but even so, the Gore Commission made no mention of aircraft as a possible means of attack. Instead, it emphasized bombs and mentioned shoulder-fired missiles. It recommended an annual budget of only $100 million to buy and install explosives detection equipment for screening luggage in airports. With so little funding, the screening of all checked bags could not be achieved in less than 20 years; this strongly implied that the commission saw no imminent terrorist threat to civil aviation.

In retrospect, particularly since 9/11, the Gore Commission's analysis of civil aviation seems cursory. Surprisingly, the 9/11 Commission report also seems ambiguous, hasty, and dismissive regarding civil aviation security from now on. We will come back to this important point.

By 2001, FAA and other federal agencies and regulated entities had made substantial progress in improving baseline security. The airlines had implemented Computer-Assisted Passenger Pre-Screening (CAPPS) for checked baggage. The bags selected by

CAPPS were either "matched" (not put on board unless the passenger was also on board) or screened by an explosives detection system (EDS), which is FAA-certified equipment capable of detecting a small quantity of explosives in a packed bag. Again, since the directors of the CIA and FBI were members of the Gore Commission, it is odd that the commission had recommended bag-matching, which is ineffectual against a suicide bomber. Either these two leaders of national intelligence thought suicidal attacks against aviation in the United States improbable or (an alternative that strains belief) they did not give much thought to the matter at all.

FAA, realizing that CAPPS was not infallible, regarded CAPPS-based checked baggage security as an interim measure, to be replaced altogether by EDS screening as soon as funding permitted, as the Gore Commission had recommended. In contrast, CAPPS was not used at the checkpoints, where everyone was screened—passengers and persons accompanying them to and from the gates, workers at concessions within the airports' "sterile areas," aircrews, other employees, and their belongings.

To improve the checkpoints' detection of weapons and especially improvised explosive devices (IEDs, bombs), which were considered the principal danger, FAA used a portion of its new $100 million annual capital budget to deploy improved X-ray sets, 420 of them by 2001. The X-ray sets incorporate Threat Image Detection (TID), which at random intervals projects fictitious images of IEDs, firearms, their disassembled components, and other weapons onto the operators' screens, thereby providing ongoing training, maintaining the operators' alertness, and measuring their performance objectively. FAA also installed 450 explosive trace detection units at checkpoints, and required that they be used continually to examine luggage and—indirectly—passengers. At the same time, FAA recognized that screening could not be improved merely by better equipment: direct, performance-based regulation and certification of the companies that conducted screening (under contracts with the air carriers) were needed. FAA expected to publish a final certification rule for screening companies in 2001.

FAA also used federal air marshals (FAMs) to deter hijacking. The FAMs were highly trained, disciplined, and prepared to use lethal force; but there were very few of them, and they were deployed almost exclusively on international flights, where intelligence indicated a much higher threat. Given the huge number of domestic flights, it was therefore highly unlikely that FAMs would be in position to defeat an actual hijacking.

FAA was not an intelligence agency, but it was expected to estimate terrorist threats to aviation, inform carriers and airports, give warnings of possible attacks, and draft the intelligence justifications for emergency amendments and directives. The 40 specialists in its security intelligence directorate received reports and other materials from the national intelligence agencies (CIA, NSA, FBI, and others), determined their relevance to aviation, and compiled the results in sanitized, useful form for distribution to the regulated entities. The intelligence staff also gave threat briefings to managers of air carriers and airport security. Significantly, in the context of 9/11, the briefings included the fact that one of the people arrested as conspirators in the Bojinka plot had thought of crashing aircraft into buildings. This raises the question why FAA did not then prepare more effective defenses against such an attack. The answer may suggest why known vulnerabilities persist in aviation security—even today, when, according to the government, al-Qaida may be active in the United States and may be planning to attack air transport again.

The first reason was ignorance of effects. FAA did not realize that an airliner's impact could cause buildings like the towers of the World Trade Center to collapse, and therefore did not appreciate how attractive such an attack would be to Usama bin Ladin.

Nor did FAA see how such an attack could succeed. It seemed impossible that an aircrew could be coerced into flying into the target—the pilots, in extremis, with guns at their heads, would surely miss deliberately—and so this form of attack seemed very unlikely. Equally unlikely was any scenario in which al-Qaida recruited qualified pilots from middle eastern or other airlines to become suicidal terrorists.

Had FAA thought more thoroughly about how al-Qaida might actually succeed with an attack of this type, it might have reasoned that the terrorists would not have to be fully competent pilots. They would not need to know how to take off or land, or how to fly in anything other than clear skies in daylight. FAA might then have alerted the intelligence community to look, at home and abroad, for indications of terrorists preparing to attack in this way. FAA might also have reasoned that in this form of hijacking, the terrorists would not need firearms, because they would never have to hold out, on the ground, against highly armed FBI or military forces when negotiations failed. Not having understood the potential new form of attack, FAA opted for the usual defense against hijacking: primarily preboarding screening of passengers and their cabin luggage, and control of access to airliners and their contents on airport ramps. FAA did not even change the decades-old policy of permitting passengers to bring small knives aboard.

Granted, if the FAA had figured out how such attacks might be made, it would still have faced considerable difficulty in changing the security program. Hardening cockpit doors—given its cost and safety effects—would have required formal rule making. Lowering the settings on metal detectors and searching for blades would have lengthened checkpoint waiting lines, particularly because the emphasis on detecting improvised explosive devices would have continued. To prevent chaos at checkpoints, escorts ("meeters and greeters") would have had to be prohibited from entering the sterile concourses. All aircrews and passengers would have had to be informed of the new threat and the necessity to resist any attempt to take control of an aircraft in flight. That would have had to be done with great care. An unruly airline passenger had already died as a result of being forcibly restrained by the crew and other passengers; any additional deaths would have been ascribed to FAA's seemingly exaggerated warnings of a threat that then never eventuated. These countermeasures, particularly hardening cockpit doors (at a cost of hundreds of millions of dollars) and educating the public about the new threat, could not have been effected unless the president had clearly told Congress and the public that the terrorist threat had risen to a dangerous level. In hindsight, that would probably not have happened in 1998, 1999, or 2000, because no credible intelligence related to this form of attack was received after 1996, because the directors of the CIA and FBI had not thought it worth mentioning in the Gore Commission's report, and because the domestic threat level (except in December 1999) was considered low. Nor was it likely to happen in 2001: the 9/11 Commission has revealed that before 9/11, the government's appreciation of the terrorist threat was uneven.

The institutional myopia and obstacles that kept FAA from understanding, and countering, the threat of airliners as missiles suggests why many vulnerabilities remain in civil aviation. We will return to this point with relation to actions since 9/11 and since the recommendations of the 9/11 Commission.

STRENGTHENING CIVIL AVIATION SECURITY SINCE 9/11

Immediately after 9/11, the executive branch responded quickly and effectively. FAA directed the regulated entities to implement security program amendments to deal with the new form of threat and permit resumption of flights. The publicly visible changes included permitting only ticketed passengers (not escorts) to enter the sterile areas, thereby giving additional time per passenger for the closer screening needed to find small blades and permitting the use of CAPPS to select passengers for secondary screening. There were other, less visible changes, such as prohibition of most cargo on passenger flights. To an unprecedented extent, general aviation operations were restricted. In sum, FAA and the regulated entities responded comprehensively and began to restore public confidence.

Perhaps understandably, since it was dealing with many immediate operational challenges, the executive branch, including FAA, was slow to produce a comprehensive new plan for aviation security. Congress filled that void, held hearings, and by November 2001 passed the Aviation and Transportation Security Act (ATSA). Since then, most effort has focused on three mandates of ATSA: (1) establish the Transportation Security Administration (TSA); (2) form a screening workforce of TSA employees, replacing by November 2002 the screeners previously employed by the airlines' contracted security companies; and (3) by December 2002 screen all checked bags with EDS.

Initially, the staff of TSA consisted of security specialists transferred from FAA. Newer members of TSA's headquarters and field staffs, which have grown large (since TSA is responsible for surface and subway transportation as well as aviation), seemed to comprise many former law enforcement and military personnel, but relatively few with experience in air transport. TSA's growing pains have been aggravated by having to reintegrate into the Department of Homeland Security (DHS), which was established later and is itself in flux; and by frequent changes among senior executives, including having three administrators in not quite three years.

PASSENGER AND BAGGAGE SCREENING

TSA did field—by the deadline set in ATSA—federal screeners (except for the screeners employed by private-sector companies at five airports, under a comparison trial required by ATSA). The hiring of 45,000 screeners (25,000 for preboarding checkpoints and 20,000 to screen checked baggage) was marred by cost overruns of human resources contractors and by mistakes in background checks. There were initial misallocations of staff; consequently, some airports had too few screeners while in others TSA was said to mean "thousands standing around."

TSA has worked through those initial problems, and the public has generally welcomed the new, apparently more diligent screeners. Improved compensation and working conditions have reduced turnover; and stability in the workforce would permit effective continuing training in the many difficult tasks screeners perform, such as interpreting X-ray images. TSA's new checkpoint equipment —1,733 walk-through metal detectors; 1,392 improved X-ray sets; 1,219 explosives trace detectors—also should boost effectiveness. It was therefore disappointing that the DHS inspector general reported to Congress in April 2004 that with regard to rates of detection (the only measure that ultimately matters), the new screeners were no better than (or just as bad as) the employees of the much-criticized screening companies before 9/11. Possibly, overall performance has been improved since the inspector general's report, but observation of checkpoints indicates strongly that their ability to detect improvised explosive devices (IEDs, bombs) in cabin luggage is still far below what it could be, given the stability of the workforce. Obviously, the effectiveness of the federal screeners should be raised to the highest sustainable level, establishing a new baseline for performance. Such a baseline is needed to evaluate the competence of the private companies that may soon take over screening at many airports, under an "opt out" (of federal screening) provision of ATSA.

In many respects, TSA and its systems integration contractors, equipment manufacturers, airports, and airlines together accomplished something astounding in deploying the systems and training the staff needed to screen nearly all checked bags at U.S. airports by 31 December 2002. The equipment included about 1,100 certified EDSs (computed X-ray tomography sets, akin to CAT scans in hospitals) and 5,400 explosives trace detectors. Its operation required selection and training of 20,000 personnel. At some airports, the objective of screening all bags was not met until later in 2003, but Congress willingly gave the extension, appreciating the real progress made in so short a time; also, at 22 airports as of mid-2004, according to the ranking member of the House Aviation Subcommittee (which very properly did not identify these airports), some bags were still not being screened. Those points are quibbles. But it is not quibbling to note that some screening procedures are insufficiently stringent and are acceptable only in the short run, as an expedient needed to cope with high volumes of bags. In the longer run they must be replaced with procedures that have a higher probability of detecting bombs in bags. And it is significant that the deadlines imposed by Congress could be met only by installing many individual screening stations in the lobbies of most airports—an inefficient, labor-intensive arrangement that creates vulnerabilities, both in the control of screening processes and by adding to crowding in the lobbies, where armed attacks and bombings are possible. It is now generally accepted that screening stations must be removed from lobbies and replaced by EDSs integrated into the airports' baggage-handling systems. This is a necessary change, but an expensive one. The installation of in-line screening systems, as they are called, will cost several hundred million dollars at each of many large airports, and the total cost for such systems in all the airports that need them is likely to exceed $5 billion.

Although TSA has taken over the screening of passengers and baggage, and although there is now a much larger corps of FAMs, aviation security remains largely a responsibility of airports and carriers, responding to TSA regulations. Screening and FAMs protect against only two possible terrorist tactics for attacking civil aviation: bombs placed in checked bags or carried into airliner cabins by passengers, and hijackings. Also, TSA's screening is confined to airports in the United States; at foreign airports from which U.S. airliners fly, screening remains as it was before 9/11—a responsibility of airlines, now regulated and inspected by TSA. (One seeming contradiction of ATSA is that it prohibits all but U.S. citizens from becoming screeners in the United States, where immigrants' trustworthiness could be established by the federal government; but it continues to permit foreign citizens to perform this function for U.S. airlines abroad, where the ability of the U.S. government to verify backgrounds and trustworthiness is severely limited, indeed non-existent in many countries, and the threat of terrorism is often high. This contrasts with the practice of El Al, which employs its own government-vetted, predominantly Israeli, screeners abroad.)

Passengers, their checked bags, and their carry-on bags are only three of many possible means, or "vectors," of terrorism. Others include air cargo and surface-to-air missiles.

AIR CARGO

Cargo carried on passenger airliners is an obvious vector. A bomb in an airliner's cargo is just as destructive as one in a checked bag. Cargo security now generally depends, as it depended before 9/11, on a "known shipper" process, under which cargo is deemed secure if the shipping company meets certain criteria of apparent trustworthiness. That is a slim reed on which to rest the lives of crews and passengers. There are some 500,000 such known shippers in the United States at any time, a shifting population as companies go into and out of business. Assuming that on average each company has two employees who have access to the cargo and know that it will be shipped by air, the effectiveness of the known shipper regime depends on the trustworthiness of 1 million people—each able to put a bomb into air cargo, but none subject to a government background check. That circumstance alone makes known shipper unreliable, but there is further cause for concern: testing has shown that bogus entities, wholly made-up fronts, could readily become known shippers. TSA, on the advice of industry representatives, has drafted stronger cargo security measures.

In 2005 TSA issues a Notice of Proposed Rulemaking to implement these measures. The proposed rulemaking would require the adoption of security measures throughout the air cargo supply chain, and would impose significant barriers to terrorists seeking to use the air cargo transportation system for malicious purposes. To secure the air cargo supply chain, TSA is developing and implementing a layered security system that uses a combination of information- and technology-based solutions, says the agency. Initiatives include:

- Creating a new mandatory security regime for domestic and foreign air carriers in all-cargo operations using aircraft with a maximum certificated takeoff weight of more than 100,309 pounds.

- Creating requirements for foreign air carriers in all-cargo operations with aircraft having a maximum certificated takeoff weight of more than 12,500 pounds but no more than 100,309 pounds.
- Creating Security Threat Assessments on individuals with unescorted access to cargo.
- Enhancing existing requirements for indirect air carriers (freight forwarders).
- Codifying and further strengthening the Known Shipper program.

TSA has also initiated prototype projects to screen a portion of the cargo shipped from five airports, using EDSs of the type used to screen checked baggage. If TSA concludes that procedures such as known shipper are inadequate and that EDS screening of cargo is needed, it may not cost quite as much as screening checked baggage, but it probably will be of the same order of magnitude: billions of dollars for equipment and installations, and hundreds of millions annually for operating costs.

SURFACE-TO-AIR MISSILES

Airliners are vulnerable to surface-to-air missiles. The Gore Commission was particularly concerned about shoulder-fired missiles and recommended that the Defense Department lead a study of the threat and possible countermeasures. The study established that the global availability of missiles, and their ease of use, indeed makes them a serious threat. It identified various countermeasures—emergency air traffic control procedures; defensive systems such as jammers that might be installed on airliners, etc.—but none had been implemented by 2001. A missile attack by al-Qaida on an Israeli airliner at Mombassa, Kenya, in November 2002 led the U.S. government to address this threat more intensively. DHS has awarded contracts to test the installation and operation of jammers on airliners. If the tests are successful, the government will have to decide whether to install the jammers on airliners, at an initial cost of billions of dollars and recurring annual costs in the hundreds of millions, or accept an unmitigated danger.

COST

At this point, a pattern of asymmetry may be apparent. Terrorists can carry out devastating attacks on airliners, using bombs (in checked bags, or carried into the cabin, or in cargo), hijackings, or missiles, at a cost of tens of thousands or at most hundreds of thousands of dollars. The cost of defending each possible attack vector effectively goes into billions of dollars. But the effects of a successful attack can be immense—in addition to loss of life, the national economic loss can be in the hundreds of billions of dollars.

Al-Qaida fully appreciates such asymmetry. In a tape made soon after 9/11, Usama bin Ladin said that "the target is the enemy's economy" and urged his followers to "strike the pillars of the enemy's economy." Al-Qaida's leaders seem to put air transport at or near the top of their list of economic pillars. They seem to grasp that air travel is to a great extent discretionary, and that many people will stop flying, at least for a few years, if terrorist attacks make it seem too dangerous. New attacks could devastate air transport. Airlines—several of which are already in financial straits—might go out of business; hotels, tourism, and aircraft manufacturers and their suppliers would be hard hit. The ripple effects, including a loss of public confidence, could put the U.S. economy into a recession.

EDUCATE PUBLIC

Threats to many vectors confront policy makers with a choice: defend them all adequately, so as to defer or disrupt attacks; or leave some with inadequate defense. Israel and its airlines defend all the vectors; the United States and its air transport industry still do not. The 9/11 Commission report suggests applying risk management to aviation security, perhaps implying that vulnerabilities should be ranked according to their gravity and their amenability to remedies, and that the least grave and most difficult to fix might be allowed to persist, with acceptance of the risk they pose. But while risk management is a rational way to deal with natural perils (storms, earthquakes, and the like), accidents, and even common crimes such as theft, it may break down in the face of al-Qaida's suicidal determination and versatility. Any vector left without adequate defense will ultimately come to al-Qaida's attention, through reconnaissance or research, and it will then become a preferred vector for terrorism. On the other hand, a comprehensive defense of all vectors is hugely expensive. El Al and the government of Israel spend $65 million every year to defend Israel's 35 airliners. The United States, which can assume a similar level of threat and has some 5,000 passenger airliners and many planes that carry only cargo, would probably have to spend about $9 billion annually—i.e., $15 per passenger flight.

The United States could afford this, but there is considerable hesitation to pay such a sum for comprehensive defense. Other factors also militate against it. There is also some reluctance to ask the public, particularly air travelers, to cooperate in reducing vulnerabilities. Even if FAA had discerned the new suicidal form of hijacking, it might have hesitated to inform the public, out of concern about fatal overreactions to unruly passengers or simply not to frighten people unnecessarily. Similarly, air passengers today are not being asked to take sensible steps to reduce their vulnerability. The national response to two forms of threat—surface-to-air missiles and attacks in airports—reveals this hesitation to engage the public in defense.

The slant range of shoulder-fired missiles is such that they can be launched from anywhere in a large ground area (hundreds of square miles) under and to the sides of an airport's approach and departure flight paths. When a missile is fired, the most useful immediate reports can, potentially, come from members of the public—if there has been some public education on what to look for and how to report it. Even more usefully, education might enable members of the public to recognize and report terrorists preparing to fire. But there is no such public education program, even though the government thinks the threat sufficiently grave to contemplate spending billions on aircraft-mounted countermeasures.

The history of terrorist attacks also tells al-Qaida that destruction of airliners is not the only way to terrorize people to the extent that they will stop flying. Demonstrated perils at any step of air travel— e.g., several bombings in publicly accessible, unsecured areas of airports—will have similar effects. Baggage claim areas for domestic flights are particularly vulnerable. They are crowded at predictable times; there are many bags on the floor and carousels; people carrying bags can come in from the street and mingle in the throngs. These baggage claim areas invite attacks with suitcase bombs. The terrorists need not be suicidal; they can leave a suitcase and walk away. As soon as practicable, domestic baggage claim should be enclosed in every airport's sterile area, where international baggage claim is now generally situated. Until then, the public should be made aware of the peril and the steps individuals should take to lessen it. For instance, by helping to reduce crowding in the claim areas, passengers make counterterrorist surveillance more practical, reduce the probability of being attacked, and lessen casualties when there is an attack. Passengers should be educated: travel light; if possible, to avoid checking bags; and don't have friends or relatives meet them inside airport terminals or accompany them into baggage claim. But there is no such public education campaign. On 9/11, the passengers on United flight 93 counterattacked; this was a dramatic demonstration that an informed public can deter an attack or blunt its effect, so it is to be hoped that public education in aviation security will soon be offered.

9/11 COMMISSION REPORT

The 9/11 Commission report is valuable in many respects. It complements earlier staff statements in vividly describing the attacks, how they were planned, and the vulnerabilities they exploited. It has a very useful section, "Institutionalizing Imagination: The Case of Aircraft as Weapons" (pp. 344–8), on how intelligence, sound reasoning, and an open mind can forestall surprise attacks. On the other hand, its brief recommendations for aviation and transportation security (pp. 390–3) seem superficial, incomplete, and ambiguous. Its treatment of funding for aviation security cannot be helpful when TSA deals with OMB and the congressional appropriations committees, which are reluctant to fund aviation security.

The 9/11 Commission report comments that over 90 percent of TSA's annual $5.3 billion budget has been spent on aviation security, mostly on screening passengers and baggage "to fight the last war"—i.e., that too much is being spent on measures no longer needed. This criticism is hardly justified. It is foolhardy to think that undefended passengers and baggage would not again become vectors of attack. Al-Qaida remains an undefeated, potent force, so one could ask when guarding against its attacks could have become "the last war." Just as ambiguously, elsewhere this same brief section recommends very expensive improvements in passenger and baggage screening.

The report asserts that hard choices must be made in allocating limited resources for transportation (including aviation) security. It does not seem to consider that the limits on resources—particularly government funding—may be overrestrictive and should be relaxed. The 9/11 Commission thus may be repeating an error of its predecessors: recommending that agencies implement a list of needed improvements, while failing to endorse the necessary funding.

Recommending a layered security system, the report says it must take into consideration the "full array of possible enemy attacks, such as insiders, suicide terrorism, or standoff attack." It goes on to say, "Each layer must be effective in its own right. Each must be supported by other layers that are redundant and coordinated." The use of *must* implies that TSA would have little discretion in responding to the report's specific recommendations concerning layers of aviation security.

INSIDER THREAT

The standoff (missile) attack has already been considered in this chapter. The insider enemy has not. That threat relates to the challenges of access controls, screening, and background checks. Access controls pertain to the secure areas of airports, such as the "security identification display area" (SIDA). They include perimeter barriers (fences, walls), controls at points of entry, identification media, challenge procedures, guards, and patrols. TSA is testing improved access control technologies at several airports, and the successful systems will ultimately be installed at most airports. But these measures only prevent unauthorized persons from entering the designated areas; they do not address the threat of terrorists who are authorized employees—insiders. This is not an insignificant concern; some 600,000 employees of airports, airlines, contractors, and other entities are an authorized unescorted presence within the SIDAs of airports, and thus have access to parked airliners or to materials (such as bags, cargo, and catering items) that will be loaded into them. These employees can readily place contraband in the aircraft; and many, including employees of federal agencies, have been arrested for moving drugs in this manner. Bombs, being smaller, could be inserted even more easily.

ATSA recognizes the "insider threat" and mandates screening of all persons, objects, and vehicles entering the air operations areas of airports, with stringency equivalent to passenger preboard screening. This goal is laudable but practically impossible. Some ramp workers need to carry tools, including knives. Packaged with care and concealed in a vehicle, the very small quantity of explosives needed to destroy an aircraft in flight cannot realistically be detected. A terrorist insider can bring bomb components into the SIDA separately, on successive entrances, and then assemble them. Bombs or their components, and weapons, can be passed through or over fences. And insiders really do not need bombs or weapons to be lethal; if suicidal, they can, for example, drive vehicles to collide catastrophically with airliners, a form of attack analogous to what happened on 9/11.

An alternative to physical screening is to establish every ramp worker's trustworthiness. The current criteria—proof of citizenship or appropriate immigration status, and a satisfactory check for a criminal history—are inadequate; al-Qaida's moles will not have criminal records. TSA has mentioned link analysis as a means of establishing trustworthiness; it may be effective, if the links of concern have been comprehensively established, and if applicants complete their personal history forms truthfully. Apparently, link analysis would have to be buttressed by background investigations of some kind. Even then, an additional layer of security, perhaps comprising surveillance and continuing investigations (including use of informants), will be needed at airports to counter the insider threat. All that will be expensive.

Establishing trustworthiness (or its untrustworthiness) is a challenge facing TSA as it complies with the recommendation of the 9/11 report to implement a successor to CAPPS. In 2002, TSA confidently predicted implementation of CAPPS II later the same year. That was not to be, and the secretary of Homeland Security recently announced the abandonment of CAPPS II, after $100 million had been spent trying to develop it. This cannot be viewed as anything other than a debacle, but it is to be hoped that the experience will help TSA develop a new passenger categorization system called Secure Flight. It is certainly needed, as a basis for implementing another of the report's recommendations: to screen passengers for explosives concealed in or under their clothing.

EXPLOSIVES

Technology is available to screen people for concealed explosives. TSA has set up explosives trace detection portals at several airports, to test their effectiveness and practicality. They will need to be augmented by additional systems, in order to resolve their alarms, which can have innocuous causes (such as the nitroglycerine prescribed for treatment of angina, and minuscule explosives traces on miners, soldiers, or construction workers) but may also have been caused by actual explosives carried by a terrorist. "Alarm resolution" requires either a full-body scan by a backscatter X-ray or millimeter wave system, to which some passengers may object because the images reveal their bodies; or a manual search (called a pat-down, but to be effective it really amounts to an insistent groping of the entire clothed body), to which even more passengers would probably object.

Although the 9/11 Commission report does not mention this, the existing checkpoints are also inherently deficient in detecting explosives in bags. Again, more effective technologies—such as EDS, now used to screen checked baggage—are available and, to be consistent with more stringent body screening, should be deployed.

Effective EDSs for passengers and their carry-on bags are much more expensive than the equipment now generally installed. The alarm resolution procedures are inconvenient, intrusive, and possibly embarrassing, and they take more time. They cannot practically be applied to all passengers, but Secure Flight, if it confidently categorizes passengers into a large safe majority whose persons and bags can be minimally screened, and a small minority requiring intensive screening, will allow real improvements in the effectiveness of checkpoints. Significant additional benefits would accrue from using Secure Flight in screening checked baggage.

With regard to screening checked baggage, the 9/11 Commission report advises TSA to remove EDSs from airport lobbies and reinstall them in-line, integrated in the airports' baggage handling systems. TSA has long been committed to this reinstallation, but the slow pace is due largely to inadequate appropriations. The report's suggestion that the air transport industry should pay a portion of the cost seems not to recognize that airports are already paying, or preparing to pay, a substantial share. This could have the pernicious effect of making appropriations committees even less willing to fund the reinstallations adequately.

The report recommends that TSA intensify its efforts to screen potentially dangerous cargo. This recommendation seems not to recognize that all cargo is potentially dangerous unless the trustworthiness of everyone who has access to it has been established. Nevertheless, the idea has considerable merit, and it may improve TSA's prospects of obtaining funds for screening cargo. There is also merit in the recommendation to deploy a hardened container on every passenger airliner that also carries cargo. These containers, called hardened unit load devices (HULDs), developed under FAA and TSA sponsorship, can now safely contain the detonation of bombs significantly larger and more powerful than the one that destroyed Pan Am 103, a Boeing 747, in flight.

HULD complements screening; in combination they provide much greater protection against bombs than the sum of both applied separately. The cost of HULD, though not trivial, is considerably less than that of some other, similarly effective measures now being implemented.

CONCLUSION

On 25 August 2004, at a hearing by the House Aviation Subcommittee on the recommendations of the 9/11 Commission, Representative DeFazio, the ranking minority member, expressed disappointment with the report's sketchy treatment of aviation security, calling it thin gruel. Commissioner Lehman did not disagree, but said that a paper written by the commission's staff, which would cover the topic thoroughly, would soon follow the report. The monograph, titled "Staff Report, August 26, 2004", has since been redacted and released to the public. It adds some detail to the commission report's description of the four fatal flights and the lapses in intelligence and security that made them so vulnerable. It does not, however, add anything to the main report's scant treatment of what now needs to be done to make civil aviation really secure. Judging by the public document, the staff, as well as the commissioners, found it easier to analyze what happened on 9/11 than to propose, even in outline form, a security strategy for the future. In any case, those responsible for aviation security must be relieved that the commission has not just handed them an unconnected list of improvements called essential, without the authority and resources needed for their implementation. Such a list would not have been the first of its kind.

In the absence of a blueprint from the commission, Congress continues to try to fill the strategic void by mandating additional measures to deal with specific threats to aviation, often without appropriating the funds needed for their implementation. And it is reported that TSA, under its fourth administrator, will soon be radically reorganized. Once again, the nation must hope that stability will be achieved in the executive branch, clear strategic vision will follow, and then—at long last—we may make steady progress in the exacting mission of defending civil aviation against our ferocious enemies.

CHAPTER 39

Port and Maritime Security

Carl Bentzel, J.D., LL.M.
Advisor for Homeland Security, DCI Group LLC;
Former Senior Advisor, U.S. Senate Committee on Commerce,
Science, and Transportation

THE U.S. MARITIME TRANSPORTATION SYSTEM

In September 1999, according to *An Assessment of the U.S. Marine Transportation System*, a report by the Department of Transportation (DOT), the United States had more than 1,000 harbor channels and 25,000 miles of inland, intracoastal, and coastal waterways, serving over 300 ports, with more than 3,700 passenger and cargo terminals. These waterways and ports linked to 152,000 miles of railways, 460,000 miles of underground pipelines, and 45,000 miles of interstate highways. Annually, the U.S. marine transportation system (MTS) moves more than 2 billion tons of domestic and international freight, imports 3.3 billion tons of domestically used oil, transports 134 million passengers by ferry, and serves 78 million Americans engaged in recreational boating, and more than 5 million cruise ship passengers. Waterborne cargo contributed more than $742 billion to the U.S. gross domestic product (GDP) and created employment for more than 13 million Americans. These figures represented a dramatic growth in waterborne commerce, and they were expected to double over the next 20 years.

Also, according to DOT,[1] the United States is the world's largest merchandise trading nation. The MTS is vital not only to U.S. retailing and manufacturing but also to the energy sector and to sectors that rely on energy-generating commodities, such as petroleum. Refineries and distribution hubs for petroleum products are centered in just a few major seaports around the United States; and over 60 percent of all petroleum used in the United States is imported by vessels into one of those hubs.

In 2001, some 5,400 commercial ships made more than 60,000 calls at U.S. ports. Most ships had foreign owners and crews; less than 3 percent of all U.S. overseas trade was carried by U.S.-flag vessels.[2] International ocean shipping is a very open trading market in which about two-thirds of the ships operate under flag-of-convenience registries such as Panama and Liberia. Often, ownership of such vessels is difficult to identify because little disclosure has been required; and legal recourse against foreign shipping lines is restricted.

The MTS is vitally important to the Department of Defense (DOD). DOT and DOD have designated 17 strategic seaports for military mobilization, which relies almost exclusively on shipping for the overseas transportation of military equipment and supplies. Military conflicts require the immediate and rapid transportation of oversize equipment, such as tanks and artillery; and the military also relies on maritime transportation for the longer-term transport of military supplies. Any impediment to utilization of U.S. ports could hamper a military mobilization.

These facts suggest the troubling issue of how to facilitate maritime trade expansion while still protecting our maritime borders from crime, threats of terrorism, or threats to our ability to mobilize our armed forces.

REGULATION OF PORT AUTHORITIES

Port authorities in the United States are instruments of state or local governments. Seaport authorities vary in size and composition: some span miles of waterfront; others are relatively compact. A seaport can exert control over business practices as an owner-operator, or can function solely as a landlord; also, some marine terminals are privately owned and operated. Control of security is even more complex to discern than operational control.

The United States has no national port authority. Jurisdiction is shared by the federal government and state and local governments. Under the Constitution, states are given regulatory authority.

However, the federal government does have the authority to regulate navigable waterways, a task largely delegated to the U.S. Army Corps of Engineers and the U.S. Coast Guard. The federal government also has the right to regulate interstate and foreign commerce, and thus to regulate port practices, though it cannot act so as to favor or disfavor any port.[3] Historically, however, the federal government has not exercised its authority to regulate or police U.S. seaports, except during wars and national security crises.

The major federal authorities at U.S. seaports are Customs and Border Protection (CBP, previously the Customs Service) and the Coast Guard. CBP ensures that all goods and persons entering the United States do so in accordance with our laws and regulations. It also has the authority to deal with violations of U.S. export laws, embargoes, and economic trade sanctions; and it can conduct warrantless searches and seizures at U.S. borders (land, air, and sea).

The Coast Guard was first given authority to protect seaports from aggression during World War I, under the Espionage Act of 1917. This act included the safeguarding of waterfront property, supervision of vessel movements, establishment of anchorages and restricted areas, and the right to control and remove people aboard ships. In June 1940, during World War II, President Franklin Roosevelt gave the Coast Guard functions that other government agencies regulating maritime commerce had previously overseen. By the end of the war, concerns about sabotage had resulted in almost exclusive federal control of shipping and access into and out of ports, and the Coast Guard's regulatory activities were supplemented by Port Security Units made up of civilian volunteers. Later, as a result of concerns about the spread of communism, President Harry Truman signed Executive Order (EO) 10173, implementing the Magnuson Act,[4] which authorized the Coast Guard to fulfill duties it had assumed during both world wars to ensure the security of U.S. ports "from subversive or clandestine attacks." The Coast Guard established security units at major ports of the United States to prevent sabotage and ensure the timely loading and sailing of merchant ships, and (controversially) had the power to check the backgrounds—and loyalty to the United States—of merchant sailors, longshoremen, warehouse employees, and harbor pilots. Beginning in August 1951 every vessel entering a U.S. anchorage had to notify the Customs Service of its intended destination and cargo 24 hours before arrival. The names of these vessels were passed to the appropriate "captain of the port," and Coast Guard patrol boats identified and checked each, boarding and examining those that appeared suspicious.[5] As the Cold War receded, so did control of port and maritime shipping. However, the Coast Guard captain of the port has wide authority to enforce security requirements related to marine safety, environmental protection, maritime law enforcement, and national security. Coast Guard personnel also have authority to exercise jurisdiction as if they were CBP officers and can conduct warrantless searches and seizures.

Because of fiscal constraints, the Customs Service traditionally focused on policing cargo entry, while the Coast Guard focused more on waterside activities. Consequently, physical or operational security functions were largely left to the state or private entities that operate and control the ports.

THE SEAPORT CRIME AND SECURITY COMMISSION

In 1999, President Clinton signed an executive memorandum establishing the Interagency Commission on Crime and Security in U.S. Seaports. The commission was to (1) analyze the nature and extent of serious crime and assess security; (2) provide an overview of the specific missions and authorities relevant to federal, state, and local government agencies as well as the private sector; (3) assess coordination among the federal agencies; and (4) recommend ways to improve the response of federal, state, and local governments to seaport crime.

General Findings

In August 2000, the commission concluded that crime was significant and extensive. Criminal activity at U.S. seaports includes importation of drugs and contraband; stowaways and alien smuggling; trade fraud and commercial smuggling; environmental crimes; cargo theft; and the unlawful exportation of controlled commodities, munitions, stolen property, and drug proceeds. Many of these actions violate federal law.

The commission also evaluated the threat posed by terrorism to U.S. seaports. It considered this threat low, but it considered vulnerability to an attack to be high. The commission believed that a terrorist attack had the potential to cause significant damage, mainly because of the openness of ports, the harm that could be caused by many cargoes, and the usual proximity of large populations living on waterways. It also found that, at the time, the general state of security ranged from poor to fair. Following is a summary:

- There were no widely accepted standards or guidelines for physical, procedural, and personnel security for seaports, although some ports were making impressive efforts.

- Often, there was little control of access to a seaport or to sensitive areas within it, either because no practices had been established or because enforcement was inconsistent. Many ports did not issue identification cards to personnel to restrict access to vessels, cargo receipt and delivery operations, and passenger processing operations. (This commission isn't mandated by the MTSA because this commission predates the MTSA.)

- At many seaports, firearms were not restricted.

- Many seaports relied on private security personnel who did not have the same expertise as regular police officers.

- Federal, state, and local law enforcement agencies frequently did cooperate with regard to security, for instance by sharing intelligence. But at some of the locations surveyed, representatives of the private sector were not sure which federal agency required reports of possible cargo thefts and other violations.

- No regular security-related local meetings were being held between law enforcement organizations (federal, state, or local), the trade, and port authorities, except at a few "strategic seaports" that had port readiness committees.

- The most prevalent and most frequently reported crime was drug smuggling. Drug smugglers seemed increasingly knowledgeable about the maritime shipping trade and were utilizing it.

- Smuggling of illegal aliens, sometimes by organized crime rings, was also a problem.

- Cargo theft—again, sometimes by organized criminals—was identified as another major problem.

- Export crime, including money-laundering and the unlawful export of controlled commodities such as munitions or arms, was also reported.[6]

The commission's major recommendation concerning crime was better data collection, which would improve the response and allow for a more targeted approach to law enforcement. Other recommendations included coordinating federal, state, and local law enforcement authorities; possibly monitoring cargo theft through the National Incident-Based Reporting System; and forming a national-level subcommittee to establish voluntary minimum guidelines for physical security at U.S. seaports.

Seaport Security and Terrorism

As noted above, the commission concluded in 2000 that the threat of terrorism to U.S. seaports was low (about the same as the threat to other U.S. infrastructure) but that vulnerability to terrorism was very high. It noted that seaports are relatively open and accessible and handle huge volumes of cargo, much of which could be sabotaged by terrorists for their own operations. Additionally, because seaports tend to be located close to large population bases and on waterway systems, terrorism at a seaport could cause widespread harm. For instance, the detonation of a bomb, the release of contaminants, or the smuggling of chemical or traditional weapons (to be used elsewhere) could affect many communities near a port; and an oil tanker or cruise ship could be taken over and intentionally crashed into critical or sensitive infrastructure.

Regarding vulnerability and security, the commission found that coordination among law enforcement officials was generally acceptable where FBI Joint Terrorism Task Forces existed. However, it emphasized that the existing task forces did not evaluate the vulnerability of U.S. seaports to secretive crimes such as smuggling and terrorism. The report recommended that the Coast Guard and FBI coordinate with relevant agencies to develop a system for categorizing physical and information infrastructure at seaports on the basis of vulnerability and threat. The commission also recommended that the FBI include seaports in the regular domestic terrorism surveys.

Finally, the commission said that the Coast Guard captain of the port
and the FBI should, annually, update and coordinate their respective
Maritime Counterterrorism Plans and Incident Contingency Plans,
and conduct exercises with other concerned federal, state, local,
and private entities.

THE ISPS CODE

In 2001–2002, the United States, through the activities of the U.S.
Coast Guard, sought an international treaty to adopt security
standards at ports throughout the world under the auspices of the
International Maritime Organization (IMO), in which the Coast Guard
is the lead U.S. entity representing the interests of the United States.
The United Nations had established IMO by treaty in 1948 to regulate
the international practices of ocean shipping; and before 9/11, IMO
had in turn concluded international treaties regulating the safe
operation of vessels. Soon after 9/11, the commandant of the Coast
Guard, Admiral James Loy, was instrumental after a yearlong effort
to have IMO adopt an international treaty on port security. In
December 2002, IMO agreed to the treaty.

The International Ship and Port Facility Security (ISPS) Code
is a comprehensive set of measures to enhance the security of ships
and port facilities, developed in response to the perceived threat after
9/11.[7] The code is implemented through the International Convention
for the Safety of Life at Sea (SOLAS, chap. XI-2, special measures to
enhance maritime security). The code has two parts, one mandatory and one not. General implementation is left to the SOLAS
contracting governments; more detailed implementation is a matter
for individual governments. Under the Law of the Sea,[8] a nation can
regulate the practices of vessels entering its ports, if such activity
affects its security. The Coast Guard (representing the U.S. government) advocated multilateral agreement that would parallel and
be consistent with U.S. enacted law; by negotiating the ISPS Code
in conformity with U.S. law, the administration was able to
avoid seeking Senate ratification of the treaty. By December 2002,
federal legislation and an international treaty regulating the
practices of shipping and ports with respect to their security
obligations had passed, and implementation of the law had been
set for 1 July 2004.

THE MARITIME TRANSPORTATION SECURITY ACT

Background of MTSA

Two years earlier, in July 2000, Senator Ernest "Fritz" Hollings, chairman of the Senate Committee on Commerce, Science, and Transportation, had introduced a bill (S. 2965) to codify many of the proposals, described above, of the Commission on Seaport Crime and Security. In October 2000, the committee heard testimony from the Coast Guard, Maritime Administration, Department of Justice, American Association of Port Authorities, and International Longshoremen's and Warehousemen's Union. The port authorities objected strongly to the bill, among other reasons, they thought that the issues did not need to be addressed at the federal level; the Longshoremen's Union argued that criminal background checks of employees were unnecessary and could deprive some innocent workers of their jobs.[9] In 2001, Hollings reintroduced a port security bill (S. 1214), and in July 2001 the committee held another hearing.[10] In August 2001, the bill was ordered to be reported favorably, without amendment. This was, of course, shortly before 9/11. The bill's passage might otherwise have been doubtful; but as a result of 9/11, S. 1214 became the Port and Maritime Security Act of 2002, which became P.L. 107-295, the Maritime Transportation Security Act (MTSA) of 2004. Immediately after 9/11, House and Senate committees held hearings on port security;[11] consequently, S. 1214 was expanded to address the threat of terrorism at seaports more directly. Also, Secretary of Transportation Norman Mineta requested some minor changes, including criminal penalties for crimes on the high seas. On 20 December 2001 the Senate approved S. 1214, though before passage it removed the criminal provisions (at the request of Senator Leahy of the Judiciary Committee).

Passage in the House of Representatives was more difficult. The major impediments were the provisions on cargo security and the issue of federal funding for the security mandates. A user fee had been proposed as a source of funds, but the industry objected; and to secure passage of the bill, Senator Hollings withdrew the fee and substituted a requirement that the administration report within six months of enactment its own proposal for funding the security mandates. (As of this writing, Congress had not received this report.) In November 2002 the House and Senate sent the act for the president's signature.

MTSA: The Final Product

The passage of MTSA reflected a need for change in U.S. policies: specifically, a greater degree of direct oversight of the practices of ocean shipping. Practically speaking, only one other mode of transportation—aviation—has been required to submit to the direct security and oversight of federal law enforcement. However, because of a long history of terrorism, aviation had evolved under the guidance of federal controls. After the passage of MTSA, port security became the second such area of transportation. In its case, though, the regulatory challenge was much greater because of the varied geography and the different constituencies involved.

MTSA directed the secretary of transportation to do the following: (1) Identify vessel types and U.S. port facilities at a high risk of a "transportation security incident," which was defined as an incident involving a significant loss of life, environmental damage, disruption of a transportation system, or economic disruption in a particular area. (2) Assess the vulnerability of U.S. port facilities and vessels that may be involved in a transportation security incident.

MTSA also required the secretary of transportation to prepare a National Maritime Transportation Security Plan for deterring transportation security incidents and for responding to any such incident that did occur. (To date, no plan has been finalized.) Components of the plan include:

1. Assignment of duties and responsibilities among federal departments and agencies and coordination with state and local governmental agencies
2. Identification of security resources
3. Procedures and techniques to be applied in deterrence
4. A system of surveillance and early notice
5. Designation of areas requiring an Area Maritime Transportation Security Plan and the identification of a federal maritime security coordinator (a Coast Guard official)
6. A plan for ensuring that the flow of cargo through U.S. ports is reestablished quickly after a transportation security

incident, including the recognition of certified Secure Systems of Transportation

MTSA has a series of planning and coordination requirements to refine the National Maritime Security plan, and requires the federal maritime security coordinator for each designated area to submit to the secretary of transportation an Area Maritime Transportation Security Plan. The Area Plans, when implemented in conjunction with the National Maritime Transportation Security Plan, must:

1. Be adequate to deter a transportation security incident to the maximum extent practicable
2. Describe the area and infrastructure covered
3. Describe its integration with other Area Maritime Transportation Security Plans
4. Include consultation and coordination with DOD

Another element of the interlocking provisions of MTSA requires owners or operators of vessels or facilities to prepare and submit to the secretary of transportation a vessel or facility security plan for deterring a transportation security incident. These plans are to be consistent with the National Maritime Transportation Security Plan and Area Plans and are to be reviewed, approved, and updated. MTSA permits a vessel or facility to operate temporarily without such a plan if the owner or operator certifies that deterrence has been ensured by alternative means, but the alternative means must be at least as effective as those applied by regulation for the vessel and facility security plans. MTSA also enabled the Coast Guard to take any necessary interim security measures immediately.

MTSA also requires the secretary of transportation to establish response plans for areas, vessels, and facilities that may be involved in a transportation security incident and to make such plans available to the director of the Federal Emergency Management Agency (FEMA), for inclusion in the director's response plan for U.S. ports and waterways. So in addition to security requirements MTSA mandates contingency response.

Specifically, MTSA, in an effort to restrict access to sensitive areas and cargoes, requires transportation security cards for entry into a secured area of a vessel or facility, and the issuance of biometric transportation security cards to individuals seeking access to secure areas. It establishes criteria (such as being convicted of a felony) for denial of a card. Information collected pursuant to criminal backgrounds checks is intended to be kept private, and individuals who are to be disqualified are entitled to a judicial review to determine whether they constitute a threat of terrorism. Additionally, MTSA requires crew members on vessels calling at U.S. ports to carry and present on demand any identification that the secretary of transportation decides is necessary, and for U.S. authorities regulating entry requirements to adopt a single set of rules governing the form of documentation necessary for foreign seafarers. The administration was encouraged to enter into international negotiations regarding a common standard for seafarers' identification.

To resolve the issue of funding, MTSA established a grant program for port authorities, facility operators, and state and local agencies required to provide security services to implement Area Maritime Transportation Security Plans and facility security plans. MTSA requires the secretary of transportation to report annually to specified congressional committees on progress in correcting vulnerabilities identified by the Coast Guard in port security and in compliance with the area and facility plans. (To date this report has not been submitted.) The report is also supposed to indicate current funding and project future funding for a number of federal port security programs. MTSA also authorizes grants for fiscal years 2003–2008 to support technological research and development.

Additionally, MTSA (following the model of aviation laws) was designed to allow U.S. authorities to review the security of foreign ports so as to determine whether vessels and cargo originating there posed a threat to the United States. MTSA directs the secretary of transportation to assess the effectiveness of antiterrorism measures maintained at specified foreign ports and make recommendations for improvements, including the establishment of a port security training program. If vessels arriving from foreign ports have ineffective antiterrorism measures, the secretary is authorized to prescribe conditions of entry or to deny entry into the United States. The secretary of transportation is required to notify the secretary of state whenever a foreign port is found not to be maintaining effective antiterrorism measures.

MTSA also had provisions for obtaining better, faster information on vessels, cargoes, passengers, and crew members entering the United States. Certain foreign and domestic vessels operating in the navigable waters of the United States are to be equipped with an automatic identification system (AIS) so that federal authorities can track their whereabouts. MTSA set a schedule for phasing in AIS. To deter transportation security incidents, the law also authorizes the secretary of transportation to develop and implement a long-range automated vessel tracking system for all vessels in U.S. waters that are equipped with the Global Maritime Distress and Safety System or equivalent satellite technology. Long-range satellite tracking is intended to supplement AIS, which is envisioned as a near-shore device. Importantly, MTSA directs the secretary of transportation to implement a system to collect, integrate, and analyze information concerning vessels operating in or bound for U.S. waters, including information related to crew, passengers, cargo, and intermodal shipments.

Section 70116 of MTSA provides for evaluation and certification of secure systems of international intermodal transportation, in order to receive recognition under the provisions of the National Maritime Transportation Security Plan for reopening ports to commerce in the event of a terrorist attack. The standards include screening cargo before loading in a foreign port for shipment to the United States, standards and procedures for securing cargo and monitoring its security in transit, standards on locking and sealing shipping containers, and standards and procedures for allowing the U.S. government to ensure and validate compliance. (To date no regulations have been issued implementing this section.)

MTSA also attempts to upgrade maritime security training and increases the Coast Guard's authority to protect shipping against terrorism. Section 109 provides for standards and curriculum for the training and certification of maritime security professionals. Section 107 amends the Ports and Waterways Safety Act to authorize the use of qualified armed Coast Guard personnel as sea marshals on vessels and public or commercial structures on or adjacent to U.S. waters to deter or respond to terrorism or transportation security incidents.

Finally, in addition to many other changes in maritime transportation and changes to laws governing how the Coast Guard operates as well as requirements for numerous reports, MTSA established a National Maritime Security Advisory Committee to: (1) advise, consult with, report to, and make recommendations to the secretary of transportation; and (2) make available to Congress recommendations that the committee makes to the secretary. (To date this committee has not been established.)

MTSA is probably the farthest-reaching legislation concerning ocean shipping and its security. However, MTSA (like the ISPS Code) has its critics, who contend many details are left to interpretation by regulatory bodies.

MTSA: Implementation and Issues

Implementing and funding MTSA may be a challenge for the Department of Homeland Security (DHS), in several regards.

Funding

Before MTSA, maritime security was largely shared between federal, state, local, and private entities and was neither well coordinated nor effective. Under MTSA there is much more federal control; and state, local, and private-sector infrastructure and facilities must meet federal requirements. What proportion of costs, therefore, should be defrayed by federal funds?

According to the Coast Guard and a "Maritime Security Notice" in the *Federal Register* of 30 December 2002,[12] the cost of implementing security in U.S. seaports will be several billion dollars. In 2004, the budget request for port security grants (the first such request) was $46 million; Congress has appropriated funds: $440 million has been released to port authorities from amounts appropriated; and $75 million was released to port authorities from amounts appropriated to the Office of Domestic Preparedness (ODP). But these amounts indicate a considerable shortfall.

Security Plans

The Coast Guard indicates that some 9,000 vessels and 3,500 facilities were supposed to have filed plans by 31 December 2003. Between that date and 1 July 2004, the private sector underwent the Coast Guard's review of security plans. During the same time the Coast Guard was expected to work with state and local officials to complete area security and contingency response plans (again, by 1 July 2004).

Significant issues remain, however, primarily concerning the lack of resources necessary for implementation. Evidently, most of the facility plans have been bare-boned; and some matters—such as identification of workers and access controls—have been postponed until the government issues final directions on credentialing employees. Another issue is whether facilities can meet the higher-level security requirements or whether they will just close down at the highest levels. The Coast Guard may eventually have to decide whether to approve substandard compliance or close down non-compliant facilities; the latter choice would of course have serious economic implications.

Regarding area plans, the Coast Guard may have to deal with situations in which ensuring the safety of surrounding structures and populations entails high costs. Current policy calls for affected owners of infrastructure to work voluntarily with the Coast Guard, but this policy leaves compliance to be addressed (or not addressed) ad hoc. The Coast Guard and Congress have established a few command and control centers where law enforcement agencies can monitor a region; this approach seems practical and attractive.

Port Security Assessments

The Coast Guard has scheduled 55 militarily strategic port areas for assessment. As of this writing it had completed 16 assessments and intended to complete the rest by the end of fiscal year 2005.

MTSA did not set a date for the completion of assessments; but the intention was that the assessments would be provided to the private sector as a basis for its security plans, which were to be completed by 1 July 2004. Thus the private sector will receive little benefit from the federal assessments. Because of the delays, the Coast Guard has revised the assessment program to involve less coverage of individual facilities and focus more on assets that would be covered by area security and contingency response plans. Also, the revised program is intended to maintain data in an integrated Geographic Information System (GIS) that will display facts about port security in a user-friendly format.

The Coast Guard is just starting to evaluate foreign seaports and has sent out some preliminary teams of DHS agents; but as of this writing it is too early to evaluate progress.

Credentialing Transportation Employees

MTSA requires a Transportation Workers Identification Credential (TWIC) for maritime employees in sensitive areas of port facilities.

TWIC involves a background check, which can be appealed by the worker or waived by the authorities. The Transportation Security Administration (TSA) is supposed to set similar requirements for other categories of transportation workers (primarily truck drivers carrying hazardous materials). However, TSA has proposed no regulations to implement this section of the law. It has announced pilot programs to test TWIC technology in the ports of Wilmington (Delaware) and Long Beach (California), and recently in Florida. But as a result of inaction, many port facility security plans have not instituted the requirements for criminal background checks.

Maritime Intelligence

Given the status of implementation of seaport security measures, good intelligence may be the most important factor in security. MTSA provides for a single maritime intelligence system to collect and analyze information concerning vessels operating in waters under the jurisdiction of the United States, but no effort has been made to coordinate commercial maritime intelligence in order to provide effective analyses. In fact, the Coast Guard, the Navy, CBP, and TSA are working on separate intelligence programs, and the latter two have invested millions in new facilities.

There has been discussion of a possible maritime center, analogous to the North American Aerospace Defense Command (NORAD). The Coast Guard and Navy have taken the lead in this endeavor, but there has been little actual progress in finding experts or in linking maritime intelligence to other information about terrorism. Also, the federal government may not be knowledgeable enough about commercial shipping to detect anomalies and irregularities that suggest possible terrorism; nor has it invested much in developing such knowledge or hiring private-sector experts.

Tracking Vessels in U.S. Waters

MTSA provided that all vessels entering U.S. waters must carry transponders. The intention was to be able to track high-interest vessels such as oil or LNG tankers and monitor shipping near sensitive infrastructure. The transponders are to be a part of the Automatic Identification System (AIS), which integrates equipment and technologies to automatically send detailed information on each ship to shore-based agencies and other ships.

Internationally, the rule about transponders has been implemented, and all large commercial vessels now carry them. But the government has requested only nominal sums for purchasing the necessary monitoring equipment. Current plans call for implementing AIS at ports that already monitor movements through Vessel Traffic Systems (VTS), but it seems unlikely that a nationwide AIS system will even be considered until fiscal year 2006.

Cargo Security Programs

DHS has two agencies with jurisdiction over various aspects of cargo security: CBP, which is responsible for cross-border transportation; and TSA, which is responsible for intermodal transportation. To facilitate the safe transportation of cargo, and to deter and detect shipments of nuclear, radiological, chemical, or biological weapons, CBP and TSA have established several initiatives.

CBP has taken a "layered" approach to the security of incoming cargo containers. After 9/11 and the passage of MTSA, it first increased accountability and information regarding cargo shipments and implemented a 24-hour rule so as to focus cargo inspections. Under this rule certain information must be given 24 hours before cargo is loaded onto a ship bound for the United States; CBP then uses the resources at the new National Targeting Center to evaluate risk and decide which cargoes to screen. CPB says that it monitors all incoming cargo in this way. However, critics point out that this procedure relies on the veracity of shippers, and furthermore that the identity of some shippers can be easily concealed.

Once a shipment is identified as high-risk, it is subject to nonintrusive inspection (NII). At the time of this writing, 12 percent of all containers received NII. The current technology—which critics consider inadequate—uses X-rays or gamma imaging systems. However, marine containers are commonly 48 feet long and can carry as much as 60,000 pounds; and if such a container has mixed contents, potential terrorism may be hard to identify. DHS has established a Science Directorate, and CBP is evaluating various new devices. But it is unclear how much is being invested in technology that would replace X-rays with scientific analysis. Also, the maritime industry is concerned that if screening policies are inadequately applied—with too few screeners, say, or poorly positioned screeners—the pace of trade will be slowed.

CBP has also developed the Container Security Initiative (CSI) and Customs-Trade Partnership Against Terrorism (C-TPAT). CSI is designed to position CBP agents at major seaports around the world to inspect U.S.-bound cargo at the point of departure; at this writing it was operating at 36 foreign seaports representing 45 percent of the total maritime cargo. CSI has been criticized as too expensive for a program offering undetermined benefits; also, there is some question about the willingness of the foreign nations to participate.

C-TPAT is a voluntary program that allows companies to apply for certification to manage their supply chain with regard to security, so that their cargoes can be expedited. As of February 2004, some 5,700 companies had submitted applications providing a security profile of their operations, and about 2,900 had been reviewed and certified. Additionally, a "smart box" concept was being considered: this would involve a locking system to prevent or reveal tampering. Critics of C-TPAT say that it should focus more on validation; that as currently conducted it is little more than a paper exercise with very little actual federal oversight; and that it does not require any verification of the contents of cargo containers.

TSA has its own program, Operation Safe Commerce, to provide grants to maritime shipping companies so that they can implement technology to secure an entire supply chain. No progress reports have yet been issued, and critics contend that the research being done is unfocused.

The Office of Cargo Security at the Border and Transportation Security Directorate is working on the Secure Systems of Transportation Program, 46 USC 70116. This is a cargo certification arrangement similar to C-TPAT but with higher standards for security, compliance, and screening. It has not advanced very far, evidently because of bureaucratic infighting.

CONCLUSION

In sum, CBP has made progress in the area of cargo security; but given the importance of overseas trade, the increasing reliance of U.S. manufacturers on "just-in-time" deliveries from overseas, and the fact that only limited resources are available to police incoming cargo, it is necessary to develop policies that will allow our ports to reopen quickly after an attack involving a cargo container.

Much still needs to be done before U.S. ports would be positioned to recover from such an attack.

N O T E S

1. U.S. International Trade and Freight Transportation Trends, U.S. DOT, p. 9.
2. "The Maritime Component," *Sea Power* (August 2001).
3. U.S. Constitution, Article I, Section 9, Clause 6: "no preference shall be given by any Regulation of Commerce or Revenue to the Ports of one State over those of any other: nor shall Vessels bound to, or from, one State, be obliged to enter, clear, or pay Duties to another."
4. Magnusson Act, 9 August 1950, chap. 656, sec. 1, 64 Stat. 427.
5. U.S. Coast Guard Web site, History of the Coast Guard at War.
6. Senate Report 107-064.
7. See www.imo.org.
8. Law of the Sea, United Nations, Section 3, Subsection A, Article 25: "the coastal state may take the necessary steps in its territorial sea to prevent passage which is not innocent."
9. Oversight Hearing on U.S. Seaport Security, 4 October 2000. Senate Committee on Commerce, Science and Transportation.
10. Hearing on Crime and Security at U.S. Seaports, 24 July 2001, Senate Committee on Commerce, Science, and Transportation.
11. House Energy and Commerce Committee, 17 October 2002, "Securing America: The Federal Government's Response to Nuclear Terrorism at Our Nation's Ports and Borders."
12. See www.gpoaccess.gov.

CHAPTER 40

Transportation Information and Security

Harold W. Neil, Jr.
Executive Assistant, Office of Transportation Security,
Department of Transportation, State of New Jersey

INTRODUCTION

This chapter discusses the importance of developing ways to fuse transportation information, that is, to let decision makers in homeland security access information from all modes of transportation. The concept of a virtual "transportation information fusion center" is presented as an important part of transportation security for the state of New Jersey.

THE NEW JERSEY TRANSPORTATION COMMUNITY AND HOMELAND SECURITY

Transportation security, like many other areas of homeland security, is complicated by the large number of public and private entities involved. The transportation sector, or community, in New Jersey, one of the highest-density transportation environments in the United States, comprises a complex array of bureaucratic structures and transportation infrastructures. Important public entities include the following:

Amtrak
Metropolitan Transportation Authority (MTA)
N.J. Transit Corporation
Port Authority Trans-Hudson (PATH)

Port Authority Transit Corporation (PATCO)

Southeastern Pennsylvania Transportation Authority (SEPTA)

South Jersey Transportation Authority (Atlantic City
  International Airport, Atlantic City Expressway)

Delaware River and Bay Authority

Delaware River Port Authority

N.J. Turnpike Authority

N.J. Turnpike Authority/Garden State Parkway Division

New York State Thruway

Port Authority of New York and New Jersey (Newark Airport,
  Holland/Lincoln Tunnels, George Washington Bridge, PATH)

South Jersey Port Corporation

Burlington County Bridge Commission

Delaware River Bridge Commission

Motor Vehicle Commission

Currently, each of these entities develops its own security plan, although this is done in conjunction with the New Jersey Domestic Security Preparedness Task Force, which provides guidelines to all critical infrastructure sectors; and with the New Jersey Department of Transportation, which has established an Office of Transportation Security.

Transportation is a particularly important sector because it profoundly affects all others. At present, the security guidelines for the transportation sector are either general or specific to a subsector or to a mode of transportation (freight rail, mass transit rail, ferry/water taxi, mass transit bus, trucks, roads and highways, bridges, tunnels, seaports, and general aviation and ports). The next phase in improving transportation security is to develop an integrated state transportation security strategy that interrelates the various modes of transportation at each phase of homeland security.

"Information fusion" is a critically important capability for achieving an integrated transportation security strategy and for supporting decision making and missions. One can understand the need for information fusion by imagining a terrorist incident that simultaneously involves several modes of transportation and several types of transportation infrastructure. Today, information about transportation security vulnerabilities, security status, traffic flow, and incidents is processed in different bureaucracies. To access that information, official requests must be submitted; the information is then "pulled" from the appropriate agency; next, it is directed through a focal point, formerly the Office of the Commissioner, now through the Office of Transportation Security of New Jersey's Department of Transportation to entities such as the task force, the New Jersey Office of Counterterrorism, and the governor. This slows information delivery and reduces its efficiency; also, piecemeal data can make patterns and situations impossible to discern.

New Jersey's Proposal for a Regional Intermodal Transportation Security System

The next phase in the evolution of transportation security in New Jersey is to integrate data from all transportation-related entities, public and private, through a virtual network. The goal is to make transportation data accessible by officials at secure Web-based portals. Decoupling information-sharing flows from bureaucratic structures— eliminating the current need for the N.J. Department of Transportation (N.J. DOT) Office of Transportation Security to "pull" information from each entity and mode of transportation listed above—will enhance the efficiency of policy makers or responders at all phases of homeland security: protection, prevention, preparedness, response, and recovery. This will apply to every mode of transportation, including freight rail, mass transit rail, ferry/water taxi, mass transit bus, trucks, roads, and highways, bridges and tunnels, seaports and general aviation, and ports, and to all hazards and incidents, particularly chemical, biological, radiological, nuclear, explosive, and cyber, anywhere in the state or region.

Therefore, transportation information fusion is a significant part of achieving N.J. DOT's planned enhancement of transportation security.

A fusion center would provide decision makers with a holistic overview of activity in all modes of transportation. Maps and video images would enable officials to detect, mitigate, and respond to threats and incidents having to do with both homeland security and general emergency management.

Transportation information, including video and sensor feeds, can be overlaid on a geographical information system (GIS), enabling officials to focus on specific roadways, bridges, etc., for the purpose of gathering data and intelligence to make decisions for prevention, deterrence, response, and recovery related to threats and incidents. Figure 40-1 illustrates how a statewide strategy for intermodal transportation security would be supported by the proposed regional transportation information fusion center and the concept of an intelligent transportation system (ITS) developed over recent decades.

In addition to sensors, human intelligence (HUMINT) plays an important part in New Jersey's transportation security strategy. In 2003, a voluntary Highway Watch Program was instituted by N.J. DOT in partnership with the American Trucking Association and the N.J. Motor Truck Association; this program enables truckers to alert law enforcement and security officials to threats and suspicious activity that cameras may not detect on the roads. The intention is to train 30,000 truckers (20,000 of whom are independents), as well as transportation maintenance workers from N.J. DOT and the state's toll-road authorities, to identify abnormalities and incidents and call in the information to a national line, to be administered by the Transportation Security Administration (TSA). Other HUMINT initiatives include the Commercial Vehicle Driver Program: if a truck is stopped in one state for suspicious activity, information regarding the vehicle will be passed on to other states or regions. (This program was initially part of the U.S. DOT Truck Stop Safety Watch. N.J. DOT plans to add elements and incorporate security aspects to fit it into the scheme of the proposed ITS fusion center, which would capture HUMINT in real time and check it against national databases to monitor vehicles for risk.)

HOW TRANSPORTATION INFORMATION CAN BE USED IN HOMELAND SECURITY

Here is a hypothetical scenario that illustrates the vital role transportation information can play in homeland security.

Planning

At the planning phase, transportation information could contribute to counterterrorist policies based on a more integrated understanding of how different modes of transportation interrelate and how they

F I G U R E   40-1

Statewide strategy for intermodal transportation.

Phase Threat	Prevention and Deterrence	Interdiction and Crisis Management	Mitigation and Consequence Management
General (all hazards)	Cameras on highways, roads, trains, bridges, tunnels, ports, airports, buses "Panic button" installed on buses for use by driver to issue warning of threat or incident GIS, GPS, AVL, motion detectors Tracking of hazardous materials Baggage screening for passenger rail, aviation, and mass transit Cargo screening for maritime vessels and freight rail Scanning of rail lines, infrastructure, and equipment Virtual security zones in the South Jersey Port area* Tracking of all trucks, buses, freight rails, and cars (to know which are missing and which ones are carrying or have the capability to carry hazardous materials) Sensors and analysis of data to determine risk level of vehicle at any point in transportation system Pre-positioned barriers and protocols to respond to vehicles determined to be at risk Driver identification verification Biometrics of transportation workers and arrested criminals Facial recognition technology to screen drivers and license plates (data will be checked against state and national intelligence databases) Data from private sector Highway watch data of incidents reported by truckers. Analysis of data to track different types of common incidents	Designated routes for emergency responders Designated evacuation routes Variable message boards on highways, roads, train and bus stations Public broadcasts to inform about threats and incidents and what actions to take for safety or evacuation	Evacuation of people based on traffic flows Dispatch of responders along routes determined by real-time data to be most efficient for arrival at scene of incident Exercise
Chemical or Biological	Vulnerability assessment Threat assessment Radiological detectors Monitoring of air and water supply for chemicals	Inspection-imaging systems throughout transportation routes	Dispatch of responders along routes determined to be flowing

(*continued*)

FIGURE 40-1
Continued.

Phase Threat	Prevention and Deterrence	Interdiction and Crisis Management	Mitigation and Consequence Management
Chemical or Biological (continued)	Monitoring of meteorological data to predict airborne spread of biochemical threat in an outbreak or accident Port-of-entry monitoring of cargo Medical surveillance Predeployed detection systems	Keep routes open to responders	Plume detection and modeling Exercise
Nuclear or Radiological	Vulnerability assessment Threat assessment Port-of-entry monitoring of cargo Radiological materials security Nuclear nonproliferation protocols	Port-of-entry detectors or discriminators Pedestrian-vehicle detection portals Quick-response technical backup teams	Computerized radiological assessment Plume modeling Deployable decontaminants WMD "war gaming" training Quick-response technical backup teams Exercise
Explosives or Fire	Scanners (e.g., X-rays) to detect explosive devices Deployment of explosive K-9 units at multi-modal facilities	Device disablement systems Containment foams Detectors for predeployed or handheld explosives Technical readiness training	Blast containment foams Explosives material tagging (for attribution) Target hardening by blast-resistant building design and materials Exercise
Cyber	Vulnerability assessment Threat assessment Technical readiness training Antivirus software Firewall protection	Statistical network traffic analysis Predictive systems Intelligence agents	Computer-assisted situation analysis and management Adaptive network countermeasures Retrospective network traffic mapping Exercise

*Note: New Jersey's DOT is creating virtual security zones in the South Jersey Port area, which encompasses the Salem Nuclear Power Plant. This virtual security zone will have a high-technology surveillance program that, if successful, will serve as an operational model for the state's intermodal transportation security strategy. The virtual security zone will rely on a defense plan designed to identify threats and communicate threat-related information to the relevant officials for effective prevention, detection, and response.

support missions such as the protection of critical infrastructure and postevent emergency management.

Threat and Vulnerability Analysis

Intelligence analysts would use transportation information to "connect the dots" having to do with potential or actual threats and terrorist activity. For example, suspect movements could be tracked from mode to mode.

New Jersey is using a tool kit for risk assessment from the Office of Domestic Preparedness (ODP) to prioritize funding for "target hardening" of critical infrastructures and for all modes of transportation in the state. These evaluations will inform the state's evolving transportation security strategy. Threats and vulnerabilities that are identified by using the tool kit would be depicted, or mapped, through the ITS fusion center. (Since the ODP tool kit is recommended by the federal government for use nationally, there is a unique opportunity to develop a uniform nationwide approach to merging data on risks and vulnerability with transportation information.) With this information, planners would be able to see the results of queries such as: "Show me all access routes that would enable a truck bomb to approach a target rated at vulnerability level x or above."

Detection

The screening of cargo containers and vehicles to detect and interdict nuclear or chemical weapons takes place along freight railways, in seaports, and at bridges and tunnels. Information from such sensors can be checked against databases and added to the "common operating picture" so that all security officials would have access to the data and could use the data as a basis for their decisions regarding prevention, detection, and response.

Tracking

Vehicles carrying hazardous materials (HAZMAT) use automatic vehicle location systems (AVLs) and global positioning systems (GPSs). To prevent and interdict terrorists' hijacking of HAZMAT vehicles, authorities need to be able to access identification such as high-risk cargo and track these vehicles. Similarly, the fusion center would enable authorities to monitor and account for parked general aviation aircraft and check that against flight data.

Dispatch of First Responders

Emergency responders would use the data to prevent or respond to incidents, optimizing the routing of responders to the scene of an incident.

Determining Evacuation Routes

In the event of an attack, the fusion center would provide authorities with the information necessary to determine which evacuation routes would be best, based on real-time information about the number of people (per mode) currently in the transportation system, what routes in each mode are relatively open, and what the throughput capacity is for each route. In the event of a biochemical or radiological attack, plume modeling and weather data would be factored into decisions about optimal evacuation routes.

CHALLENGES TO CREATING AND IMPLEMENTING INFORMATION FUSION
Problem 1: Lack of a Definition of 'Security'

In developing a state transportation security strategy that integrates the separate strategies of individual agencies and establishes common policies, procedures, and protocols, one challenge is the lack of a common definition of security. Even within N.J. DOT, the many transportation agencies that are responsible for security do not yet have a common definition of security, or even a rudimentary understanding of how security fits into the overall mission of the department. Defining security is important and will affect the allocation of resources.

Problem 2: Lack of Common Concepts

To govern the use of the virtual information fusion network, common concepts are needed: missions, goals, policies, and so on. The lack of such shared concepts is a challenge to a statewide strategy. Eventually, such concepts will become common doctrine throughout the public and private sectors, not just on paper but operationally as well, particularly since transportation-related agencies, private-sector entities, and citizens are currently cooperating to bring their unique perspectives to the creation of a statewide strategy.

Problem 3: Bureaucratic Resistance to Information Sharing

Full-scale situational awareness requires sharing of data and information that agencies gather, analyze, and produce internally; but the agencies are often reluctant to share such information. Each agency has the very legitimate desire to maintain the integrity of its information; if data are manipulated in the process of dissemination between agencies, those data could be rendered unreliable, inaccurate, and therefore useless. To address these concerns, safeguards will be needed.

Problem 4: Insufficient Funding

It will cost hundreds of million of dollars to build an information fusion center, deploy the needed sensors, and integrate the databases and information systems for all modes of transportation. Fortunately, the fiber-optics infrastructure is already available. To date, however, no federal funding has been made available for the fusion center, although TSA seems to be enthusiastic about the idea. Another potential funding strategy is to form partnerships with other states and with the private sector to spread the cost. The fusion center would have value to other states and private companies, because it would give users access to a vast network of information that could optimize infrastructure planning and transportation logistics.

CONCLUSION

All modes of transportation are vulnerable to terrorism and also serve as means of conveyance to terrorists in planning and executing an attack. Moreover, transportation systems and associated information are critical to homeland security planning and to the execution of homeland security missions. Yet today there has been too little progress in transportation security. The expectation is that better information flow and a holistic view of transportation information and incidents will improve decision making and facilitate joint action.

See also Chapter 61, **IT Architecture for Homeland Security.**

Emergency Management, Public Health, and Medical Preparedness

Introduction to Section 8

Major General Donna F. Barbisch, C.R.N.A., M.P.H., D.H.A.
Director, Chem Bio Radiological and Nuclear Defense
Programs Integration, Department of Defense;
Adjunct Professor, George Washington University;
President, Global Deterrence Alternatives, LLC

Preparedness is the word of the moment in health and medical communities across the nation. But before we can achieve preparedness, we need to have answers to several questions: Preparedness for what? Who is responsible? How much preparedness is needed? How soon is it needed? How much exists already? Where can we get scarce resources? How can we allocate scarce resources when needs grow uncontrollably? How can we organize to bring independent public and private health and medical organizations together to provide the best care for the greatest population? Finally, how can we do all this in a cost-effective manner?

In the United States there is no unifying national preparedness strategy for public health and medicine. Public health, as a component of government, has the mission to "fulfill society's interest in assuring conditions in which people can be healthy."[1] Providing for the safety and welfare of citizens is a state (rather than a federal) responsibility. State and local government public health officials are expected to prepare communities for threats such as bioterrorism as well as natural infectious outbreaks. However, while public health is a governmental function, we need to recognize that

---

Note: The views expressed are the author's and do not represent those of the Department of Defense.

the health and medical community is made up of both public and private entities.

Health care must be recognized as distinct, and different, from public health. Health care is primarily a privately run industry or "community." Hospitals, which have been given a lead in coordinating the health care community, are only one part of health care. The health care community is generally associated with health facilities (such as hospitals, outpatient centers, nursing homes, and rehabilitation facilities) and health care personnel (including physicians, nurses, pharmacists, and nursing aides).

However, many health and medical supporting functions either cross the border between public health and health care or do not belong in either category. Examples include the first-responder community (paramedics and prehospital services), allied health services, independent pharmacies, home health, hospice, food service, and supporting functions such as utilities and security.

Clearly, the entities in this array were not designed to function together to achieve preparedness with regard to homeland security. Private hospitals have relatively little experience with public health emergencies and only now are adopting operational frameworks such as the incident command system (ICS). Public health has limited experience with hospital management. Many complex and interrelated activities cross public and private areas of responsibility, so that functions become disconnected and gap-ridden.

Public health and private health care are working jointly to plan and develop programs to respond to formidable health and medical challenges in homeland security, but they have not completed this task. A systems approach is needed. The first steps are defining the mission, identifying existing capabilities, and then thoroughly examining roles and responsibilities. We must create a seamlessly responsive system that integrates existing processes and adapts to as yet unknown health and medical situations. This will also require risk management: it is not possible to build and sustain a system with unconstrained and unlimited resources for an infinite number of casualties! Saving lives in a large-scale emergency requires moving from a system of individual care to a system based on principles of population health disaster management.

The chapters in Section 8 provide insight into emergency management and public health and medical preparedness. In Chapter 42 Ray Lehr provides an overview of the role of first responders. In Chapter 43 Claire Rubin and Jack Harrald describe important coordination frameworks including the National Incident Management System and the National Response Plan. Terri Tanielian and Brad Stein present in Chapter 44 a compelling account of how an emphasis on pre- and postattack mental health can significantly reduce the impact on survivors. In Chapter 45 Elin Gursky discusses the challenges and complexities of the biological threats that face us in the new global environment. In Chapter 46 Boaz Tadmor, Lion Poles, and Shmuel Shapira describe how one country, faced with continued attacks, has developed a disaster culture and how it approaches hospital preparedness and mass casualty management.

N O T E

1. Institute of Medicine, Committee for the Study of the Future of Public Health, Division of Health Care Services, *The Future of Public Health* (Washington, D.C.: National Academy Press, 1988).

Emergency Response: An Overview

Ray Lehr
Northrop Grumman Corporation;
Assistant Chief (Retired), Baltimore City Fire Department

INTRODUCTION

Americans expect that when disaster strikes, the government will dispatch appropriate help. Depending on the size and nature of the emergency, that help could come from a firehouse down the block or a specially trained unit several states away. Firefighters, the police, and emergency medical technicians are generally called first responders. They are responsible for evaluating an incident at the outset, and the decisions they make at the scene can save lives and lessen the impact of the event. On the basis of their observations, analysis, skill, training, and instincts, they will either handle the incident or call for additional support from local, state, or federal resources.

WHO DOES WHAT?

Usually, the first notification of an incident is a call to 911. The call is received in a "public safety answering point" (PSAP) that is responsible for sending the right personnel—typically the local fire department, emergency medical services, police, or sheriff—to the scene to begin controlling the event. First responders apply standard incident command (IC) procedures so that their efforts are coordinated and information and decisions follow a predetermined protocol.

The need for standardized IC procedures derived from the difficulty of controlling wildfires in the western United States. Fast-moving fires that might consume forests, homes, and businesses require vast resources. Thousands of people with widely varying skills, from dozens of agencies and jurisdictions, must be organized on short notice and deployed to areas—often remote places—where they must maintain their organizational structure for days or weeks. After some disastrous fires in southern California in 1970, several of the agencies involved formed Firefighting Resources of California Organized for Potential Emergencies (Firescope) to develop coordination and a decision process. Firescope developed a structured incident command system (ICS), which has since been accepted by major emergency response organizations and supported by the federal government. As various agencies respond and provide support, the system expands and establishes a unified command structure that designates a single agency to lead the efforts, assigning specific responsibilities to supporting groups that have the appropriate skills. The federal government has taken the process one step further in creating the National Incident Management System (NIMS), which establishes rules for federal response in the National Response Plan (NRP) and coordination in support of local responders. Figure 42-1 shows the basic organization.

Under ICS, most jurisdictions establish a command post, usually a vehicle (e.g., a chief's car, command van, or communications bus). The incident commander assigns a staff member to record or log in support agencies and personnel when they arrive and give them a radio or frequency. Some supporting units will be put to work

F I G U R E   42-1

Basic structure of incident command system.

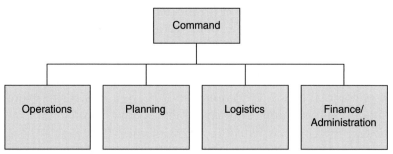

immediately. Others will be assigned to a staging area nearby or will take a position in the command vehicle to coordinate their activities in support of the lead agency. These standard procedures are documented in the jurisdiction's general emergency plans.

Civil defense agencies, first developed in the 1950s when a nuclear attack seemed possible, created and maintained such plans with input from local first responders. Today, emergency management officials are expected to develop operational plans for various natural disasters. Since 9/11, many local branches of the Emergency Management Agency (EMA) or Office of Emergency Management (OEM) have increased their staff to plan for terrorism.

In addition to an operational plan for disaster management, each agency needs a communications plan covering what information needs to be exchanged, who will talk to whom, and how updates and briefings will be conducted. Figure 42-2 is an example.

Operational and communications plans also provide a methodology for training exercises that can be modified to fit each region's unique needs. When the plans are applied frequently during exercises and routine events, they will become second nature to the responders and will help the various response agencies to develop interrelationships. Decision makers and emergency managers should not be meeting for the first time when a crisis arises; if they have already developed trust and an understanding of each other's roles and capabilities, their coordination in an emergency will be much smoother.

Many people who testified before the 9/11 Commission described the attacks as "unimaginable." That may have been true of the specifics, but emergency planners had, long before, addressed high-rise fires, mass evacuations, collapsing buildings, and rescue and recovery operations.

NORMAL OPERATIONS

Americans dial 911 about 500,000 times a day. For all kinds of calls—false alarms, fires, plane crashes, releases of hazardous materials, mass casualty events, and terrorism—the common thread is a predetermined response and a unified command system designed to coordinate activities.

When people at 911 take a call, they ask a series of questions; the resulting data determine what agencies and units are needed.

F I G U R E   4 2 - 2

Sample form for Incident Radio Communications Plan.

Incident Radio Communications Plan		1. Incident name	2. Date/time prepared	3. Operational period date/time
4. Base radio channel utilization				

System/cache	Channel	Function	Frequency/tone	Assignment	Remarks

5. Prepared by [Communications Unit]

Source: The National Wildlife Coordinating Group, www.nwcg.gov.

Larger PSAPs have a computer-aided dispatch (CAD) system, which automatically assigns units. Once the units are under way, they maintain radio contact with a dispatcher from their agency and can request additional resources until the situation is stabilized. PSAPs and dispatch centers are the command-and-control point for notification of activities, coordination with support agencies, and maintenance of awareness of all activity within the jurisdiction. If the event is prolonged, an emergency operations center (EOC, usually run by the EMA) may support the on-scene forces. Personnel from the police, fire, transportation, health, utilities, etc., may gather at the EOC, exchange information, monitor activities, and make decisions necessary to support the incident commander. Routine events usually require the coordination of only one to three agencies.

Figure 42-3 shows basic responses for first-responder agencies, and Figure 42-4 shows standard emergency operations.

F I G U R E   42-3

Basic response for three first responders.

First Responder Agency	Basic Unit/ Staffing	Normal Response Small Incident	Escalation Level 1	Maximum Response
Fire Department	Engine/pumper or truck/ladder 3–7 firefighters per unit	1 or 2 engines and 1 truck for small events 1st alarm generally consists of 4 engines, 2 trucks, and a battalion chief	Additional alarm (2nd, 3rd, etc.) usually brings a like amount of units: 4 engines, 2 trucks, and a battalion chief. Specialized units as required (Hazmat, etc.)	85–90% of total resources[1] Mutual aid from surrounding jurisdictions
Emergency Medical Service	Medic unit or ambulance 2 paramedics, EMTs, or combination	1 medic unit	1–4 additional medic units 1 supervisor	50–60% of resources Mutual aid from surrounding jurisdictions
Police/ Sheriff	Patrol car 1–2 officers or deputies	1 car with backup	5–10 cars with supervisors, detectives, specialized units such as crime lab, bomb squad, etc. as needed	10–20% of resources Mutual aid, State Police for additional support

[1] Some reserve capacity is kept in service to handle additional incidents. Large departments have "callback" plans to bring in off-duty shifts to staff reserve apparatus.

Members of the general public, unless they themselves are affected, are usually unaware of most routine calls handled by first responders. However, the news media monitor incidents through radio scanners and will send reporters if an event involves injuries or deaths or disrupts traffic or services.

COORDINATION OF ACTIVITIES

When disaster strikes, first responders respond. This sounds simple, but sorting out responsibilities and activities to ensure that the response will make the situation better, not worse, is actually a

F I G U R E   42-4

Standard emergency operations.

Type of Emergency	Lead Agency Incident Command (IC)	Supporting Agencies/Role	Total Number of Personnel
Auto Accident	Fire if persons trapped or fire danger EMS if injuries only Police if no fire or injuries	Fire: Rescue, extrication, fire control/ extinguishment, spill control/containment EMS: Victim treatment, transport Police: Traffic control, accident investigation Transportation: Traffic diversion	Fire: 4–10 EMS: 2–5 Police: 2–8 Transportation: 2–6
House Fire	Fire: Incident Command	EMS: Standby for treatment of victims Police: Control access to area and investigate if crime	Fire: 10–25 EMS: 2–5 Police: 2–8
Hazmat Incident	Fire: Incident Command	EMS: Standby for treatment of victims Police: Control access to area and investigate if crime Specialized Units: As needed	Fire: 10–25 EMS: 2–5 Police: 2–8 Specialized Units: 2–10
Bank Robbery	Police: Incident Command	EMS: Treats injured	Police: 4–10 EMS: 2–5
Hostage Situation	Police: Incident Command	Fire: Standby for tear gas, fire mitigation EMS: Standby for treatment of victims	Police: 5–20 Fire: 4–10 EMS: 2–5

complex matter. Without clear, predetermined lines of authority and responsibility, the response may be confused and haphazard, escalating the emergency and putting more people in danger. For example, a fire department should not pour water onto a crime scene when the police need to preserve evidence there; the police should not begin an evacuation when the hazardous materials team recommends "sheltering in place"; and an incident commander should not evacuate an urban area without notifying the transportation department, or else gridlock and panic may ensue.

To avoid such problems, there must be frequent and reliable communication between agencies before, during, and after an emergency. Ideally, the incident commander should already have a relationship with the response agencies. As noted above, a crisis is not the time to meet new people and bicker over who is in charge or what actions to take. Planning for disasters must be a top priority for all jurisdictions. Emergency planners should strive for as much participation as practical. Responsible leaders must ensure that emergency plans are practiced as frequently as possible.

Those managing prolonged events will need to hold a public information briefing to enlist the help of the media. In too many incidents, the media are shut out of the information flow and end up reporting rumors; the officials will then find it difficult to correct the record, and the media and the public will continue to wonder "what really happened." By scheduling press briefings at a safe distance from the scene, public safety officials can convey the facts to the public, give advice on safety, and ensure that the media have accurate details.

LARGE-SCALE EVENTS

Historically, in planning for large-scale events, the emergency management community has focused its training on perceived threats. (For instance, in the 1960s it focused on the nuclear threat, and first responders became familiar with Geiger counters, dosimeters, and potassium iodide tablets.) Thus an unanticipated event can find everybody inadequately prepared.

On 9/11, the New York City police and fire department—although they are among the world's largest and best-equipped public safety agencies, and although they did save many lives—were ill equipped to handle a disaster of such magnitude. For example, with regard to the structural vulnerability of the World Trade Center; they had no advance knowledge that might have led to different tactics. It should be noted, however, that a decade earlier, in 1991, the Philadelphia fire department was criticized for withdrawing its forces from a high-rise building believed erroneously to be near collapse.[1] In such cases, theoretically, engineers who are familiar with the structures involved and with the mechanics of the emergency should be contacted; but in reality that may not be possible. Future advances in technology and computer modeling may be the best way to provide technical expertise to incident commanders.

Another problem in New York City on 9/11 was that the convergence of many firefighters on the scene and the loss of the senior commanders when the first tower collapsed left a void in the

ICS for more than an hour.[2] Consequently, many off-duty firefighters went into action with no clear orders and no radios, so that it became difficult to verify their presence and activities. Planning for future events must consider the desire of public safety workers to do something in a disaster, and such planning must include a preordained methodology for assigning them in a way that will maximize their effectiveness without placing them in danger and will ensure that everyone is accounted for.

At large-scale events, incident commanders have a complex, taxing role: they may need to make split-second life-or-death decisions; mistakes on their part might cause the situation to spiral out of control; and they must direct an influx of well-meaning agencies.

As with military operations, the key is planning, practice, and an excellent staff. Incident commanders need a support staff capable of acting as a buffer: only the most necessary people and information should get to the incident commander. The commander's directions must be followed quickly and accurately. As an emergency escalates, routine radio transmissions should be minimized to make way for critical information. Incident commanders are frustrated when mundane reports ("We're ascending the stairs"; "We're arriving in the staging area") interfere with more important transmissions. Seasoned emergency workers know that reporting expected results is a waste of time. They should report only unexpected occurrences that need immediate follow-up. The newest generation of radios allows for emergency overrides; personnel need to practice using such technology.

Modern radio systems also use computer technology to segment communications into "talkgroups"—computer-defined groups of radios linked together for a specific incident. Well-designed talkgroups can allow work units to coordinate their activities without blocking the flow of information to commanders or to medical groups, for example.

One case where talkgroups proved their value occurred on July 18, 2001 in Baltimore. The incident was a derailment and fire in a 2-mile tunnel under a downtown business district. The fire burned for three days as firefighters uncoupled and removed the smoldering cars. At the time of the fire, a major league baseball game was beginning at Camden Yards, one-quarter of a mile from the south tunnel entrance, and the incident commander ordered an evacuation of the stadium. This complex situation was mitigated by the ability to coordinate numerous agencies, and that process was expedited due to the design of the talkgroups. The fire, police, and public works departments had considered their operational needs and had created talkgroups accordingly. Shared talkgroups such as B-11, FD-PD (fire department to police department), and B-12, FD-DPW (fire department to public works), allowed the agencies to exchange information. The system included an "all call" talkgroup that would have allowed the incident commander to communicate with all the assembled forces if a full evacuation became necessary.

WEAPONS OF MASS DESTRUCTION

Weapons of mass destruction (WMD) are a serious potential challenge to the emergency response community. First responders would need to begin control and recovery operations while evaluating the nature of the weapon and determining the best course of action. Hot zones would need to be identified. The incident commander might have to stop rescue operations if the victims have received a lethal dose of the agent. Emergency services are not accustomed to abandoning victims, and this decision would be even more difficult if there were schools, nursing homes, hospitals, and fire stations in the hot zone. Training and exercises have been conducted to prepare commanders for WMD events, but the psychological effects of making such decisions could hamper the control of an incident in the critical early stages.

Also, military units would probably be among the early responders: the Department of Defense (DOD) has given considerable attention to supporting local agencies in a WMD event. But most local governments have not trained or even met with the military units that would be deployed. Local public safety officials need to consider the worst-case scenario for their community; learn what military units are likely to be deployed; and meet with the appropriate commanders to discuss capabilities and equipment and to plan joint training exercises. Another consideration for local officials is that some full-time police officers, firefighters, and EMS personnel are also members of the National Guard. First-responder agencies must know how many of their employees are members of the National Guard and are likely to be called up in an emergency, and how such a call-up would affect the local response. If the effect is likely to leave the local community short of trained personnel, a plan for additional recruiting, supplemental staffing, or cross-training needs to be developed.

TECHNOLOGY: INTEROPERABLE COMMUNICATIONS

A basic need of first responders is communication with each other during emergency operations. Most first responders use land mobile radio systems (LMRS). Portable radios for first responders must be operable in extreme weather and high humidity, and powerful enough to penetrate concrete walls.

Since 9/11, interoperable communications (Figure 42-5) have received much attention. However, many groups were concerned much earlier about the problems of providing such communication: the Association of Public Safety Communications Officials (APCO), Public Safety Wireless Network (PSWN), and Project SAFECOM have for some time been urging the removal of barriers to interoperability. The technical challenges include the multiple bands and frequencies of public safety radio, incompatible technologies, FCC regulations, resistance from vendors, and a lack of funding. The McKinsey Report and the report of the 9/11 Commission emphasized the need to improve communications in public safety agencies; and first-responder organizations such as the International Association of Chiefs of Police (IACP) and International Association of Fire Chiefs (IAFC) have made efforts to obtain the necessary funding. However,

F I G U R E   42-5

Levels of interoperability (a simplified version).

Method of Interoperability	Degree of Complexity	Number of Agencies	Bands, Frequencies	Cost
Swap radios	Low	2–3	2–3	Low
Talkaround	Low	2–4	Same band	Moderate
Mutual aid channels	Low	2–6	Shared frequency	Moderate
Patch	Moderate	2–8	2–6	Moderate to expensive
System roaming	High	2–12	2–6	Expensive
Standards-based sharing of systems	High	2–20	Unlimited	Very expensive

Project SAFECOM predicts it will be 2008 before local jurisdictions will have some level of interoperability.[3] In the interim, public safety agencies will have to devise ad hoc solutions.

In 1997, Baltimore began to tackle its problems regarding public safety communications: old radio systems that could not penetrate high-rise buildings, high maintenance costs, and a lack of interoperability. Mayor Kurt L. Schmoke spent the money necessary to give first responders a system that solved those problems. The city's consolidated 800-MHz radio system (described above) was completed in 1999 at a cost of nearly $70 million. It provides communications between police, fire, EMS, and other city agencies through software-defined talkgroups. Each agency has up to 50 groupings available.

The city also had to reach agreements with the surrounding counties to give response entities seamless communications. For disparate systems to interoperate, it is necessary to share information that could compromise the total system if misused. Responsible parties are naturally reluctant to open their systems for the sake of events that might seldom or never occur. Thus safeguards, both technical and operational, must be institutionalized between the sharing agencies.

Before 9/11, most jurisdictions had trouble convincing political and budget officials that interoperable communications would be cost-effective. Now it is hoped that the PSWN Program, which has developed the Public Safety Wireless Interoperability National Strategy (WINS) can lead the way to interoperability among public safety wireless networks nationwide.

Interoperability technology exists today. The challenge is deciding what technology to choose and who will pay for it.

A PRACTICAL GUIDE TO PREPARING FOR INCIDENTS

First responders should always focus on rescue, containment, and control. In the future, new tools and equipment will be developed; but during a crisis, what makes the difference is not equipment but people. Although senior officials should provide first responders with the best equipment available, future events might make much new equipment useless. For example, a nuclear or radiological event could affect such a wide area that the communications infrastructure would be lost. A device placed in an urban environment could kill or injure not only civilians but a large proportion of the police, fire, and EMS forces.

How would your city recover from such an event? The only way to know is to conduct training and exercises that stretch your resources and—more important—stretch the minds of senior officials. Each community should conduct a thorough self-examination that includes the following questions:

- What are the total resources available for a major event?
- How would off-duty emergency workers be mobilized if the communications infrastructure failed?
- Where would additional (outside) support come from?
- How would additional support be requested?
- What are the chokepoints in the transportation network?
- Where would mass casualties be taken for treatment?
- Where could shelters and morgues be located?
- How would a mass evacuation be conducted?
- What critical networks would be affected by a large-scale power interruption for over a week?
- How would government continue if the senior leadership were eliminated?

CONCLUSION

This list is not exhaustive, but it can form a basis for evaluation and for planning to deal with disasters. Once the plans are completed, officials should practice them frequently and invite participation from surrounding jurisdictions. The administrative staff should periodically review and update the plans, taking experience and new threats into account. Even if no disaster occurs, the interaction of many jurisdictions and agencies will improve the working relationships that are critical to everyday life.

NOTES

1. See www.interfire.com/res_file/pdf/Tr–049.pdf.
2. See www.nyc.gov/html/fdny/pdf/mck_report/fire_operations_response.pdf.
3. *Project SAFECOM: Key Cross-Agency Emergency Communications Effort Requires Stronger Collaboration*, GAO–04–494 (Washington, D.C.: GAO, 16 April 2004).

CHAPTER 43

National Response Plan, the National Incident Management System, and the Federal Response Plan

Claire B. Rubin
President and Prinicpal, Claire B. Rubin & Associates,
Disaster Research and Consulting (www.disaster-central.com);
Senior Research Scientist, George Washington University,
Institute for Crisis, Disaster, and Risk Management, Washington, D.C.

John R. Harrald
Codirector, George Washington University, Institute for Crisis,
Disaster, and Risk Management, Washington, D.C.

HOW IMPORTANT ARE THE CHANGES IN NATIONAL RESPONSE MECHANISMS?

Two recent documents, the National Response Plan (NRP) and the National Incident Management System (NIMS), augur important changes for federal and national responses to major threats and crises in the United States.[1] They are likely to lead to significant policies and procedural changes in the coming months and years, in that their reach and impact go farther and deeper than previous federal response plans and systems. Since these are national rather than federal plans, they affect state and local agencies and nongovernmental organizations and also dictate organizational and procedural changes, right down to the street level. Additionally, these revised plans and systems will have implications for consultants and educators in the next few years.

To date, neither the community of practitioners nor the academic community has delved into the organizational changes associated with the two new systems—their theory, design, or potential impact. In fairness to those likely to perform the analyses, NRP and NIMS have been released in various drafts over a period of several months, during 2003 and 2004, and implementation probably will occur in 2005 and beyond. Nevertheless, these two new systems and documents merit closer and more detailed scrutiny than they have received to date. These two documents are likely to result in major changes in the understanding of, approach to, and practice of emergency management.

WHAT IS THE BASIS FOR THE CHANGES?

The Homeland Security Act of 2002 and Homeland Security Presidential Directive 5 (HSPD-5), Management of Domestic Incidents, issued in February 2003, set the wheels in motion for the creation of two essential frameworks which will form the underpinnings of the nation's approach to incident management for the foreseeable future.

As noted in March 2004 by Charles Hess, who was then an official with the Department of Homeland Security (DHS), the objectives of HSPD-5 were to (1) create a single, comprehensive national approach; (2) ensure that all levels of government and the private sector would work together; (3) integrate crisis and consequence management; and (4) assign the secretary of DHS as the principal federal official for managing domestic incidents. NRP and its companion NIMS will fundamentally change how the United States prepares for and responds to extreme events.

The NIMS document was completed in March 2004, and the final draft of the NRP document was issued in June 2004. One or more draft versions went out for public comment in the first half of 2004. The Department of Homeland Security formally issued the signed version of the NRP on January 6, 2005.

Given the long lead time in preparing the final version of NRP, neither the full extent of changes nor the need for new implementation mechanisms is yet fully known. Various guidelines and directives, as well as training programs, were to be forthcoming in the second half of 2004.

The relationship between NRP and NIMS is shown in Figure 43-1. NRP supersedes several existing plans, such as the Federal Response Plan (FRP), the U.S. Government Domestic Terrorism Concept of Operations Plan (CONPLAN), and the initial National Response Plan; and it integrates the National Contingency

F I G U R E   43-1

NIMS and NRP relationship.

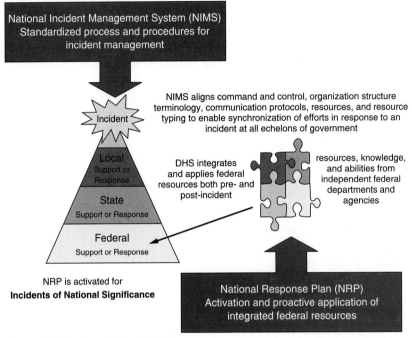

Source: U.S. Department of Homeland Security

Plan (NCP) and the Federal Radiological Emergency Response Plan (FRERP). NRP uses emergency support functions, similar to those in FRP. NIMS aligns command-and-control (C2), organizational structure, terminology, communications protocols, resources, and resource-typing on the basis of "incident command system" (ICS) concepts to enable the synchronization of efforts in response to an incident at all echelons of government.

According to Hess, the development of NRP and NIMS involved many federal agencies; stakeholders, such as state and local officials and representatives of the private sector; and the incorporation of lessons learned from a series of significant events. These events were the attacks on the World Trade Center and the Pentagon (September 2001), the anthrax attacks (October 2001), the power blackout in the eastern United States (August 2003), hurricane Isabel (September 2003), and the TOPOFF 2 Exercise (May 2003).

Regarding applicability and scope, NRP:

◆ Provides the national framework for managing domestic incidents
◆ Broadly applies to all categories of incidents
◆ Establishes protocols for monitoring and reporting incidents and potential incidents
◆ Authorizes DHS to be involved in "incidents of national significance" for coordinating operations, resources, or both

The last item above is new and important. "Incidents of national significance"—those that require DHS to coordinate operations or resources—include the following:

◆ Credible threats or indications of terrorist acts within the United States
◆ Major disasters or emergencies (as defined by the Stafford Act)
◆ Catastrophic incidents
◆ Unique situations that may require DHS to aid in coordinating incident management

The threshold for federal involvement has changed, depending on the nature and severity of the threat or hazard. Figure 43-2 shows

F I G U R E   43-2

Layered response strategy.

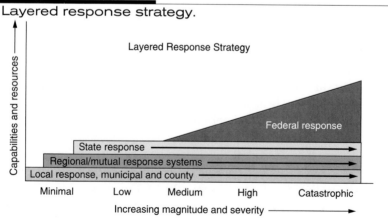

Source: U.S. Department of Homeland Security

a "layered" response strategy for the involvement of the federal government. NRP gives DHS very broad authorization for control and coordination of efforts in response to a wide range of events. The secretary of DHS becomes the nation's incident manager and will exercise this authority by appointing a primary federal official (PFO) responsible for on-scene coordination.

WHAT PROCESSES WERE FOLLOWED, AND WHO PARTICIPATED?[2]

In February 2003, the administration began the process of creating a nationwide template in order to enable federal, state, local, and tribal governments and private-sector and nongovernmental organizations to work together effectively and efficiently to prevent, prepare for, respond to, and recover from domestic incidents regardless of their cause, size, or complexity. The intent was (1) to focus national incident management policy on the terrorist threat, and in particular to integrate emergency management, law enforcement, and public health; (2) to establish the role and functions of DHS as the agency responsible for managing domestic incidents; and (3) to integrate the existing family of federal response and emergency plans and make these less conflicted.

NRP creates a new national approach to domestic incident management by merging and integrating key concepts from existing, major federal response plans: FRP, FRERP, NCP, and CONPLAN. Further, through the implementation of NIMS, NRP takes an all-hazards perspective that provides the structure and mechanisms for national-level policy and operational direction for domestic incident management.

According to DHS, NRP is intended to be truly national in scope and will result in a comprehensive system of preparedness and response. NRP will govern the federal response to a wide range of "incidents of national significance," and provide a policy framework for the coordination of federal, state, and local governments; nongovernmental organizations; and private-sector resources.

As regards stakeholders' involvement, both NRP and NIMS have been developed from the top down and centrally coordinated by DHS. Views differ on the scope and intent of stakeholders' involvement in developing NRP and NIMS. Hess and Harrald represent diverging perspectives.

Hess of DHS stated in 2004 that the development process included extensive review and participation by a broad range of partners and stakeholders. This process involved all the federal departments and agencies; state, local, and tribal government stakeholders; and the private sector.

Harrald, in July 2004, noted that the development of NRP, like all policy development, was not a pretty process to watch. When President Bush signed HSPD-5, DHS was faced with impossible deadlines driven by a perceived immediate threat of terrorism. An Interim NRP was to be issued by 1 April 2003; an NIMS by 1 June 2003; and a fully implemented NRP by September 2003. These deadlines proved to be counterproductive, and the initial documents released for review were woefully inadequate. They ignored or eliminated critical elements of the system currently in use, most notably "disaster mitigation," FRP emergency support function structure, and the process and structure of NCP as it pertained to releases of oil and hazardous substances.

The academic "hazards community" has been largely absent and uninvolved during the development of this critical national policy framework. Social scientists have examined organizational responses to large, complex events and know that open, adaptive organizational systems work best; that emergent organizations always appear; and that the most effective immediate responses are actions taken by those affected by a disaster. NRP and NIMS, however, set up a much more formal, structured system for dealing with extreme events. An ominous sign is the volume of acronyms describing new and old organizations (e.g., HSOC, NRCC, JFO, IIMG, JDCC, LEOC) and roles (e.g., PFO, SAC, FOC, FRC, FOSC). NRP has a six-page single-spaced listing of acronyms that will enable readers to decode these terms and specifies detailed, complex organizational relationships that will exist before and during extreme events. NRP recognizes and specifies that extensive training is necessary for those expected to operate within the system. This necessary training represents an implicit system boundary. Among the open questions that could concern the hazards research community are these:

- Will a centralized, highly structured, closed system entrusted solely to trained professionals work effectively for managing the preparation for and response to complex events?

- ◆ Will the hazards research community be able to evaluate and assist in the evolution of this system?
- ◆ Was such a sweeping change necessary to achieve immediate policy goals?
- ◆ What will be the unintended consequences of this policy initiative?

The authors agree that the final product was much improved after state and local review, extensive comment from within the federal government, and a restructuring of the drafting process. However, the resulting patchwork of plans and changes is dauntingly complex. NRP, for example, will maintain and expand the Emergency Support Function (ESF) structure (to include an economic stabilization, community recovery, and mitigation ESF) and retain NCP in its entirety as a supporting plan. The final NRP will supersede FRP, CONPLAN, the Interim NRP, and FRERP. NRP provides additional incident "annexes" that directly address incidents of cyber, nuclear, biological, and other terrorism. The NRP structure preserves the separate roles and responsibilities of the Department of Justice/Federal Bureau of Investigation (FBI) and the Department of Health and Human Services Centers for Disease Control and Prevention, while defining relationships and coordinating mechanisms.

NIMS INTEGRATION CENTER

The NIMS Integration Center was established by the secretary of Homeland Security in June 2004 to provide "strategic direction for and oversight of the National Incident Management System... supporting both routine maintenance and the continuous refinement of the system and its components over the long term."

NIMS is a comprehensive incident response system, developed by DHS at the request of the president. NIMS provides the core set of doctrines, concepts, principles, terminology, and organizational processes that will define the United States' approach to managing incidents involving all kinds of threats and hazards. The NIMS Integration Center will oversee all aspects of NIMS, including the development of standards and guidelines related to NIMS and the provision of guidance and support to incident-management and responder organizations as they implement the system. The center also will validate compliance with the responsibilities, standards, and requirements entailed by NRP and NIMS.

This center is a multijurisdictional, multidisciplinary entity made up of federal stakeholders and state, local, and tribal incident-management and first-responder organizations. It is situated in DHS/FEMA. (For more details, see NIMS-Integration-Center@dhs.gov. See also www.fema.gov/nims.) The center is charged with the development and maintenance of:

+ National-level training standards and course curricula
+ Materials to support implementation of NIMS (training modules, job aids, etc.)
+ Documentation and a database system for qualifications, certification, and credentialing of incident-management personnel and responders
+ A system related to standards for performance, compatibility, and interoperability of equipment
+ A repository for lessons learned

COMPLIANCE WITH NIMS

Beginning in fiscal year (FY) 2005 (September 2004–August 2005), federal departments and agencies must make adoption of NIMS by state, local, and tribal governments a requirement for federal preparedness assistance through grants, contracts, and other activities.

The NIMS Compliance Assurance Support Tool (NIMCAST) was published in the *Federal Register* on 4 June 2004. It is the assessment tool used to (1) evaluate state and local compliance with the standards and requirements of NIMS, (2) determine eligibility for federal preparedness assistance, and (3) provide management tools to strengthen incident-management programs at the department, agency, or jurisdiction level.

NIMS recognizes that most incidents are managed locally, but it is based on the premise that field command and management functions must comply with a standard set of ICS organizational definitions, doctrines, and procedures. The goal is to take advantage of this commonality to build flexible, modular, scalable response organizations supported by interoperable technology. However, the federal dictates regarding the structural and C2 aspects of incident management do not guarantee managerial effectiveness at any level.

WHAT ARE THE CHALLENGES AND OPPORTUNITIES OF IMPLEMENTATION?

Developing a standard template and a new approach to domestic incident management presents numerous challenges, including the following.

Creating a New Way of Doing Business While Keeping What Works

Early feedback on NRP stressed the need to preserve and reinforce what works well in the creation of a new approach to incident management. The challenge is to build on the multitude of existing authorities and processes, span the gaps between them, and establish a new, comprehensive system.

Combining Multiple Approaches for Incident Management into a Single System

Significant communication, and the development of significant relationships, will be necessary in order to create a single framework flexible enough to encompass the role of the federal government and adequately support state and local incident managers, while also accounting for situations where the federal government exercises direct authority and has direct responsibility for incident management. (Examples are the FBI's role in countering terrorists and the federal on-scene coordinator's role under NCP in responding to pollution incidents.)

Imposing Structure and Standards While Maintaining Innovation and Creativity

NIMS and NRP are a historic attempt by the federal government to impose standards and structure on a very diverse, complex national response system. We know that in the past, one key to success has been the ability of individuals and organizations on the ground to improvise and adapt to meet immediate needs; an example is the management of the Pentagon's response by Arlington County, as Harrald et al. noted in 2002. We run the risk of overstructuring a system that has been historically effective, and of diminishing critical innovative and creative capabilities.

Shifting the Traditional Focus on Response and Recovery

The majority of existing incident-management plans focus on response and recovery. For example, FRP was predicated on the Stafford Act to provide federal assistance after a presidential declaration of disaster or emergency. As NRP expands beyond this traditional function to focus on prevention and preparedness during an incident, efforts toward prevention and preparedness become major considerations as regards domestic terrorism. Expanding into areas with limited legislative authority and funding for preincident actions is a challenge.

Encouraging Federal-to-Federal Support in the Absence of Legislation

HSPD-5 envisions activating and using NRP as the framework for interagency mutual aid, absent a disaster or emergency declaration that would make the Stafford Act applicable. The Stafford Act authorizes the secretary of DHS and the emergency preparedness and response undersecretary (FEMA's director) to "task" ("mission-assign") supporting departments and agencies after an incident is declared an emergency or a disaster. This type of tasking authority does not exist for incidents of national significance that do not result in a presidential declaration of a disaster. When the Stafford Act does not confer authority, interagency mutual aid is in fact essentially voluntary, and agencies will need to commit themselves to some type of interagency mutual aid or assistance agreement to carry out those interagency incident-management activities that do not rise to the level of a presidentially declared disaster.

Creating a Meaningful System of Certification and Credentialing

NIMS establishes a federal role and system for "qualification, certification, and credentialing of incident management personnel and organizations." This is a massive and critical component of implementing NIMS-NRP. Incentives are built into the process, by means of funding that will be tied to certification and credentialing. Without meaningful standards and measurements, however, the system could be abused, subverted, or both.

Working Within Time Constraints

Developing a national plan is, by necessity, a collaborative process. Meeting the ambitious schedules without hindering the collaborative process may be difficult. The federal government has been unable to meet its own timelines, imposed by HSPD-5; thus it is doubtful that the state and local governments and nonprofit organizations affected by NIMS and by NRP will do any better.

CONCLUSION

These are just a few of the challenges associated with the creation of a complete, comprehensive, usable, user-friendly, all-hazards NRP. Other considerations include developing supporting "annexes," identifying the correct emergency support structure and mechanisms, synchronizing the terminology and organizational element descriptors so that everyone has a clear understanding of how the plan works, and deciding who pays and under what circumstances.

In addition, compliance with NRP is mandatory for all federal agencies. In order to remain eligible for federal funding, state governments are expected to modify existing plans for incident management and emergency operations, within a year of its becoming national policy. Local governments and nongovernmental and private-sector organizations will have to adjust their plans and procedures to operate within the context of NRP-NIMS. This is an ambitious and untested undertaking, involving a wide array of organizations and individuals not accustomed to working together. Nevertheless, it will determine the emergency management agenda for the coming decade.

N O T E S

1. The National Response Plan (NRP) and the related National Incident Management System (NIMS) can be obtained from the Department of Homeland Security (DHS) website: www.dhs.gov/.

2. Based on NHRAIC, *Hazards Observer,* July 2004. "Invited Comment" by John R. Harrald and Charles Hess.

BIBLIOGRAPHY

Harrald, John R., et al. 2002. *Observing and Documenting the Inter-Organizational Response to the September 11th Attack on the Pentagon* (15 July). George Washington University Institute for Crisis, Disaster, and Risk Management, at www.gwu.edu/~icdrm/publications/nsf911/.

Hess, Charles. 2004. "NRP and NIMS." Slide Presentation to the National Response Team (March) at www.nrt.org.

NHRAIC. 2004. *Hazards Observer* (July). See John R. Harrald and Charles Hess, "Invited Comment," at www.colorado.edu/hazards.

"NIMS Compliance Assurance Support Tool (NIMCAST)," *Federal Register,* 4 June 2004.

White House. 2003. Homeland Security Presidential Directive 5: Management of Domestic Incidents, at www.whitehouse.gov/news/releases/2003/02/20030228-9.html.

CHAPTER 44

Understanding and Preparing for the Psychological Consequences of Terrorism

Terri L. Tanielian, M.A.
Senior Research Analyst, Associate Director for Mental and Behavioral Health, Center for Domestic and International Health Security, The RAND Corporation

Bradley D. Stein, M.D., Ph.D., M.P.H.
Natural Scientist, Associate Director for Mental and Behavioral Health, Center for Domestic and International Health Security, The RAND Corporation

INTRODUCTION

Two of the various definitions of *terrorism* that have been offered are as follows:

> The illegal use or threatened use of force or violence; an intent to coerce societies or governments by inducing fear in their populations; typically with ideological and political motives and justifications; an "extrasocietal" element, either "outside" society in the case of domestic terrorism or "foreign" in the case of international terrorism.[2]

> The purpose of terrorism is not the single act of wanton destruction, it is the reaction it seeks to provoke: economic collapse, the backlash, the hatred, the division, the elimination of tolerance, until societies cease to reconcile their differences and become defined by them.[3]

What these definitions have in common is recognition that, beyond the physical damage caused by the event itself, terrorism is intended to have a psychological effect. It targets the social capital of a nation—cohesion, values, and ability to function. Therefore, successful counterterrorism and national continuity depend on effective interventions to sustain the psychological, behavioral, and social functioning of the nation and its citizens. From the impact of an attack (e.g., destruction and death) and the consequences associated with the response (e.g., economic loss and disruption) to the impact of preparedness and counterterrorism themselves (e.g., behavioral and social ramifications of new security procedures), there is an urgent need for an understanding of the development of effective intervention and tools for assessing and predicting psychological, behavioral, and social responses and counterresponses.

The attacks of 9/11 and the persistent threat of future terrorism demonstrate the importance of preparing the nation to respond more effectively. The emotional consequences of terrorism (which can include acute and long-term distress, anxiety, grief, depression, anger, etc.) pose unique challenges for government officials charged with planning prevention and response, and they raise important questions regarding the ability of the public health system to understand and prepare for such events.

The federal government has undertaken unprecedented efforts to increase the nation's ability to respond to terrorism, including the establishment of the Department of Homeland Security (DHS), the passing of the PATRIOT Act, and (to address bioterrorism specifically) the investment of over $4 billion in the public health infrastructure. However, little national or local policy has focused on the importance of addressing psychology or mental health as part of these efforts.

This chapter describes the psychological consequences of terrorism and outlines strategies for dealing with them. This information should prove useful for policy makers attempting to develop state and local response strategies.

WHAT ARE WE WORRIED ABOUT?

Much has been written about the emotional, cognitive, somatic (biological), and behavioral responses that can be expected in the immediate aftermath of terrorism. Many of these studies have focused on the incidence and prevalence of posttraumatic stress disorder (PTSD) and acute stress disorder, the impact on the use of health care services, and the impact on substance use (e.g., smoking and drinking). Many of the reactions that were identified after 9/11 (including increases in PTSD and the use of alcohol) have also been found, communitywide, after other large-scale traumas such as earthquakes, wildfires, and hurricanes. However, incidents of mass violence, such as shootings and terrorism, are intentional and are therefore the most psychologically disturbing type of disaster; thus their psychological consequences are frequently more severe.[4]

Beaton and Murphy's review of responses to terrorist events suggested that up to two-thirds of those directly affected (either as a victim or as a relative) are psychologically impaired to some degree.[5] They may experience a wide range of emotional and behavioral consequences that include PTSD, a psychiatric disorder characterized by persistent flashbacks or nightmares, extreme irritability or jumpiness, and emotional numbing or avoidance of reminders of the trauma. Others may develop other anxiety disorders, depression, and problems with substance use, as well as symptoms that do not meet the criteria for PTSD.[6]

The documented prevalence of such problems after specific events varies widely, perhaps because of differences in the populations involved, the nature of the events, and the methodologies used in the studies. Typically, the researchers have screened victims to identify symptoms of posttraumatic stress and to determine whether these symptoms meet the criteria for a clinical diagnosis of PTSD. For some victims, however, these symptoms may not initially meet the criteria; but if left untreated for some months after the first screening, they may become more severe.

WHO WILL MOST PROBABLY BE AFFECTED?

Individuals most likely to be affected, psychologically and behaviorally, by a terrorist event include those who were injured, those who were present or nearby, those (such as first responders) who were exposed to trauma as a result of their attempts to help victims, and those (such as vulnerable populations) who were already at risk of developing psychological symptoms. Also, terrorism may be more likely than other traumatic events to cause a psychological reaction in individuals who were far from the attack but are nevertheless concerned about being in danger.

Direct and Indirect Victims

Studies conducted immediately after 9/11 found a range of emotional and behavioral reactions, both in the cities where the attacks occurred and across the country. For example, three to five days after 9/11, 44 percent of a national sample of Americans reported experiencing substantial emotional stress.[7] One to two months after 9/11, 8 percent of residents sampled in Manhattan reported symptoms consistent with PTSD, and 10 percent reported symptoms consistent with depression.[8] During this time frame, estimates of probable PTSD in areas close to the attack ranged from 3 percent in Washington, D.C., to 11 percent in the New York metropolitan area.[9] Subsequent surveys of the general public found a decrease in the prevalence of severe emotional distress,[10] but—at least in New York City—such surveys also found changes in health-related behaviors, such as a persistent increase in the use of cigarettes, alcohol, and marijuana[11] and an increase in missed doses and suboptimal doses of antiretroviral therapies among HIV-positive men.[12] Such behavioral changes can have a wide public health impact and as such need to be considered as well.

First Responders

First responders—traditionally thought of as the police, firefighters, and emergency medical technicians (EMTs)—care for both survivors and the dead and also face the possibility of having to enter a dangerous environment. Thus they may witness mass carnage and destruction, and their own health and well-being may be imperiled. Considerable attention has been given to emotional repercussions among first responders, particularly those who responded to the bombing of the Murrah Federal Building in Oklahoma City in 1995 or to the attack on the World Trade Center (WTC) on 9/11. Studies by North and Herman and their colleagues[13] suggest that the experience of responding to such events significantly increases the risk of symptoms of PTSD and other psychiatric sequelae.

Vulnerable Populations

Terrorism can have an especially profound effect on vulnerable populations such as children, racial and ethnic minorities, and those with an existing psychiatric illness. Individuals in a community who are exposed to a terrorist act experience a range of psychological reactions that affect how the incident is managed. At one end of the range are behaviors of normal people under abnormal circumstances, such as wanting to return to their families immediately, regardless of official advice or orders to stay in place. These normal reactions may either help or hinder efforts to contain a threatening agent; deliver medical care; and reduce the morbidity, mortality, and costs associated with the disaster. At the other end of the range are new behaviors or exacerbated habitual behaviors that are disruptive to the community, such as refusing to be evacuated.[14]

Children are a vulnerable population of particular interest. One study found that when children were more distressed, their parents spent more time talking with them.[15] It seems likely that these parents were trying to reassure the children, but in a situation where parents as well as children may feel threatened, we cannot draw a conclusion about the implications of this finding without more information about the actual conversations. Possibly, another factor, such as the parents' own distress, causes longer parent-child conversations about terrorism and also intensifies the psychological effect of terrorism on children. Another possibility is that the correlation is not between parent-child conversations and symptoms, but rather between conversations and reported symptoms. That is, perhaps parents who spend more time in such conversations become more aware of their children's mental state and therefore report more symptoms; in other words, the conversations serve as a means for parents to find out about the psychological impact of terrorism on their children. Still another possibility is that in some cases the conversations may heighten children's worries and psychological reactions, particularly if the parents warn the children to avoid public places, take precautions against anthrax, or the like.

In studies in Israel of children repeatedly exposed to terrorism, many children evidently felt insecure, were worried about safety, and were ready to expect the worst.[16] In research in the United States several months after 9/11, children commonly remained worried about being victims of terrorism.[17] Further research is needed to determine whether such feelings might result from repeated warnings or threats of terrorism even when no actual events occur. Parents are likely to influence how children respond to terrorism, and there are few other types of traumatic events where the potential threat to both parent and child is comparable. Additional studies will contribute to an evidence base allowing better-informed recommendations to parents about how to help children cope with terrorism.

Several studies have investigated whether ethnicity and culture are predictive of psychological and behavioral reactions. Studies of residents of New York City after 9/11 found differences among populations in outcomes and in the utilization of services. In a large-scale epidemiologic study, one predictor of PTSD was Hispanic ethnicity.[18] Also, African-American and Hispanic respondents were less likely than white respondents to use services or take medications. The researchers attributed this disparity to various cultural factors, including valuing self-reliance, expressing emotions in certain ways, and having reservations about sharing emotions with others.

Individuals with preexisting psychological illnesses or mental health problems also appear to be at greater risk of experiencing psychological consequences of terrorism.[19] For example, in one study, prior depression or anxiety was associated with higher levels of posttraumatic stress symptoms after 9/11.[20]

Understanding—and mitigating—the likely consequences for vulnerable populations will be a critical component of counter-terrorist preparedness, planning, and response.

STRATEGIES FOR PREPAREDNESS AND RESPONSE

Although additional research on preparedness and response is still needed, the studies conducted so far have found that after terrorist events, community-oriented responses (such as those aimed at and based on existing community relationships) have been instrumental in managing psychological consequences. These studies examined responses in Oklahoma City in 1995[21] and in and around New York City and Washington, D.C., after 9/11.

Overall strategies for preparing the public and the appropriate resources to respond to large-scale traumatic events can be organized according to specific populations (e.g., victims, responders, vulnerable groups) and according to phases of the event (pre-event, acute, postevent, long-term postevent). The strategies can be divided into two categories with distinct but overlapping goals: (1) to provide immediate psychological management to allow for effective public health and emergency response strategies (e.g., by mitigating or preventing psychological distress and fear, and by minimizing potential, unnecessary demands on the health care system); and (2) to reduce both short-term and long-term psychological morbidity.

Traditional responses to an emergency such as a disaster typically include deploying trained mental health specialists to the place or places directly affected; this deployment can include groups such as the American Red Cross and other mental health organizations. These responders then become available to offer crisis counseling and management, screen for mental health problems, provide psychological first aid, and provide supportive counseling to those in need who ask for help. There may also be funding from the Federal Emergency Management Agency (FEMA) to provide psychoeducational materials to the community and to ensure that counseling services are available throughout the recovery process. To repeat, these traditional strategies have usually been implemented by trained mental health professionals who are available to those requesting them. However, the strategies need to be adapted and applied to other populations that may not be included in the traditional emergency response system, particularly those that, during screening, are not identified as needing such services and those that may not feel comfortable about coming forward for help. In addition, more training regarding the types of consequences, and effective strategies for mitigating them, may be needed for the special provider groups who will play a critical role in responding to the various psychological needs that are likely to arise: mental health specialists, informal care providers, and other existing social support systems within the community.

WHAT WORKS? DEVELOPING AND EVALUATING INTERVENTIONS

The nation's ability to respond to the psychological consequences of terrorism depends in part on the availability of effective interventions. We need reliable tools and strategies for assessing symptoms in different affected populations, and for distinguishing between individuals who are likely to recover and those who will require more intense interventions.[22] Once a population is identified as needing treatment, the efficacy of the available interventions needs to be understood. The needs of those who have been directly affected by an event may differ from the needs of those who were not directly affected. There is currently no universally applicable strategy. Experts in mental health following a disaster should design and evaluate clinical interventions such as psychotherapy, medication, and counseling to ensure the delivery of effective care at the right time and by the right persons.

In recent years, attention has been given to the effectiveness of psychological debriefings and "critical incident stress" debriefings. These techniques were developed to allow guided processing of a stressful event within a group of individuals having the same level of exposure to the event (such as a group of emergency responders after a fatal fire).[23] However, empirical research is inconclusive regarding the effectiveness of these interventions, and more work is needed to understand if, when, and for whom these models are appropriate and helpful. Early intervention strategies for individuals exposed to mass violence must be culturally relevant, sensitive to individual differences, and sensitive to the context in which members of specific groups (e.g., people with special needs, first responders, and minorities) have experienced the traumatic event. Based on evidence and application of best practice guidelines available, Ritchie, Friedman, Watson et al., (2004) outlined several key components for early mental health interventions following chemical, bacteriological, radiological (CBR) attacks.[24] These strategies involve prior planning and involve several key stakeholders.

WHO CAN RESPOND?
Mental Health Specialists

After communitywide disasters, including terrorism, individuals with training in mental health (e.g., licensed social workers, psychologists, and psychiatrists) have often played an important role in the immediate response. These specialists can provide psychoeducation and emotional support (such as the techniques grouped under the term "psychological first aid") and crisis counseling to people who have been directly affected by the event. People who have actually participated in such activities and in coordinating the broader response to the disaster have identified at least three areas for improvement.

First, in some cases, many local specialists in mental health and specialists from outside the area may descend on the scene of a disaster, potentially putting themselves at risk and hampering the activities of other responders. Second, many mental health specialists are not trained in, or are not even familiar with, psychological first aid or currently agreed-on best practices for working with victims in the immediate aftermath of a disaster. Third, experts in mental health in the context of disasters generally agree that many traditional interventions (e.g., psychoanalysis) are inappropriate following a terrorist event or a large-scale disaster.[25]

Accordingly, efforts are now under way in many communities (such as some in Connecticut and Massachusetts), and in the mental health field more broadly, to train individuals to respond to a disaster. One example is the American Red Cross Disaster Mental Health training program. Efforts are also being made to develop plans to restrict access to a disaster site to those individuals, identified in advance, who have expertise in "disaster mental health response."

Informal Care Providers and Community Organizations

In a terrorist attack, informal care providers (such as teachers, supervisors, and faith-based organizations) can be instrumental in providing information and support to victims and their families, and in helping to manage the psychological consequences of the event.

Schools will be in a unique position to provide grief counseling, reassure students about their safety, and monitor students with severe stress reactions.[26]

Work sites also provide an opportunity for individuals to express their concerns and receive information following an incident.[27] If response strategies include isolating employees or quarantining buildings, employers will need to understand their role in implementing a public health response, as well as in managing the psychological consequences of the event and the response.

The clergy were cited as one of the most frequently sought sources of help in surveys conducted after 9/11. They represent another important source of informal care and support. Response planners should consider how churches and other religious organizations can work together to manage the psychological consequences of terrorism.

HOW CAN WE ENSURE THAT THE RESPONDERS ARE READY?

More work is needed to prepare community-level care providers to respond to the psychological consequences of terrorism. For instance, little is known about what education and training the providers will need for responding to psychological consequences, and little is known about the skills involved.

The participation of those familiar with psychological and psychiatric issues will be critical to all phases of planning for preparedness at the local and state level. In the planning phases, such individuals can help devise appropriate strategies for communicating about risk; can help develop educational materials that are sensitive to risk perception and to emotional and cognitive responses and processing; and can help train and educate emergency response personnel with regard to detecting and treating traumatic reactions.

During the acute management phase of a terrorist event, trained mental health professionals can be part of the response team to help diagnose neuropsychiatric complications associated with some biological or chemical agents, and to distinguish between psychosomatic symptoms and organic symptoms. Over the longer term, they can provide appropriate and effective interventions for victims who have been directly affected and for others who are experiencing psychological distress, including members of the general population.

A few specific issues having to do with mental health specialists require further consideration by federal, state, and local preparedness planners: workforce size and training requirements for disaster response and terrorism specifically; the "surge capacity" of the mental health treatment system for handling psychological casualties; and effective interventions to address the needs of diverse affected populations.

CONCLUSION

Uncertainty and lack of information about the specific or unique psychological effects of terrorism may complicate the task of state officials who must develop mental health plans as part of overall preparedness. Also, the way response plans are implemented and communicated might generate or mitigate fear and anxiety in a particular population. Clearly, understanding how to manage the psychological consequences of terrorism is critical to developing and implementing realistic, appropriate response strategies.

The emergency response system, including the public health system, must be prepared for a terrorist attack and have strategies in place to minimize its psychological consequences. Initial preparation should include collaborating and coordinating with a variety of agencies involved in homeland security (emergency responders, hospitals, public health officials, etc.) to ensure the inclusion of individuals who understand and can respond to the psychological aspects of terrorism: emergency responders, health care providers, including mental health professionals, and other health care personnel. An effective communication system will be essential in order to apply recommendations for responding to and mitigating public uncertainty and distress. State and local health departments should consider developing a three-prong approach to planning, similar to that used by FEMA: education, preparedness, and action. Finally, strategies for preparedness need to address the mental health consequences of a terrorist attack as well as the issues of physical health.

N O T E S

1. The article is based on a related work in *Milbank Quarterly,* September 2004. See also B. D. Stein, T. L. Tanielian, D. P. Eisenman, D. Keyser, M. A. Burnam, and H. A. Pincus, "Emotional and Behavioral Consequences of Bioterrorism: Planning a Public Health Response," *Milbank Quarterly* 82:3 (2004): 413–55.

2. National Research Council, *Terrorism: Perspectives from the Behavioral and Social Sciences,* N. J. Smelser and F. Mitchell (eds.), (Washington, D.C.: National Academies Press, 2002).

3. Tony Blair, speech to joint session, U.S. Congress, 17 July 2003; http://news.bbc.co.uk/2/hi/uk_news/politics/3076253.stm.

4. F. H. Norris, *Fifty Thousand Disaster Victims Speak: An Empirical Review of the Empirical Literature, 1981–2001* (Rockville, Md.: Substance Abuse and Mental Health Services Administration, 2001).

5. R. Beaton and S. Murphy, "Psychosocial Responses to Biological and Chemical Terrorist Threats and Events: Implications for the Workplace," *Journal of the American Association of Occupational Health Nurses* 50:4 (2002): 182–9.

6. See the following: L. Abenhaim, W. Dab, and L. R. Salmi, "Study of Civilian Victims of Terrorist Attacks (France 1982–1987)," *Journal of Clinical Epidemiology* 45:2 (1992): 103–9; H. S. Desivilya, R. Gal, and O. Ayalon, "Extent of Victimization, Traumatic Stress Symptoms, and Adjustment of Terrorist Assault Survivors: A Long-Term Follow-Up," *Journal of Trauma and Stress* 9:4 (1996): 881–9; T. A. Grieger, C. S. Fullerton, and R. J. Ursano, "Posttraumatic Stress Disorder, Alcohol Use, and Perceived Safety after the Terrorist Attack on the Pentagon," *Psychiatric Services* 54:10 (2003): 1380–2; C. S. North, "The Course of Posttraumatic Stress Disorder after the Oklahoma City Bombing," *Military Medicine* 166:12 (Supp.) (2001): 51–2; C. S. North, S. J. Nixon, S. Shariat, et al., "Psychiatric Disorders among Survivors of the Oklahoma City Bombing," *Journal of the American Medical Association* 282:8 (1999): 755–62; and D. Reissman, E. Whitney, T. Taylor, et al., "One-Year Health Assessment of Adult Survivors of *Bacillus anthracis* Infection," *Journal of the American Medical Association* 291:16 (2004): 1994–8.

7. M. A. Schuster, B. D. Stein, L. Jaycox, et al., "A National Survey of Stress Reactions after the September 11, 2001, Terrorist Attacks," *New England Journal of Medicine* 345:20 (2001): 1507–12.

8. S. Galea, J. Ahern, H. Resnick, et al., "Psychological Sequelae of the September 11 Terrorist Attacks in New York City," *New England Journal of Medicine* 346:13 (2002): 982–7.

9. W. E. Schlenger, J. M. Caddell, L. Ebert, et al., "Psychological Reactions to Terrorist Attacks: Findings from the National Study of Americans' Reactions to September 11," *Journal of the American Medical Association* 288:5 (2002): 581–58.

10. R. C. Silver, E. A. Holman, D. N. McIntosh, et al., "Nationwide Longitudinal Study of Psychological Responses to September 11," *Journal of the American Medical Association* 288:10 (2002): 1235–44. See also B. D. Stein, L. H. Jaycox, M. N. Elliott, et al., "Emotional and Behavioral Impact of Terrorism on Children: Results from a National Survey," *Applied Developmental Science.*

11. D. Vlahov, S. Galea, J. Ahern, et al., "Consumption of Cigarettes, Alcohol, and Marijuana among New York City Residents Six Months after the September 11 Terrorist Attacks," *American Journal of Drug and Alcohol Dependence.*

12. P. N. Halkitis, A. H. Kutnick, E. Rosof, et al., "Adherence to HIV Medications in a Cohort of Men Who Have Sex with Men: Impact of September 11th," *Journal of Urban Health* 80:1 (2003): 161–6.

13. C. S. North, L. Tivis, J. C. McMillen, et al., "Psychiatric Disorders in Rescue Workers after the Oklahoma City Bombing," *American Journal of Psychiatry* 159:5 (2002): 857–9. D. Herman, C. Felton, and E. Susser, "Mental Health Needs in New York State Following the September 11th Attacks," *Journal of Urban Health* 79:3 (2002a): 322–31.

14. C. DiGiovanni, Jr., "The Spectrum of Human Reactions to Terrorist Attacks with Weapons of Mass Destruction: Early Management Considerations," *Prehospital and Disaster Medicine: The Official Journal of the National Association of EMS Physicians and the World Association for Emergency Physicians in Association with the Acute Care Foundation* 18:3 (2003): 253–7.

15. Stein et al. (forthcoming).

16. J. A. Shaw, "Children Exposed to War/Terrorism," *Clinical Child and Family Psychology Review* 6:4 (2003): 237–46.

17. Stein et al. (forthcoming).

18. Galea et al. (2002).

19. Norris (2001).

20. Silver et al. (2002).

21. B. Pfefferbaum, J. A. Call, and G. M. Sconzo, "Mental Health Services for Children in the First Two Years after the 1995 Oklahoma City Terrorist Bombing," *Psychiatric Services* 50:7 (1999): 956–8.

22. National Institute of Mental Health (NIMH), *Mental Health and Mass Violence: Evidence-Based Early Psychological Intervention for Victims/Survivors of Mass Violence—A Workshop to Reach Consensus on Best Practices* (NIMH Publication No. 02-5138) (Washington, D.C.: U.S. Government Printing Office, 2002).

23. Ritchie E. C., M. Friedman, P. Watson, R. Ursano, S. Wessely, and B. Flynn (2004) Mass Violence and Early Mental Health Intervention: A Proposed Application of Best Practice Guidelines to Chemical, Biological, and Radiological Attacks.

24. J. T. Mitchell, "When Disaster Strikes: The Critical Incident Stress Debriefing Process," *Journal of Medical Emergency Services* 8 (1983): 36–9. See also J. T. Mitchell and G. S. Everly, "Critical Incident Stress Management and Critical Incident Stress Debriefings: Evolutions, Effects, and Outcomes," in B. Raphael and J. P. Wilson (eds.), *Psychological Debriefings: Theory, Practice, and Evidence* (New York: Cambridge University Press, 2000), pp. 71–90.

25. NIMH (2002).

26. B. D. Stein, T. L. Tanielian, M. E. Vaiana, et al., "The Role of Schools in Meeting Community Needs during Bioterrorism," *Biosecurity and Bioterrorism: Biodefense Strategy, Practice, and Science* 4:1 (2003), pp. 273–81. See also M. D. Weist, M. A. Sander, N. A. Lever, et al., "School Mental Health's Response to Terrorism and Disaster," *Journal of School Violence* 1:4 (2002): 5–31.

27. W. Goldman, "Terrorism and Mental Health: Private-Sector Responses and Issues for Policy Makers," *Psychiatric Services* 53:8 (2002): 941–3.

CHAPTER 45

Moving Target: Biological Threats to America

Elin A. Gursky, Sc. D.
Principal Deputy for Biodefense, National Strategies Support
Directorate, ANSER/Analytic Services, Inc

INTRODUCTION

America is facing turbulence, disquiet, and greater complexity than ever before: the nation comprises increasingly heterogeneous cultures, religions, and ideologies; benefits from unprecedented levels of global populations and trade; and is inundated by information from the World Wide Web. The attacks of 9/11 and the anthrax-laden letters sent anonymously shortly thereafter have forced leaders and policy makers to grapple with unfamiliar biological threats and develop new protective strategies. Developments in technology, transportation, and information sharing have brought new threats against human life and civil order, including the risk that potentially lethal pathogens could be deliberately released and could cause epidemics.

A three-part paradigm for the relationship among threats, vulnerabilities, and systems can help us understand specific weaknesses, allocate resources, and improve our protective efforts.[1]

THREATS

Infection is still a leading cause of death.[2] Although the incidence of, and mortality from, many epidemic diseases declined during the

---

Note: The author would like to acknowledge the assistance of Stephen Dunham, David Higgins, and Holly Myers in preparing this chapter.

twentieth century, especially in developed nations, there is renewed concern over the threat of communicable pathogens. One-third of the world's population lives with the bacterium that causes tuberculosis.[3] Globally, there are 300 to 500 million cases of malaria annually, resulting in 1 million deaths. The Republic of the Congo had 143 cases of Ebola hemorrhagic fever from 2000 to 5 May 2003.[4] In 2004 the World Health Organization (WHO) included among its surveillance activities reports of avian influenza in Thailand; hepatitis E in Sudan; Lassa fever in Sierra Leone; Nipha virus in Bangladesh; cholera in Chad, Niger, and Mozambique; yellow fever in Venezuela and Liberia; dengue fever in Indonesia; meningococcal disease in Nigeria; and salmonella enteritidis in the United States.[5] Many previously identified infectious pathogens, including tuberculosis, malaria, and West Nile fever, have resurged by developing resistance to drugs or have expanded their geographical distribution.[6]

Besides the increasing prevalence of resistant and globally redistributed diseases, the Centers for Disease Control and Prevention (CDC) have acknowledged nearly 40 infectious diseases that emerged since the early 1970s. These include human immunodeficiency virus (HIV); hepatitis C; *E. coli* O157.H7; Ebola virus; Hanta virus; and the severe acute respiratory syndrome (SARS) virus. In the United States, the mortality rate from infectious diseases declined in the early twentieth century but is now double what it was in 1980.[7]

Newly emerging diseases are having a dramatic global effect. SARS, an atypical pneumonia, was first reported in Asia in February 2003; it spread to 24 countries in North America, South America, and Europe. Although 85 percent of cases occurred in China and Hong Kong, there were significant outbreaks in Taiwan, Canada, and Singapore.[8] Over 8,000 people became ill, and 774, including health care workers, died from this novel coronavirus that was transmitted from person to person, was airborne, or was spread by exposure to contaminated surfaces.[9] Besides the direct human toll, SARS has had an economic impact. Uncertainty about its virulence and transmission led to fear and a "crisis of confidence" in government;[10] avoidance of public places; reduction in consumption; and losses in trade, travel, tourism, high technology, and information technology, with regional effects cascading into significant global economic losses.[11] By late April 2004, the global cost of fighting SARS—including direct costs to health care systems and indirect costs associated with disrupted commerce, travel, and education—approached $30 billion.[12]

In 2003 a report from the Institute of Medicine concluded that 13 factors account for the renewed threat from infectious diseases, including microbial adaptation and change, misuse of antimicrobial drugs, human immunological vulnerability, climate and weather, changing ecosystems, advances in medical technology, economic development and land use, human demographics and behavior, and international travel and commerce.[13] One factor is the threat of bioterrorism: the deliberate release of biological pathogens on susceptible and vulnerable populations.

Disclosures regarding advanced programs in the Soviet Union,[14] producing biological weapons that may have made their way to Syria, Libya, North Korea, and elsewhere, offer compelling evidence that the ability to make such weapons can spread to rogue states and terrorist organizations.[15] Biological weapons programs are accessible, deployable, and relatively inexpensive. One CIA analyst estimated the cost at "about $10 million, compared with $100 million to develop chemical weapons capability or $2 billion for nuclear capability."[16]

The still unattributed anthrax attacks that came shortly after 9/11 resulted in 22 illnesses and five deaths and demonstrated the unique character of biological weapons. Unlike explosives or chemical and nuclear weapons, which have discernible effects, pathogens are silent and invisible, initially mimicking symptoms of routine illnesses, such as fever, cough, and respiratory distress. Bioterrorism is covert: the perpetrators can inflict harm with a weapon that leaves no "footprint" and can themselves avoid the target area during the period of disease incubation. Because the pathogens considered the most likely bioweapons are communicable, they would produce epidemics.

CDC has identified three categories of agents; those in category A are considered the greatest threat. The criteria used by CDC include the impact of illness and death on public health, the stability of the agent, the ability to produce and deliver large quantities of an agent to sizable populations, the potential for person-to-person transmission, and the potential for public fear and civil disruption. Category A includes variola major (smallpox), *Bacillus anthrasis* (anthrax), *Yersinia pestis* (plague), *Clostridium botulinum* (botulinum toxin), *Francisella tularensis* (tularemia), and filoviruses and arenaviruses (viral hemorrhagic fevers).[17] Although categories B and C are of somewhat less concern and would have less effect on health and civil order, they too would disrupt daily life and work. In fact, the deliberate or natural release of pathogens on a large scale, irrespective of category or etiology, would be a severe blow to many sectors of American society: recovery would not be swift or without human and economic loss.

The global spread of natural disease and biological threats against the United States does not depend solely on humans as vectors or hosts. Nondeliberate foodborne illnesses affect 76 million Americans annually; the estimated expenditures associated with salmonella—including medical costs and lost wages—amount to over $1 million.[18] A deliberate attack against the country's agricultural and food industries, which employ one of every eight workers, would have even greater consequences for the U.S. economy.[19]

Agroterrorism, "the deliberate introduction of a disease agent, either against livestock or into the food chain, for purposes of undermining stability and/or generating fear,"[20] would result in lost production, the destruction of diseased animals or contaminated products, costs associated with containment (such as vaccines and drugs), lost export markets, and decreased sales across agriculturally dependent businesses. Canada, France, Germany, Iraq, Japan, South Africa, the United Kingdom, the Soviet Union, and the United States had agricultural bioweapons programs during some part of the twentieth century. Egypt, North Korea, Rhodesia, and Syria may have or have had similar programs.[21]

Food production in 2001 constituted 9.7 percent of the U.S. gross domestic product (GDP), more than $991 billion.[22] Regarding the economic impact on the United States from costs associated with foot-and-mouth disease in the United Kingdom, it is projected that losses would range from $10.4 to $33.6 billion.[23] Many diseases have been eradicated from domestic animal populations; consequently, these populations are susceptible to foreign animal diseases, a situation recognized by veterinarians: "Thus, having no existing herd or flock immunity, domestic livestock populations are vulnerable. Modern high-density vertically integrated industries, livestock sale and transportation practices, and centralized feed supply and distribution systems only add to the potential for animal-to-animal or fomite transmission."[24]

Some experts consider that for terrorists, agriculture is a more likely target than humans because agroterrorism requires less sophisticated technology, terrorists could attack easily and safely, there is less public perception of wrongdoing, the outcome is more certain, and a comparatively longer period is needed for detection of the event. As a soft target, agriculture might prove attractive to foreign terrorists as well as some American radical groups. The ramifications for the world's food supplies would be devastating, as the president of Kansas State University noted in testimony before the Emerging Threats Subcommittee of the U.S. Senate: "Wheat and rice account for an astonishing 45 percent of the world's calories. A terrorist strike against the cereal crops would threaten the foundation of our food supply—the foundation of the world's food supply."[25]

Besides potential terrorism against foods and crops, experts have raised concerns regarding the security of the nation's drinking water, noting the potential for deliberate disruption of sources, distribution and information systems, and water treatment chemicals.[26] More than 160,000 public water systems nationwide serve as few as 25 to over 1 million people.

VULNERABILITIES

Life expectancy in the United States has lengthened by 30 years since 1900; much of the increase is attributable to public health interventions such as improving safety in the food supply, at workplaces, and in motor vehicles, and reducing risk factors (such as smoking) for coronary heart disease and stroke.[27]

One important achievement has been the development of vaccines, which have sharply reduced the incidence of diseases such as tetanus, diphtheria, and *Haemophilus influenzae* type B. Many dread diseases described since biblical times have been conquered by twentieth-century medical and public health science. Smallpox was eradicated worldwide in 1979; polio was eradicated from the Americas in the early 1990s.[28] Since Jenner's use of the bovine analogue to provide immunity against smallpox in humans, there have been ongoing attempts to improve adaptive immunity to many specific infectious agents. Routine childhood vaccination programs in developed countries have brought to record lows the number of cases of—and deaths and disability associated with—diseases such as pertussis, rubeola, rubella, and mumps.[29] But many diseases such as tuberculosis and malaria are rampant in large parts of the world; reversals in their mortality rates await the development of vaccines.

Concern about deliberately induced infections has aroused renewed interest in developing vaccines and other medical countermeasures. In July 2004 President Bush signed Project Bioshield into law (P.L. 108-276), making available $5.6 billion in funding and promised liability protections and some tax incentives to persuade the pharmaceutical industry to develop a range of protective measures—including vaccines, therapeutics, and rapid diagnostic tools—that might otherwise generate little interest.[30] Labor-intensive, scientifically rigorous, accelerated efforts are projected to be applied to the usual 10- to 15-year research and development cycle in the quest for biodefense vaccines meeting certain criteria: low levels of toxicity, high levels of immunity, a long immunological "memory," and cost-effectiveness.[31]

The list of FDA-approved medical countermeasures for the six agents in category A includes vaccines for two agents (smallpox and anthrax) and postexposure therapy for four (anthrax, plague, botulism, and tularemia), but rapid diagnostics for none.[32] Scientific advances can reverse human, animal, and crop vulnerabilities to disease and bioweapons, and consequently make these populations less attractive targets. The National Institutes of Health (NIH) have an aggressive agenda for developing medical countermeasures, instituting basic research on microbes, exploiting the recent identification of 40,000 genes in the human genome, and developing methods to boost innate immune responses.[33] The challenge of developing these tools is exacerbated by rapidly advancing capabilities that demonstrate the potential dark side of science: the ability to manipulate strains of bacteria resistant to antibiotics, to engineer viruses that can defeat vaccine-induced immunity,[34] and to reconstruct the poliovirus from its genetic sequence.[35]

Despite advances in vaccines, diagnostic tests, antivirals, antibiotics, and a range of pharmaceutical interventions that have contributed to longevity, concern is mounting about Americans' vulnerabilities: chronic diseases associated with lifestyle and behavioral factors that compromise adults' and children's quality of life, independence, and general fitness. Data from the National Center for Health Statistics reveal that more than 12 percent of adults must limit their activities because of one or more chronic conditions.[36] Cessation campaigns have reduced smoking, but almost 500 million deaths annually from cancer, cardiovascular disease, or respiratory disease can still be attributed to it.[37] During 1988–1994, 11 percent of children and adolescents age 6 to 9, as well as 23 percent of adults age 20 or older, were considered obese.[38] Today, 64.1 percent of adults age 20 or over are considered overweight or obese.[39] The annual costs associated with obesity—both direct medical costs and loss of productivity—are estimated to be $117 billion.[40] Data from the late 1990s showed that only 65 percent of adolescents and only 15 percent of adults engaged in the recommended amount of physical activity. The annual economic costs to the United States from alcohol abuse were estimated to be $167 billion in 1995, and the costs from drug abuse were estimated to be $110 billion. Of the 15 million new cases of sexually transmitted diseases (STDs) reported each year, almost 4 million occur in adolescents. The costs associated with the most common STDs and their complications are estimated at $17 billion annually. Almost 1 million people in the United States are infected with HIV; about one-half of new cases are people under age 25. The lifetime cost of health care for a person with HIV infection is $155,000 or more.[41] Americans with diabetes number more than 17 million, resulting in direct and indirect annual costs of $132 trillion.[42] Annually, approximately 20 percent of the U.S. population is affected by a mental illness, and more than 19 million adults suffer from depression.[43] The top three causes of death for Americans age 15 to 19 are unintentional injuries, homicide, and suicide.[44]

Disparities in health care and in access to health care contribute to the current rates of diseases that are vaccine-preventable; over 40 million Americans lack health insurance.[45] Data from 1998 demonstrated that over 25 percent of children were not receiving recommended routine immunizations and that fewer than 50 percent of persons age 65 or older had received pneumococcal vaccine. Both these trends are improving, but pneumonia and influenza together constitute the sixth leading cause of death in the United States.[46] Some 48,000 Americans die each year from diseases that are vaccine-preventable.[47]

These sobering—and costly—issues are particularly important because physical and mental resilience is crucial to preparing Americans for threats to their immune system, their psyche, and their way of life. Some would argue that these social and health needs are far more pervasive and deserving of attention and funding than the unpredictable—perhaps improbable—recurrence of bioterrorism;[48] but in any case most would recognize the enormous value of healthful modifications in lifestyle and behavior, attainable by many individuals, in improving the general quality of life.

As a critical component of domestic security, the health status of Americans must be factored into preparedness for terrorism.

For example, evacuation from contaminated areas and disaster sites will challenge individuals who need assistance because of age or disability: 6.2 percent of adults are unable to walk—or can walk only with extreme difficulty—a quarter-mile. While they wait for help, their exposure to a pathogen may be prolonged.[49]

Health status is also important in determining the safety and efficacy of pre- or postevent vaccination. During the "Phase I" civilian program, smallpox vaccination was contraindicated for first responders who had (or whose household members had) medical conditions such as eczema or severe acne, chronic viral illnesses such as herpes, a history of chemotherapy or organ transplant, or immune system disorders such as HIV-AIDS.[50] Individuals with such medical contraindications are approximately 4 percent of today's population.[51]

Another issue in preparedness is the level of individuals' self-care and self-sufficiency. During World War II, food rationing prompted Americans to cultivate yards, vacant lots, ball fields, parks, and even strips of grass between houses. By 1944, 20 million Americans had planted "victory gardens."[52] The Cold War brought fallout shelters, air raid sirens, and other measures of civil defense to protect Americans from radiological emergencies.[53]

Today, as in the past, threats reinforce the importance of courage and self-determination. If the delivery of routine civil and government services was interrupted, communities, individuals, and households might have to wait days for assistance. Since 9/11 Americans have been encouraged to prepare resources necessary to "shelter in place"; to stockpile food, water, and medications; and to have plans to reunite if family members become separated during a disaster.[54,55]

Because terrorism and bioterrorism are amorphous and unpredictable, Americans are once again being asked to play a strategic role in the nation's security and economic viability. In 2002, in *Securing the Homeland, Strengthening the Nation*, President George W. Bush noted, "The need for homeland security is tied to the underlying vulnerability of American society.... Not since World War II have our American values and our way of life been so threatened.... We will find new and important ways to encourage citizens to be more alert and active in their communities."[56]

Biological threats demand particular actions to protect individuals—and their contacts—from disease and deliberate infection. Although government will play a leading role, the importance of individuals' and communities' contributions toward reducing their vulnerabilities and risk factors cannot be discounted.

SYSTEMS

The concept of protecting the health of a community can be traced to the earliest civilizations. There is evidence of bathrooms and drains in the excavated sites of a 4,000-year-old city north of India, and of sewage systems in ancient Athens and Rome. Classical Greek manuscripts chronicle communicable diseases that we now identify as mumps, diphtheria, and malaria. The Greeks' methodical documentation was wide-reaching, and by the tenth century all the essential Greek medical writings had been translated into Syriac, Hebrew, or Arabic. In Rome, the livers of slaughtered animals had to be examined and determined to be healthy before the architect Vitruvius Pollio would consider a site suitable for habitation. In the medieval era, inhabitants of cities were instructed not to throw dead animals into water supplies if the water was used for cooking or drinking. Decrees for building slaughterhouses, paving streets, and cleaning public marketplaces were implemented to separate animal excrement and carcasses from inhabitants and discourage the presence of spoiled food.

Early strategies against disease and contagion were based on religious teachings, empirical evidence, and the perceived merits of hygiene, though also on ignorance and fear. In the Middle Ages, people who were recognized as having communicable diseases were reported to authorities and isolated. Quarantine stations were erected in the early 1300s to detain for 40 days travelers and cargoes from ships that were infected or considered suspicious. The microscope, developed in the late seventeenth century, revealed previously invisible agents of disease and validated many public health measures. During that time, there was considerable interest in counting populations and diseases; the resulting data became the foundation for statistical analysis of epidemics and were a catalyst for health policy. Health codes were formulated to control transmissible diseases, guide the care of special populations (infants, the elderly), identify types of exposure (occupational, environmental), and organize and provide medical care.[57]

Today's challenges place unprecedented demands on protective systems. Two of the most critical systems are medical care of individuals and public health, which detects and mitigates adverse health conditions in populations. Both systems would be severely challenged by a large-scale epidemic or a catastrophic event.

Over the past decade, minimally invasive, noninvasive, and nonsurgical medical interventions have significantly reduced hospital stays. In concert with aggressive cost containment, excess bed capacity has been eliminated from most of the nation's 5,000 acute-care hospitals. Hospitals are also struggling with increased regulatory burdens; revenue shortfalls; an "on-demand" climate of purchasing consumable supplies; and decreases in the critical workforce, including nurses, technicians, and food service personnel.[58] Hospital emergency rooms, possibly the first line of detection in a bioterrorist attack, have experienced an increase in volume with the closing of over 1,000 emergency departments since 1992 and are bearing the rising burden of care for the uninsured, underinsured, and vulnerable.[59]

State and local public health systems face equally serious issues of capacity and capability in the event of epidemics and catastrophic diseases. Local public health departments—long underresourced and overtasked by the demands of federal and state public health entities, elected officials, and the communities they serve—have had to assume new responsibilities of biodefense planning and response while continuing to provide a wide spectrum of public and personal services. Supplemental federal biodefense resources—at record levels—have provided some relief, but this funding has come while budgets are being cut because of state deficits. A report describing issues of preparedness among the nation's 50 state and 2,800 local health departments noted, "The resulting public health landscape is a disparate and uneven collage of resources, capabilities, and responsibilities that defy ready definition and challenge attempts to fund and build a consistent floor of preparedness and response."[60]

In fact, while the medical and public health sectors strive to improve their specific abilities to respond to a large-scale infectious biological event, it is equally important that these sectors harmonize their detection and response. For example, a biological attack might be detected through "population signals" (large numbers of people converging on health care facilities; atmospheric biosensors) or "patient signals" (unusual clinical diseases; diseases occurring during atypical seasons). Swift, appropriate intervention will depend on immediate sharing of information and on congruent decisions regarding where individuals should go if they require prophylaxis, what clinical and epidemiological criteria constitute a "case," and what information should be disseminated to avoid additional exposure of the population and health care workers.

The critical interdependency of medical and public health systems—a necessary but unattained goal—requires assistance from still other systems. Data must be received from multiple and divergent sources that continually characterize and monitor "sentinel" disease events and rely on sophisticated systems capable of providing information about illness in humans and animals, sales of over-the-counter medications, absenteeism in schools, and other signs. Early warning systems like BioWatch have been added to the tool kit of homeland security. BioWatch—funded by the Department of Homeland Security (DHS) and operated in cooperation with the Environmental Protection Agency (EPA)—consists of pathogen detectors that collect airborne particles, which are subsequently tested by state and local public health laboratories.[61] However, for any surveillance and detection system to help contain epidemics, there must be incisive analysis, robust decision making, and rapidly deployable response systems, all of which are currently in embryonic stages.

Containment of disease will also require expertise and assistance from sectors outside medicine and public health. For example, during the anthrax attacks of 2001, medical and public health experts on infectious diseases received crucial guidance from authorities in industrial hygiene and occupational safety regarding the dissemination patterns of anthrax spores; and postal authorities provided insight regarding mail distribution systems.[62] Depending on the conditions and scope of an event, the response to an outbreak will require the involvement and guidance of emergency, safety, and law enforcement personnel. The practiced capabilities of the Defense Department through its civil support teams also await deployment to civilian sites as needed.

Other systems also play roles in homeland security. Bioterrorism has challenged existing laws and legal structures regarding issues of protection—laws addressing the movement of persons and products, isolation and quarantine, vaccination, the commandeering of facilities, federal versus state authorities, emergency licensing of health care professionals, and more. In fact, research has found that the single most important factor in the unsuccessful attempt to vaccinate

500,000 first responders against smallpox was a failure to put in place adequate liability and compensation schemes for the clinical professionals and hospitals that were to administer the vaccinations.[63] The Institute of Medicine's report *The Future of Public Health in the Twenty-First Century* noted that federal, state, and local public health laws are often outdated and internally inconsistent, impeding efficient responses and contributing to a lack of coordination in emergencies.[64]

Another crucial system is communication and "risk messaging." During the anthrax attacks of 2001 there were difficulties in providing rapid, ongoing, continually updated information to the news media, the public, and clinical communities.[65] Homeland Security Presidential Directive 3 established an advisory system that designates five threat conditions by colors: low (green), guarded (blue), elevated (yellow), high (orange), and severe (red).[66] The Red Cross refined the actions citizens should take at these threat levels.[67] The message itself, however, is inadequate if it is not linguistically and culturally appropriate and sensitive to the belief systems of the community at risk. Data from the U.S. Census Bureau indicate that almost 4.5 million households are "linguistically isolated" and that 15.4 million people age 18 to 64 (5.9 percent) speak English less than "very well."[68] Research indicates that much of current planning for responding to bioterrorism was conceived without adequate input from the community and may, therefore, overestimate the degree of cooperation and consensus with regard to medical countermeasures, recommendations to remain in place, and other health directives.[69] Additional research indicates that confidence in the government's ability to prevent or respond to a terror attack has dropped to 53 percent, down from 62 percent in 2003.[70] Finally, only 68 percent of Asians and Pacific Islanders in America and 63 percent of African-Americans believe that the public health response to terrorism will result in "fairness" regarding control measures that include isolation, quarantine, travel restrictions, and distribution of medicines or vaccines.[71]

Detection and mitigation of an epidemic will require synchronous and complementary actions by most sectors inside and outside government, through predefined and practiced roles and under accepted systems of "incident command." The benefits of sophisticated science and technology will ultimately depend on the ability of organizations and systems to apply these tools. The challenge ahead requires visionary leadership, sustained support, and an unerring acceptance that biological threats require fundamental change in organizational relationships, skills, and ways of life.

AN OPERATIONAL PARADIGM

Many experts believe that the United States faces a strong probability of bioterrorism and the certainty of continued assault by natural, emerging, and mutating strains of virulent disease. There would be little disagreement that the ideal strategy regarding bioterrorism is to remove the threat. Favored options include destroying bioweapons at their source; using treaties and diplomatic and trade sanctions to impede their acquisition, stockpiling, and deployment; preventing their production by redirecting the relevant science toward beneficial ends;[72] using military intervention when necessary; and improving the ability to guard U.S. borders and ports, inspect incoming shipping containers, and identify individuals on "watch" lists. However, these measures, even if fully successful, will not protect populations from naturally occurring disease. Pathogens will continue to present a moving target, whether deployed by nature or terrorists.

The paradigm encourages consideration of mitigating the risks associated with current and future threats through manipulating vulnerabilities and systems. The events surrounding the Phase I Civilian Smallpox Vaccination Program provide a useful illustration.

Events surrounding Operation Iraqi Freedom contributed to heightened concerns regarding the threat of bioterrorism from a country suspected of manufacturing, acquiring, and hiding biological weapons, including smallpox.[73] The vulnerability of the American population to variola, the etiological agent, was well documented; because the vaccination program was curtailed in 1972, at least 119 million Americans are susceptible to smallpox, and the 157 million U.S. citizens vaccinated before that time probably now have little protection.[74] Smallpox kills one-third of its victims (it killed 300 million people in the twentieth century). However, in the period—up to four days—between exposure and the onset of symptoms, the vaccine can halt or lessen the sequelae of the disease. Because smallpox is infectious, its release by terrorists intending to cause an epidemic would very soon stress medicine, public health, and other traditional response systems, resulting in many cases, many deaths, and economic and civil disruption.

CONCLUSION

The paradigm offers two strategies to modify the effects of the threat. The first strategy would be to reduce vulnerability by giving vaccinations. Unfortunately, though, the current vaccine has side effects and is contraindicated for large segments of the U.S. population. The second strategy would focus on building robust systems of detection and surveillance, information sharing, risk messaging, and response. The cumulative effect would support actions to identify populations at risk, isolate infected people, administer vaccine to a ring of exposed contacts, and contain the spread of the epidemic. It should be understood, however, that mass vaccinations might be necessary if the level of threat rises, thrusting systems into pre-event rather than postevent actions. The paradigm must be manipulated in accordance with changing threats.

Our culture has been altered since the attacks of 2001. The complexities of the threats we face, our fundamental biological vulnerabilities, and our slowly adapting systems demonstrate the difficulties inherent in protecting Americans from bioterrorism.

N O T E S

1. The paradigm is adapted from the multiple causation model of disease (agent, host, environment).
2. *Contagion and Conflict: Health as a Global Security Challenge* (Washington, D.C.: Center for Strategic and International Studies, January 2000).
3. U.S. Department of Health and Human Services (USDHHS), *The State of the CDC, Fiscal Year 2003*.
4. "Datapoints: Killer Diseases through Time," *Scientist* (2 June 2003), www.the-scientist.com/yr2003/jun/upfront8_030603.html.
5. World Health Organization, "Communicable Disease Surveillance and Response," www.who.int/csr/don/archive/year/2004/en/.
6. *Addressing Emerging Infectious Disease Threats: A Prevention Strategy for the United States* (Atlanta, Ga.: National Center for Infectious Diseases, CDC, 1994), www.cdc.gov/ncidod/publications/eid_plan/default.htm.
7. Seth Borenstein, "World Sees an Explosion in New Infectious Diseases," *San Jose* (Calif.) *Mercury News* (4 May 2003), www.mercurynews.com/mld/mercurynews/news/5771315.htm.
8. Department of the Treasury, Australian Government, *The Economic Impact of Severe Acute Respiratory Syndrome (SARS)*, www.treasury.gov.au/documents/677/HTML/docshell.asp?URL=economicimpact_.
9. CDC Fact Sheet: Basic Information about SARS (13 January 2004), www.cdc.gov/ncidod/sars.

10. Department of the Treasury, Australian Government, *The Economic Impact of Severe Acute Respiratory Syndrome (SARS)*.

11. James Newcomb, "Biology and Borders: SARS and the New Economics of Bio-security," *Bio-era* (May 2003), www.bio-era.net/research/add_research_9.html.

12. Elin Gursky, "On the Record," *Government Executive* (1 October 2003), www.govexec.com/features/0903hs/HS0903Gursky.htm.

13. Board on Global Health, Institute of Medicine, *Microbial Threats to Health: Emergence, Detection, and Response* (Washington, D.C.: National Academies Press, 2003).

14. Ken Alibek, *Biohazard* (New York: Random House, 1999).

15. "Biological Weapons Proliferation," Report No. 2000/05, Canadian Security Intelligence Service "Perspectives" (9 June 2000), www.csis-scrs.gc.ca/eng/miscdocs/200005_e.html.

16. "War on Terrorism: Bioterrorism Inexpensive and Spreading, U.S. Says," Cox News Service (27 August 2002).

17. Lisa D. Rotz, Ali S. Khan, Scott R. Lillibridge, Stephen M. Ostroff, and James M. Hughes, "Public Health Assessment of Potential Biological Terrorism Agents," *Emerging Infectious Diseases* 8:2 (February 2002).

18. Ibid.

19. Peter Chalk, "Hitting America's Soft Underbelly" (RAND National Defense Research Institute, 2004).

20. O. Shawn Cupp, David E. Walker II, and John Hillison, "Agroterrorism in the U.S.: Key Security Challenge for the 21st Century," *Biosecurity and Bioterrorism: Biodefense Strategy, Practice, and Science* 2:2 (2004).

21. "Agroterrorism: Threats and Preparedness," Congressional Research Service (13 August 2004), www.fas.org/irp/crs/RL32521.pdf.

22. Chalk, "Hitting America's Soft Underbelly."

23. David A. Ashford, Thomas M. Gomez, Donald L. Noah, Dana P. Scott, and David R. Franz, "Biological Terrorism and Veterinary Medicine in the United States," *Journal of the American Veterinary Medical Association* 217:5 (2004): 664–7.

24. Ibid.

25. Jon Wefald (President, Kansas State University), "Agricultural Biological Weapons Threat," testimony before U.S. Senate Emerging Threats Subcommittee (October 1999).

26. John B. Stephenson (Director, Natural Resources and Environment, Government Accountability Office), "Drinking Water: Experts' Views on How Federal Funding Can Best Be Spent to Improve Security" (GAO-04-1098T), testimony before Subcommittee on Environment and Hazardous Materials, Committee on Energy and Commerce, House of Representatives (30 September 2004).

27. "Ten Great Public Health Achievements: United States, 1990–1999," *Morbidity and Mortality Weekly Review*, 48:12 (2 April 1999): 241–3.

28. Board on Global Health and the Institute of Medicine, *Considerations for Viral Disease Eradication: Lessons Learned and Future Strategies-Workshop Summary* (Washington, D.C.: National Academies Press, 2002).

29. "Infections: Mumps," *KidsHealth for Parents*, Nemours Foundation, kidshealth.org/parent/infections/bacterial_viral/mumps.html.

30. "U.S. Bioterror Plan Frustrates Industry," *New York Times* (16 October 2004).

31. Charles A. Janeway, Jr., Paul Travers, Mark Walport, and Mark J. Shlomchik, *Immunobiology* (New York: GS Garland Science, 2005).

32. Bradley T. Smith, Thomas V. Inglesby, and Tara O'Toole, "Biodefense R&D: Anticipating Future Threats, Establishing a Strategic Environment," *Biosecurity and Bioterrorism: Biodefense Strategy, Practice, and Science* 1:3 (2003): 193–201.

33. "The NIH Biomedical Research Response to the Threat of Bioterrorism," statement of Anthony S. Fauci, M.D., before House of Representatives Select Committee on Homeland Security (3 June 2004).

34. Smith, Inglesby, and T. O'Toole, "Biodefense R & D."

35. Jennifer Couzin, "Active Poliovirus Baked from Scratch," *Science* 297 (2002): 174–5, www.sciencemag.org/cgi/content/full/297/5579/174b.

36. National Center for Health Statistics, "How Healthy Are We?" (1 September 2004).

37. USDDHS—Public Health Service, *Progress Review: Tobacco Use* (14 May 2003), www.healthypeople.gov/Data/2010prog/focus27/default.htm.

38. USDDHS, *Healthy People 2010: Leading Health Indicators*, www.healthypeople.gov/Document/HTML/uih/uih_4.htm.

39. National Center for Health Statistics, "How Healthy Are We?"

40. USDDHS, *The State of the CDC, Fiscal Year 2003.*

41. USDDHS, *Healthy People 2010: Leading Health Indicators.*

42. USDDHS, *The State of the CDC, Fiscal Year 2003.*

43. USDDHS, *Healthy People 2010: Leading Health Indicators.*

44. USDDHS, *The State of the CDC, Fiscal Year 2003.*

45. Matthew L. Wynia and Lawrence Gostin, "The Bioterrorist Threat and Access to Health Care," *Science* 30 (14 May 2002), www.sciencemag.org.

46. USDDHS, *Healthy People 2010: Leading Health Indicators.*

47. USDDHS, *The State of the CDC, Fiscal Year 2003.*

48. Hillel W. Cohen, Robert M. Gould, and Victor W. Sidel, "The Pitfalls of Bioterrorism Preparedness: The Anthrax and Smallpox Experiences," *American Journal of Public Health* 94:10 (October 2004).

49. National Center for Health Statistics, "Disabilities/Limitations."

50. Centers for Disease Control and Prevention (CDC), "Smallpox (Vaccinia) Vaccine Contraindications" (28 March 2003).

51. Alex R. Kemper, Matthew M. Davis, and Gary L. Freed, "Expected Adverse Events in a Mass Smallpox Vaccination Campaign," *Effective Clinical Practice* 5:2 (March–April 2002): 84–90.

52. Deborah Holmes, "Victory Gardens," Old House Web, www.oldhouseweb.com/gardening/Detailed/757.shtml.

53. See Cold War Civil Defense Museum Web site, www.civildefensemuseum.com/docs.html.

54. "Be Prepared—American Red Cross Preparedness Information," www.redcross.org/services/disaster/0,1082,0_500_,00.html.

55. U.S. Department of Homeland Security (DHS), "Ready.gov" Web site, www.ready.gov/.

56. President George W. Bush, *Securing the Homeland, Strengthening the Nation* (2002), pp. 2, 3, www.whitehouse.gov/homeland/homeland_security_book.html.

57. George Rosen, *A History of Public Health* (Baltimore, Md.: Johns Hopkins University Press, 1993), pp. 1–167.

58. Monica Schoch-Spana, "Hospital Buckle during Normal Flu Season: Implications for Bioterrorism Response," *Biodefense Quarterly* (March 2000), www.upmc-biosecurity.org/pages/publications/archive/quarterl_4.html.

59. USDDHS, "Ambulatory Care Visits to Physician Offices, Hospital Outpatient Departments, and Emergency Departments: United States, 1999–2000," Vital and Health Statistics, Series 13, No. 157.

60. Elin Gursky, *Drafted to Fight Terror: U.S. Public Health on the Front Lines of Biological Defense* (Westport, Conn.: Smith Richardson Foundation, 2004).

61. Congressional Research Service, "The BioWatch Program: Detection of Bioterrorism" (19 November 2003).

62. Elin Gursky, Thomas V. Inglesby, and Tara O'Toole, "Anthrax 2001: Observations on the Medical and Public Health Response," *Biosecurity and Bioterrorism: Biodefense Strategy, Practice, and Science* 1:2 (2003).

63. Holly Myers, Elin Gursky, Georges Benjamin, Christopher Guzdor, and Michael Greenberger, "The Threat of Smallpox: Eradicated but Not Erased," *Journal of Homeland Security* (February 2004), www.homelandsecurity.org/journal/Articles/displayarticle.asp?article=103.

64. Institute of Medicine, *The Future of the Public's Health in the Twenty-First Century* (Washington, D.C.: National Academy Press, 2002), www.nap.edu/catalog/10548.html.

65. Gursky, Inglesby, and O'Toole, "Anthrax 2001."

66. Homeland Security Presidential Directive 3; www.whitehouse.gov/news/releases/2002/03/20020312-5.html.

67. American Red Cross Homeland Security Advisory System Recommendations for Individuals, Families, Neighborhoods, Schools, and Businesses, www.redcross.org/services/disaster/0,1082,0_500_,00.html.

68. U.S. Census Bureau, "Language Use and English-Speaking Ability: 2000," www.census.gov/prod/2003pubs/c2kbr-29.pdf.

69. Roz D. Lasker (Center for the Advancement of Collaborative Strategies in Health, New York Academy of Medicine), "Redefining Readiness: Terrorism Planning through the Eyes of the Public" (14 September 2004).

70. "Americans Don't Trust Public Health in Case of Attack, New York Poll Shows," *New York Newsday* (24 August 2004).

71. "Will Public Health's Response to Terrorism Be Fair?" (RAND Center for Domestic and International Health Security, 2004), www.rand.org/publications/RB/RB9086/.

72. Gigi Kwik, Joe Fitzgerald, Thomas V. Ingelsby, and Tara O'Toole, "Biosecurity: Responsible Stewardship of Bioscience in an Age of Catastrophic Terrorism," *Biosecurity and Bioterrorism: Biodefense Strategy, Science, and Practice* 1:1 (2003).

73. Barton Gellman, "Four Nations Thought to Possess Smallpox: Iraq, North Korea Named, Two Officials Say," *Washington Post* (5 November 2002).

74. William J. Bicknell, "The Case for Voluntary Smallpox Vaccination," *New England Journal of Medicine* 346:17 (25 April 2002): 1323–5.

Preparedness and Response in Israeli Hospitals

Dr. Boaz Tadmor
Director Cerberus Enterprises, LLC

Dr. Lion Poles
Deputy Director General, Kaplan Medical Center

Dr. Shmuel C. Shapira
Deputy Director General, Hadassah Medical Organization

Disasters and other emergencies can strain and even irreversibly damage a health care system. Consequently, the threat of terrorism—both conventional terrorism and acts involving weapons of mass destruction (WMD)—has created a relatively new need for providers of health care: preparedness and response. In preparing for and responding to terrorism, a hospital system must maintain balance and the appropriate priorities. To remain robust and flexible, the system must establish protocols, perform exercises, and learn from the experience of others. The Israeli system has conducted a great deal of training, exercises, and drills and has been tested by many terrorist events; this chapter will offer lessons to be learned from its experience and, we hope, facilitate discussion and collaboration between American and Israeli professionals.

THE ISRAELI MEDICAL SYSTEM

Israel has 27 public acute care hospitals in addition to its geriatric, psychiatric, and private hospitals. Of the general hospitals, six are level 1 trauma centers in densely populated urban areas; 14 others are sophisticated medical centers but without cardiosurgery or neurosurgery services; and the rest are remote level 3 community hospitals that can, if necessary, offer triage and surge capacity. Some of the hospitals are very much involved in social and educational community projects. There is a highly developed network of outpatient clinics; and the four HMOs have a network of primary care clinics reaching throughout Israel. The national medical insurance law mandates that every Israeli be medically insured by one of these HMOs. A single hospital system serves both the civilian population and the military population; however, the military has its own primary and secondary (expert) clinics but may use the HMOs and hospital clinics in times of need.

As for first responders, Israel has a single national emergency medical services (EMS) system, a national police system, and a national firefighting system. The national search-and-rescue unit and air evacuation systems are supervised by the Israel Defense Forces (IDF). The operational leader of the medical system, which sets priorities in peacetime, during disasters, and during wars, is the Supreme Health Authority (SHA); it represents the Ministry of Health (MOH), the IDF Medical corps, and the HMOs. An advisory committee comprising the hospitals' chief executive officers (CEOs), EMS, the Home Front Command (HFC) medical system (the operating arm of SHA), and other organizations is consulted if necessary.

Medical preparedness is funded mainly by MOH. Equipment and pharmaceuticals (e.g., physical protection, ventilators, medical drugs) and new infrastructure are also funded by MOH.

INTEGRATION AND COORDINATION

Hospital emergency rooms serve most victims of terrorism. According to the lessons learned in Israel from mass casualty events, in the first 24 hours after a terrorist incident three waves of casualties arrive: the most severely injured arrive in EMS ambulances or private cars within 30 to 40 minutes after an event in an urban location. Those moderately or lightly injured arrive within roughly two hours. Mildly injured patients, and patients experiencing acute stress reaction (ASR), tend to arrive within 24 hours. Being prepared to admit casualties at any time following any assault, the hospitals become a hub for three systems of resources: operational, medical, and informational. Hospitals need to assemble, evaluate, implement, and disseminate information quickly and accurately and deliver it to various internal and external managers and local and state agencies.

In order to be efficient in response during a crisis, a hospital must be a part of a much larger coordinated collaborative effort, sharing responsibility and delegating authority. This effort includes first responders, the media, local communities, the pathological institute (coroners), other hospitals, MOH, and HFC. There should be one communication system for alerting the public, executing orders, and disseminating information.

After emergency triage at the scene, HFC's medical command-and-control center and the EMS control center are responsible for coordinating the evacuation of casualties. They are also responsible for informing hospitals of casualties that are on the way. This notification initiates the hospitals' local protocols for preparedness and enables them to set priorities (with the help of MOH) for delivering care, identifying casualties, and communicating with victims' families and the relevant authorities.

At the time of an event and shortly thereafter, the hospital CEO may be obliged to address the media and share information with the public, providing updates on the situation. Therefore, CEOs need to learn and be trained in "risk communication" skills.

Throughout an event, every hospital must have a designated EMS representative who coordinates the arrival of ambulances and ensures that the hospital's security system is coordinated with the police and the local community. A medical representative of HFC works with the incident command system (ICS) that is based in the hospital, to coordinate most of the hospital's needs; inform the hospital network, MOH, the EMS system, and the air evacuation teams; and communicate about resources and support needed from other authorities and agencies.

In Israel, the media plays a role in medical response to a crisis by serving as a "first responder" for information. Hospital emergency plans provide for a designated media area in the hospital; and the media have the task of gathering information from patients and the staff (in compliance, however, with hospital policies about not disturbing patients or operations).

"Crisis drills" are held yearly, taking into account all the needs for collaboration and bringing all responders under the protocols of performance. Various responders share the lessons they have learned from previous crises through written materials and through personal meetings and multidisciplinary training.

EVOLUTION OF OPERABILITY OF THE HOSPITAL SYSTEM

The general hospitals have always been an integral part of Israel's national emergency response system. Most hospitals have participated in the management of injured soldiers and civilians during and between wars. Historically, lessons learned during wartime and through isolated conventional mass-casualty incidents (MCIs) were gathered, but no comprehensive doctrine was established. In the 1980s, as lessons emerged from the war of 1973 and the perceived threat of chemical warfare (CW) increased, the heads of the medical system decided that a fundamental change was needed in the way hospitals prepare for crises.

Under the auspices of the Supreme Health Authority (SHA), a trilateral system was founded. The Emergency Division of MOH (EDMOH) was given overall responsibility and funding for infrastructure and procurement; and the IDF medical corps—acting on behalf of MOH through a newly established Hospital Contingency Branch (HCB) and the Nuclear, Biological and Chemical (NBC) Medical Branch (NBCMB)—led the development of doctrine and the implementation of new procedures. Representatives of the public general hospitals participated in planning and implementation through several steering committees headed by hospital executives and comprised of subject-matter experts and representatives of the trilateral preparedness organization. These committees included a contingency committee for conventional MCIs, a contingency committee for CW, a staffing committee, and a procurement committee. The recommendations of the committees were presented and approved by SHA, becoming official policies and receiving the necessary budgets.

After Israel was attacked by Iraqi missiles during Operation Desert Storm in the Persian Gulf (1991), HCB was designated as the leader for CW preparedness. Later, the steering committees developed new directions, such as preparing for an accident at a nuclear reactor (1994) and preparing for a mass toxicological incident (1997, following the release of the nerve gas Sarin by terrorists in Japan in 1994–1995). The principles of preparedness and the interrelationships of those involved remain the same today. Concomitantly, operational missions were transferred to the medical department of HFC (established in 1994), which incorporated HCB in 1999. The emerging threat of biological warfare (BW) and a new crisis alert regarding Iraq in 1998 led to the development of an entirely new preparedness initiative—the "unusual biological incident." The evolving threats of BW, bioterror, and emerging infectious diseases necessitate different kinds of response and new partners, including the public health system, laboratory network, surveillance system, and ambulatory medical services. In the biological threat scenario, hospitals changed their role; rather than being the key factor, as in previous threats, they became just one component of a national interrelated response system that was developed within MOH.

IN-HOUSE HOSPITAL PREPAREDNESS

Israeli hospitals can be regarded as part of the first-responder system because most of the medical management of victims and nearly all decontamination procedures are planned to take place in hospitals. In addition, the last decade of EMS experience has shown that for most urban incidents, evacuation can take as much as 90 minutes. Since natural and human-made MCIs can of course occur after hours, all hospital contingency plans are required to base initial response capabilities on the emergency department, which is reinforced by any in-house staff available during those hours. Hospitals are required to develop redundant telecommunications and notification capabilities, and to provide effective triage, decontamination, and treatment in the first hour, until additional staff arrives and becomes incorporated into the crisis management activities. Specific means provided to hospitals by MOH include decontamination infrastructure (e.g., communication, architecture, entrances, decontamination sites, and negative-positive pressure environments); power-driven level 3 respiratory protection sets with universal canisters (ABEKP3 type); MOPP4 protective garments or, alternatively, standard kits to protect against airborne biological agents; and specific sets of antidotes sufficient for the first 8 to 24 hours of treatment (to be supplemented from national stocks of emergency medications).

All prehospital and interhospital activities are supervised and coordinated by the medical officer of HFC (on behalf of MOH) through an emergency response center incorporated with members of HCB. Within the hospital, all emergency contingency activity is coordinated and supervised generally by a physician. Since emergency preparedness is principally a nonprofit activity funded by the hospital, in many places this physician is the hospital's deputy general manager. Usually that physician heads an operational body—an emergency contingency committee—with representatives from nursing, logistics, security, and administration. Subcommittees are often established for specific scenarios (e.g., a bioevent committee comprising the infectious disease unit, the director of the microbiological laboratory, a security officer, and logistics and nursing executives). These subcommittees define and help to execute annual and ad hoc plans, updated according to MOH directives. They are not primarily assigned to emergency preparedness, so their activities usually reach a peak before planned or anticipated exercises or inspections. Their most difficult task is maintaining continuous readiness among the staff, through intermittent individual or institutional training, small-scale drills, and instructions.

In Israel, the public, the media, and MOH expect hospitals to be able to handle any emergency; and hospital managers perform accordingly, perhaps as a matter of self-esteem. Only recently has systematic analysis been done for the most likely wartime incidents with which hospitals should prepare to cope. There is still no official specific analysis of hospitals' missions during terrorist events and natural disasters; and no procedures have been established for assessing hospitals' individual vulnerability to internal hazards. With respect to MCIs, all Israeli hospitals are expected to provide medical assessment, treatment, and continuing care for large numbers of patients; and to identify and manage contaminated patients and patients who have been exposed to an unusual biological agent (this management includes protecting the hospital staff, patients, and others within the hospital). As of this writing, five medical centers were equipped to deal with the identification and management of patients exposed to radiation. In general, such response and mitigation activities should not interfere with everyday emergency care. Traditionally, emergency management has four phases: (1) mitigation, (2) preparedness, (3) response, and (4) recovery. Israeli hospitals have been directed to focus on phases 2 and 3. Most of the hospitals are now addressing phase 2 and are preparing for disasters (e.g., an earthquake, terrorism, or emergency evacuations) that could take place at their own facilities.

SUGGESTIONS FOR THE NEAR FUTURE

As the global and local perspective shifts from warfare to terror, and as the anticipated threats include chemical, biological, radiological, and nuclear (CBRN) disasters, certain concepts for the near future are being formulated.

Current policies—including policies for emergency preparedness—are dictated by economic pressures and tight budgets, especially in the medical system. Moreover, there is a huge array of possible human-made and natural disasters. Consequently, there is a clear need for a cost-effective approach that can find a common denominator among many threats, so as to concentrate on generic solutions. Common denominators might include decontamination; surge capacity; multifaceted, multilevel triage; communication regarding risks and crises; and public relations. It is vital to agree on low-probability versus high-probability scenarios, so that preferences and resources can be allotted to the latter (in toto) and critical steps in the response plan to the former. Hospital-specific hazards—both external and internal—should be analyzed, and emergency missions should be tailored accordingly and supported by appropriate resources.

Management and Education

Concurrently, new concepts are needed for management and education, based on the following principles.

Advance Steps
These measures involve the assembly of officially approved unified doctrines and (reviewed) local manuals; the infrastructure and equipment entailed by the doctrines. Infrastructure and equipment are to be ready in place, according to relevant considerations of time, space, and distance.

Ongoing and High-Frequency Steps
These measures include defining critical human resources (roles and professions) for the immediate response phase and training at least annually.

Medium-Frequency Steps

These include education and training for managers through annual conferences and "tabletop" exercises and simulations; and annual large-scale drills for low-probability scenarios as a measure of "collective memory."

Low-Frequency Steps

These include preparing materials (manuals, presentations, etc.) and providing instruction in just-in-time principles for most potential participants in low-probability scenarios. The scenarios can be classified as "rapid" or "slow."

Rapid scenarios involve conventional events (e.g., mass trauma from explosives or airplane crashes), chemicals (including toxins), and quickly identifiable radiological exposure. These scenarios tend to be clearly bounded in time and place, with distinct victims or exposed individuals. Most of the rapid scenarios are easily perceived by human senses or simple monitoring equipment. Victims are managed mainly within the hospital system. The initial response phase is expected to be limited to 24 hours. Common problems in rapid scenarios include surge capacity, triage, decontamination, identification of hazards, treatment protocols, control and communication, public relations, intensive care, and personnel recruitment and management. The main principles of response planning for rapid scenarios are to apply the experience gained from the terror campaign of the last 15 years and to apply the conventional MCI model (modified as necessary for victims of contamination).

Slow scenarios include biological outbreaks and unidentified radiological exposure. These scenarios are not clearly bounded in space or time nor are the victims or exposed individuals distinct. Slow scenarios are not perceptible by human senses; thus relatively advanced or sophisticated diagnostic procedures are necessary. The response to a slow scenario is beyond the scope of the hospital system, and the response phase will last for several days or weeks. The main problems are similar to those in rapid scenarios: surge capacity, triage, contaminated victims, etc. However, special consideration should be given to detecting the event, to notification, to diagnostic procedures, and to relations with external entities such as public health and ambulatory medical services. Specific criteria for a hospital's preparedness should be established. Local planning, staff training, and maintenance of emergency equipment are not funded by MOH (preparedness activities tend to add expenses but not to produce revenue); still, any new standards should be accompanied by appropriate resources or budget allocations. Finally, emergency contingency units should be founded and funded within the general hospital, ambulatory, and public health systems to ensure real commitment and productivity on the part of nonemergency medical organizations.

Some of these principles are already implemented or are expected to be implemented in the strategy of MOH.

Hospital Management of MCIs

Terrorism is a formidable challenge for the medical system, calling for crisis management by hospital administrations. Often, terrorism takes the form of MCIs that disrupt the balance between demand and resources and overwhelm medical facilities. Injuries can be conventional or unconventional (e.g., associated with WMD), may be unusually severe, and can include any combination of the following:

Penetrating

Blunt

Blast

Crush

Burns

Biological

Chemical

Radiation

Emotional reactions

The targets, settings, and weapons of terrorism can produce outcomes similar to those seen in a full-scale war, although with some variations related to shorter evacuation times and civilian victims. Cyberterror may be a primary strategy or may accompany other kinds of assault; in either case it can have severe consequences for hospitals, which depend on computers for their daily operations and in monitoring and caring for patients.

Apart from the challenge of treating MCI casualties without unduly interrupting hospital routines, terror attacks have nonmedical implications for hospitals, such as fears on the part of the staff, issues of security, and attention from the media.

Following is a checklist for the initial hospital management of MCIs. The items are discussed briefly below.

- Confirm information and notify key personnel in the hospital (a list of these people should be prepared beforehand).
- Gather data—type of event, location, estimated number of casualties, severity of injuries, estimated time of patients' arrival at the hospital.
- Evacuate current patients from the emergency department.
- Consider alerting extra medical and paramedical personnel.
- Notify operating theaters, the imaging department, and the blood bank.
- Stop elective operations.
- Set up a helipad.
- Assign a triage officer (an experienced trauma surgeon).
- Decide whether decontamination will be needed; if so, operate decontamination facilities.
- Decide whether to set up additional patient admission areas.
- Open a command station.
- Open a public information center.

Modus Operandi

MCIs should be directed by the most senior, most experienced medical officer present in-house. Sometimes the medical director who is available will start the process and be replaced later on by a more senior person.

Confirmation

One does not want to interrupt hospital routines for a false alarm. The initial message—typically from EMS—will usually reach the emergency department clerk, who should ask for the caller's telephone number and immediately call back. (This step can be skipped if the receiver is familiar with the caller, or if the call is from a direct line-to-line phone.) After confirmation, key people in the hospital (whose names will be on a list prepared beforehand) should be told.

Gathering Data

If the situation at the scene is chaotic, initial information will be limited and inaccurate; this should be taken into account. Information essential for early preparations includes:

* Location, which can affect victims' time of arrival
* Type of event, which also indicates arrival time and may entail decontamination
* Estimated number and condition of casualties

Hospital Security

Security is needed to maintain order and to prevent an assault on the hospital itself. Often, the hospital's security forces are assisted by the local police. The security staff should control the flow of arriving ambulances and helicopters; take responsibility for the helipad; screen visitors and arriving patients for weapons (some of the wounded might be the terrorists); and prevent bystanders from impeding medical teams.

Evacuation of the Emergency Department

During MCIs, patients already in the emergency department should be transferred to other departments or (if their ailments are minor) released, so that the arriving victims can be admitted quickly. If a department is overcrowded, patients may be kept in corridors or certain public areas.

Recruiting of Additional Staff

This depends on the magnitude of the event, the time of day (hospitals are typically better staffed during the day than at night), and the likelihood of injuries (e.g., burns) requiring specialists. The event director should have data about which staff members are present and which are scheduled to arrive soon.

Notification of Operating Theaters, the Imaging Department, and the Blood Bank

Elective procedures should be postponed while immediate needs are assessed. Ongoing surgeries should be finished as soon as possible; the most senior staff members available will be brought in to ensure this. Similar principles apply to the imaging department and blood bank.

Assignment of Triage Physicians

The triage physician works adjacent to where ambulances unload. Optimal triage is crucial—"overtriage" will waste scarce resources, and "undertriage" can be detrimental to victims. For a conventional MCI, the triage physician should be an experienced general surgeon. In a chemical assault, triage is based on (a) walking, (b) lying and spontaneously breathing, and (c) ventilation. In radiological or biological assaults, patients arrive more slowly and immediate triage is less important. In compound injuries—conventional and chemical or radiological—each injury is considered major.

Decontamination

The need for and type of decontamination should be determined as soon as possible, ideally before the first victims arrive. In any situation that may involve toxic chemicals, radiological agents, or early exposure to spores, decontamination is mandatory. It should arrest the victims' ongoing exposure and protect the staff against secondary contamination. Usually, undressing will suffice, but sometimes—especially when nonvaporizing materials are involved—flushing with pure water and scrubbing with detergents are also indicated. Victims' belongings should be collected in biohazard bags and marked with details about each patient or with a temporary identification number. Staff members in the "hot zone" work with full protection gear; staff members in the "clean zone" apply universal precautions.

Opening of Additional Admitting Areas

Early on, even when data are limited and uncertain, the leader must decide whether or not to open additional areas for admission and treatment. Extra spaces will increase the capacity of the hospital; but a single site is easier to control, and staff members will function best at the site where they are used to working. For a major MCI, extra admission space, such as a lobby, is usually needed. It can be best utilized if there has been timely preparation: e.g., the installation of oxygen pipes, extra electrical sockets, vacuum apparatus, stretchers, monitors, ventilators, and carts with medical supplies.

Control Station

This station will operate during major MCIs. It is typically located in a large meeting hall, staffed by the relevant directors and consultants, and chaired by the CEO or an associate. Adequate communication and computers should be accessible. So that the control station can be activated quickly, its location must be decided on, and minimal preparations made, beforehand. This control center is, mainly, in charge of communication with external authorities. To ensure rational decision making, the CEO or the associate, carrying portable communication devices, should go to each admission and treatment site.

Public Information Center

The main responsibilities of this center are to deal with the public and to help identify victims. To avoid interference with medical treatment, it should be at some distance from treatment sites. It is staffed by a team of psychologists, social workers, and nurses, including professionals who can meet relatives' needs. The hospital should dedicate several telephone lines for inquiries from victims' relatives. Some relatives will come to the hospital, so the public entrance should be part of the public information center. Victims who have died at the scene are taken directly to the forensic institute; some others may be pronounced dead on arrival (DOA) at the hospital. A few victims may be unidentified because they are unconscious or because of their age or the nature of their injuries. Digital photographs, description forms noting special signs, and personal belongings will assist identification. Data regarding arriving casualties, with an emphasis on those who are unidentified, should be distributed (through the Web) among various hospitals.

Miscellaneous Lessons

A dedicated medical team should be assigned to each patient. Staff members must avoid the "butterfly syndrome"—wandering from one patient to another because of curiosity or anxiety. Bottlenecks can occur not only in the emergency department but also in, for example, the angiography suite and the operating theaters. Therefore, the flow of inpatients must be monitored and controlled. Ideally, this flow should be unidirectional: for instance, a patient leaving the emergency department for a CT scan would not then return to the emergency department but would be transferred to the next treatment station.

The hospital's spokesperson should strike a balance between public relations on the one hand and unimpeded medical care and patients' privacy on the other.

In MCIs, acute management is considered terminated only after a thorough debriefing. All the senior medical and administrative directors who were involved, or their senior representatives, must attend this meeting. The debriefing will produce conclusions and lessons that should be disseminated within the organization and to other relevant hospitals.

Terrorism and MCIs put heavy demands on a hospital system, which often is already overstretched—but proper management can decrease mortality, morbidity, and permanent disability; decrease chaos; and enable the hospital to return quickly to its routines.

The Incident Command System (ICS)

The ICS is responsible for risk assessment and risk management. It functions as a hub, evaluating incoming information and disseminating decisions and orders. At least five hospital elements should be represented in the ICS: decision makers, logistics, administration, operational personnel, and the spokesperson. Liaisons from EMS, HFC, and the police are external elements. The protocols and procedures are generic but should be customized for each hospital, given its capabilities, expertise, and staff.

The ICS is busy, crowded, noisy, and sometimes chaotic; but it should always have a clearly designated manager, organizational operational charts, and ways to communicate. When the hospital is under a toxicological cloud, personnel should wear protective masks or hoods or should work in a preplanned positive-pressure room. Functioning in such a scenario depends on such protective equipment, and on training.

Criteria for performance of the ICS include reaction time; delegation of authority; flexibility in responding; short-, mid-, and long-term planning; information gathering and evaluation; collaboration with peers, the media, and first responders; and independence of decision making.

Operationally, the most important lessons are as follows:

- The ICS of a specific hospital does not function in isolation; it is part of a larger, more complex system to which it should be connected and with which it should collaborate.
- Decisions should be made quickly and clearly and disseminated efficiently all along the chain of command.
- In an emergency, there may be no second chances. The ICS must therefore be proactive, resilient, and swift to recover.

HOSPITAL DRILLS

Comprehensive and specific teaching, learning, training, implementation, exercises, drills, and lessons are interwoven. The main questions are the following:

1. Who is responsible for the overall preparedness—the hospital, its director, or the community?
2. Who is paying for preparedness?
3. What kinds of drill should be conducted, when, and for whom?
4. Who will conduct drills? Will those who conduct drills be inside or outside teams?
5. How can knowledge be kept current and operationally relevant?
6. What are the metrics designated to evaluate the drills?

In a hospital, the entire chain of command must be trained—including leaders, who sometimes tend to skip drills. In a drill, all components of the response teams, internal and external, should share their expertise. We believe that during a time frame of, say, two years there should be a full cycle of training and drilling: from specific "tabletop" exercises and limited drills to all-system tabletop exercises and full-scale all-system "live" exercises. Simulation centers with "smart" reactive dolls can improve clinical practices, reduce expenses, and enhance knowledge and experiences. In our experience with conventional and WMD events, simulation centers have been efficient, effective, and well appreciated.

In Israel we have one "national simulation center" (M.S.R), which garnered amazing experience in training and implementing the lessons learned, sharing it with all "hands on" operational physicians, nurses, and relevant military personnel.

Another effective practice is peer review of a drill by the staff of another, comparable hospital.

The main issues to check at a drill setting are as follows:

1. Type of drill
2. Population involved
3. Scenario
4. ICS functions
5. Risk communication
6. Collaboration with external elements
7. Surge capacity: staff and resources
8. Security and safety
9. Logistics and administration
10. Information sharing
11. Methods of debriefing

HOSPITALS AND WMD

Generic procedures and protocols should be the main elements of preparedness for WMD events. Of course, every scenario has its own unique elements, but even these are usually based on national standards of detection, identification, and physical and medical protection and treatment. Those standards are accepted by all health care facilities and entail specific training and exercises. The underlying principle is that everyone should be trained in the same way, to facilitate peer review, benchmarks, and measurement. To provide the best possible treatment, it is vital to know the answers to questions like these: In a toxicological event, how quickly can the emergency room team put on protective gear? How quickly will the decontamination area be ready for use?

Not every staff member needs to know every detail, but everyone should know the basic elements of survival, decontamination, and lifesaving procedures. For example, in a radiological exposure, it is most important to remember that radiation does not kill immediately; that treatment of severe physical injuries is more critical than specific radiological treatment (though the two can be done in parallel); and that decontamination is necessary. When an event occurs, a team of experts should come in and recommend further procedures; thus every hospital should have a list of available experts.

CONCLUSION

Hospital preparedness can be defined as organizational resilience of the staff and system through comprehensive understanding and functions in an ever-changing environment and under various constraints. Planned procedures and protocols include a "survival-renewal-recovery kit" to prevent posttraumatic stress disorder (PTSD) in the organization. Goals and actions need to be defined beforehand, on the basis of risk analysis and risk management. Collaboration at all levels is crucial, and clear priorities must be set. Generic benchmarks and measurements are needed to assess readiness and performance. Overall training and specific training are crucial. Hands-on experience is the basis for preparedness.

Role of the Private Sector

CHAPTER 47

Introduction to Section 9

Governor James Gilmore
Partner, Kelley Drye & Warren LLP

Nearly 85 percent of the nation's critical infrastructure is in the hands of private industry, much of it in the metropolitan areas where terrorist organizations are most likely to attack. After the first bombing of the World Trade Center in 1993 and the bombings of the U.S. embassies in Africa in 1998, I was named, in 1999, to chair the Congressional Advisory Panel to Assess Domestic Response Capabilities for Terrorism Involving Weapons of Mass Destruction, better known as the Gilmore Commission. After five years of work, we concluded our task on 15 December 2003 and sent to the Department of Homeland Security (DHS), the president, and Congress a total of 144 recommendations, of which 125 have been adopted wholly or in part by the federal and legislative branches of our government.

The private sector has flourished in America since our founding, but terrorism is challenging our public-private partnerships. Progress has been hampered by political debates about big versus small government, who is responsible for our security and who should pay for it, privacy concerns, whether security improvements should be voluntary or mandatory, and lingering questions of liability related to terrorist threats and incidents. A combination of carrots and sticks will be needed. For instance, American companies rely on sound insurance policies to guarantee the ability to recover from any disaster, be it natural or human-made. The insured losses incurred on

9/11 have approached $35 billion. That heavy burden threatened to put some insurers out of business.

Terrorism insurance coverage should be available to all companies that seek it. Congress must act swiftly in 2005 to renew the Terrorism Risk Insurance Act (TRIA) and establish certainty for the many sectors of the American economy that rely on this insurance. Without this affordable insurance program, companies facing skyrocketing insurance costs could be forced to forgo coverage altogether. Uninsured companies that fell victim to a future terrorist attack would then leave the government with a horrendous choice: allow vital companies and services to fail, costing thousands of jobs, or present the taxpayers with a mammoth bill to publicly fund the recovery.

Another example of this effort to connect the private and public sectors can be found on the DHS Web site, www.dhs.gov/dhspublic. The program, called "Open for Business," centralizes information to let every business in America know how to work with DHS. It is designed to assist the business community, and you will find links to contacts, grants, small-business opportunities (the heart of the American spirit and economy), research and development initiatives, and government contracts. Sharing information is the necessary ingredient in any democracy to get the private sector more involved with government—state, local, and federal—to make us safe, while still preserving our liberties.

It is in the interest of the private sector, as well as that of the federal government, to create and foster public-private partnerships. In Chapter 48 Ronald Kelly stresses the importance of major corporations in taking responsibility for their own security, which involves developing and implementing fundamental security practices; conducting risk and vulnerability assessments, emergency planning, crisis management, and employee screening; and creating and implementing critical infrastructure protection strategies to manage risks and shore up vulnerabilities. Crisis management teams are often helpful in creating, implementing, and assessing corporate emergency management plans, as Donald Schmidt explains in Chapter 49. Alan Orlob provides a case study of corporate crisis management in action in Chapter 50 on JW Marriott's response to a suicide bombing at its hotel in Jakarta in August 2003.

In addition to creating, testing, and implementing crisis management plans, a business should also address its responsibility for the psychological health of its employees. In Chapter 51 Mark Braverman points out that terrorist threats and incidents could trigger posttraumatic stress disorder among employees, which could harm the business as a whole through decreased productivity resulting, potentially, from psychological trauma. He recommends a comprehensive, integrative approach to corporate crisis management that should include "human impact planning." William Donnelly in Chapter 52 provides a case study that highlights the great potential for public- and private-sector collaboration to enhance preparedness at the county level. William C. Nicholson surveys some of the key legal issues that private businesses must bear in mind in responding to terror events in Chapter 53. Ultimately, the mission of homeland security is to protect the people of this nation from terrorist threats and incidents; this can be done only through cooperation between the public and private sectors.

Role of Corporate Security

Ronald J. Kelly
Director, IBM Corporate Security

INTRODUCTION

The terrorist attacks of 9/11 were a watershed for the United States, for the relatives of the victims, for the administration, for ordinary citizens, for American corporations worldwide, and for the people who are responsible for developing, implementing, and maintaining the security of corporate America.

Time may not yet have healed the wounds of 9/11, but it is beginning to blur the sense of threat. Or perhaps there is a growing sense of security resulting from the frantic burst of government activity afterward. This response led to the wars in Afghanistan and Iraq; the commitment of American combat forces or special forces in North Africa, Central Asia, the Philippines, and elsewhere; the PATRIOT Act; the Department of Homeland Security (DHS); the 9/11 Commission; a national "intelligence czar"; and a sense among the public that although law enforcement and intelligence communities had failed, the problems were being fixed.

There have been months of hearings on what went wrong, who failed us, who is to blame. People have asked why the American intelligence community did not prevent the attacks, assuming simplistically that all the pieces of the jigsaw puzzle were there, waiting for the CIA and FBI to communicate with each other and put them together. There has been broad support for hurriedly implementing all the recommendations of the 9/11 Commission, although no one has satisfactorily explained how the pieces of the puzzle would have come together if those recommendations had been in place before the attack.

There are many things that, as members of the public, we do not know and may not know for several years: whether the U.S. government departments reorganized under DHS are functioning better than they were beforehand; whether the country would have been better protected by a smaller, more selective reorganization; whether we should change, weaken, or strengthen the PATRIOT Act; whether the reorganization of the intelligence community will make us safer. Also, many high-profile critics tell us that the steps the government has taken to protect the national infrastructure are not enough, that the infrastructure is still vulnerable. (They are right, but why should we want to give that information to our enemies?)

Anyone who thinks seriously about this threat must conclude that there could be another terrorist attack at any time, with no warning, no chatter, no raising of the alert level, no government announcement, and none of the commentary we normally receive from experts in the media.

The effort to carry the war to certain terrorists abroad was necessary and has been helpful; the arrests of many al-Qaida operatives worldwide may have delayed a follow-up attack on the United States. The work of the Joint Terrorism Task Forces (JTTF) has made it much more difficult for terrorists to recruit, organize, and put together an operation in the United States without fear of detection and further arrests.

However, there is nothing to suggest that terrorists have given up. On the contrary, there is an ongoing barrage of threats against the West, and innumerable individuals are willing to sacrifice their lives in an attack on the United States. Preventing such an attack may be beyond the resources of federal, state, or local governments. There is a saying: "The government has to get it right 100 percent of the time; the enemy has to get it right just once." Therefore, the government needs help.

The private sector owns or operates more than 85 percent of the nation's critical infrastructure and thus should be in the forefront of governmental efforts to protect the country. Corporations must play a significant role in reducing the risk of an attack against the business infrastructure and in preparing for the consequences of an attack if one occurs. Corporate America has to help turn soft targets into tough targets and increase its own survivability.

Major corporations need to take the responsibility for developing and implementing fundamental security practices, including risk assessment, baseline security, emergency planning, crisis management, screening of employees, and protecting critical infrastructure. Corporations also need to examine their vulnerabilities, dependencies, and logistic needs and determine how they will function if they are temporarily denied the use of certain assets. Most important, DHS needs to form an interactive partnership with the private sector.

Corporations must consider how they would function during and after a catastrophic attack on the United States. How would they move people and products if air traffic was grounded for a long time? How would they handle a serious power outage? What would they do if sea cargo was delayed because of a threat against a seaport, if a truck bomb exploded in a tunnel or on a bridge, if there was a bomb or chemical attack against rail transportation, if a suicide bomber attacked the lobby of a corporate building, if the financial markets were forced to close for several days, if the supply chain was interrupted, or if manufacturing facilities were attacked and seriously damaged? Any of these situations could occur with little or no warning.

Corporations should assess how they would respond if there was a dirty bomb attack in a major American city, if their employees were too frightened to go to work or too anxious to stay on the job, if there was a rumor of an imminent nuclear threat to a large city like New York. (I refer the reader to Graham Allison's book *Nuclear Terrorism*, published in 2004.[1])

For some corporations, 9/11 changed the explicit responsibilities of their security functions; and for all corporations, it should have changed the implicit responsibilities. Corporate security has a new challenge; it must look to the future, help plan for what may be unimaginable, try to shine a light into the dark corners of extremism and see what is there to fear, what the threat is, and what actions must be taken to mitigate the threat.

I will suggest steps to improve security across the business infrastructure, starting with risk assessment.

SECURITY RISK ASSESSMENTS

Every business site should have a risk assessment. Risks to employees, facilities, and physical and intellectual assets vary from country to country and from location to location within a country. Risks can be human-made or natural; they include hurricanes, floods, earthquakes, chemical spills, and violence in the workplace as well as terrorism; but the focus here will be on terrorism.

Each site must be reviewed so that the security organization has a realistic understanding of the threat there. The risk assessment should look at the number of employees, the business mission at the site, the location, and the environment. For instance, a site near a major government building, a chemical facility, or a building that is part of the financial infrastructure may have substantially greater risk than a site in or near a residential area. Each site must be surveyed and evaluated according to comprehensive security criteria because each site is unique in some way. A risk assessment should always include input from the person or persons ultimately responsible for running the business at that location. Risk assessments often require information from noncompany sources, including consultants, media reports, security professionals, local law enforcement agencies, and the government and its intelligence organizations. When analyzing all this information, be aware that many sources have their own agenda. Consequently it is important to have access to skilled analysts and operations personnel who are not part of official policy making. Fortunately, several organizations provide straight up-and-down reporting.

One excellent source of information concerning locations outside the United States is the Overseas Security Advisory Council (OSAC), a partnership between the U.S. Department of State and the business community. OSAC has existed since 1985 and has analysts and country councils in some 60 nations. (Its Web site, administered by the Department of State's Bureau of Diplomatic Security, is www.ds-osac.org/constituents/login/login.cfm.)

Security consultants offer various services that can aid risk assessment: bulletins, newsletters, Web sites, monthly and quarterly reports, and in-depth country reports covering political, economic, and security issues. Such consultants range from one person trying to cover the globe to large well-staffed companies with impressive country or regional expertise. Many consultants provide an excellent product—timely, accurate, and well balanced. Others are little more than news clipping services offering no analysis. Thus it is important to choose wisely when information from a consultant is to be used in risk assessment. Know what type of information is needed, what the consultant can reasonably be expected to contribute, and where the consultant is situated regarding a particular issue. Consultants can often note patterns and trends and can do research for specific information, but they may have little or no ability to predict terrorist operations or targets.

Even experienced government intelligence analysts, using highly sensitive human and signal intelligence and with unrestricted access to reports of interrogations of terrorists, have not been able to consistently identify specific targets before the fact; instead, they tend to take the past as an indicator of the future.

BASELINE SECURITY

To repeat, the business community may have no warning of an attack and thus no ability to *surge*—to quickly put together a response to a threat. Therefore it is important to build and maintain a strong baseline security program, which can be enhanced if there is a significant unforeseen change in the threat. The following baseline program is a modified, abridged abstract of IBM's security manual.

Baseline security can be understood as the processes that must be in place to deal with known general threats, not specific threats. It can be conceptualized somewhat like security at an airport, where certain fundamental processes must operate day in and day out, regardless of any specific threat, to prevent aircraft from being taken over by attackers or blown up by suicide bombers, and to prevent anyone from stashing explosives on an aircraft, carrying explosives on board, or storing explosives in luggage. Similarly, a corporate baseline security program is a blueprint for protecting human, physical, and intellectual assets. It should meet the corporation's fundamental, daily security needs. It should address today's concerns. It should inspire confidence in the employees and senior management. Security at a business location must be seen not as a stand-alone process but as a fully integrated part of the business.

The corporation must develop a baseline security program that need not ride a roller coaster whenever the government or the media report a possible terrorist threat. Senior management and employees need to feel confident that the company's security program is focused, on target, comprehensive, and responsive.

Specific changes in risks can justify enhancing the baseline program. Additions can be made if there are specific threats or significant new terrorist tactics. For instance, if there were a series of truck or car bombs against a particular corporation anywhere in the world, the corporation could increase baseline security by including vehicle barriers, security fences, hydraulic wedges, fixed or retractable bollards, antiram foundation walls, heavy-duty drop bars, etc.

Some corporations have already added such measures to their baseline security. Some firms are including more stringent processing for loading dock operations; some are vetting limousine drivers and drivers of delivery trucks who have access to their facilities; some have increased the offset from vehicle parking areas to buildings; some use protective film on windows facing courtyards, parking areas, and the street. Actually, these steps are part of baseline security at certain firms, but for many corporations they would represent an addition to baseline security. Baseline security has to be tailored to each company and will depend on the nature and location of the business. The following categories (again, from an abridged version of IBM's security manual) indicate some areas that should be covered in the baseline requirements.

Perimeter Lighting

Good perimeter lighting helps reduce crime, protects employees, gives employees a greater sense of safety and security, reduces accidents, allows for better surveillance by security personnel, and allows closed-circuit television (CCTV) cameras to operate at night or in darkness or semidarkness. The lighting should meet the requirements specified in the Illuminating Engineering Society (IES) Standards, or the local equivalent.

Primary Vehicular Access Controls

Physical security at the primary vehicular entrance will depend on the nature and location of the business. Entrances to plants, laboratories, and headquarters on a campus-style site should have an installed gatehouse that is staffed during regular business hours and can be operated remotely during nonbusiness hours. Driveways should be designed and constructed to hinder or prevent a high-speed vehicle approach to lobbies or buildings, particularly where some floors of a building overhang the basic structure. Bollards, landscaping, speed bumps, and other techniques should be used to impede or prevent vehicle access to areas with high concentrations of people.

Secondary Vehicle Access Entrances

These entrances should be capable of being closed, so that access to the location is via the primary entrance only.

Possible Concealment Areas

A clear line of sight along the building perimeter should be maintained; and any containers, such as trash receptacles and recycling containers that could be used to conceal an explosive device should be removed from close proximity to the building. Also, detection devices should be installed to provide an early warning of any unauthorized entry.

Other Access Points

Less obvious entrances to a building such as grills, gratings, manhole covers, utility tunnels, skylights, and roof vents should be designed to prevent entry into the building, or to any critical utilities. Access to the roof from the ground via exterior stairs or ladders should be prevented.

Building Perimeters and Interior Security

All perimeter doors designated as emergency exits should be constructed of heavy-duty material and equipped with a locking device. The door jambs, hinges, and locks should be designed to resist forced entry. A controlled access system should be used that expedites employees' entrance but denies unauthorized entrance. There are many such systems on the market.

Tailgating is a problem that requires constant vigilance and employee education. Employees should understand that there can be business risks as well as security risks in allowing anyone to follow them through a controlled access system without proper authorization. Every employee should be vigilant in enforcing this requirement.

Lobbies

All lobbies should have a system to control access from the lobby into the company's interior space, including elevators. A security control center or a receptionist in the lobby should have an inconspicuous panic alarm, monitored by a control center that can respond to an emergency. If the alarm is activated, all doors providing entry into the building interior space should lock automatically. Doors should allow for emergency exit, and doors from the exterior to the lobby should remain unlocked to allow law enforcement or emergency response personnel to enter the lobby.

Where elevator access is from the lobby, activation of the panic alarm should cause all elevators to stop at a floor other than the lobby, and not return to the lobby until the situation has been stabilized. Facility entrances that are opened remotely or manually (or both) should have audio and visual devices for identifying individuals before allowing access to the facility. Restrooms in lobbies should be locked, and people with packages should be prohibited from taking the packages into a restroom.

Windows and Exterior Glass

Operable windows on the ground floor should be constructed to prevent unauthorized or undetected entry. Shatter-resistant glazing should be used on windows in exterior walls adjacent to the areas where there are normally large concentrations of people, and on ground-, first-, second-, and third-floor windows facing streets or in direct proximity to parking areas.

Loading Docks

The access to loading docks should be carefully controlled. Delivery trucks should be vetted in advance when possible; otherwise, they should be checked when they come on-site. Given the threat of car and truck bombs, it is poor security policy to allow any delivery vehicle onto a site and up to a loading dock without first identifying it and what it is transporting. Loading docks should have written emergency response procedures with adequate guidance for dock and security personnel. Staffed loading docks should be equipped with panic alarms that are monitored on-site or off-site by a control center. Unstaffed loading docks should have audio and visual devices to permit the identification of an individual before allowing access to the building's interior.

Mail Rooms

Access to mail rooms should be restricted to authorized individuals. Doors and windows leading into mail rooms should be constructed so as to protect against forced entry. Entry points should be monitored by intrusion detection sensors during unstaffed hours. Procedures should be in place for identifying and responding to a "suspicious mail" incident. Mail room personnel should receive semiannual training and updates as necessary. Security personnel should closely examine mail-handling procedures, including procedures for special deliveries and for after-hours deliveries that might not normally go through the normal mail room screening process. It is especially important to ensure that appropriate baseline security is observed when mail room services are contracted out.

Underground Parking Garages

Underground parking garages present a significant risk. A car, van, or truck loaded with explosives can be parked under the building, where an explosion will do the most damage to structural integrity. Consequently, a garage parking area immediately below the company's location must be carefully controlled and limited to authorized vehicles. Badge access should be required. This can be challenging in a building with several tenants, but it should be a no-compromise requirement.

Critical Utilities and Chemicals

A utility is "critical" if its destruction, or damage to it, could cause significant revenue loss or present a danger to the community. Critical utilities include electrical substations, tank farms, water chillers, utility tunnels, satellite ground stations, microwave parabolic reflectors, communications towers, waste treatment centers, water wells, and chemical storage areas, to name just a few. Such utilities must receive special attention in a risk assessment and must be adequately protected as part of baseline security.

The storage of large amounts of toxic or explosive chemicals also requires special attention. Some companies have highly trained, armed security personnel to protect chemical facilities or storage. If that is not practical, barriers, fences, and other access controls should be used to prevent or delay entry. Two layers of fencing are advisable, so that an object cannot be placed against a chemical tank or thrown over a fence in close proximity to the tank. At least one fence should be strong enough to stop a vehicle, and the second fence should be high enough to prevent anyone from climbing into the restricted area. Fences should be topped with concertina wire and alarms. CCTV should be part of the defensive perimeter; it will provide an early warning of any attempted penetration of the protected area. Local law enforcement should be informed of the chemical storage, and a plan should be worked out to ensure its prompt response in an emergency. Movement of chemicals on-site should be tracked and recorded manually or by computer.

Access to chemical storage areas by employees or contractors should be closely controlled. Trucks delivering toxic or explosive chemicals should be vetted by prenotification at least several hours beforehand. If possible, anyone delivering hazardous chemicals to the site should undergo a criminal background check. Employees or contractors with access to areas where hazardous chemicals are stored should also have a background check and should be given appropriate training.

EMERGENCY PLANNING

After risk assessment and baseline security, the next area to consider is emergency planning. Good emergency planning will save lives; poor emergency planning may cost lives.

Elements of Emergency Planning

Emergency planning is site-specific: many aspects of the plan will depend on local conditions. An emergency plan for corporate headquarters in a 40-story office building in Manhattan will be different from that of a small branch office in a rural area. Still, the basics of emergency planning are much the same everywhere. The objective is to minimize the risk of injury or death and protect intellectual and physical property. The emergency plan should include procedures for incidents such as natural and human-made disasters, threats and acts of violence against people and property, political or civil unrest, demonstrations, and catastrophic events in close proximity to the business location.

The emergency plan should include designation of a crisis management team (CMT) with alternative members, a crisis management center, and an alternative center. The CMT should normally include people from senior line management, human resources, the legal department, security, facilities management, communications, finance, the medical department (if any), and others as necessary.

The plan should also include telephone numbers for contacting the following persons: all major company business leaders at other sites in the area, the landlord if the building is rented or leased, and employee listings: home addresses; home, office, and cell phone numbers; and pager numbers. Employee listings should be sorted alphabetically, or by zip code, or—for many overseas locations— by neighborhood code. Additional listings should include all local medical personnel, ambulance services, hospitals, and other medical facilities; all local police and fire departments units; all state and county law enforcement units in the area; the local National Guard unit; the Red Cross and Salvation Army; the local office of DHS; the local and state DHS representative; the Environmental Protection Agency; the Federal Office of Emergency Management; the local FBI office; security managers from other businesses in the area; the Weather Bureau; all major local media stations, including radio and television; and the company's consultants and other contacts as necessary.

The emergency plan should provide a means to contact and account for employees who work at the site, work at home, work at other businesses, or are visiting the site from other locations. If a catastrophic event occurs outside normal business hours, employees should know where to turn for information and guidance. Also, all employees should plan how to contact family members in an emergency and should know what arrangements have been made for their children in school. If employees are worried about their families, it will be much more difficult to apply a cohesive emergency plan during business hours.

The corporation must have a security emergency plan, every site should have an emergency plan, and individual employees and their families should have an emergency plan. All employees should be aware of Web sites where they can obtain advice and guidance on preparing for and dealing with an emergency. Two outstanding Web sites are those of DHS at www.ready.gov and the Federal Emergency Management Agency (FEMA) at www.fema.gov/are youready.

There is a need for considerable redundancy in contacts because the people or offices you normally call or deal with may not be available during a serious incident—they may be preoccupied with the emergency, or it might occur after business hours or on a weekend or holiday.

Every corporation and security organization should understand the importance of evacuation drills, particularly in high-rise buildings. Such drills must be more than just planning exercises and more than just mentally stimulating; they must include stress factors, challenging scenarios, and unanticipated complications. In a crisis, employees will respond well to situations they have been trained to deal with, but less well to situations that are totally unexpected. There should be semiannual testing of facility evacuation in at least one of the following situations: an unspecified threat, a fire, an incident involving hazardous materials, a bomb threat, and an explosion.

Education

Education of employees, particularly first-line managers, is crucial to the success of an emergency plan. Well-trained, educated employees are the company's first line of defense in a life-threatening incident.

Education should include some appreciation of potential threats and possible consequences. Selected employees with key roles, such as wardens in a building evacuation, must be trained and retrained. All employees should know how to respond to a fire, a bomb threat, an evacuation, a suspicious letter or package, a power outage, and other emergencies. They should understand their site or location procedures. This information should be provided the first day they report to work at a specific location. Security personnel and all employees—including secretaries, assistants, receptionists, and mail room workers—who are responsible for receiving packages and parcels should be trained to recognize and deal with suspicious articles. (The need for such training became apparent during the anthrax threat.) Also, telephone operators, secretaries, receptionists, and security personnel should be trained in dealing with threatening calls.

CRISIS MANAGEMENT

Much of the planning for site-specific incidents is also applicable to a catastrophic attack. Corporate security experts must elevate site-specific planning to develop means for dealing with local or regional catastrophic events such as the attacks on the transportation system in Madrid and the attacks against commercial air transportation in Russia in 2004—or attacks against targets such as chemical storage areas and nuclear facilities. Is the corporation prepared to act in such an emergency? Is it prepared to respond so as to protect its employees, help its customers, protect its property, keep itself functioning, and be a good corporate citizen?

The Crisis Management Team

Every major business location should have a CMT with members as appropriate from line management, communications, human resources, facility management, finance, and security. Other executives may be called on to support the CMT as necessary. At the pinnacle of the corporation there should be a corporate crisis management team (CCMT).

CMTs work simultaneously at several levels: at the site or city level where an incident occurred, at the country or geographic level where support may be provided, and at the corporate level where policy must be made. The crisis management chain of command should be fully understood and adhered to throughout the company.

Although local and state governments and the federal government have the primary responsibility in dealing with an incident, the private sector would be involved in many ways. A city government can hardly evacuate people if the evacuation process has not already been worked out with local companies that have a large number of employees. Chaos can result if public planning and private-sector planning are not integrated.

One main responsibility of the local CMT is to account for employees in the affected areas and find ways to help employees and local customers, issue instructions to local managers and employees, warn employees of areas to avoid, instruct employees to work from home or report to other work locations, and help keep the business running.

Employees might be advised to remain at work because streets, trains, subways, or roads are dangerous. In a chemical or dirty bomb attack, it may be prudent for employees to remain at certain locations rather than be evacuated into the street. Crisis management should include steps to take during a local chemical or radiological attack. The plan should answer such questions as how the building can be secured, whether employees are safer inside a building or outside, whether (and how) heating, ventilation, and air-conditioning systems (HVACs) should be shut down, what is the safest area of the building, how to deal with people coming from an outside contaminated area into the company's secured area, how employees who have been exposed to chemicals or radiation can be decontaminated, how (and under what circumstances and authority) employees can be evacuated from a contaminated area to a clean area, and how the CMT can communicate with employees who were not at the site at the time of the incident. (Some of these issues are addressed in *Survival Handbook for Chemical, Biological, and Radiological Terrorism* by Elizabeth Terry and J. Paul Oxer, P.E., published in 2003—a book that deserves to be better-known.[2])

All members of the CMT should keep a copy of the emergency plan in their offices and at home (since an emergency may occur after business hours). All the important names, numbers, contacts, and directions should be stored on a disk or on the hard drive of a laptop, ready for instant use. At the site or business location there should be a crisis management room equipped with an AM-FM radio that can operate on batteries and several televisions connected to cable and network news. The room should have thinkpads with dial-up connection; several telephones that bypass the PBX equipment; telephone service that will leave a message simultaneously on the business telephones, cell telephones, and home telephones of key members of the CMT; a good-quality VCR with recording capability; video conferencing capability (at large locations); and a means of quickly obtaining the names of all employees and their managers working in the area.

The crisis management team leader (CMTL) at every level should be a senior line management executive with the authority to make and implement decisions. CMTLs must be able to operate across functional lines, not just represent their own line of business. There should be an alternative CMTL who can take over if the leader is not available. Local CMTs should be empowered to make immediate decisions that affect the security and safety of local employees. They should not act merely as communicators of problems to the next level of management, or as a conduit from senior management to employees. They must be empowered to act.

Communication and the CMT

In its area of direct responsibility, the local CMT should be the public face of the company to employees, customers, clients, and business partners. Its most important immediate responsibility is to get information out to local employees. The difficulty it confronts is that the situation may be unclear and the facts uncertain, with too many unknowns. CMTs may be tempted to postpone communications until they have most or all of the facts. Wrong! Communication is the glue that keeps the employees together.

Local CMTs may never have all the information they want, but employees are waiting for something—for some sign that management is aware of the incident and taking action. In a catastrophic incident, local CMTs will be racing against the rumor mill; they must take control of the situation, and they do this through communications. The local CMT should move quickly to get out a brief message to employees indicating what facts it has and reassuring employees that it is responding to the crisis and will provide frequent updates. Some immediate dialogue between the CMT and the employees, and between managers and employees, is necessary to maintain control of the situation.

However, local CMTs should not become the voice of the company. That role is usually reserved for corporate headquarters or for the CCMT. The local CMT should avoid communications that are not specific to the immediate situation, or communication that could be considered as enunciating corporate policy. It should not communicate directly with the media unless the content is approved by or coordinated with corporate communications or the CCMT.

Human Resources and the CMT

The role of human resources on the local CMT is to account for employees and ensure their well-being. In a serious attack, this can become a Herculean task. First, there must be a good method for identifying people who normally work in the affected area; this may be partially accomplished through the regular line management chain. The representative of human resources on the local CMT should set up a subgroup to help account for employees and to handle the calls that will come in to the CMT from up-line management and from the families and friends of employees. This information should be provided periodically to the local CMT and the CCMT.

The local CMT should be prepared to provide humanitarian aid to employees and in some cases to their families. This should be handled by the representative of human resources on the CMT. At the local and the corporate level, human resources should be prepared to provide guidance for employees' welfare. The CMT should have available employees, or experts on retainer, with extensive experience in dealing with people in need. The CMT must be prepared to provide medical or psychological assistance to employees or their families. Human resources should have available a database that can provide the names and locations of employees with skills that might be needed in a catastrophic incident.

One lesson of 9/11 is that accounting for and communicating with employees can be difficult. Employees should be provided with at least three contact numbers to be used in an emergency: their manager's telephone number, the security contact for the location, and an 800 number in the area. For instance, there could be one 800 number for all the employees of a company working in one city; in an emergency they could call that number and receive a message providing general instructions.

Security and the CMT

Security will have many staff roles on the CMT or CCMT. One important role is to help the CMT prepare for a major incident: good preparation is the key to responding successfully. The security organization should act as the corporation's "over-the-horizon radar," reviewing the past, looking at the present, and considering the future. Fundamental risk assessments should have been conducted for every major location in the company, and security should ensure that CMT training and emergency planning encompass these risks.

During an actual crisis, security should be the CMT's principal contact with federal, state, and local law enforcement agencies and other agencies as necessary. If the incident occurs at or near a leased facility or rented facility, security or facilities management should be in contact with the landlord. Security should act as the eyes and ears of the CMT, providing updates on significant developments and participating in any decisions. If the site does not have an in-house medical team, security should maintain contact with local medical facilities and ambulance services. Some incidents may require coordination with DHS or the Federal Office of Emergency Management. Security should have the appropriate contacts with these agencies. Once again, I stress the importance of redundancy in contacts.

One area of contacts that is often overlooked by security professionals is medicine. If the United States suffers a significant chemical, biological, or radiological attack, contacts in the medical community will be very important. If security does not already have good sources and contacts in this area, it should start developing them now. Many hospitals are at 85 percent capacity or more; they do not have much capacity to surge. In an attack involving weapons that inflict mass casualties, a great deal of the initial response may have to be organized by private companies, at least to the extent of advising their employees what immediate steps to take. This too requires good contacts within the medical community, at the local hospitals, with local medical services, at the Red Cross, with public health officials, and with specialists in chemical or biological hazards. Some companies have a medical staff that is responsible for this liaison; such a company should make sure that the medical staff has a role on the CMT. In other companies, human resources should be responsible for developing and maintaining these contacts.

During a major incident, security should be able to get a quick reading on how other local organizations are responding. A check with security representatives from these other companies will be helpful. Is everyone else responding in the same way as your company? If not, why not? This information may or may not change the CMT's response, but in any case it will help them understand how others are dealing with similar issues. In this role security is both a purveyor and an adjudicator of information to the CMT. Security should be able to judge and comment on the merits of the actions being taken by other companies.

SOURCES AND CONTACTS

In some situations a good source may be impossible to find. A primary responsibility for security is to evaluate threats as they relate to a particular business, not necessarily to the population in general. In that sense, threat assessment is company-specific. Security may start with a general threat, but at some point it must ask how, if at all, the information affects a particular business.

Corporate security organizations should consider their information requirements for at least the next 10 years. If the corporation is mostly domestic-based, its information requirements are probably narrower than those of an international corporation. Still, domestic corporations as well as international corporations need good information, from good sources. But what is a good source? Every politician, every political commentator, every media figure, every academic expert on terrorism seems able to tell us what happened yesterday and what will happen tomorrow, but never what will happen today. The best anyone may be able to say is that what has happened before will probably happen again.

Since 9/11, much attention has been focused on the likelihood of a follow-up attack. Many people wonder why there has been no such attack yet. Was the government's response after 9/11 so formidable that al-Qaida was temporarily thrown off balance, or is al-Qaida planning an attack that will not take place for several years? We do not know, of course, although the government has made the next attack much more difficult than 9/11.

As a result of this uncertainty, security directors and their staffs are continually seeking information that might provide some warning of an attack. Unfortunately, the likelihood that any contact or source will have such specific information is close to zero. The warnings provided by the U.S. government since 9/11 have been very general, and all over the map. This is not necessarily a fault. If the government has specific information concerning an attack, it will probably be shared initially with a very limited number of people, because the first objective will be to prevent the attack.

A more likely situation is that the government will have a piece or a few pieces of information suggesting a terrorist attack but not indicating the time, place, or target. Often government agencies will provide a list of possible sector targets because they do not have more specific information. Security directors must penetrate this haze to determine if their companies should take any special security measures. To do this effectively, they need more specific information, in at least three categories: (1) information concerning the terrorist group that may be planning an attack; (2) some idea of the city, location, or target of the attack; (3) most importantly, some sense of the veracity and quality of the information that led to the warning.

In addressing the first two categories, security directors need to know the name or identifying characteristics of the group, its history of targets, its recent attacks, statements it may have made on its Web sites concerning future attacks, where it has attacked before, and where it says it will attack in the future. Much of this background information is provided by the government or can be obtained from consultants. Such information can help security professionals make judgments as to whether their company fits the targeting patterns of a particular group, or if there is a perceived threat to their company. As with politics, all threats are local.

As noted, the third category—the quality of the information—is most important. Information, like every other commodity, has a shelf life and should be rated for quality. Since 9/11, there have been numerous warnings concerning possible terrorist attacks. In 2004 we were warned about attacks on or close to July Fourth, the funeral of Ronald Reagan, the Olympics, the Democratic convention, the anniversary of 9/11, the Republican convention, the presidential debates, the election, and the inauguration. As of this writing no attack has taken place. We can ascribe this to the security provided at these venues; or we can assume that no attack was planned; or we can suppose that the warning was based only on reported surveillance, "a terrorist look-see," or an increase or decrease in chatter—but in any case it raises the issue of quality and shelf life. Usually, we do not know much about the quality of information. That is the sort of question, however, that good contacts can sometimes answer.

Specifically, does a warning reflect some new information? Is the government taking additional steps to deal with the threat? What aspect of a general threat has changed, and does that change portend an attack against a particular sector or some part of the infrastructure that will adversely affect your company? The answers to these questions will help qualify the information as it relates to your company's security. Security professionals should be able to put reported threats in perspective and advise senior management on the degree of risk. Understanding the seriousness and timeliness of information can help you determine if your company should take action to protect its business.

DHS is reaching out to business organizations to provide information concerning threats, and security directors should link up with the DHS representative in their area. DHS should set up an organization like OSAC to work with the business community. The OSAC model has worked very well, so there is no need to reinvent the wheel. State and local police organizations are trying to work closely with businesses in their area and to share information about threats. Local FBI offices are very helpful and are also a barometer concerning the seriousness of a warning. If they are working in their normal mode, the situation cannot be too bad; however, if everyone is out in the street looking for bad guys, you need to be more careful.

In developing security contacts outside the United States, it is a good idea to start with the regional security officers at U.S. embassies. They are usually well informed and helpful. OSAC's country councils overseas are an excellent source of information, and their wide business membership provides access to other local country security professionals working for American business interests. Local country security managers often know the situation on the ground very well, and their perspective can be important. They often have excellent contacts with local government authorities. Several consultant services can provide good in-country reporting; and some universities and think tanks have excellent analysts, extensive data banks, and good worldwide contacts.

CONCLUSION

Immediately after 9/11, some businesses that had not been directly affected froze in place: executives were discouraged from traveling, meetings were canceled or delayed, scheduled events were postponed. Did these companies assume that there would soon be more attacks in the United States, or in other countries? Did they think that business meetings, conventions, and trade shows would be targets for terrorists? Did they believe that all commercial air travel was unsafe? Were they simply waiting for the government to signal an all-clear that never really came? Or was their temporary paralysis caused by a lack of preparation?

By now, there should be no doubt about the deadly intent of our enemies. Consequently, we must take measures to prevent another attack and to protect our share of the national infrastructure. We should also be better prepared to assist our employees, help our customers, keep the business going, and immediately return to the economic offensive if we are attacked. The keys to doing this are risk assessments, baseline security, emergency planning, crisis management, comprehension of intelligence and threats, good contacts, and a real partnership with DHS. These programs are a business necessity today and an insurance policy for tomorrow.

N O T E S

1. Graham Allison's, *Nuclear Terrorism* (New York: Times Books/Henry Holt, 2004).
2. Elizabeth Terry and J. Paul Oxer, P.E., *Survival Handbook for Chemical, Biological, and Radiological Terrorism* (Philadelphia, PA: Xlibris Corporation, 2003).

CHAPTER 49

Corporate Emergency Management

Donald L. Schmidt
Emergency Response Planning Practice Leader,
Marsh Risk Consulting

INTRODUCTION

What Is Emergency Management?

Many terms are used for emergency management in the private sector: emergency response planning, contingency planning, crisis management, disaster planning, etc. However, *emergency management*, the term used in the public sector, is more inclusive and is becoming increasingly popular in the private sector. Emergency management has four phases: mitigation, preparedness, response, and recovery. Since September 11, 2001 one more phase has emerged from mitigation: prevention or deterrence.

Emergency management begins with mitigation—identifying a threat; assessing its potential impact on people, facilities, operations, and the environment; and taking steps to reduce the probability of occurrence or the severity of consequences. Preparedness involves organizing and training people, providing facilities and equipment, and developing policies and procedures for responding. The response phase includes actions taken to safeguard people and stabilize the incident. In the private sector, recovery includes continuity of critical business functions, addressed in business continuity plans, and disaster recovery. Crisis management is an overarching executive-level plan that includes making strategic decisions;

communicating with stakeholders such as employees, stockholders, customers, and suppliers; and addressing the emotional needs and health care of affected employees and their families, i.e., the human impact.

National Preparedness Standard: NFPA 1600

The National Commission on Terrorist Attacks upon the United States (9/11 Commission) reviewed the need for preparedness in the private sector and noted in Chapter 12 of its report:[1] "the private sector controls 85 percent of the critical infrastructure in the nation [and] the 'first' first responders will almost certainly be civilians."

The commission acknowledged that lack of a standard contributed to lack of preparedness. It asked the American National Standards Institute (ANSI) to develop a standard for the private sector. After a series of workshops that included representatives from many private-sector industries and associations as well as public officials, ANSI's Homeland Security Standards Panel endorsed *NFPA 1600, Standard on Disaster/Emergency Management and Business Continuity Programs.*[2] NFPA 1600—on which this chapter is based— was promulgated by the National Fire Protection Association (NFPA) under the consensus-based process of standards development accredited by ANSI and established common criteria for emergency management and business continuity.

> Congress then acted on the recommendation of the 9/11 Commission and incorporated Section 7305, Private Sector Preparedness, into the National Intelligence Reform Act of 2004, Title VII—Implementation Of 9/11 Commission Recommendations. The Act, signed into Law by President Bush on December 17, 2004, recognizes NFPA 1600, Disaster/ Emergency Management and Business Continuity Programs, as our national preparedness standard.
>
> (a) FINDINGS.—Consistent with the report of the National Commission on Terrorist Attacks Upon the United States, Congress makes the following findings:
>
> > (1) Private sector organizations own 85 percent of the Nation's critical infrastructure and employ the vast majority of the Nation's workers.

(2) Preparedness in the private sector and public sector for rescue, restart and recovery of operations should include, as appropriate—

(A) a plan for evacuation;

(B) adequate communications capabilities; and

(C) a plan for continuity of operations.

(3) The American National Standards Institute recommends a voluntary national preparedness standard for the private sector based on the existing American National Standard on Disaster/Emergency Management and Business Continuity Programs (NFPA 1600), with appropriate modifications. This standard establishes a common set of criteria and terminology for preparedness, disaster management, emergency management, and business continuity programs.

(4) The mandate of the Department of Homeland Security extends to working with the private sector, as well as government entities.

(b) SENSE OF CONGRESS ON PRIVATE SECTOR PREPAREDNESS.— It is the sense of Congress that the Secretary of Homeland Security should promote, where appropriate, the adoption of voluntary national preparedness standards such as the private sector preparedness standard developed by the American National Standards Institute and based on the National Fire Protection Association 1600 Standard on Disaster/Emergency Management and Business Continuity Programs.

Coordinating Emergency Management, Business Continuity, and Crisis Management

In the private sector, the four phases of emergency management may be assigned to various individuals or groups. Many groups or individuals may share responsibility for emergency response, depending on the specific threat or scenario. For example, security is often responsible for dealing with bomb threats and a medical staff for dealing with medical emergencies. Business continuity, including the recovery of information technology, may be assigned to another group, on- or off-site. Crisis management, including communication, may be handled by the corporate staff, with only limited responsibilities assigned to local managers who would interact with local news media.

The resources needed for effective emergency response, business continuity, and crisis management can be significant, depending on the size and nature of the business. Each function also requires specialized skills and expertise. Therefore, responsibilities for these three functional areas are typically split among several persons or groups. But the plans must be connected and well coordinated to ensure the most effective response.

Program Development

An emergency management program is developed stepwise, but with flexibility, allowing individual entities to do what best meets their needs. A summary of the nine steps follows:

Step 1. Develop an executive or managerial policy statement that defines the organization's vision, goals, and objectives. This statement should vest authority in those charged with responsibility for development, implementation, and execution of the emergency management program. This is important during program development and is essential for critical, time-sensitive decisions such as an evacuation—which should not be delayed because of lack of authority.

Step 2. Assign a knowledgeable, capable manager to oversee the program. Organize a planning committee that includes people familiar with the facility, employees, operations, hazards, and resources. The committee may include representatives from areas such as facilities management, engineering, environmental health and safety, security, medical, risk management, human resources, finance, public relations, government or regulatory affairs, and legal.

Connectivity and coordination between the emergency planning committee on the one hand and business continuity and corporate crisis management plans on the other are essential. There are significant opportunities for sharing information or jointly assessing a terrorist threat to quantify its potential impact on facilities and business operations. Emergency response and business continuity teams can jointly determine the location and specifications of the emergency operations center. They can also jointly develop an incident command structure to facilitate effective flow of information and coordinated planning, damage assessment, and logistics. The committee should seek beyond the organization for those who can provide input, who have a role in the plan, or who must review or

approve the plan. Outside resources can include public fire departments, hazardous-materials response teams, law enforcement,
emergency medical services, the local emergency planning committee
(LEPC), contractors, and vendors. Outreach should address prompt
notification and warning of threats that may affect the organization's
facilities, coordination of response procedures, and establishment of
a unified command structure.

Step 3. Identify terrorist threats; assess the vulnerability of
people, property, and business operations; and quantify potential
severity. Develop planning scenarios to determine the necessary
organization, resources, policies, and procedures.

Step 4. Identify statutory requirements that must be addressed
in the program. Next, determine the capabilities needed to respond
effectively to identified scenarios. Assess the availability and
capability of resources including communication and notification
systems, facilities, equipment, trained personnel, and utility systems
(such as ventilation). Evaluate the response time and capabilities of
public emergency services for each scenario, especially for large-scale
or widespread incidents.

Step 5. Compare available resources and capabilities with the
resources and capabilities needed. Any gaps should be addressed in
the facility's program.

Step 6. Organize a team to execute protective actions such as
evacuation, shelter-in-place, and first aid as well as more
advanced actions such as bomb searches, firefighting, dealing
with hazardous materials, or conducting a search and rescue.
Structure the organization using the incident command system to
enable effective supervision of personnel and coordination with
external public emergency services and other internal and external
resources.

Step 7. Write threat- and facility-specific response procedures for
detection, notification, and warnings and for basic protective actions
such as evacuation, shelter-in-place, and lockdown. More advanced
capabilities and procedures—including search and rescue, firefighting, and dealing with hazardous materials—may be warranted
if public capability is lacking and the facility must therefore be more
self-sufficient. Management must support advanced capabilities, and
programs must comply with regulations.

Step 8. Train personnel and exercise the plan. Weaknesses in
the program that have been identified during exercises or during

post-incident critiques should be addressed through corrective action that strengthens the overall program.

Step 9. Audit the program periodically and add or revise components to ensure that it meets current needs.

PROGRAM MANAGEMENT
Management Commitment and Policy

An emergency management program should be supported by senior management, whose direction will enable wide participation by experts within the organization and increase the probability that planning will be completed on schedule. Management must be briefed on mandatory elements of the program (e.g., evacuation plans) as well as options for enhanced response such as medical aid, firefighting, rescue, and handling hazardous materials. Development of the plan, procurement of equipment, training, drills, and exercises require initial and long-term funding. Management must therefore be informed of options and costs.

Senior management should document the organization's vision, mission statement, goals, and objectives. Management should vest authority in those assigned responsibility for the program, and this should be clearly documented. The document should be widely distributed, so all employees know who is in command during an emergency and who is responsible for updating the plan. Management must also hold those persons assigned responsibility for emergency management accountable, to ensure adequate preparedness.

Regulations and Standards

Many laws, rules, or regulations require emergency planning (e.g., planning for evacuation), and certain standards specify the scope of emergency plans (e.g., staffing, equipment, and training of those involved in firefighting, hazardous materials response, or medical care). Regulations have been promulgated at the federal, state, and local levels. Voluntary standards are prepared by organizations such as NFPA and can be adopted and enforced by political jurisdictions. The U.S. Department of Homeland Security (DHS) is working with

ANSI to build a comprehensive, online database of standards for homeland security.

Federal requirements include Occupational Safety and Health Administration (OSHA) standards (29 CFR 1910) applicable to firms with 10 or more employees. Notable examples are 1910 Subpart E, Exit Routes, Emergency Action Plans, and Fire Prevention Plans; 1910.120, Hazardous Waste Operations and Emergency Response; and 1910 Subpart L, Fire Protection (which includes requirements for detection, alarms, fire protection equipment, and firefighting).

Numerous environmental regulations require, or specify requirements for, emergency planning. They pertain to hazardous waste, prevention of oil pollution and chemical accidents, response to spills, the community's right to know, and transportation of hazardous materials.

Since the private sector controls about 85 percent of the critical national infrastructure, federal regulations promulgated since 9/11 require assessment of terrorist risk, mitigation of threats to critical facilities, implementation of emergency response plans, and business continuity or recovery. Many industry associations—in the chemical industry, financial services, health care, telecommunications, transportation, the energy sector, maritime operations, etc.—have prepared their own guidelines to meet the federal regulations.

Approximately half of the states in the nation have adopted NFPA 1, Uniform Fire Code® (UFC); most of the remaining states have adopted the International Fire Code (IFC) developed by the International Code Council; and several states have a different code or no code. UFC and IFC require basic emergency planning for most types of facilities. They require additional protection and planning for high-hazard facilities such as those that manufacture, use, or store hazardous materials; those that have many occupants, such as high-rise buildings; and those that are public venues, such as theaters and concert halls. Numerous cities and counties have also adopted their own fire codes or have ordinances addressing local requirements.

The Life Safety Code® developed by NFPA has been adopted by 38 states. It specifies minimum standards for exits, emergency planning, etc., for new and existing structures. OSHA recognizes compliance with the 2000 edition as meeting the requirements of 29 CFR 1910.35.

Other standards and recommended practices published by
NFPA address various aspects of emergency planning. Examples
applicable to planning for terrorism include NFPA 1620,
Recommended Practice for Pre-Incident Planning; NFPA 471,
Recommended Practice for Responding to Hazardous Materials
Incidents; NFPA 600, Standard on Industrial Fire Brigades; and
NFPA 1670 Standard on Operations and Training for Technical Search
and Rescue Incidents.

THREAT ASSESSMENT

The emergency management program should be designed to protect
people and facilities against site-specific scenarios. Understanding
of site-specific scenarios requires identification of the type of threat;
point of origin (where the bomb explodes or the chemical is released);
impact area (area affected by the initial event and its subsequent
development and spread); and the vulnerability of the facility,
personnel, and operations.

Terrorist threats include chemical, biological, radiological,
nuclear, or explosive (CBRNE) attacks; cyberattacks; firebombs;
and attacks by armed intruders. The point of origin of an explosion
could be a basement parking garage (World Trade Center, 1993) or a
truck bomb outside a building (Murrah Federal Building, 1995). The
attack could destroy the building and heavily damage adjacent
buildings, or it could be limited to a portion of the building. A
hazardous chemical or biological agent released outside can spread,
depending on meteorological conditions (wind speed, direction,
cloud cover, temperature, and humidity). Anthrax spores released
from an opened package could be spread by a ventilation system to
contaminate an entire building, or be contained within a separate
package-reception facility.

The impact of each threat also depends on the vulnerability of
people, buildings, and building systems. A vulnerability assessment
will identify weaknesses in site layout; perimeter and building
security; building construction; and the arrangement of utility
systems that can compromise the ability to deter, detect, or respond
to a terrorist threat or attack. The vulnerability assessment should
identify opportunities to mitigate, prevent, or deter an attack or
reduce its scope and consequences.

The program manager must assess all credible threats and visualize possible scenarios. Plans must then address the personnel, organization, facilities, equipment, training, and other resources needed to respond to each scenario.

MITIGATION

Mitigation is reduction of the probability of occurrence or the severity of an attack. It involves physical and operational measures to prevent or delay an attack or lessen the effects of an attack that does occur. Mitigation of exposure to terrorist threats should address site selection, building design, building utilities, space planning, physical security, operational security, security policies and procedures, and computer security.

Site selection and placement of the building on the site are important decisions. Ideally, maintain at least 100 feet of separation between buildings, public streets, and parking areas. Place buildings so they are not parallel to the street or parking area. Angling a building can help deflect the blast wave of an explosion.

Buildings can be constructed to better withstand an explosion or to maintain structural stability, allowing occupants to evacuate. Laminated glass or inside curtains can contain flying glass. Critical utility systems such as emergency power supplies, potable water and water for fire protection, communications systems, and ventilation systems (including smoke exhaust and stairwell pressurization) should be protected. Redundancy should be built in if the threat of terrorism is significant.

Space planning can also protect people and critical operations within a building. Locate people away from exterior glass facing nearby streets or publicly accessible parking areas. Locate critical operations such as computer rooms in the central part of the building behind security barriers to restrict unauthorized access. Segregate potential target areas such as lobbies for visitors, package reception areas, loading docks, and areas accessible to unauthorized persons. Ideally, high-volume package reception areas should be located in a separate building or at a remote, segregated part of the building equipped with a separate ventilation system to contain any explosion or release of hazardous material.

Provide increasing levels of security from the property line to the heart of the building where critical operations are located.

Consider fencing, gates, high-visibility lighting, and surveillance or security guards at the property line. Prohibit unauthorized vehicular and pedestrian access to the property. Review grounds to identify areas where people can hide or where packages can be hidden. Lock mechanical equipment rooms to prohibit unauthorized access to air controls and fan rooms. Protect external air intakes accessible to outsiders—especially any located within reach of ground level.

Provide a combination of qualified personnel, physical barriers, intrusion detection devices, and alarm systems to prevent unauthorized access to the site, the building, and critical areas within the building. Physical barriers such as walls, locks, and electronic access control help keep people out of unauthorized areas. Intrusion detection systems include surveillance cameras (closed-circuit television with or without recording capability) and detectors that sound an alarm. A sufficient complement of qualified security personnel is critical because physical security measures can be compromised if an experienced terrorist has enough time.

RESOURCES

Many resources are essential to effective response: personnel, facilities, systems, equipment, supplies, funding, etc. Personnel include trained employees, contractors, and public emergency services (fire, law enforcement, emergency medical services, hazardous-materials cleanup, etc.). Facilities, systems, and equipment include emergency operations centers, first aid equipment, medical supplies, detection systems, fire suppression systems, occupant notification or other warning systems, communication capabilities (e.g., two-way radios, pagers, telephone systems, call centers), ventilation systems, smoke exhaust systems, and exits.

Critical resources include a system to warn occupants to take protective action, an adequate complement of properly arranged exits to facilitate evacuation, communications systems and equipment to alert public officials and members of the emergency organization, and a communication system for use by members of the emergency organization.

As a part of program development, all resources—their availability and capabilities—must be assessed. Which personnel are available to respond during normal business hours and after hours? How quickly can they be notified, and when would they arrive on-site? What are their capabilities? What is the response time of public-sector emergency personnel? What is their knowledge of the facility and are they able to deal with the scenarios identified during the threat assessment? If public emergency services are overwhelmed by a large-scale incident, what resources must the private organization have to safeguard employees?

Identify all resources available for emergency response including facilities, personnel, or equipment owned or available under a "mutual aid" agreement. Inventory these resources and document them in the plan. Identify any gaps between required resources and available resources, and adjust the plan to address these.

EMERGENCY ORGANIZATION

Every facility should organize a team to respond to emergencies. The organization may be limited to basic protective actions such as evacuation and shelter-in-place, or its response can be more extensive if the management supports and staffs a larger and more capable team.

Emergency Manager

A knowledgeable, capable emergency manager should be appointed to develop the emergency organization and threat- and site-specific response procedures. This manager should have the authority to make critical decisions during an emergency, such as when to evacuate and when to shelter in place. The emergency manager should be familiar with all facilities, building construction, utility systems, occupancy hazards, communications and warning systems, fire detection and suppression systems, exit systems, and the location of occupants within all buildings. The emergency manager should be well trained, knowledgeable about terrorist threats and scenarios, and capable of leading the emergency organization.

Emergency Response Teams

The emergency organization must at least assign responsibility for notifying public emergency services (e.g., law enforcement, fire, and emergency medical services) and warning building occupants to take protective actions. Primary and backup notification should be addressed in the plan.

The emergency organization may be limited in size and staffed only to evacuate personnel or shelter personnel in place. Larger facilities may warrant organizing teams for evacuation, shelter-in-place, first aid, firefighting, hazardous-materials response, search and rescue, and bomb searches. The role and responsibilities of each team—its structure, staffing, required equipment, and training requirements—should be written out in an organizational statement. The statement should meet OSHA requirements and specify precautions to ensure the safety and health of first responders.

Evacuation Team

A team should be organized to facilitate prompt evacuation. An emergency manager who is able to quickly assess a potential threat should have the authority to order evacuation. The following are suggested roles for the evacuation team:

- The evacuation team leader has responsibility for the evacuation plan under the command of the emergency manager.
- Floor wardens facilitate the evacuation of every floor. Wardens must ensure that all areas have been evacuated, including restrooms, storage rooms, and any areas whose occupants might not hear the evacuation order or alarm system.
- Monitors should supervise the descent down stairwells. They direct occupants to the correct stairwell and ensure that doors are open and the pathway is unobstructed. They inform evacuees to stay to the right and where to move—to the level of exit discharge (ground floor) or to a predetermined intermediate floor.
- Elevator monitors prohibit evacuees from using elevators and direct them to the nearest stairwell. Lobbies for passenger and service elevators should be monitored.
- Aides ("buddies") should be assigned to assist evacuees with special needs. Pairing a capable individual with each evacuee needing special assistance will speed evacuation. The aides should assist their charges to a safe area where they will await

rescue. Obviously, buddies should be located near those they will assist, and alternative buddies should be considered.

- ◆ Monitors should be assigned to the assembly point to record the names of people who arrive there and to confirm that everyone who was in the building has been evacuated. These assembly monitors should have access to the employee roster and visitor logs, which they should use as checklists.

Shelter-in-Place Team

A team should be organized to move occupants to the interior of the building and to close off the building from outside air. Assign building facilities or engineering personnel to shut down the ventilation system. Close all air intakes and exhaust dampers, either from a central command center or manually unit by unit.

Instruct the evacuation team to move people to the interior of the building, away from windows and doors. Assign security staff members to close the exterior doors and advise occupants to remain in the building until it is safe to move outside.

Bomb Search Team

A bomb search team includes people who are familiar with the building and its contents. They are best able to detect suspicious packages or objects that are out of place and therefore suspect. Train the bomb search team to conduct a search and to recognize suspicious objects. This includes knowing how to section a room from floor to ceiling and search each section. The search team also needs to understand precautions such as prohibiting the use of potential triggering devices (radios, cellular telephones, etc.).

Search-and-Rescue Team

The emergency organization may need to provide rescue services until the public fire department arrives on-site, or if the fire department is unable to provide required services because it is unable to reach the site or because the magnitude of the incident overtaxes its resources.

Other teams can include firefighting, medical response, property conservation, and decontamination.

INCIDENT COMMAND SYSTEM

A terrorist incident will probably require substantial resources from the private sector and the public sector, and the two must work well together. Successful control of the incident requires an incident management system that assigns roles and responsibilities and allows for effective and efficient use of all resources.

The incident command system (ICS) is a management system designed to integrate facilities, equipment, personnel, procedures, and communications within a common organizational structure. ICS is used for all types of emergencies, small or complex, by federal, state, local, and tribal government and by many private-sector and nongovernmental organizations. It normally has five major functional areas as shown in Figure 49-1: (1) command, (2) operations, (3) planning, (4) logistics, and (5) finance and administration. ICS has been designated by the National Incident Management System[3] for use in the U.S. public sector.

The roles and responsibilities of the emergency manager and emergency response teams should be defined in accordance with the five sections of ICS. Assign the emergency manager to be the facility's incident commander (IC), and assign subordinates to the three sections of the command staff: government liaison, safety, and public information. The IC (emergency manager) can handle planning for smaller incidents, but large-scale incidents will probably require another person to head the planning section. Organize evacuation, shelter-in-place, firefighting, first aid and medical aid, hazardous-materials handling, search and rescue, and other teams under the operations section. Professionals from the finance, accounting,

F I G U R E   49-1

The five sections of ICS and the three command staff positions.

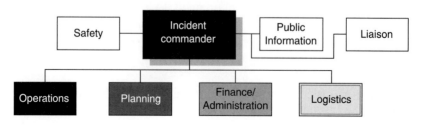

insurance, and risk management departments can staff the finance-and-administration section. Appoint staff members familiar with resource needs and methods of acquisition to handle logistics.

Incident Commander

Decisions made by the IC during the initial minutes after detection are key to safeguarding people. Recognizing critical needs and prioritizing limited resources require knowledge of the various hazards posed by terrorists' weapons. Specific responsibilities of the IC include the following:

- Activate the emergency response plan and elements of ICS
- Ensure that public emergency services and members of the emergency organization are notified and informed where to report (or not to report, if conditions are unsafe)
- Assess the situation—identify the nature of the threat and its potential impact on people, buildings, and the environment
- Determine incident goals, objectives, and immediate priorities
- Consider the threat of secondary devices
- Order building evacuation, sheltering in place, or a combination of both to move people out of danger
- Establish a perimeter around the "hot zone" where the hazard exists or could spread (e.g., the area around a suspected bomb or an area contaminated by a chemical weapon)
- Establish a command post at a safe location upwind and upgrade away from direct involvement with victims, responders, or emergency response vehicles
- Ensure that adequate safety measures are in place
- Provide a detailed situation report to management and government officials when they arrive on-site
- Manage incident operations

Operations Section

The chief of the operations section is responsible for managing all operations to protect personnel and stabilize the incident.

For small organizations, the emergency manager acting as IC
will probably assume responsibility for operations. Operations
include:

- Evacuation
- Shelter-in-place
- Search and rescue
- Decontamination, first aid and medical treatment
- Firefighting
- Site security
- Fire suppression, ventilation, and elevator systems control in
  the building

Planning Section

The chief of the planning section reports directly to the IC and is
responsible for collecting, evaluating, disseminating, and using
information about the development of the incident and the status of
resources. Planning is essential to an understanding of the current
situation and how it could develop so that alternative strategies can
be formed. This includes assessment of the nature of the incident; its
immediate impact; its actual or potential spread, risks, and hazards;
the implementation of control strategies; and the availability and
capabilities of resources.

Logistics Section

The logistics section, which also reports to the IC, provides facilities,
services, and materials. It must identify the service and support
requirements for planned and expected operations and then procure
resources.

Finance and Administration

The finance-and-administration section manages the financial aspects
of the incident within the constraints of the organization's policies,
procedures, and governance rules. This includes compiling time
records for personnel working to stabilize the incident or cleanup;

compiling a record of expenditures; communicating with all departments to compile estimates of damage and interrupted business for any insurance claims; notifying and coordinating with insurance brokers and underwriters' claims staffs to prepare and settle claims resulting from the incident; and providing a financial summary. Units under the finance-administration section include documentation, time and costs, and claims.

Command Staff

Three staff positions support the IC: liaison, safety, and public information.

The liaison officer is responsible for interacting on-site with governmental agencies, including law enforcement, firefighters, emergency medical services, environmental agencies, and public health workers. When agencies assign representatives to the incident, the liaison officer will coordinate with them. The liaison officer's goal is to provide information to the public agencies on-site or provide access to the persons who have the information that will enable these agencies to control the incident.

The safety officer is responsible for monitoring and assessing hazardous and unsafe situations and developing measures for personnel safety. The safety officer will correct unsafe acts or conditions and should be authorized to stop or prevent unsafe acts when immediate action is required. The safety officer should also investigate accidents, recommend corrective action, and prepare an accident report to submit to the compensation-claims unit.

Someone from public relations or public affairs acts as the public information officer responsible for collecting and releasing information about the incident to the news media and other agencies and organizations. The public information officer should be a competent spokesperson, familiar with the organization's media relations policies and procedures—especially policies for approving the release of information. The public information officer establishes a media briefing area and acts as the single contact person for release of information to the media and others, schedules regular press briefings, controls the release of information, and coordinates with government officials to refer specific questions that should be answered by public authorities.

Incident Command Post

An incident command post (ICP) is a place at a safe distance from the incident where the IC can observe and direct operations at the scene of the incident. It can be a place outside a building, a motor vehicle, or a convenient location within a building. It should not be confused with the emergency operations center (EOC), which is an on-site, off-site, or virtual meeting place for incident management. The IC's responsibilities include the following:

- Establish the ICP at the time of the emergency
- Communicate the location of the ICP to members of the emergency organization and responding public agencies

When public emergency services arrive on-site, they will establish their own command post. If possible, relocate the private-sector command post adjacent to it. This will enable easier communications and allow the organization to contribute to the unified command of the incident.

Emergency Operations Center

The EOC is a command and communications center with personnel who gather, retrieve, analyze, process, and display information to coordinate response to an emergency. Staff the EOC with members of the emergency organization, executive management, department managers, and support staff to receive and distribute messages, post the incident status, and track resources. Equip the EOC with the following:

- Sufficient telephone lines—direct (i.e., not switched through a PBX) and independently powered (so service will not be disrupted if primary and emergency electrical power is lost). In a severe incident, telephone service and telecommunications may be impaired, so plan for alternative communications.
- Access to electronic mail and the Internet.
- AM-FM radio, television, and emergency alert system radio.
- Dry-erase board, flip charts, or poster board with markers and erasers.
- Copies of drawings of all building utilities including ventilation (e.g., air intake locations, air-handling unit controls,

and exhaust dampers), electrical equipment (locations and areas served by transformers, substations, generators, and disconnects), natural or propane gas, water, and sewage.

+ Site plans showing the location of buildings, parking areas, roadways, and other surrounding properties.

+ Building plans showing the layout of each floor, the location of any command center for control of building utilities, the location of stairwells and their levels of exit discharge, the location of areas of refuge, and elevator lobbies.

+ Video and 35-millimeter still cameras with spare videotape, film, and batteries for documenting damage and cleanup activities.

EMERGENCY RESPONSE PLAN

Each facility should have documented, site-specific policies and procedures for response to terrorism scenarios, including events inside or outside the building, events that affect a region or the nation, and attacks that can affect the availability of required infrastructure (e.g., electricity, natural gas, steam, and potable water). Specific scenarios should include an explosion, a suspect package, a bomb threat (received by telephone, mail, e-mail, Web site, or orally), release of chemicals (industrial and warfare), a biological agent, pandemic infection, and a cyberattack.

ALERTING, WARNING, AND COMMUNICATIONS

A prompt, effective means of alerting public agencies and internal response teams to respond to a threat is critical. Establish a primary means of notification and ensure that there is reliable backup communication in case the primary system fails or is overtaxed.

Warning systems such as emergency voice communication systems or simple public address systems are important. They should have backup power, and speakers must be located so that all occupants of the building can hear important announcements. Document operating instructions in the plan, and be sure that competent persons are able to activate the system. Scripts should be prepared in advance for scenarios identified in the threat assessment, and personnel must be capable, if necessary, of speaking clearly in several languages to communicate with all occupants. Provide a means of warning occupants with impaired hearing or sight. Training should ensure that all building occupants are familiar with the sound of the evacuation signal, so they will respond immediately.

Other communications capabilities such as two-way radio systems should be interoperable between all responders who must work together. Establish a command channel for the leaders of the tactical response teams to talk with the incident commander. Assign radio channels and program radios to ensure that the teams handling evacuation, sheltering-in-place, medical aid, rescue, hazardous-materials response, security, etc., can talk as needed. Assess the reliability of the radio communications systems and prepare plans to deal with a loss of communications capabilities.

To alert public agencies, provide complete information about the emergency including specific location (site, building, and area within the building), number and location of any victims (their symptoms or injuries), the nature and spread of the hazard, and actions taken to stabilize the situation or protect life and property.

Establish notification and escalation procedures to ensure prompt notification of managers involved with business continuity, corporate crisis management, etc., as the scope of the incident grows or its impact increases.

Periodically, inspect and test all systems and equipment used for alerting, warning, and communications to be sure they are reliable. Fire alarm systems or emergency voice communication systems should be tested in accordance with applicable codes and standards such as NFPA 72, National Fire Alarm Code®. Maintenance specified by the manufacturer and by applicable codes and standards should be done.

PROTECTIVE ACTIONS
Evacuation

Every building should have an evacuation plan based on an assessment of factors such as the following:

- Construction and layout of the building
- Potential terrorist targets within the building (e.g., mailroom, lobby, loading dock, parking garage)

+ Number and concentrations of occupants, including number and location of those with special needs
+ Occupant notification systems
+ Building utility systems (especially ventilation)
+ Fire protection systems (e.g., sprinklers and smoke control systems)
+ Exits and exit routes

Plan development should include preparation of building floor plans with clearly marked paths to primary and secondary exits.

Hazards within the building such as the mailroom or a lobby where a bomb might explode should be identified, and alternative evacuation routes should be designed to avoid them.

Concentrations of occupants in auditoriums, cafeterias, and conference rooms require extra attention to ensure that exits are adequate for the maximum number of occupants. These areas are also potential targets because of the concentration of people in them.

Occupants with special needs should be identified in advance, usually voluntarily, to protect their privacy. Anyone with an obvious disability will require assistance, and plans should address this. The plans should also anticipate that there will be others who will not identify themselves as having special needs but will nevertheless need assistance. These could include people with arthritis or temporary conditions such as a sprained ankle or a broken leg. Heart disease, emphysema, asthma, or pregnancy can reduce a person's stamina to the point where assistance will be needed to descend stairs. This is especially true if there are any airborne contaminants.

A high-rise building presents two challenges: the number of occupants and the time necessary to evacuate them all safely. Evacuation plans for high-rise buildings require an assessment of the building and its exits as well as close coordination with the building's management team and the local fire department. Full evacuation of a high-rise building is not typically ordered when a fire alarm system is activated. Initially, the floor where the alarm sounds and two floors above that floor are evacuated down below the floor where the fire alarm has activated. The next zone to be evacuated would include the two floors below the fire floor because these floors would be used as staging areas by firefighters. The number and location of floors to be evacuated could change, depending on the location and spread of fire and smoke, arrangement of the ventilation system, and any vertical penetrations in the floors. The evacuation plan may call for all floors within the air-handling zone to be evacuated. Severe incidents would require full evacuation. Occupants should not be directed to the roof.

Evacuation plans should identify areas of refuge. These include oversized landings of a stairwell or fire and smoke compartments within a floor. The refuge areas should have a means of communicating with the evacuation team leader or firefighters. The number of people who can safely occupy the refuge area and the circumstances when the area would be used should be addressed in the evacuation plan.

Elevators should not be used for evacuation when there is a fire, smoke, or an airborne hazard. During a fire, elevators may be recalled automatically to the first floor. Older elevators may stop at the fire floor, putting their occupants in danger. Use of elevators during a terrorist attack that is spreading an airborne hazard into or within a building could worsen the spread.

The evacuation plan should be designed to overcome any limitations in the building's exits: limited audibility of the building's fire alarm or occupant notification systems, inadequate exits, poor marking of exits, obstructions or impediments, long travel distances, and dead ends. Once the limitations have been identified, the evacuation plan can emphasize alerting in noisy areas (or areas where the alarm system is not loud enough) and the use of extra floor marshals to move occupants along or to redirect them around bottlenecks.

A building with several tenants requires close coordination with the building's manager to ensure that building plans and the tenant plan work seamlessly. Close coordination and effective real-time communication during an evacuation are essential.

Evacuation plans must also address the shutdown of processes or equipment that would create a hazard if they were left running after their operators were evacuated. The time necessary to shut down this equipment should be determined, and the safety of operators while they are shutting down the process or equipment should be addressed.

Evacuation Scenarios

The decision to evacuate part or all of a facility depends on the nature of the emergency and the area affected. The release of a chemical or biological agent or a bombing inside the building would call for evacuation. However, an incident that occurs outside the building and does not threaten the building or its occupants would not require evacuation. In fact, evacuation of the building could put people in harm's way—for example, if a chemical, biological, or radiological hazard was overspreading the path of evacuees.

Bomb threats are another special case. There are various options for handling such threats. If a suspected device is found or there is credible information that an explosive device is in a building, the building should be evacuated. However, a telephoned bomb threat that includes no specific information may not require evacuation. Evacuation scenarios should be discussed with law enforcement authorities, who should approve all procedures.

No evacuation plan is perfect, and no plan can anticipate every possibility. Therefore, the IC has to assess the threat to the building occupants and make the best decision possible. Occupants will tend to make their own decisions if they have had prior experience in an emergency or if leadership is lacking. A thoughtful evacuation plan that is communicated clearly and practiced should work well.

Evacuation Routes and Assembly Areas

Evacuation routes should be established for every floor of each building. Each map should also indicate the location of the primary and secondary assembly areas.

Primary and secondary assembly areas should be separated from each other by direction (e.g., north and south) so that both are not subject to the same event. They should be located away from the staging area for emergency vehicles, at least a quarter-mile apart, and should not be in the path of prevailing winds.

Each assembly area should be given an easily remembered name—such as the name of a nearby local landmark. Maps showing assembly areas should be included with any emergency information communicated to employees.

Sheltering in Place

An airborne hazard (chemical, biological, or radioactive) outside a building may require sheltering in place. For instance, a hazardous plume may be moving toward an area that cannot be evacuated before it arrives. Sheltering in place is a temporary strategy designed for situations in which remaining inside is safer than evacuating. It is designed for at most one to two hours because all buildings are subject to air infiltration.

Sheltering in place was originally developed for properties near hazardous-materials sites where an uncontrolled release of chemicals could result in a dangerous, spreading plume; but today it is also applicable for terrorist threats in urban centers. In a city, large numbers of people in mid- and high-rise buildings cannot be evacuated very quickly—and even if they could, traffic congestion would make it impossible to move everyone outside the hazard zone.

Shelter-in-place procedures should be developed for these possibilities. Inside rooms such as conference rooms that are large enough for numerous people are a good choice. Preferably such rooms should be above the ground floor (most attack chemicals are heavier than air and tend to settle to the ground), should be windowless, and should have a minimal number of vents and doors (because these openings will have to be closed or sealed to prevent infiltration by airborne hazards). Supplies should be kept on hand to equip the shelters. These should include flashlights and batteries, first aid kits, several means of communication (e.g., landline and cellular telephones dedicated for emergency use with emergency telephone numbers as well as two-way radios, if available), a battery-powered radio to receive official information, and a roster of employees to identify people who may be missing.

Assign specific persons to close doors and windows to seal off the building from the exterior airborne hazard. The location of all controls to shut down the building's heating, ventilation, and air-conditioning system should be identified and marked in advance for "shelter-in-place shutoff." Determine how long it takes to shut down air-handling units and air intakes. Ensure that knowledgeable persons are responsible for shutdown, are promptly notified, and are able to complete their task within the required time.

Medical Treatment

First aid must be provided for anyone injured or sickened by a terrorist attack. However, several significant issues must be addressed, depending on the nature of the incident. For one thing, if the attack involves chemical or biological hazards, rescuers providing first aid can also become contaminated. Therefore, special personal protective equipment (PPE) is needed, but it will probably be available only from emergency services, health care professionals, or the military. Second, providing medical care for victims requires knowledge of what has caused the sickness or injuries and the proper methods of treatment. Third, rendering aid to a contaminated victim could contaminate the treatment area.

If a facility has no trained personnel and no special equipment or procedures to treat victims of chemical agents, the following actions should be taken:

- Access victims only if it is safe to do so.
- Notify police, fire, and emergency medical services, and local hospitals.
- Provide care for life-threatening conditions, if it would not expose the caregiver to the same hazard.
- Coordinate with emergency medical services and the nearest hospital to ensure that they are aware of the type of exposure and can prepare for appropriate treatment.
- Inform the local hospital of any people who may arrive on their own. These patients may have to be segregated to prevent contamination of the facility or others.
- Universal precautions should be taken to prevent exposure to bloodborne pathogens.

THREAT-SPECIFIC EMERGENCY PROCEDURES

Detection and Assessment

The initial assessment of an incident must be done as quickly as possible.

- Type of attack (e.g., chemical, biological, explosive, radio-active, nuclear, or incendiary)

- Area of release (inside or outside, exact location, proximity to air intakes)
- Containment or spread of the hazard
- Casualties

An explosion of a "dirty" weapon could release chemical, biological, or radiological hazards. The emergency manager should review and be familiar with the signs of different types of attacks to determine the nature of any attack. For example, it is important to recognize physical evidence of a chemical attack:

- Crowd panic
- Mass casualties—unusual numbers of sick or dying people with symptoms such as nausea, disorientation, difficulty breathing, convulsions, localized sweating, red eyes, and red or blistered skin
- Pattern of casualties—casualties distributed downwind outdoors or casualties grouped within a confined area (e.g., one that shares a ventilation system) indoors
- Unexplained odors—unusual smells (e.g., fruity, flowery, sharp-pungent, garlicky or like horseradish, like bitter almonds or peach kernels, like new-mown hay) that are out of character with the surroundings
- Dead animals, birds, or fish—an unusually large or noticeable number of sick or dead wildlife in the same area
- Lack of insect life—no normal insect activity on the ground, in the air, or in water. Standing water can be checked for the presence of dead insects
- Different-looking areas—trees, shrubs, bushes, food crops, or lawns that are dead, discolored, or withered, when there has been no drought
- Unusual fogs, clouds, mists, or liquids—surfaces with oily droplets or film, when there has been no recent rain. Low-lying clouds or a foglike condition not consistent with the surroundings. Pools of liquid from an unusual or unidentified source
- Low-lying clouds or a foglike condition not compatible with the weather
- Smoke or fog inside a building

- Abandoned spraying devices, such as chemical sprayers used by landscaping crews
- Unusual metal debris—unexplained bomblike or munitions-like material, especially if it contains a liquid
- Explosions that disperse or dispense liquids, mists, vapors, or gas; explosions that seem to destroy only a package or bomb device
- Unscheduled spraying or unusual application of spray

Distinguishing Between a Chemical and a Biological Release

To decide whether a release is biological or chemical, look for symptoms. A biological agent rarely causes immediate symptoms, but a chemical agent usually does. Symptoms of exposure to toxic chemicals, including chemical warfare agents, include one or more of the following:

- Pinpoint pupils, leading to a perception of darkness
- Dilated pupils (caused by some chemicals, but not chemical warfare agents)
- Dizziness
- Runny nose
- Clammy skin or perspiration
- Difficulty breathing
- Nausea, vomiting, or both
- Blurred vision or blindness
- Seizures
- Loss of bladder control
- Loss of consciousness
- Death

Again, a biological release will generally not cause immediate symptoms. Knowledge of the location and even the occurrence of a biological release will usually depend on direct observation of the release event (e.g., powder falling out of an envelope), or a warning probably from public officials. Without such evidence, detecting the source of a biological release may be impossible.

Distinguishing Between an Indoor and an Outdoor Release

The location of the source is crucial, since actions will differ, depending on whether the release occurs outdoors, indoors, or into building air intakes. See Figure 49-2.

If there is uncertainty as to where the release occurred or is occurring, look outside—if people are getting very ill inside from an outdoor source, then there will be visible evidence outdoors: dead or dying birds and wildlife, people collapsing on the sidewalks, etc. If these signs are not present, the source is probably indoors or in (or near) one of the building's air intakes. To cause immediate symptoms indoors, a very large or very toxic outdoor release near a building's air intake would be required.

Determination of Protective Actions

The location of the terrorist incident, known and potential hazards, and obvious property damage and casualties determine protective actions. The response must also anticipate the possibility of further terrorist attacks.

The location of an attack may be within the building, immediately outside, a few blocks away, or miles away. An attack that occurs miles away could still pose a threat to the site from airborne hazards such as chemical or biological agents or radio-activity.

The scope of any hazards may not be known for hours or much longer, so the initial assessment of the threat should anticipate potential hazards. Any explosion could release airborne chemical, biological, or radioactive hazards. If there are any symptoms or signs of chemical or biological agents, declare an emergency, assess what is known, and implement protective actions.

Protective actions must address all the potential hazards posed by the terrorist act including fire, structural collapse, airborne hazards, and the threat of similar or different additional attacks. A major explosion could cause significant property damage, inflict casualties, and spread airborne hazards. The target building could collapse onto adjacent buildings or onto people in the street. Airborne hazards within a building could spread throughout the building, affecting other occupants. An airborne hazard released outside could infiltrate a building.

F I G U R E   49-2

Matrix of possibilities: chemical or biological, indoors or outdoors.

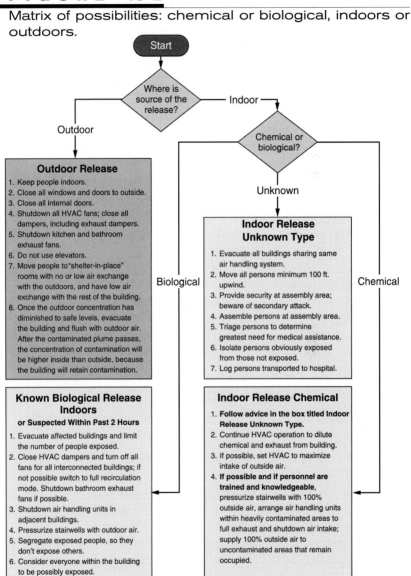

Emergency procedures should stress protection of people first. This could include evacuation from an unsafe building or environment or sheltering in place to protect people from airborne hazards outside the building. Any sick or injured people should be given first aid by a qualified emergency response team or triaged for treatment by public emergency medical services. If the safety of building occupants is properly addressed and there are sufficient trained and equipped personnel, other efforts could be undertaken. These could include firefighting, containment of hazardous materials that may have been released, salvage, and property conservation. A large-scale incident that overtaxes public emergency services may require extraordinary efforts by the emergency response team and others to assist victims.

The initial assessment of an incident requires determining the type of hazard, its source, and the extent of any spread.

Airborne Hazards

If the initial assessment reveals an actual, suspected, or potential airborne hazard, its source should be determined. If an explosion or vapor cloud is reported or observed outside the building, protective actions should be appropriate for an outside hazard. If an airborne hazard could have occurred within the building, possibly from a malicious act or the opening of a package, or if an outside airborne hazard may have infiltrated the building, protective actions should be appropriate for an inside hazard.

Outdoor Release, Biological or Chemical

Minimize exposure by taking as many of the following actions as possible:

- Indoors—move anyone who is within a 500-foot radius of the release site.
- Notify police and firefighters to evacuate areas a minimum of one mile downwind in accordance with the Emergency Response Guidebook.
- Follow shelter-in-place procedures—close all windows and doors to the outside; close all internal doors; shut off all HVAC fans and close all HVAC dampers, including exhaust dampers; do not use elevators, since they create a piston effect and can pump air into or out of the building.
- Once the outdoor concentration has diminished to a safe level (as determined by the IC), evacuate the building

and flush it with outdoor air. After the contaminated plume passes, the concentration of contamination will actually be higher inside the building than outside, because the building will tend to retain contamination that managed to enter.

Indoor Release, Biological or Chemical
Follow these procedures:

- Evacuate the building
- Gather all evacuees at assembly areas, but no closer than 100 feet from the evacuated building
- Provide security at the assembly areas to prevent a secondary attack

Have evacuees congregate at assembly points upwind of and at least 100 feet from the building (preferably much farther). As soon as possible, separate people known to be exposed from those who may not have been exposed. Account for all evacuees and provide first aid as required.

Indoor Release, Biological
A biological agent will probably not cause immediate symptoms, and the type of biological agent (or even whether it is real or a hoax) may not be known for hours or possibly days. In fact, a biological agent can be introduced into a building without the occupants even knowing about it.

Take the following protective actions if a release is known or suspected to have occurred within the past hour or two:

- Close HVAC dampers and turn off all fans. Operation of any HVAC system will exhaust air (and the biological agent) to the outdoors, possibly infecting people who do not know they are at risk.
- Pressurize stairwells with outdoor air, if possible.
- Limit the number of people exposed.
- Segregate those with symptoms, those potentially exposed, and those who have had close contact with others who have

been exposed—unless the biological agent is determined not to be contagious (e.g., anthrax).

* Log the names, addresses, and contact information of those who have been exposed.

Radiological Incident

A conventional explosion may scatter radioactive material, or an aerosol containing radioactive material could be spread over a wide area. Some people may be injured and many may be contaminated or exposed. A radiological hazard will not be known for sure until government officials assess the scene. Therefore, take the following precautions.

* Remove seriously injured people from the source of radiation, stabilize the injuries, and arrange transportation to hospitals.
* Establish a perimeter around the source, and restrict entry to rescue personnel only.
* Check everyone near the scene for radioactive contamination. Establish a decontamination area and decontaminate people whose injuries are not life-threatening (broken arms, etc.) before sending them to hospitals.
* Detain uninjured people who were near the event or who are inside the control zone until they can be checked for radioactive contamination, but do not delay treatment of injured people or transport to a hospital for this purpose.
* Inform nearby hospitals to expect the arrival of radioactively contaminated and injured people.

Fires and Explosions

When a fire or explosion is detected, notify the fire department and describe the nature of the fire, its location, and any fire alarm zones that have been activated. Advise the fire department of the building entrance closest to the scene.

If an explosion occurs, attempt to determine its cause. If an explosion is not known to be accidental, assume that it could have dispersed a chemical, biological, or radioactive hazard. Follow instructions for indoor or outdoor release of chemical or biological agents.

The IC should order evacuation of the building or portions of the building to protect the occupants. The IC should also set up a command post near the building or adjacent to the location of the fire. Direct the emergency response team to their assigned areas, as necessitated by the conditions reported. When the public fire department arrives, inform its IC of the nature of the emergency and action being taken. Building plans, a two-way radio, master keys, and other information should be provided as requested.

Supervise fire protection systems (e.g., sprinklers, fire pump, and water supply control valves) and utility systems (generators, electrical disconnects, HVAC, gas, etc.). Ensure that all sprinkler systems and fire pumps are operating properly. If there is a power outage or potential outage, monitor any generators to ensure that they have started and are running smoothly. Disconnect power to part or all of the building at the direction of the fire department's IC. Activate any building smoke exhaust system and manipulate the HVAC system at the direction of the fire department's IC. If there is no directive from the fire department's IC, shut down the air-handling system to prevent the spread of smoke.

Keep the building entrance and driveway areas free for access by the fire department. Occupants should be directed to emergency exits and assembly areas away from the building. Unauthorized persons should be kept off the property.

Suspicious Package or Letter

Terrorists might package an explosive device or a biological agent such as anthrax and send it through the mail or by courier. Everyone should be aware of the indicators of packages that may contain a terrorist weapon and of the procedures for emergency response.

General Characteristics

Following are some characteristics of suspicious incoming letters or parcels. Any one characteristic may not be reason for concern, but multiple characteristics should arouse suspicions and be a reason for taking precautions and conducting further evaluation. See Figure 49-3.

- Hand delivery.
- No postage or excessive postage.

FIGURE 49-3

Indicators of a suspicious package.

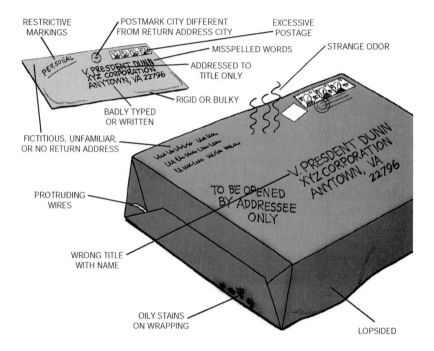

- Package is unexpected or from someone unfamiliar to the addressee.
- Receipt is followed by an anonymous call asking if the item was received.
- Package is addressed to someone no longer with the organization or is otherwise outdated.
- Address is handwritten or poorly typed; title is incorrect or appears with no name; common words are misspelled.
- There is no return address or an unverifiable return address.
- Package is marked "Personal," "Confidential," "Fragile—Handle with Care," "Rush—Do Not Delay," "To Be Opened in Privacy," "Your Lucky Day Is Here," or "Prize Enclosed."
- Package is of unusual weight relative to its size or is lopsided or oddly shaped.
- There are soft spots or bulges.

- There is a strange odor or a stain.
- There is a powdery substance on the outside.
- There is a "sloshing" sound. (Mail bombs typically do not "tick.")
- There is pressure or resistance when the package is opened; this may indicate a mail bomb.
- There is an unusual amount of tape.

Package Marked "Anthrax" or Is Powdery

If a letter or package is marked "anthrax," has a powdery substance on the outside, is leaking a powder, or contains a powdery substance when opened, the following actions should be taken:

- Notify the emergency response team immediately. Describe the location of the package and the reasons why you are suspicious. The emergency manager or another authorized person will determine if law enforcement or the fire department should be notified.
- If any contents have spilled, shut down the building's ventilation system to prevent the spread of the powder.
- Do not shake, open, or empty the contents of any suspicious envelope or package.
- Do not sniff, touch, taste, or look closely at the package or at any contents that may have spilled.
- Do not carry the package or envelope; do not show it to others; do not allow others to examine it.
- Put the envelope or package in a plastic bag or some other container to prevent leakage of the contents. Within the mail center, the package should be placed in a holding-transport container.
- If there is no container, cover the envelope or package with anything (e.g., clothing, paper, or an upside-down trash can) and do not remove this cover.
- Leave the area and section it off to prevent others from entering (i.e., keep others away).
- Wash hands with soap and water to prevent spreading any powder to the face.

When a Suspicious Item Is Found
If a suspect item is found, take the following actions:

- Notify the emergency manager.
- If the package is believed to contain a powdery substance, if a vapor or gas (e.g., aerosol) is released, or if any contents have spilled, shut down the building's ventilation system to prevent the spread of any powder or vapor and evacuate all occupants of the air-handling zone or zones that could be cross-contaminated.
- The emergency manager should direct notification of police and fire departments, which will notify additional agencies as needed.
- Alert employees in the immediate area and others located in adjacent areas that a suspicious letter or package has been found.
- If the suspicious item is believed to be a bomb, evacuate the surrounding area for 150 feet in all directions, including the floors above and below. If the package is found outside, evacuate 1,850 feet in all directions.
- Put the suspicious item in a sealed container and move it to an isolated area. If the package is believed to be a bomb, place it in a bomb-holding container. If there is no container available, leave it alone.
- From a safe distance, the person who finds the suspected package should write down any reasons for suspicion (e.g., excessive postage, no return address, rigid envelope).
- Without making direct contact with the suspicious item, record all available information from all sides: name and address of addressee, name and return address of sender, postmark cancellation date, post office codes, types of stamps, other markings or labels, other peculiarities (such as oil stains, tears, a flap sealed with tape, or a flap not glued down).
- Record all information about the suspected letter or package. If possible, photograph the package from all sides without moving it. The photographs may be used to verify the package as legitimate or to show responding emergency personnel.
- Contact the addressee to ask for identification or verification of the letter or package.

Before calling for outside assistance, attempt to find out if the sender or addressee has any knowledge of the item or its contents. If the addressee can positively identify the suspected item, it may be opened with relative safety. If the addressee cannot verify the letter or package and only the sender can be contacted, determine whether the letter or package still represents a threat.

Bomb Threats

Bombs have historically been the weapon of choice for terrorists. People carrying explosive devices are aware of the danger of a premature explosion and have a natural desire to set the explosive and leave the area. However, suicide attacks have proved that assumptions about quick entry and exit are no longer necessarily valid.

Easily accessible locations such as lobbies and unlocked doors can hide an explosive device. Other possible areas are stairwells, restrooms, janitors' closets, unused offices, and display areas.

When a bomb threat is received, the predetermined chain of command must be activated. Record all details and communicate with the emergency manager to determine whether to evacuate. The credibility of the threat must be assessed, given the available information, and the emergency manager must decide the following:

- Whether or not the building should be evacuated
- The scope of any evacuation—full or partial
- The duration of any evacuation

Bomb Threats by Telephone

Give all personnel, especially telephone operators and receptionists, a checklist to record information about bomb threats, such as the characteristics of the voice and any background noises heard during the call. Do the following:

- Keep the caller on the line as long as possible. Ask the caller to repeat the message. Record every word spoken.
- If the caller does not indicate the location of the bomb or the time of detonation, ask.

- Inform the caller that the building is occupied and detonation of a bomb could result in death or serious injury to many innocent people.
- Pay particular attention to background noises, such as motors running or music playing, that may give a clue to the caller's location.
- Listen closely to the voice (male, female), voice quality (calm, excited), accent, and any speech impediment.
- Immediately after the caller hangs up, notify the emergency manager and fill out the bomb threat form. See Figure 49-4.

Bomb Threats by Letter

When a written threat is received, save all materials, including any envelope or container. Once the message is recognized as a bomb threat, further unnecessary handling should be avoided. Every possible effort must be made to retain evidence such as fingerprints, handwriting or typewriting, paper, and postal marks. These will prove essential in tracing the threat and identifying the writer.

Although written messages are usually associated with generalized threats and extortion attempts, a written warning of a specific device may occasionally be received.

TRAINING, DRILLS, AND EXERCISES

The emergency plan is only as good as the knowledge and ability of the emergency organization and the IC. Terrorist incidents are extremely challenging and will place great demands on the emergency organization. Therefore, a high level of training is required for all members of the organization, its leaders, and all employees.

Training and drills should cover the location, controls, supervision, shutdown, and use of systems and equipment as defined in emergency procedures. This includes notification, communication, ventilation systems, smoke exhaust, stairwell pressurization, and fire suppression systems.

Knowledge of all emergency procedures, including evacuation and sheltering in place, is essential. Procedures for response to CBRNE scenarios should be covered, so all personnel understand

F I G U R E   49-4

Bomb threat form.

Department of the Treasury
Bureau of Alcohol, Tobacco and Firearms
BOMB THREAT CHECKLIST

1. When is the bomb going to explode?
2. Where is the bomb right now?
3. What does the bomb look like?
4. What kind of bomb is it?
5. What will cause the bomb to explode?
6. Did you place the bomb?
7. Why?
8. What is address?
9. What is your name?

EXACT WORDING OF THE BOMB THREAT:

_____
_____
_____
_____
_____
_____

Sex of caller: _____   Race _____

Age: _____   Length of call: _____

Telephone number at which call is received: _____

Time call received: _____

Date call received: _____

CALLER'S VOICE

☐ Calm   ☐ Nasal

☐ Soft   ☐ Angry

☐ Stutter   ☐ Loud

☐ Excited   ☐ Lisp

☐ Laughter   ☐ Slow

☐ Rasp   ☐ Crying

☐ Rapid   ☐ Deep

☐ Normal   ☐ Distinct

☐ Slurred   ☐ Whispered

☐ Ragged   ☐ Clearing Throat

☐ Deep Breathing   ☐ Cracking Voice

☐ Disguised   ☐ Accent

☐ Familiar (If voice is familiar, who did it sound like?) _____

BACKGROUND SOUNDS:

☐ Street noises   ☐ Factory machinery

☐ Voices   ☐ Crockery

☐ Animal noises   ☐ Clear

☐ PA System   ☐ Static

☐ Music   ☐ House noises

☐ Long distance   ☐ Local

☐ Motor   ☐ Office machinery

☐ Booth   ☐ Other (Please specify)

BOMB THREAT LANGUAGE:

☐ Well spoken (education)   ☐ Incoherent

☐ Foul   ☐ Message read by threat maker

☐ Taped   ☐ Irrational

REMARKS: _____

_____

Your name: _____

Your position: _____

Your telephone number: _____

Date checklist completed _____

ATF F 1613.1 (formerly ATF F 1730.1, which may still be used) (6-97)

Source: Department of Treasury; Bureau of Alcohol, Tobacco, and Firearms

their role and responsibilities. The roles, responsibilities, procedures, and activation of the ICS should be covered.

Conduct tabletop, functional, or full-scale exercises using realistic scenarios to challenge members of the emergency organization and evaluate the adequacy of response procedures. Carefully scripted and facilitated exercises offer good training and give people an opportunity to work together to manage challenging incidents. These exercises can identify weaknesses or deficiencies in the plan or in the ability to execute the plan.

All facilities must prepare an emergency action plan (EAP) as defined by OSHA. The OSHA standard requires training of designated employees to assist in the safe and orderly emergency evacuation of employees. Train all employees in the EAP when it is first developed, whenever employees' duties under the plan change, and whenever the plan itself is changed.

Training for fire brigades, rescue teams, and hazardous-materials teams must be commensurate with their duties and functions. Training requirements are spelled out in the OSHA and NFPA standards.

Train medical response teams in the protocols for treatment of chemical, biological, and radiological exposure. They should at least be able to recognize the signs of exposure and be familiar with immediate triage, treatment, segregation, and decontamination requirements.

Considerable training is available from public sources, through distance learning on the Internet, and from colleges and universities. Private contractors provide training in first aid, CPR, use of automated external defibrillators, firefighting, rescue, and dealing with hazardous materials.

Outline the scope and frequency of training in the emergency plan and the regulatory requirements (e.g., OSHA standards, fire prevention, and life safety codes). Document all training in a master file, including dates, subject material, instructor, and duration. Maintain records for review by regulatory authorities.

CRITIQUES, AUDITS, AND EVALUATIONS

At the conclusion of any incident, prepare a report documenting chronology, the use of personnel and resources, and what procedures did and did not work well. Conduct an incident debriefing with all personnel involved. Include representatives from the external agencies that were involved.

Periodically audit the facility's capability to respond to terrorist incidents. Review policies, procedures, staffing of the emergency organization, use of the incident command system, scope of training, and the results of drills and exercises. Look at record keeping. The audit should compare current capabilities with required capabilities and regulatory requirements. Review the "threat environment," changes in the facility, and vulnerabilities. Does the capability to respond to terrorist threats meet the current needs of the facility? Document any discrepancies between needed capability and actual performance.

Compile a list of actions to be taken to improve response, assign these to a responsible person, and establish due dates. Also, establish a process with management oversight to ensure that the corrective actions are completed on schedule.

N O T E S

1. National Commission on Terrorist Attacks upon the United States, *The 9/11 Commission Report* (New York: Norton, 2004).
2. National Fire Protection Association, *NFPA 1600, Standard on Disaster/Emergency Management and Business Continuity Programs* (Quincy, Mass: National Fire Protection Association).
3. On 28 February 2003 the president issued Homeland Security Presidential Directive (HSPD) 5, "Management of Domestic Incidents," directing the secretary of Homeland Security to develop and administer a National Incident Management System (NIMS). On 1 March 2004 NIMS was published by DHS; it includes ICS for use in the public sector.

CHAPTER 50

Protecting Soft Targets: How Marriott International Deals with the Threat of Terrorism Overseas

Alan Orlob
Vice President, Corporate Security, Marriott International Lodging

Of some 100 companies surveyed after 9/11, during the period of October 2002 to February 2003, by Thomas Cavanaugh, a researcher for the Conference Board, nearly 40 percent said that security was an expense which should be minimized. Almost half of these companies had not increased spending on security at all since 9/11; and in one-fourth of them, the chief executive had not met with the security chief during the past year. These surprising statistics reflect a cloud of malaise that has fallen over many companies since 9/11. For security directors, who have a mandate to provide a higher level of security, this attitude is particularly appalling.

In August 2003, the JW Marriott Hotel in Jakarta, Indonesia, was the target of a suicide bombing. Just after noon, as more than 300 people sat at lunch in the hotel's Sailendra Restaurant, a 28-year-old Indonesian who was a member of Jemaah Islamiyah drove an older Toyota Kijang to the front entrance of the hotel. Sweating profusely from Jakarta's heat and humidity, but mostly because of his mission, he was stopped at the entrance to the driveway by three security guards who were performing vehicle inspections. The guards peered into the back of the vehicle and noticed several large boxes. When they started to question the driver, he panicked and pushed a number on a cell phone, causing the explosives in the vehicle to detonate. The resulting explosion blew a hole 10 feet wide in the pavement and shattered the windows in the restaurant next to the driveway.

Windows in surrounding buildings were also blown out. Twelve people died in the attack, including security guards, taxi drivers, and the bomber himself. Only one of the victims was in the hotel—a Dutch banker living in Jakarta who was having lunch in the restaurant with a colleague. The banker had been due to leave Indonesia three days later and return home to his family in Amsterdam.

Considering that the obvious intent of the attack was to inflict mass casualties, it was quite remarkable that the security forces were able to mitigate what might have been a catastrophe. Had they not been in place and had the bomber continued to the front entrance and on into the lobby of the hotel, a much graver disaster would have resulted. In fact, if the bomber had been allowed to proceed even another 20 feet, he would have been alongside the popular restaurant with its 300 patrons.

When the JW Marriott Hotel in Jakarta opened on 18 September 2001, it had the highest level of security procedures that Marriott hotels apply. Customers were screened by a metal detector before entering the building. Vehicles were subjected to inspection at the entrance to the driveway. Only vehicles known to the hotel were allowed to park close to the entrance. Luggage was searched for explosive devices. A list of guests was stored off-site to be accessible in the event of a bombing or a major fire. These procedures were part of Marriott International's crisis program, which had been developed in the late 1980s. As we began our rapid expansion into the international market, senior management realized that many of the countries we were going into would present unique challenges for security. Bombings, kidnappings, civil insurrections, and natural disasters were commonplace in some of these countries and had to be planned for.

Intelligence is the key component of any crisis planning. We conducted a search of private security companies who could provide the type of risk assessments we needed. We wanted information about political and economic conditions in certain countries as well as trends in terrorism and security. Impending threats in Asia, coups developing in Latin America, expatriates being kidnapped in Guatemala—this was the type of information we needed. To accomplish this, we contracted with four companies. Two of the companies were based in Washington, D.C.; the third was based in London; the fourth was based in Hong Kong. We thought that using four companies would give us a broader cross section of opinion on threats than relying on a single company whose expertise might be region-specific. To enhance our intelligence reporting, we turned to the U.S. State Department's Overseas Security Advisory Council (OSAC).

OSAC was established in 1995 by George Shultz, who was then secretary of state. Shultz sought to create a forum for the U.S. government to interact with the private sector and share information on issues related to security. OSAC would be administered through Diplomatic Security, the law enforcement branch of the State Department. With regional security officers in every embassy, it was able to reach out to the private sector. The sharing of vital information went both ways. Private companies would let the regional security officer know when any of their employees were victims of crimes. Local country councils were formed with warden systems to notify expatriates immediately if there was a threat that might necessitate evacuation. Analysts were hired to monitor and report on every region in the world. And as technology increased, a Web site was developed for posting this information. Finally, OSAC formed a council in Washington and invited several representatives of the private sector to sit on the council and to interact with their peers in business and government. As Marriott's vice president in charge of security, I was invited to join OSAC as a council member in 1999 and was assigned to the Country Council Support subcommittee. At the time of the bombing in Jakarta, Indonesia was one of six countries assigned to me. I had visited Jakarta on a number of occasions and had developed a working relationship with the regional security officer, Jake Wohlmann. I had also met with the local OSAC council in Jakarta and knew many of the members. I was well aware of the threat posed by Jemaah Islamiyah, whose adherents had trained with al-Qaida and shared its ideology.

Using past experiences and a template from OSAC's manuals on crisis planning, we formulated a detailed plan. It included procedures to be followed by hotels and categorized these procedures according to color-coded "threat conditions." Under "threat condition blue," procedures would include posting one security officer at the entrance to the hotel and another—visibly—in the lobby. Guests would be required to produce identification when checking in. Doors in the nonpublic area of the hotel leading to water, electrical, or communications equipment would be kept locked. Vendors making deliveries would be closely screened before being allowed into the hotel.

As threats increased, hotels would be directed to follow the procedures of "threat condition yellow." Guests' luggage could not be stored unless it had been inspected. The list of registered guests was kept off-site. Vehicles were not allowed to park close to the building. Security patrols were increased both inside and outside the building.

At the highest level, "threat condition red," further procedures were mandated, designed to prevent vehicles or people from endangering the hotel with explosives or firearms. At this "red" level, persons observed taking photos of the hotel were challenged. Vehicles were searched; metal detectors were used to screen guests, suppliers, and associates. Any luggage accompanying a guest was inspected.

All these procedures were contained in a corporate crisis plan that was supplied to the hotels. Hotels were required to complete and send back their own local plan, which would have measures to handle specific local contingencies.

It was important for us to be assured that the procedures outlined in the crisis plan were being followed by the individual hotels. Initially, compliance was monitored by the Marriott regional security directors, but later it was decided that an outside security company could perform the task more independently and more efficiently. A company based in London, with offices throughout the world, was given the contract to complete the audits. The auditor would arrive at a hotel unannounced and would closely observe whether the procedures were being followed. The auditor would later announce him- or herself to the general manager and complete the audit with the manager's assistance. Every general manager was given directions that the procedure outlined in the crisis management plan for each threat condition had to be followed completely. Failure to follow it could result in disciplinary action.

At Marriott International's headquarters in Bethesda, Maryland, we assembled a crisis team. This was headed by Ed Fuller, the president of Marriott's international lodging group, and consisted of senior executives who had responsibility for a number of critical areas, including human resources, legal issues, risk management, finance, and public relations. A representative was assigned to handle logistics in the event of a crisis; and a recorder was appointed to ensure that if a crisis occurred, all the actions taken would be documented. This information would be useful later for assessing how the crisis team had handled a situation. In my role, overseeing security for Marriott's international operations, I was to develop this comprehensive crisis program as well as ensure that the program was ongoing and implemented at all the hotels.

As the crisis team came together, we needed a training component. We hired an outside consulting firm to develop a "tabletop exercise" that would, as much as possible, replicate an actual crisis taking place at a hotel. The crisis team spent a day forming an understanding of the dynamics of crisis management. Later, during actual crises, we found that the dynamics we had studied were very similar to those of the real events. Finally, we hired an outside public relations firm to train our general managers in handling the media during a crisis. Every year since then, the international crisis team has trained and critiqued itself. As Y2K approached, our crisis team came together and, in a tabletop exercise, went through six scenarios that had been drawn up to simulate possible real-life episodes. We spent New Year's Eve assembled in a crisis center in Newport Beach, California, watching and monitoring as the clock reached midnight around the world. Even though there were no major incidents, it was acknowledged that the exercise had provided valuable training both to the crisis team and to the general managers of the hotels. At no other time had they been able to plan beforehand for a crisis.

Marriott has been able to put the crisis team to good use since its establishment. An employee was abducted from a hotel in the Middle East in 1996. One earthquake hit San Salvador and another struck Guam. In 1995, a Tamil Tiger placed an improvised explosive device in the Marriott Hotel in Colombo, Sri Lanka. His mission was to put a device in five hotels that night. Fortunately, no one was injured in the blast. After he left the Marriott Hotel, one of the other devices exploded prematurely, killing the bomber.

In 2003, when the suicide bomber blew up his car and himself at the JW Marriott Hotel in Jakarta, the general manager called the Marriott crisis hotline and reported the incident. Someone at Kroll, a private security company that had the contract for monitoring the hotline, called me at home. It was just past midnight when I got the call. Coming out of a sound sleep, I called Fuller. Within 30 minutes, all the members of the crisis team had been wakened and were on a conference call. After I briefed the team on the situation as I knew it, the members all contributed something, depending on their areas of expertise. Risk Management made the necessary calls to Singapore to get insurance people dispatched to the scene. Public Relations began drafting a press statement. Human Resources started working on a plan to take care of the associates. More than 100 people had been injured and had been taken to local hospitals. Agents from a local security firm were sent to the hospitals with lists of guests and associates, to begin accounting for victims. At the time of the bombing, many guests of the hotel were conducting business outside. Some of them, when they heard the news of the bombing, went directly to the airport and left the country. All had to be accounted for.

There is a 12-hour time difference between Washington and Jakarta. No one on the crisis team slept that night or much of the next day; everyone was too busy dealing with issues of the bombing. A day later, as the situation stabilized, Fuller and I flew to Jakarta to survey the situation on the ground.

It was shocking at first to see the amount of destruction left by the blast—the entire facade of the building seemed to be gone. In reality, most of the damage was limited to glass and carpets; very little of the primary structure of the building was affected. However, the pain to the injured, physical and psychological, was immense. When the car exploded, it was laden with jerricans full of gas. A huge fireball blew into the driveway, restaurant, and front lobby. Most of the injured had burns and cuts and were sent to hospitals. Those who had no physical injuries would obviously require psychological counseling. Months after the bombing, some employees still could not return to their jobs, even though they had no physical problems. Some of the staff members, who adhered to traditional Indonesian culture, were afraid that there were ghosts lingering at the site. Associates were fearful that the hotel would never reopen and that they would have to find new jobs. Some people thought that the hotel might be attacked again. Some of the security team felt guilty, thinking that the bombing had occurred through their fault. All these anxieties needed to be dealt with.

The owner of the hotel is a Chinese Indonesian. He was distraught and avoided the news media, spending the first several days in isolation, dealing with his own depression. But then he acted. Making an announcement that the hotel would reopen within a month, he summoned architects and contractors to redesign the front of the building. Working seven days a week, 18 hours a day, they replaced glass and ceiling tiles, changed carpets, and painted.

Also, security measures were enhanced. All the exterior glass was laminated to prevent shattering. Heavy cement planters were placed in front of the driveway to block any vehicles from entering. The new design required cars to drive through a vehicle checkpoint located on the roadway, off the hotel's property. A canopy was erected for the vehicles to drive under, with eight security officers conducting inspections. Security cameras monitored their actions. A police officer, armed with a submachine gun, stood by, closely watching the occupants. A blast wall was erected to separate the vehicle checkpoint from the front of the hotel. Four detectors were purchased by the hotel to monitor vapors for traces of explosives in luggage or cars. A similar vehicle checkpoint was provided for any cars entering the parking garage. A bomb-sniffing dog was bought. Security cameras were added to the rest of the hotel. In case anyone was conducting surveillance on the hotel, security officers received training in countersurveillance; and a special countersurveillance team was added to the security staff. Luggage was screened away from the hotel. A walk-through metal detector was established at the entrance to the driveway. Anyone entering the hotel was required to go through the metal detector, and the security officers monitoring it were constantly tested for vigilance. Additional jersey barriers were placed on the roadway, blocking any cars from coming close to the hotel's entrance.

The hotel reopened to the public on 8 September, only four weeks after the bombing. Occupancy suffered, not only at the JW Marriott but throughout Jakarta and throughout the country. Western companies were reluctant to send their employees to Indonesia, fearing another attack from Islamic extremists. Many corporate security directors pulled their employees out of the country and made western hotels, including the JW Marriott, off-limits to their staff.

Marriott and the owner of the JW Marriott in Jakarta knew that the only way to regain business at the hotel was to offer the highest degree of security in the city. When all the security enhancements had been added, it was time to let customers know what had been done. Historically, companies faced with reporters wanting interviews on security have responded with statements such as, "We don't comment on our security procedures." This time, however, it was considered important to let people know that the hotel had mitigated a terror attack and was continuing to offer a high level of security. That philosophy was reflected in all interviews that were conducted.

The local management in Jakarta and I reached out to corporate security directors who were concerned about the level of security in Jakarta. These directors were invited to visit the hotel and see for themselves how much security was in place.

In November, I delivered a presentation to the OSAC Annual Briefing held at the State Department's headquarters in Washington. The keynote speaker was Colin Powell, secretary of state. More than 700 security professionals were in attendance, and it was useful for them to see a case study of how a company was able to defend a soft target against a suicide bombing. An obvious question was asked: "If your hotel had such a high degree of security before the bombing, why was it selected as a target?" This question had been perplexing to many within Marriott as well. The bombing at the Marriott took place two days before the defendants in the bombing attack from the previous year in Bali were sentenced. Some people said the judge involved in the sentencing was to have had lunch at the JW Marriott on the day of the bombing. Others said that CIA officers who were in Jakarta conducting interrogations of the suspects in the bombing at Bali were staying in the hotel. This was speculation and has never been confirmed, although it does make some sense.

Our strategy seemed to work. After the presentation at the State Department, one of the people in the audience, a corporate security director for a Fortune 100 company, approached me. He told me that shortly after the bombing at the Marriott his boss had telephoned him and berated him, saying that—given the inherent risk in Jakarta at the time—it had been a "security failure" to have any of the firm's employees staying at the hotel. However, after listening to the presentation, the boss had leaned over and admitted that the security director had been right: because the security procedures in effect at the Marriott Hotel were so sophisticated, and because of the way the blast had been mitigated, having their employees stay there should be considered a "security success." I spent time with another corporate security advisor who had pulled his company's employees out of the hotel and was reluctant to let them return. During a weekend in Vietnam, I was able to show him the security procedures that are specified by Marriott and that apply to all Marriott hotels. In turn, this security advisor took me on a tour of his company's facilities, helping me understand its organization and culture. Both of us had spent time in special forces units—I with the U.S. Army Special Forces and he with the British SAS. With regard to security, we spoke a common language. We then flew to Jakarta and reviewed the enhanced security in place at the JW Marriott Hotel. Soon afterward, this security advisor decided to use Marriott's "threat condition" checklist as a criterion for any other hotels that his company considered doing business with. It took almost eight months, but occupancy at the JW Marriott climbed back to the former level.

The amount of security applied at the JW Marriott Hotel in Jakarta does not come cheaply. Indeed, the money spent on security throughout Marriott International may seem exorbitant, especially because the travel industry was in decline in the months after 9/11. However, there were three important reasons for Marriott to invest in additional security.

First and most important was Marriott's commitment to protecting its guests and employees. In the early 1980s, Marriott started requiring all its hotels to install fire sprinkler systems. Fire sprinklers were relatively new at the time and were not required by codes. They are also expensive, and some senior managers, as well as some owners, were skeptical. However, the commitment was made. In more than 70 years of operation Marriott has never had a death from fire in any of its nearly 3,000 hotels.

Second, senior management at Marriott recognized the value of the brand. They understood the damage that could ensue if terrorists decided to target Marriott because of its name and its reputation as an American company. Protecting the brand was paramount. In 1999, during the war in Yugoslavia, Marriott Security was watching the political impact of the war. The Greeks were part of the NATO alliance, but for religious and historical reasons the Greek people were very much against what was going on. In fact, more than 90 percent of them opposed the war. Marriott put its hotel in Athens under "threat condition yellow," one level lower than the highest security condition—at a time when no other hotels in the city were applying additional security measures. Soon afterward, a bomb exploded at a neighboring international hotel, killing a meeting planner and severely injuring another guest. Later, it was discovered that the bomber had been considering the Marriott Hotel but had decided that there was too much security at the Marriott and had chosen the softer target instead. A similar incident took place when U.S. forces invaded Iraq. Terrorists put a small gas canister in a garbage can inside a western hotel in Amman, Jordan. They planned to ignite a fire in the can to detonate the gas canister. However, the hotel's sprinkler system went on, dousing the fire. The terrorists responsible for the attempted bombing were caught a short time later and confessed. During their interrogation, they too said that their original target had been the Marriott Hotel, but when they conducted their surveillance they were deterred by the extent of security there. These instances suggest the value of making a hotel a "hard" target when soft targets are being attacked.

Third, Marriott was concerned about investors' confidence. By far most of the hotels with the Marriott name are managed by Marriott and owned by outside investors. As Marriott pursued its goal of expansion in the market, there were strong concerns that investors would turn sour if it appeared that Marriott could not deter terrorists.

This approach to security within the Marriott organization has been directed from the top. In the weeks following 9/11, J. W. (Bill) Marriott, Jr., the chief executive officer and chairman, called on Brian Jenkins, a noted expert on terrorism, to meet with Marriott's security team. Chad Callaghan, who oversaw loss prevention for Marriott's hotels based in the United States, and I worked with Jenkins to ensure that there were no holes in the security effort. Bill Marriott invited us on several occasions to meet with him and his executive committee to brief them on security procedures. Ed Fuller ensured that I had an adequate budget to hire additional regional directors, and he fully supported the security initiatives that we put forward. In fact, Fuller was very much involved in the process, having final approval of all the threat conditions.

CONCLUSION

In a survey in 1990, travelers who were asked what they expected of a hotel put security ninth in order of preference. In a survey conducted two years after 9/11, security had moved into the number one spot. Thirty years ago, no one would have expected to have to walk through a metal detector before boarding a flight. Now such detectors are commonplace. The climate has changed. Customers not only want but demand security. In countries where terrorism is increasing, metal detectors, luggage screening, and vehicle inspections at hotels are all expected and appreciated. People who plan corporate meetings will not send their employees to a hotel without first confirming that it has the necessary security. There can be no going back. When U.S. government buildings overseas beefed up their security after the attacks against the embassies in Africa, terrorists started looking for softer targets. Hotels fit that description. Now, it is up to hotels to take the same approach as the U.S. government to defeat terrorists' plans. Hotels can no longer be the soft target that terror organizations are seeking. We need to constantly reach out for intelligence and continually refine our security procedures to counter threats. Only by doing this can we hope to deter terrorists and maintain the safe environment that travelers want.

CHAPTER 51

The Challenge to Corporate Leadership: Managing the Human Impact of Terrorism on Business Recovery

Mark Braverman, Ph.D.
Principal, The Braverman Group, LLC

Terrorism . . . is intended to coerce societies or governments by inducing fear in their populations. . . . The nation's mental health, public health, medical and emergency response systems currently are not able to meet the psychological needs that result from terrorism.[1]

INTRODUCTION: ONE COMPANY'S STORY

FashionLine,[2] in the garment district in midtown Manhattan, New York City, is a wholly owned division of EuroLine, a global company based in Europe. FashionLine sells discounted women's apparel through catalogs. It houses 80 percent of its administration, design, purchasing, and catalog production in six floors of an office building on Seventh Avenue, where it employs 325 people. Its information technology (IT) group, billing department, and call center—employing 175 people—are across the river in New Jersey. On the Monday after 9/11, FashionLine is feeling the effects at several organizational levels.

1. *Overall workforce*: 90 percent of the employees have returned to work. However, others are unwilling to return because they are afraid to use the tunnels and bridges that lead into Manhattan, or because they are reluctant to be separated from their families; they are working from home or using vacation

or sick time. Many who have returned to work say that they cannot concentrate. They check the Internet for news compulsively, feel compelled to call their families several times a day, worry about their children at school, have fears about further attacks, find their minds wandering, and keep remembering vivid details of 9/11.

2. *Management*: Line and middle managers are also experiencing shock and fear; but in addition they must deal with production deadlines, since—as the upper managers keep reminding them—this is the busiest season of the fashion year. Moreover, they are concerned, both professionally and personally, about the people who report to them. They wonder who, if anyone, can provide guidance in this unprecedented situation.

3. *Executives*: The executive managers feel, above all, unrelenting pressure from the parent company, which acquired FashionLine only recently. Calls from EuroLine express concern about 9/11, but the clear subtext is concern about deadlines and profits. Thus FashionLine's executives in turn exert pressure downward. The middle managers respond dutifully and encouragingly but have private doubts—not only about absent and shocked employees but about employees whose work depends on travel and who are still waiting for commercial flights to resume.

4. *Human resources (HR)*: The HR managers meet with the chief operating officer (COO) and pull out the "Business Continuity Plan," but it offers little to guide them, since the physical plant is undamaged, employees are physically unharmed, and access to the workplace is not impeded. Nothing in the plan seems applicable except a postincident review of evacuation procedures. FashionLine conducts a fire drill and finds that stairwells are unlit and that some floors are inaccessible because release mechanisms in the doors malfunction. The employees then demand a meeting with management and insist on immediate repairs. A fire safety expert who has been called in remarks that in some situations it is safer to remain in a building rather than evacuate; this principle proved fatal on 9/11, and many of FashionLine's employees now say they

would ignore such instructions. The next day, a few more employees fail to report to work.

TERRORISM AS A BUSINESS ISSUE

The situation at FashionLine was typical in the New York metropolitan area after 9/11; and it was even worse in the financial district, where the attack had taken place and thousands of employees had fled for their lives. At one firm, a study concluded that 43 percent of the staff were at risk of posttraumatic stress disorder (PTSD), and nine months later the rate of PTSD remained at 21 percent.[3] In Washington, D.C., government employees reacted similarly, and their supervisors and office heads—who had no plans or formal procedures to follow—responded with silence or confusion. The following excerpt suggests how terrorism can affect business functioning:

> There are other indirect costs to non-target companies, such as the fear and anxiety the threat of terrorism produces that sap employee productivity. "Terrorists wreak havoc even when they don't attack, just by implying they might," says Lisa Parker, senior vice president of The Strickland Group, a New York–based executive coaching and development firm. "There is a substantial risk of a loss of productivity from employee fear, including greater absenteeism, missed deadlines, irritability and difficulty concentrating and making decisions. The recent scare in New York [an intelligence report on terrorists' plans to target specific buildings in New York and New Jersey] dramatized this starkly. I have a colleague who had trouble sleeping and would come in to work late and go to meetings tired and frazzled. And we were not even close to the action. Fear has a way of infecting everyone."[4]

The effects of 9/11 went far beyond New York and Washington. Employers in high-rise buildings across the United States reported that people were afraid to come to work, and businesses that relied on travel had to find other ways to contact colleagues, customers, and suppliers.

Much the same had been true in 1995, when the federal office building in Oklahoma City was bombed: almost half the survivors developed anxiety, depression, and problems with alcohol; and over one-third reported PTSD.[5] A year after the bombing, Oklahomans reported increased rates of alcohol use, smoking, stress, and PTSD symptoms as compared with another city.[6]

The Challenge to Business

Because it has struck workplaces, terrorism is a critical business and management issue; and counterterrorism is especially important for industries that are likely to be targets or to be affected by damage to domestic or global communication, transportation, and security. Accordingly, companies are reviewing their plans for emergency response and business continuity. Also, an increasing number of businesses now understand the need for procedures to deal with the psychological impact of traumatic events in the workplace[7]—a need that is particularly urgent because terrorism intentionally exacts its heaviest toll through psychological effects, and because those effects can pervade entire communities.

Effects on Productivity and Health: One Company's Response

Long after 9/11, managers still needed to plan for accommodating employees' needs. The present author worked closely with one company that responded skillfully and compassionately: the TJX Corporation, based in New England, seven of whose employees were passengers on the planes that crashed into the World Trade Center. At the headquarters where these employees had worked, centers for information, counseling, and support remained in place for weeks. Also, although TJX's business relies on long-distance travel, the CEO and his representatives announced, in person, that no employee would board an airplane until he or she was individually ready to do so. Half-day meetings were scheduled for managers and traveling employees to provide information on alternative travel arrangements, on how to manage traumatic stress and grieving, on coping with family concerns such as children's fears about parents' safety, on counseling and consulting resources, and on how to adjust performance expectations. Updated information on travel security was continually transmitted on TJX's intranet, by telephone, and face to face within work units.

The Need for Special Planning

Unlike TJX—but like FashionLine—many companies, however well-meaning, had no appropriate plans in place and therefore stumbled. They found that standard business continuity and emergency response plans cannot be relied on in a terrorist event. These plans deal with recovery after the destruction of physical infrastructure and information assets, but not with emotional reactions even when the physical plant is untouched, and not with damage to the societal infrastructure that impedes communication and travel even when people appear healthy. However, there are some well-established, broadly applicable approaches to managing traumatic stress and organizational upheaval.

PSYCHOLOGICAL TRAUMA AND THE WORKPLACE

There has been substantial research on the psychological response to traumatic events, including military combat, physical and sexual assault and abuse, mass disasters, and occupational demands (as in law enforcement).[8] And since the establishment in 1971 of the National Institute for Occupational Safety and Health and the continued development in the private sector of health and stress management in the workplace, there has also been much research on the relationship between workplace conditions and stress-related health issues.[9] Private companies commonly take steps to minimize or prevent the negative effects of traumatic events on employees and on overall organizational functioning.

Most companies have disaster plans and emergency response plans, often covering evacuation, public relations, legal protections, and death benefits. Increasingly, companies are also developing plans to deal with the acute and long-term effects of traumatic events on employees' health and morale, but these plans may not be comprehensive or well integrated into crisis management and emergency response. Specific procedures for treating injured or traumatized employees are rare, even though such employees may never return to work or to full productivity—and even though researchers in psychology, occupational medicine, sociology, and law have noted a dramatic increase in disability claims relating to mental injury and consider emotional stress a very important issue,[10] especially when it is caused by terrorism. Usually, terrorism cannot permanently halt commerce or industrial production; but by impairing workers' health and productivity, it can have enduring effects on communications, production, transportation, and commerce.

Posttraumatic Stress Disorder

PTSD, which was recognized by the American Psychiatric Association in 1980,[11] results when functioning continues to be disrupted as a consequence of a traumatic experience. It is characterized by intrusive reexperiencing of the traumatic event; emotional numbness or, conversely, difficulty controlling emotions (especially anger); withdrawal from intimacy and social interaction; impaired concentration and memory; and avoidance of activities or situations that are reminders of the trauma. Its long-term consequences include severe depression, substance abuse, marital problems, and withdrawal from work and social activities.[12]

According to researchers and practitioners, a positive outcome requires a supportive environment in which survivors' feelings are accepted and can be openly discussed; otherwise, survivors may be unaware that their reactions are normal, may feel overwhelmed, and may make no further effort to process the experience. Lindemann described a tendency to "wall off" the trauma from consciousness when conscious processing fails.[13]

The Role of Group Support and Leadership

People react variously to trauma in the workplace, but many of the symptoms of PTSD can impair an organization's ability to continue business as usual, even when there is no damage to IT systems, the physical plant, communications, or the supply chain. Furthermore, morale can be undermined when leadership is perceived as uncaring, unprepared, or in denial.

After a collective trauma in a workplace, group support must be mobilized. Normally, employees are connected—and an organization is enabled to function—by informal communication and support networks within and between work groups. But group support in the aftermath of a crisis does not emerge spontaneously; therefore, leadership must plan and implement such support by explicitly permitting and fostering interpersonal communication about a traumatic event. Otherwise, employees may assume that they are not permitted to openly work through their reactions with others at work and will not do so. Similarly, information may be lacking, so that rumors and fear spread, especially when terrorism is involved. In such a situation employees' need for information, connection with leadership, and interpersonal connection must be given the highest priority. This will reduce the risk of PTSD and of general breakdown in organizational functioning.[14]

Crisis Management as a Core Business Activity

In this discussion, a *crisis* is any event or series of events that threatens an organization's survival or its finances, brand, reputation, or relationships with employees, customers, or suppliers. *Crisis management* is not simply the handling of a potentially catastrophic but transitory situation such as a product recall, an industrial accident, a natural disaster, or mass violence. Rather, it has become, increasingly, a central activity closely linked to strategic planning. How a company plans for crises is

> an expression of the organization's fundamental purpose or strategic vision.... The sociotechnical systems that we call "corporations" are so complex and interdependent that they have become extremely fragile.... A minor event, even a single individual, can now have a drastic effect on an organization as a whole and on its community and environment. These events will not diminish in this century; they are, in fact, increasing rapidly.[15]

Thus crisis management—which we will call "Human Impact Planning"—must be comprehensive and integrated with security, emergency management, business continuity, and plans to manage the impact on employees, families, and stakeholders. Below, we describe planning for human impact in particular; but it is not to be seen as a separate activity—it is part of the whole.

PLANNING FOR THE HUMAN IMPACT OF TERRORISM

Human Impact Planning is concerned with managing the effects of crises on employees, interns and students, families, the community, customers, contractors, and others. It is a key component of an over-all plan for response to and recovery from any crisis. It addresses three primary concerns:

1. *Prevention of traumatic stress.* Some employees will be at risk for PTSD; this reaction can impair general morale and the ability of the group to return to normal functioning and productivity within a reasonable time. In the mid and long term, unrecognized, untreated PTSD can permanently remove employees from the workplace through attrition, termination, and disability.

2. *Facilitating crisis-related communications.* Traumatic events in the workplace disrupt formal and informal communication, so that individual victims are "sealed over." When employees cannot talk about what has happened, and when their questions and fears are not addressed, their individual and collective productivity will suffer.

3. *Support for management.* Traumatic crises are enormously stressful for managers, whose normal functioning as leaders may be impeded. They may feel that they have lost control over operations and over employees' well-being and may be unsure about how to respond effectively when they themselves are shocked, confused, and grieving. However, employees will still look to them for direction, safety, and normality.

In general, Human Impact Planning spans the life cycle of crisis management from planning through response to recovery; and its guiding principle, throughout the process, is that attention to effects on employees and other stakeholders is crucial. Human Impact Planning will typically include the following elements. These will be discussed in more detail below:

- Identification of the team responsible for planning
- Identification of situations that may impair the health and functioning of employees and business organizations
- Review of the systems in place to prevent and respond to these impacts
- Provision of support and tools for management response

- Provision of services during and after a crisis to respond to individuals' acute psychological and physical needs
- Monitoring of the medium- and long-term effects of a crisis on organizational health and productivity

Identifying the Planning Team

A multidisciplinary team should be involved in developing a plan to protect the company from the immediate and ongoing effects of terrorism. This may be an existing team, such as crisis management or business continuity, and it should include or have an explicit mandate from executive management. In general, the team will include representatives from the following groups: human resources; risk management; legal; health, safety, and security; and operational management.

Identifying Potential Impacts

The team has two initial tasks: (1) review the range of crises and situations that may directly or indirectly threaten the health, work, and psychological well-being of employees, family members, the community, and other people; (2) understand how an impact on employees and their families might, in turn, affect the organization.

An attack may have an immediate or direct impact on operations, or an indirect effect. For example, bioterrorism may make a hospital a "hot zone," necessitating a plan for operations at an emergency site. But it may also have a direct effect on operations by causing lockdowns or disruptions in transportation and thus limiting the ability of the staff to get to work—at a time when these employees are most urgently needed for emergency services, including decontamination. What must be done to ensure that employees will be comfortable about coming to a potential hot zone? In short, it is as important to prepare for staff shortages or reduced functioning as it is to prepare for disruptions of equipment, the supply chain, or IT. For example, with regard to IT and telecommunications, it is necessary to have backup systems and emergency procedures. But all this will be useless without a trained, skilled staff, so backups and redundancies must also be established for human resources. What if human resources are reduced because of casualties or because critical staff members cannot get to work? What if there is only one shift available, and the people on this shift are working around the clock? What can be done to prevent mistakes that result from fatigue or burnout?

Reviewing and Assessing Systems

Specifically, it will be important to review plans for crisis management, business continuity, and emergency response to ensure that they can handle something as serious as a terrorist attack. "Tabletop exercises" and full-scale drills are good ways to review systems.

Here is a sampling of questions to be included in the review:

- Since normal communications may be compromised, disrupted, or nonexistent during an attack, do alternative procedures exist to account for people?
- Is there a coordinated plan with specific objectives, procedures, and resources to ensure the physical and emotional recovery of employees?
- Is there a representative of human resources on the crisis management team?
- Do policies and procedures specifically address issues that arise when employees die on the job?
- Are managers trained to recognize and deal with traumatic stress in employees?
- Does the existing business continuity plan rotate the staff during various scenarios?
- Do scenarios for business disruption take into account that members of the recovery team may also experience stress?
- Is there a communications plan for employees and families during and after a crisis, to minimize lost work time and ensure recovery of productivity?
- Are special resources in place to provide psychological first aid in scenarios involving terrorism, catastrophic accidents, and natural disasters?
- Have arrangements been made for special benefits and relief for employees and families who have been dislocated or have suffered injury or death of loved ones?

♦ Have psychological first-aid and counseling resources been evaluated? Special skills are needed to handle severe psychological impacts; also, such resources must have the capacity to handle unusually high demand.

Once the required resources and procedures are in place and integrated into or coordinated fully with existing response systems, the team will assume its role as part of ongoing response and recovery activities.

Providing Support and Tools for Managers

Managers are the key to recovery, but they are at a high risk for debilitating stress when the workforce has been traumatized. Because of their position and role, they may feel uncertain and torn. They are under internal pressures, as well as pressures from higher management, to help the company deal with damage to its infrastructure, customer base, and operations, and in many cases with temporary or long-term loss of personnel. They are also concerned about the employees for whom they are responsible. They may ask: Should I adjust my performance expectations? When should I require my sales force to resume the five-day twice-monthly travel schedule? How can I expect a 24/7 rush to meet a deadline? How hard should I push? Also, the managers themselves may be traumatized and may find that their judgment and functioning are compromised.

Middle and line managers are the group most likely to feel frustrated if top leadership is unavailable or fails to provide useful direction. They are also the group most likely to be in touch with reality "on the ground" regarding the organization's ability to meet demands imposed from the top. In the absence of established, well-designed forums for communication and data-gathering initiated by top leadership, no news, good or bad, will reach the top levels; and middle and line managers will inevitably feel beleaguered, isolated, and demoralized. From a business standpoint and from the standpoint of organizational morale and health, there is nothing more important for top leadership than establishing consistent, regular, two-way communication with middle and line managers. This practice must be literally institutionalized and made part of the culture for the short and long term in the aftermath of trauma.

A plan for management support will include:

◆ Clearly defined and mandated meetings for management groups under certain conditions such as an attack or threat
◆ Skilled consultants be available to these groups
◆ A protocol for the meetings that includes opportunities for participants to talk about their own stress and about management issues (e.g., employees' stress, performance expectations, helpful resources), and clarification of the needs of upper management (discussed below)
◆ Consulting resources available to management for guidance in the handling of individual or work-group situations immediately after a crisis and during recovery

The importance of group support for managers cannot be overestimated. Individual supervisors and managers must know that they are not alone, and that specialized knowledge and adjustments in expectations and work rules will emerge from group interaction and the input of experts. Leadership must communicate to management that the best path back to normal productivity is through short-term adjustments. To deny or ignore trauma by "pushing through" sends the wrong message and flies in the face of everything we know about recovery.

Providing Services for Acute Psychological and Physical Needs

Standard occupational health and safety systems may be inadequate or inappropriate in crises such as terrorist attacks. The capacity of resources such as employee assistance programs must be assessed before the need for these programs arises. It is a common mistake to assume that contracted counseling services can handle a company's complex, wide-ranging needs after a disaster. Furthermore, methods commonly in use to prevent or mitigate traumatic stress in survivors of or witnesses to mass disasters have recently been scrutinized to assess their efficacy and their potential to do harm.[16] Careful consideration of methods and practitioners of postincident counseling must be a part of any plan to respond to human needs. Finally, counseling and specialized crisis counseling services are only one part of a program to respond to such needs. For example, services should extend to families so that employees can work reasonably free of concerns for their families' well being. If there is widespread damage to infrastructure, public health services, and other public services, the physical needs of employees and their families may become a crucial business issue.

A full list of these services should be developed as part of a comprehensive response and recovery plan that is in place beforehand (and has been approved at the highest levels). The plan will often extend beyond standard compensation and benefits and thus will have to be coordinated with human resources and executive management. Specific services and assistance will depend on the company, its location, and the nature and severity of the impact. However, most plans will include the following components:

- *Robust systems for tracking employees after an attack*: This is necessary for operational reasons and is part of caring for coworkers and families. A disaster is worsened when a company cannot quickly generate information about casualties and deliver it to families and coworkers.
- *Family preparedness planning*: This may include information, emergency and safety equipment, and provisions for communicating between the workplace and home (e.g., satellite phones not dependent on power or on infrastructure such as cellular towers).
- *Financial and physical assistance*: This may include emergency funds and loans, electric generators, emergency food and water supplies, temporary housing, and assistance with travel in the case of full-scale evacuations or temporary relocations of families.
- *Coordination with public and private relief*: Relief agencies include the Red Cross, state and federal victim assistance programs, and public health entities.

Monitoring Medium- and Long-Term Effects of a Crisis

Psychological and other health effects, as well as lowered morale and impaired trust, may have an incubation period; some people may not recover fully for a long time, if at all. Thus executive management must assess—as a business issue—the continuing effect of the crisis on the health and functioning of individuals and work units. Productivity will not be reestablished if some employees are suffering from unrecognized stress reactions. Even if there is no immediate apparent effect such as absenteeism or medical claims, there may be "presenteeism" and poor morale, so that within the first year to 18 months, turnover will increase. This can be avoided if the steps outlined above are followed, such as providing managers with the tools to recognize and understand the effects of stress and ensuring flexibility in performance expectations. Protocols for monitoring recovery throughout the organization should be part of the comprehensive human impact plan.

CONCLUSION

Terrorism presents a considerable but not insurmountable challenge. In meeting this challenge, corporate leadership has an opportunity to create workplaces more fully committed to employees' health and to individual and group productivity. The solution described here has five fundamental components: (1) commitment by leadership to comprehensive planning; (2) thorough review of existing crisis management, business continuity, and emergency planning; (3) provision of direct support to management; (4) flexibility in work design and employment practices; and (5) monitoring medium- and long-term effects.

As 9/11 demonstrated, the American workplace can be a focus of violence, terror, and death. As those of us in crisis consulting began working with the leaders and managers of affected companies, we realized that it is not the crisis counselors, management consultants, security experts, or guards at the door who determine whether the employees of a company can recover a sense of safety and well-being—or whether the company itself will survive. It is, rather, the actions and vision of senior leadership that pull a company through, to continue its mission stronger and more vital than before.

NOTES

1. National Academies, Institute of Medicine, *Preparing for the Psychological Consequences of Terrorism* (August 2003) (report).

2. FashionLine is a fictitious name, but the case description is based on the author's experience as a consultant to a company in New York after 9/11.

3. K. Becker, "A Company at Ground Zero: Organizational Intervention over a Nine-Month Period after the 9/11 Terrorist Attack," unpublished manuscript (2002).

4. R. Banham, "Living with Risk," *Treasury and Risk Management* (2004).

5. C. North, S. Nixon, S. Shariat et al., "Psychiatric Disorders among Survivors of the Oklahoma City Bombing," *Journal of the American Medical Association* 282 (1999): 755–62.

6. D. Smith, E. Christiansen, R. Vincent, and N. Hann, "Population Effects of the Bombing of Oklahoma City," *Journal of the Oklahoma State Medical Association* 92 (1999): 193–8.

7. M. Braverman, "Posttraumatic Stress Disorder and Its Relationship to Occupational Health and Injury Prevention," in J. J. Hurrell et al. (eds.), *Encyclopaedia of Occupational Health and Safety* (Geneva: International Labor Office Press, 1998).

8. L. Hytten and A. Hasle, "Firefighters: A Study of Stress and Coping." *Acta Psychiatrica Scandinavica Supplementum* 335 (1989): 50–5. See also T. Lundin and L. Weisaeth, "Disaster Workers' Stress and Aftereffects: A Proposed Method for the Study of Psychological and Psychiatric Effects on Rescue Workers and Health Care Personnel," unpublished manuscript (1991).

9. See the following: Braverman (1998). M. Braverman, "A Model of Intervention for Reducing Stress Related to Trauma in the Workplace," *Conditions of Work Digest* 11:2 (Geneva: International Labor Office, 1992). M. Braverman, "Post-Trauma Crisis Intervention in the Workplace," in James Campbell Quick, Lawrence R. Murphy, and Joseph J. Hurrell (eds.), *Stress and Well-Being at Work: Assessments and Interventions for Occupational Mental Health* (Washington, D.C.: American Psychological Association, 1992). M. Braverman, "Preventing Stress-Related Losses: Managing the Psychological Consequences of Worker Injury," *Compensation and Benefits Management* 9:2 (Spring 1993). B. Gersons, "Patterns of PTSD among Police Officers Following Shooting Incidents: A Two-Dimensional Model and Treatment Implications," *Journal of Traumatic Stress* 2:3 (1989): 247–57. J. J. Hurrell and L. R. Murphy, "Psychological Job Stress," in W. N. Rom (ed.), *Environmental and Occupational Medicine* (2d ed.) (Boston: Little, Brown, in press).

10. See Braverman (1993). See also R. S. Schottenfeld and M. R. Cullen, "Occupation-Induced Posttraumatic Stress Disorders," *American Journal of Psychiatry* 142:2 (1985): 198–202.

11. American Psychiatric Association (APA), *Diagnostic and Statistical Manual* (3d ed.) (Washington, DC: American Psychiatric Association, 1980).

12. See the following: M. J. Horowitz, "Stress-Response Syndromes: A Review of Posttraumatic and Adjustment Disorders," *Hospital and Community Psychiatry* 37:3 (1986): 241–9. B. van der Kolk, "The Psychological Consequences of Overwhelming Life Events," in B. van der Kolk (ed.), *Psychological Trauma* (New York: American Psychiatric Press, 1987). J. Rosen and R. Fields, "The Long-Term Effects of Extraordinary Trauma: A Look beyond PTSD," *Journal of Anxiety Disorders*, 2:2 (1988): 179–91. J. L. Titchener, "Post-Traumatic Decline: A Consequence of Unresolved Destructive Drives," in C. Figley (ed.), *Trauma and Its Wake*, Vol. 2, *Traumatic Stress Theory, Research, and Intervention* (New York: Brunner/Mazel, 1986), pp. 5–19.

13. E. Lindemann, "Management and Symptomatology of Acute Grief," *American Journal of Psychiatry* 101 (1944): 141–8.

14. L. Barton, M. Braverman, and S. Braverman, "A Comparative Analysis of Organizational Response to Traumatic Stress among Workers in the Aftermath of Crisis," *Disaster Prevention and Management* 2:1 (1993). See also L. Fisher and W. Briggs, "Communicating with Employees during a Tragedy," *IABC Communication World* (February 1989): 32–5.

15. T. Pauchant and I. Mitroff, *Transforming the Crisis-Prone Organization* (New York: Jossey-Bass, 1991).

16. National Institute of Mental Health, *Mental Health and Mass Violence: Evidence-Based Early Psychological Intervention for Victims/Survivors of Mass Violence—A Workshop to Reach Consensus on Best Practices* (2002).

CHAPTER 52

Working with the Business Community to Enhance Preparedness at the County Level: A Case Study

William Donnelly
Chairman, Morris County Infrastructure Advisory Group

The federal government alone cannot protect the homeland, just as a town alone cannot rebuild itself after a hurricane or flood.

—Homeland Security Secretary Tom Ridge

INTRODUCTION

This chapter describes efforts to enhance homeland security and emergency preparedness in Morris County, New Jersey, through a partnership between the public and private sectors. Other counties across the United States may benefit from this example, which suggests useful frameworks and processes.

Morris County in northern New Jersey, 35 miles west of New York City, is the second wealthiest county in the state and the fourth wealthiest in the United States. Fifty Fortune 500 companies have headquarters or major facilities there. Morris County has an extremely productive and well-educated workforce and provides jobs to more than 250,000 people. There are 39 municipalities within the county's 469 square miles, with a population of 470,212 (according to the 2000 Census).

Morris County has a history of fostering public-private partnerships for efforts related to homeland security. The Morris

County Bioterrorism Task Force was created in 1999, and early on the Morris County Chamber of Commerce (MCCC) became actively involved in coordinating public and private resources to support it. In 2000, MCCC created a standing Preparedness Committee and conducted seminars on such subjects as how a business should handle internal and external emergency communications, weapons of mass destruction, the legal implications of planning for terrorism, and the fundamentals of planning for business continuity. These initiatives were the early stages of bringing the public and private sectors of the county together for preparedness planning.

Early in 2002, Morris County's prosecutor, Michael M. Rubbinaccio, asked MCCC to create a county Infrastructure Advisory Group (IAG), comprising private-sector companies, to help the public sector in its preparedness and counterterrorist functions by identifying industry-specific vulnerabilities and best practices. IAG became an integral part of the Morris County Counterterrorism Task Force, created in April 2002 as a public-private partnership comprising law enforcement officials, federal experts in domestic preparedness, local and county government agencies, and members of private industry. MCCC structured IAG with 10 industry-specific subcommittees: (1) Chemicals, (2) Communications, (3) Culture and Entertainment, (4) Education and Research, (5) Finance and Professional Services, (6) Food, (7) Health, (8) Real Estate, (9) Transportation, and (10) Utilities. Each of the subcommittees has a volunteer chair who manages it. To date, approximately 250 companies and community institutions are participating in IAG; eventually, MCCC expects this number to double.

Each subcommittee meets independently at least three or four times a year to achieve the goals set out by the prosecutor. Bimonthly, there is a meeting of the Preparedness Committee that includes IAG and representatives of the public sector. In addition, IAG and the public sector periodically hold "tabletop exercises" for the purpose of developing an integrated joint-action preparedness plan for the county. The prosecutor's office, the Office of Emergency Management (OEM), and the county health officer regularly participate in the IAG meetings and interact with leaders of the business community. This joint action is creating a new community with the goal of ensuring the safety of Morris County.

IAG is responsible for maintaining communication between the public and private sectors; developing standards, best practices, and emergency management plans for private industry; conducting vulnerability assessments of cyberspace; and applying "target hardening" to the county's key assets. During 2002 and 2003, OEM and the Morris County health officer recognized IAG as the organization through which they would structurally communicate and interact with the private sector.

New Jersey has an Infrastructure Advisory Committee (IAC) "to act as a liaison between the public and private sectors" (New Jersey Domestic Security Preparedness Act, p. 9, line 11). IAC comprises industry-specific subcommittees that function statewide. The chairs of Morris County's IAG are being aligned with the chairs of New Jersey's IAC. This will facilitate the mutual sharing of best practices between New Jersey and Morris County and prevent duplicative efforts. The alignment is further strengthening the joint action of the public and private sectors and integrating state and county preparedness initiatives.

Also, near the beginning of 2002, MCCC partnered with the U.S. Department of Defense (DOD) by cosponsoring the First Annual Preparedness Conference, which featured a panel of guest speakers from the office of the secretary of defense, the FBI, the New Jersey Office of Homeland Security, and the Morris County prosecutor's office. This event has continued annually in order to raise the community's awareness of security issues, provide information about preparedness, answer questions about the county's joint public-private preparedness plan, and recruit members for the 10 sector-specific IAG subcommittees.

THE NEXT STAGE OF EVOLUTION IN OUR JOINT ACTION

The public and private sectors in Morris County have acknowledged a need to create a Business Emergency Operations Center (BEOC) within MCCC, with a full-time administrator and a desk at the county's Emergency Operations Center staffed during county emergencies. The functions of BEOC would include the following:

- *Professional management:* Until now Morris County's IAG has been managed by volunteers. With the increasing participation and complexity of IAG, a full-time manager would be able to provide the day-to-day services required to enhance its mission and to increase private-sector participation.

- *Information management:* The database requirements of IAG are large, with approximately 250 participating companies. In addition to company information, contact information will have to be kept for key business personnel, including both business and personal telephone numbers, e-mail addresses, and so on. A list will also be created of countywide private assets that the public sector could use during an emergency.

- *Software and web development:* The state of New Jersey, through its department of health, has offered MCCC its Local Information Network and Communications System (LINCS) to be the backbone for the creation of BEOC's database management and Web-based communication system. New Jersey Institute of Technology (NJIT) has offered to design the home page and system to meet the needs of BEOC, and to host the site.

It is envisioned that BEOC will improve emergency communication and coordination and provide additional support to the public and private sectors. BEOC would become a national model for the county administration of joint-action preparedness functions. Funding to create BEOC is (as of this writing) being sought from local, state, and federal sources.

PUBLIC-PRIVATE PARTNERSHIPS AND THE STAGES OF PREPAREDNESS

Generally, there are three stages of preparedness for the private sector. The first stage involves plans for what to do in advance of an emergency. Most often, this relates to the hardening of assets, which can include plans for the protection of employees, the physical plant, information technology, etc. The second stage relates to those procedures that will be implemented during an emergency. Finally, the third stage involves plans for the continuation of business after an emergency, particularly when there could have been injury to its employees and damage to its physical plant, its suppliers, its customers, its distribution channels, and so on.

With regard to the first stage of preparedness—the hardening of assets—a company can assess its preparedness by comparison with the best practices of its industry, by following the recommendations of the public sector, or both. These guidelines can be learned by participating in the county committee for the relevant industry.

The assessment of a company's emergency management plans—stage two—is most often conducted in a tabletop exercise: a simulation that takes place around a table, with the participants being the likely parties to an incident. Members of the public and private sectors will be present. An incident will be described in a written scenario, and the parties will then discuss their individual responsibilities. In this way, existing plans are assessed to ensure that there is an appropriate response for each agency and private-sector company. Less frequently, tabletop exercises are also used to create plans for emergency management.

Typically, a private company will create an emergency plan based on the assumption that such critical infrastructures as utilities, water, food, communication, and transportation will continue to function if an incident occurs. But in an actual incident, such continuity may not be possible. The advantage of the tabletop exercise is that it fosters a dialogue between the private and public sectors, which will in turn foster the working relationships necessary for future joint action, particularly in response to an actual emergency.

In addition to tabletop exercises, drills are also used to assess whether preparedness plans are understood by all parties involved and are functional. The education of a company's employees as to their responsibilities during an emergency is critical to the success of a plan. Prewritten plans are preferred.

The third and final stage of preparedness planning for the private sector is business continuity after an emergency. Planning for various contingencies is critical to ensure operational success after a major natural or human-made event. The adequacy of a company's plan can be judged by comparing it with industry best practices, consulting with the public sector, or utilizing specialized consultants.

CHALLENGES FACING PUBLIC-PRIVATE PARTNERSHIPS AT THE COUNTY LEVEL

Cultural Cooperation

Anyone trying to achieve joint action between the public and private sectors realizes quickly that each sector has its unique culture, management style, and focus. However, the sectors are interdependent and must cooperate because each requires a successful, sustainable community as part of its mission. When the two sectors work hand in hand to achieve homeland security at the county level, the community will achieve "two reasons for joint action—the virtue of joint planning and the advantage of having someone in charge to ensure a unified effort." A third reason is "the simple shortage of experts with sufficient skills" (9/11 Report, p. 401).

Funding

While it is obvious that certain homeland security initiatives should be managed at the federal and state levels, counties are uniquely suited for collaboration because they have operational management. On the basis of this premise, greater funding should be given to the public- and private-sector organizations that manage homeland security at the county level.

CONCLUSION

After more than four years of experience in managing public-private partnerships to enhance homeland security, MCCC has found that several strategies have proved to be successful:

- In creating a partnership, it is important to engage the leaders of all relevant public organizations in the county who have responsibility for preparedness, such as the county prosecutor, the head of OEM, and the county health officer. When the private sector is then invited to participate in preparedness planning with the public sector, the private sector should meet with all the relevant public agencies at the same time.

- It is important to create private-sector committees by industry (e.g., communication, food, health, transportation) so that the private-sector companies in each industry can discuss strengths, weaknesses, opportunities, and threats for their particular businesses with regard to homeland security.

- The highest-level public officials and private-sector executives should be invited to participate and to give their commitment to the ongoing process of preparedness. With their support, their organizations will follow their leadership.
- Once the public and private sectors have been established, it is important to engage them in continuous communication, regular face-to-face meetings, and periodic events, such as conferences. These will create opportunities for joint action to be effective at the county level.
- Because of the increasingly difficult challenges our businesses are experiencing in our global economy, at times with decreasing human and financial resources, it is important to educate and motivate the private sector to sustain its commitment to homeland security. Terrorist organizations are patient; therefore, the private sector must be continuously vigilant.

As the 9/11 Report observed, "Private-sector preparedness is not a luxury; it is a cost of doing business in the post-9/11 world. It is ignored at a tremendous potential cost in lives, money, and national security" (p. 398).

The "new community" described in this chapter is characterized by the joint functioning of the public and private sectors, cooperating in new ways to prevent and respond to terrorism. This joint action at the county level will create a greater pool of resources to make a difference locally, where homeland security efforts matter most.

C H A P T E R 5 3

Legal Issues for Business in Responding to Terrorist Events

William C. Nicholson, Esq.
Adjunct Professor, Widener University School of Law

When an emergency occurs, the first question is, "What was that?" The answer determines the steps taken by private-sector and public-sector emergency responders and emergency management and affects the legal analysis afterward. If the answer is "a terrorist attack," the law prescribes a structure for the response and various legal actions. Failure to appreciate the legalities may lead to liability.

Terrorist attacks are not necessarily against the government. Businesspeople must keep in mind that an attack may be directed against a population center where a business is located, against an entire industry, or against one specific business. The terrorists may be foreign or domestic, and they may have various motives. Business leaders should pay close attention to threats against an industry or business and should develop a close working relationship with federal, state, and local law enforcement, which will typically track such threats.

THE LEGAL STRUCTURE FOR EMERGENCY RESPONSE

The Homeland Security (HS) Act of 2002[1] significantly modified the national approach to terrorism and all other emergencies.[2] In this act, the Department of Homeland Security (DHS) focuses on terrorism,[3] which is a federal crime.[4] Homeland Security Presidential Directive

(HSPD) 5 contains specific directions on implementing the act;[5] this directive "treats crisis management and consequence management as a single, integrated function, rather than as two separate functions" (as they had been under Presidential Decision Directive 39[6]). Under HSPD-5, the attorney general has "lead responsibility for criminal investigations of terrorist acts or terrorist threats by individuals or groups inside the United States, or directed at United States citizens or institutions abroad, where such acts are within the Federal criminal jurisdiction of the United States."[7]

Integration of crisis management and consequence management means that the scene of a terrorist event, which is a crime scene, is under the jurisdiction of federal law enforcement for purposes of gathering and controlling evidence. Almost inevitably, there is a conflict between the priorities of criminal investigation (crisis management) and emergency response and recovery (consequence management). Rapid recovery and rescue of injured victims require prompt disturbance of the crime scene, possibly impeding law enforcement. Numerous courses have been given in integrating response and informing responders other than those in law enforcement how to cooperate with investigations; but during an event, firefighters and emergency medical services (EMS) are likely to revert to their own training and ignore the concerns of law enforcement. Such conflicts can delay a response, increasing injuries, deaths, and potential liability.

HAZARDOUS MATERIALS

Terrorism may involve a release of hazardous materials (HAZMAT, or hazmat), even if the actual attack does not take that form. For example, at the World Trade Center in the aftermath of 9/11 there were plumes of smoke (visible from space) and huge quantities of minute dust particles containing many materials. There was wide-spread concern about how responders exposed to hazmat might be affected;[8] but initially, the Environmental Protection Agency (EPA) determined that the situation was environmentally safe, and thousands of emergency workers entered the ruins without personal protective equipment. Later, the dust was found to be extremely dangerous. Within a year of 9/11, 213 senior commanders had retired and 500 line firefighters were set to retire early as a result of exposure to the dust and consequent lung problems.[9]

"World Trade Center cough" was described as "characterized by a reduced lung capacity and a hyper-reactivity of the airways to inhaled particles, bacteria and viruses. The cough is dry and non-productive and can leave the sufferer gasping for air."[10] This cough was caused by breathing in microscopic glass particles and was estimated to affect hundreds, or possibly thousands, of people. These particles are not regulated by the Clean Air Act; thus they did not show up as a danger during EPA's monitoring.

Such hazards must be carefully considered by businesses after a terrorist attack. As outlined below, specific controls and requirements apply to all employers in this situation.

Hazardous Waste Operations and Emergency Response (HAZWOPER) Standard[11]

Violation of the Clean Air Act is not the sole, or even the major, potential source of liability after terrorism involving hazmat. As with any response to hazmat, the activities of responders are regulated by both the Occupational Safety and Health Administration (OSHA) and the Environmental Protection Agency (EPA).[12]

Public and private entities may have a duty to respond to a release of hazmat. Normally, internal response teams will be first on the scene at industrial incidents.[13] OSHA's rule for Process Safety Management of Highly Hazardous Chemicals—intended to prevent or minimize the consequences of catastrophic releases of toxic, reactive, flammable, or explosive chemicals—requires such teams. These teams may find themselves responding to terrorism, because hazardous materials in an industrial setting are a significant potential source of weapons for terrorists.

When a spill or an airborne release of hazmat takes place on public property (such as a highway) or travels over the borders of an industrial facility, the first response group is usually the fire service. To deal with this dangerous situation, the responders need considerable technical expertise.[14]

OSHA closely regulates the actions of emergency responders to an incident involving hazmat. Violation of the HAZWOPER requirements may result in significant liability, and penalties may ensue:

De minimis notice—no penalty[15]

Nonserious—no penalty to $7,000[16]

Serious—$1 to $7,000[17]

Repeated—no penalty to $70,000[18]

Willful—$5,000 to $70,000[19]

Failure-to-abate notice—no penalty to $7,000 per day[20]

Also, a violation of law may be used as proof in a civil trial for damages for personal injury or wrongful death. When the elements of the violation are congruent with the elements required for civil liability and the burden of proof is the same for both, the only issue in a civil trial may be the measure of damages.[21] Under OSHA, emergency responders may be seen as having "employment relations" with any entity that controls, supervises, or directs them; such entities may include the business on whose premises the release occurs, the local government, and the federal government.[22]

This is not a matter of merely academic interest. Lawsuits filed against the City of New York by firefighters alleging lung damage due to insufficient personal protective equipment during the response to 9/11 at the World Trade Center, and the cleanup afterward, exceeded $7 billion.[23] HAZWOPER requirements regarding personal protective equipment and all other aspects of the aftermath of an event apply to private-sector employers as well as to units of government.

Weapons of Mass Destruction

Legal issues that would arise after the use of weapons of mass destruction (WMD) may depend on what weapons are used or may be common to all WMD.

Nuclear Weapons

After the use of a nuclear device, as after any crime, it is vital to gather evidence, but in this case the evidence may be contaminated or destroyed by the nuclear explosion.

Existing defense polices are an outgrowth of national priorities during the Cold War and were designed for a nuclear threat. However, the threat envisioned then was a massive nuclear strike by the Soviet Union, rather than smaller strikes by terrorists using either compact "suitcase" or "dirty" bombs. Today, international controls on possession of fissionable materials seem to be breaking down at the same time as the ability to create nuclear weapons proliferates. But a nuclear bomb similar to, though more powerful than, the atom bombs that the United States dropped on Japan in World War II is still the least likely of all WMD to be used, owing to the difficulties involved in obtaining or developing a sophisticated weapon. A *dirty bomb* is more likely, because there is a lack of controls over the much more common radioactive materials that might be used in its construction, and because such a weapon can be made relatively easily—basically, by building a conventional explosive device and adding radioactive materials. The explosive disperses the radioactive substance, which will contaminate people and property for periods ranging from hours to generations, depending on the materials used.

To survive a nuclear attack, a business needs, at least, standard data backups off-site. Because such an attack may come without warning and may be very destructive, more data backup with a shorter lag time may be appropriate, e.g., a company that now uses tape backup, transported from the site every day by an employee, might consider real-time remote data mirroring. One lesson of 9/11 is that *off-site* should mean a geographically remote location. Some companies with offices in the World Trade Center found that transporting tape across the street did not suffice.

Insurance against nuclear terrorism may never be feasible; therefore, businesses must be proactive if they are to survive a nuclear attack. In addition to data preservation, lines of succession for leadership and all critical posts, as well as alternative operating locations, must be considered. If these commonsense steps are not taken, shareholders may have grounds for action against the directors and officers of an organization.

Bioweapons

These differ significantly from other WMD, and from conventional weapons. Bioweapons are often difficult to obtain or to "weaponize" properly. Some biological pathogens, such as smallpox and Ebola virus, are closely controlled. Others, like anthrax or ricin, may be readily obtained in nature, but require considerable processing.

The first challenge is to identify the use of bioweapons, which may appear to be natural events and thus raise issues of evidence. Systematic surveillance of the signs and symptoms of patients admitted to hospital emergency rooms is becoming more widespread.

Businesses may want to note patterns of employees' sickness to learn if a number of illnesses stem from a common cause, possibly bioterrorism. They should consider developing relationships with local public health authorities to expand the scope of reporting from emergency rooms to the workplace; this might allow bioterrorism to be identified more quickly.

A second challenge is identifying and charging the user of bio-weapons. Even if a terrorist group claims credit, tying the confession to the crime will be complicated and will raise issues of criminal enforcement. In this regard, businesses should consider keeping surveillance videotapes for a longer time before reusing them; increasing retention time from, say, 24 hours to two weeks may preserve evidence needed to identify a bioterrorist. The same consideration applies to e-mail, telephone messages, and other communications.

A third challenge of bioweapons is the delay between their use and their effects; this makes it difficult to gather evidence. Here too, longer retention of surveillance tapes and records of communication can be helpful.

Other challenges include illnesses such as AIDS and SARS, in which the victim is the disease vector. Such threats suggest that businesses should consider making supervisors more aware of signs and symptoms of diseases—particularly diseases that are known to occur in an area where employees travel, and particularly when there is a specific threat to an industry or an individual business.

Civil liberties issues arise from the need to isolate and quarantine contagious persons, possibly against their will. Lawsuits for false arrest and false imprisonment might ensue. While isolation and quarantine will typically take place apart from the business context, they may affect a business—e.g., if an employee returns from travel in an area that is found to be the source of a bioterrorist attack. In that case, if the illness is communicable, the entire business site may be isolated and all employees could be quarantined. Therefore, a business should have a contingency plan for legal challenges to its cooperation with these governmental actions.

Chemical Weapons

These have been used for centuries, and their availability has greatly increased since World War II. Today, formulas for chemical weapons can be found on the Internet, so the use of such weapons has become even more likely. Two types of chemical strike are possible: first, direct deployment of chemical devices against people; second, attacks on chemicals used in commerce, whether at storage sites (such as tanks) or through transportation mechanisms (such as tanker ships, trains, or pipelines).

Terrorists would probably prefer agents like VX, sarin, or mustard, which are deadly and can cause panic in those not killed outright. Such agents vary in lethality and ease of manufacture, but all require at least some scientific knowledge and sophistication to make and deploy effectively. If these are created and used, potentially liable parties could include suppliers or importers of precursor chemicals, manufacturers of laboratory equipment, laboratories handling chemical agents, and sellers of items that could be used for chemical dispersion, as well as landlords.[24]

The most readily available chemical agents are those used in large quantities in industry, such as liquefied petroleum gas, chlorine, and phosgene. These substances are closely regulated by EPA and OSHA, and businesses using them are subject to controls on planning and use. Businesses need to prepare for the possibility that terrorists will use these "found" weapons. Liable parties might include all entities involved in the extraction, transportation, storage, and distribution of a substance, as well as landlords. And a neighboring business whose employees or visitors might be affected by the release could also be sued.

Businesses near a site where potentially damaging chemicals are stored or near places where such chemicals are transported (e.g., highways or railroads) need to include a possible release in their emergency plans.

LEGAL ISSUES FOR BUSINESS "INVITEES" AND EMPLOYEES

A business may receive a terrorist threat during its regular hours, when employees and "invitees"—customers, suppliers, or other visitors—are on the premises. Alternatively, terrorists might attack without warning. In either case, there may be injuries and damage. The natural impulse for those injured would be to sue the terrorist, but the terrorist may not be found or may have no assets.

The law recognizes duties in persons controlling property toward their guests and employees. This concept, known as premises liability law, obligates those in charge of property to keep it in a reasonably safe condition. One part of this body of law is negligent-security law, which obligates owners and possessors of land to take reasonable steps toward security and to safeguard people who are legitimately on-site from foreseeable injurious actions—i.e., crimes—by third parties. The reason for imposing this duty on controllers of property is that such crime is preventable, and the people who can take steps to prevent it should do so. Landlords may be responsible for crimes committed by third parties on their property.

After 9/11, responsible business owners nationwide put additional security measures into place, including screening visitors and visitors' possessions. Airlines were sued for inadequate security, and all Americans confronted additional restrictions on travel.

Negligent-security lawsuits have historically been brought to get damages for harm caused by traditional crimes like robbery, rape, and murder. The key in these suits is frequently the foreseeability of the crime. To determine foreseeability, the courts concentrate on what knowledge the possessor of land had and take into account the "totality of the circumstances," which comprises actual notice, previous experience, and the probability that third parties' acts will endanger visitors.[25] Foreseeability is typically established by demonstrating that the defendant had actual or constructive prior notice of the kind of injury at issue.

As 9/11 demonstrated, foreseeable terrorism may be a ground for lawsuits based on premises liability. The scope of the attacks and the amount of destruction they caused pose significant potential problems for property owners and possessors. For these people, the traditional approach to negligent security is frustrating because there is no definitive list of steps that will prevent lawsuits. Whether an owner or possessor of land should adopt a particular security measure goes beyond simply analyzing the risk of litigation. Rather, this decision includes several factors: (1) considerations from a business standpoint, (2) relations with employees and customers, (3) precluding harm, (4) insurance costs, and (5) mitigating litigation. Various experts may be needed to fully evaluate these matters.

In the aftermath of 9/11, the landlord's duty of care has risen significantly. According to the concept of commonly accepted business practices, higher standards of care are set when additional steps are taken by a large number of similarly situated concerns. For instance, screening people and packages before they are allowed to enter the premises of a business has become much more common since 9/11. To the extent that many more businesses have taken such steps, as in New York City, it seems reasonable to require any given business there to follow suit. In a small urban area far from the east coast, fewer firms may have taken such steps; it might be argued, therefore, that these measures are less necessary in that area. The potential for terrorist attacks is often said to be national (hence the yellow alerts and orange alerts pronounced by DHS), but the fact that New York City has been under continual orange alerts indicates that a higher level of preparedness might be a commonly accepted business practice there. Landlords in New York City who relax security (as some are doing) are incurring a significant risk of liability if another terrorist attack occurred and resulted in injury or damage on their property.[26]

To minimize their potential liability for negligent security, property owners and possessors should, first, evaluate the steps taken by other businesses in similar circumstances, and, second, make sure to establish security measures that are at least as protective.

COMPLYING WITH EVOLVING STANDARDS FOR BUSINESS EMERGENCY RESPONSE

One legacy of 9/11 may be standards that augment the traditional approach to determining what level of protection will avoid liability for negligent security. Two important developments are the newly promulgated National Incident Management System (NIMS)[27] and the National Fire Protection Association (NFPA) 1600 "Standard on Disaster/Emergency Management and Business Continuity Programs."[28]

NIMS was adopted by DHS on 1 March 2004. It provides a consistent nationwide template to enable units of government and private-sector organizations to work together effectively and efficiently. Because much of the nation's critical infrastructure is in private hands, businesses are likely to be targets of terrorism. The private sector is expected to be a full partner in NIMS. The term *private sector* appears 37 times in the NIMS document; and although most of these references have to do with noncoercive coordination and cooperation, NIMS may well become a mandatory national standard in the future.

The 9/11 Commission recommended that NFPA 1600 be established as the "national preparedness standard" for government and business.[29] The commission further stated that NFPA 1600 should be established as the legal standard of care toward the public and employees. NFPA 1600 imposes significant requirements for planning, training, and applications. It creates a shared set of norms for disaster management, emergency management, and business continuity programs. It recognizes ways to apply plans and lists resource organizations in disaster recovery, emergency management, and business continuity planning. NFPA 1600 requires that "the program shall include, but shall not be limited to," the following plans:

1. Strategic
2. Emergency operations response
3. Mitigation
4. Recovery
5. Continuity[30]

Of concern to many businesses that might not otherwise bother with NFPA 1600 is the recommendation of the 9/11 Commission that financial institutions and insurers take compliance into consideration when determining creditworthiness and insurability.[31] For the financial and insurance industries, compliance will mean better protection of their own assets; thus they will probably adopt the recommendation. If so, businesses not in compliance would face potentially huge increases in the costs of borrowing and insurance. Conceivably, failure to comply with NFPA 1600 might mean that no loans or insurance would be available at any price.

Legislation has been introduced to enact the recommendations of the 9/11 Commission, including NFPA 1600, almost without modification.[32] The bill finds businesses largely unprepared for terrorism, partly owing to a lack of common standards for private-sector preparedness.[33] It affirms that DHS has a mandate that includes working with the private sector as well as with government entities. The legislation would set up a Private Sector Preparedness Program, amending the HS Act of 2002; it would direct DHS to endorse a "voluntary" private-sector preparedness program, using NFPA 1600 as an example. The bite of this legislation is a "Sense of Congress" finding that insurance and credit-rating industries should consider compliance with the voluntary national preparedness standard in calculating insurability and creditworthiness. In this way, the federal government is creating a system whereby business pressures will produce compliance with the NFPA 1600 standard. The standard also imposes a duty to "comply with applicable legislation, regulations, directives, policies, and industry codes of practice,"[34] which implies compliance with NFPA 1600.

To avoid liability, then, private-sector managers would be well advised to establish structures that comply with NIMS and NFPA 1600—and indeed to be ahead of the curve in both daily operations and emergency response. This step can help businesses defend themselves in court against any charges of negligence following a terrorist attack.

LEGAL ISSUES IN EVACUATION

Frequently, emergency response demands a choice among alternatives that are all unappealing. Often, different plaintiffs will see a decision as incorrect for opposite reasons, depending on their perspective on how that decision may affect them. Evacuation is one example. Evacuation may be the best protective measure, but it may prove costly and bothersome for people and businesses and may itself be risky. Thus it demonstrates the essential difficulty facing an authority who must select courses of action during a response: how to react successfully while not intruding unnecessarily into people's daily life.

State and local emergency management acts and ordinances contain the legal authority for declaring an evacuation. Such laws may confer this authority on a head of government. Whether and how widely to evacuate is the kind of public policy judgment that should ordinarily be protected by discretionary function immunity.[35]

A business facing forced evacuation because of terrorism or a threat of terrorism will quickly find out if its emergency plans are adequate. Occasionally, individuals reject evacuation. Businesses may also be tempted to do so. A business may have ongoing processes that it cannot abandon without a significant loss of funds or even damage to or destruction of equipment (as in the production of steel). If unanticipated evacuation could result in such damage, emergency plans may include contingencies that would allow properly trained and equipped employees to remain on-site. However, the increased danger to such employees could expose the business to significantly higher liability. Requiring employees to stay in place, as opposed to seeking volunteers and training and equipping them properly before an event, would be legally risky.

The choices facing an authority may be ugly. Should time be spent persuading obstinate residents or employees to evacuate when a larger number of other, more cooperative, people might be saved? How should limited resources be used? Should uncooperative people be arrested and confined (risking a possible claim for false arrest)? One solution is to require people who will not evacuate to complete a "next-of-kin" form so that the government may notify their families (the implication being that failure to depart will make death inevitable). The form also should include a waiver of liability to help the government avoid potential responsibility for the person's death.

Such a form could be strong evidence against a business that required employees to remain in place during a known danger. Balancing the costs and benefits of evacuating when told to do so versus staying in place for economic purposes and exposing employees to potential injury is a variation on the sort of cost-benefit analyses frequently made by businesses. To lessen the likelihood of liability, however, such planning should be undertaken before an event occurs.[36]

Sometimes people do not wish to leave because their companion animals are not permitted to accompany them to Red Cross shelters. Many jurisdictions are dealing with this issue by creating advance agreements with veterinarians to accommodate such animals.

Reentry to the site of an incident during an emergency may be essential in order to execute crucial tasks. The nature and importance of such tasks must be assessed to determine whether it is sensible to risk lives and legal liability by allowing such reentry. To be legally protected, absent an overwhelming reason, reentry should not be permitted until the peril is over. Again, businesses may face difficult choices when an evacuation lasts longer than was originally expected. Legal counsel should be closely involved in consideration of options at this point.

CONCLUSION

A terrorist attack may involve a release of hazardous materials, whether or not they are included as such in lists kept by EPA. This situation may result from the extreme effects of an attack on common substances, such as pulverized glass after the attacks on the World Trade Center. Or hazardous materials—nuclear, biological, or chemical—may be the actual weapon in an attack.

All businesses need to reevaluate their preparedness for catastrophic events in order to lower their potential liability afterward. Many proactive steps for businesses are being developed, and some are already required. Common industry practices for avoidance of premises liability, for example, have been considerably upgraded. Increased security undertaken by large numbers of similar companies will result in a higher standard for all in order to prevent liability. The recommended adoption of NIMS and NFPA 1600 will probably result in a new set of requirements for business, and there is pressure from the lending and insurance industries for its adoption. Proactive observance of these standards could be the step that saves lives and protects property during a terrorist attack and prevents liability afterward.

Businesses cannot afford to stand still. They must understand that legal standards for business preparedness and continuity are evolving, and that this process has accelerated since 9/11. Failure to recognize a changing environment almost always makes a company more vulnerable to failure. In contrast, understanding these factors could result in a significant competitive edge in the aftermath of a terrorist attack.

N O T E S

1. Public Law 107-296, HR 5005, 107th Congress.
2. William C. Nicholson, "Integrating Local, State and Federal Responders and Emergency Management: New Packaging and New Controls," *Journal of Emergency Management*, 1:15 (Fall 2003): 15.
3. HS Act, §01.
4. "Note: Responding to Terrorism: Crime, Punishment, and War," *Harvard Law Review*, 115 (2002): 1217, 1224. "The United States has traditionally treated terrorism as a crime. The U.S. Code contains criminal statutes that define and establish punishments for terrorism."

5. Management of Domestic Incidents (28 February 2003); www.whitehouse.gov/news/releases/2003/02/20030228-9.html.

6. U.S. Policy on Counterterrorism (21 June 1995).

7. HSPD 5, §8.

8. Robert Lee Hotz and Gary Polakovic, "America Attacked; Environmental Nightmare; Experts Differ on Peril from Smoke; Health: EPA Says the Cloud Rising from the Ruins Is Not Toxic, but Others Aren't So Sure. Rescuers Are Most at Risk for Possible Ill Effects," *Los Angeles Times* (14 September 2001): A5. "Those construction workers, firefighters and cops are being very heavily exposed to dust and asbestos. That [exposure] isn't going to end tomorrow; they'll be heavily exposed for weeks and months."

9. Alan Feuer and Michael Wilson, "Its Ranks Depleted, a Weary Fire Department Is Trying to Regroup," *New York Times* (11 September 2002); www.firehouse.com/terrorist/911/11_NYTregroup.html.

10. Laurie Garrett, "City Struggles to Contend with Widespread WTC Cough," *New York Newsday* (30 September 2002).

11. See William C. Nicholson, "Legal Issues in Emergency Response to Terrorism Incidents Involving Hazardous Materials: The Hazardous Waste Operations and Emergency Response (HAZWOPER) Standard, Standard Operating Procedures, Mutual Aid, and the Incident Command System," *Widener Symposium Law Journal* 9:2 (April 2003): 295, 298–300.

12. In 1970, Congress enacted the federal Occupational Safety and Health Act (OSH Act), 84 Stat. 1590 (codified at 29 USC 553, 651–678, 2002). It specifically authorized the secretary of labor to promulgate national health and safety standards. 29 USC 655(a). Occupational Safety and Health Standards 29 CFR '1910.120 (q) (1998) covers employees who are engaged in emergency response to hazardous substance releases no matter where it occurs except that employees engaged in operations specified in paragraphs (a)(1)(i) through (a)(1)(iv) of this section are not covered; nor are emergency response organizations that have developed and implemented programs equivalent to this paragraph for handling releases of hazardous substances pursuant to Section 303 of the Superfund Amendments and Reauthorization Act of 1986. Environmental Protection Agency (EPA) 40 CFR '372.18 (1995) deals with the enforcement and compliance guidelines for reporting toxic chemical release and the community's right to know.

13. 29 CFR, §1910.119, deals with preventing or minimizing the consequences of catastrophic release of hazardous materials in an industrial setting.

14. See Federal Emergency Management Agency, United States Fire Administration, Hazardous Materials Response Technology Assessment (2000), which discusses various technologies for control and mitigation of hazmat incidents, including training required for their application.

15. 29 USC, §568, discusses the procedure of issuing a citation to an employer who is in violation of a requirement of Section 5 or Section 6 of OSH Act.

16. 29 USC, §666. A civil penalty accessed on an employer for violation of either an employer's requirements and duties under Section 5 of the OSH Act or any violations of the Occupational Safety and Health Standards under Section 6.

17. 29 USC, §666, describes a serious violation as existing in a place of employment if there is a substantial probability that death or serious physical harm could

result from an existing condition, or from one or more practices, means, methods, operations, or processes which have been adopted or are in use.

18. Ibid.

19. Ibid.

20. Ibid.

21. See, e.g., *Meridian Insurance Company v. Zepeda*, 734 NE 2d 1126, 1130–1131 (Ind. App. 2000). "... A criminal conviction may be admitted in evidence in a civil action and may be conclusive proof in a civil trial of the factual issues determined by the criminal judgement."

22. "Note: Administrative Law—Occupational Safety and Health Act—on Multi-employer Jobsite, When Employees of Any Employer Are Affected by Noncompliance with a Safety Standard, Employer in Control of Work Area Violates Act; Employer Not in Control of the Area Does Not Violate Act, Even If His Own Employees Are Affected, Provided That the Hazard Is 'Nonserious,'" *Harvard Law Review* 89 (1976): 793, 796.

23. "Lawsuits Stemming from WTC Attack Could Cost City Billions," *New York News* (8 February 2002); www.ny1.com/ny/Search/SubTopic/index.html? &contentintid=19077&search_result=1#.

24. John M. Barkett, "If Terror Reigns, Will Torts Follow?" *Widener Symposium Law Journal* 9:2 (April 2003): 486, 500–1.

25. See *Morgan v. Bucks Associates*, 428 F. Supp. 546, 549 (ED Pa. 1977).

26. Benjamin Weiser and Claudia H. Deutsch, "Stringent Measures Gather Dust, Experts Say," *New York Times* (16 August 2004): B-1. "Without question, many companies after 9/11 took serious steps, some quite ambitious and costly, to protect their employees and their assets. Gregg A. Popkin, senior managing director of CB Richard Ellis Inc., which manages about 115 commercial buildings in the metropolitan area, says landlords in those buildings have spent a combined $50 million on scanners, turnstiles and other measures in the past three years. ... But there is much that has not changed all that dramatically. Plans that were drawn up were shelved, security machines put in place have been taken out, and computer security remains far from perfect."

27. For NIMS and related information see www.fema.gov/nims/.

28. For NFPA 1600 (2004 Edition) see www.nasttpo.org/NFPA1600.htm.

29. *9/11 Commission Report*, p. 398.

30. NFPA 1600, §5.7.2.

31. *9/11 Commission Report*, p. 398.

32. S.2774, 9/11 Commission Report Implementation Act (introduced 7 September 2004). Additional bills have been introduced in the House of Representatives.

33. S.2774, §806, Private Sector Preparedness.

34. NFPA 1600, §5.2.1.

35. See Ken Lerner, "Governmental Negligence Liability Exposure in Disaster Management,"*Urban Lawyer* 23 (1991): 333.

36. See William C. Nicholson, "Litigation Mitigation: Proactive Risk Management in the Wake of the West Warwick Club Fire," *Journal of Emergency Management* 1:2 (Summer 2003).

Academe

C H A P T E R   5 4

Introduction to Section 10

The Honorable Scott D. Bates, J.D.,
Senior Fellow, Center for National Policy;
Former Senior Policy Advisor, U.S. House Select
Committee on Homeland Security

By 1947, America was confronting a cold war with the Soviet Union. When the Soviet Union developed a hydrogen bomb and a missile program, and when it launched *Sputnik* in the 1950s, many Americans felt that they were personally imperiled and vulnerable; and they and their leaders concluded that the security of the United States depended on expertise, innovation, and preeminence in science and technology. The power and ambitions of the Soviet Union seemed to present what was, historically, perhaps the first direct threat to the safety and security of the American homeland.

In response, America mobilized for a challenge that was expected to persist indefinitely. Academe was part of this mobilization and played a considerable role in determining how the Cold War would be fought. Colleges and universities created or expanded programs in strategic studies, Soviet studies, regional studies, and the Russian language. Arguably, the strategic vision and understanding provided by academics contributed to homeland security during the Cold War, and to the ultimate outcome of that war.

Today, although America stands unchallenged in military strength, there is a new challenge to the American homeland—terrorism—and once again, academe should be a part of the current mobilization. The three chapters in this section discuss the need for academe to respond and restructure. In Chapter 55 Todd Stewart points out that with regard to homeland security the importance of academia involves not only science and technology but also education, training, outreach, and service. In Chapter 56 Joseph Vorbach and Patrick Newman offer an innovative way to apply strategic studies to homeland security. In Chapter 57 Richard Larson reviews selected operations research (OR) work in emergency response in which the resources of local first responders are overstretched.

American colleges and universities are not yet fully equipped to meet the complex challenges presented by terrorism. Developing an appropriate curriculum and encouraging interdisciplinary study and cooperation will raise academic as well as organizational issues, but this is an essential task: disciplines as diverse as management, accounting, military science, biology, and language are all central to the war on terror. The authors in this section present ways to take the first steps forward.

Academe and Homeland Security

Todd I. Stewart
Major General, United States Air Force (Retired);
Executive Director, National Academic Consortium for
Homeland Security

INTRODUCTION

This chapter regarding the roles and responsibilities of academic institutions in homeland security and defense is descriptive and prescriptive. It addresses three primary roles: academe as (1) a target of actual or threatened terrorism, (2) a resource for terrorists, and (3) a source of counterterrorist solutions.

Definitions

The following terms are defined as they will be used in this discussion.

- *Academe* (or *academia*) is defined broadly and comprehensively to include secondary schools; all types of postsecondary academic research, education, and training institutions, public and private; and academic associations, consortia, supportive organizations, and professional societies, some of which focus on homeland security and defense.
- *Terrorism* has no universally accepted definition, but here the term will refer to any threat or act of violence that changes attitudes or behavior through intimidation and fear.

F I G U R E   55-1

Terrorism event.

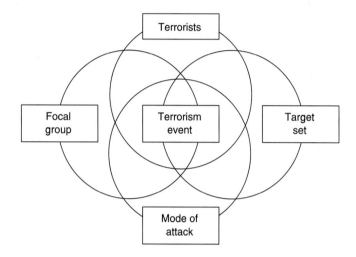

- *Terrorist event* (or *terrorism event*) means threatened or actual violence—e.g., kidnapping, assassination, or a larger attack. Such an event has four components: (1) the terrorist or terrorists; (2) the target or targets; (3) the focal group, i.e., the group to be influenced; and (4) the mode of attack (see Figure 55-1).
- *Terrorists* are individuals or groups that threaten or use violence to change the attitudes and behaviors of a focal group. Terrorists can be described in terms of intent (goals), capabilities, organization, motivation, degree of fanaticism, etc. Goals and motives are probably the most usual characterizations.
- *Target sets*, historically, have included prominent individuals or groups, individuals or groups with some political or other special significance, symbolic assets or events, large groups of people, and critical infrastructure. The *National Strategy for Homeland Security* identifies 13 sectors of critical infrastructure: agriculture, food, water, public health, emergency services, government, defense industrial base, information and telecommunications, energy, transportation, banking and finance, chemical industry, and postal and shipping.[1] A target

set can also be characterized by its value to terrorists and its vulnerability to terrorism.

* *Focal groups* are the people that the terrorists want to influence and commonly include governments and citizens. Perhaps most commonly, terrorism is intended to erode citizens' confidence in their government. Often, the ultimate goal is to change the government or its policies.

* *Mode of attack* comprises means, methods, and weapons. Of particular concern are weapons of mass destruction (WMD), which include chemical, biological, radiological, nuclear, and high-explosive (CBRNE) weaponry—and, more recently, "weapons of mass disruption and effect," e.g., cyberterrorism. Weapons can also include misappropriated industrial chemicals and other hazardous materials, aircraft, and shoulder-fired antiaircraft missiles.

* *Method of attack* means how weapons are used. One important distinction is that between suicide and nonsuicide attacks.

* *Counterterrorism* includes actions taken to deter, prevent, or disrupt attacks, and to respond to and recover from such attacks.

Counterterrorist Strategy

Figure 55-2 shows a generalized strategy for antiterrorism and counterterrorism. It suggests a "layered defense," in which the initial focus is on *deterrence*—actions taken to dissuade groups or individuals from using or threatening violence to achieve their goals. Deterrence may involve forestalling a specific terrorist event.

If deterrence is failing, the strategy next focuses on timely *prediction*—through effective *intelligence* and *warning*—that an event is imminent. Ideally, intelligence will be "actionable," allowing appropriate law enforcement or military authorities to act preemptively to *prevent* (or at least disrupt) the event.

If preemptive action is not possible, the strategy focuses on mitigating the consequences of an event. *Mitigation* is generally accomplished through protective and preparatory measures, applied beforehand, such as planning, protecting critical infrastructure, installing rapid-detection technologies, and training and equipping "first responders."

FIGURE   55-2

Counterterrorism strategy.

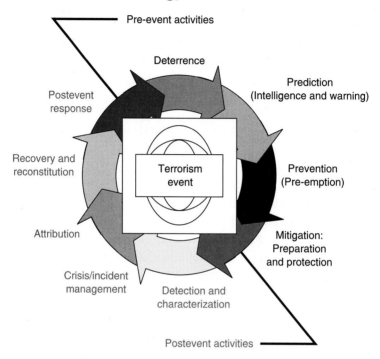

If an event cannot be deterred or prevented, the strategy calls for rapid *detection and characterization* of the attack, particularly if it involves bioterrorism or cyberterrorism and if (as is typical) the fact that a premeditated attack has occurred is not immediately evident.

Immediately following detection of an event, the strategy turns to *emergency management* or *crisis management*. Here the focus is on defeating the attack and on containing the immediate consequences: dealing with casualties and fatalities, extinguishing fires, containing the spread of disease, restoring essential utilities and services, etc. Next, the focus shifts to long-term *recovery* and *reconstitution*. This includes restoring critical infrastructure and the physical and mental health of victims.

Concurrently with crisis management and recovery, the strategy also focuses on *attribution*: determining, through intelligence, law enforcement, and forensics, who perpetrated the event. If the perpetrator was acting on behalf of, or with the support of, another nation, we will most likely be in a state of war with that nation. Otherwise, attribution will most likely involve treating the event as a crime, and emphasizing the identification and preservation of evidence, leading to prosecution.

For each element in this counterterrorist strategy, relative to a particular event, the following questions should be addressed:

- What is the goal?
- What are the required or desired outcomes or outputs?
- Who is responsible and accountable for this element of the strategy?
- What is the plan for accomplishing the required or desired outputs and outcomes?
- What capabilities and resources are needed and available to execute the plan?

When there are shortfalls in capability or resources, these further questions should be answered:

- What additional resources are required?
- What basic applied research is required?
- What technology development and transition or commercialization are necessary?
- What education and training are required?

These questions, which imply decision making, are illustrated in Figure 55-3. Again, the decision process is applicable to each element of the counterterrorism model—deterrence, prediction, prevention, detection, etc. "Research and development" and "education and training" are the elements with which academe is most commonly involved.

The model illustrated in Figure 55-3 suggests that, generally, technology is developed in response to operational requirements—this is the "requirements pull." However, in many cases the process is reversed. Basic research often leads to new technologies that offer new capabilities and allow conceptual change in operations (strategies and tactics) and even changes in operational goals. For example, the Global Positioning System (GPS), originally developed for the Department of Defense, has enabled many businesses and other nondefense government agencies to change the way they work,

F I G U R E   55-3

Counterterrorism strategy: Decision process ("requirements pull").

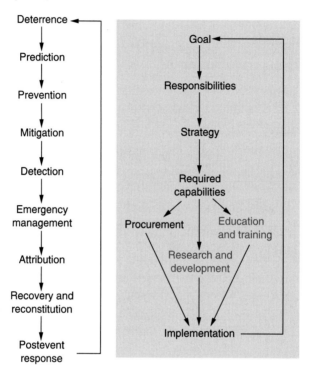

improving effectiveness and efficiency. This "technology push" is shown in Figure 55-4. "Research," "technology development," and "education and training" are the points where academe is most commonly involved in the process.

National Strategy for Homeland Security

The *National Strategy for Homeland Security* (July 2002) identifies "critical mission areas" that also serve as a conceptual framework for identifying goals, desired capabilities, and responsibilities.[2] These critical mission areas are

Intelligence and warning

Border and transportation security

F I G U R E   55-4

Counterterrorism strategy: Decision process ("technology push").

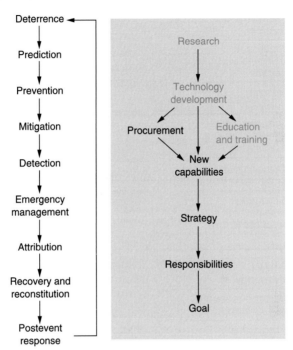

Domestic counterterrorism

Protecting critical infrastructure and key assets

Defending against catastrophic threats

Emergency preparedness and response

The *National Strategy for Homeland Security* also identifies certain "foundations":

Law

Science and technology

Information sharing and systems

International cooperation

For each critical mission area and each foundation, the strategy identifies goals, objectives, and desired outcomes or

National Strategy for Homeland Security: Decision process.

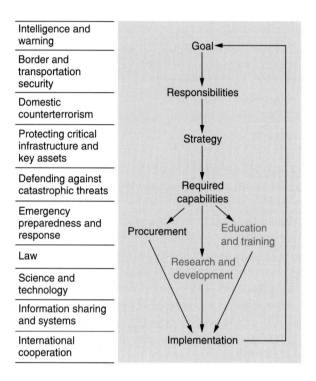

capabilities—more than 80 goals in all. For each goal, we again need to ask the questions that were illustrated in Figure 55-3. Figure 55-5 illustrates the relationship between these management-process questions and the critical mission areas and foundations.

ROLES OF ACADEME IN HOMELAND SECURITY

National Roles and Responsibilities

The *National Strategy for Homeland Security* emphasizes that homeland security is not solely the responsibility of the federal government or governments in general. It is the responsibility of individual citizens, government agencies at all levels (federal, state, and local), and nongovernmental organizations, including academe.

Citizens

Fundamentally, individual citizens are responsible for the security of the United States. In particular, through the representative process, citizens influence government policies, strategies, and programs related to homeland security and influence the enabling legislation. Ideally, this presupposes an aware, knowledgeable citizenry.

Government Agencies

Federal, state, and local government agencies have an important role in homeland security. At every level, executive-branch agencies, supported by the associated legislative branch, are responsible for providing for safety and security, within the limits of their respective jurisdictions and authorities. Additionally, government officials and activities are frequently targets of terrorists who want to change governments or governmental policies. And government agencies at all levels are involved in homeland security as employers of men and women who serve in the National Guard and Reserve and who may be mobilized for prolonged periods.

At the federal level, many executive-branch departments and agencies share responsibility for various aspects of homeland security and defense. Departments include Agriculture, Commerce, Defense, Energy, Health and Human Services, Homeland Security, Interior, Justice, Transportation, and State. Agencies include the Central Intelligence Agency and the Environmental Protection Agency. Within Congress, currently, more than 30 committees and subcommittees claim jurisdiction over some aspect of homeland security, defense authorization, and oversight or appropriation.

At the state level, the executive branch of each state has assigned homeland security to an existing or new department, agency, or office. Some states have also chartered committees or task forces to coordinate the efforts of state agencies with respect to homeland security. Similarly, many state legislatures have assigned the oversight and appropriation of homeland security to new or existing committees and subcommittees.

Government units at the county, township, and municipal levels have a particularly important responsibility. Ultimately, all disasters and emergencies, including terrorism, are local events. Preparation and response fall to local officials and agencies such as the "first responders" responsible for law enforcement, fire protection, public utilities, public health and medical care, and other essential services.

Nongovernment Organizations

Business, industry, and nonprofit organizations play several roles in national homeland security. It has been estimated that 85 to 90 percent of the critical infrastructure in the United States is owned by the private sector. Consequently, business and industry are a likely target of terrorism; and private-sector companies have a responsibility to help secure critical resources such as public utilities. Of particular concern are companies that manufacture, use, or transport hazardous materials. Prominent business executives have often been kidnapped or assassinated. Terrorists are also likely to consider private-sector companies a source of resources (e.g., aircraft and hazardous materials) necessary to attack other targets. The private-sector insurance industry is crucial because it allows commercial enterprises to operate despite the risk of terrorism and helps individuals and companies to recover from terrorist events. Moreover, businesses and industries are also employers of people in the National Guard and Reserve and are adversely affected by a prolonged mobilization.

"Government-interest" organizations, industry trade associations, and organized labor groups are often involved with homeland security and defense. These groups may be powerful voices or lobbyists influencing public policy, including homeland security. Associations representing state governors, county governments, city mayors, the chemical industry, pharmaceutical companies, public utilities, and so on have been active in shaping homeland security. These groups, particularly industry associations, are also a source of functional expertise to help government agencies establish standards for homeland security operations, equipment, and personnel.

Many other nongovernment organizations also have a role. These include the Red Cross, community-support groups (e.g., Kiwanis and Rotary), faith-based groups, and volunteer organizations (e.g., the Citizen Corps), which help victims of natural and human-made disasters.

The remainder of this discussion will focus on the three roles of academe in homeland security: (1) as a target of terrorism, (2) as a source of logistics or resources for terrorist attacks on other targets, and (3) as a source of solutions to problems of homeland security.

F I G U R E   55-6

Responsibilities for counterterrorism.

	Government				Non-Government		
	Citizens	Federal	State	Local	Industry	Other NGOs	Academe
Deterrence							
Prediction							
Prevention							
Mitigation							
Detection							
Emergency management							
Attribution							
Recovery and reconstitution							
Postevent response							

These problems include the need for better-informed public policy and strategy, more effective and less costly technologies (products and services), educated and trained professionals in homeland security and defense, and more aware citizens.

Figure 55-6 summarizes how these respective roles and responsibilities relate to the elements of counterterrorism shown earlier in Figure 55-3. The question is "What are the roles and responsibilities of academe with respect to each element of the counterterrorist strategy?" Similarly, Figure 55-7 relates the roles and responsibilities of the various stakeholders to the critical mission areas and foundations spelled out in the *National Strategy for Homeland Security.*

Academe as a Target

American colleges and universities are potential targets of terrorism. Their campuses are like small cities—in some large academic institutions the students, faculty, and staff number more than 50,000—and thus have at least the same risk of terrorism as a city

F I G U R E   55-7

Responsibilities for critical mission areas and foundations.

	Government				Non-Government		
	Citizens	Federal	State	Local	Industry	Other NGOs	Academe
Intelligence and warning							
Border and transportation security							
Domestic counterterrorism							
Protecting critical infrastructure and key assets							
Defending against catastrophic threats							
Emergency preparedness and response							
Law							
Science and technology							
Information sharing and systems							
International cooperation							

of comparable size. Actually, population density is often greater on university campuses than in cities with comparable populations. This density enhances the value of a campus as a target, increases its vulnerability, and intensifies the potential consequences of a successful attack.

Also as in cities, major universities have prominent members who are potential targets of terrorism—senior administrators and high-profile researchers and scholars. For example, scientists at universities in the United States and elsewhere who use animals in their research have become targets of harassment, threats to themselves and their families, and arson in their facilities by animal-rights activists.

Most major research institutions also have critical infrastructure that is a potentially valuable target, such as nuclear reactors and laboratories where research with hazardous biological agents is conducted. Notably, the University of Texas and Boston University are planning to construct and operate "biosafety level 4" laboratories for research on the most dangerous biological agents and pathogens. Many universities are also repositories for valuable assets such as rare books, manuscripts, and art collections. For example, several presidential libraries and National Archives buildings are on or near college campuses.

Most large universities have a significant number of foreign students. Foreign students in general, and ethnic student groups in particular, are potential targets for extremists. A large population of foreign students also provides an opportunity for foreign nonstudent extremists to blend in and gain access, inconspicuously, to potential targets at a university.

Also, many universities have sporting events, concerts, and other activities that attract large numbers of people; for example, more than 100,000 spectators may attend a football game at a large university. Such a population is highly concentrated, offering a high-value target to terrorists.

In 2003, the Office of Domestic Preparedness of the Department of Homeland Security (DHS) published a checklist of counterterrorist policies, strategies, and procedures for colleges and universities to implement.[3] This checklist, which emphasized WMD, included the following points:

- Establish a working relationship with the closest FBI field office and the regional Joint Terrorism Task Force
- Consider assigning officers to work as liaisons with international student groups on campus to build trust among such students
- Establish a team responsible for directing the campus's emergency operations plan

- Review the plan with campus officials and local, state, and federal officials to determine what staff training is needed
- Discuss with local officials ways the campus can provide help to the local community and itself, in the event of an incident outside the campus
- Review leave policies so that officers can be reassigned and plainclothes officers can be switched to uniform positions, to make them more visible, when appropriate
- Increase physical checks of critical facilities during periods of increased alert
- Establish single points of access for critical facilities and require identification checks of all people seeking to enter
- Limit public access to critical facilities and consider procedures to escort authorized persons who need to use those facilities
- Increase inspections of people entering critical facilities
- Assess the use of video monitoring of campus sites
- Assess the adequacy of physical barriers outside sensitive buildings
- Review parent communication programs and procedures for students to contact family members

Academe as a Source of Resources for Terrorists

Colleges and universities in the United States and worldwide are a source of resources or logistics for terrorists who are planning actions against nonacademic targets.

First (and perhaps foremost), academic institutions offer a pool from which young people—who are often very impressionable—can be recruited for extremist causes. Also, historically, most academic institutions in the United States and in democratic countries around the world have encouraged open communication and the free exchange of ideas, including open debate over radical political, religious, social, and economic concepts, viewpoints, and ideologies. Consequently, colleges and universities are potentially useful to an extremist group that wants to maintain or increase its membership. But this is also true of academic institutions—elementary schools, secondary schools, and colleges and universities—in nondemocratic societies, where the subject matter is controlled by the state or, say, by a sponsoring religious group. In the most extreme cases, such schools can be described as institutes of indoctrination, rather than academic institutions in the Western sense.

Colleges and universities also offer terrorists a potential source of materials that could be used (directly or indirectly) as weapons. Many major universities have research and teaching programs that involve the storage and use of potentially dangerous biological agents and pathogens, chemical agents, radiological materials, and other hazardous materials. For instance, a collection or colony of disease-infected laboratory animals, if released, could endanger public health.

Some research at colleges and universities is classified; but in keeping with the traditional openness of academe, most academic research is unclassified and unrestricted. In fact, researchers depend on the publication of their findings in the "open literature," since such publication affects promotions and tenure. As a result, there is a dilemma with respect to research on issues of homeland security and defense. While there are institutional and cultural pressures to publish the results of such research, the convenient availability of "sensitive, but unclassified" information could be of great value to a potential terrorist.

Academe as a Source of Solutions

The third major role of academe is as a developer and provider of solutions to problems of homeland security: better-informed public policy and strategies, better and cheaper technologies (products and services), educated and trained professionals in homeland security and defense, and more aware citizens. In general, academic institutions help meet national, state, and local requirements by conducting basic and applied research. Colleges and universities also transform research into relevant capabilities—such as practical, affordable products and services, and recommendations of public policy—through the development and commercialization of new technologies. Of course, academic institutions are primarily responsible for educating and training people to meet current and future challenges of homeland security, whether these people will work in government, the private sector, or academe itself. Similarly, American secondary schools and postsecondary institutions, particularly public

F I G U R E   55-8

Academic roles in developing and providing solutions for homeland security.

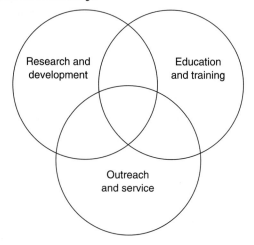

colleges and universities, have a responsibility to educate students for their role as citizens and to help them understand national issues related to homeland security. Finally, academic institutions, especially public universities and colleges, contribute to homeland security through outreach and services. This typically involves contributing a school's expertise and other resources in support of government agencies responsible for homeland security and defense.

Figure 55-8 suggests that the academic functions of homeland security—research and development, education and training, and outreach and service—are interrelated. For example, research and development inform and update related education and training programs. Also, questions and issues that arise in education and training programs suggest questions and topics for future research.

In the context of Figure 55-6, academe—again through relevant research and development, education and training, and outreach and service—supports individuals, government agencies, and nongovernment organizations responsible for each element in the counterterrorist strategy. This notion is illustrated in Figure 55-9.

Similarly, in the context of Figure 55-7, universities and colleges support individuals, government agencies, and nongovernmental organizations responsible for each critical mission area or foundation

F I G U R E   55-9

Responsibilities for counterterrorism: Academe.

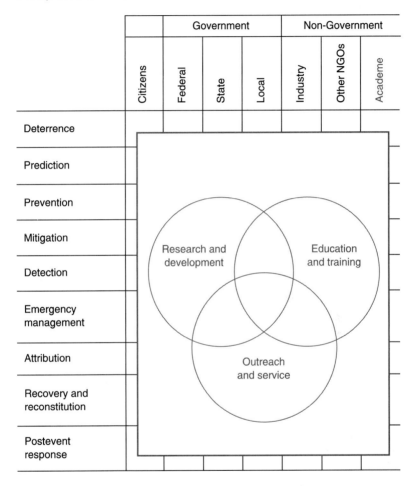

element in the *National Strategy for Homeland Security.* Figure 55-10 illustrates these relationships.

Academic Research and the Development of Solutions

A primary role of academe is to create new knowledge through basic and applied research and to share the results through publication and teaching. Currently, although some university research in homeland

F I G U R E   55-10

Responsibilities for critical mission areas and foundations: Academe.

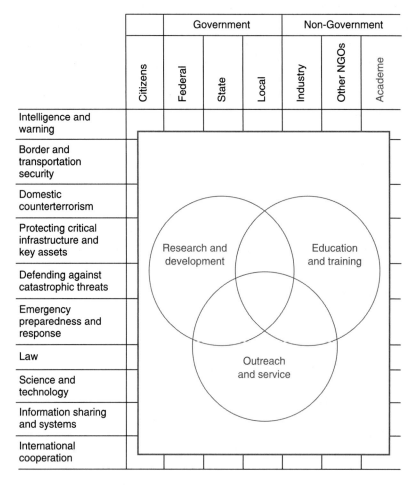

	Citizens	Government			Non-Government		
		Federal	State	Local	Industry	Other NGOs	Academe
Intelligence and warning							
Border and transportation security							
Domestic counterterrorism							
Protecting critical infrastructure and key assets							
Defending against catastrophic threats							
Emergency preparedness and response							
Law							
Science and technology							
Information sharing and systems							
International cooperation							

Research and development

Education and training

Outreach and service

security and defense is funded by the private sector and by state governments, most is funded by various concerned federal entities—including the departments of Homeland Security, Defense, Health and Human Services, Agriculture, and Justice, and agencies such as Central Intelligence and Environmental Protection. These federal departments and agencies tend to rely on existing national laboratories and previously established Federally Funded Research and Development Centers (FFRDCs) to support research, when the existing laboratories and centers have the necessary expertise. These federal agencies generally look to academe and the private sector for research and development support that is not readily available in the federal laboratories and centers. Unlike the federal laboratories and centers, which tend to focus on selected disciplines, universities and colleges can generally do research in a broader range of disciplines: e.g., mathematics and statistics, all the physical sciences, humanities, social and behavioral sciences, biological sciences, medicine and public health, law, and engineering. In addition, colleges and universities are positioned for both interdisciplinary and cross-disciplinary research. This is especially relevant to homeland security and defense, as many challenges in this area require a multidisciplinary approach.

As an exception to the federal strategy of relying primarily on organic research, the Homeland Security Act of 2002 required the secretary to establish one or more "university-led centers of excellence" in homeland security. As of August 2004, DHS had established three such centers related to terrorism and counter-terrorism:

> Risk Analysis and Economic Impact (University of Southern California)
>
> Foreign Animal and Zoonotic Diseases (Texas A&M University)
>
> Post-Harvest Food Security (University of Minnesota)

A fourth center, for behavioral and social aspects of terrorism and counterterrorism, is also being planned. These centers undertake both research and education.

There are several limitations to academic research on homeland security. Most academic research is done by faculty members and graduate students or postdoctoral fellows. Consequently, the scope of the research that can be accomplished in a timely manner at any particular institution is limited by the expertise of the faculty and the availability of graduate students. Since the research is also used to train these students, the work is commonly paced by academic schedules. As previously noted, the academic culture implies unconstrained publication of research. Faculty members need to be able to publish their work in appropriate academic journals, and graduate students need to be able to publish their theses and dissertations. Consequently, academic institutions generally have a limited capability for classified research. Also, most of the federally sponsored research in homeland security and defense is applied research—covering the application of existing or emerging technologies to specific aspects of homeland security. By contrast, much (perhaps most) university research is basic research—fundamental science that is generally independent of specific applications. In that regard, the National Research Council offered examples of areas in which research universities need to focus on basic research in homeland security:[4]

Understanding the mechanisms of human pathogenesis, response and healing

Sensor networks

Extraction of understanding from large quantities of data

Human behavior and system design

Understanding complex, adaptive systems

Intelligent, adaptive power grid

Replacing humans in hazardous situations

Reliable computer code and secure communication systems

Research in homeland security, whether conducted in the national laboratories or FFRDCs, in academe, or in the private sector, is not an end in itself. Eventually, the results should lead to solutions. Solution development for homeland security and defense generally takes two forms.

The first form is the development of technologies that become capabilities relevant to, say, counterterrorist strategy (see Figure 55-2) or to the critical mission areas in the *National Strategy for Homeland Security* (Figure 55-5). Typically, this involves the translation and commercialization of applied research to yield practical, affordable products and services. Research universities generally participate in this process in one of two ways. First (and probably most commonly), universities license the use of their (patented) intellectual property to companies involved in technology transition and in producing and delivering new products and services: e.g., new sensors and detection devices, new vaccines, or new systems for collecting, fusing, analyzing, and sharing intelligence. Alternatively, most large research universities can help faculty members start new businesses and develop new products or services based on research done at the university.

The second form of solution development relates to nontechnological research, such as research in the social and behavioral sciences, humanities, or law. Here, the solution generally is new, better-informed public policy, strategies, or programs for homeland security and defense. Academic institutions can contribute significantly in this area, as they often have expertise not generally available in the national laboratories or FFRDCs.

Education and Training

Academe plays a unique role in homeland security by educating and training people to become better-informed citizens, scholars in related disciplines, government officials, and nongovernment executives.[5] An overview of this role must consider:

- *Education and training requirements*: Who needs to be educated and trained? Who needs to know what (subject matter)?
- *Education and training resources*: Who does the education and training? What instructional methods and technologies are appropriate?

To facilitate discussion of these issues, some comments on learning in general and various types of learning will be useful. Perhaps the most familiar taxonomy of learning was formulated by Benjamin Bloom and his colleagues.[6] It identifies three general domains of learning: cognitive, affective, and psychomotor. The cognitive domain includes knowledge and intellectual skills such as the recall or recognition of specific facts, procedural patterns, and concepts. Bloom identified six major categories of cognitive learning: in order from simplest to most complex, these are knowledge, comprehension, application, analysis, synthesis, and evaluation. These categories are hierarchical in that the first (knowledge) must be mastered before the second (comprehension), and so on.

The affective domain has to do with feelings, values, appreciation, enthusiasm, motivations, and attitudes. Bloom's taxonomy identifies five major categories; listed hierarchically, they are receiving phenomena, responding to phenomena, valuing, organization, and internalizing values.

F I G U R E   55-11

Domains of learning.

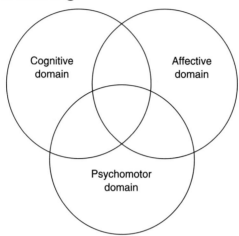

The psychomotor domain includes physical movement, coordination, and motor skills. Development of these skills requires practice and is often measured by speed, precision, distance, procedures, or techniques. Bloom did not offer a categorization of this domain, but Simpson, for example, identifies seven major categories: perception, set, guided response, mechanism, complex overt response, adaptation, and origination.[7]

The domains overlap somewhat, with no sharp line between them (see Figure 55-11). Similarly, there is no sharp distinction between education and training, either in general or with respect to homeland security (see Figure 55-12).

In considering education and training requirements for homeland security, academe needs to understand precisely who needs to be educated and what kind of competence is sought—i.e., what subject matter is to be addressed and in what learning domains. From a macro perspective, homeland security education and training requirements are illustrated in Figures 55-3 through 55-5, 55-9, and 55-10.

Perhaps the most important requirement receives the least attention. Individual citizens need to be aware and knowledgeable about homeland security issues and lawfully express their opinions to their elected representatives directly or indirectly (e.g., through lobbyists). Most citizens probably obtain information about homeland

F I G U R E   55-12

Relationship between domains of learning and education and training.

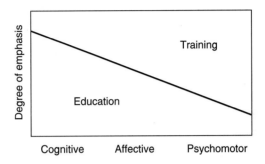

security from the media, but academe should also have a role. Government courses in secondary schools should address national security and homeland security; and postsecondary institutions, in particular public colleges and universities, also have a responsibility to prepare students to be better-informed citizens.

As Figures 55-9 and 55-10 suggest, academe needs to educate and train people for homeland-security and defense in government and the private sector. Specific needs typically depend on functional or organizational roles and responsibilities, especially concerning the elements of counterterrorism (Figure 55-9) and the critical mission areas and foundations (Figure 55-10). Following are representative (but not exhaustive) occupations or career fields in homeland security and defense that have specific education and training requirements:

Agriculture
Architecture
Aviation
Border security
Business administration
Communications
Emergency management
Emergency medical services
Engineering
Explosive ordnance disposal

Fire protection
Food science
Foreign service
Geography and geodesy
Immigration services
Information assurance and technology
Insurance
Intelligence
Law
Law enforcement (criminal justice)
Linguistics
Logistics
Medicine and allied health professions
Mental health
Military
Natural resource management
Planning
Politics
Public administration
Public health
Science
Social services
Transportation
Veterinary medicine

Each of these fields requires initial education or training and continuing education. In addition, academe also needs to provide the education and training necessary to facilitate the transition of people from unrelated career fields into positions responsible for aspects of homeland security and defense.

Academe must also be responsive to requirements for team training. This includes teams from within a discipline or functional area (e.g., law enforcement, fire protection, and public health) and multidisciplinary teams (e.g., representatives from all the functions responsible for dealing with a disaster within a particular political jurisdiction such as a city or county).

Academe, broadly, includes various institutions that provide, or could provide, resources for education and training in homeland security:

Secondary schools

Public and private postsecondary schools

Four-year colleges and universities

Two-year community colleges

Vocational and technical schools

Private-sector companies offering specialized training

Federal, state, and local government academies, e.g., for law enforcement and fire protection

Secondary schools (high schools) offer courses in government and citizenship that address the roles and responsibilities of citizens. Ideally, these courses should address, at least at the "awareness" level, the challenges to national security and the role of government and individual citizens in meeting those challenges. In particular, these courses should emphasize an informed citizenry participating in debates about public policy and strategy for homeland security and defense.

Postsecondary schools and private-sector organizations provide education and training for individuals in government agencies and nongovernment organizations. Community colleges and vocational-technical schools generally focus on basic skills necessary for entering careers such as law enforcement, fire protection, emergency medical care, allied health professions, business administration, engineering technology, and information technology—and especially first-responder careers. Community colleges generally offer two-year programs that lead to an associates degree or certificate or prepare individuals for professional licensing in certain technical fields. Community colleges also offer continuing education to upgrade the skills of practitioners in various careers or to help individuals change careers. An increasing number of community colleges are developing and offering courses directly related to homeland security, especially emergency management. Typically, community-college programs focus on practical applications of concepts and technology.

Colleges and universities typically offer undergraduate- and graduate-degree programs in disciplines directly or indirectly related

to homeland security. Undergraduate programs are usually four-
or five-year programs, leading to a bachelor's degree. Graduate
master's-degree programs take one or two years. Doctoral and
professional degree programs (e.g., medicine and law) typically take
three to four years. Many such programs now include entire courses,
or blocks of instruction within existing courses, on aspects of
homeland security: e.g., terrorism and terrorists, WMD, bioterrorism
and defense, agroterrorism and defense, and cyberterrorism and
information assurance.

There has been a significant growth in the number of undergraduate and graduate degree programs related to emergency
management and homeland security. The Web site of the
Emergency Management Institute of the Federal Emergency
Management Agency (FEMA)[8] offers related data and information
about these programs. However, with respect to undergraduate and
graduate certificate and degree programs in homeland security, there
is currently no consensus about what constitutes a common body
of knowledge. Homeland security does not yet seem to be widely
recognized and accepted as an academic discipline. The present
author, in an informal survey of introductory programs and courses
("Homeland Security 101"), found that the following subjects were
commonly included:

- The changing environments of international and national
  security
- Past and present efforts at domestic preparedness
- Antiterrorist and counterterrorist strategies, including deter-
  rence; prediction (intelligence and warning); prevention
  (preemption); mitigation, detection, and characterization of
  consequences; crisis and emergency management; attribution;
  recovery and reconstitution; and postevent response
- Current threats
- Common targets (values and vulnerabilities)
- Modes of attack (means, weapons, and methods of delivery),
  with emphasis on WMD, disruption, and effects
- Psychology of fear and terror
- Risk management
- Law, policy, and strategy

- Roles and responsibilities (individual and collective) of citizens, volunteer groups, government (at all levels), non-government organizations, and academe
- Need for cooperation, coordination, collaboration, and integration among stakeholders
- Career opportunities in homeland security and defense; homeland security as a profession
- Challenges and opportunities in homeland security

Colleges and universities tend to offer more traditional degrees, with a focus on emergency management or homeland security: e.g., public administration, with a major or concentration in homeland security; or a degree in computer science, with a concentration in information assurance. Consequently, there is still no commonly accepted standard for accrediting certificate or degree programs in homeland security.

Education and training for homeland security are provided in part by government academies and training agencies. At the federal level, these include the Department of Justice's Federal Bureau of Investigation (FBI) Academy, and DHS's Federal Law Enforcement Training Center and Emergency Management Institute. Numerous other federal departments and agencies also have education and training centers or programs. State governments (and many political subdivisions within states) operate law enforcement and fire academies. The curricula for virtually all these academies now address terrorism, particularly events involving WMD.

Finally, many private-sector companies and associations provide specialized education and training. Commonly, courses are offered to companies in the private sector, to train these companies' security forces and to educate corporate executives, particularly executives overseas, regarding the risks of kidnapping, assassination, and other forms of terrorism.

Historically, most academic institutions have been residential or, if not residential, have offered instruction only on campus. With the development of distance learning, however, nonresidential and off-campus education and training are increasing and are becoming more accepted within academe. These include regularly scheduled classes at remote sites, linked to the main campus by video-teleconferencing; and student-paced courses available online or in other electronic

media. Such methods can be particularly advantageous for continuing education, because the students may be working, may have
tight budgets, and may therefore be unable to enter a residential
program.

Outreach and Service

This aspect of academe is consistent with the general charter of most
public universities, particularly land-grant institutions. Colleges and
universities can be an important source of local expertise in many
areas of homeland security.[9] Many academic institutions routinely
provide—formally or informally—experts in homeland security as
consultants or advisors to state and local government agencies
responsible for homeland security. The present author is an advisor
to Ohio's Security Task Force, assisting its standing committees and
subcommittees, as well as the 18 state departments and agencies that
are represented on the committee; he also advises the committee
within the Ohio general assembly that is responsible for homeland
security.

Land-grant institutions also operate a university extension
system. Typically, university extension offices operate within most
counties in a state. These offices offer education, training, and technical assistance to individuals, government entities, business and
industry, and community groups. Recently, county extension agents
have been increasingly involved in promoting awareness of issues of
homeland security (e.g., agroterrorism) and providing education and
training materials and seminars related to risk-reduction strategies
and technologies.

In 2003, Ohio State University established the National
Academic Consortium for Homeland Security (NACHS) to foster
interest in homeland security within academe; to promote collaboration among academic institutions and individual scholars working in
this area; and to coordinate academic support for government
agencies and nongovernment organizations responsible for aspects
of homeland security. The public NACHS Web site[10] was established
to facilitate an exchange of information about academic programs
for research and development, education and training, and outreach
and service; it also provides a way to share information about current events, conferences, research opportunities, lessons learned, and
innovative benchmark programs in homeland security.

CHALLENGES, ISSUES, AND OPPORTUNITIES

This discussion of challenges, issues, and opportunities is as a summary. It is intended to be representative and illustrative, not all-inclusive.

Colleges and universities will continue to be potential targets of terrorism. While much progress has been made during the past few years, university and college campuses generally remain vulnerable. They are likely to be targeted by activist groups because of the nature of some academic research (e.g., research on animals). Providing more effective, cheaper security for major events on campuses (e.g., athletic events and concerts) will continue to be a challenge.

Major research universities can expect to work increasingly with biological select-agents and other hazardous materials, as more biodefense research and development are conducted. Funding the very expensive special laboratory facilities necessary to do such research safely is also likely to be a significant challenge, particularly when the budgets of public institutions are constrained. Citizens concerned about community safety are likely to oppose potentially hazardous biodefense research and the construction of the laboratory facilities for it.

Many academic programs, particularly in the physical sciences, mathematics, and engineering, have historically relied on a significant proportion of foreign students. This trend is due to several factors, including a declining interest in these disciplines among American students and a tendency for American businesses and industries to export many high-tech operations (and jobs) to foreign countries, where related products and services are cheaper. Consequently, research on homeland security in these disciplines also depends on foreign graduate students and faculty members. But increased controls on visa application and processing procedures are dramatically reducing the number of foreign students in the United States. This trend is exacerbated by an international rivalry for top students and by a fear on the part of some foreign students that they will be persecuted at American institutions because of their ethnicity or religion.

Because much of the research done at universities will be essential for national security, there will be increasing pressure to keep the results of sensitive research out of the hands of potential terrorists. This conflicts with academic openness and is not a new problem (as the National Research Council has noted[11])—it always arises in wartime, and the global war on terrorism is no exception. There will be a need for careful analysis and assessment of the information involved and of what constraints will least impair the process and progress of research while still protecting sensitive information.

There is also a need for collaboration on research, development, education, and training related to homeland security. This includes collaboration among scholars in different disciplines; collaboration among academic institutions doing similar, related, or complementary work; and collaboration among researchers in academe, in national laboratories, and in the private sector. Collaboration has traditionally been facilitated by professional societies and associations, academic and professional publications, and informal networking. Several consortia related to homeland security have recently been established. NACHS is one example; in August 2004, its membership included more than 150 colleges and universities.

CONCLUSION

The homeland security environment is dynamic, changeable, and uncertain. Thus academe will need to stay abreast of many new requirements, organizations, disciplines, and professions. Keeping up to date is likely to remain a challenge for the foreseeable future, but the challenge must be met if research, technology development, education, training, and outreach are to remain relevant.

Universities that have tended to focus on basic research will need to consider giving more attention to applied research, technology transition, and specific recommendations for better-informed national security policy and strategy. Academe and the private sector are both under pressure to "turn science into solutions" as quickly as possible. Such pressure frequently comes from agencies that fund homeland security: e.g., DHS's Homeland Security Advanced Research Projects Agency (HSARPA).

Externally funded academic research in homeland security is largely requirements-driven and shaped by the availability and allocation of grants. However, both academe and the funding agencies need to pay some attention to opportunities for technology push—the notion that new and emerging technologies might well have applications for homeland security not previously envisioned by the responsible operational units.

Regarding education in homeland security, perhaps the most important challenge for academe is preparing students to be better-informed, responsible citizens. The primary responsibility for this education in citizenship should fall to the secondary schools, whose graduates are of or nearing voting age and need to be adequately informed on the issues. But postsecondary schools, particularly public institutions, should also offer courses and seminars in citizenship and homeland security early in the curriculum.

Colleges and universities should continue to develop a wide range of education and training in homeland security, especially in homeland security as a career. This includes education and training for students who have not yet entered the workforce, continuing technical and professional education for practitioners, and transition training to help individuals move into related careers and professions. Undergraduate and graduate degree programs, as well as certificate programs, are appropriate.

Academe also needs to address team education and training. Preparing for, responding to, and recovering from terrorism involves multifunctional, multi-institutional, and multijurisdictional teams. Currently, much team training and evaluation is done through national, state, and local scripted exercise programs. However, there is also a growing need for other types of programs, in which concepts, policies, and procedures can be taught and learned before an exercise is evaluated.

State university extension programs have been established to make education and training available statewide, generally through a network of extension agents located in counties. Historically, extension programs have focused on agriculture, natural resources, family and community programs, and economic development. Recently, most extension programs have also begun to address homeland security, particularly agroterrorism. These extension systems offer a well-developed capability to deliver homeland security education and training to individual citizens and teams.

Homeland security is not yet a recognized profession; nor does it have a generally accepted common body of knowledge that would establish it as an academic discipline. Although universities and colleges are starting to offer undergraduate and graduate programs leading to degrees in homeland security, these programs vary greatly in content and emphasis, and the degrees are unlikely to be widely recognized until standard curricula have been developed. Standardization will probably be a protracted process, lasting a decade or more. Meanwhile, the focus will probably be on creating a major in homeland security or areas of concentration within more traditional disciplines and degree programs.

Progress toward homeland security as an academic discipline is likely to be paced by the development of homeland security as a recognized profession. Both the discipline and the profession would be multidisciplinary, requiring some competence in several areas. Their development could be accelerated if, for example, DHS established a cadre or corps of homeland security professionals within its ranks, requiring standards-based certification. Once the standards for certification were established at the federal level, state and local government agencies, as well as the private sector, would probably follow DHS's lead and adopt the same or similar standards and certification process.

Funding for academic programs in homeland security will continue to be a challenge. Public institutions of all types have been receiving less funding, so that they have had to raise their tuition and decrease their programs. Academic institutions must increasingly rely on external funding, particularly for research and for new programs. However, federal funding for homeland security has increased (for example, federal funding for research in biodefense, primarily through the Department of Health and Human Services, has more than doubled), and there has been an expectation that some of these funds would become available for related academic research, education, and training. Still, although the annual budget for DHS is about $40 billion, only about $1 billion is allocated to science and technology—and much of that is for applied research at the national laboratories and in the private sector. Relatively little funding has been allocated to basic research, the traditional focus of academic researchers.

Funding to support education and training in homeland security is available from several sources. Federal block grants to states and cities are available for planning, purchasing new equipment, and training (primarily training of people in law enforcement and fire protection, and other first responders). DHS's Office of Domestic Preparedness manages this grant program. Current policy requires that at least 80 percent of the funding allocated to a state is to be reallocated to local governments. This funding has stimulated many academic institutions, particularly community colleges, to develop new programs and courses focused on these training requirements. By contrast, no comparable federal funding has yet been allocated to support the development of homeland security education programs.

N O T E S

1. *National Strategy for Homeland Security*, Office of Homeland Security, White House, July 2002.
2. Ibid.
3. S. Jaschik, "Homeland Security and the American Campus," *Priorities, Association of Governing Boards*, No. 23 (Spring 2004).
4. National Research Council, "Making the Nation Safer: The Role of Science and Technology in Countering Terrorism" (Washington, D.C.: National Academy Press, 2002).
5. Ibid.
6. B. S. Bloom, *Taxonomy of Educational Objectives: The Classification of Educational Objectives* (New York: McKay, 1965).
7. E. J. Simpson, "The Classification of Educational Objectives in the Psychomotor Domain," in *The Psychomotor Domain*, Vol. 3, (Washington, DC: Gryphon House, 1972), pp. 43–56.
8. www.training.fema.gov/emiweb/edu/.
9. National Research Council, "Making the Nation Safer."
10. www.homelandsecurity.osu.edu/NACHS.
11. National Research Council, "Making the Nation Safer."

CHAPTER 56

Considering a New Paradigm for Strategic Studies

Commander Joseph E. Vorbach III, Ph.D.
Associate Professor of International Relations and Director,
Marine Transportation System Initiative,
U.S. Coast Guard Academy

Patrick N. Newman, J.D.
Program Manager, Marine Transportation System Initiative,
U.S. Coast Guard Academy

INTRODUCTION

Strategic studies in homeland security education programs that prepare leaders to design and implement national policy must be responsive to an ever-evolving environment of threat. Curricula must include classical foundations, emerging literature, and case studies that force students to address current challenges and forecast future threats and responses. Perhaps of greatest importance, these programs should be available to a diverse student body, including all who will become leaders in their communities and fields. The right students intermingled in robust residential programs will yield more leaders, across all levels of government, who are prepared to adapt flexibly to strategic conditions in a changing world.

At present in the United States, programs that even begin to address the needs outlined above are new and tentative and do not yet reflect a comprehensive discourse between those offering the programs and those who need graduates with the skills the programs

---

Note: The views expressed in this chapter are those of the authors and do not necessarily reflect the official position of the Coast Guard or the Department of Homeland Security.

provide. However, pieces of a puzzle that when assembled would represent an optimal array of strategic studies programs are in place. For example, the senior service schools of the Department of Defense (DOD) bring some of the right people together to study threats and responses; and the curricula these schools have been offering in the years after the Cold War have increasingly included the study of asymmetrical and transnational security threats. In an effort that is perhaps most reflective of a nationwide quest for new approaches in a transformed threat environment,[1] the Naval Postgraduate School, with principal support from the Department of Homeland Security (DHS), has been offering a master's program in homeland security that includes students from the federal, state, and local levels of government, including a small cadre of military officers. There are other programs as well, but it is not yet clear whether or not they are aligning actors and curricula optimally.

Without diminishing the "value added" of existing programs that prepare military officers to contribute to the formulation of grand strategies, there is a need for strategic studies in homeland security programs that will parallel the classic approaches of war colleges, cross-pollinate with them, and most importantly support the development of talent pools across a wider array of expertise at all levels of government to inform the making of national security policy. This need might ultimately be filled by a combination of public and private programs, but in any event the need must be filled.

BROADENING THE DEFINITION OF SECURITY AND STRATEGIC STUDIES

The argument for strategic studies that incorporate the new dynamics of the post-9/11 environment is an extension of debates in the field of security studies that have been under way for at least two decades, especially in the period following the Cold War. In 1983, Richard Ullman analyzed security studies by beginning with the assumption that "defining national security merely (or even primarily) in military terms conveys a profoundly false image of reality."[2] At a time during the Cold War when tension between the United States and the Soviet Union was particularly intense, Ullman drew attention to the possibility that a narrow definition of security might cause states to ignore nontraditional threats. He proposed a new definition of security that would consider a threat as any:

> ...action or sequence of events that (1) threatens drastically and over a relatively brief span of time to degrade the quality of life for the inhabitants of a state, or (2) threatens significantly to narrow the range of policy choices available to the government or a state or to private, nongovernmental entities (persons, groups, corporations) within the state.[3]

The dramatic changes in the international system that ensued with the end of the Cold War prompted further lively debate among scholars[4] and practitioners[5] about the changing security environment. These discussions, in some cases, pitted traditionalists who sought to limit the scope[6] of what would be considered a threat to security against commentators who took a broader view.[7]

Today, the debate over security studies spans a spectrum that includes a growing literature in global and human security,[8] but the argument presented here rests within the more traditional concepts of national and international security. That is, for the foreseeable future, the security "landscape" will be shaped by the manner in which nation-states, individually and collectively, work to protect themselves from internal and external threats. Richard Betts's model[9] sees military science as the innermost of three concentric rings, so that it is surrounded by strategic studies, which are in turn surrounded by security studies. This chapter takes this model as a starting point but argues that the innermost ring can no longer be constituted of military science alone. Further, the strategic-studies ring must be expanded to consider the relationship between a new, broader core of relevant preparedness and response sciences and the world of variables affecting national and international security—the outer ring. In the new model, classic (DOD-oriented) strategic studies would remain an element of the inner ring, but would be joined by the offerings of other programs that provide avenues for other leaders in entities related to homeland security to prepare for their future as shapers of national security strategy. See Figure 56-1.

The critical question that emerges from the construction of the new model is how people with backgrounds in relevant fields of homeland security science will receive opportunities to develop and apply their skills in strategic thinking for the benefit of the nation. Developments since the formation of the Department of Homeland

F I G U R E   56-1

Two models for strategic studies.

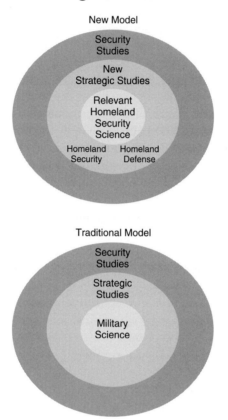

Security (DHS) in early 2003 suggest that the question has not yet been adequately addressed.

THE EMERGING ARCHITECTURE OF HOMELAND SECURITY EDUCATION

On 25 November 2002, President George W. Bush signed into law the Homeland Security Act of 2002. This act, which constitutes the foundation of the nation's evolving homeland security architecture, created the cabinet-level DHS by combining 22 federal agencies and programs with over 170,000 employees and an annual budget of approximately $40 billion.

In addition to organizational and operational changes, the act mandates significant training and education requirements. These requirements assume a high degree of interagency collaboration and integration. However, the act does not mandate a comprehensive, coordinated process or mechanism for achieving the level of education or types of educational programs that are required to carry out the missions of DHS. Nor does the act mandate the creation of high-level strategic decision-making education programs for senior managers and administrators. The prime focus is on training and education at operational levels (e.g., training "first responders"). Section 312 does authorize the establishment of a "Homeland Security Institute." However, the institute will report to the undersecretary for Science and Technology, is authorized for only three years, and has been outsourced to the private sector.

The creation of DHS instituted a structure parallel to DOD with a mandate to protect the homeland. In the White House, a homeland security advisor has functions related to homeland security that parallel those of the national security advisor. All these architectural changes suggest at least some distinctions between those who will be involved in homeland security and those who will be involved in homeland defense. Notwithstanding the difficulty of delineating what is properly one or the other, it seems clear that while traditional defense missions remain critical, there is an emerging spectrum of unique homeland security challenges. Within that spectrum, even the best and the brightest of an array of federal, state, and local personnel do not have the opportunities for strategic study that are afforded to their counterparts in the military.

A WAY FORWARD THROUGH NEW CHALLENGES

There are certain obstacles to the implementation of a strategic studies program that would do for DHS what the war colleges have done and continue to do for DOD. Cataloguing these challenges is a useful exercise that points toward the most sensible ways of proceeding over the next several years.

The first challenge is a collection of bureaucratic cultures that does not have a history of investing as lavishly as the military in the development of their best and brightest. There is a dedicated homeland security workforce, but the United States provides it with little systematic preparation above agency-centric training and participation in university-based advanced degree programs that provide, in most cases, knowledge germane to the employees' specific work. Except for modest assistance with tuition, the cost of obtaining an advanced degree is borne by the individual. In most circumstances, civilian agencies are not given the same flexibility as their military counterparts, simply because of a lack of resources—and because agency heads and members of Congress have entirely different expectations. Members of Congress tend to insist that if they give you five billets for something, they want to see five people actively working on that specific issue. A few extra billets, intended for training, are usually allocated, but when budget cuts and downsizing are going on, these billets are usually the first to go and the last to be reinstated.

A second challenge is that whereas students in the war college programs have with few exceptions been military officers employed by the federal government, the best combination for strategic studies in homeland security programs will include federal, state, and local functionaries (and ideally also some private-sector and international students[10]). State and local governments as well as other civic groups crucial to homeland security face multifaceted challenges. State and local governments face budget shortfalls; and though they are likely to recognize the inherent value of a strategic studies program made available to their employees, they will also be gauging the federal commitment. Facing tight budgets and deficits, and without federal assistance and guidance, these important communities will not be able to participate to the extent desirable.[11] Thus fiscal realities are likely to dictate the means by which homeland security strategic studies are delivered.

A third possible obstacle to the effective development of strategic studies in homeland security programs is the level of homeland security education and training taking place in the public and private domains. Though this is a daunting challenge, there is much to be gained for all concerned from an effort by DHS, working with the many people interested in the process, to speak to academe about what it seeks in strategic studies programs. All the programs that already provide opportunities for strategic studies, or that might provide such opportunities in the future, can be valuable partners in joint efforts, which should be begun immediately. In all likelihood, there is room for everyone at the table, especially if the objective—producing more leaders at all levels of government who can contribute to making better national security policy—is kept in the forefront.

Finally, some people are concerned that DHS is pursuing nationwide uniformity in a manner that jeopardizes academic freedom and might stifle innovation. DHS and its partners may need to reassure those who feel this concern. It will be important over the next several years for DHS to make clear that it seeks only to be part of the process of developing templates for programs and to ensure that academe understands what it wants its most promising future leaders to take away from a strategic studies program.

A rigorous, sequential, progressive program of professional strategic studies in homeland security is essential. Bolstering the knowledge and skills that are needed today is not enough; failure to look to the future will invite operational ineffectiveness and strategic stagnation. Despite the existence of sophisticated models of U.S. military education, there is no crosscutting, parallel degree-granting advanced education program within DHS. This notional program must be pulled together soon, and it must consist of at least three parts: (1) new curricula that acknowledge the fundamental changes in the global security environment and place a high value on inter-disciplinary study; (2) a newly structured program that takes into account the most massive reorganization of the federal government since the National Security Act of 1947; and (3) a new means of delivery that includes the progressive introduction and promotion of a culture of strategic thinking and renewal.[12] Given the challenges of the new security environment and the importance of senior-level participation and leadership, the most important initial target for this new educational program must be the executive level.[13]

What can DHS do? It is true that senior and midlevel leaders within DHS and across agencies face immense operational pressures; it is also true that trying to take a long view while managing day-to-day operations is inherently difficult. Nevertheless, the importance of establishing a coherent system of progressive education cannot be overstated. To begin with, DHS should make efforts in the near term to sponsor discussions with a wide array of potential contributors to the debate on strategic studies in homeland security.[14] DHS should be seen as being at the forefront, keenly interested in the learning that is taking place in the member institutions of homeland security academic consortia[15] and in the unique academic centers[16] that emerged during the past two decades in efforts to understand new threats. Perhaps slightly farther into the future, particularly as DHS begins to arrive at more definite plans for organizing itself regionally, the secretary might consider using his authority under Section 308 of the Homeland Security Act of 2002[17] to establish regional Centers of Excellence in Strategic Studies. These centers might become hubs that can receive leaders from across government for joint study of the homeland security environment while concurrently supporting smaller and potentially mobile programs that reach even farther into communities. Above all else, DHS should begin as soon as possible to speak with one voice about the need for programs that will develop the leaders of the future in the field of homeland security.

While much shaping remains to be done and many approaches merit consideration, strategic studies in homeland security programs must have as their objective, among other things, the development in emerging leaders of the ability to:

- Analyze comprehensively national and international trends (political, economic, social, and legal) and quickly identify threats and opportunities
- Understand and function effectively in a fluid interagency environment
- Apply a civil-military lens in the analysis of threats, when appropriate
- Think and act dynamically in both the strategic and the tactical sense
- Do all this with a sensible appreciation of organizational, fiscal, and political constraints and opportunities

In the future, an ideal approach to developing such leaders might be phased as follows.

Basic Program

A basic program, offered initially and primarily for DHS employees and interagency participants, would cover:

- Knowledge of DHS's organization
- Knowledge of national homeland security architecture to include interagency and state or local roles and responsibilities

- Knowledge of homeland security strategy and tactics
- Knowledge of transnational and national threats

Intermediate Program

A five- to six-month intermediate program, designed to develop more advanced knowledge, could include distance learning and internships. The intermediate program could enhance employees' functional knowledge of the directorate, the staff, and existing links to stakeholders and partners. This program would also include more sophisticated learning of homeland security organization and interagency–joint military operations and tactics.

Advanced Program

During an advanced learning program, modeled on the approaches of war colleges and the Foreign Service Institute, senior leaders moving toward greater responsibility would learn advanced concepts essential to the development of a strategic view and the ability to make executive decisions.

A core curriculum for this phased approach, particularly in the second and third phases, should include the study of:

- Resource optimization and management
- Classic national security and international relations—theory and practice
- Intergovernmental, interagency, joint military tactics, operations, and strategy
- Interfaces between science and technology on the one hand and policy on the other
- Intelligence sharing and information management
- Organizational behavior and cultural understanding
- Harmonization of military and interagency policy
- International and transnational threats and comparative responses
- Strategic and scenario-based (futures) planning
- Risk-based decision making
- Social and legal characteristics

The advanced phase should also include a program for research on senior management exchange programs that would allow an emerging leader to study another organizational culture and write about the experience. Finally, the advanced program should have, as a shared capstone experience, an operational crisis practicum.

CONCLUSION

Though ambitious, such a program is achievable. Planners in DHS and outside can take heart for at least two reasons: (1) similar programs undertaken during the Cold War have endured and continue to be seen as essential to the success of the Defense[18] and State[19] departments;[20] and (2) numerous public and private entities are already providing pieces of the puzzle described above. DHS can play an essential role in shaping an emerging program by funding its executive development programs, which take advantage of the best practices and offerings of people in the public and private sectors— such people are arrayed across the country. One can envision the accomplishment of various pieces of the program described as public entities such as the Federal Law Enforcement Training Center, the Emergency Management Institute, the Center for Domestic Preparedness, the Naval Postgraduate School, and the U.S. Coast Guard Academy. Meanwhile, the other objectives are achieved at private centers of excellence. Such an approach is certainly an organizational challenge, but it will encounter fewer bureaucratic roadblocks and will ensure the optimal use of existing facilities and programs. DHS must play a role in ensuring that strategic studies programs in homeland security are developed in a timely way without bureaucratic turf wars.

N O T E S

1. For an overview of the ongoing transformation in DOD, see Arthur K. Cebrowski, "Transformation and the Changing Character of War," *Officer* (July–August 2004).
2. Richard H. Ullman, "Redefining Security," *International Security* 8:1 (Summer 1983): 129.
3. Ibid., p. 133.
4. See, e.g.: Netta Crawford, "Once and Future Security Studies," *Security Studies* 1 (Winter 1991). Stephen M. Walt, "The Renaissance of Security Studies," *International Studies Quarterly* 35 (June 1991). Helga Haftendorn, "The Security

Puzzle," *International Studies Quarterly* 35 (March 1991). Joseph S. Nye, Jr., and Sean M. Lynn-Jones, "International Security Studies: A Report of a Conference on the State of the Field," *International Security* 12:4 (Spring 1988): 5–27. Peter Andreas and Richard Price, "From Warfighting to Crime Fighting: Transforming the American National Security State," *International Studies Review* 3:3 (Fall 2001): 31. Andreas and Price note a "growing gap between traditional security concepts and paradigms and the contemporary practice of security."

5. U.S. General Accounting Office (GAO), "Drug Control: Assets DOD Contributes to Reducing the Illegal Drug Supply Have Declined," GAO/NSIAD-00-9 (21 December 1999). This report confronts the issue faced by a defense department with a continually widening array of obligations related to nontraditional threats.

6. See Lawrence Freedman, "International Security: Changing Targets," *Foreign Policy* (Spring 1998): 53. Freedman articulated the concern of traditionalists: "Once anything that generates anxiety or threatens the quality of life in some respect becomes labeled a 'security problem' the field risks losing all focus."

7. See Marc A. Levy, "Is the Environment a National Security Threat?" *International Security* 20:2 (Fall 1995). See also Erik K. Stern, "The Case for Comprehensive Security," in Daniel H. Deudney and Richard A. Matthew (eds.), *Contested Grounds: Security and Conflict in the New Environmental Politics* (Albany: State University of New York Press, 1999), pp. 135–142.

8. See, e.g., Peter J. Katzenstein, *The Culture of National Security: Norms and Identity in World Politics* (New York: Columbia University Press, 1996). See also Keith Krause and Michael C. Williams (eds.), *Critical Security Studies: Concepts and Cases* (Minneapolis: University of Minnesota Press, 1997).

9. Richard K. Betts, "Should Strategic Studies Survive," *World Politics* 50 (October 1997): 9.

10. Although the term *homeland security* seems to be associated with the United States since 9/11, the lessons learned from the efforts of other nations must be a component of a robust program of strategic studies in homeland security.

11. Fiscal realities may require the augmentation of a full residential program with a combination of distance-learning approaches, a relaxation of residential requirements. A shorter "command and staff" program attended by midlevel leaders may be an appropriate, albeit incremental, strategy.

12. One example of an effort to institute strategic renewal in a public organization is the U.S. Coast Guard's Evergreen Project, which focuses on scenario-based planning and the ability to know, shape, create, manage, and position an organization for future success.

13. DHS has developed prototype courses that bring mid- and senior-level leaders together for, among other things, team building and analysis of shared challenges. These programs should be expanded and established more formally.

14. Doing so will be consistent with "DHS Strategic Plan—Securing Our Homeland," which includes the strategic goal of organizational excellence and sets out to create a leadership development curriculum for all department executive managers and supervisors.

15. For example, the Web sites of the National Academic Consortium for Homeland Security at http://homelandsecurity.osu.edu/NACHS/ and the Northern Command Homeland Security/Defense Education Consortium at www.hsdec. org/ (accessed 13 September 2004).

16. See, e.g., Center for Unconventional Security Affairs at the University of California-Irvine, www.cusa.uci.edu (accessed 14 September 2004); Matthew B. Ridgway Center for International Security Studies at the University of Pittsburgh, www.umc.pitt.edu/media/pcc020211/ridgwayctr.html (accessed 14 September 2004); and Transnational Crime and Corruption Center at American University, www.american.edu/traccc/ (accessed 13 September 2004).

17. 6 USC 188, Public Law 107–296, 25 November 2002, Sec. 308. Conduct of research, development, demonstration, testing, and evaluation. (c) Discretion of secretary.—The Secretary shall have the discretion to establish such centers and to consider additional criteria as necessary to meet the evolving needs of homeland security."

18. See David McIntyre, Ph.D., Deputy Director of ANSER Institute for Homeland Security, "Education for Homeland Security—The Critical Need," *ETS News* (Winter 2002—2003), at www.homelandsecurity.org/hlscommentary/ Education_for_Homeland_Security.htm (accessed 29 August 2004). Few civilians grasp the breadth and sophistication of the U.S. military education program. In contrast to the lack of a nationally accredited or DHS-administered advanced homeland security education program, the U.S. war colleges grant master's degrees and require graduate-level work. The most promising military officers frequently receive up to three years of full-time resident attendance in civilian master's or Ph.D. programs. The average midlevel army officer working on plans and budgets in the Pentagon has three to five equivalent years of postgraduate study—a Ph.D. program's worth of postgraduate schooling in his field. A general devotes a quarter of his career to formal preparation for his position.

19. The nine-month State Department Senior Service seminar, established by President Eisenhower in 1958 and constructed on an interagency teamwork model, should also be considered among the useful examples from the Cold War period.

20. See Captain Robert G. Ross and Commander Peyton M. Coleman, "The Way Forward: Education and Jointness in Homeland Security—Learning from the Department of Defense," *Journal of Homeland Security* (May 2003), at www. homelandsecurity.org/journal/articles/displayArticle.asp?article=90 (accessed 13 September 2004). See also Michael E. Doyle and Greg Stump, "Why We Need a Homeland Security University," *Homeland Defense Journal* (December 2003): 22–7.

CHAPTER 57

Decision Models for Emergency Response Planning

Richard C. Larson
Professor of Civil and Environmental Engineering and of Engineering Systems, Massachusetts Institute of Technology

Operations research (OR), born in World War II, has for 65 years proved invaluable as an empirical science and a technology for decisions and planning. OR uses the scientific method to assess the consequences of alternative decisions involving long-term strategic planning and shorter-range tactics and operations. Since a decision can be viewed as an allocation of resources, OR is the science of resource allocation. In World War II OR was applied successfully in (for instance) finding optimal locations for new, expensive radar installations in Great Britain and in optimal search theory—the deployment of aircraft and ships in search of enemy submarines.[1] The latter was deemed so important that the original papers by Bernard Koopman remained classified for 15 years. Today OR is ideally suited for evaluating and guiding our operational strategies and actions with regard to large-scale emergencies: terrorism, natural disasters (e.g., earthquakes, floods, tornadoes, hurricanes), and industrial accidents. After World War II, OR was widely applied in the civilian sector,

Note: This research was supported by the U.S. Department of Homeland Security through the Center for Risk and Economic Analysis of Terrorism Events (CREATE). The work was conducted through a subcontract from CREATE at the University of Southern California to Structured Decisions Corporation, West Newton, Massachusetts. For helpful comments on an earlier draft, the author thanks Andrea Allocca (New York Fire Department), Linda Green, Peter Kolesar, Lawrence Wein, Gang Yu, and David Kamien.

by private companies and nonmilitary government entities; collectively, costs of operations have been reduced by billions of dollars in this sector and the quality of services provided has improved significantly. Most Fortune 500 companies have used OR in long-, medium-, and short-term decision making. The U.S. Postal Service has used OR extensively in designing routes and a national distribution network, and in scheduling personnel. New York City used OR successfully for 30 years and accordingly created a permanent OR group within its Office of Management and Budget. The military has its Military OR Society with 3,000 members (who must have a security clearance to attend meetings).

OR is found in many unexpected places. The New England Patriots' coach Bill Belichick uses OR for football. In 2003, with the ball on the Patriots' side of the 50-yard line, on a fourth down and with 1 yard to go, he went for a first down—a decision that was contrary to what 90 percent of coaches in the NFL would have done but was supported by some 30 pages of sophisticated "Bellman equation" OR analysis by a professor at UC Berkeley.[2] The decision proved correct: the first down was achieved and the team continued to a touchdown (and later that season to a victory in the Super Bowl). Although a football game and a terrorist attack are very different situations, this example shows that OR can inform and transform decisions in the gritty complexity of the real world. OR, like electrical or mechanical engineering, is not just an academic discipline; it has numerous substantial benefits for large and small organizations, and this type of down-to-earth practical science is needed to confront the many challenges of emergency response planning and operation. (As will be discussed below, that is why OR was so valuable to New York City's firefighters on 9/11.)

The methods of OR are any part of the scientific method that sheds light on the problem at hand. Usually, though not always, mathematics is involved. A mathematical model of a system or problem is created, tested, refined, and then implemented on a computer. Next, the OR analyst runs the model under alternative assumptions, leading to optimal or near-optimal system configurations or decisions. But some famous OR studies have involved no mathematics at all, using only clever applications of common sense that led to insightful redefinitions of the problems.

Response to a major emergency requires careful planning and professional execution. Decisions involve the movement (deployment) of people, equipment, and supplies; and the development of operational policies once the people and materiel are in place. OR is nearly perfect for creating better plans for responding to emergencies and designing better operational policies when rescue efforts are under way.

This chapter reviews selected OR work in emergency response. Some of this work is recent and aimed directly at homeland security issues; but most of it has evolved over the past 50 years, motivated by other emergency applications, especially by first responders (police, fire, and emergency medical departments) in municipalities. Thus we are now building on a rich legacy of research and implementation, though only recently have we collectively refocused our energy on catastrophic events involving homeland security. The new threats posed by terrorists present new problems for OR analysts. In some ways, our situation today is analogous to that of Philip M. Morse, George Kimball, Bernard Koopman, and other OR pioneers at the beginning of World War II. There are numerous new OR-related problems to identify, frame, formulate, and solve. The end result should be the most rational deployment of our scarce national resources, so as to maximize lives saved and injuries averted if there is another terrorist attack, or in cases of human accidents and natural disasters.

For the purposes of this chapter, a major emergency is one in which the resources of local first responders are overstretched. An example is the influenza pandemic of 1918–1919,[3] when there were too few nurses, doctors, and other resources to care for the sick and dying. Historically, lack of timely responses to unfolding events and lack of disciplined management strategies have led to many unnecessary deaths. One goal of this chapter is to show that careful, systematic approaches to the operational problems associated with emergency response can lead to policies and procedures that maximize the effectiveness of the available resources, saving lives and minimizing injuries.

FIRST RESPONDERS: POLICE, FIRE, AND EMERGENCY MEDICAL SERVICES

Perhaps most relevant to emergency response planning are the 40 years of OR work focused on urban and municipal first responders: police, fire, and emergency medical forces. This work started with the Science and Technology Task Force of the President's Commission on Law Enforcement and Administration of Justice in 1966.[4] It led to the national implementation of the three-digit emergency number 911, and to a generation of research on OR emergency services. When New York City adopted its 911 system in 1970, managers discovered the usefulness and necessity of queuing theory in scheduling call takers. The original scheduling of personnel, without the benefit of OR analysis, yielded intolerable delays (30 minutes or more) on weekend evenings, with the callers hearing only an "electronic ringing sound." With OR analysis, rescheduling the existing personnel reduced the delays to within acceptable limits. The recommendations were fully implemented within 1 month of the study's completion.[5]

Queuing occurs when the available resources are not adequate to handle real-time demands; it is a type of rationing. Sometimes this rationing and its delays are deliberate, as with some private-sector call-in complaint centers. In a major emergency, queues are endemic and must be managed aggressively by using techniques such as prioritization and triaging. Triage classifies those who are injured into various categories and assigns each category a priority so that the highest priority is dealt with first; the objective is, given limited resources, to save as many lives as possible. Without triage, queues would grow boundlessly and few casualties could be treated quickly. Sometimes triage requires difficult decisions; for example, on 7 December 1941 at Pearl Harbor triage nurses decided against medical treatment other than morphine for those whose injuries seemed to be fatal. But such decisions may be the only way to direct scarce medical expertise to those whose lives can be saved. Modeling work on "cutoff priority queues" provides a methodology of setting priorities and predicting system performance under alternative triaging schemes.[6]

The present author was a member of the Science and Technology Task Force of the President's Commission and as a result of that work wrote a Ph.D. thesis on allocations of urban police patrols, which in turn culminated in a book[7] offering various OR models to examine police response times, patrolling patterns, new technologies (such as automatic vehicle locations systems), personnel scheduling, etc. This effort led to the "IRP project"—Innovative Resource Planning in Urban Public Safety Systems—a four-year research program (funded by the National Science Foundation) at the Massachusetts

Institute of Technology. The IRP project led to many graduate theses and computer-implemented models related to police and emergency medical operations and started the "public safety" OR careers of at least five doctoral students.[8]

The key model from the IRP project was "hypercube queuing." This is a detailed equation-based mathematical multiserver model of the spatial operation of urban police departments and emergency medical services.[9] It uses various analytical tools from the technical field known as stochastic processes and reflects the unscheduled nature of 911 calls by modeling them as a Poisson process. The service times of different servers (police patrol cars, ambulances) are uncertain (probabilistic) and have different average values, reflecting differing workloads and travel times. The hypercube model has been applied in designing police beats, choosing dispatcher cars, allocating patrol time, evaluating how automatic vehicle location systems reduce response time, etc.[10] By combining the spatial and temporal aspects of police and ambulance operations within one unified probabilistic framework, the hypercube model predicted the operational consequences of alternative police deployments over space and time and illustrated the inadequacy of some traditional beliefs about deployment.[11] It forecast a large number of interbeat dispatches of police cars (this was later verified in the field)[12] and showed that police cars may have an above-average workload even if their "own" beats have virtually no internally generated work. The hypercube queuing model has been implemented in New York City;[13] Boston, Massachusetts;[14] Hartford, Connecticut; Orlando, Florida; Dallas, Texas; Cambridge, Massachusetts; and elsewhere. In 1992 the Orlando police department redesigned the police beat layout of the entire city to create a new central city precinct.[15] Without the model, its planners would have had no scientific basis for making such a dramatic change; with the model, it could be confident that the new allocation would satisfy all performance standards.[16]

Various vendors have commercialized the hypercube model, but its full impact is impossible to determine because not all implementations have been documented in the open literature. For homeland security, the model is a promising way to guide response resources depleted by a major emergency. But the model needs to be generalized in order to include the impact of second- and third-tier responders from regional, state, and federal agencies, and of specialized responders such as HAZMAT and bioterrorism units. It also needs a time-dependent solution structure, with (potentially massive) data from the field. The author, with research colleagues at Structured Decisions Corporation of West Newton, Massachusetts, is building from the hypercube model a new deployment model for response to terrorist attacks and other large emergencies. The desired result is a model that will guide event managers in the dispatch and routing of heterogeneous responders on a regional interagency basis. The effort will also help local planners to identify and correct weaknesses in their response plans for major emergencies. This effort is part of the CREATE project at the University of Southern California, funded by the U.S. Department of Homeland Security (DHS).

In 1969 New York City commissioned the RAND Corporation of California to open the New York City Rand Institute (NYCRI), which assembled a team of analysts to examine a wide variety of operational problems there.[17] Its OR work on emergency services has won awards and stood the test of time; some of it is still the best available today. An example is NYCRI's fire department relocation model.[18] One large fire or several small fires in close geographic proximity will deplete the local firefighting resources. Most fire departments try to rebalance protection by temporarily moving some of the still available fire companies from more distant firehouses to firehouses left vacant by the busy companies, but this in turn creates new relative vacancies at the more distant firehouses, requiring reassignment of even more distant firefighters into the newly vacated firehouses. This wavelike process, if not carefully managed, can leave certain neighborhoods uncovered. There are literally hundreds of billions of ways to implement relocations, and no human can contemplate the consequences of each option and pick the best. But computer-implemented mathematical models such as NYCRI's relocation model are perfect for this job. NYCRI was shut down in 1975, when New York City had a budget crisis; but 30 years later its relocation model lived on in the city's fire department, and it was used to relocate firefighters on 9/11.[19] With the model, plus a "fallback 3" response strategy (meaning far less than usual number of units initially dispatched to an incident), the fire department kept its average response times to other, more routine fires at an average of 5.5 minutes, only about 1 minute above normal.

NYCRI's relocation methodology is most relevant in planning response to a terrorist attack. The attacks of 9/11 are an "existence proof." Any other terrorist attack is also likely to overwhelm nearby first responders, putting the entire city or region at risk, if resources are not managed carefully. In the event of a terrorist attack, according to Peter Kolesar of Columbia University, coinventor of the NYCRI relocation model:

> Several core principles underlying the NYFD version would probably be appropriate. First, solve the problem as it occurs rather than trying to plan in advance, since you probably cannot anticipate the dimensions of the attack and following crisis. Second, use some politically acceptable mathematical measure to define when coverage is inadequate and to evaluate alternative relocation options. Third, employ a computer-driven optimization algorithm to generate actual solutions. Fourth, allow the actual decision makers to modify or override the algorithm's suggestions.[20]

University students are becoming increasingly interested in research on emergency response. For example, Michael Metzger, a doctoral student at MIT, wrote a master's thesis on deployment of rescue and recovery resources in response to an earthquake.[21] He used data from the world's most earthquake-prone country, Iran, to illustrate the results of his OR analysis. Among other measures, his model predicts the number of hospital admissions and fatalities over the hours and days following the earthquake. The results are important, controversial, and counterintuitive; they depend on the response strategy or strategies selected, particularly when more than one community is damaged by the earthquake. Metzger shows that to save the maximum number of lives in all affected communities, it may be necessary to dispatch "local" responders from one community to a more distant community—where, say, 100 or more lives might be saved "at a cost" of saving fewer lives in the "home" community. Such sharing of resources may be politically difficult and would require considerable public education beforehand. Metzger's methodology (which in a published article) demonstrates how one can model the temporal allocation of resources following a catastrophe and thereby find ways to deploy personnel to save lives and reduce injuries.

This has been a sampling of the many OR contributions to analysis of first responders. (For additional details, see endnotes 8, 17, and 18. Also, the present author and a colleague have produced a summary book;[22] and there is prizewinning work on the scheduling of police personnel.[23]) The 40-year body of OR work on emergency response should be invaluable in building the next generation of emergency response models and methods, which will apply to terrorist attacks and to other major emergencies.

HAZARDOUS MATERIALS

Transporting hazardous materials on trains, trucks, and vessels exposes the public to risks of environmental catastrophes, and a terrorist attack on hazardous materials in transit obviously increases that risk. For example, there is much debate about using deep caves at Yucca Mountain in the Nevada desert for long-term storage of radioactive waste from nuclear power plants. Should that or another location be selected and operations started, there would be a huge transportation effort throughout the United States, hauling spent fuel rods and other radioactive wastes; and each city, town, village, or farm on a transportation route would be at risk of an accident and contamination.

Consequently, there have been OR studies of the routing and scheduling of hazardous materials, point to point on a transportation network such as the national railway system, so as to mitigate the risk, spread it equitably, or both. This work has shown that there are trade-offs between efficiency and equity.[24] The lowest total risk to the system is achieved by routing conveyances along the same path each time; but a more equitable policy uses various routes, with more people sharing the risk, at a modest increase in total risk. For nuclear waste, the routes are of course yet to be decided, but analyses suggest how efficiency and equity can be addressed in an integrated way.

Routing of hazardous materials so as to reduce risk is an example of "pre-event" OR analysis. By making improved decisions based on such analysis before a major emergency occurs, one can reduce the potential damage and sometimes even reduce the probability of the event itself.

BIOTERRORISM

Carefully planned detection of and response to bioterrorism are crucial to saving lives. This is a new area of concern and has only recently been the focus of OR analyses, but the work has been widely reported and influential nationwide. The developed models provide a consistent framework for considering operations following a bioattack. This work has changed our national policies regarding immunizations and medications following a bioterrorist attack.

With regard to a possible anthrax attack, Wein and Kaplan state:

> Two pounds of weapons-grade anthrax dropped on a large American city could result in more than 100,000 deaths, even if early cases were successfully diagnosed, antibiotics were distributed broadly and drug adherence was high. The reason for the catastrophic death toll: Not enough people would receive antibiotics quickly enough to prevent symptoms from developing, and those who developed symptoms would overwhelm the medical facilities.
>
> Any plan to cope with this scenario must include (1) immediate intervention, (2) rapid distribution of antibiotics to everyone in the affected region, (3) aggressive education to ensure adherence to the full course of treatment and (4) creation of "surge capacity" to treat the sudden influx of patients.[25]

Wein, Craft, and Kaplan[26] based their conclusions on a highly sophisticated set of mathematical models that included airborne anthrax dispersion, age-dependent dose-response, disease progression, and a set of spatially distributed two-stage queuing systems consisting of antibiotic distribution and hospital care. One of their most controversial recommendations is to have nonprofessionals disperse antibiotics very soon after an attack; or to have antibiotics in the hands of citizens at all times, prepositioned at the points of need; or both.[27] On the basis of these recommendations, the U.S. Postal Service has announced that its mail carriers will help to distribute antibiotics if a large attack occurs in the Washington, D.C., area.[28]

Kaplan, Craft, and Wein used OR methods to study response to a smallpox attack.[29] The initial federal policy had been to isolate the symptomatic victims, trace and vaccinate their contacts, quarantine others, and hope that the spread of disease could be limited by these measures. The OR analysis, again based on a highly complex but compelling set of models, indicated that this initial policy would result in many deaths. Instead, the analysis suggested a different response: as soon as the attack is recognized, undertake mass vaccination across the entire population. This recommendation caused quite a stir nationally—in the press and among physicians and policy makers—but now has been adopted as official U.S. policy.

OR is playing a major role in other aspects of medical response to emergencies. For instance, Linda Green has shown how usual measures of efficiency, defined in terms of hospital beds occupied, cause large queuing delays for beds even when demand is no more than routine; demands caused by a major emergency would overwhelm such hospitals.[30] With regard to policy, the conclusions of the work on anthrax and smallpox have been extended by Bravata et al. to regionalized or local stockpiling of drugs and response to bioterrorism.[31]

One can see the need for additional OR research on optimal locations for stockpiling drugs and equipment. Traditional location theory seeks global optimal solutions that minimize some measure of total system travel time or distance (see endnote 22). Usually, having a single facility or a few carefully positioned facilities can minimize travel time. In the locale of a major emergency, the traditional formulation of the problem may be inappropriate. Instead, one has to consider that some of the stockpile facilities may be destroyed by the emergency, or that paths leading from them may be damaged or inaccessible, or both. In such cases, one may want to have more than the usual number of facilities, each containing fewer medications and supplies, in order to increase the survivability of the system for distributing drugs and supplies. This version of the problem is somewhat similar to the p-dispersion location problem, where p is the number of facilities being dispersed. These issues are addressed in papers by Gong et al.[32] and Berman and Gavious.[33]

During a major bioterrorism event at one identified location or in one limited region, getting timely, appropriate medical care to those exposed is critical for their survival. One can imagine scenarios in which victims are first triaged, those identified as needing immediate transport are taken to nearby hospitals or other medical facilities, initial treatments are administered, and then many patients at the nearby hospitals are moved out to more distant locations—for unless there is such outward movement, the nearby hospitals will become queuing choke points and their own limited resources will be overwhelmed. The wavelike movement of patients out of nearby facilities to more distant ones is the reverse of NYCRI's model for relocating firefighters. Creating such hospital "surge capacity" (in the words of Kaplan and Wein) certainly warrants further research.

Effective responses by health care systems are essential to the total societal response to major events: terrorist attacks, natural disasters, and human-made accidents. These systems may have a large number of components; there may be many relevant factors; and the resulting interactions may be complex. Mathematical models are essential in order to understand all the complexities and trade-offs, ultimately leading to more informed decisions and allocations of scarce societal resources.

RESPONSES BY THE PRIVATE SECTOR

Emergency response is not limited to public-sector agencies. In a major emergency such as a terrorist attack, it is important for private firms whose operations have been interrupted by the emergency to resume normal operation as soon as possible. OR can play a role in that process.

There are few companies whose operations are more complex than those of airlines. With thousands of flights scheduled each day, the efficient matching of planes and crews to schedules and airports is an intricate, carefully choreographed optimization problem. When unplanned events occur, numerous decisions must be made. "Usual events" in the airline industry are "Chicago O'Hare closed by snow" or "Miami closed by a hurricane." These natural events are difficult enough to handle, as hundreds of flights and thousands of passengers may be affected; but imagine what happens when all planes are unexpectedly grounded, as happened on 9/11 to civilian airlines. Planes in the air on 9/11 were directed to land at nearby airports. At the end of the day, the planes and their passengers found themselves literally all over the country and even outside the country, often at locations far from the intended destinations. The situation of each airline was very far from what had been carefully planned. Yet, as described in award-winning work,[34] as a result of OR optimization Continental Airlines had the "best" recovery of any large airline in terms of percentage of delays and cancellations during the restart phase after the nationwide grounding of commercial aircraft. The computer-implemented OR methodology determined the least-cost sequence of decisions to get the airline up and flying again, consistent with the thousands of constraints dealing with matching crews to planes to which they are qualified, getting each plane back on schedule, adhering to maintenance schedules, obeying FAA's rules for maximum allowable flying times of crews, etc. Since then, many other airlines have adopted this proprietary OR methodology to ensure their swift recovery from major events.

The events of 9/11 affected many industries in addition to airlines. For instance, the mantra of "just-in-time" management of supply chains was abandoned on 9/11 because there was no redundancy or slack in just-in-time systems. Hundreds of trucks were lined up at the Canadian border on 12 September 2001, awaiting customs and immigration clearance before they could enter the United States. Thus factories in the United States began experiencing shortages of parts and supplies. This has led to a new type of supply-chain analysis, requiring robustness in case of emergencies and trading off just-in-time efficiencies with redundancies needed to maintain normal operations during a major event. This is another area for analytical, model-based approaches.

IMPLEMENTATION

Many of the models and methods discussed here are being used daily by first-responder emergency services throughout the United States. As noted, NYCRI's relocation model was used extensively and successfully by the fire department of New York City on 9/11. Private firms have implemented the methodologies discussed here and often extended them to real-time command and control systems, such as computer-aided dispatch systems and regional emergency management systems. The end user in such circumstances probably does not even know that "OR is inside" the computer programs. This is as it should be, just as the user of an Internet search engine such as Google does not care about the workings of the engine but cares only about the results. The final proof of the value of OR is the quality of the decisions made by those who use it.

Today, computer applications are inexpensive (relative to the past), and so we are seeing more and more databases being assembled that will assist the OR planner in preparation for emergency response. One of these is New York City's Citywide Assets and Logistics Management System (CALMS).[35] CALMS was set up for disaster response and is the only system in New York City that cuts across jurisdictional lines and retains knowledge of the whereabouts of supplies, equipment, and personnel from many different agencies. It is organized according to six asset types: (1) fleet, (2) equipment and supplies, (3) facilities, (4) contracts, (5) personnel, and (6) donated goods. CALMS automatically gets periodic uploads, to refresh its databases. And its spatially oriented data can be displayed on maps of the appropriate parts of the city via a Geographic Information System (GIS) mapping tool. Eventually we will see systems such as CALMS instilled with intelligent OR-based models and algorithms that would recommend the best movements of men, women, and materiel in response to an emergency. Also, OR may be included in the widely implemented "emergency incident management" systems, computer-based systems to coordinate the management of resources in emergencies; there is now an effort to standardize these nationally.[36]

The need for OR in homeland security is apparent. The U.S. Department of Homeland Security has job openings for professionals with OR training. New York City has hired such people. Even the taxicab system of New York City has sought such professionals, to interact with consultants who are examining the consequences of using GPS vehicle positioning technology for the taxis. OR professionals often have undergraduate degrees in electrical engineering, mechanical engineering, or computer science, so they can integrate technical engineering knowledge into the systems framework of OR.

Emergency services management is a new professional career. Emergency services managers may also be called emergency program managers or directors, operations center chiefs, and risk management experts. They coordinate equipment, emergency workers, and volunteers who move into action following a disaster. They make sure that government, volunteer, and medical personnel work together cohesively and effectively during an emergency. Knowledge of operations research is increasingly a job requirement.[37] Universities such as the University of Richmond (Virginia) offer certificates and degrees in emergency services management.

For many years, weather forecasts have exposed the public to the types of probabilistic analyses discussed here. We are all accustomed to hearing that "the probability of rain tomorrow is .4." Quantified uncertainty has become a part of our daily lives. As regards homeland security, the public is also aware of probabilities associated with hurricanes, particularly the time and place of landfall. Public preparedness for and response to hurricanes are important components of homeland security, because a hurricane of category 3, 4, or 5 in the United States certainly constitutes a major emergency as defined in this chapter. The analyses we have been discussing are used today to create a "probability risk profile" of approaching hurricanes and to make decisions about evacuations. Here additional

OR analyses may be valuable for the detailed planning of evacuations, to minimize false alarms and the consequent public apathy, and also to minimize the chance that evacuees could end up on congested roadways subject to local flooding. There is still much to do.

CONCLUSION

OR, the science and technology of aiding decisions, helped immensely in World War II. Today we face different threats—a new type of warfare described as asymmetrical. This creates a possibility of large-scale devastation similar to that caused by natural disasters and human accidents. Planning appropriate societal response to such large-scale emergencies can save many lives and reduce injuries. Hardware technology alone, without careful systems planning, is not enough; nor is there enough money in the public coffers to let us think that simply "throwing money" at a problem will solve it. OR offers a scientifically valid, integrated framework for considering all aspects of a problem and for assessing the consequences and trade-offs associated with alternative decisions. We expect to see many more results from OR in the years ahead, as the nation comes to grips with the new threats from terrorists and the old threats from nature and industrial accidents.

N O T E S

1. Philip M. Morse and George E. Kimball, *Methods of Operations Research* (Cambridge, Mass.: Technology Press, 1951); republished by Saul I. Gass (ed.) (New York: Dover, 2003).
2. David Lionardt, "Incremental Analysis, with Two Yards to Go," *New York Times* (1 February 2004). See also http://espn.go.com/nfl/columns/garber_greg/ 1453717.html.
3. John M. Barry, *The Great Influenza: The Epic Story of the 1918 Pandemic* (New York: Viking Penguin, 2004).
4. Alfred Blumstein et al., *Task Force Report: Science and Technology—A Report to the President's Commission on Law Enforcement and Administration of Justice, Prepared by the Institute for Defense Analyses* (Washington, D.C.: U.S. Government Printing Office, 1967).
5. Richard C. Larson, "Improving the Effectiveness of New York City's 911," in A. W. Drake, R. L. Keeney, and P. M. Morse (eds.), *Analysis of Public Systems* (Cambridge, Mass: MIT Press, 1972).
6. C. Schaack and R. C. Larson, "An N Server Cutoff Priority Queue," *Operations Research* 34:2 (1986): 257–66. C. Schaack and R. C. Larson,. "An N Server Cutoff Priority Queue Where Arriving Customers Request a Random Number of

Servers," *Management Science* 35:5 (1989): 614–34. In the following, we show how this would work with data from the Hartford, Connecticut, police department: Stephen R. Sacks, Richard C. Larson, and Christian Schaack, "Minimizing the Cost of Dispatch Delays by Holding Patrol Cars in Reserve," *Journal of Quantitative Criminology* 9:2 (1993): 203–24.

7. Richard C. Larson, *Urban Police Patrol Analysis* (Cambridge, Mass.: MIT Press, 1972).

8. Richard C. Larson, "Public Sector Operations Research: A Personal Perspective," *Operations Research* 50:1 (2002): 135–45.

9. Richard C. Larson, "A Hypercube Queuing Modeling for Facility Location and Redistricting in Urban Emergency Services," *Journal of Computers and Operations Research* 1:1 (1974): 67–95. Richard C. Larson, "Approximating the Performance of Urban Emergency Service Systems," *Operations Research* 23:5 (1975): 845–68.

10. Richard C. Larson and E. Franck, "Evaluating Dispatching Consequences of Automatic Vehicle Location in Emergency Services," *Journal of Computers and Operations Research* 5 (1978): 11–30.

11. Richard C. Larson, "Illustrative Police Sector Redesign in District 4 in Boston," *Urban Analysis* 1:1 (1974): 51–91.

12. Richard C. Larson, "Measuring the Response Patterns of New York City Police Patrol Cars." New York City Rand Institute R-673-NYC/HUD (1971).

13. Richard C. Larson and T. Rich, "Travel Time Analysis of New York City Police Patrol Cars," *Interfaces* 17:2 (1987): 15–20.

14. M. Brandeau and R. C. Larson, "Extending and Applying the Hypercube Queuing Model to Deploy Ambulances in Boston," in A. Swersey and E. Ignall (eds.), *Delivery of Urban Services* (New York: North Holland Press, 1986).

15. Stephen R. Sacks and Shirley Grief, "Orlando Magic: Efficient Design of Police Patrol Districts," *OR/MS Today* 21:1 (February 1994).

16. Richard C. Larson, "Hypercube Queuing Model," in Saul I. Gass and Carl M. Harris (eds.), *Encyclopedia of Operations Research and Management Science* (Boston, Mass.: Kluwer, 2001): 373–7.

17. L. V. Green and P. J. Kolesar, "Applying Management Science to Emergency Response Systems: Lessons from the Past," *Management Science* 50:8 (August 2004): 1001–14. P. Kolesar, "Ten Years of Research on the Logistics of Urban Emergency Services," in J. P. Brans (ed.), *Operational Research 1981* (New York: North Holland Press, 1982). P. Kolesar and A. Swersey, "The Deployment of Urban Emergency Units: A Survey," *TIMS Studies in Management Science* 22 (1985).

18. P. Kolesar and W. E. Walker, "An Algorithm for the Dynamic Relocation of Fire Companies," *Operations Research* 22:2 (March–April 1974): 249–74. W. Walker, J. Chaiken, and E. Ignall (eds.), *Fire Department Deployment Analysis* (New York: North Holland Press, 1979).

19. McKinsey Report, *Increasing FDNY's Preparedness*. See www.ci.nyc.ny.us/html/fdny/html/mck_report/index.shtml.

20. Peter Kolesar, personal communication, 10 and 17 August 2004.

21. Michael Metzger, "Formulating Earthquake Response Models in Iran." Master's thesis, Massachusetts Institute of Technology (2004).

22. Richard C. Larson and A. R. Odoni, *Urban Operations Research* (Englewood Cliffs, N.J.: Prentice Hall, 1981).

23. P. E. Taylor and S. J. Huxley, "A Break from Tradition for San Francisco Police: Patrol Officer Scheduling Using an Optimization-Based Decision Support System," *Interfaces* 19:1 (1989): 4–24.

24. Rajan Batta and Samuel S. Chiu, "Optimal Obnoxious Paths on a Network: Transportation of Hazardous Materials," *Operations Research* 36:1 (1988): 4–92. Oded Berman, Z. Drezner, and G. Wesolowsky, "A Routing and Location on a Network with Hazardous Threats," *Journal of the Operational Research Society* 51 (2000): 1093–9. Oded Berman, V. Verter, and Y. Bahar, "Designing Emergency Response Networks for Hazardous Materials Transportation," working paper, Rotman School of Management, University of Toronto (2004). Ram Gopalan, Krishna S. Kolluri, Rajan Batta, and Mark H. Karwin, "Modeling Equity of Risk in the Transportation of Hazardous Materials," *Operations Research* 38:6 (1990): 961–73. Honghua Jin, Rajan Batta, and Mark H. Karwin, "On the Analysis of Two Models for Transporting Hazardous Materials," *Operations Research* 44:5 (1996): 710–23.

25. Lawrence M. Wein and Edward H. Kaplan, "Unready for Anthrax," *Washington Post* (28 July 2003): A21.

26. Lawrence M. Wein, David L. Craft, and Edward H. Kaplan, "Emergency Response to an Anthrax Attack," *PNAS* 100:7 (1 April 2003): 4347–51.

27. Edward H. Kaplan, William J. Bicknell, and Lawrence M. Wein, "The Citizen as First Responder." Fox News (13 August 2003). See www.foxnews.com/story/0,2933,94665,00.html.

28. United States Postal Service, "U.S. Postal Service May Deliver Medicine in the Event of a Catastrophic Incident." News release no. 04-015 (18 February 2004).

29. Edward H. Kaplan, David L. Craft, and Lawrence M. Wein, "Emergency Response to a Smallpox Attack: The Case for Mass Vaccination," *PNAS* 99:16 (6 August 2002): 10935–40.

30. L. V. Green, "How Many Hospital Beds? *Inquiry* (Winter 2002–2003): 400–12. L. V. Green, "Capacity Planning in Hospitals," in *Handbook of Operations Research/Management Science Applications in Health Care* (New York: Kluwer Academic, 2004).

31. D. M. Bravata, K. McDonald, D. K. Owens, E. Wilhelm, M. L. Brandeau, G. S. Zaric, J.-E. C. Holty, H. Liu, and V. Sundaram, *Regionalization of Bioterrorism Preparedness and Response (Evidence Report/Technology Assessment)* (Rockville, Md.: Agency for Healthcare Research and Quality, 2003). G. S. Zaric, M. L. Brandeau, D. M. Bravata, J.-E. C. Holty, E. R. Wilhelm, K. M. McDonald, and D. K. Owens, "Modeling the Logistics of Response to Anthrax Bioterrorism," working paper, Stanford University (2004).

32. Qiang Gong, Arun Jotshi, and Rajan Batta, "Dispatching/Routing of Emergency Vehicles in a Disaster Environment Using Data Fusion Concepts," *Proceedings of the International Data Fusion Conference, Stockholm* (June 2004).

33. Oded Berman and A. Gavious. "Location of Bioterror Response Facilities: A Game between State and Terrorist," working paper, Rotman School of Management, University of Toronto (2004).

34. B. Thengvall, J. Bard, and G. Yu, "Multiple Fleet Aircraft Schedule Recovery Following Hub Closures," Transportation Research, Part A 35 (2001): 289–308. B. Thengvall, J. F. Bard, and G. Yu, "Balancing User Preferences for Aircraft Recovery during Airline Irregular Operations," *IIE Transactions on Operations Engineering* 32 (2000): 181–93. G. Yu, M. Arguello, M. Song, S. McCowan, and

A. White, "A New Era for Crew Recovery at Continental Airlines," *Interfaces* 33:1 (2003): 5–22.

35. See www.nyc.gov/html/oem/html/response/calms.html.

36. See www.dhs.gov/dhspublic/display?content=3259.

37. See www3.ccps.virginia.edu/career_prospects/briefs/E-J/EmergencyManage. html.

Science, Technology, and Information Sharing

Introduction to Section 11

Terry Janssen
Chief Technologist for Knowledge Management,
Lockheed Martin Corporation

Technology enables homeland security. Hardware, software, and human minds combine forces across the spectrum of processes and missions, from collecting intelligence to identifying people to monitoring vulnerable infrastructure. Although technology is critically important, it also presents a challenge. The technology used by the vast number of people, organizations, and systems involved in homeland security produces an astounding volume of information— geospatial intelligence data, multimedia, and text such as news and intelligence reports. The more technology is used, the more information is generated.

Processing and analyzing that information in order to predict, prevent, and respond to threats to homeland security, and then effectively sharing that information, present a huge challenge for knowledge management. Knowledge management is a process followed by organizations to (1) capture and share information, experience, expertise, and insights; (2) promote collaboration; and (3) provide broad access to the organization's information assets without regard to their source or structure. Technology supports knowledge management by fusing information from different systems; storing vast content; extracting information from text, voice, and images; integrating information into a knowledge layer; and sharing access to and visualizing that knowledge. Bureaucratic culture and procedures evolve much more slowly than technology.

The 9/11 Commission recognized this and ushered in the Intelligence Reform and Terrorism Prevention Act of 2004, which addresses this by mandating a new "information sharing environment" for intelligence. This environment will undoubtedly harness knowledge management technologies in order to effectively utilize the vast quantity of security-related information.

In Chapter 59 T. J. Allard and Nigel Hey describe the role of technology in combating terrorist threats. In Chapter 60 Fred Facemire and Mark Laustra describe the role of technology in improving checkpoint security. Gerald Metz in Chapter 61 discusses an architecture for sharing information. In Chapter 62 Don Adams presents two concepts central to intelligence technology (IT) in homeland security: sense and respond, and predictive response. In Chapter 63 David Kamien, Jean-Francois Cloutier, and Denis Ranger discuss a novel approach to information sharing needs analysis (ISNA) using peer-to-peer architecture and collaborative scenarios.

Science, Technology, and Terrorism

Thurman J. Allard
Director of Homeland Security, Sandia National Laboratories

Nigel Hey
Sandia National Laboratories

Science and technology are important in a coordinated, systematic approach to preventing terrorism, and in managing operations after a terrorist act. The collection and analysis of intelligence, aided by technology, are important in understanding how terrorism might be carried out and by whom. Also, technology is valuable in detecting terrorist activity and dealing with its consequences.

The systems and technology base supported by U.S. government agencies and private-sector companies is a source of support for homeland security directed against radiological, chemical, biological, and high-explosives threats and cyberterrorism.

The National Nuclear Security Administration (NNSA) laboratories and certain Federally Funded Research and Development Centers (FFRDCs) provide bridges between academic research, which focuses on physics, chemistry, and other scientific disciplines; and private-sector research and development (R&D), which is market-oriented. The NNSA laboratories do product-oriented research, but not the manufacturing or marketing phases. If technology developed at a national laboratory reaches the prototype stage—for example, the decontaminant foam developed at Sandia National Laboratories and used in the cleanup after the anthrax attacks—it will then be made available for license by the private sector.

TAXONOMY OF DEALING WITH A TERRORIST EVENT

A terrorist event has three overlapping chronological segments:

- *Prevention and detection:* Understanding the threat and vulnerability, detecting a motivation to use terrorist techniques, and detecting acquisition and storage of weapons. Intelligence and law enforcement are the primary keys to prevention. Intelligence analysis helps direct the requirements for technology that can facilitate prevention.
- *Interdiction and crisis management:* Intervention during the planning, acquisition, stockpiling, and deployment of the weapon.
- *Mitigation and consequence management:* Stopping or reducing effects of the attack, limiting the dispersal of toxic material, treating casualties, countering further exploitation of the situation by the perpetrator, and determining the identity of the perpetrator (attribution).

See Figure 59-1.

Technical thrusts may be described as understanding (continuing awareness) of the threat through gathering and assessing information, sensor systems, mitigation of effects, and training technology. *Response* involves detection and assessment of potential and actual terrorism, efforts to delay a terrorist act in order to provide additional response time, and countermeasures to neutralize the terrorist device and mitigate its effects. Several technologies and operations support response, including those applied in routine intelligence and law enforcement operations.

Detection and mitigation technology is now widely deployed throughout the United States. For example, at the Winter Olympics of 2002 in Salt Lake City, decontaminant foam was warehoused nearby, and NNSA technicians were operating a detection and laboratory program, Biological Aerosol Sentry and Information System (BASIS). There are several BASIS operations nationwide.

Anticipating and managing potential and actual terrorism require a systems approach, defined by the U.S. Army as "a logical process for effectively and efficiently planning which considers all elements of a system."[1] This involves "mapping" all aspects of threat and vulnerability, applying appropriate means of detection, knowing

F I G U R E   59-1

Homeland Security Technolgies

Threat/Phase	Prevention & deterrence *Prior to known terrorist activity*	Interdiction & crisis management *During movement/ storage/deployment*	Mitigation & consequence management *Following incident*
Chemical/ Biological	Vulnerability assessment Threat assessment Air-water supply monitoring Medical surveillance (i.e., RSVP, EARS) Predeployed detection systems (i.e., MicroChemLab., AURA) Port-of-entry monitoring	Quick-response technical backup teams Chem/bio sensor/alarm suites (i.e., PROTECT, BASIS, PROACT) Inspection/imaging systems	WMD "war gaming" training (i.e., WMD-DAC) Deployable decontaminants (i.e., decontamination foams) Explosives materials tagging (for attribution) Plume detection and modeling (i.e., ASPECT) Quick-response technical backup teams
Radiological/ Nuclear	Vulnerability assessment Threat assessment Port-of-entry monitoring Radiological materials security Nuclear nonproliferation protocols	Port-of-entry detector/ discriminators (i.e., Smart, RadScout) Large-area imagery Quick-response technical backup teams Pedestrian/vehicle detection portals	Plume modeling (i.e., Turbo-FRMAC-) radiological dose assessment Deployable decontaminant foams WMD "war gaming" training (i.e., WMD-DAC) Quick-response technical backup teams (i.e. NEST, RAP)
Explosive/ Fire	Vulnerability assessment Threat assessment Predeployed explosives detectors (i.e., portals)	Device disablement systems (i.e., PAN Disrupter) Containment foams Predeployed/hand-held explosives detectors Technical readiness training (i.e., Operation America)	Blast containment foams Architectural surety Blast-resistant building design/materials
Cyber	Vulnerability assessment Threat assessment Technical readiness training (i.e., SCADA Testbed) Anti-virus software	Statistical network traffic analysis Predictive systems (i.e., CIPHER) Use of Intelligence software agents Statistical network traffic analysis	Computer-assisted situation analysis/ management (i.e., NISAC) Adaptive network countermeasures Retrospective network traffic mapping (i.e. IOWA)

what to do if terrorism is detected (procedural guidelines or "conduct of operations"), and being ready to deal with an attack and its consequences.

Three examples of infrastructure protection illustrate the systems approach:

- *Ports*: These are part of the national transportation infrastructure. In 2002, the ports of Long Beach and Los Angeles formed a working group with the U.S. Coast Guard, U.S. Customs, and the maritime industry to implement Operation Safe Commerce. They contracted with Sandia National Laboratories to provide systems engineering oversight, technical project management, and support for planning, evaluating, installing, and testing security solutions and upgrades for them and for other ports and locations along the cargo path.

- *Transportation:* Numerous technologies exist within the transportation infrastructure for use along borders and at vehicular ports of entry, including traditional antismuggling technology and high-tech surveillance-detection systems derived from methods developed for securing nuclear reactors and weapon stockpiles. The R&D community is combining these and other technologies to develop a holistic, more easily manageable approach—"smart borders." Finding "bad" cargo among the good without slowing commerce is the main challenge. New sensor technologies are being evaluated; e.g., Sensor for Measurement and Analysis of Radiation Transients (SMART) was first deployed at the New York–New Jersey Port Authority.

- *Communications:* Critical infrastructures are maintained largely by computerized, networked supervisory control and data acquisition (SCADA) systems. Idaho National Engineering and Environmental Laboratory and Sandia National Laboratories offer infrastructure protection, including engineering solutions, vulnerability studies, training, test bed facilities, and research on advanced systems.

MODELING, SIMULATION, AND ANALYSIS

Computer simulation provides a holistic method for setting priorities for preparedness, detecting early indicators, assessing response and mitigation options, analyzing the performance of new technologies, and communicating insights to first responders.

The National Infrastructure Simulation and Analysis Center (NISAC), originated jointly by Sandia and the Los Alamos National Laboratories (LANL), is now an integral part of the Department of Homeland Security (DHS). NISAC provides analysis to support policy making, investment and mitigation planning, education and training, and real-time crisis management. Its distributed information systems offer virtual analysis capabilities to many users and providers.

Infrastructures are complex and therefore difficult to model. For instance, the electrical transmission infrastructure—the U.S. power grid—was put together not by plan but piecemeal, according to the demands of users and by separate companies; and as yet there is no comprehensive model. Thus planners have no way of knowing exactly what this infrastructure looks like.

TYPES OF THREATS

Terrorist threats generally fall into five categories: three types of weapons of mass destruction (WMD)—chemical, biological, and nuclear—explosives, and cyberterrorism. A "dirty bomb" uses high explosives and radioactive materials, but is mostly valuable in terrorism for its psychological effect.

Chemical and Biological Threat

Chemical weapons, in the form of mustard and other agents, were first used on a mass scale by Germany during World War I. Biological weapons were developed later, by the military in several nations. These WMD then moved into the ambit of terrorism. The best-known incident—other than attacks by agents of nation-states—was the release of sarin by the Aum Shinrikyo on the subway in Tokyo in 1995, killing 12 and injuring 1,040. This cult actually attempted eight attacks that year, using sarin, hydrogen cyanide, and botulinum. A successful attack with smallpox or anthrax is believed by many to be a more significant threat than chemical weapons or explosives. With recipes for making bioweapons readily available on the Internet, individuals or organizations can produce them with little scientific knowledge or funding.

Technical means have been developed to counter chemical and biological agents. These include threat and response analysis, environmental sensing and monitoring, facility protection and biosecurity, advanced chemoterror and bioterror warning systems, reagent design, and decontamination technology.

Nuclear and Radiological Threat

A nuclear terrorist weapon can be an improvised nuclear device (IND), purchased whole or assembled from parts and typically designed to produce a nuclear yield, or a radiological dispersal device (RDD), which would do relatively little damage but would result in radioactive contamination and could cause panic.

A counterterrorism planner must assume that terrorists with a nuclear weapon will use it if they are not stopped. Thus planners emphasize reducing vulnerability through protection, detection, identification, and interdiction of nuclear materials.

NNSA laboratories have had a primary role in providing technology for the federal response to nuclear incidents. A systems approach, which drives investments to the highest payoff areas, helps prioritize these efforts.

Explosives Threat

Terrorists' usual weapon of choice is high explosives—such as the simple truckload of fertilizer used to destroy the Murrah Building in Oklahoma City, explosives packaged for destruction (used by suicide bombers), a more sophisticated explosive such as Semtex, or highly flammable fuels such as propane or gasoline. In one recent year, 137 of 190 nonmilitary terrorist attacks involved explosives.

Explosive or fire-based weapons are relatively easy to make. In 2003, e.g., a mentally disturbed man killed 192 people on a subway in Seoul by using a cigarette lighter to ignite a milk carton filled with gasoline.[2]

Cyberthreats

As is well known, data stored and transferred on computer networks and the Internet are under constant threat from hackers, worms, and viruses. Considerably less well known are the threats to specialized digital devices—distributed control systems (DCS) or SCADAs—that control infrastructure in the United States and worldwide.

Before concern arose over cyberterrorism, hacking, and nuisance attacks, the information technology (IT) market was driven by cost considerations, features, and efficiency, with little thought to security. Although this has changed, defensive measures are hampered because product vendors and utility operators still insist on a business case and demonstrated need. Areas of technical expertise include modeling and simulation tools to identify vulnerabilities, cybersecurity assessments, capabilities for detecting and defending against possible attacks, tools to minimize damage, and "red teaming" (security works best when designed in first rather than added afterward). "Black-hatting"—in which an expert team tries to defeat friendly systems—offers insights into vulnerabilities and the detection and mitigation of hacking.

EDUCATION AND TRAINING

Education—in prevention, interdiction, crisis management, mitigation, and consequence management—is crucial to counterterrorism. Standard classroom and lab techniques (e.g., in the use of detectors and protective first-responder equipment) are complemented by more sophisticated, computer-implemented war games and red teams.

For example, the Weapons of Mass Destruction–Decision Analysis Center (WMD-DAC) at Sandia National Laboratories in Livermore, California, uses computer simulation and visualization to train policy makers, tactical personnel, and first responders in interactive, real-time "what if?" war games involving chemical, biological, and nuclear materials. WMD-DAC's simulation architecture is founded on protocols of the Institute of Electrical and Electronics Engineers (IEEE).[3] Developed by the Department of Defense (DOD), these support large, distributed simulations in which several organizations pool independently created models.

Antiterrorist personnel are using computer-aided war games developed in support of DOD missions and intelligence. These computer programs offer a capability to create attack and response scenarios, to change those scenarios in real time as an event unfolds, and to provide a running record for lessons learned. Details of an exercise are kept from the crisis management "actor," who has to decide on the spot whether to, say, apprehend suspected terrorists, tag them with an electronic identifier, or place them under immediate surveillance.

PREVENTION AND DETECTION

State-sponsored terrorism is discouraged and sometimes prevented by classic means such as possible counterstrikes against a known assailant, export controls, agreements regarding transfer of technology, and other diplomatic efforts, including the Chemical and Biological Weapons Conventions. But nonstate terrorism is little affected by such measures. Here, effective deterrence and prevention depend on effective criminal justice, making it known, credibly, that there is little chance for terrorism to succeed. Prevention and deterrence must therefore include strong elements of response, backed up by three principal elements:

- Coordinated intelligence gathering that integrates human intelligence (HUMINT) with transactional and law enforcement information and technical detection, to catch potential aggressors and identify actual ones. This requires continuous monitoring, analysis, and evaluation of suspicious activities, people, organizations, and states, by intelligence services and technical experts.
- Response capabilities to mitigate the consequences of any attack.
- An uncompromising policy of pursuit and retribution. Potential perpetrators must be aware that substantial means exist for interdiction and mitigation, without their knowing the precise nature of these processes.

Threat and Vulnerability Assessment

Threat assessment considers what type of attacks we should guard against, and vulnerability assessment considers what might be successful targets. Threat assessment and vulnerability assessment differ in approach, but they are closely connected in that, after analysis of their combined findings, a systems approach can alleviate the fact that there are not enough resources to protect everything.

Threat assessment is an important first step in homeland security and continues to change as targets of opportunity (e.g., spectator events and prominent individuals) change. It requires looking into the adversaries' mind—aided perhaps by preterrorism analysis of social-behavioral indicators—and making prioritized estimates of what they may wish to accomplish. Vulnerability assessment involves analysis of strategic national assets and consideration of how likely it is that an attack on any of them would be mounted and carried out successfully. These two processes must be integrated so that security analysts can determine where to focus their efforts. Without such an approach, homeland security officials would have such a broad set of vulnerabilities that it would be impossible to protect them all. With it, they are able to make specific, appropriate investments in people (i.e., guards and guns), equipment, facilities, and research and development.

After a threat has become apparent—e.g., from captured documents—further analysis will help determine which of various potentially vulnerable sites are the most likely targets. Security teams can then go to work at those sites, assessing what protective measures are in place and what new measures are needed. If, for example, a chemical or biological attack seems imminent, attention should be paid to air, water, and food systems.

Structures can be designed with relatively low-cost features to reduce vulnerability to terrorism. In this regard an "architectural surety" program from Sandia National Laboratories uses risk management methodologies and technical capabilities to examine the vulnerabilities of public buildings and other structures and recommend changes in architectural design, building codes, or construction standards. Sandia subsequently developed risk-based software, RAMPART, to help the General Services Administration assess risks to nearly 8,000 federal buildings.

Even more important is the nation's interlinked system of infrastructures: electric power, oil and gas, transportation, water, communications, banking and finance, emergency services, law enforcement, government, agriculture, health services, etc. Disruptions in any one of these could jeopardize the entire complex. Many are known to be vulnerable to physical threats, cyberthreats, natural forces, and system failures. Sectors in which reserve capacity has decreased in favor of increased organizational efficiency would be particularly hard hit.

Probabilistic risk assessment (PRA), first developed decades ago for high-consequence systems such as nuclear weapons and nuclear power plants, is now being applied to critical infrastructures. Laboratories of the Department of Energy (DOE) have helped utilities and industrial associations create security assessment methodologies for water utilities, chemical storage facilities, dams, power plants, and electrical power transmission systems. For example, a tool developed in cooperation with the American Water Works Association Research Foundation and the Environmental Protection Agency (EPA) has been applied at several large water utilities.

Other tools, such as AdHopNet (developed through NISAC), are designed to improve predictions of physical attacks and cyberattacks against communications. The NEVADA vulnerability database, from Lawrence Livermore National Laboratory (LLNL), automatically collects information on vulnerability and relays it to the potential targets.

Another aspect of prevention is vulnerability awareness among users of infrastructures or facilities that could become targets. With forewarning and regulations, users and managers will be able to plan for disruptive events. On 9/11, for instance, some companies had backup or redundant computer systems, but many others lost all their data. Similar vulnerabilities exist among the owners and managers of critical infrastructures such as the power transmission grid. Maintaining awareness is made more difficult by the fact that "if security works, you don't hear about it."

Intelligence

Terrorism, like natural disasters, cannot always be predicted. Nevertheless, intelligence collection and analysis are invaluable in understanding how terrorist acts might be carried out and in suggesting actions for interdiction. Also, although it is generally agreed that the indicators for detecting the acquisition and deployment of a weapon by a terrorist group (elements of preterrorism analysis) may be ambiguous, the very presence of a credible intelligence system may force groups to adopt higher-risk means that are less likely to succeed.

Technical intelligence support goes beyond the design and deployment of sensors, into techniques for discovering weapon manufacturing and weaponization as well as illegitimate acquisition and use of materials, and, again, prediction of attacks. In some instances, this requires the combined analysis of foreign and domestic information and the collective knowledge of numerous experts.

Data Fusion

Former Secretary Tom Ridge of DHS observed that counterterrorism needs the ability to conduct competitive analysis and data fusion, "having access to reports and the analytical work products not only from the CIA and FBI, but from the other government agencies that have intelligence and information gathering responsibilities."[4]

Ideally, any counterterrorism effort will have the best technical resources available so as to obtain information, analyze it, and apply it effectively as long as necessary. Today, however, information gathering is inflated by technology—in sum a helpful situation, but difficult to manage because of its sheer size. A single intelligence operation could receive information from wiretaps, aerial reconnaissance, telephone tips, credit card records, police surveillance, and security cameras. Combing through vast amounts of data for relevant material is daunting: quantitatively and qualitatively it quickly overcomes the capability for item-by-item analysis. An initial task may be to search for "shapes" (phrases of interest that occur repeatedly in a verbal stream), then to look closer if necessary. Other information, perhaps from unattended sensors, may indicate activity at a given site. A theory may result that can be the beginning, though only the beginning, of a technological investigation of possible terrorism. More information must be found to substantiate the theory, characterize it, decide what to do about it, and organize human resources until the question is resolved.

Progress in data fusion is now being made in many areas, including defense intelligence. Advances in computer technology enable one machine to process trillions of pieces of elementary binary data per second. This creates an unparalleled ability to go through large amounts of raw information in a relatively short time, so that it can be preprocessed and preselected before it reaches the desk of a human analyst.

Chemical-Biological Detection

Chemical weapons—in contrast to biological weapons—produce an immediate effect and are unlikely to be mistaken for a natural occurrence. However, chemical agents are relatively difficult to handle and deploy. Naturally volatile, they tend to evaporate, depending on their composition and the ambient temperature and air pressure; and their effectiveness depends on wind, rain, and atmospheric stability. They can cause mass casualties, but mass panic is probably a greater threat.

Significant advances have been made in chemical and biological sensors, which may be used at various phases of a threat, from weapon acquisition or development through exploitation. MicroChemLab detects a wide range of gaseous and liquid agents of chemical and biologial warfare (CBW) for in-field intelligence and site assessment. Ultraviolet fluorescence analysis of airborne CBW particulates can be undertaken from aircraft or satellites as early as the warning phase. Biochemical microsensors—small, smart, cheap microelectromechanical systems—can be used late in the threat scenario for damage assessment as well as for warnings.

Argonne National Laboratory and Sandia National Laboratories are partners in Program for Response Options and Technology Enhancements for Chemical/Biological Terrorism (PROTECT), jointly funded by DHS and the Department of Justice. Its goal is to protect public facilities, such as subways and airports, against chemical attacks. The system can rapidly detect a chemical agent and transmit readings to an emergency management information system. It has been deployed in the subways in Washington, D.C., and Boston. Other examples of protective systems are LANL's BioWatch and Oak Ridge National Laboratory's SensorNet. The latter, first deployed in Tennessee to detect water or airborne hazards, dispatches detailed information (including the projected path of a contaminant plume) to incident management centers within minutes of an event.

Bioattacks are difficult to detect because of the incubation time between exposure and the onset of symptoms; thus it is likely that many people will have been exposed before anyone is aware of an attack. The first indications are most likely to come from health care workers who report an unusual pattern of illness. Several computerized systems have been developed to keep track of such occurrences. EARS collects related information about hospital emergency departments, doctors' offices, 911 calls, over-the-counter drug sales, and employee absenteeism and makes them generally available. The Rapid Syndrome Validation Project (RSVP) uses epidemiological information, provided by physicians, to give early warning of disease outbreaks.

Threat-specific sensor technologies are also available for surveillance operations that may precede actual intervention. Advanced UV Remote-Sensing Applications (AURA) detects biological agents from an unoccupied aerospace vehicle (UAV). This system uses ultraviolet laser-induced fluorescence to discriminate between biological aerosols, which have a unique optical signature when illuminated; and other particles, such as dust or diesel fumes. Detection, mapping, and analysis take approximately 10 seconds. Ares, a van-mounted system working on the same principles, can be set up at any site, such as a high-value facility or a high-visibility event. Ares uses commercial off-the-shelf components where possible to reduce cost.

Detecting Cyberterrorism

The national laboratories share the cyberprotection knowledge and tools they have developed for use with their computer software and hardware. Organizations are given access through direct contact and collaboration and various forms of technology transfer. The laboratories provide vulnerability assessments that help organizations harden their facilities and sharpen their defense capabilities. Also available are education resources, including Sandia's Center for Cyber Defenders, which trains cybersecurity professionals and college interns; and a three-day SCADA training course for government and commercial entities offered by Pacific Northwest National Laboratory (PNNL).

Through its cyber fingerprinting project, LLNL is developing techniques for extracting evidence of an attack from clues such as subtle variations in packet arrival times and target sequencing. CIPHER, from Oak Ridge National Laboratory, allows users to quickly detect potential "low and slow" intrusions, possibly from sophisticated users. NADIR, developed and used by LANL, detects anomalies and alerts an analyst. Sandia and the other labs make extensive use of "intelligent agents" that can, in effect, roam the Internet, identifying unusual events in the data stream as possible signs of attack.

Commercial vendors are beginning to develop methods for mitigating attacks and restoring operations. The labs are assisting with preexistent and planned tools. These include the Automatic Intrusion Detection and Reaction System, which has operated effectively at LLNL for more than five years, as well as work in agent control of networks.

Detection of High Explosives

If intelligence indicates that a high-explosive bomb is likely to be detonated at a building, the normal procedure will be to restrict vehicular access, closely monitor pedestrian traffic, increase inspection of bags and packages, and search the building with dogs or electronic sniffers. Perhaps the building has been fitted with special glass that turns to powder instead of shards when it is broken, thus eliminating the most common cause of casualties from car bombs. Ideally its security force will have explosives-detection technology, intrusion detectors will be operating around the clock, and people will enter through some efficient means—e.g., badge swipe and password or retinal scan.

One device for prevention and interdiction, developed for the Federal Aviation Administration, detects explosives at the parts-per-trillion level and so can identify individuals at airports who have minute traces of explosives on their clothing. A commercially produced walk-through portal for detecting traces of explosives on a person is available for airports and other public facilities; the technology for this device was developed by Sandia National Laboratories and licensed to Barringer Instruments (now Smiths Detection). Similar technology was used in a prototype vehicle portal, and in a line of Hound portable and handheld sensors, one of which is called Microhound.

Numerous sniffer detectors for explosive materials are in use in transportation hubs, government centers, and office buildings. New technologies are also emerging. Explosives can be detected when they are exposed to a magnetic field, causing atoms of interest, like nitrogen-14, to give off weak radio waves. The frequency of the return wave identifies the chemical. Technologies using this phenomenon—nuclear quadrupole resonance (NQR)—have attracted considerable interest because radio waves can easily penetrate clothing or baggage.

Detection of Nuclear Devices and Radiation

A nuclear or radiological device emits radiation that can be detected with a sensor. Because nuclear devices may be acquired or built outside the United States and smuggled in, international safeguards and inspections are crucial to the nuclear materials control program. If a device originates in the United States, it must be detected while it is being assembled or when it is being transported to the target.

Since there are many natural, medical, and industrial radioactive materials, knowing what type of material is emitting radiation is necessary in order to avoid false alarms and nuisance alarms.

Spectral sensors, which use special algorithms to identify radioactive material automatically, provide this capability.

There are many sensor systems, from very large, fixed installations to small, rugged, portable, battery-powered units such as the pocket Radiac. The two main types of radiation detectors are gross counter detectors (usually plastic) and isotopic identifiers (usually working on a sodium iodide or germanium crystal). Gross counter detectors are simply set off when some "threshold" radiation is received; isotopic identifiers, which are larger and more expensive, identify the actual isotope, greatly reducing the likelihood of false alarms.

One isotopic identifier, SMART, was developed by Sandia before 9/11 to detect radioactive materials transported through portals at international passenger and package terminals. It uses a commercial sodium iodide scintillation spectrometer and associated electronics, along with analysis algorithms, to detect and identify radioactive materials passing within several meters of the sensor. A video image of the detection event scene is displayed on a base-station computer. The system automatically and continuously updates and recalibrates for background phenomena and can identify even a shielded radioactive source. It can be mounted as a fixed sensor or operated from a vehicle as small as a golf cart.

A portable, easy-to-use radiation detector, RadScout, which screens for dangerous radioisotopes in luggage or shipping containers and reports its results on the spot, was built and demonstrated at LLNL, then licensed to Ametek for marketing as the Detective and the Detective-EX. These radiation detectors will be used at border crossings, cargo ship docks, and transportation terminals to differentiate between potentially dangerous radioactive materials and harmless radiation sources.

To prevent terrorists from penetrating U.S. ports with nuclear weapons or the materials used to make them, a cargo container can be bombarded with neutrons, after which its radiation environment is analyzed for the signature of highly enriched uranium or plutonium. But how can this be done quickly? In view of the urgent need to keep traffic moving, the relatively old-fashioned technique of X-raying cargoes and looking for unusual shapes may prove to be the most effective.

At a much larger scale, new radiation detection equipment for cargo containers is in operation at the Global Marine Terminal in

Jersey City, New Jersey. Every cargo container taken off a ship and loaded onto a truck must go through a 20-foot-high detector array before it can leave the terminal. If the device indicates a potential hazard, the container is isolated and an emergency response is initiated. If the device remains mute, the container is free to go. Similar systems to detect chemical-biological as well as radiological materials are increasing, along with smarter, tamper-proof container locks that probably will be equipped with radio-frequency identification (RFID) technology, to sound an alert if tampering is attempted.

INTERDICTION AND CRISIS MANAGEMENT

Interdiction includes intervention during the stages of planning, acquisition, stockpiling, and deployment of weapons, as well as crisis response and management. It may occur before or after an act of terrorism. It requires collaboration between intelligence and law enforcement agencies, each—because we can assume that the adversary's technical capabilities are also increasing—supported by up-to-date technology. Law enforcement sting operations to trap people who want to obtain materials or unique technology will be supported by technologists who will provide clues as to what such individuals might seek.

The management of interdiction requires close knowledge, and observation, of conduct of operations—including procedures that must be followed in deciding what to do once something suspicious has been detected. Suppose that when officers are checking vehicles crossing a border, a radiation detector lights up. What should the officers do? Stop the vehicle and its occupants at the border? Tag the vehicle in some way and follow it? Or, as part of an approved operation, does this border point randomly divert vehicles into an inspection compound, so that when this vehicle is chosen the occupants do not know whether they have been caught or are being randomly sampled?

Intervention at any point of the interdiction or mitigation process may require neutralization, retrieval, or dismantling of a terrorist weapon. Advanced disablement tools such as Sandia's Percussion-Actuated Nonelectric (PAN) disrupter could be used against conventional high explosives, RDDs, and other WMD. PAN dismantles suspected explosives and preserves forensic evidence. It was used at the Unabomber's cabin in Montana and at Olympic events beginning with the summer games of 1996 and the winter games of 2002. It was also used by the Massachusetts state police, with the assistance of the FBI, to disable shoe bombs removed from an airline passenger, Richard Reid.

There have been several interdictions of chemical-biological agents. For example, a decontamination formulation, dispensed as a foam, was one process used to eliminate anthrax in the Hart, Dirksen, and Ford buildings on Capitol Hill, and at contaminated sites in New York and in the Postal Service (USPS). The nontoxic formulation was licensed by Sandia National Laboratories for industrial production by MODEC and EnviroFoam Technologies. Sandia also provided the USPS with equipment for decontaminating mail by irradiation.

Nationwide workshops in bomb detection and disablement have been sponsored by Sandia since 1994. Participants in Operation America, cosponsored by the Department of Justice, come from bomb squads, police and fire departments, and emergency response organizations nationwide; other government agencies; the armed forces; and security agencies in friendly countries. Participants learn applied explosives technology and advanced bomb-disablement logic, tools, and techniques.

Finally, there is a need to provide excellent personnel, equipment, etc. for the emergency operations center (EOC), which goes into action as soon as an emergency is declared, and follows through either until the operation is handed over to another agency or until it concludes the consequence management stage. A future EOC system would allow crisis managers to operate more effectively by using technology-rich, intelligence-rich crisis response and management— utilizing systems technology and maximizing collaboration and teamwork across organizational boundaries. To achieve this goal, there will need to be ways of providing new types of information and situational awareness and systems that truly constitute a deterrent to terrorism. EOC staffers will need to use existing technologies, such as war games, with other emergency units. As in other aspects of antiterrorism, there is a need to innovate, because terrorists are innovating.

MITIGATION AND CONSEQUENCE MANAGEMENT

Mitigation and consequence management are best done with an integrated system. A key to their success is a prior commitment to a response that is sustained, supported by technology, and regularly and vigorously practiced no matter how many federal agencies are involved. Guidance plans will at times be generated as a natural consequence of testing successful technical systems. For example, after developing Protective and Responsive Options for Airport Counter-Terrorism (PROACT) for the Bay Area Rapid Transport (BART) system centered in San Francisco, Sandia National Laboratories and Lawrence Livermore National Laboratory published a set of protocols for postattack response and mitigation.

Technology plays a role throughout mitigation and consequence management. Detection and protective equipment benefit first responders; advances in medical treatment benefit victims; technical intelligence and information systems benefit crisis managers and their support teams; decontamination and recovery systems benefit the public, recovery workers, and the environment; and specialized analysis equipment supports the forensics effort that is required for attribution.

Training through drills and exercises, both in the field and in computer simulations, while expensive, identifies vulnerabilities. Also, equipment and procedures that protect workers from hazardous radioactive, chemical, and biological agents need continual improvement.

NNSA offers experience to the FBI and other agencies at the consequence management and mitigation stage through its Nuclear Emergency Support Team (NEST). NEST provides technical assistance in response to terrorists' use or threatened use of a nuclear or radiological device in the United States. It also supports the Department of State in a similar role for incidents overseas, and regularly participates in DOD Northern Command exercises.

NEST maintains a fast-response capability for a radiological emergency involving dispersal of radioactive debris—for example, from a dirty bomb. NNSA's Radiological Assistance Program (RAP) provides initial responders who can be at the scene in a few hours. They will characterize the radiological environment, provide technical advice to the FBI and other emergency response agencies, and assist with decontamination and material recovery.

According to DOD, consequence management includes "measures to alleviate the damage, loss, hardship or suffering caused by emergencies. It involves measures to restore essential government services, protect public health and safety, and provide emergency relief to affected government, businesses and individuals."[5] At a more technical level, as applied to nuclear, chemical, and biological attacks, it calls for stopping or reducing effects of the agent at the time of deployment, limiting its dispersal, and countering further exploitation of the situation by the perpetrator.

Reliable methods are needed to contain, mitigate, or decontaminate people and areas exposed to contaminants. These will be supported by technical means as well as specialized training in many activities such as integrated communications, specialized triage, and the use of decontaminants. This work is supported by the DHS National Disaster Medical System, composed of teams of professional personnel who can be quickly deployed in support of local public health officials in the event of national emergency.

After a bombing, danger to human beings rapidly subsides. That is not true of a chemical, biological, or radiological attack when wind, local air currents, and other atmospheric effects will spread the attack material. Rapid analysis of plume dispersal is required in order to plan evacuations and deploy emergency personnel. Sensors help predict the effects of plume dispersal and mitigate the consequences, including environmental cleanup. DHS's nationwide BioWatch warning system detects trace amounts of biological materials in the air of urban centers. It helps determine the geographic extent of a released biological agent, allowing officials to make decisions about emergency response, medical care, and consequence management more quickly. Key partners are the Centers for Disease Control and Prevention, EPA, and (for sampling systems and training) the NNSA laboratories.

Detection and mapping of chemical plumes are also enabled by a system developed at LANL in collaboration with EPA: Airborne Spectral Photometric Collection Technology (ASPECT). The package is mounted aboard a small EPA aircraft, enabling surveillance from a safe distance. It provides information on the size, shape, composition, and concentration of gas plumes emanating from a disaster, including terrorism.

New technology is also aiding emergency personnel. As noted above, Sandia has developed a portable MicroChemLab for first responders. Originally configured to detect toxins such as ricin and botulinum, it uses microfabricated chips to isolate and identify biological and chemical agents.

Another handheld detector can identify anthrax in less than 5 minutes, rather than the hours previously necessary. It analyzes fatty-acid esters vaporized from the cell walls of bacteria and compares them with cataloged signatures indicative of anthrax or other pathogens. This technique has been used to identify pathogens at the genus level and often at the species level, identifying the bacillus in minutes. It is considered a crucial step toward developing bioattack warning systems and defenses, such as decontaminant foam dispersal systems, in public facilities. These systems are exemplified by PROTECT, described above.

Firefighters, the police, and emergency personnel will be first responders in terrorist attacks. These men and women will require considerable knowledge of technology, including information about hazardous materials (hazmat, or HAZMAT). They must be trained for an array of terrorist threats, including improvised explosive devices and WMD. More specialized training is available for first responders in, for example, bomb detection and dismantlement programs; one such program was described earlier.

The general public will benefit from receiving information about the danger, and the limits to danger, posed by radiological, chemical, and biological weapons—for example, the fact that an RDD dirty bomb, though frightening, has limited effect as compared with sophisticated weapons of mass destruction. If effectively implemented, education in such matters can be expected to assist mitigation and consequence management by reducing the likelihood of panic, enabling individuals to practice effective self-treatment, and minimizing the number of casualties.

FORENSICS AND ATTRIBUTION

Technologists must be sensitive to the criminal justice process. Technical means for investigating and evaluating any event will be hampered by activity at the scene before a forensic examination. Thus care should be taken to ensure that emergency response and consequence management do not hinder a criminal investigation process unnecessarily. When chemical, biological, or radioactive materials have been used, investigators will have to work in a contaminated environment where gathering evidence—which is complicated enough after a conventional explosion—will be especially difficult. Also, efforts by emergency responders to disable a device may destroy evidence. (To avoid this, a net or tent can be placed over the device and filled with a foam that will absorb the shock of detonation or destruction, retain forensic evidence, and decontaminate any chemical or biological substances.)

To facilitate attributing cyberterrorism, Pacific Northwest National Laboratory is building the Internet Characterization Tool, which delineates Internet transactions and information, ultimately permitting analysts to determine the identity and source of possible threats. Other tools are moving analysts toward enhanced forensic and attribution research: these include LANL's Network Rewind Button, which can replay previous network traffic; and IOWA, a product of LLNL that creates a cybermap of networks and produces graphs in response to queries.

Criminal investigation and prosecution as phases of the response to a terrorist event have typically not been addressed by the national laboratories. However, the laboratories have traditionally been involved in forensics issues involving the collection and preservation of evidence, especially in environments contaminated by radioactive, chemical, and biological agents. In this case the laboratories have developed concepts that are not expected to become commercially profitable very soon. Chemical, biological, radiological, and high-explosive attacks leave physical evidence of a type not encountered in conventional crime investigation. Thus specialized laboratory examinations, which may or may not parallel detection technologies, will be brought to bear in identifying the precise nature of an event as well as its perpetrators. In some cases, postevent investigations can be enhanced by tagging materials that are generally benign but can be used as weapons. Nitrate fertilizer, for example, can be tagged in a variety of ways so that its manufacturer, and even its distributor, can be identified.

CONCLUSION

International conflict has changed radically, so that terrorism is now considered the single greatest external threat to the peace and prosperity of the United States. Terrorism has no national borders, no integrated centers of administration, no official channels of communication, no forums at which agreements and treaties can be brought to the table. For the first time, it seems, weapons of mass destruction could be brought across national borders without forewarning, undetected and bearing no marks of identification. Critical infrastructures—water supplies, power grids, etc.—could be brought down by a carefully planned attack with commonly available high explosives. However, the intellectual and technological resources of the United States and its allies should be, with time and with participation by the general population, fully capable of managing this difficult new environment.

The U.S. counterterrorism program emphasizes worldwide intelligence gathering and analysis, in collaboration with NATO and other friendly nations. There is also some collaboration among terrorist groups, and they have, additionally, proved adept in the use of technology. But the United States and its allies have a great advantage in that most have large, well-funded science and technology enterprises capable of supporting intelligence gathering and management, crisis management including counterattack, and consequence management. Qualitatively and quantitatively, these resources are incalculably better than those available to terrorists. They include computer systems for analyzing electronic messages for hints of terrorist activity, detectors that sniff the air for dangerous materials, devices that check cargoes for terrorist supplies, software-prowling intelligence agents, advanced personnel identification systems, networked microrobots, airliner antimissile kits, and a great deal more. Such technology has already impeded terrorists and eventually may make terrorism unattractive because the avoidance of countermeasures will be too expensive, too complex, and too risky. The high-tech U.S. Strategic Defense Initiative was created in 1983 for much the same reason, after President Ronald Reagan challenged scientists "to turn their great talents now to the cause of mankind and world peace." The world has changed since then, but the sentiment retains its validity. The agents of conflict and chaos will remain in jeopardy for as long as science and technology remain at the service of peace and goodwill.

N O T E S

1. For the term "systems approach," see http://pespmc1.vub.ac.be/SYSAPPR.html.

2. Adam Dolnik, "Countering the Threat of Transport Terror," *IDSS Commentaries* (31 March 2004).

3. See www.ieee.org/catalog/olis/compsim.html.

4. Andrew Koch with Kim Burger, J. A. C. Lewis, and Paolo Valpolini, "Homeland Security," *Jane's Defence Weekly* (11 September 2002).

5. Department of Defense (DOD), Operations Directorate, Joint Staff, *Handbook of DOD Assets and Capabilities for Response to a Nuclear, Biological, or Chemical Incident* (August 1996).

Improving Checkpoint Security

Fred Facemire
Director, System Integration, Smiths Detection

Mark Laustra
Smiths Detection

Since 9/11, an increase in funding for, and a sharper focus on, security in transportation has significantly hardened the U.S. security infrastructure, particularly in the aviation industry. In this critical effort, a set of tools is enabling security professionals to become more effective in detecting and deterring threats such as explosives and metallic and nonmetallic weapons—and in detecting the terrorists who use them.

Despite this progress, security professionals have a difficult task in safeguarding the traveling public and the transportation infrastructure, because there is an ever-growing range of threats. To counter these threats, further significant strides must be made to develop and integrate new technologies and systems into the security screening process.

TRANSPORTATION SECURITY SCREENING

The goal of transportation security screening is to deter, identify, and disarm threats to the safety and security of the traveling public and the transportation infrastructure. In the aviation industry, progress toward this objective, with particular emphasis on proactively detecting explosives, is being achieved through a combination of technologies that enable greater scrutiny of luggage, cargo, and passengers boarding commercial aircraft. This article will review the challenges and opportunities involved in further improving the screening of passengers, especially those who board commercial aircraft.

Ideally, all public areas—in particular, transportation access points such as airports—would be rendered safe through general surveillance without significantly impeding the flow of commerce; but daunting problems regarding technology, logistics, and privacy must first be overcome. In the meantime, checkpoints provide a barrier to threats by consolidating the security equipment and personnel that screen each person for threatening items, and by verifying that each passenger has the proper documentation to enter a secure area. Security officials will continue to rely on screening checkpoints to mitigate threats from transportation systems, even as technology advancement enables more of the security screening process to occur before the passenger reaches the checkpoint's physical barrier.

CHECKPOINTS
Deterrence and Detection at Checkpoints

The ability of checkpoints to deter attacks is extremely important in transportation security, because the array of threats is so broad that the complete elimination of every threat is impractical. Effective deterrence in this environment depends both on displaying a strong physical barrier to those with hostile intentions and on implementing advanced technology to create uncertainty in terrorists about the probability of passing through the checkpoint undetected. Therefore, checkpoints that contain unfamiliar new technologies and exhibit high levels of coordination and automation increase the perception of risk by would-be terrorists.

If a checkpoint fails to deter a terrorist, then it must have the capability to detect, identify, and respond to the array of threats. No single screening technology alone is sufficient for this task, because of the complexity of the transportation security environment and the variety of threats against it.

Today, a number of new and existing complementary technologies are beginning to help security professionals raise the level of protection. For example, there are continuing advances in data acquisition and image processing in X-ray systems for inspecting baggage. The result is better resolution and sharpness of X-ray images, enabling better recognition and identification of threats in baggage and personal items. Recent technological progress has increased the sensitivity of metal detectors to ever-smaller metallic objects while at the same time allowing these detectors to discriminate between threatening objects and innocuous items. Explosive trace detection (ETD) machines, which back up X-ray systems in screening checked and carry-on baggage, detect and identify microscopic quantities of explosives in just a few seconds, with very few false alarms. ETD whole-body passenger screening portals, which find traces of explosives on people by gently puffing them with air and analyzing the particles collected from their bodies and clothing, are being introduced at airports. This significant improvement in detection closes a security gap by mitigating the threat of explosives carried by a person. Document processing and biometric technologies are further expanding the role of technology in security screening to include verifying passengers' identity.

Such new technologies in screening provide opportunities to improve overall checkpoint efficiency. Some ETD whole-body passenger screening portals, for example, have been integrated with archway metal detectors to automatically control traffic flow through both devices while screening passengers for explosives and metallic weapons. Such integration, as part of a comprehensive screening process, has significant potential to allow screeners to focus on finding threats because it reduces burdensome tasks like directing traffic.

But despite the wide application of promising new technology in screening, more work is still needed to effectively counter current and emerging threats.

The National Intelligence Reform Act of 2004, signed into law by President Bush last year provides important resources along these lines to improve checkpoint security. The legislation provides funding to improve current checkpoints as well as research promising new technologies.

Improving Checkpoints: Gaps and Interim Steps

Current "legacy" equipment for screening generally provides high-detection performance for the threats the equipment was designed to detect. However, there are several well-publicized shortcomings, including:

- Ineffective detection of readily available threats (items such as ceramic weapons and explosives)
- High rates of false alarms
- High costs associated with dedicating screening personnel to operate equipment
- Lack of coordination between stand-alone detection systems

The government, national and university laboratories, and commercial equipment companies are devoting tremendous resources to solving these problems through the development and application of technology.

While new technologies promise to address many challenges of transportation security, low-cost improvements can maximize systems that are already deployed. For example, enhancements to conventional X-ray image processing and display software can quickly and automatically improve complicated or dense areas of an image without compromising its overall quality, and can assist a screener in making decisions about the contents of bags. Optimizations to the baggage conveyor system that enable rapid prescreening divestiture and then quickly clear bags to their owners are also being installed in some high-traffic airports. In addition, some vendors are installing automatic return container stalls to efficiently pass containers for bags and personal items from the back to the front of the checkpoint.

A number of security operators are now significantly improving screening efficiency from these types of simple, low-cost, easily implemented methods.

EMERGING DETECTION TECHNOLOGIES

Although existing checkpoint systems can be optimized to make screening more efficient, new technologies must move from the laboratory to the field to close gaps in the detection of threats.

Such technologies will expand the list of detectable threats and will simultaneously make it possible to detect existing threats in new ways.

Microsensors

One applied technology is microsensors: miniaturized components that convert tailored interactions with the environment (i.e., the surroundings) into electrical signals for data analysis. When micro-sensors are applied to threat detection, each sensor is engineered to alter its output signal in a repeatable way based on the presence of trace quantities of substances of interest. Special polymers can be integrated with the sensor to limit the substances that interact with it; however, the chemical properties of most "threat substances" have enough similarity with other substances (potential interferents) that a single polymer is incapable of preventing interference. This problem is overcome by constructing arrays of sensors with different attractive properties and processing their output signals with sophisticated pattern-recognition algorithms. These sensor arrays can be fabricated on semiconductors with integrated microelectronics and assembled in compact packages for low-power portable or remote environmental monitoring applications. Microsensors hold the promise of making threat detectors ubiquitous in public security.

Terahertz

Another promising technology is based on terahertz light, which has wavelengths of roughly 10 microns to 3 millimeters and occupies the nonionizing region of the electromagnetic spectrum between micro-waves and infrared light. Terahertz light has been known for some time to possess unique properties that make it attractive for security screening. For example, metals, ceramics, and explosives can be imaged when concealed behind common clothing and packing materials (e.g., cotton, wool, paper, and plastics), which are transparent at terahertz frequencies. Terahertz energy also interacts with many explosives and drugs in ways that produce characteristic spectra for automatic identification of substances. However, only recently has the technology required to capture these effects become sufficiently advanced to support the development of systems for field use.

Terahertz technology is making an early entry into security screening as a handheld wand capable of detecting metallic and nonmetallic objects as well as explosives in real time. Continuing advances will enable the development of practical nonintrusive whole-body walk-through portals for detecting weapons and explosives. These advances may also facilitate the development of baggage screening capabilities to complement existing and emerging X-ray systems. Terahertz technology is bridging the gap between concealed object imaging and automatic threat detection and identification.

Body Scanning

Body-scanning technologies that use either backscattered X-rays or millimeter wave radiation for imaging potential threats, such as concealed weapons, have been tested for several years. However, these systems have not been widely deployed, primarily because they involve complicated interactions with passengers and are able to "undress" the passenger, raising concerns about the invasion of privacy and about legal liability. A solution to the problem of privacy is technological. One method being developed by several organizations is the separation of threats from the underlying body: the threats are displayed on a simplified human figure to indicate their location. Another is to add "fig leaves" to the image, blurring out areas that people consider private. These approaches depersonalize the image but also can reduce the ability of operators to identify threats. A body-scanning system based on terahertz technology could enhance this technological method by providing spectroscopic information on objects in addition to image data. Thus, a terahertz-based body scanning system could automatically identify explosives on the body without operator interaction.

Biometrics

Biometric technologies are also important in security. Biometrics can verify a person's identity as stated on travel documents, personalize screening information by security equipment, and compare an individual passenger with names on a "watch" list. Electronic identity verification has been successfully implemented in border control through such programs as US-VISIT and INSPASS and is already used to screen passengers on some high-security commercial flights. These implementations have relied on relatively mature biometric methods: fingerprinting or hand geometry. Other prominent biometrics such as facial and iris recognition are also beginning to gain acceptance as problems with their performance and usability are overcome.

FROM SYSTEMS TO SOLUTIONS

As new technologies are being refined, transportation security is also on the verge of shifting from collections of stand-alone sensors to integrated systems of systems. This evolution is vital because threats are increasingly complex. Integrated systems will provide tailored information that is more complete and timely than any that can be provided by just a single piece of screening equipment. Applying information technology to integrated security systems will clarify understanding, and at the same time facilitate the rapid insertion of new technologies.

People who are responsible for acquiring security equipment are sometimes skeptical about an "integrated system," asking how much value is actually provided by the additional cost. Integrated systems should address the end user's needs in several areas, including:

- Improved operational efficiency, because information is available where and when it is needed
- Reduced turnaround times and fewer screening delays, because the system is better able to resolve abnormal events
- Reduced staffing, because equipment is automated and screening functions are consolidated
- Improved response to threats because of greater opportunity to plan rather than merely react
- Less quantifiable benefits, such as increasing customers' satisfaction and enhancing the reputation of security providers

When a system is conceptualized and created, the technology developer should determine which benefits are important to the security operator and tailor the integrated system to achieve these.

Once deployed, such integrated systems can significantly improve the flow of information between security professionals.

With current stand-alone systems, information available at one station about a threatening situation is directly available only to a screener or his or her supervisor. Other security personnel learn of the situation through a convoluted communication process, which is time-consuming and imperfect.

LESSONS FROM THE MILITARY

Information technology applied to military air defense operations provides an example of intelligently integrating data from sensor systems to significantly improve operators' understanding of a threat. These "command and control" (C2) capabilities give military decision makers at all levels of command intuitive views of their environment that highlight problems requiring attention. The same approach to integration can be used to tailor information for transportation security screeners, so that they are able to respond more quickly to a threat and to recognize threats that would not be revealed by a single system.

INTEGRATED CHECKPOINTS

Integrated checkpoints, often referred to as "checkpoints of the future," enable security professionals to use shared information to identify and respond to threats faster, more accurately, and more effectively. In contrast, a traditional checkpoint is a collection of stand-alone detection machines with operators coordinating the flow of passengers. Such a segmented operation makes each station a point of delay in moving the passenger and his or her belongings through the screening process; and the screeners can only partially assess the threat associated with each passenger because information from other screening stations must be passed by word of mouth.

In a checkpoint of the future, the equipment will integrate two processes: (1) verification of passengers and their documents and (2) traffic control. Thus the screeners will not be burdened with the task of exchanging and integrating data. Moreover, intelligently tailored information on the environment and on threat indicators will allow screeners to better apply their skills in recognizing abnormal behavior, judging potential threats, and making decisions.

INTEGRATING SYSTEMS

Several commercial providers of network equipment and software offer systems to integrate security. With these networking tools X-ray systems can be connected to trace detectors or metal detectors; however, the real benefits of integration are achieved when data from detection systems are processed and presented so as to address specific screening requirements. For example, conventional X-ray images containing annotated suspicious objects can be exported automatically to secondary baggage screening areas to guide directed trace or hand searches. System developers are best able to identify, and implement, specific opportunities for integration when they collaborate closely with security operators to understand particular screening requirements.

Integration can be categorized as related to system operation or system management. System-operation functions are an integrated part of the security system that is necessary for the system to perform its primary function. The implementation of these functions generally follows restricted, often proprietary, protocols of data exchange because the functions are closely tied to subsystems. By comparison, system management functions, such as managing users' accounts, will typically span multiple systems and databases. If the benefits of true integration of security equipment are to be realized, the transportation security community needs to adopt open interface standards for integrating system management functions. In the absence of such standards, getting equipment from multiple vendors to communicate typically requires either specially developed pro-prietary interfaces or nondisclosure agreements. This limits the entry of new technological players into the marketplace, deters the develop-ment of C2 systems, and adds significant expense for customers who, for instance, want to utilize more than one vendor of a technology. Again, open interface standards are commonplace in markets where information technology is a significant presence. Transportation security needs to adopt a similar approach to enable the integrated security systems that are necessary to meet emerging threats.

FIELD TESTING

Another innovation that will make screening more effective and screening equipment more reliable is the early introduction of prototype equipment into the real-world environment. Security screening is fraught with vagaries that cannot be modeled, or even clearly identified, in an office or laboratory; consequently, before any equipment is widely deployed it must be evaluated in the hands of security operators in real screening environments to identify areas (technical, operational, ergonomic) that need refinement. During the evaluation, the system developer and security operators need to interact closely to ensure a correct understanding of the system's capabilities and the factors affecting its effective use.

Again, transportation security can draw lessons from the military about the rapid transition of new technologies into the hands of the front-line operator. The military has successfully deployed many systems by instituting cross-functional, cross-organizational teams, commonly called integrated process teams (IPTs), and by moving the developers of technological solutions close to operators during the later stages of system development.

IPTs and the coupling of developers and operators have the same goal: enabling collaboration between the participants to ensure a successful solution to a challenging problem. IPTs composed of program and technical leaders from key stakeholder organizations (e.g., regulatory agencies, operators, providers of transportation services, commercial developers, testing and evaluation agencies, and international security partners) provide needed insight into the issues of defining, developing, demonstrating, and delivering advanced systems. These teams also help educate the stakeholders on the important considerations in each area of the project—whether that project is technical, operational, regulatory, or commercial.

In civil transportation, similar development programs that physically place engineers together with operators yield tremendous benefits and more effective systems.

CONCLUSION

Security operators and technology developers can most effectively protect the traveling public when they are partners in applying current and emerging technologies to meet challenges. Screening technologies are vital to transportation security for keeping threats such as explosives from being introduced into modes of transportation, but the application of today's technologies can go only so far toward protecting borders against terrorists. To screen more effectively for an increasingly complicated arsenal of explosives, metallic and nonmetallic weapons, and other threats, developers of detection systems and devices must work closely with the security operators. Low-cost improvements can maximize the value of existing technologies, and constant feedback from operators can help shape more effective future technological solutions. Advances in detection are only as valuable as the information they provide to the security operators who evaluate risks each day. When that information—derived from openly interfacing technologies and permitted by appropriate regulatory controls—can be shared among coordinated teams, airports will deliver the most sophisticated, expedient, and effective solutions possible against present and future threats.

CHAPTER 61

IT Architecture for Homeland Security

Gerald Metz
Technical Director, Mission Systems C2I Programs,
Northrop Grumman Mission Systems

OVERVIEW

A common theme in the 9/11 Commission Report is the need to improve how information is shared among the diverse public and private-sector agencies that play a role in our emergency services, public health and safety, law enforcement, transportation, intelligence, and national defense. The report makes the case for a paradigm change from "need to know" to "need to share" in the interest of better serving public safety and the public good. This chapter, based on work being done by Northrop Grumman Corporation, describes the problem and how a "network-centric" service-oriented architecture such as the one being developed for the military by the Defense Information Systems Agency (DISA) supports information sharing across the homeland security community.

THE CHALLENGE OF SHARING INFORMATION

Sharing information is a daunting technical and organizational task, even within a single enterprise. In large corporations or government agencies, a chief information officer (CIO) typically takes charge of assessing the organization's needs for managing and moving information, and for defining a cohesive infrastructure of hardware, software, and data communications elements, which might be called information technology (IT) architecture, to meet those needs in a unified way. Transferring information effectively among the diverse parts of a large enterprise is challenging enough. Figuring out how to move information across the external boundaries of diverse organizations, presumably for the common good, is formidable. The technical issues are easier to solve than social and organizational issues, because each organization has its unique reasons to be protective of its information.

Consider the diverse players who have a role in providing for our homeland security. There is no one CIO who acts as overlord to provide uniform technical direction. There is no single, common mission among the players. There is no clear understanding of who has what information, who needs that information, or why one organization has an interest in making its information available to others.

The political realities of this challenging environment provide the context for this discussion of IT architecture. The organizational obstacles to sharing data have to be overcome through policy adjustments and cooperative arrangements; the IT architecture has to enable those agreements by ensuring that each participant's security, privacy, need to know, and other concerns can be addressed.

IT architecture to enable interoperability among contributors to homeland security addresses a different set of needs from those of a large corporation or enterprise, for we are talking about exchanging information among many diverse enterprises. Technology alone cannot motivate decision makers to support the IT needs of stakeholders outside their respective organizations, but it can be instrumental in dismantling barriers to information sharing. For that to happen, IT experts have to understand and provide technical solutions to the real and varied institutional issues that impede the exchange of information. IT architecture should address those institutional concerns in a way that not only is technically convincing but gives decision makers confidence that they can authorize the exchange of valuable information with others without compromising their own organizations' interests.

Institutional Challenges

Sharing information across organizations for the common good seems like a good idea, until you try to do it. Getting approval from

Northrop Grumman to contribute this chapter is a small case in point. After first presenting a business case for contributing it, the author had to submit it for reviews to make sure that it did not disclose proprietary information or infringe on anyone's intellectual property, and that no information contained in it violated federal restrictions on the export of technology. These reviews are appropriate and necessary in our commercial environment, much as those who work in health care are obligated by law to safeguard patients' private information. Investigators in law enforcement agencies are trained to safeguard the integrity of evidence for potential use in court, and to hold information close to the vest in general lest they compromise the effectiveness of their investigations. Facility managers who identify vulnerabilities in security and devise ways to mitigate them cannot allow a potential attacker to know about those vulnerabilities or how they are protected. Those in the Department of Defense (DOD) and other federal agencies who handle sensitive information are trained to classify it as "secret" or "top secret" and to keep it locked in an approved safe. But as the 9/11 Commission put it, "Even the best information technology will not improve information sharing so long as ... personnel and security systems reward protecting information rather than disseminating it."[1]

Sharing information across organizational boundaries requires people who can see its value and are willing to make the effort, even when on the surface it appears to benefit someone else. It calls for people at senior levels who are willing to invest some personal and political capital to build "win-win" partnerships with their peers in other organizations. Then, these working relationships have to develop into standardized operational procedures, supported by formal or informal agreements. With a little perseverance, this author did receive approval from Northrop Grumman to contribute this chapter, illustrating that it can be done.

Technical Needs

The primary technical challenge in being able to share information across so many diverse, independent organizations is the very fact that they are independent. Since there is no single CIO, there is no unified approach. No two organizations have the same requirements, budgets, or priorities. Each organization values and protects its independence, and so IT architecture designed to enable interoperations must acknowledge and support that independence. Enterprise approaches generally do not do this. Despite the technical challenges, this diversity offers vast opportunities for win-win exchanges of information that promise to enrich the participants' understanding of situations.

What follows is an outline of the kinds of issues that need to be addressed to accomplish this vision of being able to share even sensitive information, with appropriate safeguards, so that all the stakeholders in homeland security have a better understanding and awareness of the whole situation and everyone's role in it.

Secure Internetworking

The call by the 9/11 Commission for a paradigm change from "need to know" to "need to share" does not diminish the importance of protecting sensitive information. Each participating organization has its own policies, sometimes mandated by law, that constrain the release of information. It is therefore essential that the architecture enable each organization to retain control of what information is released, and to whom.

The standard IT first line of defense is to build a private network for an organization (its intranet), with a firewall around it to keep unauthorized people out. Need to share calls for ways to exchange information with authorized external parties, so we need internetworking strategies that enable us to make reliably controlled exceptions:

* Delivering, with appropriate authorization, information from computers within one organization's intranet to computers on external networks
* Similarly, providing a way to request and receive information from known sources outside the organization's intranet
* Ensuring that these internetworking capabilities are highly available, especially during a disaster when public networks are congested

Interoperability of Computers and Software Applications

Thanks to the Internet's mature and widely accepted standards for data communications, applications have ways of exchanging messages over the network regardless of what kind of computer they run on. But there are other obstacles to making applications compatible with each other, including choice of programming language and operating system. The use of Web services extends the Internet's strategy for interoperability into the applications themselves to surmount these remaining barriers.

Beyond that, there remains the matter of interoperability between comparable applications from different vendors. Agencies will continue to make independent purchasing decisions, each on its own schedule and budget. To share information with its neighbors, each agency needs its applications to be compatible with what the others are using.

Consistency of Information Content

Organizations with diverse missions, such as the police, firefighters, and emergency medical services (EMS), do not have a common vocabulary, even concerning the same incident:

- Similar applications, such as incident management systems, might not have comparable information content and capabilities.
- Agreement among applications on data format and semantics is needed. In the long term, working groups or standards organizations can help with this. Meanwhile, in the near term, we need tools to address the differences.

Scalability

Some designs work well on a small scale, but slow down or fail entirely when the amount of data or number of users exceeds some limit. The architecture for homeland security (HLS) must anticipate the ongoing shift from "need to know" toward "need to share," offering the ability to add users, computers, agencies, and application features without degrading the existing ones.

Extensibility

Extensibility is the ability to introduce new capabilities easily. Terrorists are always changing their tactics. As soon as we learn to defend against one sort of attack, they devise a new one. We cannot afford to build every new capability from scratch or to allow the system to grow in complexity as we add or modify capabilities. New capabilities have to be developed quickly and economically, be able to join in with little or no integration, and be easy and inexpensive to deploy widely.

THE ROLE OF ARCHITECTURE

When the architect Yoshio Taniguchi set out to design the new home for New York City's Museum of Modern Art (MOMA), his objective was to facilitate encounters between its collection and museumgoers. This required him not only to identify and understand the unique needs of displaying modern art and the needs of the public but to provide an environment that would encourage people and art to interact. Taniguchi would have no role in selecting the art itself. That is not what architects do. Architecture is the catalyst, not the content. Taniguchi was asked to define a new environment for displaying MOMA's collection, and to imagine and anticipate what might be required to accommodate future museum acquisitions in an art form that is experimental by definition. As if this weren't challenging enough, he also had to satisfy aesthetic expectations, for as an art museum, the building itself is expected to be a work of art.

As with buildings, systems architecture does not specify what the applications do or how they work. It describes the environment in which applications will operate, enables them to carry out their respective tasks, and provides services designed to enhance their ability to interact with each other and with their users. Our needs and expectations for the things we want computers to do for us continuously grow in scale and complexity. Computer architecture must continuously evolve to meet these growing expectations, which include finding new ways to manage and avert the growth in complexity. Complexity is the enemy of reliability, of budgets, and of the ability to get something working quickly and maintain it throughout its life cycle.

Specific objectives for HLS architecture are

+ To meet the unique and diverse needs of the homeland security community and its computer applications

- To facilitate and encourage interaction among diverse users and their computer systems
- To avoid or mitigate "system of systems" complexity issues

Managing Complexity

Divide and conquer is a general approach to reducing complexity that can take on many forms. Good architecture identifies small, well-bounded parts of the problem and isolates them in discrete modules. Each module keeps all its complexity to itself, and presents the result to the rest of the system on a simple, well-understood interface. By carving out parts of the problem and solving each part separately within its own enclosed module or "black box," these small chunks of complexity are hidden from the rest of the system. This has a number of benefits:

- Hiding the details of each separable part of the problem within its own black box allows other parts of the system to ignore those details and focus on their own challenges.
- Black boxes make it possible to improve on or replace the solution to one part of the problem by upgrading one black box without touching, and without breaking, the rest of the system.
- When one black box is upgraded, the parts of the system that use it inherit the benefits of the improvement.

A classic example of architecture using "divide and conquer" is the Open Systems Interconnection (OSI) Reference Model for data communications networks, shown in Figure 61-1.

Each layer in this "stack" of services has a well-defined and well-bounded role in how networks deliver messages and documents. Because networks use this model, applications (at layer 7) can ask the network to deliver a message or document without needing to know or care about all those details. Because of this layered architecture, an organization can replace its local area network's Cat-5 wiring with a new wireless LAN (a change in the physical layer), and have the applications that use it continue to work with no other modification required. Operating systems like Windows and Linux also offer services to applications, enabling them to print or save a

F I G U R E   6 1 - 1

Responsibilities of each layer of the OSI Reference Model.

OSI Layer	Examples of Responsibilities to the Layer Above
7. Application	***Word processing, E-mail Alarm monitoring, Air traffic control*** Responsible for meeting all the users' needs and expectations.
6. Presentation – Formats – Protocols	***XML, HTML, ASN.1, MPEG*** Define the organization or structure of documents carried over a session, and present the document in the format the application expects. ***Telnet, FTP, HTTP, SMTP*** Responsible for organizing data carried over a session into messages or documents. Encryption and authentication features may be offered here.
5. Session	**DNS, SSL** Responsible for establishing, synchronizing, maintaining and terminating communication sessions between systems using the transport protocol.
4. Transport	***TCP, UDP, SPX, vines*** Responsible for end-to-end delivery of data using network layer services. Some services (e.g., TCP) guarantee delivery; some (e.g., UDP) do not.
3. Network	***IP-V4, IP-V6, IPX*** Responsible for addressing and routing "packets" of data using the data link layer. Provides cross-platform (hardware-independent) delivery.
2. Data Link	***Ethernet, PPP, 802.2, HDLC, SDLC*** Responsible for how ones and zeros are encoded and carried by the physical layer.
1. Physical	***Wireless, Cat-5, Coax, Fiber, Microwave Satellite*** The means of physically interconnecting computers, switches, and routers.

document without needing to know anything about the particular printer or storage device that is installed.

Promoting Collaboration

Architecture cannot make people decide to collaborate, but it can and must remove the technical obstacles that impede the sharing of information. It must also offer solutions to the issues that make decision makers reluctant to authorize the release of information even to those having a need to know. In the community of organizations engaged in homeland security and defense, the architecture has to provide for the protection of sensitive information, and must do so in a way that gives the leaders in those organizations confidence that the information will be handled in accordance with their policies and intent.

Architecture must address the various interoperability issues, or at least make them easy to overcome. It must offer strategies to enable different applications to exchange data, and to understand each other's data. Standards would be a big help; but in the absence of standards, applications will need tools that enable them to translate and use data from external sources.

SERVICE-ORIENTED ARCHITECTURE FOR HOMELAND SECURITY

In 2003, the CIO of the Department of Defense (DOD) outlined his vision for a "net-centric data strategy."[2] He offered a metaphor: "The network is the computer." In a concept that leverages the success of the OSI network architecture, the premise is that it does not matter where data reside on the network or if all the components of an application reside on the same computer, as long as the application components and the data can find each other and interact over the network. The resulting Network-Centric Enterprise Services (NCES) architecture is all about sharing data by posting it somewhere on the network and then advertising it for other applications to find and use.

DOD expects its NCES architecture to provide a way to move information quickly and effectively from intelligence applications to decision-making applications to engagement applications, creating a seamless flow of information from actionable intelligence to decisive action. Northrop Grumman has been developing network-centric services and promoting their use within DOD since before the memorandum of 2003 on NCES. In 2004 we began an independent research and development project in cooperation with the Communications-Electronics Research Development and Engineering Center (CERDEC) at Fort Monmouth, New Jersey, to show how NCES concepts can be applied to homeland security. We were pleased to see a recent report by Stevens Institute of Technology that independently recommended application of DOD's NCES approach to promote regional information sharing for homeland security in the Port of New York and New Jersey and the surrounding region.[3] Applying the

DOD concept to the civilian environment, however, is not a simple cut-and-paste exercise. The applications are different; the civilian user communities have different needs and expectations; and these communities, unlike DOD, have no single CIO to orchestrate design and implementation.

In practice, NCES is a suite of application-layer services built on the commercial success of applications built for the Internet. The World Wide Web Consortium (W3C) is in the process of doing for the application layer what OSI accomplished with its stack of data communications protocols. W3C is developing standards for how applications interact with other applications over the network. Like the OSI Reference Model, these protocols work on any computer, with any operating system, and with applications written in any programming language. For example, W3C has specified:

> XML (Extensible Markup Language), a text-based data format compatible with any kind of computer and available to applications written in any programming language.
>
> SOAP (Simple Object Access Protocol), the means by which one application can ask another to provide a service. SOAP messages are written in XML.
>
> WSDL (Web Services Description Language), a protocol for one computer to tell another about a service that it provides and how to use the service. A WSDL document, also written in XML, defines a set of related services and tells a programmer how to construct SOAP messages to use each service.
>
> UDDI (Universal Description, Discovery, and Integration), a directory service enabling applications that provide a service to register the service, and applications that need the service to look up where on the network to find it and how to use it (using WSDL). Metaphorically, a UDDI directory provides "yellow pages," "white pages," and "green pages" directories for network services.

Simplifying the Application Layer

The W3C specifications for SOAP, WSDL, and UDDI, supporting the application layer of the OSI stack of protocols, are the tools needed to construct network-centric, service-based applications. All three protocols use XML, the data format developed for the Web that can be used with all types of computers, operating systems, and programming languages. These W3C tools make it possible to assemble applications using software modules that are distributed across the network. An application can receive a notification from one computer, ask a second computer to contribute additional information, and invoke a software service on a third computer to aggregate the information and take some action based on plans hosted on a fourth computer.

A Business-to-Business Example

Online banking is one convenience offered by the World Wide Web. Bank Web sites offer customers access to their account information and forms for various transactions using a Web browser. The Vanguard Group's Web site goes a step further in customer service. It gives customers the ability to securely enter their account and access information for other institutions' Web sites. Vanguard then uses Web services provided by the other banks, with the customer's authorization, to prepare a single portfolio report that describes all of the customer's investments—those at Vanguard merged with those at the other institutions.

Dividing and Conquering the Application Layer

Like Yoshio Taniguchi's new museum, the environment at the application layer is intended to encourage the interaction of a collection of independently developed pieces. This application-layer architecture, illustrated in Figure 61-2, is loosely organized into three levels: NCES core enterprise services (CES), integration services, and specialized services. Web services are the independent components that divide and conquer the complexity of, and encourage interaction among, homeland security applications.

Core Enterprise Services
Core services are those that every application is likely to need. These are things that might be taken care of by the operating system on an individual computer, such as how to store and retrieve data, or how two applications communicate with each other. In this architecture where "the network is the computer," we need network services to perform these operating-system services. The concepts of core

FIGURE 61-2

Dividing and conquering the application layer.

7. Application Layer	
Specialized Services	**Traffic event notification, Alarm filtering, Map services** Responsible for implementing application-specific tasks, and making those implementations available for reuse in other applications.
Integration Services	**Semantics, Legacy support** Responsible for facilitating the interoperability of applications.
NCES Core Enterprise Services	**Discovery, Enterprise service management, Security, Mediation, Messaging, Collaboration, User assistance, Storage, Applications** Responsible for providing applications with generalized services, such as those provided by the operating system of an individual computer.

enterprise services from NCES are reused for this architecture. Remember that this is about architecture, so each of the following describes a category or collection of services, not a particular service.

1. *Discovery*: Services that enable applications to find information or services on the network using known directory and registry assets.

2. *Enterprise service management*: Services for maintaining the health and status of network resources and for managing the network addresses of users and services.

3. *Information assurance and security*: Services that provide for the security, integrity, and continuity of information and who has access to it. These services include *authentication* (verifying that users and information services on the network are who or what they say they are, e.g., password, signature, and certificate services); *authorization* (managing what information and services a particular user has been granted access to); and *encryption* (making information unreadable by everyone but the intended recipient).

4. *Mediation*: Services that figure out and convert (translate, merge, correlate, rename, etc.) information from the offered form into a form that is usable by its recipient.

5. *Messaging*: Services that support the exchange of information among users and machines on the network.

6. *Collaboration*: Services that enable users to work together, interacting through shared applications or services on the network (e.g., chat, online meetings).

7. *User assistance*: Automated capabilities that learn and apply users' preferences and patterns to enhance users' productivity.

8. *Storage*: Network services for storing and retrieving information.

9. *Applications*: Housekeeping services that support the network-services environment by configuring and maintaining application services and making them available to applications.

Integration Services

These include semantics and legacy support.

1. *Semantics*: Services that help one application understand data from another. These services would address differences in what things are called, what units they are expressed in, and more complicated or specialized data conversions that may be needed.

2. *Legacy support*: In this context, a legacy application is any application that does not use this architecture. Adapter services are needed to acquire and normalize information from legacy applications, to make that information available for sharing.

An adapter is a specialized code that exchanges data with an application using its native interface, and then exposes the application's data to the network using Web services. Northrop Grumman has developed adapters for the U.S. Army to provide backward compatibility between legacy applications and a newer service-oriented system of systems.

Specialized Services

Finally we come to the information services that help meet specific needs of homeland security, including applications used for training for, planning for, detecting, responding to, and recovering from a crisis. Shared information promotes consistency from planning to training to execution. Shared services provide opportunities to integrate these applications seamlessly; and the ability to leverage existing services in building a new application or capability reduces cost and schedule. The following are examples of specialized services that may be useful to support homeland security applications.

1. *Traffic event notification*: Having information about the operational status of the transportation infrastructure is important in the management of any emergency.

2. *Alarm filtering*: As new automated-sensor surveillance systems are deployed on a large scale, their effectiveness depends on avoiding false alarms. Rule-based filters are needed to recognize any routine, benign occurrences that may be mistaken for alarm conditions.

3. *Map services*: Geographic information systems (GIS) technology plays a growing role in emergency management. Shared map services will facilitate the sharing of geospatial (map-related) data and will promote a common understanding and awareness of those situations that require a coordinated response.

CONCLUSION

In spite of the many well-supported recommendations in the report of the 9/11 Commission concerning the importance of improving how we share information, reward systems continue to discourage sharing information beyond the boundaries of one's own organization. We continue to be trained to withhold information as a rule and release it only in special cases; and when there is any doubt, the practice is still not to release it.

Recent success stories in public safety and transportation[4] can serve as models for information sharing in HLS. The Integrated Incident Management System (IIMS) is one example. Developed with funding from the U.S. Department of Transportation and managed by the New York State Department of Transportation, it implements the "Common Incident Management Message" standards, known as IEEE-1512,[5] to enable the eight participating agencies listed below to notify each other of scheduled and unscheduled highway incidents, contributing to improved safety, reduced congestion, improved mobility, and increased efficiency and productivity.

New York State Department of Transportation

New York City Department of Transportation

New York City Police Department

New York City Fire Department/EMS

New York City Department of Sanitation

New York City Department of Environmental Protection

Metropolitan Transportation Authority–New York City Transit

New York City Office of Emergency Management

The Transportation Operations Coordinating Committee (TRANSCOM), serving major highway routes in the greater New York–New Jersey–Connecticut area, is another success story. In an implementation that predates the IEEE-1512 standards, TRANSCOM uses traditional IT techniques to collect and disseminate information about traffic incidents among its 17 member agencies. TRANSCOM's board of trustees consists of the chief operating officers of each member agency, a structure that addresses in a formal and very effective way the need for cooperation and executive-level concurrence on how their information is managed and shared.

The same capabilities and practices that transportation authorities use to manage everyday planned and unplanned incidents such as lane closings and motor vehicle accidents will prove invaluable in responding to catastrophic incidents. The awareness, habits, and skills developed through everyday exchange and use of information in the course of routine operations are key to making these practices available and useful.

The Regional Information Joint Awareness Network (RIJAN) is a vision by John P. Pazckowski, the New York and New Jersey Port Authority's director of operations and emergency management. RIJAN's mission would be to do for homeland security what IIMS and TRANSCOM have done for transportation.

Northrop Grumman has been a leader in the use of network services to make the mission-critical information systems of our armed forces interoperable. The same technology offers solutions to the technical challenges described in this article, to support interoperability among the diverse civil and military agencies that secure and defend our homeland. A unified national strategy for interoperability in homeland security is needed. Our hope is that regional networks for HLS such as RIJAN will be implemented, will validate the approach, and will be extended nationwide.

N O T E S

1. *The 9/11 Commission Report*, ch. 3, "Counterterrorism Evolves," p. 88.
2. John P. Stenbit, "Department of Defense Net-Centric Data Strategy," DOD CIO memorandum (9 May 2003).
3. Stevens Institute of Technology, *Securing the Port of New York and New Jersey: Network-Centric Operations Applied to the Campaign against Terrorism* (September 2004).
4. *Sharing Information between Public Safety and Transportation Agencies for Traffic Incident Management*, National Cooperative Highway Research Program (NCHRP) Report 520, Transportation Research Board of the National Academies, Washington, D.C. (2004).
5. *Guide to the IEEE 1512™ Family of Standards*, Standards Information Network, IEEE Press (April 2004).

Two Critical Concepts for Information Technology in Homeland Security

Don Adams
VP, Chief Technology Officer–Government and
Chief Security Officer, TIBCO Software

This chapter examines two modern concepts in information technology, or IT—(1) sense and respond and (2) predictive response—and their application to critical challenges facing practitioners and citizens concerned with homeland security. These methodologies come from the best of evolving commercial practices and emerging trends in real-time logistics and even defense initiatives. Both methods have been applied to counterterrorism and to the Herculean effort required to make the U.S. Department of Homeland Security (DHS) successful. However, not all challenges can be met with technology, and many methodologies that can play a key role in homeland security call for no high tech at all.

SENSE AND RESPOND
The Methodology

Sense and respond is becoming common jargon in a rapidly increasing number of mission-critical environments, including medicine, logistics, network-centric operations other than warfare (NCOW), and, it is to be hoped, all levels of defense. The simplest example of sense and respond is the brain and nervous system. If your finger touches something hot, your nerves sense the threat and pass a message to your brain, which tells your body, arm, hand,

and finger to recoil. Such a response to a threat can be good or bad: you may appropriately recoil slightly, escaping the original threat of bodily harm without creating additional threats; but you may overreact, so that your head, shoulder, arm, or hand hits another object and is injured.

Note that in sense and respond, you may not actually have to touch or consciously perceive the threat to which your senses react. In fact, the possibility of responding to sensory input without having to think about it seems reassuring. This once happened to me high in the Sierra Nevada, after a trout fishing expedition. As I was following a friend along a narrow, overgrown streamside trail, for no conscious reason I jumped up and away from it. When I recovered from the shock of such a violent change in trajectory, I looked down at an enormous timber rattler that my friend had walked over and irritated. My subconscious sense-and-respond mechanism had almost certainly saved me from a snakebite in a remote, inaccessible place. Implementations of sense and respond in, for example, logistics and medicine attempt to re-create this subconscious response to sensory input.

By using computer systems with monitoring software and an array of sensors you may be able to identify a threat more rapidly than you could otherwise. This is a good first step in a defensive response. The sooner you know that there is a problem, the better your chance of minimizing the impact of the threat.

In a recent issue of *Military Medical Technology*, Commander William J. Upham wrote: "A model for monitoring the warfighter's health status—vitals (pulse, respiration), voice stress, temperature, EKG/EEG, and environmental exposure to potential chemical hazards—requires robust and fully networked remote sensing technology to facilitate real-time data exchange between the warfighter and the health risk assessment team."[1] This is a classic sense-and-respond scenario, and the methodology need not be perfect in order to yield advantages. Upham continues:

> Combatant commanders must learn to live with uncertainty and ambiguity on the battlefield. Recognizing that the fog and friction of war will never be entirely eliminated, network-centric battle management, including medical sense and respond technology, must include advanced information/data exchange technology that is fully networked, integrated at the joint level, and reliable to achieve information and decision superiority.[2]

While recognizing and accepting the imperfection and ambiguity of the environment, Upham still considers the objectives of a medical sense-and-respond implementation achievable.

Using Sense and Respond in Counterterrorism

Professionals in counterterrorism are natural candidates for sense-and-respond methodology. By using as many sources as possible from public and sensitive environments and by applying analytics in real time, they can respond quickly, even immediately, to a threat or incursion. Their response can have both intended and unintended outcomes, depending on their level of preparation for a specific scenario. For example, consider the U.S. Coast Guard, which is stretched thin by the challenge of counterterrorism. A network of sensors spanning the country's ports, tied to tools of business activity management (BAM) and with additional sources at carriers, insurers, and law enforcement and intelligence agencies, would allow the Coast Guard to apply its limited resources more efficiently, inspecting the highest-risk vessels before they enter populated areas. This was very effectively demonstrated for the Coast Guard in San Diego, California (see Figure 62-1).

Unfortunately, however, the possibility of adequate if not perfect information does not always result in perfect decisions or execution. For instance, the National Law Enforcement and Corrections Technology Center in Charleston, South Carolina, has a team responsible for a pilot reaction to and interdiction of vessels believed to be carrying nuclear materials. But although they have discussed the capabilities a sense-and-respond infrastructure might provide, they are unable even to set up a prototype of such an approach because their funding barely covers the basic boots, clothes, and protective and sensing equipment for the teams who would respond.

Another attempt at sense and respond, the second Computer-Assisted Passenger Prescreening System (CAPPS II), was terminated because of unintended or unplanned consequences. CAPPS II was developed and initially deployed with every good intention and with what were considered adequate safeguards for privacy, accuracy, and accountability. As 9/11 faded from memory, civil libertarians already disturbed about the PATRIOT Act attacked the system, creating public consternation and eliciting further attacks by the media against the

F I G U R E   62-1

U.S. Coast Guard port security prototype.

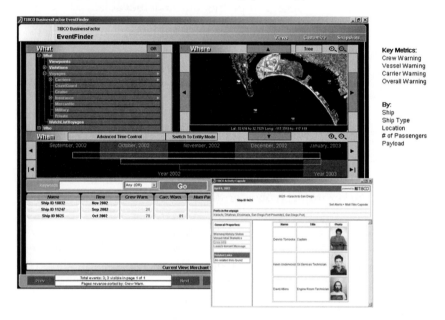

airlines that had participated in the test deployment. Ultimately DHS canceled CAPPS II, with little rationale (or with little that was made public), illustrating the power of protest over the best intentions of the government. A comparable example is "Total Information Awareness" (TIA); the interested reader can find its history by searching on the Internet.

Still, sense and respond has had some successes in the federal government. A recent example is the Sense and Respond Logistics solution for the Department of Defense Office of Force Transformation (OFT). The solution demonstrates how a sense-and-respond environment can increase the speed of command and adapt to an evolving situation and to changes in commanders through a "publish and subscribe" paradigm and distributed business rules that implement priorities and guidance. Moreover, the value of the Sense and Respond Logistics (SRL) approaches taken by OFT and the vendor Synergy, Inc., was proved by the U.S. Marine Corps (see Figure 62-2).

All these approaches and concepts have broad validity in counterterrorism, critical infrastructure, and other aspects of

F I G U R E   62-2

How SRL adapts its operations.

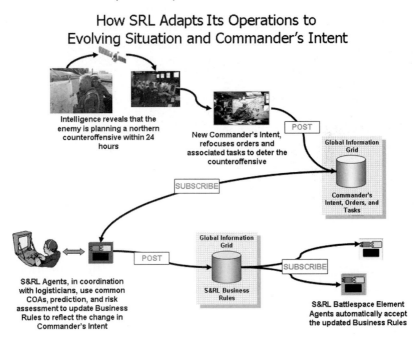

homeland security. In particular, publish and subscribe provides a highly efficient environment for national, regional, and local interactions with and among first responders. Recently, agencies of the Finnish government held discussions with vendors about the possibility of linking nuclear monitoring with the national police (for guidance) and local law enforcers (for crisis planning and execution) as part of a sense-and-respond environment using publish and subscribe and BAM. This approach would allow all participants to visualize scenarios, formulate strategies, and set horizontal and hierarchical tasks for responding to any category of crisis.

Using Sense and Respond to Secure Borders and Protect Critical Infrastructure

The securing of borders seems to be moving toward sense-and-respond methods. In the U.S. Visit program, current and planned initiatives for collecting information at border crossings are evidently gathering steam without major attacks from American civil libertarians. (There have been interesting responses outside the United States, but these are beyond the scope of this chapter.) As U.S. Visit proceeds to "increment 2b," where it truly gains the necessary access to sources, we will probably hear the same hue and cry as with Total Information Awareness (TIA), a DOD data-mining program for counterterrorism intelligence that was derailed as a result of privacy concerns and CAPPS II. In the interim, though, it is only an extension of the earlier immigration effort that conveniently collects biometric proofs of identity for foreign visitors to the United States. This is not as threatening as the collection and analysis of Internet traffic or information on people's itineraries. In a free society, many people seem to do or say things that they are not proud of, or that they believe violate current law.

Studies and Research on Securing Critical Infrastructure has a history going back to the President's Commission on Critical Infrastructure Protection (PCCIP) in the mid-1990s and even earlier. The final document, *Critical Foundations: Protecting America's Infrastructures*, was delivered to the president by this blue-ribbon committee. The members had been asked to look at national-level government and commercial infrastructures, including energy creation, distribution, and management; the financial sector; transportation systems and their management; information and communications; and vital human services. The paper was supposed to be a national call to arms for cooperative research and development and collaborative responses to threats to the national security in each of the targeted industries.

Presidential Decision Directive 63 (PDD 63) was a result of *Critical Foundations*. PDD 63 directed government agencies to work to resolve the vulnerabilities identified by PCCIP. The Critical Infrastructure Assurance Office (CIAO) was also created as a result of the report. CIAO—originally based at the FBI and now part of DHS—has wandered, looking for roles and responsibilities that did not overlap those of other organizations. It has not been considered a resounding success; its activities did little other than try to make people feel reassured that the problem was being studied and that there was a hotline to call if a critical infrastructure was attacked. Most of what modest funding came out of this effort went to government agencies' pet projects and to academic studies and research, with no meaningful involvement of other stakeholders such as the owners and operators of the affected critical infrastructures.

Until there is a real-time sense-and-respond infrastructure for the power grid, little progress will be made in detecting and responding to a problem that may or may not be caused by a terrorist act. Innovative research (partially funded by the University of California, the California Power Commission, and the Department of Energy) on using sense and respond to monitor the power grid may show the way for the electric industry and subsequently find applicability in other critical infrastructures. This initiative, begun in early 2004, is being undertaken by a consortium including California ISO; PG&E; the University of California-Berkeley; Silicon Valley Power; a number of experts on power, integration, and business processes, led by Dr. Ali Vojdani of UISOL; and other partners.

Using Sense and Respond in the Department of Homeland Security

The Department of Homeland Security (DHS) is working on several of the largest challenges ever undertaken (comparable in scale to, say, the Manhattan Project). For one, it has perhaps the largest and most diverse task of integration in history, along with having to become operational as an amalgamation of 23 previously separate agencies. It also faces a nearly incredible challenge with regard to budget, because many problems of the former agencies were related to inadequate or misallocated budgets for both mission operations and the underlying IT.

DHS needs an internal sense-and-respond environment if only to keep track of often competing initiatives in its aggregate of organizations. Such a system could track budget, procurement, finance, and personnel systems across the organizations; and it could perform analytics using BAM or similar technologies to give DHS executives more real-time insight into initiatives and expenditures that are redundant or that might be leveraged more broadly than originally envisioned. A sense-and-respond environment could also be a model for other governments and agencies. If it could be tied to funding controls in Congress and to OMB initiatives like the Federal Enterprise Architecture, it might provide transparency regarding how our tax dollars are spent.

Beyond this, DHS needs to carefully exploit sense-and-respond methodology in many areas. Especially, it needs to foster and fund measurable programs for the National Law Enforcement Council

(NLEC) and other entities that have a real problem to solve and no other obvious source of funding. DHS also needs to pursue initiatives in cooperation with other stakeholders in the protection of critical infrastructure. This should no longer be basic academic research but initial limited deployments by consortia of concerned parties, like the activities in California described above. We have plenty of innovative technology; what we need is funded efforts for innovative deployment and utilization of that technology. Industry can work with academia to create new technologies when such collaboration makes sense, technically and in terms of business. When fundamental research does not yet make business sense, the Department of Defense has an organization and methodology, through The Defense Advanced Research Projects Agency (DARPA), to fund and manage it. DHS needs to focus on operationally deployable solutions: the integration and exploitation of existing intellectual capital; sense and respond at borders and critical infrastructure; and the training, equipping, and organizing of first responders.

Using Sense and Respond in Cooperation with Community Health Care and Education

Health care providers and educators, including the school nurse, can be a significant part of sense and respond. International efforts like those of Voxiva (Voice of Life) in the third world are initial models for such a solution. If a biological agent is released, school nurses are perhaps the people most likely to see its initial impact: an increased number of children exhibiting patterns of symptoms. These symptoms could be input to a sensor messaging and monitoring system and could then be evaluated and correlated with input from other sources (caregivers and people in law enforcement or intelligence) to produce the desired subconscious sense-and-respond scenario. Before any group was aware of significantly anomalous patterns, the system could alert affected responders to a potential terrorist event. This could minimize further exposure or at least mitigate the situation through early detection and response.

A Pattern for Utilization of Sense and Respond

OFT's program for a sense and respond logistics concept (SRLC) developed a formal model for sense and respond logistics to create a joint adaptive capability. Developers also are examining the behaviors, mathematics, and science of networks to translate them into operational concepts and procedures. Researchers have found that tactical SRLC applications must be flexible, featuring self-synchronization and the ability to network to achieve a larger outcome. These local efforts then tie into larger actions on the battlefield.

In an article in *AFCEA Signal Magazine* (February 2004), Captain Linda M. Lewandowski, USN, chief transformation strategist with the Office of the Secretary of Defense, Force Transformation, says:

> Studies of SRLC capabilities during operation Iraqi Freedom detected a growing gap between networked combat systems and current logistics applications. Battlefield operations moved so quickly that they outpaced their supply lines. The goal is not only to develop a faster command and control loop, but also to create the ability to out-adapt a flexible enemy. However, to be effective, the system must reach down to the tactical level. Today this capability does not exist.[3]

There is an effort to move away from top-down, centralized decision-making hierarchies to a more decentralized model. The system may have a profound impact on command and control because it promotes more decision making at the tactical level, in the distributed elements of a force. Lewandowski notes: "You're going to command by establishing and communicating the context. That's really your control. You are dictating orders less and establishing the commander's intent and making sure everybody is operating within the same context."[4] She adds that SRL is a substantiation of network-centric warfare. The effort takes information-age theory and principles and applies them to a large U.S. Defense Department environment. Lewandowski says: "What hasn't been done yet is we haven't taken [network-centric warfare] theory and principles and translated them into a more military and conceptualized context."[5] She also notes that when the program began, its developers realized that SRLC was really a larger translation of network-centric warfare.

But network-centric warfare is only a step toward the concept of full joint warfare, according to Donald L. Zimmerman, chief executive officer of Synergy, Inc., which is developing the SRLC software component. Within the Defense Department there is ongoing competition among different concepts of "warfighting." Zimmerman says: "Some of those concepts are [aimed at] trying to get the network-centric flow-down and some aren't yet. There's a lot of work still to be done."[6]

PREDICTIVE RESPONSE
The Methodology

The account above of the author's nearly being bitten by a snake was used as an example of sense and respond. Actually, it was also a predictive-response scenario. My body responded to the presence of the snake without thought or conscious sensory input. My subconscious defense mechanisms detected and responded to the threat before I was aware of it. This is an example of a predictive response.

Some innovative leaders in the IT industry are making great strides and will have solutions in the market before this book goes to press. Suppose that a major money-laundering attempt is about to occur, in violation of the PATRIOT Act. How would you like to determine this beforehand, on the basis of a set of analytics and sensor inputs related to elements of a developing pattern that has a high likelihood of precipitating money laundering? How about programmatically raising a terrorism threat warning, on the basis of analytics of a distributed sensor net across multiple communications infrastructures that predict a higher-than-normal risk profile? Or consider a threat indicator for a car bomb near the green zone in Baghdad, based on inputs from all intelligence sources, correlated with a set of rules and processes updated over the past four hours with input from an operative captured last night. And, by the way, all this should proceed without a human driver until an exception is noted and an alert is raised.

Complex event processing software technology will provide increasingly robust analytical capabilities. From financial trading to customer support to homeland security, the ability to execute a predictive response to changes in the environment will fundamentally change the playing field. An example of high-level architecture for complex events processing is shown in Figure 62-3, as a model. A key to the power of complex events processing is the temporal base for events, processes, rules, and the inference engine itself. There are a number of different inference engines in use in industry and

F I G U R E   62-3

Complex events architecture.

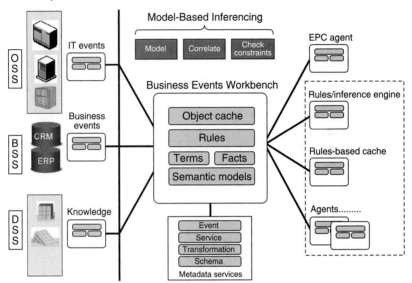

government today, but most do not have a temporal (time) basis. A collection of, say, 17 events will have an entirely different implication if they happen in 3 hours as opposed to 24 hours. The system has to be able to identify and respond to these differences. In financial systems the temporal differentiator can be in seconds or even milliseconds. Missile defense experts understand this, and many currently use an earlier-generation inference engine with temporal capabilities.

Using Predictive Response in Counterterrorism

Probably, any future success in counterterrorism will be in part because predictive-response methodologies and the technologies that make them possible have been adopted. We will still need all the sources, methods, and indicators that we have worked with over the past two decades, but all this information can be effective data for a predictive-response infrastructure. The ability to make better and better predictions will evolve from cooperation and collaboration among disparate resources and assets. Just as there was a breakdown in intelligence because of perceived and real legal barriers to cooperation, different elements of counterterrorism could perceive limitations or restrictions on their sharing of information. The inference infrastructure and the predictive-response methodology will not be perfect at first; but with increased data sources and over time, the predictions will become far more accurate. This is much more than any reasonable analyst or group of analysts can claim. No one is going to consider the 1,500 events spread across a five-day window occurring at 700 different locations in finance, transportation, border crossings, traffic stops, e-mail, or telephony that may lead to an alert for a predictive response. In such a scenario, the counterterrorism forces need to analyze the prediction, weigh it for rationality, and be prepared to respond.

Predictive Response and Critical Infrastructure Protection

Many people lie awake at night thinking about threats to our critical national infrastructure. We should not dwell on this, but it is something to be concerned about. Just as I was writing this chapter, I read a piece in a periodical which stressed that cybersecurity protection for electric power grids (one of the critical infrastructures specified in PDD 63) was lagging because ongoing issues of maintenance and reliability were being given priority. Another major issue is the industry's unwillingness to impose additional cybersecurity mandates on itself when it does not know if the technology required to fulfill the mandates exists. A predictive-response solution connected to present and next-generation sensors throughout the power grid could not only predict and respond to natural or systemic power anomalies but also detect patterns of cybersecurity attacks within the technical infrastructure.

Predictive Response in the Department of Homeland Security

Predictive response could serve DHS well. Typically there are two or more models for visualizing event-related or event-correlated occurrences. Two of the most widely envisioned models for examining complex events are related to business processes and technical infrastructure. The first has to do with events that did or did not happen as anticipated in a complex workflow or business process as defined by management; the second has to do with a technical environmental sensor "trigger" or status change in a large group of monitored hardware devices.

DHS takes both these views of events, and many other views. It also has a unique need for predictive-response methodology: this is what DHS is all about. DHS is in business, spending our taxes, in order to get inside the decision loop of any potential enemy of the American people. Predictive response could help it get so far inside terrorists' decision loop that it could prevent rather than simply respond to anomalous events. This presupposes that DHS has sources to monitor and patterns for which to establish sets of rules that can evolve with every new piece of data. We would not want this to remind us of the famous acronym GIGO—garbage in, garbage out. The defining feature of a predictive-response system is that, unlike individual analysts or groups of analysts, it can nearly perfectly represent and respond to new sets of rules as collective awareness increases. It can also act as a sounding board for trying out potential

F I G U R E   62-4

Driving toward predictive response.

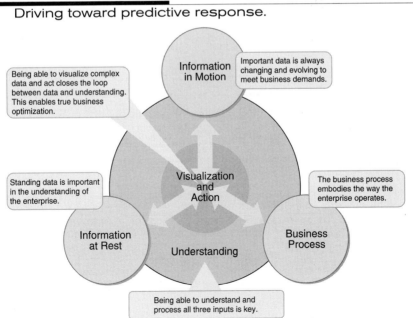

scenarios without having to wait for the indicators to actually occur. This makes it both an objective amplifier of thought processes and a generator of artificial crises for response scenarios.

A Pattern for Utilization of Predictive Response

There are few models of predictive response, since this concept is so new; but Figure 62-4 shows certain components of such a model. Elements of information at rest and in motion are combined with complex event processing in business processes as part of a bridge to predictive response.

CONCLUSION

This chapter has merely highlighted certain possibilities. Sense and respond and predictive response are technical methodologies that I consider timely, and critical for homeland security. This chapter has highlighted the potential contribution of sense and response and predictive response technical methodologies to homeland security. It is imperative that the United States and its allies harness these technical methodologies, and enhance our capabilities to detect and prevent future attacks.

N O T E S

1. Commander William J. Upham, *Military Medical Technology*, Volume 8, Issue 4 (May 19, 2004).
2. Ibid.
3. Henry S. Kenyon, "Defense Supply System to Out-Maneuver a Flexible Enemy," *Signal Magazine, AFCEA Journal* (February 2004).
4. Ibid.
5. Ibid.
6. Donald L. Zimmerman, chief executive officer of Synergy, Inc., in George Cahlink, "Sense-and-Respond Logistics," *Air Force Magazine Online* Volume 87, No. 11 (November 2004).

Needs Analysis for Information Sharing

David G. Kamien
President and Founder, Mind-Alliance Systems

Jean-Francois Cloutier
CTO, Mind-Alliance Systems

Denis Ranger
Product Architect, Mind-Alliance Systems

INTRODUCTION

Fundamental to homeland security is the need to share information between international, federal, state, local, and private-sector entities. The critical need to enhance information sharing (IS) in homeland security was expressed in the Intelligence Reform and Terrorism Prevention Act, passed on 17 December 2004. The section headed "Information Sharing" requires the president to establish a secure "information sharing environment" (ISE) for data related to terrorism. The act also establishes an Information Sharing Council "to assist the president and the ISE program manager with ISE-related duties."[1] In essence, this section of the act aims to implement the recommendation of the 9/11 Commission, which called for replacing "need to know" with "need to share" as the paradigm for IS.[2] We believe that if ISE is to be developed successfully, an analogous paradigm shift is required in Information Sharing Needs Analysis (ISNA) itself. This chapter outlines a new paradigm.

In IT projects, needs assessment has traditionally been a finite phase. To the best of their ability, systems designers develop an analysis of users' current needs and potential future needs. At a certain point, this is translated into a scope of work that is "frozen" so that the "building" can begin. The quality of the needs analysis is bounded not only by time but also by the ability to understand the end users' business logic and information needs. Because IS is so fundamental to homeland security, and because IS needs are complex and dynamic,[3] we believe that ISNA must be carefully managed not as a phase in a project but rather as an ongoing—that is, an evolving—process. We also believe that, to a much greater extent than traditional needs analysis, ISNA must involve the sharers of information: the end users of the system.

In homeland security, needs related to IS vary greatly by agency, group, and mission. Disparate agencies will resist a centralized, "one size fits all" approach to IS; and a uniform set of data requirements will satisfy no one. Therefore, ISNA must be decentralized, nonhierarchical, and bottom-up. Groups of sharers should be empowered to determine what their own "private" IS needs are; this empowerment will provide traction against several problems and issues: bureaucratic competition over turf and over the control of information and authority; concerns about legal liability, accountability, and possible accusations of infringement of civil liberties (such as privacy); fear of information overload; inadequacies in the information management system;[4] and concern about strain-limited analytical resources. See Figure 63-1 for a list of impediments to information sharing.

Our concept of distributed ISNA is a key to addressing these significant concerns and achieving the desired outcomes. In short, each sharing group (i.e., an intra- or interagency group of people who have decided to share information among themselves and their systems) crafts its own IS policies, procedures, and collaborative environments.

SCENARIO-BASED ISNA

We use the term *scenario* to refer to a "chronothematic" sequence of events and activities that drive the IS needs of the sharing group. A scenario is a chronology of all the important pre- and postattack factors that are relevant for planning IS and coordinating joint action. The scenario itself is developed collaboratively by the entities involved.

Scenarios strengthen awareness of the interdisciplinary, collaborative nature of regional homeland security. They provide a context and rationale for uncovering and communicating information

F I G U R E   63-1

Impediments to information sharing.

- Organizational fragmentation and compartmentalization
- Culture of bureaucratic competition over *turf*—the authority and political power that goes with control of information
- Distrust of other agencies and their use of information
- Accountability and liability exposure concerns
- Parochial traditions, fear of change, and lack of initiative
- Concern about disinformation and leaks or malfeasance that could compromise sources and methods
- Security clearance and classification issues
- Absence of joint concept-of-operations and businesses processes that require sharing
- Legal impediments, such as concern that sharing might taint information for trial
- Civil liberties issues stemming from privacy protection concerns
- Absence of an information sharing needs and gap analysis methodology capable of handling dynamic information resources, needs, and complex requirements
- Federal-centric focus and state and/or local distrust of federal government
- Technology issues, such as the lack of secure communications links, incompatibility of databases and applications, and inadequate budget or staff to remedy system disconnects and incompatibilities
- Ignorance about whether information is important
- Inadequate information interpretation
- Concern about information overload

sharing needs and capabilities. A scenario-based methodology and software environment will help groups of agencies to rapidly "scope out" the following:

- Missions and tasks that drive the need to share information
- What information is shared
- When IS should occur
- How information is to be delivered

This process specifies IS needs at an unprecedented level of detail, laying a basis for improved and better-integrated information.

SOFTWARE "ARCHITECTURE" FOR ISNA

ISNA is not a onetime effort but a continuous process. It is collaborative and information-intensive, with a potentially large number of scenarios, involving multiple agencies. The process is also communication-intensive, if only because the participants may be geographically dispersed. Clearly, a software environment is needed to support collaboration and to capture, manage, and communicate a continually growing and changing body of knowledge about agency profiles, scenarios, needs for sharing, capabilities, channels, etc. Participants engage in negotiations to hammer out sharing agreements and specify and plan the implementation of channels over which sharing will take place.

The high-level requirements for this software environment are perhaps surprisingly demanding: what an agency needs to know or is able to share can itself be sensitive information. The environment must support secure and fine-grained access control and enforceable dissemination policies on all sharing-related information.

Structurally, IS will rarely be a simple hierarchy or hub-and-spokes arrangement; most often it will be isomorphic with the complex social networks of the communities that built it. The environment must support the construction, representation, and navigation of arbitrarily complex IS formats.

If (to change the metaphor), we think of IS as a map, or as mapping, then revealing the map or doing the mapping should be a bottom-up, opportunistic, discovery-driven process; it does not lend itself to centralized control. Nevertheless, the environment must allow for oversight in order to evaluate whether an IS map, in its shape and details, conforms to stated policy, and to track the implementation of the prescribed sharing channels.

The environment must also allow for descriptions of a wide variety of information, systems, sources, protocols, etc. Additionally, it must integrate seamlessly with any number of loosely coordinated pilots and projects.

Each scenario represents a consensus among agencies as to the context and rationale for IS. A scenario can be quite complex, with alternative outcomes and sub-scenarios. Each agency may have its own idiosyncratic culture and set of priorities. The environment must support a multicultural, collaborative process of composing and modifying possibly complex scenarios.

Cognitive overload is a persistent concern, given the abundance of information about sharing that must be gathered, analyzed, managed, and tracked. Interfaces between end users must allow participants to move back and forth easily between the "big picture" and the many details of scenarios, sharing channels, agreements, and so on.

These difficult requirements are not easily addressed by traditional, centralized software. A centralized design, in which all IS knowledge is stored in and accessed from a central location, is inadequate for a number of reasons:

Agencies are unlikely to cede control over the storage and management of information they consider sensitive.

Centralization limits scalability and creates a single point of failure.

ISNA is itself a form of information sharing (if only about IS itself).

The Intelligence Reform and Terrorism Prevention Act dictates a "decentralized, distributed" IS environment.

We believe that a system—whether it is conceptualized as architecture, a map, or something else—should eschew centralization. We envision a peer-to-peer (P2P) system in which peers form "sharing spaces." Each sharing space is under the control of a "sharing community," with its members either within a single agency or spread across several agencies. The community collaboratively constructs within its sharing space a local segment of the global IS arrangement. A community may elect to give other communities access to some content of its sharing space, subject to dissemination policies set by community members.

The sharing spaces are allowed to grow, discover each other, and interconnect securely and as needed, all with no need for centralized control. Some sharing spaces will be created by communities for the purpose of developing or specifying sharing needs and capabilities; other sharing spaces will be set up by oversight agencies to import this information and evaluate its "fitness" to policy.

To enable the rapid growth of a P2P network, the installation of a peer and attendant software must be a very simple and trustworthy process. We believe it can be made no more complicated than opening a Web page on a software distribution server, clicking on a button to download and install the software, and then following a guided configuration script. To instill confidence, the software would be delivered with source code and would log all activities as well as enable security audits.

The creation and configuration of sharing spaces must be simple to support agile information sharing; new information sharing communities must be able to form easily and quickly and disband as soon as the need for them disappears.The information (about IS) held in each sharing space would be encoded in "atomic" form, not as files. A uniform knowledge representation format, such as W3C's Resource Description Framework, would be used to enable open-ended querying of all information and provide the opportunity for rule-based analysis, such as determination of fitness to policy.

The peers in a sharing space collaborate and share their computing and storage resources while carrying out ISNA functions such as managing scenarios, recording sharing needs and capabilities, and discovering information sharing opportunities and gaps.

Peers expose service interfaces for remote access by Web applications or stand-alone tools through which end users collaborate in composing scenarios, analyzing needs and capabilities, and negotiating information sharing agreements.

CONCLUSION

The end result is a networked environment for ISNA that does not depend on a central controlling entity, gives each participant complete control over security and privacy, imposes minimal initial IT costs, and grows opportunistically to fit the demands of IS communities. We advocate a comprehensive approach to defining IS needs and to designing supporting IS policies and mechanisms to ensure that practices comply with policy.

Finally, we should note that much of this is very similar to "results management" as a framework for homeland security. The elements of results management are management system standards, scenario-based planning, risk management, and development of capabilities, with the goal of devising strategies for homeland security and assessing progress. As applied to homeland security, both results management and IS must be flexible, so as to respond effectively to changes—sometimes very dramatic changes—in threats or in operations. Goals, priorities, activities, partnerships, and allocations of resources may need to be reviewed or reconsidered very quickly; and the system must immediately take into account any new terrorist weapon or capability that threatens domestic targets, or any significant change in counterterrorist technology.

See also Chapter 16 **Homeland Security's National Strategic Position: Goals, Objectives, Measures Assessment.**

N O T E S

1. Intelligence Reform and Terrorism Prevention Act, P.L. 108-458, 2004, Section 1016.
2. Final Report of the 9/11 Commission, p. 417.
3. IS needs evolve over time, as do various factors in homeland security, such as threats, personnel, initiatives, geopolitics, standards, and technologies.
4. For example, construction of the FBI's Virtual Case Management System has been delayed despite available funding. See Curt Anderson, "FBI Computer Overhaul Hits Another Snag," Associated Press (13 January 2004).

Domestic Security and Civil Liberties

Introduction to Section 12

K. A. Taipale
Executive Director, Center for Advanced Studies in
Science and Technology Policy, World Policy Institute

Within the public discourse, concerns about domestic security and civil liberties are often asserted as competing and potentially incompatible policy interests requiring the achievement of some tolerable state of balance. Implicit in this notion of balance is the smuggled assumption of a dichotomous rivalry in which security and liberty are traded one for another in a zero-sum political game. But the notion is misleading, for there is no fulcrum—as is implicit in the metaphor of a balance—at which point the correct amount of security and liberty can be achieved. Rather, security and liberty are dual obligations of civil society, and each must be maximized within the constraints imposed by the other. "In a liberal republic, liberty presupposes security; [and] the point of security is liberty."[1]

Because metaphor affects not just how we communicate but also how we structure our understanding and perception from the outset, challenging the prevailing metaphor of balance is not simply a semantic game. Metaphor has suasive power, particularly in policy debates, because it sets the expectations that can presuppose the outcome. The notion of balance pits security against liberty in a presumed Jacobin antagonism: those seeking to maintain civil liberties can then be said to be against collective security, and those seeking security can be accused of being too easily willing to forgo individual liberty. Often invoked—but rarely parsed—is a comment attributed to Benjamin Franklin: "Those who would give up Essential

Liberty to purchase a little temporary Safety, deserve neither Liberty nor Safety."[2] Inherent in Franklin's rejection of purchasing temporary security by giving up essential liberty, however, is the presumption not of tension between the two, but rather of a duality of concern with security on the one hand, and with liberty on the other.

Nevertheless, in policy debates about security and liberty, the need for achieving balance is often invoked in response to perceived challenges to the doctrinal status quo. The primary challenge to existing doctrine—that is, the presumed imbalance to be righted—in the current debate results from a blurring of the traditional line between reactive domestic law enforcement policies and preemptive national security strategies in response to the changed nature of the threat posed by transnational terrorism.[3] Because the exercise of law enforcement and national security power has previously been governed by disparate—and potentially irreconcilable—doctrines and laws, this blurring requires determining which set of existing principles, or what new principles, will govern in these changed circumstances.

New security policies are necessary because the seed value of potentially catastrophic outcomes to national security has devolved from other nation-states (the traditional target of national security power) to organized but stateless groups (the traditional target of law enforcement power), and the consequences of failing to prevent attacks before they occur have become politically unbearable. Thus a general consensus to take a preemptive rather than a reactive approach to counter these threats has emerged: even the most strident civil libertarians concede the need to identify and stop terrorists before they act. Preemption, however, requires *actionable intelligence*—that is, information useful in predicting and countering future behaviors. Actionable intelligence can generally be obtained only through forms of *surveillance*—the selective observation of precursor behaviors that are usually ambiguous and often resemble lawful behavior. Although surveillance is an accepted national security strategy, when it is applied in the context of domestic security it has the potential to conflict with traditional policy doctrines and legal structures premised in part on protecting individual liberty and based on the presumption of innocence. The policy question becomes when and under what circumstances selective government attention can be properly focused on a particular group or individual, and what standard such intelligence must meet before it is actionable for counterterrorism sanctions, particularly for sanctions that may not be subject to traditional judicial due process: for example, restrictions on travel or deportation for unrelated infractions.

Reconciling these conflicting needs, however, does not necessitate slighting one for the other if security and liberty are accepted as dual obligations. Indeed, there is no inherent policy conflict at all between security and liberty within the constitutional framework of reasonableness. Strategies that place an unreasonable burden on liberty—for example, demonizing a minority or engendering suspicion of everyone—are not just unacceptable outcomes for liberty but measures that provide little or no security because they are ineffective at identifying terrorists and they undermine the public cooperation and confidence needed for success. On the other hand, liberty incurs responsibility,[4] and unfettered liberty at the expense of security that can potentially result in catastrophic outcomes impinges not just on collective security but also on the very foundation of liberty for all individuals and is itself, therefore, unreasonable. However, *effective* security strategies—strategies that actually help locate, target, and preempt terrorists before they act without unduly burdening the vast majority of innocent people—are by definition not unreasonable, since individual liberty is not synonymous with permitting plotters to commit terrorist acts free from sanction.

Providing both security and liberty requires an informed policy debate in which the nature of the new challenges to traditional civil liberties doctrine is better understood and where the security strategies at hand for resolution are examined within the construct of the dual obligation to provide both security and liberty. The chapters in this section discuss these issues.

In Chapter 65 Paul Rosenzweig examines some of the changing base conditions presented by the transnational terrorist threat and various counterterrorism strategies. Abraham Foxman (Chapter 66) and Laura Murphy (Chapter 67) examine the changing nature of the threat to civil liberties and identify constraints imposed by civil liberty concerns on security strategies. Finally, in Chapter 68 Newton Minow and Fred Cate examine how new technologies challenge privacy but also present new opportunities to protect both civil liberties and security. Together, these chapters help inform a process that can—and must—lead to fulfilling both obligations: improved security and protected liberty.

NOTES

1. Thomas Powers, "Can We Be Secure and Free?" *Public Interest* 151:3 (Spring 2003): 5.

2. Pennsylvania Assembly: Reply to the Governor, 11 November 1755. See Leonard W. Labaree (ed.), *The Papers of Benjamin Franklin*, Vol. 6 (1963), p. 242.

3. U.S. Department of Justice, "Fact Sheet: Shifting from Prosecution to Prevention, Redesigning the Justice Department to Prevent Future Acts of Terrorism" (29 May 2002).

4. See the following: Amitai Etzioni, *The Spirit of Community: Rights, Responsibilities, and the Communitarian Agenda* (New York: Crown Publishers, 1993), 323 pp. George Bernard Shaw, *Man and Superman* and *Maxims for Revolutionists: Liberty and Equality* (Cambridge, Mass.: The University Press, 1903). ("Liberty means responsibility. That is why most men dread it.")

Thinking About Civil Liberty and Terrorism

Paul Rosenzweig
Senior Legal Research Fellow, The Heritage Foundation,
Adjunct Professor of Law, George Mason University,
School of Law

In any civilized society the most important task is achieving a proper balance between freedom and order. In wartime, reason and history both suggest that this balance shifts in favor of order—in favor of the government's ability to deal with conditions that threaten the national well-being.

—William Rehnquist[1]

INTRODUCTION

Not everyone would agree with Chief Justice Rehnquist about the balance between liberty and order. Since 9/11, a movement has emerged that might be called anti-antiterrorism. Its argument is that certain steps being taken domestically against potential terrorist attacks are too intrusive and threaten civil liberties. This movement has criticized many aspects of the domestic legal response to terrorism, but one focus in particular is the PATRIOT Act,[2] which was passed with overwhelming support by Congress soon after 9/11. Various provisions of the act are said to have seriously infringed on American liberties, while failing to deal effectively with the threat of

---

Note: Portions of this chapter are from the author's "Civil Liberties and the Response to Terrorism," 2004, and are used with permission. Paul Rosenzweig, "Civil Liberties and the Response to Terrorism," 42 *Duquesne L. Rev.* 663 (2004).

terror. Actually, the public concept of the PATRIOT Act is somewhat broader than its actual provisions. Nevertheless, its very name has come to symbolize, for some commentators, all areas of domestic antiterrorist law enforcement. It seems to have become a convenient shorthand term for all questions that have arisen about the alteration in the balance between civil liberty and national security.

Two overarching themes can perhaps be identified in the criticism of the PATRIOT Act, in itself and as a symbol. First, its critics frequently decry the expansion of executive authority as such. At least sometimes they seem to equate the potential abuse of authority by the executive branch with actual abuse. They may argue, implicitly or explicitly, that growth in executive power is a threat, whether or not the power has in fact been misused. In essence, these critics come from a long tradition of limited government that fears any expansion of executive authority because potential abuses of power outweigh any potential benefits.

The second theme might be described as a fear of greater efficiency. As part of its counterterrorist program, the government has begun to explore ways of applying technology to manage data and facilitate law enforcement. New technologies offer two advantages over current investigative practices: they can, potentially, expand the information available to federal law enforcement and intelligence agencies; and they can enhance the efficiency with which those agencies are able to examine and correlate existing information. Both possibilities are of concern to critics of the programs. Expanded access to information increases executive power, and with greater efficiency comes more effective use of power.

Proponents of the PATRIOT Act (again, in itself and as a symbol) argue that, for one thing, its critics fail to make certain important distinctions. According to this argument, criticism of the act often blurs potentiality and actuality. Although many aspects of the act do expand governmental power, its advocates say that the potential for abuse has proved to be far less than what the critics assumed.[3]

A second argument advanced by these advocates of the PATRIOT Act is that much of the belief in the potential for abuse stems from a misunderstanding—and an exaggeration—of the true nature of the new governmental powers involved.

A third argument offered by the advocates is more fundamental: they say that what the critics are proposing is a prohibition against expansion of executive power, and that in the context of a war on terrorism any such prohibition would be a mistake. Whereas we could afford such a solution with regard to traditional criminality, we cannot afford it in combating the threat of terror. In our current circumstances (the proponents' argument goes), the correct response is vigilance and oversight, enforced through legal, organizational, and technical means. To prevent excessive encroachment on civil liberties, we need only remain watchful.

This chapter (as the reader may have already surmised from the author's affiliation) is on the side of the proponents of the PATRIOT Act. From this viewpoint, the chapter will discuss the public debate on the threat posed to civil liberty by the expansion of executive power. It will outline some theoretical constructs that, in the author's opinion, should guide analysis of the PATRIOT Act and of related expansions of government power. It will also summarize some of the relevant history and will attempt to identify similarities and differences between past experiences and the contemporary situation. It will then offer some basic principles for assessing the potential threat to civil liberties posed by various legal and technological changes.[4]

CONTEXT: THE CHANGING NATURE OF LAW ENFORCEMENT AND INTELLIGENCE

Counterterrorism as it exists today needs to be placed in its historical context. To at least some degree, assessment of the PATRIOT Act depends on that context—on how one views the nation's responses in times of war, what one considers the constitutional constraints on executive power, and whether one puts the threat of terror into the "law enforcement" box or the "intelligence" box for legal analysis. Arguably, the war on terror is not a classic law enforcement problem, and thus most of the difficulties in contemporary analysis arise from trying to fit a square peg—law enforcement practices—into a round hole, the reality of terrorism.

THE LESSONS OF HISTORY

Some people caution against repeating past excesses in current counterterrorism. They see in history a series of lessons about overreactions and overzealousness in the face of war. The tension between civil liberty and national security is but one example of how we repeatedly return to the same fundamental issues. Consider the following episodes.[5]

In 1798, during the Napoleonic wars in Europe, President John Adams, a Federalist, effectively brought the United States into a state of undeclared war on the side of Britain against France. Thomas Jefferson and the Democratic Republican Party opposed these measures as likely to provoke an actual, unnecessary war. The Federalists, in turn, accused the Jeffersonians of treason. The Federalist Congress exacerbated the situation by passing the Alien and Sedition Acts of 1798.[6] The Alien Act authorized the president to deport any noncitizen he judged dangerous to the peace and safety of the United States; the deportee would have no right to a hearing and no right to present evidence. The Sedition Act prohibited the publication of false, scandalous, and malicious writings against the government, Congress, or the president with intent to bring them into contempt or disrepute. These were, in effect, aggressive efforts to suppress political criticism of Adams, his policies, and his administration. The acts expired, and Jefferson, after succeeding Adams as president, pardoned all those who had been convicted under it. Though never tested in the Supreme Court, these acts are widely regarded as having been unconstitutional and a stain on the nation.

During the Civil War, President Abraham Lincoln suspended the writ of habeas corpus on eight occasions. The broadest such suspension declared that "all persons ... guilty of any disloyal practice ... shall be subject to court martial."[7] Under this authority as many as 38,000 civilians were imprisoned by the military.[8] In 1866, a year after the war ended, the Supreme Court ruled that the president was not constitutionally empowered to suspend the writ of habeas corpus, even in time of war, if the ordinary civil courts were functioning.[9] This suspension too is considered by some an excessive response to a crisis and has come to be regarded as an unfortunate wartime error.

In 1917, the United States entered World War I. Thereafter, federal authorities, acting under the Espionage Act,[10] prosecuted more than 2,000 people for their opposition to the war. As a result, virtually all antiwar sentiment was suppressed. The Supreme Court initially approved most federal actions in support of the war,[11] but over the next half-century it overruled every one of the decisions it had made during World War I, in effect repudiating the excesses of the wartime period.[12]

On 19 February 1942, during World War II, President Franklin Delano Roosevelt signed Executive Order (EO) 9066,[13] authorizing the army to "designate military areas" from which "any persons may be excluded." Over the next eight months, more than 110,000 people of Japanese descent were forced to leave their homes in California, Washington, Oregon, and Arizona. Although the Supreme Court upheld the president's action,[14] it has come to be recognized as a grave error. In 1988, President Ronald Reagan offered an official presidential apology and reparations to each of the Japanese-American internees.[15]

Geoffrey Stone has said of all this: "In time of war—or, more precisely, in time of national crisis—we respond too harshly in our restriction of civil liberties, and then, later, regret our behavior."[16]

However, proponents of the PATRIOT Act and related measures maintain that reading too much into this history is a mistake that could have grave consequences. First, it disregards necessity. As Justice Arthur Goldberg said, "While the Constitution protects against invasions of individual rights, it is not a suicide pact."[17] And although some of these historical reactions were overreactions (nobody argues today that the internment of the Japanese served a useful military purpose), others were not.

Many people, for example, think that Lincoln's suspension of habeas corpus was essential to the prosecution of the war.[18] Some argue that it was necessary to protect the troops, save Maryland for the Union, and secure the safety of Washington, D.C.[19] Lincoln himself made this argument, in a special address to Congress on 4 July 1861.[20] Later in the war, the draft riots in New York threatened to deprive the Union of conscripts.[21] Lincoln feared that this might bring the war to a premature end, leaving the United States divided and slavery still legal.[22] Using the authority granted by Congress in the Habeas Corpus Act,[23] he directed the draft boards to ignore writs of habeas corpus issued to them by state courts seeking release of the conscripts.[24] It seems reasonable to argue that even if Lincoln's acts were de jure improper, they were de facto justifiable, and perhaps praiseworthy.

The first lesson here, we can argue, is that we should not be too harsh in our retrospective judgments—hindsight is always 20/20. And as for ourselves and our own time, we must perhaps be at least somewhat generous in our self-review. We may not know for many years whether or not our current fears were well-founded.

CONTEMPORARY OVERSIGHT

Actually, the historical episodes described above can be seen as offering comfort. Many people today think that we are on a downward spiral toward diminished civil liberties. But possibly a better view of this history will show that the balance between liberty and security is more like a pendulum: it may be pushed far in one direction by significant events (such as 9/11) but will eventually swing back toward the center, after the catastrophe has ended, the threat has receded, and people have recovered from their initial reaction.

We should acknowledge the historical reality that when a wartime crisis passes, the balance swings back in favor of freedom and liberty. And since World War II, our society has matured, so that the pendulum is unlikely to swing as far as has happened in the past. For example, whatever one may think of the detention of three Americans as enemy combatants, there is a difference in degree from the detention of over 100,000 Japanese-Americans. Perhaps there is also a difference in kind, since the detention in the former case was based on some individual suspicion, but this was not true with regard to the Japanese-Americans.[25] Chief Justice Rehnquist has said:

> There is every reason to think that the historic trend against the least justified of the curtailments of civil liberty in wartime will continue in the future. It is neither desirable nor is it remotely likely that civil liberty will occupy as favored a position in wartime as it does in peacetime. But it is both desirable and likely that more careful attention will be paid by the courts to the basis for the government's claims of necessity as a basis for curtailing civil liberty.[26]

What accounts for this seeming change in the contemporary context? Though little empirical evidence exists, a rough analysis can identify a number of factors, all of which contribute to greater oversight in the exercise of executive authority, constraining the greatest excesses:

- *A more activist Court*: The present-day Court seems far more willing to overturn executive branch actions and thus acts as a limit on excessive power. Earlier crises occurred before the "rights revolution" of the 1960s and the growth of judicial power. Indeed, the Rehnquist Court had invalidated more acts of Congress than any previous Court,[27] suggesting a high degree of involvement in curtailing authority.[28]

- *A more partisan Congress*: Though partisanship is sometimes deplored, its growth has brought at least one benefit—a greater "market" for oversight of the executive branch. Since the Watergate era, we have seen an increasing use of congressional investigative authority; and the prospect of aggressive congressional oversight, such as the prospect of public censure, can act as a check on executive power.

- *Investigative journalism*: Since Watergate, the press has focused more on exposing activities that some might prefer to keep secret from the public. It is hard to imagine a return to the days when the press actively participated in concealing Franklin Roosevelt's disability or Kennedy's dalliances. This trend may reduce the possibility of secret prosecutions and secret searches and seizures.

- *Public interest groups*: Americans now form public interest groups, such as the American Civil Liberties Union (ACLU), to a greater extent than ever before. These organizations, through their public information and litigation activities, also act as a check on executive authority. They are like the "canary down the mineshaft," serving as an early warning system of abuse.[29]

- *An increase in the public's ability to monitor government*: Technology, which offers greater opportunity for the government to monitor citizens' activities, also promises greater governmental accountability by making governmental functions more transparent.[30]

- *Greater awareness of civil liberties*: The public seems far more educated about civil liberties today than at any time in the past. The "information age" and the Internet allow individuals to gather the information necessary to make decisions and, if necessary, to organize a response to governmental power. Many Americans are vitally concerned about freedom, liberty, and governmental action and exercise their franchise with those concerns in mind.[31]

Admittedly, there is little more than anecdotal evidence to support this analysis, but it appeals to common sense and seems consistent with contemporary experience. We may indeed have strengthened, substantially, our ability to examine, oversee, and correct abuses of executive power. The public is in a stronger position today than it ever has been before. And, arguably, that power of oversight gives us freedom to grant the government great powers when the need arises, secure in the knowledge that we can restrain their exercise as appropriate. In short, one possible lesson from history is that we should not be utterly unwilling to adjust our response to liberty and security for the sake of counterterrorism, since we have the capacity to manage that adjustment, and to readjust it as necessary.[32]

THE CONSTITUTIONAL STRUCTURE

The Constitution weighs heavily in both sides of the debate over national security and civil liberties. The president and Congress must respect and defend the individual civil liberties guaranteed in the Constitution; but they should not fail to act when we face a serious threat from a foreign enemy.

The Preamble to the Constitution acknowledges that the U.S. government was established in part to provide for the common defense. Presumably, the war powers were granted to Congress and the president in order to be used. Congress was also granted the power to "punish ... Offenses against the Law of Nations,"[33] which include the international law of war, or terrorism. In addition, serving as chief executive and commander-in-chief, the president also has the duty to "take Care that the Laws be faithfully executed," including laws pertaining to national security and immigration.

Thus, it can be argued that as we consider questions of civil liberty it is important not to lose sight of one goal of government—personal and national security. In this regard, it is worth noting that under settled modern Fourth Amendment jurisprudence, law enforcement may secure without a warrant (through a subpoena) an individual's bank records, telephone toll records, and credit card records, to name just three of many sources of data. Other information in government databases (e.g., arrest records, entries to and exits from the country, and drivers' licenses) may be accessed directly without even the need for a subpoena.

In 1967, the Supreme Court said that the Fourth Amendment protects only those matters in which someone has a "reasonable expectation of privacy" and, concurrently, that anything one exposes to the public (i.e., puts in public view or gives to others outside his or her own personal domain) is not something in which he or she has a "reasonable" expectation of privacy—that is, a legally enforceable right to prohibit others from accessing or using what has been exposed.[34] So, for example, federal agents need no warrant, no subpoena, and no court authorization to do the following:

> Have a cooperating witness tape a conversation with a third party (because the words of the third party have been exposed to the public)[35]
>
> Attach a beeper to someone's car to track it (because the car's movements are exposed to the public)[36]
>
> Fly a helicopter over a house to see what can be seen[37]
>
> Search someone's garbage[38]

Thus, an individual's banking activity, credit card purchases, flight itineraries, and charitable donations are information that the government may access because the individual has voluntarily provided it to a third party. According to the Supreme Court, no one has any constitutionally based enforceable expectation of privacy in them. The individual who is the original source of this information cannot complain when another entity gives it to the government. Nor does the individual have a constitutional right to be notified of the inquiry.[39] Some thoughtful scholars have criticized this line of cases, but the issue has been fairly well settled for decades.[40]

Congress, of course, may augment the protections that the Constitution provides and has done so with respect to certain information. There are privacy laws restricting the dissemination of data held by banks, credit card companies, and the like.[41] But in almost all these laws (the census being a notable exception),[42] the privacy protections are good only as against other private parties; they yield to criminal, national security, and foreign intelligence investigations.

One caveat should be made here: the foregoing discussion has identified principally the restrictions that apply to domestic law enforcement officials. There are additional restrictions on the authority of foreign intelligence agencies to conduct surveillance or examine the conduct of American citizens. However, the courts have recognized that the Fourth Amendment applies somewhat differently to national security as distinct from domestic law enforcement.[43]

TYPE 1 AND TYPE 2 ERRORS: THE REALITY OF TERRORISM

Terrorism remains a potent threat to international security. The U.S. State Department has a list of over 100,000 suspected terrorists or people suspected to have contact to terrorists worldwide.[44] Before its camps in Afghanistan were shut down, al-Qaida evidently trained at least 70,000 people.[45] Jemaah Islamiyah in Indonesia (an organization linked to al-Qaida) has been estimated to have 3,000 members across Southeast Asia and still to be growing.[46] Although estimates of the number of al-Qaida terrorists in the United States have varied since 9/11, the figure provided by the government in recent, supposedly confidential, briefings to policy makers was 5,000.[47] This figure may include many who are raising funds for terrorist organizations and others who have been trained for the Jihad, whether or not they are actively participating in terrorist cells. But these and other publicly available statistics probably support two conclusions: (1) no one can say with much certainty how many terrorists are living in the United States; and (2) many who want to enter in the foreseeable future will be able to do so. Given the porousness of our borders and the potential availability of catastrophic weapons, one scholar (Graham Allison, who was an official in the Defense Department during the Clinton administration) has predicted that there is a 50-50 chance that a nuclear weapon will be exploded on American soil within the next 10 years.[48]

The threat is not exclusively internal. The newest terrorist target may be global shipping. The world is particularly vulnerable to maritime terrorism, and maritime piracy is already increasing.[49] *Lloyd's List* has reported that terrorists might be training maritime pilots in the Malacca Strait in order to capture a ship, pilot it into a port or chokepoint, and detonate it.[50]

Virtually every terrorism expert in and out of government believes that there is a significant risk of another attack. During the Cold War, U.S. analysts assessed the capabilities of the Soviet Union, on the assumption that its capabilities limited the threat it posed. But today the threat of a terrorist attack is asymmetric. Because terrorists use low-tech means (e.g., box cutters), their capacity for harm is, in a sense, limitless. The United States therefore faces the far more difficult task of discerning their intentions. Whereas the Soviet Union created "things" that could be observed, the terrorists create only transactions that are difficult to sift from the noise of everyday activity. This may be a problem of unprecedented scope, and one that must be solved if American lives are to be saved.

Terrorism cannot be suppressed by military means alone. Effective law enforcement intelligence may be the key to forestalling new terrorist acts, if recent history can serve as a guide.[51] In fact, the police have arrested more terrorists than military operations have captured or killed. Police in more than 100 countries have arrested more than 3,000 people whom they suspect of being linked to al-Qaida,[52] while the military has captured some 650 enemy combatants.[53] Equally important, the situation may require a different form of policing: preventive rather than reactive. This is because some terrorists are willing to perish in an attack.

Thus, we can maintain, the traditional model of law enforcement needs to be modified (or, in some instances, discarded) in the context of investigating terrorism. The traditional model is highly protective of civil liberty, in preference to physical security. The maxim "It is better that 10 guilty go free than that one innocent be mistakenly punished"[54] embodies a moral judgment about criminal law. To put this maxim another way, American society is less willing to accept false positives—type 1 errors—than false negatives, type 2 errors.[55] One factor in that preference is a historical distrust of government (as noted earlier, this distrust motivates some critics of the PATRIOT Act). Another factor, at least implicitly, is a comparative valuation of the social costs of type 1 errors (punishing the innocent) and type 2 errors (freeing the guilty): we tend to see a great cost in any type 1 error. And, although we realize that type 2 errors also have a social cost (since they return the guilty to the general population), we have a commonsense understanding that type 2 errors do not threaten large numbers of citizens or the American polity itself.

But 9/11 has, for some people, changed the calculation. First, they say, it changes the cost of type 2 errors. According to this argument, whatever the cost of freeing a member of the Mafia such as John Gotti or an individual criminal such as the sniper John Muhammad, it must be substantially less than freeing a member of al-Qaida and thus failing to stop a terrorist assault. It follows that our law enforcement system must be modified to meet the new reality. In other words, we cannot accept the rule that "Better 10 terrorists go free than that one innocent be mistakenly punished."[56]

Second, 9/11 has changed the nature of type 1 errors. In traditional law enforcement the "liberty interest" is personal liberty, freedom from the unjustified application of governmental force. We have as a model the concept of an arrest, the seizure of physical evidence, or the search of a tangible place. As we move into the information age, and deploy new technology to track terrorists, that model is probably no longer wholly valid.

Rather, we now add a distinct, though related, concept of liberty: the liberty that comes from anonymity.[57] Anonymity is a possibly weaker form of liberty. The American understanding of liberty interests tends to acknowledge that the personal data of those who have committed no criminal offense can be collected for legitimate governmental purposes. Typically, outside the criminal context, such collection is done in the aggregate and under a general promise that uniquely identifying individual information will not be disclosed. Examples include individual data collected by the census and by the Internal Revenue Service (IRS) (the latter can be disclosed outside of IRS only with the approval of a federal judge based upon a showing of need).[58] These examples suggest, not that Americans expect absolute privacy, but that government scrutiny that impinges on our liberty is expected to occur only with good cause, even in a criminal or terrorism investigation.[59]

This concept of the liberty interest at stake (the interest that will be lost when type I errors occur) emphasizes one other point about privacy: new counterterrorist laws and systems are not necessarily an unalloyed diminution of privacy. Rather, such laws and practices may substitute one intrusion (for example, a search of electronic data about an individual) for another intrusion (a physical body search at an airport). This implies that legal analysts cannot make broad value judgments, because individuals evaluate their own privacy differently. For many Americans, the price of less electronic privacy might not be too great if it resulted in more physical privacy, but some might conclude otherwise. This does not suggest much that could resolve the tension; but possibly it suggests that we should not allow the tension to be resolved by unrepresentative institutions like the courts but should, rather, entrust the evaluation of privacy preferences to more representative institutions, like the legislature.

Not all solutions necessarily trade off type 1 and type 2 errors. Some novel technological approaches to counterterrorism might reduce the incidence of both types of error.[60] More commonly, we will alter both values but the comparative changes will be the important factor. Where many critics of the PATRIOT Act and other governmental initiatives go wrong is, it seems to me, in their absolutism—they refuse to admit that we might need to accept an increase in type 1 errors. To me, their reasoning simply cannot be right, because liberty is not an absolute value; it depends on security (both personal and national). As Thomas Powers has written: "In a liberal republic, liberty presupposes security; the point of security is liberty."[61] If (as I believe) type 2 errors have become more dangerous, then we must be more tolerant of type 1 errors—and this is true even though our goal should be to minimize both types.

SOME GENERAL PRINCIPLES

If Congress and the president have a constitutional obligation to act forcefully to safeguard Americans against foreign attacks, this does not mean that everything they might attempt is necessarily prudent or within their power. Core American principles would seem to require that any new counterterrorism technology (deployed domestically) should be used only within the following bounds:[62]

- No fundamental liberty guaranteed by the Constitution can be breached or infringed upon.
- Any increased intrusion on American privacy interests must be justified through an understanding of the particular nature, significance, and severity of the threat being addressed by the program. The less significant the threat, the less justified the intrusion.
- Any new intrusion must be justified by a demonstration of its effectiveness in diminishing the threat. For example, if a new system or technology creates many false positives, it is suspect. If it "fits" the threat—if it effectively predicts or thwarts terrorism—it should be more willingly embraced.
- The full extent and nature of an intrusion must be understood, and appropriate limits applied. Not all intrusions are justified simply because they are effective. For example, strip searches at airports would prevent people from boarding planes with weapons, but at too high a cost.
- Whatever the justification for an intrusion, if there are less intrusive means of achieving the same end at a comparable

cost, the less intrusive means should be preferred. There is no reason to erode Americans' privacy when equivalent results can be achieved without doing so.

- Any new system must be designed to be tolerable in the long term. The war against terror may have no immediately foreseeable end; thus excessive intrusions may not be justifiable as emergency measures that will soon lapse. Policy makers must be restrained, because the nation might have to live with the consequences of their decisions for a long time.

From these general principles can be derived certain specific conclusions regarding new technology:

- No new system should alter or contravene existing legal restrictions on the government's ability to access data about private individuals. Any new system should mirror and implement existing legal limitations on domestic or foreign activity, depending on its sphere of operation.
- No new system should alter or contravene existing operational system limitations. Development of new technology is not a basis for authorizing new government powers or new government capabilities. Any such expansion should be independently justified.
- No new system that materially affects citizens' privacy should be developed without specific authorization by Congress, or without provisions for congressional oversight.
- Any new system should be as tamperproof as possible.
- Any new system should have built-in safeguards to reveal and trace abuse.
- Any new system should, as far as possible, incorporate technological improvements in the protection of American civil liberties.
- No new system should be implemented without a full array of protections against its abuse.

CONCLUSION

As James Madison told the Virginia ratifying convention: "There are more instances of the abridgment of the freedom of the people by gradual and silent encroachments of those in power than by violent and sudden usurpations."[63]

These theoretical considerations and operational guidelines will be of real value only in their application to actual problems and proposed solutions. With regard to counterterrorism, it is not sensible either to condemn every governmental initiative or to give the government a blank check. Each program and proposal must be carefully assessed on its own merits. Measured against these standards, the PATRIOT Act and related governmental programs can be said to hold up fairly well. By and large, I believe, they post little practical threat to civil liberty and promise significant benefit.

Rather than focus on the possibility of executive abuse, America may need to construct suitable oversight and response mechanisms that will both empower executive action and suitably check abusive practices. That effort, in the long run, is far more likely to enhance Americans' security and liberty.

N O T E S

1. William Rehnquist, "All the Laws But One: Civil Liberties in Wartime," *Online Newshour* (11 November 1998); www.pbs.org/newshour/gergen/november98/gergen_11-11.html.

2. See USA PATRIOT Act, P.L. 107-56, 115 Stat. 272 (26 October 2001).

3. According to the inspector general for the Department of Justice, there have been no instances in which the PATRIOT Act has been invoked to infringe on civil rights or civil liberties. See Report to Congress on Implementation of Section 1001 of the USA PATRIOT Act (27 January 2004). See also "Report Finds No Abuses of PATRIOT Act," *Washington Post* (28 January 2004): A2.

4. For more details, see Paul Rosenzweig, "Civil Liberties and the Response to Terrorism," *Duquesne Law Review* 42 (2004): 63.

5. This summary is based on Geoffrey Stone, "Civil Liberties in Wartime," *J.S. Ct. Hist* 28 (2003): 215. However, Stone reaches different conclusions.

6. See Fifth Congress, Second Session: An Act Concerning Aliens, 1 Stat 570-72; An Act Concerning Enemy Aliens, 1 Stat 577-78 (the Alien Acts); An Act for the Punishment of Certain Crimes against the United States, 1 Stat. 596-97 (the Sedition Act).

7. Roy P. Balser et al. (eds.), *The Collected Works of Abraham Lincoln* (Newark, N.J.: Rutgers University Press, 1953–1955), pp. 436–7.

8. Mark E. Neely, Jr., *The Fate of Liberty: Abraham Lincoln and Civil Liberties* (New York: Oxford University Press, 1991), pp. 113–38.

9. *Ex parte Milligan*, 71 U.S. 2, 1866.

10. Act of 15 June 1917, chap. 30, title I, §3, 40 Stat. 219.

11. For example, *Schenck v. U.S.*, 249 U.S. 47, 1919; *Debs v. U.S.*, 249 U.S. 211, 1919.

12. For example, *Brandenburg v. Ohio*, 395 U.S. 444, 1969.

13. *Federal Register*, Vol. 7, 1942, p. 1407.

14. *Korematsu v. United States*, 323 U.S. 214, 1944.

15. Civil Liberties Act of 1988, 102 Stat. 903, P.L. 100-383 (10 August 1988).

16. Stone, 2003, p. 215.

17. *Kennedy v. Mendoza-Martinez*, 372 U.S. 144, 160, 1963. Justice Goldberg was quoting Justice Robert Jackson, who made the same observation in *Terminnelo v. Chicago*, 337 US. 1, 1949.

18. See, e.g., Harry V. Jaffa, *A New Birth of Freedom: Abraham Lincoln and the Coming of the Civil War* (New York: Rowman and Littlefield, 2000), p. 364; and William Rehnquist, "Civil Liberty and the Civil War," Gauer Lecture, NLCPIS (1997).

19. See Neely (1991); Rehnquist (1991).

20. See Don Fehrenbacher (ed.), *Speeches and Writings: 1859–1865* (1989), pp. 246–62.

21. See James G. Randall and David Donald, *The Civil War and Reconstruction*, 2nd ed. (1961), p. 361.

22. Neely (1991), pp. 69–70.

23. An Act relating to Habeas Corpus, and Regulating Judicial Proceedings in Certain Cases, chap. 81, §1, 12 Stat. 755, 1863.

24. See Neely (1991), p. 72, for the text.

25. Michael Chertoff, "Law, Loyalty, and Terror," *Weekly Standard* (1 December 2003), pp. 15, 16.

26. Rehnquist (1998). See also Jeffrey Rosen, *The Naked Crowd* (New York: Random House, 2004), p. 131.

27. Remarks by Akhil Reed Amar, Heritage Foundation (9 July 2002). See also Cass Sunstein, "A Hand in the Matter," *Legal Affairs* (March–April 2003).

28. For example, the Supreme Court has already reviewed executive decisions relating to the detention of "enemy combatants." See *Hamdi v. Rumsfeld*, 124 S.Ct. 2633, 2004; *Rumsfeld v. Padillia*, 124 S.Ct. 2711, 2004; *Rasul v. Bush*, 124 S.Ct. 2686, 2004; *Ex parte Milligan*, 1866.

29. See Michael Kinsley, "An Incipient Loss of Freedom," *Washington Post* (15 June 2003): B07.

30. See Dennis Bailey, *The Open Society Paradox: Why the Twenty-First Century Calls for More Openness, Not Less* (Brassey, 2004). See also David Birn, *The Transparent Society* (Perseus Books Group, Philadelphia, PA, 1999), p. 378.

31. See Amatai Etzioni and Deidre Mead, *The State of Society: A Rush to Pre-9/11*; www.gwu.edu/~ccps/The_State_of_Society.html. They cite evidence from surveys that fewer respondents now think it necessary for average citizens to give up civil liberties.

32. There may also be technological factors. See, e.g., K. A. Taipale, "Data Mining and Domestic Security: Connecting the Dots to Make Sense of Data," *Columbia Science and Technology Law Review* 5:2 (2003); www.stlr.org/cite.cgi?volume=5&article=2.

33. U.S. Constitution, Article I, §8.

34. *Katz v. U.S.*, 389 U.S. 347, 1967.

35. *U.S. v. White*, 401 U.S. 745, 1971.

36. *U.S. v. Karo*, 468 U.S. 705, 1984.

37. *Florida v. Riley*, 488 U.S. 445, 1989.

38. *California v. Greenwood*, 486 U.S. 35, 1988.

39. *SEC v. O'Brien*, 467 U.S. 735, 1984. See also 743, citing *U.S. v. Miller*, 425 U.S. 435, 443, 1973.

40. For example, James X. Dempsey, "Communications Privacy in the Digital Age: Revitalizing the Federal Wiretap Laws to Enhance Privacy," *Albany Law Journal of Science and Technology* 8 (1997): 65.

41. For example, 12 U.S.C. §3402, §3403, §3407.

42. For example, 13 U.S.C. §8, §9, §214.

43. See, e.g., EO 12333, 3 C.F.R. 200, 1982; reprinted at 50 U.S.C. §401 note; *U.S. v. U.S. District Court (Keith)*, 407 U.S. 297, 1972; *In re Sealed Case*, 310 F.3d 717.

44. Eric Lichtblau, "Administration Creates Center for Master Terror 'Watch List,'" *New York Times* (17 September 2003): p. A20, col. 01.

45. See remarks by U.S. Senator Bob Graham, *Meet the Press* (13 July 2003) (televised interview).

46. Terence Hunt, "Bush Shows Resolve by Visiting Bali," *Chicago Sun-Times* (22 October 2003): 36.

47. Bill Gertz, "5,000 in U.S. Suspected of Ties to al Qaeda," *Washington Times* (11 July 2002).

48. See Graham Allison, *Nuclear Terrorism: The Ultimate Preventable Catastrophe* (Times Books, 2004).

49. For example, William Langewiesche, "Anarchy at Sea," *Atlantic* (September 2003).

50. "Asia Pirates Training for Terrorist Attack," *Lloyd's List International* (15 October 2003).

51. For example, Dana Dillon, "War on Terrorism in Southeast Asia: Developing Law Enforcement," *Backgrounder*, No. 1720, Heritage Foundation (22 January 2004).

52. Peter Slevin, "U.S. Pledges Not to Torture Terror Suspects," *Washington Post* (27 June 2003): A01.

53. Francis Taylor, "State Dept Official Says War against Terrorism Continues" (9 June 2003) (transcript); http://usembassy.state.gov/tokyo/wwwh20030611a6.html.

54. For example, *Furman v. Georgia*, 408 U.S. 238, 367 n. 158, 1972 (J. Marshall, concurring). For the aphorism, *Blackstone, Commentaries*, Vol. 4 (Wait, 1907), chap. 27, p. 358.

55. *In re Winship*, 397 U.S. 357, 372, 1970 (J. Harlan, concurring).

56. See William Stuntz, "Local Policing after the Terror," *Yale Law Journal* 111 (2002): 2137, 2183–4.

57. See Phillip Kurland, "The Private I," *University of Chicago Magazine* (Autumn 1976): 8; quoted in *Whalen v. Roe*, 429 U.S. 589, 599 n. 24, 1977.

58. For example, 26 U.S.C. §7213.

59. See Paul Rosenzweig, "Privacy and Consequences: Legal and Policy Structures for Implementing New Counterterrorism Technologies and Protecting Civil Liberty," in Robert Popp and John Yen (eds.), *Emergent Information Technologies and Enabling Policies for Counter Terrorism* (IEEE Press, forthcoming).

60. See Taipale (2003), p. 31.

61. Thomas Powers, "Can We Be Secure and Free? *The Public Interest* (Spring 2003); www.thepublicinterest.com.

62. See Paul Rosenzweig, "Principles for Safeguarding Civil Liberties in an Age of Terrorism," *Executive Memorandum*, No. 854, Heritage Foundation (January 2003).

63. Speech to the Virginia Ratifying Convention, 16 June 1788, reprinted in Matthew Spalding (ed.), *The Founders' Almanac*, Heritage Foundation (2002), p. 133.

Security and Freedom of Speech

Abraham H. Foxman
National Director, Anti-Defamation League

INTRODUCTION

Arguably, counterterrorism should include a system of law enforcement in which the police not only can pursue terrorists after they strike but—more importantly—can stop them before they act. But to achieve this, we may need to recalibrate the existing balance between individual liberty and national security.

Many Americans believe that even under the threat of terrorism we must start any reassessment of the relationship between civil rights and security from the premise that the United States has a set of basic principles of freedom and equality that must not be compromised. Among these is freedom of speech. They argue that the First Amendment protects even, or especially, wicked and hurtful speech, "ideas that we hate."[1] One line of reasoning in this regard is that only through a free exchange of ideas can society test its beliefs and rid itself of destructive ones[2]—that free speech is conducive to tolerance and social progress, especially in a diverse culture such as ours.

However, this chapter will advocate an opposing view, which has been held by many other Americans, including Justice Robert Jackson of the Supreme Court. Jackson once observed, during the 1940s, "The choice is not between order and liberty. It is between liberty with order and anarchy without either." He invoked "the oft-forgotten principle" that civil liberty "exists only under law and not independently of it" and warned that if we did "not temper ... doctrinaire logic with a little practical wisdom, [we would] convert the constitutional Bill of Rights into a suicide pact."[3]

Extremists have often used freedom of speech as a weapon against liberty. Whether by soapbox harangues, cross burnings, meetings in basements, or, more recently, the Internet, extremists in America have found ways to spread their hateful and seditious ideas. This extremist speech has largely been tolerated by law enforcement authorities. Meanwhile, over time, the rules governing free speech in the United States have developed in response to real threats to safety and public order, and a conceptual distinction between "advocacy" and "action" has evolved as the boundary for regulating such discourse.[4]

Today, Islamist terrorists are of primary concern. They use sophisticated methods to wreak widespread death and destruction, and their worldwide network of cooperating cells and interlocking groups has enormously increased the threat to innocent lives. Consequently, the conceptual distinction between advocacy and action may need some practical fine-tuning.

Take, for example, the words of Imam Fawaz Damra, a Muslim cleric who was convicted by a federal court in Ohio of submitting a fraudulent application for naturalization.[5] In 1988, addressing an audience in St. Louis, Missouri, he said:

> The first principle in which I believe—and it is also found in the words of Allah the Almighty, in the Holy Qur'an—this first principle is that *terrorism and terrorism alone is the way to liberation*. ... Our struggle with the Israeli enemy is the heart of the struggle. ... Get in touch with those young men who went to Afghanistan, and make them open a front in Palestine. [Direct] all the rifles at the first and last enemy of the Islamic nation and that is the sons of monkeys and pigs, the Jews.

This is standard hate speech. Although it is inflammatory, and although it advocates possibly criminal violence, it contains no incitement to imminent lawlessness and so is still protected by the First Amendment.

By contrast, in 1991, in a speech in Cleveland, Ohio, Damra exhorted the audience to "donate to the Islamic Jihad ... for the Intifadah! ... The Jihad!" He called for someone who "would leave his house with a knife to stab the Jews—12 Jews after the events of the Gulf War." When audience members gave money, he asked for more: "Brothers, the Intifadah calls you. Five hundred dollars! ... *If you write a check, write it for the Islamic Committee for Palestine, I.C.P.*"

This second example does not seem to be abstract advocacy. People who think that such speech should not be punished may be dangerously mistaken. Nor does it seem sensible to conclude that Damra's remarks related only to a foreign country's domestic conflict, and therefore did not directly affect the national security of the United States. In 1995, the Justice Department publicly identified Damra— along with Usama bin Ladin—as a possible unindicted coconspirator in the bombing of the World Trade Center in 1993.[6] We may once again cite Justice Jackson, who maintained that those who believe the Constitution should protect such extremism under the rubric of "free speech" have embraced "doctrinaire logic" over "practical wisdom."[7]

The U.S. government, at any rate, has begun to grapple with this threat, on the assumption that the First Amendment does afford sufficient flexibility so that security agencies can respond effectively to terrorist organizers and their supporters. Also, Congress has enacted antiterrorism legislation, including provisions of the USA PATRIOT Act, to authorize law enforcement action; the official assumption in this regard is that the PATRIOT Act will be applied carefully and responsibly and will respect free expression.

Another challenge, then, is to synchronize counterterrorism in a way that respects another fundamental right: freedom of religion.

AMERICAN FREE SPEECH JURISPRUDENCE

Historically, as American courts have considered the limits of free speech, they have not done so in a vacuum but have been influenced by the world around them. Threats—of sedition, of communism, of terrorism—have prompted efforts to constrain freedom of expression. Perhaps remarkably, First Amendment jurisprudence has been characterized by the concept that freedom of expression should not be constrained lightly or without justification. Limitations that have been imposed have been presented as exceptions to the basic guarantee. Nevertheless, another Supreme Court justice, Arthur Goldberg, famously restated Justice Jackson's admonition: "The Constitution is not a suicide pact."[8]

Understanding what recalibration may be necessary today requires some background on the history of free speech jurisprudence in the United States. Although this history dates back to the earliest years of the republic, the most significant case law developed in the twentieth century.

The first Sedition Acts in the United States were passed in 1798[9] and proved so unpopular that the next ones were not passed until World War I.[10] Consideration of the constitutionality of these later statutes set the terms for our modern understanding of the government's ability to limit free speech in wartime. The case, *Schenck v. United States*,[11] concerned two anarchists who were charged with conspiracy to violate the Espionage Act of 1917 for having "wilfully conspired" to circulate a document "calculated to cause . . . insubordination and obstruction" among men who had been called for military service. Justice Holmes's opinion upheld their convictions:

> We admit that in many places and in ordinary times the defendants in saying all that was said in the circular would have been within their constitutional rights. But the character of every act depends upon the circumstances in which it is done. . . . The question in every case is whether the words are used in such circumstances and of such a nature as to create a clear and present danger that they will bring about the substantive evils that Congress has a right to prevent. It is a question of proximity and degree.

Within the year, Holmes became uncomfortable with the Court's development of the "clear and present danger" test. In the Court's next noteworthy decision in this area, he dissented from affirming a conviction for conspiracy to violate the Espionage Act. This case, *Abrams v. United States*, concerned an individual convicted under the statute for printing a leaflet with "language intended to bring the form of government of the United States into contempt, scorn, contumely, and disrepute."[12] In its ruling, the majority relied on Holmes's opinion in *Schenck* and upheld the conviction, finding no violation of the defendant's right to free speech. But Holmes maintained that advocacy for a general strike that "urged curtailment of production of things necessary to the prosecution of the war" was not enough to prove that such advocacy was done, as required by the statute, "with intent by such curtailment to cripple or hinder the United States in the prosecution of the war." He said that although he did not doubt the questions of law decided in *Schenck*, even in wartime "it is only the present danger of immediate evil or an intent to bring it about that warrants Congress in setting a limit to the expression" of public issues; he concluded that "Congress certainly cannot forbid all effort to change the mind of the country."

Clear and present danger continued to be used in the 1950s, most notably in anticommunist cases.[13] Even in that context, however, doubts about the correctness of this standard grew. In *Dennis v. United States*,[14] the crime charged under the Smith Act was advocating violent overthrow of the government and conspiracy to advocate violent overthrow—not an actual conspiracy to overthrow the government. Neither the charge nor the evidence had anything to do with whether plans had actually been laid for an uprising. The Supreme Court, by a 6–2 vote, upheld the convictions of 11 Communist Party leaders. Justice Douglas, dissenting, argued for a narrow understanding of "clear and present danger" and held that free speech should be the rule, not the exception, and only "when conditions are so critical that there will be no time to avoid the evil that the speech threatens, is it time to call a halt." Justice Black, also dissenting, stated that these convictions could not be supported even under "clear and present danger."

In 1969, in *Brandenburg v. Ohio*,[15] the Court, adopting Justice Douglas's formulation, articulated the modern standard for when advocacy by itself is unprotected by the First Amendment: "Constitutional guarantees of free speech and free press do not permit a State to forbid or proscribe advocacy of the use of force or of law violation except where such advocacy is directed to inciting or producing imminent lawless action and is likely to incite or produce such action." Douglas concurred in *Brandenburg*, and focused on a corollary concern: that in order for speech to be punishable, there has to be something more to the speech itself than just words. There must be "speech plus" something, and the "plus" itself must be punishable: "The line between what is permissible and not subject to control and what may be made impermissible and subject to regulation is the line between ideas and overt acts." Douglas's position eventually won the day and was adopted by the Court three years later in *Healy v. James*.[16]

There remain some contexts in which pure speech can be punished. First, speech can lay a foundation for a criminal act, particularly criminal conspiracy.[17] Second, a speech or an expressive component does not immunize otherwise criminal behavior from punishment.[18] Third, speech can also be evidence of intent or motive, and be used to prove a crime.[19]

FREE SPEECH POST-9/11

Not surprisingly, how to respond to potentially harmful speech has become an issue since 9/11. This issue involves speech that constitutes incitement to imminent violence and therefore is not protected. It also involves expressive activity accompanied by potentially harmful conduct. Given the historical background, do recent events require further modification of the standards? Specifically, (1) is the *Brandenburg* incitement test still appropriate; and (2) is the United States moving effectively as a nation to punish harmful conduct when it accompanies advocacy of terrorism?

With regard to question 1, although incitement to violence is not protected speech, it is sometimes extremely difficult to determine what constitutes incitement—particularly under the *Brandenburg* test. This test requires a likelihood that the incitement will lead to imminent violence, and particularly when the speech is a form of religious advocacy or takes place in a religious setting.

Seeking to limit such speech may also raise concerns regarding the religion clauses of the First Amendment: the "free exercise" clause and the "establishment" clause. Not only does the Constitution protect free speech but it also protects the free exercise of religion and mandates the separation of church and state. These constitutional provisions require additional sensitivity on the part of law enforcement officials seeking to curtail or sanction advocacy in a religious setting such as a mosque.

Although most Muslims oppose terrorism and violence, some Islamic fundamentalists have sought to incite violence against Americans. A strong case could be made that in places like Iraq, where Americans are in fact being killed, such incitement should be punishable. It might also be argued that a battlefield is not the place for freedom of speech. In Iraq, the circumstances do not involve American law. But should the United States ever face a similar state of lawlessness, similar violent rhetoric would probably not be protected by the First Amendment.

Inside the United States, where the concern is mainly about plotting by secret terrorist cells, it is much harder to support an argument that anti-American preaching by Islamic fundamentalists, in and of itself, should be punishable, or an argument that Islamic fundamentalist Web sites advocating violence against the United States should be censored or forbidden. In both examples, the imminence of the threat that gives rise to unlawfulness is more difficult to establish. Also, any attempt to censor religious leaders would represent a dramatic change in American law; and there is little evidence that Americans are ready to accept such a change. Furthermore, it is not clear that censoring radical clerics would prevent terrorism within U.S. borders.

The key question, then, is question 2: are we moving effectively as a nation to punish harmful conduct that accompanies advocacy of terrorism?

A fundamental principle of constitutional law is that "violence or other types of potentially expressive activities that produce special harms distinct from their communicative impact . . . are entitled to no constitutional protection."[20] This principle predates 9/11 and underlies the concept of hate crimes. It now underlies provisions of the Anti-Terrorism Effective Death Penalty Act of 1996 (AEDPA), enacted after the first attack on the World Trade Center and the bombing of the Murrah Federal Building in Oklahoma City, and provisions of the PATRIOT Act, which expanded earlier prohibitions against material support for terrorism.

This constitutional principle seems sound and consistent with the First Amendment. Not speech as such but "speech plus" is limited. The question, then, is not whether the limitation is constitutional but whether it is adequate and how well it is being implemented in the post-9/11 context.

Section 303 of AEDPA, as modified by Section 810 of the PATRIOT Act, imposes criminal sanctions for anyone under the jurisdiction of the United States who "knowingly provides material support or resources to a foreign terrorist organization, or attempts or conspires to do so." "Material support or resources" is defined as "currency or monetary instruments or financial securities, financial services, lodging, training, expert advice or assistance, safe houses, false documentation or identification, communications equipment, facilities, weapons, lethal substances, explosives, personnel, transportation, and other physical assets, except medicine or religious materials."[21]

There have been some prosecutions, and portions of the definition of material support have already been challenged in court on First Amendment grounds. Specifically, "training," "expert advice and assistance," and "personnel," have been questioned, and at least two lower courts have found these provisions too vague. Probably, additional prosecutions will give rise to additional legal challenges.

It can be argued that as a matter of policy and common sense, providing tangible, material assistance to terrorists is and should be punishable. Providing such support may be a form of advocacy—communicating a message—but is apparently more than just advocacy and thus can be considered "speech plus." (Assault, for instance, also communicates a message but is clearly punishable.) Another point is that money is fungible, so if someone provides funding to underwrite social or presumably humanitarian efforts of a terrorist group, the group is able to use other assets for its terrorist activities. This is also a reason for regarding raising money as "speech plus," unprotected by the First Amendment.[22]

Historically there has been some question about whether giving money should be regarded as expressive activity; but the Supreme Court recently determined—in a different context, the financing of election campaigns—that there are limits to the protection afforded by the First Amendment to donations. If that interpretation ultimately applies as well to funding for groups designated as terrorist, the current law would appear to be sufficient. However, one part of the United States' strategy for preventing terrorism is to curb the funding of terrorist groups; therefore, any future court ruling that viewed such funding as protected expressive activity should probably raise serious questions.

Most other forms of material support listed in AEDPA seem punishable without raising First Amendment issues. Knowingly providing lodging, communications equipment, or weapons to terrorist groups does not seem to be an expressive activity. However, providing personnel, training, and expert advice or assistance, under certain circumstances, could be expressive activity. Suppose, for example, that a group identified as terrorist disagreed with the designation and wanted to obtain legal or public relations advice or expertise as to how to challenge it. Would an American offering such advice be violating the statute? Is that an appropriate application of the statute?[23]

Such questions deserve thoughtful analysis. Judicial determinations that certain definitions are too vague do not necessarily mean that providing personnel, training, or expert advice can never be prohibited; these findings mean only that the courts are going to require greater specificity from the legislature. One can readily think of examples that would clearly constitute material support for terrorists—pilot training is one example. These instances underscore the importance of the language in the statute which specifies that the individual must "knowingly provide" the assistance. A proprietor of a flight school would be subject to prosecution for providing expert assistance to an individual if the proprietor knew or should have known that a student was learning how to fly in order to operate a hijacked plane. If the current language of the statute ultimately is found to be too vague, it should be changed but probably not abandoned altogether, because the underlying concept makes sense.

The word *knowingly* in the current law would typically be interpreted by courts to mean that an individual providing support "knew or should have known" that the recipient was a terrorist group. This requirement protects those who were truly unaware. It thus strengthens the constitutional underpinnings of the statue as punishing more than just expressive activity. But in the post-9/11 context, one can reasonably ask whether it goes far enough. Should inadvertent assistance to terrorist groups also be punishable? Or, alternatively, if it is not punishable—and it probably should not be, because there is no criminal intent—how much of an impediment is this to law enforcement agencies newly charged not only with punishing but also with preventing crimes? And are there alternative strategies?

Another important question relates to the Internet. Would, and should, the law view an Internet Service Provider (ISP) that provides a platform for a terrorist Web site as offering material assistance to terrorism? Some ISPs voluntarily reject hate sites, and as private companies they have every right to establish terms of service and to ban pages that do not comply. Such ISPs could also reject sites advocating terrorism. However, it is not clear whether the government could legally prosecute, under the material-assistance laws, an ISP that hosts such a site.

Some ISPs, no doubt, would compare themselves to public utilities, such as telephone companies, and would argue that a telephone company is not held liable for allowing its technology to be used in the planning of a crime. But many ISPs require users to sign agreements regarding the content of the user's site and can accept or reject those clients seeking to use their technology for purposes contrary to corporate policy. Thus, ISPs are not directly analogous to utilities.

Moreover, as regards "material support," the question arises whether the nature of the Internet requires a particularized First Amendment analysis. Although the Supreme Court has made clear that its prior cases "provide no basis for qualifying the level of First Amendment scrutiny that should be applied" to the Internet, the applications of those settled standards of constitutional analysis to technological innovations are evolving.[24] The Court has consistently acknowledged that "each medium of expression ... may present its own problems"[25] and that "differences in the characteristics of new media justify differences in the First Amendment standards applied to them."[26] Along similar lines, Justice Breyer has maintained that "the Constitution permits legislatures to respond flexibly to the challenges future technology may pose to the individual's interest in basic personal privacy."[27] Arguably, the same approach should apply to national security and public safety.

In fact, at least one federal appellate court has upheld the regulation of speech on the Internet under the "speech plus" doctrine, in part reasoning that the Internet's technological capacity to disseminate worldwide computer programs that promote the piracy of copyrighted works warranted a more deferential constitutional standard of review.[28] The Internet's power to solicit financial support for terrorist causes from an untold number of individuals and to recruit terrorist operatives from every region of the globe might likewise inform the proper meaning of "material support" in the post-9/11 world.

To return to question 2, are we moving effectively to punish harmful conduct associated with advocacy of terrorism? Clearly, we are moving in that direction. It is not yet clear how effective the new laws are, but for now the question seems to be implementation, not First Amendment principles.

STRIKING A BALANCE: ADDITIONAL CONSIDERATIONS

We may now return to fanatics like Imam Damra. Faced with the current counterterrorism efforts of law enforcement agencies, other radicals are unlikely to be as explicit in their public statements as he was. They therefore will be harder to find. That being the case, what steps, if any, can law enforcement officers appropriately take in order to root them out? Should these officers, say, randomly investigate mosques and Muslim organizations around the country in the hope of uncovering criminal activity?

These questions represent another tricky intersection between practical attempts to ensure or enhance security and principled efforts to protect civil liberties. There are conflicting views on where to strike this balance. In May 2002, the Justice Department revamped its guidelines for permissible investigations of religious groups, including rules governing covert monitoring of religious gatherings.[29] These guidelines relieved federal investigators of an earlier requirement to show a reasonable suspicion of specific criminal activity by a group's members in order to justify starting an undercover investigation. Some commentators have strenuously objected to the new guidelines, arguing that the withdrawal of the "reasonable suspicion" requirement invites law enforcement agents to engage in discriminatory religious profiling.[30] Again, the right approach to the problem probably lies somewhere in between.

Stereotyping and scapegoating are unacceptable; we must ensure that no ethnic or religious minority in the United States is singled out for blame. Even when law enforcement officials are dealing with the threat of international terrorism, they should never engage in discriminatory profiling on the basis of ethnicity or religion. Suspicions must be grounded in factual evidence.

A different path might lead to, or toward, unlawful suppression of religious practice. For example, the fear of arbitrary infiltration of mosques by undercover law enforcement officers may already have caused reduced attendance at Muslim religious services, rewording of Islamic passages spoken at religious services that merely mention the word *jihad*, and a decrease in contributions to Muslim charities.[31] If the reports of such effects are true, they reveal a significant problem. An acceptable strategy to maximize security should not inhibit innocent religious observations. If a strategy does cause such inhibition, it probably contravenes the "principle that government, in pursuit of legitimate interests, cannot in a selective manner impose burdens only on conduct motivated by religious belief"—a principle which the Supreme Court has described as "essential to the protection of the rights guaranteed by the [Constitution's] Free exercise Clause."[32]

On the other hand, the requirement that the police demonstrate a reasonable suspicion of ongoing criminal activity before they may investigate the operations of a particular religious institution should not be interpreted so strictly as to hinder law enforcement unreasonably. Remember that Damra's invective against Jews and his calling generally for the murder of innocents was not and still is not criminal, by virtue of the free speech guarantee of the First Amendment.[33] And if such lawful sermons were the only basis for suspecting terrorist activity—under a strict reading of the "reasonable suspicion" requirement—the police arguably would not have enough evidence of criminal activity to open an undercover investigation into the operations of his mosque.[34]

However, today any such reading of the "reasonable suspicion" requirement would seem irresponsible, at best. Because the Constitution is not a suicide pact, the police should investigate radical clerics, even though their sermons may not alone constitute a crime. Responding to statements that support homicidal fanaticism is, we can argue, neither stereotyping nor religious profiling but, rather, both sensible and constitutional. And to the extent that any of these radical clerics are also engaged in fund raising which could constitute material support for terrorism, the situation would be considered even more serious. As the Supreme Court has recognized, "even the exercise of religion may be at some slight inconvenience in order that the state may protect its citizens from injury."[35]

That said, any remaining burden on religious practice should not be taken lightly. Because the United States professes equal treatment for all under the law, Americans owe it to fellow citizens who may be adversely affected by necessary security measures to safeguard their liberties as vigorously as possible. This commitment will keep us a cohesive society.

CONCLUSION

Constitutional safeguards are critical. Any expanded police powers must be continually checked by all branches of government. Law enforcement authorities must police themselves. The courts must be watchful so that investigative powers are not abused. And close legislative oversight of law enforcement activity is also warranted. In sum, the best way to fashion effective and appropriate security measures is to rely on the constitutional structure that those measures are designed to protect. In that way, we can strike the right balance between safety and civil liberty.

N O T E S

1. *Healy v. James*, 408 U.S. 169, 188 (1972), quoting *Communist Party v. Subversive Activities Control Board*, 361 U.S. 1, 137 (1961, J. Black, dissenting).
2. *Abrams v. United States*, 250 U.S. 616, 630 (1919, J. Holmes, dissenting).
3. *Terminello v. City of Chicago*, 375 U.S. 1 (1949, J. Jackson, dissenting); see 31, 37.
4. *Healy v. James*, 192.
5. Marilyn H. Karfeld, "Tape Shows Local Imam Supported Terror Groups: The Spiritual Leader of a Parma Mosque Once Raised Funds for the Palestine Islamic Jihad," *Cleveland Jewish News* (26 September 2001): 18. The quotations from Damra are all from this source. When interviewed for this article, he denied that he was in any way involved in Palestine Islamic Jihad.
6. Ibid.
7. *Terminiello v. City of Chicago*, 37.
8. *Kennedy v. Mendoza-Martinez*, 372 U.S. 144, 160 (1963).
9. Commonly known as the "Alien and Sedition Acts." They were passed by the Fifth Congress in 1798, lapsed by their own terms, and were not reenacted. The Supreme Court never ruled on their constitutionality.
10. Espionage Act of 1917 and the Sedition Act of 1918.
11. 39 U.S. 247 (1919). The subsequent quotation is from 249 and 252.
12. *Abrams v. United States*, 250 U.S. 616, 617 (1919). Subsequent quotations are from 621.
13. For example, *American Communications Association v. Douds*, 339 U.S. 382 (1950); *Dennis v. United States*, US. 494 (1951).
14. 341 U.S. 494. Subsequent quotations are from 561, 579–81, and 585.
15. 395 U.S. 444 (1969). Subsequent quotations are from 447.
16. 34 408 U.S. at 169 (1972), holding that the right to establish a campus branch of Students for a Democratic Society could not be abridged because of disagreement with the group's beliefs about the appropriateness of lawbreaking absent overt illegal activity.

17. *Yates v. United States*, 354 U.S. 298, 344 (1957).

18. *Dennis*, 341 U.S. 575.

19. *Wisconsin v. Mitchell*, 508 U.S. 476, 489 (1983).

20. Ibid., 476, citing *Roberts v. U.S. Jaycees*, 468 U.S. 609 (1984).

21. 18 U.S.C.A. §2339A, B (2004).

22. *United States v. Al-Arian*, 308 F. Supp. 2d 1322, 1342 (M.D. Fla. 2004).

23. *United States v. Sattar* 272 F. Supp. 2d 348, 359 (S.D.N.Y. 2003).

24. *Reno v. A.C.L.U.*, 521 U.S. 844, 870 (1997).

25. *Southeastern Promotions, Ltd. v. Conrad*, 420 U.S. 546, 557 (1975).

26. *Red Lion Broadcasting Co. v. FCC*, 395 U.S. 367, 386 (1969).

27. *Bartnicki v. Vopper.* 532 U.S. 514, 541 (2001 J. Breyer, concurring).

28. *Universal City Studios, Inc. v. Coreley*, 273 F.3d 429, 451-52 (2d Cir. 2001), rejecting a First Amendment challenge to Digital Millennium Copyright Act.

29. U.S. Department of Justice, *The Attorney General's Guidelines on General Crimes, Racketeering Enterprise and Terrorism Enterprise Investigations*, 22 (USDOJ, 2002); www.usdoj.gov/olp/generalcrimes2.pdf.

30. See Lininger, "Sects, Lies, and Videotape: The Surveillance and Infiltration of Religious Groups," *Iowa Law Review*, 89:1201 (2004).

31. Ibid, 1233–4.

32. *Church of the Lukumi Babalu Aye, Inc. v. City of Hialeah*, 508 U.S. 520, 543 (1993).

33. *Brandenburg*, 395 U.S. 449.

34. See Lininger, 1283–4.

35. *Cantwell v. Connecticut*, 310 U.S. 296, 306 (1940).

CHAPTER 67

Principled Prudence: Civil Liberties and the Homeland Security Practitioner

Laura W. Murphy
Director, Washington Legislative Office
American Civil Liberties Union (ACLU)

INTRODUCTION

One effect of 9/11 is renewed attention in America to questions of foreign affairs and domestic security. After the Cold War ended, certain academic and professional disciplines that had been developed to address it found themselves with no raison d'être. Since 9/11, the domestic security and foreign affairs sectors of government (and private industry) have experienced a renaissance, but with a focus different from the earlier sovietology and nuclear strategy. That new focus is expressed by the terms *homeland security, asymmetric threat* and *international terrorism.*

Consequently, as compared with the Cold War, the campaign to prevent and eliminate global terrorism today implies broader questions of domestic policy and constitutional law. Because the new homeland security professionals—FBI agents, homeland security intelligence analysts or customs officials, the CIA's counterterrorism specialists, corporate vendors—must necessarily work among and with the American people in tracking their targets, the whole constitutional superstructure of the way America protects itself within

Note: Nothing in this chapter should be construed as endorsing any position counter to ACLU policy. This chapter is meant as an objective look at the general discourse on the subject.

its borders is being looked at anew. Some argue that the peculiar threat of terrorism—in which minimal personnel, using minimal materiel, can stage catastrophic attacks that can kill or injure thousands of Americans—justifies blanket revisions of basic constitutional norms and protections, especially the First, Fourth, Fifth, Sixth, and Fourteenth Amendments. Others argue that the constant perception of threat in America, with the steady drumbeat of dire predictions about future attacks, is overwrought and unrealistic, and that there is no need for dramatic, expensive security initiatives. Both positions seem unwise. Thus the challenge for the new homeland security professional is to accommodate the two extremes. It is a challenge both practical, in terms of new federal initiatives, expenditures, and bureaucratic reorganization, and moral in that it requires FBI agents and CIA analysts to reconcile traditional concepts of liberty in America with the external pressures of the "threat matrix" faced by the United States.

It is also an unenviable pursuit; and as in many national security and law enforcement contexts, successes remain classified while failures are trumpeted. Moreover, politics intrude: homeland security experts must accommodate their operations to open government laws; constitutional guarantees of free speech, association, and religion; constitutional protections against the arbitrary application of government power; and the checks and balances that diffuse powers among the executive, legislative, and judicial branches.

How should a homeland security expert think about these abstract concerns? And how should they be applied in creating and implementing policy? This chapter attempts to address both questions so as to provide practical guidance for the homeland security practitioner in a subject that invariably strays into more philosophical territory. A security professional in government is going to face these constitutional issues in gritty, ambiguous, real-world situations. Nevertheless, understanding the larger constitutional and ethical framework is essential.

Accordingly, this chapter takes an inductive approach to the problem of how to protect civil liberties in the aftermath of 9/11, by presenting three case studies. The first case involves the proposal to create a national identification card. My intention is not—necessarily—to convince the reader of the propriety or impropriety of a national ID card but to provide a framework for thinking about the legal, ethical, practical, and constitutional issues of such a system.[1]

The second case applies this analysis to bioterrorism, allowing the reader to see the proposed test in action in an emergency. One can judge whether civil liberties work only by testing them on the margins; a hypothetical bioterror attack presents the opportunity for a stress test. The third case considers whether, when, and how a homeland security professional can take a person's faith or ethnic group into account when investigating terrorism (or other national security matters).

THE DEBATE

The basic debate over civil liberties today centers on two general propositions. The argument in favor of abridging liberties through aggressive policing and intelligence collection is that the immediate, asymmetric threat—terrorism like that of al-Qaida—is so grave, and the potential harm so calamitous, that traditional constitutional presumptions in favor of the individual (versus the collective need) must be rethought. The intelligence chief at the Department of Homeland Security (DHS) expressed this argument in remarks at Harvard University in 2003:

> What I'm about to say is very arrogant—arrogant to a fault. Set aside what the mass of people think. Some things are so bad for them that you cannot allow them to have them. One of them is war in the context of terrorism in the United States. Therefore, we have to abridge individual rights, change the societal conditions, and act in ways that heretofore were not in accordance with our values and traditions, like giving a police officer or security official the right to search you without a judicial finding of probable cause. Things are changing, and this change is happening because things can be brought to us that we cannot afford to absorb. We can't deal with them, so we're going to reach out and do something ahead of time to preclude them. Is that going to change your lives? It already has.[2]

The common response to such an argument is often expressed somewhat as follows:

> The choice between security and liberty is a false one. Our history has shown us that insecurity threatens liberty. Yet if our liberties are curtailed, we lose the values that we are struggling to defend.[3]

Or, as is often asserted by the ACLU: "If we give up our freedoms, the terrorists win."

In practice, things are rarely as simple as either of these statements suggests. Still, security professionals should understand civil liberties principles so that their decisions can strike a balance between principle and prudence. The framework presented below resembles that put forward in the Constitution, where a balance is struck in the allocation of powers among the different branches, so as to create tension between expedience and caution and allow governmental functions—like commerce, foreign affairs, and domestic security—to serve, not oppress, individual liberty and prevent abuses.

THE TEST

The 9/11 Commission struggled with this issue at length in its final report. Though it proposed broad expansions of federal authority, it also recognized the need for safeguards.[4] Some of the checks are direct, like the proposed creation of an independent civil liberties watchdog within the government (p. 395). Others are more functional, like the recommended declassification of the intelligence community's top-line budget figures (p. 416). Perhaps the most significant safeguard is the legalistic balancing test the commission formulated in response to the debate over proposals to expand the USA PATRIOT Act. Two commissioners testified that:

> The test is a simple but important one. The burden of proof should be on the proponents of the measure to establish that the power or authority being sought would in fact materially enhance national security, *and* that there will be adequate supervision of the exercise of that power or authority to ensure the protection of civil liberties. If additional powers are granted, there must be adequate guidelines and oversight to properly confine their use.[5]

I propose an essentially similar test, but with two additional factors to consider in weighing the propriety of proposed actions (at the level of national policy or in the course of individual investigations). The first three elements of the test are normative and utilitarian. That is, they require the tester to apply certain societal value judgments about the relative importance of security and liberty, but also have a strong effectiveness component. The fourth element of the test is something that good homeland security practitioners should always be thinking about; it involves political and public relations repercussions. This fourth test is often overlooked, but it can sink a program or initiative, even one that does not compromise civil liberties.

Part 1 of the Test

Do the costs of liberty outweigh the potential benefits to public safety? If so, the security measure should probably be rejected and replaced with a less constitutionally suspect alternative.

For instance, we could strip-search every airline passenger and confiscate any implement that could possibly be used as a weapon. The security benefit would be high—indeed, terrorists would probably abandon hijacking altogether—and such a search could be considered a minor imposition, relative to the potential harm of a terrorist attack. But this measure would offend passengers' personal dignity and might violate the First Amendment, which has been interpreted to include the right to travel. Also, other quite effective measures are available (e.g., baggage matching, hardened cockpit doors, armed air marshals, and greater airport security). These are issues that the homeland security practitioner must struggle with.

Part 2 of the Test

Will the measure call for, or result in, discrimination based on religion, ethnicity, race, or other group characteristics? This part of the test is perhaps the most controversial in the post-9/11 context. It requires some hard thinking about the nature of the threat facing America.

Many people contend that, to quote the comedian Bill Maher, "when you're color-blind, you're blind."[6] In other words, it is evident that the threat today is exclusively from the Muslim world; the personal representatives of this threat are all going to be Arabs, south Asians, or members of some other ethnic group with a large Muslim population; and therefore they should suffer added scrutiny. According to a more sophisticated version of this argument in favor of profiling, in certain limited circumstances, the threats to America— and to liberty—are so great that race, ethnicity, or other immutable characteristics should be taken into account. Paul Rosenzweig argues that "in *very limited* circumstances, the balance might change when the object of our activity is to prevent terrorism, and the use of national origin data and characteristics is much more narrowly applied."[7]

Others, such as the ACLU, would argue that this formulation of the problem proceeds from a false premise. Certainly, if the authorities know an individual suspect's ethnicity or race, it can be used as one of several descriptors for investigators. But to subject all Muslims and Arabs to special scrutiny merely because of their ethnicity or religion, even in the context of counterterrorism, disregards the basic American moral and constitutional commitment to equality under the law. Moreover, it ignores the fact that terrorists belong to numerous different ethnic groups (they include European-looking Chechens, for instance, and Filipinos) and that many could easily pass as "ordinary" Americans. Whichever side one takes, it seems evident that this issue should be a consideration in creating and implementing homeland security policy.

Part 3 of the Test

Is the measure properly tailored to the desired mission, or could it result in unintended and possibly abusive consequences?

The best examples of this concern involve broad delegations of investigative power to the executive branch without appropriate checks by the courts or congressional oversight. Historically, for instance, the executive branch had complete discretion to conduct electronic and physical surveillance of suspects in national security investigations. The rationale was that the president alone possessed secret knowledge and operational ability to fight the Cold War. The executive, however, extended this authority to domestic contexts, including the FBI's counterintelligence program (COINTELPRO), which conducted covert operations against civil rights and antiwar activists; and the CIA's Operation CHAOS, which spied on law-abiding American citizens in an eventually futile attempt to determine whether foreign agitators were behind the upheavals on college campuses during the late 1960s and early 1970s.[8]

This element of the test is particularly important in what is called the war on terrorism, because the enemy is largely undefined and because broad law enforcement or domestic intelligence authority could be used against lawful dissidents or opponents of the administration in power.

Part 4 of the Test

How will the public probably react to the measure?

Homeland security practitioners, when dealing with sensitive civil liberties issues, sometimes ask themselves, "Would I be offended if someone did x or y to me?" But the proper question is how the program, initiative, or tactical operation is likely to be received by the community affected and the public at large. For instance, even if an overall policy is salutary, the specifics may be reminiscent of Big Brother, and in that case the initiative is going to be attacked. Time and money can be saved by thinking carefully about the political and public ramifications of homeland security operations.

THE NATIONAL ID CARD

Proponents of a national identification (ID) card have suggested three general types. One is a plain card, issued by a centralized bureaucracy, which would serve no other purpose but to identify the holder. It would contain, at minimum, name, address, date of birth, a fingerprint or another biometric, a photograph, and a unique number. The second is a de facto national ID: a federally standardized driver's license. It would look very much like the plain card but would also establish that the holder may operate a motor vehicle. The third card would be voluntary, but nonparticipants would be subject to heightened scrutiny at airports and other sensitive facilities. Let us consider arguments on both sides of this issue.

First, will the card be effective? This question turns on empirical limitations of technology in establishing identity. Even if a card is technologically infallible, can it also be infallible in the sense of absolutely ensuring that the holder is actually the person that the card identifies? Although there are arguments either way, experts tend to doubt that infallibility is possible.[9] The national ID card would have to be based on "breeder" documents already used by applicants to establish their identity: birth certificates, social security cards, passports, etc. These are notoriously easy to forge or acquire fraudulently. Even if the ID card itself were error-proof, there would still be a possibility of identity theft.[10] Until this problem is addressed, a national ID card, as a practical matter, cannot be an effective tool in establishing identity. In particular, a terrorist organization like al-Qaida would expend considerable resources to obtain national ID cards for its operatives.

Another consideration regarding effectiveness is that the card could engender a false sense of security. Legislators and policy makers might use the existence of the national ID system to downsize other security measures, such as the additional security personnel stationed at airports since 9/11. The voluntary ID card might pose especially significant risks. What happens, for instance, if a potential terrorist acquires a card and consequently is subjected to fewer security checks at airports, government facilities, and other sensitive locations?

Second, will the card entail discrimination? Proponents of a national ID card frequently suggest that it would result in less discrimination based on race, ethnicity, or other similar characteristics. Alan Dershowitz of Harvard, for instance, argues that when student IDs began to be issued there, African-American students were less likely to be harassed by the campus police. Even though they were asked for their ID more frequently than other students (Dershowitz recognizes that this is unacceptable), they were able to present the card, and the encounter ended.[11] Dershowitz argues that the same would be true of Arab and Muslim Americans. Opponents of a national ID card are generally skeptical about this argument. Dershowitz seems to be asserting that the possession of a national ID card would establish one's authenticity as a member of society. At Harvard, the campus police stopped harassing African-American students because the card established the students' specific right to be on campus. But that would not necessarily hold true in an airport or government facility, where—even if people had national ID cards—security personnel might still continue the harassment just to "play it safe." In addition, as Dershowitz admits, the national ID card would not stop the disproportionate singling out of Arabs and Muslims by security personnel. Arguably, there is also a danger that eventually the police would begin to use failure to carry one's card as a rationale for continuing and escalating law enforcement encounters.

Third, does the card serve a narrow purpose, and will it result in unintended consequences? Proponents argue that America in the information age cannot exist without a mechanism to prevent people from remaining anonymous. A national ID card is that mechanism. By its nature, a system of national identification would spill over into many other sectors of government (taxation, the census, selective service, voter registration, etc.). Private industry might also begin to use one's card for purposes such as credit reporting and market research. And, to be effective at all these tasks, a national ID card would have to consolidate terabytes of information about Americans into a central data storage repository. Misuse or abuse of this information is a real possibility, especially if the personal identifiers on the card become linked somehow with highly sensitive information such as medical records or ethnic and religious affiliation.

This becomes troublesome as regards the census, which was misused to violate personal liberties during World War II, when the Census Bureau helped the War Department intern Japanese Americans.[12] In the summer of 2004, a request made under the Freedom of Information Act revealed that the Census Bureau had compiled statistics on large middle eastern populations around the country and had given the information to DHS.[13]

Proponents of the card often counter these concerns about efficacy, discrimination, and potential abuse with a difficult question: Wouldn't even an imperfect card at least make it more difficult for terrorists to operate? Perhaps the only way to answer this is to have Congress commission cost-benefit studies. Undoubtedly, the financial cost of the system would be high: some 300 million Americans would have to go to local "identity bureaus," present previous identity documentation, be processed, and then receive the card.[14] Human costs would be harder to calculate. Over time, many false positives would probably result from mistaken identity, technological limitations, and the necessary linkages between the identity system and the thousands of names currently in government terrorist and criminal watch lists; such errors, if retained in one's government identity record, could impede finding employment, opening a bank account, or accessing government services.

Fourth, what about public relations? Probably, the negative reaction to a national ID card in the United States would be significant. Americans have traditionally supported individual and privacy rights; also, there are strong institutional interests on both the left and the right that would vehemently oppose the card. Whether this is a compelling argument is a question for the policy makers, but it should surely be a factor in the discussion.

The debate over a national ID card is likely to continue. The threat of terrorism persists; the technology that would underpin the card system continues to mature; and the potential government design and maintenance contracts for a national ID card present an appealing entrepreneurial opportunity for the private sector. Conversely, public mistrust of a national ID card, as well as organized opposition, is also likely to persist. I hope that the four-element test presented here provides a framework for debate that takes into account both principle and prudence.

THUGS AND BUGS—CIVIL LIBERTIES AND BIOTERRORISM

Consider these facts, from the Centers for Disease Control and Prevention, about the smallpox virus. The last confirmed case of the smallpox virus appeared in Somalia almost 30 years ago. The disease last occurred naturally in the United States in 1949. Almost no Americans under the age of about 30 have been vaccinated against the virus, and vaccination is the only possible defense. The most common strain of smallpox kills almost one in three infected persons; other strains have even higher mortality rates. The disease itself is horrible. After about a week of incubation, infected persons begin to develop a severe fever and other flu-like symptoms. After a few days, they start to develop raised bumps all over their bodies, which harden into pustules, eventually scab over, and, if the person lives, fall away leaving extensive scarring. The most common strain spreads only through extensive personal interaction, especially the handling of blankets and clothing used by a victim. Hardier strains spread through airborne contact. The only two remaining samples of the disease are kept in tightly controlled laboratories in the United States and Russia. There is strong concern, however, that the breakup of the Soviet Union might have resulted in the creation or theft of some off-the-books samples of the virus.

Now suppose that some hypothetical terrorists have obtained a weaponized form of the virus. They release it in the middle of New York City. Since this particular strain of the disease has an approximately 30 percent mortality rate, hundreds of thousands will die. What can the government properly do to contain such an outbreak?

Bioterrorism, along with biotechnology, free speech and the Internet, and privacy in the information age, is an issue on the cutting edge of civil liberties. If certain viruses or other biological agents were introduced into the global population, especially in developing countries, they could cause untold harm. However, containing an outbreak poses unique challenges to democratic governments, because it necessarily involves extraordinary emergency powers. Forced quarantine and forced inoculation are invasive abridgments of personal freedom.

Accordingly, smallpox represents a particularly illustrative civil liberties situation, because the only possible defense is vaccinating everybody within a certain radius of the initial outbreak. Vaccination is quite effective when delivered within three days after exposure; it helps lessen the severity of the symptoms if administered within seven days after exposure. Once the skin rash begins to form, however, palliative care is the best that medicine can offer.

From a civil liberties perspective, this is perhaps not an especially difficult case. The ACLU's general rule for deciding when extraordinary state measures are warranted is that the intrusiveness and duration of such measures must be proportional to the threat posed by the disease, and the emergency measures must be the least restrictive possible for civil liberties.[15] So, for instance, if a hemorrhagic fever, like the Ebola virus, were to start spreading, and health officials had evidence that the disease was airborne, quite stringent emergency actions could be taken. In the case of acquired immune deficiency syndrome (AIDS)—and the ACLU has policy to this effect—stringent emergency actions could not be taken. Actually, highly restrictive measures were often proposed when AIDS first emerged; this experience suggests why caution is necessary in allowing the government extraordinary powers (arrest, quarantine, etc.) in a medical emergency. In the case of smallpox, as long as they were the least restrictive measures possible, quarantine, compulsory testing, mandatory admission to hospitals, and the collection of private medical information to track the carriers of the disease could be acceptable. Though the general rule would have to be applied case by case (an urban outbreak would be assessed differently from a rural outbreak, for instance), the ACLU recognizes that emergency measures might have to be taken in extraordinary situations.

That said, the state takes on certain obligations once it exercises its emergency power. First, individuals affected by the medical emergency must have the option to elect any alternative treatment that is equally effective. Second, patients' privacy must be assiduously protected. Patients must retain control over their medical records, and the doctor-patient privilege cannot be abridged. Third, the emergency measures must be subject to independent review, and the findings disseminated to the public. Fourth, extraordinary measures must never be applied in a discriminatory fashion. As mentioned, one need look no further than the early days of the AIDS virus, and the not infrequent calls for the quarantine of gay men, to see the danger. Fifth, effective due process protections should be in place to protect persons wrongly quarantined, and a fair compensation mechanism should be established for the appropriation or destruction of private property. These conditions would not detract from the containment of the bioterrorism attack but would ensure that fundamental notions of fairness and individual liberty were protected, even in the face of the panic engendered by bioterror.

Notice how this discussion of bioterrorism applies the four-element test. It is explicitly based on a rational cost-benefit analysis. It bars discrimination. It requires government officials to make their emergency conduct commensurate with the severity of the threat. And it requires the government to tailor its response narrowly to the actual extent of the threat, and to take steps to compensate individuals affected, increasing public confidence in the necessity and legitimacy of the containment measures. Indeed, one could apply this model response to many similar catastrophe scenarios, including the detonation of a radiological dispersion device or "dirty bomb," the release of a chemical agent like VX or ricin, or even natural disasters.

PROFILING BASED ON RACE, ETHNICITY, OR SIMILAR CRITERIA

In the context of counterterrorism since 9/11, whether race, ethnicity, national origin, or religion can be used to inform law enforcement activity and intelligence gathering is a vexing issue. Arguments for and against tend to revolve around one question: does the targeted group, in an absolute sense, have a proclivity toward the activities being investigated? For many on the left and the right, the question whether Arabs, Muslims, and south Asians are, in fact, more likely to be terrorists is simply answered "yes." Briefly, here is the argument.

> After 9/11, the FBI investigated hundreds of thousands of terrorist tips and ultimately picked up a mere 1,200 men, mostly illegal immigrants, for questioning. The government detained some for

weeks or sometimes months, checking out their backgrounds, before deporting or releasing them. The vast majority of the men were Muslim. And any investigation of Islamic terror cells worth its salt will turn up...Muslims! But so charged and distorted has the debate about policing and race become over the last decade that it is now professional suicide to say that, in hunting Islamic terrorists, one is going to look for and find Muslims.[16]

This statement seems to imply the following reasoning: all the terrorists on 9/11 were Muslims; therefore the target of terrorist investigations should be Muslims. Here again it is worth applying the four-part test. I will explore some of the arguments on either side, to suggest ways in which the homeland security practitioner should think about the issue of profiling based on nonbehavioral criteria such as race or religion.

First, is it effective to take such criteria into account when deciding how to allocate and focus investigative resources? The arguments in favor of such an approach include the contention that modern international terrorism is almost exclusively perpetrated by Islamic fundamentalists; thus it makes sense for counterterrorism to target Muslims. This argument is similar to defenses of domestic racial profiling of African-Americans and Latinos. George Will once wrote, "Felons are not evenly distributed across society's demographic groups. Many individuals and groups specialize in hurling accusations of racism, and police become vulnerable to such accusations when they concentrate their efforts where crime is."[17] The problem with this position, however, is that—if taken to heart by law enforcement—it becomes a self-fulfilling prophecy. Minorities are seen as more criminally inclined because they are arrested more often. Why are they arrested more often? Arguably, because law enforcement and the public begin to believe that they commit more crimes. How do law enforcers and the pubic know this? Because minorities are arrested more often.

There is some empirical evidence suggesting that criminal proclivities may be less linked to race or ethnicity than Will asserts. For instance, there have been studies done of the racial dynamics of cocaine and crack abuse. In 1991, during what was called a crack epidemic, a survey conducted by the National Institute on Drug Abuse (NIDA) found that 75 percent of users of powder cocaine and 52 percent of users of crack cocaine were white.[18] But although more whites use cocaine or crack, in absolute terms, African-Americans and

Latinos make up a disproportionately high number of felony arrests and convictions for cocaine and crack offenses. According to a report by the United States Sentencing Commission in 1995, 96.5 percent of federal crack offenders were persons of color (including Latinos). In 2000 the percentage was lower, but still greatly disproportionate: 84.7 percent.[19] The overrepresentation of blacks and Latinos in the federal and state criminal justice systems helps perpetuate the myth that persons of color commit more drug crimes.

The same problem recurs in the context of counterterrorism, but possibly with higher stakes in terms of American lives. If the government is using nonbehavioral profiles, terrorists will try to fool the profile. Consider the "black widows" in Russia, women who lose their husbands in the fighting and are recruited as suicide bombers; or the use of teenagers or women by Palestinian militants against Israel. An overemphasis on Muslims or Arabs also ignores the fact that, before 9/11, two of the three most significant terrorist attacks against civilians on American soil had been committed by American white male extremists: the bombings in Oklahoma City and at the Atlanta Olympics. (The third was the bombing at the World Trade Center in 1993.).

Furthermore, there is little evidence that the sweeps of the Arab and Muslim populations in America since 9/11 have borne much fruit. For instance, pursuant to the investigation in the aftermath of 9/11, more than 1,000 primarily Muslim and middle eastern men were detained under various rationales (e.g., some were held for minor immigration violations and others as material witnesses). Only one of the 762 detainees surveyed by the Justice Department's inspector general in 2003 has been charged with a terrorism-related crime. That one case is Zacarias Moussaoui, and he was in custody before 9/11.[20]

Another practical concern about using nonbehavioral characteristics is exactly that: they are nonbehavioral. In November 2001, eight former FBI officials expressed concern that the new emphasis on dragnet tactics at the Justice Department under John Ashcroft was perhaps unwise. The former FBI director William H. Webster said that a policy of preemptive arrests and detentions "carries a lot of risk with it. You may interrupt something, but you may not be able to bring it down. You may not be able to stop what is going on."[21]

The ethnic selectivity of the Justice Department's response to 9/11, including what were described as voluntary interviews of more than 5,000 middle eastern men throughout the country, additionally demonstrates the public relations pitfalls of racial or ethnic profiling. Webster touched on this as well: "We used good investigative techniques and lawful techniques. We did it without all the suggestions that we are going to jump all over the people's private lives, if that is what the current attorney general wants to do. I don't think we need to go that direction."

Generally, in considering race, ethnicity, religion, or national origin so as to make decisions about domestic security, the principle is that it is of course permissible to use such criteria to specifically describe a specific suspect. But the real issue is how central that criteria may be to the entire profile of a suspect. If race, ethnicity, religion, or national origin are the only bases for suspicion, the pool of suspects will be prohibitively large.

Here is another hypothetical situation. The National Security Agency intercepts a cell phone conversation in Morocco that provides two pieces of intelligence: (1) an al-Qaida group is planning an attack in a shopping center somewhere in the Midwest; (2) the perpetrator is a Yemeni. The alert is passed along to the FBI and DHS. How should their agents respond?

Simply detaining every Yemeni from Chicago to Detroit, aside from the obvious civil liberties implications, would probably be ineffective and would deflect resources from more promising investigative techniques. A better approach would be to try to collect more detailed information on the suspect, find out additional details about the actual attack, and increase security at midwestern shopping malls. The chances would then be better than even that the FBI and DHS would be able to add additional details to the suspect's description. The amount of work necessary to interdict the attack would be lessened, and the chance of success heightened.

In this hypothetical situation, would it (for the sake of argument) be acceptable to stop every brown-skinned Arab-looking person entering a midwestern mall? The liberty interests of the mall patrons would have to be balanced against the reliability and specificity of the intelligence, the possible unintended consequences of the overt profiling, and the chance that by stopping only brown-skinned possible Yemenis, the authorities might miss the actual terrorist, who looked different. The ACLU would say that race or ethnicity should never be used, absent other more specific behavioral indicators, as a justification for initiating a law enforcement encounter. Others would argue that, in this case, the interests of security outweigh the individual rights of innocent Arab-looking men who would be subjected to heightened scrutiny. At the very least, I personally would counsel the homeland security practitioner to seek additional individual clues to or leads on the identity of the possible terrorist. This is especially important, again, because a policy of stopping and frisking every brown-skinned visitor to the malls would create a huge, unwieldy suspect pool.

There is no formula for addressing the problem of profiling in a constitutional democracy. The best plan is to use commonsense investigative tools to narrow the investigative focus. If the only thing an investigator can say about a suspect is that he (or she) is a Saudi, an Indonesian, or an Iranian, there is a serious problem, not just for civil liberties, but for the potential success of that investigation. If the investigator can instead say that the suspect is a Saudi, about 6 feet tall, with salt-and-pepper hair, traveling with a woman, the profile is approaching appropriateness and effectiveness. Given the vast reach and resources of the American homeland security establishment, and its high level of talent, we can focus on best practices that serve to identify specific suspects, not suspect groups or classifications.

I would also note the potential public relations problems that come with ethnic, religious, racial, or national origin profiling. One reason why homeland security is an unenviable vocation is that police power engenders mistrust in certain communities and demographics. For racial minorities and the American Arab and Muslim population, heavy-handedness can elicit an "us versus them" mentality and a consequent reluctance to cooperate with investigations or to come forward with tips or leads. A more appropriate approach to homeland security operations that involve sensitive questions of race or ethnicity is to focus, to the greatest extent practicable, on means and methods that seek to involve the community to allay its fears about arbitrary law enforcement or national security efforts. The best way to accomplish this is to focus on individual suspicion, based on behavioral characteristics and specific intelligence.

CONCLUSION

Often, public pressure to do something about a particular threat pushes law enforcement professionals to adopt less particularized investigation techniques. For instance, as former FBI director Webster noted, the Justice Department publicized several initiatives that targeted Arab and Muslim communities. The homeland security practitioner should equally be cognizant of this institutional and bureaucratic factor and, especially if pressure appears unwise or potentially ineffective, should resist it whenever possible.

N O T E S

1. However, the ACLU does oppose a national identification card, including a federally standardized driver's license. See Hearing on Driver's License Security Issues, 107th Congress, 2002 (statement of Katie Corrigan, ACLU legislative counsel). The ACLU also takes a position on the issues represented by the other two cases; but I will present the arguments pro and con.

2. Patrick M. Hughes, "Future Conditions: The Character and Conduct of War, 2010 to 2020," guest presentation for Program on Information Resources Policy (July 2003); see http://pirp.harvard.edu/pubs_pdf/hughes%5Chughes-i03-1.pdf).

3. Justin Rood, "Homeland Intelligence Chief Hughes Warned Civil Rights Would Have to Be 'Abridged' to Prevent Another Terror Attack," *Congressional Quarterly* (28 October 2004).

4. *The Final Report of the National Commission on Terrorist Attacks upon the United States* (9/11 Commission Report) (2004), pp. 394–5. For subsequent quotations from this source, page numbers are given parenthetically).

5. Prepared Statement of Richard Ben-Veniste and Slade Gorton, National Commission on Terrorist Attacks upon the United States, before the Subcommittee on National Security, Emerging Threats, and International Relations of the House Committee on Government Reform, 108th Congress, 2004.

6. Bill Maher, *Victory Begins at Home*, HBO television broadcast (July 2003).

7. "Anti-Terrorism Efforts, Civil Liberties, and Civil Rights," testimony of Paul Rosenzweig, Senior Fellow at the Heritage Foundation, before the United States Commission on Civil Rights (19 March 2004); see www.heritage.org/Research/LegalIssues/tst031904a.cfm.

8. See *Final Report of the Select Committee to Study Governmental Operations with Respect to Intelligence Activities*, S. Rep. 94-755, 94th Congress, 1976.

9. Testimony by Professor Ben Schneiderman, U.S. Public Policy Committee of the Association for Computing Machinery, to the House Subcommittee on Government Efficiency, Financial Management, and Intergovernmental Relations, 107th Congress, 2001; see: www.acm.org/usacm/National.htm.

10. Committee on Authentication Technologies and Their Privacy Implications, National Research Council, *IDs—Not That Easy: Questions about Nationwide Identity Systems*, Stephen T. Kent and Lynette I. Millett (eds.) (2002), pp. 34–35; see www.nap.edu/books/030908430X/html.

11. For example, Alan Dershowitz, "Identification, Please," *Boston Globe* (11 August 2002): 14.

12. Edwin Black, *IBM and the Holocaust: The Strategic Alliance between Nazi Germany and America's Most Powerful Corporation* (Three Rivers Press, 2001), p. 346.

13. Audrey Hudson, "Census Bureau Restricts Release of Arabic Analysis," *Washington Times* (31 August 2004): A04.

14. See Robert A. Rosenblatt, "Fraud-Proof Cards for Social Security Pegged at $10 Billion," *Los Angeles Times* (23 September 1997).

15. ACLU Policy Guide, "Communicable Diseases and HIV/AIDS," Policy No. 268.

16. Heather MacDonald, "The Hunt for Terrorists Runs Up Against Political Correctness," *New York Sun* (5 November 2002).

17. George Will, "A Defense of Racial Profiling," *Seattle Post-Intelligencer* (19 April 2001) B7.

18. King E. Davis and Tricia B. Bent-Goodley (eds.), *The Color of Social Policy* (Council on Social Work Education, 2004), p. 111.

19. Ibid.

20. Steve Fainaru, "Report: 9/11 Detainees Abused," *Washington Post* (3 June 2003): A1.

21. Jim McGee, "Ex-FBI Officials Criticize Tactics on Terrorism," *Washington Post* (28 November 2001): A1.

CHAPTER 68

Government Data Mining

Newton N. Minow
Senior Counsel, Sidley Austin Brown and Wood

Fred H. Cate, J.D.
Distinguished Professor and Director, Center for Applied
Cybersecurity Research, Indiana University;
Senior Policy Advisor, Center for Information Policy
Leadership at Hunton and Williams

INTRODUCTION

Government data mining is widespread and expanding. In 2004, the Government Accountability Office (GAO)[1] found 42 federal departments—including every cabinet-level agency that responded to the survey—engaged in or planning to engage in data mining involving personal information, by accessing data from the private sector or through sharing among federal agencies.

- The Department of Defense (DOD) announced that it was working on "Total Information Awareness"—later renamed "Terrorism Information Awareness"—a research and development program that included technologies to search personally identifiable transaction records and recognize patterns across separate databases for the purpose of combating terrorism.[2]

- The Advanced Research and Development Activity center, based in the National Security Agency, has a project—Novel Intelligence from Massive Data—to develop tools to examine large quantities of data to "reveal new indicators, issues, and/or threats that would not otherwise have been found due to the massiveness of the data."[3]

- Section 201 of the Homeland Security Act, signed into law in November 2002, requires the Department of Homeland Security to "establish and utilize ... data-mining and other advanced analytical tools," to "access, receive, and analyze data to detect and identify threats of terrorism against the United States."

- The Army defense contractor Torch Concepts, with the assistance of DOD and the Transportation Security Administration (TSA), obtained millions of passenger records from U.S. airlines to study how data profiling can be used to identify high-risk passengers. For many of the passengers, Torch Concepts was able to buy demographic information including gender, occupation, income, social security number, home ownership, years at current residence, number of children and adults in the household, and vehicles.[4]

- TSA has announced that it is deploying the second generation of the Computer-Assisted Passenger Prescreening System (CAPPS II, now being developed under the name Secure Flight), which compares airline passengers' names with private- and public-sector databases to assess the level of risk a passenger might pose.[5]

- The USA PATRIOT Act expands the power of the Treasury Department's Financial Crimes Enforcement Network—FinCEN—to require financial institutions to report suspected money laundering or terrorist activities by their customers. The act also mandates new "Know Your Customer" rules which require financial institutions to (1) verify the identity of any person seeking to open an account; (2) maintain records of the information used to verify the person's identity and; (3) determine whether the person appears on any list of known or suspected terrorists or terrorist organizations.[6]

- The police in Florida have created a database—Multistate Antiterrorism Information Exchange (MATRIX)—to link law enforcement records with other government and private-sector databases and "find patterns and links among people and events faster than ever before." Eight states and DHS are now participating in MATRIX, which is funded by the Justice Department and DHS.[7]

These and similar government programs present vexing legal and policy issues about the government's access to, and use of, personal information, especially when that information is obtained from the private sector or another government agency or when it concerns individuals who have done nothing to warrant suspicion. Surprisingly, many of these issues have not yet been addressed by statutes or judicial decisions, or the applicable law is uncertain or unclear.

In this chapter we will examine the technological and geopolitical factors that have raised—and complicated—this question, and helped to render existing law inadequate. We then present that law, followed by a description of the legal and other issues posed by data mining, but not resolved by existing law. We end with a summary of the recommendations of the DOD Technology and Privacy Advisory Committee (TAPAC), which as of this writing were under consideration by Congress and the secretary of defense.

The Broad and Changing Definition of Data Mining

Determining the law applicable to data mining is made more difficult because it is defined broadly and the definition is continually changing. Most definitions include searches of one or more databases of personally identifiable information, by or on behalf of an agency or employee of the government. That definition describes a variety of activities.

Criminal investigators have long made use of subject-based data mining, which looks for information about a specific individual: it starts with known suspects and searches for information about them and the people with whom they interact. The law applicable to such searches, discussed below, is fairly clear, although quite complex, and focuses on the type of information sought, the target of the investigation, whether the target has a "reasonable expectation of privacy" in the information, the evidentiary grounds on which it is sought, whether it is sought from the individual target or a third person, and the purpose for which it is sought. Depending on the answers to these questions, investigators may need no legal authorization for the search, may need a warrant or wiretap order issued by a traditional state or federal court, or may need authorization by the Foreign Intelligence Surveillance Act (FISA) court. The law applicable to subject-based searches may be convoluted, but it is generally settled.

Many new government data-mining programs, especially in the law enforcement and national security arena, however, feature pattern-based searches. These involve developing models of what criminal or terrorist behavior might look like and then examining databases for similar patterns. A pattern-based search is similar to commercial data-mining techniques. Businesses develop a pattern of attributes or behaviors that their good customers have in common and then search databases to find people matching those patterns. The government's programs are potentially far more powerful, given the range of data to which it has access and the capacity of data mining to eliminate the need to aggregate data before searching them.

Moreover, the power of data-mining technology and the range of data to which the government has access have blurred the line between subject- and pattern-based searches. The broader the search criteria, and the more people other than actual criminals or terrorists who will be identified by those criteria, the more patternlike these searches become. Even when a subject-based search starts with a known suspect, it can be transformed into a pattern-based search as investigators target individuals for investigation solely because of apparently innocent connections with the suspect. The more tenuous the connection, the more like a pattern-based search it becomes.

Whether a search is characterized as subject-based, pattern-based, or a hybrid of the two, the fundamental legal question remains the same: To what extent does—and should—the law permit the government to conduct sophisticated computerized searches of transactional records and other private-sector databases of U.S. citizens and permanent residents in an effort to detect and prevent terrorist attacks, for national security, and for law enforcement purposes?

This question has become more urgent—and the applicable law less clear—in the face of three developments. First, dramatic advances in information technology have greatly increased the government's ability to access data from diverse sources, including commercial databases. New technologies also allow the government to engage in data mining to search vast quantities of data for the purpose of identifying people who meet specific criteria or otherwise present unusual patterns of activities.

Second, these technologies have exponentially increased the volume of data available about individuals and greatly reduced the financial and other obstacles to retaining, sharing, and exploiting those data in both the public and the private sector. One of the most immediate challenges facing U.S. antiterrorism is separating out the "signal" of useful information from the "noise" of all those data.

Third, as 9/11 made clear, the United States faces a new threat: the power of terrorists to strike from within; their willingness to sacrifice their own lives; their demonstrated ability to turn technologies into weapons that can cause mass destruction; and their use of advanced information technologies to launch highly coordinated, well-financed, and painstakingly rehearsed attacks.

INFORMATION PRIVACY AND ITS PROTECTION FROM INTRUSION BY THE GOVERNMENT

Information privacy is protected in the United States by a variety of constitutional, statutory, administrative, and common-law provisions. Here, we address only the most important of these that are applicable to data mining.

Constitutional Protections

Privacy is not explicitly protected in the Constitution. The Supreme Court, however, has interpreted much of the Bill of Rights as protecting various elements of privacy, including an individual's right to be free from unreasonable searches and seizures by the government; the right to make decisions about contraception, abortion, and other "fundamental" issues such as marriage, procreation, child rearing, and education; the right not to disclose certain information to the government; the right to associate free from government intrusion; and the right to enjoy one's own home free from intrusion by the government, from sexually explicit mail or radio broadcasts, or from other intrusions.

In the context of protecting individual privacy from intrusion by the government, the Supreme Court has found protections for privacy in the First Amendment provisions for freedom of expression and association, the Third Amendment restriction on quartering soldiers in private homes, the Fourth Amendment prohibition on unreasonable searches and seizures, the due process clause and guarantee against self-incrimination in the Fifth Amendment, the Ninth and Tenth Amendment reservations of power in the people and the States, and the equal protection and due process clauses of the Fourteenth Amendment.[8]

Two constitutionally based privacy protections are most applicable to information privacy: the Fourth Amendment and the protection against government disclosure of personal matters.

The Fourth Amendment

One of the colonists' most serious grievances against the British government was its use of general searches. The hostility to general searches found powerful expression in the Fourth Amendment. As interpreted by the Supreme Court, this provision prohibits "unreasonable" searches and seizures, requires that most searches be conducted only with a warrant issued by a court, makes the issuing of warrants conditional on the government's showing "probable cause" that a crime has been or is likely to be committed and that the information sought is germane to that crime, and generally requires that the government provide the subject of a search with contemporaneous notice of the search.

The protection afforded by the Fourth Amendment, while considerable, is not absolute. The Supreme Court has determined, for example, that warrants are not required to search or seize items in the "plain view" of a law enforcement officer,[9] for searches that are conducted incidentally to valid arrests,[10] and for searches involving national security. Smith and Howe have written:

> The national security exception has been narrowly drawn to apply only in instances of immediate and grave peril to the nation and must be invoked by special authorization of the Attorney General or the President. The national security exception is available only in cases of foreign security, not domestic security, and the contours of the exception are more specifically outlined by statute.[11]

In the areas where the Fourth Amendment does apply, what makes a search or seizure "unreasonable"? In 1967, concurring in *Katz v. United States*, Justice Harlan wrote that reasonableness was defined by the individual's "actual," subjective expectation of privacy and the extent to which that expectation was "one that society was prepared to recognize as 'reasonable.'"[12] The Court adopted that test for determining what was "private" within the meaning of the Fourth Amendment in 1968 and continues to apply it today, with somewhat uneven results.[13]

Most pertinently for government projects that could involve accessing data about Americans from commercial databases, the Supreme Court held in 1976 in *United States v. Miller* that there can be no reasonable expectation of privacy in objects or information held by a third party. The case involved bank records, to which, the Court noted, "respondent can assert neither ownership nor possession." Such documents "contain only information voluntarily conveyed to the banks and exposed to their employees in the ordinary course of business," and therefore the Court found that the Fourth Amendment was not implicated when the government sought access to them:

> The depositor takes the risk, in revealing his affairs to another, that the information will be conveyed by that person to the Government. This Court has held repeatedly that *the Fourth Amendment does not prohibit the obtaining of information revealed to a third party and conveyed by him to Government authorities, even if the information is revealed on the assumption that it will be used only for a limited purpose and the confidence placed in the third party will not be betrayed.*[14]

Congress reacted to the decision by enacting a statutory right of privacy in bank records,[15] but this logic has served as the basis for another important exclusion from the protection of the Fourth Amendment: information about (as opposed to the content of) telephone calls. The Supreme Court has found (in *Smith v. Maryland*) that the Fourth Amendment is inapplicable to telecommunications "attributes" (the number dialed, when the call was placed, the duration of the call, etc.), because that information is necessarily conveyed to, or observable by, third parties involved in connecting the call:

> Telephone users, in sum, typically know that they must convey numerical information to the phone company; that the phone company has facilities for recording this information; and that the phone company does in fact record this information for a variety of legitimate business purposes.

As a result, under the Fourth Amendment, the use of "pen registers" (to record information about outgoing calls) and "trap and trace" devices (to record information about incoming calls) does not require a warrant, because they collect not the content of a call but only information about the call that is necessarily disclosed to others.

Because virtually all transactions and communications, especially if they have any electronic component, require disclosing information to a third party, the scope of Fourth Amendment protection is dramatically reduced. This is especially apparent in the context of the Internet, because anonymous transactions are technologically difficult and even the most secure, encrypted communications require the disclosure of significant communications attributes. As with information disclosed to a third party, Congress reacted to the Supreme Court's decision by creating a statutory warrant requirement for pen registers.[16]

The exclusion from Fourth Amendment protection of information disclosed to (or possessed by) a third party raises significant issues when applied to government mining of commercial databases and other government efforts to aggregate personally identifiable information held in the private sector. Such information, by definition, will be held by third parties, so government use of those data, under the Supreme Court's current interpretations, is unlikely to be limited by the Fourth Amendment, no matter how great the intrusion into information privacy.

The Fourth Amendment applies to searches and surveillance conducted for domestic law enforcement purposes within the United States and those conducted outside the United States if they involve U.S. citizens (although not necessarily permanent resident aliens). The Fourth Amendment also applies to searches and surveillance conducted for national security and intelligence purposes within the United States, if they involve Americans who have no connection to a foreign power.[17] The Supreme Court has not yet addressed whether the Fourth Amendment applies to searches and surveillance for national security and intelligence purposes, if they are conducted wholly outside the United States or involve Americans who are connected to a foreign power.[18] Appellate courts have found, however, that there is an exception to the Fourth Amendment's warrant requirement for searches conducted for intelligence purposes within the United States that involve only non-U.S. persons or agents of foreign powers.[19] Statutory protections, discussed below, fill some of the gaps in the Fourth Amendment's scope and impose additional restrictions on government searches and seizures.

Protection Against Government Disclosure of Personal Matters

The Supreme Court has extended the protection of privacy from government intrusion beyond the Fourth Amendment to a more general constitutional right against government-compelled "disclosure of personal matters." In 1977, the Supreme Court heard *Whalen v. Roe*, a case involving a New York statute requiring that copies of prescriptions for certain drugs be provided to the state, which was challenged on the basis that the requirement would infringe patients' privacy rights. In his opinion for the unanimous Court, Justice Stevens wrote that the constitutionally protected "zone of privacy" included "the individual interest in avoiding disclosure of personal matters."[20] Nevertheless, having found this new privacy interest in nondisclosure of personal information, the Court did not apply strict scrutiny—which it typically reserves for cases involving "fundamental" interests. Instead, applying a lower level of scrutiny, the Court found that the statute did not infringe the individuals' interest in nondisclosure. The Court also explicitly rejected the application of the Fourth Amendment right of privacy, writing that Fourth Amendment cases "involve affirmative, unannounced, narrowly focused intrusions."

The Supreme Court has never decided a case in which it found that a government regulation or action violated the constitutional privacy right recognized in *Whalen*. Lower courts have used *Whalen* to strike down government actions on the basis that they violated individuals' right in nondisclosure.[21] Courts in the Fourth and Sixth Circuits have severely limited the scope of the *Whalen* nondisclosure privacy right. [22] Even those courts that have relied on the right of nondisclosure, however, have applied only intermediate scrutiny, instead of the strict scrutiny typically used to protect fundamental constitutional rights.[23]

Other Protections for Information Privacy in the Public Sector

Most of the provisions that protect information privacy from intrusion by the government are statutory rather than constitutional.

Privacy Act of 1974

Congress has enacted various statutory provisions limiting the power of the government to compel the disclosure of personal information and protecting against misuse of personal information possessed by the government. The broadest of these is the Privacy Act of 1974.[24] It requires federal agencies to store only relevant and necessary personal information and only for purposes required to be accomplished by statute or executive order; collect information to the extent possible from the data subject; maintain records that are accurate, complete, timely, and relevant; and establish administrative, physical, and technical safeguards to protect the security of records. The Privacy Act also prohibits disclosure, even to other government agencies, of personally identifiable information in any record contained in a "system of records," except pursuant to a written request by or with the written consent of the data subject, or pursuant to a specific exception. Agencies must log disclosures of records and, in some cases, inform the subjects of such disclosures when they occur. Under the act, data subjects must be able to access and copy their records, each agency must establish a procedure for amendment of records, and refusals by agencies to amend their records are subject to judicial review. Agencies must publish a notice of the existence, character, and accessibility of their record systems. Finally, individuals may seek legal redress if an agency denies them access to their records.

The Privacy Act is less protective of privacy than may first appear, because of numerous broad exceptions.[25] Twelve of these are expressly provided for in the act itself. These include:

1. An agency can disclose its records to officers and employees within the agency itself, the Bureau of the Census, the National Archives, Congress, the comptroller general, and consumer reporting agencies.

2. Information contained in an agency's records can be disclosed for "civil or criminal law enforcement activity if the activity is authorized by law."

3. Under the "routine use" exemption federal agencies are permitted to disclose personal information as long as the nature and scope of the routine use were previously published in the *Federal Register* and the disclosure of data was "for a purpose which is compatible with the purpose for

which it was collected." According to the Office of Management and Budget (OMB), "compatibility" covers uses that are either functionally equivalent or necessary and proper.[26]

In addition, the Privacy Act has been subject to judicial interpretations, which have created new exceptions. For example, courts have found that the following special entities do not constitute an "agency": a federally chartered production credit association, an individual government employee, state and local government agencies, the White House Office, and those components of the Executive Office of the President whose sole function is to advise and assist the president, grand juries, and national banks.

Moreover, the Privacy Act applies only to information maintained in a *system of records* defined as a "group of any records under the control of any agency from which information is retrieved by the name of the individual or by some identifying number, symbol, or other identifying particular assigned to the individual."[27] As a result, the D.C. Circuit Court held that "retrieval capability is not sufficient to create a system of records. . . . 'To be in a system of records, a record must . . . in practice [be] retrieved by an individual's name or other personal identifier.'"[28] Fogarty and Ortiz have noted that "[a] number of courts have held that private notes written by government agents are not considered a 'system of records' when kept in personal files and are consequently exempt from the Act."[29]

Sectoral Protections

In addition to the Privacy Act and the privacy exceptions to the Freedom of Information Act, there are also many more focused privacy laws applicable to specific sectors of the government or types of government activities. Many of these apply to information, people, or settings left unprotected by the Supreme Court's interpretation of the Fourth Amendment. For example, the Right to Financial Privacy Act, enacted in response to the Supreme Court's decision in *United States v. Miller*, restricts the government's access to bank records.

Federal statutes prohibit the Department of Health and Human Services from disclosing social security records except as "otherwise provided by Federal law" or regulation. Similarly, federal law prohibits the Internal Revenue Service (IRS) from disclosing information on income tax returns and the Census Bureau from disclosing certain categories of census data.

Some statutes protecting privacy in commercial sectors also impose limits on government access to personal information. For example, the Cable Act of 1984 prohibits cable companies from providing the government with personally identifiable information about their customers, unless the government presents a court order. Stewart Baker writes that such an order can be obtained only on "'clear and convincing evidence' that the customer was suspected of engaging in a crime and if the order afforded the customer an opportunity to contest the government's claim."[30] The PATRIOT Act amended this provision to apply only to records about cable television service and not other services—such as Internet or telephone—that a cable operator might provide. The Video Privacy Protection Act prohibits video rental companies from disclosing personally identifiable information about their customers unless the government presents a search warrant, court order, or grand jury subpoena. The Family Education Rights and Privacy Act of 1974 contains a similar provision applicable to educational records.

Electronic Surveillance

Perhaps the most significant sectoral protections for information privacy apply to electronic surveillance and other searches. Title III of the Omnibus Crime Control and Safe Streets Act of 1968, as amended by the Electronic Communications Privacy Act (ECPA) of 1986, sets forth statutory guidelines for obtaining a warrant to conduct surveillance for domestic law enforcement purposes. These requirements go beyond the protections provided by the Fourth Amendment. The additional protections include restricting the use of wiretaps to investigations of serious crimes; requiring law enforcement agencies to exhaust less intrusive techniques before turning to eavesdropping; limiting the duration of wiretaps and requiring procedures to minimize the interception of innocent conversations; establishing a statutory suppression rule; requiring detailed annual reports to be published on the number and nature of wiretaps; and subjecting the entire process to judicial oversight.[31]

The PATRIOT Act subsequently weakened some of these protections. Even before that, however, courts rarely refused the government a wiretap order. Between 1968 and 2003, courts approved a total of 30,692 wiretap orders (10,506 federal and 20,186 state). Those figures have increased fairly steadily since 1980. Over the past 35 years, courts have refused only 32 wiretap orders sought by the government.[32]

ECPA's restrictions on wiretaps are greatly weakened in the case of pen registers and trap-and-trace devices that seek only identifying information about calls. In those situations, the government must merely certify that the "information likely to be obtained is relevant to an ongoing 'criminal investigation.'" The PATRIOT Act extended these provisions to "addressing and routing" information about Internet communications. To obtain more detailed information about communications, such as where a particular cell phone is located, the government must obtain either a search warrant or a special court order known as a section 2703(d) order. To obtain a section 2703(d) order, the government must present "specific and articulable facts" that the information sought is relevant to an ongoing criminal investigation.[33]

To obtain access to e-mail stored by a service provider (to which the Fourth Amendment does not apply because the information is in the hands of a third party), ECPA requires that the government obtain a warrant if the e-mail has been stored for 180 days or less. If the e-mail has been stored for more than 180 days, the government need only present a subpoena, which the Federal Bureau of Investigation (FBI), the IRS, and grand juries are empowered to issue themselves.[34]

Intelligence Gathering

Although the above statutes apply when the government seeks information for law enforcement purposes, the Foreign Intelligence Surveillance Act (FISA) of 1978 governs surveillance and, since being amended in 1994, physical searches conducted within the United States for the purpose of gathering foreign intelligence. FISA regulates certain electronic surveillance and physical searches in the United States against foreign powers and agents of foreign powers, including Americans, when a significant purpose of the surveillance or search is to obtain foreign intelligence information.

As amended by the PATRIOT Act, FISA creates a special eleven-judge court—the Foreign Intelligence Surveillance Court. An application approved by the attorney general is submitted to this court for authorization, setting out the facts to support a finding by the judge that there is probable cause to believe that the proposed target is a foreign power or an agent of a foreign power and describing the premises or property to be the subject of the search or surveillance. Each application includes "minimization procedures" as the term is defined in the act, setting out the procedures to be followed to minimize the acquisition, retention, and dissemination of the information. Surveillance and searches are authorized for periods of 90 days (to target an American agent of a foreign power) up to a year (to target a foreign government). In certain limited circumstances, the attorney general may authorize electronic surveillance or physical searches without court authorization when the means of communication or premises are used exclusively by certain foreign powers as defined in the act (e.g., a foreign government). Between 1979 and 2003, FISA judges approved 16,971 FISA warrants—all but five that the attorney general had sought.[35]

Executive Order (EO) 12333, issued by President Ronald Reagan in 1981, established the framework within which U.S. intelligence activities are conducted today. This EO explicitly recognized that "timely and accurate information about the activities, capabilities, plans, and intentions of foreign powers, organizations, and persons and their agents, is essential to the security of the United States," but that intelligence must be gathered in a "responsible manner that is consistent with the Constitution and applicable law." The EO restricts government surveillance of Americans outside the United States, even for foreign intelligence purposes, unless the persons involved are agents of a foreign power or the surveillance is necessary to acquire "significant information that cannot reasonably be acquired by other means."

EO 12333 is implemented within each agency by procedures that require the approval of the agency head and the attorney general. These procedures address in detail the collection, retention, and dissemination of information about Americans, and provide extensive guidance as to when and how DOD officials may engage in collection techniques such as electronic surveillance and nonconsensual physical searches; but they provide little direct guidance concerning data mining.

The *Attorney General's Guidelines on General Crimes, Racketeering Enterprise, and Terrorism Enterprise Investigations*, first adopted in 1976 by Attorney General Edward Levi and most recently (as of this writing) revised by Attorney General John Ashcroft in May 2002, provide guidance to FBI officials concerning surveillance and other searches, including the terms under which the FBI may use publicly available sources of information. According to the guidelines, the FBI "may draw on and retain pertinent information from any source permitted by law, including publicly available information, whether obtained directly or through services or resources (whether nonprofit or commercial) that compile or analyze such information[,] and information voluntarily provided by private entities."[36]

The guidelines specifically authorize the FBI to carry out "general topical research, including conducting online searches and accessing online sites and forums as part of such research on the same terms and conditions as members of the public generally," but require that such research not include searches by "individuals' names or other individual identifiers." The guidelines authorize "online search activity" and "access [to] online sites and forums on the same terms and conditions as members of the public generally," without any restriction as to subject-based searches, for "the purpose of detecting or preventing terrorism or other criminal activities." Finally, the guidelines provide that for "the purpose of detecting or preventing terrorist activities," the FBI may "visit any place and attend any event that is open to the public, on the same terms and conditions as members of the public generally."

These guidelines are supplemented by the *Attorney General's Guidelines for FBI National Security Investigations and Foreign Intelligence Collection* that Ashcroft revised in October 2003.[37] These more recent guidelines, large portions of which are classified, focus on the activities of the FBI in "preventing, preempting, and disrupting terrorist threats to the United States" and authorize widespread sharing of information necessary to achieve this purpose. The sections concerning how this information may be collected are classified, but given the subject of these guidelines, it is reasonable to assume that they are no more restrictive than the guidelines on general crimes.

The number and variety of statutes applicable to government collection and use of personal information highlight the special sensitivity in the United States regarding government use of personal information, but also suggest the complexity of laws in this area. Moreover, in every case the protection for information privacy is subject to significant exemptions to accommodate other public interests.

Government Privacy Policies

The privacy protection most recently adopted in the public sector, reflecting an earlier development in the private sector, is the reliance on privacy policies posted on government Web sites. On 2 June 1999, Jack Lew, the director of OMB, issued a memorandum (M-99-18) to federal agencies instructing them to post privacy policies providing users with basic information about the nature of personally identifiable information collected on the Web site and the uses to which that information might be put.

In 2002, Congress passed the E-Government Act of 2002 requiring that federal government agencies post privacy policies on their Web sites. Those policies must disclose:

- What information is to be collected
- Why the information is being collected
- The intended use by the agency of the information
- With whom the information will be shared
- What notice or opportunities for consent would be provided to individuals regarding what information is collected and how that information is shared
- How the information will be secured
- The rights of the individual under section 552a of title 5, United States Code (commonly referred to as the Privacy Act), and other laws relevant to the protection of the privacy of an individual

The E-Government Act also requires that agencies conduct and, where feasible, publicize "privacy impact" assessments before developing or procuring new information technologies or instituting new information collection programs. On 26 September 2003, OMB released a memo (M-03-22) to heads of executive departments and agencies providing guidance on application of the new law. Information technologies used for national security are exempt from having to provide the privacy impact assessment.[38]

SPECIAL CHALLENGES PRESENTED BY GOVERNMENT DATA MINING

Government data mining entails many potential practical risks—for example, the risk of chilling innocent behavior and protected expression; erroneously targeting innocent people for sanction or further investigation owing to errors in the data, their aggregation, or the algorithms used to analyze them; and embarrassing or harming people through inadvertent or wrongful disclosure or misuse of the data. These risks are significant and are inherent in any mining of personal information, especially when the government does it. Recent government data mining by national security authorities makes some of these concerns even more acute or presents special issues of which legal advisors should be aware. We conclude by highlighting three of these.

Individual Identification

The first concern is how to identify individuals for purposes of aggregating data about them and then link those data with the right person. Business and government have long struggled with how to ensure that information about one person is correctly attributed to that individual and only to that individual. Many factors contribute to the difficulty of integrating data accurately:

- Names may be recorded differently in different records (e.g., J. Smith, J. Q. Smith, John Q. Smith).
- Individuals, especially women, change their names. There are approximately 2.3 million marriages and 1.1 million divorces every year in the United States, often resulting in changed last names (and also changed addresses).[39]
- Many people have the same name.
- Many individuals have more than one address (e.g., home, office, vacation home, post office box), and are likely to change addresses. As of 1998 there were 6 million vacation or second homes in the United States, many of which were used as temporary or second addresses. And, according to the U.S. Postal Service, about 43 million Americans—approximately 17 percent of the U.S. population—and 2.6 million businesses change addresses every year.[40]
- Social security numbers (SSNs) improve the likelihood of a correct match to the account holder; but even when accounts include SSNs, identification may be difficult because accounts for the same household may reflect different primary SSNs

(e.g., husband, wife, minor beneficiary) and because of transcription errors in recording strings of numbers.

Integrating data accurately is especially difficult in the context of counterterrorism, which often involves matching data from disparate systems over which the intelligence community has no control, from intercepts and other sources where little or no identifying information is provided, and in ways that prevent seeking or verifying additional identifying information.

In addition, even when data are accurately aggregated, the file must then be linked to the right person. This has so far proved a significant challenge in the national security environment, for a number of reasons. The problems associated with misidentifying people, including well-known figures such as Senator Ted Kennedy, on the current "do not fly" lists are well documented. These problems are exacerbated by the poor quality of most identity documents and the ease with which fraudulent documents may be obtained. The 9/11 hijackers had false identification documents, either forgeries or legitimate driver's licenses issued by states to the wrong person. Moreover, photographs on driver's licenses and passports, which are issued for terms of between four and ten years, often provide poor verification of identity. Better forms of identification, such as biometric identifiers (e.g., fingerprints or retinal scans) are not widely used today, and pose significant issues about cost, reliability, and impact on privacy.

During an investigation in 2002–2003, GAO found that U.S. border guards failed 100 percent of the time to spot counterfeit identity documents that GAO agents were using to enter the country illegally. Similar results were found before 9/11, when GAO agents tried to gain unauthorized access to federal buildings, airports, and military bases.[41]

False Positives and Data Correction

Inaccuracies in matching and linking data pose many risks. If they lead to failures to detect potential terrorists, they pose security risks. If they lead to misidentification of people as possible terrorists who in fact are not, they pose other risks, including significant privacy concerns. The latter risks may be the most likely, because of the certainty that data-mining systems will generate false positives, both as a result of inaccuracies in the data and how they are matched and linked, and as a result of the inevitable inability of the system to distinguish in every case between innocent and suspicious behavior.[42] False positives impose many economic costs to information privacy, to national security (which is undermined when scarce resources are spent investigating nonthreats), and in public annoyance and undercutting public support for counterterrorism.

Given the inevitability of false positives, government data mining must evaluate the number and percentage of false positives that any system generates and the consequences of a false positive. Those efforts must also provide some system, consonant with the purpose of the data mining, to correct errors and screen out false positives. To date, however, the government has not developed such a system. Quite the contrary: in March 2003, the Justice Department exempted the FBI's National Crime Information Center from the Privacy Act's requirements that data be "accurate, relevant, timely and complete"; and in August 2003, DHS exempted the TSA's passenger screening database from the Privacy Act's requirements that government records include only "relevant and necessary" personal information. Mismatched data and misidentified individuals pose a grave risk for both privacy and security, and this risk is exacerbated by the failure of national security officials to address it.

Accessing Private-Sector Data

Since 9/11, government agencies have stepped up efforts to access personally identifiable information from the private sector for a variety of uses designed to enhance public and national security. The GAO report of 2004 on government data mining found that more than one-fourth of all government data-mining projects involved accessing data from the private sector. The government has broad powers for doing this. It can access publicly available data on the same basis as any member of the public; it can contract for data; and it can exercise its unique power to issue subpoenas, search warrants, wiretap orders, "national security letters," and FISA (Section 215) orders that require the product of personal data, usually in secret.

This enhanced reliance on private-sector data, usually obtained from third parties, raises significant privacy issues regarding not just the government's conduct but also that of the private sector. While there has been growing attention to the government's access to, and use of, private-sector data (e.g., the DHS chief privacy officer's report concerning Jet Blue, the Technology and Privacy Advisory Committee report, and the GAO's report on government data mining), little thought has been given to the legal principles that should guide the private sector when it responds to government requests for access to personally identifiable information, or to the legal protection that applies, or should apply, when it does so.

CONCLUSION

Government data mining can pose risks to individuals and institutions alike. Those risks include infringing on legally protected privacy rights; undermining national security by targeting innocent individuals, failing to identify real suspects, or otherwise misfocusing scarce resources; creating liability for businesses and others that provide, or fail to provide, the government with requested data, or otherwise fail to comply with often detailed and burdensome laws; and interfering with transnational data flows or subjecting U.S. companies to liability under foreign national laws.

These and other risks are exacerbated by the escalating pace of technological change. Scott Charney of Microsoft testified before the DOD Technology and Privacy Advisory Committee in 2004 that technological innovation is leading to less expensive storage capacity for digital data, cheaper and more advanced tracking technologies, steady advances in computer processing power, and increased standardization in data formats. See Figure 68-1 for a summary of the recommendations of the DOD Technology and Privacy Advisory Committee. Taken together, these developments mean that more personally identifiable data will be created and stored and will be easier to access, and that it will be increasingly possible to aggregate and match these data quickly and affordably. The privacy risks and other risks associated with government data mining will increase as information technologies develop.

F I G U R E   68-1

Impact of TAPAC recommendations on government data mining (i.e., searches of one or more electronic databases of information concerning U.S. persons, by or on behalf of an agency or employee of the government).

Type of Information	New Recommended Requirements
Data mining that is *not* known or reasonably likely to involve **personally identifiable** information about **U.S. persons** (i.e., U.S. citizens and permanent residents)	No new requirements
Data mining limited to **foreign intelligence** that does *not* concern **U.S. persons**	No new requirements
Data mining known or reasonably likely to involve **personally identifiable** information about **U.S. persons**:	
If based on **particularized suspicion** about a specific individual, including searches to identify or locate a specific individual (e.g., a suspected terrorist) from airline or cruise ship **passenger manifests** or other lists of names or other nonsensitive information about U.S. persons	No new requirements
If concerning **federal government employees** that is solely in connection with their employment	No new requirements
If limited to searches of information that are **routinely available without charge or subscription to the public**—on the Internet, in telephone directories, or in public records to the extent authorized by law	1. Administrative authorization (set forth in Rec. 2.1), which may be granted on a "per program" or "per search" basis; and 2. Regular compliance audits (set forth in Rec. 2.5).
If conducted with **deidentified data** (i.e., data from which personally identifying elements such as name or Social Security number have been removed or obscured)	All new requirements apply (i.e., administrative authorization, compliance with technical requirements, special rules for third-party databases, and regular compliance audits, as set forth in Recs. 2.1, 2.2, 2.3, and 2.5), *except for* need to obtain a Foreign Intelligence Surveillance Court order (set forth in Rec. 2.4).
If conducted with **personally identifiable information**	All new requirements apply (as set forth in Recs. 2.1–2.5), *including* application to the Foreign Intelligence Surveillance Court (Rec. 2.4), which can be made on a "per program" or "per search" basis.

NOTES

1. *Data Mining: Federal Efforts Cover a Wide Range of Uses*, GAO-04-548 (May 2004), pp. 3, 27–64, tables 2-25; see www.gao.gov/new.items/d04548.pdf.

2. DOD Technology and Privacy Advisory Committee, *Safeguarding Privacy in the Fight against Terrorism* (March 2004), pp. 15–20; www.sainc.com/tapac/final Report.htm.

3. See ic-arda.org.

4. Department of Homeland Security (DHS) Privacy Office, *Report to the Public on Events Surrounding JetBlue Data Transfer—Findings and Recommendations* (20 February 2004); available at www.dhs.gov/interweb/assetlibrary/privacy_ rpt_jetblue.pdf.

5. Privacy Act; System of Records, 68 Fed. Reg. 45,265, 2003, DHS, TSA (interim final notice). See also GAO, *Computer-Assisted Passenger Prescreening System Faces Significant Implementation Challenges*, GAO-04-385 (February 2004).

6. Transactions and Customer Identification Programs, 68 Fed. Reg. 25,089 (2003).

7. Thomas C. Greene, "A Back Door to Poindexter's Orwellian Dream," *The Register* (24 September 2003); Robert O'Harrow, Jr., "U.S. Backs Florida's New Counterterrorism Database," *Washington Post* (6 August 2003): A1; see also www.matrix-at.org/.

8. Fred H. Cate, *Privacy in the Information Age*, (Brookings Institution Press, Washington, D.C., 1997), pp. 49–66.

9. *Coolidge v. New Hampshire*, 403 U.S. 443, 1971.

10. *U.S. v. Edwards*, 415 U.S. 800, 1974.

11. Jeffrey H. Smith and Elizabeth L. Howe, "Federal Legal Constraints on Electronic Surveillance," in Markle Foundation Task Force, *Protecting American's Freedom in the Information Age* (2002), p. 136, n.16; www.markletaskforce.org/documents/ Markle Report Part3.pdf.

12. 389 U.S. 347, 361, 1967.

13. The Court has found "reasonable" expectations of privacy in homes (*Camara v. Municipal Court*, 387 U.S. 523, 1967); businesses (*G.M. Leasing Corp. v. United States*, 429 U.S. 338, 1977); sealed luggage and packages (e.g., *United States v. Chadwick*, 433 U.S. 1, 1977); and even drums of chemicals (*United States v. Knotts*, 460 U.S. 276, 1983)—but no "reasonable" expectations of privacy in voice or writing samples (*United States v. Dionisio*, 410 U.S. 1, 1973), phone numbers (*Smith v. Maryland*, 442 U.S. 735, 1979), conversations recorded by concealed microphones (*United States v. White*, 401 U.S. 745, 1971), and automobile passenger compartments (*New York v. Belton*, 453 U.S. 454, 1981), trunks (*United States v. Ross*, 456 U.S. 798, 1982), and glove boxes (*South Dakota v. Opperman*, 428 U.S. 364, 1976).

14. 425 U.S. 435, 443 (emphasis added).

15. Right to Financial Privacy Act, 12 U.S.C. §§3401–3422.

16. 18 U.S.C. §§3121, 1841.

17. *U.S. v. U.S. District Court for the Eastern District of Michigan*, 407 U.S. 297, 1972 (commonly referred to as the *Keith* decision).

18. Smith and Howe, op. cit., p. 133.

19. See *U.S. v. Bin Laden*, 126 F. Supp. 2d 264, 271–72, S.D.N.Y., 2000.

20. 429 U.S. 589, 599–600, 1977.

21. *Tavoulareas v. Washington Post Company,* 724 F.2d 1010 (D.C. Cir.), 1984; *Barry v. City of New York,* 712 F.2d 1554 (2d Cir.), 1983; *Schacter v. Whalen,* 581 F.2d 35 (2d Cir.), 1978; *Doe v. Southeastern Pennsylvania Transportation Authority,* 72 F.3d 1133 (3d Cir.), 1995; *United States v. Westinghouse Electric Corporation,* 638 F.2d 570 (3d Cir.), 1980; *Plante v. Gonzalez,* 575 F.2d 1119 (5th Cir.), 1978; *Doe v. Attorney General,* 941 F.2d 780 (9th Cir.) 1991.

22. *J.P. v. DeSanti,* 653 F.2d 1080 (6th Cir.), 1981; *Walls v. City of Petersburg,* 895 F.2d 188, 192 (4th Cir.), 1990.

23. *Doe v. Attorney General,* 941 F.2d, 796.

24. 5 U.S.C. §§552a(e)(1)–(5). For the three exceptions cited below see §552a(b), (b)7, and (b)3.

25. Sean Fogarty and Daniel R. Ortiz, "Limitations upon Interagency Information Sharing: The Privacy Act of 1974," in Markle Foundation Task Force, op. cit., pp. 127, 128.

26. Ibid., pp. 129–30. See also "Guidance on the Privacy Act: Implications of 'Call Detail' Programs to Manage Employees' Use of the Government's Telecommunications Systems," 52 *Fed. Reg.* 12,900, 12,993, 1987 (OMB).

27. 2*U.S. v. Miller,* 643 F.2d 713 (10th Cir.), 1981, § 552a(a)(5). See also Fogarty and Ortiz, op. cit., p. 128.

28. *Henke v. United States DOC,* 83 F.3d 1453, 1461 (D.C. Cir.), 1996, quoting *Bartel v. F.A.A.,* 725 F.2d 1403, 1408 n.10 (D.C. Cir.) 1984.

29. Op. cit., p. 129, citing *Bowyer v. United States Department of Air Force,* 804 F.2d 428 (7th Cir.), 1986; *Chapman v. NASA,* 682 F.2d 526 (5th Cir.), 1982.

30. Stewart A. Baker, "The Regulation of Disclosure of Information Held by Private Parties," in Markle Foundation Task Force, op. cit., pp. 161, 167.

31. See *Internet Security and Privacy,* hearing before the Senate Judiciary Committee, 25 May 2000 (statement of James X. Dempsey, Senior Staff Counsel, Center for Democracy and Technology); www.cdt.org/testimony/000525dempsey. shtml.

32. Administrative Office of the United States Courts, *2003 Wiretap Report,* table 7; www.uscourts.gov/wiretap03/contents.html. See also Electronic Privacy Information Center, Title III Electronic Surveillance 1968–2002; www.epic.org/ privacy/wiretap/stats/wiretap_stats.html.

33. 18 U.S.C. §2703(d).

34. Baker, op. cit., p. 163.

35. Center for Democracy and Technology, "The Nature and Scope of Governmental Electronic Surveillance Activity" (June 2004); www.cdt.org/wiretap/wiretap_ overview.html. See also Electronic Privacy Information Center, Foreign Intelligence Surveillance Act Orders 1979–2002; www.epic.org/privacy/wiretap/ stats/fisa_stats.html. See generally Smith and Howe, op. cit. pp. 140–1.

36. U.S. Department of Justice, Office of Legal Policy, *Attorney General's Guidelines on General Crimes, Racketeering Enterprise and Terrorism Enterprise Investigations* (2002), pp. 21–2; www.usdoj.gov/ag/readingroom/generalcrimea. htm.

37. U.S. Department of Justice, Office of Legal Policy, *Attorney General's Guidelines for FBI National Security Investigations and Foreign Intelligence Collection* (2003); www.usdoj.gov/olp/nsiguidelines.pdf. The quotation is from p. 1.

38. A "national security system" is defined as " an information system operated by the federal government, the function, operation or use of which involves: (a) intelligence activities, (b) cryptologic activities related to national security, (c) command and control of military forces, (d) equipment that is an integral part of a weapon or weapons systems, or (e) systems critical to the direct fulfillment of military or intelligence missions, but does not include systems used for routine administrative and business applications, such as payroll, finance, logistics and personnel management."

39. National Center for Health Statistics, *National Vital Statistics Reports*, 51:8 (19 May 2003): 1, table A.

40. U.S. Postal Service Department of Public Affairs and Communications, *Latest Facts Update* (24 June 2002).

41. Amitai Etzioni, "Reliable Identification for Homeland Protection and Collateral Gains," in Markle Task Force Report, op. cit, appendix A.

42. Paul Rosenzweig, *Proposals for Implementing the Terrorism Information Awareness System*, Heritage Foundation Legal Memorandum 8, 2003; www.heritage.org/ Research/HomelandDefense/lm8.cfm.

Politics and Accountability

CHAPTER 69

Introduction to Section 13

The Honorable Warren Rudman
Counsel, Paul, Weiss, Rifkind, Wharton and Garrison LLP
Former U.S. Senator from New Hampshire

In January 2001, the United States Commission on National Security/21st Century, which I cochaired with Gary Hart, predicted:

> The combination of unconventional weapons proliferation with the persistence of international terrorism will end the relative invulnerability of the U.S. homeland to catastrophic attack. A direct attack on American citizens on American soil is likely over the next quarter century.[1]

People didn't pay much attention to that report until 9/11. Then they paid a lot of attention.

The 9/11 Commission concluded that the failure to prevent the attacks was due to diffusion of responsibility and accountability among various agencies, and it recommended changes in federal government organizational structure. Establishing the Department of Homeland Security (DHS) realigned responsibilities that had sprawled across outdated concepts of boundaries. In January 2005 the House of Representatives approved the creation of a permanent standing Committee on Homeland Security, following the 9/11 Commission's recommendation that both the House and the Senate should create "a single, principal point of oversight and review for homeland security" across the federal government. The change to the House Rules established a committee with primary jurisdiction over governmentwide counterterrorism policy and primary jurisdiction over the counterterrorism mission of DHS. The new committee will have by far the most significant responsibility for homeland security policy of any committee in the House or Senate, but it will not have jurisdiction over all aspects of immigration, over the Coast Guard, the FBI, or intelligence. However, because homeland security missions cut across different parts of DHS, are shared by the military and state and local government, and extend to the private sector, accountability, responsibility, and authority in homeland security remain significant challenges. Oversight and accountability systems should be developed and applied not only to individual agencies but also to collaboration among multiple agencies and sectors. Oversight should address contributions to joint actions, and all participants in homeland security must be accountable to the American people for a realistic set of performance measures.

At the root of our efforts to secure the nation against terrorism there are political questions regarding values, principles, doctrine, the distribution of power, and historic constitutional challenges. These political questions must be addressed through leadership, dialogue, deliberation, debate, and voting. In Chapter 70, Anne Khademian discusses the political questions at the core of homeland security for national debate and discussion. In Chapter 71 Charles Wise and Rania Nader discuss the critically important need to establish an effective accountability system for homeland security. Finally, in Chapter 72 William Rosenau addresses the important issue of the ideological differences between the United States and al-Qaida and the necessity to win the war of ideas.

N O T E

1. United States Commission on National Security/21st Century, *Road Map for National Security: Imperative for Change*, Phase 3 Report. Washington, D.C. (31 January 2001), pp. viii.

CHAPTER 70

The Politics of Homeland Security

Anne M. Khademian
Associate Professor, Center for Public Administration and Policy,
Virginia Polytechnic University

At the core of efforts to secure the nation against terrorism are political questions regarding value, principles, doctrine, the distribution of power, and historic constitutional challenges. These questions cannot be answered by applying scientific knowledge, strategic planning, or performance measures but must be addressed through dialogue, deliberation, debate, and voting in communities, counties, and states.

WHERE DOES ACCOUNTABILITY FOR HOMELAND SECURITY REST?

A terrorist act of any kind is first and foremost a local disaster requiring a local response from firefighters, the police, rescue and health workers, and others. But where does accountability—as distinguished from response—rest? Who is accountable for preparing for, reacting to, and indeed preventing terrorism?

Homeland security is a complex mix of activities, which some analysts classify as "crisis management" and "consequence management." Crisis management involves predominantly law enforcement and intelligence. It is focused on anticipating and preventing terrorism through intelligence, surveillance, border security, and tactical operations; and on investigation and forensics afterward. Consequence management focuses on efforts to respond effectively and to recover.[1] What policies or strategies should guide these efforts? How should these responsibilities be distributed and integrated across federal, state, and local governments and agencies? And who should be accountable for ensuring the effectiveness of the efforts?

Locating Accountability and the U.S. Constitution

The *National Strategy for Homeland Security* states that the American federal system provides both "opportunity" and "challenges" for defending the country from terrorism. Opportunities come from the expertise, initiative, and organizational excellence of many state and local governments and federal agencies. The challenge is to put all the pieces together so as to enhance rather than complicate prevention, preparedness, and response, and to clarify accountability for these various elements of homeland security.[2]

This is no small task. Much of American constitutional history involves political struggles between the federal, state, and local governments. More than 87,000 local governments are responsible for running schools, collecting property taxes, managing waste, regulating economic development, providing safe water, managing the environment, running parks and recreation facilities, building roads, and organizing, planning, preparing for, and responding to natural and human-made disasters. While we recognize these functions as local responsibilities, we do not necessarily hold local governments exclusively accountable for them. Often, there is debate over what role, if any, the federal government or a state government should have.

The Government Accountability Office (GAO) has argued persuasively that the federal government should take the lead in developing a national strategy for homeland security, and in setting comprehensive national standards for providing essential equipment, preparing and training first responders, protecting power grids, securing containers for shipping, bolstering port security, establishing hospital capacities, and formulating building codes.[3] A national strategy, it is claimed, would clearly delineate the responsibilities of federal agencies and federal, state, and local governments and would also establish a base level of preparedness for every community.[4]

The recent history of American federalism supports this argument. There has been a gradual transition from a federal system with strong boundaries between the work of local governments, states, and the federal government to a mixed and even top-heavy federal system in which states and local governments share in (or perhaps shoulder the burden of) implementing programs determined by the national government.[5] This has varied, depending on the presidential administration, but the long-term trend toward national efforts to define policy for the country as a whole is clear.[6]

National, Local, or Mixed Standards of Accountability

Should there be national standards for homeland security? In theory, each state or locality could be accountable for determining what constitutes adequate planning, training, and equipment; adequate protections for infrastructure; adequate standards for hospitals and public health systems; and adequate communication between responders, public officials, and the public. This approach would be contingent on local circumstances, practices, and experiences.[7] There is strong philosophical precedent for a more localized approach to federalism. According to the "states' rights" argument, states and local governments are closer to the people, more directly involved in daily affairs, and better able to represent as well as protect the public.[8] In 1787, the Antifederalists held that simple government, close to the people, would be most conducive to freedom. Essentially, such government is more readily controlled by the people and more accurately reflects local priorities.[9]

Is this an argument for making state and local governments accountable for homeland security? Or should the priorities and goals of homeland security be established by state and local government organizations working with federal agencies? If there is an "opportunity" to utilize the expertise and experience of state and local agencies, can accountability for safety, security, and civil liberties be assigned with any clarity among different governments and government agencies? Question 1, then, involves fundamental assumptions about the "best" way to govern, and it may entail trade-offs.

WHAT CONSTITUTES A "COMMUNITY" FOR PURPOSES OF PREPAREDNESS?

Cities, towns, districts, counties, states, and countries are formally defined by geographic boundaries within which some form of government has legal authority. But a community is not necessarily defined in this way. Communities are defined by collective decision making and common interests—one of which is security. In colonial America defensive stockades were often built around clusters of residents and government officials. Later, the states became large communities with a common interest in security; the right of each state to a well-regulated militia was guaranteed by the Second Amendment to the Constitution. But the concept of a community is taken to the national level in the preamble to the Constitution, which specifies that the new government will "provide for the common defense" of the nation.

How should we define a community for purposes of homeland security? Should we focus on cities and towns, on regions and urban areas, on states, or on the nation? The answer will affect not only how we approach homeland security, but what impact policies for homeland security will have on communities and their members. First, homeland security policy will interact with communities, often in unanticipated ways. Second, our view of community membership and its obligations will affect how policies for homeland security policy are developed.

Communities, Public Policy, and Unanticipated Consequences

However we define *community*, there will be consequences for the members of a community beyond receiving grant money for homeland security, receiving assistance with planning and training, or mandates for organizing and responding to terror alerts. Communities are not inert and, as noted above, are not always defined by legal boundaries. Communities expand and contract in population, reflect changing priorities and concerns, and grapple with the challenges of collective living. Some communities thrive and grow; others stagnate and die. One factor in these dynamics is the relationship between communities and public policy—such as policies for homeland security. Policy analysts may try to estimate the impact or consequences of a public program on a community: if, for example, $1 million is spent in community A to train, equip, and plan for homeland security, how much more prepared will the community be? Often, however, the consequences of public policy are unanticipated or are not captured by analyses.[10]

Consider a public program with federal funding that defines communities as regions, or metropolitan areas, for purposes of homeland security. To secure and spend federal grant money, local governments throughout a region or metropolitan area will need to communicate with neighboring jurisdictions to identify regional resources and vulnerabilities, set common priorities, and engage in joint planning. Potentially, interests that cross geographic boundaries can be identified or developed, expanding the concept of the community beyond its traditional limits. One example is the National Capital Region (NCR), the cities and counties around Washington, D.C.: while Virginia, Maryland, and the District of Columbia have interests that differ, their efforts to plan and prepare for terrorist attacks as a region have reinforced regional governance. Their Council of Governments (COG)—the main forum for collaboration—has grown in strength and influence not only as regards homeland security but also for transportation, general planning, housing and development, health and human services, and the environment.

However, an emphasis on regional collaboration for homeland security could also have negative effects. Differences, disagreements, and historical struggles between various jurisdictions could be highlighted and reinforced.

Communities, Membership, and Homeland Security

Another question about the community is what it means to be a member of a community that is focused on homeland security. What obligations does the government have toward members of the community, and what obligations do members of the community have concerning homeland security?

If we ask, "What must governments do to protect citizens?" we might focus on how governments plan, train, conduct exercises, and equip the police and other first responders and emergency managers to prevent, prepare for, and respond effectively to a terrorist attack.

We might also focus on the need to limit governmental authority so that civil liberties are not compromised. This approach focuses on the obligation of governments to protect and serve members of communities, and to limit its own exercise of powers.

We can also view membership in a community as an obligation to participate in governance. As regards homeland security, consider federal funding for Citizen Corps Councils at the county and local levels of government. Just as the police try to engage the public in keeping communities safe, Citizen Corps Councils engage volunteers from the community to serve—in the event of an emergency—as responders, in medical reserve squads, and in other capacities. Several commentators have suggested community policing as a model for building relationships for homeland security at a community level; this can strengthen the response to possible terrorism and can lessen fear by letting residents share information—a form of counterterrorism.[11] Resources for homeland security are used not only to equip and train professional first responders and emergency managers but also to build a community capacity to identify security interests from the bottom, up, and to play a role in community-based protection.

How we define communities for the purposes of homeland security, and how we conceptualize membership in a community, will influence how communities develop counterterrorist programs and policies. More fundamentally, this can influence how communities practice governance.

HOW DO WE DEFINE HOMELAND SECURITY?

A national strategy for homeland security implies clear priorities and a comprehensive understanding of necessary resources and technologies. What should a national program for homeland security look like? What framework should guide efforts to prevent, prepare for, and respond to terrorism? Historically the federal government has sometimes emphasized natural disasters—an "all-hazards" approach or framework—and sometimes emphasized civil emergencies: an attack on America or an act of terrorism.[12] There are important differences between these emphases, affecting how funding is distributed and how communities organize for homeland security.

All-Hazards Versus Terrorism

In an all-hazards framework, professionals focus on the basic functions of managing any emergencies: hurricanes, tornadoes, toxic chemical spills, fires, or terrorism. These functions are mitigation (reducing the impact of a potential disaster); preparedness (training, technical assistance, and exercises); and response and recovery (immediate action following a disaster, then restoration of the community).[13] In the 1990s the Federal Emergency Management Agency (FEMA)—now the DHS Directorate of Emergency Preparedness and Response—spearheaded an "all-hazards" approach at the federal, state, and local level, and among nonprofit organizations involved in relief and recovery.[14]

After 9/11, resources devoted to all-hazards were reallocated to counterterrorism—i.e., to responding to and preventing terrorist attacks. Actually, many first responders and emergency managers consider counterterrorism a natural extension of the all-hazards framework. Firefighters and rescue teams, for example, need to know how to deal with a collapsing building or a chemical explosion regardless of whether it was due to a terrorist attack or an accident. In this view, terrorism is one more hazard for which the country must prepare; and DHS has frequently supported this idea, calling for a "single all-discipline, all-hazards plan."[15] But in fact it is not entirely clear how counterterrorism fits within the all-hazards, all-disciplines framework.

The difference is one of emphasis. Consider, in particular, state and local law enforcement officials. If homeland security is framed primarily as counterterrorism, these officials must focus on such matters as identifying threats and building interagency relationships domestically and with foreign intelligence agencies for information sharing and investigation. Tremendous resources currently go toward preventing a possible terrorist attack when the color-coded homeland security warning system for state and local governments shifts from yellow to orange. Police patrols are increased around landmarks, government buildings, and critical travel areas, and in some cities cars and trucks are randomly searched. The U.S. Conference of Mayors estimated that under "code orange," cities spent $70 million per week.[16] Also, after a terrorist attack, law enforcement resources and capabilities must be focused on securing and investigating the crime scene. By contrast, in an all-hazards framework, prevention and investigation are less important for law enforcement officials than efforts to secure roads, evacuate citizens, and prevent looting after a disaster.

The emphasis also influences the equipment, training, exercises, and personnel needed to address particular types of terrorist attacks. Some level of preparedness is necessary for all-hazards, but identifying and responding to, say, bioterrorism or chemical terrorism requires special detectors, a means to distribute pharmaceuticals to victims, protective gear and breathing apparatus for first responders, decontamination facilities, and specialized training.[17] Should we view terrorism as an extension of all-hazards—another specific hazard which the nation must address? Or should we focus primarily on homeland security, deliver specialized equipment and training to first responders for terrorist attacks involving weapons of mass destruction, build the capacity of law enforcement agencies at all levels of government to engage in counterterrorism and investigation, and approach existing all-hazards systems as the response component of homeland security? In the latter case, homeland security and all-hazards (mainly natural disasters) compete directly for the same resources.

Suppose, for example, that County A in a northern state needs to upgrade its basic emergency response capabilities. Its 911 system is antiquated; its firefighters need new equipment and clothing; its emergency rescue units need access to a helicopter. County A has no major metropolitan area, no large power plants, no major airport, and does not border on Canada. In response to a state request for homeland security priorities and needs, it asks for money to buy firefighting gear and to upgrade its 911 system. In County B, farther north, on the border with Canada, officials have requested money for radios that would allow law enforcement officials to communicate with their Canadian counterparts to patrol the border and enforce security. Funds are limited, and the state must choose between the two sets of priorities. A terrorist attack in County A, which has minimal capacity to respond, would be devastating. Yet the ability of County B to enhance border security could directly affect the war on terror. Thus although many factors influence the allocation of funds for homeland security, determining the framework for homeland security will be crucial.

Implications for Funding and Organizing Homeland Security

The two primary sources of state and local funding within DHS reflect the division between all-hazards and terrorism. In the budget for fiscal year 2003, homeland security functions focused on terrorism were to be directed through an all-hazards framework. Specifically, FEMA was to direct and manage $3.5 billion in funding for training and equipping first responders, for exercises, and for statewide planning.[18] As part of DHS, the newly named Directorate of Emergency Preparedness and Response was to "protect the Nation from all-hazards by leading and supporting the Nation in a comprehensive risk-based emergency management program."[19] But in the budget for fiscal year 2004 and again in 2005, this emphasis changed. Funding for homeland security preparedness functions—training first responders, equipment, planning, and exercises—went primarily to the Office of Domestic Preparedness (ODP).[20] Recently relocated to the Office of State and Local Government Coordination in the Office of the Secretary, ODP has the "primary responsibility within the executive branch of government for the preparedness of the United States for acts of terrorism."[21]

In structuring homeland security, governors and state emergency management personnel will focus on the money available through ODP to prepare for terrorist attacks.[22] Separating the source of all-hazards funding (FEMA) from the agency charged with preparing the nation for terrorism (ODP) will probably influence the approach that state and local governments take to establishing regional organizations for receiving and distributing funds, for planning, and for preparation. Determining which of the two offices is more "efficient" or speedy in its distribution of grant money does not answer the more fundamental question of what framework ought to guide the development of homeland security policy and the distribution of money.

WHAT SHOULD BE THE RELATIONSHIP BETWEEN CIVIL LIBERTIES AND SECURITY?

The USA PATRIOT Act (Uniting and Strengthening America by Providing Appropriate Tools Required to Intercept and Obstruct

Terrorism), passed in the immediate aftermath of 9/11, has become a focal point in the political struggle to define and protect civil liberties in the context of counterterrorism. From the perspective of the Department of Justice and other advocates of the legislation, the law is essential for security. The law makes it easier for federal agencies to share intelligence, strengthens the ability of the government to prosecute terrorism, removes what were viewed by government officials as obstacles to the investigation of terrorism, and facilitates enforcement efforts in light of new technologies such as cell phones and Internet communication.[23]

From the perspective of its critics, the PATRIOT Act is a direct threat to civil liberties. In particular, the authority to track Internet use, check library records, conduct "sneak and peek" searches of suspects' homes when they are not present, and use roving wiretaps are considered dangerous tools that can be applied without sufficient checks and balances to protect individual liberties. When the Department of Justice declares that the "fight against terrorism is now the first and overriding priority" and that the PATRIOT Act "has played a vital role in the Department of Justice's efforts to preserve America's system of ordered liberty for future generations," the emphasis seems to be on sacrificing some liberties today for greater security tomorrow.[24]

But are liberty and security necessarily competing values? Is it true that "our liberties make us vulnerable and if we will give up some of these liberties, at least temporarily, we will be more secure"?[25] Or can the two values be "mutually reinforcing"?[26] It depends on how we define liberty and how we pursue security.

Security Versus Liberty: Two Sets of Guidelines

If the relationship between liberty and security is framed as a trade-off, American history offers numerous examples: the passage of the Alien and Sedition Acts of 1798, in part to restrict opposition to the government during a time of impending war with France; the internment of more than 110,000 Americans of Japanese descent during World War II; the targeting of possible members of the Communist Party in the United States by Senator Joseph McCarthy's hearings during the Cold War; and the investigation by the FBI of hundreds of civil rights activists and protestors opposed to the Vietnam War. These are viewed as violations of individual liberties in the government's pursuit of national security.

We interpret these events, however, within a particular understanding of liberty—specifically, freedom *from* government, or at least from excessive government. To preserve liberty, government must be restrained.[27] As critics of the PATRIOT Act argue, there must be checks and balances to limit governmental intrusion. Without restraints, it is argued, government grows in strength and liberties gradually erode. Consider cameras to photograph drivers who run red lights. Once cameras are placed at traffic lights, it is argued, cameras can more easily be placed in other locations to detect speeders or even to capture on film the liquids drivers might consume in a restaurant or bar before getting into a car.[28]

But we also understand the historic events in the context of a particular approach to security: to prevent or limit the unpredictable by setting standards, monitoring behavior, and in some cases locking people up. In each instance the government policy sought to restrict individual action or speech—through intimidation, regulation, or, in extreme situations, imprisonment or internment—or to gather information about individual actions and associations so as to discover a pattern or intent. With this approach to security, and an understanding of liberty as freedom from government, the relationship between the two is inevitably a trade-off. An increase in one means a reduction in the other.

But an alternative approach to liberty—"government is us"— suggests an alternative approach to security. Liberty is seen not as freedom from government but as emerging from participation in governance.[29] Rather than focus on restraining government, this concept of liberty focuses on encouraging and ensuring the people's access to the work of government. Within this concept, suggestions have been made for enhancing security. One such suggestion is, as noted earlier, the model of community policing. Another suggestion is to rely on members of the community to report suspicious activities, and even to help uncover terrorist cells. The suggestion raises the question whether there should be a boundary between the work of police officers and the community. If the police act in partnership with the community, is there a distinction between governmental actions and the actions of the public? How might a community prevent vigilantism, or the use of close relationships with law enforcement to promote individual prejudices?

Targeting Security More Effectively to Protect Liberty

Some observers have argued that another alternative is to work for security in more productive ways that pose no threat to civil liberties. Rather than surveillance of individuals (tracking Internet use, gathering information in databases, using roving wiretaps), there should be "surveillance of means."[30] The emphasis would be on conducting "surveillance of the means that terrorists could use to wreak destruction, such as tracking purchases of chemicals, fertilizer, and other raw components of bombs or biological warfare or watching who is trying to rent crop-dusting aircraft."[31] This would mean, in part, securing chemical, biological, and nuclear materials at the source within the United States and elsewhere.[32] The diminution of rights and freedoms does not, according to this argument, guarantee security.[33] In fact, the competition of ideas, freely expressed, and the pursuit of technologies that focus on surveillance of means are believed to promote security.[34]

ARE WE AT WAR AGAINST TERRORISM DOMESTICALLY? IF SO, WHAT DOES THAT MEAN FOR THE WAY WE FIGHT THE WAR?

Since 9/11 political leaders have frequently said that the nation is fighting a war on terror. As a symbol, the term "war on terror" mobilizes public support; but it also has important legal implications for the resources used in the fight. If we are at war against terrorism domestically, as well as abroad, what is the role of the military and its vast resources for pursuing terrorists and responding to terrorism within our borders? American law and history make a case for separating domestic law enforcement from military activities, but the line has blurred over the years. Homeland security raises the question whether or not the resources of the military should be used directly to fight terrorism at home; it also raises fears of the slippery slope. If military resources are used domestically to fight terrorism, does it become easy to "invent a security threat and turn [every] job over to the military"?[35]

The Posse Comitatus Act

The Posse Comitatus Act prohibits the use of American military equipment and personnel to enforce civilian laws "except in cases and under circumstances expressly authorized by the Constitution or Act of Congress."[36] The law was passed after a controversial presidential election in which President Grant sent troops as *posse comitatus* ("the power of the county") to oversee the polls as federal marshals in three southern states. The presidential order capped years of a military presence in the South during Reconstruction—a presence that spread to civilian law enforcement. Southern legislators sponsored the Posse Comitatus Act to reestablish the line between civilian law enforcement and national defense.[37]

The legislation represents a strong historical opposition to standing armies. The Declaration of Independence focused on abuses of power by King George III associated with the use of the British military to enforce colonial law; and the Constitution created civilian control over the military and, by protecting militias, put checks on the military.

But the boundary between civilian law enforcement and military activities blurs rapidly. While the law prohibits the military from participating in arrests, searches and seizures, collection of evidence, and other police-like activities on U.S. soil, the military can provide "passive" support to law enforcement officials in the form of surveillance, logistical and technical support, training, and information.[38] Several other exceptions are also in place, including use of the military to enforce particular civil rights laws; to support the enforcement of customs laws (especially drug laws); and to assist law enforcement officers in crimes against members of Congress, crimes involving nuclear materials, and the imposition of quarantines.[39] Most important, the president can issue a proclamation to deploy the military to quell an insurrection or restore public order.[40] In 1992 the marines and the army were ordered to work with the federalized California National Guard to quell unrest in Los Angeles following the acquittal of police officers accused of beating Rodney King. The army had a controversial supporting role in the siege of

David Koresh's Branch Davidian compound in Waco, Texas, in 1994. Also, the involvement of the military has been extended to the war on drugs and to border patrols, and military personnel have replaced striking postal employees and air traffic controllers. Each extension of the military into domestic efforts is controversial.

What should be the passive role of the military in homeland security? If we are at war on the home front, does the limitation on the use of the military still apply?

The Military and Homeland Security

When the primary threat to homeland defense was the standing armies and navies of foreign enemy nations, the case for separating military and civilian law enforcement was obvious. Today, threats take the form of weapons of mass destruction such as chemical and biological agents and nuclear weapons, dirty bombs, suicide bombers, and planes that are used as weapons. "What legal bar does the *Posse Comitatus* Act present today to using the military to prevent or respond to a biological or chemical attack on the soil of the United States?"[41] According to legal and military experts, "not much."[42]

The use of military resources to fight terrorism on the home front has two possible consequences that require careful consideration. First, it could dilute and diminish military expertise. One Marine Corps analyst has written:

> Continued reliance upon active-duty military for ancillary missions, such as counter-drug operations and WMD (weapons of mass destruction) consequence management, will almost certainly have the effect of degrading the nation's active military with regard to its raison d'être.[43]

Second, this application of military resources may gradually wear down distinctions between domestic law enforcement and the military. The military is for fighting enemies from countries or locations outside the United States or enemies posing a threat to the United States. Domestic law enforcement is for protecting and regulating the activities of members of the public who have constitutional protections such as the right to remain silent, the right to an attorney, and protection from unreasonable searches and seizures. But as the military becomes more involved in law enforcement, this distinction can blur. Critics note that in the war on drugs, free use of military equipment by civilian law enforcement agencies and the creation of U.S. military joint task forces have had this effect, which is sometimes called the militarization of law enforcement.[44]

Therefore, what limits should be placed on the role of the military in homeland security, particularly in crisis management or the prevention of terrorist attacks? Should military resources be used for intelligence and surveillance? Should the military provide support in cities when the homeland security alert system is raised from yellow to orange, or red? And to what extent should the military assist in restoring order and control following a terrorist attack?

WHAT IS THE BEST ORGANIZATIONAL STRUCTURE FOR HOMELAND SECURITY?

Consider the three recent changes Congress has made to consolidate the structure and oversight of homeland security programs and policies. First, in 2003 Congress established the Department of Homeland Security as the fifteenth cabinet-level department. Creation of the department was one of the largest reorganizations in U.S. government history bringing 22 agencies and more than 180,000 employees under one roof. Second, following recommendations made by the 9/11 Commission, Congress passed the Intelligence Reform and Terrorism Prevention Act of 2004 to create a Director of National Intelligence (DNI) of the National Intelligence Program (NIP) to coordinate and direct the resources—or "connect the dots"— of the many agencies involved in intelligence gathering, support for operations, and analysis.[45] Third, the 109th Congress granted permanent status to the House Select Committee on Homeland Security in an effort to consolidate oversight for the counterterrorism mission of the Department of Homeland Security and national counterterrorism policies.[46] The Senate made a similar move toward consolidation by adding "homeland security" to the title of an existing committee—now named the Committee on Homeland Security and Governmental Affairs.[47]

The question, however, is should consolidation drive the organization of homeland security? Do structural adjustments aimed at centralization produce coherent and effective homeland security policies?

Two forces in the U.S. government compete in reorganization efforts. The first is pluralism. In *Federalist* No. 51 James Madison wrote that multiple interests and sources of power help maintain a strong republic.[48] Competing ideas and competing factions in a large country would prevent any one idea from dominating for very long. The congressional committee system, for example, could be viewed as facilitating the access of numerous competitive interests to the legislative process and generating multiple sources of expertise. Indeed, despite the creation of a permanent committee on Homeland Security, issues of jurisdiction over transportation as it relates to homeland security, cybersecurity, and immigration will remain in competitive tension between the new committee and established committees with jurisdiction in these areas.[49] From a pluralist perspective, this shared authority creates a healthy "competition of ideas" or a creative tension.

Running counter to the argument for pluralism are concerns for clarity and focused accountability—particularly in the wake of failed policies. The case for consolidation as a way to make policy implementation visible is bolstered by historic and theoretical arguments in favor of hierarchical public organizations with leadership visible at the top. The Progressive reformers at the turn of the twentieth century argued that more consolidation in the executive branch would enhance accountability and performance, making government more efficient and effective.[50] Competing sources of influence, in other words, would be replaced with focused expertise.

These two points of view have influenced the debate over the structure of federal government agencies and departments and over the structure of the congressional committee system. Identifying the right approach, or finding the right mix between these two priorities is essential for effective homeland security.

Balancing Legislative and Executive Priorities

Central to the debates over the structure of organizations involved in homeland security and the structure of congressional committees are competitive tensions between the legislative and executive branches of government. Different approaches to organization have implications for the relationships that build between the Congress, the White House, and the organizations responsible for homeland security. Consider creation of the Office of Homeland Security in 2001 and the eventual creation of DHS in 2003.

The Office of Homeland Security (OHS) was established within the Executive Office of the President in 2001, shortly after 9/11. This new office signaled two concerns. First, the White House wanted to leave in place the pluralistic structure of 46 agencies involved in homeland security, with OHS as a point of coordination.

The second concern was to place OHS close to the president. By creating it through an executive order and putting it in the Executive Office of the President—without legislative authorization—the White House sought to limit congressional influence over the coordination efforts of OHS. Indeed, Tom Ridge, director of OHS and eventually named the first Secretary of Homeland Security, resisted formally testifying before Congress before legislation converted the office to a department.

Pressure from Congress, and revelations of the mishaps leading up to 9/11, prompted the president to support consolidation within the executive branch to establish a separate cabinet department.[51] But there were other organizational possibilities. The president and Congress could have created an independent agency,[52] for example, located outside any cabinet department and governed by a number of commissioners appointed for five or more years at a time. Such an agency, perhaps modeled on the Federal Reserve Board, could play the role of coordination, as OHS was initially intended to do, or work to define homeland security for federal, state, and local regulatory agencies. If the agency had regional authorities, like the Reserve Banks, the coordination might be regional. Without a direct connection to a cabinet department, independent agencies have traditionally developed bases of political support with the constituencies they oversee, with professionals represented inside the agency, or with the congressional committees with jurisdiction over the agency.

The question is: which structural approach with its implications for congressional and executive branch oversight and influence best supports homeland security?

WHAT IS THE "DISTINCTIVE COMPETENCE" OF DHS IN HOMELAND SECURITY?

The sociologist Phillip Selznick argues that one difference between an organization and an institution is the "distinctive competence" that emerges in the latter—the capability for which it is known and valued.[53] The legislation creating DHS sets out seven mission areas, including preventing terrorism, reducing the United States' vulnerability to terrorism, mitigating the effects of attacks that do take place, assisting in the response, and maintaining the department as a focal point in planning for all natural and human-made disasters and emergencies. DHS is also charged with balancing security concerns and the demands of free commerce and economic growth, and contributing to the campaign against illegal drug trafficking and the links to terrorism.[54]

No matter how explicit legislation is, agencies have to make decisions. What specific tasks should DHS undertake to prevent terrorism? How should it assist in responding to acts of terror? How does it balance economic growth and free commerce with security? Those decisions will facilitate DHS's distinctive competence: its unique contribution to counterterrorism. Here again, there are no obvious answers. The matter rests with leadership within and outside DHS, the capacities and experiences of its employees, its own technological capabilities and those of its partnering organizations, and the standard operations inherited from the 22 agencies that today form DHS.[55]

Choices to Make, Balances to Strike

To define its distinctive competence, DHS must find ways to balance or support what can appear to be conflicting priorities. In April 2004 DHS created a committee to advise and guide it on data integrity, privacy, and interoperability.[56] The tricky part, however, is balancing security and privacy, as TSA found when it tried to launch the Computer-Assisted Passenger Prescreening System (CAPPS II) to check the personal information of airline passengers against commercial and government databases; concerns about inaccuracy, failure, and compromising use of the information sent the program back to the drawing board.[57] Similarly, how should DHS balance economic growth and free trade with security? Should all containers coming into the United States be examined? Or should only those containers deemed high-risk or those with suspect cargo be examined? Should all trucks coming across the Mexican and Canadian borders be examined, or only those not registered with DHS? Every security regulation has commercial implications.

Finally, as DHS develops its distinctive competence, it must build tasks around the question of risk. This effort has several layers. The first is making determinations about the kind of risks faced by the nation. What methods will terrorists use to attack and what could be the potential damage? Will the next terrorist attack involve airplanes, railroads, subways, or nuclear power plants? Will it involve a dirty bomb, a biological agent injected into the water supply, a chemical gas, or something unanticipated? Determining how to prevent terrorism, how to mitigate attacks that do occur, and how to respond requires careful thought about potential types of attacks. It also entails thinking about how competently DHS can prepare for and respond to the unexpected. DHS must consider what capacities are essential for an agile and effective response to circumstances for which nothing was written or planned.

The second layer of risk has to do with the likelihood of different scenarios, where they might occur, and what "assets" are threatened in a particular scenario. Efforts to identify potential targets and determine the vulnerabilities of those targets fall into this category. Here too there is no obvious, indisputable way of making the determination. If DHS determines that certain geographic locations such as New York City and Los Angeles have more potential targets and face a higher likelihood of being hit, then should it consider allocating more tasks, personnel, and resources toward counter-terrorism there? If DHS proceeds on the assumption that any part of the United States is vulnerable to attack or has resources that could be exploited in an attack, the challenge would be to distribute tasks, personnel, and resources equally across the country—every location should have money and means to prepare and respond. A state with a prominent farm economy, for example, may not offer evident targets for terrorist attacks, but it could have many small airfields with crop dusters capable of spreading chemical or biological agents. Securing these assets could be deemed as important as beefing up the radiation-detection capacity in New York City's subways. Both funding scenarios are reflected in the battles over the distribution of homeland security grants to states, localities, ports, and transportation authorities.[58]

The third layer of risk requires a judgment about how much risk Americans can accept. How far should DHS go in reducing the risk of an event? As Don Kettl writes:

> No official wants to suggest publicly that full protection is impossible or that even the smallest amount of risk is acceptable. At the same time, no public official could long survive the furor that would come from imposing the costs and restrictions required to truly bring the risk as low as theoretically possible.[59]

How DHS screens airline passengers, patrols borders, regulates shipping containers, monitors foreign visitors, and develops policies to protect critical infrastructure will rest in part on an organizational understanding of what is an acceptable level of risk, and in part on the practices and priorities the DHS agencies and employees bring to the job.

Task Definition

The Immigration and Customs Enforcement (ICE) agency, within DHS, has responsibility for the internal enforcement of immigration laws. Approximately 8 to 12 million illegal immigrants are in the United States, but ICE concentrates its 2,300 agents on 80,000 criminal aliens and 320,000 absconders—people who escaped after a deportation order.[60] This narrow focus sets ICE off from the Customs and Border Protection agency (CBP). CBP patrols the borders, but once an illegal immigrant passes the border, ICE takes over. The result is a de facto determination by DHS that an illegal immigrant not recognized as a criminal or an absconder poses a minimal risk of supporting or conducting terrorism. Defining the task of ICE has to do partly with resources: how can 2,300 agents best be utilized? It also has to do with issues of turf between two agencies whose personnel and responsibilities are similar, and with the need to balance law enforcement and the economic benefits provided by a large immigrant population that works in millions of jobs needed in the U.S. economy.

CONCLUSION

In defining its distinctive competence, DHS is buffeted by past turf wars, existing procedures, economic concerns, conflicting congressional and executive-branch priorities, and demands to protect civil liberties. Its challenge is to clearly define its role in homeland security, and to identify tasks that can facilitate its role. In the effort to prevent, mitigate, and respond to terrorist attacks and other types of disasters, should DHS play a dominant, centralizing role across the federal government and with state and local governments, or should it play a role of coordination and facilitation? Should DHS aggressively utilize its authority to solicit and analyze intelligence data in competition with other intelligence services, or gather, store, and analyze data in a way that spans various sources? And should DHS focus on addressing known threats or on coping with the unknown?

Any distinctive competence that emerges in DHS will reflect resolutions of many of the questions posed in this chapter. But will these questions be resolved by reliance on what has been tried and institutionalized in the past, and on compromises between powerful political interests, or through debate and discussion to develop consensus at the community, state, and national level?

See also Chapter 16 **Homeland Security's National Strategic Position: Goals, Objectives, Measures Assessments.**

N O T E S

1. General Accounting Office (GAO), "National Preparedness: Integration of Federal, State, Local, and Private Sector Efforts Is Critical to an Effective National Strategy for Homeland Security," testimony by Randall Yim before Subcommittee on Economic Development, Public Buildings and Emergency Management, Committee on Transportation and Infrastructure, House of Representatives (22 April 2002), GAO-02-621T. But see HSPD-5: "In these efforts, with regard to domestic incidents, the United States Government treats crisis management and consequence management as a single, integrated function, rather than as two separate functions."

2. Office of Homeland Security, *National Strategy for Homeland Security,* (July 2002), p. vii.

3. Siobhan Gorman, "Homeland Security: Spreading the Faith," *National Journal* (11 October 2003); GAO, testimony of Randall Yim (11 April 2002).

4. GAO, "Combating Terrorism: Intergovernmental Partnership in a National Strategy to Enhance State and Local Preparedness," testimony of Paul Posner before Subcommittee on Government Efficiency, Financial Management, and Intergovernmental Relations, Committee on Government Reform, House of Representatives (22 March 2002).

5. Donald Kettl, *Regulation of American Federalism* (Baltimore, Md.: Johns Hopkins University Press, 1983). Daniel Elazar, *American Federalism: A View from the States* (3rd ed.) (New York: Harper and Row, 1984). Morton Grodzins, "The Federal

System," in *Goals for Americans* (Englewood Cliffs, N.J.: Prentice Hall, 1960). Martha Derthick, "Federal Government Mandates: Why the States Are Complaining," *Brookings Review* (Fall 1992), pp. 50–3.

6. Consider recent legislation and policy initiatives. "No Child Left Behind" sets national standards for school performance and national rules governing poorly performing schools. Similarly, efforts to pass a constitutional amendment banning gay marriage would take the decision away from the states.

7. Matt Statler, Johan Roos, and Bart Victor, "Illustrating the Need for Practical Wisdom," working paper, 2004, p. 26.

8. J. W. Peltason, *Understanding the Constitution* (11th ed.) (New York: Holt, Rinehart and Winston, 1988), p. 17.

9. Herber J. Storing, *What the Antifederalists Were For: The Political Thought of the Opponents of the Constitution* (Chicago, Ill.: University of Chicago Press, 1981).

10. Helen Ingraham and Steven Rathgeb Smith, *Public Policy for Democracy* (Washington, D.C.: Brookings Institution, 1993).

11. William Lyons, "Partnerships, Information, and Public Safety: Community Policing in a Time of Terror," *Policing: An International Journal of Police Strategies and Management* 25:3 (2002), pp. 530–42(13). Matthew Scheider and Robert Chapman, "Community Policing and Terrorism," *Journal of Homeland Security* (April 2003); www.homelandsecurity.org/journal/articles/Scheider-Chapman.html.

12. Keith Bea, *Proposed Transfer of FEMA to the Department of Homeland Security.* Congressional Research Service (29 July 2002) (from CRS Web).

13. Ben Canada, *Homeland Security: Standards for State and Local Performance.* CRS Report for Congress (8 October 2003), pp. 24–5. (Congressional Research Service, Library of Congress, from CRS Web.)

14. National Academy of Public Administration (NAPA), *Coping with Catastrophe: Building an Emergency Management System to Meet People's Needs in Natural and Manmade Disasters* (Washington, D.C.: NAPA, 1993). Sandra Schneider, *Flirting with Disaster: Public Management in Crisis Situations* (Armonk, N.Y.: Sharpe, 1995).

15. DHS, *Initial National Response Plan* (30 September 2003), p. 1.

16. U.S. Conference of Mayors.

17. Richard Danzig, "Battling Bioterrorism," *Government Executive* (15 July 2004), p. 17.

18. Office of Management and Budget, Budget of the United States Government: Fiscal Year 2003, pp. 933–8. White House press release, "President Announces Substantial Increases in Homeland Security Budget" (24 January 2002), www.whitehouse.gov/news/releases/2002/01/20020124-1.html.

19. PL 107-296, Section 507.

20. The important Emergency Management Performance Grants are still allocated through FEMA. The FY04 budget also gives FEMA responsibility for several public health initiatives, including the Metropolitan Medical Response Program, as well as grants for planning and preparation of major metropolitan health systems for disasters and cash stockpiles for emergency pharmaceuticals and training of public health personnel. FY 2004 Budget Fact Sheet, Office of the Press Secretary, White House (1 October 2003). www.dhs.gov/dhspublic/display?content=1817.

21. PL 107-296, Section 430.

22. National Governors' Association, Center for Best Practices, Vol. 2, *Homeland Security: A Governor's Guide to Emergency Management* (2002), p. 12.

23. Department of Justice, "Report from the Field: The US PATRIOT Act at Work" (July 2004), pp. 1–2.

24. Ibid., p. 29. Prepared remarks for U.S. Mayors' Conference (25 October 2001). Development of a passenger prescreening program to increase security for airline travel has drawn criticism from advocates of privacy, from passengers, and from members of Congress. The Transportation Security Administration (an agency within DHS) argues that airline travel will be more secure if the government has private information about passengers—such as name, address, phone number, and birth date—that can be verified with other commercial and government databases. Such information can also be checked against terrorist "watch" lists. But critics argue that the loss of privacy is dramatic while the gains in security are unknown.

25. Gilmore Commission, *Forging America's New Normalcy,* Fifth Annual Report to the President and Congress of the Advisory Panel to Assess Domestic Response Capabilities for Terrorism Involving Weapons of Mass Destruction, December 2003, p. 22.

26. Ibid., p. 4.

27. Michael Sandel, *Democracy's Discontent* (Cambridge, Mass.: Harvard University Press, 1997).

28. Ellen Alderman, "Homeland Security and Privacy: Striking a Delicate Balance," *Carnegie Reporter* 2:1 (Fall 2002); www.carnegie.org/reporter/05/homeland/index.html.

29. Michael Sandel distinguishes between these two types of liberty and the forms of government that support them. In the American experience, he argues, the procedural state has grown to protect individual liberties from intrusions by government; the alterative is republicanism, or the realization of liberty through participation in governance. The former emphasizes the individual, the latter the community.

30. Alderman, "Homeland Security and Privacy: Striking a Delicate Balance." Christopher Connell, *Homeland Defense and Democratic Liberties: An American Balance in Danger? Carnegie Challenge 2002* (New York: Carnegie Corporation, 2002).

31. Connell, p. 4.

32. Ibid.

33. Working Paper Prepared by Human Rights First for the International Conference on Terrorism and Human Rights, Cairo (January 20), pp. 226–8, www.humanrightsfirst.org/us_law/after_911/after_911_09.htm

34. Gilmore Commission, *Forging America's New Normalcy.* See also *Annual Report, Vol. 5*: Forging America's New Normalcy: Securing our Homeland, Protecting Our Liberty. The Advisory Panel to Assess Domestic Response Capabilities for Terrorism Involving Weapons of Mass Destruction. Rand (15 December 2003), pp. 33–4.

35. James Fallows, "Military Efficiency," *Atlantic* (August 1991): 18.

36. 18 U.S.C. §1385, 1994.

37. "The Posse Comitatus Act: A Principle in Need of Renewal," 75 *Wash. U. L.Q.* 953 (Summer 1997), http://law.wustl.edu/WULQ/75-2/752-10.html#fnB11.

38. Ibid.

39. Ibid.

40. 42 U.S.C. 5170b, reference (f).

41. Major Craig T. Trebilcock, "The Myth of the Posse Comitatus" (October 2000), www.homelandsecurity.org/journal/articles/Trebilcock.htm.

42. Ibid.

43. Aaron Weiss, "When Terror Strikes, Who Should Respond?" *Parameters* (August 2001): 117–33, http://carlisle-www.army.mil/usawa/Parameters/01autumn/Weiss.htm.

44. David Kopel and Paul Blackman, "Can Soldiers Be Peace Officers? The Waco Disaster and The Militarization of American Law Enforcement." *30 Akron L. Rev.* (1997): 619–59, http://i2i.org/SuptDocs/Waco/cansoldiersbepeaceofficers.htm#fnb23.

45. Public Law No: 108-458 Intelligence Reform and Terrorism Prevention Act of 2004.

46. H. RES. 5, Adopting rules for the One Hundred Ninth Congress. Within the House and Senate Appropriations Committees, separate subcommittees for homeland security were created in the 108th Congress.

47. S. Res. 445, Senate Committee Reorganization for Homeland Security and Intelligence Matters.

48. E. M. Earle (ed.), *The Federalist* (New York: Modern Library, 1937), No. 51.

49. Shaun Waterman, "New Homeland Security Committee Off to a Shaky Start."

50. Jack Knott and Gary Miller, *Reforming Bureaucracy: The Politics of Institutional Choice* (Englewood Cliffs, N.J.: Prentice Hall, 1987).

51. Donald Kettl, *System Under Stress: Homeland Security and American Politics* (Washington, D.C.: CQ Press, 2004).

52. "Independence," however, refers to the location of an agency outside the executive branch, not necessarily to absence of oversight and influence of elected officials. The history of independent agencies, for example, suggests greater congressional influence than presidential influence.

53. Philip Selznick, *Leadership in Administration: A Sociological Interpretation* (Evanston, Ill.: Row, Peterson, 1957).

54. Public Law No. 107-296.

55. See James Q. Wilson, *Bureaucracy: What Government Agencies Do and Why They Do It* (New York: Basic Books, 1989).

56. Chris Strohm, "Homeland Security Creates Privacy Advisory Committee, Govexex.com," *Daily Briefing* (26 April 2004), www/govxec.com/dailyfed/0404/042604c1.htm.

57. Chris Strohm, "DHS Scraps Computer Pre-Screening System, Starts Over," Govexec.com, *Daily Briefing* (15 July 2004), www.govxec.com/dailyfed/0704/071504c1.htm.

58. Anne Khademian, "Strengthening State and Local Terrorism Prevention and Response," in Kettl (ed.), *The Department of Homeland Security's First Year* (The Century Foundation, 2004): 152.

59. Kettl, *System Under Stress*, p. 76.

60. Jerry Seper, "Limits Set on Border Patrol," *Washington Times* (17 August 2004): A01.

CHAPTER 71

Accountability and Homeland Security

Charles R. Wise
Professor, School of Public and Environmental Affairs,
Indiana University

Rania Nader
School of Public and Environmental Affairs, Indiana University

Scrutiny of U.S. homeland security departments and agencies has indicated a need for greater accountability, but a balance must be struck between oversight and innovation. The 9/11 Commission Report stated that citizens are "entitled to some standards of performance so they can judge, with the help of their elected representatives, whether the objectives are being met"; it concluded that the failure to prevent the attacks was due to diffusion of responsibility and accountability among various agencies, and it recommended changes in federal government organizational structure.[1] This call for accountability has received priority in part because elected officials and the public have been unable to identify, among all the agencies and programs ostensibly responsible for homeland security, those prepared for and capable of effective counterterrorism.

Citizens and public officials have always been concerned about the performance of public programs in general,[2] "and today, citizens expect government to produce results. They are no longer tolerant of inefficiency or ineffectiveness."[3] For example, the Government Performance and Results Act (P.L. 103–62, Sug. 3, 1993) requires federal agencies to develop a strategic plan and to establish performance measures.[4]

A SEARCH FOR ACCOUNTABILITY

"Effective accountability is crucial for meeting citizens' reasonable expectations that government bureaucracies operate in accordance with law and core ethical values."[5] But a general expectation or demand does not guide political overseers or program administrators in achieving accountability. The phrase "hold government accountable" is often used as if its meaning were obvious, but how will we hold whom accountable for what?[6] Harvard University professor Robert D. Behn, an expert in public policy notes:

> When we hold someone or some organization accountable for something, what do we really do? In some ways, it means that we want to be able to identify who is responsible for the organization's outputs or outcomes, for its successes or failures. But then what? That answer does not really clarify things. What does it mean to hold people responsible for success? What does it mean to hold people responsible for failure? I know of no definitive answer, either theoretical or empirical. But I bet I know what the managers who are to be held accountable think. I believe they believe, from their own empirical experience, that "holding people accountable" means that when they fail they are punished and when they succeed nothing significant happens.[7]

Accountability for homeland security cannot be achieved by relying on the existing governmental mechanisms and procedures. It must, instead, result from implementing political and management design—from adaptation and creation.

One might first turn to the literature of public administration. A difficulty here is that "the scope and meaning of 'accountability' [have] been extended in a number of directions well beyond its core sense of being called into account for one's actions."[8] The core sense is useful,[9] implying that those involved in homeland security should answer to an outside authority; but the question remains, "To what authority?" In the American system, with its separation of powers, numerous authorities can claim that agencies owe them accountability. In addition, accountability for homeland security at any level of government must adapt to the multiorganizational, intergovernmental nature of homeland security itself.

ACCOUNTABILITY IN HOMELAND SECURITY

Accountability systems must apply to multiagency, collaborative homeland security activities as well as to individual agencies.

Otherwise, important dimensions of homeland security will remain unexamined and neglected. That is, developing an accountability system for homeland security at the federal level is not coterminous with developing a system for the Department of Homeland Security (DHS), because federal homeland security is not the sole province of DHS. For example, before 9/11 the General Accounting Office (GAO) identified 40 federal agencies involved in counterterrorism,[10] and 22 agencies were merged to form DHS. For fiscal year 2005, the Office of Management and Budget (OMB) received requests for funding for homeland security from 35 agencies, of which DHS was only one. At the federal level, agencies outside DHS with homeland security functions include the Department of Defense, Central Intelligence Agency, Department of Justice (encompassing the FBI), and Centers for Disease Control and Prevention.

The 9/11 Commission called for integrated joint action by the federal agencies responsible for homeland security.[11] Thus a starting point for accountability at the federal level is that it should be aimed at joint action rather than the activities of individual agencies. The same could be said for the state and local level. State governments, for example, have multiple agencies that need to integrate their activities: e.g., the office of emergency management, the state police, and the National Guard.

Accountability will also need to recognize that homeland security is intergovernmental. For example, an official of GAO commented to a congressional committee, "To develop this essential national strategy, the federal role needs to be considered in relation to other levels of government, the goals and objectives for preparedness, and the most appropriate tools to assist and enable other levels of government and the private sector to achieve these goals."[12] For instance, a federal agency cannot achieve its goals without supporting state and local agencies and integrating its activities with theirs. Thus the FBI has created 66 Joint Terrorism Task Forces nationwide that involve state and local law enforcement officers, FBI agents, and other federal agents and personnel. Accountability for the FBI in homeland security cannot focus just on how FBI agents perform investigations; it also needs to focus on how the FBI is integrating its activities, sharing information and resources, and assisting in the development of capabilities at the state and local level. In short, homeland security is inherently collaborative. Its environment is complex, unstructured, and rapidly changing; and it has so many dimensions that it should be described not as a network but as "networks."[13]

The approach chosen to achieve accountability will affect the ability of agencies to form collaborative networks. The approach used for a single agency is inappropriate for multiagency activities:

> The traditional administrative accountability design involves a single agency linked to a single (if complex) result, or set of efforts, for which it alone is to be held accountable by some sub-set of elected officials nominally acting on behalf of the citizenry as a whole.... But substantial adjustments to the canonical design may be necessary or desirable to accommodate the fact that in a collaborative the efforts and, quite possibly, the budgetary resources of the individual agencies *jointly* produce at least some of the desired (and often the undesired) results.[14]

The wrong approach may preclude adapting security efforts to differing conditions:

> While collaboration offers the ability to increase government's responsiveness to diverse circumstances and changing conditions, it lends itself more to certain kinds of relationships than to others. Because collaborators thrive on discretion, strong hierarchical or legal controls are likely to make their work considerably more difficult.[15]

FOSTERING INITIATIVE AND ENTREPRENEURSHIP FOR HOMELAND SECURITY

Homeland security officials and professionals will need to exercise entrepreneurial leadership and take risks. Barriers to entrepreneurship, including some embedded in current accountability systems, will need to be examined and altered.

The 9/11 Commission concluded that a major factor in the inability of the intelligence and law enforcement communities to "connect the dots" was a "failure of imagination."[16] Two years earlier, a joint congressional inquiry had found that "there was a dearth of creative, aggressive analysis targeting Bin Ladin and a persistent inability to comprehend the collective significance of individual pieces of intelligence."[17] For example, the FBI's assistant director for counterterrorism said, "We are a reactive bunch of people, and reactive will never get us to a prevention.... Is there anybody thinking and where's al-Qa'ida's next target?"[18] The 9/11 Commission observed that government agencies "are often passive, accepting what are viewed as givens, including that efforts to identify and fix glaring vulnerabilities to dangerous threats would be too costly, too controversial, or too disruptive."[19]

The assertion that public managers are less likely to take risks than their private counterparts has not received much empirical support.[20] However, accountability policies and practices can have a significant effect on public servants in this regard. Often, higher-level officials hold lower-level officials accountable; and research has found that top managers can influence perceptions of risk as legitimate or illegitimate and what behavior is acceptable concerning risk.

There seems to be a widespread perception that aversion to risk was prevalent before 9/11. In a letter addressed to Congress and published in *Atlantic Monthly*, an anonymous writer who had spent 22 years in the CIA noted an "unwillingness of senior leaders across the Intelligence Community to remedy fixable problems if it meant ... alarming political leaders who might ask the Community to take risks." The joint inquiry of 2002 found that intelligence agencies were perhaps overly "risk averse," restricting the sharing of critical information with FBI criminal investigators beyond what the Justice Department's policy of 1995—commonly referred to as the "wall"—required.

ANALYZING AVERSION TO RISK

Factors contributing to passivity and risk aversion among intelligence and law enforcement officials fall into three categories: institutional constraints, weak incentives, and low tolerance for error.

Institutional Constraints

Recruitment by the CIA and FBI was evidently hampered by the red tape associated with accountability. The CIA's efforts to recruit international sources who may have been engaged in illegal activities encountered much resistance within the agency. Recruiting such individuals required special waivers; and several CIA officers in the field reported, "Their concerns were not that waivers were denied, but that they were not career enhancing and that the process by which requests were brought forward was cumbersome and resulted in disincentives to work to recruit anyone who might have been involved in proscribed acts." FBI agents recruited in the United States had to go through a tedious approval process that could take as long as six months.[21]

Weak Incentives

The 9/11 Commission noted, "Imagination is not a gift usually associated with bureaucracies," and added that it was "crucial to find a way of routinizing, even bureaucratizing the exercise of imagination."[22] A culture of innovation requires incentives and rewards—not necessarily material, but positive. However, external rewards are rare in government; innovation often entails personal costs for a bureaucratic entrepreneur, who is seen as a "boat rocker" in conventional agencies.[23] Thus government executives need to send a signal that new ideas are welcome, and they need the budgetary and managerial flexibility to implement good ideas and reward entrepreneurs (with, say, public recognition or a choice of assignments). There is evidence that managers currently lack such flexibility. In his testimony before the joint inquiry, Lee Hamilton, the vice-chairman of the 9/11 Commission, said:

> There is too much rigidity in the system. There is not enough allowance for incentive.... We've got to work through this matter so that managers can manage more effectively.... I would absolutely assure you ... that you would not tolerate in your office the kind of management restrictions that operate today in the federal government.[24]

Low Tolerance for Failure

It seems logical that if we do not give public officials room to fail, they will not take the sort of risks necessary to solve problems but will fall back into "the safety zone of standard operating procedures."[25]

For example, in his briefing to the joint inquiry, Richard Clarke, who was the terrorism coordinator for the National Security Council, said:

> I think if you look at the 1980s and 1970s, the individuals who held the job [of Deputy Director of Operations], one after another of them was

either fired or indicted or condemned by a Senate Committee. I think under those circumstances, if you become Director of Operations, you would want to be a little careful not to launch off on covert operations that will get you personally in trouble and will also hurt the institution.... I think that they institutionalized a sense of covert action as risky and as likely to blow up in your face. And the wise guys at the White House who are pushing you to do covert action will be nowhere to be found when the Senate Select Committee on Intelligence calls you up to explain the mess that the covert action became.[26]

On the other hand, entrepreneurship in government can raise ethical concerns. Although, arguably, "public entrepreneurship can be, and at its best is, ethical,"[27] critics worry that if public servants become entrepreneurial, "individualism, profit, selfishness and shrewd calculation become the norms for public agencies as well as private business."[28] Also, in homeland security, overagressiveness can lead to violations of civil liberties; the 9/11 Commission noted that "while protecting our homeland, Americans should be mindful of threats to vital personal and civil liberties. This balancing is no easy task, but we must constantly strive to keep it right."[29] However, these legitimate concerns do not preclude a proactive, responsible bureaucracy if initiative is an integral part of the overall accountability system. Cohen and Eimicke examined several presumed failures of public-sector entrepreneurship but concluded that the problems could have been avoided if the individuals had followed some simple ethical guidelines.[30] This suggests that if ethical guidelines are specified by top officials and oversight mechanisms are in place to ensure that the guidelines are followed, a balanced approach is achievable.

ACCOUNTABILITY: A MULTIFACETED IMPERATIVE

Accountability is often discussed as if it were a singular phenomenon, but various mechanisms exist and are applied to individual agencies even within the same governmental jurisdiction. Those choosing an accountability system for homeland security will need to adapt an array of mechanisms designed to support its objectives and will need to decide which mechanism to emphasize.

Romzek and Dubjick identify four types of accountability systems in the public sector: bureaucratic, legal, professional, and political.[31] Each type emphasizes different values and different bases for accountability. The bureaucratic mechanisms are characterized by intense scrutiny from an internal source, such as a supervisor or rules of operation; and the prevailing value is efficiency. Legal accountability involves intense scrutiny from an external source such as an auditor or a court; the prevailing value is the rule of law. Professional accountability involves a low level of scrutiny, with emphasis on internal sources of control; the prevailing value is deference to expertise. Political accountability involves a low level of scrutiny from external sources, such as a clientele group or elected officials; the prevailing value is responsiveness. Under bureaucratic and legal accountability, public servants have less flexibility: they are constrained by standard operating procedures, rules, or court rulings. In professional and political accountability, they have more flexibility and discretion.[32]

These types of accountability are equally legitimate, and an agency will typically have various concurrent systems representing two or more of the categories. Also, multiple systems will probably be operating within a category. Rosen describes accountability systems in the federal government as "an awesome armada of policies, mechanisms, and processes for overseeing government bureaucracies" that provide a great deal of redundancy.[33]

More accountability is not necessarily better; multiple methods do not necessarily lead to an effective overall system. In fact, the numerous, sometimes contradictory demands emanating from multiple approaches may be counterproductive. Failures and ethical lapses in the federal government have sometimes led to a public outcry and then to additional accountability mechanisms, resulting in disincentives to initiative. As Rosen has noted of the federal government, "If all accountability mechanisms worked as they could, they would probably hobble bureaucracies in their essential work."[34]

Reformers who introduce new accountability mechanisms for homeland security run the risk of impeding accountability altogether, if the reforms are contrary to the existing mechanisms and if no adjustment is made in the array of methods.[35] New mechanisms must be aligned with existing mechanisms to create appropriate incentives and thereby achieve the desired performance.

ACCOUNTABILITY AND INITIATIVE

The choice and alignment of accountability mechanisms for homeland security will determine if the system creates incentives or disincentives for risk-taking, entrepreneurship, and initiative.

Performance objectives related to homeland security are directed at managing risk. The U.S. comptroller general told a congressional committee, "Managing risk requires us to constantly operate under conditions of uncertainty, where foresight, anticipation, responsiveness, and radical adaptation are vital capabilities."[36] In other words, it requires acting entrepreneurially.

If initiative is desired, the accountability mechanisms must overcome the normal tendency of bureaucrats toward caution and self-protection. Levin and Sanger note that public managers are typically cautious and are constrained by budgets, political factors, and broader oversight and accountability mechanisms that discourage risk-taking. They argue that to create a balanced system, it is important to develop incentives for managerial discretion and innovation while holding managers accountable for achieving well-defined organizational goals. However, discretion is a precondition. The problem is that innovation and initiative thrive in environments that encourage autonomy and risk-taking and eschew hierarchy, centralization, and routines, whereas accountability requires an environment that allows for a continuous flow of information about an agency's operations, resulting in standardized procedures and decision points and many rules and regulations.[37] Thus to balance accountability and entrepreneurship, trade-offs must be made.

An important task of entrepreneurial leaders is to motivate subordinates.[38] In one study, the main approach used by entrepreneurial managers was teamwork rather than monitoring and control.[39] It is important to encourage innovation throughout the workforce. A study of innovations in government found that the most frequent initiators of innovation were not politicians or even agency heads, but career public servants who were middle managers and front-line staff. Innovative behavior did not come at the expense of accountability; the innovative public servants worked through bureaucratic channels and respected due process.[40]

An emphasis on control of public servants' behavior cannot be assumed to increase organizational success and in fact may decrease it.[41] In homeland security, strict requirements for obtaining prior approvals and for prompt reporting can discourage initiative. Consequently, risk-taking and adaptivity will slow down to the pace of hierarchical decision making.

In contrast, an environment conducive to initiative can be created by actions that increase tolerance for error and risk-taking, reduce layers of hierarchy to share power and information, increase budgetary flexibility, and reward behavior that supports initiative. This does not eliminate accountability; on the contrary, analysis and evaluation are still emphasized, because innovative organizations are shaped, refined, and reoriented by continual formal and informal analysis. The key is to focus analysis and evaluation on progress of defined goals, so that managers have discretion as regards implementation and accountability for performance.[42]

ACCOUNTABILITY SYSTEMS FOR HOMELAND SECURITY

Accountability systems that encourage collaborative interagency and intergovernmental action will emphasize performance, results, goals, and measurements. The question is which type of accountability— bureaucratic, legal, professional, or political—will be most suitable for homeland security operations and agencies.

The overall task of policy makers is to align the accountability systems so as to provide incentives for homeland security professionals. Policy makers seeking entrepreneurial behavior will have to choose accordingly; in addition, the multiagency, intergovernmental nature of homeland security will require consideration. The accountability system will need to encourage interagency and intergovernmental collaboration; this requires discretion and accommodation on the part of management. Therefore, low-control accountability relationships based on professional norms and politics would seem more appropriate than the high-control relationships in legal and bureaucratic systems.[43]

Bureaucratic accountability, which is strongly control-oriented, is unlikely to suit homeland security; nor is it likely to encourage entrepreneurial behavior. Nonetheless, this approach was emphasized in the creation of DHS. Proponents of DHS, such as the Hart-Rudman Commission, felt it necessary to have a cabinet department, with a secretary serving as the focal point for accountability, and argued for the power of legal authority. The proposals did not address two questions that still remain largely unanswered: how to achieve coordination and integration of activities with agencies outside DHL, and how to develop accountability for multiagency, intergovernmental activities.

Before DHS was created, prominent commissions issuing reports on homeland security did recognize political accountability. The Hart-Rudman Commission and the Gilmore Commission both recommended consolidating jurisdiction in a congressional committee.[44] Political accountability could be enhanced if the legislature arrived at some method in which oversight was consolidated: the Permanent Select Committee on Intelligence in the House and the Select Committee on Intelligence in the Senate are examples of consolidated oversight for the departments and agencies with intelligence functions. Political accountability can also be more effective if mechanisms are found for an ongoing dialogue with the agencies to be held accountable, in which the oversight committees communicate clear goals.

Professional accountability can also be effective for homeland security; because homeland security has a multiagency nature, accountability to professional peers is logical. Bardach and Lesser note that when collaborating agencies are providing initiative and resources, it is necessary to establish certain outsiders to whom these agencies are accountable, and one set of outsiders is the various partners within the collaborative. Partner agencies are in many senses accountable to one another, and they use various means to project this sense of accountability. Formal interagency agreements may be used, but professional norms, interpersonal loyalties, and a shared desire to work together in the future can promote peer accountability. Also, partners at all organizational levels are in a position to act as the loyal opposition—they are informed because they have been close enough to the operations of their partner agencies to understand the important details of their work, and they are not as encumbered as insiders might be by a desire not to upset existing personal relationships.[45]

Steps policy makers take to demand collaborative, integrated activity among homeland security agencies can bolster such professional accountability, especially if the members of the collaborative will have to report on their own contribution to its success.

Policy makers should clarify goals so as to direct collaborative activity and to help homeland security managers sort through the many voices making demands on them. The challenge of accountability for every public manager is the multiple, conflicting, and shifting expectations for performance, emanating from multiple legitimate sources.[46]

Both collaborative action and entrepreneurial initiative will be enhanced by accountability systems that emphasize results rather than control. Both can benefit from managers who maintain strong relationships with political and professional constituencies as well as have the capacity to measure results.[47]

An emphasis on results implies specified goals that serve as the basis for measurement. This is not an easy matter; there is an inherent tension between simple verifiable goals and more complex performance measures, and between the capacity and adaptability of the measurement systems.[48] Nonetheless, the confrontation over goals is necessary to obtain accountability: "The two enemies of accountability are unclear objectives and anonymity."[49] Specifying goals guides management and also eliminates anonymity by high-lighting a specific agency's responsibility.[50]

At the federal level, defining goals for homeland security has just begun. The Gilmore Commission concluded that there has been too little clear strategic guidance from the federal government about the definition and objectives of preparedness and how states and localities will be evaluated in meeting those objectives.[51] Similarly, the comptroller general reported:

> The federal government is well short of where it needs to be in setting national homeland security goals, including those for intelligence and other mission areas, to focus on results—outcomes—not inputs and outputs which were so long a feature of much of the federal government's strategic planning.[52]

Setting realistic goals is a complex process involving external stakeholders and overseers, organizational managers, and professionals. Otherwise, an executive agency that does not want to offend any stakeholders or neglect any values could simply formulate multiple, vague goals.[53]

Managers in homeland security must see measurement as furthering their mission.[54] Collaborators can track results (such tracking should be a commitment for managers) so as to allay fears that they are exercising discretion for unintended purposes.[55] They may then be able to claim the discretion they need.[56] When the policy of using performance measures comes from within the organization, the measures are more likely to be adopted.[57]

GUIDELINES FOR ACCOUNTABILITY FOR HOMELAND SECURITY

Policy makers choosing types of accountability should consider the following points:

- Multiple accountability systems exist in government. Existing systems may or may not facilitate homeland security. A layering of accountability systems will not necessarily produce more accountability and may produce less.
- Policy makers need to align accountability systems, decide which types to emphasize, and decide which types can be used in combination.
- Homeland security officials and managers need to identify key stakeholders (this answers the question "To whom am I accountable?") and engage them in dialogue to identify values (this answers the question "For what am I accountable?").
- While accountability systems need to be developed and applied to individual agencies, these systems also need to address collaboration among multiple agencies. Oversight should address contributions to joint actions.
- Accountability systems need to assess how homeland security units at one level of government are supporting or detracting from activities at other levels of government.
- Accountability systems need to adapt to changes in homeland security. They should be designed to encourage entrepreneurial leadership, initiative, and discretion.

Ethical guidelines are necessary to safeguard democratic values and human rights. Nonetheless, guidelines are unlikely to cover all contingencies and should be supplemented by ongoing dialogue among homeland security personnel and stakeholders. A balance must be struck between risk-taking and preserving democratic values.

Evaluation focused on specific goals and results enhances accountability. Managers should have discretion for implementation and be held accountable for performance.

Homeland security overseers (the people "to whom" managers are accountable) should focus and communicate their expectations for performance. Conflicting, changing expectations cause confusion, risk-aversion, and diminished accountability.

High-control, hierarchical accountability is unlikely to produce entrepreneurial leadership or collaboration among homeland security agencies. Political accountability and professional accountability are more likely to provide the necessary flexibility.

If accountability is focused on results, goals must be developed jointly by overseers, officials, and managers.

See also Chapter 16 **Homeland Security's National Strategic Position: Goals, Objectives, Measures Assessment.**

N O T E S

1. *9/11 Commission Report* (New York: Norton, 2004), pp. 365, 400.
2. David Osborne and Peter Plastrik, *Banishing Bureaucracy* (Reading, Mass.: Addison-Wesley, 1997). See also B. Guy Peters, *The Future of Governing: Four Emerging Models* (Lawrence: University Press of Kansas, 1996).
3. Robert D. Behn, "The New Public Management Paradigm and the Search for Democratic Accountability," *International Public Management Journal* 1:2 (1999): 131.
4. Bernard Rosen, *Holding Government Bureaucracies Accountable* (3rd ed.) (Westport, Conn.: Praeger, 1998), p. 207.
5. Ibid., p. 210.
6. Behn (1999), p. 142.
7. Robert D. Behn, "Linking Measurement and Motivation: A Challenge for Education," *Advances in Educational Administration* 5 (1997): 17.
8. Richard Mulgan, "Accountability: An Ever-Expanding Concept," *Public Administration* 78:3 (2000): 555.
9. Ibid. See also G. W. Jones, "The Search for Local Accountability," in S. Leach (ed.), *Strengthening Local Government in the 1990s* (London: Longman, 1992).
10. Raymond J. Decker, "Combating Terrorism," statement prepared for U.S. House of Representatives, Subcommittee on Economic Development, Public Buildings, and Emergency Management. Hearing on Combating Terrorism: Options to Improve the Federal Response, 107th Congress, 1st Session (24 April 2001).
11. *9/11 Commission Report*, pp. 400–1.
12. Paul L. Posner, "Combating Terrorism: Intergovernmental Partnership in a National Strategy to Enhance State and Local Preparedness," testimony

before the U.S. House Committee on Government Reform, Subcommittee on Government Efficiency, Financial Management, and Intergovernmental Relations. Washington, D.C.: GAO-02-547T (22 March 2002), p. 7.

13. Charles R. Wise and Christian Freitag, "Accountability and Risk: The National Fire Policy," *Journal of Public Administration Research and Theory* (2002): 141.

14. Eugene Bardach and Cara Lesser, "Accountability in Human Services Collaboratives: For What? And to Whom?" (1996), p. 203.

15. Stephen Paige, "Measuring Accountability for Results in Interagency Collaboratives," *Public Administration Review* 64:5 (2004): 541.

16. *9/11 Commission Report*, p. 339.

17. U.S. House Permanent Select Committee on Intelligence and U.S. Senate Select Committee on Intelligence (Joint Committee), *Report of the Joint Congressional Inquiry into Intelligence Community Activities before and after the Terrorist Attacks of September 11, 2001* (Washington D.C., 2002), p. 62.

18. Ibid., p. 66.

19. *9/11 Commission Report*, p. 352.

20. Wise and Freitag (2002).

21. Joint Committee, p. 99.

22. *9/11 Commission Report*, p. 344.

23. Martin A. Levin and Mary B. Sanger, *Making Government Work* (San Francisco, Calif.: Jossey-Bass, 1994), p. 59.

24. Joint Committee, p. 73.

25. John J. DiIulio, Jr., Gerald Garvey, and Donald F. Kettl, *Improving Government Performance: An Owner's Manual* (Washington, D.C.: Brookings Institution, 1993), p. 232.

26. Joint Committee, p. 105.

27. Linda DeLeon, "Ethics and Entrepreneurship," in Van R. Johnston (ed.), *Entrepreneurial Management and Public Policy* (New York: Nova Science, 2000), p. 222.

28. James A. Stever, *The End of Public Administration: Problems of the Profession in the Post-Progressive Era* (Dobbs Ferry, N.Y.: Transnational, 1988), p. 99.

29. *9/11 Commission Report*, p. 394.

30. Stephen Cohen and William Emicke, "Is Public Entrepreneurship Ethical?" *Public Integrity* 1:1 (1999): 54–74.

31. Barbara Romzek and Melvin Dubjick, "Accountability in the Public Sector: Lessons from the Challenger Tragedy," *Public Administration Review* 47:3 (1987): 227–38.

32. Barbara Romzek and Melvin Dubjick, "Issues of Accountability in Flexible Personnel Systems," in Patricia Ingraham and Barbara Romzek (eds.), *New Paradigms for Government* (San Francisco, Calif.: Jossey-Bass, 1994), pp. 263–93.

33. Rosen (1998), p. 209.

34. Ibid., p. 210.

35. Romzeck and Dubjick (1994), p. 88.

36. David M. Walker, "9/11 Commission Report: Reorganization, Transformation, and Information Sharing," testimony before the Committee on Government Reform, U.S. House of Representatives (3 August 2004) (GAO-04-1033T), p. 24.

37. Levin and Sanger (1994), pp. 17, 214.

38. John Brehm and Scott Gates, "Donut Shops and Speed Traps: Evaluating Models of Supervision on Police Behavior," *American Journal of Political Science* 37 (1993): 555–81. See also Gary Miller, *Managerial Dilemma: The Political Economy of Hierarchies* (Cambridge: Cambridge University Press, 1992).

39. Paul Teske and Mark Schneider, "The Bureaucratic Entrepreneur: The Case of City Managers," *Public Administration Review* 54:4 (1994): 337.

40. Sandford Borins, " Loose Cannons and Rule Breakers, or Enterprising Leaders? Some Evidence about Innovative Public Managers," *Public Administration Review* 60:6 (2000): 500, 504.

41. See the following. Peter Blau, *The Dynamics of Bureaucracy* (2nd ed.) (Chicago: University of Chicago Press, 1963). Barbara Koremenos, "Leadership and Bureaucracy: The Folk Theorem and Real Folks," *Rationality and Society* (2004). Donald Warwick, *A Theory of Public Bureaucracy: Politics, Personality, and Organization in the State Department* (Cambridge, Mass.: Harvard University Press, 1975).

42. Levin and Sanger (1994), pp. 248, 276.

43. Paige (2004). *See also* Beryl Radin and Barbara Romzek, "Accountability Expectations in an Intergovernmental Arena," *Publius* 26:2 (1996): 59–81.

44. Advisory Panel to Assess Domestic Response Capabilities for Terrorism Involving Weapons of Mass Destruction (Advisory Panel), *Forging America's New Normalcy*, Arlington, Va. (15 December 2003).

45. Bardach and Lesser (1996), pp. 205–6.

46. Jocelyn M. Johnston and Barbara Romzek, "Contracting and Accountability in State Medicaid Reform: Rhetoric, Theories, and Reality," *Public Administration Review* 59:5 (1999): 388.

47. Paige (2004), p. 593.

48. Robert S. Kravchuk and Robert W. Schack, "Designing Effective Performance-Measurement Systems under the Government Performance and Results Act of 1993," *Public Administration Review* 56:4 (1996): 349–58.

49. Sandford Borins, "The New Public Management Is Here to Stay," *Canadian Public Administration* 38:1 (1995): 121.

50. Behn (1999), p. 158.

51. Advisory Panel (2003).

52. Walker (2004), p. 17.

53. Behn (1999), p. 156.

54. William Gormley and David Weimer, *Organizational Report Cards* (Cambridge, Mass.: Harvard University Press, 1999). See also Robert Kaplan and David Norton, "The Balanced Scorecard: Measures That Drive Performance," *Harvard Business Review* 70:1 (1992): 71–9.

55. Bardach and Lesser (1996).

56. Paige (2004), p. 603.

57. Patria De Lancer Julnes and Marc Holzer, "Promoting the Utilization of Performance Measures in Public Organizations: An Empirical Study of Factors Affecting Adoption and Implementation," *Public Administration Review* 61:6 (2001): 693–708.

Waging the "War of Ideas"

William Rosenau, Ph.D.
Political Scientist, The RAND Corporation, Washington Office;
Adjunct Professor, Security Studies Program,
Georgetown University

INTRODUCTION

"Wars of subversion and counter subversion are fought, in the last resort, in the minds of the people," a leading British authority on counterterrorism concluded in 1971.[1] More than three decades later, there is growing recognition among U.S. government officials, journalists, and analysts of terrorism that defeating al-Qaida— arguably the preeminent challenge to U.S. security—will require far more than "neutralizing" leaders, disrupting cells, and dismantling networks. From its inception in the mid-1990s, al-Qaida has been both a terrorist organization and an international revolutionary movement, which today stretches across North America, western Europe, and the global south.[2] That organization, driven from its redoubt in Afghanistan in late 2001, continues to demonstrate its potency, as shown by the deadly railway attack in Madrid in March 2004. However, the much greater threat is posed by the global jihadist movement that Usama bin Ladin continues to inspire. That movement, characterized by some observers as a worldwide insurgency,[3] threatens the United States' interests in regions as diverse as central Asia, the Middle East, and Southeast Asia.

The views expressed in this chapter are the author's and do not necessarily reflect
those of RAND or its sponsors.

The extremist ideology articulated by bin Ladin and his circle ties together this widely dispersed, multiethnic extremist movement, characterized by one specialist as an "idea-based network, self-organizing from below, inspired by postings on the Internet." Al-Qaida, in the words of another scholar, "is the ideological organization par excellence."[4] Al-Qaida's message, disseminated widely and effectively through all forms of mass media, including the Internet, has a powerful appeal in much of the Muslim world.[5] Cutting off the supply of recruits to this movement, eliminating its financial support networks, and preventing it from metastasizing into new regions will thus require a campaign to undermine its ideological appeal. As the 9/11 Commission concluded in its final report, eliminating al-Qaida as a formidable danger ultimately requires "prevailing in the longer term over the ideology that gives rise to Islamist terrorism."[6]

But as Clausewitz famously observed, in war everything is simple, but even the simple things are extremely difficult. Although the United States and its allies have waged successful campaigns to discredit totalitarian ideologies such as fascism and communism, these operations have never come readily to liberal democracies. Part of the explanation can be found in the uneasiness open societies tend to have about engaging in psychological manipulation, lying, and other mendacious and "underhanded" practices that are likely to be part of any full-scale campaign against a hostile ideology.[7] That this campaign would necessarily involve efforts to discredit a religious viewpoint—no matter how extreme that viewpoint might be—also clashes with liberal notions about the importance of religious liberty and the need to maintain the separation of church and state. More fundamentally, waging a blatantly ideological struggle seems quite unnatural to Americans and other Westerners, who tend to downplay intangible factors such as ideas, history, and culture as political motivators, preferring instead to stress relatively more concrete driving forces such as personal security and physical well-being.[8]

Whatever the explanation, it is clear to most informed observers that the United States has so far failed to conduct anything approaching an effective counterideological campaign against al-Qaida. What during the Cold War George Kennan and others called "political warfare," and what of late has been euphemistically called "strategic influence," is today simply not a significant part of the "global war on terrorism." Or rather, it is a part of that war—but it is being employed effectively only by our adversaries.

In this chapter we will take the first tentative steps toward suggesting an ideological counterstrategy. To provide a context for the subsequent discussion, this chapter will outline the ideology promulgated by al-Qaida and associated terrorist groups. Second, it will examine recent attempts by the United States to combat al-Qaida's worldview and compare this effort with America's global propaganda campaign against the Soviet Union. The chapter will conclude with some preliminary ideas about waging an effective counterpropaganda campaign against al-Qaida, including potential themes and approaches.

But first, some words on terminology are in order. There is no single word or phrase in English that fully captures the concept of a campaign to combat a hostile ideology. The two terms mentioned above, *political warfare* and *strategic influence*, have clear shortcomings. The word *warfare* has obvious military connotations. Among other things, its use implies that we are engaged in a conflict with a clear beginning, middle, and end, when in reality the struggle against terrorism is likely to persist for generations, as a number of U.S. policy makers have suggested.[9] *Strategic influence*, defined by one military officer as "the deliberate, conscious coordination ... of all government informational activities designed to influence opinions, attitudes, and behavior of foreign groups in ways that will promote U.S. national objectives,"[10] is both euphemistic and politically tainted as a result of the Pentagon's ill-fated attempt to establish an Office of Strategic Influence (OSI), an organization accused by its bureaucratic detractors of spreading "disinformation."[11]

Similarly, the word *propaganda*, with its unwholesome connotation of Orwellian "Newspeak," is probably too corrupted to be useful as anything other than a term of abuse. International broadcasting, cultural exchanges, conferences, and other forms of "public diplomacy," defined by the now-defunct U.S. Information Agency (USIA) as "promoting the national interest ... through understanding, informing, and influencing foreign publics,"[12] is too narrow for our purposes, since it does not include the full range of political, military, economic, and intelligence measures that might usefully be employed to hinder the spread of al-Qaida's worldview. The term *psychological operations* (PSYOP) has similar difficulties. The traditional focus of PSYOP is on the battlefield and includes activities such as producing and distributing leaflets to encourage enemy forces to lay down their arms. Thus, the term is also too narrow and, like propaganda, is burdened with unhelpful connotations of "mind control." What we are left with, then, is a variety of words and phrases, no one of which is sufficient for capturing the essence of our objective, that is, "prevailing in the longer term over the ideology that gives rise to Islamist terrorism."

AL-QAIDA'S IDEOLOGY

What is the worldview embraced by al-Qaida and its international affiliates? A leading scholar cogently describes this ideology as "jihadist-salafism," that is, a profound "respect for the sacred texts in their most literal form [combined with] an absolute commitment to jihad."[13] A Sunni reformist movement with origins in the encounter of the Muslim world with the West in the second half of the nineteenth century, *Salafiyya* (from the Arabic *salaf*, "devout ancestors") advocates a return to Islam as practiced by the Prophet.[14] For Salafis, the Quran and the Prophet serve as the highest (indeed the only) source of theological, social, and political truth.[15] This puritanical strain of Islam, spread through mosques, Islamic centers, and *madrassas* (religious schools), is rapidly gaining adherents across the Muslim world.[16]

While most Salafis do not support the use of violence to achieve key goals such as the reestablishment of sharia ("divine law"), the radical jihadist-salafism tendency is an "armed doctrine" that combines theological orthodoxy with a political agenda that includes the destruction of "apostate" regimes such as Saudi Arabia, Egypt, and Pakistan. Sayyid Qutb (1906–1966), a theorist for the fundamentalist Muslim Brotherhood and a leading intellectual influence on al-Qaida's Egyptian inner circle, described the entire world—including the nominally "Islamic" republics—as engulfed in *jahiliyyah*, that is, the ignorance, sin and barbarism that characterized the world before the arrival of the Prophet.[17] To subscribers of jihadist-salafism like bin Ladin, the world is divided into two camps: the Islamic community (*umma*) and the enemy, that is, the unbelievers, led by the United States and other Western "crusaders" and their Zionist allies. "[T]here are two parties to the conflict," bin Ladin told the al-Jazeera satellite channel in 1999: "The first party is world Christianity, which is allied with Zionist Jewry and led by the United States, Britain, and Israel; while the second party is the Muslim world."[18]

In the judgment of bin Ladin, these sinister forces seek nothing less than the destruction of Islam. As he declared in 1996, the United States after the end of the Cold War "escalated its campaign against the Muslim World in its entirety, aiming to get rid of Islam itself."[19] In Bin Laden's view, the persecution of Muslims in Chechnya, the Palestinian territories, Kashmir, and elsewhere offers ample evidence that the *umma* is facing an existential threat, and that the United States, through its regional satraps, is working toward the eradication of Islam.

This conceptualization leads bin Ladin and his followers to what one analyst has described as "a theoretical legitimization for ruthless political action" in which the detested "'other' . . . becomes a perfectly legitimate target in the war for the glory of Islam."[20] The United States, according to bin Ladin, has created "an ocean of oppression, injustice, slaughter and plunder," and has thus merited responses like the 9/11 attacks.[21] Furthermore, waging jihad is not simply the obligation of the Islamic paladins of al-Qaida. According to bin Ladin, contributing in some way to violent, defensive jihad is the solemn obligation of every Muslim.[22] Striking at the United States is particularly important, in his judgment, since without American support, the United States' client regimes in the Middle East and elsewhere will "wither away."[23]

Thus the belief in the transformative power of violent political action is a central component of the worldview articulated by al-Qaida. In this, al-Qaida has much in common with those in the West—from the Jacobins to the Nazis to the European radicals of the 1970s—who believed that terror could serve as the midwife to revolution.[24] For all its condemnation of the West, al-Qaida is a distinctly modern syncretic creation that has borrowed heavily from the hated "crusaders" in areas such as technology (e.g., the Internet), ideas (e.g., political violence and revolution), and operational approaches (e.g., fashionable management nostrums, such as the use of "flat" or "virtual" structures).[25]

Indeed, al-Qaida shares many features with twentieth-century totalitarianism, particularly its Marxist-Leninist variant. In addition to their shared views on the role of violence, and their Manichean outlook, common features include:

- The centrality of the ideological component in their struggle against their adversaries
- A global strategy that seeks to bring about a universal transformation[26]
- An internationalist stance that rejects national borders, class hierarchies, and racial distinctions
- A belief that imperialism and a lust for natural resources is the impetus behind the West's presence in the developing world[27]
- A stress on what communist parties referred to as "agitation and propaganda," including the rhetorical demonization of their perceived enemies (e.g., al-Qaida's vilification of Jews as the offspring of apes, and of Hindus as "worshipers of cows")[28]
- A conspiratorial mind-set, and a belief in the central role of a "vanguard" that drive the masses toward revolution[29]

Finally, the al-Qaida worldview shares with communism a utopianism characterized by what one expert describes as "unprogrammatic simplicity."[30] Just as Moscow called for the creation of a dictatorship of the proletariat, al-Qaida urges the reestablishment of the caliphate (*khilafah*, the unified Islamic state, whose last vestige was abolished by Kemal Atatürk in 1924). As with the utopian Marxist-Leninist vision, al-Qaida's dream lacks specifics about the most fundamental questions of governance, such as how political decisions would be made, how the state should be structured, and how fundamental public needs such as security would be met. In other words, both movements offer a vague image of some future paradise to be achieved through armed struggle, discipline, and revolutionary rigor, but no concrete plan for that glorious prospect, or how it will actually take shape.

To spread this ideological vision, al-Qaida relies heavily on information technology. Indeed, in the words of one analyst, al-Qaida "loves the Internet."[31] Relatively cheap, largely unregulated, and able to reach millions of people, the Internet serves as an ideal instrument for disseminating ideological themes, vilifying opponents, providing moral inspiration, and recruiting new supporters. Web sites, chat rooms, and bulletin boards can also serve a more operational purpose. The Internet, according to a senior U.S. Defense Department official, functions as a "cybersanctuary" for al-Qaida and other terrorists, allowing them to "conceal their identities, to move large amounts of money, to encrypt messages, and to plan and even conduct operations remotely."[32]

THE U.S. GOVERNMENT'S CAMPAIGN

During the Cold War, the United States and other Western powers (Britain, most notably)[33] developed a robust infrastructure for waging a "war of ideas" against the communist ideology being promulgated by the Soviet Union and its allies. During the Truman and Eisenhower administrations, the so-called golden age of U.S. propaganda, counterpropaganda, and public diplomacy operations,[34] the U.S. government carried out a sophisticated program of overt and covert activities designed to shape public opinion behind the Iron Curtain, within European intellectual and cultural circles, and across the developing world.[35] Broadcasting by Voice of America (VOA) and Radio Free Europe/Radio Liberty (RFE/RL) brought news and cultural programming to target audiences abroad. At the height of their international popularity, "the radios" (as they were called) reached 50 percent of the Soviet population and 70 to 80 percent of the eastern European public every week.[36] Cultural exchanges brought foreign academics, journalists, and politicians to the United States to give them direct exposure to American citizens, ideals, and institutions. Reading rooms at American consulates and embassies gave foreigners access to newspapers, books, magazines, and other media. Through secret funding by the Central Intelligence Agency (CIA), the U.S. government supported organizations like the Congress for Cultural Freedom, an international association of prominent artists, writers, and scholars opposed to totalitarian ideologies. Aggressive political warfare campaigns in Western Europe went beyond simply countering communist propaganda with pro-American messages. In France, for example, the United States worked with local authorities to limit the power of communist-controlled unions, to deny communists access to social welfare benefits, and to restrict the supply of newsprint to communist presses.[37]

High-level interest in such operations waned during the 1970s, but received renewed emphasis under President Ronald Reagan, the "Great Communicator," who, like Eisenhower, was a firm advocate of the informational component of America's Cold War strategy.[38] However, with the end of the Cold War official interest once again plummeted. During the 1990s, Congress and the executive branch disparaged informational activities as costly Cold War anachronisms. The budget for State Department informational programs was slashed, and USIA, a quasi-independent body that reported to the secretary of state, was disestablished, and its responsibilities were transferred to a new undersecretary of state for public diplomacy. By the late 1990s, according to one critic, the once mighty VOA had been reduced to the "Whisper of America,"[39] and in the words of another observer, "public diplomacy was left to wither without strategic focus or organizational direction."[40] Things were no better within the CIA, the organization responsible for carrying out covert informational activities—e.g., disinformation, and secret support to foreign organizations and institutions—where political warfare was widely viewed as a career dead end. According to one press account, the officers and staff conducting foreign "influence operations" shrank to one-tenth of the level it had reached in the 1980s.[41]

The attacks of 9/11 convinced many both inside and outside of the government that far more needed to be done to reach Muslim audiences, explain the United States' policies, and dry up the ideological stream contributing to the growth of violent Islamic extremism. President George Bush has correctly described the "war on terrorism" as "a long-lasting ideological struggle."[42] So far, however, little progress has been made in "winning the war of ideas." Since 9/11, the surge in federal national security spending has been greater than at any time since the Korean War,[43] yet the State Department's public diplomacy budget remains stuck at its pre-9/11 level of $1 billion per year, a mere 0.3 percent of the U.S. defense budget.[44] Across the Muslim world, particularly since the war in Iraq, public opinion views the United States, its policies, and the global war on terrorism in increasingly unfavorable terms.[45] As mentioned above, OSI was strangled in its bureaucratic cradle. VOA, according to one estimate, reaches a mere 2 percent of the world's Arabs.[46] Other international media initiatives, such as Radio Sawa, appear to have little influence in the Arab "street."[47] Most notoriously, the State

Department's "Shared Values" campaign, intended to promote a benign view of the United States by distributing short documentaries that highlighted the benefits enjoyed by Muslims in America, failed when television stations in key Islamic countries failed to carry the U.S. programming.[48] Sometimes our adversaries stumble onto the truth. One al-Qaida Web site did in November 2002 when it concluded that "America's means of propaganda are no longer influential in the same way they were for decades."[49]

NEW APPROACHES

How should the United States approach the challenge of combating jihadist-salafism? The recognition by the president that defeating al-Qaida and other international terrorists requires an ideological weapon is an important first step, but much more needs to be done. As one prominent theorist has wisely cautioned, this weapon cannot be used "as a substitute for policy, as a way of looking as if one is doing something when one doesn't really have a clear understanding and grasp of the goal one is trying to achieve."[50]

In the interest of strategic clarity, the U.S. government should abandon the assertion that the U.S. government and its partners are engaged in a global war against terrorism per se, as some American officials have suggested,[51] and declare that the struggle is in fact against al-Qaida and the ideology that sustains it. The United States does not have the resources to combat all manifestations of terrorism, and what is more, not all terrorists threaten the United States. To be sure, acknowledging al-Qaida as the paramount adversary will lead its ideologists and their fellow travelers to claim that the West is locked in a "war against Islam." But the resulting strategic clarity will likely outweigh any risks associated with this approach; also, the ideologues of jihadist-salafism are already making this charge about a "clash of civilizations," as discussed above. With the focus on al-Qaida, policy makers can marshal their resources in a more focused and effective manner.

Themes

Central to any effective counterideological campaign is a coherent and powerful set of themes. What follows is not intended to be systematic or comprehensive; rather, these themes are meant to suggest in a general way what the campaign might look like and how it might be orchestrated. The Islamic world, made up of more than one billion people, is obviously diverse, and so it will be critical to tailor these themes to Muslims in specific nations or regions and Islamic traditions. The focus here is on elite and intellectual opinion, although some of these themes might be adapted for a broader audience:

Jihadist-Salafism as an Alien Ideology

As mentioned earlier, al-Qaida's worldview is a relatively recent, highly politicized intellectual construct that has borrowed liberally from European extremism, most notably Marxism-Leninism. Although the al-Qaida ideology has an appeal throughout the Muslim world, it is well outside Islam's mainstream Sunni, Shiite, and Sufi traditions. Al-Qaida's ideologues are eager to position themselves as contemporary manifestations of Islam's heroic past.[52] Highlighting the imported, foreign nature of the ideology could help undercut al-Qaida's Islamic credentials.

Jihadist-Salafism as a Threat to Islam

Throughout east Africa and Pakistan, Sufis are confronted by ideological extremists who declare that their branch of Islam is a heretical assault upon the faith. While many Sufis (like other Muslims) detest aspects of U.S. foreign policy, many also loathe the extremists who rant in their mosques and prevent them from expressing themselves culturally. Assistance to the "enemies of our enemies" may therefore prove to be a useful stratagem. For example, support for Sufi music—an important part of their religious practice—through festivals and radio broadcasts could help empower Muslims who are under attack by ideological extremists. Counter messages should also mention attacks on Shiite mosques in Iraq carried out by al-Qaida affiliates. The intention of course is not to foment sectarian strife, but to reinforce the idea that al-Qaida's ideology is fundamentally anti-Muslim.

Al-Qaida and Nationalism

Al-Qaida rejects the modern nation-state as a godless Western invention, yet for some Muslims nationalism continues to exert a powerful pull, as demonstrated during the uprisings in Iraq against the coalition's occupying forces. Faith, clan, tribe, and other forces may trump nationalism in many cases, but it may be useful in some circumstances to portray al-Qaida, with its dreams of a new caliphate, as a threat to national identity.

Al-Qaida as a Threat to Key Values

Although the Bush administration believes that fostering a "global democratic revolution" is the key to defeating international terrorism,[53] this approach is problematical. The president is part of a long U.S. tradition according to which "American liberal values and institutions constitute a generalizable model that promotes human rights and prosperity."[54] However, other models of legitimacy may in fact be more applicable and suitable to the non-Western world.[55] While the administration argues that liberal democracy is a universal value, many in the Muslim world view democratization as a distinctly American priority. At the very least, the democratization strategy is likely to take decades to bear real fruit, and in the meantime it may be wise to focus on more expedient approaches, given the urgent nature of the threat from al-Qaida. The focus therefore should be on stressing the danger that jihadist-salafism poses to core human values, as the U.S. national security advisor suggested in August 2004 when she characterized the ideology as one of "death and hatred" that must be fought by the "appeal of life and hope."[56]

Methods and Instruments

Neither American officials nor American Muslim leaders have enough credibility in the Islamic world to articulate these themes in a way that will resonate with significant audiences. Unfortunately, "people in other countries don't see America as [a] beacon of idealism[,] but as something menacing," as one journalist concluded recently.[57] American policy for the Middle East, including support for Israel as well as for repressive regimes in the region, makes it nearly impossible for the U.S. government to wage an effective counter-ideological campaign unilaterally.

For these reasons, it is essential that the ideological counter-message be articulated by Muslims outside the United States. As suggested in the preceding section, jihadist-salafism has adversaries in the Islamic world, and these individuals and organizations should be given the resources to carry out a counteroffensive. This support should not be linked directly to the U.S. government. Rather, other governments, private foundations, and international organizations with greater credibility in the Muslim world should play a much greater part than they have played so far in helping voices opposed to jihadist-salafism to be heard. This is not to say that the United States' traditional tools, such as international broadcasting, should be discarded. However, they should be used more widely as a "megaphone" for Muslims who reject the worldview being spread by al-Qaida. Many of these voices are likely to be strongly opposed to U.S. foreign policy, particularly with respect to the Middle East. The radical scholar Shaykh Salman al-Oadah, a Saudi once admired by bin Ladin, has criticized the 9/11 attacks for killing noncombatants, and in 2002 he coordinated an open letter written by Saudi intellectuals that called for greater dialogue with the West.[58] The potential value of such figures as persuasive opponents of the al-Qaida ideology far outweighs whatever potential danger they might pose as detractors of the United States or Israel.

Support to writers, scholars, journalists, and other intellectuals should be central, since in ideological struggles, intellectuals by definition play an essential part in creating and articulating ideas that can be marshaled against one's enemies. Encouraging a freer intellectual climate by supporting universities, publishing houses, Web sites, newspapers, and research institutions in the Islamic world would give Muslim intellectuals a base from which to create and disseminate antitotalitarian ideas, much as the Congress for Cultural Freedom did during the Cold War. Already, Muslim intellectuals are mounting sophisticated attacks on the distortions of Islam being made by bin Ladin and his followers, and these counterarguments should be given a wider hearing across the Islamic world.[59]

As important as the Internet is in terms of spreading extremist ideology, the United States and its allies should resist the temptation to deal with al-Qaida Web sites by simply pressuring Internet service providers (ISPs) to shut them down.[60] Terrorists and their supporters are usually able to find new hosts with little difficulty. In addition, these Web sites serve as a window into the movement's strategy, operations, and recruitment techniques that might not otherwise be available to intelligence analysts, law enforcement personnel, and other experts.

At the same time, the United States should work closely with its friends and allies to restrict the ability of ideologues of jihadist-salafism to spread their message in other ways. Such an approach runs counter to Western liberal traditions, and to the belief that a "marketplace of ideas" is the best antidote to despotic notions. Moreover, such an approach could play into the hands of tyrannical but useful governments, like the Karimov regime in Uzbekistan, that cites the "global war on terrorism" as an excuse for persecuting real or imagined opponents of the state.

But as discussed at the beginning of this chapter, defeating al-Qaida requires an attack on an ideology. To be effective, this counterpunch will require more than just allowing alternative worldviews in the Muslim world to be more widely disseminated, as important as that task is. In the Middle East, state-sponsored or state-run magazines and newspapers routinely publish the most hateful diatribes against "infidels," Jews, "crusaders," and other alleged "enemies" of Islam. In an article that appeared in a journal produced by the Religious Affairs Department of the Saudi armed forces, for example, it was charged that "World Jewry has established a shadow government run by 300 Satans who call themselves 'elders.'"[61] Such publications serve as transmission belts for jihadist-salafism. The United States must do much more to pressure the leaders of Saudi Arabia and other governments to eliminate their support for such extremist expression, regardless of whatever political price these other states might be forced to pay domestically by attacking extremism.[62] Similarly, all ideologues promoting jihadist-salafism should be dropped from government payrolls, forbidden to travel abroad, denied access to media outlets, stripped of welfare benefits, and denied other privileges. Advocates of suicide bombing, such as the Egyptian-born extremist Dr. Yusuf al-Qaradawi, who attended a conference in Britain in July 2004, should as a matter of policy be denied further opportunities to spread their ideological message to audiences in the West.[63] Again, such measures inevitably raise questions of civil liberties, and every care must be taken to avoid the suppression of legitimate dissent. That said, these measures are certainly no harsher than many of the other widely used tools in the global campaign against al-Qaida, such as detention without trial, psychological and physical pressure against prisoners during interrogations, and the use of special operations forces and other military power against terrorist cadres.

CONCLUSION

Great powers have been hated throughout history. During a visit to Paris in 1903, in the aftermath of the second Boer War, King Edward VII of Great Britain, when told by a companion that "the French don't like us," replied, "Why should they?"[64] Today, as the world's preeminent power, pursuing often highly unpopular policies, the United States is confronting swelling numbers of people around the world who don't like us. But while we should never expect to be universally loved—as many Americans seem to expect—neither should we be oblivious of the fact that al-Qaida's legions, and the millions of people in the Muslim world who support them, would like to see large numbers of Americans dead. As bin Ladin declared in 1998, it is an "individual duty for every Muslim who can do it in any country" to "kill Americans and their allies."[65]

To defeat al-Qaida, such notions must be fought far more effectively. Al-Qaida's inner circle, and the dedicated cadres who make up the ranks of affiliated terrorist groups like Jemaah Islamiya in Southeast Asia, the Islamic Movement of Uzbekistan in central Asia, and the Group for Salafist Preaching and Combat in north Africa, are almost certainly immune to counterideological messages. Instead, informational tools and strategies must be aimed at larger groups that may be receptive to the murderous message of jihadist-salafism. This approach, together with the full range of other forms of political, military, economic, and intelligence power, is essential if the West is to cut off the flow of terrorist recruits, money, and other resources, and halt the further spread of al-Qaida.

N O T E S

1. Frank Kitson, *Low Intensity Operations: Subversion, Insurgency, and Peacekeeping* (London: Faber and Faber, 1971), p. 78.

2. For more on the nature, structure, and operations of al-Qaida, see Jason Burke, *Al-Qaeda: Casting a Shadow of Terror* (London and New York: Tauris, 2003), particularly chapters 1–2.

3. See, e.g., John Mackinlay, Globalisation and Insurgency. International Institute for Strategic Studies Adelphi Paper 352 (Oxford: Oxford University Press, 2002), p. 79; and "Point Man of the Pentagon," *American Legion Magazine* (August 2004): 30.

4. Michael Doran, "The Pragmatic Fanaticism of al Qaeda: An Anatomy of Extremism in the Middle East," *Political Science Quarterly* 117:2 (Summer 2002): 187.

5. Anonymous [Michael Scheuer], *Imperial Hubris: Why the West Is Losing the War on Terror* (Washington: Brassey's, 2004), pp. 209–12.

6. National Commission on Terrorist Attacks upon the United States, The 9/11 Commission Report (Washington, D.C.: U.S. Government Printing Office, 2004), p. 363; hereafter cited as 9/11 Commission Report.

7. "Strategic Deception in Modern Democracies: Ethical, Legal, and Policy Challenges," Conference Brief, U.S. Army War College Strategic Studies Institute, n.d., p. 2.

8. Carnes Lord, "The Psychological Dimension in National Strategy," in Frank R. Barnett and Carnes Lord (eds.), *Political Warfare and Psychological Operations* (Washington, D.C.: National Defense University Press, 1989): 22.

9. As U.S. Army Chief of Staff Peter Schoomaker has concluded, this conflict "is a little bit like having cancer. You may get in remission, but it's never going to go away in our lifetime." Quoted in Robert Burns, "Army Chief Says Islamic Extremist Threat Is Like a 'Cancer' That Will Linger," Associated Press (15 June 2004).

10. Susan L. Gough, "The Evolution of Strategic Influence," USAWC [U.S. Army War College] Strategy Research Project, Carlisle Barracks, Pa. (7 April 2004), p. 1.

11. See, e.g., Andrew Buncombe, "Threat of War: Pentagon to Target Allies with Covert Propaganda," *Independent* (London) (17 December 2002): 11.

12. Quoted in "Changing Minds, Winning Peace: A New Strategic Direction for U.S. Public Diplomacy in the Arab and Muslim World," Report of the Advisory Group on Public Diplomacy for the Arab and Muslim World, Washington, D.C. (1 October 2003), p. 20.

13. Gilles Kepel, *Jihad: The Trail of Political Islam* (Cambridge, Mass.: Harvard University Press, 2002), p. 220.

14. Ibid., p. 219. The movement's Saudi strain, known as Wahhabism, serves as kingdom's state ideology. In general, "Muslims view the Western usage of the term...as carrying negative and derogatory connotations." Febe Armanios, "The Islamic Traditions of Wahhabism and Salafiyya," CRS [Congressional Research Service] *Report for Congress*, 22 December 2003, p. 1.

15. Febe Armanios, "The Islamic Traditions of Wahhabism and Salafiyya," CRS Report for Congress (22 December 2003), p. 3. The term *"wahhabism,"* which has derogatory connotations for many Muslims, is a version of Salifiyya practiced in Saudi Arabia (p. 1).

16. Ibid., p. 3.

17. Sayyid Qutb, *Milestones* (Cedar Rapids, Iowa: Mother Mosque Foundation, n.d.), p. 12.

18. "Usamah Bin-Ladin, the Destruction of the Base," al-Jazeera (10 June 1999), Foreign Broadcast Information Service (FBIS).

19. "Mujahid Usamah Bin Ladin Talks Exclusively to Nida'ul Islam about the New Powder Keg in the Middle East," Nida'ul Islam (October–November 1996), www.islam.org.au/articles/15/LADIN.HTM, accessed 1 September 2004.

20. Maha Azzam, "Al-Qaeda: The Misunderstood Wahhabi Connection and the Ideology of Violence," Royal Institute of International Affairs, Briefing Paper No. 1 (February 2003), p. 4.

21. See, e.g., "Azzam Exclusive: Letter from Usamah Bin Muhammad Bin Ladin to the American People," Waaqiah (Internet) (26 October 2002), FBIS.

22. See, e.g., "Bin Laden's Sermon for the Feast of the Sacrifice," Middle East Media Research Institute [MEMRI], Special Dispatch Series No. 476 (5 March 2003), p. 10.

23. "Pakistan Interviews Osama Bin Laden," Pakistan (Islamabad) (18 March 1997), FBIS.

24. John Gray, "Living with Bin Laden," *Independent on Sunday* (London) (18 May 2003): 25.

25. This point is made in Bruce Hoffman, "The Leadership Secrets of Osama Bin Laden: The Terrorist as CEO," *Atlantic Monthly* (April 2002): 26–27.

26. John Gray, "How Marx Turned Muslim," *Independent* (London) (27 July 2002): 16.

27. "The Arabian Peninsula," according to bin Laden, "has never ... been stormed by any forces like the crusader armies spreading in it like locusts, eating its riches and wiping out its plantations." "Bin-Laden, Others Sign Fatwa to 'Kill Americans' Everywhere," *Al-Quds al-Arabi* (London) (23 February 1998), FBIS.

28. See, e.g., "About the Heroes' Will and the Legitimacy of the New York and Washington Operations," Alneda (Internet) (24 April 2002), FBIS.

29. Paul Berman, *Terror and Liberalism* (New York and London: Norton, 2003), p. 118.

30. Reuel Marc Gerecht, "The Gospel According to Osama Bin Laden," *Atlantic Monthly* (January 2002) (online edition).

31. Timothy L. Thomas, "Al Qaeda and the Internet: The Danger of Cyberplanning," *Parameters* 33:1 (Spring 2003): 112.

32. "Opening Statement of Deputy Secretary of Defense Paul Wolfowitz before the House Armed Services Committee" (10 August 2004), armedservices. house.gov/schedules/2004.html, accessed 18 October 2004.

33. See, e.g., J. Vaughn, "'Cloak without Dagger': How the Information Research Department Fought Britain's Cold War in the Middle East, 1948–1956," *Cold War History* 4:3 (April 2004): 56–84.

34. Gough, "The Evolution of Strategic Influence," p. 16.

35. For various perspectives on these activities, see Scott Lucas, *Freedom's War: The American Crusade against the Soviet Union* (New York: New York University Press, 1999); Frances Stoner Saunders, *The Cultural Cold War: The CIA and World of Arts and Letters* (New York: New Press, 1999); Walter L. Hixson, *Parting the Curtain: Propaganda, Culture, and the Cold War, 1945–1961* (New York: St. Martin's, 1998); and Kenneth A. Osgood, "Form before Substance: Eisenhower's Commitment to Psychological Warfare and Negotiations with the Enemy," *Diplomatic History* 24:3 (Summer 2000): 405–33.

36. Anthony J. Blinken, "Winning the War of Ideas," *Washington Quarterly* 25:2 (Spring 2002): 105.

37. Lucas, *Freedom's War*, p. 137.

38. Gough, "The Evolution of Strategic Influence," pp. 20–4.

39. Newton N. Minow, "The Whisper of America," Decision Memorandum, Foundation for Defense of Democracies (August 2003).

40. "Shays Hearing on Public Diplomacy in the Middle East," press release (10 February 2004), www.house.gov/shays/news/2004/February/febdip.htm, accessed 15 March 2004.

41. J. Michael Waller, "Losing a Battle for Hearts and Minds," *Insight on the News* (22 April 2002): 18.

42. Quoted in Bill Powell, "Struggle for the Soul of Islam," *Time* (13 September 2003): 46.

43. 9/11 Commission Report, p. 361.

44. Powell, "Struggle for the Soul of Islam," p. 46.

45. See, e.g., Pew Research Center for the People and the Press, "A Year after Iraq War: Mistrust of America in Europe Ever Higher, Muslim Anger Persists" (16 March 2004), http://people-press.org/reports/display.php3?ReportID=206, accessed 8 September 2004.

46. Blinken, "Winning the War of Ideas," p. 105.

47. Derek Kinnane, "Winning Over the Muslim Mind," *National Interest* (Spring 2004): 94.

48. Hady Amr, "The Need to Communicate: How to Improve U.S. Public Diplomacy with the Islamic World," Analysis Paper, No. 6, Saban Center for Middle East Policy, Brookings Institution (January 2004), pp. 31–2. For more on the failure of the U.S. battle for Muslim "hearts and minds," see David E. Kaplan, Aamir Latif, Kevin Whitelaw, and Julian E. Barnes, "Hearts, Minds, and Dollars," *US News & World Report* (25 April 2005): 22.

49. "Commentator Analyzes Recent Bin Ladin Tapes, Sees U.S. as Losing 'Information War' against al-Qaeda," Al-Ansar (Internet) (20 November 2002), FBIS.

50. Abram N. Shulsky, "Comment," in Barnett and Lord, *Political Warfare*, p. 106.

51. See, e.g., White House, The National Security Strategy of the United States of America (Washington, D.C.: White House, September 2002), p. 6.

52. Anonymous, *Imperial Hubris*, p. 136. For a useful discussion on countering transnational revolutionary ideologies, see Mark N. Katz, "Speaking Freely: Defeating Islamic Fundamentalism," *Asia Times Online*, 26 February 2005, www.atimes.com/atimes/Middle_East/GB26Ak01.html, accessed 3 March 2005.

53. See, e.g., White House, Office of Management and Budget, "Department of State and International Assistance Programs" (7 September 2004), www.whitehouse.gov/omb/budget/fy2005/state.html, accessed 7 September 2004.

54. Zachary Selden, "Neoconservatives and the American Mainstream," *Policy Review* (April–May 2004), www.policyreview.org/apr04/selden.html, accessed 7 May 2004. For a representative expression of the administration's views, see "State of the Union Address," 2 February 2005, www.whitehouse.gov/news/releases/2005/02/print/20050202-11.html, accessed 13 June 2005.

55. John Gray, "Global Utopias and Clashing Civilizations: Misunderstanding the Present," *International Affairs* (London) 74:1 (1998): 149.

56. White House, "Dr. Rice Addresses War on Terror" (19 August 2004), www.whitehouse.gov/news/releases/2004/08/20040819-5.html, accessed 24 August 2004.

57. David Ignatius, "A Copernican Foreign Policy," *Washington Post* (7 September 2004): 23.

58. Paul Eedle, "Terrorism.Com," *Guardian* (London) (17 July 2002): 4.

59. See, e.g., "Liberal Muslim Scholar: The Term 'Jihad' Is Misunderstood by Islamist Clerics," MEMRI Special Dispatch Series, No. 699 (23 April 2004), www.memri.org/bin/articles.cgi?Page=subjects&Area=reform&ID=SP69904,

accessed 8 September 2004; and "Arab Liberal: Most Islamic Ideologues, Organization Leaders Advocate Violence," MEMRI Special Dispatch Series, No. 696, www.memri.org/bin/articles.cgi?Page=subjects&Area=reform&ID= SP69604, accessed 8 September 2004.

60. See, e.g., Paul Eedle, "Al-Qaeda Takes Fight for 'Hearts and Minds' to the Web," *Jane's Intelligence Review* (August 2002): 25.

61. "Saudi Armed Forces Journal on the Jews: 'The Fabricated Torah, Talmud, and Protocols of the Elders of Zion Command Destruction of All Non-Jews for World Domination,'" MEMRI Special Dispatch Series, No. 768 (20 August 2004), www.memri.org/bin/articles.cgi?Page=subjects&Area=antisemitism&ID= SP76804, accessed 9 September 2004.

62. The Saudi authorities have made progress in this direction, having banned hundreds of extremists from preaching in mosques. Max Rodenbeck, "Unloved in Arabia," *New York Review of Books* (21 October 2004), www.nybooks.com/ articles/17477, accessed 26 October 2004.

63. "Muslim Cleric Faces New Attack Over Visit," *Daily Telegraph* (London) (11 July 2004), www.telegraph.co.uk/news/main.jhtml?xml=/news/2004/07/ 12/ucleric.xml&sSheet=/portal/2004/07/12/ixportaltop.html, accessed 20 October 2004.

64. Kevin Myers, "The Fishy Heart of the Entente Cordiale," *Sunday Telegraph* (London) (4 April 2004): 22.

65. "Usama Bin-Ladin, Others Sign Fatwa to 'Kill Americans' Everywhere," *Al-Quds al-Arabi* (London) (23 February 1998), FBIS.

Glossary

9/11	The al-Qaida terror attacks of September 11, 2001
AEDPA	Antiterrorism and Effective Death Penalty Act of 1996
ANSI	American National Standards Institute
APHIS	Animal and Plant Health Inspection Service
AT	Antiterrorism
ATA	Antiterrorist Assistance (State Department Program)
BAM	Business Activity Monitoring
BT	Biological Terrorism
BWC	Biological Weapons Convention
CAPPS	Computer-Assisted Passenger Prescreening System
CAPPS II	Computer-Assisted Passenger Prescreening System, version 2
CBO	Community-Based Organization
CBPA	Capabilities-Based Planning and Assessment
CBP	Customs and Border Protection
CBRNE	Chemical, biological, radiological, nuclear (high-explosive)
CCTV	Closed-Circuit Television
CDC	Centers for Disease Control and Prevention
CDRG	Catastrophic Disaster Response Group
CERCLA	Comprehensive Environmental Response, Compensation, and Liability Act

CERDEC	Communications-Electronics Research Development and Engineering Center
CERT	Community Emergency Response Team
CES	Core Enterprise Services (context: NCES)
CI/KR	Critical Infrastructure/Key Resources
CIAO	Critical Infrastructure Assurance Office
CIO	Chief Information Officer
CIP	Critical Infrastructure Protection
CISR	Center for Islamic Studies and Research (al-Qaida's official media organ)
CMC	Crisis Management Coordinator
CMT	Crisis Management Team
CMTL	Crisis Management Team Leader
COG	Center of Gravity
CONPLAN	U.S. Government Interagency Domestic Terrorism Concept of Operations Plan
COOP	Continuity of operations
COP	Common Operating Picture
CROP	Common Relevant Operating Picture
CSG	Counterterrorism Security Group
CT	Counterterrorism
CTC	Counterterrorism Committee (United Nations)
C-TPAT	Customs-Trade Partnership Against Terrorism
DARPA	Defense Advanced Research Projects Agency
DBT	Design Basis Threat
DCE	Defense Coordinating Element
DCI	Director of Central Intelligence
DCO	Defense Coordinating Officer
DEST	Domestic Emergency Support Team
DFO	Disaster Field Office
DHS	Department of Homeland Security
DIA	Defense Intelligence Agency
DISA	Defense Information Systems Agency
DMAT	Disaster Medical Assistance Team
DMORT	Disaster Mortuary Operational Response Team
DOC	Department of Commerce
DOD	Department of Defense
DOE	Department of Energy
DOI	Department of the Interior
DOJ	Department of Justice

DOL	Department of Labor
DOS	Department of State
DOT	Department of Transportation
DPA	Defense Production Act
DRM	Disaster Recovery Manager
DSCA	Defense Support of Civil Authorities
DTRA	Defense Threat Reduction Agency
DTRIM	Domestic Threat Reduction and Incident Management
EAS	Emergency Assistance Personnel or Emergency Alert System
EMS	Emergency Medical Services
EOC	Emergency Operations Center
EPA	Environmental Protection Agency
EPCRA	Emergency Planning and Community Right-to-Know Act
EPLO	Emergency Preparedness Liaison Officer
EPR	Emergency Preparedness and Response
ERL	Environmental Research Laboratories
ERT	Environmental Response Team (EPA)
ERT-A	Emergency Response Team—Advance Element
ERT-N	National Emergency Response Team
ESF	Emergency Support Functions
ESFLG	Emergency Support Function Leaders Group
EST	Emergency Support Team
ETA	Basque Nation and Freedom
ETD	Explosive Trace Detection
EU	European Union
FAMS	Federal Air Marshall Service
FAS	Freely Associated States
FBI	Federal Bureau of Investigation
FCO	Federal Coordinating Officer
FEMA	Federal Emergency Management Agency
FIRST	Federal Incident Response Support Team
FMC	Federal Mobilization Center
FMEA/CIL	Failure modes and effects analysis and critical items list
FNS	Food and Nutrition Service
FOC	FEMA Field Operations Center
FOG	Field Operations Guide

FOUO	For official use only
FRC	Federal Resource Coordinator
FRERP	Federal Radiological Emergency Response Plan
FRP	Federal Response Plan
GAO	Government Accountability Office (formerly Government Accounting Office)
GAR	Governor's Authorized Representative
GIA	Armed Islamic Group
GIS	Geographical Information System
GSA	General Services Administration
HAZMAT	Hazardous Material
HAZWOPER	Hazardous Waste Operations and Emergency Response
HHS	Department of Health and Human Services
HLD or HD	Homeland Defense
HLFRD	Holy Land Foundation for Relief and Development
HLS	Homeland Security
HQ	Headquarters
HSAS	Homeland Security Advisory System
HSC	Homeland Security Council
HSIN	Homeland Security Information Network
HSOC	Homeland Security Operations Center
HSPD	Homeland Security Presidential Directive
HULDs	Hardened Unit Load Devices
HUMINT	Human Intelligence
IAIP	Information Analysis and Infrastructure Protection
IC	Intelligence Community
ICE	Immigration and Customs Enforcement
ICP	Incident Command Post
ICS	Incident Command System
IEEE	Institute of Electrical and Electronics Engineers
IEEPA	International Emergency Economic Powers Act
IIMG	Interagency Incident Management Group
IIMS	Integrated Incident Management System
IMINT	Imagery Intelligence
IMO	International Maritime Organization
IMT	Incident Management Team
INRP	Initial National Response Plan
IOF	Interim Operating Facility
IPT	Integrated Process Teams

IRTPA	Intelligence Reform and Terrorism Prevention Act of 2004
IS	Information Sharing
ISAO	Information Sharing and Analysis Organization
ISNA	Information Sharing Needs Analysis
IT	Information Technology
JFO	Joint Field Office
JIC	Joint Information Center
JIS	Joint Information System
JOC	Joint Operations Center
JTF	Joint Task Force
JTTF	Joint Terrorism Task Force
LAN	Local area network
LEGATs	Legal Attachés
LES	Law enforcement sensitive
LTTE	Tamil Tigers of Tamil Eelam
MAC Entity	Multiagency Coordinating Entity
MACC	Multiagency Command Center
MASINT	Measurements and Signatures Intelligence
MERS	Mobile Emergency Response Support
MOA	Memorandum of Agreement
MOU	Memorandum of Understanding
MTSA	Maritime Transportation Safety Act
MWCOG	Metropolitan Washington Council of Governments
NAHERC	National Animal Health Emergency Response Corps
NASA	National Aeronautics and Space Administration
NAWAS	National Warning System
NBC	Nuclear Chemical and Biological
NCES	Network-Centric Enterprise Services
NCOW	Network-Centric Operations Other than Warfare
NCP	National Contingency Plan; National Oil and Hazardous Substances Pollution Contingency Plan
NCR	National Capital Region
NCS	National Communications System
NCSD	National Cyber Security Division
NCTC	National Counterterrorism Center
NDMS	National Disaster Medical System
NEP	National Exercise Program
NFPA	National Fire Protection Association
NGA	National Geospatial-Intelligence Agency

NGB	National Guard Bureau
NGO	Nongovernmental Organization
NICC	National Infrastructure Coordinating Center; National Interagency Coordination Center
NID	National Intelligence Director
NIMS	National Incident Management System
NIPP	National Infrastructure Protection Plan
NIRT	Nuclear Incident Response Team
NJTTF	National Joint Terrorism Task Force
NMRT	National Medical Response Team
NOAA	National Oceanic and Atmospheric Administration
NORAD	North American Aerospace Defense Command
NORTHCOM	Northern Command
NRC	Nuclear Regulatory Commission
NRCC	National Response Coordination Center
NRCS	Natural Resources Conservation Service
NRO	National Reconnaissance Office
NRP	National Response Plan
NRT	National Response Team
NSA	National Security Agency
NSC	National Security Council
NSRP	National Search and Rescue Plan
NSSE	National Special Security Event
NVOAD	National Voluntary Organizations Active in Disaster
NWCG	National Wildland Coordinating Group
NYPD	New York Police Department
OASD	Office of the Assistant Secretary of Defense
OCT	Overseas combating terrorism
ODP	Office of Domestic Preparedness
OFT	Office of Force Transformation
OHS	Office of Homeland Security
OIA	Office of Imagery Analysis
OMB	Office of Management and Budget
OR	Operations Research
ORCON/OC	Originator Controlled
OSAC	Overseas Security Advisory Council
OSC	Operation Safe Commerce; On-Scene Coordinator
OSHA	Occupational Safety and Health Administration
OSI	Open Systems Interconnection
OSINT	Open Source Intelligence

OSLGCP	Office of State and Local Government Coordination and Preparedness
PACOM	Pacific Command
PCC	Policy Coordination Committee
PDA	Preliminary Damage Assessment
PDD	Presidential Decision Directive
PFLP	Popular Front for the Liberation of Palestine
PFO	Principal Federal Official
POC	Point of Contact
PPE	Personal Protective Equipment
PRA	Probabilistic Risk Analysis
PTSD	Posttraumatic stress disorder
RA	Reimbursable Agreement
RAID	Rapid Assessment and Initial Detection
RAMP	Remedial Action Management Program
RCP	Regional Contingency Plan
RCRA	Resource Conservation and Recovery Act
RECP	Regional Emergency Coordination Plan
REPLO	Regional Emergency Preparedness Liaison Officer
RFI	Request for Information
RICCS	Regional Incident Communications and Coordination System
RIJAN	Regional Information Joint Awareness Network
RISC	Regional Interagency Steering Committee
ROC	Regional Operations Center
RPN	Risk Priority Number
RRCC	Regional Response Coordination Center
RRT	Regional Response Team
SA	Situational Awareness
SAC	Special Agent-in-Charge
SAR	Search and Rescue
SCC	Secretary's Command Center (HHS)
SCI	Sensitive compartmented information
SCO	State Coordinating Officer
SFLEO	Senior Federal Law Enforcement Official
SFO	Senior Federal Official
SHSI	Sensitive homeland security information
SIGINT	Signals Intelligence
SIOC	Strategic Information and Operations Center
SOA	Service-oriented architecture

SOAP	Simple Object Access Protocol
SOG	Standard Operating Guideline
SOP	Standard Operating Procedure
SRL	Sense-and-respond logistics
START	Scientific and Technical Advisory and Response Team
TRANSCOM	Transportation Operations Coordinating Committee
TSA	Transportation Security Administration
TSC	Terrorist Screening Center
TTIC	Terrorist Threat Integration Center
UASI	Urban Area Security Initiative
UDDI	Universal description, discovery, and integration
UNSCR	United Nations Security Council Resolution
US&R	Urban Search and Rescue
USACE	U.S. Army Corps of Engineers
USCG	United States Coast Guard
USDA	U.S. Department of Agriculture
USD-I	Undersecretary of Defense for Intelligence
USSS	U.S. Secret Service
UTL	Universal Task List
VMAT	Veterinarian Medical Assistance Team
W3C	World Wide Web Consortium
WAWAS	Washington Area Warning System
WMD	Weapons of Mass Destruction
WSDL	Web Services Description Language
WTC	World Trade Center
XML	Extensible Markup Language

INDEX